# Encyclopedia of
# Urban America
## The Cities and Suburbs

# Encyclopedia of
# Urban America
## The Cities and Suburbs

Volume 2
M–Z

Neil Larry Shumsky
Editor

**ABC-CLIO**

Santa Barbara, California
Denver, Colorado
Oxford, England

Library of Congress Cataloging-in-Publication Data

Encyclopedia of urban America : the cities and suburbs / Neil Larry Shumsky,
    editor
        p.   cm.
    Includes bibliographical references and index.
    Contents: vol. 1. A–L   —   vol. 2. M–Z.
    1. Cities and towns—United States—Encyclopedias.    2. Suburbs—
United States—Encyclopedias.    3. Cites and towns—United States—History.
4. Suburbs—United States—History.  I. Shumsky, Neil L., 1944– .
    HT123.E5     1998                                    98-11698
    307.76'0973'03—dc21                                  CIP

ISBN 0-87436-846-4 (alk. paper)

04  03  02  01  00  99  98      10  9  8  7  6  5  4  3  2  1

ABC-CLIO, Inc.
130 Cremona Drive, P.O. Box 1911
Santa Barbara, California 93116-1911

This book is printed on acid-free paper ∞.

# Contents

# Encylopedia of
# Urban America
## The Cities and Suburbs

# List of Entries
# Volume 1: A–L

# List of Entries
## Volume 2: M–Z

# Encyclopedia of
# Urban America
## The Cities and Suburbs

## Mail-Order Merchandising

The mail-order catalog industry entails a system of merchandising that distributes goods to consumers when it receives orders that a customer has placed by mail after consulting a listing of salable items and then delivers the goods using various modes of transport. While some historians trace this business practice to Benjamin Franklin, who promoted his Pennsylvania fireplaces by mail order in 1744, most credit Montgomery Ward with the distinction of having established the first modern mail-order business in 1872.

Although initially directed at rural consumers, many nineteenth-century mail-order businesses had an urban base. For example, the two Chicago giants—Montgomery Ward (founded in 1872) and Sears, Roebuck (1886)—could not have expanded as they did without that city's central position in a national railroad network. Both Ward and Sears claimed that an "entire city's shopping district" was conveniently compressed within the 500 pages of their semiannual catalogs. They also called the catalog a "department store in a book." It has been estimated that 10 million Americans shopped by mail in 1910.

Several actions of the U.S. Post Office—cheaper bulk mailing rates, postal money orders, rural free delivery (RFD began in 1896), and parcel post (1913)—enormously expanded mail-order profits. Championed by the Grange and other farmers' organizations, these postal innovations were fought bitterly by express companies, local storekeepers, and the National Association of Grocers. However, by 1920 a package weighing 50 pounds could be sent by parcel post anywhere in the country from Chicago and a 70-pound package could be sent anywhere in the city's first three postal zones. In 1913, as another example of the importance of mail ordering, when 787 Wisconsin farm families were sampled about their consuming habits, 38 percent bought an average of 17 mail-order parcels a year.

Unlike the country store, where customers could inspect products, mail-order merchandising required constant attention to its credibility. Firms used their catalog covers to de-pict their urban distribution centers and warehouses as efficient, well-planned beehives of clerks who diligently filled thousands of orders a day from a seemingly inexhaustible cornucopia of products. Sears sold cheap sets of stereopticon slides depicting his Chicago headquarters, branch offices, plants, and warehouses in cities throughout the country. In 1924, the Sears catalog claim as "The World's Largest Store" was applied to radio advertising as the company adopted WLS as its call letters.

Catalogs prompted heated conflicts. Country storekeepers and small-town editors waged a prolonged and vitriolic campaign against catalogs. Local merchants urged townspeople and farmers to bring catalogs to "Home Town Industry Jubilee and Bonfires," where country store owners paid a dollar in trade for every new catalog used as fuel for the huge bonfire they burned in the town's public square. Prizes of up to $50 were offered to those folks who collected the largest number of "Wish Books" for public immolation.

Catalogs influenced other aspects of everyday rural life. Installment buying came to the countryside through mail-order merchandising. The "Farmer's Bible" doubled as an encyclopedia in many rural schoolhouses. Children practiced arithmetic by adding up orders, did geography from its postal zone maps, and tried figure drawing by tracing the catalog's models. The "Big Books" (1,064 pages in 1921) served as home almanacs, since they usually contained inspirational readings, poetry, and farming and household tips.

—*Thomas Schlereth*

### References
Latham, Frank B. *A Century of Serving Customers: The Story of Montgomery Ward.* Chicago: Montgomery Ward, 1972.
Schlereth, Thomas J. "Country Stores, County Fairs, and Mail-Order Catalogs: Consumerism in Rural America." In Simon J. Bonner, ed., *Accumulation and Display: Consumerism in America.* New York: W. W. Norton, 1987.
———. *Cultural History and Material Culture: Everyday Life, Landscapes, Museums.* Charlottesville: University of Virginia Press, 1992.
Stevenson, Katherine C., and H. Ward Jandl. *Houses by Mail: A Guide to Houses from the Sears, Roebuck Company.* Washington, DC: Preservation Press, 1986.

## The Main Line (Philadelphia, Pennsylvania)

Ironically, the Philadelphia Main Line, one of the best-known and most prestigious suburban areas in the United States, takes its name from humble origins. The first of these is the "main line" of public works, a system of railroads and canals, constructed in the 1820s and 1830s and owned by the state of Pennsylvania, which ran westward from Philadelphia to Pittsburgh. Later, the "main line" of the Pennsylvania Railroad coincided with or paralleled this route, thereby opening land along its right-of-way for suburban living. It was the straightening and improvement of this railroad in the late 1860s, combined with post–Civil War prosperity, that made the Main Line a Mecca for well-to-do Philadelphians who wanted to escape the more unpleasant aspects of the city while they continued to earn substantial incomes by commuting the ten or so miles downtown every day. In fact, much of the land along the Pennsylvania route was developed by the railroad itself or by executives connected with the company.

Actually, the Main Line is a collective term for a succession of suburban communities that radiate out from various stations along the old Pennsylvania Railroad (now owned by Conrail and used by the South East Pennsylvania Transportation Authority, or SEPTA, for its commuter trains). The most important of these stations, which correspond by and large with the various suburbs' names, are Overbrook, Merion, Wynnewood, Ardmore, Haverford, Bryn Mawr, Rosemont, Villanova, Radnor, St. David's, Wayne, Devon, and Paoli. During the late nineteenth and early twentieth centuries, these suburbs, and particularly those further out from the city, were renowned for their large country houses and surrounding acreage, as well as for their Episcopal churches, country clubs, cricket grounds, golf courses, and even fox hunting clubs—Anglophilic customs and pursuits that were attractive to the Anglo-American social elite up and down the East Coast.

By the mid-twentieth century, the Main Line was a favorite setting for novels, plays, and movies about upper-class suburbia. The most celebrated of these was *The Philadelphia Story*, a comedy by Philip Barry (1942), which was the basis for a movie of the same name and later a musical entitled "High Society." More precisely, Barry's play was based on life at a large estate in the suburb of Villanova. The Main Line's rolling hills and reputation for healthful country living have also made it an attractive site for institutions of higher learning, such as Bryn Mawr College, Haverford College, Rosemont College, and Villanova University.

During the post–World War II period, with the proliferation of automobiles and the construction of fast commuter highways into Philadelphia, the Main Line suburbs grew less dependent upon the railroad. Consequently, residential development began to sprawl into every conceivable open space in the area, including many of the large country estates whose owners, beset by higher taxes, inflation, and the disappearance of cheap servants, could no longer afford to maintain them.

As the twentieth century comes to an end, many parts of the Main Line contain tract housing that differs little from its counterparts elsewhere. These coexist, however, with some remaining large estates and thousands of older dwellings that have retained the ambiance of wealth and good taste. The Main Line thus remains a prestigious address for Philadelphia suburbanites as well as an important example of early railroad suburbs.

—*David R. Contosta*

### References

Baltzell, E. Digby. *Philadelphia Gentlemen: The Making of a National Upper Class*. New York: Quadrangle, 1971.

Farris, John T. *Old Roads out of Philadelphia*. Philadelphia: J. B. Lippincott, 1917.

Farrow, Barbara Alyce. *The History of Bryn Mawr*. Bryn Mawr, PA: Committee of Residents, 1962.

Maier, Phyllis C., and Mary Mendenhall Wood, eds. *Lower Merion: A History*. Ardmore, PA: Lower Merion Historical Society, 1988.

Townsend, J. W. *"The Old Main Line."* Philadelphia: n.p., 1922.

## Mariemont, Ohio

In 1914, Mary Emery, a prominent philanthropist in Cincinnati, Ohio, decided to memorialize her late husband by constructing a new town to provide decent housing for the working poor of her city. With the aid of Charles Livingood, a friend of her deceased son, she quietly and gradually acquired almost 400 acres of land by 1921 on a site overlooking the Little Miami River valley about ten miles east of downtown Cincinnati. Livingood commissioned John Nolen (1869–1937) to plan Mariemont, which Emery named after the family's vacation estate in Rhode Island.

Nolen's planning background included numerous designs for company towns and replanning projects for suburbs throughout the United States. He intended Mariemont to be his first new town explicitly based on the garden city idea put forth by Ebenezer Howard in England in 1898. Using the garden cities of Letchworth (1903) and Welwyn (1920) in Britain as models, Nolen devised a plan for his new town "in accordance with American ideas."

His plan combined a radial baroque town center with several residential neighborhoods of curvilinear design. Nolen designated the town center as the site of commercial and retail activities and located municipal offices and services here. He advised Emery and Livingood to construct a variety of housing types including row houses, duplexes, and detached homes. He supplied each neighborhood with parks and public spaces, churches, and wide streets free of overhead wires. Mariemont had its own steam-heating facility and sewage-disposal plant in the "industrial park" below the Little Miami River bluff just south of the community. Nolen hoped that these utilities would create income for the Mariemont Development Company by selling services to the adjacent towns of Madisonville and Fairfax. Unlike orthodox English garden cities, Mariemont had no permanent reserve of rural land other than a short-lived model farm. The Norfolk and Western Railway ran south of the village, through the industrial park, and the main east-west axis of the plan used the Wooster Pike highway to connect Mariemont with downtown Cincinnati. An electric street railway already served the adjacent town of Madisonville, within easy walking distance of Mariemont's town center.

Mariemont represents the way in which Nolen's planning philosophy emphasized both the local and the metropolitan nature of any place. By understanding the metropolis as a collection of contiguous communities, the neighborhood became an essential element in Nolen's planning vocabulary. Mariemont stood as Nolen's solution to the problem of suburban isolation and alienation rather than as a solution to Cincinnati's big-city slum problem.

On the surface, the layout of Mariemont is strikingly similar to the plans for the British garden cities of Letchworth and Welwyn, drawn by Unwin and Parker. But read more deeply, the Mariemont plan contradicts one of the fundamental tenets of English garden city planners. Because Nolen designed Mariemont as a small suburban town with the intention of encouraging metropolitan expansion, the underpinnings of the plan were essentially at odds with Ebenezer Howard's garden city. Nolen did not build Mariemont to contain Cincinnati; rather he designed it to draw the metropolis beyond its existing borders and connect new suburban development with other parts of the city.

Mariemont exemplifies the "Americanization" of the garden city idea from one that saw large cities as problems to one that found a solution in the metropolis. Rejecting the idea that the metropolis had to be contained, Nolen adapted the garden city form to the problem of organizing urban and suburban growth. He designed Mariemont as a garden city according to American ideas of metropolitanism, but in doing so he did not abandon what he thought were the socially beneficial aspects of Howard's ideal city. He tried to create community both in the suburb of Mariemont and in the larger metropolitan arena of Cincinnati.

—*Bradley Cross*

**See also**
Nolen, John.
**Reference**
Nolen, John. *General Plan of Mariemont: A New Town.* Cambridge, MA: John Nolen, 1921.

## Marsh, Reginald (1898–1954)

Reginald Marsh created nearly 1,000 paintings, over 200 prints, and hundreds of drawings, cartoons, and magazine and book illustrations during a career centered in New York City. After he graduated from Yale in 1920, his cartoons and illustrations for the *New York Daily News,* the *New Yorker,* and *Vanity Fair* in the 1920s presaged his most significant urban themes, which pervaded his paintings and prints from about 1928 on.

Particularly during the 1930s, his subjects covered the full range of urban life, from opera house to burlesque hall, from Broadway to the Battery, from the Bowery underworld, where the maimed bodies of its denizens are hemmed in by the girders of the elevated railroad, to the edge city of Coney Island, where muscled men and corpulent women find libidinous release. The energy of his line and the occasional garishness of his colors were well suited for depicting the city as a performance space for display and for voyeurism, where grand gestures and minute details are equally significant. Able to depict the skyscrapers of Wall Street and lower Manhattan, he focused especially on the details of urban life: the rivets of bridge girders, the flutings of fire hydrants, the crumbled fedoras of men in breadlines. Advertising signs, salacious newspaper headlines, theater marquees, and sideshow banners surround the taxi dancers, sailors on leave, laborers, strippers, and subway riders who populate his images.

In many of his works, women are the objects of a male gaze, yet their position gives them a power over men who seem able only to watch rather than to possess them. One can thus read his images for their thick documentary description, for their sociological suggestiveness, and for their ability to convey the psychological complexity of urban life; his crowded, even claustrophobic, scenes infuse the diverse vitality of urban life with undercurrents of alienation, anonymity, and vulnerability.

Marsh's comfortable family background could easily have insulated him from the crush of this urban population, but he sought it out, establishing his studios on or near Fourteenth Street and Union Square and constantly wandering the city and its Coney Island retreat with sketchbook or camera in hand, celebrating and satirizing the crowds around him, at one point writing, "I felt fortunate indeed to be a citizen of New York, the greatest and most magnificent of all cities in a new and vital country whose history had scarcely been recorded in art."

—*Richard N. Masteller*

**References**
Cohen, Marilyn. *Reginald Marsh's New York: Paintings, Drawings, Prints and Photographs.* New York: Whitney Museum of American Art in association with Dover Publications, 1983.
Goodrich, Lloyd. *Reginald Marsh.* New York: Harry N. Abrams, 1972.

Laning, Edward. *The Sketchbooks of Reginald Marsh*. Greenwich, CT: New York Graphic Society, 1973.

Sasowsky, Norman. *The Prints of Reginald Marsh: An Essay and Definitive Catalog of His Linoleum Cuts, Etchings, Engravings, and Lithographs*. New York: Clarkson Potter, 1976.

## Mass Transit

Mass transit consists of multipassenger conveyances that operate along fixed routes, with regular stops, on frequent schedules, and with set fares. There are now more than 1,190 mass transit systems in the United States that carry a total of 8.1 billion passengers annually. The major transit service, or mode, today is the bus, which accounts for 67 percent of all passengers. Electric railways, subways, trolleys, and ferryboats are also important and have been more important in the past.

Mass transit is a relatively new phenomenon. Before the early nineteenth century, no city anywhere in the world had a mass transit system. In the preindustrial city, most people got around on foot. The preeminence of pedestrian traffic set the radius of the preindustrial city at about two miles, a distance that men and women could walk in about half an hour.

The world's first mass transit vehicle was the omnibus. Introduced in Nantes, France, in 1826, the omnibus was a horse-drawn wagon that carried 12 to 20 passengers and reached a speed of five miles per hour. Filling the demand for improved transportation that had been created by urban population growth, the omnibus became a business success. By the 1830s, the omnibus had spread to Paris, London, and such American cities as New York, Boston, Philadelphia, Brooklyn, Washington, D.C., and New Orleans. In 1832, more than 100 coaches were running in New York City.

In the United States, omnibus service was usually initiated by entrepreneurs in related enterprises—such as livery stables and teamsters—and operated as small businesses. Private omnibus companies received franchises from local governments that entitled them to use city streets. In return, the companies had to pay licensing fees, pass vehicular safety inspections, and meet other rudimentary operating standards. An omnibus ride usually cost 10 cents, a high price that confined its ridership to middle-class residents.

Another transit mode, the horse railway, was pioneered in New York City in November 1832. Like the omnibus, the horse railway was a wooden box on wheels that was pulled by horses. But unlike the omnibus, which ran directly on the rough, poorly maintained city streets, horsecars glided on iron rails that had been sunk below the surface of the street. The use of iron rails reduced friction to a minimum and brought about marked service improvements. Horsecars made speeds up to eight miles per hour, about one-third faster than the omnibus; hauled three times more passengers for the same investment of energy; and allowed for more com-fortable rides. By the 1850s horse railway lines had been introduced in Boston, Philadelphia, Pittsburgh, Cincinnati, St. Louis, Chicago, and Newark. The new service surpassed the omnibus in total ridership and became the country's dominant urban transit mode.

The horse railway became the first mode to reveal mass transit's great impact, the reshaping of urban form. Although the omnibus had moved too slowly to have much impact on urban geography, the faster horsecar enabled residents to live farther from their places of employment without having to spend more time traveling. Consequently, the horsecar stimulated residential construction in outlying sections of such cities as Boston, New York, Pittsburgh, and St. Louis and led to the development of a ring of suburbs three to four miles from the center.

As they became indispensable to urban life, horse railways were increasingly blamed for a range of urban problems. Urbanites complained that the cars aggravated traffic congestion, caused accidents, and fouled the streets with wastes from horses. Horse railways also contributed to social tensions by throwing all kinds of people together in crowded spaces, thus heightening class, racial, ethnic, and gender tensions. With an average fare of 5 cents, horse railways were patronized by working-class as well as by middle-class riders.

In the mid-nineteenth century, businessmen and inventors began to search for mechanical forms of propulsion that might replace the horse railway. In 1873, Andrew S. Hallidie inaugurated the world's first cable railway on San Francisco's steep hills. Although the cable railway became a dominant form of transportation in only a few places, such as San Francisco and Chicago, it was adopted by more than 25 other American cities. Cable railway track peaked at 305 miles in 1893. This proliferation of cable railways was due as much to the horse railway's shortcomings as to its own strengths. High capital costs restricted the location of cable railways to built-up areas, and frequent breakdowns impaired cable operations. When a superior source of mechanical propulsion became available at the end of the nineteenth century, most cable railways were scrapped. In the 1990s, the only surviving cable railways are three short lines in San Francisco that cater mostly to the tourist industry.

The single most important innovation in mass transit history was that of electrical power. In 1888, Frank J. Sprague, a former U.S. Navy officer, successfully electrified a railway in Richmond, Virginia. Sprague's line proved that electrification was a clean, fast, inexpensive, lightweight, and mechanically reliable source of energy that was superior to alternative propulsion systems. Electric railways—called trolleys—had lower capital costs than cable railways, lower operating costs than horse railways, and higher speeds than either. In the

*The Metro Center subway station in Washington, D.C., in 1995.*

1890s, electric railway construction boomed, and trolleys became the dominant transit mode in American cities. By 1902, electric railways accounted for 97 percent of the country's total street railway track of 22,577 miles. Private electric railway companies carried nearly 7.8 billion riders per year. Electricity also increased the "riding habit"—people rode more frequently as travel became more convenient. Between 1890 and 1902, per capita ridership more than doubled, from 32 to 79 trips a year.

Electrification fostered monopolistic tendencies within the industry. The pattern was that the small, independent businesses were consolidated into gigantic corporations that controlled nearly all of a city's transit lines. The rise of powerful corporations that were unresponsive to popular demands for better service, combined with growing ridership, led to widespread public disenchantment with mass transit.

In the 1920s electric railway companies encountered financial problems. One difficulty was that the inflation following World War I increased the fuel and equipment costs that companies paid. Long-term franchise agreements prohibited companies from raising their fares. Private companies that did petition for fare increases and service reductions often found their requests rejected by regulatory commissions that defined transit as a public service rather than as a private business and that reflected the popular resentment of poor passenger service.

A second reason for the decline of mass transit was the emergence of the automobile as a competitor. The number of private automobiles in the United States climbed from 458,000 in 1910 to 22.9 million in 1930. The competition between mass transit and the automobile was shaped by distorted public policy definitions. Although transit companies were defined as self-supporting, profit-making businesses, privately owned automobiles were thought to be a public entity that deserved government support through highway construction and cheap fuel prices. This belief distorted patterns of public spending and provided heavy subsidies to automobiles that were denied to mass transit. As a result, patronage of mass transit dropped from 23 billion riders in 1926 to 7.3 billion in 1970. Most railway companies abandoned track or discontinued routes; many disappeared as profit-making businesses as their lines were taken over by public authorities.

Since the 1970s mass transit has experienced a modest revival. This resurgence was initiated by the Urban Mass

Transit Act of 1964, which represented a shift in federal planning and funding priorities, and it was propelled by the rising gasoline prices of the 1970s. From its lows in the early 1970s, mass transit patronage climbed to 8.5 billion in the 1990s. Despite these gains, however, mass transit remains a secondary source of transportation. In 1990 there were only three large cities in the United States—New York, Washington, D.C., and San Francisco—where at least one-third of the workers used mass transit to commute to work. Elsewhere, and particularly in suburbs built on the metropolitan periphery since World War II, the automobile remains the chief source of urban and suburban transportation.

—*Clifton Hood*

**See also**
Buses; Cable Cars; Horsecars; Interurban Transit; Omnibuses; Rapid Transit; Streetcars; Subways.

**References**
Barrett, Paul. *The Automobile and Urban Transit: The Formation of Public Policy in Chicago, 1900–1930.* Philadelphia: Temple University Press, 1983.
Cudahy, Brian J. *Cash, Tokens, and Transfers: A History of Urban Mass Transit in North America.* New York: Fordham University Press, 1990.
Holt, Glen E. "The Changing Perception of Urban Pathology: An Essay on the Development of Mass Transit in the United States." In Kenneth T. Jackson and Stanley K. Schultz, eds., *Cities in American History,* 324–343. New York: Knopf, 1972

## Master Plan

A master plan is a document designed to provide a generation-long, comprehensive strategy for the development of a particular city. Introduced shortly after 1900, the master plan is a uniquely American concept that has played an important role in city planning practice for much of the twentieth century. The master plan was conceptualized as a means of imposing order on the turn-of-the-century industrial city and has been used by planners as a means of pulling the disjointed elements of the city together into a coherent whole.

From the earliest plans, such as those of Henry Wright for St. Louis (1907) and Daniel H. Burnham for Chicago (1909), master plans have exhibited a standard format. They generally have contained coordinated schemes involving the transportation system, placement of public facilities, land use issues, and calls for greater municipal control. In this way, master plans have sought to guide the reshaping of the city into a single functional unit.

What differentiates the master plan from other planning tools has been a conscious effort to treat the city in a holistic fashion. Reflecting a belief that the city and its inhabitants exist as a unified whole, the binding of the plan itself has come to symbolize the conviction by master planners that the city must exist as a community.

The first generation of master planners—Burnham, Wright, Harland Bartholomew, John Nolen, and Frederick Law Olmsted, Jr.—were excited by turn-of-the-century European experiments in large-scale urban transformation such as the Ring Strasse in Vienna. But realizing that projects like this had been accomplished in authoritarian states, American planners saw the master plan as a means to achieve a new urban order within a democratic framework. For them, the master plan could operate as an urban constitution. While the plan might call for taking private land, it provided a rationale for such action. According to the early master planners, even though the plan originated with the planner, it became the will of the people once it was adopted as the plan of the people.

The master plan, however, went through a fundamental shift during the late 1910s and early 1920s. For the second generation of master planners, the master plan embodied the potential for control that they, as planners, could exercise over the city. Armed with new tools like zoning, master planners believed that through the plan they could mold the city into any shape they desired. So while the plan still contained all of the same elements that it originally possessed, these master planners saw the plan more as an expression of their scientific expertise than as an act of democracy.

Although virtually every American city had prepared a master plan by the end of the 1920s, master planner visions of grandeur disappeared with the Depression. Since most American cities had trouble remaining solvent, long-term master plans ceased being a priority. But World War II and the postwar period brought about a resurgence of the master plan. As city after city in the United States attempted to come to grips with urban blight and the challenge of suburbanization, the master plan returned to favor. Containing glossy visions of the city-of-tomorrow, the master plan supplied the justification for the massive urban renewal projects of the 1950s and early 1960s.

In the late 1960s, though, the master plan came under increasing fire. With racial unrest and accelerating urban decay, the hope of urban control and community faded away. Indeed, the notions of control and community were the very things that critics of the master plan railed against. For opponents of the idea of master plans, such as urban critics Neil Anderson, Robert Goodman, and Jane Jacobs, it was an ineffectual effort to gain control of the city. For such thinkers, planners were unable to determine the future of the city in the next six months, let alone 25 years. Moreover, for them, the master plan denied the pluralistic nature of the city and did not acknowledge that the city existed as many communities. Consequently, the attempt to fashion the city into a single entity made the plan an instrument of domination by the city's elites.

By the end of the 1960s, even planners were moving away from the idea of the master plan. They no longer believed that the city could exist as a cohesive whole and gravitated toward solving individual, short-term problems. Thus, the master plan has played a limited role in American planning in recent years.

—*Mark Abbott*

**See also**
Zoning.
**References**
Abbott, Mark. "The Master Plan: A History of an Idea." Ph.D. dissertation, Purdue University, 1985.
Kent, T. J., Jr. *The Urban General Plan*. San Francisco: Chandler Publishing, 1964.
Scott, Mel. *American City Planning since 1890*. Berkeley: University of California Press, 1971.

## Matthews, Mark Allison (1867–1940)

Mark Matthews, a Presbyterian clergyman and political activist, had a ministry marked by a unique combination of evangelical fundamentalism and social gospel activism. Born in Calhoun, Georgia, on September 24, 1867, Matthews received his education at the local academy and was initially ordained in the Cumberland branch of the Presbyterian Church. Beginning his ministry in Calhoun, Matthews immediately began engaging in civic reform and social issues. He accepted a pastorate in Dalton, Georgia, in 1893 before moving to Jackson, Tennessee, in 1896. There, at the First Presbyterian Church, Matthews spearheaded efforts to establish a hospital, night school, humane society, and town library.

Called to Seattle's First Presbyterian Church in 1902, Matthews quickly established himself as a powerful voice in city affairs. Believing that the "church is my force and the city is my field," Matthews immersed himself in urban issues ranging from investigating the city's red-light district to civic reform. He waged vigorous campaigns against Seattle mayors, police chiefs, business leaders, saloonkeepers, and anyone else he believed corrupt. His church played a major role in recalling Seattle's mayor in 1910. As in Tennessee, Matthews's congregation became the model of an institutional church. From night schools and unemployment bureaus to kindergartens and antituberculosis work, Matthews never ceased working to build what he considered a more righteous community.

Exercising autocratic authority and delivering a compelling message, Matthews built First Presbyterian into the denomination's largest congregation in the country with nearly 10,000 members, and Presbyterians elected him national moderator of the church in 1912. He founded the first church-owned and -operated radio station in the country, led efforts for a major hospital in Seattle, and was elected to be a freeholder for reform of city government.

Matthews ranks as the most influential clergyman in the Pacific Northwest during the first half of the twentieth century. In a region that had, and still has, the lowest percentage of church membership in the nation, Matthews's ministry stands as remarkable testimony to his influence on an urban community.

—*Dale E. Soden*

**References**
Russell, C. Allyn. "Mark Allison Matthews: Seattle Fundamentalist and Civic Reformer." *Journal of Presbyterian History* 57 (1979): 446–466.
Soden, Dale E. "Mark Allison Matthews: Seattle's Minister Rediscovered." *Pacific Northwest Quarterly* 74 (1983): 50–58.

## Mayor-Council Government

Diversity is a hallmark of American politics, and nowhere is this more evident than in the ways the nation governs itself locally. There are some 80,000 units of local government in the United States, few of which are exactly alike. To some extent, this variety is a function of the size of the country, the variety of local and regional cultures, and a commitment to the principle of self-government. But the diversity also reflects differing understandings of the democratic creed, and disagreements about the appropriate role of the public in the governing process. And it reflects, also, an enduring faith in the efficacy of institutional engineering, a belief that the organization of government has a profound impact on who wins and who loses politically.

These ideological and institutional differences are evident, for example, in the perennial debates over the kind of charter a municipality should adopt. Charters are one of the wellsprings of a city's corporate life, and an important statement about political values. As such they are frequent targets of those seeking to legitimate their particular vision of democratic politics.

Over the years, two radically different visions of democratic politics have dominated the debate. One of these is the mayor-council form of government; the other the council-manager plan. Today, some variant of these two plans operates in roughly 90 percent of the nation's communities larger than 2,500 in population.

The mayor and manager plans were late-nineteenth and early-twentieth-century American inventions. Both were part of efforts to adjust democratic institutions to the twin realities of urbanization and industrialization. These two revolutions posed new challenges to local government and resulted in vastly expanded municipal responsibilities and budgets. Unfortunately, although the challenges had increased, local government's capacity to deal with them had not. This, at least, was a common theme among a generation of reformers, as was the assumption that municipal government suffered from a number of structural deficiencies. One deficiency was too much democracy—too many elected offices and too frequent elections—itself the result of haphazard growth during the nineteenth century. As new problems had arisen, new agencies had been created, often with their own independent electoral base and seldom with any mandate to cooperate, one with the other, for the sake of the common good.

Nor, it was said, could one expect much from the general institutions of government. Mayors, for example, were typically secondary figures; indeed, for much of the century, they were little more than adjuncts of the city council. Councils, on the other hand, were major actors, at least on paper, with extensive charter authority over the affairs of the community. But the councils themselves were of little help; in fact, they were part of the problem, weakened, as they were, by parochialism and partisanship. At-large and nonpartisan elections, both of which were introduced at the time, helped alleviate these problems somewhat. But many of the most serious problems were more fundamental, rooted in the very nature of legislative assemblies. The council was a collective body, consisting of coequal members. And while perhaps freed from parochial and partisan constraints, they were often limited by differing visions of the common good and how best to achieve it. To move legislation through this kind of institution often required time-consuming bargaining and vote trading—logrolling of the sort that gave legislatures the reputation, often well-deserved, of being irresponsible and incoherent.

Municipal systems were also flawed by relatively short electoral cycles. By the late nineteenth century, the one-year term of office had been expanded to two, but officials still had difficulty accomplishing much in such a short period. Worse yet, the electoral cycle made officials far too dependent on political parties, which, though often corrupt, nonetheless controlled nominations to office and the grassroots organizations needed to win.

The remedy, according to reformers, was to simplify government by eliminating the myriad of independent municipal bodies and by centralizing authority in the hands of the city's executive and city council. This was the major thrust of both the council-manager and mayor-council plans. Proponents of both schemes agreed that structure was a large part of the problem, and both agreed it could be fixed. They disagreed, however, in two important respects: ideologically, with respect to their outlook on politics, and institutionally, with respect to the appropriate role of elections and elected public officials in the governmental process.

The mayor-council form came first. In 1899, the newly organized National Municipal League adopted a Model City Charter that called for a strong mayor–council form of government as part of its reform platform. As envisioned by the league, the mayor-council form would be an uncluttered, hierarchical arrangement. Policymaking would be the responsibility of a small, single-chambered city council (by this time, most communities had abandoned bicameralism) and a mayor.

The centerpiece of the model, however, was the mayor. The mayor would be chief executive in fact as well as in name. Unlike mayors earlier in the century, the new mayor would be elected by the people, not appointed by the council, and would have important administrative and legislative powers: the executive budget, for example, and the two-thirds veto. Department and agency heads would be directly accountable to the mayor, not, as before, to city council committees or to various boards and commissions. Finally, other public employees would be appointed and evaluated on the basis of their competence and performance rather than on the basis of their political connections.

What made the strong mayor–council system so attractive to its champions was its promise of more efficient and more accountable democratic government. The mayor was a "single mind and a single will" who would be able to coordinate municipal affairs. The office would also be more intelligible to an electorate that had been all too easily confused by divided authority and all too easily manipulated by political parties. Since voters understood that a great deal depended on the character of the mayor, party leaders would henceforth be constrained in whom they nominated for the office.

Despite early successes, the ideal of strong mayoral leadership has never been fully accepted. For some, the model ignores the nation's constitutional tradition by investing too much power in one office and paying too little heed to the necessity of a strong system of checks and balances. For others, the concerns are as much substantive as structural, a belief, especially among minorities with strong opinions about policies and programs, that their interests would be better served if entrusted to a specialized agency at some distance removed from the mayor, the council, and elections generally.

Even among early reformers, the mayor-council plan eventually fell from favor. The problem, in brief, was politics. Whatever their merits, mayors and councils were, above all else, political officials, subject to the vagaries and uncertainties of the electoral process and always at risk of losing office. Success, moreover, was often contingent on cultivating voter support, a political imperative that often caused mayors and other elected officials to promote a more active role for government than reformers considered proper, wise, or economical. What was needed, instead, was a plan that insulated the governmental process from elections and indeed from elected officials.

The answer lay in the manager-council plan, which the National Municipal League endorsed in its 1915 Model City Charter. The plan embodied a radically different vision of democratic politics. There would be an elected council responsible for setting broad policies. But council members would be part-time citizen legislators who would be paid only token salaries and thus forced to divide their attention between tending the city's affairs and their own. Full-time responsibility for implementing council policy, and for handling day-to-day matters, was entrusted to a professional manager who was appointed, not elected, accountable to the council, not the voters, and (in theory at least) indifferent to politics and policymaking.

Although the ideal of strong mayoral leadership has never been universally or fully accepted, the office today is generally far stronger, in terms of charter authority, than it was when the National Municipal League first endorsed it at the turn of the century. The most impressive powers, the line-item veto, for example, and the executive budget, enhance the mayor's role in the legislative process, something that reflects the reformers' uneasiness with representative assemblies. Less impressive, but nevertheless substantial, are the mayor's powers over the executive branch. These include the authority to hire and fire key department heads and to shape, through staffing decisions and the budget process, agency priorities and spending programs.

Of all the features of the office, however, none surpasses in importance the mayor's electoral base. The electoral connection is critical. Mayoral elections, for example, are typically high stimulus ones, and no other local election is as consistently able to focus as much attention on as wide a range of issues. None affords citizens the opportunity to scrutinize as intensely the policies and personalities of aspirants to office. And having survived the scrutiny, no other local official can speak as authoritatively as can the mayor in the role of elected representative and political symbol of the entire community. These are powerful assets in a democratic society.

Mayors have used these assets to expand the role of the office far beyond the boundaries set forth in municipal charters and legal commentaries. Over the years, mayors have assumed responsibility for defining what is important to the community and for proposing appropriate agendas for public action. Equally important, mayors early on used their electoral connection to forge direct links to the electorate—links that were independent of party, just as reformers had hoped, but independent of reformers as well. And by making the office the focal point of popular and elite expectations, mayors also moved the office stage center in municipal arenas.

Mayors have also assumed a leadership role in the broader arenas of state and national politics. Accountable to the voters, and not to the state legislature, governor, or presi-dent, mayors have often been an independent force for local communities. As such, they have embraced a vision of the office that includes, in addition to managing such municipal services as water, sewerage, public safety, and public works, promoting the social and economic well-being of the community's population.

This has been a defining characteristic of the office, evident, for example, during the 1920s and 1930s, in mayoral attacks on resurgent nativism in northern cities and in mayoral initiatives to alleviate the severe economic hardships that plagued the country during the three and one-half years between the onset of the Depression and the advent of the New Deal. The issues differ today, but mayors remain important actors in the national dialogue on such questions as nuclear power, child abuse, racial and ethnic tensions, poverty, environmental degradation, and the economic viability and livability of the nation's older communities. On occasion they have even been major voices in national debates over defense and foreign policy, as was the case during the war in Vietnam.

Being a player in these broader arenas is important partly because both the problems and their solutions often transcend municipal boundaries. But there is another factor, frequently overlooked, that gives mayoral leadership in these arenas special meaning—namely the structure of urban governance. Local governments are created by the state, and the state (and increasingly the federal government as well) determines how public authority and public resources are to be distributed.

As it turns out, municipalities are usually only one of several government units operating within the geographic boundaries of a town or city. States differ in this respect, but more often than not municipalities, and mayors, have little if any fiscal or administrative control over such key programs as education, transportation, or welfare. States typically delegate responsibility for these programs to other units of local government, such as counties, special districts, independent school districts, or public authorities.

Although they have little if any jurisdiction in these areas, mayors often are very much a part of the public (and private) dialogue about what these governments do, and how they go about doing it. And they are major actors, more generally, in the competition among governments to control scarce resources. Local tax dollars are the most obvious of these, but so too, especially since the 1960s, are state and federal program funds.

The mayor-council plan today is a far different system of government than that envisioned by the National Municipal League in its 1899 Model City Charter. The major difference is the mayor's expanded political role, something that is at some distance removed from the ideal outlined by the league. The office has expanded, and the mayor today is usually the single most influential actor in municipal affairs. Much of this has been at the expense of city councils, which is not to say that councils are everywhere and always "burned-out volcanoes," as some claim they are. In larger cities especially, the council remains a formidable legislative presence, ignored only at considerable peril. But even in larger cities, the mayor is at the center of a community's political and governmental life, and the mayor is the one, above all others, to whom citizens look for that difficult-to-define, but no less important, quality—leadership.

—*Russell D. Murphy*

**See also**
Council-Manager Government.

**References**
Banfield, Edward C., and James Q. Wilson. *City Politics.* Cambridge, MA: Harvard University Press, 1963.
Beard, Charles Austin. *American City Government: A Survey of Newer Tendencies.* New York: The Century Company, 1912.
Coleman, James S. *Community Conflict.* Glencoe, IL: Free Press, 1957.
Dahl, Robert. *Who Governs? Democracy and Power in an American City.* New Haven, CT: Yale University Press, 1961.
Goodnow, Frank J. *Municipal Government.* New York: The Century Company, 1909.
Kotter, John P., and Paul R. Lawrence. *Mayors in Action.* New York: Wiley, 1974.
Morgan, David R., and Sheilah S. Watson. "Policy Leadership in Council Manager Cities." *Public Administration Review* 52 (1992): 438–446.
Munro, William Bennett. *Municipal Government and Administration.* New York: Macmillan, 1923.
Murphy, Russell D. "The Mayoralty and the Democratic Creed: The Evolution of an Ideology and an Institution." *Urban Affairs Quarterly* 22 (1986): 3–23.
Pressman, Jeffrey. "The Preconditions of Mayoral Leadership." *American Political Science Review* 66 (1972): 511–524.
Rowe, Leo S. "A Summary of the Program." In *Report of a Committee of the National Municipal League, Adopted by the League, November 17, 1899.* New York: Macmillan, 1900.
Sayre, Wallace, and Herbert Kaufman. *Governing New York City: Politics in the Metropolis.* New York: Russell Sage Foundation, 1960.
Svara, James H. *Official Leadership in the City: Patterns of Conflict and Cooperation.* New York: Oxford University Press, 1990.
Yates, Douglas. *The Ungovernable City.* Cambridge, MA: MIT Press, 1977.

## McPherson, Aimee Semple (1890–1944)

The flamboyant life of Aimee Semple McPherson, who founded the Church of the Foursquare Gospel, brought her worldwide fame. Born on a Canadian farm on October 9, 1890, McPherson was introduced to Christianity through the Salvation Army, in which her mother was active. While still a teenager, McPherson became a Pentecostal, and after feeling a call to preach, she bought a tent and began to barnstorm around the United States. With healings occurring in her ministry, she rapidly gained a following.

In the early 1920s she moved to Los Angeles, California, where she settled permanently. She also built the Angelus Temple, which cost $1.5 million. She developed a distinctly urban style of revival, as opposed to the more common tent and open air gatherings held in rural locations. Her sermons were highly dramatic—theatrical, in fact—and she would preach in costumes that mirrored her sermons. On one occasion, she titled the sermon "God's Law" and delivered it dressed as a police officer.

Aimee Semple McPherson was an enigma to many. She founded a church that condemned divorce, yet she was divorced. She preached the love and peace of Christ, yet she was involved in one stormy lawsuit after another. A few years before her death, she punched her mother and broke her nose. The scandal that scarred her ministry and haunted her until her death was her mysterious disappearance on May 18, 1926, while she was swimming in the sea off Ocean Park, California. McPherson was presumed drowned, but five weeks later she appeared and told a story about being kidnapped and held for ransom. Her tale, including her masterful escape and a perilous flight across the desert, made headlines around the world and McPherson the most famous woman in the United States. The Los Angeles district attorney was suspicious, however, claiming that she had run off with her radio engineer. A grand jury investigated; charges were brought against her but then dropped, and the matter was never solved.

The Angelus Temple remained McPherson's headquarters for nearly 20 years until she died in 1944. The church that she founded was expected to fold when she died, but it has confounded the pundits and flown in the face of Aimee Semple McPherson's scandal-scarred and troubled life, remaining her legacy.

—*James Henslin*

**References**
Blumhofer, Edith L. *Aimee Semple McPherson: Everybody's Sister.* Grand Rapids, MI: William B. Eerdmans, 1993.
Epstein, Daniel Mark. *Sister Aimee: The Life of Aimee Semple McPherson.* New York: Harcourt Brace Jovanovich, 1993.
Thomas, Lately. *Storming Heaven: The Lives and Turmoils of Minnie Kennedy and Aimee Semple McPherson.* New York: William Morrow, 1970.

## Megalopolis

In popular usage, *megalopolis* alternately describes a very large city or an expansive regional conurbation. As invented by the ancient Greeks and reinvented by the French geographer Jean Gottmann (1915–1994), however, the term refers to peopled places rather abstract spaces. For their part, the Greeks projected a Great City (Megalopolis) in the Peloponnesus that never lived up to its name; for his, Gottmann identified a "super-metropolitan" conurbation on the northeastern Atlan-

*The lights of Chicago and the surrounding area give only a faint idea of the extent of this megalopolis.*

tic seaboard of the United States that revolutionized the study of urbanization.

What Gottmann dubbed Megalopolis in 1957 was an "almost continuous stretch of urban and suburban areas" extending from Maine to Maryland. A linked "chain of metropolitan areas," including Boston, New York, Philadelphia, Baltimore, and Washington, anchored Megalopolis. But, transcending its "polynuclear origins," this "constellation of large cities" and suburban satellites had become an urban galaxy. Form followed function in the making of Megalopolis, as history and geography conspired to create a new urban form: the "dynamics of urbanization" on the northeastern Atlantic coast traced a trajectory from colonial "town" settlement and maritime trade-related growth to urban industrial development and suburbanization. If the unprecedented "concentration of population, of industrial and commercial facilities, of financial wealth and cultural activities" in Megalopolis is the result of its uniquely American history, this "pioneer area" pointed toward the future as well. "Although unique today," wrote Gottmann in 1957, "*Megalopolis* obviously has been and still is an extraordinarily interesting laboratory *in vivo* where much of what may well be accepted as the 'normalcies' of the advanced civilization of the latter part of the twentieth century is slowly shaping." Urbanists the world over soon put this proposition to the test, but none more successfully than the Japanese. Focusing their attention on the conurbation that stretched 500 kilometers along Honshu's Pacific coastline from Tokyo to Osaka, they pronounced it Tokaido Megaroporisu.

Antiurban critics of megalopolitan life in the 1960s upbraided Gottmann for his positive characterization of Megalopolitans as the world's "richest, best educated, best housed, and best serviced group of similar size"; others, who falsely identified a trend toward "counter-urbanization" and mistakenly projected the demise of Megalopolis, challenged his bold predictions in the 1970s. But, through it all, the concept of Megalopolis remained Gottmann's *idée fixe*. Not only did he continue to study megalopolises-in-the-making, he began to tinker with the concept itself. Having earlier identified Megalopolis as the "hinge" of the national economy, based on its extraordinary concentration of commercial, industrial, and financial activities, Gottmann later observed that "central cities" worldwide had begun to marshal the power of information. In the 1980s, this observation led him to envision "transactional cities," whose horizons extended beyond national borders to the global information society. Today, urban visionaries continue to envisage ecumenopolises (ecumenical cities) and global cities. Their urban dreams arguably owe, in large measure, to Jean Gottmann and his conceptualization of Megalopolis.

—*Jeffrey E. Hanes*

**References**

Gottmann, Jean. *The Coming of the Transactional City.* College Park: University of Maryland Institute for Urban Studies, 1983.

———. "Megalopolis; or, The Urbanization of the Northeastern Seaboard." *Economic Geography* 33 (1957): 189–200.

———. *Megalopolis: The Urbanized Northeastern Seaboard of the United States.* New York: The Twentieth Century Fund, 1961.

———. "Megalopolis Revisited: Twenty-Five Years Later." Institute for Urban Studies, Monograph No. 6. College Park: University of Maryland, 1987.

Gottmann, Jean, and Robert A. Harper, eds. *Since Megalopolis: The Urban Writings of Jean Gottmann.* Baltimore: Johns Hopkins University Press, 1990.

Konvitz, Joseph W., ed. Special Issue on Megalopolis. *The Journal of Urban History* 19 (1993).

## Memphis, Tennessee

Located on the Mississippi River and resting atop the Fourth Chickasaw Bluff approximately one-third of the way between the Missouri River and the Gulf of Mexico, Memphis grew out of various forts and settlements that belonged alternately to French, British, and Spanish governments in the eighteenth century. In 1818 General Andrew Jackson and a former governor of Tennessee, Isaac Shelby, purchased land from the Chickasaw Indians; the following year, Jackson and two other speculators, John Overton and James Winchester, founded Memphis, surveyed the town, and divided lots for sale.

In its early years, the city grew along with the flourishing Mississippi River trade. Served by flatboats, steamboats, and, finally, railroads, Memphis became an entrepot for the Mid-South—an area encompassing western Tennessee, northern Mississippi, eastern Arkansas, and the boot heel of Missouri—and the marketing capital for the region's growing cotton trade. Its fortunes entwined with King Cotton and, as the site of a lucrative slave market, the city evidenced southern sympathies in the antebellum years and voted overwhelmingly for secession after Fort Sumter.

Prior to the Civil War, a number of ethnic groups, most notably the Irish and Germans, gave Memphis a heterogeneous demographic makeup. But in the 1870s, a series of yellow fever epidemics, which led to a fiscal crisis and the substitution of a state-administered taxing district for local government, dramatically changed the city's population. Municipal records show that thousands of whites, especially Germans, fled the city and never returned, while most of the Irish remained and suffered staggering casualties.

After the last major epidemic in 1878, Memphis grew almost entirely by immigration from the surrounding countryside. By the end of the nineteenth century, Memphis's population was roughly half black and half white with virtually no first-generation immigrants. The steady influx of a native-born, rural population made Memphis, in H. L. Mencken's phrases, the "most-rural-minded city in the South"

and the "buckle of the Bible Belt" (a reference to the fundamentalist Christianity predominant in the rural environs).

Nevertheless, Memphis became the economic and cultural center for blacks living in the Mid-South. Beale Street, the "Main Street of Negro America," became the city's entertainment and vice center as well as the primary commercial district for the African-American community. In the early twentieth century, W. C. Handy, a black musician who moved to Memphis from nearby Clarksdale, Mississippi, wrote the "St. Louis Blues" and the "Memphis Blues" and made his adopted city internationally renowned as the birthplace of this new musical genre. From his real estate office on Beale Street, Robert R. Church, Sr., became the South's first black millionaire; his son, Robert R. Church, Jr., used the family fortune to underwrite his own political activities and became, by the 1920s, the nation's most powerful black Republican. Such fame belied the fact that Memphis's large black population continued to endure second-class citizenship in a segregated city.

For almost the entire first half of the twentieth century, Memphis government and politics were dominated by the powerful Democratic machine of "Boss" Ed Crump. Born and raised in Holly Springs, Mississippi, Edward H. Crump parlayed his insurance underwriting firm and a host of other business ventures into a sizable fortune. As one of the city's most prominent citizens, he came to dominate the local Democratic party. Although he seldom held elective office himself, he established an autocracy through a series of surrogate mayors. While providing adequate public services and winning national acclaim for city beautification, under machine rule Memphis allowed vice a free hand, imposed strict censorship, and curbed dissent. A paternalist dedicated to preserving white supremacy, Crump allowed blacks to vote—a rarity in the Jim Crow South—but used patronage and coercion to ensure that the substantial black electorate kept his candidates in office. Crump controlled the Memphis and Shelby County governments and exerted considerable influence in statewide politics until elimination of the poll tax and other electoral reforms resulted in a stunning defeat for the boss's gubernatorial candidate in 1948. However, Crump continued to rule Memphis unilaterally until his death in 1954.

One legacy of Crump's prolonged control of local government was the lack of attention to city planning. The boss ignored a comprehensive city plan prepared in 1924 that advocated improved access to the central business district and downtown riverfront renovation. Crump's preoccupation with low property taxes and his refusal to increase expenditures led him to delay road building and downtown construction. Suspicious of the federal government, he refused to allow the city to participate in early urban redevelopment and renewal programs. Shortly after Crump's death, an updated comprehensive plan called for many of the same changes for the city. However, a conservative coalition blocked the attempts of local reformers to apply planning principles to urban growth.

Meanwhile, the city pursued an aggressive annexation policy, adding 250 square miles of land and an estimated 350,000 people after World War II. By 1980 only two suburban communities remained autonomous, and Memphis engulfed virtually all of the metropolitan area. As Memphis spread across the landscape, retail establishments, commercial office buildings, and movie theaters vacated downtown locations for suburban shopping centers. In the 1970s, efforts to save the beleaguered central business district included creating a pedestrian shopping mall and developing Mud Island.

White flight to the urban fringe and the deterioration of the downtown underscored the serious racial problems that plagued Memphis. The city's failure to respond to the Supreme Court's order to desegregate public education left the schools essentially unchanged after the *Brown v. Board of Education* decision in 1954. When the Court mandated busing in 1974, a cadre of community leaders formed Citizens Against Busing (CAB) to resist. Within a few years, church-affiliated "white flight" academies multiplied, with the Baptist, Church of Christ, and Presbyterian denominations leading the way. By the 1980s Memphis possessed one of the nation's largest private school enrollments, and an almost exclusively black student body remained in the public schools.

Racial polarization surfaced dramatically in 1968 when a labor dispute, a strike by garbage workers, turned into a volatile civil rights confrontation. The assassination of Dr. Martin Luther King, Jr., who had come to Memphis to aid the striking garbage workers, touched off an orgy of looting, arson, and gunfire and intensified racial polarization in the city. Race relations remained strained in the Bluff City for many years, and, despite the existence of a black electoral majority, voters refrained from electing a black mayor until 1990, well after most other cities with a comparable population composition.

By the late twentieth century, Memphis was a city very much shaped by the importance of the automobile after World War II, exhibiting low population density, central city decay, and suburban sprawl. Still the unofficial capital of the Mid-South, the city's massive medical complex provided health care for millions of people in the region; the University of Tennessee Center for the Health Sciences, the University of Memphis, Rhodes College, LeMoyne-Owen College, and Christian Brothers University made the city an educational center as well. Along with Elvis Presley's mansion, Graceland, the restoration of Beale Street's historic "blue light" entertainment district reflected civic leaders' efforts to capitalize on the city's rich musical heritage. The conversion of the Lorraine Motel, where King was assassinated, into the National Civil Rights Museum represented a similar attempt to attract tourist dollars while also reconciling the city's troubled racial past.

—*Roger Biles*

**See also**
Crump, Edward H.
**References**
Biles, Roger. "Epitaph for Downtown: The Failure of City Planning in Post–World War Two Memphis." *Tennessee Historical Quarterly* 44 (1985): 267–284.
———. *Memphis in the Great Depression.* Knoxville: University of Tennessee Press, 1986.
Capers, Gerald A. *The Biography of a River Town: Memphis, Its Heroic Age.* Chapel Hill: University of North Carolina Press, 1966.
McKee, Margaret, and Fred Chisenhall. *Beale Black and Blue: Life and Music on America's Main Street.* Baton Rouge: Louisiana State University Press, 1981.
Miller, William D. *Memphis during the Progressive Era.* Memphis, TN: Memphis State University Press, 1957.
Sigafoos, Robert A. *Cotton Row to Beale Street: A Business History of Memphis.* Memphis, TN: Memphis State University Press, 1979.
Tucker, David M. *Memphis since Crump: Bossism, Blacks, and Civic Reformers, 1948–1968.* Knoxville: University of Tennessee Press, 1980.

## Metropolis

The word *metropolis* derives from the ancient Greek and means mother city, or a parent city-state like Athens that sent out people to plant new colonies. It also refers to the chief city of a civilization or country. From the eighteenth century on, London was the metropolis of the Western world, to be replaced by New York early in the twentieth century. The characteristics of this kind of city were dramatically captured in Fritz Lang's film *Metropolis* (1926).

The great age of the metropolis in the United States was the century from the 1850s to the 1950s, with New York and Chicago as the major examples. Industry was the key to urban growth and the center of the economy. A chief attribute of the metropolis was an intense concentration of people and functions, often reflected in the form of concentric rings: commercially, a cluster of office towers at the core; industrially, a zone of factories surrounding the core; and residentially, a suburban residential ring of the more affluent who could escape the congestion of the two inner rings. The result was a sharp separation between work and residence and a severe segregation of people based on class and race. Another attribute of the metropolis was the "metropolitan" role in which it acted as an imperial power in economic and cultural activities at the regional, national, and even international levels.

From at least the middle of the twentieth century, the metropolis has been surrounded by an increasingly dispersed population. These "city-regions" are recognized statistically by being designated as Standard Metropolitan Statistical

Areas (SMSAs), but political forms have not developed equally with these regional changes. The metropolis is usually isolated politically from its surroundings, and new regions have successfully fended off proposed forms of "metropolitan" municipal government.

The older metropolitan core no longer contains the industry, the retail trade, or most of the office functions, all of which have become dispersed through city-regions or the even more dispersed "urban fields." The metropolis has not disappeared, however, and has often become a new type of vital center, specializing in corporate headquarters, high culture (museums, concert halls, theaters), and communications (media and publishing).

—*Gil A. Stelter*

**References**

Fox, Kenneth. *Metropolitan America*. London: Macmillan, 1985.

Galanty, Ervin, ed. *The Metropolis in Transition*. New York: Paragon House, 1987.

Kasinitz, Philip, ed. *Metropolis, Center and Symbol of Our Times*. New York: New York University Press, 1995.

Scott, Allen J. *Metropolis: From Division of Labor to Urban Form*. Berkeley: University of California Press, 1987.

Sharpe, William, and Leonard Wallock, eds. *Visions of the Modern City*. New York: Columbia University Press, 1982.

Sutcliffe, Anthony, ed. *Metropolis, 1890–1940*. Chicago: University of Chicago Press, 1984.

## Metropolitan Area

Since 1910 the Bureau of the Budget has used different terms to describe places that are clearly urban but whose political boundaries are not adequate to describe the area that includes the entire population because the whole population overlaps those boundaries. The purpose of the bureau has been to standardize statistical information and make it both comparable and compatible with statistics gathered and used by the many different federal, state, and local agencies that collect information and produce data about cities and urban places.

The preferred terminology for such an area has been Metropolitan Area (MA) since 1990. The current definition of an MA is a place having at least one city with a population of at least 50,000 (the central city) and a metropolitan population of 100,000 (75,000 in New England, which does not use the county-level rule described below). The county containing the largest city is considered a central county, and the MA includes contiguous counties in which at least 50 percent of the inhabitants live in the urban area surrounding (but outside of) the central city. Other counties can be included in the MA if they meet certain levels of commuting and have specific metropolitan characteristics.

The problem of finding appropriate terminology and definitions for these places began early in the twentieth century. In the federal censuses of 1910, 1920, 1930, and 1940

the term Metropolitan District was used as the official designation for metropolitan areas, or places that overlapped city boundaries. Then, in 1949, the Bureau of the Budget introduced the concept of the Standard Metropolitan Area (SMA). The bureau defined an SMA as the entire county in which a central city was located.

Ten years later, in 1959, the bureau changed the terminology to Standard Metropolitan Statistical Area (SMSA). To qualify as an SMSA, an area had to contain one or more cities with a population of at least 50,000. This could be either one city with 50,000 residents or two adjacent cities with a combined population of 50,000 if the smaller city had at least 15,000 residents. The county (or counties) in which the city or cities were located was now called a central county if it had a residential labor force that was at least 75 percent nonagricultural. An adjacent county could be included in an SMSA if at least 15 percent of its labor force worked in the county containing the central city and if 25 percent of those working in the second county lived in the county that contained the central city.

In 1983, the SMSA was renamed the Metropolitan Statistical Area (MSA), and that was changed in 1990 to Metropolitan Area (MA), the term now in use.

—*Craig Pascoe*

**References**

Duncan, Joseph W. "Metropolitan Areas for the 1980s." *American Demographics* 1 (1979): 25–33.

Forstall, Richard L., and Philip N. Fulton. "The Official SCSA/SMSA Definition: Concept and Practice." *Statistical Reporter* (1976).

Short, John R. *An Introduction to Urban Geography*. London: Routledge & Kegan Paul, 1984.

U.S. Bureau of the Census. *1990 Census of Population and Housing: Supplementary Reports—Metropolitan Areas as Defined by the Office of Management and Budget*. Washington, DC: Government Printing Office, 1993.

Yeates, Maurice, and Barry Garner. *The North American City*. New York: Harper & Row, 1976.

## Miami, Florida

Miami, the largest city in Florida, is unique, a city of contrasts, contradictions, and extremes. Presidential aspirations have begun and ended here. Few cities serve as headquarters for both international revolutionary and counterrevolutionary activities. The Contra war in Nicaragua was plotted in restaurants and coffee shops in the area called Sweetwater, and clandestine attacks on Cuba continue to be launched from Miami. The city has served as a refuge for the famous and infamous, including gangsters during Prohibition, serial killers, deposed Latin American dictators, sheiks, rock stars, artists, writers, athletes, and just about anyone starting over. As political conditions in the Western Hemisphere fluctuate, Miami continues to be a destination for waves of refugees.

Miami now has the largest percentage of foreign-born residents of any metropolitan area in the United States. With over half its population of Hispanic origin and more than one-fifth black, many from the Caribbean, Miami *is* multiculturalism. Here, immigrants are reluctant to buy the expectation that starting at the bottom, working hard, and playing by the rules will benefit their children in the future. Whether Cuban, Nicaraguan, or Haitian, Miami's immigrants want their piece of the pie sooner. What is more, enough succeed to make this "American dream" more than just rhetoric.

Miami has never been ordinary. It did not develop along a well-traveled river or railroad route, and it never attracted industrial capital; nor did it emerge as a seaport. From its inception at the turn of the twentieth century until World War II, Miami was a frontier city. Newer and less traditional, its culture defied classification as either southern or northern. With a largely transient population and a high proportion of first-generation residents, the city has always lacked a consolidated sociopolitical structure and a substantial core of established elites. In most respects, it has always welcomed newcomers, particularly if they possessed money, dreams, and panache.

Miami grew from the visions of eccentric speculators. In the 1880s, Henry Flagler, millionaire partner of John D. Rockefeller, moved to Palm Beach for health reasons and established a new career as a railroad and real estate magnate. A decade later, Julia Tuttle, an unconventional widow who had come from Cleveland, persuaded him to extend his railroad to Miami. She built a house on the northern bank of the Miami River, which eventually became the hub of downtown Miami. Her dreams and persistence were critical to Miami's early development, making it the only major American city conceived by a woman. Her tenacity, coupled with an offer of free land, convinced Flagler to extend his railroad south, providing the necessary transportation link for Miami's emerging tourist and citrus industries.

The area grew at a dizzying pace between 1910 and 1925 as it exploded from 5,000 to 146,000 residents. After a causeway was built across Biscayne Bay, and a mangrove swamp was filled to develop Miami Beach, growth began full throttle, and the area was soon covered with the palatial mansions of rich northerners. Inland, the grandiose plan of developer George Merrick produced the upscale suburb of Coral Gables. Commercial farming developed in remote areas south of Miami in what would become the towns of Homestead and Florida City.

Crises have always played important parts in shaping Miami, and the first economic boom ended abruptly in 1926 when a major hurricane devastated the city. The Depression soon followed. One effect of this economic downturn was that Jews, previously barred from many hotels and private clubs on Miami Beach, were welcomed with open arms now that their resources were needed. By the mid-1930s, a significant influx of Jewish working-class and middle-class migrants from the Northeast had arrived. Their coming led to the proliferation of small hotels and apartments, particularly in the southern end of Miami Beach, which became the Art Deco district 40 years later.

The next economic boom began with World War II and gathered steam in the postwar decade. Many servicemen and servicewomen stationed in south Florida during the war returned here to live. Commercial air travel was launched with the establishment of Pan American and Eastern Airlines, and communities like Miami Springs and Hialeah sprang up near the airport. Retirees came to escape northern winters and settled throughout the area. While the wealthy continued to build winter homes, affordable transportation made Miami vacations affordable to middle-class families and boosted development of a year-round hospitality industry.

Jobs in the area attracted blacks from the rural South and the Caribbean. Between 1940 and 1950, the population of metropolitan Miami nearly doubled, rising to 505,000; by the 1960s, it had reached nearly 1 million. With its transplanted groups from north and south, as well as the Bahamas, Miami was becoming an "ethnic cauldron." The next wave of development was spurred by migration from Latin America and the Caribbean, usually as the result of political regimes rising and falling.

South Florida has always had close ties with Cuba, and by 1948, Cuba led all countries in the world in the volume of passengers exchanged with the United States. Two deposed Cuban presidents lived in Miami, and a prominent Cuban politician of the 1940s built Miami's first baseball stadium. Fidel Castro spent time in Miami in the 1950s, and some of his family live there today. Following the 1959 Revolution and the failed Bay of Pigs invasion, Cuban exiles began arriving in mass. Some settled in New York and New Jersey, but most preferred the already Latin atmosphere of Miami. By 1980, 52 percent of all Cuban Americans lived in Dade County. The number of Cubans in Miami rose dramatically once more in 1980 after the Mariel boat lift.

Miami's emergence as the "capital of the Caribbean" has reinforced these trends. Miami is the preferred destination of migrants from the Caribbean and Central America, especially for the elite and middle classes. As the United States abandoned the Contra war (which was largely based in Miami) in the late 1980s, a flow of working-class immigrants began, first from Nicaragua, then from other Central American nations, as well as Colombia, the Dominican Republic, Puerto Rico, and Cuba. Meanwhile, the frustration of democracy in Haiti increased emigration pressures there, despite American policies designed to discourage Haitian crossings.

At the same time that immigration was increasing dramatically, the influx of northern Anglos slowed and became negative after 1970. This demographic change was especially evident among the elderly and the Jewish. In 1950, for example, Miami Beach was 50 percent Jewish, by 1970 it was 80 percent, but by 1990 it had fallen to only 40 percent. The elderly population, while still about 30 percent, has also decreased, largely because retirees began to settle in more affordable parts of Florida. The tourist industry stagnated as vacationers discovered they could afford Caribbean destinations, and families flocked to Walt Disney World. At the same time, many longtime residents reacted to the growing multiculturalism by leaving—a 24 percent reduction in the number of Anglos occurred between 1980 and 1990. From its peak of 85 percent in the 1950s, the proportion of Anglos has decreased since 1960 and is expected to decline to around 30 percent by 2000. This trend is most dramatic in the inner city, but it has occurred throughout the entire metropolitan area.

Generally, when people speak of Miami, they really mean Dade County, not the smaller incorporated City of Miami at its hub. Within the county there are 26 incorporated municipalities. Miami is the largest, but other well-known towns include Miami Springs, Hialeah, North Miami, North Miami Beach, Miami Beach, Coral Gables, Homestead, and Florida City. Most of the area's population and sprawling territory lies outside these incorporated communities. The largest governmental body is Metropolitan Dade County. As constituted by "good government" reform in 1957, this strong county government has an appointed manager and, until recently, was administered by a nonpartisan commission. Within Dade County, each municipality retains some local autonomy; however, in most areas it must accept standards set by the county.

By 1995, the estimated population of Dade County exceeded 2 million, and the area had become truly multicultural. Nearly 45 percent of its residents were born outside the country; about one-half had arrived since 1980. Cubans accounted for 30 percent of Dade's population in 1990, and all persons of Hispanic origin made up 49 percent of the total. About 60 percent of Hispanics are Cuban with others coming from the Caribbean and Americas. In comparison, more than 20 percent of Dade residents report their race as black, about 20 percent of them from the Caribbean.

As south Florida became a large metropolis, its economy diversified, and the area became an important port for Caribbean and Latin American markets. Over the last 30 years, Miami has displaced New Orleans as the country's principal trade entrepot with Latin America. By the early 1980s, 100 multinational corporations had their Latin American headquarters in Miami, and it stood behind only New York as an international banking center.

Yet some elements of the old Miami have not disappeared. Anglo men still control the largest firms and dominate many important political bodies. Major newspapers and radio and television stations continue to be owned and operated by nonminorities. Interestingly, the "white flight" from Dade County has been class-selective. While Anglo laborers and production workers have left, executives and managers have tended to remain or even move into the area. The affluent city of Coral Gables remains principally Anglo, while Jewish influence continues strong in Miami Beach. Black Miamians have fought a continuous struggle to gain economic and political power, but that struggle has taken a particular form in Miami. To understand the sociopolitical climate of Miami, it is necessary to consider two of its significant demographic features: the Cuban enclave and the continued isolation and subjugation of black Miamians.

Miami's Cuban community is regarded as the foremost example of a true ethnic enclave in the United States. An ethnic enclave is a distinct economic region characterized by the spatial concentration of immigrants who organize a wide variety of enterprises to serve their own ethnic group and the general population. The foundation of the enclave is not simply its size or scale but its highly differentiated nature. In Dade County, 42 percent of all businesses are owned by Hispanics, a percentage exceeded only in Los Angeles. However, they generate far more revenue here. Three-quarters of the Hispanic-owned enterprises are controlled by Cubans. The second and most important overall feature, however, is the institutional completeness. The range of sales and services controlled by Cubans, as well as their penetration into the professions, is so extensive that Cubans can live and deal completely within their own ethnic group in Miami.

The completeness of the enclave somewhat insulates new arrivals from the usual vicissitudes of the secondary labor market. In contrast to Mexican immigrants, for example, who join the labor market in peripheral sectors dominated by Anglos and with little informal support, many recent Cuban immigrants enter the labor market through businesses owned or operated by earlier arrivals. While wages may not be higher in the enclave, ethnic bonds provide informal networks of support that facilitate learning new skills, access to resources, and the whole process of economic adjustment. These positive implications have resulted in a socioeconomic position that is relatively high in comparison with most other immigrant groups.

While Cuban entrepreneurialism is impressive, most businesses are small and family-owned. Only one out of seven Hispanic businesses had paid employees in 1990, and together they created only 30,000 paid jobs. Latinos remain underrepresented in the fastest-growing industries, especially financial services. Although their representation has increased, they continue to be outnumbered by Anglos in professional and executive occupations.

Cubans have begun to establish pivotal political power in Miami, which they exercise through a growing number of elected officials and influential organizations, such as the Cuban American National Foundation, the Latin Builders Association, the Hispanic Builders Association, and the Latin Chamber of Commerce. By the late 1980s, the mayors of Miami, Hialeah, Sweetwater, West Miami, and Hialeah Gardens had been born in Cuba. Miami's city manager and Dade County's manager were Cuban as were the majority of Miami's commissioners. More than one-third of the county's current delegation to the state legislature is Cuban, and their coalition has become influential. Their success has spread to the national level, where two Cubans serve in the U.S. House of Representatives. Nowhere else in the country, nor even in American history, have first-generation immigrants achieved political power so quickly and so thoroughly.

From the cavalier way in which ancient Indian burial mounds were destroyed to the creation of modern black apartheid, Miami has grown and developed on the clear basis of white superiority even though the economy of south Florida has always depended on black labor. The earliest construction and railroad workers were Bahamian, and black migrants from northern Florida, Alabama, and Georgia formed the core of the agricultural labor force. During the years before the Hispanic influx, most hotel workers were black. But while their labor was needed, their voices were unwanted.

Blacks in Miami were expected to "stay in their place." When Miami was chartered in 1896, Florida law required a petition signed by at least 300 citizens, but there were only about 200 white residents at the time. Henry Flagler took care of this by having his black railroad workers brought to the meeting. After voting for the charter—i.e., in Flagler's best interests—the workers were sent back over the tracks and their disenfranchisement renewed. City officials quickly impressed upon blacks, especially Bahamians who considered themselves social equals, the appropriate behavior for "southern Negroes."

Strict segregation was rigidly enforced in Miami, and its legacy has been hard to erase. At first, most blacks lived in "Colored Town" (later renamed Overtown), just north of downtown Miami. When Overtown became too small, a new black neighborhood, Liberty City, was constructed to the northwest, complete with a wall to separate it from white neighborhoods; a similar wall cordoned off the black section of Coconut Grove. As other black settlements developed, including Brownsville, Opa Locka, and, in the southern part of the county, Perrine, Princeton, Goulds, and Florida City, segregation was maintained. Before the civil rights legislation of the 1960s, the only blacks allowed to live permanently in Mi-

ami Beach were servants who lived with employers. Workers in hotels and restaurants were required to carry identification cards and return home across the bay each night. Entertainers who performed in Miami Beach had to stay in hotels in Overtown. Apartheid endured into the early 1960s, when Miami scored about 99 on the index of residential segregation (where 100 signifies total segregation), making it the most segregated metropolitan area in the United States.

For the most part, the civil rights movement came quietly to south Florida, doing away with formal, legal segregation. But just when the black minority seemed to have new opportunities for upward mobility, Cuban refugees transformed the city. The quest by black Miamians for political strength has confronted two debilitating conditions, weak community leadership and an unresponsive political system. The first was a by-product of urban renewal programs in the 1960s, especially freeway construction. As in many cities, one positive result of segregation was the emergence of Overtown as a vibrant center of small businesses and professionals serving the local black population. Urban renewal virtually destroyed Overtown, displacing much of the black middle class to newly desegregated suburbs, new black suburban developments, or away from Miami altogether—often to southern cities such as Atlanta that offered greater economic opportunity. The result was an early split between more affluent black suburbs and a black underclass in the inner city.

These socioeconomic cleavages within the black community are often apparent and are reflected in a belief that black leaders do not support grassroots racial issues and contribute to an inability to unify the black population. At the same time, black neighborhoods, although segregated, are spread throughout Dade county. As a result, it is very difficult to develop a common agenda and unified political action. In contrast, Hispanic communities are joined in a wide band extending west from downtown Miami. Taken together, this all adds up to the "Miami Syndrome"—a black community divided by class, culture, and geography that must function under subordination to both Anglos and Cubans.

Dade County's metropolitan government has traditionally provided little possibility for redressing black concerns. The movement to reform local politics in the late 1950s by developing the nation's first metropolitan government, including at-large elections for all commissioners, effectively squelched any effective forum to address neighborhood and minority differences. With some 60 percent of the area's black population living in unincorporated Dade County, and much of the remainder living in Miami with its large Hispanic majority, the chance of generating effective black political representation was nonexistent.

Four riots during the 1980s revealed the widespread anger among black Miamians about their failure to keep pace with other groups economically and their lack of a political voice that was heard. City elites responded by creating a set of economic and social programs to assist and improve black neighborhoods. The task of rejuvenating the black community was daunting, but there were some successes. Compared to ten years previously, the number of black businesses had more than tripled by 1987. Under a set-aside program, black contractors began receiving county work. In general, development projects have met limited success, and gains in employment have been modest. In 1991, there were about 6,800 black businesses in Dade County, but their average sales and receipts ($40,934) was only about half that reported for Hispanic businesses. Black firms accounted for only 0.5 percent of the total sales and receipts in Dade County—a considerably lower share than is typical of black-owned business statewide or nationwide. It could be generalized that most of the limited benefits from special programs and incentives were received by black professionals and middle-class businesspeople.

The gains by blacks in Miami pale in comparison to the economic and political success of Cubans. When Dr. Martin Luther King, Jr., visited Miami in 1966, he noted the racial hostilities in Miami and cautioned not to pit Cuban refugees against blacks in competition for jobs. While competition is difficult to document, Cubans were clearly more successful than blacks in the area of government contracts awarded to minorities. Between 1968 and 1980, the Small Business Administration (SBA) cumulatively dispersed 46.6 percent of its loans in Dade County to Hispanics and only 6 percent to blacks. The situation actually worsened after the riots, when nearly 90 percent of SBA loans were awarded to Hispanics or whites.

While Miami's racial and ethnic structure is often portrayed as a tripartite division among Anglos, Hispanics, and Blacks, it is important to note once again the cultural diversity within black Miami. The second major immigrant group in Dade County is Caribbean blacks. Largely because of Caribbean immigration, Dade's black population grew by 47 percent between 1970 and 1980 (a growth rate exceeded only in Atlanta) and another 42 percent in the succeeding decade. About 14 percent of Miami's black population in 1990 were Haitian.

The first refugees from repression and poverty in Haiti arrived by boat in 1963. Their request for political asylum was denied, and another boatload did not arrive until ten years later. As conditions in Haiti worsened between 1977 and 1981, it is estimated that as many as 80,000 Haitians came by boat or plane. Those not forcibly returned to Haiti received a cold welcome in south Florida. Not officially recognized as refugees, most were ineligible for social services or work permits. Ill equipped to succeed in competitive south Florida, the average Creole-speaking Haitian immigrant has less than six years of formal education and possesses few marketable skills. No well-established enclave has received them, and most assistance to them has come from churches and private organizations.

In one respect, Haitian immigration mirrored Cuban—an early wave of middle- and upper-class refugees in the 1960s and 1970s followed by poorer immigrants. While shops, restaurants, and other small businesses have developed, Haitians have not emulated the success of the Cuban enclave. The reality of their situation, including immigration policies that bar them, the lack of official refugee status with its concomitant social and financial assistance, and the social discrimination linked to being black in America, has resulted in a very different structure of opportunity.

Relations between Haitians and Miami's native blacks have been strained by cultural differences and the perception of economic competition. Rather than recognizing the racism experienced by Haitians, many African Americans view them as unwanted competitors in a tight job market. In general, Haitians have tried to avoid being identified with Miami blacks because they want to rise above what they perceive to be a downtrodden group.

In the 1990s, several developments have begun to unite the black community. A major incident resulted from the treatment of Nelson Mandela when he visited Miami in 1990. Unlike the civic honors bestowed on him in other cities, the official reception in Miami was decidedly cool—the product of Cuban and Jewish outrage at Mandela's refusal to disavow cordial relations with Fidel Castro and Yassir Arafat. The mayors of Miami Beach and Miami, as well as the Metro-Dade Commission, refused to honor or meet him, much to the anger of local black leaders. Most black elected officials did not take a stand on this issue, an example of the divisions within the black community. Then, a week later, in front of a store in Little Haiti where a customer had fought earlier with the Cuban proprietor, the Miami police violently broke up a large Haitian demonstration.

In the wake of these events, a group of black professionals and community leaders organized a boycott and called on national organizations not to schedule conventions in Miami. The Boycott Coalition demanded an apology from Miami's elected officials to Mandela, an investigation into police conduct during the Haitian demonstration, a series of economic measures to promote black economic interests (especially in the tourist industry), and changes in Miami's political system to provide for greater black representation.

The boycott had an impact. Before the end of 1990, 13 organizations, including the American Civil Liberties Union and the National Organization for Women, had canceled conferences scheduled for Miami. In all, the city is estimated to have lost over $60 million in convention-related business. The Greater Miami Convention and Visitors Bureau, with local corporate sponsorship, eventually established a scholarship program for black students to receive training and subsequent management-level employment in the tourist industry, and the Miami Beach Commission agreed to promote a new, black-owned hotel. Meanwhile, the mayor of Miami Beach and the Metro-Dade Commission issued retroactive statements honoring Mandela, and the Cuban-American mayor of Miami admitted that the situation may not have been handled well. The boycott was lifted in 1993.

Recent electoral reform has been the most promising development in furthering the interests of the black community. A federal court ruling in late 1992 ordered Metro-Dade to replace its at-large commission immediately with members elected from individual districts in order to guarantee minority representation. Following the establishment of 13 districts, the next election produced a new Metropolitan Dade County Commission composed of four African Americans (including the chair), six Hispanics, and three Anglos—a representative commission after all these years. South Florida currently has two African Americans serving in the U.S. House of Representatives and six state legislators. Blacks serve on the current city commissions or councils of Miami, El Portal, Opa Locka, and Florida City, and the latter two black communities also have black mayors.

Increased representation does not translate easily into political power, as became abundantly clear when a new Metro-Dade county manager was chosen in 1994. To select a replacement for the outgoing Cuban American, both the Hispanic and black communities mobilized. Going into the election, the five Cuban-American commissioners lined up behind a Hispanic candidate, and the four African Americans and one Anglo backed an African-American candidate. The deciding vote for the Cuban candidate was cast by a politically astute Anglo who had been supported by the Cuban community three years before in her successful bid to become the first woman president of the Florida Senate.

In a metropolitan area in which ethnic groups—especially blacks—are spatially segregated, the existence of a powerful, institutionally complete community among Cubans makes it difficult to create a common agenda for all the citizens.

—*Guillermo J. Grenier*

### References

Allman, T. D. *Miami: City of the Future.* New York: Atlantic Monthly Press, 1987.
Grenier, Guillermo J., and Alex Stepick. *Miami Now: Immigration, Ethnicity, and Social Change.* Gainesville: University Press of Florida, 1992.
Muir, Helen. *Miami USA.* Miami, FL: Pickering Press, 1990.
Parks, Arva Moore. *Miami: The Magic City.* Miami, FL: Centennial Press, 1991.
Peters, Thelma. *Miami 1909.* Miami, FL: Banyan Books, 1984.
Portes, Alejandro, and Alex Stepick. *City on the Edge: The Transformation of Miami.* Berkeley: University of California Press, 1993.

## Middle Class in Cities

The term *middle class* developed during the nineteenth century as a way of referring to two somewhat different phenomena. Since that time, the phrase has frequently served as an essential part of two partly contradictory conceptions of the nature of American society and culture, especially urban and suburban society and culture. One use of the term describes the United States as almost uniformly, or at least predominantly, middle class. The other use of the term identifies the middle class as a separate and distinct formation in a hierarchically organized, and not necessarily consensual, society and culture.

The former, more inclusive conception of a middle-class society and culture that encompasses all Americans reflects a long-standing perception, dating in some respects from the colonial era, that America was populated disproportionately from "middling sorts" of Europeans, that no formal aristocracy developed within American political institutions, that American economic and geographic conditions nurtured the ambitions and self-esteem of ordinary people, and that the aristocratic styles and social and political claims of the "better sort" were increasingly modified and eventually defeated by the challenge of a democratically informed populace. That the triumph of the democratic "common man" should have become equated with the emergence of a dominant "middle-class" culture reflects the further perception that the industrialization of the United States in the nineteenth century did not produce a deeply alienated and highly self-conscious working class—that the opportunities of a vast, thinly populated continent; the fluidity of social arrangements in a highly mobile society; and the persuasiveness of democratic rhetoric in a society in which white workingmen were entitled to vote gave nearly every white American, and hence white America as a whole, the sense of being "middle class." The visibility of an African-American proletariat, both before and after the abolition of slavery, only made more plausible the attachment of the adjective *middle-class* to many general propositions about white America.

Although the term *bourgeois* has occasionally substituted for *middle class,* this essentially consensual formulation has never focused on the populations of cities, or on urbanization as a force for change in American society and culture. Especially with respect to the nineteenth century, it was (if anything) the small town, set within, serving, and in essential accord with its surrounding countryside, that provided

*Since the mid-ninetenth century, middle-class Americans have filled their homes with material possessions in order to display their social status.*

the nurturing environment of an American "middle-class" (or "bourgeois") society and culture. This association has changed somewhat with the massive twentieth-century suburbanization of urban and rural populations alike. With respect to the period following World War II especially, the suburb has joined, and even largely replaced, the small town as the characteristic incubator and protector of national middle-class lifestyles and values.

The second use of the term *middle class* differs in essential ways from, and is even in some ways contradictory to, the first. By specifying a distinct middle class within a larger social hierarchy, some scholars, especially in recent years, have challenged not only the idea of a national middle-class culture but also the notion of a broad national consensus of any sort. According to this view, American lifestyles and values have varied, and significant variations have proceeded from differences of many kinds, including those of social class. Thus, *middle-class,* when used as an adjective modifying *society* or *culture,* means something more limited and more precise than it does in the broader formulation where it does little more than substitute for the adjective *American.* And it is immediately suggestive of the power of parallel constructs—upper class, working class, and the like—that together with middle class provide a more complex understanding of the way Americans have lived than does any simple conception of a middle-class (i.e., classless) national consensus.

A corollary of this challenge to the broader use of *middle class* is a recognition that the middle class (the term can now be used as a noun) has a separate history of its own that can be understood as a distinct part of the larger history of the nation as a whole. It is a history, moreover, that historians have thus far located primarily within the nation's larger and smaller cities, and within its emerging nineteenth- and twentieth-century suburbs. The emergence of a relatively

well-defined middle class in the nineteenth century was embodied in a wide array of new experiences and circumstances on the part of urban (and somewhat later, suburban) middling folk, including the new, postartisanal alignment of business ownership, salaried employment, and nonmanual work; the increasing separation of manual from nonmanual work environments and the progressive refinement of the latter; and the diverging real income levels of manual and nonmanual members of the workforce. At the same time these developments were occurring the cities of the United States began to experience the increasing articulation of wealthy, middling, and working-class residential neighborhoods and neighborhood institutions; the increasing size and growing refinement of the homes of families with middling incomes; the careful cultivation of a more refined domestic life and the adoption of child-rearing strategies designed to preserve status within those homes; and the pursuit of entertainment and sociability in commercial and voluntary institutions increasingly divided by class. Reflecting their more distinct and enclosed quotidian worlds, small- and medium-scale businessmen, salaried employees, and the families of such "headworkers" (the term *white collar* would emerge only at the end of the nineteenth century) became more aware of themselves as a distinct middle class, and of the different experiences and values that distinguished them from those above and below them in the social hierarchy.

The articulation of the urban middle class, according to this narrower formulation, was a nineteenth-century phenomenon. During the twentieth century, a number of developments have somewhat eroded the boundaries between social classes. The most notable of these concern income and work. Rising real incomes among manual workers, especially in the decades following the New Deal, and the proliferation throughout the century of low-paying nonmanual jobs in offices and stores, have created a significant overlap between "white collar" and "blue collar" incomes, and to some extent have eliminated the distinction between middle-class and working-class standards and styles of living. In addition, there has been a rapid increase, mainly within the service sector of the economy, of jobs that are not clearly identifiable as white collar or blue collar, which further confounds a distinction upon which much class identification was historically based.

It can be argued, moreover, that modern mass media, especially television, tends to erode distinct class cultures. These cultures, and the economic and social experiences that undergird and support them, have not disappeared, but they are less distinct than they were a century ago. Today, middle class, especially when encountered in political discourse, is used most often to distinguish between a putatively welfare-dependent underclass and the vast majority of the remainder of American society, including regularly employed manual workers. Middle-class Americans do preserve significant aspects of traditional class distinctions in their daily lives, but in public discourse it is the comprehensive formulation of an American middle-class culture that largely prevails.

—*Stuart M. Blumin*

### References

Blumin, Stuart M. *The Emergence of the Middle Class: Social Experience in the American City, 1760–1900.* Cambridge, England: Cambridge University Press, 1989.

Ehrenreich, Barbara. *Fear of Falling: The Inner Life of the Middle Class.* New York: Pantheon Books, 1989.

Gilkeson, John S., Jr. *Middle-Class Providence, 1820–1940.* Princeton, NJ: Princeton University Press, 1986.

Greenwood, Janette Thomas. *Bittersweet Legacy: The Black and White "Better Classes" in Charlotte, 1850–1910.* Chapel Hill: University of North Carolina Press, 1994.

Mills, C. Wright. *White Collar: The American Middle Classes.* New York: Oxford University Press, 1951.

Ryan, Mary P. *Cradle of the Middle Class: The Family in Oneida County, New York, 1790–1865.* Cambridge, England: Cambridge University Press, 1981.

## Middle Class in Suburbs

Two contrasting themes dominate the experience of the American middle class in suburbs. First is the idea of "suburban accessibility," an embodiment of the middle-class values of upward mobility and economic opportunity for anyone who works hard enough. For urban families, the detached house surrounded by a white picket fence has long symbolized the material and social validation of acceptance into middle-class suburban society. In contrast to suburban accessibility is "suburban privatism." From this perspective, suburbia is an elitist enclave protecting its residents from the negative influences of lower-class urban life.

This tug-of-war between accessibility and privatism is paralleled by the ambiguous status of the middle class itself. For example, the term *middle class* has been used inclusively; the overwhelming majority of Americans consider themselves middle class. At the same time, *middle class* has had exclusive connotations, particularly when used in contrast to those lower down the socioeconomic scale. Given the uncertainty over who and what constitutes the middle class, it is not surprising that similar tensions have long been evident in the suburban environment of the American middle class.

The middle-class suburban experience in the United States can be divided into four periods, the first marked by an initial burst of suburban separatist fervor, followed by two periods of long, steady increases in accessibility, and then ending with a sharp reversion to privatism:

1. Between 1815 and 1874, the first wave of middle-class suburbanization occurred, largely among business and professional families who could afford the costs of outlying residences.
2. Between 1874 and 1945, technological innovations in transportation and construction opened suburbia to a wider segment of the middle class.
3. Suburban accessibility reached its height in the mass suburban migration between 1945 and 1960.
4. Finally, the period since 1960 has witnessed a return to separatism and privatism in suburban communities marked by the appearance of walled, gated communities.

Obviously, this periodization is most applicable for eastern and midwestern cities, which have a longer history of middle-class suburbanization. Nevertheless, the recent experiences of newer suburbs in the South and West have also been punctuated by debates about accessibility and privatism, suggesting that these issues have national relevance.

In the middle decades of the nineteenth century, increasing numbers of urban middle-class families moved to suburbs. These new communities on the urban fringe appealed largely to businessmen and professionals. Places such as Brooklyn Heights, which in 1814 became the first commuter suburb of New York City, offered more land, more open space for children to play, and a more relaxed and relaxing lifestyle than that available in the congested city.

These years were marked by the ascendance of a middle-class "suburban ideal" that combined Jeffersonian notions of agrarianism with Victorian idealization of the virtuous home. Acquiring a suburban residence became one of the major goals that businessmen and others in the growing middle class strived for; it represented success, not just ideologically but also spatially. Large lots and winding streets, a hallmark of early landscape architects and designers like Frederick Law Olmsted and Alexander Jackson Davis, evoked pastoral images of the rambling country estates of the gentry.

Parroting the landed gentry also served other purposes. Because the generally high costs of commuting, both in time and money, limited suburban residence to an elite upper-middle class, an aura of exclusivity surrounded the ownership of suburban homes. From this perspective, suburbia took its value from the lack of many of the noxious elements of urban life: dense neighborhoods, foul air, and ethnic immigrants, particularly after the 1840s. Olmsted's Riverside and other similar communities were attractive not only because they allowed people to live among neighbors of similar circumstances, but because they shielded their residents from those of lesser circumstances and made it unnecessary to live among them.

Separatist attitudes among middle-class suburbanites also affected politics in metropolitan areas. After Boston had successfully annexed several surrounding communities, the independent suburb of Brookline voted in 1874 not to merge politically with its larger neighbor. Campaign literature opposed to annexation emphasized Brookline's distinctiveness; the suburb was not like Boston and did not experience its urban problems and social heterogeneity. Brookline's successful resistance sparked a series of similar revolts against annexation in other cities across the country.

Although Brookline's independence was a triumph for suburban separatists, the next seven decades saw a gradual decline in suburban exclusivity. New transportation and construction technologies enabled many middle-class families who had previously been excluded to participate in the suburban lifestyle. Innovations in transportation (during this second era of suburbanization) began with the electric streetcar in the late 1880s and included the mass-produced automobile a few decades later. Both technologies expanded the range of commuting while keeping time and cost factors relatively low. Meanwhile, new and affordable building techniques, such as the balloon frame, made the construction of new dwellings easier and more economical than it had been. Local governments assisted the new suburban expansion by providing essential services, e.g., gas and sewer lines, to developing areas. The convergence of accessible transportation, cheaper construction, and available government services distinguished these suburbs from those of an earlier era. Instead of exclusive, privately developed neighborhoods, suburban homes were now constructed by individual builders who generally built only a few houses at a time on speculation. This unplanned development meant that anyone who could afford to build a house in suburbia could become a suburbanite.

Ironically, with more people seeking the middle-class suburban ideal, the ideal itself was reshaped. In Boston suburbs such as Roxbury or Mattapan, land costs rose as neighborhoods became populated, forcing new residents to build duplexes or triplexes instead of the previously characteristic single-family houses. Similarly, the social exclusivity of suburban living began to evaporate. In Detroit, for example, increasing numbers of immigrant groups were represented in suburban communities between 1880 and 1920. One group excluded from suburbanization was blacks; through a combination of racism and economics, they were barred from most newly settled neighborhoods. This pattern would continue for most of the twentieth century.

The Depression and World War II put middle-class suburban expansion on hold. Only a small percentage of families made the move from city to suburb during this period, reinforcing the waning image of suburbia as an elite environment. But even though economic and political events limited actual migration to suburbia, middle-class desires to live in suburbs and achieve suburban respectability continued to grow unimpeded.

The years after World War II saw added democratization of suburbs for the middle class as they became affordable and available. After 15 years of pent-up demand for new houses, an entire industry dedicated to creating middle-class suburban society sprang up in the 15 years after the war. Mass-construction techniques, perfected by companies such as Levitt and Sons and replicated by thousands of lesser-known developers, eliminated the need to construct and finance one's own house. Government-backed mortgages reduced the costs and risks of buying a new home. Manufacturers of consumer goods began supplying suburban families with new products deemed essential to a proper suburban middle-class lifestyle—no new house was complete without a washing machine, dishwasher, electric range, and, of course, a television. The demands would ultimately include dryers, lawn mowers, food processors, and a host of other machines and appliances. By 1960, new suburban communities had grown by almost 20 million people, or 46 percent. In contrast, with few exceptions the 20 largest cities in the United States had static or declining populations between 1950 and 1960.

The sheer size and speed of the suburban migration was not lost on the country. Some social critics downplayed the cultural significance of the process, arguing that middle-class suburbia was neither socially satisfying nor architecturally attractive. Studies of the "Organization Man" and the "Lonely Crowd" suggested that middle-class suburban life was nothing more than a "rat race" to "keep up with the Joneses." Ignoring these cultural criticisms, middle-class families voted with their moving vans, their Chevrolets, and their FHA mortgages to create a new suburban society.

Suburban accessibility, though much greater in this period, continued to be unavailable to the black community. Much of the suburban migration, in fact, originated in urban neighborhoods that white families were abandoning precisely because they feared the prospect of black neighbors. Builders like Levitt capitalized on these fears by enforcing restrictive racial covenants in new suburban developments. Even when the Supreme Court declared these formal racial restrictions unconstitutional in 1948, developers, real estate companies, and mortgage brokers continued informal racial policies designed to ensure that neighborhoods remained lily-white. When middle-class blacks did move into suburban areas, they often relocated to predominantly black communities that abutted older urban neighborhoods.

The mass migration of middle-class families to suburbs in the 1950s meant that suburban society would dominate the national agenda for the remainder of the century. But even as middle-class suburban culture captured the attention of politicians, corporate businessmen, and moviemakers, a backlash against suburban accessibility reintroduced patterns of separatism and privatism within suburbia.

From one perspective, the creation of a national suburban middle class brought a diverse nation closer together. Certain distinctly "suburban" features could be found in almost every metropolitan region. With more and more families moving each year, the strains of relocation were eased by the knowledge that each new city contained suburban neighborhoods similar to the one left behind. Architectural styles might have differed—mission and stucco ranches in southern California, aluminum-sided Cape Cod colonials in the East—but the basic environment of culs-de-sac, two-car garages, and chain-link fences prevailed.

Similarly, the ever-present shopping mall was a cultural and commercial link among suburban communities. Fundamentally dedicated to the values of middle-class consumers, malls became the public space of suburbs after 1970. Mothers walked with babies there, older adults congregated there, and teenagers "hung out" there. In fact, suburban teen culture and mall culture became so synonymous that they provided the subject of several movies in the early 1980s. The centrality of malls to suburban middle-class society was reinforced with the development of regional centers combining office, commercial, retail, and recreational activities in a single location. By the end of the 1980s, many of these suburban downtowns, or "edge cities," had replaced the urban downtown and become suburbia's economic and entertainment hub.

While suburban shopping malls and office complexes did a brisk business with consumers and workers, they also represented another prominent trend within middle-class suburban society, a return to privatism. Critics of enormous malls, or regional supercenters, noted their artificiality and controlled environments. Malls might have replaced the town square as a place for people to gather, but they nevertheless remained privately owned spaces and, through the vigilance of private security officers, limited access to "undesirables."

The private control of suburban space also extended to other areas. In many middle-class subdivisions, walls, gates, and speed bumps announced that outsiders were unwelcome and attempted to re-create the original "exclusive" suburban environment. Many communities even hired private police firms to supplement regular police patrols. Restrictive zoning and high property taxes continued to carve out socially isolated communities; and some communities, like Mount Laurel, New Jersey, or Yonkers, New York, even went to court to try to protect their right *not* to provide low-cost housing. Other communities fought court battles to avoid school busing programs that linked their schools with school districts of different social, economic, or racial composition. Critics attacked these practices as outright racism or, at the very least,

as restricting individual choices and freedoms. Defenders of privatism countered that suburban homeowners had the right to choose their own neighbors and their children's classmates and friends.

This rapid return to suburban privatism might continue to dominate the middle-class suburban agenda in the twenty-first century. After all, most young, middle-class Americans are now second- or even third-generation suburbanites. Middle-class families today will never know the experience of moving to suburbia (they have always been there), nor will they know the social and economic opportunities afforded by earlier suburbanization because it has already passed. Instead, the American middle class, having grown up in suburbs, will most likely focus its energies on sorting itself out and arranging itself in politically, socially, and economically distinct and homogeneous neighborhoods.

In the end, the dominance of middle-class suburban culture within American society has produced tensions between accessibility and privatism in national political debates as well. Questions about affirmative action, minority rights, and ethnic and cultural pluralism share the themes of making political, economic, social, and cultural avenues more or less accessible to certain groups in society. If the history of the suburban middle class is any indication, these national questions will linger for many decades before a solution is found.

—*Etan Diamond*

**See also**

Annexation; Brookline, Massachusetts; Davis, Alexander Jackson; Levittown; Llewellyn Park, New Jersey; Olmsted, Frederick Law; Riverside, Illinois; Suburban Ideal; Transportation; White Flight.

**References**

Binford, Henry C. *The First Suburbs: Residential Communities on the Boston Periphery, 1815–1860.* Chicago: University of Chicago Press, 1985.

Fishman, Robert. *Bourgeois Utopias: The Rise and Fall of Suburbia.* New York: Basic Books, 1987.

Garreau, Joel. *Edge City: Life on the New Frontier.* New York: Doubleday, 1991.

Jackson, Kenneth T. *Crabgrass Frontier: The Suburbanization of the United States.* New York: Oxford University Press, 1985.

Kelly, Barbara, ed. *Suburbia Re-examined.* New York: Greenwood Press, 1989.

Marsh, Margaret. *Suburban Lives.* New Brunswick, NJ: Rutgers University Press, 1990.

Polenberg, Richard. *One Nation Divisible: Class, Race, Ethnicity in the United States since 1938.* New York: Viking Press, 1980.

Riesman, David. *The Lonely Crowd.* New Haven, CT: Yale University Press, 1961.

Stilgoe, John R. *Borderland: Origins of the American Suburb, 1820–1939.* New Haven, CT: Yale University Press, 1988.

Warner, Sam Bass, Jr. *Streetcar Suburbs: The Process of Growth in Boston, 1870–1900.* Cambridge, MA: Harvard University Press, 1962.

Whyte, William H., Jr. *The Organization Man.* New York: Touchstone, 1956.

Zunz, Olivier. *The Changing Face of Inequality: Urbanization, Industrial Development, and Immigrants in Detroit, 1880–1920.* Chicago: University of Chicago Press, 1982.

# Middletown

Middletown is the pseudonym for Muncie, Indiana, which has come to be regarded as the typical American small city. The name is the one that Robert and Helen Lynd used when they studied Muncie in the mid-1920s and is also what they called their first study of the city.

The impetus for the study came from the Institute for Social and Religious Research, which John D. Rockefeller, Jr., funded and which sought to unify all American Protestant churches into a single vast social service network. The institute gave its highest priority to a Small City Study that would analyze the total religious activities of a single industrial city. Among the requirements set by the institute and its first study director were that the city had to be located in the industrial Northeast or Midwest region of the country, that it contain between 25,000 and 50,000 residents, that it have a high proportion of foreign-born residents, that it have a minimum population growth rate of 35 percent in the previous decade, that it be a county seat, and that it have members of all the major religious denominations in the United States.

Before the study even began, a new director, Robert S. Lynd, assumed control. After an abortive effort to conduct the study in South Bend, Indiana, he changed the criterion regarding foreign-born residents to native-born, and picked Muncie, Indiana, as the site. Moving there with his young wife in 1924, Lynd, who had no previous experience in community surveys, floundered for a time before he adopted a scheme originated by the British social anthropologist W. H. R. Rivers to study primitive societies. The Lynds gathered data by means of participant observation, interviews, document examination, and statistical manipulation.

When the results were put in book form, the Lynds had great difficulty finding a publisher before Harcourt, Brace accepted it. *Middletown: A Study of American Culture* appeared in 1929 and has remained in print ever since. The book contained a wealth of detail concerning everyday life that has become the stock of social history; its main theme was the pernicious impact of industrialization and modernization on an American community and its people. According to the Lynds, the town had been transformed from a rural, pre-industrial community to an industrial one. Starting as a happy town whose population consisted largely of skilled workers, Muncie had become an unhappy one divided between a business class and an anxious working class, mostly unskilled, caught in the toils of a heartless industrial system. Industrialization had produced a society divided into classes but unaware of that division. Industrial workers now suffered from blocked mobility as skilled workers were either reduced to the level of unskilled operatives or never able to rise above that level. The workers, however, were not rebellious; they were willing to support and fit into the system because they had bought into the values of a consumer society. But the desire to consume was common to all levels of society, as the entire population believed that consumer goods reflected social status and social position.

The book has had a tremendous impact on American intellectual life and has stimulated continued study of the town. The Lynds wrote a sequel, *Middletown in Transition: A Study in Cultural Conflicts,* in 1937, and a team of sociologists using the name Middletown III published two books, *Middletown Families* (1982) and *All Faithful People* (1983), detailing 50 years of change in the town. Finally, a five-part film on Middletown appeared on public television in 1982. It is described in *Middletown: The Making of a Documentary Film Series.*

—*Dwight Hoover*

**See also**
Lynd, Robert S. and Helen M.
**References**
Caplow, Theodore. "The Gradual Process of Equality in Middletown: A Tocquevillean Theme Re-examined." *Tocqueville Review* 1 (1979): 114–126.
Caplow, Theodore, and Howard Bahr, et al. *All Faithful People.* Minneapolis: University of Minnesota Press, 1983.
———. *Middletown Families: Fifty Years of Change and Continuity.* Minneapolis: University of Minnesota Press, 1982.
Hoover, Dwight. *Magic Middletown.* Bloomington: Indiana University Press, 1986.
———. *Middletown: The Making of a Documentary Film Series.* Philadelphia: Harwood Academic Publishers, 1992.
———. "Middletown Again." *Prospects* 15 (1990): 445–486.
Janis, Ralph. "Middletown Revisited: Searching for the Heart of Mid-America." *Indiana Magazine of History* 78 (1982): 346–361.

# Migration from Rural to Urban Areas

Throughout the history of the United States, rural-to-urban migration has occurred continually, transforming the nation from one that was overwhelmingly rural in 1820 to one that is now only marginally so. While the existence of this migration has itself been consistent, its dimensions, causes, and consequences have changed significantly over time. These patterns are related in understandable ways to structural economic, demographic, and social changes in both urban and rural areas. Because of the close relationship between urban conditions and rural population change, and the effect of rural out-migration on urban economic growth, an understanding of rural-to-urban migration is crucial to the story of urban development.

The term *rural-to-urban migration* usually refers to net migration from rural to urban areas, or migration from rural to urban areas not including migration from urban to rural areas. Theoretically, this migration should be able to be measured at the national, state, or local level, but data constraints complicate measurement below the national level since the destinations of rural out-migrants are generally unknown; they may be headed for urban areas or for rural areas in other states or localities. At these lower levels, measurement of "net rural out-migration" must suffice. These restrictions exist because migration from rural to urban areas, like most forms of internal migration, are largely undocumented and must be estimated indirectly. Unlike international migration where customs procedures and the variable of birthplace provide reasonably reliable measures of migration, internal migration usually occurs informally and in ways that are not measured. In a highly mobile society like the United States, even data on the state of birth help little since rural-to-urban migration can occur within the same state, and migration between states is not necessarily from rural to urban areas.

In the absence of special survey data that is specifically designed to measure migration, rural-to-urban migration must be measured indirectly. The most common method is to examine a rural population at two different times and then consider the difference between the actual population at the time of the second count and what that population would have been expected to be if the entire population change had occurred only because of births and deaths. The difference between the actual and the expected population at the second count can then be attributed to net migration, although the reliability of these estimates depends on the quality of the population figures themselves as well as on the assumptions made about the expected levels of fertility and mortality in the intervening years. This "census survival procedure" can be applied to both historical and contemporary data, although reliability is clearly lower for past events about which there is less accurate knowledge of fertility and mortality rates. While rural-to-urban migration can be estimated with this technique on a national level, at local levels these estimates measure net rural out-migration more fairly since the destinations of people leaving a rural area may have been either urban or rural.

An additional complication to obtaining an accurate historical perspective on rural-to-urban migration is the changing meanings of the terms "rural" and "urban." The census bureau currently defines the urban population as those people living in an incorporated place with 2,500 or more inhabitants, or in an unincorporated but "census designated" place of 2,500 or more inhabitants, as well as those residing in other territory included in "urbanized areas." The rural population consists of everyone else. These definitions have not been consistent over time, with a major change occurring when the concept of the "urbanized area" was introduced in 1950. In addition, communities that cross the 2,500 threshold between censuses are reclassified as urban; this greatly complicates measuring rural-to-urban migration since there

can be significant negative change in rural population due to community growth rather than out-migration.

Yet, despite these methodological difficulties, some sense of the magnitude of the population shift to cities can be gained by looking at the table below. Needless to say, these data do not represent migration figures per se, but only changes in the relative shares of the population that are rural or urban. Even in the absence of rural-to-urban migration, these shifts can occur because of differential rates of fertility and mortality in rural and urban areas, as well as international immigration, which can (and did) contribute disproportionately to the populations of rural and urban areas. Yet the table, while a simplification, provides insight into the temporal pacing of the shift to a distinct rural minority in population share. Obviously, one critical year is 1920 when the census first shows that more than 50 percent of the population lived in urban places.

While rural-to-urban migration occurred in the early and mid-nineteenth century, this movement was masked to a certain extent by the simultaneous expansion of the western frontier. Although some rural people in the New England and Middle Atlantic states gravitated to large, coastal eastern cities like Boston and Philadelphia, others went west, to settle in the Midwest or beyond. Yet, by the late nineteenth and early twentieth centuries, as the availability of new agricultural land diminished, and as changing agricultural technologies permitted the average size of farms to increase while the demand for farm labor was decreasing, migration out of

**Proportions of Urban and Rural Population in the United States, 1880–1990**

| Year | Percentage | |
|------|-------|-------|
|      | Urban | Rural |
| 1880 | 28.2 | 71.8 |
| 1890 | 35.1 | 64.9 |
| 1900 | 39.6 | 60.4 |
| 1910 | 45.6 | 54.4 |
| 1920 | 51.2 | 48.8 |
| 1930 | 56.1 | 43.9 |
| 1940 | 56.5 | 43.5 |
| 1950 | 64.0 | 36.0 |
| 1960 | 69.9 | 30.0 |
| 1970 | 73.6 | 26.4 |
| 1980 | 73.7 | 26.3 |
| 1990 | 72.8 | 27.2 |

**Note:** A change in the definition of "urban" occurred in 1950 because of the inclusion of the creation of the concept of an "urbanized area."
**Source:** *Current Population Reports—Population Characteristics, Series P-20, No. 457,* Table B.

rural areas began to surpass movement into rural places. Much of the migration to rural and frontier areas in the nineteenth century was undertaken by entire families, but the surging rural out-migration of the late nineteenth and early twentieth centuries was concentrated among single adults and was aimed at the large cities of the East and Midwest.

A reduction in agricultural opportunity was a major determinant of this migration, but probably more important were the growing opportunities in cities, particularly in the burgeoning manufacturing sector. Manufacturing jobs provided economic independence for both men and women, and cities provided a host of social amenities unavailable in rural communities. While rural blacks remained largely trapped by sharecropping and tenancy in the South, young whites left rural areas in great numbers, particularly during the first two decades of the twentieth century, and joined European immigrants in the major cities.

Progressive Era reformers, already concerned about what they viewed as the unwholesome nature of rapidly growing cities, viewed this migration away from farms and rural areas with alarm. Nostalgic attachment to rural farm life by the native-born, white, farm population led many to view rural depopulation with alarm. The perception that rural out-migration was selective caused great concern that the farm population was declining both quantitatively and qualitatively. One early response was the appointment of a Commission on Country Life by President Theodore Roosevelt in 1908. Its major objective was to study the so-called "rural problem" and find ways to increase the rewards of farm life in order to reduce migration. The YMCA started rural outreach programs to encourage rural Christian leadership and community building. The U.S. Department of Agriculture created the Cooperative Extension Service, which with 4-H clubs for youth and various services for adults endeavored to raise rural standards of living and encourage positive thought about agricultural life. Yet, this combination of propaganda and reform had little effect on migratory flows, which continued in the same direction after World War I.

In the late 1910s and on into the 1920s, the substantial flow of whites to urban areas was joined by a significant out-migration of rural blacks from the South, a movement that has come to be known as the "Great Migration." In a direct sense, this migration was motivated by economic factors; one was the increased demand for urban labor caused by restrictions on foreign immigration in the early 1920s, while another was the effect of the boll weevil on the cotton economy of the South. But noneconomic factors also played a role, particularly the desire of African Americans for the social and political freedoms they associated with northern life and the news of northern economic opportunities that was increasingly relayed by earlier migrants. Although this migration

slowed by approximately 50 percent during the 1930s, it regained momentum after World War II and played a significant role in population redistribution through the middle of the 1960s.

Although there had been a black presence in some cities since the nineteenth century, the migration after World War I led to the rapid growth of black urban communities in most northeastern and midwestern cities. The implications were profound and multifaceted. On a cultural level, the national awareness of black musicians such as Muddy Waters and Robert Johnson was greatly enhanced by the migration, particularly the movement between the southern Delta and Chicago, and blues became an important form of musical entertainment for all Americans. Political ramifications of the migration were significant as well and differed in each city as urban political machines that had originally been designed by and for European immigrants responded to the presence of a new group of voters. From a national political perspective, the move out of the Jim Crow South and into the North transformed many blacks from nonvoters to voters and accordingly pressed the federal government to reconsider its position on civil rights. President Franklin D. Roosevelt's tentative movement in favor of broader rights was one of many factors influencing the widespread abandonment of the Republican Party by blacks during the 1930s, a transition that has had significant political consequences ever since.

Both academicians and policymakers have treated the migration of blacks and whites to urban areas quite differently. Because of the intense poverty and perceived backwardness of the rural South, there was little weeping about the population depletion of rural southern communities, and the consequences of black migration for northern cities have received much more attention. The development of racially segregated residential neighborhoods has elicited much comparison to European immigration. In the 1960s, concerns about black urban poverty produced many studies of "ghettoization" that attempted to analyze the effects of racial prejudice and the political and economic structures of cities on the process of black community formation. Recent research has brought a more sophisticated understanding of spatial and temporal variations in urban economic opportunities and a heightened awareness and understanding of the importance of kinship structures and the migratory process itself in shaping black urban settlement.

During the 1950s and 1960s, rural-to-urban migration continued among both blacks and whites. One major cause of this population movement was the continued mechanization and specialization of agriculture, and a corresponding dearth of alternative opportunities in rural areas. Yet opportunities for unskilled workers in urban areas also declined after World War II, and there was a growing awareness of rural poverty and the lower availability of education and health care in rural than urban areas. The federal government increasingly realized that the problems of rural America were not synonymous with those of agriculture and that out-migration was not a panacea. The development of nonagricultural programs for rural areas began during the Eisenhower administration in the 1950s. Some were aimed at moving rural residents out of unprofitable, small-scale agriculture and into other kinds of employment. Federally funded highway construction, for example, aided many rural communities but placed others at a severe disadvantage. During the Kennedy and Johnson administrations, the rural poor received particular attention, and the federal government attempted to improve education, nutrition, and sanitation, as well as to diversify economic opportunities in rural communities to slow further out-migration. These efforts continued during the Nixon and Carter administrations, but they were curtailed significantly during the Reagan presidency when agricultural subsidies dominated federal rural policy, partly because of the farm crisis of the 1980s.

As farms have become larger and more productive, the farm population has declined, from more than 24 million in 1945 to fewer than 5 million in 1990. The word "rural" is no longer equivalent to "farm," and far fewer than half of today's rural areas are primarily agricultural.

Since the 1970s, rural areas have restructured themselves in significant ways. Dependence on natural resource industries such as agriculture has decreased, and growth has occurred in manufacturing and government employment. Improvements in communications and transportation have blurred social and economic distinctions in certain respects, and some rural places on the urban fringe function largely as suburbs. Rural communities today are diverse in both their economic structure and well-being. Some have successfully developed manufacturing and public employment sectors while others have become popular destinations for retirees and vacationers. Many others have stagnated economically, and in the 1970s and 1980s many of the gains in rural manufacturing were lost to overseas competitors. Currently, rural poverty rates exceed those of urban areas, and migration to urban areas offers few prospects to poorly educated rural residents.

A brief turnaround in the otherwise persistent rural out-migration occurred during the 1970s, when rural areas experienced a net in-migration of 4 million people. A desire for rural amenities by urban commuters and the revitalization of the rural economy were primary factors. However, this trend did not persist during the 1980s even though rural areas grew slightly; in 1990, almost 67 million Americans, approximately 27 percent of the population, lived in rural places. Recent population growth in rural areas is thought to be primarily due to the expansion of metropolitan areas into the rural communities on their fringes. But as this expansion persists, rural communities cross the line between urban and rural population and become reclassified as part of metropolitan areas. Such changes in categorization complicate measuring rural migration, but it nevertheless appears that while the wholesale depopulation of rural areas that occurred in the first half of the twentieth century has abated, the current population growth of rural areas is essentially stagnant and is closely linked to the growth of metropolitan areas.

—*Katherine Hempstead*

**See also**
Metropolitan Area.
**References**
Dahmann, Donald C., and Laarni T. Dacquel. "Residents of Farms and Rural Areas: 1990." *Current Population Reports—Population Characteristics, Series P-20, No. 457,* Appendix A. Washington, DC: Government Printing Office, 1991.
Lapping, Mark, Thomas L. Daniels, and John W. Keller, eds. *Rural Planning and Development in the United States.* New York: Guilford Press, 1989.
Trotter, Joe William, Jr., ed. *The Great Migration in Historical Perspective: New Dimensions of Race, Class and Gender.* Bloomington: Indiana University Press, 1991.

## Military and Cities

Warfare and militarism have profoundly affected urban development and city life in the United States. The nature of the relationship, however, has varied with changes in the American warfare state. Prior to the twentieth century, the urban impact of militarism was generally temporary or episodic, occurring most forcefully in times of war. But with the rise of the United States as a global power after 1890, as historian Roger N. Lotchin has pointed out, American cities have entered into more permanent partnerships with the military and its civilian contractors. Since World War II and throughout the permanent mobilization of the Cold War, the military has played a pivotal role in shaping metropolitan development around the country.

In early American cities, defense against intruders—either Indians or foreign aggressors—was of critical importance. Spanish military forts, or presidios, founded in the eighteenth century, were the crucibles of urban growth in several western locations including San Antonio, San Diego, San Francisco, and Los Angeles. In the Ohio Valley and Great Lakes regions, Pittsburgh, Cincinnati, Detroit, Louisville, and other cities developed around fortified French trading posts. Even some of the major commercial seaport cities like New York, Charleston, and New Orleans featured defensive walls and fortifications that revealed these cities' martial character. But as the frontier receded and foreign powers withdrew,

*In a major naval port like San Diego, California, the presence of the military is always obvious.*

the defensive orientation of these cities gave way to civilian control and commercial development.

A number of American cities, however, maintained their martial character well into the twentieth century. With the establishment of naval shipyards in Charlestown, Massachusetts (1800), Norfolk, Virginia (1800), Brooklyn, New York (1801), Vallejo, California (1854), and other ports, the navy became a major local employer, attracting other businesses and transportation operations to these areas. Army posts like Fort Riley, founded in 1853 near Junction City, Kansas, and Fort Sam Houston, established in 1873 outside San Antonio, Texas, outlived their frontier origins to become economic pillars of their respective communities.

The number of long-term urban-military partnerships increased in the twentieth century as the United States became a global power. The naval buildup that began in the 1890s gave rise to a fierce urban rivalry for future home port sites and other naval facilities. Over the next few decades, Norfolk, San Diego, Charleston, Bremerton, and other cities that landed such plums became self-proclaimed "navy towns" and did whatever they could to accommodate the fleet. With the advent of airborne warfare, similar urban-military partnerships developed in communities that successfully attracted new air stations and air force bases. The powerful urban-military coalitions that developed in these cities skillfully used their initial assets as a basis for wooing future military operations to an area. But despite the rise of this "metropolitan-military complex," as Roger Lotchin calls it, few American cities were heavily dependent on defense before World War II.

Through much of the nation's history, the military had its greatest impact on cities during wartime, when mobilization, migration, and warfare dramatically affected urban centers. As centers for military recruitment and enlistment, cities became sites of both patriotic ceremony and violent resistance. During the Civil War, Union cities like Springfield, Massachusetts, paid unprecedented sums in cash bounties to attract local recruits, and city fathers in Philadelphia sponsored elaborate civic pageants to promote enlistment. In New York City, however, widespread antidraft sentiment among the city's Irish working class led to three days of bloody rioting in 1863, a phenomenon repeated in several other northern cities. During the Vietnam War, antidraft violence was also common in American cities, especially those with large universities. Moreover, as sites of wartime troop embarkation, many coastal cities became raucous boom towns where male service personnel sought entertainment, vice, and other diversions.

More importantly, war changed the physical and economic infrastructure of cities, disrupting trade and development in some cities while accelerating them in others. During the Revolution, the British occupation of New York and the economic stability that resulted permanently benefited that city at the expense of Philadelphia and Boston. During the Civil War, Chicago profited from the closing of the lower Mississippi and seized much of the western trade previously controlled by St. Louis. At the same time, the burning of Atlanta and other Confederate cities devastated much of the urban South, crippling the region for years after the Civil War.

In the twentieth century, military production for World War I and World War II boosted urban economies throughout the country by bringing federal defense contracts, expanding industrial operations, and generating an influx of migrant workers. To accommodate this growth, the federal government intervened directly in urban affairs: it provided temporary housing and community facilities, built roads and airfields, policed vice, and directed other activities associated with the war. Much of the wartime growth and federal activity took place along the urban periphery, thus accelerating the process of suburbanization.

Wartime developments also transformed urban social relations. During all major American wars, the influx of migrants and refugees taxed urban communities and resulted in social stress and dislocation. Competition for food, housing, employment, transportation, and other services contributed to the Richmond bread riot of 1863, the New York Draft Riot the same year, and the many wartime and postwar race riots that struck U.S. defense centers in 1917, 1919, 1943, and 1946. Ultimately, black urban migration was one of the most significant legacies of the two world wars.

In the nuclear age, military-urban relationships became more institutionalized as the United States entered a state of permanent mobilization. During World War II, federal authorities located many new military bases, shipyards, aircraft plants, and atomic research centers in the South and West, away from the congested and strategically vulnerable cities of the Northeast. With the escalation of the arms race and the Cold War, many of these facilities stayed open and became the foundation of the nuclear, aerospace, and electronics industries. Such defense-related growth boosted the fortunes of Los Angeles, San Diego, Phoenix, Dallas–Fort Worth, and other Sunbelt (or, as some would say, "Gunbelt") cities at the expense of older industrial centers in the Northeast and Midwest.

With the end of the Cold War, however, many of these same Gunbelt cities have experienced painful economic contractions as bases closed and plants laid off workers. Other cities like Hanford, Washington, and Rocky Flats, Colorado, have encountered serious environmental problems caused by toxic waste. Yet despite these setbacks, some form of institutionalized urban-military relationship is likely to continue as long as defense remains a key function of the American state.

—*Marilynn S. Johnson*

**See also**
Civil Defense.
**References**
Bernstein, Iver. *The New York City Draft Riots: Their Significance for American Society and Politics in the Age of the Civil War.* New York: Oxford University Press, 1990.
Gallman, J. Matthew. *Mastering Wartime: A Social History of Philadelphia during the Civil War.* New York: Cambridge University Press, 1990.
Johnson, Charles W., and Charles O. Jackson. *City behind a Fence: Oak Ridge, Tennessee, 1942–1946.* Knoxville: University of Tennessee Press, 1981.
Johnson, Marilynn S. *The Second Gold Rush: Oakland and the East Bay in World War II.* Berkeley: University of California Press, 1993.
Kirby, Andrew, ed. *The Pentagon and the Cities.* Newbury Park, CA: Sage Publications, 1992.
Lotchin, Roger N. *Fortress California, 1910–1961: From Warfare to Welfare.* New York: Oxford University Press, 1992.
———, ed. *The Martial Metropolis: U.S. Cities in War and Peace.* New York: Praeger, 1984.
Miller, Marc Scott. *The Irony of Victory: World War II and Lowell, Massachusetts.* Urbana: University of Illinois Press, 1988.

## Mill Towns

One of the unique settings in the history of American urban development is the mill town where a single steel mill, lumber mill, coal mill, or textile mill constructed, owned, and controlled an entire town. The aim in creating these instant communities was to attract, house, and ultimately control a workforce. From the late eighteenth century until the middle of the twentieth, mill owners governed both mill and town, sometimes with benevolent paternalism. For workers living in these industrialized communities, the mill town became the political, social, economic, and religious center of their lives. The story of textile mill towns typifies the mill town experience as well as any.

Textile mills began appearing in late-eighteenth-century New England as part of America's expanding economy and population. Because they were water-powered, the first textile mills were constructed along swiftly flowing rivers often far from any settlement. Samuel Slater built the first textile mill in Pawtucket, Rhode Island, in the early 1790s, and he used the traditional New England village as a model for his new mill community. The basic layout of the mill village consisted of cottages and company stores haphazardly built next to a mill located by a river. Only later, as the town became established, did the mill owner add a church and school. Slater and most other owners of small mills hired entire families, including wives and small children, to work in their mills. This setting was duplicated at other nearby locations, and by 1815 more than 170 mill villages surrounded Pawtucket.

Although some mill towns would be much larger later on, mill owners continued to imitate the design of New England towns for their communities. In 1813, the Boston Manufacturing Company, directed by Francis Cabot Lowell, established communities like Waltham, and later Lowell, Massachusetts. These towns resembled New England college campuses, like Harvard, more than factory communities. Instead of employing entire families like earlier, smaller mill villages, the mills at Waltham and Lowell were staffed by young, female operatives from rural New England. Work, good cash wages (from $1.85 to $3.00 a week), and family ties attracted young women from farms in Massachusetts, Vermont, New Hampshire, and Maine. These young women, whose average age was about 16, worked in the mills for four or five years. Mill owners promised parents that their daughters would live and work in a strict religious and morally pure environment.

Boardinghouses served as one way of controlling the young operatives. Although contemporary critics complained about dirt, poor ventilation, and overcrowded conditions, the housekeepers served as moral police who imposed curfews (usually 10:00 P.M.), enforced rules against alcohol, and tattled to mill owners about the women's deportment and church attendance. Evening schools, libraries, charities, lectures, and self-improvement clubs added to the reputed quality of the environment.

Larger towns like Lowell differed greatly from typical mill villages of the 1840s. An average mill town like Ludlow, Massachusetts, remained small, situated in a rural area, and used entire families for labor. Unlike proprietors of large mills, owners of smaller works usually lived and worked in the villages themselves. The cluster of hamlets scattered around Rockdale, Pennsylvania, represents the typical mill town experience during this period. Each settlement resembled a New England village, and the mill owner lived in a great house on a hill where he could look down on tenements that he had provided for his workers near the mill.

In the 1830s, some textile mills and mill communities expanded. To meet increased competition, mill owners reduced wages, instituted speedups, and ignored the maintenance of boardinghouses. Strikes in the 1830s and the movement in the 1840s for a ten-hour working day signaled growing discontent with deteriorating conditions in mills and mill towns. Mill owners in Lowell and other mill towns replaced young female operatives with newly arrived immigrants who worked for lower wages. By 1860, immigrant Irish women who provided their own housing and no longer lived in company-owned boardinghouses made up most of the workforce.

In the antebellum, cotton-growing South, there had been some attempts to construct mills and mill towns. In 1846, William Gregg of South Carolina copied the New England mill village by providing housing, company stores, a school, and a church for workers and their families. But textile manufacturing did not flourish in the South until after the Civil War, when northern mill owners began building factories in the southern Piedmont. Entrepreneurs built textile factories and mill communities from southern Virginia to Alabama. As in the North, mill owners built homes and mill towns to attract and control a labor force. Because of the devastated economy in the South, many whites chose to work in the mills and live in the adjacent villages. Like early New England operatives, southern mill workers came from the rural society that surrounded the new mills. Most of the early southern factory workers were widows with children, yeoman farmers unable to compete in the growing market economy, mountain people looking for steady incomes, and anyone who already had family in the mill towns.

The low wages paid by the mills forced family members to pool their earnings. Mill owners, in order to clear as much as possible from the housing they provided, required at least one worker per room per house. Families without enough children or adults often took in boarders. Children older than 12 were expected to supplement the family income and observe mill rules. Families faced eviction for not filling their quota of workers, disturbing the peace, drinking, and pregnancy outside of marriage. By 1900, about 92 percent of southern textile families lived in villages owned by mills.

A typical southern mill village consisted of the superintendent's residence, single-family dwellings, one or more frame churches, a schoolhouse, and a company store. Owners of mill towns considered these facilities necessary for workers and a way of maintaining their own authority. The company store, where workers redeemed their payment of script, kept operatives constantly in debt. Even when owners provided housing in an already established town, the mill community remained apart. Although some Piedmont mill towns provided modern services, like electricity and indoor plumbing, these facilities remained rare in mill towns until well into the twentieth century.

Rarely did a mill village have a church from its inception. Only when a mill town grew large enough did the mill owner construct a church and determine which denominations, usually only Protestant, could use it. Southern mill owners, like their New England counterparts, imposed rigid moral codes on their workers. Mill owners appointed a sheriff to maintain order even if the mill community was part of an established town with a law enforcement bureaucracy.

In the late nineteenth and early twentieth centuries, mill owners commonly tried to improve their towns: they built libraries and churches; provided cultural centers like the YMCA; installed modern conveniences like electricity, indoor plumbing, and paved streets; offered improved educational facilities; and embarked on beautification campaigns. While mill town owners remained paternalistic and relied on codes of morality to control workers, they also began to recognize the importance of better living and working conditions; they also dealt with public health issues like mild plagues.

After World War I, a less paternalistic, more corporate-minded mill management emerged. Increased production in the 1920s caused a vicious cycle of price-cutting, wage-cutting, and layoffs. Workers lost jobs to new technologies, and owners faced renewed foreign competition. In the 1930s, mill owners relinquished company housing and other property and began to abandon the village system. They offered workers the choice of purchasing their homes or leaving the mills.

Mill communities continued to exist where mills remained in operation. Most mill towns were no longer owned by mills, but their existence continued to depend on the mill's success. Textile mills, once considered the economic salvation of the rural South, began closing in the 1970s and 1980s because of automation and international competition. Mill towns faced unemployment, failed businesses, and the out-migration of residents. Other communities centering around steel mills or lumber mills confronted similar problems. Once the mainstay of industrialization for a growing economy and the means of urbanization for a rural society, the mill town has largely disappeared from the American landscape.

—*Craig Pascoe*

**See also**
Coal Towns; Company Towns.
**References**
Carlton, David L. *Mill and Town in South Carolina, 1880–1920.* Baton Rouge: Louisiana State University Press, 1982.
Dawley, Alan. *Class and Community: The Industrial Revolution in Lynn.* Cambridge, England: Cambridge University Press, 1976.
Hall, Jacquelyn Dowd, et al. *Like a Family: The Making of a Southern Cotton Mill World.* Chapel Hill: University of North Carolina Press, 1987.
Hareven, Tamara K., and Randolph Langenbach. *Amoskeag: Life and Work in an American Factory City.* New York: Pantheon, 1978.
Hartford, William F. *Working People of Holyoke: Class and Ethnicity in a Massachusetts Mill Town, 1850–1960.* New Brunswick, NJ: Rutgers University Press, 1990.
Kulik, Gary, Roger Parks, and Theodore Z. Penn, eds. *Documents in American Industrial History; Volume II: New England Mill Village, 1790–1860.* Cambridge, MA: MIT Press, 1982.
Wallace, Anthony F. C. *Rockdale: The Growth of an American Village in the Early Industrial Revolution.* New York: Knopf, 1978.

## Milwaukee, Wisconsin

From its beginning as a wilderness trading post in the early 1800s to its rise as a major manufacturing city by the middle of the twentieth century and then to its struggle to adapt to the emerging postindustrial world, Milwaukee has experienced stunning growth and also, for many, devastating decline. Long an ethnically diverse city, Milwaukee experienced explosive growth, and arguably its most prosperous years, between 1920 and 1970 when its population grew from less than 500,000 to more than 740,000. Despite setbacks during the Depression, the massive in-migration that began around 1900, annexation, and the development of a manufacturing base made Milwaukee a thriving community during the middle decades of the twentieth century.

Historically, Milwaukee has been characterized by a large number of foreign-born citizens, particularly from Germany. Germans accounted for one-fourth of the city's residents as the nineteenth century ended, and while they account for less than 10 percent of the population in the 1990s, German culture remains a significant influence. By 1960, blacks accounted for over 8 percent of the population, and currently about one-third of the city's population is African American. During the last two decades of the 1900s, the city lost much of its manufacturing base, its population declined, and the black population has endured an inordinate share of the costs of these transformations.

During the post–World War II years, Milwaukee experienced a dramatic decline in manufacturing and a rise in service employment. As in other cities, redevelopment initiatives focusing on downtown revitalization generated pockets of prosperity amidst growing poverty. As the year 2000 neared, downtown Milwaukee and its suburbs thrived while many communities throughout the balance of the city were suffering. Inequality, particularly along racial lines, was exacerbated during those years. Thus, the case of Milwaukee concretely illustrates the dynamics of uneven development in urban America since World War II.

Milwaukee emerged from World War II as a growing and prosperous city. That prosperity was rooted in the city's durable goods manufacturing industries. By the start of World War II, Milwaukee was a world leader in the production of heavy manufacturing equipment. During the war itself, Milwaukee's machine shops did most of the metalwork required for the atom bomb project. And while Milwaukee's economy was sound at the conclusion of hostilities, its downtown was deteriorating as in many other cities.

In 1948 business leaders organized the Greater Milwaukee Committee to revitalize the central business district. Formally, this partnership operated through private channels until 1973, when it created the Milwaukee Redevelopment Corporation to direct increasing amounts of local and federal dollars for urban development into private development projects. In urban redevelopment circles, "public-private partnership" became economic buzzwords in the 1970s, 1980s, and 1990s, and Milwaukee has been no exception. In 1986, Milwaukee's commissioner for city development stated, "Partnership. That word seems to apply to nearly every significant accomplishment of the Department of City Development." Downtown Milwaukee has indeed been revitalized. But there is far more to the story.

During the mid-1950s, Milwaukee's manufacturing base began to decline. The decline took a sharp turn from the mid-1970s to the mid-1980s. Household names like Allis-Chalmers, Allen Bradley, Schlitz, and American Motors shut down, reduced operations, or shifted production to other places. As research by Milwaukee's Department of City Development, the Urban Research Center of the University of Wisconsin-Milwaukee, and others has shown, Milwaukee lost 27,000 manufacturing jobs between 1975 and 1985. Although the rate of loss declined in subsequent years, the loss of jobs has continued. The number of service jobs has increased, but overall the city lost 3 percent of its job base in the 1980s, while the suburbs experienced a 20 percent increase during those years.

While this was a particularly acute time in the restructuring of Milwaukee's economy, these changes reflect longer-term trends that go back to the early 1950s and continue today. The number of manufacturing jobs in Milwaukee dropped from almost 125,000 in 1954 to less than 64,000 in 1994. And while the total number of jobs in the city increased from 284,000 in 1950 to 318,000 in 1990, Milwaukee's share of metropolitan area jobs during those years dropped from 66 percent to 28 percent.

In response to the loss of manufacturing jobs, the city focused its redevelopment efforts on the central business district. As Jack Norman, business reporter for the *Milwaukee Journal* has observed, Milwaukee's "comeback" was kicked off in the early 1980s with the opening of the Grand Avenue Mall, a 250,000-square-foot indoor shopping mall that involved renovating buildings on three city blocks and constructing skywalks to connect the stores and the mall with surrounding office buildings. The partnership making the Grand Avenue Mall possible involved a $12.6 million Urban Development Action Grant, a $20 million contribution that the city raised by issuing municipal bonds and creating a tax-increment finance district, over $15 million invested by the Rouse Corporation, and $20 million provided by 47 local corporations. The mall was followed by many other downtown developments, including the Bradley Center, the Milwaukee Center developed by Trammel Crow featuring a luxury hotel and several restaurants and theaters, a Hyatt Regency Hotel, several new corporate office buildings, and other small commercial establishments. In addition, Northwestern Mutual Life Insurance is developing one major office tower while a Washington, D.C., developer will build two more. Plans are also being considered for expanding the Grand Avenue Mall. A key justification for downtown development in Milwaukee continues to be the assumption that revival of the central business district will spill over into the inner city and other residential neighborhoods.

Downtown is booming, and so are the suburbs. Between 1972 and 1987, while total employment in the city of Milwaukee declined by 3 percent (from 352,180 to 340,390), employment in the suburbs increased by 33 percent (from 396,720 to 531,510). Even manufacturing employment increased 12 percent in the suburbs between 1983 and 1987.

What has not changed is the racial isolation of the Milwaukee metropolitan area. While the black population has grown considerably since the 1950s, it has remained highly concentrated and segregated. The Milwaukee Urban League found that 98.5 percent of the area's black population lived in the city of Milwaukee in 1970. By 1980, 97.5 percent remained within the city limits. More recently, census data reveal that in 1990, 96.7 percent of all black residents in the metropolitan area still lived within the city. While this meant a slight increase in the black suburban population, it meant little in terms of integration. Much of the black suburban growth resulted from the growth of a small black community on the city's north side into a single suburb bordering the city.

Several social costs have been associated with the uneven development of Milwaukee. Following the national trend, average incomes have declined. Department of City Development research showed that between 1977 and 1984 the buying power of median household income in the city declined by 12 percent. In part, this reflects the restructuring of the local economy. The 27,000 manufacturing jobs that the city lost between the mid-1970s and mid-1980s paid an average salary of $23,600 while the 24,000 service jobs it gained during those years paid only $13,000. Compounding these problems is the fact that, as the Social Development Commission found, there are at least seven job seekers for each available job.

There are also other costs. One critical consequence of the declining economic status of many Milwaukee families is the growing cost of housing. Between 1977 and 1984, the median percent of household income spent on rent increased from 26 percent to 32 percent while the proportion of renters spending more than 50 percent of their income on rent increased from 15 percent to 32 percent. As in many other cities, homelessness has subsequently become a problem in Milwaukee, with estimates of the homeless population ranging from 11,000 to 20,000. In 1989, Milwaukee experienced a record high of 112 murders. This was 31 more than in the previous year and 20 more than the previous record of 92 set in 1987. This was only the beginning, as the number of murders in the city increased to 155 in 1990 and 165 in 1991 before decreasing slightly by the middle of the 1990s.

The spatial segregation of racial minorities in Milwaukee (one of the 16 cities Douglas Massey and Nancy Denton labeled "hypersegregated" in their book *American Apartheid*) reflects and reinforces other barriers that confront the city's minority population. According to its executive director, the Metropolitan Milwaukee Fair Housing Council routinely finds racial steering on the part of local realtors. In the mid-1980s, Milwaukee had the highest black-to-white mortgage loan rejection rate among the nation's 50 largest cities, and the city continued to be among the "leaders" in the early 1990s as black applicants were rejected for mortgage loans three or four times more often than whites (according to Home Mortgage Disclosure Act reports). The racial composition of neighborhoods also continues to influence accessibility to homeowners' insurance and other financial services. And, during the 1980s, black unemployment nearly doubled while other groups experienced only a slight increase. The rate of black unemployment persists at approximately 20 percent compared to 3 or 4 percent for whites.

Milwaukee has experienced many of the social costs of uneven economic and spatial development, including greater inequality. Some "partners" are clearly doing better than others. As in other cities, the growing racial inequality reflects both the effects of structural changes and intentional racial discrimination. As the sales manager of the largest property/casualty insurance company in the city advised one agent, "Very honestly, I think you write too many blacks. You gotta sell good, solid premium-paying white people . . . they own their own homes, the white works . . . black people will buy anything that looks good right now, but when it comes to pay for it next time, you're not going to get your money out of them."

Milwaukee is struggling to adapt to the emerging postindustrial world. In this process, uneven development and the social costs of race and class continue to plague the community.

—*Gregory D. Squires*

Portions of this article are reprinted from *Capital and Communities in Black and White* by Gregory D. Squires. By permission of State University of New York Press. © 1994.

**References**

McNeely, R. L., and Melvin Kinlow. *Milwaukee Today: A Racial Gap Study.* Milwaukee, WI: Milwaukee Urban League, 1987.

Norman, Jack. "Congenial Milwaukee: A Segregated City." In Gregory D. Squires, ed., *Unequal Partnerships: The Political Economy of Urban Redevelopment in Postwar America.* New Brunswick, NJ: Rutgers University Press, 1989.

Orum, Anthony M. *City Building in America.* Boulder, CO: Westview Press, 1995.

Trotter, Joe. *Black Milwaukee: The Making of an Industrial Proletariat.* Champaign: University of Illinois Press, 1985.

Wells, Robert W. *This Is Milwaukee.* Milwaukee, WI: Renaissance Books, 1970.

## Mining Towns

American cities can be categorized fairly easily. There are single industry towns; industrially diversified cities; agricultural villages; commercial, mercantile, and banking centers; government and bedroom cities; and mining towns. These last named are places apart, if only because they were literally built to be self-consuming. In his acclaimed novel, *English Creek,* Ivan Doig has one of his characters, a young, rural Montanan, describe the mining town of Butte. Butte, Jack McCaskill says, was a place "where shifts of men tunneled like gophers." Montanans were "a little scared of Butte. There seemed to be something spooky about a place that lived by eating its own guts."

Only mining towns became ghost towns; only mining towns were "site specific" in the sense of being tied to the resource that gave them life. The factors that influenced other urban locations—markets, available workforce, transportation, amenities of sundry sorts—were irrelevant. Industries could move; mines could not. They were fixed, and while the mines ran, the towns continued to eat their own guts. They became daily less livable, more clogged by the heaped slag of their own self-destruction. There were hundreds of such places in America, no other as large or as dominating as Butte, but each spooky in its own way.

That men would tunnel underneath the streets of their city was only one characteristic of mining towns. Just as important was the fact that mining, whether hard rock or coal, was the single most dangerous occupation in America. Men took great risks of injury, even greater risks of diseases like pneumoconiosis, frequently called black lung or miners' con. These were tough and/or desperate men, and their towns mirrored that toughness and some of that desperation. But their willingness to incur these risks also gave miners a special status. Not only did mining town merchants and professionals economically depend on the miners, they took their definitions of justice and community, even of "manliness," from them as well.

That miners came from almost everywhere on earth also contributed to the unique character of their camps and towns. Mining towns were more racially, ethnically, and culturally mixed than other American urban areas. Mining workforces were also younger, more likely to be unmarried, more willing to engage in worker militancy, and more footloose than all but a handful of other trades. All of this gave to mining towns an ephemeral, almost an evanescent, quality. It is not coincidental that they were called camps until such time as they had proven their stability and staying power and earned the label "town." Some of them, such as Butte, became major industrial centers; others, Cripple Creek, Colorado, for example, lived fast, fitfully—and briefly. Little wonder that they were home to more bars and houses of prostitution than any other

*A new city was expected to spring up rapidly at this site where gold was discovered in 1927.*

American cities except seaports—with which mining towns had certain striking similarities.

If their varied "amusements" distinguished them, it was the corporate dominance that marked most of them that truly typified American mining communities. A transient work-force put a premium on company ownership of boarding houses and stores; unpredictable markets forced companies to seek greater efficiencies of scale, whether in the anthracite fields of Pennsylvania or the copper mines of Montana, Arizona, and Utah. Whether this *had* to mean corporate consolidations and consequent corporate dominance can be debated; that it meant it *in fact* cannot.

There is one final point. For all these reasons and more, there are no surviving American mining towns, at least of the sort that distinguished the nineteenth and early part of the twentieth centuries. Some were victims of the same economic forces that broke the steel towns; others simply self-destructed. Butte survives but its deep mines are shut down and filled with water. Leadville, Colorado; Goldfield, Nevada; Mahanoy City and Shamokin, Pennsylvania; and most of the villages of Harlan County, Kentucky, and other coal-mining counties of Appalachia are either idled or seriously "deindustrialized." Aspen, Park City, Telluride, Crested Butte, Alta, Lead, Kellogg, and scores of other mining/smelting towns have become ski resorts. Still others, Garnet, Polaris, Elkhorn, Caribeau, Little Chicago, and Bodie, are inhabited only by ghosts. All of them, regardless of their present circumstance, are victims of the postindustrial blues, of the deindustrialization of America.

—*David M. Emmons*

**References**

Lingenfelter, Richard. *The Hardrock Miners: A History of the Mining Labor Movement in the American West, 1863–1893.* Berkeley: University of California Press, 1974.

Mann, Ralph. *After the Gold Rush: Society in Grass Valley and Nevada City, California, 1849–1870.* Stanford, CA: Stanford University Press, 1982.

Rohrbough, Malcolm. *Aspen: The History of a Silver Mining Town, 1879–1893.* New York: Oxford University Press, 1986.

Smith, Duane A. *Mining America: The Industry and the Environment, 1800–1980.* Lawrence: University Press of Kansas, 1987.

———. *Rocky Mountain Boom Town: A History of Durango.* Albuquerque: University of New Mexico Press, 1980.

# Mobile Home Communities

Between one-fifth and one-quarter of all single-family housing built over the last three decades consists of mobile homes. At less than half the cost per square foot of site-built housing, mobile homes are a primary source of unsubsidized, affordable housing in the United States.

Mobile homes are completely assembled, equipped, and even furnished in enclosed factories. Built on chassis with their own axles and wheels, they are transported from factory to site where they are tied down with anchors or set on foundations and then hooked up to utilities. Today, fewer than 10 percent of mobile homes will ever move once they are brought to a site. Indeed, the term *mobile* is misleading, and the federal government has adopted the industry's preferred term *manufactured housing* in legislation passed since 1979.

Because of their virtually permanent attachment to a site, the development and design of mobile home communities have been integral to the market success of this form of housing. Community design must support the lifestyle requirements of residents, but it must also appeal to residents and officials of the larger community where prejudice against mobile home communities must be placated.

The modern mobile home evolved from the automobile travel trailer, which had achieved enormous popularity by the mid-1930s, when an estimated 10 million Americans were taking to the road annually on trailering vacations. The demand for adequate campsites created the basis for the trailer park industry. The 1937 edition of the *Official Directory of Trailer Parks and Camps* estimated the total number of trailer parks in the United States at 3,300. Several proposals for franchised trailer parks with names like Gliderville and Trailer Town were developed, but few were actually constructed until the 1950s. For the most part, trailer parks were "mom and pop" operations, often attached to some other enterprise like a gas station or vacation cottages. Since contemporary trailers did not contain their own sanitary facilities, parks provided these along with picnic tables and electricity. For their part, local community officials discouraged trailer park developments because of concern that the transient population would set down roots. Ordinances were passed to assure that parks were confined to less desirable areas of town and their patrons' stay limited.

The onset of World War II rapidly and radically transformed the use of automobile trailers. Gasoline rationing reduced trailer vacationing, but the demand for housing for war workers found ready response in house trailers. During the war, the federal government became the major purchaser of trailers, deploying them as temporary war workers' housing. These trailers typically included toilet facilities and kitchens adequate for year-round living. The government specified the design of the trailers it purchased and also developed site plans for the communities it constructed for their placement. These communities offered larger sites than private parks, and included ample laundry, bathing, and recreation facilities and, where necessary, boardwalk streets. Private parks were also developed, typically to lower design standards, but often preferred by "trailerites" because they imposed fewer regulations, such as restrictions on constructing site-built additions.

Mobility was regarded as a major advantage in using trailers to house war workers because they could be deployed rapidly and because they could also be removed quickly and completely after the war. Removal was especially important, since most local governments continued to oppose the use of trailers as permanent housing even though such restrictions were eased in light of wartime demands.

The end of the war generated renewed demand for vacation trailers, but also an unexpectedly large demand for trailers as year-round housing. The primary market for permanent housing came from military personnel and itinerant construction workers. Military demand was accommodated, in part, by constructing trailer parks for married personnel on military bases. Many universities, with enrollments swollen by returning GIs, also constructed trailer parks. Likewise, large-scale parks were developed in conjunction with major construction projects, such as nuclear armament and power facilities. The development of private parks also flourished during this period. The typical park had about 100 spaces with limited community facilities. Most remained mom-and-pop operations, with the owners/managers living on-site. Often, a mobile home dealership operated in conjunction with a park.

In many parts of the country, park sites were difficult to find, and park owners who also had dealerships could restrict space to their buyers. Owners who wanted to sell their units in the park might be required to pay commissions on the sale. Eventually, states made these so-called "closed park" practices illegal, but they illustrate the limited rights of mobile home owners in rental parks.

By the 1960s, the travel trailer and mobile home markets had become largely differentiated. Communities served one type of user, but rarely both. Clear differentiation had also emerged among types of mobile home communities, especially between parks that were housing-oriented or service-oriented. Housing-oriented parks are designed for the affordable housing market, and generally attract younger, smaller, and less-affluent households. They offer limited community amenities, modest lots, and gridiron street arrangements. They are often located at the periphery of rapidly urbanizing areas where land is inexpensive and zoning restrictions minimal. Service-oriented parks generally attract a seasonal and/or retired population of largely middle-class households. They feature extensive community amenities, including clubhouses, swimming pools, and even golf courses. Well landscaped, these parks often employ curvilinear street arrangements characteristic of contemporary site-built housing subdivisions. Located primarily in Sunbelt areas, service-oriented parks accommodate larger homes ("double-wides") and often include such site-built additions as enclosed patios and carports.

Both housing and service-oriented communities are larger than the mobile home parks of the 1950s, averaging 250 to 300 spaces. They are typically designed and managed by professionals. Management continues to restrict what residents may do on their sites, but these restrictions are usually accepted as a way of maintaining community quality.

Today, approximately 45 percent of manufactured homes are located in parks. There are over 24,000 parks in the United States, and they provide more than 1.8 million homesites. Manufactured housing communities still correspond to either a housing or service orientation, but there is a large range of park types. Land ownership has become increasingly popular, and mobile home subdivisions and cooperative parks have developed to meet this demand. It has become increasingly common for homes to be sold on and with a site, using a single mortgage for both. In these sales, units are permanently affixed to the site and provided with extensive site-built additions.

Sociological studies of park life generally conclude that residents have a strong sense of community. Population homogeneity and close physical proximity appear to support positive social interaction, especially in service-oriented parks. Improved park design has also helped to make mobile homes more acceptable to the general public, but strong reservations remain because of the perception that mobile home residents do not pay property taxes equivalent to the costs of providing them with services. Many local communities still use zoning to restrict and even exclude manufactured housing, but 22 states now require local governments to provide for the placement of mobile homes, including their siting on individual lots.

With almost 10 percent of the American people now living in mobile homes, community design plays an important role in providing user satisfaction and community acceptance. The general evolution of community design approximating that of conventional site-built community standards will undoubtedly help assure acceptability, but at a price. The consumer of affordable housing who has been a mainstay of the industry may be squeezed out of the market in new developments. At the same time, older parks are being eliminated by pressure to convert land to more profitable use. Local governments may have to step in and provide homesites to fill this growing gap,

but in order to do this they will have to overcome their significant bias against factory-built housing and the communities they foster.

—*Allan D. Wallis*

### References
Bernhardt, Arthur. *Building Tomorrow: The Mobile/Manufactured Housing Industry.* Cambridge, MA: MIT Press, 1980.
Nutt-Powell, Thomas E. *Manufactured Homes: Making Sense of a Housing Opportunity.* Boston: Auburn House, 1982.
Wallis, Allan D. *Wheel Estate: The Rise and Decline of Mobile Homes.* New York: Oxford University Press, 1991.

## Moral Reform

It is a truism that Americans periodically go on moral binges in which some citizens try to act as moral arbiters for all citizens. It is less obvious, however, that these sprees commonly reflect bitter resistance to extensive social change. Yet that has certainly been the case with the rapid urbanization of the nation. Secularization, loosening family ties, an increasingly multilingual populace, and new modes of pursuing pleasure undermined the village culture of an earlier era, and traditionalists responded in the first half of the twentieth century with various strategies intended to restore the moral guidelines of a village past in the urban nation.

Some of these reforms were meant to provide an institutional framework in which to teach proper morals and behavior to the urban poor. The playground movement early in the century, for instance, aimed to steer the children of immigrants away from the crude life of the streets and onto playgrounds where supervised team play would train them in both the cooperative and the competitive values needed to make them into good citizens. This "positive environmentalism" not only focused on what was wrong but also offered a constructive moral alternative.

A very different approach to moral reform was expressed in various repressive movements that sought not to teach the proper but to outlaw what was objectionable. Prostitution was one obvious target of social control, the sleazy urban dance hall another. But by far the most significant of these efforts was the war on the saloon.

Spearheaded by the Anti-Saloon League (ASL), the Prohibition movement reached its goal when the Eighteenth Amendment to the Constitution was ratified in 1919. In its effort to dry up the nation the ASL drove people with clashing cultural styles into hostile camps and exposed the severe social strains of the era. The patrons of the saloon were largely urban workers—Catholics, Jews, and Eastern Orthodox recently arrived from the cultures of Southern and Eastern Europe where alcohol was a normal part of communal life. The middle-class ASL, on the other hand, was rooted in traditional Protestant views of family, social order, work, and the deferment of pleasure, and it perceived its foes as threats to this moral order. There were thus bitter ethnic, religious, and class feelings at work on both sides of the dry divide.

Although Prohibition did curtail drinking to a significant degree, it did not stem the tide of social change that had triggered the movement for moral reform in the first place. Thus, when Prohibition ended in 1933, other expressions of moral reformism flourished. Among these were pressures to influence the content of movies. Although censorship laws were already on the books in several states and dozens of towns and cities by the 1920s, movies grew more and more lurid, especially after the Depression cut into revenues in the early 1930s. Many believed that the new films posed a fundamental challenge to family, religion, patriotism, and general decency. Finally, in the face of a growing public outcry, congressional rumblings about "regulating" the industry, and threats by the newly organized Catholic Legion of Decency to boycott "condemned" films, the producers of movies agreed in 1934 to abide by the Motion Picture Production Code they had ignored since they approved it in 1930.

In general, the code had an extremely low tolerance for sex, profanity, gratuitous violence, and incitement to criminal behavior. The boundaries were so narrowly defined that the censors even tried to change Clark Gable's famous line, "Frankly, my dear, I don't give a damn," in *Gone with the Wind* to, "My dear, I don't care." Fortunately, they relented. Family values were promoted by banning any reference to prostitution, abortion, adultery, "perversion," and birth control. The code had a positive side to it as well. It insisted that "correct standards of life ... be presented" in motion pictures. Flag, country, and religion, for instance, had to be treated respectfully. Proper films, it claimed, would lead to proper character and proper ideals. Thus, the code expressed both the positive and the repressive aspects of earlier moral reform movements. Not until the 1950s was it effectively challenged.

Moral reformism touches upon some of the most sensitive issues of a relatively open society. Should personal morality be regulated by law? What is the proper balance between the will of the majority and the rights of a minority, or between the rights of the community and the rights of an individual? These have been vexing questions since the founding of the Republic, and there is no sign of easy answers in the near future.

—*Don S. Kirschner*

**See also**
Playgrounds; Prohibition; Prostitution; Temperance Movement.
**References**
Boyer, Paul. *Urban Masses and Moral Order in America, 1820–1920.* Cambridge, MA: Harvard University Press, 1978.
Cavallo, Dominick. *Muscles and Morals: Organized Playgrounds and Urban Reform.* Philadelphia: University of Pennsylvania Press, 1981.
Clark, Norman H. *Deliver Us from Evil: An Interpretation of American Prohibition.* New York: W. W. Norton, 1976.
Leff, Leonard J., and Jerold L. Simmons. *The Dame in the Kimono: Hollywood Censorship and the Production Code from the 1920s to the 1960s.* New York: Grove Weidenfeld, 1990.

## Mormons

The Church of Jesus Christ of Latter-day Saints (better known as the Mormon Church) has historically been ambivalent in its attitudes about urbanization and cities. On the one hand, the noted urban historian John W. Reps has called the Mormons "the most successful city builders" of "all the religious and utopian societies" in nineteenth-century America. This was reflected in the fact that members of this denomination, first under the leadership of Mormon founder Joseph Smith and later under his successor, Brigham Young, established several hundred cities and towns of varying size, first in the American Midwest and then in the far western United States. But at the same time, from its founding in the 1830s until the present, spokesmen for the Mormon Church have expressed deep-seated anxieties, and sometimes outright fear, about the negative, corrupting effects of cities. These concerns, of course, have reflected those of other Americans.

Mormon ambivalence was initially evident in the Book of Mormon, a work believed by the church to be a sacred history of the pre-Columbian inhabitants of the Western Hemisphere. This book, revealed by Mormon founder

*Since its construction (1853–1893), the gigantic Mormon Temple has dominated Salt Lake City.*

Joseph Smith in 1830, served as the basis for the formal establishment of the Mormon Church. Essentially, the Book of Mormon is the story of struggles between two groups both believed to have descended from one of the "Lost Tribes of Israel." The first group, the fair-skinned "Nephites," was righteous and divinely favored, living in or near cities, which they established as centers of civilization. They earned their livelihood through skilled trades and agriculture. The second group, the dark-skinned "Lamanites," were wild, ferocious, wicked, nomadic, and generally organized in small groups or tribes. They lived in the wilderness and provided for themselves by hunting wild animals. The ambivalence of the Book of Mormon about cities and urban society is most evident in its presentation of the Lamanites as the ultimate survivors of these struggles and as the ancestors of the American Indians. In contrast, the light-skinned, urban Nephites degenerated into such extreme wickedness and decadence that they were annihilated as a people and their civilization destroyed.

At the same time, Joseph Smith promoted urban life for his own growing Mormon movement in the United States and attempted to gather his followers in a "New Jerusalem," which is initially described in the Book of Mormon. By 1831, Smith had moved to Kirtland, Ohio, which was already a flourishing community of people who were not Mormons. The large influx of Smith's followers helped make Kirtland a major center of Mormonism, dramatized by construction of the church's first temple, completed in 1836. At the same time, Smith established a second gathering place for the faithful in Independence, Missouri.

Smith projected the future of this small, frontier community as Mormonism's Zion, or principal gathering place, where all of his followers would ultimately come together in preparation for the Millennium and the Second Coming, which he believed imminent. In a carefully prepared "Plat of the City of Zion," Smith designed every detail of this projected "City of God," including the disposition of land, water rights, uniformly wide streets arranged in a gridiron pattern, and the division of the town into ecclesiastical wards. Smith's plans, however, were discontinued in 1833 when non-Mormon settlers, alarmed by Smith's extensive urban planning and angered over the increasing number of Mormons who claimed that the community was theirs exclusively, ousted the Mormons from Independence.

The besieged Mormons made their way into the frontier of northwest Missouri. Here, Joseph Smith's "master plat" in urban planning served as the basis for a new community, Far West, the Mormons' gathering place in the late 1830s. Just as in Independence, Mormon plans were aborted, and the so-called Missouri War of 1838–1839 resulted in expulsion of the Latter-day Saints from Missouri, forcing them into Illi-

nois. Here, Smith realized more of establishing a Mormon Zion based on his carefully drawn plans. Known as Nauvoo and located along the Mississippi River, it flourished into a community of some 12,000 people. Smith implemented many details of his "master plat," including the gridiron arrangement of uniformly wide streets and the division of the town into ecclesiastical wards designed to define or create social neighborhoods.

Smith's basic concepts of urban planning survived his own violent death at the hands of an anti-Mormon mob in 1844. His plans also sustained the Mormons' enforced abandonment of Nauvoo two years later and their migration west to Utah. Smith's successor, Brigham Young, followed his predecessor's basic concepts as he established some 350 communities throughout the Great Basin and other parts of the Far West. These cities and towns featured gridiron streets of uniform width; division into ecclesiastical wards; the reservation of strategic blocks for public buildings and grounds such as schools, churches, and parks; and community control of land distribution and water rights—the latter of particular importance in the arid regions of the Far West.

At the same time that Young and other Mormon leaders promoted new cities and towns, they and their followers also expressed deep anxieties and, indeed, strong negative feelings about urbanization. This ambivalence has continued down to the present, despite the paradox of the Mormon Church itself becoming more urban as its general membership increasingly lives in cities. Thus, the Mormons continue to reflect attitudes and demographic trends evident in American society at-large.

—*Newell G. Bringhurst*

**See also**
Young, Brigham.
**References**
Arrington, Leonard J. *Great Basin Kingdom: An Economic History of the Latter-day Saints.* Cambridge, MA: Harvard University Press, 1958.
Arrington, Leonard J., Feramorz Y. Fox, and Dean L. May. *Building the City of God: Community and Cooperation among the Mormons.* Salt Lake City, UT: Deseret Book Company, 1976.
*Dialogue: A Journal of Mormon Thought* 3 (Autumn 1968): 37–92. This special issue contains 11 articles by various authors under the general title "Mormons in the Secular City."
Reps, John W. *The Making of Urban America: A History of City Planning in the United States.* Princeton, NJ: Princeton University Press, 1965.

## Morrison, DeLesseps Story (1912–1964)

DeLesseps Story Morrison was mayor of New Orleans, Louisiana, from 1946 to 1961, a time of great change in the city. In 1946, as candidate of the Independent Citizens' Committee, he used his dynamic energy and a reform platform to eke out a narrow victory. He defeated the incumbent, Robert S.

Maestri, head of the regular Democratic organization, the political machine that had controlled the city since the nineteenth century.

Unlike previous reform leaders, Morrison combined political acumen with a reform orientation. He created his own political organization, the Crescent City Democratic Association (CCDA), and he recruited several members of the regular Democratic Party into its ranks. Moreover, Morrison fashioned an enviable image for running a reform administration that supported major construction projects, especially the Union Terminal, the Civic Center complex, improved streets, and a nationally recognized recreation program. Additionally, he extended services and facilities to the expanding suburbs and sought to bring new industry into the metropolitan area.

One of his most acclaimed programs attracted international trade, mainly from Latin America, to New Orleans. Morrison also managed to fend off the state forces of Earl Long, Huey's brother, on several occasions. Unlike previous Crescent City politicians, he openly courted the black vote. Although he himself supported segregation, he believed strongly in creating facilities for and extending services to African Americans.

Although he never attained state office (he ran unsuccessfully for governor in 1956, 1960, and 1964), he retained power in the city despite a major scandal in the police department. According to most scholars, his was the last successful political machine in New Orleans. After he left office in 1961, he served as ambassador to the Organization of American States during the administration of John F. Kennedy. On May 22, 1964, at the age of 52, he died in a plane crash.

—*Edward F. Haas*

References

Haas, Edward F. *DeLesseps S. Morrison and the Image of Reform: New Orleans Politics, 1946–1961.* Baton Rouge: Louisiana State University Press, 1974.

Parker, Joseph. *The Morrison Era.* Gretna, LA: Pelican Publishing, 1974.

## Moses, Robert (1888–1981)

Robert Moses, the New York City park commissioner, highway builder, and construction czar, was born in New Haven, Connecticut, the second son of wealthy German Jewish parents. He graduated from Yale College in 1909 and then attended Oxford University where his studies of the English civil service earned a Ph.D. from Columbia University in 1914. His work for the New York City Bureau of Municipal Research caught the attention of Governor Alfred E. Smith, who chose the good-government Republican to help fashion his strong Democratic executive coterie. In 1924, Smith

appointed Moses president of the New York State Parks Council and the Long Island State Park Commission. By 1930, Moses was building 9,700 acres of parks on Long Island, including the lido at Jones Beach, and miles of suburban parkways. Ironically, a man who never learned to drive shaped the region's future behind the wheel.

In 1933, Mayor Fiorello H. La Guardia of New York City named Moses his park commissioner, a post Moses redefined to control the five-borough agency. (He bypassed civil service rules against holding multiple public offices by accepting sumptuous perks instead of a salary, eventually holding 12 city and state offices simultaneously.) Moses scrounged city contributions to match New Deal work-relief grants and was employing 80,000 people by 1936 on projects that included refurbishing the Central Park Zoo; building 255 playgrounds, 11 outdoor pools, and oceanfront beaches; and designing parkways in the outer boroughs of the city. In 1934, La Guardia appointed Moses to head the toll-collecting authorities that built the Triborough and Marine Parkway Bridges. Moses plowed Triborough surpluses into a highway network that stretched from upper Manhattan to the Shore Parkway around Brooklyn (completed in 1940). He expected Triborough revenues to fund a suspension bridge between the Battery and Brooklyn in 1939 but settled for control of a combined Triborough Bridge and Tunnel Authority (TBTA), which built the Brooklyn-Battery Tunnel.

In 1938, Moses urged Mayor La Guardia to put the New York City Housing Authority (NYCHA) under a board to coordinate housing and recreation. The mayor sidestepped naming Moses housing czar but endorsed his talks with Metropolitan Life Insurance Company and other fiduciaries to invest in medium-rent projects on the Lower East Side. When La Guardia appointed Moses to the City Planning Commission in late 1941, Moses used Triborough resources to prepare a list of postwar projects, including highways, parks, hospitals, and (behind the back of the NYCHA) housing sites. In 1943 Moses handed Metropolitan Life slum clearance authority and tax relief on East 14th Street to begin building the 8,755 units of Stuyvesant Town, the prototype for "urban redevelopment." Already city housing coordinator and the expediter of postwar plans, Moses was named city construction coordinator by Mayor William O'Dwyer in early 1946.

To this Promethean job, Moses brought an urgency to rebuild New York according to the needs of the automobile. He knocked down blocks of tenements to carve expressways across the South Bronx and South Brooklyn and to access tracts of land for garden apartments in the outer boroughs. In 1955, he reached agreement with the Port Authority of New York and New Jersey that constructed the lower deck of the George Washington Bridge, the Staten Island Expressway, and the mammoth Verrazano-Narrows Bridge. As construction coordinator and TBTA chief, Moses built 13 vehicular spans and gave the city more miles of superhighway (eventually 416 miles) than Los Angeles.

Moses changed the environment where New Yorkers lived and worked. Insisting on public housing that cleared slums, Moses concentrated the NYCHA's austere 12- and 14-story structures in sections of Harlem, Brownsville, Brooklyn, and the South Bronx that were already black or Puerto Rican. As construction coordinator, he facilitated the land deal with the Rockefeller family that located the United Nations on East 42nd Street; as park commissioner, he allowed New York University to encroach on Washington Square; and, as city planning commissioner, he agreed that NYU and Bellevue Hospital should collaborate on a medical center at East 34th Street. Appointed by William O'Dwyer to chair the Mayor's Committee on Slum Clearance, Moses huddled with private redevelopers to exploit Title I of the Housing Act of 1949. Moses unveiled projects for Corlear's Hook on the Lower East Side, Washington Square South, Manhattantown on West 97th Street, and half a dozen other sites that required thousands of blacks and Puerto Ricans to move to NYCHA projects in Brooklyn and the Bronx. His bulldozers touched off protests in Greenwich Village and Manhattantown where corrupt redevelopers removed 15,000 tenants. Undaunted, Moses plowed ahead at the Lincoln Center for the Performing Arts and at Seward Park and Penn South, where the garment industry's United Housing Foundation sponsored medium-rent cooperatives. By 1959, 16 Title I projects had replaced 314 blighted acres with towers that contained 28,000 units.

By then, Moses' high-handedness had run up against a city rediscovering small-scale neighborhood life. The Manhattantown Title I project sparked a preference for brownstone rehabilitation, which resulted in the West Side Urban Renewal. As park commissioner, he enraged residents of Greenwich Village with his plan to let cars run through Washington Square, and he affronted East Siders by putting parking lots in Central Park. He resigned as park commissioner and from the Mayor's Committee on Slum Clearance in 1960 and was forced from his other state appointments by Governor Nelson A. Rockefeller in 1962. He left his last stronghold, the TBTA, in 1968.

For 40 years Moses was New York's master builder. He gave the city postindustrial redoubts like NYU-Bellevue and Lincoln Center, and he rooted white-collar professionals on Washington Square and the Upper West Side. He cleared East Side tenements for trade-union cooperatives, hospital complexes, and the United Nations. His Cross-Bronx Expressway eviscerated one borough, while the bridges and motorways opened up Queens and Staten Island to the masses.

Moses believed that the people of the city shared his hatred of slums, admiration for high-rise structures, and freedom to drive. And at the time, most New Yorkers applauded the sprawling metropolis that was his legacy.

—*Joel Schwartz*

### References
Caro, Robert A. *The Power Broker: Robert Moses and the Fall of New York.* New York: Knopf, 1974.
Moses, Robert. *Public Works: A Dangerous Trade.* New York: McGraw-Hill, 1970.
Schwartz, Joel. *The New York Approach: Robert Moses, Urban Liberals, and Redevelopment of the Inner City.* Columbus: Ohio State University Press, 1993.

## Motels

A motel is traditionally defined as inexpensive housing for automobile travelers in low-rise buildings that emphasizes convenience, principally with parking immediately outside each room; avoids entry through formal lobbies; and abjures many traditional services of hotels, the motel's major rival. In actuality, motels resembled hotels in size, rates, and location by the 1950s.

The first motel in the United States is generally agreed to have been Askins Cottage Camp, which opened in 1901 on the outskirts of Douglas, Arizona. The word *motel,* it is almost unanimously agreed, was first used by James Vail in 1925 for his Motel Inn at San Luis Obispo, California. Before general acceptance of the term in the late 1940s and early 1950s, various alternatives vied for common usage, most often tourist camp, tourist court, cottage court, and, rarely, autel.

Motels began to appear more commonly along intercity highways in the open countryside and in small towns in the late 1920s. There they benefited from cheap land, the absence of hotels, easy access for automobiles, and the absence of municipal codes often strongly influenced by hotel competitors. Motels evolved as private businesses distinct from the publicly owned campgrounds that were usually available free or at minimal cost to facilitate local tourism and promote local identity. By the early 1930s, public agencies relinquished the provision of roadside lodging to private enterprise because of the fear that undesirable vagrants were taking advantage of public campgrounds.

"Mom and pop" motels—individually owned, family operated, and small—structured the new industry from the first and dominated it through the early 1950s. Consequently, despite the motel's profound public influences, individualism and mostly voluntary standards have prevailed. At first, owners were eager to overcome their business's notoriety as a haven for illicit romance and criminal activity, and they cooperated to gain business by referrals from other owners. Thus, "referral" chains mushroomed by the late 1930s, the best advertised at the time being United Motor Courts, founded in 1933 and operating until 1955. Better-known survivors are Quality Courts United and Best Western, founded in 1941 and 1946, respectively.

An article, "Camps of Crime," written by J. Edgar Hoover, head of the FBI, in 1940 charged the existence of widespread immorality and criminality in motels, and it received considerable attention. This necessitated a renewed, increased effort by motel owners to develop a decent reputation for their businesses. Nonetheless, the vast majority of the 9,848 motels counted for the 1935 federal census and the 13,521 in 1939 remained outside of any formal motel organization.

Representation of their collective interests was slow to develop. The first trade organization was short-lived (1933–1934) and induced by the federal government's desire to stimulate codes for industry under the National Industrial Recovery Act. The American Motor-Hotel Association grew slowly from its inception in 1941, but it was bolstered by the advent of strong statewide affiliates during the late 1940s. Motels and hotels became sufficiently reconciled by 1963 that motels joined, and added their name to, the American Hotel & Motel Association to represent the collective interests of the lodging industry.

Starting in the 1950s, wealthy investors dominated the motel trade. Amidst America's legendary affluence after World War II and the demand for travel that had been bottled up since the Depression, the number of motels peaked at an all-time high of 44,699 in 1972. A Memphis house builder, Kemmons Wilson, who headed the entrepreneurial team for Holiday Inn, is commonly credited with pioneering the modern motel. Returning from his own family vacation in 1951, Wilson started planning an alternative to the "mom and pop" motels that had proliferated in the late 1940s among people seeking easy work in retirement. He envisioned a place for travelers to stay that would overcome the inadequacies he perceived in motels, carry reasonable prices, and provide invariably good accommodations verified by a brand-name in an extensive chain; these plans coincided with trends in American mass marketing that had begun at the end of the nineteenth century. Wilson built the first Holiday Inn in 1952, started franchising in 1954, and made the venture a public stock corporation in 1957. Underlying this private investment opportunity were strong inducements flowing from public policy—accelerated depreciation for motels in the federal income tax code (1954) and the beginnings of the interstate highway system (1956). By 1963, Holiday Inn number 400 had opened, and by the early 1970s the chain had three times as many rooms as either of its chief competitors, Ramada and Sheraton.

Motels contributed significantly to America's demographic decentralization in the second half of the twentieth century. Although urban renewal in the mid-1950s briefly encouraged reinvestment in central cities by hotels and motels offering similar services and prices, investors in motels consistently found better opportunities alongside the new highways and interstates that were also encouraging suburban growth. As suburbs changed from being dormitory communities into places of work as well as residence, motels were among the suburban services provided for local businesses and passing travelers. To many cultural critics, motels also symbolized what they perceived as the negative tendency of suburbs to privatize society and alienate people.

Segmentation, the strategy of distinguishing brands under common ownership according to a hierarchy of prices and services targeted at specific populations, evolved to bring new consumer groups into the market as it became glutted in the 1980s. In the census of 1987, motels numbered only 26,066, and the total number of motel rooms available reached 1,275,435.

—*Keith A. Sculle*

**See also**
Hotels.
**References**
Belasco, Warren James. *Americans on the Road: From Autocamp to Motel, 1910–1945.* Cambridge, MA: MIT Press, 1979.
Jakle, John A., Keith A. Sculle, and Jefferson S. Rogers. *The Motel in America.* Baltimore: Johns Hopkins University Press, 1996.

## Motion Pictures and Cities

In American films, images of the city fit into various categories, each representing a different extreme. American cities have been portrayed as centers of vice, corruption, warfare, and immorality; denizens of urban neighborhoods have often been pictured as stupefied, embodying their days as the walking comatose full of despair and hopelessness. Or urban people have been shown to be in love with city life despite, or perhaps because of, the darker side of that world. Indeed, this last category of people is often made up of those who have immigrated from even darker lives in the "old country" and who see American cities as respites from pogroms, political revolutions, or economic devastation, even if only temporarily.

What is even more ironic about the relationship between filmmaker, studio, and audience in American films is the voyeuristic tendency endemic to cinema itself. Perhaps no one who is horrified by urban decay, immorality, or strife in the United States would be so aghast if he or she would look back clearly at the country from which America derived so much of its cultural, political, and economic structures and see or read the images of cities in England. William Blake's London, like T. S. Eliot's view of that city in "The Waste Land" or Charles Dickens's descriptions in *Hard Times* or *Oliver Twist,* is filled with corruption, overcrowded living conditions, and people doing whatever they must to survive.

Sweeping surveys of cities in American film must reduce the vast number of movies about cities to manageable categories—categories that flirt with the same cultural stereotypes depicted in films themselves. For their films to "play in Peoria," American moviemakers have filmed cities according to the widespread image that these places are like Sodom and Gomorrah, urban jungles and nightmarish wastelands that are filled with violence (mainly from gangs and gangsters, although natural disasters have their role) or that present immoral temptations to those prone to gambling, illicit sex, or simply fast-paced life—an affirmation of the disasters that befall anyone seeking bright lights, big city.

A second important type of city depicted in American films is more positive. In big city films that proclaim the rags-to-riches myth, the glamour and the footlights of Broadway or Hollywood—the artistic-cultural Meccas of the country—often provide a way to see and dream about a life that they might want but never know, or might want and then pursue.

A third category of American cinematic cities, perhaps somewhere between the first two, examines the theme of melting pot versus cultural diversity as people from various ethnic groups or social classes meet, make love, and war against each other. In watching these films, audiences from a predominantly white America can live vicariously with groups that they choose never to meet in reality or never have the chance to associate with in fact.

Since most American films about cities are set in the largest or most famous of them—New York and its vicinity, Los Angeles, Chicago, San Francisco, Philadelphia, and New Orleans—this entry is primarily concerned with them. Some urban settings in films are unidentified; they simply depict the primordial fear of and desire for the abstract "city." And since the categories are not absolute, many movies identified with one type of film easily fall into one or more of the other categories as well.

In any mention of big cities in the United States today, one almost inevitably hears words related to "crime," "violence," or "gangs." Films have certainly contributed to the continuing dialectic between crime and large cities, so closely that cultural conservatives believe that gang and gangster films engender and provoke more violence. Since the first showing of D. W. Griffith's *The Musketeers of Pig Alley* (1912), gangland crime, whether petty or organized, has been a Hollywood staple. In Hollywood's earliest forays into this genre, gangsters proliferate in New York City and Chicago. Of course, many of these films are based on true stories. *Little Caesar* (1930), *Scarface* (1932), and *Al Capone* (1959) are all set in Chicago and portray America's most famous gangster as he makes his mark and leaves it on urban America. Chicago is

also the setting for *Call Northside 777* (1948), a more obscure film based on a true crime story, and *The Man with Golden Arm* (1956), a vehicle for Frank Sinatra that, for its day, dealt realistically with drugs and organized gambling.

In New York City, gangsters and gang violence abound. From *Lights of New York* (1928), dubbed the first 100 percent all-talking film, to *New York Knights* (1929), which marked the sound debut of Norma Talmadge, to *Gangs of New York* (1938), to *The Roaring Twenties* (1939), which depicts an out-and-out gang war, to *Out of the Fog* (1941), in which gangsters terrorize a Brooklyn family, to *The Naked City* (1948), filmed on actual street locations in New York, the image of New York as an urban jungle was clearly established in Hollywood's golden age.

Crime or gang dramas with generic city settings include *Underworld* (1927), the first major motion picture that had a gangster as its protagonist, as well as *Public Enemy* (1931), *The Asphalt Jungle* (1950), and *The Big Heat* (1953).

In more recent years, urban violence, released from the Motion Picture Production Code, has erupted on the screen. In New York, especially since the 1970s, the "mean streets" have been depicted as exactly that. From *Little Murders* (1971), *Superfly* (1972), *Across 110th Street* (1972), *The Warriors* (1979), and *Ft. Apache, the Bronx* (1980) to Martin Scorsese's *Mean Streets* (1973), *Taxi Driver* (1976), and *Goodfellas* (1989), urban gangs and crime have horrified and perhaps titillated American audiences who, when they think of New York City and its surrounding boroughs, imagine nothing less than a war zone. In movies set in Los Angeles, urban crime stories are as disparate as the sci-fi epic *Blade Runner* (1982), which takes an overcrowded L.A. to a new, acid-rainy plateau; the Eddie Murphy vehicle *Beverly Hills Cop* (1984) and its successors; *Bugsy* (1991), which concerns Hollywood's most beloved gangster, Bugsy Siegel; and the more topical and contemporary realities of urban minority gangs depicted in *Colors* (1988), *Boyz n the Hood* (1991), *Menace II Society* (1993), and *Falling Down* (1993), the last being, perhaps, every white person's dream or nightmare of confronting the minority gangs of Los Angeles.

San Francisco is also forcefully represented in the gang/crime genre with *The Maltese Falcon* (1941), *Bullitt* (1968), *Dirty Harry* (1971), *The Organization* (1971), and *48 Hours* (1982). Not to be left out, Miami logs in with *The Miami Story* (1954), *Miami Exposé* (1956), *Tony Rome* (1967), another Sinatra vehicle, *Black Sunday* (1977), in which international terrorists descend on the Super Bowl, and the remake of *Scarface* (1983). Also within this genre, New Orleans is represented by *Angel Heart* (1986), *The Big Easy* (1986), and David Lynch's *Wild at Heart* (1990).

More complex than films depicting cities as ridden with crime are those that show great cities as industrial or moral wastelands. Since vast numbers of people began migrating to American cities in the nineteenth century, overcrowding and its resulting tensions and acts of economic desperation have characterized life in big cities. Charlie Chaplin directed several films that depicted the strife between economic and social classes in American cities, as well as the desperate measures that some citizens took to avoid homelessness and starvation. From the short *Easy Street* (1917) to *The Kid* (1921), Chaplin portrayed inner-city slum life and raised moral questions about the lengths some people would go to in order to survive (such as child abandonment), as well as the sacrifices other people made despite their own straitened circumstances (like taking in a stranger's child). Later, *City Lights* (1931) and *Modern Times* (1936) portrayed, respectively, the inequities between rich and poor in the sprawling city—a poor, blind woman sells flowers to pay her rent while a rich man throws money away on drunken sprees—and the effects of industrialization on city workers who are variously characterized as sheep being herded to work daily or as automatons who can't stop tightening screws even after the assembly line stops operating. Even more pointed is *The City* (1939), Ralph Steiner's documentary about overcrowded urban centers. Other films set in and concerning urban slum life include *The Bowery* (1933); *Hallelujah, I'm a Bum* (1933), starring Al Jolson as a Central Park tramp; *Dead End* (1937), which introduced the "dead end kids" of New York's Lower East Side to American audiences; *Angels with Dirty Faces* (1938), set in Brooklyn; and *Panic in Needle Park* (1971), a film that depicted drug life in New York's ghettos.

The wasteland of slum life is matched by the immoralities of city life in films from a variety of urban settings. New Orleans enters the picture prominently with its Bourbon Street night life. *Gambler from Natchez* (1954) and *The Cincinnati Kid* (1965) both depict gamblers who make it, or try to make it, in the city known as the "Big Easy." But brothels also are a claim to fame in New Orleans, as Jane Fonda and Laurence Harvey show in *Walk on the Wild Side* (1962) and Brooke Shields, Susan Sarandon, and Keith Carradine reveal in *Pretty Baby* (1978). Even Oliver Stone's *JFK* (1981) depicts prostitution in New Orleans, albeit as part of the gay underground. As if New Orleans didn't have enough problems, Elia Kazan's *Panic in the Streets* (1950) brings bubonic plague to the city below sea level.

Of course, immorality abounds in Los Angeles, especially in the white-collar, executive world. From *Sunset Boulevard* (1952) to *Chinatown* (1974) to *Body Double* (1984) and *The Player* (1991), friends, colleagues, writers, stars, directors, fathers, lovers, and daughters engage in the most illicit and taboo actions. And then there is the L.A. pornography industry, as seen in *Hardcore* (1978), which lures teenage runaways from all parts of the country. Even *Jimmy Hollywood* (1994) shows that success comes via vigilantism.

In San Francisco, things get even stranger, and not for obvious reasons. While *The Maltese Falcon* (1941) depicts the standard crime and betrayal of love, the remake of *Invasion of the Body Snatchers* (1978), which moved to the big city from the small-town setting of the original version, and *Time after Time* (1980) ask the question: "What if aliens from the future or Jack the Ripper out of the past were to invade contemporary big cities?" Films like *San Francisco* (1936), which chronicled the 1906 earthquake and fire in San Francisco and for that matter *In Old Chicago* (1937), which depicted the great Chicago fire of 1871, pale by comparison to the manufactured evils loosed on the city by Hollywood. But the archetypal San Francisco film, portraying the city's scenic wonder amidst love, betrayal, and white-collar crime, is Alfred Hitchcock's *Vertigo* (1958). From the roofs of buildings to San Francisco Bay, the city never looked the same after the projector showed this gem.

New York City contributes, of course, to the "immorality" plays with such diverse fare as *The Apartment* (1960); *Cruising* (1980), which also has one of the most violent screen murders in film history; and *Midnight Cowboy* (1969), which won the Academy Award for best film of that year even though it had an X rating and which, more than any other film, shows the corrupting power of New York City on individuals from every class and region of America. *On the Waterfront* (1954) shows the influence and corruption of big city unions on the individual and glorifies naming names to boot. *Klute* (1971) deglamorizes prostitution and turns its whore (Jane Fonda again) into a sympathetic heroine, while *The Lost Weekend* (1945) foreshadows contemporary concern with alcoholism. *Marathon Man* (1976) brings Nazis to New York, a sobering thought, while *King Kong* (1933) brings to the Empire State Building the great ape that would later save Tokyo from Godzilla in *King Kong vs. Godzilla* (1962). It seems that America and Japan are rivals in yet another way.

Washington, D.C., also enters the fray, realistically, with *All the President's Men* (1976), which shows how most Americans' confidence in the presidency, and perhaps in government altogether, was severely undermined through the Watergate scandal.

Disaster movies are always set in crowded cities to maximize potential human catastrophe. Films like *Earthquake* (1974), *The Towering Inferno* (1974), *Die Hard* (1989), and *Backdraft* (1991) make one fearful of entering a building more than two stories high, while *After Hours* (1986) transforms every corner of lower Manhattan into a comic nightmare. And Philadelphia is the setting of the most frightening industrial wasteland nightmare in David Lynch's audacious *Eraserhead* (1977).

After this lengthy account of the evil, danger, and corruption of American cities revealed in film, it is difficult to present a positive analysis. And yet, in many other American films, large cities do offer some people glamour, fame, and in one particular filmmaker's case, an ongoing love affair.

Chicago seems a more attractive city in *The Front Page* (1931), *The Benny Goodman Story* (1955), and even in *The Sting* (1973), even though the last depicts crime and corruption, albeit with the Newman-Redford touch. New Orleans, the birthplace of American Jazz, is shown more positively in *The Birth of the Blues* (1941) and *New Orleans* (1947). Baltimore of the 1950s is nostalgically beautiful in Barry Levinson's *Diner* (1982) and in the more contemporary *Sleepless in Seattle* (1993). The glitter of the nightlife and the open beaches of Miami are well shown in *The Heartbreak Kid* (1972). Philadelphia, despite David Lynch, is shown as a site of historical importance, especially for the underdog, in *Rocky* (1976), and as a place of comic romance in *The Philadelphia Story* (1940). But more recently, this old American city has been propelled into a different sort of limelight in Jonathan Demme's *Philadelphia* (1993), in which the city of brotherly love provides the setting for Hollywood's first look at the AIDS epidemic. While Philadelphia might not want this sort of attention, the very positive depictions of homosexual love, familial support, and (ultimately) professional respect, if not love, provide the audience with another, more challenging view of life in the great city.

Despite its political corruption, Washington, D.C., looks positively glowing at night as Jefferson Smith explores its parameters and monuments in *Mr. Smith Goes to Washington* (1939). Nashville is flattered in *Coal Miner's Daughter* (1980) and *Nashville* (1975), even if the most enduring image from the latter movie is Geraldine Chaplin's journalistic odyssey through an automobile graveyard and not the exuberance of the Grand Ole Opry. Seattle is very attractive in *Sleepless in Seattle* (1993) and its nighttime view of Puget Sound, and in the examination of its alternative/grunge crowd in *Singles* (1992). San Francisco has its own charm in romantic comedies like *What's Up, Doc?* (1972), *Play It Again, Sam* (1972), and *Foul Play* (1978).

The last film brings up the movies of that director most in love with one particular city, Woody Allen, who has set most of his films in New York City. Though teeming with crowds, Manhattan's atmosphere, its seemingly endless opportunities for aesthetic delights from movies, the theater, delis, museums, the Upper East and West Sides, Greenwich Village, and Central Park are evocatively captured in films ranging from *Take the Money and Run* (1968) to *Annie Hall* (1977); from *Broadway Danny Rose* (1984), where the Carnegie Deli forms the locus of action, to the architectural tour of Manhattan taken in *Hannah and Her Sisters* (1986); from *Alice* (1990)

and *Husbands and Wives* (1992) to *Manhattan Murder Mystery* (1993). But Allen's true love poem to the city is *Manhattan* (1979), in which New York's skyline, streets, Central Park, and planetarium, filmed in vivid black and white, never looked so romantic.

Still other positive views of New York are found in *Applause* (1929); *The Clock* (1945), which uses real locations at Grand Central Station; *Fame* (1980); *Funny Girl* (1968); *Going My Way* (1944), a "positive" look at slum life; *On the Town* (1949); *One Sunday Afternoon* (1933); *Splash* (1984), which gives shopping at Bloomingdale's a whole new meaning; *Big* (1988), which does the same for the F.A.O. Schwartz toy store; *Stage Door* (1937); *When Harry Met Sally* (1989); *The Hudsucker Proxy* (1994); and, again, *Sleepless in Seattle* (1993), the best falling-in-love-on-the-Empire-State-Building film since *King Kong*.

The final thematic element of large cities in American film is the depiction of racial and ethnic minorities—a portrayal that is, both for many viewers who live in these filmed cities and for many who live out of them, uncomfortably synonymous with urban life. Recently, the feeling of Detroit was well captured in its turbulence and romance between blacks and Jews in *Zebrahead* (1992). Baltimore once again becomes a nostalgic setting as Barry Levinson sensitively looked at four generations of immigrant Russian Jews in *Avalon* (1987). San Francisco provided one of the earliest views of interracial romance in *Guess Who's Coming to Dinner* (1967), and it also shows the joys and pain of the gay community of the Castro district in the documentary *The Times of Harvey Milk* (1984). Los Angeles is the setting for a sensitive portrayal of black-white relations in the midst of urban tensions in *Grand Canyon* (1992), as well as black, Latino, and Vietnamese gang violence in *Colors* (1988), *Boyz n the Hood* (1991), and *Menace II Society* (1993).

However, it is left to New York, including Brooklyn and the Bronx, to be the most prolific setting for racial and ethnic themes. Films with particularly Jewish themes and characters range from *His People* (1925), *The Jazz Singer* (1927), and *Crossfire* (1947), to *The Pawnbroker* (1965), *Bye Bye Braverman* (1968), *Me, Natalie* (1969), *Hester Street* (1974), and *Crossing Delancey* (1988), not to mention Woody Allen's films. Italian life is not confined to Scorsese's *Mean Streets* (1973). *Love with the Proper Stranger* (1964) depicts Italian families on the Lower East Side; *Marty* (1955) shows the hard life of a Brooklyn butcher; and *Saturday Night Fever* (1978) gives Italian Americans the dubious distinction of raising the temperature of disco to well above normal. African Americans were exploited in film's like *Shaft* (1971) and *Superfly* (1972), but more fully embodied in *Shadows* (1959), *The Brother from Another Planet* (1984), and Spike Lee's provocative *Do the Right Thing* (1989), *Jungle Fever* (1991), and *Crooklyn* (1994).

*Do the Right Thing, Jungle Fever,* and Robert DeNiro's *A Bronx Tale* (1993) also vividly capture the tensions between African Americans and Italian Americans, recalling the tensions between the white Jets and the Puerto Rican Sharks in *West Side Story* (1961).

Though violence reigns in this latter group of films, they nevertheless hold out hope of allowing and encouraging Americans to see more complex pictures of ethnic groups of all backgrounds—to see all the racial and ethnic groups in American cities living, loving, and even fighting each other, realistically, day after day. Given that the realities of capitalist constraints have always lured or forced ethnic minorities into large American cities, blaming these victims—whose entire world is often confined to ethnic neighborhoods like Bensonhurst, Chinatown, Harlem, south-central Los Angeles, and Crown Heights—for violence and danger in large cities is like blaming a movie camera for capturing images that one prefers not to see. There is always some greater force in control.

—*Terry Barr*

**See also**
Bogart, Humphrey; Chaplin, Charlie; Gangster Films; Keaton, Buster; Nickelodeons; Robinson, Edward G.; Sennett, Mack.

**References**
Friedman, Lester D. *The Jewish Image in American Film.* Secaucus, NJ: Citadel Press, 1987.
Halliwell, Leslie. *Halliwell's Film Guide.* 5th ed. New York: Scribners, 1986.
Thompson, Kristen, and David Bordwell. *Film History: An Introduction.* New York: McGraw-Hill, 1994.

## Motion Pictures and Suburbs

The motion picture industry has been depicting American suburban life for over 90 years. During this period, it has produced approximately 400 films that interpret the evolution of the suburban landscape and lifestyle. Invariably, movies based in suburbia are family melodramas: relations between children and their parents and between husband and wife—an almost complete focus on the nuclear family—mark them. With few exceptions, suburban-oriented films do not deal with larger social, economic, or political issues. Moreover, these films are almost always about the privileged lifestyle of upper- or upper-middle-class Americans.

The earliest suburban film identified so far is *The Suburbanite* (1904). This movie is a prime example of the film practice of viewing suburbs as a symbolic landscape of upper-middle-class domesticity marked by familiar icons and motifs such as the detached house, lawn, and separation of domestic and economic functions. It also exemplified how time and place would be depicted in later films. The place depicted in *The Suburbanite* is a suburb of houses with no center, no shops, no street traffic, and, above all, no community. Like virtually all suburban movies, this one is set in the contemporary present. Filmmakers have had great difficulty depicting the suburban past or envisioning a future suburban landscape. Lacking a past and a future, suburban movies do not depict the symbols of change found in many other film genres.

However, the present is not a static time frame in films for it changes with each age. In the 1930s, during the experimental stage of suburban film, the middle landscape or suburb, located between urban and rural locations, was depicted as the home of rich and powerful families in such films as *It Happened One Night* (1934), *Dark Victory* (1939), and *The Philadelphia Story* (1940). Here, grand homes are surrounded by open land but no neighbors and no community. In the tradition of the English gentry, these families seem to have been part of the suburban landscape forever.

Returning to the theme of *The Suburbanite,* the films of the 1940s depicted upper-middle-class families leaving cities and moving to suburbs. The main characters sought to follow the gentrified existence of the wealthy on a modified scale that befit their class. In *George Washington Slept Here* (1942) and *Mr. Blandings Builds His Dream House* (1948), the characters sought to purchase unique "historic" homes in agrarian settings that would give them roots in the American past but still allow a daily commute to the city. The move to suburbia was depicted as involving tremendous sacrifices, but these families were buying a "suburban dream" appropriate to their station in life. This dream primarily involved owning a unique home in a pastoral setting. Yet, the historic houses they purchased were ultimately unsatisfactory and had to be transformed or ripped down to incorporate modern conveniences. Once more, the needs of the present overcame the psychological and patriotic requirements of maintaining an agrarian and historic past.

Adult gender roles in films about suburbs are also significant. Women have not always shared the dream of moving to suburbs. In *Christmas in Connecticut* (1945), Barbara Stanwyck was quite content with an independent life in the city while writing a magazine column about her fantasy world as a country housewife. In *Miracle on 34th Street* (1947), Maureen O'Hara portrayed a divorced business executive living in New York City where she was raising her daughter to face the reality of the world without coloring it with fantasy. However, these films demonstrated that women must believe in fantasy, and this critical illusion was now firmly attached to the domestic bliss of suburbia. There was no doubt that both women would abandon their urban lives to become full-time, full-fledged suburban homemakers. However, the ambiguity of women toward suburbia and enforced domesticity would be a continuing theme in film and ultimately lead to motion pictures such as *The Stepford Wives* (1974).

Suburban films also exemplify the transitional nature of men's image in the twentieth century. Men invariably favored the move to suburbia. However, there are few patriarchs in the suburbs of movies. Clifton Webb in *Cheaper by the Dozen* (1950) comes closest to this role. Virtually all the men in these films are responsible for families, and they are generally portrayed as coping breadwinners like Robert Young in *Sitting Pretty* (1948), or confused fathers like Jim Backus in *Rebel without a Cause* (1955). Actors who played adult male roles in these movies usually portrayed mild-mannered men trying to contend with life as best they could.

By the end of the 1940s, films set in suburbs had reached their classical stage of development. The suburbia depicted in them was an adult world where parents often appeared middle-aged and children did not usually play a significant role in the plot. A degree of affluence demonstrated by homeownership and ample creature comforts was an essential element of these films. However, expectations of suburban life had been lowered to allow the portrayal of middle-class characters living in a middle landscape. The suburban house was no longer depicted as a mansion or a historic dwelling. Instead, it was a Cape Cod, a colonial, or a ranch house in the midst of many other houses in the nonpastoral setting.

The suburban dream of a unique house was now de-emphasized in favor of the "suburban ideal." The goal of this ideal was to create an environment that would assist people in following a prescribed pattern of behavior, on a voluntary basis, without any coercive laws aimed at behavior management. This ideal became the hallmark of the professional/managerial class who populated the suburbs depicted in movies. (In general, movies have shown suburbia as being inhabited only by the middle classes and above.) Surrounded by children and material rewards, they sought the good life. This classical stage of suburban films was epitomized by such movies as *Cheaper by the Dozen* (1950), *Father of the Bride* (1950), *Father's Little Dividend* (1951), and *Here Come the Nelsons* (1952). In these movies, women accepted their domestic role willingly, and men no longer dreamed about the life of the gentry. Children were respectful, if not exactly responsible; they would clearly grow up to lead lives exactly like their parents.

Just as Hollywood was working out this classical image of suburban life, television absconded with it in such series as *The Adventures of Ozzie and Harriet, Father Knows Best, Leave It to Beaver,* and *The Donna Reed Show.* For this and other reasons, the motion picture industry began to depict suburban life more comprehensively. This self-reflective stage of development began to refine or question some of the suburban film genre's own conventions.

The father's role in suburban film was refined by Gregory Peck in *The Man in the Gray Flannel Suit* (1956). Here, Peck portrays Tom Rath, a suburban family man unable to provide the type of house and consumer goods his wife felt the family deserved, nor could he develop the ambitious career he seemed qualified to attain. Rath finally chose to settle for a career that would provide material comfort for his family but be limited in scope. *The Man in the Gray Flannel Suit* enhanced the contemporary view of middle-class men as "organization men" who had limited ambition or creativity in their professional lives. Instead they sought freedom in the private, family realm. Thus, the suburban ideal became even more important to these male characters. A suburban home and the accompanying consumer goods offered compensation for his regimented professional life. The acceptance of this solution became so ingrained that suburban films rarely focused on the father's job, and a number do not even mention how he earned a living. As a contemporary review stated, Tom Rath settled for "a comfortable 9-to–5 o'clock job and an untroubled suburban life with his wife and three kids."

The smooth and untroubled nature of suburban life was opened to question, especially in terms of women's roles. True, Hollywood produced a whole series of films portraying contented housewives, often played by Doris Day or Doris Day–lookalikes in such films as *Please Don't Eat the Daisies* (1960), *The Thrill of It All* (1963), and *Send Me No Flowers* (1964). But even in these films, an undercurrent belies the tranquillity of suburban life, and filmmakers began to depict women challenging the ideal. In *All That Heaven Allows* (1955), Jane Wyman portrays an upper-middle-class suburban widow with grown children who refuses to live the hollow life dictated by convention, family, and friends in her closed suburban community. Despite strong opposition, she embarks on an affair with a younger man of lower social status. Women's roles still primarily involved being a suburban wife and mother, but the variety of styles depicted is intriguing. They range from adaptive homemaker in *The Grass Is Always Greener over the Septic Tank* (1978) to a cold, unfeeling mother in *Ordinary People* (1980) to fierce protectors of husband and family in *Fatal Attraction* (1987) and *The Hand That Rocks the Cradle* (1991).

The most dramatic shift in suburban family roles was depicted in *Rebel without a Cause*, starring James Dean. Except for the restless daughters depicted in films of the 1930s, suburban children had been obedient and generally obscure members of these family melodramas. Most films blamed juvenile delinquency on the environment of urban slums and poverty—a problem not supposed to exist in the affluent world of suburbia. Thus, while the title of the film offered some reassurance, this motion picture unnerved middle-class Americans. *The Saturday Review* summarized the widespread attitude when it described *Rebel without a Cause* as "a study of modern youth that is frightening in its unfamiliarity." The themes of unhappiness, corruption, and rebellion among suburban youth because of the lack of parental and community spiritual values or an overwhelming concern for material pleasures recurred in later films such as *The Graduate* (1967), *Goodbye Columbus* (1969), *Over the Edge* (1979), and *The Breakfast Club* (1985).

Yet this story line had serious problems. How could teenagers and young adults permanently rebel against the affluence that constituted an essential part of their suburban world? Soon, youthful rebellion in the middle landscape became the arrogance of children flaunting parental, school, and other institutional rules but never endangering the affluent, if absurd, world of their parents, as seen in motion pictures such as *Risky Business* (1983) and *Ferris Bueller's Day Off* (1986). These independent but rich kids are shown mastering slow-witted, lower-class types even in urban settings. In *Adventures in Baby-Sitting* (1987), an inexperienced teenaged suburban girl faces down two minority gangs on a subway train, outwits thieves and gangsters, and manages to spontaneously sing the blues in an African-American nightclub. The extreme of sadistic class arrogance by a suburban youth is best exemplified in the films *Home Alone* (1990) and *Home Alone 2* (1992). The suburban ideal would never again apply to children in any meaningful way.

Moviemakers were now depicting affluence and the concern for material well-being as a troubling aspect of suburban life that was disrupting marriages and families. In *Divorce American Style* (1967), a married couple work hard to achieve the American dream of a suburban lifestyle with all its material rewards. However, "success" is depicted as the emptiness of the suburban landscape and the unhappiness of the married couples portrayed. This line of filmmaking eventually led to *The War of the Roses* (1989). The Roses were a married couple so attached to their house and possessions that their divorce produced a war in which house and possessions were wrecked as the husband and wife maimed and finally killed each other. Such hatred, spite, and misdirected values do not remind us of Ozzie and Harriet but are so compelling that the film usually unnerves its viewers.

Even the prized icons of house, shopping mall, and the very land turn on terrified suburbanites as Hollywood brought horror into suburbia in films such as *The Incredible Shrinking Man* (1957), *The Amityville Horror* (1979), *The Dawn of the Dead* (1979), and *Poltergeist* (1982). The deconstruction stage of suburban film reached its highest point when filmmakers began to deliberately parody the genre in such movies as *Polyester* (1981), *The History of White People in America* (1985), *The Burbs* (1989), and *National Lampoon's Christmas Vacation* (1989).

The challenge to the classic film image of suburban life avoided issues of economic class, ethnicity, and race. The benefits of suburbia were still depicted almost exclusively for the white middle and upper-middle classes. The urban poor or ethnic working class were set apart. In *City across the River* (1949), a working-class family named Cusack had the modest "dream" of moving to the suburbs to buy a "little grocery store with rooms upstairs." Lacking the money, the family was forced to meet its inevitable fate in the slums of Brooklyn.

It took 12 more years and the civil rights revolution before a black family was portrayed as sharing the dream of moving to a suburban-like neighborhood in *Raisin in the Sun* (1961) and another 27 years before *Moving* (1988) showed a black family actually living in the middle landscape. To date, only one movie has been identified that briefly portrays an Asian wishing to live in suburbia. There seem to be no films about Hispanics in suburbia. In fact, there are probably a greater number of friendly creatures from outer space living or visiting suburbs in the movies than lower-class whites, blacks, Asians, and Hispanics combined.

The evolution of suburban film has serious limitations. Lacking a past and without a future, how can the present be improved? What are the alternatives? Only three movies out of approximately 400 show suburbanites moving back to the city. In *Consenting Adults* (1992), a couple moves out of suburbia and builds a single-family house in the vast emptiness of what seems to be the Great Plains. Several films depict the suburban ideal as no longer voluntary but enforced. In *The Stepford Wives* (1974), men give up trying to convince their spouses about the bliss of suburban domesticity and replace them with robots. *Serial Mom* (1994) depicts a perfect housewife whose absolute commitment to the suburban ideal transforms her into a serial killer. She murders neighbors for improper behavior such as not recycling their garbage.

Perhaps the best answer to the question of alternatives to suburban life was given in *The Swimmer* (1968), starring Burt Lancaster as Neddy Merrill. This aging, upper-class Lothario decides to swim home across the country. As he moves from one neighbor's pool to another, he is forced to face the shallowness of the upper-middle-class suburban lifestyle and his own misdeeds. Merrill's vulnerability grows as his physical strength diminishes. The audience begins to learn that he has lost his job, his wife has left him, and his children never really respected his pretentious fatherhood. Finally, Merrill reaches home only to realize he doesn't live there anymore. Locked out of his house, in the pouring rain, with only a bathing suit for cover, Neddy Merrill has been cast out of suburbia with nowhere to go. The meaning was clear. There is no film alternative to suburbia. To those movie characters scripted to live in the middle landscape, and to those cast out like Neddy Merrill, suburbia, with all its imperfections, is really the Paradise Lost of the Silver Screen.

—*Philip C. Dolce*

**See also**
Suburban Ideal.
**References**
Basinger, Jeanine. *A Woman's View: How Hollywood Spoke to Women, 1930–1960*. New York: Knopf, 1993.
Loukides, Paul, and Linda K. Fuller, eds. *Locales in American Popular Film*. Bowling Green, OH: Bowling Green State University Popular Press, 1993.
Porton, Richard. "Suburbia: American Dreams, Suburban Nightmares." *Cincaste* 20 (1993): 12–15.
Quart, Leonard, and Albert Auster. *American Film and Society since 1945*. 2d ed. New York: Praeger, 1991.
Rollins, Peter C., ed. *Hollywood as Historian: American Film in the Cultural Context*. Lexington: University of Kentucky Press, 1983.

## Mt. Lebanon, Pennsylvania

Mt. Lebanon is located in a region of hills and valleys six miles south of Pittsburgh, Pennsylvania. Its large lots, curvilinear streets, and exclusive nature reflect design characteristics of the early automobile suburbs of the 1920s.

Originally settled as an area of scattered farms, Mt. Lebanon was initially developed as a streetcar suburb when a trolley tunnel was built under a large hill south of Pittsburgh in 1902, and was incorporated as an independent township in 1912. Mt. Lebanon was located too far from the city to experience much growth, however, until an automobile tunnel, the Liberty Tubes, was constructed in the early 1920s. With the opening of the tunnel, the number of building lots platted in Mt. Lebanon increased dramatically from 895 between 1901 and 1920 to more than 4,500 during the 1920s.

The introduction of the automobile brought Mt. Lebanon within easier commuting distance of Pittsburgh and increased the amount of land available for development; it also changed residential land use patterns. When housing was no longer tied to half-mile-wide strips of land along streetcar routes—about the distance commuters would walk to trolleys—Mt. Lebanon's developers took advantage of the freedom provided by automobiles to create a new kind of suburb. Subdivisions were dispersed along major roadways, and lot sizes increased substantially. Instead of straight streets in a rectangular grid with small, narrow lots and the relatively high densities characteristic of streetcar developments, Mt. Lebanon boasted curvilinear streets with larger, wider lots and relatively lower densities. Lots expanded from 25–30 feet by 100–150 feet to 50–75 by 140–250. In Mission Hills, one of Mt. Lebanon's premier subdivisions, housing density was only half that of earlier subdivisions.

Like most early automobile suburbs, Mt. Lebanon developed as a socially and economically homogenous community. By offering modern urban conveniences such as gas, electric, and sewer connections, platting larger lots, forbidding multifamily dwellings, and specifying minimum construction costs, the developers of Mt. Lebanon sought to attract wealthier members of the middle class. In 1930, the median value of houses in Mt. Lebanon was $14,746, more than twice that of Pittsburgh. Like their counterparts elsewhere, Mt. Lebanon's developers used restrictive deed covenants to maintain an exclusive nature for their communities. In addition to restricting sales to whites, a common provision ultimately ruled unconstitutional by the Supreme Court, one subdivision dictated that homes had to be designed by architects and built of brick or stone; in addition, to hide the more debased and utilitarian aspects of suburban living, no garages were to be visible from the street.

Although they were influenced by large developers like J. C. Nichols of Kansas City, Mt. Lebanon's "community builders" adhered to earlier traditions of smaller developers who lived on the urban fringe during the streetcar era. Even from its inception as a streetcar suburb in 1902, the developers of Mt. Lebanon's Clearview subdivision described it as a community of large lots with all the modern amenities, including sewers, gas, and water. By 1916, they were advertising that it carried all the "proper restrictions," a code phrase indicating its exclusive nature. Rather than clearly breaking with past development practices, Mt. Lebanon's developers during the 1920s, along with their counterparts elsewhere, combined new forms with old, even as they pioneered new land use patterns that would become ubiquitous in the highway suburbs that developed after World War II.

—*Steven J. Hoffman*

**References**
Hoffman, Steven J. "'A Plan of Quality': The Development of Mt. Lebanon, a 1920s Automobile Suburb." *Journal of Urban History* 18 (1992): 141–181.
———. "The Saga of Pittsburgh's Liberty Tubes: Geographical Partisanship on the Urban Fringe." *Pittsburgh History* 75 (1992): 128–141.
Weiss, Marc A. *The Rise of the Community Builders: The American Real Estate Industry and Urban Land Planning*. New York: Columbia University Press, 1987.
Worley, William S. *J. C. Nichols and the Shaping of Kansas City: Innovation in Planned Residential Communities*. Columbia: University of Missouri Press, 1990.

## Muckrakers

At the beginning of the 1900s, the names of the muckrakers and their stories about corruption, greed, monopolies, slumlords, and the exploitation of the masses were known to almost every literate American. Today, they and their stories are largely forgotten, dug up every now and then by a professor trying to instill a sense of justice and social action in his or her students. But for about three decades, beginning in the 1880s, the muckrakers were the finest journalists in the country, well-educated writers who cared about the society and people they wrote about. Many had college degrees, at a time when the average American had a fifth-grade education; many had studied philosophy and the creative arts in Europe. Many were socialists, seeing the problems of capitalist America not in its people but in the social, political, and economic institutions that allowed exploitation. They asked the country if a person had to compromise principles to succeed. They believed that reporting society's problems through the mass media would bring abuse to light and lead Americans to reclaim their country.

There weren't many muckrakers, but even the few became part of the social conscience of an urbanizing society. They brought about sweeping state and federal reforms and laws that allowed urban lower and middle classes to reduce the amount of exploitation of the country by robber barons and corrupt political machines.

Like society itself, most publishers supported establishment policies, becoming supporters of big business and the nation's economy. A few, however, provided a forum for the media to become the cutting edge of social change. Horace Greeley, editor of the *New York Tribune* and a strong supporter of unions and the working class, had shown an antebellum nation how a strong newspaper could objectively present the news while also benefiting mankind and promoting social change. Although other newspaper and magazine editors—especially Joseph Pulitzer and William Randolph Hearst after Reconstruction—put significant resources into investigating urban exploitation, it was Samuel S. McClure who provided a national forum that became synonymous with muckraking. In the pages of *McClure's* magazine, Ida Tarbell exposed the corruption of John D. Rockefeller's Standard Oil, Lincoln Steffens explored problems of the cities, and Ray Stannard Baker looked at questions raised by the existence of the railroad trusts.

In *Packingtown* (1899), A. M. Simons wrote about exploited workers who packed diseased meat for sale to the public; within a year, the Hearst empire began crusading against issues of diseased food, unfair labor competition, and corruption in the meatpacking industry that led directly to the establishment of the Department of Agriculture. A few years later, in 1906, Upton Sinclair carried the campaign even further. In newspaper articles and a novel, *The Jungle,* he shocked a complacent America to demand that the Pure Food and Drug Act, bottled up in Congress, be brought to the floor and passed. Sinclair's exposés of big business, organized religion, education, and journalism itself established him as the greatest of the muckrakers. The same year *The Jungle* was published, Hearst's *Cosmopolitan* magazine published David Graham Phillips's vicious exposé of corruption and greed within the U.S. Senate. His series of magazine articles eventually produced a constitutional amendment establishing the direct election of senators.

In the era of Progressivism and concern for massive social change brought on by President Theodore Roosevelt, the muckrakers (only a small part of journalism) recognized that the reform movement would support their efforts. But Roosevelt, who admired and respected the press, also coined the phrase "muckraker" in 1906 when, upset with some of the journalists' excesses, he quoted John Bunyan's *Pilgrim's Progress* and said that like the pilgrim, there were some journalists who raked the muck from the earth always looking down, while rejecting a celestial crown. These muckrakers, said Roosevelt, were necessary and important, but they saw only a small part of life and never the glory that could be America.

The year Roosevelt gave the muckrakers their name was the high-water mark of the movement as series after series pointed out problems in America's social structure, exposing intertwining corporate trusts and corruption, inhumane prison conditions, the exploitation of workers, and even organized religion for owning slum tenements.

Two of the most respected muckrakers, defending the journalists' concern about what had happened to the American dream, tried to put their decade into perspective. Upton Sinclair pointed out that the muckrakers wrote "not because they love corruption, but because they hate it with an intensity that forbids them to think about anything else while corruption sits enthroned." A socialist with a mission not only to reform but to improve upon the social conditions of the world, Sinclair clearly explained what the muckrakers were all about:

As a rule, the Muckrake Man began his career with no theories, as a simple observer of facts known to every person at all "on the inside" of business and politics. But he followed the facts, and the facts always led him to one conclusion; until finally he discovered to his consternation that he was enlisted in a revolt against capitalism.

He is the forerunner of a revolution; and, like every revolutionist, he takes his chances of victory and defeat. If it is defeat that comes; if the iron heel wins out in the end—why, then, the Muckrake Man will remain for all time a scandal-monger and an assassin of character. If, on the other hand, he succeeds in his efforts to make the people believe what "everybody knows"—then he will be recognized in the future as a benefactor of his race.

Ray Stannard Baker, another well-known social critic, wrote that the muckrakers

. . . really believed in human beings. We "muckraked" not because we hated our world but because

Upton Sinclair's 1906 novel, The Jungle, *publicized the appalling conditions in Chicago's meatpacking plants and led to government regulation of the industry.*

**See also**
Hearst, William Randolph; Pulitzer, Joseph; Sinclair, Upton; Steffens, Lincoln; Yellow Journalism.
**References**
Baker, Ray Stannard. *An American Chronicle.* New York: Scribners, 1945.
Brasch, Walter M. *Forerunners of Revolution: Muckrakers and the American Social Conscience.* Lanham, MD: University Press of America, 1990.
Chalmers, David. *The Muckrake Years.* New York: Van Nostrand Reinhold, 1974.
Faulkner, Harold U. *The Quest for Social Justice, 1898–1914.* New York: Macmillan, 1931.
Filler, Louis. *Crusaders for American Liberalism.* New York: Harcourt, Brace, 1939.
Harrison, John M., and Harry H. Stein. *Muckraking: Past, Present and Future.* University Park: Pennsylvania State University Press, 1973.
Hofstadter, Richard. *The Age of Reform.* New York: Knopf, 1955.
Josephson, Matthew. *The Robber Barons.* New York: Harcourt, Brace, 1934.
Lyon, Peter. *Success Story: The Life and Times of S. S. McClure.* New York: Scribners, 1963.
McClure, S. S. *My Autobiography.* New York: Frederick A. Stokes, 1914.
Reiger, Cornelius C. *The Era of the Muckrakers.* Chapel Hill: University of North Carolina Press, 1932.
Shapiro, Herbert, ed. *The Muckrakers and American Society.* Boston: D. C. Heath, 1968.
Weinberg, Alvin M., and Lila Weinberg. *The Muckrakers.* New York: Simon and Schuster, 1961.
Wilson, Harold S. *McClure's Magazine and the Muckrakers.* Princeton, NJ: Princeton University Press, 1970.

we loved it. We were not hopeless, we were not cynical, we were not bitter. . . .

One . . . man, no matter how obscure, quiet, simple, can get results amazing in their importance; one such man is worth about four thousand so-called respectable citizens who stay at home and talk about the shame of boss-rule. . . . If this republic is to be saved it must be saved by individual effort.

By 1910, the muckrakers, who were used to threats, found that big business had found new ways to end challenges to its power and authority. The banks, controlled by a series of interlocking directorates, began closing credit options for publishers, then secretly cut deals with the nation's periodical distributors, essentially forcing publishers either to cease muckraking or face financial ruin.

By 1912, only a few journalists were still unafraid to challenge corruption and stupidity, journalists who believed in America but tried to force it to recognize and attempt to solve its problems. There were still some investigations; there were still some changes. But now, in a different age, as people once again became restless, with a war approaching in Europe, the muckrakers no longer seemed relevant. A new era approached, one less concerned with the ills of a capitalist society and more concerned with getting on with life. The muckrakers had done their job and done it exceedingly well. But their time was up, and no one could change that.

—*Walter M. Brasch*

## Multicentered Metropolis

The multicentered metropolis can be defined as a metropolitan area with several core cities. Other terms for this metropolitan form include the "polycentric city" and the "multi-nodal city." The multicentered metropolis evolved out of the classic hub-and-spokes metropolitan form that arose with the development of mass transit in the middle of the nineteenth century. Horsecars, commuter railroads, and later electric streetcars produced the multiplication of suburbs linked to and dependent on a single core city. Mass transit also allowed the sorting of residents by class and the rise of distinct areas for housing, government, finance, manufacturing, and retail.

The hub-and-spokes metropolitan form predominated until the rise of the automobile. Beginning in the 1920s, the automobile, the motorized truck, and new highways stimulated the relocation of some industries to the suburbs by allowing the construction of factories away from railroad junctions or waterways. Around these suburban industrial locations arose residential developments and commercial strips. As suburban areas diversified, they became known as "satellite cities," which indicated their growing autonomy from core cities and their transformation from purely residential suburbs into truly urban areas.

While evidence of the multicentered metropolis was apparent in some urban areas before World War II, particularly around Los Angeles, it was after the war that the new metropolitan form flourished. National policies such as tax breaks on mortgage interest and low-interest loans to veterans encouraged homeownership and stimulated the construction of suburban housing. Developers took advantage of cheap, suburban land made accessible by newly constructed highways. In southern California, Arizona, New Mexico, Texas, and Florida, this postwar suburban trend was particularly evident. In the so-called Sunbelt, express highways, mild climate, hydroelectric power, and vast open areas combined with a booming economy to produce rapid urban growth. Companies relocated to the Sunbelt because of lower taxes, fewer unions, and at the whim of executives who preferred the mild climate. Once there, officials built plants on the fringes of urban areas alongside freeways, creating horizontally sprawling cities.

Southwestern urbanization also resulted from state lobbying that drew defense-related industries in increasing numbers. Relying on government contracts rather than on natural resources, port, or railroad connections, company officials were free to locate their enterprises wherever they desired. Many preferred suburban sites where they encountered less traffic, lower taxes, and cheaper land. Areas of lower population were also beneficial for safety and security since many of these companies produced research in rocketry, aerospace engineering, and atomic weapons. These defense-related industries contributed greatly to the development of suburban areas in the Southwest.

Two important transportation developments furthered the creation of new urban centers outside traditional city centers. First, because of urban congestion and high land costs, federal policy encouraged the construction of new freeways that avoided central cities. These "beltways," which eventually encircled major metropolitan areas, effectively linked the suburban cities. Drivers could travel rapidly throughout a region without venturing through the central city. Because the sites where several freeways met offered speedy connections to all parts of the metropolitan area, these interchanges became desirable locations for housing and business.

Second, the growing popularity of air travel encouraged the rapid growth of suburban areas around airports. The areas alongside freeways in the immediate vicinity of airports became prime locations for hotels, offices, shopping, and convention facilities. By doing business in these areas, executives benefited from lower hotel rates and avoided having to fight traffic into and out of the city.

By the 1970s, new communications technologies also propelled the urbanization of suburbs. The ability of workers to send information via computers over telephone lines and telecommunication satellites allowed companies to locate almost anywhere in the metropolitan area. As a result, suburbs became home for many workers in so-called "back-offices" where they processed data for firms located in central cities.

The university research park, pioneered by Stanford University in Palo Alto, California, lured defense contractors, high tech companies, and their professional employees, particularly engineers, to suburban locations. These growing suburban communities attracted newcomers by providing new, upscale residential areas and other cultural amenities. The combination of these elements produced concentrations of high tech companies in several locations, particularly Silicon Valley near San Jose, California, and along Route 128 near Boston. With their own industries, downtowns, shopping areas, and cultural institutions, these suburbs became largely autonomous from central cities.

Numerous benefits followed the rise of the multicentered metropolis. Residents had greater freedom to choose where they lived, worked, and relaxed as cities competed for residents, shoppers, and employers. Increased competition between suburban cities and traditional core cities resulted in the duplication of performing arts centers, convention facilities, and shopping districts. Competition also spurred innovative solutions to transportation problems, and increased suburban employment helped reduce commuting times for some suburbanites.

However, numerous problems also came with the rise of the multicentered metropolis. Foremost was the difficult problem of traffic. The rise of hinterland cities increased the number of commuters traveling between suburbs on roads not originally designed to carry high volumes of traffic. The rise of reverse-commuting (from an urban residence to a suburban job) taxed mass transit systems designed primarily to bring residents to the city in the morning and return them to suburban homes after work. Urban rivalries between several large cities in a single metropolitan area undercut regional planning efforts. The relocation of jobs to suburbs placed an additional burden on poorer central city residents who had to commute to hinterland jobs even though they lacked private automobiles or access to efficient mass transit.

Multicenteredness also contributed to the withering of social life in some core cities whose merchants competed with new suburban establishments for shoppers, tourists, and theater, bar, and restaurant patrons. The loss of large companies to suburbs hurt the urban tax base. Racial and social class bifurcation also intensified as cities became dominated by the very rich and the very poor, with the middle class leaving for the suburbs where they also worked. By the 1980s most Americans assumed that the central city was wracked by crime and poverty, and that image only served to further the trend toward suburban growth and economic and political autonomy.

By the 1960s these problems helped launch an era of mass transit construction typified by Bay Area Rapid Transit (BART) in and around San Francisco, which represented an attempt to reassert the role of older cities within metropolitan areas. Despite BART's high cost, low ridership, and technological glitches, new rapid transit projects were constructed in Baltimore and Washington, D.C. More recently cities have turned to light-rail lines, which have been constructed in San Jose, San Diego, Portland, St. Louis, Pittsburgh, and Los Angeles. The effectiveness of these systems in solving traffic congestion and increasing the competitiveness of downtowns is questionable given their low ridership, inability to serve more than a small portion of a metropolitan region's geographic area, and high capital and maintenance costs.

But the suburbs increasingly had problems as well. The urbanization of suburbs aroused critics who castigated the suburbs as sprawling, unplanned new cities typified by characterless mass-produced housing and hyperconsumerism. Automobile-induced metropolitan expansion into agricultural land and open space furthered the degradation of the environment. Increased traffic, crime, and noise threatened to destroy the image of suburbia as a residential utopia. In response, suburban residents formed political associations through which they demanded regulations on growth.

The continued tensions between the social and technological forces encouraging the diversification of the suburban economy and the problems inherent in the urbanization of the hinterland makes it likely that the multicentered metropolis will continue to be a particularly contentious form of metropolitan development.

—*Joseph A. Rodriguez*

**References**

Abbott, Carl. *The Metropolitan Frontier: Cities in the Modern American West.* Tucson: University of Arizona Press, 1993.

Banham, Reyner. *Los Angeles: The Architecture of Four Ecologies.* New York: Harper & Row, 1971.

Findlay, John M. *Magic Lands: Western Cityscape and American Culture after 1940.* Berkeley: University of California Press, 1992.

Garreau, Joel. *Edge City: Life on the New Frontier.* New York: Doubleday, 1991.

Muller, Peter O. *The Outer City: Geographical Consequences of the Urbanization of the Suburbs.* Washington, DC: Association of American Geographers, 1976.

Vance, James E., Jr. *Geography and Urban Evolution in the San Francisco Bay Area.* Berkeley, CA: Institute of Governmental Studies, 1964.

## Multiple Nuclei Theory

The multiple nuclei theory is a model of the internal spatial structure of urban areas proposed in 1945 by Chauncy Harris and Edward Ullman. Harris and Ullman sought to pro-vide a realistic model that avoided the geometrical oversimplifications of Ernest W. Burgess's concentric zone theory and Homer Hoyt's sector theory, while still retaining the key insights of these influential works.

Harris and Ullman argued that the internal structure of cities reflects the locational requirements of different activities and that urban areas develop around multiple centers of production, trade, and transportation functions. Typically, the initial nucleus of an urban settlement focused on the city's *raison d'être*—the retail district if the city emerged to serve a consumer hinterland, the port if established as a transshipment point, or the mine or factory if founded as a production center. Some cities developed with two or more initial cores, but in all cases the specialized locational needs of new activities tended to stimulate the growth of multiple nuclei away from the city's point of origin. Subsequent patterns resulted from the sorting out of land uses within the city, as activities with similar locational needs clustered together while incompatible uses (e.g., upper-class residential areas and industrial districts) gravitated away from each another. A city's land use pattern at any one time reflected unique site and situation characteristics, resulting in any one of an innumerable number of possible spatial configurations.

Harris and Ullman's model was influential through the 1960s. It added insights drawn from economic and regional geography to the theories of Burgess, a sociologist, and Hoyt, whose work was sponsored by the Federal Housing Administration, both of which ignored the city's relationship with surrounding cities and regions and focused primarily on residential land.

—*Elvin Wyly*

**See also**

Burgess, Ernest W.; Concentric Zone Theory; Sector Theory.

**Reference**

Harris, Chauncy D., and Edward L. Ullman. "The Nature of Cities." *Annals of the American Academy of Political and Social Science* 242 (1945): 7–17.

## Mumford, Lewis (1895–1990)

Social philosopher, historian, biographer, architectural critic, and moral reformer, Lewis Mumford was one of the outstanding public intellectuals of the twentieth century. Born in New York City on October 19, 1895, he produced a body of writing that is unmatched in modern American letters for its range and richness. "It may be," the writer Malcolm Cowley has suggested, "that Lewis Mumford is the last of the great humanists." In the course of his 60-year career as an author and insistent public advocate, Mumford did more than anyone else in this era to heighten awareness of the role that architecture, cities, and technology play in everyday life. Author of two landmark books on urban civilization, *The Culture of Cities* (1938) and *The City in History* (1961), his pioneering work on the evolution of urban culture helped establish the city as a subject for scholarly concern. He is also one of the founders of the academic fields of American Studies and the History of Technology.

An activist as well as an intellectual, Mumford played a central role in some of the major public policy debates of the twentieth century, including those on highways, urban development, nuclear disarmament, and the problems and promise of technology. And as a founding member of the Regional Planning Association of America (RPAA) in the 1920s, he helped fashion a program of urban decentralization that resulted in the building of two model communities, Radburn, New Jersey, and Sunnyside Gardens in Queens, New York.

Mumford's ideas about the city were powerfully influenced by Patrick Geddes, the Scottish botanist who became a city planner. Geddes was particularly sensitive to the connections between city and country, and he insisted that urban problems could be successfully attacked only on a regional basis. He saw the entire city-region as an interconnected ecosystem that one had to understand before suggesting alterations that might upset the delicate natural balance. Mumford's writings exemplify this holistic, ecological approach to the study of human communities. Geddes taught Mumford a new approach to looking at the city, an approach based on direct observation and a biologist's sensitivity to organic relationships. Almost from the moment he encountered Geddes's writings as a student at the City College of New York, Mumford began to use New York itself as his university, exploring the metropolitan region on foot, absorbing as much as he could of its history and habits from its buildings, terrain, and people. All of his later writing about cities is grounded in these early firsthand surveys of his native city and region.

In a steady succession of books and essays—and his popular "Skyline" column in *The New Yorker*—Mumford pointed out and emphasized a new way of looking at the built environment, brilliantly establishing the connections between architecture and civilization. "Each generation," he once remarked, "writes its biography in the buildings it creates." He also taught his readers how to approach buildings, what to expect from them, and what to demand of those who design them. The most influential architectural critic of his time, Mumford consistently urged architects to shape their work to the social, psychological, and physical needs of human beings. For him, the chief mission of architecture was to make "a new home for man."

Mumford's close attention to human needs and human scale led him to denounce the massive urban renewal, highway, and high-rise building projects that have disfigured and damaged the downtowns of America's major cities. Mumford charged that Robert Moses, New York's czar of public works, had inflicted more damage on New York—and by his far-spreading example on other cities—than anyone else in his era by bringing multitiered expressways directly into the heart of New York City and moving the poor into dispiriting concrete towers. Beginning in the 1940s, for nearly 20 years Mumford fought almost every one of Moses' major highway and urban renewal projects. He also lost nearly all of these battles, but in the process he slowly helped change ideas about highways, mass transit, and urban renewal. His work led eventually to important policy revisions, although not nearly to the kind of comprehensive reforms he advocated in his hard-hitting articles. Until he died in 1990 in Leedsville, New York, the secluded village where he had lived with his family since the 1930s, Lewis Mumford was America's urban conscience.

—*Donald L. Miller*

**See also**

Moses, Robert; Regional Plan of New York and Its Environs; Regional Planning Association of America.

**References**

Miller, Donald L. *Lewis Mumford, A Life.* Pittsburgh, PA: University of Pittsburgh Press, 1992.

———, ed. *The Lewis Mumford Reader.* Athens: University of Georgia Press, 1995.

Novak, Frank, Jr., ed. *Lewis Mumford and Patrick Geddes: The Correspondence.* London: Routledge, 1995.

## Municipal Bonds

A municipal bond, often referred to as a "municipal" or "muni" in financial circles, has two distinguishing features. First, it represents a debt issued by a public entity for a public purpose. Second, the interest earned by the bond is free from federal income taxes, and usually free from state and local taxes if the bondholder lives in the issuer's state. Beyond these general characteristics, there are a multiplicity of variations. The municipal bond market in the 1990s is huge, with well over $1 trillion worth of bonds having been issued by states, cities, counties, school districts, and a vast array of public agencies. The public purposes range from constructing schools, roads, and sewer systems to lending funds to corporations and college students. Municipal bonds are issued in two forms. One variety, general obligation bonds (often abbreviated as "GO" bonds), are backed by the "full faith and credit" of the borrowing jurisdiction and are repaid from tax revenue. The other, revenue bonds, are backed by the income from a particular project.

Since New York City first issued GO bonds in the early 1800s, they have been regarded as one of the safest long-term investments in the United States. They finance projects that provide the greatest and most diverse social benefits, and from which no individual profits directly. Examples of such projects include roads, bridges, and sewers. These bonds possess the "full faith and credit" feature because the pledge to make timely interest and principal payments is strong. That strength derives from the jurisdiction's taxing power—for most local governments, the property tax—which can be viewed as a lien on all property owned by the government and the residents within its jurisdiction. These bonds have been major sources of capital fund-raising and are likely to continue as such well into the twenty-first century. They currently constitute about 35 percent of all municipal issues.

Revenue bonds, compared to GO bonds, finance projects somewhat more narrow in their benefits. These projects fall within the general category of municipally owned businesses, including parking garages, airports, hospitals, and stadiums. At a minimum, revenues from these projects must cover operating expenses and debt payments. Since the early 1970s, revenue bonds have become popular for several reasons: their reliance on user fees rather than unpopular property taxes that create a lien on people's homes, the limited capacity of local governments to issue GO debt, and market innovations that favor revenue bonds.

—*Anthony L. Loviscek*

### References
Kohn, Meir. *Financial Institutions and Markets.* New York: McGraw-Hill, 1994.
Lipkin, Donald R. "Municipal Bonds: A Decade of Change." In William H. Baughn, Thomas Storrs, and Charles E. Walker, eds., *The Bankers' Handbook,* 518–531. Homewood, IL: Dow Jones-Irwin, 1988.
Miller, Gerald J. *Handbook of Debt Management.* New York: Marcel Dekker, 1996.
Moody's Investors Services. *Moody's Municipal and Government Manual.* New York: Moody's Investors Services, 1996.
Poterba, James. "Municipal Bonds." In Peter Newman, Murray Milgate, and John Eatwell, eds. *The New Palgrave Dictionary of Money and Finance.* New York: Stockton Press, 1992.
Standard & Poor's Corporation. *Municipal Finance Criteria.* New York: McGraw-Hill, 1993.

## Municipal Government

During the course of American history, the needs, desires, and ideals of the nation's city dwellers have changed markedly. The history of municipal government is largely a story of adaptation to these changes. The burgomasters of New Amsterdam in the seventeenth century, the aldermen of nineteenth-century Chicago, and the city managers of the myriad suburban "Heights," "Parks," and "Forests" ringing twentieth-century urban centers have faced notably different problems and demands, and the structure of municipal government has evolved in response. Though at times much criticized, municipalities have adapted, providing many of the basic services vital to America's urban development.

During the colonial era, relatively few localities received royal charters granting them the status of municipal corporation. Moreover, the functions and structures of the earliest municipal corporations differed greatly from those of the nineteenth and twentieth centuries. In some municipalities, the city government was a closed corporation with members of the board of aldermen enjoying unlimited tenure and with vacancies being filled by the board itself. The local electorate had no voice in the selection of municipal officials. In the late seventeenth and early eighteenth centuries, the management of the municipal corporation's property and the regulation and promotion of commerce were the chief business of the city aldermen. The leasing of the municipality's wharf property and market stalls, the regulation of prices and weights and measures, and the protection of local traders from outside competition preoccupied the municipal authorities.

By the mid-eighteenth century, however, municipalities were expanding their responsibilities, focusing increasing attention on street lighting, fire protection, and the elimination of such nuisances as stray livestock and lumber blocking thoroughfares. Moreover, the American Revolution brought an end to the closed corporate structure of municipal rule. Henceforth, municipal aldermen were to be chosen by the urban electorate and supposedly be responsible to them. By 1800, then, municipal corporations were less managers of property and more units of local government operating in accord with the political ideals of the young nation.

In the early nineteenth century, state legislatures and courts further redefined municipal government in the United States. Rather than being a privilege bestowed on a relatively few localities, municipal status became a right available to virtually every crossroads community petitioning the state legislature. For example, from 1803 to 1848 Mississippi's legislature incorporated 105 municipalities, granting 71 municipal charters during the 1830s alone. Meanwhile, at both the state and federal levels, judges were differentiating between municipal corporations and business corporations. Whereas the courts viewed business corporations as private entities protected from state interference, judges regarded municipalities as agents of the state, serving a public purpose. According to a number of nineteenth-century court decisions, a municipal charter could be repealed or amended at the will of state lawmakers without concurrent approval of the municipality affected. As early as 1819 in *Dartmouth College v. Woodward,* the U.S. Supreme Court ruled, in the opinion by Chief Justice John Marshall, that "if incorporation be a grant of political power . . . the legislature of the State may act according to its own judgment."

The fact that municipalities depended on state legislatures for their authority did not hinder the growth of municipal responsibilities. Instead, state solons generously approved volumes of special laws expanding the powers and functions of city governments. During the mid-nineteenth century, the largest cities created full-time professional police and firefighting forces to replace the night watch and volunteer brigades of the past. Moreover, they purchased or constructed waterworks and initiated sewerage projects. With the widespread introduction of the horse-drawn streetcar in the 1850s and 1860s, municipal councils also found themselves spending more time debating the grant of franchises for use of the public thoroughfares. Franchise agreements with gas, electric, and telephone companies as well as streetcar syndicates were to become the subject of increasing controversy during the remainder of the century.

The expanding army of municipal employees and the increasing value of public franchises were also to result in mounting cries of corruption. More jobs meant more patronage for city politicians who often seemed more concerned about building a corps of loyal supporters on the public payroll than creating effective and efficient municipal services. Streetcar or gas franchises could reap a fortune for those lucky enough to acquire the privilege, and public utility promoters were willing to pay aldermen for a vote in their favor. Rumors and reports of bribery became commonplace, and many city dwellers were aware of the possible misuse of patronage.

As early as the 1850s, the New York Board of Aldermen became known as the Forty Thieves because of the members' willingness to line their pockets with bribes. In 1884, New York City's municipal council members engaged in similar chicanery, awarding a transit franchise in exchange for bribes of $25,000 to each lawmaker. During the 1890s, journalists nicknamed a corrupt band of Chicago aldermen the Gray Wolves because of their proclivity to sell franchise privileges to the highest briber.

Similarly, abuse of patronage powers was evident in one city after another and especially undermined professionalism in urban police forces. Before 1887, Philadelphia's mayor personally appointed all policemen, and the law enforcement officers were naturally expected to be loyal followers of the mayor and his party. In 1869, when the mayor's office shifted from Republican to Democrat, the new executive fired almost the entire force, and three years later when a Republican mayor assumed power, he dismissed virtually all of the 700 officers appointed by his Democratic predecessor. Throughout the nation, good relations with political leaders were necessary if one wanted a promotion within the police force. Moreover, policemen were known to overlook bribery, intimidation, and ballot-box stuffing at polling places on election day if the malfeasance served the party that had appointed them.

The most notorious and best-publicized scoundrels in municipal government during the nineteenth century were the members of the Tweed Ring. Led by William M. Tweed, chief of the local Democratic Party organization, the ring controlled New York City government from 1868 to 1871 and robbed the city of an estimated $30 million to $100 million. It reaped its largest profits from padded contracts. The city paid far above the market price for supplies and services with the difference going into the pockets of Tweed and his henchmen. Especially notorious was the fraud associated with construction of a new courthouse. Originally estimated to cost $250,000, the final bill amounted to $14 million. Tweed went to jail for his misdeeds, and memories of his crimes have tarnished the reputation of nineteenth-century city government ever since.

Urban Americans did not passively accept the abuse of patronage, the bribery, or the padded contracts. Instead, during the late nineteenth century, a steady stream of good-government committees arose in one city after another, each dedicated to cleansing municipal administration of its supposed evils. New York's reform Committee of Seventy, a coalition of wealthy business leaders, ousted the Tweed Ring in the early 1870s. During the 1880s, Philadelphia, Cincinnati, and New Orleans each was subjected to the reform influence of a Committee of One Hundred. In these cities, the most respected citizens were rebelling against existing conditions and banding together to rid municipal government of corruption. Such committees might succeed in electing a slate of "clean" candidates or push through revisions of the municipal charter. But most often, they were short-lived phenomena that arose in momentary outrage against the municipal status quo. Finally, in 1894, good-government advocates from throughout the nation combined to form the National Municipal League, a permanent organization dedicated to a national crusade for better urban rule.

In the contemporary literature on municipal government, the reform committees and leagues found reinforcement for their opinions. Journalists and students of urban government repeatedly lambasted the state of affairs in City Hall. Reform journalist Edwin Godkin contended that "the present condition of city governments in the United States is bringing democratic institutions into contempt the world over, and imperiling some of the best things in our civilization." Likewise, James Bryce, a British observer of American government, claimed that "there is no denying that the government of cities is the one conspicuous failure of [government in] the United States."

Yet, in their condemnations of American municipal government, reformers chose to ignore the manifold achievements of urban rule in the late nineteenth century. There were payoffs, and many aldermen did place their brothers and cousins on the city payroll, but at the same time American municipalities were adapting to the new technology of the age, hiring distinguished experts to aid in the development of parks, sewerage systems, and waterworks, and developing a body of professional employees who provided municipal services at least comparable to any in the world. During the late nineteenth century, America's cities built and maintained expansive water and sewerage systems, surpassing in magnitude the systems of Europe. Moreover, New York, Boston, and Chicago employed the best available engineers to design these public works. Municipalities did not hire the brother-in-law of the local party chieftain to plan their reservoirs or draw the blueprints for their dams. For those tasks, city fathers turned to prominent experts. American fire departments readily adopted the latest firefighting technology and effectively limited the loss of life and property. Fire insurance companies made sure that municipal fire brigades were as effective as possible and lobbied successfully to curb the detrimental effects of partisan meddling. City chieftains employed the best of the emerging corps of landscape architects, including the new profession's greatest practitioner, Frederick Law Olmsted. As in the case of water and sewerage systems, party hacks were not in charge of designing the great public parklands developed in the late nineteenth century. Throughout the United States the monuments to municipal enterprise were readily apparent. Had observers of American municipal government wanted to present a positive picture, they could have found ample evidence to support their case.

The respectable good-government elite, however, chose to emphasize the negative. Municipal government may have achieved a good deal, but the means of urban rule hardly seemed to justify the ends. In the eyes of native-born, well-to-do, leading citizens, municipal government was a tawdry affair, a compromise with the uncouth and unprincipled. Plebeian Irish-born aldermen and ward heelers were among the prominent participants in municipal government, and the "better sort" had to share power with these people whom the elite considered unworthy of holding public office. Experts and professionals may have secured places on the public payroll, but so did party hacks whose very presence in City Hall seemed an offense against the basic principles of good government. Moreover, the moralistic middle class was offended by a government that provided ample water but too often ignored the equally ample supply of whiskey corrupting the city. Drinking on the Sabbath, prostitution, and gambling were all too evident, arousing the ire of moral reformers. In the 1890s, an irate Presbyterian preacher indicted New York City's Democratic politicians as a "lying, perjured, rum-soaked, and libidinous lot"; he called them "polluted harpies that, under the pretense of governing this city, are feeding day and night on its quivering vitals." New York City's aqueducts matched those of ancient Rome, but in the minds of God-fearing Presbyterians the city's moral decay likewise equaled that of the depraved empire.

To create purer and more efficient municipal governments, reformers of the Progressive Era stepped up their efforts to cleanse and restructure urban rule. During the first two decades of the twentieth century, municipal reform rose to the top of the national agenda, and good-government advocates loudly touted a variety of plans for altering the local polity. Many advocated strengthening the powers of the mayor and curbing the authority of the city council. Some sought nonpartisan municipal elections in order to eliminate party influence over city government. Another popular proposal was the small, at-large city council. Rather than having a council composed of 20 or 30 neighborhood representatives preoccupied with the parochial concerns of their own section of the city, reformers advocated a 7-member or 9-member council with each member elected at-large and representing citywide interests.

Such proposals were too modest for some reform advocates. They wanted to discard completely the traditional mayor-council framework and favored the adoption of the commission plan. This plan concentrated policymaking and administrative authority in a commission, usually of five members. Each member was responsible for one area of municipal administration. Thus, one served as commissioner for finance, another as commissioner of public works, and yet another as commissioner of public safety. Ideally, these commissioners were elected at-large. According to advocates of the plan, commission government clarified lines of authority and enabled voters to fix blame for incompetence or inefficiency readily. Crime prevention was the responsibility of the commissioner of public safety, and voters would hold that official accountable for a rash of unsolved robberies or the prevalence of prostitution. Moreover, at-large elections would eliminate the ward-based representatives of the past, who supposedly lacked an adequate understanding of citywide interests. Superficially resembling the board of directors of a business corporation, the city commission also appeared to promise the application of business efficiency to municipal government.

First adopted in Galveston, Texas, in 1901, this plan spread throughout the country during the following 15 years. By 1915, 423 municipalities had switched to the commission scheme. Yet the plan suffered from certain shortcomings. Elected commissioners were not necessarily experts in the areas of municipal endeavor they were supposed to administer. A popularly elected commissioner of public works without engineering knowledge could prove a poor alternative to an expert commissioner appointed by a mayor. Moreover, under the commission plan no one person was ultimately in charge of city government. There were five equal executives, a situation that could result in the division of city government into functional fiefdoms commanded by commissioners zealous in defending their domains and subject to no unifying overlord.

During the second decade of the twentieth century, many reformers turned to a seemingly better alternative, the council-manager (or city manager) plan. Rather than relying on amateur commissioners, the council-manager plan concentrated administrative authority in the hands of a single professional hired by the city council. The council continued to make basic policy, but the hired administrator was in charge of day-to-day municipal operations. The city manager was expected to be a nonpartisan figure trained in municipal administration who would rise above political clashes among council members and objectively implement council policy. In 1908 Staunton, Virginia, appointed the first city manager, and 11 years later 132 municipalities were operating under the plan. By the close of the second decade of the twentieth century, the council-manager plan had superseded the commission scheme as the favorite device of municipal reformers, and the number of council-manager municipalities continued to rise throughout the 1920s and 1930s. In 1933, 448 municipalities employed city managers to administer their affairs.

Manager rule, however, was not a panacea for municipal ills. Too often, managers became embroiled in municipal politics, and in some cities a new manager took office every time the political composition of the council changed. The division between administration and politics was not as clear-cut as reformers believed, and many managers discovered this fact the hard way when they fell victim to a disgruntled council.

During these same years of the early twentieth century, municipalities were gaining significant new powers over land use. Though municipalities had always been able to restrict or prohibit obnoxious uses of property within their boundaries, they did not exercise zoning powers prior to the twentieth century. Concern about unplanned growth, urban beautification, and the need to protect property values, however, resulted in demands for comprehensive land use planning. In 1907 Hartford, Connecticut, established the first permanent municipal planning commission to guide the future development of the city. Yet the commission did not exercise broad authority over the use of private property. Its chief concern was the placement of public thoroughfares and the distribution and development of such municipal facilities as parks, playgrounds, and police stations.

Not until the following decade did cities acquire broad zoning power over privately owned land. In 1913 the state legislatures of New York, Illinois, Wisconsin, and Minnesota passed laws authorizing municipalities to define residential zones from which business and industry could be excluded. Then, in 1916, New York City adopted the first comprehensive zoning plan that classified all land within the metropolis as residential, commercial, or unrestricted. Moreover, this plan restricted the height and area of buildings to be constructed, thereby ensuring that property owners left some open space around their structures and did not erect skyscrapers that impeded the flow of air and blotted out the sun. By the mid-1920s more than 400 municipalities had followed New York's example and adopted comprehensive zoning ordinances.

Yet many Americans questioned the constitutionality of these restrictions on the rights of private property owners. In a nation dedicated to individual freedom and entrepreneurial liberty, zoning seemed an extraordinary exercise of government authority. In 1926, however, in *Euclid v. Ambler Realty Company*, the Supreme Court upheld the constitutionality of this new municipal power, opening the way to further land use planning. Henceforth, zoning would be one of the most significant municipal powers, and municipal corporations were to have a heightened impact on urban development.

Zoning and land-use planning were especially useful tools for a growing number of suburban municipalities that were fashioning reputations as elite residential havens. During the 1920s the suburban population soared, and scores of new municipal corporations appeared just beyond the boundaries of the older central cities. Many of these municipalities represented a new phenomenon in the history of municipal government, having been created to preserve a semirural atmosphere rather than to provide services necessary for urbanization. For example, between 1920 and 1933, 46 communities incorporated in Nassau County, just east of New York City. In many of these cases, wealthy estate owners chose municipal rule in order to perpetuate low-density settlement and to block subdividers or other unwanted outsiders from disturbing their manorial lifestyle. Moreover, they sought to avoid the higher taxes that would result from development. Consequently, as Nassau County developed, some of its incorporated areas remained less densely populated than its unincorporated areas. In this instance, the municipal corporation was not an instrument for governing cities but rather a tool to prevent their development.

The emergence of suburban cities and villages also generated increased conflict between municipalities. Annexation wars were to become commonplace in many metropolitan areas, as each municipality sought to grab tax-rich territory before neighboring municipalities could do so. At the same time, intergovernmental agreements for the provision of shared services became more common as some communities contracted with others for fire or police protection or water and sewage treatment. The fragmentation of metropolitan America into scores of adjoining but independent municipal corporations meant that intermunicipal diplomacy became a more significant part of the job of mayors and other local officials. Successful suburban mayors had to threaten, bully, cajole, and often compromise with leaders of neighboring municipalities in governmentally divided suburbia.

Suburbanization would continue throughout the remainder of the twentieth century, but the pace of growth in both the urban core and along the fringe slowed considerably during the Depression. Just as individuals and businesses suffered from economic woes, so did municipal corporations. The rate of tax delinquency rose as residents and businesses were unable to pay their property levies. Moreover, as property values plummeted, assessments dropped, and the local tax base eroded. Between 1929 and 1933, the assessed value of property in Cleveland and Los Angeles declined more than 40 percent. Revenues thus fell short of expectations, and city governments were hard-pressed to meet their payrolls. Especially hard hit were municipalities that had accumulated a large bonded indebtedness during the prosperous 1920s. To satisfy demands for new streets and bridges and extended water mains and sewer lines, America's municipalities had engaged in large-scale borrowing, but with the advent of the Depression some proved unable to pay the interest on their debt. By the beginning of 1935, 851 municipalities were in default, or 5.2 percent of the nation's total. Among those failing to make debt payments were Cleveland, Detroit, and Miami. Florida led the nation in the number of defaulting municipalities with 165 of its 289 municipal corporations in this category.

Faced with economic woes, America's cities turned to the federal government for help. Municipalities are creations of the states, and lawmakers in Albany, Harrisburg, and Sacramento have traditionally heard appeals from troubled cities. Throughout most of American history, the federal government had assumed no responsibility for local government. In the 1930s, however, America's mayors and the Roosevelt administration forged a new link between Washington and City Hall. Congress enacted a Municipal Debt Adjustment Act to aid defaulting municipalities, and the Roosevelt administration sponsored public works programs that funneled millions of dollars to America's cities in an effort to create jobs. Streets, sidewalks, sewage treatment plants, and municipal airports were constructed with federal public works money, and city parks also benefited from Washington's generosity. To ensure that the cash kept flowing, the newly created U.S. Conference of Mayors lobbied Congress. As early as 1934, one city official observed that "mayors are a familiar sight in Washington these days. Whether we like it or not, the destinies of our cities are clearly tied in with national politics."

During the post–World War II era, this new federal-municipal relationship resulted in further legislation and more money from Washington. Perhaps the most notable federal program for cities formulated during this period was urban renewal. Created by Title I of the Housing Act of 1949, this program provided federal funds for local government agencies to purchase and clear slum property. Localities could thus rid themselves of blighted tracts that produced little tax revenue and redevelop them with valuable new apartment houses, factories, or office buildings. During the quarter-century following World War II, this scheme was just one in a long list of federal programs to deal with the problems of decaying older cities. Despite the programs, the cities continued to decay, but beleaguered mayors welcomed the federal dollars and increasingly looked to Washington for financial salvation.

Meanwhile, municipalities were taking action on their own to solve their financial woes. Traditionally, municipal governments in the United States had depended on the property tax as their chief source of revenue. In the mid-twentieth century, municipal leaders sought to wean themselves from their dependence on this tax and develop new means of raising money. In 1939 Philadelphia levied the nation's first municipal income tax, and in 1948 Saint Louis followed suit with an earnings levy. During the post–World War II era, an increasing number of cities imposed income taxes in an effort to relieve the burden of property owners. Sales taxes, cigarette taxes, amusement taxes, and taxes on hotel rooms all produced a growing share of municipal revenues. Whereas in 1945 the property tax accounted for 64 percent of New York City's general revenues, in 1984–1985 its share had fallen to less than 19 percent. The drop for Detroit was from 67 percent to 13 percent and for St. Louis from 61 percent to 7 percent. In the course of four decades, America's major municipalities had revolutionized their revenue base, raising money through a broad range of taxes and not relying so heavily on property levies.

Yet these new revenue sources did not stave off financial ills, and many of the nation's major cities faced repeated fiscal crises. Especially serious were the financial debacles of the mid- and late 1970s. In 1975 New York City in effect went bankrupt, and a state agency took control of the municipality's finances. The nation's largest municipal corporation had failed to manage its own affairs adequately, and now it became a ward of the state. Likewise, Boston, Philadelphia, and Detroit faced awesome deficits and resorted to emergency tax hikes or sought state aid to keep themselves seemingly solvent. Then, in 1978, Cleveland actually defaulted, the first major city to suffer this humiliation since the Depression. Again the state was forced to intervene, as one more municipality proved unable to govern itself.

Easing the fiscal stress somewhat was an influx of federal money during the 1970s. In 1972, Congress approved general revenue sharing, annually distributing federal funds to every municipality in the country. Moreover, a rising number of federal grant programs for urban redevelopment, local law enforcement, combating poverty, and numerous other purposes provided additional funds for municipal treasuries. More than ever before, cities were depending on federal money and on the will of lawmakers and bureaucrats in Washington. By 1977–1978, 33 percent of Cleveland's general revenues came from Washington, as did 27 percent of Chicago's income and 26 percent of Buffalo's.

The era of federal largesse, however, was short-lived. Beginning in the late 1970s Washington cut its aid to municipalities, and during the following decade the federal government retreated from its prior commitments to subsidize municipal affairs. In 1977–1978, the federal government accounted for 15.6 percent of the revenues of the 19,000 municipalities in the United States; by 1989–1990, this figure had dropped to 4.8 percent. In fact, by the 1980s Uncle Sam had changed from a sugar daddy to a harsh taskmaster. He was no longer generously distributing money, but he was still imposing costly mandates on states and localities. For example, municipalities had to conform to federal environmental mandates, but to an increasing extent they had to pay for compliance out of their own pockets.

By the late twentieth century, many of the reform panaceas of the past were losing their appeal. There was new enthusiasm for neighborhood power and heightened demands for increased representation of ethnic minorities. Consequently, at-large election of city councils came under attack, and many crusaded for a return to old-fashioned ward-based representation. In the minds of some urban residents, at-large elections no longer seemed the road to good government. They represented, instead, an elite ploy to deprive poor neighborhoods, and especially African Americans, of a voice in local rule. Meanwhile, the commission form of government appeared headed for extinction. By the late 1980s, only 171 municipalities with a population of more than 2,500 retained the commission plan, whereas 2,385 operated under council-manager government and 3,664 were mayor-council cities.

Many also questioned the pretensions of "professionals" in city government. During the 1960s angry city residents criticized urban planners for dictatorially imposing their plans on rebellious neighborhoods. From the 1960s through the 1990s many urban dwellers sought greater political control over city police who too often seemed to indulge in unnecessary brutality, especially when dealing with ethnic minorities. The police attempted to shield themselves under the mantle of professionalism, attacking so-called political influence that threatened their independence. In the minds of many, however, professionalism was just another word for unwarranted privilege.

At the close of the twentieth century Americans thus continued to search for kinds of municipal rule that were conducive not only to efficiency but also democracy. In the course of three centuries, self-elected aldermen had yielded to ward-based, popularly chosen municipal legislators who in turn were superseded by commissioners or at-large council members, city managers, and mayors. Federal involvement had compromised state control, but during the late twentieth century, the federal government was unable to continue its role as financial benefactor. In its internal structure and intergovernmental relations, the municipality had adapted to the changes in American society and politics, and the process of adaptation persists as urban dwellers seek a form of local rule best suited to current realities.

—*Jon C. Teaford*

**See also**
Annexation; Bosses and Machines; Civil Service; Commission Government; Consolidation; Council-Manager Government; Councils of Governments; Counties and Cities; Default; Federal Government and Cities; Fire Departments; Fragmentation of Municipal Government; Home Rule; Incorporation; The Legal Basis of Municipal Government; Mayor-Council Government; Municipal Bonds; Police and Police Departments; Property Tax; Social Services; States and Cities; Urban Law.

**References**
Hartog, Hendrik. *Public Property and Private Power: The Corporation of the City of New York in American Law, 1730–1870.* Chapel Hill: University of North Carolina Press, 1983.

Rice, Bradley R. *Progressive Cities: The Commission Government Movement in America, 1901–1920.* Austin: University of Texas Press, 1977.

Teaford, Jon C. *The Municipal Revolution in America: Origins of Modern Urban Government, 1650–1825.* Chicago: University of Chicago Press, 1975.

———. *The Unheralded Triumph: City Government in America, 1870–1900.* Baltimore: Johns Hopkins University Press, 1984.

## Murphy, Frank (1890–1949)

During a long and distinguished public career, Frank Murphy served as a judge on Detroit's Recorder's Court from 1924 to 1930 and as mayor of Detroit from 1930 to 1933. While Murphy was one of its judges, the Recorder's Court was probably the most distinguished municipal criminal court in the nation. It had a unified criminal jurisdiction, rare at the time, the first adult psychological clinic of any court in the nation, and one of the best court probation systems. Murphy's experience on the court taught him to see life through the eyes of the least fortunate members of society. He dispensed "justice with mercy" and reduced the jail population by the use of sensible bail procedures. He won national attention in 1925 with a report resulting from a one-man grand jury investigation of irregularities in several city government departments, his use of a sentencing board in felony cases, and the fair-minded manner in which he presided in 1925 and 1926 over the famous murder trials of a black family, the Sweets, who had defended their newly acquired home in a white neighborhood against a threatening mob.

As a young man, Murphy had dreamed of "ruling cities in our great land," and he was given the opportunity to do so as Detroit's mayor from 1930 to 1933. Mayor Murphy helped restore faith in the city's government at a time when civic morale was at low ebb; provided Detroit with honest, economical, and efficient government; made excellent appointments that accorded recognition to blacks, Jews, and the city's white ethnic minorities; extended the city's merit pay system; improved the city's police force; ousted the last remaining competitor of the city-owned transportation system; initiated a process leading to lower utility rates; and protected the rights of free speech and freedom of assembly in a time of troubles. He had close ties with the Detroit Federation of Labor and favored the unionization of some city employees.

The dominating event of the Murphy mayoralty was the Depression. No mayor in the nation did more to deal with the problem than Murphy. Detroit was one of the few cities at the time that provided public relief, and Murphy extended city aid to the needy to the extent that funds permitted; the Welfare Department, at one point, assisted 229,000 persons. Its efforts were supplemented by a Murphy-created Mayor's Unemployment Committee that registered the unemployed, maintained a free employment bureau, distributed clothing and emergency relief to those in need, maintained emergency lodges for homeless men, initiated a school lunch program for indigent children, provided legal aid for the poor, and sponsored a successful thrift garden program. As Detroit neared bankruptcy—the city defaulted on its bonds in 1933—Murphy convened a conference of U.S. mayors in an effort to secure federal aid. This action led to the establishment of the U.S. Conference of Mayors, with Murphy as its first president. He resigned as mayor in 1933 to become governor-general of the Philippines. He later served as governor of Michigan and as an associate justice on the U.S. Supreme Court.

—*Sidney Fine*

### References
Fine, Sidney. *Frank Murphy: The Detroit Years*. Ann Arbor: University of Michigan Press, 1975.
Levine, David. *Internal Combustion: The Races in Detroit, 1915–1926*. Westport, CT: Greenwood Press, 1976.
Lunt, Richard D. *The High Ministry of Government: The Political Career of Frank Murphy*. Detroit: Wayne State University Press, 1965.

## Museums

The museum is a social institution that can be examined from three perspectives: its role in the changing cultural matrix of high art, its organizational form, and its constituency, the art public. The economic and legal character of the museum is also important and should not be overlooked.

The source of legitimacy and recognition of museums in American society can be traced to a distinction between art and non-art. For most of the twentieth century, the line between art and non-art was drawn fairly clearly. On the one hand, original artworks and those with historical value were distinguished from artifacts of folk, popular, or mass culture and from commercial products. Thus, the purpose of the museum has been to store, preserve, authenticate, and exhibit original contemporary works along with works from the past that have artistic and historical value. As art, these pieces are evaluated in terms of a canon of high culture that resembles the canon for opera, ballet, symphonic works, and other types of classical music. Consistent with this convention, commercial products and amateur or folk works, and even performing arts, had no place in the museum.

However, the line between art and non-art is always being tested by artists, critics, and scholars. It was so with the emergence of the avant-garde and increasingly so with art-

*The skeleton of a dinosaur at the Field Museum of Natural History in Chicago, Illinois.*

ists who extended their work beyond conventional boundaries. In response, the canon of art has become more open-minded to admitting vernacular works (such as graffiti), film, and performance art into the accepted canon and is increasingly open to debates about political and social issues, such as the Holocaust, the atomic bomb, feminism, and debates about colonialism. This means that museum culture is more responsive to contemporary concerns that are not purely aesthetic and more democratic in the sense that many more people can relate to art. Thus, at the end of the twentieth century, museums are less for the privileged few than in the past, but it also means that artworks are more controversial.

Looked at from a long historical perspective, this is nothing novel. Aesthetic evaluations and the boundary between art and non-art were contested in France with the emergence of Impressionism at the end of the nineteenth century, and other fairly recent reconfigurations of the canon can be traced to the Arts and Crafts movement, the Art Deco movement, the Bauhaus, and in America the social realists or the "Ashcan School." Still, any major urban museum responsible for preserving art and having public education as one of its missions is less responsive to changes in art conventions than those museums devoted exclusively to contemporary works.

As an organizational form, the public museum can be traced to the Louvre in Paris, France, which opened its doors to the public in 1793, a year after the overthrow of Louis XVI. However, not until the late nineteenth century were the majority of today's most widely recognized public museums founded, including those in both Europe and America. The Boston Museum of Fine Arts, the Metropolitan Museum of Art in New York, and the Art Institute of Chicago all opened to the public in the 1870s, and before long almost every American city had established a museum with a public mission.

Today, even when central cities lose population and economic activities, museums are among the important urban institutions that continue attracting tourists. Most museums are financed by a combination of foundation grants, private donations, small government grants, and the public (in the form of memberships and admission fees). Some museums have also discovered that opening shops and selling replicas of museum artifacts can be profitable. In addition, museums usually have the official legal status of nonprofit organizations. That is, like many universities and colleges, all churches, unions, and many hospitals, they are privately supported and not administered to make a profit.

Any museum depends on philanthropists and the public interest broadly conceived. In the late nineteenth century, wealthy patrons played a critical role in establishing museums and acquiring collections. In the twentieth century, however, professional museum staffs have acquired considerable autonomy from wealthy philanthropists, who are, after all, amateur art lovers. The curatorial and educational missions of museums have expanded as acquisitions, exhibits, scholarship, public education, and "outreach" programs have become important public functions, while boards of directors, often working with museum directors and separate fund-raising staffs, are responsible for the financial well-being of the museum.

Based on surveys of art audiences, the average museum-goer can be described as fairly well educated and relatively affluent. The same is true of audiences for the theater, classical music, ballet, and opera. This is consistent with the history of American museums, namely that the wealthy elite have been the major source of support. A taste for high culture is a form of what Pierre Bourdieu, the French sociologist, calls "distinction." On the other hand, with the proliferation of specialized museums—such as museums for children and museums devoted to the art of particular ethnic groups—museum patronage is becoming more diverse. The middle class, not the elites of American cities, are increasingly becoming the main members of the large and growing audience for the arts.

—*Judith R. Blau*

### References
Blau, Judith R. *The Shape of Culture.* Cambridge, England: Cambridge University Press, 1989.
Bourdieu, Pierre. *Distinction.* Richard Nice, trans. Cambridge, MA: Harvard University Press, 1994.
DiMaggio, Paul. "Nonprofit Organizations in the Production and Distribution of Culture." In Walter W. Powell, ed., *The Nonprofit Sector.* New Haven, CT: Yale University Press, 1987.
Feldstein, Martin, ed. *The Economics of Art Museums.* Chicago: University of Chicago Press, 1991.
Taylor, Joshua C. *America as Art.* New York: Harper & Row, 1976.
Zolberg, Vera L. "Tensions and Missions in American Art Museums." In Paul J. DiMaggio, ed., *Nonprofit Enterprise in the Arts,* 184–198. New York: Oxford University Press, 1986.

## Nashville, Tennessee

James Robertson and John Donelson founded Nashborough around 1780. Nashborough (named for General Francis Nash of North Carolina) was one of many trans-Appalachian outposts that appeared after pioneers discovered the Cumberland Gap in 1750. In 1788 the settlement consisted of only 300 largely Scots-Irish settlers from North Carolina, a courthouse, two taverns, a distillery, and a handful of crude cabins. In the wake of the American Revolution, however, explorers and men on the make poured into the Middle Tennessee area. Among them was a 21-year-old lawyer named Andrew Jackson.

Renamed Nashville in 1784, until the 1820s the settlement remained a small rough-and-tumble frontier town whose chief appeal was its location on the banks of the Cumberland River. This waterway provided easy access to the Mississippi River, which made Nashville a vital link between trans-Appalachian North America and the bustling entrepot of New Orleans. Nashville was also the northern terminus of the Natchez Trace, the 450-mile overland route used before the steamboat made upstream travel manageable in the Mississippi Valley. Tobacco, cotton, grains, livestock, and colorful boatmen all passed regularly through the city. Although Tennessee became the sixteenth state to enter the Union in 1796, Nashville's population stood at only 2,000 as late as 1810.

The city's fortunes changed dramatically in the 1820s, primarily because one of its native sons, Andrew Jackson, became a national figure without equal. When Jackson was elected president in 1828, he led a team of Nashvillians into Washington (John Eaton, Felix Grundy, William B. Lewis, John Bell, James K. Polk, Sam Houston) that gave the small town a degree of notoriety and power quite out of proportion to its size. The strong-willed Jackson and his friends, dubbed the Nashville Junto, turned Nashville from a frontier backwater into a thriving town. The steamboat enhanced the town's importance as well. By the mid-1830s, steamboats enabled merchants to make the round-trip from Nashville to New Orleans in 15 days.

Jackson was also first responsible for the town's nickname as the "Athens of the South." His enthusiastic embrace of frontier democracy led many to see Nashville as a latter-day Athens, a veritable birthplace of American democracy. As if to affirm this faith, Jackson added pillars and Greek touches to the Hermitage, his home near Nashville. Architect William Strickland similarly designed the Tennessee capitol building in Nashville as a Greek temple, eschewing the more common motif of a Roman dome. Phillip Lindsley, president of the University of Nashville, brought both Greek educational ideals and Greek architecture to his campus. This combination of Neoclassical architecture and the legacy of Jacksonian democracy caused the "Athens of the South" moniker to stick.

On the eve of the Civil War, Nashville was a bustling southern city with a population of 17,000 whites and 3,200 slaves. The town played a critical role in transporting goods between inland farmers and the port of New Orleans. Like other border-state southerners, however, Nashvillians took a dim view of secession. Most locals were moderates who had backed John Bell's middle-of-the-road Constitutional Union Party in the presidential election of 1860. Tennessee seceded once the shooting began, but Nashvillians' ambivalence toward the Confederate States of America would become clear later. Union soldiers captured Nashville in 1862, did little physical damage to the town, and turned it into a Union supply center. Nashville's merchants cooperated with the occupying army, so much so that the city probably benefited from the years of war. While many southern cities lay in ruins in 1865, Nashville was virtually unscathed and had formed close business relationships with northerners. With a population of 25,000 in 1870, the city entered its Golden Age.

Postbellum Nashville became a Mecca for northern philanthropists hoping to remake the South and for educators eager to work with the freedmen. To this end, many colleges were founded in the following years. Wealthy railroad and shipping magnate Cornelius Vanderbilt founded Vanderbilt University in the 1870s. The University of Nashville received a sizable gift from philanthropist George Peabody in the 1870s, and the school (later called the George Peabody School for Teachers) became a national leader in the field of education. Fisk University was founded as a college for African Americans, accepted its first students in 1886, and soon became one of the preeminent black universities in America. The city's Central Tennessee College would later evolve into Meharry Medical College, which by 1940 could boast that one-half of all black physicians in the United States were alumni. Added to these schools were David Lipscomb College (1891), a school associated with the Church of Christ, and Tennessee Agricultural and Industrial State University (1912), the state's one publicly funded institution of higher learning for African Americans. Proud Nashvillians now had even more reasons to call their city the Athens of the South.

These universities had at least two lasting effects on the city. First, they made Nashville an unusually urbane and cosmopolitan southern city. This became evident in the 1950s when the civil rights movement proved that white Nashvillians were somewhat more "progressive" than other white southerners. Second, the presence of Fisk and Meharry helped create an unusually powerful black community in the city. Whites in the city afforded blacks more respect than was typical in other southern cities, and Nashville became a seedbed for black civil rights activism.

Besides "Athens of the South," Nashvillians took to calling their city "the Wall Street of the South" during the 1920s. The city's insurance, banking, and brokerage industries boomed following World War I. Times were flush for Nashville's 150,000 residents; the city's prosperity resembled that of New York City or Chicago rather than that of Birmingham or Charleston. The aggressive insurance industry, in an attempt to sell more policies to rural Tennesseans, embarked upon an innovative marketing strategy. It founded radio stations and began playing the country and bluegrass music that appealed to potential customers. These radio stations were a smashing success, and Nashville's insurance tycoons had unwittingly founded a new industry—the country music business. The city became home to the Grand Ole Opry, a country-and-western alternative to the more staid Grand Opera of New York City. Nashville's insurance and banking industry collapsed during the Depression and never again regained its position of supremacy. However, the city remained the place to be for aspiring country music stars.

Like many southern cities, Nashville suffered less from the Depression than northern cities. Nashville's investment-heavy insurance companies and banks collapsed, but the city's economy, based on foodstuffs and commerce, proved better able to withstand the lean years than the more industrialized economies of northern cities. Nor did World War II transform the city. Few war-related businesses relocated to the city, one notable exception being Consolidated Vultee Aircraft.

In the years after World War II, the city became home to a handful of religious publishing houses, and several large Christian denominations (most notably the Southern Baptist Convention and the National Baptist Convention) located their national offices in Nashville. As the postwar record industry boomed, the New York monopoly on music copyrights was broken, and studios recording country music flourished along the city's Music Row. The entertainment industry became a staple in the local economy, and in recent years many Christian contemporary music recording studios have flourished in the city.

In the postwar years, however, Nashville established itself as a most atypical southern city. Nashville was the first city to apply for federal urban redevelopment funding as established in the Housing Act of 1949. Nashvillians used the money to renovate a 100-acre downtown area near Capitol Hill, demolishing the city's notorious red-light district in the process. Most remarkable was the willingness of city leaders to accept federal funding and federal oversight of a local project. Perhaps more than any other region in the United States, the South had resisted federal intervention in local affairs, and Nashville was breaking with the status quo when it eagerly cooperated with federal urban renewal officials.

Nashville also played a critical role in the black civil rights movements of the 1950s and 1960s. Many black students who organized the Student Nonviolent Coordinating Committee, led the sit-in movement, and planned freedom rides studied at Fisk University and the Vanderbilt Divinity School. Marion Berry, Diane Nash, John Lewis, and James Lawson were among this new breed of black student activists trained in Nashville.

Nashville integrated its public schools long before most southern cities and with far less violence, largely due to the leadership provided by the city's Jewish community. A 1950s march by local blacks on City Hall resulted in a showdown with Mayor Ben West. In other southern cities, mayors in this situation resorted to water cannons, the national guard, and similar acts of defiance. West, on the other hand, publicly conceded that racial discrimination was reprehensible. In 1967 Vanderbilt University's Percy Wallace became the first African-American basketball player in the Southeastern Conference. In short, Nashville was different from Birmingham or New Orleans. Perhaps because of the well-established and highly respected black community associated with Fisk and Meharry, white Nashvillians accepted racial integration more willingly than other southerners.

Third, Nashville's quest for good government led to the political consolidation of the City of Nashville and Davidson County in 1963. Like other American cities, Nashville had suffered the problems attendant to suburban growth since at least 1940. The city did not enjoy home rule until the 1950s, which meant that rural interests in the state legislature, not elected municipal officials, controlled policymaking for the city. Duplicate municipal services (e.g., a City Health Department and a separate County Health Department) were inefficient, but entrenched political factions usually prohibited substantive reform. Nashville joined only a handful of other American cities (most notably Miami-Dade County) in experimenting with the most radical of solutions—wholesale consolidation of the city and surrounding county. Ever since the successful 1962 referendum, Nashville and Davidson County have functioned under a consolidated government. The scheme proved not to be the panacea that many thought it was in the 1950s, but neither has the arrangement proved deleterious to either the city or the county.

In the late 1990s Nashville had about 600,000 residents and remains more commercial than industrial. The recording industry is thriving, and the Grand Ole Opry attracts many tourists, reasons why Nashville is known as "Music City, USA." Banking and insurance remain important components of the local economy, although they have never regained the significance they had before the Depression. The new managed health-care industry is also strong in Nashville, and several national health-care providers have their headquarters there.

—*Robert G. Spinney*

**References**

Blumstein, James F., and Benjamin Walter, eds. *Growing Metropolis: Aspects of Development in Nashville.* Nashville, TN: Vanderbilt University Press, 1975.

Doyle, Don H. *Nashville in the New South, 1880–1930.* Knoxville: University of Tennessee Press, 1985.

———. *Nashville since the 1920s.* Knoxville: University of Tennessee Press, 1985.

Hawkins, Brett W. *Nashville Metro: The Politics of City-County Consolidation.* Nashville, TN: Vanderbilt University Press, 1966.

Wiltshire, Susan, Charles W. Warterfield, Jr., Christine Kreyling, and Wesley Paine. *Classical Nashville: Athens of the South.* Nashville, TN: Vanderbilt University Press, 1997.

## Nation, Carry Amelia Moore (1846–1911)

Carry Nation, one of the most famous of all American temperance reformers, was born in Garrard County, Kentucky, the daughter of George Moore and Mary Campbell. Her father was a rootless slaveholding planter who moved his family across Kentucky, Missouri, and Texas. Along the way Carry had little schooling but did have a religious conversion experience. Her mother had delusions of being Queen Victoria and, like several relatives, died insane. At the end of the Civil War, the impoverished family settled in Missouri where Carry married Dr. Charles Gloyd in 1867, an alcoholic whom she quickly left. Shortly afterward, he died, leaving Carry with a child who became insane. Carry taught school and in 1877 married David Nation, a lawyer and preacher. For ten years the Nations moved around Texas, while Carry largely sup-

ported the family by operating hotels. She also had religious visions. In 1889, the Nations moved to Medicine Lodge, Kansas, drifted into Oklahoma for a while, and then returned to Medicine Lodge. They divorced in 1901.

Although liquor sales were illegal in Kansas, dealers used a loophole to import alcohol into the state. In 1892, Carry Nation organized the Barber County Woman's Christian Temperance Union to oppose these illicit saloons. Aided by divine visions, in 1900 Nation began a violent antisaloon crusade by throwing rocks through windows of the bars in Kiowa, forcing the dealers to close. Pleased with this result, Nation moved on to Wichita, where she first used a hatchet to smash that city's saloons, including one in a leading hotel. In later years, she attacked drinking establishments in cities as large as New York, Pittsburgh, and San Francisco. Although frequently arrested, jailed, and fined, she continued her campaign. Nearly six feet tall and, when aroused, filled with fiery language, she terrified saloonkeepers. Certain of her mission, she in turn knew no fear, even though many other advocates of temperance opposed her lawless methods. She paid her fines by selling souvenir hatchets and with fees from lecture tours. Earning considerable income, she lacked business sense and gave much of her money to charity; her last years found her in poor health and of unclear mind.

—*W. J. Rorabaugh*

**References**

Asbury, Herbert. *Carry Nation.* New York: Knopf, 1929.

Taylor, Robert L. *Vessel of Wrath: The Life and Times of Carrie Nation.* New York: New American Library, 1966.

## National Urban League

The National Urban League is a nonprofit, nonpartisan civil rights organization that advocates for African Americans and provides services to the African-American community through its affiliates in 113 cities. Founded in New York City in 1910 as the Committee on Urban Conditions Among Negroes, it merged a year later with two other service agencies to create the National League on Urban Conditions Among Negroes. The organization's mission is to achieve economic and social equality for African Americans, and it has an interracial board of directors composed of prominent persons in many fields.

The league's increased presence and growth in cities generally mirrored that of African Americans in the twentieth century. Its affiliates became the principal citywide agencies promoting the interests of an increasingly urbanized black population. The league was not a mass-membership or community-based organization, but it was instead an agency staffed by black social workers who provided direct and referral services to black southerners newly arrived in northern cities. The organization also worked to break the "job ceiling" confronted by upwardly mobile blacks, and it contested discrimination in the availability of municipal services. Building on the foundation laid by black women's work in churches and settlement houses, the league helps migrants obtain employment, housing, health and child care, and recreational facilities. In addition to lending valuable aid, Urban League workers felt it their duty to dispense moral advice. For example, in Chicago the league organized "Stranger Meetings" and had black club women securing pledges from migrants to maintain appropriate public dress and deportment. Such efforts reinforced the social distance between middle-class providers and their poor and working-class clients.

The Urban League experienced strong growth during President Lyndon Johnson's Great Society, which sponsored a myriad of urban programs. Under Whitney Young's leadership (1961–1971), the number of its affiliates increase from 63 to 98. Young also strengthened the league's finances by securing corporate donations, foundation grants, and government contracts. The league aggressively presented its goals to corporate and government officials as the most reasonable alternative to the demands made by black nationalists.

The urban riots of the late 1960s prompted the Johnson and Nixon administrations to solicit Young's advice about providing new programs for alienated, inner-city blacks. Partly in response, Young developed a comprehensive "New Thrust" program to provide poor blacks with job and social skills. This program, along with the league's domestic Marshall Plan, represented a policy shift by the league. It deviated from its traditional goal of seeking only equal opportunity (its former motto was "Not Alms, But Opportunity") by demanding racial parity in the distribution of resources. After 1970 the league increasingly called attention to racial disparities in its annual report, *The State of Black America,* and it opened an office in Washington to lobby on behalf of black interests.

Although the domestic Marshall Plan remains a key component of the National Urban League's agenda, the organization today increasingly promotes its "self-help" tradition. In this, the league echoes its earlier efforts to instruct black migrants about proper behavior and devises programs that instruct black youth about personal responsibility. Hugh Price, the current president of the league, has called upon the black middle class to contribute greater financial and volunteer support to programs designed to "rescue" troubled youth. The league's pragmatic focus on self-reliance implies that individuals must assume responsibility for alleviating the social crisis of urban black communities. Today, at a time of private and public disinvestment in the black community, and the diminishing political significance of America's inner cities, the league is redefining its role in black politics.

—*Preston Smith*

**References**

Moore, Jesse Thomas, Jr. *A Search for Equality: The National Urban League, 1910–1961.* University Park: Pennsylvania State University Press, 1981.

Strickland, Arvarh E. *History of the Chicago Urban League.* Urbana: University of Illinois Press, 1966.

Weiss, Nancy J. *The National Urban League, 1910–1940.* New York: Oxford University Press, 1974.

———. *Whitney M. Young, Jr., and the Struggle for Civil Rights.* Princeton, NJ: Princeton University Press, 1989.

## National Youth Administration

The National Youth Administration (NYA) was a New Deal program established in 1935 to provide relief to youths between the ages of 16 and 25. During its eight years of existence from 1935 to 1943, the NYA offered more than relief. Under the directorship of Aubrey Williams and the watchful eye of First Lady Eleanor Roosevelt, the NYA also acted as an agent of social justice, offering educational opportunities and training in marketable skills to disadvantaged youth without discrimination on the basis of race. The NYA worked through state offices with close monitoring by the national headquarters, and the official who worked to ensure nondiscrimination was Mary McLeod Bethune, a prominent African-American educator. Many of the work relief projects developed to aid approximately 4.8 million beneficiaries contributed significantly to maintaining and developing American cities during the 1930s.

The NYA operated two major divisions to achieve its objectives, the student work program and the out-of-school work program. The student work program employed youth part-time on their high school or college campuses; high school students often performed clerical, maintenance, or library work and college youths conducted surveys, prepared laboratory materials for science classes, or constructed buildings. The out-of-school work projects included activities such as supervising playgrounds, building roadside parks, or remodeling hospitals. After its first two years of operation, the NYA began to develop projects offering youths training in marketable skills. For example, it taught secretarial skills to young women and instructed young men in masonry and carpentry.

Besides providing disadvantaged youth with work relief and long-term opportunities for education and training, NYA construction projects made valuable contributions to financially strapped cities. Cities benefited from NYA youth, who built or repaired streets and who constructed or remodeled a variety of buildings, including auditoriums, youth centers, hospitals, libraries, and band shells. In some communities, NYA projects built new landing fields and aircraft hangars, and across the nation NYA youth placed more than 1 million street signs and markers. These undertakings, and a wide range of others, such as repairing sewers and constructing sidewalks, improved urban facilities and infrastructure.

In developing urban projects, the NYA found cosponsors among municipal governments, civic organizations, recreational agencies, and charitable programs. In these, as in other NYA projects, cosponsors paid for materials and some supervision, and the NYA funded primary supervisors and wages for the youth. The national office also had the services of an architect and an assistant to oversee the quality and design of major construction projects, and many state offices employed architects as well.

One of the most impressive NYA municipal endeavors was restoring *La Villita* (the Little Village) in the heart of San Antonio. Originally built next to the Alamo, *La Villita* had deteriorated into a slum by the 1930s. The San Antonio council supported a plan to cosponsor the project in conjunction with the NYA to revitalize this historical and cultural site, and once it was completed and the NYA had developed an arts and crafts workshop there, *La Villita* became an important part of the tourist center. The NYA proved itself to be not only an important benefactor to millions of youth but also a valuable asset in improving the structural features of cities and adding to the economic opportunities of urban areas.

—*Carol A. Weisenberger*

### References
Reiman, Richard A. *The New Deal and American Youth: Ideas and Ideals in a Depression Decade.* Athens: University of Georgia Press, 1992.
U.S. Federal Security Agency. *Final Report of the National Youth Administration, Fiscal Years, 1936–1943.* Washington, DC: Government Printing Office, 1944.
Weisenberger, Carol A. *Dollars and Dreams: The National Youth Administration in Texas.* New York: Peter Lang, 1994.

## Native American Towns

Cities and towns were certainly not universal among the Native Americans living in what would become the United States. Indeed, settlements in which significant numbers of people lived permanently—what Europeans considered towns—were relatively rare because most tribes north of Mexico depended on a variety of food sources and moved during the year to exploit those sources more effectively. There was, however, a range of Native American urban patterns extending from smaller, semipermanent towns, which to Europeans often seemed mere camps, to established cities with thousands of residents. Some of these communities were as large as those of the European colonists, and many took distinctive forms that echoed their builders' worlds and values as clearly as Philadelphia or Santa Fe did theirs. Moreover, Indian towns served the same range of functions as their Euro-American counterparts. Nearly all were trade centers in which residents and visitors exchanged goods. Some were also ceremonial centers to which the surrounding population made regular visits, administrative centers from which a ruling elite directed its people, or strongholds in which the residents, and sometimes the outlying rural population, could defend themselves from attack.

Contact with Europeans had a variety of effects on pre-Columbian settlements. Increased warfare, growing reliance on white traders, and conversion to Christianity led some Indians to settle more closely together for defense or for proximity to a trading post or mission. Other natives became less urbanized as the European demand for skins and furs, or the new mobility provided by horses, turned those who had split their time between hunting and farming into full-time hunters. And in some cases, tribes and their villages disappeared completely in the wake of new diseases.

The two most urbanized Native American cultures in what is now the United States flourished in the prehistoric era and were already vanishing when Europeans arrived in North America. The more familiar of these lost cultures is the Anasazi, who built and abandoned dozens of towns in the desert Southwest between A.D. 500 and 1500, including the spectacular cliff dwellings at Mesa Verde (Colorado) and the haunting pueblos of Chaco Canyon (New Mexico). Both Mesa Verde and Chaco Canyon date from the zenith of Anasazi culture (A.D. 900–1200), and each illustrates how fully urbanized that culture had become. Corn was the staple of Anasazi life, and its successful cultivation in the arid Southwest depended on an extensive network of reservoirs and canals. These took hundreds of workers decades to construct and needed constant maintenance, so Anasazi towns were both large and permanent. In Chaco Canyon, for example, Pueblo Bonito grew into a complex of 800 rooms built according to a unified design and developed over a century and a half. A large community such as Chaco or Mesa Verde consisted of numerous pueblos fairly close to each other. Individual pueblos varied in size, but they all shared common features derived from Anasazi cosmology, which emphasized continuing links between an underworld, a skyworld, and the earth itself, and from the importance of community efforts to overcome a hostile environment.

Pueblos were multiroomed, communal structures built of stone and adobe around a central plaza. House blocks were several stories high, though banked like stairs so that front rooms on one level opened onto the flat roof of the level below. This arrangement provided year-round living and storage space for hundreds, even thousands, of people, plus a symbolic bridge between earth and sky. In or around the plaza of each pueblo stood its kivas—circular chambers, usually underground, that recalled the Anasazi's mythic subterranean origins and in which various subunits of the community conducted ceremonial functions.

The other great urban culture of the pre-Columbian United States, Mississippians, lived between the Mississippi River and the southern Appalachian Mountains. Like the Anasazi, they planted extensive fields of corn, but they also relied on streams and forests for a significant portion of their food. As a result, Mississippians generally lived on scattered homesteads or in small villages. Theirs, however, was a culture of ranked chiefdoms, and alongside its homesteads and villages were an impressive number of towns and cities that served as local or regional centers of religion, trade, and defense. The best known of these was Cahokia, near present-day St. Louis, which was the largest pre-Columbian settlement north of Mexico. At its height, around A.D. 1100, Cahokia had beween 30,000 and 40,000 residents and covered five square miles. Like other towns of the Mississippians, it was built around a plaza that was the scene of communal religious ceremonies. The plaza alone covered approximately 200 acres at Cahokia and was surrounded by 19 platform mounds on which public buildings or high-status residences might have stood. This ceremonial core was enclosed by a defensive palisade, and around it were numerous residential precincts with their own smaller plazas and mounds. Beyond the central city was an agricultural hinterland with several local urban centers and dozens of villages and farmsteads.

By the time Europeans arrived in the United States, both the Anasazi and the Mississippians had vanished as distinct cultures, and their descendants, among historic tribes, were living in much smaller communities. They were still, however, among the most urbanized tribes of the era and retained important elements of their ancestral culture. Key aspects of Anasazi town planning, for example, have continued until today among the Pueblo Indians of Arizona and New Mexico. After contact, the Pueblo continued to live on all three levels of their cosmos—above, on, and below the earth—and continued to emphasize community solidarity. Their adobe houses surround a central plaza, rising in stairsteps as one moves outward, and in or near the central space are the underground kivas of the community or particular groups within it.

Similarly, many Muskogean tribes in the southeastern United States continued to build towns similar to those of their Mississippian forebears until Euro-American influences altered, displaced, and nearly destroyed them. Like most smaller Mississippian towns, those of the Creek and Cherokee consisted of family farmsteads around a central place that served functions that were more ceremonial and administrative than residential. Creek town centers included a ball court, a meeting house in which the sacred fire burned during the winter months, and a courtyard in which it burned during the rest of the year and where it was surrounded by four clan beds aligned on the two perpendicular axes of the Creek cosmos. Cherokee ceremonial complexes were generally smaller, just a meeting house, but they were sometimes built on mounds like those found at Mississippian sites.

Elsewhere in the United States, most tribes were somewhat less—some a great deal less—urbanized at the time of contact. The least urbanized regions were the Arctic, the Subarctic, and the Great Basin, where food supplies simply would not support large communities for more than a few weeks at several times of the year. Abundant supplies of food, however, did not lead inevitably to a more urbanized culture. California had perhaps the richest natural environment in America and the densest population north of Mexico, but it also had few communities larger than a village. California Indians lived in what scholars have called "tribelets," each inhabiting a small number of principal villages that had a larger number of satellite villages or camps around them. Even the principal villages, however, were relatively small. They typically contained up to several dozen family homes, a number of sweat houses, acorn granaries, an assembly or dance house, and a menstrual lodge. Little is known about the arrangement of these structures beyond the fact that sweat houses were usually close to a stream, assembly houses tended to be central, and menstrual lodges were invariably on the outskirts. Villages were usually occupied during the winter, and during the rest of the year members of the tribe moved through their territory exploiting the natural food supplies.

A similar pattern prevailed in the Pacific Northwest, with its abundant seafood and edible plants; villages there were also quite small and usually occupied only in winter. A typical settlement in what would become Oregon or Washington was a row of large, plank houses, each inhabited by several nuclear families or members of an extended family, along a coastal or riverain beach, with a potlatch house, a menstrual hut, and one or more sweat houses.

On the other side of the continent, in the Northeast and Middle Atlantic regions, Iroquoian and Algonquian peoples followed settlement patterns distinctly different from those on the Pacific coast. While these eastern groups did obtain significant amounts of their food by hunting and fishing, they also practiced agriculture, except for the northernmost Algonquian tribes. Most, therefore, spent much of the year in relatively compact towns around which they planted corn, beans, and squash and from which they scattered to family camps for hunting or fishing at a few specific times of year, especially during the winter. Principal villages might house 1,000 people and were often occupied for a decade or more before declining soil fertility and wood supplies forced their residents to move. Surprisingly little is known about the internal arrangement of either Iroquoian or Algonquian towns. In both cultures, towns generally consisted of residential units, longhouses among Iroquoians and wigwams among

*Cliff dwellings of the Anasazi tribe at what is now Mesa Verde National Park.*

Algonquians, with few if any communal structures. Coastal Algonquians, who had relatively little contact with the Iroquoians, seem to have built less-defensive villages; houses were more widely scattered and less likely to be surrounded by a palisade. Farther west, however, the two cultures often came into close and violent contact, and settlements were more likely to be compact and enclosed by protective walls.

Between east and west, on the prairies and plains of the central United States, late prehistoric tribes were generally hunter-gatherers who also farmed, living in small, loosely organized communities along rivers and streams. The arrival of Europeans, however, exerted a profound influence on this settlement pattern. Increasing pressure from eastern tribes who had either been displaced by Europeans or turned into more aggressive hunters by them, plus the horses reintroduced to the continent by Europeans, made Plains Indians both more and less urbanized. Some tribes, such as the Sioux, Cheyenne, and Crow, used newly acquired horses to move

west and adopt a more mobile lifestyle based on hunting buffalo. For much of the year, they moved their tipis constantly as they followed the herds that supported them. Only in winter did they remain settled for extended periods of time. Other tribes, such as the Mandan, Hidatsa, and Pawnee, remained in their settlements along the Missouri River and its tributaries, but in many cases their villages grew larger in size but smaller in number in response to the greater threat of mounted raiders equipped with firearms. Village Indians also moved to more sheltered locations during the winter, and some undertook extended hunts on the Plains during the summer or fall. For most of the year, they lived in their principal settlements, farmed the floodplain, and hunted on the adjacent plains.

Both Plains lifestyles resulted in relatively large communities with symbolic internal arrangements. Sioux or Cheyenne villages often contained hundreds of tipis in a great circle opening toward the east. Both the circle and its orientation reflected the importance of the sun, their principal deity; the circle followed its course through the day and year, and the opening faced the point from which it began its daily journey. Within the circle, Sioux and Cheyenne villages were divided by moieties, just as their larger cultures were; clans associated with one moiety stood on the north side, while those of the other moiety filled the southern half.

The Mandan, too, arranged themselves in circles, but in their case the shape evoked memories of the circular palisade with which their culture hero, Lone Man, had saved them from a great flood. Mandan towns were generally surrounded by a palisade and dry moat. Each contained a circular plaza in which the residents erected a cedar post, representing Lone Man, inside its own small palisade. A ceremonial lodge stood on the north side of the plaza, and arranged around the other sides were lodges of individuals with important roles in the rituals performed there. Beyond this ceremonial space stood as many as 150 hemispheric, earthen lodges, sometimes organized in concentric circles and sometimes scattered randomly.

*—Charles E. Chandler, Gregory Mitchell, Kelli N. Sparrow, Daniel B. Thorp, and Ian M. Urbina*

### References

Goodwin, Gary C. *The Cherokees in Transition: A Study of Changing Culture and Environment Prior to 1775.* Chicago: University of Chicago Department of Geography, 1977.

Meyer, Roy W. *The Village Indians of the Upper Missouri: The Mandans, Hidatsas, and Arikaras.* Lincoln: University of Nebraska Press, 1977.

Muench, David, and Donald G. Pike. *Anasazi: Ancient People of the Rock.* Palo Alto, CA: American West Publishing, 1974.

Nabokov, Peter, and Robert Easton. *Native American Architecture.* New York: Oxford University Press, 1989.

Smith, Bruce D. *Mississippian Settlement Patterns.* New York: Academic Press, 1978.

Sturtevant, William G., ed. *The Handbook of North American Indians.* Washington, DC: Smithsonian Institution, 1978.

Wedel, Waldo R. *Central Plains Prehistory: Holocene Environments and Culture Change in the Republican River Basin.* Lincoln: University of Nebraska Press, 1986.

## Nativism

As a social and political attitude and disposition, American nativism grew from citizens' anxieties about the intersection of national and personal character. Popular concern about national character descended from the origin of the United States as an "invented" nation that lacked the characteristics regularly regarded as conferring nationhood. Absent was a long, shared history, but present from the first was considerable ethnic and cultural diversity. The most widely shared cultural inheritance—England's—was too discredited by the Revolution to be celebrated as a source of unity. Anxiety about the nation's future was exacerbated by the newness of its re-

publican form of government, the loudly voiced doubts of European critics, and such evidence of fragility as nascent sectionalism. Later, after the Civil War and the initial phases of industrialization, nationalist concerns refocused, transformed into questions about the sort of nation the United States had become, about how its emerging power should be used, and about who would control its tendencies. In either case, for some Americans, ethnic and cultural diversity provoked doubts about national unity, character, and direction.

None of this would have produced a powerful social movement that lasted from the 1780s through the 1920s if nationalist anxieties had not become intertwined with anxieties about personal character. These concerns were initially provoked by a republican ideology that stressed the necessity of personal autonomy and freedom from manipulation. The very definition of citizenship became uncoerced participation in public affairs. This meant that from the first there was a popular suspicion of combination and power, on the one hand, and exclusion and dependence, on the other. Later on, it would mean ambivalence about large organizations as a means to magnify one's personal effect but also as agents of oppression. Authentic nativism, then, exaggerated perceived cultural differences associated with ethnic and religious diversity into threats to both individual autonomy and national identity.

American nativism was not strictly an urban movement, but it found its greatest strength in cities. As the center of economic and social change, cities were places where personal identity was most likely to be challenged. It was also in cities that the increasing numbers of the non-English foreign-born and their children were most likely to produce powerful—and to some, threatening—institutions. This does not mean that nativism was strictly a phenomenon of New York, Philadelphia, Boston, Baltimore, or even Chicago, St. Louis, and New Orleans. It thrived in smaller cities like Lawrence, Massachusetts; Clinton, Iowa; and Kokomo, Indiana.

From the 1780s through the 1820s, a sort of protonativism emerged in cities along the Atlantic seaboard from Baltimore to Boston. Democratic-Republican political societies, patriotic fraternities like the Order of Red Men, and tradesmen's associations harped on the necessity of individual economic autonomy as well as freedom from political manipulation, and they occasionally castigated "outsiders"—usually the non-English foreign-born—for taking away jobs, luring politicians with their votes, or having political loyalties that lay outside the United States.

But it was in the 1830s and 1840s that heightened fears about the loss of economic and political autonomy produced nativist organizations with mass memberships that were committed to imposing disabilities on the "foreigner." These fears were most acute in cities. Sometimes they were political, as in New York City and Brooklyn, where elements of a fractured Democratic Party reaching out to new immigrant voters provoked a rival Native Democratic Association (1835), or in Boston, where authorization of an Irish-American militia company led to allegations that the state government was truckling to the power of the Roman Catholic Church and inspired an invigorated nativism in militia units and volunteer fire companies.

Sometimes the fears had economic origins. Working men largely blamed their declining wages (up to one-third in cities like Philadelphia and New York between 1836 and 1842) on immigrants and ignored the transformation of the economy and depressions. They responded with an enlivened Protestant evangelism, enthusiasm for the temperance movement, and the hope that public education based on the Bible might save the next generation. In city after city, but especially in Philadelphia, political and sometimes physical tumults took place between native-born, Anglo-American Protestants and largely Irish-American Catholics over the place of the "Protestant" Bible in public schools and the nature of citizen control over public school curricula. Though nothing as violent as the "Bible Riots" of May and July 1844 in Philadelphia was repeated elsewhere, friction between Protestants and Catholics over schools was prevalent in such disparate cities as St. Louis, Baltimore, and even frontier Milwaukee. In 1845, representatives of urban nativist organizations gathered in Philadelphia to try to create a national "Native American" party that denounced naturalized voters, the politicians who pursued them, and the sacrifice of public schools to a "foreign potentate." As a remedy, they proposed that immigrants wait as long as 21 years before receiving the right to vote and that the foreign-born be excluded from elected office altogether.

In the mid- to late 1840s—in cities—nativists discovered the perfect vehicle for mass political mobilization, the fraternal benefit society. New York City's Order of United Americans (1845), Philadelphia's Order of United American Mechanics (1845), or the Patriotic Order, Sons of America, fused "equality" in brotherhood, assistance in adversity, and education for citizenship with a sort of "open" political primary (that is, in contrast to allegedly "managed" local party nominating conventions) for members. When the Order of United Americans began exercising political clout in New York's municipal elections in 1852, the journalist Horace Greeley began calling it a "Know Nothing" movement because of the obscurity of its members, who frequently replied, "I know nothing," when asked about their involvement. Fraternal organizations like these proliferated rapidly, chapter by chapter, first along the Middle Atlantic and Northeast seaboard, then in the Great Lakes and Mississippi Valley states, and subsequently in the South. Populating major cities first,

they soon moved into secondary, and even tertiary, towns and reached as far west as Davenport, Iowa, and even San Francisco, California.

The use of fraternal organizations for political purposes was perfected by activists from the Order of United Americans who, in 1852, turned the preexisting Order of the Star-Spangled Banner into the basis for a national, nativist political party. Strengthened by a fraternal "second degree" oath, which committed members to political loyalty, "American" tickets swept elections in the most urbanized states in 1854 and 1855. Emboldened, the American Party launched a presidential campaign in 1856, but the candidacy of Millard Fillmore carried only Maryland. A combination of actual achievements in reforming naturalization, ineffective nativist officeholders, and the appropriation of the language of threatened autonomy by pro- and antislavery activists led to the demise of the American Party in all but a few urban strongholds like Baltimore and New Orleans.

The Civil War seemed to resolve the question of whether a self-governing republic could survive as a nation and rendered many Americans much less wary of the power of organization (organization, after all, had won the war). The emerging power of the United States, however, compelled the question of which combinations would control the nation's destiny. And certainly, postwar America organized with a vengeance—into corporations, labor unions, farmers' alliances, and fraternal societies. Almost immediately, distress was apparent as the middle-class, Anglo-American, Protestant community believed that the urban Irish had learned the power of organization too well. The urban Roman Catholic Church was just beginning to show its institutional muscle with a nationwide system of parochial schools that a bishops' council authorized in 1864 and with agitation to remove the Protestant King James Bible from public school curricula in cities like Cincinnati and Cleveland between 1869 and 1875. The urban Irish showed a remarkable facility for political organization, providing the power base for New York's "Boss Tweed" and electing the nation's first big city Catholic mayors in New York in 1880, Boston in 1884, and in industrial Lawrence and Lowell, Massachusetts, soon thereafter. The raids by the Irish-American Fenian order on British Canada in 1866 and 1870 drew men and money from New York, Cleveland, Detroit, and Buffalo and filled some native-born Anglo-Americans with dread that the American Irish continued to have loyalties abroad—and were armed to boot.

Such fears were held widely enough to create a great wave of what nativists liked to think of as "counter-organizing" in the 1880s and 1890s. The prewar American Protestant Association, Order of United Americans, and Patriotic Order, Sons of America, survived or were revived. The Masons and the Knights of Malta underscored their anti-Catholic aspects, and the Loyal Orange Institution revised its constitution in 1884 to address specifically American issues. New organizations like the Loyal Women of American Liberty and the Order of the Little Red School House took on the Bible and public school issues and aggressively promoted a proposed constitutional amendment to tax the assets of parochial schools. The Knights of Pythias and the Improved Order of Red Men sought to eliminate German-speaking chapters from their orders and, by implication, promote English as the nation's "official" language. At the same time, organized labor became exercised about the "imported" foreign labor allegedly sought by employers to undercut American wage rates. The Knights of Labor and then the American Federation of Labor agitated this issue into the 1890s, despite the outlawing of "contract" labor by the Foran Act of 1884. In cities throughout the United States, the Women's Christian Temperance Union and the Anti-Saloon League diverted attention from individual drinkers to "organized" liquor distributors and putatively "foreign" networks of saloonkeepers.

The effort to marshal these forces into a mass political movement in the 1890s was led by the American Protective Association. Founded by Henry Bowers in the Mississippi River town of Clinton, Iowa, in 1887, it thrived when it came under the leadership of the Detroit nativist organizer William Traynor and moved into big cities. An umbrella organization for nativist fraternities that consistently overestimated its true membership, the APA sought to control the Republican Party's national convention of 1896 and fizzled when it failed. In part, it was undone by the very success of contemporaneous "progressive" urban reform, which tended to take power away from ethnic voters and place it in the hands of Anglo-American elites.

While the mainstream of the nativist movement worried most about incompletely assimilated immigrants and their appropriation of American politics to promote "foreign" causes, a variant branch emerged in the 1890s that fretted about increasing ethnic diversity and the alleged inability of whole classes of newcomers to assimilate. The Immigration Restriction League of Boston (1894) became the first chapter of the American Association of Immigration Restriction Leagues, which spread through major eastern cities. Members of the leagues doubted the suitability for citizenship of the increasing number of southern and eastern European immigrants and were especially disturbed about the concentration of the foreign-born in cities. They noted with alarm that by 1880 three-quarters of Chicago's population were immigrants or the children of immigrants and that 20 years later 2 million immigrants and 2 million of their offspring lived in New York City. In response, the league favored use of a literacy test for admission to the country as an exclusionary device. Repeatedly stymied in Congress or vetoed by presidents, a literacy test finally became law over President Wilson's veto in 1916, its support increased by antiforeign phobias before the United States entered World War I.

Most nativist interest, however, was less in exclusion than in control and assimilation as validations of Protestant, Anglo-American, middle-class superiority. During the first two decades of the twentieth century, the predominant manifestation of nativism was "Americanization," a bureaucratic partnership between private organizations and the government. New York's Committee for Immigrants in America or the Ford School of Dearborn, Michigan, combined cultural indoctrination of immigrants with patriotic political science and instruction in the English language. "Americanization" took on new urgency as part of "preparedness" before World War I, and the National Security League (1914) and the American Defense Society (1915) continued to pursue coercive assimilationist education. They labeled cultural nonconformists as dangerously disloyal, and the organizations enthusiastically supported wartime Immigration and Sedition Acts, which led to serious infringements of civil liberties.

"Americanization" absorbed what proponents viewed as quick shocks in the aftermath of World War I. A variety of Euro-American ethnic groups took President Wilson's championship of self-determination seriously and used whatever political weight they had to enlist American support for the nationalist claims of their ancestral peoples. The success of socialist political candidates, especially in what were seen as urban, "ethnic" communities, alarmed those who felt menaced by the new Soviet Union's commitment to international communism. Distressed by strikes in the shipyards of Seattle and throughout the steel industry, as well as by what were perceived as an unprecedented strike of policemen in Boston and a "general" strike in Lawrence, Massachusetts, stunned Americanizers were among the first to concur in the response to a "Red Scare," prosecuted by the Department of Justice, that assaulted the civil liberties of "aliens" regarded as political radicals. At the same time, Catholics and Lutherans alike, defending both religious and civil traditions, mounted strong opposition to a proposed federal Department of Education that might homogenize school curricula. Would-be Americanizers also blamed immigrants and their children for the failure of Prohibition to shrink crime, especially urban crime, and reform public morality.

From these fears emerged the nativist appeal of the Ku Klux Klan. Formed in its early-twentieth-century incarnation in Atlanta during 1915 by capitalizing on an anti-Catholic, anti-Semitic, and antiblack message, it developed into a mass movement in the Midwest and Great Lakes states when it fused with urban and suburban Protestant apprehension that political and cultural leadership was slipping into other hands. Once thought to be a small-town, rural phenomenon, the Klan of the 1920s was a movement of activists in cities and towns who sought reaffirmation through political action and the unity and good feeling that emanated from the fraternal organization. The Klan fizzled, though, when, as previous nativist organizations had demonstrated, it became apparent that putting "Americans" in office was no guarantee that cultural homogeneity would spontaneously result, nor was it a guarantee (as some lurid crimes by Klan leaders demonstrated) that public morality would be transformed.

The federal immigration restriction laws of 1921 and 1924 proved to be the death knell of organized nativism in the United States. These laws were not the consequence of the nativist movement itself but were actually a denial of its tenets. It was widespread public disillusion with the traditional nativist goals of Anglo-American, Protestant assimilationism that generated support for legislation to reduce the number of immigrants and regulate immigration according to ethnicity that owed much more to pseudoscientific racism than nativist plaints about the need to inculcate immigrants and their children with a common "national character." In fact, the 1930s experienced the emergence of racist organizations rather than nativist ones. Father Coughlin, the "radio priest," and the Silver Shirts of William Dudley Pelley spoke a language less permeated with American nationalism than with international Aryan racism.

—Dale T. Knobel

See also

Anti-Semitism; Ku Klux Klan; Racism and Discrimination.

References

Bennett, David H. *The Party of Fear: From Nativist Movements to the New Right in American History.* Chapel Hill: University of North Carolina Press, 1988.

Higham, John. *Strangers in the Land: Patterns of American Nativism, 1860–1925.* New Brunswick, NJ: Rutgers University Press, 1963.

Knobel, Dale T. *'America for the Americans': The Nativist Movement in the United States.* New York: Twayne, 1996.

Moore, Leonard J. *Citizen Klansmen: The Ku Klux Klan in Indiana, 1921–1928.* Chapel Hill: University of North Carolina Press, 1991.

Solomon, Barbara Miller. *Ancestors and Immigrants: A Changing New England Tradition.* Chicago: University of Chicago Press, 1956.

Wallace, Les. *The Rhetoric of Anti-Catholicism: The American Protective Association, 1887–1911.* New York: Garland, 1990.

## Natural Environment and Cities

Cities and metropolitan areas have major effects on the natural environment. While this has been true since cities first appeared, the impact of urban areas intensified with the development of industrialism and the rapid urbanization of the last two centuries. The extensive growth of world cities since the end of World War II has affected the environment to an unprecedented extent. In the United States also, urban development has accelerated, and today a majority of the population lives in sizable metropolitan areas. As a result, the tension between natural and urbanized areas has increased. City builders have reshaped and often destroyed natural landscapes, although urbanites have attempted to reassert the importance of nature within the city itself. Over time, the relationship between the city and the natural environment has been interactive, with cities having massive effects on the natural environment, while the natural environment, in turn, has profoundly shaped urban configurations.

Americans founded cities in locations where nature offered various attractions, such as on coastlines where the land's natural contours created harbors; on rivers and lakes that could be used for transportation, water supplies, and waste disposal; and in fertile river valleys with extensive food and animal resources. Rather than being passive, the natural environment frequently played an active and even destructive role in the life of cities. Urban history is filled with stories about how city dwellers contended with the forces of nature that threatened their lives, their built environments, and their urban ecosystems. Nature not only caused many of the annoyances of daily urban life, such as bad weather and pests, but it also gave rise to natural disasters and catastrophes such as floods, fires, and earthquakes. In order to protect themselves against the forces of nature, cities built many defenses, including flood walls and dams, earthquake-resistant buildings, and storage places for food and for water. At times, such protective steps sheltered urbanites against the worst natural furies, but often their own actions—building on floodplains and steep slopes, under the shadow of volcanoes, or in earthquake-prone zones—exposed them unnecessarily to danger from natural hazards.

Cities have always placed demands on their sites and their hinterlands. In order to extend their sites territorially, urban developers often reshaped natural landscapes, leveling hills, filling valleys and wetlands, and creating huge areas of made land. On this new land, they constructed a built environment of paved streets, malls, houses, factories, office buildings, and churches. In the process they altered biological ecosystems for their own purposes, killing off animal populations, eliminating native species of flora and fauna, and introducing new and foreign species. Thus urbanites constructed a built environment that replaced the natural environment, creating a local microclimate, with different temperature gradients and rainfall and wind patterns than those of the surrounding countryside.

Cities need food, water, fuel, and construction materials, and in order to fulfill these needs urbanites increasingly had to reach far beyond their boundaries. In the nineteenth century, for instance, the demands of city dwellers for food produced rings of garden farms around cities and eventually drove the transformation of distant prairies into cattle ranches and wheat farms; in the twentieth century, as the urban population increased, this demand powered the rise of large factory farms. Cities also required freshwater supplies in order to exist—engineers, acting at the behest of urban elites and politicians, built waterworks, thrust water intake pipes ever further into neighboring lakes, dug wells deeper and deeper into the earth looking for groundwater, and dammed and diverted rivers and streams to obtain water supplies for domestic and industrial uses and for firefighting. In the process of obtaining water from water-rich but distant locales, they often transformed them, making deserts where there had been fertile agricultural areas (e.g., the Owens Valley and the Los Angeles water supply) and flooding many towns and farms (e.g., the construction of Boston's Quabaan Reservoir in 1928 flooded 28 towns).

City entrepreneurs and industrialists were actively involved in the commodification of natural systems, putting them to use for purposes of urban consumption. The exploitation of water power from rivers and streams, for instance, provided power for manufacturing cities, but it also sharply altered river dynamics, destroying fish populations and depriving downstream users of adequate and unpolluted supplies. For materials to build and to heat the city, loggers stripped the countryside of forests, quarrymen tore granite and other stone from the earth, and miners dug coal to provide fuel for commercial, industrial, and domestic uses.

Urbanites had to seek locations to dispose of the wastes produced by their construction, manufacturing, and consumption. Initially, they placed them on sites within the city, polluting the air, land, and water with industrial and domestic effluents and modifying and even destroying natural biological systems. In the post–Civil War period, as cities grew larger, they disposed of their wastes by transporting them to more distant locations. Thus, cities constructed sewerage systems for domestic wastes to replace cesspools and privy vaults and to improve local health conditions. They usually discharged the sewage into neighboring waterways, often polluting the water supply of downstream cities. In order to avoid epidemics of waterborne disease such as typhoid and cholera, downstream cities sought new sources of supply, building protected watersheds in distant areas or using technological fixes, such as water filtration (1890s) or chlorination (1912). Industrial wastes also added to stream and lake pollution, and urban rivers often became little more than open sewers.

The air and the land also became "sinks" for waste disposal. In the late nineteenth century, bituminous (or soft) coal became the preferred fuel for industrial, transportation, and domestic use in cities such as Chicago, Pittsburgh, and St. Louis. But while providing an inexpensive and plentiful energy supply, bituminous coal was also very dirty. The cities that used it suffered from air contamination and reduced sunlight, while the cleaning tasks of householders were greatly increased. Industry also used land surfaces for disposal of domestic and industrial wastes, and open areas in and around cities were marked with heaps of garbage, horse manure, ashes, and industrial wastes such as slag from steel-making or copper smelting. Such materials were often used to fill in "swamps" (wetlands) along waterfronts.

In the late nineteenth and early twentieth centuries, reformers began campaigning for urban environmental clean-ups and public health improvements. Women's groups often took the lead in agitating for clean air, clean water, and improved urban "housekeeping," showing a greater concern than men with such quality of life and health issues. Many Progressive reformers believed that the moral qualities of good citizenship were related to environmental improvements and to exposure to nature. They pushed for reduction of pollution and for construction of urban parks and playgrounds as a means to acculturate immigrants and upgrade working-class citizenship. Coalitions of reformers, urban professionals such as engineers and public health officials, and enlightened businessmen spearheaded drives for improvements in water supply and sanitary services. The replacement of the horse, first by electric traction and then by the automobile and motor truck, as a prime means of power for urban transport brought about substantial improvements in street and air sanitation. Campaigns for clean air and reduction of pollution of waterways, however, were largely unsuccessful. On balance, urban sanitary conditions were probably somewhat better in the 1920s than in the late nineteenth century, but the cost of improvement often was the exploitation of urban hinterlands for water supplies, increased downstream water pollution, and growing automobile congestion and pollution.

During the post–World War II decades, city environments suffered from heavy pollution loads as they sought to cope with increased automobile usage, pollution from industrial production, new varieties of exotic chemical pesticides and herbicides such as DDT, and the wastes of an increasingly consumer-oriented economy. Cleaner fuels and smoke-control laws largely freed cities during the 1940s and 1950s of the dense smoke from which they had previously suffered. Improved urban air quality resulted largely from the substitution of natural gas and oil for coal as urban fuels and the replacement of the steam locomotive by the diesel-electric. However, great increases in automobile usage in areas such as Los Angeles and Denver produced the new phenomena of photochemical smog, and air pollution replaced smoke as a major concern. Another improvement that proved temporary involved the replacement of the open dump and the pig farm by the sanitary landfill as a disposal place for urban garbage beginning in the 1950s. By the 1970s, however, it had become clear that the sanitary landfill often had substantial polluting qualities. In addition, some metropolitan areas ran out of land for landfills, beginning an expensive search for non-polluting and environmentally sound alternatives.

In these years also, the suburban out-migration, which had begun in the nineteenth century with commuter trains and streetcars, accelerated in the 1920s with the automobile, and in the 1970s increased to a torrent, putting major strains on the formerly rural and undeveloped metropolitan fringes. To a great extent, suburban layouts ignored environmental considerations, making little provision for open space, producing endless rows of resource-consuming and polluting lawns, contaminating groundwater with septic tanks, and consuming excessive amounts of freshwater and energy. The growth of the edge or outer city since the 1970s reflected a continued preference on the part of Americans for space-intensive single-family houses surrounded by lawns, for private automobiles over public transit, and for greenfield (not environmentally polluting) rather than brownfield (environmentally polluting) development. Even though today's environmental regulations prevent some of the environmental abuses of the past, without greater land use planning and environmental protection, urban and suburban America will, as it has in the past, continue to damage and to stress the natural environment.

—*Joel A. Tarr*

**See also**
Air Pollution; Land Pollution; Water Pollution.
**References**
Cronon, William. *Nature's Metropolis: Chicago and the Great West.* New York: W. W. Norton, 1991.
Melosi, Martin V. "The Place of the City in Environmental History." *Environmental History Review* (1993): 1–23.
Rosen, Christine Meisner, and Joel Arthur Tarr, eds. *The Environment and the City: A Special Issue of the Journal of Urban History* 20 (1994).
Tarr, Joel A. *The Search for the Ultimate Sink: Urban Pollution in Historical Perspective.* Akron, OH: University of Akron Press, 1996.

## Naturally Occurring Retirement Communities

The term *naturally occurring retirement community* (NORC) has been increasingly used to describe a concentration of older people living in a setting not purposely planned or designed for older residents. It has been estimated that 27 percent of Americans aged 55 and older live in NORCs; in contrast, only 5 percent to 7 percent live in planned retirement communities.

NORCs have a variety of physical characteristics and demographic origins. Physically, NORCs can be apartment and condominium complexes, or neighborhoods and older parts of towns. NORCs can even be rural areas or small towns.

The demographic origins of NORCs may be described as (1) aged-left-behind, (2) aging-in-place, and (3) in-migration.

Aged-left-behind NORCs have typically experienced significant economic decline and become relatively unattractive places to live. Concentrations of older residents in these NORCs typically occur for two reasons—the departure of many younger residents seeking better employment and living conditions elsewhere, or the residential immobility of older residents. The elderly who remain do so because of strong ties to the area and a feeling that they are economically or emotionally incapable of living elsewhere. These areas are often distinguished by declining housing stock, increasing social ills, and an elderly population in need of a range of medical, social, and personal services.

Aging-in-place NORCs are distinguished by the residential immobility of older residents rather than by the out-migration of younger residents. These NORCs have also been referred to as *de facto* retirement communities. They may consist of poorer housing stock and an older population at risk of losing the ability to live independently, or they may consist of wealthier elderly residents in higher-priced homes. In both cases, the older residents are often overhoused, very satisfied with their housing conditions, and intent on remaining for the foreseeable future in their homes of many years.

In-migration NORCs are distinguished by the movement into an area of older residents seeking a more convenient lifestyle or an amenity-oriented lifestyle. Older people attracted to a more convenient lifestyle tend to be the older elderly, or widowed women seeking the companionship of age peers in a setting convenient to shopping and services. These NORCs are often particular buildings or building complexes found nationwide. In contrast, older people attracted to amenity-oriented in-migration NORCs tend to be relatively young, independent, married, and affluent retired people seeking a more hospitable climate, a greater range of activities, and a more leisurely life. These NORCs are often vacation or resort areas and some initially attract older migrants on a seasonal basis. Seasonal locations tend to be in the southern United States and attract migrants from northern states and Canada.

Examples of in-migration NORCs that have attracted older people seeking a more convenient lifestyle are usually apartment or condominium complexes. Residents of these NORCs benefit from a socially supportive and convenient environment while living independently in an age-integrated setting. These localities have often attracted older residents without the benefit of advertising, payment subsidies, age segregation, or special design considerations. There appear to be three factors contributing to the attraction of such NORCs: location, management, and design. Location is often the first main attraction of these NORCs. Since alleviating social isolation is a key motive for the move, two main aspects of location are important—proximity to friends and family and the availability of good shopping and service facilities. High-quality and caring management is critical to maintaining a stream of referrals to the NORC since older people are often attracted by word of mouth from older residents. Finally, the architectural design of a NORC is generally not a major initial attraction but a potential barrier to continued independent living.

Other examples of in-migration NORCs are rural areas and small towns. Rural in-migration NORCs represent specialized retirement destinations that can be differentiated by the characteristics of the older migrants they attract and the NORC attributes these migrants find attractive. Three types of rural in-migration NORCs have been identified: amenity, convenience, and bifocal.

Rural amenity NORCs typically attract younger, healthier, better-educated, and more-affluent older migrants who move as couples to a sparsely populated rural area rich in natural amenities such as lakes and forests. Accessible health care, community services, shopping, and churches are secondary attractions to these areas. Since these moves are often made to escape an urban lifestyle, amenity NORCs tend to be the most distant from urbanized areas. Migrants are often seasonal residents prior to relocating permanently and are not likely to have family or personal ties in the area. Amenity migrants are the least likely to move into housing specifically for older residents and the most likely to leave the area due to the death or illness of a spouse.

Rural convenience NORCs tend to attract older, less-educated, and less-affluent local people who are moving a short distance from a rural area to a nearby rural community that offers more conveniences. The convenient lifestyle being sought emphasizes attractive and well-maintained housing in a desirable neighborhood and improved accessibility to health care, grocery shopping, restaurants, and churches. Migrants to convenience NORCs are the most likely to live alone and tend to retain proximity to family and friends. These migrants also have the highest likelihood of moving to housing specifically for older residents and subsequently moving to nearby health-care facilities. These NORCs tend to be the least distant from urbanized areas.

Rural bifocal NORCs are specialized retirement destinations that attract a unique type of migrant sharing similarities and differences with both amenity and convenience migrants. They are not merely NORCs that attract both amenity and convenience migrants. Bifocal NORCs tend to attract younger, healthier, older migrants who move as couples to sparsely populated areas for the rural lifestyle and recreational opportunities while remaining fairly close to family and friends. These migrants tend to be less affluent than amenity

NORC migrants, but they are attracted by many of the same attributes (i.e., natural beauty, woods, lakes, health care, churches, and grocery shopping). However, bifocal migrants move shorter distances than amenity migrants, and bifocal NORCs tend to be closer to urban areas than amenity NORCs. The move to bifocal NORCs is unlikely to be triggered by declining health, and these migrants are not likely to move into housing meant specifically for older residents. While they are rarely seasonal residents prior to relocating, some bifocal migrants will have vacationed in the area before they move. Due to the likelihood of having nearby family and friends, these migrants are more likely than amenity migrants to remain in the area after the death or illness of a spouse.

The examples of in-migration NORCs in apartment and rural settings illustrate that they are not only desirable to their older residents but to their hosts as well. Apartment NORCs are desirable to resident managers and management companies because older residents tend to be long-term tenants who pay their rent and cause minimal wear and tear on the apartment. Rural NORCs are attractive to their host communities largely because of the economic benefits they provide. There have been reports that rural communities whose economies are based on retirees have outpaced other communities in the growth of per-capita income. This mutual attraction between community and resident often produces a highly desirable living environment for older people.

—Michael E. Hunt

See also
Retirement Communities.
References
Golant, Stephen M. Housing America's Elderly: Many Possibilities/Few Choices. Newbury Park, CA: Sage Publications, 1992.
Hunt, Michael E., and Gail Gunter-Hunt. "Naturally Occurring Retirement Communities." Housing for the Elderly 3 (1985): 3–21.
Hunt, Michael E., and Leonard E. Ross. "Naturally Occurring Retirement Communities: A Multiattribute Examination of Desirability Factors." Gerontologist 30 (1990): 667–674.
Litwak, Eugene, and Charles F. Longino, Jr. "Migration Patterns among the Elderly: A Developmental Perspective." Gerontologist 27 (1987): 266–272.
Speare, Alden, Jr., and Judith W. Meyer. "Types of Elderly Residential Mobility and Their Determinants." Journal of Gerontology 43 (1988): 74–81.
Wiseman, Robert F. "Why Older People Move: Theoretical Issues." Research on Aging 2 (1980): 141–154.

# Neighborhood

A neighborhood is a place of local orientation for urban dwellers, a spatial entity whose residents share the same ethnic or socioeconomic characteristics, use the same local institutions, perceive themselves as having a distinct identity (symbolic awareness), and interact socially on a frequent basis. Its size can range from a street crossing to a multiblock area to an entire suburb annexed by an adjoining city. However, neighborhoods defy easy definition, existing as products of social relations, as states of mind, and as spatial units possessing place-names and physical boundaries.

Sociologists have long held an urban neighborhood to be the archetypal local community, a place of close or even intimate social relations with fellow residents more than with outsiders. As the size and social diversity of emergent cities increased during the nineteenth and twentieth centuries, urban sociologists sought to identify residential enclaves with sharply different population characteristics. Working in the 1920s and 1930s, Chicago school sociologists Robert Park, Harvey Zorbaugh, and Louis Wirth studied "natural areas" with exotic names like the Gold Coast, the Ghetto, and the Slum. Starting in the late 1940s spatial ecologists, following the lead of Esref Shevsky and Wendell Bell, used census tract data to chart differences in urban subareas on the basis of social rank, ethnicity, and what they labeled "urbanism" (e.g., lifestyle). In the 1990s, studies of social networks by Claude Fischer and Barry Wellman have questioned whether neighborhoods function as bounded communities in which geography determines local social attachments, although there is no definitive answer.

For historians, neighborhood community has also proved a vital institution to urban democracy. The historical debate over neighborhood has focused on which factors most shaped residence—class or ethnicity—as well as whether transience inhibited the development of neighborhood communities. Studies of Chicago, Philadelphia, Pittsburgh, and Detroit have underscored the importance of neighborhoods in anchoring ethnic communities through local church parishes, voluntary institutions, political machines, and employment. Scholars of class have likewise treated neighborhoods as repositories of working-class consciousness as industrial capitalism tore apart the social fabric of nineteenth-century cities. The separation of work and residence early in the century and the subsequent arrival of immigrants undoubtedly created distinctive enclaves, many of which mirrored European peasant villages in structure.

Still, American neighborhoods have always remained highly fluid. Only in the mid-nineteenth century did city dwellers come to divide urban space cognitively into districts whose names described the character of their inhabitants. Well into the century, for example, New York City remained socially diverse in composition and functioned only marginally as communities serving mainly the nonmobile.

By the early twentieth century, urban residents showed strong local attachments, and areas like Boston's Jamaica Plain became places whose rich public life of homes, churches, schools, and businesses mediated between the impersonal metropolis and the private family. But there is also increasing historical evidence that, for many, social ties operated independently of space. Furthermore, urban sprawl and political consolidation has, to a large extent, robbed neighborhoods of their earlier vitality. Nevertheless, many urban neighborhoods continue to function as centers for community organization and local orientation, particularly for newly arrived immigrants.

—*Kenneth A. Scherzer*

**See also**
Community.
**References**
Mooney-Melvin, Patricia. *The Organic City: Urban Definition and Neighborhood Organization, 1880–1920.* Lexington: University Press of Kentucky, 1987.
Park, Robert E., Ernest W. Burgess, and Roderick D. McKenzie. *The City.* Chicago: University of Chicago Press, 1925.
Scherzer, Kenneth. *The Unbounded Community: Neighborhood Life and Social Structure in New York City, 1830–1875.* Durham, NC: Duke University Press, 1992.
von Hoffman, Alexander. *Local Attachments: The Making of an American Urban Neighborhood, 1850–1920.* Baltimore: Johns Hopkins University Press, 1994.
Wirth, Louis. *The Ghetto.* Chicago: University of Chicago Press, 1928.
Zorbaugh, Harvey W. *The Gold Coast and the Slum: A Sociological Study of Chicago's Near North Side.* Chicago: University of Chicago Press, 1929.
Zunz, Olivier. *The Changing Face of Inequality: Urbanization, Industrial Development, and Immigrants in Detroit, 1880–1920.* Chicago: University of Chicago Press, 1982.

## Neighborhood Protective Association

The membership of a neighborhood protective association includes residents of a neighborhood who have banded together in response to a perceived threat to their neighborhood or to preserve their neighborhood; the association protects the community against unwanted intrusions from external political, social, and economic forces. These associations use various names that reflect the specific nature of their concerns: neighborhood improvement association, neighborhood beautification association, taxpayers' association, property owners' association, homeowners' association, or neighborhood watch group are all common terms.

The neighborhood watch program is instituted to curtail a growing crime rate or to prevent criminal activities from entering a relatively crime-free neighborhood. The neighborhood watch also provides some basic neighborly services to residents who are sick or elderly. The local police force generally supports watch programs enthusiastically, provides educational support, and encourages close communication between the watch group and the police. Beautification associations campaign for the improvement or introduction of parks, sponsor beautiful yard competitions, give awards for cosmetic improvements, direct cleanup projects, and demolish abandoned or older buildings that they consider an eyesore. Neighborhood preservation groups are concerned with saving older homes, businesses, and other buildings that they consider historic landmarks. These organizations are most active in the zone in transition of cities where there is constant change and neighborhood encroachment. Historic preservation groups also campaign against radical change (for example, the introduction of retail businesses into a residential neighborhood) by protecting the present use of a building or area.

Property owners' or homeowners' associations are concerned with preserving property values and the continued viability of a neighborhood. These groups support zoning to protect the integrity of neighborhoods and also fight local statutes that might threaten the identity of neighborhoods. At times, neighborhood organizations have used zoning to prevent racial or ethnic minorities and lower-income families from buying businesses or homes in an area. In the past, the restrictive deed covenant was used for this purpose, but it has been replaced with more subtle means like club memberships, building restrictions, and excessive homeowners dues in neighborhoods with strong neighborhood associations.

—*Craig Pascoe*

**See also**
Restrictive Deed Covenants; Zone in Transition.

**References**
Boyte, Harry C. *The Backyard Revolution: Understanding the New Citizen Movement.* Philadelphia: Temple University Press, 1980.
Laska, Shirley Bradway, and Daphne Spain, eds. *Back to the City: Issues in Neighborhood Renovation.* New York: Pergamon Press, 1980.
Robin, Peggy. *Saving the Neighborhood.* Rockville, MD: Woodbine House, 1990.
Rohe, William M., and Lauren B. Gates. *Planning with Neighborhoods.* Chapel Hill: University of North Carolina Press, 1985.
Skogan, Wesley, and Michael Maxfield. *Coping with Crime: Individual and Neighborhood Reactions.* Beverly Hills, CA: Sage Publications, 1981.
Williams, Michael R. *Neighborhood Organizations: Seeds of a New Urban Life.* Westport, CT: Greenwood Press, 1985.

## New Deal: Urban Policy

Between 1933 and 1941, President Franklin D. Roosevelt and his New Deal administration in Washington forged a close link between the federal government and the nation's cities that endured for over a half-century. The basis of the federal-urban relationship was money. New Deal funding of public works, low-income housing, and programs for the poor and the unemployed saved the nation's cities from bankruptcy. These urban-related federal programs were, for the most part, regarded as emergency activities and never coalesced into a comprehensive or even coherent urban policy during the 1930s. They did, however, lay the basis for permanent legislation that over the next 40 years expanded the federal role in cities into a vast array of urban programs involving billions of dollars. As a result, the nation's urban voters became loyal adherents of the Democratic Party, especially in the older cities of the Northeast and the Midwest.

The development of the federal-municipal relationship in the 1930s was an unforeseen consequence of the virtual collapse of state and local government finances. Prior to the 1930s, American cities had successfully financed their governmental activities with the local property tax and other municipal taxes and fees. This ended with the stock market crash of 1929. As the private economy deteriorated, state and local finances were shattered. The tax base in many cities declined by 30 or 40 percent. Even with drastic reductions in essential public services, most cities faced insolvency. The nation's municipal leaders pleaded for federal help since state governments were unwilling or unable to offer significant aid. From the beginning of the New Deal, Roosevelt and his chief administrators showed a strong willingness to help the cities but refused to simply give them the cash. Knowing the propensity of many city political machines to squander public funds, FDR provided almost all of the aid through federal agencies, which oversaw the expenditures.

Federal aid to cities came in five areas: (1) unemployment relief programs, (2) public works projects, (3) home mortgage refinancing and new home mortgage underwriting, (4) low-income public housing projects, and (5) welfare funding for the poor and disabled. All these programs were nationwide in scope, with suburbs and small towns sharing them with large central cities, but funding was targeted especially to the great metropolises since they faced the most serious social consequences of massive unemployment, poverty, and bankruptcy. Also, it became apparent to the Democrats that federal aid to cities brought them the loyalty of urban political machines and voters. As small town and rural America became more conservative and critical of the New Deal after 1936, urban voters became the New Deal's most ardent and consistent supporters. Unemployment relief in the cities was administered by the Public Works Administration, the Civil Works Administration, and later by the Works Progress Administration. Important as these programs were to the cities, they were always regarded as temporary expedients until the private urban economy rebounded. The same was true of the Home Owners Loan Corporation (HOLC), which refinanced home mortgages and thus allowed urban homeowners (and local lending institutions) to tide themselves over until the Depression lifted.

The more permanent contribution of the federal government to cities in this era came with the public works projects, the low-income housing program, and the welfare programs administered under the Social Security Act of 1935. The public works projects were primarily for unemployment

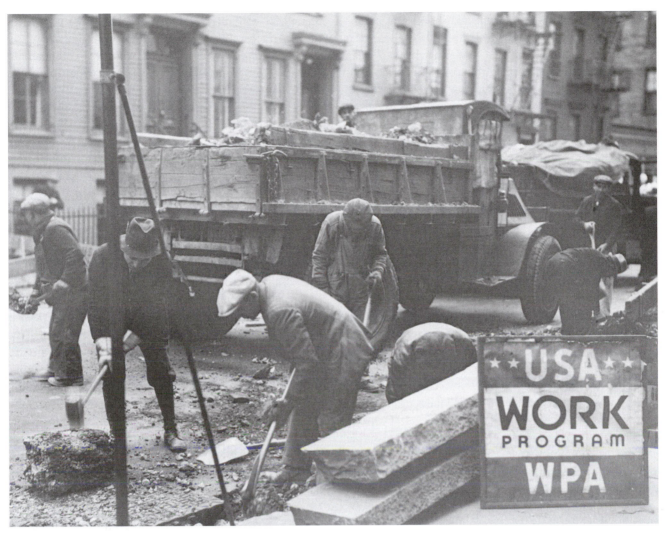

*A WPA street crew at work in New York City during the Depression.*

relief, but they also made a substantial contribution to improving the physical plant of urban America during a decade when it would have otherwise seriously deteriorated. A wide variety of urban projects was undertaken. The list included streets, highways, bridges, subways, schools, parks, sewage treatment plants, even a municipal dog pound. While valuable as individual accomplishments, these projects were not always coordinated into larger urban or regional plans. They were often pet schemes of local political bosses or projects that could be started quickly to get people employed.

When it came to addressing the fundamental and enduring problems of the cities, three federal housing programs presented the most direct and coherent response, although even in this case the programs may have harmed cities as much as they helped them. The Home Owners Refinancing Act (1933) was a temporary expedient to help homeowners refinance their mortgages, and during its three years of operations, it saved almost a million homes from foreclosure. The two permanent housing programs were those of the Fed-

eral Housing Administration (1934) and the U.S. Housing Authority (1937). They formed the first enduring links between the federal government and cities, and both have exerted a very significant impact. The U.S. Housing Authority was empowered to fund the construction of low-income housing projects in cities and towns through locally appointed public housing authorities. While the majority of projects have been built in smaller towns, the most massive and controversial ones were developed in the nation's biggest cities. By providing poor families with structurally safe, sanitary dwelling units, these projects have been of great value, but their concentration in the inner city also contributed to the general decline of the central city. In fairness to the New Deal's housing reformers, the placement of the great majority of public housing on inner-city slum sites was not their preference, but a program that would have dispersed low-income families into the urban fringe or the suburbs was adamantly opposed by a wide variety of groups and would certainly have killed the entire New Deal public housing program.

In contrast to the U.S. Housing Authority project for low-income renters, the Federal Housing Administration's program of mortgage insurance for prospective home buyers tended to facilitate the escape of white, middle-income families from the central city. The Federal Housing Administration was reluctant to insure mortgages in economically modest or declining neighborhoods, especially those adjacent to slums or minority housing, but it was willing to underwrite mortgages for what were often structurally inferior houses on the urban fringe or the suburbs. In this way the Federal Housing Administration accelerated, rather than slowed, the white, middle-class exodus from the central cities.

In hindsight, the basic problem of the New Deal's housing programs was their inability or unwillingness to address directly what most urban experts of the 1930s considered the greatest problem facing urban America: the decline of central cities as upper- and middle-income families began moving to the suburbs. The New Deal's greenbelt town program, three small suburban "new towns" for moderate-income families, provided examples of a more rational, balanced, and fair-minded program of urban dispersion, but due to their unpopularity with Congress and private real estate interests, the New Deal did not consider including them in its permanent federal housing program, and they have never become a significant factor in public housing or federal planning policy. Therefore, the New Deal's housing programs, by allowing the middle classes to leave for the suburbs more easily and reinforcing the concentration of low-income families in the inner cities, where a substantial number became supported (some say enmeshed or trapped) in the government's welfare programs, contributed in part to the great central city disasters of the 1960–1990 era.

Some of the blame for all this rests with President Roosevelt. FDR was certainly not opposed to the development of a coordinated urban program that would have addressed the deeper and more enduring problems facing central cities, but it was not a high priority in the first place; and its more radical aspects, such as the greenbelt towns, proved to be politically unpopular. In the press of more immediate and demanding crises, FDR never got around to seriously considering the long-term problems of central cities. The chief example of this was his failure to take any action on the thoughtful and broad series of recommendations on American cities formulated by the Committee on Urbanism of the National Resources Committee, the New Deal's chief planning agency. The report, *Our Cities: Their Role in the National Economy,* was issued in 1937 and called for a comprehensive, coordinated series of federal programs for urban America to eliminate slums, help finance and direct urban welfare and crime programs, and protect central cities from what it called "urban blight" through comprehensive city planning. The report also recommended the control of suburban expansion through metropolitan and regional planning and use of the new town concept. Taken together, these recommendations envisaged a permanent, coordinated program of urban reconstruction and metropolitan control.

The *Our Cities* report was ignored by both Roosevelt and the Congress, but various pieces of its more specific recommendations continued to be debated over the next several years by government, business, and real estate leaders. The issue that stimulated the most thought and action was the subject of slums and blight. In 1941 both government housing experts and private real estate leaders recommended a large-scale, federally funded program of urban redevelopment to physically eradicate slums and thus, it was hoped, prevent even larger areas of the nation's cities from further deterioration. These recommendations were written into legislation in a 1943 bill called the "Neighborhood Development Act." The bill never got out of committee, but six years later the Housing and Urban Renewal Act of 1949 embodied its essential goal. It was this legislation, based on one of the key recommendations of the *Our Cities* report, that moved the federal-city relationship from one that focused almost exclusively on slum clearance and public housing to the more comprehensive urban redevelopment programs of the years from 1960 to 1990.

Sadly, almost no one recognized until the 1950s that the nation's central cities were in far deeper trouble than had previously been thought. Certainly in the years before 1950 no one except perhaps Lewis Mumford anticipated that over the next half-century most of the so-called "central cities" would be marginalized and largely discarded by both residents and employers, who have moved to the gigantic suburbanized regions that have replaced them. To blame the government officials of the 1930s for failing to see into the future when almost no one else did is clearly unfair. It can also be argued that the New Deal's urban programs responded accurately to the desires of the majority of Americans through its attempts to make inner-city housing more livable for low-income families who were already being concentrated there by 1933, while enabling those with moderate or middle incomes to join the affluent in the general escape to the suburbs. It was clear in 1933, and beyond any doubt by the 1980s and 1990s, that the overwhelming majority of Americans have rejected the old compact central city as a place of work or residence. They desire to live most of their lives in the new decentralized suburban regions that now dominate the American landscape and economy. Therefore, the nationally financed and directed urban programs born during the New Deal era, with their primary focus on the central city and the issues of low-income housing, welfare, and inner-city decay, appear remote to the interests of most suburbanites and are, in the 1990s, being dismantled.

—*Joseph L. Arnold*

**See also**
The Depression and Cities; Greenbelt Towns; Hoovervilles; National Youth Administration; Resettlement Administration; Tugwell, Rexford Guy.
**References**
Argersinger, JoAnn E. *Toward a New Deal in Baltimore: People and Government in the Great Depression.* Chapel Hill: University of North Carolina Press, 1988.
Arnold, Joseph L. *The New Deal in the Suburbs: A History of the Greenbelt Town Program, 1935–1954.* Columbus: Ohio State University Press, 1971.
Dorsett, Lyle W. *Franklin D. Roosevelt and the City Bosses.* Port Washington, NY: Kennikat Press, 1977.
Friedman, Lawrence M. *Government and Slum Housing: A Century of Frustration.* Chicago: Rand McNally, 1968.
Gelfand, Mark I. *A Nation of Cities: The Federal Government and Urban America, 1933–1965.* New York: Oxford University Press, 1975.
Leuchtenburg, William. *Franklin D. Roosevelt and the New Deal, 1932–1940.* New York: Harper & Row, 1963.
Smith, Douglas L. *The New Deal in the Urban South.* Baton Rouge: Louisiana State University Press, 1988.
Trout, Charles A. *Boston, the Great Depression and the New Deal.* New York: Oxford University Press, 1977.

## New England Town Meetings

A town meeting is an assembly of all the qualified voters in a town for the purpose of engaging in town legislative and electoral activities. English Puritan colonists created the town meeting shortly after they arrived in the Massachusetts Bay Colony in the early seventeenth century. It is direct democracy in its purest form. Though town meetings have probably never been, in practice, as democratic as the contemporary popular mind imagines, the popular American political culture often preserves a romantic and nostalgic view of the New England town meeting. When some early-twentieth-century Progressives campaigned for direct democracy (the popular initiative and referendum), they often argued that they were building on the New England town meeting and bringing a new form of direct democracy to modern cities and states.

The origins of the town meeting in the early seventeenth century can be traced to the Congregational Church, which accorded all power to the local congregation of self-chosen citizens who authored their own written covenants such as the Mayflower Compact of 1620. Since each new town in New England was, at least partly, an extension of its church, and membership in the congregation usually overlapped with citizenship, the self-governance of the town church extended to town government. While the members of a congregation met to select clergy and govern their church, similar political behavior emerged in town governance. These English colonists

may have loosely built upon the parish governance some of them had known in England, but since most English villages had been governed by local lords and squires rather than parish meetings, the English roots for the New England town meeting were thin. The English colonists, basically, invented the town meeting.

Seventeenth-century town meetings did not encourage the individualism that later became so much a part of American political values. Instead, they sought a politics of consensual communalism, i.e., conformity and consensus rather than diversity and dissent. Nevertheless, the structure of town meetings proved compatible with the growth of popular democracy in the eighteenth and nineteenth centuries. Since the town meeting theoretically had ultimate and nearly unlimited power in town affairs, it became more democratic as the franchise, property ownership, and secular life became more widespread. Thus developed the town meeting as a symbol of democracy, the image that exists in the political legend of American popular culture today.

However, the New England town meeting proved best suited for smaller communities. As towns grew into cities in the nineteenth and twentieth centuries, the town meeting form of government was replaced in many communities. Today, it exists mostly in northern New England towns, especially in Maine and Vermont. Although some midwestern communities settled by New Englanders had town meetings, this form of government remained almost entirely a New England institution.

Although the town meeting originally met weekly or monthly, today it is an annual spring meeting in most towns that have retained this form of government The selectmen/selectwomen may call special meetings, and the town's citizens may petition for special meetings. For each town meeting a "warning" (agenda) is issued, and generally the town meeting can vote only on items included on the warning. Each meeting elects its own moderator. Even though the town meeting proved unsuitable for governing large cities and suburbs, it is still an integral part of many smaller New England towns. Although some twentieth-century commentators once labeled the town meeting an anachronism, it is firmly established and still popular in many smaller New England towns.

—*Rod Farmer*

**See also**
New England Towns and Villages.
**References**
Lingeman, Richard. *Small Town America: A Narrative History 1620–the Present.* Boston: Houghton Mifflin, 1980.
Lockridge, Kenneth A. *A New England Town, The First Hundred Years: Dedham, Massachusetts, 1636–1736.* New York: W. W. Norton, 1970.
Zuckerman, Michael. *Peaceable Kingdoms: New England Towns in the Eighteenth Century.* New York: Vintage Books, 1970.

## New England Towns and Villages

In the seventeenth century, New England towns varied from other towns that fit somewhere on the continuum between villages and cities, serving commonly as market centers for provision of low-order goods and services. In New England, towns, like their successor townships elsewhere in North America, referred both to geographical spaces and also to the communities that inhabited those spaces.

New England town communities were exclusive; they formed the established church congregation, the basic unit in which political expression was exercised by means of the town meeting, and, most importantly during settlement, the vehicle for distributing land to families intent on farming. New England towns were not marketplaces themselves, though a town in New England might have developed into such a direct descendant of English towns. It is worth nothing, nevertheless, that many New England towns were named for English market towns.

Like New England towns, New England villages were both spaces and the communities that inhabited those spaces. And, as villages have always been secondary to towns, so it was in New England where towns took precedence over villages. The distinction is important. Colonial villages were secondary parishes or districts of towns that might in time become towns in their own right. Salem, Massachusetts, offers an apt illustration. Within the New England town of Salem, there developed early on both the town of Salem (the port and marketplace that became the core of present-day Salem) and also the village of Salem, where farmers who settled on dispersed, enclosed farmsteads soon petitioned for their own parish and church, found and persecuted witches within their community, and eventually received a charter as the town of Danvers.

The role of New England towns and villages became especially significant after the American Revolution. As towns and their villages had evolved between the 1630s and the 1780s, they had taken on a conventional shape and size, largely square and averaging about 36 square miles in New England. The Congressional Township and Range Survey System perpetuated exactly these dimensions across much of the federal lands west of the Appalachians, and cities thereafter were built on the ever-present, unyielding grid of parallel and perpendicular streets.

If New England towns of the colonial period were preurban spaces, New England villages were protourban places. With the quickening of commerce after 1790, increasing numbers of permanent nonfarmers congregated at points of high accessibility to engage in trade. Throughout New England, these places were colonial town and village centers, often located on hilltops where townspeople had placed their meetinghouse and burying ground and to which they had built their town roads. The nineteenth-century gathering of commercial activities and residences around meetinghouse lots at town centers and junctions of town roads created a protourban system. Nineteenth-century religious disestablishment separated the meetinghouse and burial ground from the remainder of the meetinghouse lot to form the secular village common.

As urban sorting played itself out in the nineteenth century, many of these places became important cities and towns, like Pittsford, Massachusetts, or Bristol, Connecticut, and others, like Cummington, Massachusetts, literally and figuratively slid downhill, often to mill sites or turnpike crossings. Some also became early suburbs, like Roxbury, Massachusetts, enveloped by expanding Boston, while others inspired suburban design, like Litchfield, Connecticut. Today, New England villages continue to inspire suburban development. One need only read the real estate pages of any local newspaper to find repeated references to the New England town and village landscape in subdivision names, landscaping, and domestic architecture.

—*Joseph S. Wood*

**See also**
Community; New England Town Meetings; Township; Villages.
**References**
Wood, Joseph S. " 'Build, Therefore, Your Own World': The New England Village as Settlement Ideal." *Annals of the Association of American Geographers* 81 (1991): 32–50.
———. *The New England Village.* Baltimore: Johns Hopkins University Press, 1997.

## New Federalism

New Federalism was an ambitious set of domestic policy initiatives conceived and proposed by President Richard Nixon in the early 1970s. It was also the name given to a major effort by President Ronald Reagan to restructure federal-state relations in the 1980s. Taken together, the proposals called for a dramatic restructuring of American federalism by placing renewed emphasis on state and local governments and decreasing the power of the federal bureaucracy, especially the power of individuals responsible for administering various urban and social welfare programs.

The theoretical rationale for the programs was that American government had become too centralized and that too much power rested in the hands of Washington bureaucrats. In addition, it was argued that this increased centralization caused an overreliance on Washington for leadership, that it reduced the role of local and state decision-making bodies, and that the various programs of Lyndon Johnson's Great Society overtaxed the American people without providing the efficiency and effectiveness needed to solve the complex problems they addressed.

Politically, the New Federalism of the Nixon era was supported by a coalition of leaders who wanted to reduce the budgetary and the programmatic authority of the Washington bureaucracy and the national political establishment. Local and most state leaders supported the program strongly, and President Nixon, on signing a key piece of legislation, argued that it set the stage for a "second American Revolution." The various programs were seen as major new initiatives and did result in major changes affecting local and state governments.

Two programs were central components of the New Federalism of the Nixon years. The first, officially called the State and Local Fiscal Assistance Act of 1972 but commonly referred to as "general revenue sharing," had the federal government redistribute its revenues using preset formulas that measure a variety of factors affecting state and local governments. The intent of general revenue sharing was to increase the flow of federal money to general-purpose units of government without increasing the federal restrictions on the use of those funds. This was a popular program, and it lasted until the mid-1980s.

The second program that was central to Nixon's New Federalism was "special revenue sharing." This was a new way for the federal government to deliver funds to a recipient unit. By consolidating various grant programs into more general uses (urban development rather than separate, special funds for sewerage, housing, and so on), special revenue sharing was intended to provide more money for specific program improvements while reducing administrative costs and increasing local autonomy over the use of the money.

Federal expenditures for New Federalism programs peaked in the mid-1970s, and when Ronald Reagan was elected president in 1980, he maintained that his New Federalism package would reduce the federal deficit and get big government off the back of the average citizen. Politically, Reagan's New Federalism, often referred to as New Federalism II, emphasized reducing all governmental involvement while Nixon's New Federalism had wanted to shift the involvement of government from the federal level to state and local governments. So while the two programs had the same name, they were vastly different, both in what they wanted to accomplish and how they planned to accomplish it.

Under President Reagan, a variety of federal programs were ended and domestic expenditures reduced. General revenue sharing, which had been reduced since the middle of the 1970s, was allowed to conclude, and the various special revenue sharing programs were greatly reduced. There were several attempts at instituting new initiatives, the most important of which involved federal and state governments exchanging responsibility for welfare and various medical programs. None of these was adopted, and most were actually never debated seriously since the majority of state and local officials did not favor New Federalism II.

Clearly, both New Federalism programs were logical extensions of a leading theoretical point of view that argued that government activity was doomed to fail and that government should therefore not be permitted to undertake such programs. This approach also argued that local decision-makers were the most competent to determine policy and make decisions that influenced their communities. Both were seen as providing alternatives to the contending approach, which argued that government action was not only needed but essential if social programs were to be reduced and that it was the federal government's responsibility to establish national norms.

As a concept, New Federalism is likely to resurface in the next decade since it involves a fundamental way of looking at the domestic political process and specifically the American intergovernmental arena.

—*David A. Caputo*

**References**

Caputo, David A., ed. "General Revenue Sharing and Federalism." *The Annals* 419 (1975).

Conlan, Timothy. *New Federalism: Intergovernmental Reform from Nixon to Reagan.* Washington, DC: Brookings Institution, 1988.

Kincaid, John, ed. *Amerian Federalism, the Third Century.* Newbury Park, CA: Sage Publications, 1990.

Murray, Charles. *Losing Ground: American Social Policy, 1950–1980.* New York: Basic Books, 1984.

Nathan, Richard P. *The Plot That Failed: Nixon and the Administrative Presidency.* New York: Wiley, 1975.

Palmer, John L., ed. *Perspectives on the Reagan Years.* Washington, DC: Urban Institute Press, 1986.

## New Orleans, Louisiana

New Orleans is a multiracial, multiethnic, historically Catholic city located on the fringes of the Bible Belt. Founded by Jean Baptiste Le Moyne, Sieur de Bienville, in 1718 as a French fortification near the mouth of the Mississippi River, the original city (now the French Quarter or *Vieux Carre*) was modeled after La Rochelle in France. The heart of this area was originally called the Place d'Armes but was renamed Jackson Square in 1849. The mosquito-infested, disease-ridden site combined with French neglect to retard growth and make New Orleans an economic liability for much of the French reign. Ceded to Spain at the end of the Seven Years' War, effective in 1764, the city began to prosper as its new administrators spurred colonization by permitting British and American settlers into the region. Spain ceded New Orleans and the rest of the Louisiana Territory back to France only to see Napoleon sell the territory to the United States in 1803.

It was during the French and Spanish regimes that New Orleans's distinctive community of freemen and women of color came into being. Numbering nearly 20,000 at its peak in 1840, two decades of precipitous decline still left the city with almost 11,000 free people of color on the eve of the Civil War. Representing as much as 29 percent of the city's population in 1810, 23 percent in 1820, 25 percent in 1830, and 18 percent as late as 1840, New Orleans's free people of color composed a fully articulated community with a complex class structure that occupied far more than the fringes of society. Holding nearly $2.5 million of real estate by 1850 (an amount 50 times greater than the holdings reported by African Americans in Boston), some 650 free blacks owned land in New Orleans. Only three other American cities had as many as 100 black landowners, and no other had even 200. When counted with the city's slaves, New Orleans's free people of color constituted a nonwhite majority that greeted the Americans at the time of the Louisiana Purchase and remained intact down to the 1840s. With the largest black urban community in the United States, New Orleans's social order was unique in North America.

The antebellum era was a golden age for New Orleans. The War of 1812 brought cooperation between Americans and Creoles (colonial French and Spanish descendants of Louisiana birth) against the British; afterward, following development of the steamboat and the regional boom based on cotton, land, and slaves, the city became an even more important trading center. Land speculation fueled development of commercial enterprises in the heart of the city, particularly in the growing "American" sector uptown. Residential settlement crowded the higher areas along the natural levees and ancient ridges left by the Mississippi River as steam railroads extended commuting distances. The bursting of this speculative bubble and a subsequent depression slowed growth for about a decade beginning in the late 1830s.

The continuing stream of French and West Indian immigrants meant that New Orleans remained predominantly French-speaking virtually throughout the antebellum period and that French influence would not be obliterated as completely as in the other French colonial outposts of Chicago, Detroit, and St. Louis, despite the growing influx of Americans. When the English-speaking Americans came to predominate numerically, the shrewd manipulation of constitutional devices and legislative gerrymandering by the Creoles produced a political impasse that was only resolved by the division of New Orleans into three semiautonomous municipalities in 1836. Based in the residential enclaves that tended to split uptown Americans from Creoles in the two downtown municipalities, the arrangement emulated the Parisian model of city government and helped calm ethnic rivalries until New Orleans was reconsolidated and joined by the suburb of Lafayette in 1852.

At the same time, a massive wave of immigration, led by thousands of Irish and Germans, made an already cosmopolitan population even more heterogeneous. St. Louis Cathedral, on Jackson Square, had been the only Catholic church in the city until 1832 when the Irish established St. Patrick's; ensuing years saw both the Irish and German immigrants further institutionalize their presence in New Orleans. A resultant spate of Know-Nothingism and political nativism in the 1850s emphasized American ascendancy and began a tradition of violence and disorder related to elections that antedated the Civil War and Reconstruction. Still, the city's unique cultural tapestry produced an exciting blend of music, food, and festivity—as evidenced by the emergence of the first modern Mardi Gras "krewes" in 1857—that absorbed its ethnic fragments as much as it held them in suspension. By 1860 economic and cultural growth had made New Orleans the largest city in the South (population 168,675) and the fifth largest in the United States.

The city was not as fortunate during and after the Civil War. Federal forces occupied New Orleans between 1862 and 1865, but its now overwhelmingly white majority resisted Reconstruction by electing Democratic mayors after 1870 who were determined not to share power with freed blacks. Divided before the Civil War by color, culture, law, occupation, and neighborhood, nonwhites faced Reconstruction with a sense of their distinctive histories and a forced awareness of their mutual interests.

The imposition of segregation at the dawn of the twentieth century symbolized the ascendance of a new, Americanized racial order and accelerated the subordination of ethnicity—both black and white—as a stark racial duality held sway. The state constitutions of 1879 and 1898, and the subsequent avalanche of segregationist legislation, sanctioned a rigid system of social subordination as the norm. Protests emanating from New Orleans's Creoles of color could not stop the trend, and the unsuccessful challenge to Jim Crow that Homer Plessy took all the way to the U.S. Supreme Court simply enshrined the principle of "separate but equal" for longer than the next 50 years.

In the Gilded Age, New Orleans stagnated economically, saw race relations deteriorate, and succeeded only in adding another layer to its polyglot population through a large Sicilian immigration. By 1880, New Orleans's population of 216,090 ranked it no higher than ninth in the United States; by 1900, its population had swollen to 287,104, but cities growing even more rapidly pushed it down into twelfth place.

The construction of James B. Eads's famous jetties in the mouth of the Mississippi River allowed the river to scour itself out to a depth that accommodated the most modern oceangoing vessels by 1880; connections to the Southern Pacific Railroad tied the city to California in 1883; and the Cotton Centennial Exposition held in the new Audubon Park the next year seemed to herald better times. But the fair's bankruptcy proved a better indicator of what lay in store. Competing cities prevented New Orleans from regaining its lost preeminence, sanitation problems promoted recurrent outbreaks of cholera and yellow fever, and New Orleans's unique legacy of race relations produced a sporadic experiment with interracial cooperation among waterfront workers that alternately bedeviled employers and dissolved in violent disorder. The city remained primarily a place of commerce within a rapidly industrializing country, never quite adapting to the new age. Within this troubled context, however, New Orleans demonstrated its cultural vitality by developing jazz as a popular music form. Early practitioners, such as cornetist Buddy Bolden, and later stars, such as Louis Armstrong, earned richly deserved reputations for their virtuosity and pioneered what has been called the United States' only original art form.

In the twentieth century, New Orleans possessed one of the South's rare urban political machines, which dominated the city from 1904 until its defeat by DeLesseps S. Morrison in 1946. It emerged from an era of closely contested municipal elections after Reconstruction that pitted a growing cadre of ethnic, professional "Ring" politicians against a group of "silk-stocking" interests that identified themselves as "reformers." All were nominally Democrats after the overthrow of Reconstruction and the Battle of Liberty Place on September 14, 1874, that united most of white New Orleans under the party's banner and the cause of white supremacy. For the rest of the century, disorderly, violent, and corrupt elections practices were the rule rather than the exception and produced a precarious balance of power that saw significant "reform" victories in the mayoral campaigns of Joseph Shakspeare (in 1880 and again in 1888) and Walter C. Flower (1896).

Their administrations proved notable in professionalizing the city's fire and police departments, respectively, and in developing creative approaches to crime and vice. The former pursued the "Shakspeare Plan," a policy that exacted tribute from open, but illegal, gambling operations in an attempt to shore up a depleted treasury and provide needed public services; the latter oversaw creation of New Orleans's famed Storyville (1897–1917), a segregated vice district that tried to accommodate and regulate prostitution.

Shakspeare's second term, however, was marred by the murder of police chief David C. Hennessy and the subsequent lynching of 11 Italians in 1891 by an aroused citizenry—an incident that caused an international furor and helped popularize the concept of a "mafia." Most significantly, periods of "anti-Ring" success by business-dominated coalitions with influence in state government witnessed the creation of new agencies (e.g., the Board of Liquidation, the Sewerage and Water Board, and the Dock Board) that pulled the power to control tax rates, development, and the waterfront out of City Hall and into more insulated, appointive agencies. Losing what was, at best, their tenuous grip on the city's electoral politics, a succession of "reform" groups found other means of protecting and pursuing their interests.

John Fitzpatrick, an Irish ward leader of working-class origins and sympathies, was elected mayor in 1892 and epitomized early "Ring" leadership. Nearly impeached after he supported laborers in massive strikes in 1892 and 1894, he helped organize the Choctaw Club, a new Democratic organization, after Walter Flower's victory, and thus facilitated the emergence of the New Orleans "machine." Martin Behrman, who served as mayor from 1904 to 1920, and from 1925 until his death in 1926, consolidated the machine's control of the city through his use of patronage and by striking accommodations with the local business community and state political leaders. The Choctaws retained power until Governor Huey Long broke their organization during the Depression, and they then resurrected themselves by allying with Long's followers in the administration of Mayor Robert Maestri (1936–1946).

After World War II, New Orleans was fundamentally reshaped by the long-delayed process of suburbanization, changing racial demographics, and the onset of the civil rights revolution. Not until the 1920s did A. Baldwin Wood's heavy-duty pumps, coupled with a new system of canals that carried swamp and floodwater out of the city, break the chokehold with which nature had thwarted New Orleans's development for the first 200 years of the city's existence. At the same time, the Orleans Levee District tamed the forbidding lakeshore that served as the city's northern boundary, and the new lands opened for development there facilitated the drive toward racial segregation and polarization by enabling white movement out of the city. The Depression and World War II halted further growth, but postwar transportation improvements—especially new bridges across the Mississippi River and the construction of Interstate 10—inaugurated a new era. Between 1960 and 1980, New Orleans's white population declined by 155,627 while its nonwhite population grew by 85,854. Whites again became a minority, representing only 42.5 percent of the city's 557,482 inhabitants. With 70 percent of whites in the metropolitan area living in the suburbs, the city-suburban, black-white cleavage became the region's most striking social development.

DeLesseps S. Morrison, mayor from 1946 until 1961, a racial "moderate" who presided over the city's postwar construction and economic booms, destroyed the Choctaws as an effective political organization but ultimately proved unable to cope with the new forces unleashed by the civil rights movement. Demonstrations along the city's main shopping thoroughfare, Canal Street, and disorders that accompanied court-ordered school desegregation in 1960 and 1961 doomed the ambitious Morrison's gubernatorial candidacy and set the stage for the caretaker regime of Victor H. Schiro (1961–1970) that followed. Having survived Hurricanes Betsy (1965) and Camille (1969) during the Schiro years, the city finally eased into the civil rights era with the election of Maurice (Moon) Landrieu in 1970 and the city's first African-American chief executive, Ernest N. (Dutch) Morial, in 1978 following Landrieu's two terms.

Though Morial did better with blacks and less well with whites than Landrieu, effects of the Voting Rights Act of 1965 could clearly be seen in each of their campaigns as they were initially elected by overwhelming black majorities but received only a minority of the white vote. For the first time, Landrieu brought African Americans into the highest levels of city government and energetically pursued federal assistance that had previously gone begging. His renovation of the French Market, construction of pedestrian malls around Jackson Square, and creation of the aptly named Moonwalk overlooking the Mississippi River in the French Quarter—along with his sponsorship of the Superdome and new construction in the central business district—were all designed to bolster a burgeoning tourist trade and accompany economic activity in the port and the oil and petrochemical industries.

Dutch Morial, an attorney who was one of the prime architects of the civil rights revolution in New Orleans, went beyond Landrieu in trying to open the oligarchic boards and independent agencies to black participation. He successfully put down a police strike early in his first term, and he pursued economic diversification and the expanding tourist trade as the central business district boomed. The construction of new venues such as the convention center and the emergence of new attractions such as the French Quarter Festival to accompany older ones (such as the Jazz and Heritage Festival) testified to the reorientation of the city's economy. The slashing of federal support that followed Ronald Reagan's election as president in 1980, the collapse of the oil patch in the mid-1980s, and the unsuccessful attempt to solve long-term fiscal problems cast a pall over Morial's second term. Increasing racial polarization doomed his attempt to remove the two-term limit, and New Orleans slid into another era of economic stagnation.

According to the 1990 census, the city's population had officially dipped below the half million mark to 496,938. Whites constituted little more than a third of the total (173,305, or 35 percent) while the number of blacks had grown to 308,364, or 62 percent. Within the metropolitan area, racial polarization remained almost as great as ever. Of the total population of 1,238,816, more than seven of every ten blacks lived in the central city while nearly eight of every ten whites resided in the suburbs. In 1994, Dutch Morial's son, Marc H. Morial, was elected the city's third African-American mayor, and the city seriously flirted with casino gambling and other gaming operations as a possible solution to the long-standing economic problems. However, the licensing of casinos was no panacea, and in late 1997 an $830 million casino under construction sat unfinished. More and more, however, New Orleans appeared to be losing its distinctive, historic character even as it took on the more common aspect of a deindustrialized, racially segmented American metropolis.

—*Arnold R. Hirsch*

See also
Armstrong, Louis; Behrman, Martin; French Colonial Towns; Morrison, DeLesseps Story.

**References**
Armstrong, Louis. *Satchmo: My Life in New Orleans.* New York: Prentice-Hall, 1954.
Arnesen, Eric. *Waterfront Workers of New Orleans: Race, Class, and Politics, 1863–1923.* New York: Oxford University Press, 1991.
Clark, John G. *New Orleans, 1718–1812: An Economic History.* Baton Rouge: Louisiana State University Press, 1970.
Haas, Edward F. *DeLesseps S. Morrison and the Image of Reform: New Orleans Politics, 1946–1961.* Baton Rouge: Louisiana State University Press, 1974.
Hirsch, Arnold R., and Joseph Logsdon, eds. *Creole New Orleans: Race and Americanization.* Baton Rouge: Louisiana State University Press, 1992.
Jackson, Joy. *New Orleans in the Gilded Age: Politics and Urban Progress, 1880–1896.* Baton Rouge: Louisiana State University Press, 1969.
Logsdon, Joseph. "Immigration through the Port of New Orleans." In Mark Stolarik, ed., *Forgotten Doors: The Other Ports of Entry to the United States.* Philadelphia: Balch Institute Press, 1988.

## New Professionalism

In the 1890s, when squalor, congestion, disease, crime, and general inefficiency were approaching nightmarish proportions in American cities, a group of well-heeled amateurs emerged with a variety of reforms intended to humanize urban conditions. As their numbers increased and their efforts matured, these reformers created such new professions as public health, social work, and city planning, all of which treated matters of social policy in the twentieth century.

In important ways, the model for these reformers was the medical profession. Actually, medicine came to the late nineteenth century with a bad reputation. Because medical practice and practitioners had been virtually unregulated for decades, almost anyone could do almost anything in the name of healing the sick; it was a golden age of medical incompetence and quackery. Only under heavy pressure from the American Medical Association (AMA) did this situation change after the turn of the century. A rigorous medical education became mandatory, strict licensing requirements were implemented, and admissions into the field were zealously restricted. In this way, the medical profession assumed the characteristics by which it claimed professionalism: (1) extensive training in knowledge, especially scientific knowledge, that was arcane to the general public; (2) a presumed ethic of public service; and (3) insistence on the right of professionals to define and regulate their own affairs through organizations of their own making. In the first half of the twentieth century, as deaths from childbirth and communicable diseases (perhaps also from medical incompetence) declined and life expectancy lengthened, the prestige and incomes of physicians rose dramatically.

Public health developed along roughly parallel lines, but because of its special focus on contagion and epidemics it was more concerned with the community than the individual, and with preventive rather than curative procedures. In addition, along with the other emerging new professions, it shared the basic assumption that a flawed environment had caused many urban problems. As medical and social knowledge expanded, the field of public health became increasingly specialized (e.g., epidemiology, sanitation, vital statistics) and its activities were increasingly defined and integrated by the American Public Health Association (APHA). The AMA and APHA thus made similar claims to professionalism—expertise, service, and autonomy—but they differed fundamentally about the significance and responsibility of the social environment and, increasingly over the years, on the need for national health insurance, which the AMA bitterly opposed after 1920.

At the same time, social workers were confronting the consequences of poverty, immigration, and economic insecurity. With social workers, the process, if not always the results, of professionalization was much the same as with health workers. They presided over an expanding body of technical knowledge that emerged from what they considered to be scientific investigations of urban problems; they divided their field into areas of specialization (e.g., delinquency, housing, social insurance); and they organized an association to elevate their professional standards and advance their own interests.

City planning was originally concerned primarily with the "city beautiful"—with how the city looked. Only later did planners concentrate on how the city functioned and finally on the general pathology of cities. This latter interest once again led to increasing specialization (e.g., transit, zoning, housing) and brought them into intimate contact with the other new professionals in common concerns about poverty, housing, health, and congestion.

Unlike the medical profession, the new policy professions essentially followed social paths to their objectives. Whereas physicians aimed primarily at healing individuals, policy professionals dealt with social ills and therefore tended to prescribe treatment for the entire community. Indeed, one of the hallmarks of these new professionals was their insistence on the controversial idea that the rights of the community must take precedence over the rights of the individual. This commitment impelled them to identify readily with movements of liberal social reform, and, despite frequent conflicts among them, to help formulate the policies that have shaped the welfare state since the 1930s.

Medical and policy personnel continue to follow the internal dynamics of their respective professions. Medicine quickly adapts to scientific and technological change, but it is generally steadfast in preserving the one-on-one relationship between physician and patient, slow to concede much to environmentalism, and reluctant to tolerate government involvement in its affairs (which it thinks of as "interference"). The policy professions also adapt easily to science and technology, but they perceive their clientele as social aggregates, pay homage to environmental causation, and commonly seek solutions through government mediation. For all their similarities, therefore, the medical and policy professions have followed separate, and not always amicable, paths into the late twentieth century.

—Don S. Kirschner

**See also**
City Planning; Social Services; Social Welfare.
**References**
Boyer, M. Christine. *Dreaming the Rational City: The Myth of American City Planning.* Cambridge, MA: MIT Press, 1983.
Kirschner, Don S. *The Paradox of Professionalism.* Westport, CT: Greenwood Press, 1986.
Leiby, James. *A History of Social Welfare and Social Work in the United States.* New York: Columbia University Press, 1978.
Numbers, Ronald L. "The Fall and Rise of the American Medical Profession." In Nathan O. Hatch, ed., *The Professions in American History,* 51–72. Notre Dame, IN: University of Notre Dame Press, 1988.
Rosenkrantz, Barbara Gutmann. *Public Health and the State.* Cambridge, MA: Harvard University Press, 1972.

## New York, New York

New York City—the "Empire City," the "New World Metropolis," the "Modern Babylon," the "city of Giants," the "New Cosmopolis," the "Big Apple," "Gotham"—has been the dominant urban center in North America since 1800. During that time, the city and its surrounding territory attracted the largest population in the United States, and by some measures the entire world. New York's economic institutions eclipsed not only its American competitors by the early nineteenth century but also the rest of the world by 1920. The accumulation of capital in the region attracted an ever-growing population that was the most polyglot in world history. At various times, New York was the largest Irish, Jewish, Italian, and African city in the world.

The first human settlers of the New York metropolitan region migrated from Asia sometime after 25,000 B.C. By 1600, the Lenape Indians, part of the Delaware tribe and the Algonquin language family, lived on an island 12.5 miles long and 2.5 miles wide that they called "Manhatta," an Indian term for "hilly island" or "small island." Nearby, tribes of Canarsies resided in what was later called Brooklyn, Matinecooks in Flushing, Rockaways in Queens, and Weckquaeegecks (Mahican) in Yonkers.

Viking and Norse explorers probably visited the region as early as the eleventh century but left no written evidence of their journeys. In 1524, Giovanni da Verrazano became the first European known to enter New York harbor. He sailed through the narrows later named after him, looked around, and left. Nearly a century later, 1609, Henry Hudson, an English explorer-for-hire seeking a water passage to Asia for the Dutch West India Company, entered the harbor, cruised past Manhattan, and proceeded northward along the river later named after him. Hudson never found a route to Asia, and his voyage was labeled a failure. But, unlike what happened after the earlier European visitors, settlers soon followed Hudson.

In 1624, representatives of the Dutch West India Company built a fort off the tip of Manhattan (later Governor's Island). During the next two years, either Willem Verhulst or Peter Minuit "purchased" Manhattan from the Indians. Historians remain divided on the subject, but the traditional story claims that Minuit paid the Canarsies 60 florins for the island. In fact, the tribe never held title to the land, lived on Long Island, and used Manhattan only to hunt and fish. Whether Minuit bought the island or not, his enterprise, christened New Amsterdam, was imagined to be the gateway to the Dutch colony of New Netherland and a way station to the Orient. Of the earliest European settlements in North America, only Quebec (established by the French in 1608) became a significant city, making New York the oldest major city in what became the United States.

Muddy shorelines and swampy hinterlands characterized the New Amsterdam region, best witnessed by lower Manhattan, the New Jersey Meadowlands, and Jamaica Bay. Nevertheless, the settlement enjoyed a variety of geographical advantages. At the foot of the island, a huge, landlocked, deepwater harbor, protected by reefs, opened to the Atlantic. With more than 770 miles of shoreline (measuring the entire shorelines of the areas and regions that constitute the five boroughs of New York today—the Bronx, Brooklyn, Manhattan, Queens, and Staten Island), the harbor was surrounded by flatland, usually free from ice and fog, and situated at the confluence of three tributary systems—the Hudson, East, and Passaic rivers. The Hudson River was not only wide and deep, it also allowed Atlantic tidal waters to extend more than 100 miles north as far as the city of Troy. Furthermore, a geology of Manhattan schist and Fordham gneiss near the surface of the island later provided a sturdy bedrock for intensive, high-rise, skyscraper development.

However, these physical advantages did little to spur substantial growth before 1780. Indeed, uneasy relations and violent conflict between the first Dutch settlers and native inhabitants characterized New Amsterdam's early history and culminated in "Kieft's War" between 1643 and 1645. Thereafter, under the leadership of Petrus Stuyvesant, director-general from 1647 to 1664, the Dutch built a densely packed "medieval" city. Narrow, irregular streets, canals, and slips (Broad Street in lower Manhattan was originally a canal) were constructed on the southern tip of the island. Protective walls were erected at the north end of the city, first in 1635 (later removed and named Wall Street) and then, after the British takeover, just south of the Collect Pond. Open space inside the walled community permitted residents to grow crops and allowed pigs to forage.

New Amsterdam developed as a seaport, sustaining itself on Europe's growing demand for agricultural exports like timber, grain, potash, and especially furs. The seal of New Netherlands even depicted a beaver. For more than a century, a "saltwater elite" whose wealth derived from ships, wharves, warehouses, and real estate dominated the local economy. Dutch rule ended in 1664 when a British warship sailed into the harbor and demanded its surrender. The Dutch complied, and the port was renamed after James, the Duke of York and brother of King Charles II.

From its Dutch origins, New York emerged as the most heterogeneous of the original 13 British colonies. As early as 1643 the Jesuit missionary Isaac Jogues complained about the "confusion of tongues" and counted 18 different languages spoken by the 400 or 500 inhabitants of New Amsterdam. For Jogues, the community was "Babel." Outside the wall, European settlers lived in scattered settlements and farms, resisting the comparatively ordered, tight, homogeneous villages of Puritan New England. Religious differences among Anglicans, Quakers, Congregationalists, Presbyterians, Jews, Huguenots, and Catholics proved more intense than any other colonial city in the Americas. The English even delayed founding the first Anglican congregation until 1698 when they established Trinity Church.

Religious tensions, however, were never as violent as racial conflicts. In 1626, the first Africans were brought to the city, mostly as slaves. Working primarily as domestic servants and artisans, enough of them were emancipated to establish the first free black community in 1644. Between 1650 and 1750, Africans comprised 20 to 25 percent of the settlement's population, and New York was second only to Charles Town, South Carolina, in both the number of slaves and the number of slaveowners in any North American city. Unsuccessful slave "revolts" in 1712 and 1741 resulted in the execution of more than 20 slaves and their sympathizers on each occasion, including several who were burned to death. Legal slavery endured until 1827.

During the American Revolution, British troops occupied New York, supported by a large Loyalist, or Tory, population among the city's merchant class. After battles at Brooklyn Heights and Harlem (later Morningside) Heights in 1776, Revolutionary troops abandoned the region. The only American city to suffer British occupation for the entire war, New York attracted Loyalists from other colonies, briefly swelling its population to 30,000. Ironically, New York experienced more physical damage than any other city during these years because of fires in 1776 and 1778 that destroyed over half the city, including Trinity Church.

With the British departure in 1783, New York became a center of commercial innovation and economic enterprise. The population doubled in three years and stood at 33,131 in 1790, second only to Philadelphia's 42,520. In 1784, Alexander Hamilton founded the Bank of New York, the first such institution in the young republic, and speculators in securities and other risky financial instruments opened a stock exchange on Wall Street in 1792. As early as 1797, New York's total tonnage in imports and exports led the nation. By the 1820s, customs duties collected in New York were large enough to subsidize the entire operation of the federal government, excepting interest.

New York's most important "planning" decision during these years resulted from the Commissioners Plan of 1811. Previously, streets in the city were irregular and followed patterns parallel to the waterfronts on both sides of Manhattan. But in 1811, the city imposed a "grid" over the island from Houston to 155th Street. All future real estate development was controlled by 2,028 rectangular blocks separated by avenues running north-south and streets east-west. Property was sold in small, uniform, 100-foot by 25-foot lots, theoretically providing affordable housing for the city's mechanic and artisanal classes. The grid abolished all existing rights-of-way (Broadway being the major exception). The island's existing topography with its numerous hills, streams, swamps, and even farms and houses north of 14th Street was simply ignored. The grid, in the words of surveyor John Randel, facilitated "buying, selling and improving real estate on New York Island." City leaders also assumed that the scale of the city would never exceed six stories. New York thus pursued a rigid, highly ordered plan during the apogee of its growth, a dramatic visual contrast with other world cities like London, Paris, Rome, or Tokyo, all characterized by comparatively chaotic, irregular street patterns.

A variety of forces catapulted New York to national dominance in the first half of the nineteenth century. First, the Treaty of Ghent (1815) ended the War of 1812 with Great Britain. The following century of peace, during which European countries were not vying for additional territory in North America (with the major exception of France's incursion into Mexico in 1863), markedly contrasted with the many wars among colonial powers, colonists, and Native Americans during the previous 200 years. Second, New York proved more hospitable to economic innovation and new commercial elites. The adoption of an auction system in 1817 ensured a prompt discount on imported commodities, so European merchants began "dumping" goods through New York. For over two decades, auctioning offered smaller profits but stimulated business by ensuring rapid turnover and the quick sale of goods. In 1818 the Black Ball packet ships initiated the first regularly scheduled shipping line between the United States and Europe. By punctually sailing on a preordained date and time, and following a fixed route, with a full cargo or not, New York attracted the most lucrative trade, especially "fine freight" of small size and high value. The packets simultaneously generated a "triangular trade." Ships bearing cotton from the American South sailed to Europe, then to New York filled with immigrants, freight, and news, and finally returned to the South laden with American and European manufactures.

Finally, the Erie Canal (1817–1825) dramatically expanded the city's hinterland to the far western end of the Great Lakes. The brainchild of Governor DeWitt Clinton, the 40-foot-wide, 4-foot-deep, and 363-mile-long canal was the first all-water route to the American West. Derided as "Clinton's folly" or "DeWitt's ditch" by cost-conscious critics because of its $7 million price tag, the Erie Canal was one of the largest public works projects of the nineteenth century. But the enterprise generated nearly $1 million in income during its first full year of service. Most importantly, freight rates dropped from $100 per ton to $5 per ton and travel time from 20 days to 8 days between the Atlantic seaboard and the West. By 1867 the canal carried two-thirds of all American commerce, doubling that of all railroads in the country combined. Even as late as 1890 the canal's freight tonnage still equaled that of *all* railroads in the United States.

The canal made New York the continental entrepot of North America. Consider journalism and the marketing of agricultural commodities. Since products such as flour and cotton were stored along the waterfront before being transshipped to Europe, a "commission system" emerged whereby New York merchants and financial institutions advanced a large part of the purchase price to farmers and planters for several months, effectively paying for the commodity before it reached New York and literally indebting farmers to New York merchants. The same merchants then enjoyed first call on many products from the hinterland, further encouraging storekeepers across the country to replenish their stocks with New York merchandise. Similarly, New York's location between Europe and the American West made it the central place in the circulation of business, political, and journalistic information. By 1860, one-third of the nation's printers and publishers called New York home. By 1920, New York employed more people in printing and publishing than Chicago, Philadelphia, Boston, and St. Louis combined. The Erie Canal thus unified the economy of the northern United States; at the same time it stimulated development of a regional network of cities linking Europe, the Atlantic seaboard, and the Midwest in an east-west direction and generating a distinctive urban-industrial culture.

These developments gave New York unrivaled advantages that it did not lose for 150 years. From 1820 to 1960 (when it was surpassed by Rotterdam), New York remained the world's busiest port, the value of its trade usually outranking nearby Boston, Philadelphia, and Baltimore combined. By 1850, over 70 percent of the nation's imports and exports passed through New York City. This exorbitant volume of trade induced the nation's largest banks to keep reserve deposits in New York, thereby generating ever more capital accumulation.

New York's dominance of the national economy manifested itself in the city's physical development. The one-mile strip of waterfront between Delancey and 14th Streets was the nation's shipbuilding hub. Along South Street, the young republic's most successful merchants and shippers—A. A. Low, Preserved Fish, William E. Dodge, John Jacob Astor—established their offices. Pearl Street, lined with auctioneers and textile jobbers, became the dry goods center of the country. By the middle of the nineteenth century, New York's stock, produce, and cotton exchanges surpassed all national competitors. Wall Street, now a lane with plentiful banks, marine insurance companies, and attorney's offices, was equated with financial services. The 1842 Greek Revival buildings of the Merchants Exchange and the Custom House aptly symbolized the prominence of business in the city. Building the Custom House structure required demolishing historic Federal Hall where the Stamp Act Congress met, the Continental Congress debated American independence, and George Washington was inaugurated as the first president of the new republic. Later generations revered the site as sacred, hallowed ground. For antebellum New Yorkers, however, tradition and history took a backseat to trade.

The economic base of New York in the nineteenth century gradually shifted from a reliance on commerce and small-scale manufacturing by artisans to light industry. Like medieval Bruges and Venice and early modern Paris and London, textile production proved a key stimulus. Between 1850 and 1950, clothing and garment manufacturing employed 25 to 50 percent of the city's workforce. By 1925, New York produced more than one-half of the nation's clothing, not to mention 10 percent of the entire national manufacturing output. A new garment district constructed between the two world wars (from 30th to 42nd Streets between Sixth and Ninth Avenues) had the world's largest concentration of apparel manufacturing, employing more workers than Detroit's entire automobile industry in the 1940s. In contrast to the mammoth factories constructed in South Chicago, Detroit, or Pittsburgh, these "light" industries operated for a consumer market in small plants requiring little space.

New York's growing economic supremacy made it a magnet for cheap labor. As early as 1850, nearly 60 percent of Manhattan's population—a "heterogeneous compound" of humanity—had been born elsewhere. National and global forces such as famine in Ireland, agricultural consolidation in Italy, industrialization in Northern Europe, pogroms in Russia, natural population growth throughout North America, and declining economic opportunities in rural America propelled an unprecedented wave of human migration to New York. In the 50 years after 1820, New York's population (within the five boroughs of the future city) grew almost tenfold, from 152,056 in 1820 to 1,478,103 in 1870. Between 1820 and 1860, 3.7 million Europeans, roughly two-thirds of the total entering the United States, passed through New York. Whereas only 10 percent of the city's population was foreign-born in 1835, by 1860 the figure reached 47 percent, one-quarter of whom where Irish. The city's Irish and German immigrants and their children were so numerous from 1855 to 1880 that the city easily surpassed Dublin as the largest Irish city in the world; only Berlin and Vienna counted more German-speaking residents.

The explosive economic and demographic growth generated equally impressive physical development. An absence of space and transportation facilities forced real estate interests not only to construct five- or six-story factories, countinghouses, and warehouses along the riverfronts but to "manufacture" land itself. In 1795, Water Street bordered the East River. Over the next 15 years, landfill expanded the city another full block into the East River, setting South Street on the river's rim. A decade later, still another man-made block put Front Street at the water's edge. Soon, irregular docks—200- to 300-foot-long "slips"—dotted a waterfront full of barrels, boxes, and lumber, not to mention the ankle-deep mud, snow, slush, and dust.

By mid-century, landmarks like Colonnade Row on Lafayette Place (1833), Gramercy Park (1834), the Astor House (1836), Greenwood Cemetery (1836), City Prison, or "The Tombs" (1838), Trinity Church (1846), Grace Church (1846), and A. T. Stewart's Marble Emporium (1846) were completed. The Croton Water system (1842) and Central Park

(1857–1873) became models for similar public works nationwide. The country's initial cast-iron building, constructed of precast, uniform materials bolted together, appeared in 1848. Five years later Elijah Gray Otis displayed the first elevator or "safety hoister" at the Crystal Palace (1853), and in 1857 the Haughwout Building became the nation's first edifice to incorporate both innovations.

The multiplying population produced a new housing form—"tenant houses" or "tenements." After 1830, renting became the common form of housing for over 80 percent of New Yorkers. Initially, single-family row houses were converted to "double" tenements, followed by "railroad" tenements and finally "dumbbell" tenements from 1879 to 1901. The latter was shaped like a dumbbell; the 28-inch indentations on each side extended about 50 feet in length and supposedly provided a 5-foot well for light, air, and ventilation when two of these buildings were placed next to each other. Tenements covered 90 percent of their lots (in contrast to row houses, which only occupied about 50 percent), went up six stories, contained about 25 small units, and sheltered as many as 300 people. In other North American cities, housing rarely exceeded three stories in height and was spread over larger areas. Few tenements included bathing facilities; most had one water closet per floor. The unsanitary conditions generated contagious diseases; in some years in the 1850s, deaths in the city exceeded births. By 1865, over 55 percent of the city's residents lived in tenements. The 82,000 tenements in 1900 housed two-thirds of New York's inhabitants, "packed together like herrings in a barrel."

These tenements enabled Manhattan to become the most intensely developed piece of American real estate, making New York the most densely populated city in the history of the world. By 1894, New York had a density of 143 people per acre south of 110th Street, surpassing Paris, in second place, at 125 per acre. The Eleventh Ward of Lower Manhattan had 986 people in each of its 32 acres, a figure overwhelming the most densely populated slums of Asia (Bombay at 760 per acre in 1881) and Europe (Prague at 485 per acre in the 1890s). The densities became even more astounding. In 1905, 30 blocks in Manhattan had densities greater than 1,000 per acre, and parts of the Lower East Side averaged 967. In the Bronx, 3 blocks accommodated over 600 people per acre. Even when Manhattan's density declined to 162 people per acre in the 1920s, it still remained two and one-half times that of London. By then, the New York region contained 10 percent of the total population of the United States. As late as 1950, when Los Angeles averaged 4,391 residents per square mile and Chicago 16,165, Manhattan counted a staggering 86,730, with an average of 26,395 for the entire city.

Well into the twentieth century, the majority of this human conglomeration remained the foreign-born and their offspring. Between 1880 and 1920, 17 million of the 23 million immigrants who entered the United States disembarked in New York. The largest groups were East European Jews and Italians. By 1910, more than 1 million Jews comprised 25 percent of New York's population and made it the world's largest Jewish city. Not far behind were Italian immigrants and their children. Exceeding 800,000 by 1920, New York had more Italians than any city in Italy.

New York's African-American population also experienced a resurgence. After declining from 25 percent in the colonial era to less than 2 percent by the 1860s (only 10,000 in 1865), there were 90,000 blacks in 1910. By 1930, that figure had more than tripled to 327,706, nearly 5 percent of the total population of the United States. Two-thirds of New York's African Americans lived in Harlem, making it, in James Weldon Johnson's words, "the recognized Negro capital" of the world.

Overcrowded tenements, massive in-migration, and sweatshops produced vibrant labor union and reform movements. Since clothing workers dominated the industrial workforce, the International Ladies Garment Workers Union (1900) and the Amalgamated Clothing Workers Union (1914) were among the most powerful unions in the country, the former having a membership of more than 200,000 in 1935. In 1914, the United Hebrew Trades represented more than 100 local unions with a membership exceeding 250,000 workers. Two years later, 464,000 of New York's 1.4 million workers had joined the American Federation of Labor. Some of the nation's first settlement houses appeared with the University Settlement (1886), the College Settlement (1889), and the Henry Street Settlement (1893), their volunteers working to improve conditions through housing reform, public health services, kindergartens, summer camps, and playgrounds.

The poor, crowded living conditions endured by the majority of New Yorkers never hindered the city's phenomenal growth. In the half-century after 1895, New York emerged as the dominant city in the world. In 1898, a political consolidation united Manhattan, the Bronx (earlier portions were annexed in 1874 and 1895), Brooklyn, Queens, and Staten Island into a single political and governmental unit. Overnight, New York grew to 299 square miles. Greater New York remained the national headquarters for the new, modern business organization, the corporation. Of the 185 largest industrial combinations in the United States, 69 had their headquarters in New York. The city had 298 mercantile and manufacturing enterprises valued at more than $1 million— more than Chicago, Philadelphia, Boston, San Francisco, Baltimore, and St. Louis combined. By 1900, the total deposits in New York banks equaled those in the rest of the United States. Wall Street investment banking firms became a national institution, due in large part to service bankers like J. Pierpont

Morgan, Sr., James Stillman, George Baker, and Jacob Schiff as they pioneered new financial instruments. The metropolitan region boasted over 1,500 millionaires, 45 percent of the total in the United States. For the first third of the century, New York continued to hold on to one-fourth of the entire wholesale business and nearly one-fifth of the hotel receipts in the country. By every important measure—from population to density to industrial output to bank deposits to wholesale trade—New York ranked first in the country. And unlike other world cities such as London, Paris, Berlin, Tokyo, or Vienna, New York was not a national or even a state capital.

Midway through the twentieth century, New York remained simultaneously the world's richest city, busiest port, and most populous metropolitan area. Over 1,200 corporations with $1 million in assets called New York home, including 136 of the 500 largest industrial corporations, 11 of the 50 largest banks, 19 of the 50 largest merchandising firms, 13 of the 50 largest utilities, and the seven largest insurance companies in the nation. Of the 70 corporations with at least $1 billion in assets, 29 were in New York; the rest had branch offices there. Without exaggeration, New York was "the capital of capitalism." The location of the United Nations (1947) in New York made Gotham and the surrounding 40 million-person "megalopolis" the symbolic capital of the world.

This vast influx of capital and people found form in tall buildings. As early as 1915, the Equitable Building had a daytime population of 16,000, larger than most American towns. At various times, the world's tallest building was in New York: the Park Row Building (1899), the Singer Tower (1908), the Metropolitan Life Tower (1909), the Woolworth Building (1913), the Chrysler Building (1931), the Empire State Building (1931), and the World Trade Center (1974). By 1930, 188 of the 377 American buildings over 200 feet in height were on Manhattan Island. As late as 1974, New York had as many 60-story buildings as the rest of the world combined and twice as much office floor space as any other central business district on earth.

Similarly, New York's bridges and tunnels were the engineering marvels of their age. Upon completion, the Brooklyn Bridge (1883), the Williamsburg Bridge (1903), the George Washington Bridge (1931), and the Verrazano-Narrows Bridge (1964) were the world's longest suspension bridges. The Holland Tunnel (1927) was the world's longest underwater passage. The Bayonne Bridge (1931) was the world's largest arch span bridge. Their prodigious size accentuated the immense scale of the region's waterways even if none of them possessed the quaint charm of the Pont Neuf in Paris, the Ponte Vecchio in Florence, or Tower Bridge in London.

Tall buildings, long bridges, and deep tunnels told only part of the story. The New York region witnessed a variety of architectural and urban patterns in their most sophisticated, advanced, and numerous form: the garden city (Forest Hills Garden in 1913 and Radburn, New Jersey, in 1927), the garden apartment (developed by Andrew Thomas in the 1920s), the cooperative apartment (Amalgamated Houses in the Bronx in 1927), the superblock (Rockefeller Center in 1935), the postwar suburb (Levittown in 1947), even the warehouse (Brooklyn's Army Supply Base in 1919). Municipal leaders and planners experimented with the first housing and building codes (the Tenement House Act of 1901 and the Multiple Dwellings Law of 1929), the high-rise housing complex (Parkchester in the Bronx, 1938–1942), the comprehensive zoning law (1916 and 1961), the fair housing law (1944), the limited-access highway (Bronx River Parkway in 1912–1925), the urban highway (Henry Hudson Parkway in 1934), and the city planning commission (1936). After erecting the initial public housing project in the nation (First Houses in 1935), New York proceeded to construct public housing on an unmatched scale. In less than five decades, the municipality built nearly 180,000 apartments in 330 projects and provided shelter for 600,000 New Yorkers, more than the total populations of Boston and Cleveland in 1980. By 1970, New York managed 18 municipal hospitals; Chicago and Los Angeles had one each. The city bureaucracy of 300,000 was the country's most extensive. The City University of New York was the nation's largest municipal university and the third largest overall. Taken together, the number and scale of New York's public and private services were unmatched anywhere in the United States. New York was, in the words of the architect Le Corbusier, "the jewel in the crown of universal cities."

The metropolitan region experienced another dramatic spatial reconfiguration after 1900. After peaking in 1910 at 2.3 million, Manhattan's population steadily declined during the remainder of the century, to 1.4 million in 1990. By contrast, the outer boroughs experienced a demographic explosion. In 1890, the Bronx was a bucolic, semirural county of 89,000 inhabitants. By 1940, it was a mixed, densely populated commuter zone of 1.4 million. Similarly, Queens was reputedly the fastest-growing community in the world by the 1920s, jumping from less than 90,000 in 1890 to nearly 1.3 million in 1940. By 1925, Brooklyn had replaced Manhattan as the most populous borough, passing the 2 million mark and eventually peaking at more than 2.7 million in 1960. In 1970, with nearly 2 million people, Queens held a quarter of the city's people.

The dispersion of New York's population was aided and abetted by new transit systems. In 1904, New York inaugurated the world's first subway system with fully integrated express and local lines. By 1920, New York's 202 route-miles of subways and els surpassed the lengths in London (157), Chicago (71), Paris (59), Boston (22), and Berlin (22). When completed, the 722 miles of subway lines, enough to stretch from New York to Chicago, was the longest in the world. By 1940, the combined system of steam railroads, elevated and underground rapid transit lines, and electric streetcars was the prototypical public transportation system of the world. Measured by riders in number or per capita, route mileage, track mileage, and capital investment, it was second to none. At the end of the twentieth century, New York's subways carried 46 percent of all New Yorkers to work daily and accounted for 11 percent of all mass transit passengers nationwide.

Traffic congestion generated a new political entity—the authority—to facilitate the movement of goods and people throughout the region. In order to build and operate transit, water, and harbor systems efficiently, the Port Authority of New York and New Jersey (1921), the Triborough Bridge Authority (1933), New York City Transit Authority (1953), and the Metropolitan Transit Authority (1968) were created. Together, they assumed responsibility for building or operating the Holland and Lincoln Tunnels, the George Washington Bridge (1931), the Triborough Bridge complex (1936), La Guardia Airport (1939), the Verrazano-Narrows Bridge (1964), the World Trade Center (1974), Port Elizabeth, the subway, and commuter railroad lines.

The leading figure in the ascendancy of the authority and the physical growth of the city was Robert Moses. Between 1924 and 1968, Moses held as many as 12 municipal and state positions simultaneously, including the city's parks commissioner, construction coordinator, and chairman of the Triborough Bridge and Tunnel Authority. Acting on behalf of developers, planners who advocated deconcentration, and middle- and working-class New Yorkers seeking affordable, subsidized housing, Moses improved 3,522 hectares of parks, increased neighborhood playgrounds from 119 to 374, planted over 2 million trees, opened Jones Beach and Orchard Beach, and built nearly every highway, bridge, and public housing project in the area. New York's arterial highway system was eventually copied throughout the United States. Moses oversaw the construction of Lincoln Center for the Performing Arts, Shea Stadium, the Coliseum, the United Nations, Co-op City, and the World's Fairs of 1939 and 1964. The $27 billion he spent on these and other projects convinced even his severest critic, Lewis Mumford, that "in the twentieth century, the influence of Robert Moses on the cities of America was greater than that of any other person."

Improved transit systems, highway construction, federally insured mortgage insurance, and the mortgage interest deduction on personal income taxes gave birth to another wave of massive suburbanization. Between 1940 and 1970, 2.5 million (mostly white) New Yorkers migrated to suburbs, allowing Nassau and Suffolk counties to quadruple their populations. The most affluent migrated to the lush, tree-lined streets of Bronxville and Scarsdale in Westchester County,

Greenwich and New Canaan in Connecticut, Short Hills and Morristown in New Jersey, and the North Shore of Long Island. The city's Jewish population alone dropped from 2.1 million at its height in 1957 to 1 million by 1981. At the same time, the new suburbanites were replaced by migrants from Puerto Rico and African Americans from the South. In 1957, New York became the first city in the world with over 1 million residents of African descent.

The demographic decline barely affected New York's economic fortunes. In 1960, New York had 25 percent of the 500 largest corporate headquarters in the United States, while 69 percent of the rest at least had sales offices in New York. New York was still home to six of the world's ten largest banks. By some measures, New York enjoyed the greatest concentration of manufacturing jobs the world had ever known, making Brillo soap pads, Kirkman's laundry soap, Eberhard-Faber pencils, Topp's chewing gum, Rockwell chocolate bars, even leis eventually sold in Hawaii. By 1970 the 20 million residents of the metropolitan region made it the largest in the world, comprising 10 percent of the total U.S. population. The 8 million city residents were as many as Chicago, Los Angeles, Houston, and Pittsburgh combined. Mayor Robert F. Wagner proclaimed that New Yorkers "make more, sell more, buy more, eat more, and enjoy more than the citizens of any other city in the world." He was right.

Yet, dramatic global changes at that very moment were weakening New York's economic fortunes. Between 1950 and 1990, New York lost nearly 70 percent of its manufacturing jobs. Whereas the five boroughs employed nearly 1.1 million blue-collar workers (out of its total population of 6 million) in 1950, 40 years later only 315,000 blue-collar jobs existed for 7 million residents. Although state, municipal, and federal governments added 200,000 employees, another 250,000 jobs in wholesale and retail trade left New York. The major areas of occupational growth were 500,000 new jobs in nongovernment services, one-third of which were in finance, real estate, and insurance. Even here, however, the record was mixed. From 1988 to 1995, 43,000 banking industry jobs, 36 percent of those in the city, disappeared. Some left New York, and others were "downsized" out of existence.

After 1955, New York was plagued by perpetual "urban crises"—growing fiscal indebtedness, a declining tax base due to "white flight" and industrial deconcentration, an increasing demand for city services, rising welfare rolls, deteriorating infrastructure, and ever greater disparity between rich and poor. By 1964, 20 percent of New Yorkers lived in poverty, a figure that changed little over the next three decades. In 1975, the municipality nearly went bankrupt before New York State intervened. Nevertheless, the municipal debt reached $22.5 billion in 1992, forcing annual payments of $2.5 billion, or $300 per citizen. Destitution echoed that found among the

Irish population 150 years earlier or the Italians in 1890, best symbolized by the shorter life expectancy for black males in Harlem than adult men in Bangladesh.

Brooklyn experienced the most severe hits. The Brooklyn Navy Yard, which had opened in 1801 and remained the largest in the nation for most of its history, employing 70,000 at its height during World War II, closed in 1966. The Brooklyn docks fell victim to the modernization and containerization of competitors in New Jersey. Breweries, which numbered 132 in 1940, had vanished by 1976. The *Brooklyn Eagle,* where Walt Whitman once worked, ceased publication in 1955. Three years later, the baseball Dodgers did the unthinkable—they moved to Los Angeles.

New York's transformation from an industrial city to a service-oriented metropolis coincided with a dramatic demographic metamorphosis. Whereas the descendants of European immigrants accounted for almost 95 percent of New Yorkers in 1940, by 1990 they constituted less than 50 percent. After dropping from 34 percent to 18 percent between 1930 and 1970, the foreign-born population rose to 33 percent by 1995. More than ever before, these immigrants were an ethnic and racial kaleidoscope, a "magic cauldron" of polyglot communities. While most originated in the Caribbean, Asia, and the Middle East, over 150 countries were represented annually among the city's legal newcomers. In 1990, for the first time in New York's history, no single racial or ethnic group constituted a majority. New York had become the most ethnically and racially diverse city in world history.

Portents of doom have a rich history in New York; critics have long thought it a dying city. Alexis de Tocqueville predicted armed uprisings. Mark Twain complained that it was simply "too large." Rudyard Kipling described New York as a "long, narrow pig-trough." Since 1800, jammed-together buildings, unbearable congestion, overcrowded housing, out-of-sight taxes, maldistributed wealth, violent street crime, and epidemic disease have convinced soothsayers in every generation that the Empire City's reign was disintegrating. They were always wrong. More apt was E. B. White. Manhattan, he wrote in 1949, is a "poem whose magic is comprehensive to millions of permanent residents but whose full meaning will always remain elusive."

—*Timothy J. Gilfoyle*

**See also**

Beame, Abraham David; Bowery; Broadacre City; Chrysler Building; Coney Island; Dinkins, David N.; Dumbbell Tenement; Empire State Building; Erie Canal; Greenwich Village; Harlem; Hempstead, New York; Henry Street Settlement; Koch, Edward Irving; La Guardia, Fiorello; Levittown; Lincoln Center for the Performing Arts; Moses, Robert; Regional Plan of New York and Its Environs; Rockefeller Center; Scarsdale, New York; Smith, Alfred E.; Tammany Hall; Tin Pan Alley; Veiller, Lawrence Turnure.

**References**

Albion, Robert Greenhalgh. *The Rise of New York Port, 1815–1860.* New York: Scribners, 1939.

Bender, Thomas. *New York Intellect: A History of Intellectual Life in New York City, from 1750 to the Beginning of Our Own Time.* New York: Knopf, 1987.

Binder, Frederick M., and David M. Reimers. *All the Nations under Heaven: An Ethnic and Racial History of New York City.* New York: Columbia University Press, 1995.

Caro, Robert. *The Power Broker: Robert Moses and the Rise and Fall of New York.* New York: Knopf, 1974.

Gottman, Jean. *Megalopolis: The Urbanized Northeastern Seaboard of the United States.* Cambridge, MA: MIT Press, 1961.

Jackson, Kenneth T. "The Capital of Capitalism: The New York Metropolitan Region, 1890–1940." In Anthony Sutcliffe, ed., *Metropolis, 1890–1940.* London: Mansell, 1984.

Kessner, Thomas. *Fiorello H. La Guardia and the Making of Modern New York.* New York: McGraw-Hill, 1989.

Kouwenhoven, John A. *The Columbia Historical Portrait of New York.* New York: Columbia University Press, 1953.

McNickle, Chris. *To Be Mayor of New York: Ethnic Politics in the City.* New York: Columbia University Press, 1993.

Plunz, Richard. *A History of Housing in New York City: Dwelling Type and Social Change in the American Metropolis.* New York: Columbia University Press, 1989.

Regional Plan Association. *The Regional Plan of New York and Its Environs.* 10 vols. New York: Regional Plan Association, 1929.

Stern, Robert A. M., Gregory Gilmartin, and John Massengale. *New York 1900: Metropolitan Architecture and Urbanism, 1890–1915.* New York: Rizzoli, 1983.

Stern, Robert A. M., Gregory Gilmartin, and Thomas Mellins. *New York 1930: Architecture and Urbanism between the Two World Wars.* New York: Rizzoli, 1987.

Stern, Robert A. M., Thomas Mellins, and David Fishman. *New York 1960: Architecture and Urbanism between the Second World War and the Bicentennial.* New York: Monacelli Press, 1995.

Still, Bayrd, ed. *Mirror for Gotham: New York as Seen by Contemporaries from Dutch Days to the Present.* New York: New York University Press, 1956.

Stokes, I. N. Phelps. *The Iconography of Manhattan Island, 1498–1909.* 5 vols. New York: Robert H. Dodd, 1915–1928.

White, E. B. *Here Is New York.* New York: Harper & Row, 1949.

# Newspapers

For 300 years, the newspaper has been part of the American city, but the city has not always been part of the newspaper. Only gradually did newspapers discover that the city that provided their readers and revenue could also provide their news. The history of the American newspaper, then, is in part an urban history, a history of discovering, building, and finally reimagining the city.

The American newspaper was born in Boston, the largest city in England's American colonies in the late seventeenth century. The first newspaper, suppressed after one issue, was *Publick Occurrences* (1690). The first successful newspaper was the *Boston News-Letter* (1704), and it set the pattern for those that followed in Boston, Philadelphia, and New York. Modeled on the *London Gazette,* the *News-Letter* linked local political and mercantile elites with the outside world of European politics, trade, and war. A few items of local news appeared in these early papers: ship arrivals, government proclamations, the odd news item on disease, fire, or accident. But most news came from abroad. As political and business enterprises, the first American newspapers were rooted in their cities, but their gaze was outward.

Gradually the city impinged upon the newspaper. In Boston, controversy over smallpox inoculation erupted in the city's three newspapers in 1721. In Philadelphia, Benjamin Franklin occasionally used the *Pennsylvania Gazette,* which he took over in 1729, to call for action on his favorite city causes: charity, fire control, and a hospital. After the Revolution, American newspapers increasingly carried items on local civic events, as well as local shipping notices and advertisements. Philadelphia papers devoted 11 percent of their space to local news in 1781 and 23 percent in the 1790s. By the 1820s newspapers carried a daily flow of news on the activities of local governments and voluntary associations. In the 1810s and 1820s, for example, the *New York Evening Post* carried discussions of poor relief, sewage disposal, streets, ferries, parks, and water supply. Still, what defined a great metropolitan newspaper in the 1820s—a paper like the *New York Courier and Enquirer*—was the most recent, most dependable, most copious news—from elsewhere.

As newspapers spread westward, the pattern persisted. For any frontier village that aspired to be a city, a newspaper was essential. And the newspaper business grew rapidly in the trans-Appalachian West. The first western papers were founded at Pittsburgh (1786), Lexington (1787), and Cincinnati (1793). Quickly, newspapers flowered everywhere. By the 1830s, the United States had some 900 newspapers (mainly weeklies), twice as many as Great Britain, its nearest rival. Though these newspapers served as political, economic, and cultural focal points for their communities, they still imported the bulk of their news from the East Coast and abroad.

Then, in the 1830s and 1840s, some newspapers in eastern cities began to look inside their own cities for a much wider variety of news. Led by the *New York Sun* (1833) and the *New York Herald* (1835), these new "penny papers" learned to pry news from corners of the city that had been overlooked before: the churches, the sporting and social clubs, the police stations, the criminal courts, the avenues and alleys, and mansions and hovels of the metropolis. In the penny press, the city itself became news, and urban readers became gawkers at an endlessly fascinating, and often appalling, urban spectacle.

The newspaper grew into an immensely popular urban institution in mid-nineteenth-century America. Between 1850 and 1880, the number of daily newspapers grew 300 percent, from 254 to 971; circulation grew more than 400 percent. The greatest growth occurred in the major cities. By the end of the 1870s, New York had 29 daily papers, and these papers circulated one copy a day for every 1.58 people in the city. Philadelphia had 24 dailies, Chicago 18, and Boston 11. Newspapers and periodicals in the ten largest cities in the late 1870s were turning out more than 1 billion copies a year. Each copy was growing fatter as well. The typical metropolitan newspaper set a lavish smorgasbord of local news for its readers. Indeed, the complexity, diversity, and disorder of the modern city was mirrored in the miscellaneous nature of the news. The *Chicago Times,* for example, carried as many as a thousand items of news every day, many of them one-sentence bits jumbled together into long columns of tiny print. This journalistic principle of "infinite variety," as *Times* proprietor Wilbur Storey called it, seemed well suited to the heterogeneity of modern urban life.

At the same time, a new approach to urban journalism was beginning to emerge in the industrial cities of the Midwest, led by the *Detroit Evening News* (1873), the *Chicago Daily News* (1875), and the *St. Louis Post-Dispatch* (1878). This second wave of small, popular dailies was similar to the penny press of the 1830s, but with a difference. These new urban papers treated the city less as a bizarre spectacle and more as an organic, interdependent community. They sought collective action, including expanded government, to confront

*It was common for young boys, "newsboys," to sell papers on city streets in the early twentieth century.*

the social chaos of the city. In news coverage, they emphasized a few prominently played, continuing stories that would focus the attention of all readers in the city. Melville Stone's *Chicago Daily News,* for example, called not only for voluntary collective action and government reform but also for increased government action, including utility regulation, large-scale public works, and expanded human services. In a remarkable editorial in 1876, the *Daily News* even called on the city to provide a job for every person who needed one. The community owed its least-fortunate members help in time of need, the newspaper argued, for their misfortune was the community's misfortune as well.

The great exemplar of this kind of activist urban journalism was Joseph Pulitzer's *New York World* (1883). Pulitzer tried to achieve popularity and influence through both diversity and commonality. Like the *Chicago Times,* the *World* appealed to a heterogeneous audience with "infinite variety." Like the *Chicago Daily News,* the *World* sought to build the city as well as to reveal it. Pulitzer made the *World* a voice for public works, for active government, and for the collective life of the city.

Pulitzer's blend of news smorgasbord yet common core remained the standard style of urban newspaper journalism throughout most of the twentieth century. Local news, in its infinite variety, was prime. Yet newspapers also sought to focus upon common, unifying themes that would tie their diverse readers and their fragmented cities together. Even politically conservative publishers who hated federal government activism routinely promoted major public works and active government at the local level.

In the years after World War II, urban newspapers faced a new form of metropolitan heterogeneity as advertisers and readers fled to the suburbs. Many papers responded to this challenge with more heterogeneity of their own. Some joined the rush to the suburbs, with special zoned editions for different suburban areas. Many dailies died, despite desperate efforts to reimagine their audiences. The successful ones remembered Pulitzer. They learned to serve up a smorgasbord of new suburban news, but they also remembered that the center city was a crucial common denominator; indeed, it was all that their suburban readers had in common. Through the pages of the *Chicago Tribune* or the *Philadelphia Inquirer,* residents of Schaumburg or Lansdale could still "live" in Chicago or Philadelphia, though they never set foot in the city.

For the newspaper and its readers, the city has become a vital, if imaginary, symbolic center, a place of professional sports teams, downtown convention centers, tourist restaurants, summer festivals, and refurbished waterfront promenades. Thus has the urban history of American journalism come full circle. While once the newspaper reported to city people news from elsewhere, now the paper reports city news to people from elsewhere.

—*David Paul Nord*

**See also**
Hearst, William Randolph; Pulitzer, Joseph; Riis, Jacob August; Yellow Journalism.
**References**
Baldasty, Gerald J. *The Commercialization of News in the Nineteenth Century.* Madison: University of Wisconsin Press, 1992.
Baughman, James L. *The Republic of Mass Culture: Journalism, Filmmaking, and Broadcasting in America since 1941.* Baltimore: Johns Hopkins University Press, 1992.
Clark, Charles E. *The Public Prints: The Newspaper in Anglo-American Culture, 1665–1740.* New York: Oxford University Press, 1994.
Clark, Charles E., et al. *Three Hundred Years of the American Newspaper.* Worcester, MA: American Antiquarian Society, 1991.
Griffith, Sally Foreman. *Home Town News: William Allen White and the Emporia Gazette.* New York: Oxford University Press, 1989.
Juergens, George. *Joseph Pulitzer and the New York World.* Princeton, NJ: Princeton University Press, 1966.
Kaniss, Phyllis C. *Making Local News.* Chicago: University of Chicago Press, 1991.
Nord, David Paul. *Newspapers and New Politics: Midwestern Municipal Reform, 1890–1900.* Ann Arbor, MI: UMI Research Press, 1981.
Schudson, Michael. *Discovering the News: A Social History of American Newspapers.* New York: Basic Books, 1978.
Steele, Janet E. *The Sun Shines for All: Journalism and Ideology in the Life of Charles A. Dana.* Syracuse, NY: Syracuse University Press, 1993.

# Nicholson, Francis (1655–1728)

Francis Nicholson, the country's first great patron of architecture, landscape design, and town planning, designed Annapolis, Maryland, in 1694 and Williamsburg, Virginia, in 1699, and he set the stage for the founding of Manakintown, Virginia, and Darien, Georgia.

Born in 1655 at Downholme Park near Richmond, Yorkshire, in England, he received some education and in his youth was page to Mary Paulet, wife of Charles Paulet, Lord St. John of Basing, later Marquis of Winchester. In 1678, he was commissioned an ensign in the King's Holland Regiment and served at Nieuport, Flanders. Reassigned to the 2nd Tangier Regiment in 1680, he was promoted to lieutenant and sent to Morocco. From 1682 to 1684, as a courier, he made at least three overland trips between Morocco and England. His travels took him to Cadiz, Toledo, Madrid, and Paris and exposed him to varieties of architecture and town planning. Among his other posts, Nicholson was lieutenant governor of Maryland from 1693 to 1698 and governor of Virginia from 1698 to 1705, and in those colonies he designed the new capital cities of Annapolis and Williamsburg, respectively.

Probably inspired by plans for the rebuilding of London in 1666, Nicholson brought baroque planning principles to North America with his plans for Annapolis and Williamsburg. Indeed, the awkward placement of Annapolis's baroque elements, the way its radiating avenues intersect with two squares and two circles off-center, suggests the hand of an ambitious amateur. Public Circle, meant to be the location of state buildings, and Church Circle, designated for those of the church, are linked only by one very short street, School Street; the symbolic isolation of two buildings that epitomize church and state indicates Nicholson's thought. The plan also included a market square and a residential square, Bloomsbury Square, modeled on those of London but new to the colonies. Annapolis, as a name, speaks again to Nicholson's penchant for classical allusions and is the first American town designated a "polis." In 1699 Maryland clergyman Hugh Jones wrote that "Governour Nicholson hath done his endeavour to make a towne . . . [H]ad Governour Nicholson continued there some years longer he had brought it to some perfection."

After Nicholson became governor of Virginia, legislation was approved on June 7, 1699, to move the government of the colony from Jamestown to a new site called "Williamsburgh" in honor of the king. Only one broad street, 100 feet wide, is shown on Theodorick Bland's survey. Known as the Duke of Gloucester Street, it links the College of William and Mary, whose charter of 1693 owed much to Nicholson, and the new statehouse. Once again influenced by the classical world of ancient Greece and Rome, Nicholson, inspired by the Temple of Jupiter Capitolinus in Rome where the senate met, caused the statehouse to be renamed "The Capitoll" in 1699, the first known use of this term. The first surviving survey shows no other streets, but several contemporary sources stated that Nicholson used various streets to lay out divers "W" and "M" ciphers, intended to celebrate both the monarchs and the college. The specific configuration of these streets remains speculation. It is also likely that Market Square and Palace Green were part of Nicholson's original plan, since a house for the governor was authorized in 1701.

Nicholson's penchant for using ancient Roman ideas in his designs is unmistakable in the plan of Williamsburg. The town resembles a Roman *castrum,* or army camp; Duke of Gloucester Street serves as the *decumanus* and North and South England Streets as the *cardo,* with Market Square in the position of a forum and the powder magazine functioning as a *praetorium.*

In 1700 Nicholson also selected the site for the extinct community of Manakintown, Virginia, a town established for Huguenot refugees. Its plan has been attributed to William Byrd, and featured a large square named in honor of Nicholson. Appointed governor of Nova Scotia in 1713, Nicholson renamed its capital Annapolis Royal, and received credit for improving its defensive fortification, Fort St. Anne. Later, as governor of South Carolina, he sought to embellish Charleston by resurveying its lots and streets. He also over-

saw the layout of a fort and town on the Altamaha River in what became Darien, Georgia; it had 200 half-acre lots and 600 acres of "Common ground . . . to build the town upon." He saw Fort King George built there in 1725.

But it was Nicholson's key role in the creation of Williamsburg and its earliest public buildings and gardens that are his greatest urban legacy. Williamsburg is the first truly American town built in the colonies. The two major public buildings in Annapolis, the statehouse and the church, both represented and housed traditional institutions brought from Europe. But in Williamsburg, buildings that housed more American interests—the capitol, college, market square, and powder magazine—were as prominent as those representing the British monarchy (the governor's palace and the church).

Nicholson's Williamsburg also held great portents for later architecture and town planning in the United States. Washington, D.C., dominated by the Capitol, is not only located between Annapolis and Williamsburg but in many ways is a composite of their plans, and the specific location of its major buildings relied on the example of the two tidewater towns. George Washington called L'Enfant's attention to Annapolis, and Jefferson, who constantly communicated with L'Enfant, knew Williamsburg well. Under Nicholson between 1699 and 1705, architecture, landscape design, and town planning first emerged as fine arts in what became the United States.

—*James D. Kornwolf*

### References
Kornwolf, James D. " 'Doing Good to Posterity,' Francis Nicholson, First Patron of Architecture, Landscape Design, and Town Planning in Virginia, Maryland, and South Carolina, 1688–1725." *Virginia Magazine of History and Biography* 101 (1992): 333–374.
Reps, John W. *Tidewater Towns: City Planning in Colonial Virginia and Maryland.* Williamsburg, VA: Colonial Williamsburg Foundation, 1972.

## Nickelodeons

Nickelodeons were primitive movie theaters established in American cities by 1905 and took their name from the 5-cent admission fee. Before 1905, motion pictures were usually shown as a cheap novelty in vaudeville theaters before the stage acts. Gradually, small storefront nickelodeons appeared in New York City, Chicago, Boston, and other large cities. For a nickel, 100 to 200 patrons could view five or six short black-and-white silent movies, usually a comedy, a melodrama, an adventure, and a chase or travelogue. These quickly made shorts were generally between 10 and 30 minutes long.

Some nickelodeon entrepreneurs, like William Fox and Marcus Loew, recognized the enormous profits these small movie houses could produce. By 1908, more than 10 million

Americans paid nickels and dimes each week to see a series of short movies. Most patrons were urban children, often working-class immigrants eager for inexpensive and convenient entertainment. The topics varied, required no literacy, and provided views of America that most city people had never seen.

From 1908 to 1913, D. W. Griffith made more than 400 "shorts" for the nickelodeon circuit. As he learned the craft, he experimented with new film techniques, such as panoramas, close-ups, visual symbolism, and new lighting methods. As owners of nickelodeons accumulated sufficient capital, they established movie studios that produced films to satisfy the expanding American appetite for motion pictures.

Before then, no film made in America was longer than 30 minutes, and most were shorter. And then, a New York furrier and amusement arcade entrepreneur, Adolph Zukor, made a one-hour French film, "Queen Elizabeth," starring Sarah Bernhardt. It was successful with middle-class audiences, so Zukor hired Edwin Porter to make similar feature movies with American actors, such as "The Count of Monte Cristo" with James O'Neill.

Griffith's controversial masterpiece, "The Birth of a Nation" (1915), a three-hour epic of the Civil War and Reconstruction Era, marked the end of nickelodeons. The full-length feature movie made the short film program obsolete. World War I curtailed the European movie industry, giving American movie producers time and opportunities for technical innovation, consolidation, and commercial growth. The feature film and the sound picture made movie theaters more expensive to operate by 1929, but a few nickelodeons continued to serve small towns until the 1930s. Nickelodeons did, however, introduce millions of Americans to the downtown cinema as a new form of mass entertainment, and they created the Hollywood film industry.

—*Peter C. Holloran*

### References

Bowers, Q. David. *Nickelodeon Theatres and Their Music.* Vestal, NY: Vestal Press, 1986.
Gabler, Neal. *An Empire of Their Own: How the Jews Invented Hollywood.* New York: Crown, 1988.
Harpole, Charles. *History of the American Cinema.* New York: Scribners, 1990.

## Nixon Administration: Urban Policy

The platform on which Richard Nixon ran for the presidency in 1968 promised that his administration would enlist the public and private sectors in a "vigorous effort" to meet "the crisis of the cities." Urban interests were highly encouraged when one of Nixon's first acts as president was to establish an Urban Affairs Council to (in Nixon's words) "advise and assist . . . in the development of a national urban policy." The president asked Daniel P. Moynihan, then a well-known Democratic academic, to be his counselor on urban affairs.

Moynihan soon produced a ten-point proposal for a national urban policy, calling for vigorous federal action to assist "the transformation of the urban lower class into a stable community." Although Nixon embraced Moynihan's plan at first, it soon became evident that federal activism on behalf of central cities ran counter to Republican political interests and ideology. Nixon had won only 12 percent of the black vote in 1968 and thus had no political incentive to craft a program benefiting central city minorities. Furthermore, the notion of federal activism was anathema to a party committed to solving public problems by using the private sector and to devolving federal responsibilities to state and local governments. The only substantial idea to develop from the Moynihan effort was Nixon's attempt to reform welfare, the Family Assistance Plan, which called for a guaranteed minimum income. After passage in the House of Representatives, however, it died in the Senate.

Although the Nixon administration declined finally to develop a comprehensive urban policy, cities were nevertheless deeply affected by Nixon's commitment to devolution, known as the New Federalism. The fundamental idea underlying the New Federalism was to dismantle the hundreds of national categorical grant programs designed by Congress and implemented during the Great Society years of the Johnson administration (1964–1968). Responsibility and some resources would be turned over to state and local governments, which, it was argued, knew better how to solve their problems than Washington. Nixon, who faced a Congress controlled by Democrats, spoke often of "returning power to the people." State and local officials of both political parties favored the idea.

The New Federalism agenda produced two major initiatives affecting urban governments. One was general revenue sharing (the 1972 State and Local Fiscal Assistance Act), which annually returned $5 billion in federal revenues to approximately 30,000 general-purpose local governments and the states. The rationale for revenue sharing was to use the superior tax-raising capabilities of the federal government to offset chronic state and local fiscal problems and at the same time provide a high degree of local discretion in spending that money. There were virtually no strings attached to shared revenues. The state portion of the program was terminated in 1980; local revenue sharing ended in 1986.

The second initiative involved a proposal to consolidate 129 separate categorical grant programs into six broad functional block grants, which Nixon called "special revenue sharing." Once again, the administration argued that local governments, freed of the detailed regulations and restrictions that characterized categorical grants, would have much greater discretion in spending federal money that came in the form of block grants for law enforcement, job training, education, transportation, and community and rural development. In addition, block grants would simplify an increasingly cumbersome and duplicative system of federal grants.

In the end, Congress passed only two of the Nixon block grant proposals. The Comprehensive Employment and Training Act (CETA) of 1973 consolidated a number of job training programs. It lasted only until 1982, when Congress replaced it with the Job Training Partnership Act. The more lasting contribution was the Housing and Community Development Act of 1974 (actually signed by President Gerald Ford shortly after President Nixon resigned), which consolidated the old urban renewal program, Model Cities, and several other programs to create Community Development Block Grants (CDBG). This program constitutes the major Nixon urban legacy.

Popular with the nation's mayors, CDBG provides federal dollars on an annual entitlement basis directly to all cities with populations of at least 50,000 people. Funds are distributed according to a formula that considers a city's poverty level, the age of its housing stock, and its growth rate. Cities may use this money for a wide range of purposes, including the construction of community facilities such as pedestrian malls, historic preservation, economic development loans, and land acquisition and clearance.

Ironically, for all his intentions to cut the size of the federal government, Nixon presided over a steady increase in federal intergovernmental fiscal aid. Though his administration shared responsibility for this increase with a Democratic Congress, it is nevertheless true that when Nixon entered office in 1969, federal grants to states and cities amounted to 2.2 percent of the gross national product. When he left office in 1974 the percentage stood at 3.1.

—*Peter Eisinger*

### See also
Community Development Block Grants; New Federalism; Revenue Sharing.

### References
Conlan, Timothy. *New Federalism: Intergovernmental Reform from Nixon to Reagan.* Washington, DC: Brookings Institution, 1988.

Harrigan, John J. *Political Change in the Metropolis.* 5th ed. New York: HarperCollins, 1993.

Peterson, Paul. *The Price of Federalism.* Washington, DC: Brookings Institution, 1995.

## Nolen, John (1869–1937)

As an early-twentieth-century proponent and practitioner of city planning, John Nolen produced nearly 400 town plans in the United States. Born in the turbulent era of Reconstruction following the American Civil War, he received a degree in the newly established social sciences from the University of Pennsylvania in 1893. While there, he studied constitutional law, politics, and "contemporary affairs," equipping him with sociological theory and a framework with which to identify social problems around him. After a decade of traveling to European cities, embarking on graduate work at the University of Munich, teaching adult education at several American universities, and taking on the job of executive secretary for the Society for the Extension of University Teaching at the University of Pennsylvania, he entered the newly established Harvard School of Landscape Architecture. He graduated with his M.L.A. degree by 1905 and soon labeled himself a "town planning consultant," taking on planning jobs and public speaking engagements promoting the necessity of "modern town planning principles."

In addition to dozens of articles in journals and newspapers, Nolen published four books: *Replanning Small Cities* (1912); *City Planning* (1916), which Nolen edited; *New Ideals in the Planning of Cities, Towns and Villages* (1919); and *New Towns for Old* (1927). Like many of his colleagues, Nolen believed that "the existing methods of haphazard building . . . were not only socially bad, but expensive." He sought to rid his clients' cities of overcrowding, traffic congestion, high crime rates, and lagging economies through the "scientific" study of a specific place, and by developing a regularized and efficient design based upon modern planning principles.

Nolen's early planning practice mainly turned on replanning parts of cities or towns. But around 1920, when he accepted a commission to design the new town of Mariemont, Ohio (near Cincinnati), Nolen's philosophy of town planning shifted from merely correcting specific problems through replanning to one that advocated the creation of entirely new communities as the best solution for society's ills. Rather than tinkering with malfunctioning parts of a mechanical city, he wanted to create a more organic city in which all its parts were intimately interrelated—a homeostatic organism rather than a mechanical assemblage. *New Towns for Old* embodied Nolen's changed philosophy, which understood old cities to be irrevocably contaminated, necessitating the construction of well-planned towns from scratch.

Nolen's association with the International Garden City Federation became explicit with the construction of Mariemont, Ohio, by 1925, the first garden city built "in accordance with American ideas." Other communities Nolen planned or replanned include Kingsport, Tennessee (1915); Union Park Gardens, Delaware (1915), Kistler, Pennsylvania (1916); Overlook Colony, Pennsylvania (1917); Venice, Florida (1926); Madison, Wisconsin (1926); and Naples, Florida (1926).

—*Bradley Cross*

**See also**
Mariemont, Ohio.
**References**
Glass, James Arthur. "John Nolen and the Planning of New Towns: Three Case Studies." M.A. thesis, Cornell University, 1984.

Hancock, John Lorentz. "John Nolen and the American City Planning Movement: A History of Culture Change and Community Response, 1900–1940." Ph.D. dissertation, University of Pennsylvania, 1964.

## Office Work

Office work grew along with American cities. In the early nineteenth century, office work was a relatively uncommon occupation and usually one sought by men aspiring to rise though a business to a position of prestige and wealth. By the early twentieth century, office work had become a ubiquitous feature of urban life with hundreds of thousands of mostly young women engaging in a wide variety of tasks called office work. Office work was numerically the most important occupation for women in the twentieth century, and even though not all office work and workers were found in cities, no cities could be found without them.

Throughout the nineteenth century, office work was almost exclusively an all-male occupation. Managers, fellow employees, and the larger society considered office work men's work and assumed that men would fill these positions. Employers believed that men possessed the qualities necessary to succeed in office jobs, and men could find appropriate clerical jobs at every stage of their working lives. Lower-level office jobs were stepping stones to careers within a firm, and higher-level positions in offices promised the possibility of earning a wage large enough to support a family (family wage).

The office and business districts of the largest American cities had almost no accommodations for female white-collar workers. The men who occupied these positions worked in what was considered a male space—the office. During much of the nineteenth century, offices contained relatively undifferentiated space, assuming only male employees working closely together. Men's space extended beyond the office into the city where patronizing saloons and drinking in general seems to have been part of the work life of some male clerical workers. Male clerks and secretaries frequented saloons in their buildings for a drink and for the free lunch that often accompanied it.

During the late nineteenth century, however, changes in the economy and the city altered this masculine world forever. Office work, a service occupation, was growing along with industrial capitalism. Firms were not only increasing in size but were also differentiating the various functions of the company or corporation, developing planning and managerial departments, and physically separating these functions from production. Regardless of the firm or industry, clerical workers were not directly involved in either production or planning. The "output" of an office worker, however, serviced both the "brain" and the "hands" of a firm and often connected production and planning with each other. The growth of clerical occupations was directly related to the differentiation and growth of these two functions.

The firms employing the largest number of office workers were found in the booming cities of the late nineteenth and early twentieth centuries, and many of the entrants into this new kind of employment were women. Women first became stenographer-typists, a position new to offices, when the typewriter became a ubiquitous piece of office equipment by the 1890s. They then entered all other office jobs (bookkeeping and a variety of clerk positions) by the early years of the twentieth century. The women who first took advantage of this new occupational opportunity were usually young, white, single, and native-born, but, over time, they were increasingly the daughters of immigrants. During those years, working in an office was usually thought to be a good position for a respectable daughter before she married and began her own family. Of course, many young and not-so-young women in this relatively well paid employment saw these jobs as a way to support themselves and their families.

The entry of women into office work began the redefinition of office space into male and female activities and spheres, and it also signaled the first significant appearance of women in the downtown business district. During the late nineteenth century, a visitor to any large city in the United States would have looked in wonder at the many strange sights: skyscrapers; the bustling, congested streets; large department stores teeming with goods for sale; noise, smoke, and smells; and women working in offices.

Even though reformers and commentators often portrayed cities as evil, dangerous places for vulnerable girls on their own (and this was certainly sometimes true), cities often facilitated women's entry into office work by offering them a wide range of possible activities, services, and institutions. Besides the obvious lure of jobs, urban settings also provided business training at private business colleges and public high schools; presented private and philanthropic boarding houses; provided educational and recreational services oriented to young white-collar women on their own; and offered services, like downtown lunchrooms, oriented to a "respectable" female clientele. As a result, by the 1930s, when the majority of office workers in the United States were female, the office girl appeared to be a typical feature of the American urban scene.

—*Lisa M. Fine*

### References

Aron, Cindy Sondik. *Ladies and Gentlemen of the Civil Service: Middle-Class Workers in Victorian America.* New York: Oxford University Press, 1987.

Davies, Margery. *Woman's Place Is at the Typewriter: Office Work and Office Workers, 1870–1930.* Philadelphia: Temple University Press, 1982.

DeVault, Ileen. *Sons and Daughters of Labor: Class and Clerical Work in Turn-of-the-Century Pittsburgh.* Ithaca, NY: Cornell University Press, 1990.

Fine, Lisa M. *Souls of the Skyscraper: Female Clerical Workers in Chicago, 1870–1930.* Philadelphia: Temple University Press, 1990.

Kwolek-Folland, Angel. *Engendering Business: Men and Women in the Corporate Office, 1870–1930.* Baltimore: Johns Hopkins University Press, 1994.

Strom, Sharon Hartman. *Beyond the Typewriter: Gender, Class, and the Origins of Modern American Office Work, 1900–1930.* Urbana and Chicago: University of Illinois Press, 1992.

## Olmsted, Frederick Law (1822–1903)

The career of Frederick Law Olmsted, as well as those of his sons Frederick, Jr. (1870–1957), and John Charles (1852–1920), is so intertwined with the history of landscape architecture that it is virtually impossible to consider their careers apart from the larger context. Their work ranged from Olmsted's first association with Calvert Vaux when they submitted their successful design in 1858 to the competition to plan New York's Central Park, through the founding of the American Society of Landscape Architects in 1900 by his sons, and includes more than 500 projects with which they were associated.

Olmsted has a tremendous reputation and is frequently considered one of the founders of modern landscape architecture and the landscape of many of the great parks that were built in American cities during the nineteenth century. However, the central roles played by Olmsted's two sons in creating the profession of landscape architecture has exaggerated the importance of Olmsted, Sr., in the history of America's designed environment. Olmsted personally did little or no actual design work. But before academic programs to train landscape architects had been developed, Olmsted's successive firms functioned as *ateliers* where many notable designers served apprenticeships, just as Olmsted's collaboration with Calvert Vaux forged his own new career in landscape design after his career in literature, especially travel writing.

Because of Olmsted's reputation, and the prestige he has been accorded, there is a common perception, both publicly and professionally, that he deserves credit for any noteworthy planned landscape created in the late nineteenth or early twentieth century. In fact, Olmsted's most significant contribution was as an administrator, promoter, and writer—not as a designer. This is made clear by the simple fact that after Olmsted and Vaux dissolved their partnership in 1872, Olmsted's new firm amassed more than 550 commissions before he retired in 1895. Olmsted himself could not possibly have prepared the necessary plans, and it was the mostly anonymous but highly talented brigade of young designers working in his studio who executed these projects.

In fact, Olmsted's major contribution to urban design was creating the large, multidisciplinary design firm. His was almost certainly the first to follow the model currently emulated by American design firms in which the identity of the actual designers is subsumed under the company name and masked by it. The praise lavished on Olmsted has had positive benefits in promoting the preservation and restoration of historic landscapes, but only recently have those efforts impelled research into the work of the many other pioneering landscape designers.

—*Blanche M. G. Linden*

### See also
Central Park; Riverside, Illinois.

### References

Barlow, Elizabeth. *Frederick Law Olmsted's New York.* New York: Praeger, 1972.

Fabos, Julius G., Gordon T. Milde, and V. Michael Weinmayr. *Frederick Law Olmsted, Sr.: Founder of Landscape Architecture in America.* Amherst: University of Massachusetts Press, 1968.

Fein, Albert. *Frederick Law Olmsted and the American Environmental Tradition.* New York: Braziller, 1972.

———, ed. *Frederick Law Olmsted's Plans for a Greater New York City.* Ithaca, NY: Cornell University Press, 1968.

Glodgett, Geoffrey. "Frederick Law Olmsted: Landscape Architecture as Conservative Reform." *Journal of American History* 62 (1976): 869–889.

Roper, Laura Wood. *FLO: A Biography of Frederick Law Olmsted.* Baltimore: Johns Hopkins University Press, 1973.

Rosenzweig, Roy, and Elizabeth Blackmar. *The Park and the People: A History of Central Park.* Ithaca, NY: Cornell University Press, 1992.

Stevenson, Elizabeth. *Park Maker: A Life of Frederick Law Olmsted.* New York: Macmillan, 1977.

Zaitzevsky, Cynthia. *Frederick Law Olmsted and the Boston Park System.* Cambridge, MA: Harvard University Press, 1982.

## Olmsted, Frederick Law, Jr. (1870–1957)

Frederick Law Olmsted, Jr., once wrote that he had "had many opportunities—in the office conducted by my father and elder brother—to practice landscape architecture in the broad sense." A designer, planner, conservationist, and public servant, Olmsted's career records an extraordinary half-century of leadership in the professions of both landscape architecture and comprehensive planning. As a founding member and president of the American Society of Landscape Architecture (president, 1908–1909, 1919–1923), the National Conference on City Planning (president, 1910–1919), and the American City Planning Institute (president, 1917), and as professor of the first classes in landscape architecture and city planning in an American college (Harvard University, 1901–1914), Olmsted lent authority and legitimacy to these new disciplines.

Olmsted's renowned father schooled him to take his place in the family firm with study trips here and abroad and apprenticeships on the elder Olmsted's final great projects before he retired in 1895—the World's Columbian Exposition in Chicago in 1893 and development of the Biltmore Estate in Asheville, North Carolina. In 1898, young Olmsted was taken into partnership in the family firm in Brookline, Massachusetts, by his half brother, John Charles.

Olmsted soon took an important role on the national scene. In 1901, he assumed what would have been his father's position (had he been well) as landscape architect on the Park Improvement Commission for Washington, D.C., commonly known as the McMillan Commission. Charged with restoring L'Enfant's vision to the monumental core of the nation's capital, the commission put forth a visionary plan to guide development of the city. Olmsted's recommendations—creating neighborhood parks and playgrounds, reserving open space in suburban areas before their development, and connecting urban open space to existing natural scenic areas with a system of regional parkways—established major themes that he would develop in subsequent reports on city and park planning. Frequently recalled to Washington for public service, Olmsted was among the inaugural group of appointees to the Fine Arts Commission (1910–1918), served as manager of town planning for the U.S. Housing Corporation during World War I, and was one of the original members of the National Capital Park and Planning Commission (1926–1932), established to coordinate planning for greater Washington.

Olmsted's prominence on the McMillan Commission, combined with his distinguished name, gave him a leadership role in the emerging field of urban and suburban planning. Between 1905 and 1915, he produced seven of the earliest comprehensive planning reports for city centers: Detroit (1905 and 1915); Utica, New York (1907); Boulder, Colorado (1908); Pittsburgh (1909–1910); New Haven, Con-
necticut (1910); and Rochester, New York (1911). His residential community plans, most notably for the later parts of Roland Park, Maryland, and the garden suburb of Forest Hills Gardens, New York, in the early 1900s and for the waterfront communities of Mountain Lake, Florida, and Palos Verdes Estates, California, in the 1920s, became prototypes for the development of later suburbs. The neighborhood center concept, differentiation of street width according to type of traffic, use of deed restrictions to enforce maintenance and preserve architectural and other standards, and emphasis on providing various other amenities to help create a sense of place are hallmarks of Olmsted's suburban designs.

Olmsted devoted much of his later career to his long-standing interest in park and wilderness preservation and to encouraging regional planning for land use and resource conservation. His concerns for planning the physical environment to meet the demands of modern life, while protecting open spaces and wilderness areas, are once again at the forefront of the two professions that he helped guide and nourish.

—*Susan L. Klaus*

**See also**
Olmsted, Frederick Law.
**References**
Klaus, Susan L. "Efficiency, Economy, Beauty: The City Planning Reports of Frederick Law Olmsted, Jr., 1905–1915." *Journal of the American Planning Association* 57 (1991): 456–470.
———." 'Such Inheritance as I Can Give You.' The Apprenticeship of Frederick Law Olmsted, Jr." *Journal of the New England Garden History Society* 3 (1993): 1–7.
Olmsted, Frederick Law, Jr. "The Basic Principles of City Planning." *American City* 3 (1910): 67–72.

## Omnibuses

Large, horse-drawn vehicles known as omnibuses dominated city transit between about 1830 and 1855. They were ancestors of the modern motor bus, and like their present-day descendant, the omnibus operated over a fixed route on a short headway. Riders paid a uniform fare whether the trip was one block or thirty blocks long. Most lines operated within city limits, but there were a few suburban routes. Every major American city in existence much before 1900 had omnibuses, and this type of vehicle was also used by hotels and resorts as depot connectors.

The first omnibus operation that proved more than a temporary experiment began service in Paris in 1819. London and New York copied the idea a decade later. New York showed considerable enthusiasm for the bus because of the city's rapidly growing population. The city itself was physically expanding as street after street was developed beyond the old city wall to the north, creating a problem. Horse-drawn taxis, called Hackneys or Hackney coaches, were far too expensive for ordinary citizens. Wealthy folks traveled in private carriages, but most other citizens, including the middle class, generally walked. When the town expanded much beyond village size, walking became burdensome. Bus fares were reasonable, ranging from 5 to 10 cents, and schedules were frequent as buses followed one another every few minutes. And so the omnibus became very much a part of the city scene. By 1835, New York had about 100 in service, and that number multiplied yearly until it peaked in 1853 at 683 buses. In that peak year, omnibuses carried 120,000 passengers each day.

Of course, what was good for Manhattan proved equally good for other large East Coast cities. Philadelphia's first line opened in 1831, Boston's in 1835, but Baltimore's waited until 1844. Enthusiasm for horse-drawn buses jumped the Alleghenies, and a line was incorporated in St. Louis by 1838. Twenty-five years later, this system had expanded to 145 buses carrying 14,000 passengers a day.

The expansion of service in St. Louis and elsewhere did not mean that the buses were universally admired. In fact, there was a great deal of criticism aimed at the people's vehicle. Indeed, all forms of public transit seemed to generate considerable animosity, be it a simple bus or a high-speed subway. Critics of the omnibus considered it uncomfortable, unsafe, slow, and costly. Its drivers were rude, dishonest, and abusive. There was surely some truth to all of these allegations. The bus sat high off the ground, and the only egress was through a rear door. Athletic young men no doubt found the rear steps no obstacle, but most of the population found them a challenge both on entering and departing from the vehicle. Persons of more than normal girth found the narrow door something of a squeeze, as did ladies in full skirts. The hard bench seating along both sides of the bus proved less than comfortable. There was no heating and only a tiny lamp to provide illumination. The driver sat on the forward end of the roof, and to pay the fare passengers reached through a hole cut in the top of the front end of the vehicle. The driver reached down to collect money and offer change through the same hole. If a passenger was shortchanged, it was difficult, if not impossible, to reconcile the problem verbally because neither party could hear the other. The driver worked the rear door with a leather strap looped around his legs. Between driving the two-horse team, braking with his right foot, watching traffic, working the door, and making change, the driver had little patience with passengers' complaints. He sat out in the weather, rain or shine, boiling hot or freezing cold. He worked six or even seven days a week, 16 hours a day, with breaks of only 20 minutes for lunch—all for a wage of $2 a day. It is no wonder that these poor fellows raced their vehicles and locked hubs with rival drivers in frustration.

Transit passengers soon had something new to complain about, for the jolting omnibus was made obsolete in the 1850s and 1860s by the horsecar. Street railways, in which horses pulled cars along rails in city streets, rapidly took over urban transit after the Civil War. By 1865, New York, which had been the capital of omnibus operations, had only 231 of these vehicles. In a few years, the omnibus was limited almost entirely to the Fifth Avenue Line, which converted to motor buses in 1908. The age of the omnibus was over in less than a century.

—*John H. White, Jr.*

**See also**
Cable Cars; Horsecars; Streetcars.

**References**
Berkebile, Donald H. *Carriage Dictionary.* Washington, DC: Smithsonian Institution, 1980.
Miller, John Anderson. *Fares Please! A Popular History of Trolleys, Horse-Cars, Street-Cars, Buses, Elevateds, and Subways.* Reprint ed. New York: Dover, 1960.
Rowsome, Frank. *Trolley Car Treasury.* New York: McGraw-Hill, 1957.

## Opera Houses

From its origin in Florence, Italy, about 1600 to the present day, opera has been an urban art and amusement. In North America, too, its transformation from a courtly and aristocratic to a popular entertainment has been mostly due to the influence of cities and towns.

The first American operatic performance of which we have a dependable record took place in Charleston, South Carolina, in 1735. For the next century, opera was performed in English in theaters built for spoken drama. English opera was small in scale, with an orchestra of only a few instruments, spoken dialogue, and relatively simple music. Therefore, the markets and warehouses, taverns and local courthouses in which itinerant groups of actors performed were adequate for this purpose. As early as the 1740s, theaters specially built for opera came into existence, and by the end of the eighteenth century more substantial ones had been built in the leading cities of the new nation. The Southwark, built in Philadelphia in 1766, was the first American theater to be called an opera house. No city was more theatrically minded than New Orleans where theater building and French-language opera were part of the fabric of city life.

Along with the introduction of Italian-language opera to New York City by the Garcia Company in 1825 came a specialized kind of theater, the opera house. Italian in origin, this horseshoe-shaped auditorium circled by a tier of boxes had accompanied the diffusion of Italian opera throughout Europe. The Italian Opera House built in New York City in 1833 was the first of these in the United States, soon followed by the Astor Place Opera House in 1847. The St. Charles Theater of 1835 in New Orleans was another early specialized theater.

The second half of the nineteenth century saw the building of immense, opulent, privately owned opera houses: the

New York City Academy of Music of 1854, the New Orleans French Opera House of 1859, and the Metropolitan Opera House of 1883 in New York. There were also notable buildings in Boston and Detroit. Two opera houses stand out. Eugene Le Brun's handsome Philadelphia Academy of Music (1857), still in use, has proved the most enduring. In Chicago, Adler and Sullivan's Auditorium Building (1889) served the city magnificently for 40 years, survived the Depression, and was restored in the 1960s.

Less well known in American urban history is the proliferation of small-town opera houses in the last quarter of the nineteenth century. In every region of the country, medium-sized and small towns built all-purpose theaters, small in scale, with a rudimentary stage, movable sets, and perhaps an orchestra pit. Opera was only occasionally, even rarely, performed in them, but the idea of the opera house was more important than its material form. It exemplified the aspiration of these communities to be part of an international tradition of culture. Served by the numerous traveling theatrical and operatic companies of the day, the opera house was a crucial means to transmit urban culture before radio, movies, and television.

The first third of the twentieth century was a period of mixed success and failure. In New York City in 1906 with the Manhattan Opera House, and in Philadelphia in 1908 with construction of an imposing structure, Oscar Hammerstein built opera houses as part of his challenge to the Metropolitan Opera Company. In Boston, an opera house designed by Parkman B. Haven opened in 1909. Important seasons of opera took place in all three, but the Hammerstein houses were abandoned for operatic purposes within a few years. The Boston Opera House lasted until 1958 when it was ruthlessly demolished. Samuel Insull built the Civic Opera House in Chicago in 1929, vacating the Auditorium Building, and though his opera company failed in the 1930s, the Civic remained the site of operatic performances in that city. Historically, the most important urban enterprise was San Francisco's War Memorial Opera House (1932), the first municipally owned and operated opera house in the United States. Its inauguration coincided with the decade when, at last, federal, state, and municipal governments built auditoriums for the performing arts in the guise of unemployment relief.

The last half of the twentieth century has sustained the tradition of American urban operatic building, both public

*Opening night at New York City's Metropolitan Opera House on November 8, 1954, drew more than 4,000 of the city's social elite.*

and private. Among the most notable are the New York State Theater (1964) designed by Philip Johnson for Lincoln Center, which is also the site of the second Metropolitan Opera House (1966) by Wallace Harrison; the Santa Fe Opera House (1956, rebuilt 1972); the opera house in the Kennedy Center for the Performing Arts in Washington, D.C. (1971), by Edward D. Stone; and the Wortham Center in Houston (1987) by Eugene Aubry. In many other cities, nineteenth- and early-twentieth-century theaters have been restored to their original glory and are now used as houses for opera.

American urban culture has shaped opera in another respect: the flowering, between 1925 and 1965, of a distinctive form of American opera, the Broadway musical or "light opera," which has always reflected New York City's diversity and dynamism.

—*John Dizikes*

**References**
Dizikes, John. *Opera in America: A Cultural History.* New Haven, CT: Yale University Press, 1993.
Forsyth, Michael. *Buildings for Music: The Architect, the Musician, and the Listener from the Seventeenth Century to the Present Day.* Cambridge, MA: MIT Press, 1985.
Marion, John Francis. *Within These Walls: A History of the Academy of Music in Philadelphia.* Philadelphia: Restoration Office, Academy of Music, 1984.

## Orchestras

An orchestra is an aggregation of four main families of musical instruments (strings, woodwinds, brass, and percussion) that play together. The traditional orchestra performs music written during the eighteenth, nineteenth, and twentieth centuries, and its repertoire includes symphonies, concertos, suites, and tone poems. Modern orchestras range in size from the smaller chamber orchestra of only 20 to 30 players up to the larger symphony orchestra of 90 or more.

Most American orchestras fall into one of three main categories: amateur orchestras, part-time professional orchestras, and full-time professional orchestras. Also known as "community orchestras," amateur orchestras are sometimes associated with colleges and universities. Although musicians in a part-time professional orchestra are paid for each rehearsal and concert they play, they usually supplement their income by teaching their instruments, freelancing, or holding other jobs. Musicians in full-time professional orchestras contract for a full year of employment and receive a salary and benefits. Of course, some orchestras combine the characteristics of more than one category, such as the "core orchestra," which blends a "core" of 15 to 30 full-time musicians with 50 to 60 part-time players.

While orchestras were common in Europe during the eighteenth century, they were not established in the United States until the latter half of the nineteenth century. The first American orchestras were founded with a sense of civic pride in major cities such as Boston and Chicago and were considered a sign of higher culture.

The longest continuous orchestra in the United States is the New York Philharmonic, which began performing in 1842. The founding of orchestras in the United States continued throughout the twentieth century, even during the economic turmoil of the Great Depression. According to the American Symphony Orchestra League, there are now approximately 1,650 orchestras in the United States.

Today, most American cities, and even some towns, have an orchestra, and large cities may have two or more. The full-time professional symphony orchestras tend to reside in larger cities, while part-time professional and amateur orchestras usually reside in smaller ones. It is not uncommon for a major urban area to have both a full-time professional symphony orchestra and also a part-time professional chamber orchestra located in the city itself, while one or more amateur orchestras are based in the suburbs.

Orchestras in major cities can have annual operating budgets in excess of $10 million. Most orchestras in the United States, however, have annual budgets of less than $260,000. Orchestras receive their funding through a combination of ticket sales, corporate sponsorships, government grants, and private donations. A major urban orchestra can attract people from the suburbs to the downtown of a city, and patrons of a concert directly benefit the downtown economy by eating in restaurants, sleeping in hotels, parking in lots or garages, and buying at stores.

Orchestral concerts are considered an important cultural amenity of urban life, and overall concert attendance in the United States has been rising during recent years. According to the American Symphony Orchestra League, 25 million people attended orchestral concerts in the United States during the 1992–1993 season. This was an increase over the 22 million who attended during the 1983–1984 season.

—*Steven Lee Winteregg*

**References**
Craven, Robert R., ed. *Symphony Orchestras of the United States.* Westport, CT: Greenwood Press, 1986.
Hart, Philip. *Orpheus in the New World.* New York: W. W. Norton, 1973.
Peyser, Joan, ed. *The Orchestra: Origins and Transformations.* New York: Scribners, 1986.
Seltzer, George. *The Professional Symphony Orchestra in the United States.* Metuchen, NJ: Scarecrow Press, 1975.

## Organized Crime

Organized crime is a nonideological enterprise involving a number of people in close social interaction, organized on a hierarchical basis to secure profit and power by engaging in illegal and legal activities. Permanency is assumed by group members, who strive to keep the enterprise integral and active in pursuit of its goals. It eschews competition and strives for monopoly on an industry or territorial basis. There is a willingness to use violence and/or bribery to achieve ends or maintain discipline. Membership is restricted, although nonmembers may be involved on a contingency basis. There are explicit rules, oral or written, which are enforced by sanctions, including murder.

Organized crime provides illegal goods and services, such as gambling, drugs, commercial sex, and loan-sharking (usury), while it also engages in extortion and business and labor racketeering. In the United States, organized crime is a peculiarly urban phenomenon that developed from the interactions among immigration, machine politics, and Prohibition.

Immigrants were forced into slum housing reserved for their own ethnic group. Americans of older stock virulently attacked their cultures, customs, and religious beliefs and practices. Immigrants gradually discovered that they possessed at least one commodity that some "native" Americans coveted—their vote. A new breed of urban broker—the political boss—emerged and channeled these votes into a powerful entity known as the "machine." With the help of corrupt practices and street gangs that proliferated in urban ghettos, machine politicians delivered lopsided votes that enabled them to dominate the city. Politicians frequently employed gangs for such legitimate purposes as distributing campaign literature, hanging posters, and canvassing for votes. They were also used as "repeaters," who voted early and often, and as "sluggers," who attacked rival campaign workers and intimidated voters.

The acrimony between rural and urban America, between Protestants and Catholics, between Republicans and (nonsouthern) Democrats, between "native" Americans and recent immigrants, and between business and labor reached a pinnacle with the ratification of the Eighteenth Amendment in 1919. While America had had organized crime before Prohibition, it was intimately associated with shabby local politics and corrupt police forces. The "Great Experiment" provided an extraordinary level of criminal opportunity that caused organized crime, especially in violent forms, to blossom into an important force in American society. Prohibition acted as a catalyst for the mobilization of criminal elements in an unprecedented manner. Crime before Prohibition, insofar as it was organized, centered around corrupt political machines, vice entrepreneurs, and, at the bottom, gangs. Prohibition unleashed an unparalleled level of competitive violence and reversed the power order between criminal gangs and politicians. It also produced an unparalleled degree of organization.

With the onset of the Depression in 1929 and the subsequent repeal of Prohibition in 1933, the financial base of organized crime narrowed considerably. Many "players" dropped out; some went into legitimate enterprises or employment and others drifted into conventional criminality. Bootlegging had required trucks, drivers, mechanics, garages, warehouses, bookkeepers, and lawyers—skills and assets that could be converted to noncriminal endeavors. For those who remained in the "business," however, reorganization was necessary. Most of the former bootleggers were still young men with wealth and nationwide contacts that had grown out of their bootlegging enterprises. They had substantial investments in restaurants, nightclubs, gambling, and other profitable businesses. In the 1930s and 1940s they used their national contacts, diverse interests, and available capital to cooperate in a variety of entrepreneurial activities, both legal and illegal.

During the decades following World War II, organized crime changed considerably. It became increasingly clear that organized crime was dominated mainly by Italians; the Irish, except for small pockets in New York and Boston, were no longer involved. And while the sons of Jewish immigrants played a vital role in organized crime, by the third generation the Jews had moved on, too.

The pool of available candidates for membership in organized crime dwindled in Jewish communities. In Italian communities, it remained adequate enough because the large-scale organizations needed to profit from Prohibition were no longer necessary. In Chicago, for example, at the height of Prohibition, Al Capone is reputed to have employed 700 gunmen for an organization that involved thousands of persons, while contemporary estimates of the size of the "Chicago Outfit" have ranged only as high as 130. The largest of the crime families, New York's Gambino Family, is estimated to have about 400 members. These core members, however, have associates, and the total number of criminal actors participating directly or indirectly in a crime group's enterprises is many times the size of the core membership at any given time.

In recent years, the ranks of organized crime have been thinned by successful federal prosecutions using the RICO (Racketeer Influenced and Corrupt Organization) statute—particularly the long, double-digit sentences typically handed down. Whether or not the Italian-American community will be able to provide sufficient replacements to keep traditional organized crime viable in the years to come remains an open question. In the meantime, new criminal groups are emerging that may prove more powerful and difficult to combat than those of traditional organized crime.

One element that characterizes most nontraditional criminal organizations is drug trafficking as their primary enterprise. Some of these organizations are native to the

United States, some were formed by recent immigrants, and others have their headquarters in countries such as Mexico and Colombia. These criminal organizations are developing in the United States in the absence of the corrupt political machines that provided a protective incubator for the Irish, Jewish, and Italian organized crime groups of an earlier era.

Nontraditional or emerging organized crime includes recent groups from southern Italy, Latin America, Asia, the former Soviet Union, Africa, and Jamaica, as well as outlaw motorcycle clubs. In the early 1960s, criminal organizations in southern Italy came under intense pressure, the result of a murderous factional conflict, and a number of Mafia families *(Mafiosi)* fled to the United States. The struggle flared up again during the 1980s, especially between 1980 and 1983. Scores of members were arrested and held for trial, and in a pattern reminiscent of the early years under Mussolini, many *Mafiosi* fled southern Italy. Some of these new arrivals to the United States were absorbed into existing crime families, while others remained loyal to their original families in Sicily and formed the nucleus of independent organizations in the United States.

Most Latino organized crime groups import their criminal organizations along with the drugs they sell. Most active among them are groups based in Mexico and Colombia, Cuban exiles, and more recently, Dominicans. The Medellin and Cali cocaine cartels of Colombia are particularly important because of the wealth and power they have amassed. A number of unrelated Asian groups are also involved in organized crime. Some, such as the Yakuza, are more of a problem in Japan, although there is potential for overseas expansion. Others, such as the Triads, have been an international problem for many years. A variety of black criminal groups exists throughout the United States; some are homegrown, such as the El Rukns of Chicago; others, such as Nigerians and Jamaicans, are imported.

With the breakup of the Soviet Union, organized criminal activity has emerged on a large scale there. Nascent capitalism, relaxation of totalitarian law enforcement, and liberalization of travel have provided a fertile environment for criminals who were schooled in a Soviet system ripe with corruption and an underground economy. Members of these groups have been found throughout Eastern and Western Europe, and they have sent members to New York to set up operations. Some have entered the United States for contract crimes—murder, extortion, fraud—after which they return home before authorities can detect and apprehend them. After the experience of criminal life in the Soviet Union, where police were feared and treatment of lawbreakers harsh, they view the United States as a haven.

There is one facet of organized crime in which ethnic identity is unimportant—the biker subculture, although it is overwhelmingly white and working class. The outlaw motorcycle club is a uniquely American organization, although several of them now have chapters in countries throughout the world. They date from the years after World War II when many combat veterans, particularly those residing in California, sought new outlets for feelings of hostility and alienation. Some found release in the motorcycle and in association with others in motorcycle clubs. At least four of these groups—the best known being Hells Angels—eventually developed criminal enterprises and took on the attributes of an organized crime group.

—*Howard Abadinsky*

**See also**
Gangsters.
**References**

Abadinsky, Howard. *Organized Crime*. 4th ed. Chicago: Nelson-Hall, 1994.
Fox, Stephen. *Blood and Power: Organized Crime in the Twentieth Century.* New York: William Morrow, 1989.
President's Commission on Organized Crime. *The Impact: Organized Crime Today.* Washington, DC: Government Printing Office, 1986.

## Parades

Parades are complex phenomena that have been identified variously as cultural, political, social, recreational, and economic in their nature and outward display. As one element of the substantial repertoire of American public spectacles, parades are also an enduring element of urban life. Although parades may be as old as American urbanization itself, most scholarly attention has been directed to parades and other public displays during the late eighteenth and nineteenth centuries when cities were changing from a mercantile to an industrial economic base. Since the late 1970s, historians of cities have eschewed the perspective that parades are straightforward representations of community solidarity and pride and interpret them instead as a sophisticated commentary on American urban life invented and produced by immigrants and the native-born alike.

Indeed, the notion of "invention" is perhaps the most revolutionary interpretation of ethnicity and ethnic cultural features of the last two decades. Most important in this regard has been the work of the English social historian Eric Hobsbawn, who maintains that the concept of ethnicity is itself an invention very much connected to the rise of nations and nationhood in the eighteenth and nineteenth centuries in both Europe and North America. Ethnicity and the "traditions" that accompany it were devised to support politically articulated sentiments of separate peoplehood. Thus, recent social historiography has tended to look more closely at modern cultural symbols and practices that seem self-evident and have generally been taken for granted in order to understand the reasons for their invention and the impact they have had. Parades, especially ethnic parades and other public expressions of ethnicity, have become part of this exercise.

Most urban scholars would agree that parades—ethnic and otherwise—are a spectacular public manifestation of the relationships among classes, cultures, generations, and, more recently, sexualities and genders. As public events, parades temporarily change the world in which they are orchestrated and enable both the participants and their audience to view everyday life from very different perspectives. Additionally, most scholars would concur that processions and pageantry are likely to have different meanings for their participants and observers; furthermore, they may present a very specific and possibly limited view of the community they purport to depict. Indeed, it has been argued that a single procession may project several very different messages about the community being portrayed.

The sensational parades of native-born Americans during the early years of the republic were often publicly expressed political sentiments or commemorated national events involving the military, volunteer fire companies, private associations and clubs, local elected officials and other dignitaries, and bands. As industrialization accelerated, craftsmen and other skilled workers often organized parades to protest the impact of manufacturing on their livelihood. During the nineteenth century, parades also formed an important component of the public culture of the burgeoning immigrant population in American cities. Much of the research on urban social history that has addressed itself to vernacular collective gatherings such as parades and other street ceremonies has attempted to determine the meaning of parades for various social groups and how that meaning has been produced and understood by both the performers and their audience.

Susan Davis has analyzed parades using concepts drawn from folklore, social history, and communications. She argues that parades in the eighteenth and nineteenth centuries were both practical and symbolic mechanisms for shaping as well as challenging social relations. Davis stresses that it is essential to situate parades and similar public enactments within a social and historical context in order to understand them as more than mere reflections of social life. "As dramatic representations, parades and public ceremonies are political acts. They have pragmatic objectives, and concrete, often material results. People use street theater, like other rituals, as tools for building, maintaining, and confronting power relations." For Davis and other students of American urban

*Parades are one way by which cultures maintain their distinctive identity in urban societies. Here, Greek* evzones *(a special branch of the infantry) march in Chicago in 1993.*

life, parades are political statements, political strategies, and political acts intended to address the distribution of power in society. Furthermore, as Sallie Marston has shown, the parade may itself be as contested among the various performers and members of the audience as it is between audience and the performers.

An alternative perspective on parades is the view that they are instrumental expressions of ethnic festival culture. Thus, parades should be seen less as political statements and more as a ritual celebration of community. In describing German Americans, Kathleen Conzen contends that their parades and public pageantry during the nineteenth century actively affected the emotions of participants by freeing them from the constraints of the social structure and creating a foundation for comradeship and communion. Conzen employs the notion of *communitas*—human relationships where the burden of social status, class, and roles is suspended—to describe the liberating impact of invented ethnic celebrations on German Americans. Pointing to the fact that German Americans were a diverse ethnic group without a common religious, regional, class, or political identity, Conzen regards their festive culture as a unifying force. Parades and other forms of ethnic celebration enabled German Americans to override their dif-

ferences and conceptualize a commonality in ethnic terms. In short, it was as lovers of sociability, group performances, and festivity that German Americans invented parades and other forms of public culture to construct and solidify a common identity in the socially, culturally, and politically alien American context.

Ethnic parades—from the early days of American urbanization to the present—are complex community inventions that both constitute and comment upon the challenges of life in a new land. They can be seen as expressions of conflict and solidarity as well as playfulness or rage. Their public messages are often directed as much to an external audience as to the internal participants. Like Washington's birthday and the Fourth of July, ethnic parades are constructed out of competing interpretations of the past and present as well as visions of the future, and they serve as spectacular counterpoints to the everyday world in which they are staged.

The end of the twentieth century has witnessed a marked decline in ethnic public theater despite the continuing arrival of new waves of immigrants. Some urban scholars have pointed to the inhibiting effect of the lack of public spaces in the suburbs, the emergence of a mall culture that has replaced the street culture of previous centuries, and the pacifying impact of television as fatally damaging to the social meaning, and thus the continued production and public consumption, of ethnic pageantry. While it is true to a significant degree that ethnic processions have noticeably diminished, it is also true that older forms have been reimagined and new ones exploited. An example of the former is the St. Patrick's Day parade where participation has been hotly contested as gay and lesbian Irish immigrants and Irish Americans have demanded (and been refused) a place in the procession. As with the St. Patrick's Day parades of the nineteenth century, issues and definitions of "the middle class" and "respectability" are still very much at play. Ultimately, "taking it to the street" is still a viable though perhaps decreasingly popular medium for broadcasting social meaning and commenting upon social relations. And while the extensive public spaces of the nineteenth-century city are being filled in or reconfigured (thus discouraging various forms of public congregation and theater), the streets are still available and still occupied by ethnic and other groups for the purpose of suspending the realities of everyday life and offering improvisational alternatives.

—*Sallie Marston*

### References

Conzen, Kathleen N. "Ethnicity as Festive Culture: Nineteenth-Century German America on Parade." In *The Invention of Ethnicity.* New York: Oxford University Press, 1989.

Davis, Susan. *Parades and Power: Street Theater in Nineteenth Century Philadelphia.* Philadelphia: Temple University Press, 1986.

Hobsbawn, Eric, and Terence Ranger. *The Invention of Tradition.* Cambridge, England: Cambridge University Press, 1983.

Marston, Sallie. "Public Rituals and Community Power: St. Patrick's Day Parades in Lowell, Massachusetts, 1841–1874." *Political Geography Quarterly* 8 (1989): 255–269.

Ryan, Mary. "The American Parade: Representations of the Nineteenth-Century Social Order." In Lynn Hunt, ed., *The New Cultural History.* Berkeley: University of California Press, 1989.

## Park, Robert Ezra (1864–1944)

Along with W. I. Thomas, Robert Park exerted the dominant influence in creating the Chicago School of Sociology, although some include Ernest W. Burgess and Louis Wirth as core members. Many of his students, such as Herbert Blumer and Ralph Turner, believed that Park was the most influential sociologist of his generation. Park provided the germinal insights for later theoretical and empirical developments in the fields of human ecology, collective behavior, and race relations, among others.

Robert Park had a most interesting career. He did not actively participate in a university program until he was 49 years old, appointed at that time to become a lecturer in the Department of Sociology at the University of Chicago. He had previously been a journalist for a dozen years, working on newspapers in Detroit, Minneapolis, Denver, New York, and Chicago. He later claimed that his work as a newspaperman helped develop his career as a sociologist, particularly an urban sociologist, because he had spent so much time roaming the streets and observing the people in urban centers. Park had also spent time in Germany, where he received his doctoral degree for a dissertation entitled "The Crowd and the Public." This work signaled his interest in studying collective behavior and laid the foundation for his own subsequent research, as well as that of his students. His training in Germany, where he was influenced by both Max Weber and Georg Simmel, also influenced his later ideas, particularly his contentions about the city.

After he came to the University of Chicago, Park began an enormous agenda of research and instruction. His basic intention was developing the field of sociology as a type of empirical inquiry, thereby improving on the work of many others who had treated sociology as a speculative and philosophical inquiry. Park chose the urban environment, specifically Chicago, as the setting within which to pursue his vast empirical agenda. A number of colleagues contributed to this effort, among them Ernest Burgess who would become a lifelong collaborator, Vivien Palmer who would provide the research underpinnings for the development of the Community Factbook on Chicago, Louis Wirth who under the tutelage of Park developed his own seminal writings on the city, and a host of graduate students who produced studies of life in the city.

With Burgess, Park developed a graduate seminar that plunged into field studies of Chicago. Together, the two men also wrote a book that conveyed their view of sociology, *Introduction to the Science of Society.* Because he was 22 years younger, Burgess was always overshadowed by the more dynamic and prolific Park. Together, they helped introduce and extend a number of important ideas and techniques in the field of sociology, including such methods as the life history of individuals and the use of quantitative data to study such phenomena as land values. Moreover, they believed strongly in using case studies to examine important topics, thinking that the results of such works could be generalized, in a tentative fashion, and explored in other cases to determine the degree of their accuracy and generality.

Perhaps Park's major theoretical contribution lay in his effort to provide a unique way of conceptualizing and studying urban social phenomena. Along with Burgess and Roderick McKenzie, he developed the field of human ecology. Park maintained that human life in cities resembled life among plants and animals. As with plants and animals, people lived interdependently with each other; therefore, they displayed the same "web of life." Moreover, the same kinds of processes evident in the plant and animal kingdoms, such as competition for survival and the emergence of dominant groups in particular areas, also showed important parallels to life in the city. Given the overwhelming parallels, Park proceeded to distinguish two levels of human life in cities. One was the biotic level, at which one observed competition, and the other was cultural, at which one observed the phenomenon of consensus. Indeed, to Park it was the consensus among humans that distinguished them from other forms of life.

Given this general perspective, a number of ideas and specific pieces of research followed. For example, Park came to see certain natural areas of the city as places that emerged independently of human will or action. Here, one would find certain dominant groups. There were natural areas of slums as well as natural areas of financial districts. Moreover, one could also observe the succession of different groups in particular areas over time, especially as immigrant groups moved into and out of areas.

Although later students criticized these conceptions of the city for being too scientific—that is, for leaving out the important elements of human and political action in the making of cities—Park's ideas remain influential today, especially among human ecologists and demographers interested in the city.

—*Anthony M. Orum*

### References

Bulmer, Martin. *The Chicago School of Sociology.* Chicago: University of Chicago Press, 1984.

Park, Robert E. *The Crowd and the Public and Other Essays.* Henry Elsner, Jr. ed. Chicago: University of Chicago Press, 1972.

———. *Human Communities: The City and Human Ecology.* Glencoe, IL: Free Press, 1952.

———. *On Social Control and Collective Behavior: Selected Papers.* Ralph H. Turner, ed. Chicago: University of Chicago Press, 1967.

Park, Robert E., Ernest W. Burgess, and Roderick D. McKenzie. *The City.* Chicago: University of Chicago Press, 1925.

## Parks

The municipal park movement in the United States can be dated from the passage of legislation in 1852 to create Central Park in New York City, the first time the public had ever decided to spend money specifically for a park. Before then, outdoor recreation took place in small pockets and central areas that existed primarily for other reasons: cemeteries, plazas, markets, gardens, tenement courts, school yards, and streets, or commercial establishments like beer gardens, ocean beach resorts, and amusement parks.

The municipal park movement can be roughly divided into four chronological stages, although in some newer American cities these occurred simultaneously. The phases of development are the pleasure ground (1850–1900), the reform park (1900–1930), the recreation facility (1930–1965), and the open space system (1965–1995). The later stages influenced earlier ones; for example, a playground or stadium might be inserted in a large pleasure ground, and a stadium could have a sculpture installed decades later. Moreover, the newer types do not replace existing ones; instead they are layered one over another. Finally, each stage was designed in direct response to experience with its predecessor, so this slow dialectic, combined with various insertions and layers, produces a complex and variable picture that varies from city to city. This analytic typology helps one to see through the complexities to understand the similarities between cities' approaches to parks.

Parks should not be considered only physical entities, that is, as designed objects and a subject of design history and analysis, but also as a social movement with a social program. A naive assumption is that parks are just plots of land preserved in their original state, and laymen often surmise that parks are bits of nature created only in the sense that it was decided not to build on the land. A less naive view perceives parks as aesthetic objects and sees their history in terms of evolving artistic styles, more or less independent of social forces. In fact, parks are artifacts conceived and deliberated as carefully as public buildings with both physical shape and social usage taken into account.

The pleasure ground is typically a large park located on the periphery of a city and is intended as an antidote to the stresses of city life. Its principles of composition are curvilinear. Typically, circulation paths define meadows to create a pastoral landscape. Native trees rather than exotic species are used so that the designer can shape both space and the user's path without evoking intellectual attention as a user is being directed through the park. Initially, the architectural style was rustic, but citizens did not like spending money on unassuming buildings, so the next style was the more substantial Romanesque championed by Henry H. Richardson. In the final stages of this period, wealthy donors preferred Neoclassical buildings. Water in pleasure grounds was characteristically kept in smooth ponds rather than in brooks—whose rush was considered too stimulating—so that tranquillity could be maintained and an illusion of infinity be created where sky was reflected in water. Ideally, flowers were limited to two settings, either at the base of buildings or in naturalistic bands; elsewhere, they would have suggested "the hand of man," which in pure pleasure ground theory was to be minimized. The purpose of these physical arrangements was to create what Frederick Law Olmsted, the father of landscape architecture, called "a class of opposite conditions," referring to the need to provide a counterpoint to the city's regular streets and its finite, rational way of life always dominated by considerations of means and ends.

Ideal activities in a pleasure garden included walking; boating; listening to classical music concerts; racing or watching horse-drawn carriages; playing lawn tennis, croquet, and baseball in summer; ice skating in winter; generically "spending a day" and picnicking as a family or as part of a religious group; in practice, the list of activities was expanded to include ethnic celebrations. The most significant divergence between the ideal and the real was the class difference in usage. The wealthy built homes nearby, used park roads for riding, and displayed their wealth in promenades, or dress parades. By contrast, the working poor could seldom afford the time or money to travel to the park. This split was a major impetus for creating the next park type.

In order to make parks accessible to the working class, park commissioners decided to purchase land in tenement districts where workers lived. This meant reducing their size to a few square blocks or less, a sharp drop from vast parks like Central Park in New York and Prospect Park in Brooklyn; Franklin Park in Boston; Washington, Lincoln, Douglas, and Jackson Parks in Chicago; and Golden Gate Park in San Francisco. The designers of these smaller parks quickly renounced picturesque landscape principles and embraced a Neoclassical aesthetic instead. The border was not planted to create the illusion of being in the country; trees were used to mark the edge of the park but not to screen it. Circulation was at right angles, and the composition of the park was usually bilaterally symmetrical. Age and sex segregation often rationalized the division, boys and girls being separated as were men and women. Buildings were not hidden behind trees or berms but placed centrally and prominently; in their interiors, they too were bilaterally symmetrical with gender rationalizing the layout. Water was not a key feature of these parks, but reform park planners wanted to encourage the working class to bathe, so they introduced swimming pools. In short order, swimming became so popular that recreation departments had to plan for it as an activity in its own right. Flowers were no longer restricted but used in flower boxes and the formal beds created by the orthogonal composition of the plan. The overarching purpose of this styling was to rationalize the urban environment, which in turn implied its acceptance as a permanent feature of American life.

Activities were structured and organized in these parks, and they no longer followed the model of spontaneous family life. Developmental theory from psychology introduced the idea that each age and sex group had different recreational needs that required planning and supervision. Therefore, a new occupation, the recreation worker, developed as an offshoot of social work. The greatest discrepancy between the ideal and real was that people mentally associated these parks with children and the poor, even though they were intended for everyone. The next model attempted to correct that perception.

In the 1930s, the era of the recreation facility, park administrators abandoned idealistic attempts to use parks as a mechanism of social reform. Instead, Robert Moses, park commissioner in New York City, wrote in his first annual report, "We make no absurd claims as to the superior importance and value of the particular service we are called on to render." Parks were no longer justified as accomplishing necessary social change. Rather, they were accepted as an established municipal institution, no longer a zealous reform movement. Simply expanding parks into the new suburbs became the most important goal; quantity was the byword of the day. The frequent use of the term *recreation,* rather than *play,* came to signify the importance of serving all age groups, not just children in playgrounds. The term *facility* signified that new construction was not necessarily a building. It might be a stadium, band shell, gigantic swimming pool with bleachers, or a checkerboard and tables. Otherwise, no new building type was developed exclusively for parks; the most common construction was a replica of the field house. Landscaping received less attention than ever before, with most attention going to maintenance rather than decorative effect.

During the national crises of the Depression and World War II, parks served as a conduit for public works spending and sustained morale. Women's role in wartime production stimulated a short-lived experiment with day care. By the 1950s, concern for the physically handicapped and the elderly had emerged. Professionalization, standardization, and suburbanization affected park programming and ideology by displacing references to class, by emphasizing banal efficiency at the expense of site-specific variety, and by emphasizing the quantitative aspects of extending recreation services. Planners treated the city as a mechanical system and city planning as a problem of system management. They viewed parks as one of many elements essential to an overall balance, along with schools, hospitals, transit systems, housing, shopping centers, and industrial sectors.

While active recreation was a byword of this era, ironically, big spectator sports events at stadiums and ballparks attracted massive numbers of people. This discrepancy between ideology and practice was addressed in the next era by emphasizing participation.

In 1965 when John Lindsay ran for mayor of New York City, he issued a paper on urban parks that set the tone for the entire era of the open space system. In it, he proposed that parks once again be actively used as an instrument of social reform. Prominent designers and architects, rather than in-house staff, were hired to plan parks, small lots, and plazas. The importance of narrowly defined parks diminished while the significance of open and green space gathered strength from the new concept that parks, streets, plazas, and empty lots were parts of a continuous system. Citizens and professionals viewed all unbuilt "open space" as potential sources of psychic relief.

The newest park type is characterized by the adventure playground, tot lot, and urban plaza, all of which use small bits of land previously thought unusable because of their size, shape, grade, or proximity to busy streets and incompatible land uses. The open space philosophy saw every piece of land as a potentially valuable gem in a network of open space. Social programming also became more inclusive in order to retain middle-class shoppers (with pleasant lunch spots) and workers, while simultaneously attracting poor youth used to popular culture (rock concerts, expanded hours for swimming, "happenings"). The underlying ideology of the open space system is that the city is an art form, and the park itself a performance artist—versatile and interacting with both the audience and environment. Probably the greatest discrepancy of these parks involves the understanding of "open"; research and debate about issues of who should be allowed to use public and private open spaces raises class issues once again, this time around the homeless.

Park form always reflects immediate social goals, an ideology about order, and an underlying attitude toward the city. Yet today no one is quite sure what parks are for and whom they should serve, so park planners favor a scattershot approach. A closer look at contemporary society and a realistic analysis of social problems and attitudes about cities might crystallize park policies based on contemporary needs. The global environmental crisis is certainly one of the most fundamental problems of our time, as much a sociocultural problem as a biological or technological one. Creating ecologically sustainable cities means that human attitudes and behaviors need to change, and city parks could help bring that about. However, environmental designers, politicians, and citizens do not yet view the problem with the urgency of war. Eventually, the fifth park type will most likely emerge out of concerns for living at high densities in new ways. Urban parks could model ways to practice ecological landscaping, composting and vegetable gardening, household or neighborhood recycling, and environmental (true) cost accounting that considers the environmental consequences of business activity.

—*Galen Cranz*

**See also**
Central Park; Golden Gate Park; Moses, Robert; Olmsted, Frederick Law.

**References**
Bender, Thomas. *Toward an Urban Vision: Ideas and Institutions in Nineteenth-Century America.* Lexington: University Press of Kentucky, 1975.
Chadwick, George F. *The Park and the Town.* New York: Praeger, 1966.
Cranz, Galen. "Environmental Power in Human Transition: Sustainable Development and Environmental Design Research." In Environmental Design Research Association, *Power by Design,* 27–31. Oklahoma City, OK: Environmental Design Research Association, 1993.
———. *The Politics of Park Design: A History of Urban Parks in America.* Cambridge, MA: MIT Press, 1982.
Curtis, Henry S. *The Play Movement and Its Significance.* New York: Macmillan, 1917.
French, Jere S. *Urban Green: City Parks of the Western World.* Dubuque, IA: Kendall/Hunt, 1973.
Rainwater, Clarence E. *The Play Movement in the United States: A Study of Community Recreation.* Chicago: University of Chicago Press, 1922.
Rutledge, Albert J. *Anatomy of a Park: The Essentials of Recreation Area Planning and Design.* New York: McGraw-Hill, 1995.
Seymour, Whitney North, Jr., ed. *Small Urban Spaces.* New York: New York University Press, 1969.
Steiner, Jesse F. *Americans at Play.* New York: McGraw-Hill, 1933.

## Pattern Books

The architectural historian Henry-Russell Hitchcock seems to have originated the term *house pattern book* in 1946. He used it to distinguish these nineteenth-century publications of designs for suburban and country houses from earlier *builders' guides* that were handbooks of the classical orders, structures, and designs for urban buildings.

While builders' guides were handcrafted publications intended for artisans, pattern books were products of industrialized technologies for printing and illustration that were directed at a lay audience. Pattern books proved to be hugely successful and surpassed builders' guides as the predominant form of American architectural literature by the 1840s and 1850s.

The first pattern book was *Rural Residences* (1837–1838) by the architect Alexander Jackson Davis. Although his collection of designs for simple cottages and elaborate villas was a financial disaster, it inspired Andrew Jackson Downing, a landscape gardener and architectural critic, to publish a series of immensely popular books on country houses, their gardens, furnishings, and gadgets between 1841 and 1853.

While Downing saw the designs he published as models to be developed by professional architects, his successors, like George Woodward and Amos Bicknell, sold detailed plans and specifications to builders, thus saving an architect's fee. Their hardbound books were, however, replaced by the late nineteenth century with an even less expensive alternative, periodicals like the *Scientific American Building Monthly* (1885–1905).

Pattern books have survived into the twentieth century in the form of real estate supplements to Sunday newspapers and stock plan books sold in hardware and hobby stores. Although condemned by the architectural elite as shoddy and crass, they are a popular genre and a challenge to professional authority.

—*Mary Woods*

**See also**
Davis, Alexander Jackson; Downing, Andrew Jackson.

**References**
Davies, Jane B. "Introduction." *Rural Residences.* Reprint ed. New York: Da Capo Press, 1980.
Gutman, Robert. "Architects in the Home-Building Industry." In Judith Blau, Mark LaGory, and John Pipkin, eds., *Professionals and Urban Form,* 208–223. Albany: State University of New York Press, 1983.
Hitchcock, Henry-Russell. "Introduction." *American Architectural Books.* Reprint ed. New York: Da Capo Press, 1976.
Tatum, George Bishop, and Elisabeth Blair MacDougall, eds. *Prophet with Honor: The Career of Andrew Jackson Downing, 1815–1852.* Philadelphia: Athenaeum of Philadelphia; Washington, DC: Dumbarton Oaks Research Library and Collection, 1989.
Upton, Dell. "Pattern Books and Professionalism." *Winterthur Portfolio* 2–3 (1984): 107–150.

## Pedestrian Malls

Pedestrian malls were constructed in a large number of American downtowns during the 1960s and 1970s. A pedestrian mall is a downtown corridor—usually a few linear blocks of the main shopping street—where pedestrians have a higher priority than any other activity.

Three major types of pedestrian malls have been built. The most common is the traditional pedestrian street from which automobiles and transit vehicles are banned; the vast majority of malls built in the 1960s and 1970s were of this type. A second kind is the shared mall (also called semimall), which is primarily a pedestrian thoroughfare on which limited automobile traffic at reduced speeds is allowed. Finally, a transit mall is designed primarily for pedestrians, but transit vehicles, usually buses, are also permitted on these malls; private automobiles, however, are forbidden.

The successful reservation of central city streets for pedestrians in several European countries, most notably West Germany, caught the attention of American city officials and downtown businessmen in the late 1950s. The first American city to construct a pedestrian mall was Kalamazoo, Michigan, in 1959, and dozens of other cities followed in the 1960s, including Fresno, California; Providence, Rhode Island; Miami Beach, Florida; and Burbank, California. The single purpose of most of these early malls was revitalizing downtown retail activity. The planning and design of the early malls was heavily influenced by the downtown business community, which was primarily concerned with increasing retail traffic, not improving the quality of downtown life. Malls built in the 1970s, when the majority of them were constructed, expanded their purpose to include enhancing the downtown environment and image. To encourage people to spend more time downtown, new pedestrian malls included playgrounds, larger seating areas, and landscaping that encouraged people to stay and use the mall, not merely look at it.

The degree to which pedestrian malls have been successful is debatable. Although good design can permit a mall to improve the quality and quantity of open space in a downtown, other factors must also be in place for a healthy volume of pedestrians to be maintained. First, the timing of construction is crucial. If a mall is built after most downtown retailing has already been abandoned, for example, the chances of failure are high. Second, the mall must have a sound organizational structure to coordinate, promote, and manage it after construction. A good example is the Denver Partnership, which manages activities on the highly regarded 16th Street Mall. Third, a mall works best when it is carefully coordinated with other downtown development strategies, such as improving or developing transportation, tourism, housing, and office space. Finally, if a mall can be integrated with some nearby activity that generates pedestrian traffic—a university, hospital, or government center—the chances for success are greatly enhanced. For example, many of the more successful American malls are in college towns such as Burlington, Vermont; Charlottesville, Virginia; Boulder, Colorado; and Madison, Wisconsin.

While no clear-cut consensus exists, many urban planners and city officials currently think that pedestrian malls

*Pedestrian malls have become a pleasant feature of many cities as streets like this section of Sixteenth Street in Denver have become walkways lined with restaurants and shops rather than just roadways for vehicles.*

have failed to stimulate downtown retailing, as indicated by a 1987 headline in the *Wall Street Journal,* "City Pedestrian Malls Fail to Fulfill Promise of Revitalizing Downtown." Of course, it was probably unrealistic to expect the conversion of a single street to overcome decades of economic, social, and spatial changes that contributed to the decline of many downtowns. Nevertheless, the dissatisfaction with pedestrian malls has meant that few new malls were built in the 1980s and 1990s (Denver being a notable exception), and some cities (such as St. Cloud, Minnesota; Providence; Norfolk, Virginia; and Eugene, Oregon) have converted pedestrian corridors back to streets allowing motor vehicles.

—*Kent A. Robertson*

**References**

Houstoun, Lawrence. "From Street to Mall and Back Again." *Planning* 56 (1990): 4–10.

Robertson, Kent A. *Pedestrian Malls and Skywalks.* Brookfield, VT: Avebury Press, 1994.

———. "Pedestrianization Strategies for Downtown Planner: Skywalks versus Pedestrian Malls." *Journal of the American Planning Association* 59 (1993): 361–370.

Rubenstein, Harvey M. *Pedestrian Malls, Streetscapes and Open Spaces.* New York: Wiley, 1992.

## Perry, Clarence Arthur (1872–1944)

Known for developing the concept of neighborhood planning, Clarence Arthur Perry interjected some of the social concerns identified with the Progressive Era into the planning profession. Initially directed toward improving citizenship through the purposeful location of essential civic facilities, over time neighborhood planning assumed other, less socially constructive purposes.

Perry's interest in neighborhood planning originated in the community school movement, which he promoted from the time he joined the recreation department of the Russell Sage Foundation in 1909 until World War I. In *Wider Use of the School Plan* (1910), Perry urged schools to make their facilities available for civic purposes, including town forums, adult education, and a variety of recreational activities. Closely linked with social reformers in the playground and settlement house movements, Perry shared the belief that physical changes in the urban fabric could improve social life and enhance citizenship. For Perry, it was a simple step from using the school as a civic center to making it the focus of all planning.

Perry unveiled this expanded concept of neighborhood planning at the annual meeting of the National Conference of Social Work in 1924. Perry claimed that a planned unit (determined by the distance a child could walk to school) "with its physical demarcation, its planned recreational facilities, its accessible shopping centers, and its convenient circulatory system—all integrated and harmonized by artistic designing—would furnish the kind of environment where vigorous health, a rich social life, civic efficiency, and a progressive community consciousness would spontaneously develop and permanently flourish." Perry elaborated the concept in 1929 in the volume he wrote for the Regional Plan of New York.

Neighborhood planning found wide acceptance by the early 1930s, achieving special prominence at President Herbert Hoover's 1931 Conference on Home Building and Home Ownership, where it was embraced by four different committees. It provided the underlying rationale for the new town of Radburn, New Jersey, the partially built garden city that provided a model for the New Deal's greenbelt program. The small but influential Regional Planning Association of America, with whom Perry met in the mid-1920s, made the concept the centerpiece of its proposal for a national housing policy in 1933.

Perry envisioned application of his concept not just to new development on open land but in reordering space in older urban places. Using new arterial highways as boundaries, planners could coordinate the provision of services in distinct residential quarters. As older urban areas declined physically, Perry embraced a concept of redevelopment that involved not just piecemeal rehabilitation but wholesale rebuilding. This approach, combined with Perry's stress on the importance of planning for homogeneous populations, found immediate favor with the National Association of Realtors, which commissioned planner Harland Bartholomew to prepare a "Neighborhood Improvement Act" in 1937 that would give builders tax breaks and powers of eminent domain to encourage the redevelopment of whole residential areas. Embraced under Title I of the Housing Act of 1949, this approach ultimately proved sharply divisive. Perry's death in 1944 shielded him from some of the ill effects of redeveloping whole neighborhoods and the wide-scale social displacement that accompanied the policy. Even so, by the time he retired from the Russell Sage Foundation in 1937, his purposeful effort to devise an instrument for social and civic rehabilitation had assumed new and less progressive intent.

—*Howard Gillette, Jr.*

**See also**

Greenbelt Towns; Regional Planning Association of America.

**References**

Gillette, Howard, Jr. "The Evolution of Neighborhood Planning: From the Progressive Era to the 1949 Housing Act." *Journal of Urban History* 9 (1983): 421–444.

Silver, Christopher. "Neighborhood Planning in Historical Perspective." *Journal of the American Planning Association* 51 (1985): 161–174.

## Philadelphia, Pennsylvania

For more than three centuries Philadelphia has stood at the confluence of the Delaware and Schuylkill rivers in southeastern Pennsylvania. Founded by William Penn in 1682, the city pins the midsection of the nation's eastern seaboard to the Atlantic coast and holds a prominent place in the political, economic, and social history of the United States. Geography, demography, and economic competition have shaped its history. Together, they powered its growth from a commercial center in colonial times to an industrial city that became a workshop to the world in the nineteenth century. In the twentieth century, the shift from a manufacturing to a service economy in the United States transformed Philadelphia, turning its historic strength to weakness and placing a premium on innovation and adaptation to economic, social, and political change. A crossroads at first, the city's people and institutions quickly became and still remain diverse. This has been both a blessing and a curse, prompting disorder even as it generates energy for change.

By the middle of the eighteenth century, Philadelphia was the most prosperous city in England's North American colonies. An entrepot, it tied the fertile farmlands of eastern Pennsylvania to markets in the West Indies and Europe. Its central location facilitated access to the sugar islands while sparing the city the worst effects of the contest between Britain and France for supremacy in North America. By the 1760s, Philadelphia had outstripped Boston as the busiest port in the colonies. Demand for labor attracted a flood of immigrants, sparking a construction boom that stoked the city's economy. With the coming of the American Revolution, Philadelphia briefly became a political giant. It housed two Continental Congresses during the war, the Constitutional Convention afterward, and the federal government of the United States from 1790 to 1800.

The Industrial Revolution turned Philadelphia from a commercial to a manufacturing city. Before embracing this role, Philadelphia struggled to retain its place as the hub of trade. But the opening of the Erie Canal in 1825 gave New York City better access to the trans-Appalachian West. Together with a superior harbor and relative proximity to Europe, the canal made New York the destination of choice for agricultural products coming from the West and immigrants and goods moving in the opposite direction. Opened in 1834, the Pennsylvania Main Line defeated the barrier of the Allegheny Mountains by combining a pair of canals with a portage railroad, but for convenience and efficiency this hybrid was no match for the man-made waterway farther north. Only a railroad could link Philadelphia with its hinterland and the nation's interior. Built between 1846 and 1854, the Pennsylvania Railroad gave the city access to Pittsburgh and the Ohio River, preparing the way for massive industrialization.

During the second half of the nineteenth century, Philadelphia became the industrial capital of the United States. Supplied by the Reading Railroad, soft and hard coal mined in eastern Pennsylvania fueled the city's growth and transformation. Chemicals, tools, machinery, and paper poured from hundreds of factories. Philadelphians manufactured precision instruments, paint, and pharmaceuticals; they produced vast quantities of beer, cigars, and candy. But textiles and apparel were the foundation of the city's economy. Companies like Park Carpet Mills, Quaker Lace, and Stetson Hat held the key to its prosperity.

Along the arc of the Delaware River north of the colonial city, neighborhoods like Kensington, Bridesburg, and Tacony became smokestack communities, offering jobs and housing to thousands. Connected to an expanding transportation network, the port grew rapidly but without planning or coordination. Traction, banking, and retail businesses fed upon the city's industrial base and profited handsomely. Men like Peter A. B. Widener, William L. Elkins, and John Wanamaker achieved distinction as models of the city's entrepreneurial spirit. In his department store, Wanamaker sold the products of the world, teaching the lessons of capitalism and consumerism to all who entered his mercantile domain.

Philadelphia's industrial economy reached its peak at the beginning of the twentieth century. Slowed by the Depression, it revived during World War II only to falter in the years afterward. High labor costs and antiquated plants led manufacturers to depart for the suburbs, other states, and overseas. Symptomatic of deindustrialization, the relocation of the Baldwin Locomotive Works to suburban Eddystone deprived the city of an employer that had first hired Philadelphians in the 1830s. But it was the makers of nondurable goods who took the heart out of the city's manufacturing economy. Between 1955 and 1985, such basic industries as clothing and electronics went elsewhere, their owners claiming they could no longer be competitive in Philadelphia. Left behind, vacant and hazardous, were hundreds of work sites on 4,000 acres—nearly two-thirds of the land zoned for industrial use. The service sector became predominant; finance, law, education, and health care assumed primary responsibility for the welfare of the economy. Hospitals and universities turned into Philadelphia's largest and most important employers. Graduates of Temple, LaSalle, St. Joseph's, Drexel, and the University of Pennsylvania are now among the city's chief products.

In the 1950s, reformers and businessmen made plans to redevelop the downtown. Hoping to reverse years of private exploitation and public neglect, Mayor Joseph S. Clark, Jr., and his successor, Richardson Dilworth, tried to turn the city's heritage into an economic asset. Independence Hall took on a new appearance, framed by a mall that emerged when the commonwealth of Pennsylvania demolished dozens of nineteenth-century buildings perched on its doorstep. But attracting more tourists was just part of the plan. Public policymakers and private investors also reclaimed a decaying neighborhood near the central business district. Society Hill exchanged working-class for affluent residents by transforming decrepit colonial houses into showplaces.

Symbolic of the transition from an industrial to a service economy, the demolition of the Pennsylvania Railroad's Broad Street Station in 1955 cleared the way for a new complex of office buildings for lawyers, accountants, and businessmen. According to Edmund Bacon, the director of the Philadelphia City Planning Commission at the time, the future of the city depended upon the economic health of the downtown. He called for the revitalization of Market Street, the main east-west thoroughfare, an idea that became reality, at least in part, in the 1970s. Financed jointly by the city and the Rouse Corporation, the Gallery Mall on East Market Street brought middle-class shoppers back to the downtown. To get there, they could use the new Center City Commuter Tunnel that linked the suburban networks of the old Reading and Pennsylvania Railroads. In the 1980s, Philadelphia's power brokers continued searching for ways to strengthen the economic pull of downtown. Under Mayor Wilson Goode, the city abandoned its long-standing opposition to skyscrapers, but the resulting office towers in the southwest quadrant of the central business district have yet to prove their worth, and the vacancy rate in commercial real estate remains high. Completed in 1994, the Pennsylvania Convention Center may invigorate the city's economy by bringing thousands of visitors to Philadelphia. But it remains to be seen whether prosperity at the center will extend to the depressed neighborhoods surrounding the downtown.

Throughout its history Philadelphia's economy has affected its people, influencing both the size and composition of its population. Although William Penn and his followers welcomed newcomers irrespective of faith, it was commerce that made Philadelphia the largest and most diverse city in the British colonies on the eve of independence. Over the next 75 years, manufacturing and trade combined to propel its population forward. The English, Scots-Irish, and Germans who composed the bulk of the city's people in 1780 had to make room for the flood of immigrants from Ireland and southern Germany who arrived after 1820. The African-American community grew as well. While it was small consolation to the city's businessmen and civic boosters, in 1850 Philadelphia trailed only New York among American cities in population.

Industrialization drove the city's demographics in the second half of the nineteenth century. The demand for labor brought unskilled and semiskilled workers from Southern and Eastern Europe in ever-increasing numbers. Italians, Poles, and Russian Jews helped swell the number of Philadelphians to nearly 1.3 million by 1900. Attracted by the prospect of jobs in the city's wartime economy, many African Americans left southeastern states like North Carolina and Georgia for Philadelphia after 1915. By the time the Depression undercut the demand for industrial labor, the city's population was approaching 2 million, and Philadelphia called itself the workshop of the world.

Between 1930 and 1950, Philadelphia's population increased by only 6 percent. The city had reached the top of its demographic curve, and thereafter its population would steadily shrink, falling from 2.07 million in 1950 to less than 1.7 million 30 years later. By 1992, its population had dipped well below 1.6 million. However, many who left the city remained in the region. Jobs that fled Philadelphia often settled in its suburbs, and the middle class followed them. The census of 1960 revealed that Philadelphia no longer accounted for a majority of those living in its eight-county metropolitan area. The city's share of jobs in the region fell below 50 percent in the 1970s. Unlike the city itself, Philadelphia's SMSA (Standard Metropolitan Statistical Area) was hardly in decline, and it continues to vie with Houston for the honor of being the fourth largest in the United States.

Increasingly, Philadelphia became a city divided by race. While blacks always faced discrimination in housing and employment, it was not until after the rapid growth of the city's African-American population in the first half of the twentieth century that vast stretches of Philadelphia became racially segregated. Denied access to credit by the policies of banks and the federal government, blacks concentrated in two large areas, north and west of downtown, that quickly became economically depressed. Along with discrimination, Philadelphia's African Americans were the victims of bad timing. Earlier generations of immigrants benefited from the city's enormous appetite for unskilled and semiskilled labor, but after 1945 the city had fewer and fewer places for newcomers without education or capital. Between 1960 and 1990, the proportion of blacks in the city's population nearly doubled, amounting to almost 50 percent by 1994. Many live in the shadow of factories that once employed thousands but now stand idle.

Philadelphia's public schools reflect the city's racial imbalance. Thirty percent black in 1950, the schools now enroll almost two African Americans for every child of another race. Whites have largely abandoned the public schools, most choosing to send their children to private or parochial schools if they still live in the city. Hispanic students account for almost 10 percent of the school population, up dramatically since 1970. East Asian enrollment stands at about 4 percent, twice what it was a decade ago. What began as a system of education for paupers in 1818 has come nearly full circle; half the families that patronize the public schools are on welfare. In 1968, the state ordered the School District of Philadelphia to desegregate, but despite the persistent efforts of the Pennsylvania Human Relations Commission, segregation remains firmly entrenched. The schools have been no match for segregated housing patterns, and the enhanced presence of minority and underclass students in the district's demographic profile has made integration more unlikely than ever.

The growth of Asian and Hispanic enrollment in the public schools corresponds to an important trend in the city's population as a whole. Since the early 1970s, Philadelphia has received thousands of immigrants from Europe, Asia, and Latin America. Compared to those who came at the beginning of the twentieth century, recent arrivals from Poland and the former Soviet Union are more often political refugees. In 1990, Hispanics, mainly from Puerto Rico, Colombia, and Central America, composed 6 percent of the city's population and East Asians, 3 percent. Koreans far outnumber the Vietnamese, Cambodians, and Filipinos, and, not unlike the city's small but visible population of East Indians, they possess more skills and resources than most immigrants, either past or present. Some are sufficiently well educated to move into high-paying jobs in the service economy; others have enough capital to open their own businesses. Even though many of the new immigrants are more independent than those who came earlier, they still must contend with prejudice and discrimination. In Philadelphia, the contest for work and space among ethnic and socioeconomic groups remains as competitive and complex today as it was when the Irish faced off against nativist mechanics and artisans in the Bible Riots of 1844.

For a brief time in the 1850s, Philadelphia ranked geographically as the largest city in the world. The consolidation of the city and county of Philadelphia in 1854 brought together an area measuring 130 square miles, a vast expanse by the standards of the day. Then, as now, the face of the city was marked by contrast; within its new boundaries there were urban, suburban, and rural settings. Such extremes were fitting. In a city that was fragmented in countless ways, and becoming more so every day, it was appropriate that its landscape, too, should be distended, differentiated, and diverse. However, it was not always so.

Colonial Philadelphia was densely settled and compact. William Penn and his surveyor, Thomas Holme, imagined something else. Squared off into a grid, their city was to have been spacious and open, but it soon became a tight concentration of people and buildings wedged against the Delaware River. Blocks intended for one or two homes filled in with row houses. Land use was undifferentiated; Philadelphians lived, worked, and played in the same place. Not everyone enjoyed the same lifestyle. The social structure was stratified, but each citizen participated in a world that was familiar to one and all.

During the first half of the nineteenth century, Philadelphia began to assume its modern form. Although still a walking city, it spread out, and functional distinctions in the physical environment started to appear. By the 1850s, settlement stretched from the Delaware to the Schuylkill Rivers. Residential neighborhoods were taking shape and, within them, social class sorted the population, relegating the hovels of the poor to alleys behind the grand townhouses that faced the principal streets. In business districts, production parted company with sales, nonmanual work with that done by hand. A middle class was emerging, distinguished as much by what it did for a living as by where it went at the end of the day.

The differentiation of space by function, ethnicity, and social class continued unabated after the Civil War. Built halfway between the Delaware and Schuylkill Rivers, a new City Hall pulled the central business district toward it, expanding the area of the city devoted exclusively to work. A revolution in mass transportation divided the city even further. Commuter railroads first connected satellite communities like Germantown and Chestnut Hill to the business district in the 1850s. Affluent Philadelphians could now travel long distances to work. The introduction of electric streetcars made possible the development of middle-class suburbs north and west of the downtown, while the construction of the Market Street Elevated and the Broad Street subway extended the scope of functional differentiation and geographic decentralization after 1900. Even the working class could now commute.

But it was the automobile that made Philadelphia sprawl and crawl. It detached Philadelphians from their roots, enabling them to live and work far from the central business district. Completed in the 1920s, the Benjamin Franklin and Tacony-Palmyra Bridges spurred the suburbanization of Burlington and Camden Counties in New Jersey. Meanwhile, cars and trucks quickly became a major problem in downtown Philadelphia. Standing at the intersection of the city's most important thoroughfares, Broad and Market Streets, the new City Hall impeded the flow of motor vehicles and, according to some, deserved to be demolished. By the 1940s, engineers and government bureaucrats were recommending expressways to diminish traffic congestion, while local politicians and planners, led by Edmund Bacon, argued that such roads would revitalize the economy of the downtown. Built between 1950 and 1958, the Schuylkill Expressway linked the inner city with the Pennsylvania Turnpike, but instead of promoting economic growth in the central business district, it had the opposite effect. Traffic jams plagued the route almost from the outset, prompting shoppers to avoid the downtown. At the junction of the expressway and the turnpike, the King of Prussia Mall became the biggest in the region. The city had come to the suburbs, but along with convenience and excitement it brought diversity and disarray.

Of course, Philadelphians were sensitive to the dangers of overdevelopment long before the last decades of the twentieth century. In the 1850s, the city fathers acquired more than 150 acres for what would soon become the largest urban park in America. Along the banks of the Schuylkill River, north of the Fairmount Water Works, open land was set aside to protect the city's water supply and provide citizens with a common retreat from the stresses and strains of urban life. But far from a haven, Fairmount Park became a Mecca, welcoming the world when the Centennial Exposition was held there. Expanded to almost 3,000 acres in the 1860s, the park afforded ample space for such an event. Fifty nations mounted displays, and more than 10 million people visited the fair between May and November 1876.

As one of Philadelphia's most important assets, Fairmount Park was responsible for a major alteration in the city's landscape at the beginning of the twentieth century. To connect it with the downtown, the business and political elites authorized construction of a grand avenue between the entrance to the park and City Hall. Laid out between 1908 and 1918, the Benjamin Franklin Parkway laid waste to a densely populated, working-class neighborhood. It became home to many of the city's leading cultural and educational institutions including the Free Library of Philadelphia, the Franklin Institute, the Rodin Museum, and the Philadelphia Museum of Art. Opened to the public in 1928, the Neoclassical complex that houses the Art Museum still anchors the west end of the Parkway, an impressive tribute to the values of the Philadelphia upper class. But it was the more modest Rodin Museum that captured the meaning of the Parkway for this divided metropolis. Built to house the art collection of movie theater mogul Jules Mastbaum, its collection quietly symbolized, and to astute observers revealed, the gulf between elite and popular culture in a city split by space, race, and class.

By the 1920s Fairmount Park and the Benjamin Franklin Parkway were just the latest in a long line of political and social features that maintained an illusion of community in Philadelphia. Led by men like Israel Durham, Boies Penrose, and Edwin, George, and William S. Vare, the Republican Party commanded the allegiance of voters in the city for more than a half-century. Between 1870 and 1920 the Republicans lost the mayor's office only twice. The party thrived on political favors and patronage, forging an awkward alliance between its affluent leaders and the rank and file. It parceled out contracts to construct and maintain public works and distrib-

uted franchise rights in transportation, communications, and utilities. The public jobs it created and the private wealth it sustained easily silenced its critics. In 1910 there were only 15,000 registered Democrats in the city, but the Republican hegemony would not last forever. The Depression turned the political tables and transformed most Philadelphians into Democrats. By the 1950s, the Democratic Party was firmly in charge of the government, if not at peace with itself.

Neighborhood differences made city council a Democratic battleground. Ethnic groups vied for control of the party. Between 1951 and 1991, the Democrats elected two patricians, two Irish Americans, an Italian American, an African American, and a Jewish American to the office of mayor. Not even the political about-face of former Democratic mayor Frank Rizzo could make the Republicans winners. In Philadelphia almost everyone has something superficial in common; they are Democrats.

Regardless of their party affiliation, reformers have yet to make a lasting impact on the power structure of the city. Reform administrations such as those of Rudolph Blankenburg (1911–1916) and Joseph Clark (1952–1956) were short-lived. To compensate for poverty, ignorance, and injustice, Philadelphians have relied heavily on voluntarism since colonial times. Building on the work of the Quakers, the Protestant elite organized a host of charitable institutions in the nineteenth century. They brought private interests and resources to bear on education and social welfare through such organizations as the Magdalen Society (1800), the Western Soup Society (1837), and the Philadelphia Society to Protect Children (1877). Settlement houses arrived in the city in the 1890s, and by 1906 there were enough to justify formation of a Greater Philadelphia Federation of Settlements. But the urge to organize did not stop there. Founded by the city's political and social leaders in 1920, the Welfare Federation set in motion the complete bureaucratization of charity in Philadelphia. The merger in 1959 of the federation's two legatees, the United Fund and the Community Chest, put in place a comprehensive structure to rationalize the collection and distribution of all charitable dollars. But unity has proved elusive. Today, federations representing women and minorities compete with the United Fund, now called the United Way, for the support of donors in Philadelphia and its Pennsylvania suburbs.

From the perspective of the present, Philadelphia appears to be in decline. Buffeted by winds of social and economic change, the city is struggling to maintain its balance. Regionalism is touted as the latest panacea. The nucleus of a metropolitan area that is home to more than 4 million people, Philadelphia participates in a much larger whole. Likewise, the suburbs benefit from the presence of the city, and the two must learn to work together, say policymakers and planners.

Tension between the center and the periphery is nothing new. But the diversity and fragmentation that exist today are unprecedented. Will they feed upon themselves, leading to still more parochialism and increasing levels of distrust, disorder, and decay? Or, will they drive recovery, providing the stimulation that comes from encounters with the unknown? On this score, the past is a poor predictor of the future. Diversity is a relative phenomenon. Levels of heterogeneity and discontinuity that once might have seemed intolerable are now taken for granted. Suffice it to say that Philadelphians have always managed to cope with diversity, conflict, and change.

—*William W. Cutler, III*

**See also**

Benjamin Franklin Parkway; Centennial Exposition of 1876; Chestnut Hill, Pennsylvania; The Main Line (Philadelphia, Pennsylvania).

**References**

Adams, Carolyn, et al. *Philadelphia: Neighborhoods, Division, and Conflict in a Postindustrial City.* Philadelphia: Temple University Press, 1991.

Cutler, William W., III, and Howard Gillette, Jr., eds. *The Divided Metropolis: Social and Spatial Dimensions of Philadelphia, 1800–1975.* Westport, CT: Greenwood Press, 1980.

Davis, Allen F., and Mark Haller, eds. *The Peoples of Philadelphia: A History of Ethnic Groups and Lower-Class Life, 1790–1940.* Philadelphia: Temple University Press, 1973.

Hershberg, Theodore, ed. *Philadelphia: Work, Space, Family and Group Experience in the Nineteenth Century.* New York: Oxford University Press, 1981.

Scharf, J. Thomas, and Thompson Westcott. *History of Philadelphia.* Philadelphia: L. H. Everts, 1884.

Toll, Jean B., and Mildred S. Gillam, eds. *Invisible Philadelphia: Community through Voluntary Organizations.* Philadelphia: Atwater Kent Museum, 1994.

Warner, Sam Bass, Jr. *The Private City: Philadelphia in Three Periods of Its Growth.* 2d ed. Philadelphia: University of Pennsylvania Press, 1987.

Weigley, Russell, ed. *Philadelphia: A Three Hundred Year History.* New York: W. W. Norton, 1982.

## Philanthropy

From the days of the Puritans, the philanthropic impulse in American life has had a two-sided existence. Encouraged to give alms for the sake of a moral life and community, Americans have always harbored the suspicion that charity also required close monitoring. "Instead of exhorting you to augment your charity," Cotton Mather told Bostonians in 1698, "I will rather utter an exhortation . . . that you may not *abuse* your charity by misapplying it." In the same fashion, Benjamin Franklin, an auger of all sorts of civic and educational philanthropic projects, struck a policy theme that has never disappeared from American life when he argued for abolishing English-style poor laws on the grounds that publicly administered charity pauperized rather than aided its recipients.

City life naturally concentrated philanthropic need. In Benjamin Rush and Stephen Girard, Philadelphians a generation younger than Franklin, two archetypes of urban philanthropy can be seen, the peripatetic liberal reformer determined to remake society and the flinty-eyed businessman who bequeathed vast sums for targeted needs such as orphanages, hospitals, and municipal improvements.

Fueled by the religious revival of the early nineteenth century, philanthropic efforts grew with antebellum cities. Boston merchants like Amos and Abbott Lawrence, convinced that their worldly fortunes imposed God-given responsibilities of social stewardship on them, disbursed contributions to many of the myriad charities that made up the "Benevolent Empire" of homes for fallen women, Bible distribution societies, Sunday schools, and temperance societies. Yet the era also produced innovation. In reformers such as the Boston clergyman Joseph Tuckerman (1778–1840), the traditional mistrust of indiscriminate almsgiving coexisted with a concrete understanding of poverty's structural causes. "I am ready," he wrote in 1828, "to maintain, and to act upon, the principle, 'if a man *will not* work, neither shall he eat.' But if he *cannot* work, or cannot obtain employment—and strange as it may seem to some, this is a very possible case—nor eat, except he obtain the bread of charity, shall it be witholden?" Tuckerman promoted savings banks and other self-help schemes for the poor and inaugurated the social worker's practice of home visiting through his Ministry at Large. His work underscored the division of the poor into "deserving" and "undeserving," which in turn corresponded to a *de facto* division of labor between private and public charity.

Activists like Horace Mann and Dorothea Dix put other antebellum philanthropic causes, such as public education and treatment of the mentally ill, on a new and stronger footing. They produced detailed empirical investigations while persistently and skillfully lobbying legislatures. Yet suspicion of using public resources remained strong. In 1854, President Franklin Pierce vetoed a bill that Dix had strenuously promoted through Congress that would have authorized federal land grants to states to build hospitals and asylums for the insane. Pierce feared that the law would have eventually led to a "transfer to the Federal Government of the charge of all poor in all the states."

The Civil War recast institutions, policies, and attitudes in unexpected ways. The U.S. Sanitary Commission, established in 1861, became a vast umbrella agency for war-related medical practices, drawing on the skills of talented individuals such as Frederick Law Olmsted. The great wartime sanitary fairs of 1863 and 1864 enlisted women from northern cities to raise funds for the commission. Postwar philanthropy drew liberally from the experience and authority wartime philanthropy had given thousands of men and women. The era of "scientific philanthropy" extended wartime principles of organization into institutions like state boards of charities (modeled after the example of Massachusetts in 1863), which amalgamated into the quasi-public National Conference of Charities and Correction. Private religious philanthropies underwent a similar rationalization. The United Hebrew Charities, for example, combined Jewish organizations in Philadelphia and New York in the early 1870s.

Ideologically, the London-based Charity Organization Society provided the model for American "scientific philanthropy." Seeking to promote efficiency, avoid duplication of services, and above all discourage pauperism, Gilded Age philanthropists borrowed the principles, if not the wisdom, of Joseph Tuckerman, liberally ascribing poverty to defective character and urging the spiritual reform of the individual as the answer to need. Yet, the empirical, fact-finding "science" of scientific philanthropy, intended to root out fraud, inevitably dug up information about the causes of poverty unrelated to questions of character. This dynamic created a new generation of idealistic reformers whose understanding of poverty contradicted the ideologically driven assumptions of scientific philanthropists.

In a society now urbanizing rapidly and absorbing hundreds of thousands of immigrants, a nascent domestic market struggled to keep pace with overproduction, and industrial cities faced seemingly endemic social dislocations. Late-nineteenth-century philanthropic efforts responded by adapting old ideas and inventing new ones. Settlement houses, staffed by eager, middle-class, college-educated men and women, sought, as the constitution of New York's University Settlement House put it, to "bring men and women of education into closer relationship with the laboring classes for their mutual benefit." Encouraged by figures like Jane Addams, who founded Chicago's Hull House, and Mary Richmond, who worked in Baltimore and Philadelphia before becoming director of the Russell Sage Foundation's Charity Organization Department, social work emerged as a credentialed profession with the opening of the New York School of Applied Philanthropy (later the Columbia School of Social Work) in 1904.

Undercutting ideological assumptions about poverty and individual character, settlement house workers in the Progressive Era advocated state action—such as enacting child labor laws, establishing pension and social insurance plans, and providing parks, libraries, and schools—to ameliorate environmental conditions and allow the collective needs of the urban poor to be addressed. Simultaneously, some of the huge fortunes accumulated during the great industrial expansion were channeled into what John D. Rockefeller called the "business of benevolence," an emerging world of trusts and foundations based on the social Darwinist idea of "trusteeship" articulated by Andrew Carnegie in his famous 1889 essay, "The Gospel of Wealth."

The Carnegie Corporation (1911) and the Carnegie Foundation for the Advancement of Teaching (1905), the Rockefeller Foundation (1913) and Rockefeller Institute for Medical Research (1901), the General Education Board (1902), and numerous others thus represented a new and crucial institution in private American philanthropy. Some in the trust-busting era suspected the "tainted money" of industrial titans, but their largesse and their implications for the future were equally enormous.

While those implications would not become fully apparent until after World War II, the Depression brought the structure of American philanthropy, and time-honored philanthropic assumptions, to a watershed. Herbert Hoover had come to the presidency in 1928 riding a well-deserved reputation as an able administrator of the vast philanthropic projects that channeled millions of dollars of aid into postwar Europe. Faced with the unprecedented social travails attendant upon a collapsed industrial economy in 1930 and 1931, Hoover clung to the principles of voluntarism and the intrinsic moral worth of private charity. As the suffering continued and existing structures proved incapable of solving the problems, suspicion of well-heeled philanthropists who insisted on the complete sufficiency of voluntary institutions intensified. Advocates of federal unemployment benefits ridiculed those who preferred private breadlines and soup kitchens to the dreaded public "dole."

The New Deal legislation that followed under FDR—minimum wage laws, social security, and unemployment insurance—created the skeleton of an American welfare state. The "War on Poverty" in the 1960s vastly expanded these structures, principally through the establishment of the 1965 Medicare and Medicaid programs for the elderly and the poor and the enlargement of social security benefits in 1967. Postwar prosperity and the gradual broadening of state services necessarily redefined private philanthropy in the 1950s and 1960s. Rather than the traditional focus on subsistence relief, now assumed by the state, charities increasingly turned to causes like eradicating specific diseases or providing counsel to the distressed. The great foundations also extended their activities. The most notable was the Ford Foundation, which held 90 percent of the stock of one of the wealthiest corporations in the world. Established in 1936, it was poised by the early 1950s to embark on a program of massive organized giving with national and international consequences. In the mid-1960s, the foundation responded to the explosion of racial violence in American cities by targeting minority advocacy groups and housing, employment, and legal aid societies for grant money.

At century's end American philanthropy may again be at a turning point. The welfare state is contracting, and the gains won by successful advocacy politics of the 1960s and 1970s are being steadily rolled back. Private, individual giving, always the single largest source of philanthropy, has continued to grow, often channeled through umbrella agencies like the United Way. The foundations continue their work, including newcomers like the MacArthur Foundation, established in 1978 and best known for its "genius grants" to scholars, scientists, artists, and social activists. Corporate sponsorship of philanthropic projects have assumed a larger share of the spotlight. But the sustained political assault on state-sponsored philanthropy that began in 1980, the implications of which far outweigh the illusory benefits of corporate image-making, still gathers momentum. As the state role in providing a social safety net slowly recedes and old arguments about poverty and individual character are revived, vigorous as ever, the voice of Cotton Mather again can be heard, exhorting Americans not to abuse their charity by misapplying it.

*—Howard M. Wach*

**See also**
Charity.
**References**

Bremner, Robert H. *American Philanthropy.* 2d ed. Chicago: University of Chicago Press, 1988.
———. *From the Depths: The Discovery of Poverty in the United States.* 2d ed. New Brunswick, NJ: Transaction Publishers, 1991.
Ehrenreich, John H. *The Altruistic Imagination: A History of Social Work and Social Policy in the United States.* Ithaca, NY: Cornell University Press, 1985.
Wach, Howard M. "Unitarian Philanthropy and Cultural Hegemony in Comparative Perspective: Manchester and Boston, 1827–1848." *Journal of Social History* 26 (1993): 539–557.

## Phoenix, Arizona

In 1867, pioneers entered the Salt River Valley in central Arizona and admired what remained of an ancient canal system built by the Hohokam, a people who had lived there before 1400. Homesteading the land, clearing out old irrigation ditches, planting crops, and negotiating supply contracts with nearby army posts and mining camps, the pioneers created an economic base for their community. Realizing that they were revitalizing the land of an ancient agricultural people, the settlers named their townsite Phoenix in 1870, a fitting symbol of life rising anew from the remains of the past. Growth was slow but steady, and by 1900 the town contained a population of 5,544 and offered an impressive array of urban goods, services, and amenities. By then it was a railroad hub, the seat of Maricopa County, and the territorial capital.

Along with progress came problems. In 1900, little rain fell in the nearby mountains, and the Salt River dwindled to a trickle. Thousands of acres of land were forced from cultivation, and many of the farmers and townspeople moved away in search of a more promising place. Those who remained recognized that growth would be limited unless they provided an adequate water supply. After much debate, they decided that a storage system was the answer. Joining together, residents of the valley formed the Salt River Valley Water Users' Association, and this organization, taking advantage of the National Reclamation Act of 1902, supported the federal government in constructing Roosevelt Dam, completed in 1911. Water management projects brought vital stability to the area, allowed irrigation control, and assured agricultural growth and prosperity. And as the valley prospered, so did Phoenix. In the decade following 1910, its population almost tripled, increasing from 11,134 to 29,053, and by 1920 it had surpassed Tucson and established itself as the largest city between El Paso and Los Angeles.

Business and civic leaders, proud of their city and eager to see its continued development, conducted promotional campaigns to attract visitors and new residents to the area. These campaigns emphasized the opportunities and amenities available in Phoenix, especially its climate. As a result, thousands of people arrived in the resort city during the 1920s. Phoenix also served as the center of activity for towns, farms, ranches, and mining settlements in its hinterland, and by 1930 the city had become a regional urban center with a population of almost 50,000. The Depression retarded progress, but the city's population nevertheless surpassed 65,000 in 1940.

During the 1930s, the federal government helped alleviate distress in the city and the valley with its New Deal programs, and during and after World War II the relationship between Washington and the entire area grew stronger as Arizona's capital became a major center for the military and high technology enterprises. Business leaders worked closely with the state's representatives in Washington to secure valuable assets for the area. Many inducements and other forms of cooperation were extended, and federal funds and projects stimulated the local economy.

During the Cold War, installations such as Luke and Williams Air Force Bases served as important parts of the national defense, and former war plants looked not only to the military but also to civilian markets. A multiplier effect took hold, and the coming of some manufacturers to the area attracted others. Electronics firms predominated.

Phoenix climbed to the top of the urban hierarchy in the desert Southwest during the 1950s, and it tightened its grip on that position during the next 20 years as a center of manufacturing, agriculture, and tourism. The mass production and widespread use of air conditioners in the 1950s turned Phoenix into a year-round city, and as the population rose the need for services increased.

Census returns reflected the widespread appeal of Phoenix's opportunities and amenities. Its population reached 789,704 in 1980, up from 439,170 in 1960 and 65,414 in 1940. By 1980, it was the ninth largest city in the nation, up from twentieth in 1970, and it was recognized as a growth leader in the new urban America. An aggressive annexation policy helped; the city increased its physical size from 17.1 square miles in 1950 to 324.1 in 1980. As in the past, the population was largely white in 1980. African Americans and Hispanic Americans (mostly Mexican Americans) accounted for less than 20 percent of the city's population. Hispanics continued to be the largest minority group, 14.3 percent of the population, while African Americans constituted only 4.7 percent.

In 1949, a group of boosters—business and civic leaders—organized the Charter Government Committee (CGC). It endorsed charter revision and supported the election of nonpartisan candidates. Business-minded, growth-oriented, and pragmatic enough to turn back serious opposition, the CGC and its successful candidates controlled local government for 25 years. Critics continued asking for structural change in the political system, and in 1982 Phoenix voters approved expansion of the city council from six to eight members, all elected from districts, although the mayor continued to be elected at-large. The phenomenal growth of Phoenix clearly demanded more inclusive political representation, and most voters approved of the change.

Over the years, downtown Phoenix, with its high-rise buildings, continued to serve as the governmental, legal, and financial center of the urban area, but the sprawling city, a product of the automobile age, kept spawning new focal points as residential dispersal and the decentralization of business and industry increased. Nearby towns and cities, including Tempe, Scottsdale, and Mesa to the east and Glendale to the west, became large satellites of Phoenix. Small communities in 1940, these places thrived during the next 40 years, and as a result there emerged a single vast, metropolitan complex connected by automobiles to the capital city in the middle.

In the 1950s and 1960s each town retained its own distinct identity. Tempe was the home of Arizona State University, Mesa remained the "Mormon Capital of Arizona," and Glendale continued to be a farming community. Scottsdale billed itself as "The West's Most Western Town" and became famous as a winter resort for affluent tourists. By the 1970s, however, it became increasingly difficult for these towns to maintain unique identities as they each experienced population explosions and building booms. Under the rush of more people, automobiles, housing developments, shopping centers, and office and industrial parks, the urbanization of the desert continued.

Low-density urban sprawl remained part of Arizona's lifestyle; since World War II, many newcomers to the sprawling Sunbelt metropolis had left decaying, high-density, heavily industrial areas, and they welcomed the change, preferring Phoenix to the cities they had left. This feeling and the atmosphere it encouraged helped the Phoenix Standard Metropolitan Statistical Area (SMSA) increase its population more than 700 percent between 1940 and 1980, easily continuing it as the metropolitan center of the desert Southwest. In 1980, the Phoenix metropolitan area was growing more rapidly than any other of the 30 largest SMSAs in the country.

The rapid rise of this metropolis produced significant problems as well as benefits. One major difficulty continued to be the conflict between two of the area's most cherished values—growth and the good life. Growth seemed inevitable, but the quality of life was not assured. The great challenge facing metropolitan Phoenix increasingly focused on achieving a workable balance between growth and the quality of life in the city and region.

—*Bradford Luckingham*

### References
Johnson, G. Wesley. *Phoenix: Valley of the Sun.* Tulsa, OK: Continental Heritage Press, 1982.
Luckingham, Bradford. *Phoenix: The History of a Southwestern Metropolis.* Tucson: University of Arizona Press, 1989.
———. "Trouble in a Sunbelt City." *Journal of the Southwest* 33 (1991): 52–67.
———. *The Urban Southwest: A Profile History of Albuquerque, El Paso, Phoenix, and Tucson.* El Paso: Texas Western Press, 1982.

## Pingree, Hazen S. (1840–1901)

Hazen S. Pingree, a shoe manufacturer who served as mayor of Detroit from 1890 to 1897 and governor of Michigan from 1897 to 1901, was born on a hardscrabble farm near Denmark, Maine, and had less than eight years of education in local schools. From humble beginnings as a leather cutter and itinerant cobbler, Pingree moved to Detroit where, by 1890, he had become proprietor of a large shoe factory with annual sales exceeding $1 million. He married a Michigan schoolteacher named Frances Gilbert and fathered three children, two of whom survived to adulthood.

Running as a political neophyte on the Republican ticket, Pingree won the Detroit mayoral election in 1889 and held that office until 1897. His four successive elections transformed the city's normally Democratic majorities to Republican victories with the help of foreign-born and ethnic voters whom he courted assiduously. Deeply sympathetic to the plight of unemployed workers, he became the nation's first prominent social reform mayor. He began a depression relief program (urban farming in 1893) and engaged in heated controversies with the city's traction, gas, electric, and telephone companies and forced them to reduce rates. He won public approval for a citizen-owned electric power plant, which he used as a "yardstick" to measure what he believed were overcharges by the privately owned utility.

Pingree's tempestuous political career in Detroit launched him as a leading urban spokesman for municipal ownership and (later) state regulation of utilities. He received national acclaim as the foremost, and one of the few, social reform mayors of his time. Pingree doubted the efficacy of both charter reform and structural reform—tinkering, he called them—which were the passions of municipal reformers at the time.

Elected governor of Michigan in 1896, Pingree served as chief executive of both the state and the city of Detroit until a judge vacated his municipal office. As governor, he fought continually with the powerful federal wing of his party but forced measures through the state legislature to correct the most flagrant tax evasions by large corporations. In one of his most notable battles, he pushed through legislation that brought about the first significant state reappraisal of railroad and corporate property; this law helped establish a rational basis for regulation and taxation, a measure that would later be emulated by Progressive reformers in other states, such as Wisconsin.

Choosing not to run for reelection in 1900, Pingree embarked for Africa to hunt elephants and look in on the Boer War where he hoped to voice his anti-imperialistic sentiments. Falling ill with dysentery, he died when he reached London on June 18, 1901. His reputation rests upon his work as the nation's first "social reform" mayor.

—*Melvin G. Holli*

Reference
Holli, Melvin G. *Reform in Detroit: Hazen S. Pingree and Urban Politics.* New York: Oxford University Press, 1969.

## Pittsburgh, Pennsylvania

Pittsburgh, the second largest city in Pennsylvania, has been known throughout most of its history as an industrial powerhouse and the center of the American steel industry. After World War II, an urban renewal program polished its gritty, smokestack image, but it took the virtual collapse of the American steel industry to wean Pittsburgh away from its dependence on heavy manufacturing. During the 1980s and 1990s, the city turned toward service but continued to grapple with the problems presented by an aging infrastructure and population, a regional exodus, and slow economic growth.

Pittsburgh emerged in the eighteenth century as a frontier fortress. Built on the point of land where the Monongahela and Allegheny rivers flowed together to become the Ohio, and bounded on both sides by hills, Fort Pitt (1759) provided the English with an ideal location from which to fend off attacks from the French and Native Americans. During the late eighteenth century, settlement gradually extended into the Golden Triangle, the 250-acre wedge of land that forms present-day downtown. By the time Pittsburgh was incorporated in 1816, the city had developed into a busy commercial center. Merchants and manufacturers catered to settlers passing through en route to the Ohio River Valley, and boat building became one of the region's earliest industries.

By the 1840s, the character of Pittsburgh's economy had begun to shift from commerce to manufacturing. Iron foundries, glassworks, brick refractories, and tin shops created a diverse manufacturing base and attracted thousands of skilled artisans from Ireland, Germany, Scotland, and England. The city's dense concentration of Ulster Protestants, most of whom arrived during frontier settlement, earned Pittsburgh's reputation as the Belfast of North America. These Scots-Irish Presbyterians came to dominate the social, political, and economic life of the city into the twentieth century; and many scions of Pittsburgh industry and finance, including the Mellon banking family, were of Scots-Irish descent. Today, despite successive waves of Catholic immigration, Presbyterian churches abound, and the city still forms the largest presbytery in the United States.

After the Civil War, the national demand for iron and steel, coupled with Pittsburgh's proximity to natural resources and transportation routes, contributed to its emergence as the "Forge of the Universe." Coal was mined from nearby hills, including Mt. Washington, the prominent bluff that overlooks downtown Pittsburgh. Between 1860 and 1910, the city produced over one-third of the nation's steel and over one-half of its glass and iron. Many of these foundries and factories spread from Pittsburgh southeast throughout the Monongahela Valley, the region's legendary steelmaking valley. Intent on cornering the market in steel rails, Andrew Carnegie established his formidable Carnegie Steel empire in industrial satellite towns like Braddock, Homestead, and Duquesne during the 1870s and 1880s. Pittsburgh was a boon to other industrialists, including George Westinghouse, Henry Clay Frick, and H. J. Heinz, the "pickle king." Many prominent American corporations, including Gulf Oil and Alcoa, were started in Pittsburgh during this period, often with the backing of financiers Andrew and R. B. Mellon.

Pittsburgh's intensive industrialization during the late nineteenth and early twentieth centuries exacted a heavy price. As early as 1868, the city appeared to be enveloped in a dense blanket of smoke, a condition that prompted James Parton to describe Pittsburgh as "hell with the lid off." To compensate for the pervasive soot and grime, downtown street

*Pittsburgh's downtown is known as the Golden Triangle because of its location where the Monongahela and Allegheny Rivers flow together to form the Ohio River.*

lights remained on during the day, and office workers carried an extra white shirt to wear after lunch.

Pittsburgh's smoke-belching mills also cast a foreboding pall over labor relations. Between 1887 and 1894, only New York and Chicago experienced more labor disturbances, and Pittsburgh led the country in the number of lockouts and the amount of wages lost because of them. The railroad strike of 1877 dramatically underscored worker discontent throughout the city, but the pivotal labor dispute was the Homestead Strike of 1892. With Carnegie's consent, Henry Clay Frick hired Pinkerton detectives to break the hold of the Amalgamated Association of Iron and Steel Workers at Carnegie's plant in Homestead. After a prolonged and bloody siege, Frick managed to reopen the plant and crush the union, an act that signaled the end of the "craftsmen's empire" in Pittsburgh and across the country.

After 1890 immigrants from Southern and Eastern Europe poured into Pittsburgh to satisfy the demand for unskilled labor in its expanding steel plants. By 1910 one-fourth of the city's residents were foreign-born, and another one-fifth had foreign-born parents. Many ethnic groups clustered in already densely settled city neighborhoods and built their own churches and mutual aid societies. Today, Pittsburgh

serves as national headquarters for the Croatian Fraternal Union, Polish Falcons, German Beneficial Union, Serb National Federation, and other ethnic fraternal organizations. Other than backbreaking work, industrial Pittsburgh offered new immigrants few rewards. In 1908, investigators for the Pittsburgh Survey, an exhaustive study of social conditions undertaken by the Russell Sage Foundation, found that most Slavic immigrants lived and worked in Dickensian conditions. Squalid, overcrowded housing contributed to high rates of infant mortality and the highest typhoid rate in the country. Pittsburgh also led the nation in the number of industrial accidents, a consequence of the steel industry's brutal 12-hour-day and 7-days-a-week work schedule.

Pittsburgh's phenomenal wealth did leave its mark, and examples of industrial-era munificence abound. Businessmen like Andrew Carnegie, Henry Clay Frick, and Andrew Mellon built libraries, churches, and other public institutions, most of them clustered in the city's fashionable East End. The Carnegie Library and Institute (1895) became the centerpiece of the Oakland civic center, home of some of the finest City Beautiful–inspired architecture and planning in the country. Located here are the campuses of Carnegie-Mellon University (formerly Carnegie Tech) and the University of

Pittsburgh, the planned residential development of Schenley Farms (1906), and Schenley Park (1889), a landscaped park appointed with bridle paths, fountains, and the nation's largest conservatory, donated by Henry Phipps, a Carnegie associate, in 1893. Prominent architects such as Frank Nicola, Henry Hornbostel, and Henry H. Richardson all played a hand in designing Pittsburgh's eclectic collection of civic buildings and private homes. Among the best examples of the latter is Clayton, the meticulously preserved home of Henry Clay Frick on "Millionaire's Row" in Point Breeze, opened to the public in 1990.

Living and working conditions for the majority of Pittsburgh's residents did not begin to improve until late in the 1930s and in the 1940s. Energized by New Deal legislation friendly to organized labor, the Congress of Industrial Organizations (CIO) chose Pittsburgh for its first meeting in 1938 under the leadership of John L. Lewis. Lewis in turn appointed Philip Murray to head the Steel Workers Organizing Committee, later the United Steelworkers of America (USWA). Having reached a contract with U.S. Steel before World War II, the USWA emerged as one of the nation's most powerful unions during the 1940s. Steelworkers' wages, traditionally among the lowest of all industrial occupations, rose considerably after the war.

Pittsburghers also benefited from improvements sponsored by the so-called Renaissance, a comprehensive urban renewal project launched after the war by city businessmen and politicians. Under the leadership of Richard King Mellon (a nephew of Andrew Mellon) and Mayor David Lawrence between about 1945 and 1960, the Renaissance implemented smoke abatement, slum clearance, and other public works projects designed to ameliorate urban blight. A later phase of redevelopment, often known as Renaissance II, resulted in several skyscrapers and a more modern-looking downtown. Thanks in part to postwar environmental improvements, Pittsburgh today boasts the highest proportion of green space of any major American city.

Physical improvements notwithstanding, Pittsburgh was still perceived, with much justification, as a steel town during the 1960s and 1970s. As early as 1963, one study determined the city to be perilously dependent on heavy manufacturing. Fully 40 percent of Pittsburgh's workers were employed in the metal trades, and the region continued to rely on U.S. Steel for jobs and economic stability. The recession of the early 1980s dramatically altered the status quo. Following an epidemic of plant shutdowns, employment in the steel industry dropped from 33 percent of the city's workers in 1979 to 5 percent in 1986; in all, some 90,000 manufacturing jobs were lost. City landmarks like the Eliza Furnaces and J&L (LTV) Steel on the South Side were closed or razed. Between 1983 and 1988, U.S. Steel shut down most of its plants in the Monongahela Valley, leaving behind boarded-up communities, aging populations, and some of the highest unemployment rates in the country. Historian Roy Lubove likened the region's social and economic collapse to "a wrenching industrial revolution in reverse." By 1990, Pittsburgh's population had declined by one-half from its peak in 1950.

Since the mid-1980s, Pittsburgh has attempted to refocus its economy around service and advanced technology. Research universities like Carnegie-Mellon University, the University of Pittsburgh, and Duquesne University have played a key role in this economic transformation. The University of Pittsburgh is considered a world leader in transplant technology and, along with Carnegie-Mellon, has launched several high technology ventures, including one center constructed on the site of a former steel mill. During the 1980s and 1990s, the University of Pittsburgh and its medical facilities became the city's largest employer, a title that had traditionally been held by U.S. Steel (now USX).

As heavy manufacturing disappeared, traditional working-class neighborhoods also changed. On the South Side, mill-gate taverns and nationality churches have given way to coffeehouses and art galleries, and hillside homes are being renovated into upscale lofts. Pittsburgh's industrial landscape is also being transfigured; during the 1990s efforts were under way to provide greater public access to the city's once polluted rivers and to build upscale housing on the site of an abandoned slag heap.

Despite these changes, present-day Pittsburgh defies many modern urban trends. The city boasts one of the highest persistence rates in the country and leads all other major cities in the percentage of residents who have lived in the same house for the past 30 years. Despite being cut off from recent migration (it has one of the smallest Hispanic populations in the country), ethnic identity remains strong. Residents still attend "nationality days" at Kennywood Park, a popular local amusement park, and patronize the world-famous Duquesne Tamburitzans, a musical troupe that showcases Eastern European traditions. A recent travel article described Pittsburgh as "a city where people go home to their parents for Sunday dinner," a localistic orientation that is borne out by Pittsburgh's low attendance at movie theaters but its perpetual enthusiasm for public festivals. (Pittsburgh's Saint Patrick's Day parade is the second largest in the nation.) Topography has played an underappreciated role in maintaining Pittsburgh's tightly knit neighborhoods; hills provide natural boundaries between neighborhoods, inhibit the untrammeled development of strip malls and megastores, and contribute to the city's abundant green space.

In recent years, Pittsburgh has received considerable attention from outsiders impressed by the city's mix of the traditional and the modern. In 1985 Rand McNally declared

Pittsburgh the most livable city in the country, citing the region's low cost of living, low crime rate, and impressive collection of modern amenities, including a world-class symphony and several nationally recognized museums (among them a new museum showcasing the work of native son Andy Warhol). Pittsburgh's visual diversity has attracted Hollywood film companies who have used the city as a location for such movies as *Silence of the Lambs* and *Hoffa*. In 1990 Brendan Gill hailed Pittsburgh as "a model of survival against high odds" and an example of the type of city that reflects an integrity "based not so much upon age . . . as upon the survival of cultural traditions that have been handed down for at least a few generations." Whether Pittsburgh can maintain that quality without the benefit of steel, and the way of life it supported, is uncertain.

—*Curtis Miner*

**See also**
Lawrence, David L.; Mt. Lebanon, Pennsylvania.
**References**
Bodnar, John, Roger Simon, and Michael P. Weber. *Lives of Their Own: Blacks, Italians, and Poles in Pittsburgh, 1900–1960*. Urbana: University of Illinois Press, 1982.
Couvares, Francis G. *The Remaking of Pittsburgh: Class and Culture in an Industrializing City, 1877–1919*. Albany: State University of New York Press, 1984.
Hays, Samuel P., ed. *City at the Point: Essays on the Social History of Pittsburgh*. Pittsburgh: PA: University of Pittsburgh Press, 1989.
Lubove, Roy. *Twentieth Century Pittsburgh*. 2 vols. New York: Knopf, 1969.
Toker, Franklin. *Pittsburgh: An Urban Portrait*. State College: Pennsylvania State University Press, 1986.

## Planned Community

A planned community is generally thought of as the result of a developer's attempt to go beyond simply developing land and constructing housing to create an entire integrated district or locality whose infrastructure contains certain physical characteristics that are not absolutely necessary but are expected to create a desirable environment for living. These features might include a street plan that differentiates between residential and arterial streets, underground utilities such as electrical and telephone wires, and the provision of cable television service or computer hookups in houses.

Moreover, planned communities contain amenities that are supposed to bring together in a convenient fashion many, or most, of the facilities needed in modern life (except work). These might consist of shopping, schools, recreational facilities, libraries, or even government offices (if the community is large enough to have them). A planned community might be as large as Columbia, Maryland, or Reston, Virginia, contain different residential neighborhoods, and have a discrete political existence, or it might just be a large development that includes a grocery store, convenience store, school, gas sta-

tion, and a few other retail outlets located in a small shopping center, such as Hethwood in Blacksburg, Virginia.

Of course, at least to some degree, all communities are planned, whether consciously or unconsciously. The choice of a site with freshwater, good farmland nearby, building materials, and an adjacent river for transportation have always been elements of any planned city—and city planning is a broader way of conceiving planned communities. Then, too, there are the more formally structured communities whose planning suggests that sites were selected to suit a plan and not the reverse. There is an aura of utopia about places consciously thought of as an attempt to form a more perfect environment, one that directly contrasts with existing communities. These utopian attempts are often reactions to previous experiences: where there was darkness, there is now light; where there was oppressive density, there is now openness; where there was filth and disease, there is now clean water, fresh air, and good health.

It is simplistic to suggest that planned communities are only reactions to the past. The motivation for creating a more humane environment has been pure, even if frequently predicated on the profit motive. The assumption is that new communities can be safer, more healthful, more functional, and more profitable. By the beginning of the twentieth century, the profit motive had been supplanted by what can be called "demonstration projects"—new and physically better environments to improve the quality of life. Of these demonstration projects, some began on raw sites where nothing existed; there were also proposals that utilized an existing urban place, including its infrastructure, which would be changed over time to become a new structure for urban life, in many cases less physically influenced by contemporary technology. The basic assumption animating these plans was that technology can change; therefore, a community's plans should be flexible enough to fully accommodate changes in technology as they evolve, but only to the extent that the quality of life continues to improve.

The altruistic (read paternalistic) characteristics of most (if not all) planned communities, alas, seem to contain the seeds of their own destruction. In actuality, such communities are predicated on a shortsighted understanding of both the problem and the history. Fortunately, this "problem" can be, and is being, overcome. The mechanism for doing this is returning to a kind of planning based on ecology, as the earliest settlements were based on an understanding of what is now called environmental planning. By returning to first principles, proponents of the contemporary planned community hope to return urban development to harmony with the environment, an especially difficult task because of an ongoing infatuation with technology among some members of society, in general, and among some planners, specifically.

The problem is quite simple. The designers of planned communities are not asking the right questions: to what end is planning undertaken? why does a paternalistic attitude toward the process take over? and why are alternatives to present conditions so difficult to articulate? If an alternative future cannot be imagined, how can a new paradigm be developed? It can only be hoped that the cycle, once begun, will turn upon itself and come full circle—that planning will once again become a humane and life-giving enterprise.

—*David A. Spaeth*

### References

Bacon, Edmond. *Design of Cities*. New York: Viking Press, 1967.

Davis, Mike. *City of Quartz: Excavating the Future in Los Angeles*. New York: Verso, 1990.

Hayden, Dolores. *Seven American Utopias: The Architecture of Communitarian Socialism*. Cambridge, MA: MIT Press, 1976.

Hilberseimer, Ludwig. *The New Regional Pattern*. Chicago: Paul Theobald, 1949.

Howard, Ebenezer. *Garden Cities of Tomorrow*. London: Faber and Faber, 1946.

Reps, John W. *The Making of Urban America: A History of City Planning in the United States*. Princeton, NJ: Princeton University Press, 1965.

## Playgrounds

Although the word "play" is difficult to define, in ordinary discourse, a playground is an outdoor place to play. In the twentieth century, the term is usually limited to places set aside and developed for children's play, frequently in a public park or as part of an elementary school.

Playgrounds for children began as part of educational and urban reform in Germany and other parts of Europe in the nineteenth century. The first playgrounds for children in the United States, consisting of sandboxes for young children and swings and seesaws for older children, were built in New York City and Boston in the 1870s and 1880s. Playgrounds were part of the emerging reform movement that valued physical exercise, sports, and organized games.

The first playgrounds were privately funded. In 1906, Joseph Lee, Luther Gulick, Jane Addams, and other reformers organized the Playground Association of America (PAA). The following year, the PAA began publishing a monthly journal, *The Playground,* which advocated the use of municipal funds to build playgrounds and train playground supervisors. City governments were generally more willing to pay for swings, slides, and jungle gyms than for staff, but recreation professionals worried that immigrant children would be corrupted by movies, saloons, and amusement parks. These reformers rejected the idea that a playground was just a place to play, and they sought to control the space with supervisors trained to teach "fair play" and obedience to rules. They also wanted playgrounds to be fenced and segregated by sex to protect children from bad influences.

*Originally developed as a way of promoting physical fitness in children, playgrounds have become common in cities. Some of their equipment can be very complex, as at this elementary school playground in Seattle, Washington.*

In the 1920s and 1930s, manufacturers of playground equipment such as Spalding sold a wide variety of apparatus to municipal parks and recreation departments as playgrounds spread from ghettos to middle-class neighborhoods to new suburbs. Well-equipped playgrounds with steel pipes supporting a variety of swings, slides, seesaws, trapezes, sliding poles, giant-strides, and merry-go-rounds became a familiar part of the landscape of every city and town in America. After World War II, the expansion of suburbs, where even tract houses had backyards large enough for scaled-down versions of traditional playground equipment, caused a major transformation of playgrounds.

City playgrounds have been perceived as dangerous even though new equipment, designed to look like the theme parks that were popping up in the 1950s, was installed. Climbing apparatus took on the outlines of castles, stagecoaches, and rockets. A growing concern for child safety led to placing rubberized mats, wood chips, and other soft material underneath the equipment to cushion falls. Influenced by Scandinavian theories of child development, some reformers advocated adventure playgrounds that were essentially vacant lots with scrap lumber to encourage children to build their own play structures. The Adventure playground never became popular in the United States, although in the 1970s almost all metal apparatus were replaced by wood structures, which adults considered safer and more beautiful. By the 1980s, landscape architects were providing kits for communities that wanted to build their own "customized" playgrounds. A phenomenon of the 1990s was the "Discovery Zone," privately owned play spaces in suburban shopping malls where parents are encouraged to watch their children swing and climb above a pit filled with plastic balls.

A century of discussion and experiment has produced few firm conclusions about the efficacy of playgrounds. Boys and girls of different ages may use playground apparatus differently, but no children play on the equipment for more than a small percentage of their total playtime. Clearly, it is good for children to have some open space in which to play, but it is less obvious that a particular playground design has any measurable benefit over any other. Playgrounds are convenient visual symbols of changes in attitudes toward children, as well as toward urban life in general.

—*Bernard Mergen*

### References

Brett, Arlene, Robin C. Moore, and Eugene Provenzo, Jr. *The Complete Playground Book.* Syracuse, NY: Syracuse University Press, 1993.

Harden, Pat, and Ellen O'Sullivan. "ABCs of Programming Recreation." *Parks and Recreation* 29 (1994): 30–35.

Mergen, Bernard. *Play and Playthings: A Reference Guide.* Westport, CT: Greenwood Press, 1982.

## Police and Police Departments

The development of modern police forces in American cities exemplifies the enhancement and growing complexity of municipal authority. At the same time, it reveals a shift in the basis of community order from a general consensus on moral and religious rules to reliance on a criminal justice system—of which the police force is only a part—to control an environment viewed by many urbanites as inherently deviant and contentious.

The earliest police arrangements in the English colonies were European carryovers. Until the early nineteenth century, towns and cities relied mostly on constables and night watchmen. The former were usually appointed officials whose responsibilities included both criminal and civil matters. The night watch was a duty for which all adult males under the age of 45 were eligible to be called. Often more alert to the deadly threat of fire, night watchmen offered only a small measure of crime control. Overall, this rudimentary police system was not proactive, as officials usually responded only to citizen complaint or public outcry.

By the middle of the nineteenth century, the rapid growth and increased heterogeneity of city populations, along with street disorders and perceived surges in day-to-day crime, focused new attention on what were still minimal police arrangements. The model for the development of modern American forces was the Metropolitan Police of London, created in 1829. As American police forces developed during the second and third quarters of the nineteenth century, led by New York, Philadelphia, and Boston, they developed similarities to the English model. The constables and night watch were combined into a single force of uniformed men who were armed with a baton or mace, expected to keep order through regular street patrols, and given new meaning by the emergence of more well defined urban land use. However, unlike the English, Americans were wary of letting a distant regional or central office control the new police; instead, they placed control of police in the municipality, usually the ward-based city council. Efforts to impose a system similar to London's did have a brief period of success during the second half of the nineteenth century with the establishment of a number of state-run "Metropolitan" systems including ones in New York (1857), Detroit (1863), San Francisco (1877), and Boston (1885). However, for the most part, these systems were short-lived, and by the end of the century most municipalities had reasserted control. At that point, modern police departments were being established in cities of small size but high aspirations and self-image. Having a police department was a badge of sophistication.

Because the new police officers represented local rather than regional or national authority, their work was caught up in the social conflict unleashed by the population diversity of American cities in the middle of the nineteenth century. Waves of foreign immigrants, particularly Irish and Germans, along with migrants from the American countryside, poured into cities. The resulting mosaic produced clashes—at the ballot box as well as in the street—over distinctive sociocultural behaviors and such issues as the opening of taverns and saloons on Sundays. When combined in larger cities with the emergence of well-defined central business districts, fashionable residential areas, and crowded blocks dominated by the emerging bachelor subculture of boarding houses, saloons, pool halls, and brothels, police forces took on different meanings for different urbanites. Buffeted about in this political and cultural maelstrom, the new police forces often experienced wholesale personnel changes, ineffective or inconsistent law enforcement from neighborhood to neighborhood, corruption and political interference, and inadequacies in dealing with riot and street disorder. Indeed, the massive New York draft riots of 1863 at once reflected these inadequacies and also showed the potential of the urban police as a valuable antiriot force, leading in turn to the fuller adoption of a military-type command structure after the Civil War.

Although many of the challenges faced by police forces in the middle of the nineteenth century were rooted in day-to-day neighborhood and ethnic-group tensions, the rapidly advancing industrialization of the country created more "modern," episodic forms of conflict, such as violence related to strikes. The use of urban police to combat strikes placed patrolmen in a difficult position. Usually members of the working class themselves, whose entry into the police force represented socioeconomic mobility (the annual pay of nineteenth-century patrolmen exceeded that of most, if not all, manual workers), patrolmen were tested in their professionalism. The extent to which police departments acted on behalf of the propertied classes may well have depended on the size of the city and its level of industrial sophistication; for example, the larger and more complex the city, the more vigorous the police were in controlling strikes in the interests of industrialists.

By the turn of the twentieth century, Progressive reformers looked critically at urban police forces as weak and obstructive institutions in which patrolmen's jobs were political prizes, resulting in a lack of police diligence and evenhandedness. At the same time, police forces were burdened with a variety of other "service" activities that were unintended consequences of departmental growth, e.g., lodging homeless men in police stations overnight. In response, Progressivism transformed urban policing. The drive for professionalism led to the emergence of more formal and stringent requirements to select and promote police officers. The establishment of the International Association of Chiefs of Police and

the emergence of practitioner-theorists like August Vollmer, head of the Berkeley, California, police department (1905–1932), reflected the drive for more centralized and independent police authority. The military model that had thrived earlier now competed with a civil service model that was reflected not only in new hiring and leadership practices but also in the creation of specialized department units covering vice, traffic, and internal matters, and the relocation of some functions to agencies such as departments of health, welfare, and housing.

Most importantly, police departments increasingly viewed their role as fighting crime, not providing services and monitoring public morals or street-corner behavior. This new view was highlighted by the many crime commissions of these years—notably the Wickersham Commission appointed by President Hoover in 1929—and eventually epitomized in the data on felonies that local police departments reported to Washington. There, the new Federal Bureau of Investigation, itself produced by the new ideal of a professional police force, publicized them as Uniform Crime Reports. In the course of this transformation, the arrest patterns of urban police changed dramatically, with far fewer apprehensions for ordinary offenses against the public order, such as drunkenness and disturbing the peace. In the meantime, the police station no longer functioned as an overnight flophouse for the homeless, handing that role to newly created municipal lodging houses in at least some cities. With side arms now standard issue, police officers had become frontline warriors in the battle against urban crime.

The professionalization of police forces produced mixed results by the middle of the twentieth century. Certainly blatant corruption, incompetence, and lawless discretionary behavior declined. However, police departments in large cities still drew most of their personnel from the white, lower-middle class, and suburban populations who looked less and less like the population groups most encountered by cops on the beat. More importantly, the police could hardly be said to have brought crime under control. Although the data suggest an overall decline in the rate of violent and property crimes between the 1880s and 1960s, the perception of a growing crime problem continued, partly because of the publicity constantly generated by the Uniform Crime Reports and partly by the public's fascination with gangsters and organized crime. Finally, the professionalization movement compromised relations between the police and the public by deemphasizing the noncriminal service work that urbanites valued in their police departments.

During the middle and late twentieth century, urban policing was further complicated by new technology. The automobile and the two-way radio have decreased the amount of street contact between police officers and the public and placed policemen in roving patrol cars with sophisticated communication devices. The automobile has also dramatically changed the urban environment in which policemen operate, breaking apart the dense and relatively compact industrial cities and creating instead the multicentered city— a vast complex of diverse communities, ranging from the lower-class, still somewhat dense inner cities populated mainly by minorities, to sprawling middle-class and upper-middle-class suburbs of detached houses on large lots.

As a result, the day-to-day relations between police officers and urbanites are less personal and direct, although not necessarily less positive. Preventive policing is more difficult, even with the mobility afforded by the patrol car, because of urban sprawl and the fact that criminals in automobiles have comparable mobility. Different styles of police departments have emerged to accommodate public expectations and the political realities of wholly different kinds of metropolitan communities. These have been best described by James Q. Wilson, who distinguishes among "service," "watchman," and "legalistic" departments. Ordering and disciplining automobile traffic has also brought police officers into a new relationship with citizens, who frequently interact with the police only in this context. At the same time, however, the police virtually serve as an army of occupation in the volatile inner cities.

While the professionalization movement during the twentieth century has focused the attention of the police on crime fighting, it has also regulated the behavior of the police. During the 1970s and 1980s, for example, the establishment of new procedures regarding the use of firearms reduced the number of people shot by the police. Nevertheless, the urban police retain considerable discretion in dealing with citizens, with the result that abuses remain, as graphically revealed in the highly publicized Rodney King episode in Los Angeles in 1991. The current state of police-community relations has prompted some to suggest that the twentieth-century professional model of policing is as inherently flawed as the nineteenth-century military model. Instead, the police should adopt what is called the "hospital model." This focuses on personalizing the relationship of police officers—the "physicians"—with the aggrieved citizenry—the "patients"—thus presenting a range of responses that give officers a chance to "succeed" without arresting and booking suspects, actions that have to date been used to measure effectiveness.

—*John C. Schneider*

**See also**
Crime and Criminals.
**References**
Fogelson, Robert M. *Big-City Police*. Cambridge, MA: Harvard University Press, 1977.
Guyot, Dorothy. *Policing as Though People Matter*. Philadelphia: Temple University Press, 1991.
Harring, Sidney L. *Policing a Class Society: The Experience of American Cities, 1865–1915*. New Brunswick, NJ: Rutgers University Press, 1983.
Miller, Wilbur R. *Cops and Bobbies: Police Authority in New York and London, 1830–1870*. Chicago: University of Chicago Press, 1977.
Monkkonen, Eric H. *Police in Urban America, 1860–1920*. New York: Cambridge University Press, 1981.
Moore, Mark H., and George L. Kelling. "'To Serve and Protect': Learning from Police History." *Public Interest* 70 (1983): 49–65.
Walker, Samuel. *The Police in America: An Introduction*. New York: McGraw-Hill, 1983.
———. *Taming the System: The Control of Discretion in Criminal Justice, 1950–1990*. New York: Oxford University Press, 1993.
Wilson, James Q. *Varieties of Police Behavior: The Management of Law and Order in Eight Communities*. Cambridge, MA: Harvard University Press, 1968.

## Polish Americans in Cities

Polish immigration to North America dates back to the early years of the Jamestown colony. Small numbers of Polish immigrants appeared throughout the colonial, revolutionary, and early national periods of American history, but large numbers of Poles did not arrive until after the Civil War. The six decades after 1865 experienced the greatest migration from Poland. During the same years, technological and economic forces transformed Polish peasants into industrial workers as part of the larger process that resulted in the industrialization of parts of Eastern Europe and the metamorphosis of the old agricultural system. Polish and other East European farmers lost their share of the European grain market to American farmers at the same time that American industries were seeking new sources of cheap labor. One result was the migration of some 3 million Poles to the United States. Economic changes also caused the migration of many Poles to other parts of the Western Hemisphere, Europe, and the Russian Empire.

Poles basically came to the United States in three waves before World War I. The first wave arrived between 1860 and 1890 from sections of Poland occupied by Germany. This was followed by Poles from Galicia, which was occupied by Austria, and then by Poles from the Russian Empire between 1890 and 1920. About 30 percent of all Polish immigrants returned to Poland.

While the vast majority of Polish immigrants lived in large cities, some settled in small industrial towns or in coal mining towns, and still others bought farms. After 1880, Chicago quickly became the cultural capital for Polish immigrants, and by 1920 it was the center of Polish America. By then, it housed 400,000 first- and second-generation Polish Americans while New York (St. Mark's Place on the Lower East Side, but especially Brooklyn's Greenpoint neighborhood), Pittsburgh, and Buffalo each had 200,000, and Milwaukee and Detroit had 100,000 each. Cleveland and Philadelphia each contained about 50,000 Polish Americans in 1920, and Omaha, Baltimore, Rochester, and the cities of southern New Jersey also developed substantial Polish-American communities.

In whatever towns and cities Polish immigrants settled, they attempted to re-create the communal life they had left behind in Poland. Their communities are often referred to collectively as Polonia, and many settlements took on Polish regional characteristics, reflecting the process of chain migration. The first institution to appear in most Polish colonies was a Roman Catholic organization created to form a Polish parish. These parishes re-created the Polish Catholic calendar in the United States. Traditional observances of Roman Catholic holy days were given Polish interpretations, and residents also celebrated Polish national holidays. The importance of the parish was furthered by the creation of Polish parochial schools staffed by orders of Polish nuns. These educational institutions maintained the Polish language and cultural traditions among the children of immigrants, and they also provided another base for community solidarity. This unity was especially important since Polish immigrants generally settled in cities with diverse ethnic populations. Urban neighborhoods often contained many different ethnic groups, which tended to be spatially integrated but socially segregated; Poles might live next door to Lithuanian or Irish Americans but attend different churches, send their children to different schools, and drink in different taverns. For these reasons, the parish system with its own parochial schools and allied institutions was of great consequence to Polish immigrants.

The fear that this system might be destroyed or co-opted caused various disputes in the Catholic Church and the establishment of a rival church in 1904, the Polish National Catholic Church. The Roman Catholic Church eventually responded by naming the first Polish bishop in the United States in 1908, Bishop Paul Rhode of Chicago and, later, Green Bay. The schism that resulted in the Polish National Catholic Church shook Polish-American settlements and created competing communities within Polonia.

Catholic parishes were hardly the only institutions that surfaced in Polish neighborhoods. Their populations also included many professionals who provided a middle-class base for institutional development. Small businesses flourished in Polish neighborhoods, especially funeral parlors, small grocery stores, and saloons. These served not only as places of commerce but as sources of communal life. Furthermore, Polish fraternal organizations, especially local branches of large national organizations such as the Chicago-based Polish Roman Catholic Union (1873), Polish National Alliance (1880), Polish Falcons (1894), and Polish Women's Alliance

(1898), appeared in every settlement. The creation of an ethnic press was also extremely important. The first Polish newspaper *Echo z Polski (Echo from Poland)* appeared in New York in 1863, but all the major Polish settlements had at least one newspaper. Local building-and-loan associations also emerged in every major settlement. These financial institutions played a vital role in Polish neighborhoods, and it is estimated that by 1901 about one-third of all Polish-American families owned their own homes.

Polish neighborhoods generally developed near large industrial areas such as the Bush area adjacent to the Illinois Steel South Works in Chicago. The cathedral-like St. Michael the Archangel Church, built in 1907, stood just a few blocks from the South Works' gate. St. Josaphat's Church dominated the skyline of Milwaukee's Polonia. The physical dominance of these churches was not unusual for Polish neighborhoods in the late nineteenth and early twentieth centuries, and the pattern would be repeated over and over again in cities like Pittsburgh, Detroit, and Brooklyn. By one estimate, 517 Polish parishes existed nationwide by 1900. Polonia was attempting to carve out its own space in the increasingly impersonal world of the American industrial city.

These Polish industrial communities suffered from the same conditions frequently identified with American industrial cities after the Civil War. Poor and crowded housing conditions prevailed. On Chicago's North Side, Poles lived in tenements with a housing density of about 340 people per acre. Families with an average of six children apiece in 1900 added to the crowding by taking in boarders, partly to supplement their incomes but also to help family members and friends who had recently arrived. This custom was part of the process of chain migration.

Until the 1940s, most Polish families had low incomes. Many families supported themselves with several sources of income, including the paycheck of the household head, income from boarders, child labor, and occasional working wives. Generally speaking, women with children did not work outside the home, but they added to family resources by taking in boarders or washing clothes for nonfamily members. Many families also planted gardens or kept livestock, even in cities. When Polish families bought homes, they often bought income property that also helped provide for their families.

As in most poor urban neighborhoods, crime, vice, and juvenile delinquency provided problems. The preservation of the family was extremely important to the community, and despite the observations of outside observers, Polish Americans tried hard, and were largely successful, in maintaining stable families. Much of this resulted from the intricate institutional system created by Polonia.

The second response of Polonia to the American city was an extracommunal one. Polish Americans reached out to other groups to have an impact on their neighborhoods. Polish participation in the labor movement was an important part of this response. Poles demanded better living and working conditions and tied these demands to increased safety and higher pay. Poles were involved in strikes throughout the years from 1886 to 1922, and they later played an important role in organizing the CIO during the 1930s. This extracommunal response increased as Poles acted together with others in neighborhood organizations, political parties, and professional associations. This would have been impossible without the important community building that preceded it.

The end of World War I resulted in the resurrection of an independent Poland, and the relationship between Poland and Polonia changed fundamentally. During the war itself, Polonia helped raise a Polish army to fight in France, but after the war Polonian concerns centered more on America and cultural preservation. The 1920s saw increased attacks on immigrants and the cutting off of immigration from Eastern and Southern Europe. As a result, Polonia turned inward and tried to maintain its solidarity in the United States. The economic collapse of the next decade brought even greater challenges to Polish Americans.

The Depression was hard on the Polish community. Many Poles had just begun in the 1920s to move out of old core neighborhoods to outlying districts where they were re-creating their institutional base or becoming assimilated. New Polish Catholic and Polish National Catholic parishes had begun to appear in these outlying neighborhoods, but the economic collapse after 1929 slowed and even stopped this trend. It also brought Polish Americans into the Democratic Party in large numbers. The Depression hit immigrant neighborhoods hard, and their residents rallied to President Roosevelt and the New Deal.

World War II, in turn, brought prosperity and a good deal of assimilation to the generation born in America. Unlike World War I, Polonia did not raise an army to fight for the homeland. Instead, Polish Americans collected money strictly for humanitarian aid. The American entrance into the fighting in 1941 brought large numbers of Polish Americans into the armed forces of the United States.

The creation of an independent Poland after World War I (and the resultant weakening of ties between Polonia and the homeland as Polish Americans felt less urgency about helping Poland), the impact of the Depression and the New Deal, as well as World War II, proved to be forces for Americanization. However, the aftermath of World War II saw the revitalization of Polish neighborhoods as countless numbers of displaced persons arrived in American cities. The displacement caused by the war and the subsequent Communist takeover of Poland caused a new wave of Polish immigration. The crisis also resulted in the creation of yet another important

Polish-American institution in 1944, the Polish American Congress. This new organization united the various Polish fraternal institutions and organizations into a powerful political force that was dedicated to the liberation of Poland and the cultural preservation of Polonia.

According to statistics from 1936 to 1977, 101,000 Poles came to the United States under the immigration quota system, 19,430 arrived as refugees, and 135,302 entered the United States as displaced persons under special legislation enacted between 1954 and 1977. Many of these immigrants came from the intellectual and middle classes of prewar Poland. This new immigration revived many Polish-American institutions and inner-city Polish neighborhoods despite the continued movement of earlier Polish Americans or their children to the outskirts of cities and suburbs.

Even with this rejuvenation, the American Polonia continued to change. Assimilation, intermarriage with other ethnic groups, and the trek to suburbs all jarred the institutional base created by the immigrant generation. Acculturation and even assimilation became a fact of life. After 1945 Polish Americans were more likely to attend high schools, colleges, and professional schools. Still, in general, the group tended to remain part of the working class through the 1960s. After 1970, however, more upward mobility took place and, with it, inner-city neighborhoods and membership in traditional Polish institutions declined. By 1990, 65 percent of all residents in the Chicago area who claimed Polish ancestry lived in suburbs.

Once again, however, another wave of immigration from Poland, both legal and illegal, had a serious impact on the American urban Polonia. The "Solidarity" immigration, composed largely of middle-class Poles and intellectuals, occurred after the declaration in 1981 of martial law in Poland. Once again, a thriving Polish culture appeared on the streets of Chicago, New York, Buffalo, and other traditional centers of Polonia. These new immigrants, however, have assimilated easily compared to the first wave of peasant immigrants and the second wave of displaced persons. What their arrival means for the continuance of an urban Polonia is a question that only the future will answer.

—*Dominic A. Pacyga*

**References**
Bukowczyk, John J. *And My Children Did Not Know Me: A History of the Polish-Americans.* Bloomington: Indiana University Press, 1987.
Greene, Victor. *For God and Country: The Rise of Polish and Lithuanian Ethnic Consciousness in America, 1860–1910.* Madison: State Historical Society of Wisconsin, 1975.
Kantowicz, Edward. *Polish Politics in Chicago, 1888–1940.* Chicago: University of Chicago Press, 1975.
Lopata, Helena Znaniecka, with Mary Patrice Erdmanns. *Polish Americans.* 2d rev. ed. New Brunswick, NJ: Transaction Publishers, 1995.

Pacyga, Dominic A. *Polish Immigrants and Industrial Chicago: Workers on the South Side, 1880–1922*. Columbus: Ohio State University Press 1991.

Parot, Joseph. *Polish Catholics in Chicago, 1850–1920*. DeKalb: Northern Illinois University Press, 1981.

Pula, James S. *Polish Americans: An Ethnic Community*. New York: Twayne, 1995.

## Population and Population Growth

As in most industrialized nations, population growth in the United States has largely occurred in the urban rather than in the rural sector. At the time of the first federal decennial census in 1790, only 24 places could be called urban, that is, having at least 2,500 residents—the basic census definition of "urban" for many decades. Altogether, those two dozen places had a combined population of 201,655, only 5 percent of the nation's total population at that time. The largest city, New York, had 49,400 inhabitants, and the average size of all the urban places was 8,400—hardly what we think of in terms of city sizes today. Although the U.S. Census Bureau's definition of "urban" has been slightly modified during the last 40 to 50 years, in 1990 there were thousands of urban places with an aggregate population exceeding 187 million, encompassing 75 percent of all U.S. citizens. Almost 85 percent of the nation's population growth since 1860 occurred in urban places as the United States changed from a predominately agricultural to an industrialized society.

To professionals and scholars specializing in population and its growth or decline (demographers), the urban population consists of a relatively large number of persons who live, work, and play together in a relatively small area with a concentrated population and whose economies largely center on nonagricultural activities. What is "urban" though, does not center just on numbers and densities but also upon social, economic, and political characteristics. Urban centers are also thought of as centers of trade and commerce, industrial production, and self-identity as social and political units.

Ordinarily, cities are thought of not just as urban places but as large urban places. There is wide variation in the size and nature of urban places, ranging all the way from small towns of 2,500 persons, which may be far removed from larger urban centers, to the immensely large urban centers (cities) themselves, such as New York City proper in which more than 7.3 million persons were officially enumerated in 1990. While most people intuitively distinguish between cities and small towns, there is probably no real demographic consensus about the specific population that separates a city from the smaller urban places that we call "towns." Most professionals would probably agree that a municipality of 50,000 or more persons would constitute a city and a place with fewer than 15,000 or 20,000 would more aptly be described as a town. When we think of cities, we not only think of relatively large populations but of cultural and entertainment centers, crime and vice, a labyrinth of streets, traffic, skyscrapers, commerce, retail trade, and general hustle and bustle. Cities have also served traditionally as residential areas where protection exists in terms of numbers.

In the 1990 census, more than 8,500 places were identified and classified as "urban" by the census criterion of 2,500 residents, and more than 900 smaller places were also classified as urban under a special definition; of these 8,500 urban places, only 500 had 50,000 or more inhabitants, only about 6 percent of all urban places. These places with at least 50,000 inhabitants who live within the legal or generally accepted boundaries (city limits) have come to be called "central cities." Of the people living in the United States in 1990, more than one-third, 88,375,000, resided in the central cities. This percentage has not significantly changed over the last 40 years, and central city populations are becoming more concentrated in smaller cities located in the Sunbelt.

Since the early 1950s, the population of urban places having 50,000 or more inhabitants has not grown significantly with the one exception of those places in the Sunbelt—the southern and western parts of the United States. The 229 cities with populations of 50,000 or more in 1950 had grown barely 16 percent by 1990, in contrast to the overall national population growth that exceeded 60 percent and the overall urban population growth of 94 percent during the same period. These 229 cities grew at a rate only slightly larger than that of places defined as rural, even though rural areas had shrunk in size over the 40-year period. The very largest cities, those with populations larger than 500,000 in 1950, had experienced substantial losses by 1990—2,650,000 people or 10 percent of their 1950 populations. The central city of St. Louis declined from 857,000 to 397,000 (54 percent); Cleveland from 915,000 to 506,000 (45 percent); Pittsburgh from 677,000 to 370,000 (45 percent); and Detroit from 1,850,000 to 1,028,000 persons (44 percent). Only 2 of the 18 cities having populations over 500,000 in 1950 experienced gains by 1990, Los Angeles and Houston, both Sunbelt cities. Although the number of central cities having 500,000 or more persons had increased from 18 to 23 by 1990, a much smaller percentage of Americans lived in metropolises this large, 12 percent in 1990 versus almost 18 percent in 1950. The era of the large central city appears to be over.

Lack of growth and even population losses were not restricted to the largest central cities. Even among the smallest 123 central cities with populations ranging from 50,000 to 100,000 in 1950, 53 lost population between 1950 and 1990. Of the remainder, only 26 grew at rates higher than the nation at-large. Virtually all of the growth, even in the smaller cities, was in the Sunbelt or consisted of cities with limited or even nonexistent industrial bases. Despite the substantial increase in the number of central cities as a result of smaller places attaining a population of 50,000 or more between 1950 and 1990, the proportion of U.S. residents located in central cities did not increase. It could be concluded that the maintenance of the proportion of Americans living in central cities resulted from population growth in the smaller cities and towns with fewer than 50,000 persons that subsequently surpassed 50,000.

The period from roughly the end of the Civil War through World War II was an era of great central city growth in the United States. Central cities increased their populations primarily through net in-migration—more persons moved into them than moved away. Central cities acted as magnets attracting people from rural areas, where farm economies were rapidly becoming less labor-intensive as mechanized production and harvesting became common, while at the same time labor-intensive industrial economies were rapidly expanding in the country's cities. Foreign immigrants to the United States headed for cities, not rural areas, and cities became a mosaic of different cultures and ethnicities with their "Chinatowns" and "Little Italies." There were, to be sure, persons and families who moved from central cities to areas far removed from cities' legal boundaries. These "suburbanites" or "exurbanites" were largely affluent and primarily of Anglo and Western European ancestry. Many commuted relatively long distances from serene residences to work at professional, managerial, and administrative occupations in central cities, or else they lived lives of leisure removed from the routines of city life. In the period of central city growth before World War II though, their numbers were dwarfed by the massive influx of blue-collar and lower-level white-collar newcomers who both worked and resided in central cities. Thus, central cities rapidly expanded in population before World War II.

Following the massive immigration to the country before World War I and its substantial decline in the 1920s, out-migration from central cities became more visible, and central city population growth began to subside. Taken as a whole, central cities now experience net out-migration. Because those who leave are relatively more affluent and consist of young families with children, central cities are not only losing population but are becoming relatively poorer and older, despite the increasing number of "gentrified" neighborhoods. For the most part, those central cities that have escaped these and similar problems are located in the Sunbelt and have diversified economies including banking, high tech industry, education, entertainment, tourism, and an active convention business.

It seems intuitively clear that the idea of cities may also include more than simply populations contained within the legal boundaries of large settlements (i.e., city limits). Since the early 1900s, it has been recognized that the social, economic, and political influence of central cities usually extends beyond, often far beyond, the confines of legally defined city limits. As a result, by 1950 the United States Bureau of the Census had recognized 168 Standard Metropolitan Areas (today known as Metropolitan Areas) essentially consisting of counties with central cities and adjacent counties if they met certain criteria of being socially and economically integrated with the county containing the central city. In many instances, the population outside of the central city was widely dispersed and even defined as rural by census definitions. Thus, metropolitan areas were *not* exclusively urban. The population outside the boundaries of the central city ("the ring") was clearly not homogeneous in either social or economic terms. It is to the growth of urban places over 2,500 in population in the metropolitan ring that the term *suburbanization* has often been applied. These are places that initially were self-sufficient but that slowly developed a residential character and, since 1950, have increasingly attracted both retail and wholesale trade as well as manufacturing and other commercial undertakings. As a result, the "metropolitan" definition has undergone several modifications since 1950.

In 1950, the metropolitan population was enumerated at 84.5 million, and more than one-half (56 percent) of U.S. residents were located there; of those living in metropolitan areas at the time, the majority (58 percent) were living in the central cities of the 168 areas. By 1990, the number of metropolitan areas had doubled to 336 with a combined population approaching 193 million. Over three-fourths of all Americans lived in metropolitan areas in 1990. Most of these residents (86 percent) were classified as urban, but, consistent with the stagnation of population growth in central cities, only 40 percent of them were now living in central cities—a reversal of the 1950 central city/ring balance. Over one-half (53 percent) of ring residents now lived outside of central cities in smaller urban places or else in the "fringe" area closely adjacent to central cities.

Growth of population in metropolitan rings has been phenomenal and has resulted from several factors. One of these factors is the net out-migration of people from central cities to areas sometimes quite far removed but still in the metropolitan area served by the central city. Another is the relative cessation of in-migration to central cities from rings as jobs have increasingly moved away from decentralizing cities. Yet a third factor involves formerly nonmetropolitan counties being redefined as metropolitan as they have become increasingly integrated with established metropolitan areas. For example, in 1950 the Atlanta metropolitan area, one of the fastest growing in the nation since that time, consisted of the populations of Cobb, DeKalb, and Fulton Counties, 720,000 persons. Of those, 331,000 lived in the central city of

Atlanta, somewhat less than one-half of the total metropolitan population. By 1990, the Atlanta metropolitan area consisted of 18 counties with a combined population exceeding 2.8 million; the central city of Atlanta had increased to 438,000 (it was 497,000 in 1970 but then decreased to the 1990 level), but five out of every six metropolitan residents in 1990 lived outside Atlanta itself in the metropolitan ring. The addition of 15 additional counties obviously contributed to Atlanta's population growth. At the same time though, population was also rapidly increasing *within* the added counties. Of the 15 newly added metropolitan counties, 8 more than doubled their populations between 1970 and 1990. Gwinnett County, a bedroom suburb of Atlanta, increased in population from 72,000 to 353,000 during the 20 years—an increase of almost 400 percent clearly due to massive net inmigration to the county!

The rapid expansion of the metropolitan sector over the period from 1950 to 1990 was also accompanied by metropolitan areas "bumping" into each other and thus consolidating into what could be thought of as "megalopolitan" areas. By 1990 the Bureau of the Census had recognized 20 "Standard Consolidated Statistical Areas" consisting of 72 of the 336 metropolitan areas. The largest of these, the New York-Northern New Jersey-Long Island consolidated area, had a population in excess of 18 million and consisted of 12 smaller metropolitan areas. The geographical merging of metropolitan areas has resulted in a continuous metropolitan population extending from Norfolk, Virginia, to beyond Boston, Massachusetts; almost the entirety of southern and eastern Florida; and two-thirds of the state of California.

In several respects, the concept of metropolitan areas goes beyond what is considered a city—a population concentration with relatively high population density. Because metropolitan areas use county boundaries to define the geographical extent of areas as well as having an urban place of 50,000 persons, the population *outside* of the central city or cities may be small and dispersed with low density. Even in 1990, more than 26 million metropolitan residents were classified as rural—that is, living in places having fewer than 2,500 inhabitants at some distance from central cities or else living in open countryside. For instance, of the 18 counties making up the Atlanta metropolitan area, 12 have a majority of rural residents—populations residing in places smaller than 2,500 or in open countryside. Only a small percentage of these rural denizens live on farms or work at farm occupations. Significant proportions commute to "core" metropolitan counties where they hold urban jobs. However, from a strictly demographic standpoint, it can hardly be said that they live in cities.

Traditionally, most cities have grown from the inside outward as their populations have expanded, often spilling over into adjacent territory beyond city limits. Part of central city growth has involved the annexation of this spillover population as the geographical area of central cities expanded. However, since World War II, cities have increasingly encountered barriers to annexation as many unincorporated parts of metropolitan counties now provide services (police, fire, garbage collection, etc.) that in the past were found mainly in cities. In 1950 the Bureau of the Census recognized 157 "Urbanized Areas" that consisted of central cities with populations of 50,000 or more plus the densely settled "urban fringe" in close proximity to the central city but not included in the city limits. The urban fringe could include smaller urban places or even places of fewer than 2,500 persons. In many cities, city limits often run through neighborhoods; they are demarcated by streets or streams, and one cannot easily tell where the limits of the legal city end. What one observes in air travel at night flying over a large city is essentially the urbanized area, not just the central city. Urbanized areas are thus defined almost completely in terms of population and population density rather than county boundaries and socioeconomic integration as is the case with metropolitan delineations. In all but a few cases, urbanized areas form the population core(s) of metropolitan areas. The 1990 census definition of "Urbanized Area" is similar to that for 1950; in 1990, if the population of a "central place" (or places) plus the fringe totaled 50,000, it was defined as an urbanized area.

In 1950, 69 million Americans lived in the 157 urbanized areas—about 46 percent of the nation's population. Of the persons living in urbanized areas, 70 percent were located in central cities, the balance in a rapidly expanding urban fringe. By 1990, the population of the urbanized areas had grown to 158 million people living in almost 400 urbanized areas, and of them, slightly more than 50 percent lived in the fringe, not a central place. The increase in the population of urbanized areas resulted from net out-migration from cities to fringes, greater attractiveness of the fringe for those moving from one city to another, and the growth of smaller places and their fringes into the 50,000 population class. It should be noted that the lack of growth of central cities having 50,000 or more inhabitants cannot be generalized to include populations residing in the urban fringe. While Detroit's population declined by over 800,000 between 1950 and 1990, the city's fringe population increased by 1.7 million persons in the same period.

The 1950s and 1960s witnessed the rapid growth and expansion of the nation's urbanized areas. In those 20 years, the nation's total population increased by one-third, but the 157 urbanized areas of 1950 increased at even a greater clip, 7 percent per year. Twenty-four of the areas more than doubled their population, all of them located in the South and West.

The growth of urbanized areas from 1950 to 1970 was not due to the growth of population in central cities, which barely increased at all (3 percent), but to the growth and expansion of fringe areas surrounding large cities. For the country as a whole, the fringe population of urbanized areas more than doubled, but the fringe population of St. Petersburg, Florida, increased fifteenfold; Orlando, Florida, by nine times; Fort Worth, Texas, by eight times; San Jose, California, by seven times; and Denver, Colorado, more than six times. In fact, only 50 of the fringe areas did not double their population, and in many of those cases annexation of fringe territory by central cities was sufficient to recapture population escaping to the fringe. Nashville, Tennessee; Jacksonville, Florida; and Indianapolis, Indiana, conducted extensive consolidations with the counties in which they were located. By 1970, there were 238 urbanized areas as smaller urban concentrations increased from below to above 50,000 population.

The 1970s and 1980s experienced several changes in the growth patterns of urbanized areas—primarily a trend toward smaller cities. In 1950, 55 percent of people in urbanized areas lived in 12 metropolises having more than 1 million persons; fewer than 5 percent lived in urbanized areas having fewer than 100,000. By 1970, 25 urbanized areas of more than 1 million persons had increased their share of all residents of urbanized areas to 60 percent, and the smallest still had less than 5 percent. However, by 1990, the trend had shifted. Although the number of urbanized areas with a population of 1 million had increased to 33, their share of the total population had slightly decreased from that of 1970. Urbanized areas smaller than 100,000 increased their share beyond 7 percent. The older "rust belt" urbanized areas having more than 1 million persons in 1950 showed minimal population gains in the 1970s and 1980s, and several actually lost residents.

The era of the large industrial city has peaked in central cities, urbanized areas, and metropolitan areas. Population in the United States is redistributing itself toward smaller cities, fringe areas of cities, and suburbs in the metropolitan ring, especially in the South and the West. Even since the early 1970s there has been renewed population growth in nonmetropolitan America as population is also decentralizing beyond metropolitan boundaries. Ironically, this redistribution also contributed to the growth of metropolitan and urbanized areas as smaller towns, cities, and fringe areas grew to such an extent that they are no longer defined as nonmetropolitan. These urban populations are no longer as clearly tied to employment as they were in the past, when home and work were ordinarily only a short distance from each other. The many new urbanized areas and metropolitan areas, such as those in Florida and California, serve not merely as job centers but also as recreational, educational,

and retirement areas and bring with them jobs and occupations related to those activities.

—C. Jack Tucker

See also
Birth Control; Census; City-Size Distribution; Fertility; Immigration in the Late Twentieth Century; Megalopolis; Metropolis; Metropolitan Area; Migration from Rural to Urban Areas; Urban Fringe.
References
Abu-Lughod, Janet L. Changing Cities. New York: HarperCollins, 1991.
Golden, Hilda. H. Urbanization and Cities. Lexington, MA: D.C. Heath, 1981.
Gutman, Robert, and David Popenoe, eds. Neighborhood, City, and Metropolis. New York: Random House, 1970.
Hatt, Paul K., and Albert J. Reiss, Jr. Cities and Society. Glencoe, IL: Free Press, 1957.
Long, Larry. Migration and Residential Mobility in the United States. New York: Russell Sage Foundation, 1988.
Masotti, Louis H., and Jeffrey K. Hadden, eds. The Urbanization of the Suburbs. Beverly Hills, CA: Sage Publications, 1973.
Schwab, William A. The Sociology of Cities. Englewood Cliffs, NJ: Prentice-Hall, 1992.
Tisdale, Hope. "The Process of Urbanization." Social Forces 20 (1942): 311–316.
Tucker, C. Jack. "Changing Patterns of Migration between Metropolitan and Nonmetropolitan Areas: Recent Evidence." Demography 13 (1976): 435–443.
Weeks, John R. Population. New York: Wadsworth, 1996.

## Postmodernism

The emergence of postmodern architecture and urban design has been part of a broader reconfiguration of social and cultural values that appeared along with the reconfiguration of the political economy of developed countries. Since the middle of the 1970s, postmodernism has been manifest in many aspects of life—from architecture, art, literature, film, and music to urban design and planning. Postmodernism refers to the philosophical underpinnings and cultural sensibilities that impel specific outcomes (postmodernity). An important distinction can be made between postmodernisms of resistance (that seek to challenge the cultural sensibilities of modernism and therefore undermine the status quo) and postmodernisms of reaction (more superficial responses to modernity, seeking merely to displace one style, fashion, or system of practices with another). The "postmodern turn" reflected in the physical development of American cities overwhelmingly results from postmodernisms of reaction. Playful, ephemeral, anarchic, spectacular, combinatorial, and androgynous motifs have displaced—or at least compete with—the universalistic, rationalistic, purposive, hierarchical, ascetic, and machismo motifs of modernity.

Postmodernism itself can be disaggregated into three components: a postmodern epoch, a postmodern method, and a postmodern style. Postmodernism can be interpreted as an epochal change, the "cultural clothing" of a shift in political economy from Fordism (the process of trying to provide the working class with enough income and leisure time to consume what they produce) to more flexible, globalized, neo-Fordist processes of accumulation. This perspective holds that, although the reconfiguration of both high culture and popular culture had been under way for some time, it was not until the economic "stagflation" of the mid-1970s that the relationship between art and society was sufficiently shaken to allow full expression to postmodernism. This, it should be noted, is philosophically a modernist interpretation, since it is founded on a metatheoretical view that reads cultural sensibilities from the underlying dynamics of economics and politics.

This brings us to postmodernism as a method. Here, metatheoretical perspectives are eschewed in favor of a strategy of deconstruction, a mode of critical interpretation that seeks to understand a "text" (a narrative, a movie, a building, or an urban landscape) through the specific positions of "authors" (makers, designers, builders) and the various experiences of different "readers" (viewers, users) in terms of their class, gender, culture, and so on. Postmodernism as method is thus a postmodernism of resistance, the emphasis on the variability in the range of meanings of a "text" being used to dissolve the authority of modernist theory.

Postmodernism as style, on the other hand, is principally a postmodernism of reaction. Its tropes are eclecticism, decoration, scenography, pastiche, parody, double-coding, and a heavy use of historical and vernacular motifs—all rendered with a self-conscious stylishness. The modernist aphorism "Less Is More" is itself parodied—"Less Is a Bore." Because postmodern architecture has fostered a wide variety of stylistic variants (from straight revivalism through radical eclecticism), the iconic structures of postmodern architecture are not easily established. Some of the examples cited most often include the AT&T Headquarters in Manhattan (architects Philip Johnson and John Burgee), the Piazza d'Italia in New Orleans (architect Charles Moore), and the Portland Public Services Building (Portland, Oregon) and Humana Building in Louisville, Kentucky (architect of both, Michael Graves).

It is clear from all this that postmodernism constitutes a complex and highly contested set of phenomena. It is inherently Janus-like. One face is exciting and liberating; it invites us to abandon the security of modernity's emphasis on economic and scientific progress and, instead, to live for the moment. The other face is grimly imprisoning; it makes us dependent on the constant recycling of themes, robbed of our cultural capacity to address the future, and confronted with dystopian scenarios of increasing violence, pornography, corruption, economic instability, and social polarization.

It is postmodern style that has left the greatest imprint on American cities and suburbs, however, and in this context postmodernism is, above all else, consumption-oriented and pluralistic. This has made for a sociocultural environment in which the emphasis is not so much on ownership and consumption per se, but rather on the possession of particular combinations of things and on the style of consumption. Contemporary urban society can thus be interpreted as a "society of the spectacle," wherein the symbolic properties of urban settings and material possessions have assumed unprecedented importance. Hedonism and immediacy have come to challenge the established notions of progress and development. In terms of the fabric and appearance of contemporary American cities, one important consequence is that the idea of comprehensive urban planning and design has foundered, along with utopian ideals. Instead, planning and design have come to focus on the creation of artful fragments: set-piece, high-style, mixed-use megastructures; "cover-shot" architecture; reclaimed and luxuriously rehabilitated structures; and highly packaged, neotraditional residential settings.

—*Paul Knox*

**References**

Dear, M. "Postmodernism and Planning." *Environment & Planning D: Society and Space* 4 (1986): 367–384.

Debord, G. *Society of the Spectacle.* Detroit: Red and Black Books, 1983.

Foster, H., ed. *Postmodern Culture.* London: Pluto Press, 1985.

Harvey, D. *The Condition of Postmodernity.* Blackwell, England: Oxford University Press, 1989.

Jameson, F. "Postmodernism, or the Cultural Logic of Late Capitalism." *New Left Review* 146 (1984): 53–92.

Jencks, Christopher. *What Is Postmodernism?* New York: St. Martin's Press, 1986.

Knox, Paul L. "The Postmodern Urban Matrix." In Paul L. Knox, ed., *The Restless Urban Landscape*, 207–236. Englewood Cliffs, NJ: Prentice-Hall, 1993.

## Progressivism

The Progressive Era (1890–1920) was characterized by the most widespread, multifaceted, and sustained municipal reform efforts in American history. It marked the last time that civic associations, business and professional organizations, and municipal and state governments undertook urban reform without the involvement of the federal government.

Municipal reform in the Progressive Era was a response to the rise of the "industrial" or "radial" city, which produced central congestion and outlying sprawl, sorted urban land use by cost and function, segregated populations according to socioeconomic and ethnocultural factors, and exacerbated the inherent mobility and instability of city life. Large-scale, heavy industry proliferated around the central business district, greatly inflated land values, and intensified noise and pollution. The burgeoning industrial workforce crowded into substandard housing near factories, producing crises in sanitation, public health, crime, vice, and poverty. More affluent residents flocked to outlying residential areas along electric railway lines that provided easy access to the central business district, which contained virtually all of the city's amenities, except for residences.

Between 1890 and 1920, many cities doubled or tripled their area while the country's urban population nearly quadrupled, increasing from 28 percent to 51 percent of the total. A large part of this population increase resulted from Southern and Eastern European immigrants and from African-American migrants who possessed little capital, education, or industrial skills, were trapped in low-level occupations, segregated in substandard housing, and disproportionately represented among the victims of a bewildering variety of "social problems."

This explosion of the urban population generated an exponentially increasing demand for myriad public services; brutal conflicts over how, by whom, where, and in what order these "utilities" would be delivered; and bitter strife over how they would be financed, and by whom. Cities were seriously constrained by the socioeconomic and ethnocultural fragmentation of their populations; the diffusion of governmental authority; charter restrictions on their taxing, borrowing, and regulatory powers imposed by malapportioned legislatures; and a pervasive animus directed at cities. Political power quickly passed to professional politicians ("bosses") and their party organizations ("machines"), which coordinated the city's disparate elements. Machines provided entrepreneurs and corporations with lucrative franchises and contracts, criminals and vice merchants with protection from the law, and the urban masses with material and psychic benefits, as well as an accessible career ladder for some immigrant groups. As government spending and property taxes escalated to meet proliferating demands, and as revelations of political corruption and "corporate arrogance" multiplied, affluent, "respectable" city residents clamored for "reform."

Upper-class reformers, variously dubbed "patricians," "mugwumps," or "goo-goos" (a term derived from the phrase "good government"), dominated the scene in the 1880s. Pressing for "good government" through the rule of the "best men," they advocated fiscal retrenchment, civil service laws, the short ballot, disfranchisement of the lower class, and crusades against vice. They indicted the unholy trinity of partisan professional politicians, "vicious elements," and "ignorant masses" who conspired to squander revenue on "needless" public services and raise taxes to "unbearable" levels. Although patrician reformers rarely won office or reelection, their perspectives influenced later reformers.

The devastating depression of 1893–1897 stimulated the formation of organizations combining a more sophisticated analysis with more politically appealing programs and strategies. These organizations included the League of American Municipalities, the American Society for Municipal Improvements, and the American League for Civic Improvement. The most influential of them was the National Municipal League (NML), founded in 1894, which coordinated the activities of hundreds of local affiliates, gathered a plethora of data on the urban condition, published *Municipal Affairs,* and held national conferences to promote good city government. Dominated by patricians, social scientists and urbanologists, municipal officials, and businessmen, the NML combined moral indignation and boosterism with systematic investigation and analysis. Without rejecting honesty, morality, or economy, the NML emphasized "efficiency" as the highest civic virtue, experimented with various alterations in the "structure" and "mechanics" of urban government, and adopted a model municipal charter by 1899.

The model charter featured a strong mayor and a moderately sized, unicameral city council whose members were elected for terms of six years in nonpartisan contests, on an at-large basis, in elections separate from those for state and federal offices. Structural reformers aimed to remove politics from city administration via the short ballot and civil service so that cities could be entrusted with home rule, especially in matters of property valuation, taxation, and bonded indebtedness. Carrying the machine metaphor and corporate model of efficiency even further, they presented the commission form of government and the city manager plan, particularly for small and medium-sized cities. They supported municipal research bureaus, like the one founded in New York City in 1906, to discover and publicize scientific, businesslike, objective standards of urban governance.

Although they insisted that their goals and methods were apolitical, objective, and professional, structural reformers worked "a revolution in the theory and practice of city government" that significantly altered "the occupational and class origins of decision-makers." Proposals to adopt at-large or nonpartisan elections, the short ballot, and the commission or city manager plan were generally espoused by business and professional elites with "cosmopolitan" interests and fiercely resisted by ethnic, working-class, and lower-middle-class "parochials." These structural reforms typically facilitated the election of native-born, Protestant, middle- and upper-middle-class candidates at the expense of foreign-born, working-class candidates, while engendering parallel alterations in public policy.

The increasing emphasis on efficiency and professional expertise also animated two other closely related movements. The first, city planning, stemmed from the belief that land use could be determined and managed scientifically and rationally. Challenging the deep-seated, widely held conviction that maximization of profit was the only criterion for allocating resources, urban planners strove to interject considerations of public convenience, human welfare, and aesthetics into policymaking. Their ideas gained significant backing from those convinced that inner-city congestion was the primary cause for a wide range of urban ills, as well as from businessmen and civic leaders who savored enhanced property values and profits. Planners envisioned both the "city efficient" and the "city beautiful," firmly establishing urban planning as a profession and a strategy for making the industrial city more habitable.

The second movement involved efforts to impose "social control" on the heterogeneous urban masses. Reformers who favored and advocated social control infused their crusades with efficiency and professional expertise, and they were frequently motivated by the fear of revolution from below. The Charity Organization Society advocated the "scientific" and businesslike dispensation of relief benefits that were minimal, temporary, and tied to work; they carefully screened applicants to determine their "worthiness" and tried to regulate and morally "uplift" recipients. Residents of settlement houses frequently engaged in Americanization drives, religious proselytizing, and moral purity crusades. Many educational reformers viewed public schools as agencies of Americanization and Protestantization, and thought that schools would be ideal for socializing the lower classes and immigrants into accepting a subordinate station. The organized play movement, Children's Aid Societies, juvenile courts, and other "child saving" institutions joined "in extending governmental control over a whole range of youthful activities that had previously been ignored or dealt with informally." Many urban reformers proposed public libraries, night schools, settlement houses, and athletic programs as substitutes for saloons, vaudeville houses, movie theaters, and other kinds of working-class leisure. Pressures for prohibition, Sunday blue laws, censorship of motion pictures, and crusades against gambling, prostitution, and professional athletics permeated the urban atmosphere.

Outside the mainstream of Progressive Era municipal reform stood "social reform" and "urban liberalism." The former involved efforts by old-stock, middle-class Protestant activists and politicians to mobilize and empower the urban masses to improve their socioeconomic and environmental conditions. Urban liberalism consisted of a similar agenda pursued by leaders from within the ranks of the urban, immigrant, working and lower-middle classes, whether "machine" politicians or "municipal socialists" advocating public ownership of utilities. Humanistic, empirical, and pragmatic, having emotional and political ties to the lower classes, the

three groups analyzed urban malaise "from the bottom up," casting the city masses far more as victim than cause. They placed primary responsibility for urban problems on municipal utilities and other businesses that benefited from lucrative franchises and contracts, tax breaks, special privileges, political corruption, and also on those structural and social control reformers who tried to scapegoat the lower classes.

Social reformers, urban liberals, and municipal socialists focused on concrete solutions to pressing socioeconomic problems: mandating better service at lower costs from utilities, under the threat of municipal ownership; supporting housing and factory codes; demanding a more equitable distribution of taxes; and advocating public health and sanitation measures, municipal parks, public baths and playgrounds, unemployment relief, and improvements in public schools. They eschewed Sunday blue laws, enforced temperance, the curtailment of gambling and prostitution, and censorship, except in the most blatant cases. They sought to increase the participation and influence of the urban masses through patronage, ticket-balancing, and recognition politics, while opposing at-large elections, nonpartisanship, the short ballot, civil service, and the commission and city manager forms of government. They catered to the ethnic and religious sensibilities of their diverse constituencies and rarely missed an opportunity to defend "personal liberty." They endeavored to shift many functions of political machines to the public treasury and to finance them with taxes based on one's "ability to pay."

Frustrated by charter restrictions and intraurban conflict, municipal reformers of every kind thrust themselves into state politics in the early twentieth century. Proposals for home rule, legislative reapportionment, the regulation or municipal ownership of public utilities, the popular election of U.S. senators, tax revision, structural reform of city government and politics, housing and factory inspection, prohibition, Sunday blue laws, and a copious number of other measures aimed at cities dominated legislative politics in most urban, industrial states by 1910.

Lawmakers and governors who came from cities were a major force behind Progressive reform in every major industrial state. Much of the success of the "federal-city partnership" forged in Washington during the New Deal in the 1930s derived from the efforts of those who had gained their political experience and their policy orientation in the cauldron of municipal reform during the Progressive Era.

—*John D. Buenker*

**See also**
Addams, Jane; City Beautiful Movement; City Efficient Movement; Commission Government; Council-Manager Government; Home Rule; Mayor-Council Government; Settlement House Movement; Social Gospel; Steffens, Lincoln; Veiller, Lawrence Turnure.

### References
Bernard, Richard M., and Bradley R. Rice. "Political Environment and the Adoption of Progressive Municipal Reform." *Journal of Urban History* (1975): 149–174.

Boyer, Paul. *Urban Masses and Moral Order in America, 1820–1920.* Cambridge, MA: Harvard University Press, 1978.

Buenker, John D. *Urban Liberalism and Progressive Reform.* New York: Scribners, 1973.

Ebner, Michael H., and Eugene M. Tobin. *The Age of Urban Reform: New Perspectives on the Progressive Era.* Port Washington, NY: Kennikat Press, 1977.

Hays, Samuel P. "The Politics of Reform in Municipal Government in the Progressive Era." *Pacific Northwest Historical Quarterly* 55 (1964): 157–169.

Holli, Melvin G. "Urban Reform in the Progressive Era." In Lewis L. Gould, ed., *The Progressive Era,* 133–151. Syracuse, NY: Syracuse University Press, 1974.

Schiesl, Martin J. *The Politics of Efficiency: Municipal Administration and Reform in America, 1800–1920.* Berkeley: University of California Press, 1977.

## Prohibition

The movement to outlaw the manufacture, sale, and distribution of alcoholic beverages in the United States began in 1838 when Massachusetts made it illegal for liquor dealers to sell quantities of distilled spirits smaller than 15 gallons. Widely defied, the law was repealed in 1839, but in the 1840s opponents of alcoholic beverages persuaded many towns and counties to adopt prohibition locally. Large cities, however, rarely voted to ban liquor, and residents of dry towns frequently bought their alcohol in wet places nearby. To stop the importation of alcohol into places where most residents did not want it, Neal Dow, the dry mayor of Portland, Maine, demanded statewide prohibition, and Maine became America's first dry state in 1851. Although several other states followed, all of them, including Maine, quickly rescinded their action, which lacked both public support and mechanisms to enforce it.

After the Civil War, Americans increasingly disputed liquor policy along cultural and geographic lines. Rural, old-stock Protestants embraced prohibition, but urban European immigrants, many of them Catholic, accepted alcohol. In addition, city political machines used saloons to organize immigrant votes. Fearing a politically powerful, wet, urban, and immigrant working class, and blaming saloons for crime, vice, and poverty, the Woman's Christian Temperance Union (WCTU), led by Frances Willard, and the Anti-Saloon League condemned saloons, especially those in large cities, and demanded national prohibition. By the early 1900s, most Progressive reformers generally favored banning liquor. The dry strategy was to win rural areas and small towns to their cause with local option and then to attack the cities with statewide prohibition. In the long run, the Anti-Saloon League favored a constitutional amendment designed to guarantee that Congress could not interfere with prohibition in the future.

The principal effective opponents of prohibition were the brewers, who were major employers in many cities and who owned a large number of urban saloons. The distillers had been discredited by the Whiskey Ring scandal in 1875 and played only a small role in the struggle. Virtually all of the brewers had German ancestry, and, when the United States entered World War I against Germany in 1917, the brewers suddenly lost influence. As the opposition to prohibition crumbled, Congress moved quickly to consider a constitutional amendment outlawing alcoholic beverages.

American entry into the war helped the antiliquor movement in another way. Because American food was needed to feed the Allies, Congress, fearing food shortages, prohibited distilling or brewing grain as an emergency wartime measure. Congress also banned alcohol on or near military bases. Because Americans accepted wartime prohibition as a patriotic duty in 1917, the advocates of a constitutional amendment dictating prohibition argued that they merely wanted to continue a policy that the public had already accepted.

In late 1917, Congress submitted the Eighteenth Amendment to the states. Declared ratified in 1919, it took effect in January 1920. Although the war had ended in November 1918, wartime prohibition continued until the constitutional amendment superseded it. The Eighteenth Amendment had several curious features. First, although it made the production, sale, or transportation of intoxicating beverages illegal, it did not outlaw their possession or use. Thus, it was legal to store prewar alcohol for personal consumption. Second, the amendment did not ban alcohol used for medicinal or religious purposes. In Chicago, prescription drug stores whose main business was dispensing liquor sprang up throughout the city, and in California, the Christian Brothers winery survived by providing wine for sacramental purposes. Third, the amendment allowed Congress to define "intoxicating beverage." Therefore, in 1919 Congress passed the Volstead Act, which defined any beverage containing more than one-half of 1 percent alcohol as intoxicating.

Finally, the amendment provided for joint, concurrent enforcement by federal and state governments. The drys correctly feared that many states, especially those with large cities, would ignore the law, and so they wanted federal jurisdiction. At the same time, prohibitionists wanted to ensure that if the federal government failed to act, local enforcement would still be possible. Bureaucratic conflict over this dual jurisdiction caused trouble. Local enforcement was spotty, and most big cities gave up after the middle of the 1920s. Only one prosecution ever took place in San Francisco, and that case ended in a mistrial after the jury retired to the jury room and drank the evidence.

Although liquor consumption may have fallen by more than half, millions of otherwise law-abiding Americans re-

*Federal agents poured more than 900 gallons of seized wine into a Los Angeles gutter on October 26, 1920.*

fused to give up alcohol. Demand was enormous, ranging from small-town American Legion halls that maintained bars for their members to President Warren G. Harding, who openly imbibed in the White House. Because beer was bulky and difficult to hide, bootleggers preferred to supply hard liquor made in makeshift stills. Of varying and dubious quality, it was generally called "gin" because it was clear, not aged, and unfiltered. Possessing a harsh bite, it was often flavored and generally mixed with fruit juice or soft drinks.

Importing distilled spirits from Canada became a major business that benefited that country's distillers. The Detroit River, just outside Detroit, Michigan, was a major port of entry. The small boats that carried liquor were faster than the Coast Guard's ships. On the East Coast, a crowd at a beach in New Jersey cheered when a rum runner escaped. On the West Coast, alcohol was landed on countless remote beaches along Puget Sound.

Because alcohol was illegal, it was scarce, and its price was high, with bottles of imported distilled spirits commanding as much as $20. With low production costs and no taxes, bootleggers, even after payoffs, made large profits. In Chi-

cago, it was estimated that Al Capone took in $100 million a year in the late 1920s. The result was unregulated, cutthroat competition in which suppliers, organized into gangs, sought to seize territory from their rivals and, because they were unable to use the legal system, defended themselves with weapons. Philadelphia mobsters finally established an informal court to settle disputes among themselves. Gang wars in Chicago led to hundreds of murders that were never solved. Police departments dared not investigate gang murders because so many officers were taking bribes. For the first time in American history, organized crime became a major force. After Prohibition ended, these criminal syndicates pushed drugs and moved into legitimate businesses, including liquor sales and gambling.

By the late 1920s, many Americans had become disillusioned with Prohibition. Although Herbert Hoover, a dry Republican, had called the ban a noble experiment, and he had defeated Al Smith, a wet Democrat, for the presidency in 1928, the issue was far from settled. The Anti-Saloon League had collapsed, and politicians no longer felt pressure from drys. Mabel Walker Willebrandt, the official in charge of enforcement, expressed reservations, and Hoover appointed a commission headed by George Wickersham to study Prohibition. Acknowledging the policy's failure, this group called for a new constitutional amendment to allow beer and, perhaps, light wine, but many people found this solution too timid.

By 1932, when Franklin D. Roosevelt defeated Hoover for the presidency, the Democrats were committed to ending Prohibition. In early 1933, Congress swiftly passed the Twenty-first Amendment repealing the Eighteenth. To ensure speedy action, Congress asked each state to elect conventions to consider ratifying the new amendment. Of the 37 states that voted, only North Carolina favored continuing Prohibition. Ratified in record time, the amendment repealing Prohibition became effective in December 1933. Legal beer and imported liquor were available immediately, but Americans had to wait several years for aged American whiskey. Roosevelt celebrated repeal by drinking martinis with his staff in the oval office. Eleanor, a teetotaler, did not attend.

—*W. J. Rorabaugh*

**See also**
Nation, Carry Amelia Moore; Temperance Movement; Willard, Frances Elizabeth Caroline.
**References**
Blocker, Jack S., Jr. *Retreat from Reform: The Prohibition Movement in the United States, 1890–1913.* Westport, CT: Greenwood Press, 1976.
Bordin, Ruth B. A. *Woman and Temperance: The Quest for Power and Liberty, 1873–1900.* Philadelphia: Temple University Press, 1981.
Clark, Norman H. *Deliver Us from Evil: An Interpretation of American Prohibition.* New York: W. W. Norton, 1976.
Epstein, Barbara L. *The Politics of Domesticity: Women, Evangelicalism, and Temperance in Nineteenth-Century America.* Middletown, CT: Wesleyan University Press, 1981.
Hamm, Richard F. *Shaping the Eighteenth Amendment: Temperance Reform, Legal Culture, and the Polity, 1880–1920.* Chapel Hill: University of North Carolina Press, 1995.
Kyvig, David E. *Repealing National Prohibition.* Chicago: University of Chicago Press, 1979.
Tyrrell, Ian R. *Woman's World/Woman's Empire: The Woman's Christian Temperance Union in International Perspective, 1880–1930.* Chapel Hill: University of North Carolina Press, 1991.

## Property Tax

The property tax, sometimes called an *ad valorem* tax, is an annual tax levied on the value of real or personal property. Although unpopular and controversial, it is a major source of revenue for local governments and provides cities in the United States with slightly more than one-half of their tax revenue. It serves as security for general obligation bonds, and assessed property values are often used in formulas for distributing aid to local governments or as the basis for limitations on taxes and expenditures.

At one time, efforts were made to tax all kinds of property—real and personal, tangible and intangible—at uniform rates, but today most kinds of intangible and many kinds of tangible personal property are excluded from the base. In nine states, only real estate is taxed. In a number of other states, taxable property is divided into several classes assessed or taxed at different percentages of their market value.

Usually, property used for religious, charitable, educational, or government purposes is exempt from taxation. Also, a variety of arrangements protects low-income or older people from overtaxation, and many exemptions or preferences exist for promoting economic growth.

Administrative arrangements vary from state to state, but in many cases the county is the primary administrative unit. County assessors or appraisers, with some supervision from state agencies, list and value all parcels of taxable property within the jurisdiction of each city or other taxing unit. The governing board of each taxing unit decides the amount of money to be raised from the property tax, and the county clerk or another official computes the rate to be applied to the assessed value of each piece of property.

The property tax is well suited for local levy and collection. Every unit of government has property within its boundaries. Property, especially real property, is visible and difficult to move, and the tax becomes an automatic lien on the property when levied. The *in rem* (against the property) nature of the tax makes local collection feasible. The name of the owner does not need to be known, and real property owners cannot transfer clear title until all taxes have been paid. This greatly reduces the need for unpleasant, politically unpopular collection procedures by local officials.

In spite of its advantages as a source of revenue for cities and other local governments, the property tax is very unpopular. It is highly visible, paid in large annual or semiannual installments, and unrelated to the current income of a property owner. In metropolitan areas, there are often large discrepancies in the per capita tax base available to local governments. This unpopularity has led to the spread of various kinds of limitations on its uses or amounts. Sometimes, a state limits tax rates to a certain percentage of value or freezes the dollar amount of tax increases. The most publicized tax limitation is the voter-imposed Proposition 13 in California. This measure limits total taxes to 1 percent of assessed value and requires the state legislature to apportion tax revenues among the various local governments that can tax the same property. As a result, state aid has been increased and local governments have lost much of their autonomy.

No other country depends as heavily on property taxes to support local government as the United States, but a number are moving to strengthen the property tax as a way of strengthening local governments. By contrast, Great Britain has greatly reduced the use of the property tax and weakened the autonomy of local government.

—*Glenn W. Fisher*

References

Bland, Robert L. *A Revenue Guide for Local Government.* Washington, DC: International City Management Association, 1989.

Fisher, Glenn W. *The Worst Tax? A History of the Property Tax in America.* Lawrence: University Press of Kansas, 1996.

Lo, Clarence Y. H. *Small Property versus Big Government: Social Origins of the Property Tax Revolt.* Berkeley: University of California Press, 1990.

Youngman, Joan. *Legal Issues in Property Valuation and Taxation: Cases and Materials.* Chicago: International Association of Assessing Officers, 1994.

## Prostitution

The first recorded sale of sexual intercourse for financial gain in North America occurred in seventeenth-century colonial cities; little prostitution, if any, existed among Indians. By the late eighteenth century, prostitutes were found primarily in the waterfront districts of eastern and southern seaboard cities.

In the century after 1810, all American cities and many towns experienced dramatic increases in prostitution. Social and economic changes associated with urbanization generated conditions hospitable to prostitution. The boarding house supplanted the craft household, and the peer group superseded the family. The "moral economy" of the preindustrial city was replaced by a more individualistic market economy. Prostitution became a common, commercial, public activity as sex became a consumer commodity in the urban marketplace.

Nineteenth-century prostitution was structured around several overlapping subcultures. First, single underemployed women, suffering from low incomes and poor living conditions, resorted to commercial sex to support themselves. Prostitutes consistently earned in just a few evenings what female factory laborers earned in a month. In large cities, prostitution became a temporary stage of employment for as many as 5 to 10 percent of the working-class female population. Most were single, native-born (although a majority may have had immigrant parents), 16 to 22 years of age, and migrants to the city. A few achieved remarkable success in the sexual underworld. In the early nineteenth century, one prostitute in Philadelphia, Catherine Belabrega, married William Penn, the great-grandson of Pennsylvania's founder. In New York, Eliza Bowen abandoned her trade and married the wealthy French wine merchant Stephen Jumel. Upon his death, she became the richest female in antebellum America. In the smaller community of Virginia City, Nevada, census records reveal that 24 of the 63 white women identified as prostitutes owned property in 1870. Similarly, St. Paul's Mary Robinson eventually

used her profits as a madam and invested in real estate after 1875. And, at the turn of the twentieth century, New Orleans's Lulu White reputedly possessed more than $100,000.

A second urban subculture that encouraged and supported prostitution was the prominent "sporting male" subculture. Numerous leisure institutions frequented by men after 1820 fostered pugilism and verbal bravado, gang life, and heavy drinking. This subculture valorized sexual promiscuity and heterosexual indulgence while rejecting the values of monogamy, frugality, and postponement of pleasure. The poet Walt Whitman commented that "nineteen out of twenty of the mass of American young men, who live in or visit the great cities, are more or less familiar with houses of prostitution and are customers to them." The worst feature of this sporting male fraternity were the "pimps," who first appeared in New York after 1835; by 1870 they were even in small cities like St. Paul.

Finally, prostitution was the most blatant embodiment of the underground urban economy in the nineteenth century. Antebellum proprietors of theaters in New York, Chicago, Philadelphia, Boston, St. Louis, Cincinnati, Mobile, and New Orleans routinely permitted prostitutes to sit, solicit, and conduct business in the "third tier" of their establishments. By mid-century, the brothel was the preeminent institution in urban America's vice economy; New York had over 500 at the time of the Civil War, and other large cities counted several hundred.

The prominence and public visibility of prostitution begot legalization movements between 1850 and 1920. Physicians, labeling prostitution and venereal disease a public health risk, actively supported such measures. New Orleans from 1857 to 1859 and St. Louis from 1870 to 1874 authorized some form of commercial sex. San Francisco from 1911 to 1913 instituted a system of medical inspection of prostitutes. More often, municipal officials resorted to *de facto* regulation. Periodic arrests, raids, and fines were so common that they constituted a form of taxation.

This underground economy proved extremely profitable between 1870 and 1920. New Orleans prostitutes annually generated revenues estimated at $10 million. In San Francisco, cheap cribs (small rented spaces facing the street) alone are said to have made $127,000 annually, while citywide commercial sex supposedly garnered annual profits in excess of $3 million. By 1911 Chicago's Ada and Minna Everleigh were reportedly millionaires in their exclusive South Side bordello. In New York, "syndicates" like the Independent Benevolent Association organized prostitution on the Lower East Side. The 100 to 200 members, including landlords, politicians, brothel doctors, and madames, gave a percentage of their profits to the syndicate; in return, it paid protection fees, bonds, legal costs, and acted as a board of arbitration to settle disputes.

The prominence of commercial sex generated periodic campaigns against prostitution. During the second quarter of the nineteenth century, reformers like Philadelphia's Ezra Stiles Ely and New York's John McDowall founded Magdalene societies to aid in reforming prostitutes. Female moral reform societies, hoping to expunge brothels from the city, spread throughout New York and New England towns. In eastern and midwestern cities, the Roman Catholic Sisters of Charity established Houses of the Good Shepherd to assist fallen women. Although these and other "purity crusades" were sporadic and ineffective in curtailing prostitution, they consistently defeated efforts at legalization.

After 1890, antivice activities grew increasingly more common and successful. Protestant ministers Charles Parkhurst in New York, Isaac Lansing in Boston, and William Knight in Cleveland led movements that eventually allied Progressive Era reformers, social hygienists, and opponents of "white slavery." Between 1900 and 1920, more than 40 vice commissions recommended eliminating urban sex districts. Beginning with Iowa in 1909, more than 30 states passed red-light abatement laws that permitted private citizens to obtain injunctions and close buildings housing prostitutes. Various municipalities instituted special courts (notably Women's or "Night" Court), "vice squads" in police departments, and "ma-trons" in prisons. Federal legislation in 1903 and 1907 outlawed bringing prostitutes into the country and permitted deporting immigrant prostitutes. The Mann Act of 1910 criminalized transporting women across state lines for "immoral purposes," resulting in 1,537 convictions from 1910 to 1916. Most importantly, the Commission on Training Camp Activities led by Raymond Fosdick during World War I successfully closed the red-light districts in the nation's major ports.

By 1920, prostitution had become a clandestine, underground activity. Brothels did not advertise their existence. Prostitutes no longer plied their trade openly in cabarets and nightclubs, and streetwalkers disappeared from major avenues and boulevards. Prostitutes thereafter worked more secretly in tenements, dance halls, massage parlors, and "call houses." From 1920 to 1933, Prohibition encouraged closer ties of prostitution with the illegal alcohol trade and ultimately organized crime, and it hardly vanished. Robert and Helen Lynd's famed study of *Middletown* (1929) discovered as many as 50 brothels in a community where prostitutes were simultaneously ignored and feared by townspeople. In 1948, Alfred Kinsey concluded that 69 percent of white American males born after World War I had some experience with prostitutes.

Prostitution regained visibility after 1965. Downtown realtors, suffering from high vacancy rates in commercial

*Prostitutes walking the streets near Times Square in New York City in 1971.*

property, rented to various sex industries. Cities like New York (1967–1973) eliminated licensing requirements for massage parlors, leading to their proliferation as fronts for prostitution. In 1971 Nevada became the first state to legalize prostitution. Nationally, however, estimates of the number of prostitutes remained at about the same level as those for the 1920s (100,000 to 500,000). Studies revealed elaborate hierarchies among prostitutes, the most glaring being class divisions: streetwalkers came from working-class or low-income families while call girls and massage parlor workers enjoyed comparatively more affluent backgrounds.

Prostitutes themselves grew more assertive. In 1973, San Francisco's Margo St. James founded the first known labor organization for prostitutes, COYOTE (Call Off Your Old Tired Ethics). Similar organizations quickly followed in New York (Prostitutes of New York, or PONY), Massachusetts, Washington, Hawaii, Colorado, and Florida. These groups defended prostitution as a privacy issue and demanded its acceptance as legitimate women's work. A decade later, this libertarian view brought them into conflict with feminist groups like WHISPER (Women Hurt in Systems of Prostitution Engaged in Revolt). Finally, growing fears and uncertainty regarding the AIDS epidemic threatened prostitutes with greater regulation and discrimination at the end of the twentieth century.

— *Timothy J. Gilfoyle*

**See also**

Moral Reform; Red-Light District.

**References**

Gilfoyle, Timothy J. *City of Eros: New York City, Prostitution and the Commercialization of Sex, 1790–1920.* New York: W. W. Norton, 1992.

Hobson, Barbara Meil. *Uneasy Virtue: The Politics of Prostitution and the American Reform Tradition.* New York: Basic Books, 1987.

Rosen, Ruth. *The Lost Sisterhood: Prostitution in America, 1900–1918.* Baltimore: Johns Hopkins University Press, 1982.

Symanski, Richard. *The Immoral Landscape: Female Prostitution in Western Societies.* Toronto, Ontario: Butterworths, 1981.

## Pruitt-Igoe Housing Complex

The Pruitt-Igoe housing complex in St. Louis, Missouri, was among the most notorious public housing projects in the United States and became a symbol for the failures of public housing, especially in the form of high-rise buildings, and even of modern architecture. Soon after completion of the complex's 33 buildings, each of them 11 stories high with elevators, in 1956, government agencies began pouring millions of dollars into the project to solve the disrepair, vandalism, and crime that were plaguing it. Seventeen years after it was built, government agencies began destroying the buildings in a highly publicized demolition that became a national event.

Actually two adjacent housing projects, the Wendell Oliver Pruitt Homes and the William L. Igoe Apartments,

Pruitt-Igoe was part of a major effort to revive the city of St. Louis, which had been losing population, and particularly the middle class, since the Depression. The site of Pruitt-Igoe was located in what many considered the worst neighborhood in the city, which had long been slated for public housing. The Housing Act of 1949 provided for slum clearance and new public housing projects, and St. Louis's newly elected mayor, Joseph M. Darst, made sure that his city was among the first to apply for and receive federal funds.

In 1949 the chairman of the St. Louis Housing Authority, with the mayor's blessing, hired the architectural firm of Hellmuth, Yamasaki, and Leinweber (later Hellmuth, Obata, and Kassabaum) to design modern-looking public housing projects for the city. The rising star of the firm was Minoru Yamasaki, a young architect who had made a specialty of tall building construction while he worked for the New York firms that had designed the Empire State Building and the United Nations headquarters. (He would cap his career by designing the World Trade Center in Manhattan.)

After Yamasaki's design for the first high-rise housing project, John J. Cochran Garden Apartments, won honors in architectural circles, the authority approved his more ambitious design for the Pruitt-Igoe projects, which included a combination of row houses and eight-story-high buildings with elevators. For the apartment buildings, Yamasaki employed a straight line or slab design and skip-stop elevators that stopped only at every third floor, with stairways connecting the floors above and below. Along one outer wall were deep hallways or "galleries" that were meant to function as playground, porch, and entrance to laundry and storage rooms, thereby attracting residents and creating "vertical neighborhoods" for them. Outside the high-rise buildings, Yamasaki proposed a winding park of trees and grassy lawns.

As built, however, Pruitt-Igoe fell far short of the architect's vision. Caught between the project's soaring building costs—apparently caused by inflated construction contract bids—and cost limits set by the federal Public Housing Administration, the St. Louis Housing Authority scaled back Yamasaki's plans. Pruitt-Igoe's apartment buildings grew to 11 stories, and the row houses were omitted. The number of dwelling units increased to 2,870, creating a density of just under 50 dwellings per acre. In order to save money, the authority eliminated insulation on steam pipes, screens over the gallery windows, paint on the concrete block walls of the galleries and stairwells, and public toilets on the ground floors. Landscaping was reduced to a minimum.

After changing its mind about the racial composition of the housing complex, the St. Louis Housing Authority designated Pruitt for African-American tenants and neighboring Igoe for whites. Following a U.S. Supreme Court order, the authority designated Igoe as a racially integrated project.

Since it was unable to attract white tenants, however, the entire Pruitt-Igoe project soon had only black residents.

Pruitt-Igoe quickly gained a reputation as an unpleasant and dangerous place to live. Children fell to their death from the windows, and delivery men and workers were regularly robbed. The features that Yamasaki had designed as amenities were vandalized: children used the elevators as toilets, and the washing machines and locks on storage rooms in the galleries were always broken. The tenants renamed the galleries where hoodlums gathered "gauntlets." Not surprisingly, the complex had a high vacancy rate, which further reduced the funds available for maintenance.

In 1965 the U.S. government allowed the St. Louis Housing Authority to spend its funds to cure the ailing housing project, the first such expenditure for rehabilitating a public housing project. After spending over $5 million to redesign and repair Pruitt-Igoe, the housing authority decided to consolidate residents of the occupied apartments and raze three of the high-rise buildings.

The demolition gained national attention because it was the first time a public housing project had been razed, and it involved the experimental use of dynamite to demolish large buildings. Newspapers, national magazines, and television news broadcasts reproduced and replayed sensational pictures of the demolition. In 1973, the St. Louis Housing Authority and the U.S. Department of Housing and Urban Development declared Pruitt-Igoe unsalvageable and razed the remaining buildings. The dramatic and well-publicized demolitions helped make Pruitt-Igoe a national icon event. Most journalists reported the story as symbolic of a crisis in the nation's public housing program. The sociologist Lee Rainwater, who had conducted a study of Pruitt-Igoe's low-income tenants, asserted that the project exemplified the government's misguided treatment of the poor.

Many critics condemned the design of Pruitt-Igoe, especially its use of high-rise apartment buildings for family residences. The architect Oscar Newman asserted that the design of Pruitt-Igoe encouraged crime. Another critic, Christopher Jencks, blamed the project's failures on modern architecture and claimed that the destruction of Pruitt-Igoe signaled the end of modernism.

Although many large public housing projects experience critical safety and maintenance problems today, Pruitt-Igoe was the harbinger of the troubled housing project. Long after its destruction, it lives on as a symbol of failure.

—*Alexander von Hoffman*

### References

Bristol, Katharine G. "The Pruitt-Igoe Myth." *Journal of Architecture Education* 94 (1991): 163–171.

Comerio, Mary C. "Pruitt-Igoe and Other Stories." *Journal of Architectural Education* 34 (1981): 25–31.

Meehan, Eugene J. *Public Housing Policy—Convention versus Reality.* New Brunswick, NJ: Center for Urban Policy Research, 1975.

———. *The Quality of Federal Policymaking: Programmed Failure in Public Housing.* Columbia: University of Missouri Press, 1979.

Montgomery, Roger. "Pruitt-Igoe: Policy Failure or Societal Symptom." In Barry Checkoway and Carl V. Patton, eds., *The Metropolitan Midwest, Policy Problems and Prospects for Change,* 229–243. Urbana and Chicago: University of Illinois Press, 1985.

Montgomery, Roger, and Katherine Bristol. *Pruitt-Igoe: An Annotated Bibliography.* CPL Bibliography 205. Chicago: Council of Planning Librarians, 1987.

## Public Baths

Public baths were facilities, usually showers in buildings called public bathhouses, where individuals who lacked those facilities in their private dwellings could bathe. By the 1890s, public baths were considered an important amenity that progressive American cities should provide for poor citizens. Personal cleanliness had become a necessity, not only for social acceptance and public health, but as a symbol of middle-class status, good character, Americanization for immigrants, and membership in the civic community. If slum tenements failed to provide the poor with bathing facilities so that they could follow the proper standards of cleanliness, it was thought that cities had a responsibility to provide them, either free or for a small charge.

The American obsession with personal cleanliness began in the mid–nineteenth century. Many factors, including the burgeoning urban slums of Irish immigrants, the water-cure craze and other health reforms that connected cleanliness to well-being, and the threat of epidemics, contributed to the growing demand for public baths. The provision of water and sewage systems as well as technological developments, such as bathtubs with attached plumbing, gave private baths to the affluent and made public baths for the poor feasible. The systems of public baths in large European cities, especially in England and Germany, provided examples for American cities. New waves of Southern and Eastern European immigrants and the increasing acceptance of the germ theory of disease in the 1880s added impetus to the movement.

All of these factors coalesced during the Progressive Era, and the public bath movement peaked and achieved success. By 1920, more than 40 American cities had public bath systems, either constructed at municipal expense or acquired through private philanthropy. Among America's largest cities, the 25 public baths in New York comprised the most elaborate and expensive system in the country, and many of its public baths contained swimming pools as well as showers. In Boston, most municipal baths were combined with gymnasiums and supported more enthusiastically by its Irish machine mayors than by its Progressive reformers. In Chicago, a group of women reformers (mostly physicians) formed the Free Bath and Sanitary League, led the municipal bath movement, and convinced the municipal government to build modest baths in slum neighborhoods. Philadelphia's public baths, which also provided public laundries, were built and maintained by the Public Baths Association, an organization of affluent and prominent citizens. And in Baltimore, the city's wealthiest citizen donated a public bath system to the city.

Public bathhouses were usually located in slum neighborhoods, especially those with large immigrant populations, and in vice and entertainment districts. Bath reformers recommended that public bathhouses be small, simple, and unpretentious. But some cities, such as New York and Boston, built large, imposing, expensive, and even monumental public baths. New York City's neo-Roman East 23rd Street Bath (now renovated and renamed the Asser Levy Recreation Center) contained over 100 showers and a swimming pool, cost $259,000 in 1908, and has been designated an official landmark by the Landmarks Preservation Commission.

The leaders of the national public bath movement were a diverse group united by their interest in this single issue. They included physicians, businessmen, settlement house workers, women acting as "municipal housekeepers," philanthropists, reform mayors, political bosses, and occasionally even the poor themselves. These reformers formed a national network even before they formally organized the American Association for Promoting Hygiene and Public Baths in 1912, an organization that united bath reformers and administrators of public bath systems.

The public bath movement must be considered a success insofar as it achieved its primary goal—establishing public baths so the poor could attain middle-class standards of personal cleanliness. However, little evidence indicates that the poor themselves had any sustained interest in having public baths in their neighborhoods. The baths (except for those connected to recreational facilities such as swimming pools or gymnasiums) were never utilized to nearly their capacity except on the hottest summer days, and after 1915 attendance declined even further.

What the public bath movement did succeed in accomplishing permanently, however, was disseminating the gospel of cleanliness. Tenement house legislation, growing affluence, and the inexpensive galvanized bathtub brought the private bathroom to most urban Americans. By the 1950s, American cities closed their public baths as the need for them had virtually disappeared. The private bathroom and not the public bath is the bath reformers' monument.

—*Marilyn Thornton Williams*

### References

Hanger, G. W. W. "Public Baths in the United States." In U.S. Department of Commerce and Labor, *Bulletin of the Bureau of Labor* 9 (1904): 1245–1367.

Williams, Marilyn Thornton. *Washing "The Great Unwashed": Public Baths in Urban America.* Columbus: Ohio State University Press, 1991.

## Public Disorderliness

Public disorderliness was a major feature of life in cities of the northeastern, mid-Atlantic, and midwestern states during the nineteenth century. Police used the term as a catchall to signify various kinds of drunken, loud, aimless, brawling, ruffian, suspicious, intemperate, and vagrant behavior in the early industrial walking city. But the police did not invent the term or the perceived need to formally reprimand undesirable behavior in particular places. The concept has roots in the unease expressed by Anglo elites as they increasingly placed city fortunes in the hands of capitalist entrepreneurs who needed thousands of workers to perform physically demanding labor.

During the period of early industrial growth—roughly 1820 to 1860 for large northeastern cities, and as late as 1890 for small and medium-sized cities—most attention was given to this "problem." New laws, new "preventative" police forces, and the expansion of criminal justice institutions allowed for the identification of "disorderly" persons. In the first decades, politicians, police, and judges hoped to use their new power to reprimand undesirables in an attempt to avert more serious criminality.

A larger social transformation lay behind this new use of criminal justice authority. Especially after the influx of Irish immigrants in the 1840s, an unparalleled diversity of values, subcultures, and generations began to break apart the smug, homogeneous Anglo-Protestant communities of the preindustrial era. As industry attracted foreign job seekers, different types of people confronted each other on city streets, urban space began to segment, and the middle and upper classes increasingly moved to the outer edges of cities. In many cities, this combination left inner cities to be contested by a new type of fashionable elite and a new type of working poor. Unskilled workers clustered in marginalized sections of the city and were soon characterized as the "dangerous" or "disorderly" class. Identification of an outcast class simultaneously distanced elites from the perceived vulgarity of newcomers and proclaimed the superiority of Anglo-Protestant values, which had, by this time, fused the older religious morality to the newer business values of efficiency and regimentation. There was, therefore, a cultural clash within the cities—specifically, as police and court records show, the bravado, competition, mutuality, and drunkenness of mobile young Irish men affronted the sensibilities of genteel, bourgeois, evangelical, and settled Anglo-Protestant citizens.

This phenomenon also had economic underpinnings. The laws of disorderliness were enforced only in the most valued sections of the newly configured inner city. Most arrests were made in and around residential pockets of the fashionable elite, the central business district, and the industrial yards. The specific fear in those places was the theft or destruction of the valuable materials and private property that were becoming virtually sacred in the emerging capitalistic industrial economy. As the police apprehended suspicious-looking, drunken young men roaming around stacks of processed lumber, for instance, they defended at the same time the entrepreneurial vigor of the privileged owners of lumber-processing firms and upheld the hopes for city improvement through industrial growth.

Disorderliness, as a phenomenon identified and criminalized by Anglo elites, had at its core the fear of suspicious-looking young foreigners and the vulnerability of private property in the inner city. Arrests for disorderliness were not only attempts to impose middle-class and upper-class behavior on the minority poor but also messages from elites that they would guard the material fruits of the new city. As the menace of transient young Irish men became a seemingly permanent concern, Anglo reformers and government officials increasingly found the inner city filled with vice, crime, and disease. In relative terms, the authority of law, police, and criminal justice began to command greater respect than the authorities of religion and public education. The spatial, cultural, and economic foundations of the trend toward suburban homeownership and the marginalization of certain parts of the inner city had begun.

—*Michel Martin*

### References

Gorn, Elliott J. " 'Good-Bye Boys, I Die a True American': Homicide, Nativism, and Working-Class Culture in Antebellum New York City." *Journal of American History* 74 (1987): 388–410.

Martin, Michel. " 'A Class of Persons Whose Presence Is a Constant Danger': Progress, Prohibition, and 'Public Disorderliness' in Burlington, 1860–1880." *Vermont History* 62 (1994): 148–165.

Monkkonen, Eric H. "A Disorderly People? Urban Order in the Nineteenth and Twentieth Centuries." *Journal of American History* 68 (1981): 539–559.

Schneider, John. *Detroit and the Problem of Order, 1830–1880: A Geography of Crime, Riot, and Policing.* Lincoln: University of Nebraska Press, 1980.

## Public Health

In the colonial era, American cities were ravaged by intermittent outbreaks of smallpox and yellow fever. During severe epidemics, most individuals fled to the countryside, and the economic life of the city ground to a standstill. Cities attempted to prevent epidemics by quarantining ships and erecting isolation hospitals (often called pest houses). In order to allay fears and revitalize trade, city governments sometimes published false reports minimizing the danger they knew was in their midst.

Colonial procedures for quarantine and isolation were modeled on European precedents, but inoculation, the next great advance in the battle against epidemic diseases, was an American innovation. Inoculation was first used on a large scale in 1721 during a smallpox epidemic in Boston that killed 900 people out of a population of 10,000. In the procedure, pus taken from the pustules of someone convalescing was injected under the skin of a healthy person. The fatality rate for people who had been inoculated was only 2 percent, but for individuals who contracted the disease naturally, i.e., from other people, it was 14 percent. Because people who were inoculated could spread the disease, a number of colonial legislatures forbade the practice, but as the effectiveness of inoculation became established, city and colonial governments began to regulate rather than forbid its use. By the time vaccination replaced inoculation in the 1790s, smallpox was no longer a serious public health concern, although the disease continued to flare up occasionally among the poor.

If the battle against smallpox yielded one of the most potent weapons yet developed in the war against disease, yellow fever provided the touchstone of epidemiological debate in the late eighteenth century and most of the nineteenth century. Except for smallpox and measles, most acute, communicable diseases did not appear to be transferable. Some diseases, like malaria and yellow fever, had a seasonal incidence. Medical attendants who cared for yellow fever victims often escaped the disease, while people who secluded themselves at home during epidemics were frequently stricken. Because of their experience with a wave of yellow fever epidemics that decimated Atlantic seaports in the 1790s, the nation's leading public health authorities concluded that yellow fever and most other epidemic diseases broke out when a miasma emitted from decomposed organic wastes, such as those abundantly found in every city, poisoned the atmosphere. Because of the miasmic theory of disease, cities enacted ordinances requiring homeowners and local businesses to clean up their wastes, but the laws were poorly enforced.

The rapid urbanization of the nineteenth century caused serious public health problems. In particular, cities are vulnerable to diseases spread by contact and insect vectors, such as tuberculosis and typhus, and to other diseases transmitted by contaminated water supplies, such as typhoid fever. Throughout the period, the death rate for urban dwellers was considerably higher than for residents of rural areas.

Cities were unprepared to accommodate the hordes of impoverished European immigrants who began arriving about 1830. The housing conditions of the poor deteriorated sharply, and the sanitary condition of cities degenerated, with the disposal of animal and human wastes arousing the most concern. In the absence of indoor plumbing, the poor were compelled to use outdoor privies, cesspools, and wells. Slaughterhouse, tannery, brewery, and kitchen wastes littered the streets, on which were also deposited the offal, and sometimes the carcasses, of the hundreds and thousands of horses that provided the city's main means of transportation.

During epidemics, municipal governments appointed boards of health to conduct emergency sanitary campaigns, but once a threat receded the boards disbanded or their authority lapsed. Antebellum boards of health were more concerned with preventing harm to the city's commerce than with saving lives. When permanent boards of health were established after the Civil War, they became enmeshed in the political patronage and partisan politics of the period, which, at times, greatly limited their effectiveness.

In 1832 cholera, a dread new disease, invaded American cities. The disease spread with terrifying speed, its modes of transmission a mystery. In New Orleans, it may have killed as many as 6,000 persons, or one-sixth of the population. Everywhere it struck, people fled in panic.

At first municipal authorities attributed the epidemic to the alleged filthy and dissolute habits of the poor. In the 1850s, however, John Snow, an English physician, demonstrated that cholera was an intestinal disease transmitted by water contaminated with feces. In 1866 cholera threatened to invade New York City for the third time. Lacking faith in a board of health riddled with patronage, a group of prominent citizens prevailed upon the state legislature to appoint a metropolitan board of health for the duration of the crisis. The board appointed by the state quickly brought the disease under control with far fewer deaths than had occurred before.

This success, together with the accomplishments of the U.S. Sanitary Commission during the Civil War, inspired a sweeping sanitary reform movement. Local businessmen who feared that a reputation for unhealthful conditions would deter people from living or doing business in their city vigorously supported the movement. It was also gently aided by the growing demand of urban residents for modern water supply systems and a sanitary means of waste disposal.

Cities were cleansed of organic filth, and, although the miasmic theory of disease was fallacious, the public health was greatly improved. As swamps were drained, wells closed, privies boarded over, garbage removed, and safe water made available, waterborne and vector-spread diseases such as typhoid, cholera, malaria, and typhus were eliminated or brought under control.

The advent of bacteriology and the germ theory of disease in the late nineteenth century revolutionized public health. As the microbial causes of several of humanity's worst scourges were identified, public health officials became less concerned about cleaning the environment and began to focus on conquering specific diseases with vaccines, serums, and other bacteriological products. Between 1894 and 1910, the bacteriological laboratory became the nerve center of municipal public health work. Bacteriological tests were developed for the early diagnosis of tuberculosis, syphilis, and typhoid fever; an antitoxin was produced to treat diphtheria; and the transmission of malaria and yellow fever by mosquitos was demonstrated. As medical science began to play a larger role in preventing disease, public health was professionalized. Municipal departments of public health gained more freedom from political interference, and control of public health shifted from laymen to medical professionals.

Not every disease could be attacked by eliminating insect vectors or by using biological products developed in laboratories. These measures had only limited effectiveness in dealing with tuberculosis and infant mortality, which together accounted for about 30 percent of all deaths annually. To combat these urgent conditions, a new approach to public health would have to be adopted—one that emphasized educating the public about personal health care and organizing medical services to ensure the early diagnosis and treatment of disease. Joining forces with voluntary public health organizations, municipal departments of public health established tuberculosis sanitariums and baby health centers that gave medical advice to poor women and provided free examinations of their infants. The death rate from tuberculosis fell from 200 per 100,000 population in 1900 to 97.6 in 1921. Similarly, the infant mortality rate was also halved. While public health initiatives accounted for some of this extraordinary improvement, a rising standard of living was also significant.

In the last 70 years, the federal government has assumed more responsibility for safeguarding the health of the American people. In 1912 the federal government established the Children's Bureau to study infant mortality, and in the 1920s it provided federal matching funds for maternal and child care. In 1935 the Social Security Act provided money to hard-strapped city and state departments of public health. Under the leadership of Surgeon General Thomas Parran, local public health officials were encouraged to remove the veil of Victorian morality that shrouded venereal disease. With the introduction of sulfa drugs and antibiotics in the 1930s and 1940s and the money provided by the federal government to track sexual contacts, local public health authorities appeared to be winning the battle against syphilis and gonorrhea in the 1950s.

In recent decades, some older health problems have resurfaced and a new public health menace has appeared. In the 1960s, changed sexual mores and slackening efforts to control venereal diseases put Americans at greater risk from sexually transmitted diseases. In addition to gonorrhea and syphilis, herpes, chlamydia, and genital warts became endemic. The most frightening development has been the appearance of a fatal new communicable disease, AIDS (acquired immune deficiency syndrome). Moreover, because AIDS weakens the body's natural defense mechanisms, it has triggered a resurgence of tuberculosis and the appearance of drug-resistant strains of tubercle bacilli. Municipal public health authorities must also contend with medical problems arising from violence, drug use, and out-of-wedlock births, all of which have increased dramatically in the last three decades.

—*Stuart Galishoff*

### References

Cassedy, James H. *Charles V. Chapin and the Public Health Movement.* Cambridge, MA: Harvard University Press, 1962.

Duffy, John. *A History of Public Health in New York City.* 2 vols. New York: Russell Sage Foundation, 1974.

Ellis, John H. *Yellow Fever and Public Health in the New South.* Lexington: University Press of Kentucky, 1992.

Galishoff, Stuart. *Newark, the Nation's Unhealthiest City, 1832–1895.* New Brunswick, NJ: Rutgers University Press, 1988.

———. *Safeguarding the Public Health: Newark, 1895–1918.* Westport, CT: Greenwood Press, 1975.

Leavitt, Judith Walzer. *The Healthiest City: Milwaukee and the Politics of Health Reform.* Princeton, NJ: Princeton University Press, 1982.

## Public Housing

Public housing originated as federal policy during the Depression when American cities faced a terrible overcrowding of housing caused by an epidemic of evictions and mortgage foreclosures. By 1974, the year President Richard Nixon declared a moratorium on the construction of conventional public housing, approximately 1.4 million units of federally built, low-income housing sat in communities, large and small, across America.

In 1933, motivated as much by the need to resuscitate the building trades as by the plight of ill-housed city residents, New Deal policymakers rebuffed opposition from the real estate industry and opted to "experiment" with "European-styled" conventional—that is, government built and managed—public housing. Like the Depression housing crisis itself, the public housing decision was rooted in late-nineteenth- and early-twentieth-century Progressive environmentalism, the idea that good housing made good people. Housing reformers (often called "housers") such as Helen Parrish, Jacob Riis, and Lawrence Veiller (the author of the 1901 New York City Tenement House Law) decried the sunless, overcrowded, and unsafe multiple-family buildings that housed a large number of urban working-class families.

While many housing reformers such as Veiller championed regulation and abjured the idea of government-built shelter, Washington's World War I experiment with government-built housing for shipyard workers and the serious postwar housing shortage caused interest in public housing to survive during the 1920s. In fact, the 1920s witnessed a growing number of housers embrace "new town" concepts and espouse federal intervention to achieve the goal of good, "modern" affordable housing for the masses. Communitarian housers such as Catherine Bauer, Lewis Mumford, Henry Wright, Clarence Stein, and John Nolen—many members of the Regional Planning Association of America (RPAA)—promoted the development of planned, decentralized communities for "working class" families similar to the garden city designs of Britain's Ebenezer Howard and Raymond Unwin.

The Depression horribly exacerbated the existing shortcomings of America's private housing distribution system. After 1929, President Herbert Hoover's "Own Your Own Home" crusade fizzled amidst an avalanche of bank failures and mortgage foreclosures. Meanwhile, the ranks of those who supported government housing, led by social workers and labor unions, swelled. By 1933, convinced that it would generate jobs, Roosevelt's aide and close associate Harold Ickes created a Housing Division within the Public Works Administration (headed by RPAA member Robert Kohn), which undertook a series of "housing demonstration projects." In 1937 the Wagner-Steagall Act created the U.S. Housing Administration, making the PWA "housing experiment" permanent policy.

Although the Wagner-Steagall legislation gave public housing decisions about tenant selection and site location to local housing authorities (LHAs), final power resided in Washington, which dictated the terms of the annual contribution contract (ACC) that funded up to 90 percent of the 60-year amortized cost of public housing projects. LHAs used rent receipts to cover operating costs and "in lieu of" taxes to pay municipalities an annual fee for schools, trash collection, and other city services. Thus, while local authorities retained some latitude over the composition of tenant populations and project environments, Washington's budget control deeply imprinted both the design and character of public housing. Consistent with New Deal philosophy, early public housing, although usually well designed and solidly built, excluded any frills that might tempt tenants to consider project living a way of life.

Outside of New York City, most prewar projects were low rise. Like the Bauhaus architecture of the German Weimar Republic, New Deal architects before World War II arranged public housing in superblocks. Befitting their communitarian orientation, their projects featured community buildings, nurseries, classrooms, auditoriums, and outside play areas with spray pools. Despite these amenities, projects were spartan. Cost-conscious design standards bequeathed tight ten-foot bedrooms, skimpy dining areas, and open closets. Paradoxically, while stable architecturally and sound physically, New Deal policymakers created socially shaky places. By establishing income guidelines for continued occupancy, and issuing rigid rules for tenant behavior, they defined public housing as way stations for the temporarily poor, not communities to grow and flourish over time.

Although World War II aggravated conservative reaction to New Deal social programs, the gigantic shift of workforce populations to centers of military production intensified housing shortages. The wartime National Housing Agency built thousands of units of defense and war housing. But, much to the chagrin of housers such as Catherine Bauer, the agency bequeathed to postwar America thousands of acres of ramshackle barracks housing, Quonset huts, and dull cinder-block villages. However, some "permanent" war housing exceeded housers' expectations and contributed significantly to the publicly owned stock. War housing such as the Pittsburgh area's Aluminum City Terrace was designed by renowned modern architects, in this case Walter Gropius.

The Cold War aftermath of World War II, culminating in McCarthyism's "witch hunts," deepened the assault on New Deal "socialized housing." In the 1950s tenants were forced to sign loyalty oaths and swear that they were not members of a long list of organizations condemned as subversive by the attorney general. Nevertheless, by linking public housing to the rebuilding of America's notoriously blighted downtowns, the program survived. Indeed, the 1949 Wagner-Ellender-Taft law and its 1954 successor transformed public housing into the handmaiden of the urban renaissance. At the end of the 1950s, public housing in large cities such as Philadelphia, Chicago, Baltimore, and New York had already devolved into a refuge or receptacle for poor, often black, families uprooted by urban renewal. Harnessed to urban renewal, public housing increasingly occupied either slum or remote peripheral sites. Instead of the creative architecture of the 1930s, postwar projects increasingly took the form of grim, antiseptic Corbusian towers decried by social and architectural critics alike.

Architecture alone did not invite the critics' wrath. By congressional edict, public housing in the late 1940s and early 1950s deliberately purged upwardly mobile families. Frequently, these families were replaced by "problem families" whose low income, family structure, and record of substance abuse and criminality made housing in the private sector unattainable. By 1957 once passionate disciples of public housing such as Catherine Bauer branded it a "dreary deadlock" and called it "supertenements." Dedicated reformers lost their faith in the rehabilitative powers of good housing. More-over, formerly dedicated supporters of public housing charged that public housing abetted ghettoization in addition to physical dreariness and social pathology, and they branded Mayor Richard Daley's Chicago as the worst case. Like other cities, Chicago located public housing to reinforce the boundaries of the black ghetto and protect the integrity of white neighborhoods.

Not all cities pursued grossly segregative public housing polices. In 1956 government officials in Philadelphia attempted to use public housing as an instrument to batter down the wall of segregation by dispersing low-rise public housing on the city's periphery. The public outcry against the plan was so loud that public housing in Philadelphia, just as in Chicago, Detroit, and other cities, came to buttress ghettoization. At last the 1966 decision in the case of *Gautreaux v. Housing Authority of Chicago* barred the Windy City from its deliberate policy of ghettoizing African Americans in gigantic projects such as the notorious Robert Taylor Homes.

Although the administrations of John F. Kennedy and Lyndon Johnson attempted to utilize public housing as command centers in the war on poverty, the projects inevitably became engulfed by the urban crisis of the late 1960s and the black revolution. Not only did the projects visibly isolate the minority poor spatially and architecturally, they increasingly isolated them socially. By 1970 St. Louis's Pruitt-Igoe projects epitomized the bankruptcy of linking public housing and urban renewal. According to sociologist Lee Rainwater, these and other high-rise projects not only stigmatized the poor and greatly compounded the task of managing children, they also created a "fearful world" steeped in hopelessness.

At the same time that the Kennedy administration was using social service centers as experiments, it was simultaneously leading the retreat from conventional public housing. Kennedy's public housing chief, Marie McGuire, launched

*Many public housing projects, such as the Ida B. Wells homes in Chicago, looked more like penitentiaries than like residential developments.*

a vigorous campaign to refurbish the image of public housing, with an emphasis on elderly rather than family housing. By 1965, the inaugural year of the Department of Housing and Urban Development (HUD), units for the elderly comprised half of the 26,000 annual public housing starts. That same year, through such programs as Turnkey and Section 23, HUD moved swiftly to involve the private sector in supplying low-income housing. In these programs, either private developers built projects to be turned over to LHAs or the LHAs contracted with landlords and developers for units that the LHA then leased and managed. In all cases, the authority compensated private suppliers with the difference between a tenant's ability to pay and the "fair market rent" of a unit.

In 1974, President Richard Nixon announced a moratorium on the further construction of conventional public housing. Section 8 now replaced conventional public housing as the vehicle for enlarging the supply of low-income housing. Under Section 8, low-income tenants shopped in a presumably "open" market for suitable low-rent shelter certified by the LHA as safe and sanitary. Like Section 23, Section 8 paid landlords the difference between the rent that families could afford and the unit's fair market rent. It differed from Section 23 by reducing the LHA's role, so that it was responsible only for certifying tenants and dwelling units. During the presidencies of Ronald Reagan and George Bush, pressure grew to further limit the domain of LHAs by giving tenants vouchers to secure their own housing in the marketplace. Anti–public housing forces viewed vouchers or "housing allowances" as a way of removing the federal government altogether from the housing business and placing greater emphasis on the private sector in implementing public policy. Although similar policies were adopted in several states, they were never enacted by Congress. A 1987 law made it possible for LHAs to sell existing public housing to qualified private management corporations. Few were sold.

Meanwhile, the financial noose that kept the housing authorities of big cities strapped for funds tightened. The 1969 Brooke Amendment, which aimed to relieve the rent burden of the urban poor by limiting public housing rents to 25 percent of tenant family income, further trapped LHAs in a funding conundrum that ignored the rising maintenance costs of buildings that were 30 and 40 years old, and the very limited ability to pay rent of a largely dependent, increasingly female-headed tenant population. Several big city housing authorities—Philadelphia's, for example—existed in or at the edge of bankruptcy. Thousands of units in cities such as Philadelphia—indeed, whole high-rise buildings—sat vacant, the maintenance costs too burdensome to warrant rehabilitation.

In 1994, the future of public housing both as policy and also as a large component of the urban housing stock for low-income Americans remained obscure. A significant need for "safe and sanitary" low-rent shelter remained, as witnessed by such publicized urban issues as the existence of an underclass, the abandonment of inner-city housing, and the chronic problem of homelessness, all three conditions exacerbated by the ongoing restructuring of the urban economy. Yet, contrary to the Pruitt-Igoe image, many urban public housing projects afforded good community living. Indeed, in 1994 a number of architecturally distinctive public housing projects built in the 1930s and early 1940s merited inclusion on the National Register of Historic Places in addition to serving as sound physical and social environments for tenant families. Public housing as a social policy continued to be extolled by many as a worthy solution to a chronic urban dilemma of housing low-income families decently.

—*John F. Bauman*

**See also**

Bauer, Catherine; Pruitt-Igoe Housing Complex; Regional Planning Association of America; Stein, Clarence S.

**References**

Bauer, Catherine. "The Dreary Deadlock of Public Housing." *Architectural Forum* 105 (1957): 140–142, 219, 221.

Bauman, John F. *Public Housing, Race, and Renewal: Urban Planning in Philadelphia, 1920–1974.* Philadelphia: Temple University Press, 1987.

Bauman, John F., Norman Hummon, and Edward Muller. "Public Housing, Isolation, and the Urban Underclass." *Journal of Urban History* 17 (1991): 264–293.

Bowly, Devereux, Jr. *The Poorhouse: Subsidized Housing in Chicago, 1895–1976.* Carbondale: Southern Illinois University Press, 1978.

Bratt, Rachel G. "Public Housing: The Controversy and Contribution." In Rachel G. Bratt, Chester Hartman, and Ann Meyerson, eds., *Critical Perspectives on Housing,* 335–361. Philadelphia: Temple University Press, 1986.

Fairbanks, Robert. *Making Better Citizens: Housing Reform and the Community Development Strategy in Cincinnati, 1890–1960.* Chicago: University of Illinois Press, 1988.

Fisher, Robert Moore. *Twenty Years of Public Housing: Economic Aspects of the Federal Program.* Westport, CT: Greenwood Press, 1959.

Hays, R. Allen. *The Federal Government and Urban Housing: Ideology and Change in Public Policy.* Albany: State University of New York Press, 1985.

Lubove, Roy. "Homes and 'A Few Well-Placed Fruit Trees': An Object Lesson in Federal Housing." *Social Research* 27 (1960): 469–486.

Marcuse, Peter. "The Beginnings of Public Housing in New York." *Journal of Urban History* 12 (1986): 353–390.

Meehan, Eugene J. *Public Housing Policy: Myth versus Reality.* New Brunswick, NJ: Center for Policy Research, 1975.

Stegman, Michael A. "The Role of Public Housing in a Revitalized National Housing Policy." In Denise DiPasquale and Langley C. Keyes, eds., *Building Foundations: Housing and Federal Policy.* Philadelphia: University of Pennsylvania Press, 1990.

## Public Works

A wide range of service networks collectively known as public works and including sewerage, cable systems, and electric, gas, telephone, and water lines link urban homes and businesses today. It is hard to imagine, but a century ago few of these services were available to most homes and businesses in American cities.

Until early in the nineteenth century, urban Americans relied on private sources to provide water. Most households got their water from wells, streams, lakes, rivers, or cisterns that collected rainwater. Additionally, wealthy residents of cities could purchase spring water from businesspeople who delivered it to private homes. But as early as the decade after the American Revolution, problems with this private and individualistic approach to supplying a basic necessity had already appeared. As communities grew, many households could no longer rely on a readily available source of clean water. Either they lacked access to a private well, or they were too far from a stream, river, or lake. Moreover, the problem of water quality became evident as science developed a better understanding of how disease was transmitted. Although bacteria was not discovered until the 1880s, many doctors and public health advocates connected disease with unclean water long before that. Epidemics of cholera and yellow fever during the late eighteenth and early nineteenth centuries spurred local communities to improve and increase their water supplies. While these problems worried residents, the threat of fire more often led to solutions for problems of water supply. The possibility of fire threatened everyone, but it most endangered large property owners. As a result, the business elite often called loudly for water systems that could help avert total disaster if a fire broke out.

Initially, most cities allowed private companies to supply water. Private companies supplied water to Boston between 1796 and 1848, to Baltimore between 1807 and 1854, and to New York between 1798 and 1842. But as the population of cities grew in the nineteenth century, residents discovered that private companies lacked the economic interest or the large amounts of capital needed to construct massive water systems. As a result, cities themselves assumed responsibility for providing water. In the United States, the percentage of publicly owned waterworks grew from 6.3 in 1800 to 53.2 in 1896. Population seems to have determined if waterworks were publicly or privately owned—the larger a city, the more likely it was to have a public water system. By 1896, only 9 of the country's 20 largest cities still relied on private waterworks.

The increasing size of American cities, and the development of large-scale waterworks, created a crisis in disposing of wastewater by the 1850s. Population density in the largest cities had increased substantially by the middle of the century, and overflowing privies and cesspools became a health hazard. The constant flow of water provided to households by the new public water systems exacerbated sanitation problems as the wastewater flowed into existing cesspools, yards, and alleys.

In some towns and cities, the homeowners on a single street banded together to build a private sewer. But this solution was neither practical nor realistic; to be effective, any solution had to include an entire community. Therefore, municipalities such as Brooklyn and Chicago constructed the first planned municipal sewerage systems in the late 1850s. Residents of New York City and Washington, D.C., began constructing sewerage systems in the years after the Civil War. However, extensive sewerage construction did not begin until researchers settled certain basic design questions, including the separate versus combined sewer question, around the turn of the century.

In the 1930s, the Public Works Administration (PWA) helped many smaller cities and towns construct sewerage systems. The Roosevelt administration assigned two goals to the PWA: improving the urban infrastructure and fostering economic recovery. But even with the federal aid that began to become available during the Depression, many rural and suburban communities have avoided the tremendous expense of sewerage systems and still rely on private septic tanks.

As with sewerage and water, solid waste disposal was a private function well into the nineteenth century. Households disposed of garbage by feeding it to animals, dumping it outside the city limits, or just throwing it into yards and streets. As population—and concurrently population density—increased, municipalities contracted with private firms to haul their garbage away. By the 1890s, many towns and cities had begun establishing solid waste departments to improve, serve, and guard the public health. Open trucks hauled garbage to city dumps, and private scavengers collected recyclable materials such as paper, glass, iron, and rags. Closed trucks were introduced after World War II. In the last several decades, there has been a shift back from the public provision of garbage disposal to contracting with private companies.

For centuries, streets served as the basic circulation system tying homes and businesses together. Until after the Civil War, people in cities primarily used streets for walking or for riding on horses or in carriages. The streets were public, but providing transportation was a private matter. During the nineteenth century, though, new systems of transportation developed in the largest cities: omnibuses, commuter railroads, streetcars, cable cars, and elevated railroads. While most city residents continued walking to work throughout the 1800s, public transportation was becoming increasingly available.

Between 1890 and 1917, streetcar systems expanded tremendously in the United States. The number of riders on street railways jumped from 2 billion in 1890, to more than 5 billion in 1902, and then to 11 billion in 1917. During those years, virtually all the streetcar systems in the United States were privately owned and controlled. The shift from private to public ownership of mass transit systems began as some transit companies experienced financial difficulty. In 1912, San Francisco was the first city to enter the electric street railway business by taking over a bankrupt private system; Seattle followed in 1919, Detroit in 1922, New York in 1932, Cleveland in 1942, and Boston and Chicago in 1947. By 1975, publicly owned transportation companies carried over 91 percent of the riders in the United States.

Like streets, street lights are a visible part of the infrastructure. Today, virtually all communities in North America have electric street lights that make night travel safer and easier. In eighteenth-century communities, both large cities and small villages, darkness was the rule after sundown. Spurred by the example of London, where oil lamps lit the streets, some of the largest communities in the United States began installing street lamps by the end of the eighteenth century. A major improvement came in the early nineteenth century with the use of gas for illumination. In 1816 Baltimore, Maryland, became the first city in the United States (and only the third in the world) to install a gaslighting system, and by 1850 there were more than 300 gaslight companies in the country.

The use of electricity to light streets grew rapidly after Thomas A. Edison developed the incandescent lamp in 1878. San Francisco first adopted the new technology in 1880, and New York lit Broadway with electric lights in the same year. By 1882 New York had its first central generating station (powered by steam) and 5,500 street lights in operation. By 1892 there were 235 municipally owned electric systems in the United States.

The telephone became a fixture in many urban and suburban areas after 1880. Within 50 years, by 1930, wires and switches crisscrossed the United States. New Haven, Connecticut, housed the first commercial telephone switchboard in 1878 when the 21 households and businesses with telephones were linked by a central switchboard. Only two years later, 138 exchanges were operating in the United States, and they served 30,000 subscribers. By 1887, 1,000 exchanges had more than 150,000 subscribers.

The latest infrastructure network in American cities is cable television. Over the last 20 years, cable television systems have begun operating in most major cities. As with water or sewerage systems, head-to-head competition between firms involves wasteful duplication of capital investment. Instead, most towns and cities have granted an exclusive franchise to a single cable company to provide service. The current debates over franchise agreements and the process of installing this service provide a sense of the historical debates surrounding the installation of earlier services. Questions about where the system would go, when it would be introduced, and how it would be financed are similar to those raised with earlier services.

—*Ann Durkin Keating*

**See also**
Garbage and Garbage Collection; Sewerage and Sanitation Systems; Street Lighting; Telephone; Water.

**References**
Armstrong, Ellis, Armstrong, Ellis L., Michael C. Robinson, and Suellen M. Hoy, eds. *History of Public Works in the United States, 1776–1976.* Chicago: American Public Works Association, 1976.

Keating, Ann Durkin. *Invisible Networks: Exploring the History of Local Utilities and Public Works.* Melbourne, FL: Robert E. Krieger, 1994.

Konvitz, Josef W. *The Urban Millennium: The City-Building Process from the Early Middle Ages to the Present.* Carbondale: Southern Illinois University Press, 1985.

Moehring, Eugene P. "Public Works and Urban History: Recent Trends and New Directions." *Essays in Public Works History* 13 (1982): 1–60.

Tarr, Joel A., and Josef W. Konvitz. "Patterns in the Development of the Urban Infrastructure." In Howard Gillette, Jr., and Zane L. Miller, eds., *American Urbanism: A Historiographical Review,* 195–226. New York: Greenwood Press, 1987.

## Pulitzer, Joseph (1847–1911)

Voted by journalists in 1934 as their craft's most respected figure, Joseph Pulitzer's reputation rests as much on his bequests as his accomplishments. With $1 million he established the annual Pulitzer Prizes given by the School of Journalism at Columbia University for excellence in the field.

After immigrating from Hungary, Pulitzer wrote for a German-language newspaper and then purchased the *St. Louis Post-Dispatch* in 1878. With the profits from this venture, he bought the struggling *New York World* in 1883, and his policies of sensationalism and reform soon turned the *World* into a moneymaker.

During the Gilded Age, large cities filled with immigrants from abroad and migrants from the rest of the nation. They wanted newspapers that were readable and covered the events they cared about. Department stores and other retailers wanted to advertise to this audience at the same time technological advances allowed newspapers to acquire presses with huge capacities to print on cheaper newsprint. Pulitzer capitalized on this nexus by providing content to attract the masses. He streamlined the makeup of the paper, while his staffers, some imported from St. Louis, wrote colorful stories about crime, sex, and disasters. Headlines were punchier, often featuring alliteration. Compared to its competitors, the *World* published more cartoons and drawings. The paper also pioneered in establishing society and sports sections, and its editorials had a reformist tone.

Until Pulitzer arrived in New York, the Democratic Party had lacked a dependable voice in the nation's largest city, a role that the *World* would soon play. Pulitzer sponsored all sorts of promotions and blanketed the paper with ads. His efforts paid off, and the *World* soon surpassed all New York papers in circulation. However, William Randolph Hearst arrived in 1895, and for the next few years his *New York Journal* battled the *World* for readers by emphasizing crime and other sensations. By then, Pulitzer had suffered a nervous breakdown and had had to relinquish direct control of his paper, but he oversaw every detail from his yachts, sending endless cables to his editors daily. The competition between the two journalists peaked during the Spanish-American War when all the major papers invested heavily in coverage. After the war, however, Pulitzer renounced sensationalistic journalism.

When Joseph Pulitzer died in 1911, his newspapers in St. Louis and New York passed to his sons. The *Post-Dispatch* still publishes today, but the *New York World* was discontinued in the 1930s.

—*John D. Stevens*

**Reference**

Juergens, George. *Joseph Pulitzer and the New York World.* Princeton, NJ: Princeton University Press, 1966.

## Pullman, Illinois

Pullman is a community, located south of Chicago on the Illinois Central railroad, that was started by George M. Pullman, the founder and head of Pullman's Palace Car Company, as a model industrial town. At the end of the 1870s, increased demands for every type of railroad conveyance led the prosperous sleeping car company to consider expanding its manufacturing and repair facilities. High real estate prices in Chicago and St. Louis, plus a desire to avoid Chicago's slums, forced Pullman to look elsewhere. Eventually, the company picked a site 14 miles south of Chicago between the west shore of Lake Calumet and the tracks of the Illinois Central. While Pullman bought over 4,000 acres and turned most of it over to the Pullman Land Association, he kept 500 acres for the Pullman Palace Car Company where he built his model town.

He envisioned development of an industrial complex along with a community (to house its workers) whose appearance would receive constant maintenance. Rents would repay the construction and upkeep costs. Pullman believed he would attract better workers whose lives would be enhanced by healthier conditions and superior surroundings, which would reduce absenteeism and alcoholism while rendering workers less likely to heed labor agitators. Thus, employees would be removed from the evils of inner-city life and live in middle-class surroundings, but still be close to their work.

In January 1880 he hired Solon Beman, an architect, and Nathan F. Barrett, a landscape designer, to collaborate on a master plan for the intended community. Work began in April 1880. The modified Queen Anne style brick dwellings, many with pressed red brick facings, went up rapidly. Generally, the shops and major buildings were round arched, or Romanesque. The residences, each with a basement or cellar, were placed in rectangular blocks laid out in a gridiron pattern along broad tree-lined streets. Thanks to the community's sewer and water systems, all houses had gas and running water, while 10 percent had bathtubs. Shops, factories, public buildings, and the better dwellings also had steam heat. Rents averaged about $14 per month, although half the cottages were let for between $6 and $10 per month.

The town also possessed the Florence Hotel (named for Pullman's eldest daughter) and a church, together with a block-long arcade building containing shops, library, theater, meeting rooms, and professional offices. Pullman also maintained a school and even an artificial lake. All of these amenities gave the town a parklike appearance, especially since the industrial buildings were separated from the residential section.

The new plant began operating on April 2, 1881, when Florence Pullman activated the Corliss Engine (purchased from the 1876 Philadelphia Centennial Exposition) that powered it. Although hailed as a philanthropist for his showplace community, Pullman denied any such intent as he became increasingly removed from his employees. On the surface, all appeared to run smoothly; nevertheless, the workers grew disillusioned with living in dwellings they could never purchase in a community they did not govern. After the depression of the 1890s had begun, Pullman reduced wages, but not rents, causing extreme hardship among his tenants. The workmen struck in May 1894, probably realizing that they had lost control of their working lives; those who lived at Pullman also saw that they had very little say about their personal existence.

Pullman received increasingly bad publicity thanks to his obstinate refusal to negotiate with his employees. Even his fellow industrialists criticized him. He broke the strike, in July 1894, but shortly afterward a commission investigating its causes censured him. Then, five years later, the Illinois Supreme Court ordered the firm to divest itself of any real estate not absolutely necessary for the manufacture of Pullman cars. The Pullman Company complied immediately, and by 1910 only the town's architecture made it different from neighboring industrial communities.

Pullman slumbered as an industrial village for much of the twentieth century. Then, in 1960, Chicago announced plans to clear and rebuild areas, including Pullman, that appeared to be in a state of decay. This attempt, along with others aimed at replacing old buildings with new ones, caused Pullman's residents to organize against such measures. In

1969 they secured National Historic Landmark status for their community. Later, they also received designation as a City of Chicago Landmark District. In 1973 the Historic Pullman Foundation, a nonprofit organization, came into existence and purchased several of the community's historic public buildings, including the Florence Hotel. Since that time the foundation has continued to help the residential community rehabilitate its old buildings and maintain its historic status.

—*Liston E. Leyendecker*

## References

Buder, Stanley. *Pullman: An Experiment in Industrial Order and Community Planning, 1880–1930.* New York: Oxford University Press, 1970.

Leyendecker, Liston E. *Palace Car Prince: A Biography of George Mortimer Pullman.* Niwot: University Press of Colorado, 1992.

Lindsey, Almont. *The Pullman Strike: The Story of a Unique Experiment and of a Great Labor Upheaval.* Chicago: University of Chicago Press, 1964.

White, John H., Jr. *The American Railroad Passenger Car.* Baltimore: Johns Hopkins University Press, 1978.

## Race Riots

What have been termed *race riots* have been a feature of an American tradition of violence since the early nineteenth century. Such episodes have often taken the form of white, racist, physical aggression against the persons and property of African Americans, resulting in numerous deaths, injuries, and widespread destruction of homes. Over time, the aggression encountered increasing resistance by blacks, making the point that violent acts of racism were not without some cost to those perpetrating them. White mobs, especially between 1880 and 1900, regularly engaged in the practices of lynching and torturing African Americans. Aware that racial tensions might at any time explode in such terrorism, blacks repeatedly appealed to the federal government to act against lynching, and such crusaders as Ida B. Wells exposed the lie that this barbarism was necessary to protect white women from black sexual assault. Black resistance to racist aggression had to contend with the fact that white policemen frequently participated in (and sometimes initiated) racial rioting, and that the judicial system did little to punish white rioters.

American history before the Civil War included numerous slave rebellions, most extensive of which was the Nat Turner insurrection of 1831. Consistent with that heritage of rebelliousness, the twentieth century has been marked by episodes in which African Americans have mounted urban rebellions against discrimination, governmental indifference, and police brutality. An early event in this sequence was the 1935 episode in Harlem, when blacks took to the streets, smashing storefronts and clashing with police in an outburst of fury in which three persons were killed. This violence was triggered by false rumors that a black teenager had been killed after he was arrested on shoplifting charges. Subsequently, the report of an investigating committee appointed by Mayor La Guardia determined that the rioting did not stem from the agitation of radicals but from the context of poverty, inadequate education, mass unemployment, and substandard medical care that enveloped black residents of Harlem. For several years, as blacks hoped the New Deal would respond to their needs, there was no repetition of the Harlem uprising. In 1943, and repeatedly in the 1960s, however, blacks rebelled against racial oppression, both in the segregated South and in the North, where informal systems of discrimination continued even while federal legislation outlawed overt segregation and disfranchisement. In the 1970s, the setting of conflict extended to the prison system as convicts, many of them black, rose up against dehumanizing conditions.

In the nineteenth century, antiblack rioting erupted in a number of cities. Cincinnati's history before the Civil War was marked by several incidents. In 1829, city authorities moved to implement Ohio's notorious Black Laws that required people of color to post a $500 bond. In the wake of this decision, gangs of whites terrorized blacks living in the "Bucktown" section of the city. Approximately half of Cincinnati's black population soon migrated elsewhere, many to Canada. Rioting occurred again in Cincinnati in 1836, 1841, and 1843. In 1841, at the beginning of September, a Cincinnati mob lashed out initially at blacks and then proceeded to assault white abolitionists, too. In other cities, blacks and white abolitionists also alternated as targets of racist fury, with blacks sometimes the initial targets and other times white abolitionists. In Cincinnati, blacks had some access to guns and ammunition and offered armed resistance to the mob.

Along with Cincinnati, white mobs were active in such varied cities as New York, Utica, and Philadelphia. Between 1832 and 1849, Philadelphia mobs rioted against blacks on five occasions. In July 1834 a mob invaded the city's black section, destroying homes, churches, and meeting halls, and forced hundreds to flee. Following the violence, a citizens' committee urged blacks "not to be obtrusive." On August 1, 1842, a mob attacked a parade of blacks commemorating the abolition of slavery in the West Indies. Acts of violence included the beating of many blacks and the burning of a new African Hall and the Colored Presbyterian Church. In the wake of the 1849 violence, Frederick Douglass declared: "No man is safe—his life—his property—and all that he holds dear, are in the hands of a mob, which may come upon him at any moment—at midnight or midday, and deprive him of his all." Relevant to understanding antebellum race riots is the reality that, even though some native-born and immigrant whites (especially Germans) opposed slavery and disdained racial violence, many among the successive waves of immigrants considered identification with racism part of the process of Americanization and believed there would be tangible rewards for that identification.

Racist mobs were active during the Civil War and Reconstruction periods. In 1863, racial rioting erupted in Detroit and New York. In Detroit, the alleged molestation of two white girls by a black man produced an attempted lynching. Prevented from carrying out the lynching, the mob invaded the city's black area, and before the clash was over two blacks had been killed, more than a score seriously injured, 30 to 35 homes razed, and 200 blacks left homeless. According to David Katzman, historian of Detroit's preghetto era, the riot destroyed much of black Detroit.

The so-called New York Draft Riots of July 1863 were the climax of civilian racial rioting during the war. Encouraged by the agitation of Copperhead "Peace Democrats" for a negotiated end to the war, thousands of New Yorkers rioted against the new Conscription Act, under which those with money could avoid military service by providing substitutes or paying $300. Before the violence was finally ended with the aid of troops brought from Gettysburg, the death toll reached at least 105. In his account of the riot, Iver Bernstein notes that the "horrifying slaughter of black men" suggested a campaign to erase the postemancipation presence of the black community. The violence included razing the Colored Orphan Asylum, many brutal assaults against black people, and lynchings marked by sexual mutilation, drowning, and burning of victims. Many workers joined the mobs, although the violence did not take root in centers of antebellum labor protest or among the most proletarianized poor in the sweatshop district.

Mob attacks against blacks were a feature of postwar attempts to maintain the system of racial subordination. During 1866 large-scale antiblack rioting took place in Memphis and New Orleans. The New Orleans violence was in large measure a police riot as law officers killed black and white delegates to a state constitutional convention likely to extend the voting franchise to former slaves. At the end of the century, the ongoing struggle to define the position of blacks in American society culminated in the 1898 Wilmington, North Carolina, riot. In it, white supremacists followed up a statewide election victory by trying to destroy any remnants of the Republican-Populist coalition that had given a share of political power to the state's black population. Racist leaders asserted that control of government was the prerogative of the state's propertied interests. Attacks by companies of "white guards" resulted in the deaths of at least 25 blacks. In an atmosphere of sheer terror, elected city officials were forced to turn the city's government over to the champions of white rule, and many in the black community fled for their lives. Despite receiving numerous appeals for federal intervention, the McKinley administration, its energies focused on consolidating the new American empire, did nothing. A racial system based on segregation, disfranchisement, and terror was now in place that would last until well beyond World War II.

The early years of the twentieth century brought repeated racist rioting against blacks in cities of the South and North, underscoring the national dimensions of the race question. Riots occurred in New York City (1900), Atlanta (1906), Springfield, Illinois (1908), East St. Louis (1917), and Washington D.C., Chicago, and Omaha during the horrific "Red Summer" of 1919. In Tulsa, during 1921, mass racial violence erupted as thousands of whites, some armed with machine guns, terrorized the city's "Little Africa" section. Definitive of the riots during these two decades was the role of whites as aggressors, the influence of racist propaganda in generating violence, and the complicity of the police. There was some spontaneity in these confrontations, but the violence was often well organized, impelled by specific political and economic objectives. Racist assaults in this period, however, were increasingly met with black resistance, and the white mob suffered some causalities.

The Harlem Riot of 1935 was the harbinger of an era, lasting until the present, of black rebellions against the persistence of the complex, diffuse system of racial oppression dominating most American cities. During World War II, major riots exploded in Detroit and Harlem. In June 1943, responding to rumors that whites had killed a black mother and her child, hundreds of Detroit blacks took to the streets and began attacking automobiles driven by whites and stoning white-owned businesses. Whites also joined the violence, but police intervention was mainly directed at one side of the confrontation, and all 17 persons shot and killed by the police were black. The violence in Harlem, also in 1943, was triggered when a white policeman shot a black serviceman who wanted to protest the arrest of a black woman. Harlemites were further angered by reports from blacks in army camps about incidents of white racial aggression. The level of violence was somewhat restrained by the La Guardia administration, which held out credible prospects of responsiveness to the black community's needs.

In addition to the Detroit and New York violence in 1943, there were also the so-called zoot suit riots in Los Angeles against black and Latino youth. As best described by Robin D. G. Kelley in his book *Race Rebels,* white servicemen reacted with fury to the rejection of subservice and the assertion of masculinity manifested by the zoot suiters.

*Los Angeles police officers apprehend and search African-American youths following an afternoon of rioting in the Watts area of the city in 1966.*

Major urban confrontations gripped national attention once again during the 1960s. Rebellions in Birmingham (1963) in the wake of a racist bombing, an eruption in Harlem (1964) triggered by police brutality, and violence in the Watts section of Los Angeles (1965) touched off by police harassment symbolized the escalation of racial confrontation. During the next few years Newark, Detroit, Cincinnati, Cleveland, and Chicago were high on the list of cities in which incidents of rebellion broke out. In 1968, after the assassination of Dr. Martin Luther King, Jr., blacks in many cities took to the streets and clashed with police. In Chicago, confrontation between blacks and police set the stage for the violent police response to antiwar demonstrators assembled in the city during the Democratic Party convention. The decade of the 1960s was a high-water mark in the record of American violence, compelling thoughtful observers to focus upon the existence of a substantial and enduring American tradition of violent racism.

Whatever evaluation is made about changes in the American racial pattern since the late 1960s, the 1992 Los Angeles violence, following the acquittal of police officers charged in the Rodney King assault, demonstrated the intensity of racial polarization that still exists in the United States. At the start of a new millennium, white racism is reinforced by those arguing that equality is negated by affirmative action, that whites are victimized by "reverse discrimination," and that more police and more prisons are the answer to high rates of black unemployment. A finely honed, sophisticated racism sets forth the view that blacks are inherently intellectually inferior to whites and therefore it is pointless to invest in social programs meant to compensate for the damage inflicted by segregation and discrimination.

Many of the nation's race riots have been followed by a variety of official investigations, often undertaken by commissions using the work of researchers in the social and behavioral sciences. The studies generated by such inquiries have often provided considerable information concerning the sources of violence and programs of effective action to avoid repetition of such incidents. Among the more valuable reports have been the Chicago Commission on Race Relations's study, *The Negro in Chicago: A Study of Race Relations;* the New York Mayor's Commission report on the 1935 riot, *The Negro in Harlem;* and the findings, published in some 2 million copies during 1968, of the Kerner Commission, the first presidential-level, federally funded examination of race relations nationwide. At the heart of the commission's conclusions was the declaration that, "Our nation is moving toward two societies, one black, one white—separate and unequal." Read in the light of American history since the late 1960s, this warning provides evidence that even the most extensive, well-researched investigations have too often been transformed into substitutes for effective remedial action.

The large majority of race riots have been confrontations between whites and African Americans, but Asians have also been the targets of such violence. Chinese immigrants, originally welcomed to California as mine laborers and railroad construction workers, were victims of the 1871 Los Angeles riot, actually a massacre in which 18 Chinese were either shot or lynched. Other incidents of anti-Chinese rioting took place in Denver (1880), Rock Springs, Wyoming (1885), and Seattle-Tacoma (1885–1886). In 1907, the Anti–Asian Indian "Hindu" Riot occurred in Bellingham, Washington.

In *The Souls of Black Folk,* published in 1903, W. E. B. Du Bois wrote that "the problem of the twentieth century is the problem of the color-line." If the twenty-first century is not also to be marked by the color-line, resolve is needed to eliminate the sources of race riots and other forms of racial violence.

—*Herbert Shapiro*

### References

Bernstein, Iver. *The New York City Draft Riots: Their Significance for American Society and Politics in the Age of the Civil War.* New York: Oxford University Press, 1990.

Capeci, Dominic J. *The Harlem Riot of 1943.* Philadelphia: Temple University Press, 1977.

————. *Layered Violence: The Detroit Rioters of 1943.* Jackson: University Press of Mississippi, 1991.

Daniels, Roger, ed. *Anti-Chinese Violence in North America.* New York: Arno Press, 1979.

Harris, Fred, and Roger Wilkins, eds. *Quiet Riots: Race and Poverty in the United States.* New York: Pantheon Books, 1988.

Platt, Anthony, ed. *The Politics of Riot Commissions, 1917–1970.* New York: Macmillan, 1971.

Prather, H. Leon. *We Have Taken a City: Wilmington Racial Massacre and Coup of 1898.* Rutherford, NJ: Fairleigh Dickinson University Press, 1984.

Richards, Leonard L. *"Gentlemen of Property and Standing": Anti-Abolition Mobs in Jacksonian America.* New York: Oxford University Press, 1970.

Rudwick, Elliot M. *Race Riot at East St. Louis, July 2, 1917.* Carbondale: Southern Illinois University Press, 1964.

Shapiro, Herbert. *White Violence and Black Response: From Reconstruction to Montgomery.* Amherst: University of Massachusetts Press, 1988.

Tuttle, William M. *Race Riot: Chicago in the Red Summer of 1919.* New York: Atheneum, 1972.

U.S. National Advisory Commission on Civil Disorders. *Report.* New York: Bantam Books, 1968.

Waskow, Arthur L. *From Race Riot to Sit-In, 1919 and the 1960s: A Study in the Connections between Conflict and Violence.* Garden City, NY: Doubleday, 1966.

## Racism and Discrimination

Ideological racism is a set of ideas and beliefs that explains and legitimates racial stratification and is based on the notion that some racial or ethnic groups are superior and others inferior to them. Although a minority race or ethnic group could theoretically discriminate against a majority, the nature of power relationships makes this eventuality extremely unlikely, if not impossible.

In its more traditional form, ideological racism centers on physical characteristics. A group's unchangeable physical characteristics are perceived as directly and causally linked to psychological or intellectual characteristics, thereby distinguishing between superior and inferior racial groups. In more symbolic racism, a group's cultural heritage is perceived as directly and causally related to socioeconomic well-being, therefore distinguishing between morally inferior and superior racial and ethnic groups. Despite increasing support for the broad principles of racial and ethnic integration, demonstrated in attitude surveys since the 1940s, Anglo Americans are considerably less likely than other Americans to endorse policies intended to achieve integration and combat racism and discrimination, thereby yielding a paradox in contemporary racial relations.

Discrimination is the behavioral manifestation of ideological racism—individual, organizational, and institutional practices that have a differential and harmful impact on members of a subordinate racial or ethnic group, or otherwise restrict their access to scarce societal resources and rewards. The various forms of discrimination are the mechanisms by which a dominant racial group preserves its position in the racial or ethnic hierarchy of society.

Discrimination is often defined as covarying along two key dimensions, the intention of the discriminator and the level of society at which the discriminator operates. The discriminator may or may not be motivated by prejudice, a deep and persistent antagonism toward people because of their racial or ethnic heritage. Prejudice is embodied in a cognitive component (a stereotype) and an affective component (an intense hostility). The discriminator may be an individual or a small, informal group. Institutional racism involves discriminatory racial practices built into such prominent structures as the political, economic, and social systems (particularly education). Many analysts focus on institutional racism as the prime factor in maintaining a racialized society as all facets of individual well-being are affected by access to employment, education, justice, health, and political power.

The character of individual and institutional discrimination is shaped by the spatial context in which it occurs, and the spatial context is critical for understanding racism and discrimination. This is because racial and ethnic groups, and also opportunities and rewards, are distributed differentially across the American landscape. The degree and the form of individual discrimination depends on historical and current variations in the spatial distribution and concentration of groups, which plays a major role in determining intergroup contact. The degree and form of institutional discrimination depends directly on the opportunity and reward structure of each urban or suburban place. Although national urban and industrial policies, as well as societal beliefs, expectations, and attitudes, clearly shape the character of racism and discrimination, competition between racial and ethnic groups is realized in the immediate community. Institutional discrimination varies by place in accordance with the racial and ethnic composition of an area and the structure of opportunities to acquire adequate employment, housing, political power, education, and health.

Discrimination by individuals or small groups encompasses harmful action, whether intentional or unintentional, taken by a member or small group of members of a dominant racial or ethnic group against members of a subordinate group. These actions may or may not be sanctioned by societal norms or by most members of the dominant group in the local community. Individual discrimination that occurs without the explicit intent to harm may seem like a relatively more benign form of discrimination. Its very insidiousness, however, reflects the intractability of racism. Despite the absence of a basis in prejudice, unintentional discrimination by individuals perpetrates the unequal treatment of members of subordinate groups. For example, well-meaning guidance counselors may unconsciously steer black and Latino Americans away from high tech magnet schools, while steering Asian Americans toward them. Homeowners unintentionally discriminate when they incorrectly assume that property values inevitably decrease when African Americans or Latinos move into a neighborhood, and move out when a neighborhood integrates. Inaccurate or stereotyped perceptions of Asian Americans as a "model minority" may exacerbate the resentment of other subordinate groups, sometimes making Asian Americans a target of hate crime.

Individual discrimination with the intent to harm is the most visible and dramatic form of discrimination. That segment of American society contending that racism has been eliminated typically considers only overtly intentional discrimination by individuals and argues that its apparent decline shows the demise of all racism. Yet the number of hate crimes is increasing, racial slurs remain common, and African Americans, Latinos, and Asians are continually kept out of the queue for good jobs and promotions. The Department of Justice has relied on "auditing" procedures to determine whether an individual employer or landlord restricts employment or housing opportunities for members of a subordinate group. For example, an African-American couple and an Anglo couple, identical in every qualification for homeownership, are sent into the real estate market. Discrimination is evident when representatives of the real estate industry declare that the housing preferred by the African-American couple is unavailable even though they offer it to the Anglo couple who made a lower bid after the African-American couple. Key individuals in financial institutions can reinforce this trend by regulating access to mortgages and homeowner's insurance in a discriminatory fashion.

Small, informally organized groups also discriminate intentionally, violating not only social norms but also laws. For example, members of one small town in Texas defied the Public Housing Authority's efforts to integrate a public housing unit and declared that African Americans were not welcome in their town.

Individuals may discriminate intentionally when they endorse (either explicitly or covertly) political candidates who promise racially based changes if elected; this is one instance in which members of a minority group have been seen as expressing racism or discriminatory attitudes toward a majority group or another minority. Candidates for mayoralties and other local government offices are especially prone to this form of discrimination when voters see their own lifestyles threatened. The most blatant form of intentional discrimination by individuals is highlighted in the incidents of bias generally deemed most newsworthy. For example, the white public's memory of racially based violence is easily triggered by names such as Howard Beach, the Central Park jogger, Rodney King, Vincent Chin, and Bensonhurst. But for Americans of color, discrimination is an everyday matter, not just a few isolated incidents that make the news media.

Institutional discrimination has a profound and serious impact on members of subordinate racial and ethnic groups and is surpassed in its harm only by physical violence or genocide. Substantial injury results from restricted access to the avenues that determine life chances. Institutional discrimination prevents members of subordinate groups from integrating fully into the reward structures of society, compromising the physical, financial, and sociopsychological well-being of countless subordinate individuals. Direct institutional discrimination is overt when it is formally established and sanctioned by both social custom and the legal structure. Indirect institutional discrimination is more difficult to detect and thus to eradicate.

Direct institutional discrimination includes those actions by organizations or institutions that have been explicitly designed to affect subordinate racial and ethnic groups differentially and negatively. The legal or informal norms of the immediate organization or community routinely establish and legitimate discrimination. Real estate practices that regularly steer African-American and Latino home buyers away from Anglo neighborhoods and suburbs are a striking example. The well-documented residential segregation is maintained, in part, by these tactics. Explicitly employing only white salespersons because management feels that their predominantly white clientele prefers white assistance provides another example of organizational discrimination.

Historically, the poll taxes and literacy tests that deterred minority political participation and maintained segregated public schools illustrate other mechanisms through which subordinate groups have been treated differently by explicitly, racially biased institutional practices. The ongoing attempts to rid public schools of bilingual curricula and declare English the "official" state language provide more current examples of direct institutional discrimination. The judicial and policing systems apply direct institutional discrimination when they explicitly create racial profiles of likely criminals, who are disproportionately likely to be detained as suspicious. The physical well-being of subordinate individuals is compromised by targeting specific racial and ethnic groups for cigarette and alcohol advertising. For example, billboards leased by cigarette companies are often deliberately located in neighborhoods because of their racial and ethnic composition. Moreover, the disproportionate concentration of toxic dumps or dangerous factories in minority neighborhoods may result from direct institutional discrimination.

Indirect institutional discrimination occurs when organizations and societal institutions use practices that seem to be free of bias but nevertheless have a differential and harmful impact on members of subordinate groups. The individuals and groups who carry out these discriminatory practices are unlikely to consider themselves discriminators. Consequently, individuals from both dominant and subordinate groups are easily persuaded that members of subordinate groups are responsible for their own disadvantages. For example, organizational practices that have a differential impact on the employment of subordinate group members include access to internal labor market queues through personal connections ("good ole boy" networks), hiring and promotion criteria that accentuate test-score qualifications, and seniority systems that determine promotions and terminations. Moving workplaces and retail establishments to sub-

urbs and outlying urban areas limits the opportunities for employment and consumption among subordinate groups concentrated in inner-city areas.

In addition to residential segregation sustained by direct institutional discrimination, members of subordinate groups are diverted away from affordable, adequate housing through the attrition of low-cost housing in the process of urban gentrification. The widening gulf between the location of affordable housing and employment disproportionately affects subordinate racial group members. Public transportation between the two areas is often limited and usually explained by the higher cost of providing services to inner-city areas. The spatial distribution of employment opportunities is mirrored in the variable quality of educational facilities according to place. The dependence of individual school systems on local property taxes accentuates the existence of a two-tiered system of public education—the wealthier suburban and dominant-group neighborhoods in contrast to the poorer inner-city and subordinate-group neighborhoods.

The physical well-being of subordinate-group members, relative to that of dominant-group members, is compromised by seemingly race-neutral organizational and institutional practices. For example, the criminal justice system disproportionately metes out the death penalty to members of subordinate racial and ethnic groups. The concentration of toxic waste sites and hazardous industries in minority neighborhoods already mentioned aggravates the incidence and prevalence of morbidity and mortality among subordinate groups.

In 1981, the U.S. Commission on Civil Rights separated organizational discrimination from what it called structural discrimination. Organizational discrimination is part of an organization's way of doing business, such as seniority rules, use of academic tests, and credit policies. Structural discrimination refers to the linkages among employment, education, housing, and government institutions and their representatives. The process of discrimination has its origins in past events (e.g., genocide aimed at native peoples, the enslavement of Africans, regulation of Asian and Latino entry into the United States), but structural discrimination ensures the survival of racism in the society. The self-perpetuating process of structural discrimination routinely bestows an advantage in one institution that guarantees an advantage in another institution, thereby allowing advantage (or disadvantage) to compound across employment, education, and housing opportunity structures.

The immense, seemingly intractable nature of racial and ethnic discrimination, especially institutional discrimination, frustrates efforts to deracialize American society. Diversity instruction in the classroom, consciousness-raising workshops in the workplace, strong and clear legal sanctions against perpetrators of racial discrimination and hate crimes, and diligent regulation of media portrayal of racial and ethnic groups are suggested strategies for addressing individual discrimination. Recommendations for changing the organizational and institutional levels range from race-neutral macroeconomic and labor market policies to race-specific programs to eliminate ghettos, reconstruct urban areas, and promote affirmative action.

*—Joe R. Feagin*

**See also**
Blockbusting; Housing Segregation; Nativism; Redlining.
**References**

Doob, Christopher Bates. *Racism: An American Cauldron.* New York: HarperCollins, 1993.

Feagin, Joe R., and Clairece Booher Feagin. *Discrimination American Style: Institutional Racism and Sexism.* 2d ed. Malabar, FL: Robert E. Krieger Publishing, 1986.

Feagin, Joe R., and Hernan Vera. *White Racism: The Basics.* New York: Routledge, 1995.

Jaynes, Gerald David, and Robin M. Williams, Jr., eds. *A Common Destiny: Blacks and American Society.* Washington, DC: National Academy Press, 1989.

Massey, Douglas S., and Nancy A. Denton. "Trends in the Residential Segregation of Blacks, Hispanics, and Asians 1970–1980." *American Sociological Review* 52 (1987): 802–825.

Schuman, Howard, Charlotte Steeh, and Lawrence Bobo. *Racial Attitudes in America: Trends and Interpretations.* Cambridge, MA: Harvard University Press, 1985.

Steinberg, Stephen. "The Underclass: A Case of Color Blindness." *New Politics* 2 (1989): 42–60.

U.S. Commission on Civil Rights. *Affirmative Action in the 1980s.* Washington, DC: Government Printing Office, 1981.

Wilson, William Julius. *The Truly Disadvantaged: The Inner City, the Underclass, and Public Policy.* Chicago: University of Chicago Press, 1987.

## Ragtime

In 1915 Hiram Moderwell of *The New Republic* called ragtime music "the one original and indigenous type of music of the American people" and the "folk music of the American city." Recognizing the music's roots in African-American culture and its popularity in urban America, Moderwell believed that it expressed the energy of the American people and the "jerk and rattle" of the nation's cities.

By the time Moderwell's remarks appeared, ragtime music had been printed and popular in the United States for about two decades. Its most distinctive element, sustained syncopation, came from black musicians, who improvised it in the late nineteenth century. They produced this rhythm by juxtaposing lilting melodies with misplaced accents in the treble clef against steady chords in the bass.

The "Missouri style" of ragtime, perfected by Scott Joplin and Tom Turpin, established a pattern for ragtime compositions. Made up of four separate melodies of 16 bars each, the classic rag repeated each motif once and inserted the first strain between the second and third parts (AABBACCDD).

The resulting music was ideal for brass bands and popular dances and inspired exuberant hand clapping and toe tapping. Ragtime songs gained favor in the early 1900s with their lively melodies and raucous lyrics, which were ideally suited to musical comedies on the urban stage.

The rise of ragtime music coincided with the growth of large-scale popular music publishing in the early 1900s. Dominated by "Tin Pan Alley" in New York, the sheet music industry looked for novel, catchy songs they hoped could be adapted to the stage. Though fashioned largely by black musicians like Joplin, Turpin, James Scott, and Scott Hayden, ragtime was embraced by white and black alike, and was written by white musicians such as Irving Berlin and Joseph Lamb. African-American elements in the music were never completely lost, but as composition of popular rags became increasingly formulaic, some musicians sacrificed complexity to marketability.

Not all composers were interested in simplifying the music. Scott Joplin, though known as the King of Ragtime because of such popular pieces as "Maple Leaf Rag" (1899) and "The Entertainer" (1902), wrote a ragtime ballet and two operas that contained ragtime elements. In 1913, Charles Wakefield Cadman composed a trio in D major for violin, cello, and piano in which the last movement was described as "idealized ragtime." Two decades earlier, Bohemian composer Antonin Dvorak had urged Americans to build an American school of music on an African-American musical foundation.

Ragtime became the focus of serious cultural and musical criticism by the 1910s because of the increasing number of ragtime songs that featured vulgar, suggestive lyrics, and because it was performed in saloons, brothels, musical theaters, and dance halls. Perhaps more importantly, many Americans in the era of Jim Crow laws and lynching parties found it troubling to embrace the music of African Americans as representative of the national temper. The popularity of ragtime was matched only by the steady stream of attacks on its musical and moral character. Its popularity began to wane during World War I, and ragtime gave way to jazz—another African American–inspired musical form—in the 1920s.

*—Susan Curtis*

**See also**
Joplin, Scott.
**References**

Berlin, Edward A. *Ragtime: A Musical and Cultural History.* Berkeley: University of California Press, 1980.

Blesh, Rudi, and Harriet Janis. *They All Played Ragtime: The True Story of an American Music.* New York: Knopf, 1950.

Curtis, Susan. *Dancing to a Black Man's Tune: A Life of Scott Joplin.* Columbia: University of Missouri Press, 1994.

Hasse, John Edward. *Ragtime: Its History, Composers, and Music.* New York: Schirmer Books, 1985.

Jasen, David A., and Trebor Jay Tichenor. *Rags and Ragtime: A Musical History.* New York: Seabury Press, 1978.

Schafer, William J., and Johannes Riedel. *The Art of Ragtime: Form and Meaning of an Original Black American Art.* Baton Rouge: Louisiana State University Press, 1973.

## Railroad Stations

From the late nineteenth century to the mid-twentieth century, railroad stations were a central component of almost every American city and town. Those towns that the railroads bypassed languished, while in virtually all other cities and towns the railroad station became a center of urban life.

In simplest functional terms, railroad stations provided waiting space, sheltered outdoors or enclosed indoors, at or near the side of the tracks. The metaphor of the "street" has sometimes been used to describe the railroad station program—neither a beginning nor an end, but rather a temporary stopping point on the way from somewhere else to somewhere else.

The degree to which this essential program was embellished depended upon the station type. The simplest stations were no more than small wood shelters used at flag stops (places so small that local passenger trains did not stop regularly but had to be "flagged"). Almost all stations were larger than this and included one or two passenger waiting rooms, rest rooms, a ticket agent's office, and one or two rooms for baggage and small-lot freight. (If the town grew and traffic increased, freight operations would often be moved to a separate freight station.) In the nineteenth century, when traffic supported two waiting rooms, these were typically sexually segregated. The ticket agent's office was located at trackside and featured a bay window providing a view of the tracks. Railroad stations were usually one story, although larger stations might have second floors with railroad offices or living quarters for the agent. Some larger stations also included kitchens and dining rooms, and the largest stations in major cities featured even more complex programs with additional passenger amenities and railroad offices and facilities.

The chief exterior feature of most stations was the broad overhanging roof that provided shelter at trackside. In some locations, the roof extended in the form of platform sheds paralleling the tracks. Larger stations could include additional platform sheds or a single shed sheltering multiple tracks.

*New York's old Pennsylvania Station dwarfed everything around it, emphasizing the significance not only of the railroad but of the station itself.*

American common carrier railroad development began about 1830. The oldest station in America, built by the Baltimore & Ohio Railroad at Ellicott City, Maryland (1830–1831, now a museum), displays the basic functional elements of the station and shows how rapidly the railroad station building type coalesced. Once the basic program had been determined, it remained largely unchanged for the next century.

However, in addition to meeting functional requirements, the railroad station also played a dual symbolic role. Each station simultaneously presented the image of a railroad company and was also the symbolic gateway to the adjacent city, town, or suburb. A twofold design problem resulted: the similarity of functional requirements and the image of each particular railroad company demanded elements of similarity among stations, while particular site conditions and the individual character and identity of each city, town, or village required variable design. The many ways in which each railroad met this challenge are reflected in the wide variations of architectural character of the more than 80,000 stations built across the United States in the nineteenth and early twentieth centuries.

Most stations were wood-frame structures, and they usually reflected architectural styles prevailing for contemporary residential construction. However, some railroads invested in more substantial masonry structures. The railroad's own staff often designed stations and repetitively used standardized designs, particularly on the Plains and in the Far West. Architects were also commissioned to design railroad stations and sometimes entered long-term relationships with individual railroad companies. For example, Henry H. Richardson and his successors served as architects for the Boston & Albany Railroad, and Frank Furness filled the same role for the Pennsylvania Railroad. In addition, some railroads also engaged in extensive gardening or landscaping programs for their stations.

In the largest cities, stations were designed as significant urban monuments and were commissioned to nationally recognized firms. Among the most notable urban terminals were Union Station, St. Louis (1891–1895), by Link & Cameron; Pennsylvania Station, New York (1902–1910), by McKim, Mead & White; Grand Central Station, New York (1903–1913), by Reed & Stem and Warren & Wetmore; Union Station, Chicago (1916–1925), by Daniel. H. Burnham's successors, Graham, Anderson, Probst & White; and Union Terminal, Cincinnati (1929–1933), by Fellheimer & Wagner.

Although railroad passenger travel peaked during World War II, competition from automobiles and commercial airlines thereafter led to the demise of railroad passenger service. Railroad stations, once lively centers of American life, became functionally obsolete. Beginning in the 1950s, many were closed and some demolished. Those that survived have

*The grandiose design of its interior spaces also reflected and revealed the important role of Pennsylvania Station in the development of New York City.*

remained empty or have been adapted for a variety of purposes including restaurants, museums, shops, offices, or residences. In a few cases, mainly in and near large cities, stations may even still serve continuing railroad service.

—*Jeffrey Karl Ochsner*

**See also**
Burnham, Daniel H.; Richardson, Henry Hobson.

**References**
Alexander, Edwin P. *Down at the Depot: American Railroad Stations from 1831 to 1920.* New York: Clarkson Potter, 1970.
Anderson Notter Finegold, Inc. *Recycling Historic Railroad Stations: A Citizen's Manual.* Washington, DC: Department of Transportation, 1978.
Educational Facilities Laboratories and National Endowment for the Arts. *Reusing Railroad Stations, Book Two.* New York: Educational Facilities Laboratories, 1975.
Grow, Lawrence. *Waiting for the 5:05: Terminal, Station, and Depot in America.* New York: Main Street Press/Universe Books, 1977.
Meeks, Carroll L. V. *The Railroad Station: An Architectural History.* New Haven, CT: Yale University Press, 1956.
Ochsner, Jeffrey Karl. "Architecture for the Boston & Albany Railroad, 1881–1894." *Journal of the Society of Architectural Historians* 47 (1988): 109–131.
Stilgoe, John R. *Metropolitan Corridor: Railroads and the American Scene,* 189–243. New Haven, CT: Yale University Press, 1983.

## Railroad Suburbs

The rapid development of the American railroad system after 1840 made possible a new type of settlement on the outskirts of American cities. Called railroad suburbs, they were bedroom communities built for business and professional families who depended on commuter railroad connections to urban centers. Most railroad suburbs were established between 1850 and 1890; many flourished during the twentieth century as high-status residential enclaves.

Four factors interacted to create railroad suburbs. The first was the construction of intercity rail lines that terminated on the edges of emerging downtown office cores. The second was the railroads' realization that lines designed for long-distance freight and passenger service could also profit by carrying day passengers between city centers and the first outward stops. The third were the deliberate efforts of railroad managers to foster this business with reduced-fare season tickets or package tickets ("commutation" tickets) for frequent passengers, with stations designed for daily "commuters," and with schedules that suited the needs of those passengers. Fourth was the response of land developers, who began to lay out and promote subdivisions and towns along the rail lines at distances from five to thirty miles from the city center. By the 1870s, railroads and developers were not only exploiting existing lines but also cooperating to build special spur and branch lines to new communities such as Garden City, on Long Island, and Chestnut Hill, north of Philadelphia.

Railroad suburbs appeared on the landscape as a series of discrete settlements dotted along railroad lines—as beads on a string, to use the common metaphor. In East Coast cities such as Boston, they might be overlaid on an existing network of rural communities. In the West, they were likely to be "greenfield" developments. Among the most important of these strings were the North Shore suburbs along the Chicago and North Western Railroad line that ran north from Chicago (Evanston, Wilmette, Kenilworth, Winnetka, Glencoe, Highland Park, Lake Forest); the Westchester County suburbs along the New York Central and New Haven Railroads north of New York (Mount Vernon, Bronxville, Larchmont, Mamaroneck); and the Main Line suburbs built along the main stem of the Pennsylvania Railroad west from Philadelphia (Ardmore, Haverford, Bryn Mawr, Villanova, Radnor, Paoli).

The most elegant of the railroad suburbs offered mass-market versions of the semirural villas designed and promoted by Andrew Jackson Downing. A number of railroad suburbs were designed in the romantic landscape style of the mid-nineteenth century. Examples include Glendale, Ohio; Lake Forest, Illinois; and Riverside, Illinois, designed by Frederick Law Olmsted. The ideal suburban environment offered curving streets and green open spaces complemented by the cumulative effect of individual landscaping decisions that expressed a common taste for grassy lawns, flowering shrubs, and trees. The invention of the "country club" in the 1880s served the most affluent residents of railroad suburbs and epitomized the new upscale lifestyle. At the other end of the social spectrum, many of the larger communities have always housed substantial numbers of support workers such as domestic servants, shop clerks, and park attendants; many of these residents have lived in inexpensive housing tucked into odd corners or deliberately located on the wrong side of the tracks.

Railroad suburbs were largely an eastern and midwestern phenomenon. They appeared in cities like New York, Boston, Philadelphia, Cincinnati, and Chicago that were already sizable by the 1850s and 1860s. Younger cities like Dallas, Denver, or Portland were able to rely on electric streetcars to open new land for development from the 1880s, resulting in contiguous rather than separated locations for new upper-income neighborhoods.

In older cities, the innermost railroad suburbs were ultimately engulfed by the spread of streetcar neighborhoods and frequently absorbed into the central city in the later nineteenth century. Examples include the Germantown district of Philadelphia; Chicago's Hyde Park neighborhood, a railroad suburb on the Illinois Central annexed in 1889; and the neighborhoods of southern Westchester and Queens Counties, consolidated with New York in 1898. These embedded neighborhoods have often lost their social distinctiveness.

In contrast, many outlying railroad suburbs used the power of incorporation to maintain enduring identities as communities of high social status. Such railroad suburbs were and are run in the interests of their business and professional residents. Through their control of local government, with its power over land use changes and schools, the dominant residents have been able to preserve affluent islands within changing metropolitan regions.

—Carl Abbott

**See also**

**References**
Binford, Henry C. *The First Suburbs: Residential Communities on the Boston Periphery, 1815–1860.* Chicago: University of Chicago Press, 1985.
Contosta, David R. *Suburb in the City: Chestnut Hill, Philadelphia, 1850–1990.* Columbus: Ohio State University Press, 1992.
Ebner, Michael H. *Creating Chicago's North Shore: A Suburban History.* Chicago: University of Chicago Press, 1988.
Jackson, Kenneth T. *Crabgrass Frontier: The Suburbanization of the United States.* New York: Oxford University Press, 1985.
Stilgoe, John R. *Metropolitan Corridor: Railroads and the American Scene.* New Haven, CT: Yale University Press, 1983.

# Railroads

During the transition of the United States to an urban society between the 1870s and the 1910s, railroads dominated transportation between American cities. The constraints and requirements of railroad technology broadly shaped the immense urban growth of this period. Although their major impact ended before 1920, the enormous transformation of the railroad industry during the past two decades is resulting in new impacts on urban and suburban form.

Antecedents of the American railroad can be traced back to German coal mines of the early sixteenth century. There, seeking a means of pushing heavily laden wagons in coal mines more easily, miners adapted wagons to run on parallel wooden rails, spaced the same distance (the gauge) apart as the wagon wheels. Other modifications transferred responsibility for steering the wagon from the pusher of the wagon to the rails. These changes included substituting a fixed axle for the steering axle and adding a means of keeping wagons on the rails, such as putting flanges on either the wheels or the rails, or extending a vertical rod from the wagon into a slot between the rails. Centuries later, Americans called such modified freight wagons "cars," while the English called them "wagons" or "trams" (from keeping the axles in tram, or perpendicular to the rails).

The expense of building "track" (rails and their supports) limited early railway use to locations where wagons moved heavy loads over relatively short distances, primarily in collieries. After the early seventeenth century, mine tramway technology slowly spread in English coal mining districts, particularly in the vicinity of Newcastle. As coal mines opened farther up the slopes from navigable rivers, railways up to ten miles long, worked by gravity and horsepower, emerged to carry coal from mines to boats. The pace of expansion accelerated further in the eighteenth century, as the developing Industrial Revolution's burgeoning demand for coal spurred a tenfold increase in English coal production between 1700 and 1830. By 1800, hundreds of miles of English tramways were operating, some with large wagons, iron rails, and wagons coupled together into trains. Experiments using steam engines to move trains were also beginning.

In the early nineteenth century, soaring passenger and freight traffic between many of England's mushrooming cities offered new markets for coal tramway technology. In 1821, a group of entrepreneurs organized a corporation for the sole purpose of building a 35-mile railway to carry coal and general freight traffic between the small towns of Darlington and Stockton. Powered by a combination of (mostly) horses, stationary steam engines, and a steam locomotive, the Stockton & Darlington opened in 1825 and connected several collieries with water transportation. In addition to freight shippers, occasional contractors who carried passengers in horse-drawn trams also used the line.

The modern English railroad was born when several entrepreneurs refined the idea of the Stockton & Darlington and applied it to an intercity setting. Opened in 1830, their line, the Liverpool & Manchester, operated its own steam-powered freight and passenger trains between its namesake cities according to published schedules, and any person or shipper could use the trains by paying the rates set in published tariffs. The company was a financial success, and imitators throughout England rapidly followed.

American railway technology branched from English before the Liverpool & Manchester opened, and as James E. Vance, Jr., argues, its further development in the United States diverged considerably from English practice. From the outset, the English built railroads of high quality to serve preexisting dense markets, while the Americans built crude railroads into lightly populated areas and improved the lines gradually as traffic developed, in part as a consequence of the appearance of the railroad. Three significant mineral tramways opened in Massachusetts and Pennsylvania in 1826, 1827, and 1829. Beginning in 1827, groups of merchants in cities along the Atlantic seaboard chartered private and government corporations to build cheaply constructed railroad lines into the West to move freight and passengers, usually with the intent of displacing western trade from competing ports and gathering it for themselves. The Baltimore & Ohio Railroad opened the first of these lines in 1830 with a 13-mile route running west from Baltimore. The B & O extended west gradually, following the National Road that had been completed as far west as the Ohio River in 1817. As the railroad stretched west (it did not reach the Ohio until 1851), traffic diverted from the road or stimulated by local economic growth taxed the railway's capacity to move it. By eliminating bottlenecks in locomotive and track design, shops, yards, and management structure itself, the B & O's managers gradually fashioned an increasingly efficient as well as longer railroad. Many other short lines quickly began operation and followed similar patterns of development.

Railroad corporations first linked different regions of the United States in 1841, when two affiliated companies began running trains between Boston, Massachusetts, and Albany, New York. A decade passed before the next service between regions was inaugurated, but by the early 1850s several companies were running trains between several cities on the eastern seaboard (Portland, Boston, New York, Philadelphia, Baltimore, and Charleston) and points in the Great Lakes and Mississippi drainages.

Tracks expanded with extraordinary speed thereafter, but before the Civil War they failed to constitute a national system. Different companies adopted track gauges of different width, important rivers remained without bridges, and in many cities, large and small, companies did not connect their tracks. Freight moving between the trains of different companies often had to be unloaded onto wagons, hauled across town, and then reloaded into cars of the second railroad.

The Civil War hastened the unification of railroads into a national system managed by subcontinental corporations. The exigencies of moving troops and war material affected a uniform track gauge in the North and led to building bridges and constructing connecting tracks through and around cities in both the North and the South. Railroad companies also formed accounting and engineering associations to create design standards that would let the cars of one company use the rails of another and to accept uniform billing conventions that made companies financially responsible for interchanging cars. When tracks of the Union Pacific and Central Pacific Railroads touched at Promontory Point, Utah, in 1869, completing the first transcontinental railroad, they linked into a set of lines in the Midwest and East that functioned as a subnational system. The South gained entry in 1886 when its railroads changed the gauge of their track to match that used in the rest of the country.

From the 1870s until the 1910s, private railroad corporations dominated freight and passenger transportation between cities. Few would disagree that during these years railroads greatly influenced the development of America's economy, industrial structure, and system of cities, but whether railroads had a "revolutionary" impact has been debated. In a controversial statistical analysis of how America's economy might have developed if the United States had relied only on improved canals and roads without railroads, Robert Fogel has concluded that railroads contributed a social savings no larger than 5 percent of the nation's gross national product by 1890. This conclusion conforms to other historical research. In 1790, most trade in the United States was between its cities and Europe, because the high cost of internal transportation precluded much traffic between cities. By 1830, the situation had already changed dramatically. There were many more cities in the United States, most were growing rapidly because of immigration and the beginnings of industrialization, and the very large prerailroad trade among them dwarfed the trade with Europe. These developments occurred as toll companies, despite their lack of financial success, improved roads and reduced the cost of wagon movement; as steamboats began plying the nation's rivers and lakes; and as canals began joining river and lake systems that had previously been isolated. Thus, according to this analysis, the railroad was more of an incremental improvement in a long line of transportation improvements that took place before the railroad arrived.

The railroad's contribution to the nation's economic development still was immense. Where river boats and canals already existed, railroads further lowered transportation costs and speeded movement, quickly putting coastal and inland water transportation out of business. Speed mattered, particularly for passengers and perishable foodstuffs. Railroads also brought the benefits of cheap, relatively fast transportation to the arid and mountainous West, where providing water transportation would have been unprofitable if not altogether impossible. During this time, railroad productivity improved at the rate of about 3.5 percent per year compared to 1.3 percent for other activities in the country, so railroad costs and rates continued falling into the twentieth century.

The availability of cheap steel rails beginning in the 1880s had the greatest impact because they enabled trains to carry much heavier loads. The adoption of air brakes at about the same time also made possible longer and heavier trains. From the 1880s through World War I, railroad cars increased in size and carried heavier loads as ever-longer trains snaked across the country. Locomotives swelled in dimensions and power to match. As trains grew larger and heavier, railroads invested hundreds of millions of dollars to rebuild their tracks and smooth out grades and curves to ease transportation, particularly between the end of the business depression in 1897 and about 1910.

After 1870, the melding of individual railroads into a national system with ever-lower costs figured importantly in creating national producer- and consumer-oriented firms. Exploiting economies of scale made possible by a market the size of a continent, such firms provided producers and consumers all over the country with standardized products at lower prices than goods produced in homes or by small proprietorships. During these years, Americans began consuming mass-produced, nationally advertised, and nationally distributed fresh meat, fruits, vegetables, cereals, clothing, canned foods, cosmetics, drugs, and other sundries.

The production and distribution of these products continued the high rate of urbanization that had persisted since 1790. Large-scale, mechanized agriculture reduced the price of food and began pushing the family farm out of many regions, reducing the rate of rural population growth. At the same time, new jobs of all types appeared, and most were located in larger towns and cities. To finance what some called factories-in-the-field, new banks were formed, and new packing, canning, and cold-storage houses appeared, as did new grain mills, warehouses, and retail outlets. Modern department stores appeared in larger cities in the 1880s, and Sears, Roebuck and Montgomery Ward both began mail-order merchandising. Large manufacturing companies multiplied. New service industries, such as advertising and accounting, also appeared, and, as society became ever-more specialized and reliant on contractual relations, the business of law assumed greater importance. Not to be overlooked, real estate speculation, land development, and construction industries boomed everywhere, and as Thomas Cochran points out, they continued to account for fully half of the nation's business income during this age of big business.

Railroads contributed to urbanization in still another way. They invented the salaried, white-collar, office bureaucrat, a new kind of urban worker who characterized much downtown employment by 1910. When railroad construction began in the United States in 1830, no large enterprises existed, but as railroads moved into new regions, the size of their workforces mushroomed and spread over larger and larger areas. To manage a large labor force scattered over an area as large as 2,000 miles long and 500 miles wide, and to obtain needed capital, railroad managers through trial and error pioneered a corporate form that separated ownership from management. By the 1870s, railroads had created the embryo of the modern, multidivisional corporation that now characterizes big business throughout the world, financed with stocks and bonds traded in markets in Boston, New York, London, and other world cities. Hundreds of mid-level "white collar" employees controlled the operations of these companies from their corporate headquarters, and hundreds more did so from divisional offices scattered throughout the service territory of the corporation.

In the 1880s, steel, oil, merchandising, and electrical goods companies began adopting the multidivision corporate structure as they grew immense, and by 1920 automobile and chemical companies had embraced it as well. By 1910 most larger American cities contained at least one corporate headquarters, and some cities contained many. In addition, they housed corporate divisional offices and specialized insurance companies, banks, labor organizations, accounting firms, and legal offices that dealt with corporate headquarters and divisional offices in one way or another.

During the period of railroad domination, the country's population grew from 39 million in 1870 with about one-quarter living in cities, to 92 million in 1910 with almost one-half living in cities. The addition of more than 50 million urban residents during these 40 years severely strained the nation's cities, particularly before the development of practical mechanized urban transportation in 1888. Before then, railroads serving Boston, New York, Philadelphia, and Chicago ran commuter trains that encouraged the formation of suburbs, but only the very wealthy could afford to ride commuter trains. This limited their impact on urbanization. Horse-drawn streetcars had a somewhat greater impact, but they also were too costly for most urban workers and, in addition, too slow to have a significant impact on urban form. Attempts to adapt steam and cable power to urban railways had only limited success. Before Frank J. Sprague invented a practical electric streetcar in 1888, walking and riding wagons remained the primary modes of urban transport. Consequently, the huge growth of the urban population before 1888 took place within relatively short distances of warehousing districts and factories served by railroads. Population densities rose dramatically, different classes and races lived cheek-by-jowl, and all manner of work mingled with residence.

After 1888, the speed and low cost of electric streetcars (and electric railways in subways and on elevated structures in Boston, New York, Philadelphia, and Chicago) changed urban form and began the process of net urban population deconcentration that is still continuing. At first, the middle class moved into new, homogeneous suburbs but continued to work in the city where their jobs remained. The working classes continued to occupy housing within walking distance of factories, though, and most retail jobs also remained near railroad yards because hauling by wagon was too costly for businesses to disperse. After 1917, however, motor trucks eliminated this constraint, and retailing jobs quickly scattered to suburbs, beginning the job deconcentration that also persists today.

Most urban growth in the Northeast and Midwest took place in cities that existed before the coming of the railroad, and most of them maintained roughly comparable positions in the urban hierarchy during the railroad era. In 1790 the nation's largest city, Philadelphia, dominated commerce in the new republic, but New York's superior port and inland water connections ended Philadelphia's supremacy. After 1815 New York very quickly gained a stranglehold on most trade between the Midwest and eastern seaboard cities, as well as between the United States and Europe. The completion of the Erie Canal in 1825 gave New York additional advantages in trade and communications that no subsequent transportation investment could overcome. Boston's commercial interests hoped that initiating rail service between Albany, New York, and Boston in 1841 would divert traffic on the Great Lakes from New York to Boston, but their hopes vanished as the new railroad had little impact on established trading patterns. Merchants in Philadelphia and Baltimore were similarly disappointed when railroads between their cities and the Ohio River began running in the early 1850s. From 1870 to 1910, New York, swelled by European immigration, remained the country's largest city and increasingly dominated corporate finance, advertising, and publishing.

The railroads had their greatest impact on the urban networks in the South and West. It is difficult to assess the railroad's importance exactly in these regions—which would have developed without the railroad, but differently. Still, several cities stand out in terms of their growth related to their place in the railroad network. Chicago displaced Philadelphia as the nation's second largest city. The Illinois city did not even exist before the railroad arrived, but its location at the southern end of Lake Michigan made it a convenient meeting point between eastern and western railroad lines. For that reason, many railroads located their corporate headquarters in Chicago, which then attracted the head offices of many more major corporations, some housed in imposing buildings designed by the nation's leading architects. Chicago also became a major center for manufacturing; the operations of grain shippers, milling companies, and national meatpackers; and a great market for all varieties of western commodities destined for eastern markets. The great merchandising firms of Sears, Roebuck and Montgomery Ward also settled in Chicago, while railroad operations and shops added thousands of jobs to the city's employment.

Another quintessential railroad city, Atlanta, Georgia, altered the urban hierarchy of the South. Located where railroad lines swung around the southern end of the Appalachian Mountains, Atlanta had better connections than any other southern city to the cotton-growing coastal plains and piedmont of the Old South as well as to the New South with its industries and cities, to the nation's granary in the Midwest, and to the industrial might and capital of the Northeast. It was a natural entrepot, and large cotton markets and wholesaling establishments grew up there. As a consequence, Atlanta realized large size while Charleston and Savannah languished and even the importance of New Orleans declined. Dallas and Ft. Worth grew at rail junctions where they served similar, but much less important, functions in north-central Texas.

In the Far West, Los Angeles mushroomed after 1887. A new railroad linking Los Angeles directly to Chicago that year precipitated a fare war and allowed the area's unusually aggressive promoters to market the region's ideal climate successfully. By 1910 Los Angeles was already challenging the water-oriented San Francisco for hegemony in the West. Originally lacking a natural site for shipping, but now possessing the world's largest artificial harbor, Los Angeles today is perhaps the one major city in the United States where the importance of the railroad preceded that of water transportation.

Other cities that sprang from nothing or near nothing to prominence during this period largely because of railroad connections included Pittsburgh, which specialized in steel production; Birmingham, Alabama, which became a secondary center of steel production; Denver, Colorado, a center for Rocky Mountain mining; and Minneapolis/St. Paul, Kansas City, and Omaha, centers of grain milling and meat processing as well as regional entrepots.

The very presence of railroads influenced the form of most cities. Larger cities featured huge, sometimes beautiful, sometimes ostentatious passenger terminals in the center of their downtowns, more reflecting corporate vanity than the earnings produced by passenger trains. In some cities, hundreds of daily passenger trains fanned out from terminals onto different routes, occasionally hidden in tunnels but usually crossing bridges over the city's major boulevards or, more often than not, crossing streets at grade level, where they fascinated and horrified at the same time. Railroad yards appropriated huge tracts of land near city centers, with multistory warehousing districts abutting them. Locomotive and car shops housed in imposing structures added to the urban industrial landscape. Railroad shops ranked among the nation's larger manufacturing industries in 1910, accounting for about 7 percent of the country's manufacturing employment. Some of the largest shops, such as the Pennsylvania Railroad's works in Altoona, Pennsylvania (which still employed 11,000 people in 1930), or the Southern Railroad's shops at Spencer, North Carolina, dominated smaller towns, but large complexes existed in many larger cities as well. Water and coal towers, roundhouses, bridges supporting banks of colorful semaphore signals, signal towers, and the dense clouds of smoke and steam rising from scores of moving and motionless steam engines complete the picture of the railroad's physical presence in many American cities around 1910.

Along railroad trunk lines everywhere, but most noticeably in the Plains, deserts, and mountain districts where towns were few and far between, a unique type of town arose to support railroad division points. Occurring about every 100 miles, the division point defined the limit of a train crew's day and the point where engines needed changing. All trains stopped regularly for servicing, requiring yards, roundhouses, coal and water towers, car repair shops, light locomotive repair shops, and sometimes huge ice-making plants and platforms to chop blocks of ice from the tops of refrigerator cars. Beaneries and company hotels served crews away from home. Freight and passenger stations, sometimes with restaurants to serve train passengers, and sometimes designed by prominent architects, opened windows to the outside world for farmers and small-town folk for miles around. Banks of grain elevators and multistory cold-storage warehouses also contributed to the urban landscapes of many division points.

Railroad dominance ended when business interests in an increasingly competitive and interdependent economy rebelled against private railroad corporations that used discriminatory rate and service policies to dictate the horizons of business opportunity. Business unhappiness led not only to state and national railroad regulation but also to federal and state governments getting back into the transportation business, following the model that the railroads had interrupted in the 1830s. In this model, government provided a transportation infrastructure, which was available for use by competing private transportation firms as well as by private individuals. In the 1890s, the federal government began improving ports and internal navigation, and it completed the Panama Canal in 1912. These actions revived coastal and inland water service that seized significant transcoastal, transcontinental, and Mississippi Valley freight traffic from the rails. By 1920 the majority of freight leaving Los Angeles for the East traveled by water, and as late as 1928 two-thirds of the freight between California and Oregon did also. In 1900, most of this would have moved by rail. Some states organized highway bureaucracies to improve the transportation infrastructure; California's legislature, for example, adopted the State Highway Act of 1909 to construct a statewide network of concrete wagon roads to compete with railroads. The mass production of high-quality, low-cost automobiles beginning in 1910 quickly changed the impact of the highway program, which began construction in 1912 and linked all of the state's major cities with concrete roads by 1920.

A long decline in the railroad's share of freight and passenger traffic ensued, and although the railroad industry remained private, its rate of return generally hovered far below the cost of capital until the 1980s. Between 1920 and 1933, long before the widespread use of airlines, the nation's railroads lost about 70 percent of their passenger revenue (80 percent in the West). In 1933, they attracted less than 10 percent of intercity passenger traffic whose total magnitude had increased with adoption of the automobile. Automobiles accounted for most of the loss, intercity buses for the remainder. Railroads also lost money on passengers between the late 1920s and the present. Freight traffic still earned profits before World War II, but the railroads' share of total freight movement declined yearly as truck, water, and pipeline competition intensified.

Conditions deteriorated still further in the 1950s and 1960s. Airline competition decimated the remaining passenger market except for commuter rail and intercity traffic between Washington, Philadelphia, New York, and Boston. Freight profits also decreased because of deindustrialization, the relocation of many remaining industrial plants to suburbs away from rail lines in the West and South, the replacement of anthracite home heating coal with cheap Venezuelan oil, and the growing use of bigger, more efficient trucks on interstate highways. By the late 1960s, the size of the railroad's physical plant far exceeded the needs of the remaining traffic in much of the country, especially the Northeast, and private railroad companies lacked the cash flow needed to maintain a healthy network. Curtailing the maintenance of track and equipment from the late 1950s on, company after company in the East and Midwest declared bankruptcy during the late 1960s and early 1970s, unable to meet their daily payrolls, let alone pay their debt.

Because the railroad system was still too important to let vanish, but the federal government was loathe to nationalize it, Congress reacted by passing several measures. Beginning in the early 1960s, the Department of Housing and Urban Development began to subsidize commuter rail service around Philadelphia, New York, and Boston, leading in 1967 to the creation of the Urban Mass Transit Administration (UMTA) in the Department of Transportation. Although UMTA (more recently renamed the Federal Transit Administration) became involved primarily with urban transit systems, it continued subsidizing commuter rail lines. In the 1970s and 1980s, it facilitated the transfer of commuter trains from freight railroads to heavily subsidized regional governmental bodies, not only in Boston, New York, and Philadelphia but also in Chicago and San Francisco. Congress also created an agency financed by the federal government, the National Railroad Passenger Corporation (now officially known as Amtrak) to which, in 1971, most railroads transferred responsibility for running the few remaining intercity passenger routes in the nation. In the mid-1970s, Congress created another heavily subsidized government corporation, the Consolidated Rail Corporation, or Conrail. Conrail was authorized to acquire most of the assets of bankrupt railroads in the Northeast and New England and to reorganize the companies into a viable freight operation with a modern physical plant whose capacity would complement the much-reduced industrial capacity of the Northeast and Midwest. Finally, in a series of bills that culminated with the Staggers Act of 1980, Congress greatly lessened the regulatory apparatus affecting the railroad industry, giving it the ability to abandon lines easily, lay off redundant employees, and enter into private contracts with shippers. Railroads could also raise rates with much greater freedom on captive traffic, primarily moving coal to power and steel plants.

These measures revived the rail freight industry and precipitated a restructuring that still continues. After receiving billions of dollars in government investment, Conrail became profitable and was privatized in 1987 when the Department of Transportation sold its 85 percent equity in the largest initial public stock offering in American history. Bankrupt lines west of Chicago were liquidated, but solvent companies or state governments generally picked up track that was still needed, sometimes forming new regional railroads to operate lines they had taken over. The railroads that remained solvent in the West and South in the early 1970s raised sufficient capital by increasing rates on captive traffic to rebuild their deteriorating physical plants. They also began merging, and in the process they liquidated huge chunks of their former selves. Many of these pieces were absorbed by new regional rail companies and new short lines that could profit because of less-restrictive labor agreements. Today, two major rail corporations serve the territory west of Chicago, and two serve the remainder of the country. Many regional carriers and an even larger number of short line railroads, most begun in the last decade, also operate profitably. Collectively, these railroads have been increasing their share of the nation's freight traffic since 1985 and carry about 40 percent of ton-miles (from a low of 30 percent), although gross revenues have fallen to about 10 percent of national freight revenue as railroad corporate strategy focuses on low-value traffic. Despite the low revenues, railroads in the United States earn a far greater share of traffic than railroads elsewhere in the Western free-market world. While their owners remain unsatisfied with these rates of return, American railroads have earned sufficient profits to continue investing in their physical plants, though not at a rate fast enough to keep traffic moving quickly through increasingly congested terminals.

The government's policies for passenger trains have been less successful. Congress gave Amtrak capital grants to replace rolling stock and to purchase and rebuild the northeastern railroad corridor between Washington, D.C., and Boston, Massachusetts, in which Amtrak operates fast, frequent trains that recover most of their operating costs from revenues and carry a significant part of the passenger load. Elsewhere, Congress gives Amtrak just enough of a subsidy to run a thin network of infrequent, slow, and delay-prone long-distance trains over freight railroad tracks. These seem routed to pass through as many congressional districts with as few train miles as possible and lose about 50 cents on each dollar of revenue. A few states, most notably Alabama, California, Illinois, Michigan, Mississippi, New York, North Carolina, Oregon, Pennsylvania, Virginia, Washington, and Wisconsin, provide Amtrak with additional subsidies to operate short-distance trains, but these are generally too slow and infrequent to be effective. There is, however, some sentiment to develop some of the short distance corridors more fully, and a federal study indicates that doing so would increase social profit for the nation. Overall, Amtrak's passenger traffic grew from 3 billion passenger miles in 1972 to 6 billion in 1990, or just about 2 percent of the nation's airline traffic. The recession of the early 1990s, competition from low-cost airlines, and the congressional reduction in subsidies has depressed traffic somewhat since 1990. As the 1990s progressed, Congress cut Amtrak's subsidies even further, and its future has been in doubt.

The other aspect of railroad passenger operations, the old commuter lines, are undergoing a remarkable transformation with help from federal and state grants. Regional authorities have rebuilt the physical plant of several traditional commuter systems, and ridership has been growing faster than that of urban bus systems and generally at a considerably lower deficit per passenger-mile. In addition, as freight railroads have rebuilt their physical plants, they have rendered redundant many of their terminals, yards, shops, and even main lines in large metropolitan areas, sometimes replacing them with modern facilities located far from urban areas. Some regions have organized new authorities to buy this superfluous plant and convert it into the infrastructure for new regional rail services. The largest of the new regional rail systems, Metrolink in Los Angeles, runs commuter trains where none operated before 1994 over about 300 miles of track that it bought and rebuilt at a tremendous cost. (Electric interurban trains covered some of the same territory before the 1950s.) Smaller but similar new commuter rail services now operate or are being constructed in San Diego, south Florida, northern Virginia (suburban Washington), Dallas-Ft. Worth, and Seattle. Today, commuter trains account for about 20 percent of the passenger miles carried by all of the nation's urban bus and rail transit systems.

Redundant railroad facilities have been redeveloped in other ways. They have been used for rapid transit lines and new suburban streetcars (light rail) in several places. Amtrak also encourages local governments to take responsibility for stations, and since the late 1970s Congress has made federal money available to rehabilitate or build new railroad stations for Amtrak or commuter trains as well as for local buses. Across the country, scores of cities and towns have organized special districts to obtain this money and have created showcase stations. In addition, various government bodies or the railroad companies themselves have rebuilt grand old passenger terminals in Washington, D.C., St. Louis, Los Angeles, Cincinnati, and Cleveland as restaurant and shopping centers, sometimes connected to new office buildings on adjacent land. New high-rise office buildings have also been constructed on vacated freight yards in cities that are now served by rapid transit lines. Crystal City, near Washington's National Airport, is one example, and similar projects are planned for Los Angeles, San Francisco, San Diego, and perhaps other cities.

The future prospects for railroads remain unclear. Competitive and volatile, the freight side of the business is in constant flux. Monopoly is becoming a significant political issue again, and large shipping interests are mounting pressure to force arrogant and unresponsive railroad managers to open access to their lines to any company willing to pay rent to operate trains. Railroad corporations, forgetting painful political lessons from the beginning of the century, are digging in their heels to resist. They fear creating a technical and economic disaster that would choke off the constant capital infusions necessary for railroad infrastructure to remain competitive, but their credibility is evaporating as they prove incapable of moving traffic being presented to them. Just as easily, open access could put railroads on a competitive footing with trucks and barges, allowing railroads to increase their profitability and market share further. On the passenger side, mounting government deficits limit future development. If public-sector managers can operate commuter and high-speed corridor trains profitably, disregarding the capital costs of infrastructure, they are likely to be able to obtain capital grants to build new lines. If they fail to do so, as currently, there will be little additional development. Because of their less favorable economics, prospects for long-distance trains are less bright.

—*Gregory L. Thompson*

### See also

Dummy Lines (Steam Street Railways); Elevated Railways; Interurban Transit; Mass Transit; Railroad Stations; Railroad Suburbs; Rapid Transit; Streetcars; Subways.

### References

Chandler, Alfred D., Jr. *The Visible Hand: The Managerial Revolution in American Business.* Cambridge, MA: Harvard University Press, 1977.

Cochran, Thomas C. *Railroad Leaders, 1845–1890.* New York: Russell & Russell, 1966.

Fishlow, Albert. "Productivity and Technological Change in the Railroad Sector, 1840–1910." In Conference on Research in Income and Wealth, *Output, Employment and Productivity in the United States after 1800,* 626–641. New York: National Bureau of Economic Research, 1966.

Fogel, Robert William. *Railroads and American Economic Growth: Essays in Econometric History.* Baltimore: Johns Hopkins University Press, 1964.

Kirby, M. W. *The Origins of Railway Enterprise: The Stockton and Darlington Railway, 1821–1863.* Cambridge, England: Cambridge University Press, 1993.

Perkin, Harold James. *The Age of the Railway.* London: Newton Abbott David & Charles, 1971.

Pred, Allan R. *Urban Growth and the Circulation of Information: The United States System of Cities, 1790–1840.* Cambridge, MA: Harvard University Press, 1973.

Salsbury, Stephen. *The State, the Investor and the Railroad.* Cambridge, MA: Harvard University Press, 1967.

Stilgoe, John R. *Metropolitan Corridor: Railroads and the American Scene.* New Haven, CT: Yale University Press. 1983.

Taylor, George Rogers. "The Beginnings of Mass Transportation in Urban America: Part I and Part II." *Smithsonian Journal of History* 1 (1966): 35–50, 31–54.

———. *The Transportation Revolution 1815–1860.* New York: Holt, Rinehart and Winston, 1951.

Taylor, George Rogers, and Irene Neu. *The American Railroad Network, 1861–1890.* Cambridge, MA: Harvard University Press, 1956.

Thompson, Gregory L. *The Passenger Train in the Motor Age: California's Rail and Bus Industries, 1910–1941.* Columbus: Ohio State University Press, 1993.

Vance, James E., Jr. *The North American Railroad: Its Origin, Evolution, and Geography.* Baltimore: Johns Hopkins University Press, 1995.

## Rapid Transit

The term *rapid transit* became commonly used in the United States during the 1870s to describe fast, public transportation in built-up sections of cities. Underground and elevated railways provided the earliest forms of rapid transit. These "subways" and "els" were powered either by steam locomotives, such as the London subway, which opened in 1863, or increasingly by steam-generated electricity, as were the Boston (1897) and New York (1904) subways. Several other cities built cable car systems in which cars started and stopped by engaging or disengaging an underground cable kept in continual motion by a central steam engine. Beginning in the late 1880s, the electric trolley, named for the overhead wires that brought power from a distant coal-fired generator, provided the most ubiquitous and profitable form of rapid transit. By 1902, 22,000 miles of urban railways had been electrified.

More than doubling (at 12 miles per hour) the speed of horse-drawn street railways and opening vast new tracts of suburban real estate, the trolley accelerated residential suburbanization. A variety of factors, from an aversion to manufacturing and a fear of immigrants to the cultural importance of proprietorship and domesticity, made the United States the world leader in rapid transit and the suburbanization it made possible. Contrasting the unusually low population densities of American cities to those around the globe in the 1890s, the pioneer urban statistician Adna Weber rejected the technological determinism that viewed trolleys as the cause of suburbanization. It was the "American penchant for dwelling in cottage homes" in contrast to the European preference for townhouses that was the cause; the trolley was simply the effect. Rapid transit reflected a desire to escape the industrializing city.

But rapid transit also facilitated a larger reorganization of the city, a reorganization that segregated the disagreeable aspects of industrial production from its consumer benefits. Eclipsing the nineteenth-century walking city (named for its chief means of transit and characterized by a heterogeneous mixing of classes and functions), rapid transit not only opened the suburban periphery but widened access to, represented significant capital investment in, and consequently raised the cost of land in the urban core. The value of real estate inside Chicago's "Loop" of elevated railways, for example, increased by 700 percent between 1877 and 1892 and more than doubled again by 1910. As skyrocketing real estate values forced out both housing and industry, a central business district (CBD) devoted to administrative, financial, and high-class commercial and cultural functions became the headquarters and showcase of a new industrial order. The surrounding ring of speculative real estate, crowded with poorly maintained tenements, stood ready to be demolished should CBD expansion come its way. The trolleys further served to transport workers back and forth between tenement districts and sprawling industrial plants located on cheaper, peripheral real estate. By 1920, the new metropolitan form of CBD, inner-city working-class neighborhoods, industrial satellites, and exclusive suburban dormitories, had taken shape.

Rapid transit became a symbol of the new metropolis, alternately praised as a technological marvel and force for progress and condemned as a destructive and corrupting blight on the city and the republic. Expanding the city's reach and raising land values throughout the region, rapid transit generated handsome profits and attracted $2 billion in capital. But it was also a major focus of wasteful financial speculation, and it corrupted municipal governments, the source of lucrative franchises to operate in the public streets. Rapid transit also intensified a century of conflicts between the benefits of mobility and the requirements of settlement. Viewing streets as sources of light and air and as public space for recreation, petty commerce, and politics, in short as an integral part of local settlements, inner-city residents (both rich and poor) resisted the transformation of the street into a traffic artery. Steam-powered automobiles and locomotives, bicycles, and smoother, speed-enhancing pavements met (occasionally violent) opposition throughout the nineteenth century. By the end of the century, however, a powerful coalition of transit operators, realty interests, and suburban commuters had generated formidable support for improved mobility.

Ironically, it was a group of early-twentieth-century social reformers, self-styled advocates for the inner-city poor, who completed the transformation of the street from public space into traffic artery. These social reformers (of whom Cleveland's Tom Johnson was the most famous) hoped to enhance residential and employment opportunities for the poor and therefore promoted cheap, rapid transit as a panacea. But their support for mobility (empowering municipal engineers and bypassing abutters to finance street improvements out of general revenues) also underwrote the revolution in street pavements that literally paved the way for the internal-combustion automobile. By the 1920s, public transit, burdened with financial manipulation, political corruption, labor disputes, deteriorating structures, declining profits, and an increasingly lower-class clientele, had lost favor with the middle class. The private automobile now inherited the dream of escaping the city once associated with rapid transit. While public transportation starved from a lack of public funds and was expected to pay its own way, the automobile benefited from lavish public subsidies in the form of new and improved roadways, parking facilities, and auto-friendly traffic regulations and technologies. Not only did the deterioration of public transit limit the mobility of inner-city residents just as jobs and commerce were moving to the periphery, but the automobile claimed an ever-increasing share of the limited public space in the inner city, congesting the CBD and blighting neighborhoods.

While the United States was a world leader in the first wave of rapid transit development, its commitment to private automobiles made it a laggard in the second wave after World War II. While the first wave had been motivated primarily by a desire to escape the inner city, the second wave was part of an effort to use it more efficiently. In traffic-choked and resource-poor cities, rapid transit offered less congestion, greater speed, and better fuel efficiency. Major capitals around the world, from Toronto (1954) and Mexico City (1969) to Stockholm (1950) and Beijing (1969), built extensive subway systems. Since the 1970s, and especially since the oil shocks and rising environmental concerns, the United States has begun to catch up. Washington, Baltimore, Atlanta, Buffalo, and other cities have constructed subways in recent years. The most ambitious is San Francisco's Bay Area Rapid Transit (BART), a computer-controlled system. A light rail, energy-efficient, faster version of the old streetcar is another rapid transit alternative that some cities have adopted. Although government officials regularly emphasize the possibilities of public transit, it remains to be seen whether Americans will find the political will to overcome the privatism of the automobile culture and revitalize their cities.

—*John D. Fairfield*

**See also**
Buses; Central Business District; Elevated Railways; The Loop; Streetcars; Subways; Walking City.

**References**

Barrett, Paul. *The Automobile and Urban Transit: The Formation of Public Policy in Chicago, 1900–1930.* Philadelphia: Temple University Press, 1983.
Cheape, Charles W. *Moving the Masses: Urban Public Transit in New York, Boston, and Philadelphia, 1890–1912.* Cambridge, MA: Harvard University Press, 1980.
Fairfield, John D. *The Mysteries of the Great City.* Columbus: Ohio State University Press, 1993.
McShane, Clay. *Down the Asphalt Path: The Automobile and the American City.* New York: Columbia University Press, 1994.
Miller, Zane L. *Boss Cox's Cincinnati.* Chicago: University of Chicago Press, 1968.
Smerck, George M. *The Federal Role in Urban Mass Transportation.* Bloomington: Indiana University Press, 1991.
Stilgoe, John R. *The Metropolitan Corridor.* New Haven, CT: Yale University Press, 1983.
Warner, Sam Bass, Jr. *Streetcar Suburbs: The Process of Growth in Boston 1870–1900.* Cambridge, MA: Harvard University Press, 1962.

# Rauschenbusch, Walter (1861–1918)

Walter Rauschenbusch was the most important of the theologians who formulated and expressed the social gospel as organized Protestantism's response to urban, industrial problems at the beginning of the twentieth century. Like many of his contemporaries, Rauschenbusch rued the destructive competition of industrial capitalism and the social consequences of irresponsible business practices. Through his writings and actions, he contributed to a growing social consciousness that found public expression in early-twentieth-century Progressivism.

Born in 1861, the son of a German Baptist minister and theologian, Rauschenbusch followed his father into the ministry in the 1880s. After being turned down for a post in Illinois because of his liberal beliefs, Rauschenbusch accepted the call to a congregation in a section of downtown New York City known as "Hell's Kitchen." In this community of immigrants and workers, he introduced a number of social programs designed to meet the needs of people struggling for a decent existence. He opened a day nursery for the children of working mothers, soup kitchens to feed the hungry, and public bathing facilities in a district where these were rare. Rauschenbusch was not one to remain uninvolved; during an epidemic in 1888, he ministered to the sick himself, fell ill, and lost his hearing. In the aftermath of that experience, he became fully committed to what became known as the social gospel.

Rauschenbusch attained national significance when, after he joined the faculty of the Rochester Theological Seminary, he began writing about America's social problems and the responsibility of the church to address them. *Christianity and the Social Crisis* (1907) identified particular social problems stemming from an impersonal business-driven society, and *Christianizing the Social Order* (1912) outlined important steps churches could take to address the social crisis. His *Theology for the Social Gospel* (1917), which appeared a year before his untimely death, was the first work of its kind produced by an advocate of the social gospel.

—*Susan Curtis*

### References

Curtis, Susan. *A Consuming Faith: The Social Gospel and Modern American Culture.* Baltimore: Johns Hopkins University Press, 1991.

Handy, Robert T. *The Social Gospel in America, 1870–1920.* New York: Oxford University Press, 1966.

Landis, Benson Y., ed. *A Rauschenbusch Reader.* New York: Harper, 1957.

Sharpe, Dores Robinson. *Walter Rauschenbusch.* New York: Macmillan, 1942.

## Reagan Administration: Urban Policy

A national urban policy is a comprehensive, coherent framework for the coordination and integration of all federal programs affecting cities and their inhabitants. Aimed at marshaling national efforts and focusing federal resources on urban problems, such a policy had been announced only in March 1978. The administration of President Ronald Reagan (1981–1989) reconceptualized national urban policy as a by-product of its national economic policy and reformulated intergovernmental relations as the New Federalism.

Urban policy, rarely mentioned in the president's State of the Union addresses to Congress, was not an explicit, independent priority of the Reagan administration, even though it was formed and reformulated.

President Reagan built his domestic strategy and policy on creating economic stability and growth. According to his first *President's National Urban Policy Report* (1982), "the key to healthy cities is a healthy economy." His administration's last report (1988) asserted that "the private sector has been and will continue to be the primary satisfier of social needs" and that "the importance of economic growth to a national urban policy cannot be overemphasized." (A decentralized federal system dominated by market forces logically and practically contradicts a comprehensive, coordinated approach to any domestic policy arena.)

Pivotal to the so-called "supply side" economic strategy were two tax measures with significant urban impacts. The Economic Recovery Tax Act of 1981 stimulated private investment through tax incentives, notably accelerated capital depreciation. The resulting boom in commercial construction peaked in 1985 partly because the Tax Reform Act of 1986 reduced tax rates and eliminated many tax breaks, including real estate tax shelters. It also enacted a new tax credit for low-income rental housing. The unlimited deduction of mortgage interest for first and second residences, the deductions for state and local income and property taxes, all valuable tax breaks for homeowners and the suburban middle class, were retained.

These policies were consistent with President Reagan's New Federalism, which in part reordered government functions and relationships, rejected direct federal interaction with cities, and recognized the growing role of suburbs in contemporary urban life. In short, President Reagan substantially reversed 50 years of increasing, direct federal engagement in urban problems. In practice, this shift meant reducing preexisting federal urban programs and funding, shifting responsibilities to state and local governments, and reducing the institutional voice of urban interests in national government.

The main policy objectives enumerated in the urban report of 1986 were federal deregulation; pushing decision making down to state and local governments and the private sector; block grants in preference to narrow, highly specific grants; and federal "budgetary restraint on domestic programs." At least to some degree, the administration accomplished all these objectives.

Among the successful initiatives, the Omnibus Reconciliation Act of 1981 redistributed some responsibilities by merging (by official count) 57 separate federal grant programs into 9 block grants, including a Small Cities Block Grant and a revamped social services block grant. Again according to the 1986 urban report, "these block grants were used by the Administration to ameliorate the effects of reduced Federal funding by allowing the States and localities to focus the limited resources on their highest priority needs." The combined economic and intergovernmental strategies emphasized regulatory reform and relief from what were perceived as "overly burdensome" federal regulations.

Urban enterprise zones, a major urban initiative that was proposed in President Reagan's first State of the Union address, combined both economic and federalism strategies but met with only marginal success. Using incentives such as tax and regulatory relief, the goal was to foster the economic redevelopment of targeted urban areas. The largely symbolic legislation of 1987 permitted the designation of 100 federal enterprise zones, but the legislation provided no incentives and the authority was never used. Nonetheless, by 1986, 32 states had established enterprise zones, with generally mixed results. Mayors, urban public interest organizations, and others vigorously opposed and ultimately defeated another proposed initiative: a "swap" of selected functions and financial responsibilities.

The administration firmly believed that financing and undertaking domestic policy are best left to states and localities. In fact, the flow of federal dollars to cities plummeted from $11.3 billion to $7.3 billion during Reagan's presidency, from 1981 to 1989. By 1989, federal funding as a percentage of general city revenues fell to less than one-half of what it had been in 1981. In particular, three major programs (Urban Mass Transportation Administration, Community Development Block Grants, and Urban Development Action Grants) sustained deep cuts. Congress repeatedly approved substantially larger budget allocations for the Department of Housing and Urban Development (HUD) than the president requested. Nor was the Reagan administration providing urban assistance by taking alternative routes; federal funding to nonprofit programs declined by more than 20 percent in 1980–1988, even when adjusted for inflation.

The administration sought to offer aid that complemented private market forces and efficiently targeted workers' skills and mobility rather than jurisdictions or locales. The urban reports of 1982 and 1988 repeated that "Improving the general quality and mobility of the workforce is often better for promoting economic growth than providing Federal aid to specific urban areas." The move toward vouchers, rent support, and transfer payments targeted to needy individuals (almost two-thirds of whom live in metropolitan areas) was consistent with the shift from capital investment, location-specific grants, and direct intervention. As federal budgetary pressures worked in tandem with the president's policy preferences, revenue sharing (dating back to 1972 as direct federal assistance to other governmental jurisdictions and best known for its lack of "strings" or conditions and

from which cities especially had benefited) was scaled back, first in 1980 when states were cut off, and then canceled entirely in 1986.

Significant changes in the Department of Housing and Urban Development, the institution most directly concerned with urban policy and the leading federal agency for urban action, illustrate the decline of urban policy as a priority in the Reagan administration. While the total civilian workforce in the executive branch of the federal government increased more than 8 percent between 1980 and 1988, HUD's workforce declined by more than 20 percent, from almost 17,000 at the beginning of the decade to about 12,000 in 1986. Employment at HUD declined from 0.91 percent of nondefense, civilian, executive branch employees to 0.67 percent from 1980 through 1988. The department's budget authority also declined; by the end of the administration, it was approximately 45 percent of the figure eight years before. Actual outlays, fueled in part by past commitments and preexisting authority (money in the "pipeline"), somewhat increased.

The scandals associated with HUD provide dramatic evidence of the decline in HUD's organizational capacity. In 1990, after intensive investigation and testimony, the House Committee on Government Operations concluded that "During much of the 1980s, HUD was enveloped by influence peddling, favoritism, abuse, greed, fraud, embezzlement and theft. In many housing programs objective criteria gave way to political preference and cronyism, and favoritism supplanted fairness." The cost of this "monumental waste and gross mismanagement," attributed primarily to political appointees and contractors, was estimated to be in excess of $2 billion. Eleven high-ranking HUD officials, including three assistant secretaries, were convicted of criminal activity. The scandals prompted three pieces of legislation in 1989—the HUD Reform Act, the Clean Consultants Act, and the Ethics Reform Act.

With their concentrations of poor residents and older housing, central cities have greater housing problems than other areas. The Reagan years experienced a substantial increase in housing assistance by providing rent supplements and vouchers, but these efforts neither kept pace with the problem nor addressed the supply of affordable housing. Subsidized housing starts declined about 90 percent, from more than 180,000 units in 1980 to 17,000 in 1986. More than 4.5 million low-income housing units disappeared from the nation's housing stock between 1973 and 1988. The 1988 urban report notes, "The Tax Reform Act of 1986, in eliminating widely abused tax shelters, reduced major tax incentives that generated private investment in low-income housing" and that 10 percent of housing units in cities were physically inadequate.

Data from the American Housing Survey in 1989 show that the percentage of those assisted by federal programs increased as the number of eligible families rose from 8.8 million in 1979 to 10.2 million by 1989. According to HUD's *Annual Report* of 1991, 12 percent of all renters, or more than 4 million households in 1989, were in rental units assisted by HUD, 1.4 million of them in public housing

Homelessness emerged as a nationally recognized public policy issue during the 1980s. A one-week census conducted by the Urban Institute in March 1987 estimated the number of homeless at or above 500,000. The major targeted federal effort is the Stewart B. McKinney Homeless Assistance Act of 1987 as amended in 1988, and there are at least another 70 federal programs providing some assistance to the homeless.

President Reagan's urban policy succeeded on its own terms by reducing federal support for urban programs and shifting many domestic responsibilities to state and local governments. However, an assessment of impact of the policy on cities necessarily accents distributional issues and registers continuing, even deepening, urban social problems. The president's 1988 report itself details social disorganization and urban problems—crime, unemployment, housing and homelessness, drug abuse, and poverty—that were neglected, unsuccessfully addressed, or accentuated during President Reagan's administration. Federal disengagement contributed to a legacy of deteriorated urban conditions.

—*Carol W. Lewis and Morton J. Tenzer*

**See also**

Community Development Block Grants; Housing and Urban Development, Department of; New Federalism; Revenue Sharing; Urban Development Action Grant Program.

**References**

Peterson, George E., and Carol W. Lewis, eds. *Reagan and the Cities.* Washington, DC: Urban Institute, 1986.

Wolman, H. "The Reagan Urban Policy and Its Impacts." *Urban Affairs Quarterly* 21 (1986): 311–335.

## Real Estate Developers and Development

Real estate development is the process by which agents known as developers change parcels of land to other uses, usually in order to sell it. From the earliest European settlements of North America, land agents and speculators developed frontier territory as farms and other agriculture-related uses, but similar investors also developed America's towns and cities. Since the colonial period, urban real estate development has involved transforming land, typically farm or vacant land, for commercial, industrial, residential, governmental, institutional, or recreational purposes.

Although the techniques of real estate development have changed and grown more complex over time, the process always includes land acquisition, subdivision of land into lots or parcels, construction, and disposition of developed property by selling or renting. Historically, the activities associated with real estate development are divided among several agents—property owners, investors, lenders, surveyors, engineers, architects, builders, real estate brokers, and sometimes others—who specialize in one or more aspects of development. Nonetheless, subdividers and builders play the key roles by initiating and guiding the process from the first to the final sales.

Throughout American history, the growth of population and economic activity have encouraged urban real estate development by promoting the land markets of cities in North America. In colonial cities, growing demand encouraged real estate investment. In booming eighteenth-century Philadelphia, for instance, demand was so high that landowners subdivided the large blocks designed for William Penn with lanes and alleys. Benjamin Franklin created Franklin Court from the land behind his Market Street house by building three additional houses, which he rented to others.

During the late eighteenth and early nineteenth centuries, growing demand for urban land encouraged specialization of the real estate market in the eastern seaports. Where demand was highest—in central areas adjacent to most important wharves and docks—commercial offices and warehouses displaced the earlier mix of shipyards, shops, and residences for merchants, artisans, and sailors.

Large landowners, such as Trinity Church in lower Manhattan, realized that they could make greater and more predictable profits by leasing rather than selling their properties. Acting as *rentiers,* they left it to leaseholders to build upon and rent their property to third parties. As the embryonic business districts evolved into full-fledged downtowns during the nineteenth century, the practice of leasing valuable holdings for terms as long as 50 or 99 years became established, and it persists today.

In large cities, investments in downtown real estate could produce enormous returns, a fact that inspired many town officials and businessmen to campaign for growth and trumpet a glorious future for their towns. Among the ranks of America's boosters and real estate entrepreneurs, William B. Ogden of Chicago is legendary. He arrived in Chicago in the 1830s, and in the following years he indefatigably promoted the city's public works, industries, railroads, banks, and educational institutions. In the 1840s, he invested thousands of dollars in downtown Chicago real estate, which he sold for millions several years later.

Similar stories can be told about early-twentieth-century boom towns, such as Houston, Texas, where Jesse Jones played the role of leading promoter and developer. After a pause caused by the Depression and World War II, the development of America's downtowns resumed, producing an endless string of skyscraper office buildings, hotels, department stores, and luxury apartment buildings.

The king of postwar downtown real estate development was William Zeckendorf, who changed Webb and Knapp from a sleepy New York real estate management company into the nation's premier development company during the 1950s and 1960s. Among Zeckendorf's contributions to the real estate business was the revolutionary Hawaii technique, which entails mortgaging and leasing different sections and functions of an office building. Frequently working with his chief architect, I. M. Pei, Zeckendorf developed such major downtown ventures as Mile High Center in Denver, Century City in Los Angeles, L'Enfant Plaza in Washington, D.C., and urban renewal projects such as Society Hill Towers in Philadelphia. In recent years, such giants of downtown development as the firms of Trammell Crow and Olympia and York have followed in the Zeckendorf tradition.

At the same time that downtown real estate development became specialized, so too did the residential real estate market. In the early nineteenth century, a number of factors, including a growing preference for the separation of workplace from home and diversification of the occupational structure, encouraged the emergence of distinct housing markets, stratified and geographically distributed by ability to pay.

The changes came most noticeably in the burgeoning city of New York. In Manhattan, real estate development for the wealthy created relatively homogeneous clusters of upscale housing, often accompanied by landscaped parks, on the Bowling Green and lower Broadway as early as the 1790s. By the 1830s it had already moved to Greenwich Village, and from there the affluent began their march north up Fifth Avenue.

For those with fewer financial resources, the real estate business provided row houses with progressively smaller apartments, fewer amenities, and lower prices. By the 1830s, builders began to construct multiunit structures called tenement buildings; at first these included respectable residences for the middle classes, but by the late nineteenth century they were associated with the working poor. In the outer city, developers produced a similar range of housing, but instead of row houses, this took the form of detached single-, two-, and multifamily structures.

In the nineteenth century, residential real estate development tended to be small in scale, involved relatively rudimentary site planning, and was a long-term process. Typically, a subdivider would organize the surveying, grading, and division of land into lots. Only the largest subdivisions exceeded 100 house lots, and even these became more frequent only at the end of the century. Even when auctions were used, a subdivider often took years to sell all of a subdivision's lots, which

typically lacked houses on them. The actual construction of a residence was the responsibility of a building contractor, who was hired by a lot purchaser to build his or her home or who built houses on lots he had purchased for resale. Yet, as Sam Bass Warner, Jr., has noted, the average builder rarely built more than a few houses a year.

Some nineteenth-century developments did defy the normal practice. Llewellyn Park, New Jersey, designed by Llewellyn Haskell and Andrew Jackson Davis in 1857, and Riverside, Illinois, designed by Frederick Law Olmsted and Calvert Vaux in 1869, were laid out and landscaped as complete suburban communities. In late-nineteenth-century Chicago, Samuel Elberly Gross subdivided and sold more than 40,000 lots and built 7,000 houses. But these exceptions were rare.

During the twentieth century, suburban development grew larger in scale and complexity. Beginning in 1915, Jesse Clyde Nichols developed the Country Club district outside Kansas City as an automobile suburb; by the late 1940s, it covered 5,000 acres and contained 10,000 houses. On each property throughout the entire district, Nichols imposed detailed deed restrictions that covered floor plans, facades, and external color schemes. He organized homeowner associations to maintain the extensive public parklands, and in the 1920s developed Country Club Plaza, a prototype of the modern shopping center.

After World War II, the firm of Abraham Levitt and Sons pioneered large-scale vertical integration in the field of real estate development. At the first Levittown on Long Island, New York, the Levitts not only planned and subdivided the site but also used assembly-line techniques to construct over 17,400 houses. Pricing their houses modestly, they opened suburbia to the urban middle classes and inaugurated the era of community builders such as Phillip Klutznick, the developer of Park Forest, Illinois, and more recently, the Irvine Ranch Company in southern California. Despite the rise of the community builders, however, most residential developers are still local entrepreneurs who operate on a relatively small scale.

Commercial real estate development has also helped create the postwar suburban milieu. Large shopping centers oriented to automobiles have evolved into indoor malls. Among the best-known shopping center developers of the 1950s and 1960s was James Rouse, who developed Cherry Hill shopping center, a 78-acre complex outside Philadelphia; in the 1970s Rouse shifted his attention downtown where he translated the concept of shopping center into festival marketplaces in Boston, Baltimore, and New York. The development of suburban industrial, office, and wholesale parks fueled the growth of such firms as Cabot, Cabot and Forbes in Boston and Trammell Crow in Texas.

Access to capital, especially in the form of credit, has always been crucial to the process of real estate development. Few, if any, developers are wealthy and audacious enough to use their own money to pay for the high costs of projects that will not show a financial return until an unknown future date. The methods for acquiring credit for real estate projects have also evolved over time. During the nineteenth century, downtown developers tapped the wealth of commercial banks, but usually only for short-term loans, and developers of all but high-class residences often lacked access even to these sources of capital.

Hence, land subdividers often were forced to create complex financing arrangements that involved multiple mortgages obtained from landowners, business partners, or relatives. In some cases, subdividers formed land companies as a way of pooling the resources of a group of shareholders. Developers also mortgaged house lots to building contractors, who agreed to construct houses on them. Such a financing technique was employed in the development of Boston's Back Bay section; contractors who filled the marshlands of the Charles River on their own account received building lots in exchange.

In the late nineteenth century, new means of financing the purchase of land aided urban real estate development. Real estate agents who acted as mortgage brokers helped operate citywide mortgage markets in which individuals, such as widows, with money to invest offered mortgages to buyers of unimproved or improved house lots.

The formation of savings and loan associations, sometimes called cooperative banks, allowed residents of a neighborhood to pool their savings and then loan them to each other for building and buying homes. Over time, savings and loan associations evolved into mainstream banking institutions and, despite a crisis in the 1980s, continue to function as a mainstay of the home mortgage field.

During the twentieth century, other innovations in financing have ensured the liquidity of credit upon which real estate development depends. These include the expansion of investments by commercial banks in urban real estate development and the growth of a national primary mortgage market.

Federal government policies, frequently promoted by the National Association of Real Estate Boards (a forerunner of today's National Association of Realtors), have contributed greatly to the organization and availability of credit in the real estate industry. Chief among these are the federal insurance of residential mortgages initiated by the Federal Housing Administration and the more recent organization of secondary mortgage markets, initially operated by the Federal National Mortgage Association (1938) and later by the Government National Mortgage

*Donald Trump, real estate developer and tycoon, in 1985 exhibits a model of Television City, a huge television and film production complex in New York.*

Association (1968) and the Federal Home Loan Mortgage Corporation (1970).

—*Alexander von Hoffman*

See also
Federal Housing Administration; Land Developers and Development; Real Estate Speculation.
References
Blackmar, Elizabeth. *Manhattan for Rent, 1785–1860.* Ithaca, NY: Cornell University Press, 1989.
Davies, Pearl Janet. *Real Estate in American History.* Washington, DC: Public Affairs Press, 1958.
Hoyt, Homer. *One Hundred Years of Land Values in Chicago: The Relationship of the Growth of Chicago to the Rise in Its Land Values, 1830–1933.* Chicago: University of Chicago Press, 1933.
von Hoffman, Alexander. "Weaving the Urban Fabric: Nineteenth-Century Patterns of Residential Real Estate Development in Outer Boston." *Journal of Urban History* 22 (1966).
Warner, Sam Bass, Jr. *Streetcar Suburbs: The Process of Growth in Boston, 1870–1900.* Cambridge, MA: Harvard University Press, 1962.
Weiss, Marc. *The Rise of the Community Builders: The American Real Estate Industry and Urban Land Planning.* New York: Columbia University Press, 1987.
Worley, William S. *J. C. Nichols and the Shaping of Kansas City: Innovation in Planned Residential Communities.* Columbia: University of Missouri Press, 1990.

## Real Estate Speculation

Although commonly used in a pejorative way, the term *real estate speculation* is imprecise. In the sense that real estate speculation is trading in real estate for a profit, virtually all real estate investment is speculative.

Another definition of real estate speculation resembles that of other forms of speculation, the trading of a commodity during times of abnormal price fluctuation. During booms in real estate, prices rise quickly, sometimes far above their true value. As in stock investment manias or "bubbles," a spreading belief that prices will rise indefinitely attracts casual investors who help inflate prices still further. Eventually, real estate property is so overpriced that the market can no longer sustain prices. Prices then deflate, often causing losses just as dramatic as their earlier gains.

Throughout American history there have been numerous real estate booms, including ones in Chicago in the mid-nineteenth century and Los Angeles in the early twentieth century. Perhaps the best known is the Florida land boom of the 1920s, immortalized in the Marx Brothers' movie, *Coconuts.* The Florida mania became infamous for unscrupulous land dealers who sold land that upon closer inspection was found to be located underwater.

The most recent real estate boom took place in the 1980s when rents and housing prices rose rapidly in most major urban areas, most spectacularly in California. This boom lured the officials of many savings and loan associations into extending too much credit for high-risk projects, and the ensuing collapse produced a wave of bankruptcies and investigations of the easy-lending scandals, including one that implicated at least one prominent U.S. senator, Alan Cranston of California.

—*Alexander von Hoffman*

## Recreation

In 1857 Edward Everett Hale, a Unitarian minister and champion of urban reform, published a lengthy review in the *Christian Examiner* on the subject of public amusements and public morality. "In an age of increased competition, increased demands," and "increased labor," he noted, it was no wonder that workers of all ranks sought recreation and amusement. As Hale saw it, work and leisure were two sides of the same coin. "All this complicated labor question, the discussion of ten-hour systems, of the work of women, of the work of children, asks what men, women and children are to do with the hours of rest."

Hale's question was not new. European settlers had wrestled with issues or labor, leisure, and recreation from their earliest days in the New World. John Smith complained of Jamestown settlers who spent "four hours each day . . . in worke, the rest in pastimes and merry exercise." Puritans and Pilgrims struggled continuously to protect their commonwealths from "profane customs" and "misspence of time." In 1682, Pennsylvania Quakers banned all "rude and riotous sports," but the sheer increase and diversity of immigrants and their customs ensured that colonial communities would contend endlessly with the appropriate hours of work and rest. On the eve of the Revolution, the First Continental Congress resolved to "discountenance every species of extravagance and dissipation, especially all horse-racing, and all kinds of gaming, cockfighting, exhibition of shows, plays and other expensive diversions and amusements."

Virtuous republics had to strike a balance between work and leisure, but what was that? If one defines leisure as any freely chosen activity, unfettered by obligations of work, family, or culture, then America—at least outside the rural South—has not easily embraced anything like a "leisure ethic." Commercial and industrial capitalism promoted a "work ethic that rippled," as Daniel Rodgers has noted, with "countless warnings against the wiles of idleness and the protean disguises of the idler." This has not, however, proscribed all nonwork activities. Even the Puritans "countenanced" some nonwork, nonchurch activities as useful. William Burkitt, an English Puritan whose works were popular in New England, carefully outlined the prospects in a seventeenth-century "self help" guide. God never intended endless toil for his people, Burkitt argued, and so God "adjudged some Diversion or Recreation (the better to fit both Body and Mind for the service of their maker) to be both needful and expedient."

But who would sanction and approve the nonwork activities that developed in the expanding towns and cities? Who would gauge the legitimacy of dancing, gambling, bowling, or drinking? Puritans and Quakers had their opinions, but so did later immigrants who imported diversions along with their religions and politics. Over the last two centuries, such questions have been at the heart of life in the city, the immigrant's great entrepot, weigh station, processing center, and (for many) permanent home. As Edward Everett Hale recognized in 1857, cities exuded more than economic opportunity. Most newcomers came not because "they think they will grow rich," but rather because "they are tempted by the excitement of crowds, of concerts, of bands, of theaters, of public meetings, of processions, of exhibitions, of parties, of clubs, or in general of society." The struggle for control of these activities has remained part of an even greater struggle over space, time, and behavior in cities.

The nineteenth century pushed urban growth and urban problems to center stage. As Paul Boyer has masterfully argued, from 1820 to 1920 cities became a "potent catalyst for social speculation and social action. Fears about industrialization, immigration, family disruption, religious change, and deepening class divisions all focused on the growing cities." The statistics are still staggering. In the three decades before the Civil War, the urban population grew from 500,000 to almost 4 million. The next 50 years saw no letup. The number of cities larger than 100,000 increased from 9 to 50; "small cities" (between 10,000 and 25,000) grew from 58 to 369. Worse yet, the inhabitants seemed less and less "American," their ghettos and tenements a study in creeping squalor, their votes for sale to the highest-bidding ward boss. Josiah Strong captured the sentiments of respectable "native" Americans in his best-selling book *Our Country* (1885). Cities, he argued, had become a "serious menace to our civilization." Similar sentiments continued unabated in the nineteenth century. Government reports, pulp fiction (in print or later on screen), and daily newspapers all pointed to cities as the source of crime, vice, and disease—the rotting core of America.

And yet, as Hale also recognized, cities are fountains of cultural renewal. The very density, mix, and flow of population—despite the segregation of housing by class, ethnicity, and race—has ensured a constant interaction of ideas, behaviors, and beliefs. Factories, offices, warehouses, stores,

churches, and schools have all been swirling and often tense caldrons of cultural convergence. But such places of obligation and order unaided could never unleash the creative forces found in the domains of leisure and recreation. Here was the true heart of the city.

Streets have always been a principal venue for urban leisure—strolling or cruising downtown, sitting on the apartment stoop to catch a soft evening breeze, lining sidewalks with kids on shoulders to catch a peek at a parade, or just "hanging out" on the corner. Fifth Avenue, Lenox Avenue, Taylor Street, Hollywood Boulevard—all share with back alleys of the barrios and ghettos the constant inversion of private and public, intimacy and alienation, integration and segregation, power and hopelessness that mark social life in cities. While the fear and incidence of crime and violence may reduce street life in the largest cities, the processions, pageants, and tableaus described by Walt Whitman continue to invite residents onto the broad avenues of cities across the country.

The vibrancy of urban street life has continually enticed entrepreneurs of leisure and recreation who have recognized the profits available in concentrated markets of discretionary time and income. From the earliest days of American

*Sailors pay 50 cents per dance in this undated woodcut of a dance hall in New Orleans.*

towns and cities, entrepreneurs helped to shape and institutionalize the "free time" activities of their customers in the expanding domain of what Perry Duis has called "semi-public" space. Some, like Phineas T. Barnum, gained fame and fortune from their ability to attract a paying audience. But Barnum also lost several fortunes, and most of his counterparts have receded into historical oblivion. Their collective efforts, however, continually changed and challenged the meaning of social life and social order in cities across the country.

For example, dancing has always inflamed guardians of virtue. As early as 1684, Increase Mather published a tract entitled "An Arrow against Profane and Promiscuous Dancing, Drawn Out of the Quiver of the Scriptures," which was aimed at a recently opened French dancing school. Dance was especially problematic because it publicly threatened sexual and gender mores. Two centuries later, there was no letup on dancing or its critics. Entrepreneurs recognized the attraction of public dancing, especially to young, single, working women who made up an expanding part of the labor market. By 1910 New York boasted at least 500 public dance halls, most featuring the latest "tough" dances that had emanated from San Francisco brothels: the "turkey trot," "bunny hug," and "lover's two step." The dance craze hit other cities of the day. Milwaukee had an estimated 13,000 dancers on Saturday night, and Chicago had over 80,000. The venues and the dances have changed over time—from the Charleston in a speakeasy to the frug in a go-go club—but the movement goes on.

Urban crowds have also flocked to theaters and music halls to watch others perform. In the early nineteenth century, most theaters offered a wide-ranging bill of attractions to attract audiences from all classes, who were carefully segregated by the type and cost of their seats. Within a few decades, entrepreneurs developed a host of theater types targeting special audiences, usually segmented by class, ethnicity, and race. If museum theaters and opera houses played to the "better" classes, concert saloons and vaudeville houses opened their doors to the "people." The phonograph and motion picture brought a swell of local arcades and parlors. By the mid-1890s, State Street and Wabash Avenue in Chicago, Market Street in San Francisco, and Canal Street in New Orleans had kinetoscope parlors where women might chance peeking at a near-nude Eugen Sandow, and men might linger over the whirling image of Little Egypt. If the grand movie "palaces" of the 1920s or the suburban drive-ins of the 1950s aimed at homogenizing the audience, movie content has continued to threaten the social order.

Gambling and drinking cast a darker shadow in the urban sketches of moralists. Gambling had long spiced interest in horse races, cockfights, bear baits, and card games. Cities took the old tavern wager to new dimensions in the faro halls, pool parlors, and backroom casinos that were there. As Ann Fabian has noted, by the 1850s professional gamblers had joined "the pantheon of dangerous types waiting to seduce country youths new to the city." But gambling syndicates thrived through the graft and patronage of local politicians. Their common ground was the saloon, a central social and political institution of cities late in the nineteenth century and early in the twentieth century. One headcount by Boston police in 1897 suggested that daily patronage of the city's 600 saloons amounted to almost half the population. In the 50 years before Prohibition, the saloon was at the center of debates about politics, sports, crime, assimilation, and education. Again quoting Perry Duis, "the swinging doors seemed to be a ubiquitous symbol of urban life."

Public debates about saloons, dance halls, and peep shows resonated with basic, critical issues of free enterprise, government regulation, race and gender relations, and immigration. One still finds the same controversies in contemporary disputes over "combat zones," strip joints, and adult video parlors. Then as now, both conservatives and liberals try to protect other people's virtue with Societies for the Suppression of Vice or Committees on the Amusements and Vacation Resources for Working Girls. One group seeks to suppress, the other to reform. The common theme, however, focuses on the critical role played by leisure time in maintaining social mores and order.

Shrewd entrepreneurs like Moses Kimball and P. T. Barnum aggressively positioned themselves as reformers by eliminating both the "pit" and the "third tier" from their museum theaters in Boston and New York. Matinees, "orchestra" seats, and temperance plays attracted respectable Victorians, especially women, who had avoided the rowdy and raucous crowds of old. An ad for Baltimore's Holliday Street Theater in 1853 even noted that the old third tier had been remodeled for "the commodious accommodation of the reputable colored residents." Barnum promoted a special formula for leisure both at his own museum and on the road with Jenny Lind, the "Swedish Nightingale," or Tom Thumb and a host of circus animals; he abolished "all vulgarity and profanity" so that parents and children would not be "shocked or offended." Barnum has had a host of successors over the years—leisure-time entrepreneurs who have created nightclubs, roller rinks, and sports bars where "respectable" groups can taste urban nightlife in a segregated, secure environment.

The reform efforts have not all been directed at private enterprise. Public parks provided the first important entry point for government into the world of urban recreation. More than any other development, they dramatize the tensions between the dreams of reformers and the realities of city life and the battles over space, time, and behavior. In blueprint, public parks have always stood for grandeur and order—like museums and cathedrals. American designers Andrew Jackson Downing and Frederick Law Olmsted clearly articulated the refining functions of parks, a vision shared by all urban boosters. As early as 1854, the *San Francisco Herald* compared its local "swampy" and "half-graded" streets to Europe's and the East's "beautiful squares, noble avenues, and tasteful promenades" that were "devoted to parades, meetings, and holidays."

By the Civil War, squares and promenades were not sufficient for eastern cities. In the 1850s, New Yorkers debated a huge public park project. Two decades in the making, Central Park triggered similar projects in Boston, Buffalo, Chicago, San Francisco, and smaller cities like Worcester, Massachusetts, in the last quarter of the nineteenth century. Olmsted's vision was obvious. He wrote endlessly on the role and significance of parks—in reports to client cities, in professional essays, and in letters. Parks, he said, were a form of "receptive" recreation, quite distinct from the "exertive" recreation of sports or commercial amusements. They counteracted the barrage of stimuli that energized urban life; they were a "mitigative" influence that brought nature's serene bounty to the eyes and ears of city dwellers. Moreover, parks were the "lungs of the city" whose expanses of greenery could somehow exchange and purify the foul, miasmic air that carried disease and despair. In wholesome, serene surroundings, the families of plutocrats and hod carriers could share a moment of democratic and ennobling refinement.

The theory did not unfold as Olmsted and others planned. Park plans and park grounds became contested terrain as workers and their political allies fought to bring more active and "exertive" enterprises onto public space. By the early 1900s, many park areas included tennis courts, golf courses, restaurants, photo tents, vending machines, and even horse tracks. Today's urban parks continue to evolve as dynamic spaces for recreation; today's picnickers are apt to share space with an outdoor rock concert or an ethnic festival. Despite their association with crime, public parks continue to generate visions of healthy communities and of outdoor recreation in the midst of densely populated cities.

The quest for "exertive" recreation, especially among inner-city youth, spawned the organized play movement in the late nineteenth century. Most parks had been located in distant suburbs, a source of contention in the voting for bond issues. Residents of Boston's North End, Chicago's South Side, or New York's Lower East Side had little time or means to reach the distant zones of "receptive" recreation. When Jacob Riis interviewed 48 schoolboys for *How the Other Half Lives* (1890), only 3 had ever been to Central Park. Similar conditions in other cities sometimes joined ward politicians and reformers in a drive for local play space. Reformers, however, wanted to control the space with experts trained in the latest theories of child development, adolescence, and play supervision. They firmly believed that team sports and other creative games could reduce gang activities and speed the assimilation of immigrants.

In 1906, hundreds of delegates gathered in Washington, D.C., for the founding convention of the Playground Association of America. Riis, Jane Addams, and Lillian Wald shared the spotlight with rising play experts like Luther Gulick and Joseph Lee; Theodore Roosevelt eagerly served as honorary president. The momentum built for several decades. By 1915, cities across the country had hired 744 full-time play directors; by 1930, 695 cities had built a total of 7,240 playgrounds, most of them stocked with the latest equipment and expertise. Even the Depression did not reduce the interest in public funding. The Works Progress Administration spent about $1 billion on recreation facilities between 1935 and 1941, including over 5,000 new fields and playgrounds and more than 8,000 new recreation buildings.

There were limits both to this vision and its results. In New York during the Depression, black neighborhoods received just 2 of the 255 new playgrounds that were built. When blacks strayed into "white" space, the results were often deadly. The 1919 Race Riot in Chicago was touched off when a black swimmer was stoned for encroaching on the "white" waters of the Twenty-Ninth Street Beach. The Detroit Riot of 1943 stemmed from conflicts in the parks. Only the Supreme Court's decision in the case of *Brown v. Board of Education* in 1954 opened Houston's public golf courses and Baltimore's public beaches to African Americans. But even the force of law could not reduce the tensions on Boston's Carson Beach, a transition zone between white South Boston and black Dorchester. Nor could organized play easily reduce ethnic tensions or juvenile delinquency. Recreation surveys and urban ethnographies since the 1930s have recognized the staying power of gang loyalty and turf protection.

Parks and playgrounds could not escape the tensions of urban life. The yearning to escape, however, has suffused the recreation and leisure time of city people. Since colonial times, wealthy Americans had escaped cities during the summer, often traveling to spas known for their curative waters. Bedford Springs, Pennsylvania, and Hot Springs, Arkansas, among others, acted like magnets and attracted elites from distant areas. After the Civil War, the expanding middle classes created markets for entrepreneurs of "decent" resorts such as Chautauqua and Lake Mohonk in New York, Old Orchard Beach in Maine, and Ocean Grove in New Jersey. As one Asbury Park promoter emphasized, most Americans desired "clean amusements for their children, pure literature, decent theaters, and reputable surroundings." The theme at these early bourgeois resorts was "It Pays to Be Decent." Disneyland, Disney World, Busch Gardens, and Six Flags retain this tradition.

By the late nineteenth century, improved roads and mass transit made closer escapes possible in the form of amusement parks, many near ocean or lake or river, most served by train or trolley. Andrew Culver's Prospect Park and Coney Island Railroad, completed in 1875, finally provided a cheap (35 cents), rapid, dependable means of getting to the beach at Coney Island. Within two years, 3 million passengers had used the service, followed closely by hotels, gamblers, prostitutes, and various con artists. In 1897, George Tilyou began to develop Steeplechase Park, an enclosed haven of thrills and titillation including a mechanical horse race, a Barrel of Love, and a Human Roulette Wheel. Coney Island's attractions soon included Luna Park, Dreamland, the boardwalk, freak shows, the "Original Turkish Harem," and a beach full of scantily clad youth. The Coney experience was duplicated in various degrees at trolley parks around the country, including Boston's Revere Beach, Pittsburgh's Kennywood Park, St. Louis's Forest Park Highlands, and San Francisco's The Chutes. Among the roller coasters, the bandstands, and the carousels, the masses and the classes mixed and mingled in a carnival of sensual pleasure. As John Kasson has written of Coney Island, such parks "tested and transformed accustomed social roles and values" and "mocked the established social order." The reverie lasted only a short time at most of these parks. Prohibition, the Depression, and the suburban exodus after World War II left most of them in zones of transition. Television and the automobile offered new dreams and means of the leisure escape.

Perhaps the greatest chapter of urban escape was the bicycle boom in the late nineteenth century. Although the "velocipede"—a front-cranked, wooden-framed vehicle—had stirred a brief craze in the late 1860s, cycling really took root in the 1880s with the high-rise "ordinary" whose durability and speed spawned many clubs and even a national League of American Wheelman. The dropped-frame, chain-cranked "safety" bicycle, however, opened the vehicle to more than hearty, courageous men and thereby generated enormous interest and sales. Between 1890 and 1896, the number of bicycle manufacturers increased from 27 to 250; output of new machines rose from 40,000 to over 1 million. Most of the sales came in cities and towns, which had both superior roads and denser markets. The overwhelming image in bicycle literature was escape. As one wheelman's verse argued, clerks, artisans, lawyers, or domestics could escape the grime, stench, and strain of urban din.

> On a steed of steel
> I have the wheel of life
> Soiled from my city's dust
> from the struggle and the strife
> Of the narrow street I fly

> To the road's felicity
> To clear me from the frown
> Of the moody toil of town.

There was a recurring irony in all these urban escapes—whether a picnic in Central Park, an evening at Kennywood, a Sunday ride on a bicycle or in a car. Every mode of flight was supported by the technology, rationality, and organization that were part of the life to be left behind. Despite their appearance, Olmsted's parks were not natural; they were carefully engineered with the latest knowledge of hydraulics, botany, and construction. Coney Island and its counterparts depended on the most up-to-date technology to transport their patrons, feed them, and amuse them. The bicycle, like the better-known automobile, was a pioneering product of American mass production. Moreover, cyclists increasingly favored escape routes lined with hotels, restaurants, and shops. As one old Mainer explained the traffic jams of tourists in Kennebunkport, "They do it because it reminds them of home."

Leisure and recreation have offered no easy escape from the realities of urban life. But neither have they been a simple tool of exploitation—by reformers, politicians, or entrepreneurs. Scholars have tended to lament the rise of mass media and mass commercial leisure in the form of movies, television, professional sports teams, record labels, theaters, and even restaurant chains dominated by corporations. While these trends suggest a convergence of forms and opportunities toward some "mainstream," they do not preclude popular alternatives. The blues, punk or grunge rock, reggae, and ska music are all examples of urban leisure forms that have resisted corporate domination. City playgrounds spawned new styles of basketball that challenged and transformed long-standing orthodoxies. The struggle to control leisure and recreation will continue in American cities, but there will always remain some freedom in "free" time.

—*Stephen Hardy*

**See also**
Amusement Parks; Barnum, Phineas T.; Bars and Saloons; Baseball; Basketball; Boxing; Burlesque; Circuses; Country Clubs; Gambling; Museums; Nickelodeons; Opera Houses; Orchestras; Parks; Playgrounds; Sports in Cities; Television; Theme Parks; Vaudeville.

**References**
Adams, Judith A. *The American Amusement Park Industry: A History of Technology and Thrills.* Boston: Twayne, 1991.
Boyer, Paul. *Urban Masses and Moral Order, 1820–1920.* Cambridge, MA: Harvard University Press, 1978.
Butsch, Richard, ed. *For Fun and Profit: The Transformation of Leisure into Consumption.* Philadelphia: Temple University Press, 1990.
Click, Patricia. *The Spirit of the Times: Amusements in Nineteenth Century Baltimore, Norfolk, and Richmond.* Charlottesville: University of Virginia Press, 1989.

Cranz, Galen. *The Politics of Park Design.* Cambridge, MA: MIT Press, 1982.

Duis, Perry. *The Saloon: Public Drinking in Chicago and Boston, 1880–1920.* Urbana: University of Illinois Press, 1983.

Erenberg, Lewis. *Steppin' Out: New York Nightlife and the Transformation of American Culture 1890–1930.* Chicago: University of Chicago Press, 1981.

Fabian, Ann. *Card Sharps, Dream Books, and Bucket Shops: Gambling in Nineteenth-Century America.* Ithaca, NY: Cornell University Press, 1990.

Hardy, Stephen. *How Boston Played: Sport, Recreation, and Community, 1865–1915.* Boston: Northeastern University Press, 1982.

Kasson, John. *Amusing the Millions: Coney Island at the Turn of the Century.* New York: Hill and Wang, 1978.

Nasaw, David. *Going Out: The Rise and Fall of Public Amusements.* New York: Basic Books, 1993.

Peiss, Kathy. *Cheap Amusements: Working Women and Leisure in Turn-of-the-Century New York.* Philadelphia: Temple University Press, 1986.

Riess, Steven. *City Games: The Evolution of American Urban Society and the Rise of Sports.* Urbana: University of Illinois Press, 1989.

Rodgers, Daniel. *The Work Ethic in Industrial America, 1850–1920.* Chicago: University of Chicago Press, 1978.

Rosenzweig, Roy. *Eight Hours for What We Will: Workers and Leisure in an Industrial City, 1870–1920.* Cambridge, England: Cambridge University Press, 1983.

Tobin, Gary Alan. "The Bicycle Boom in the 1890s." *Journal of Popular Culture* 7 (1974): 838–849.

Uminowicz, Glenn. "Recreation in a Christian America: Ocean Grove and Asbury Park, New Jersey, 1869–1914." In Kathryn Grover, ed., *Hard at Play: Leisure in America, 1840–1940.* Amherst: University of Massachusetts Press, 1992.

Withington, Ann. *Toward a More Perfect Union: Virtue and the Formation of American Republics.* New York: Oxford University Press, 1991.

## Red-Light District

Red-light districts were sections of American cities during the nineteenth and twentieth centuries that were noted for containing particularly high levels of illegal recreational activities. Prostitution was the most common of these, although gambling, narcotics, and unlicensed saloons also flourished.

The origin of the term is unclear. Most attribute its beginnings to red entry lights on row houses serving as brothels. What is clear, however, is that these areas were the physical embodiments of an underground economy. For groups excluded from the legitimate urban workplace because of racial or gender discrimination, poor job skills, little education, or few capital resources, red-light districts provided an alternative market economy.

The typical red-light district was defined only informally. Municipal officials rigidly suppressed illegal activities in most communities but tolerated them in a few others, resulting in *de facto* regulation. These neighborhoods were usually located near the heart of the city, adjacent to business centers and transportation termini. Railroad stations, hotels, rooming houses, and nighttime leisure institutions dominated the area. In western frontier towns such as Chicago, St. Louis, and Cincinnati, the districts were initially called "levees," referring to their proximity to wharves. From 1880 to 1910, most large cities had red-light districts that became popular tourist attractions: the Tenderloin in New York, the Levee in Chicago, the Barbary Coast in San Francisco, the Block in Baltimore, and the Stingaree in San Diego. Even small communities such as Moscow (Idaho), Lancaster (Pennsylvania), and Sioux City (Iowa) had similar districts.

One of the most famous red-light districts, New Orleans's Storyville, thrived from 1898 to 1917. Its activities became legal when Councilman Sidney Story drafted an ordinance prohibiting prostitution everywhere in the city except for a small, defined area adjoining the old French Quarter. By 1914 Storyville's economy employed an estimated 12,000 workers and generated annual revenues of about $12 million. Musicians who worked in the district's brothels, like Jelly Roll Morton, created new, indigenous forms of music, particularly jazz. The French-born photographer E. J. Bellocq captured many residents of Storyville on film, thus creating a rare visual legacy of urban America in the early twentieth century that is comparable to the images of prostitutes painted by Edouard Manet and Henri Toulouse-Lautrec in Paris, or John Sloan and George Bellows in New York.

Most of these districts were shut down between 1910 and 1917. Antiprostitution campaigns led by Protestant church federations, antivice societies, and municipal reform committees induced states to pass "red-light abatement acts" allowing citizens to sue landlords who rented property to prostitutes. The final blow came during World War I when the federal government's Commission on Training Camp Activities prohibited prostitution within five miles of any military facility.

Sex districts enjoyed a brief revival after 1970. Communities as diverse as Detroit, Boston, Dallas, Prince George's County in Maryland, Fairfax County in Virginia, Marion County in Indiana, and Santa Monica and Los Angeles in California used zoning laws to create "adult entertainment districts." The proliferation of open pornography and prostitution in Boston's "Combat Zone" and New York's Times Square generated considerable comment and controversy. In 1976, the Supreme Court upheld such regulatory measures in *Young v. American Mini Theaters.*

—*Timothy J. Gilfoyle*

**References**

Gilfoyle, Timothy J. *City of Eros: New York City, Prostitution and the Commercialization of Sex, 1790–1920.* New York: W. W. Norton, 1992.

Rose, Al. *Storyville, New Orleans: Being an Authentic, Illustrated Account of the Notorious Red-Light District.* University: University of Alabama Press, 1974.

Rosen, Ruth. *The Lost Sisterhood: Prostitution in America, 1900–1918.* Baltimore: Johns Hopkins University Press, 1982.

Shumsky, Neil L. "Tacit Acceptance: Respectable Americans and Segregated Prostitution, 1870–1910." *Journal of Social History* 19 (1986): 665–679.

Shumsky, Neil L., and Larry M. Springer. "San Francisco's Zone of Prostitution, 1880–1934." *Journal of Historical Geography* 7 (1981): 71–89.

Symanski, Richard. *The Immoral Landscape: Female Prostitution in Western Societies.* Toronto, Ontario: Butterworths, 1981.

Wendt, Lloyd, and Herman Kogan. *Lords of the Levee: The Story of Bathhouse John and Hinky Dink.* Indianapolis, IN: Bobbs-Merrill, 1943.

## Redlining

Redlining is the practice of refusing to provide financial services (primarily mortgage loans and property insurance) or of providing them on more stringent terms in selected neighborhoods for reasons not related to any reasonable definition of risk. The term originated with the practice of some lenders and insurers who literally drew red lines on maps indicating areas that were not eligible for their services. A major consideration in delineating such neighborhoods has been the racial composition of an area. Redlining has contributed to the segregation of the nation's metropolitan areas, the decline of urban communities, and the uneven development of city and suburban communities generally.

Historically, the race of a buyer and the racial composition of a neighborhood have been used explicitly in determining property values and evaluating eligibility for home loans, insurance, and other real estate–related services. Even if the explicit utilization of race has been declared illegal, it has not disappeared, and a variety of traditional industry practices continue to adversely affect racial minorities and minority neighborhoods. Underwriting rules that limit eligibility for lower valued or older homes, marketing practices that focus on suburban rather than urban communities, and the prevalence of racial stereotypes within financial industries are among those practices that serve to discriminate against racial minorities, minority neighborhoods, and older urban communities generally.

In recent years federal laws like the Fair Housing Act, the Home Mortgage Disclosure Act, and the Community Reinvestment Act and active community organizing efforts by civil rights groups, nonprofit developers, and other neighborhood groups have begun to turn this process of disinvestment into a process of reinvestment. Using the leverage provided by federal law, community groups have negotiated over $60 billion in reinvestment commitments from lenders since the Community Reinvestment Act was passed in 1977. While several partnerships have been formed involving financial institutions and community groups, industry trade associations have increased their efforts to dilute fair lending requirements in recent years. Redlining, therefore, remains a highly contentious issue, with each stage of the battle having serious implications for urban development throughout the United States.

—*Gregory D. Squires*

### References

Goering, John, and Ron Wienk, eds. *Mortgage Lending, Racial Discrimination and Federal Policy.* Washington, DC: Urban Institute, 1996.

Munnell, Alicia H., Lynn E. Browne, James McEneaney, and Geoffrey M. B. Tootell. "Mortgage Lending in Boston: Interpreting HMDA Data." *American Economic Review* 86 (1996): 25–53.

Squires, Gregory D., ed. *Insurance Redlining: Disinvestment, Reinvestment, and the Evolving Role of Financial Institutions.* Washington, DC: Urban Institute, 1997.

## Regional Plan Association

A group of influential business and civic leaders formed the Regional Plan Association in 1929 as a private, nonprofit organization to carry out the proposals of the monumental Regional Plan of New York and Its Environs. The massive Regional Plan covered the 22-county area centering on Manhattan and comprising parts of New York, New Jersey, and Connecticut.

The Regional Plan Association (RPA) should not be confused with the Regional Planning Association of America (RPAA). Both originated in New York City in the 1920s, but they were different organizations and had no connection to each other. The Regional Plan Association completed a draft Second Regional Plan in 1968 and issued a Third Regional Plan, *A Region at Risk,* in 1996.

The impacts of these plans on the region and its planning efforts is a matter of debate and controversy. But it cannot be denied that during its history, the RPA has significantly and constructively influenced many major public capital decisions. Its greatest successes have been leading the fight to acquire more public open space in the region and saving and augmenting rail transportation for commuters. RPA has been less successful in reducing urban sprawl, providing jobs for minorities, and preventing the degradation of inner-city neighborhoods. Some critics have argued that the RPA was actually responsible for the collapse of New York City's economy and its downtown in the 1980s by encouraging office development in Manhattan rather than labor-intensive manufacturing firms and factory space. However, it is likely that manufacturing in New York would have declined even without the activities of the RPA.

The Regional Plan Association has also significantly influenced specific proposals emanating from state and federal agencies. It has generally supported the policies and projects of the bistate Port Authority of New York and New Jersey, but on occasion it has been adversarial, such as when the RPA successfully opposed the Port Authority's proposal in the 1960s to build a fourth jetport in the region.

Unlike Paris, Tokyo, or London, the tristate New York metropolitan region has never enjoyed truly effective metropolitan government. The RPA provides valuable research, analysis, and policy recommendations, but as an unofficial, unelected private body, it is only a partial substitute for effective regional governance.

—*David A. Johnson*

**See also**
Regional Plan of New York and Its Environs.
**References**
Hays, Forbes B. *Community Leadership: The Regional Plan Association of New York.* New York: Columbia University Press, 1965.
Johnson, David A. "Seventy-Five Years of Metropolitan Planning in the New York–New Jersey Urban Region: A Retrospective Assessment." *New York Affairs* 9 (1985): 95–112.

## Regional Plan of New York and Its Environs

The Regional Plan of New York and Its Environs, completed in 1931, was perhaps the most extensive and best-funded plan undertaken in the history of American urban and regional planning. The plan was the brainchild of Charles Dyer Norton, a banker and civic leader associated with the J. P. Morgan interests. Norton had previously sponsored Daniel Burnham's 1909 Plan for Chicago and hoped to do for the 22-county, tristate (New York, New Jersey, and Connecticut) New York metropolitan region what Burnham had accomplished for Chicago and its region.

The Regional Plan of New York was formulated on the basis of a detailed, comprehensive survey of conditions and trends in the New York region: the *Regional Survey of New York and Its Environs.* This survey, consisting of eight volumes, explored physical conditions, land uses, transportation, buildings, neighborhoods, and government. In all, the published *Regional Plan* consisted of two large volumes: *The Graphic Regional Plan,* published in 1929, and *The Building of the City,* published in 1931. The plan was developed under the direction of Thomas Adams, a Scottish planner and surveyor, who had previously been associated with the New Town of Letchworth in England and had also been a consultant for planning the Canadian capital of Ottawa.

Produced under private philanthropic and business auspices, the plan was underwritten by the Russell Sage Foundation, which provided grants of $1,186,768, a very large sum in the 1920s. The New York metropolitan region has never had metropolitan government, and the purely advisory plan had no official status. However, it greatly stimulated the adoption of zoning by local governments. The plan's sponsors hoped that its proposals would be realized through the aggregation of local zoning decisions and state capital expen-

ditures. The Regional Plan Association (RPA), a private organization of business, academic, and professional leaders, was formed in 1929 to carry out the recommendations contained in the plan itself. The RPA continues to play a significant advisory and watchdog role in the tristate area.

Lewis Mumford criticized the plan severely when it was published for a lack of robustness and coherence, and for reinforcing trends that Mumford and others regarded as destructive and mechanistic. Later critics have charged that the plan was responsible for the decline of New York City's manufacturing base and subsequent economic distress, while others have argued that the plan had little impact on the New York region. Robert Moses, for example, vehemently denied that the plan influenced him in any way, although it is remarkable how closely Moses' highway network followed the proposals contained in the plan. No doubt the plan provided a ready-made list of public works for the pump-priming alphabet agencies of the New Deal. Moreover, the Regional Plan and its authors stimulated the emergence of professional planning education at universities and influenced the practice of city and regional planning in the United States.

—*David A. Johnson*

**See also**
Regional Plan Association.
**References**
Hays, Forbes B. *Community Leadership: The Regional Plan Association of New York.* New York: Columbia University Press, 1965.
Johnson, David A. *Planning the Great Metropolis: The 1929 Regional Plan of New York and Its Environs.* London: Chapman and Hall, 1996.

## Regional Planning

The central idea of regional planning is what the French call *amenagement du territoire* (the management of territory). The key questions for regional planning are what kind of management? for what ends? by whom? for whom? and over what territory? These questions have been answered in many different ways.

The roots of regional planning in the United States go back to the beginnings of the nation. Thomas Jefferson laid its groundwork in the federal Land Ordinance of 1785, which determined how federal lands would be surveyed. The law later resulted in the gridiron platting of the land in the Louisiana Purchase and left its extraordinary physical imprint on the middle third of the nation, an imprint that can still be seen clearly in aerial views.

In the early twentieth century, regional planning emerged as a vital concept once again; it grew from two diverse sources, metropolitan growth and southern regionalism. City planning, an accepted tool of public management, became increasingly difficult in the 1920s as urbanized areas expanded beyond city boundaries. Annexation was not always possible, so business and civic leaders thought of metropolitan regional planning as a possible solution. Since metropolitan regional government was not generally acceptable politically, metropolitan regional planning usually came to mean only voluntary, cooperative coordination without mandates or other requirements, a weak reed with which to control land and its development. Metropolitan regional planning continues in many urban areas, usually with a relatively narrow emphasis on coordinating highway development and providing open space.

A second major intellectual foundation of regional planning in the 1920s came from the Southern Regionalists, a group of social scientists centered at the University of North Carolina at Chapel Hill. They promulgated the related themes of regional cultural and historical identity, rural-urban interdependence, and integrated land management. These ideas came together in the 1930s to produce the Tennessee Valley Authority (TVA), the most important regional planning experiment in American history.

The TVA has used several definitions of region—the Tennessee River and its tributaries, the river's drainage basin, the power region to which the TVA supplied electricity, and the aggregated cluster of the seven contiguous southeastern states served by TVA. The regional boundaries have always been drawn with difficulty because the region's edges have never been clear. Defining regions requires drawing boundaries—but these are almost always artificial and create barriers between what a region includes and what it excludes. Regional definition also creates centers, and these, too, can be artificial, though centrality is sometimes defined more easily than boundaries.

Regions have been defined in many ways, most frequently on the basis of economic, industrial, or agricultural characteristics. Lagging versus leading economic indicators have been used, as have common ethnic, religious, cultural, and linguistic characteristics. Geomorphic features have defined regions, as in the case of river basins (TVA) and mountainous areas (Appalachian Regional Commission). Finally, each state is, in some ways, a political and economic region that frequently includes widely differing substate areas simply by historical accident. The conclusion must be that no single definition of region can serve all purposes. The conception of region thus depends on the purposes and objectives of regional planning in each particular case.

It is important to note at the end of the twentieth century that the need for economically based regional planning has diminished due to the shrinking of space/time distance in the United States and the decrease of large economic differences between various parts of the country. But on the other hand, the emergence of environmental problems spilling across political boundaries has impelled a renewed interest and call for regional planning based on environmentally sound principles of land management. This environmentally based regional planning faces the same obstacles that economically oriented regional planning faced earlier—the fact that appropriate regions do not usually coincide with political boundaries, making policy and project implementation extremely difficult. Another obstacle to regional planning in the United States is the growing distrust of all government.

The United States has never implemented intelligent regional planning very effectively and has paid a high price in soil deterioration, dust bowls, human neglect, and exploitation of natural resources throughout its history. Remediation has occurred from time to time, usually at additional costs that might have been avoided if thoughtful regional planning had been conducted before the damage was done. Other industrialized countries such as France and the Netherlands have been more successful in managing their territory.

—David A. Johnson

See also

City Planning; Regional Plan Association; Regional Plan of New York and Its Environs; Regional Planning Association of America.

References

Friedmann, J., and W. Alonso, eds. *Regional Development and Planning. A Reader.* Cambridge, MA: MIT Press, 1964.
———. *Regional Policy: Readings in Theory and Applications.* Cambridge, MA: MIT Press, 1975.
Friedmann, J., and C. Weaver. *Territory and Function: The Evolution of Regional Planning.* Berkeley: University of California Press, 1980.
Glassine, John. *An Introduction to Regional Planning: Concepts, Theory and Practice.* London: Hutchinson, 1974.
National Resources Committee. *Regional Factors in National Planning.* Washington, DC: Government Printing Office, 1935.
So, Frank S., Irving Hand, and Bruce D. McDowell. *The Practice of State and Regional Planning.* Chicago: American Planning Association and the International City Management Association, 1986.

## Regional Planning Association of America

The Regional Planning Association of America was an informal group of talented, energetic individuals active in the 1920s whose ideas and projects influenced American and international planning thought in the following decades. The RPAA, as it became known, was founded in New York in 1923 and met periodically but informally—often at Hudson Guild Farm in Netcong, New Jersey—until 1933. Its membership roster reads like a Who Was Who of American planning and housing: Benton MacKaye (1879–1975), forester and conservationist; architects Clarence S. Stein (1882–1975) and Henry Wright (1878–1936); housing activists Catherine Bauer Wurster (1905–1964) and Edith Elmer Wood

(1871–1945); resource economist Stuart Chase (1898–1985); architectural writer Charles H. Whitaker (1872–1938); and not least, the critic and author Lewis Mumford (1895–1990), whose writings widely publicized the work and thought of the association. A more talented array of American designers and planners had probably never assembled in one place.

The RPAA group, diverse though it was, agreed on a central principle—a profit-centered, overconcentrated, metropolitan society produced urban blight, unbalanced budgets, and symptoms of decay that were "the first warnings of a much greater collapse," in the prophetic words of Lewis Mumford. The solution, according to the group, was a more decentralized and socialized society composed of environmentally balanced regions. Within such a regional framework, community and neighborhood design could flourish and support a life-sustaining economy and a social ecology that functioned within nature, not against it. New towns and garden cities were seen as ways of achieving these goals.

The origins of RPAA's social thought have been traced to the Scottish botanist Patrick Geddes and to Ebenezer Howard, Frederick Le Play, Peter Kropotkin, and others. But the RPAA itself deserves credit for generating original ideas about the appropriate form of settlements in the emerging technological age, ideas that took shape on the ground as well as on paper. Perhaps the most renowned of the group's tangible achievements—mostly the work of Wright and Stein—was Radburn, a planned, partially completed, garden village in Fair Lawn, New Jersey, near New York City. Radburn's special features—culs-de-sac and connected green spaces—were designed to cope with negative impacts of the automobile. Sunnyside Gardens, in the Queens borough of New York City, with its interior greenswards, was another influential development designed by Wright and Stein according to RPAA precepts.

The Depression of the 1930s halted enlightened private construction like that at Radburn. But with the advent of the New Deal, the people and ideas of the RPAA found alternative outlets for realization in pump-priming development agencies such as the Tennessee Valley Authority, the Public Housing Administration, and the Resettlement Administration. Benton MacKaye's brief tenure with TVA in Knoxville, for example, helped shape that agency's foundations in integrated resource management. It also led MacKaye to create the Appalachian Trail. And it was no accident that the TVA's first new town, Norris, Tennessee, closely followed the ideas of Wright and Stein, as did the greenbelt towns built by the Resettlement Administration in the 1930s.

Quantitatively, the impact of the RPAA on settlement patterns in the United States was relatively minor. But the robust ideas of the RPAA still have resonance today, more so,

perhaps, because the problems foreseen by Lewis Mumford have not disappeared but have only deepened.

—*David A. Johnson*

**See also**
Bauer, Catherine; Greenbelt Towns; Mumford, Lewis; Stein, Clarence S.
**References**
Lubove, Roy. *Community Planning in the 1920's: The Contribution of the Regional Planning Association of America.* Pittsburgh, PA: University of Pittsburgh Press, 1963.
MacKaye, Benton. *The New Exploration: A Philosophy of Regional Planning.* New York: Harcourt Brace, 1928.
Sussman, Carl. *Planning the Fourth Migration: The Neglected Vision of the Regional Planning Association of America.* Cambridge, MA: MIT Press, 1976.

## Religion in Cities

When John Winthrop insisted in 1630 that the Puritans en route to Massachusetts Bay Colony must be "a Citty upon a Hill," he was expressing a worldview that fused religious order and urban society in the American mind for centuries after. Winthrop's city would be a city in a physical sense—a community where people gathered to work and live, a refuge from attack, a seat of government and civilization facing the wilderness. It also would be a city of God—a place where people would gather to worship and serve others in ways that would bring harmony to the community and glory to God.

Visions like Winthrop's informed much subsequent thinking about planning towns and cities in North America, from German-speaking Moravians settling Bethlehem, Pennsylvania, and Salem, North Carolina, or English Quakers such as William Penn laying out his "greene country towne" of Philadelphia in colonial America to religious communitarians such as the Shakers in towns across New England and New York, the Amana commune in Iowa, and the Mormons in Nauvoo, Illinois, and Salt Lake City, Utah, in the nineteenth century. Even the "New Age" religious impulses of the 1960s and later have produced new errands into the wilderness, as gatherings of various New Age groups in towns in the American Southwest and Hawaii attest. That dissent and disorder often disrupted these plans in no way mitigates the central role that religion played in peopling and defining urban America. To be sure, the swaying masts of commerce soon rivaled church steeples on the cityscapes of colonial America, just as the department store, the skyscraper, the train depot, and other cathedrals of commerce cast shadows over the great neo-Gothic churches of the late nineteenth and early twentieth centuries, but well into the twentieth century the idea persisted that religious institutions had a vital role to play in building urban community. Values derived from religion also have persisted in shaping the ways that urban and suburban people organize their families, define neighborhoods, approach local politics, and judge the morality of the workplace, the school, and society in general. Indeed, the particular makeup of religious affiliations in any city or suburb has been, and can be, as critical an index of a place's character and culture as any other factor. From the creation of sacred space to the delivery of social services, religion and religious institutions have made distinct imprints on the public life and civic culture of urban America. How else can one understand the Irish-Catholic politics in Boston, the Slavic parish schools in Cleveland and Chicago and the Italian ones in Philadelphia, the Dutch Reformed businesses in Grand Rapids, Michigan, the Jewish investment in public schools and services in New York, and social reform impulses virtually everywhere, not to mention the differences between the political and public cultures of Lutheran Minneapolis and Catholic St. Paul in Minnesota?

Religion has been instrumental in steering people to urban places. During the colonial period, whole congregations sometimes migrated from old England to New, founding a host of towns. The church congregation as the urban

*The prominence and distinctiveness of the Russian Orthodox Cathedral in San Francisco indicate the diversity of religious belief likely to exist in any urban area.*

foundation was taken for granted when the Massachusetts Bay Colony granted town charters to congregations rather than individual developers during the seventeenth century. Separate congregations of German Reformed, Lutheran, or pietist colonists settled towns from Pennsylvania to the southern backcountry during the eighteenth century and gave them a religious imprint that persisted for centuries.

More important than the specific migration of entire church groups in peopling urban America has been the more general provision of city-forming functions by religious bodies. The congregating of a particular denomination in a place has often attracted others of that faith to settle there. Thus, for example, an infrastructure of Moslem mosques and Islamic organizations has made the Detroit area inviting to Muslims during the past 20 years. Similarly, the chain migrations of Polish and Slovak Catholics to coal and steel towns in Pennsylvania and of Eastern European Jews to New York City during the late nineteenth and early twentieth centuries were facilitated by the presence of priests or rabbis who spoke the immigrants' languages, corresponded about conditions and prospects in America with relatives and villagers they had left behind, and arranged passage and adaptation to America for later newcomers. By helping peasants and rural migrants adapt to urban places, ethnic churches and religious organizations made massive sustained immigration and urban growth possible.

To cite just one example, whatever qualms they might have had about the "foreign" Jewish Orthodoxy and the poverty of Eastern European Jews coming to America in the late nineteenth and early twentieth centuries, Reformed and Conservative Jewish congregations in the United States provided practical advice and relief to the "new immigrants" through such organizations as the Hebrew Emigrant Aid Society. By doing so, they remade not only American Judaism but also the culture of numerous American cities.

The ways in which religious institutions smoothed movement to and settlement in American cities abound. Churches historically have sponsored families and refugees coming to America and have interceded on their behalf with authorities to complete admission procedures and find work—a practice continued recently in the case of Soviet Jews escaping communism who have been sponsored by American Jewish congregations, or in the case of Salvadorans, Nicaraguans, and other Spanish-speaking refugees fleeing political persecution who have gained access to the United States through the sponsorship of Quakers and other church groups.

It has been common for religious bodies to recruit people to settle in their own communities. During the Great Migration of southern blacks to the industrial, urban North from the time of World War I through World War II, for example, northern African Methodist Episcopal (AME) churches sent flyers, Sunday programs, and religious newspapers to churches in the South as an invitation for their congregants to come north. These announcements reassured prospective migrants that they would have a church home in a new, strange place. Black Baptist churches did likewise by publishing notices in religious and black-owned papers.

Religious bodies also underwrote or encouraged migration to new urban places in other ways. In an effort to plant Free-Soilers in Kansas during the 1850s, for example, antislavery Protestant churches in New England raised money to outfit settlers to Lawrence and other Kansas towns. After the Civil War, several black ministers led their congregations from the war-ravaged, racist South to form all-black towns in Kansas as part of the "Exoduster" movement.

In a more general way, the presence of places of worship has been an essential selling point for new developments. In their advertisements describing the amenities of "streetcar suburbs" during the nineteenth century, real estate promoters often mentioned easy access to churches as one benefit of moving to a new community on the edge of a city. Suburban developers in the transient automobile culture also have relied on at least the promise of denominational efforts to establish suburban churches as a draw.

The presence of religious institutions has made cities seem amenable and orderly, a good place to live. In the early New England mill towns, the presence of churches and the promise of moral oversight in boarding houses enabled mill owners to recruit the daughters of New England farmers, otherwise suspicious about the morally debilitating effects of industrial urban life, to work in the textile factories. Work and worship were intertwined in the images of early Lowell, Massachusetts, among several mill towns. As one former "mill girl," Lucy Larcom, recalled in her memoir, *A New England Girlhood* (1889), "the church was really the home-centre to many, perhaps to most of us; and it was one of the mill regulations that everybody should go to church somewhere." Likewise, from the 1880s into the 1920s, factory owners built churches along with workers' housing in the cotton mill villages that dotted the southern Piedmont, both as an inducement for farming families to move there and as a means to discipline workers to the clock-time habits of morality and industry. Across America, city governments and boosters still encourage and sponsor such public rituals as religious holiday festivals, Easter parades, and the lighting of the city-owned Christmas tree as ways of projecting the image of the city as the home of God-fearing people. Likewise, the passage of blue laws and the relaxation of parking restrictions on Sundays, among other devices, have helped make the Christian Sabbath holy and have kept city churches in town, not only to the profit of merchants and city boosters but also to the religious vigor of such places and the spirituality of urban life.

In fundamental ways, creating sacred space has ordered public space. At the heart of Puritan sacred space stood the town square, which symbolized the professed unity of the community, and standing over the town square was the meetinghouse, where the community gathered to hear the Word and to unite in prayer and fellowship. The central location of the church provided the focal point for community identity and life in numerous towns and small cities across America for two centuries. In southern and western towns, the church stood alongside the courthouse (and opposed to the saloon) as the symbol of moral order and one of the few places large enough to hold assemblies. Indeed, much public business was conducted in church buildings during the formative periods of many towns and cities. When the church population incorporated most of the town population, as happened in many early New England towns, and later in southern, midwestern, and western towns established by a particular religious group, church discipline became the discipline of the community. In those circumstances, the meetinghouse was sometimes literally as well as symbolically the government house. In the countryside, the location of a church often became the seed from which a crossroads town grew. Well into the twentieth century, before the department store and the shopping mall became the town square and "church" for a consumer culture, churches were also the only public places where men and women regularly came together. Moreover, they were the principal place where women exercised community authority. The regular comings and goings to worship and to club and other meetings at the church established one of the most public rhythms of urban life, just as the church bell rang out a reminder that the Sabbath was a day of rest from the work-a-day world of commerce and industry.

Modern transportation reshuffled metropolitan spatial patterns by segregating space according to use. In doing so, it spun many churches and synagogues away from city centers toward the residential neighborhoods cropping up along the streetcar lines and, later, the highways. But many old religious buildings, and church graveyards and gardens, survived the wrecking ball of urban renewal. Their presence in city centers has provided visual and psychological relief from the congestion and impersonality of looming buildings—a physical fact seized upon by modern city planners trying to bring people back to "walking cities." In slums, churches are often the only properties with greenery and without graffiti; they function as ecological as well as spiritual oases in otherwise run-down areas. Likewise, the "rural" cemetery, with its winding paths, overhanging trees, and religious statues and gravestones, which was laid out at the edges of many cities during the nineteenth century (e.g., Laurel Hill in Philadelphia, Spring Grove in Cincinnati, and Hollywood in Richmond) to provide retreat and repose from urban ills, dirt, and noise, continues doing so in modern cities that long ago enveloped the cemetery grounds. Sacred space that has become public space has not wholly lost its contemplative, spiritual effect. In more practical terms, by raising the amenity level, well-maintained churches and religious properties have kept up property values in surrounding neighborhoods.

Religion's role in shaping cities was pivotal to the public park movement that attempted to tear down urban congestion as a way to build up morality. Believing in the redemptive power of the natural landscape, such architects and designers as Frederick Law Olmsted, H. W. S. Cleveland, and George Kessler planned public parks as places of recreation and spiritual renewal. Olmsted's Central Park in New York City had an unabashedly Christian purpose and became the model for a park-building craze that swept across nineteenth-century America to Cincinnati, Indianapolis, Chicago, Minneapolis, Kansas City, and San Francisco—all in an effort to "tame" base instincts and, in Olmsted's words, provide "a distinctly harmonizing and refining influence . . . favorable to courtesy, self-control and temperance." The later efforts of playground builders, settlement house workers, and such organizations as the Young Men's Christian Association (YMCA) and the Young Women's Christian Association (YWCA) to create healthful urban space remained imbued with Protestant notions about the spiritual benefits of well-ordered nature.

Similarly, nineteenth-century suburban architects and real estate developers enlisted Christianity in the cause of suburban growth. In doing so, they followed the lead of architect Andrew Jackson Downing, whose enormously influential book *The Architecture of Country Houses* (1850) mixed Protestant piety with mortar in designing the suburban "cottage." The country home, he preached, would calm unrest and ensure the moral health of the family. Extolling the Christian virtues of lawns and tree-lined boulevards, and even the opportunity to build a muscular morality by trimming shrubs and raking leaves, became a mantra for suburban promoters for generations. The presence of a church along with a school promised to anchor each community in Protestant order and uplift. The appeal of suburbs thus was as much to conscience as to comfort.

Religious institutions have also been important as sources of investment for the building process of cities and suburbs. Decisions to build churches in particular areas have affected the character and property values of those places, as noted previously, but churches have taken more direct roles in neighborhood development by lending money to their parishioners for homes and businesses, by buying and consolidating property for public use or rental income, and by underwriting other real estate projects. Catholic savings and loan societies brought homeownership within the reach of

countless immigrants and their children and further implanted the American idea that owning one's home was morally beneficial to one's family and to society. At the same time, by encouraging homeownership with preaching and money, churches encouraged community identity and neighborhood cohesion. Neighborhood churches and synagogues could not survive unless members of their congregation lived nearby. To save the historical and financial investments in a synagogue, with its social commitment to the city, many Jewish congregations resisted the pull of suburbs during the 1960s and 1970s, when they became racial and religious minorities in changing urban neighborhoods. Businesses run by churches, such as the hotels, restaurants, and service centers of Father Divine enterprises, have helped stabilize inner-city neighborhoods in several American cities. For three-quarters of a century, the AME, Baptist, and other black churches along Auburn Avenue in Atlanta have supported local businesses, built residence halls for seniors, funded home improvements, and underwritten neighborhood rehabilitation and development while still supporting a program of vigorous social activism.

Religious institutions can take property off city tax rolls, but they can also provide employment and maintain the property values of nearby structures. After the reunification of its northern and southern branches in 1983, the Presbyterian Church merged its new headquarters on property along the waterfront in Louisville, Kentucky. This action brought millions of dollars of investment and jobs to Louisville in the 1990s at the same time that it took money and jobs away from the former headquarters cities of New York and Atlanta.

The administrative, publishing, educational, and health facilities of religious bodies are major employers in urban and suburban America and responsible for the development of huge tracts of real estate. The Oral Roberts broadcasting, educational, and health care enterprises, along with its administrative offices, gave Tulsa, Oklahoma, a substantial economic boost during the 1970s and 1980s, as have Pat Robertson's properties and investments in the Norfolk, Virginia, area since the 1970s, including the Christian Broadcasting Network and Regent University.

In order to protect their real estate and institutional investments, religious bodies have become active in civic associations and government agencies that lobby for improved city services, the upgrading of infrastructure, the enforcement of local ordinances, and greater attention to quality-of-life issues. At the same time, by absorbing large amounts of real estate and demanding increased services for their expanding operations, schools, hospitals, and other institutions run by churches have strained city coffers. The issue of taxing church property has animated local politics in Denver and a host of other cities during the 1980s and 1990s. In sum, investment decisions of churches have affected the direction and depth of city growth, or retrenchment, in many significant ways, and still do.

Religious bodies have provided social services to their own congregants and to the larger community as well. Until the common school movement of the early nineteenth century, much of the formal education in towns and cities was in church-run schools or schools sponsored by religious bodies. The Protestant emphasis on moral discipline and learning to read the Bible provided a key rationale for public education in New England and elsewhere. The Protestant control of public school boards and curriculum made urban public education an instrument of Protestant morality, much to the dismay of Catholics during the antebellum period. Anti-Catholic violence erupted in Boston, Philadelphia, and other cities during the 1830s and 1840s, especially when Catholic parents protested against using the Protestant Bible in public schools. In the 1850s, the Catholic Church in New York City, under the leadership of Archbishop John Hughes, responded by launching a major effort to build a full array of Catholic institutions (parish schools, hospitals, asylums) to parallel the public ones ruled by Protestants. They also wanted to wrap Catholics in a cultural cocoon that would insulate them from Protestant evangelizing while nurturing a Catholic identity and regimen among Catholic immigrants. Building similar Catholic institutions became the rule in virtually every American diocese by the end of the century. Other denominations did likewise, thereby reinforcing their own distinctiveness, as with the Lutherans in several midwestern cities. But these institutions also broadened the number, variety, and reach of educational, charitable, and other social service institutions in urban America.

Before state and secular organizations assumed responsibility as the primary providers of social services ranging from adult education to health care to death benefits, benevolent societies and mutual-aid societies organized by churches and synagogues often offered the only such services available to the poor and to new city dwellers. During hard times, such as the Panic of 1893 and the Depression of the 1930s, church relief was the public assistance of first and last resort for countless people out of work. During the 1880s and 1890s, even as many prominent ministers of affluent churches were railing against the supposedly intemperate poor who were said to want handouts when what they really needed was moral discipline, many churches reached out to aid and encourage the working and immigrant populations. As Reverend Josiah Strong of Cincinnati explained in *The Challenge of the City* (1907), rather than fleeing the cities, middle-class Protestants should follow Christ's example, which was "not to be ministered unto but to minister" by becoming "the center and source of all beneficent and philanthropic effort."

The social gospel movement—led by such activists as Strong, the Congregational minister Washington Gladden of Columbus, Ohio, and the theologian Walter Rauschenbusch of New York City—spurred a social conscience among Protestants that built community centers to provide relief, recreation, and the three R's. Churches influenced by the social gospel ran nurseries, kindergartens, clinics, and dispensaries, among other services, in cities across urban America. Likewise, the YMCA and YWCA sought to ameliorate the suffering, ease the social adjustment, and invigorate the physical and moral health of young American men and women coming to the city.

Many of the settlement houses established before and during the Progressive Era had an avowedly religious basis and purpose, often drawn from social gospel imperatives and experience. Some settlement house reformers, such as Jane Addams of Hull House, cut their ties to specific religious groups as a way of opening their houses to the immigrant and poor populations in their neighborhoods who were mostly not Protestant and of freeing themselves from any denominational control. Even so, religion infused much of the settlement house movement's ethos and effort. In any case, Protestant, Catholic, and Jewish settlement houses vastly outnumbered the nonsectarian ones and often lasted longer as independent outreach and community centers.

Religion magnified its impact on the health and social cohesion of cities in the various women's societies, boys' brigades, girls' guilds, labor unions, men's lodges, athletic clubs, and other associations that churches and synagogues sponsored and encouraged. These organizations and activities mediated between their members and the larger society while they provided valuable services to members and nonmembers alike. Religiously owned or sponsored schools, health facilities, and charities laid the foundation for public services in numerous cities and continue to supplement public and private secular efforts. As a study by the Lilly Foundation of churches and synagogues in Philadelphia, New York, Indianapolis, Chicago, San Francisco, and Mobile reported in 1997, urban congregations remain the "essential providers" for the very poor. They sacrifice maintenance on their own buildings to run, on average, four community service programs each, serve four times more people than they have members, and provide, on average, $140,000 annually worth of services, staff support, and meeting space each to their neighborhoods.

Religion has further encouraged city building by promoting social reform. The great revivals of the nineteenth century, from those of Charles G. Finney to those of Dwight Moody and stretched into the twentieth century with the likes of Billy Sunday, preached social obligation along with individual conversion, though all of them emphasized soul saving over social service. Such recent mass movements of religious conversion and social responsibility as Promise Keepers echo similar concerns and have found large audiences among suburban dwellers who have felt spiritually starved and isolated from community and any sense of civic duty. At the same time, the powerful message of social duty as a demonstration of spiritual conversion resounds from inner-city churches of all faiths. Much of the evangelical message has focused on throwing off individual sin, especially intemperance, but a host of social reform flowed from calls to spread the Word by good works as much as by good preaching. During the nineteenth century, religiously inspired reformers organized to provide shelter and Scripture for prostitutes, orphans, alcoholics, and the mentally and physically ill. Such reform efforts often led to demands to redeem morality by improving the physical environment of the city through public policy. The asylum movement that built penitentiaries, mental hospitals, and orphanages was premised on Protestant ideas and ideals of "Christian nurture."

The city itself became a laboratory for building a moral society. The revivals that swept America in the 1830s, 1850s, and during the years after the Civil War generally originated in new or growing cities that experienced strains from rapid economic and social change. They appealed to all segments of society, but they especially attracted converts from the rising middle class of merchants, manufacturers, lawyers and other professionals, and retailers ambivalent about their place in a new urban order and anxious to succeed. The market economy, which equated success with moral rigor, put great pressure on these individuals to stand upright as moral exemplars even as they scratched and clawed for economic advantage. Joining a church promised self-discipline, as it also brought one into association with other responsible and rising businessmen and professionals of one's class. Significantly, during the nineteenth century, as revealed in such cities as Rochester, New York, those "reborn" middle-class people who joined churches tended to remain in their communities and to support both civic improvement and social reform.

Women, too, became agents of urban betterment and social reform. The so-called "cult of true womanhood" purveyed by nineteenth-century woman's magazines, advice books, and popular literature emphasized a woman's duty to build a Christian home in the city as a refuge from the corruptions of the marketplace and countinghouse. Therein, the argument went, the pious wife and mother would redeem her husband while instructing her children in republican and Christian truths. Such ideas informed the design and interiors of the Victorian urban "home," which frequently included sacred space such as sitting rooms or alcoves for reading the Bible and reflecting on spiritual matters.

Rather than removing religious influences from the public sphere, the emphasis on the Christian home propelled moral obligation outward in efforts to embrace the whole community. Emanating from such environments were a host of voluntary associations committed to saving fallen women, abandoned or orphaned children, and wayward husbands and fathers. A principal thrust of the temperance movement, embodied for example in Frances Willard's powerful Women's Christian Temperance Union (WCTU), was the Protestant emphasis on extending private, Christian space into the public realm. Willard argued that this could only be achieved by enfranchising women who might then defeat the corrupt and corrupting saloon-centered city machines and pass the kind of reform legislation that would save the family by reshaping the city.

Religion informed urban politics in countless ways. Questions of public morality have invariably been framed in religious terms. The debates over weights, measures, and the just price that raged in eighteenth-century cities experiencing the first social and political tremors of entering a market economy were just one of many public issues cast in religious terms. So, too, were issues of licensing taverns and places of recreation, access to public space, and proper public behavior. Clashes over sabbatarian laws wracked numerous cities with large German Lutheran or Catholic and Irish-Catholic populations during the nineteenth century. Indeed, much of the political tension in nineteenth-century urban America had a religious dimension, as evangelical Protestants pressed for moral reform through public policy—e.g., temperance laws—and Catholics, Lutherans, and others emphasized personal salvation and hands-off policies from the government. Almost any issue could break along religious lines. Supporters of labor unions, for example, were as likely to invoke religion to rally support and justify their actions as were their opponents. According to students of voting behavior, religion was the best single predictor of voting patterns in the nineteenth-century city.

Churches were mobilizing stations for many forays into local politics. This has been most visibly evident in the significant role that black churches played in the modern civil rights movement, which led not only to the desegregation of public places and facilities in the American South but also to attacks on *de facto* segregation and discrimination in northern cities. Fair housing legislation that fundamentally altered the distribution of race in urban America during the 1960s and later was a direct product of social activism that emanated from urban churches. Black Protestant churches especially have opened their pulpits to political candidates and urged political activism among their members, but Catholic and Jewish congregations also have long histories of political activism.

At the same time, the apolitical orientation of many evangelical and fundamentalist Protestants skewed politics in favor of other religious groups and secular interests in places where these Protestants comprised a significant proportion of the potential electorate. Across urban America during the 1980s and 1990s, issues such as public assistance for abortion, sex education, freedom of religion in public schools, vouchers for use in private schools, and the scope and stringency of criminal codes awakened evangelical and fundamentalist Protestants to politics and made all religious groups and interests increasingly important in defining issues, raising money, and electing candidates.

Religion even became a training ground for political advancement. One of the reasons Irish Catholics enjoyed disproportionate strength in late nineteenth and early-twentieth-century city "machines" was their mastery of the many bureaucratic and political intricacies of the American Catholic Church, which they had come to rule during the nineteenth century by the sheer force of their numbers and the predominance of Irish clergy. Irish-Catholic tribalism combined with institutional experience to give Irish-Catholic candidates a voting bloc and a political savvy that few other groups matched for years. During the 1960s mainline Protestant churches organized urban action training programs for clergy and laity in most major cities to mobilize political action for such inner-city concerns as substandard housing, poverty, gang warfare, and local economic development. From these efforts came both an urban political agenda and a cadre of skilled local activists. Just by encouraging or discouraging civic activism, religion helped form the civic culture.

Religion has been a principal instrument for extending urban culture beyond city boundaries. During the nineteenth century, religious publishing houses based in cities, such as the American Tract Society and the American Bible Society, purveyed a Protestant ethos of self-discipline and morality that fit well with the rising market economy of urban America. The adaptation of religion to the new consumer culture occurred first in cities before it was transmitted to the countryside in the advice columns of magazines, catalogs of department stores, and even the periodicals of churches. As already noted, revivals often started in cities and spread outward through organized missions and religious publications. The voluntaristic nature of American religion, based on the lack of any public support for an established religion and the need for churches to recruit and hold their followers in a religiously competitive but secularizing environment, has fed strong evangelizing efforts in America over the past two centuries. To a significant extent, that effort has had both urban roots and, despite its criticism of materialism and the corruptions of the modern world, has relied on the wealth and communications capabilities of urban society to sustain itself.

During the nineteenth century, at least, the connection between urban culture and evangelical outreach was clear. Laypeople have played a significant role in that process. Two mercantile brothers in New York City, Arthur and Lewis Tappan, underwrote missionaries, the publication of tracts, and social reform (including the abolition of slavery) during the antebellum era, and the premier retailer of Philadelphia, John Wanamaker, founded missions and churches for workers and laced his advertisements with moral advice as well as sales information during the late nineteenth century. The Tappan brothers and Wanamaker were but two of a type.

The accommodation of religion to modern urban America became a point of controversy within various faiths. The pentecostal and holiness movements that broke away from mainline Protestantism during the late nineteenth and early twentieth centuries, for example, were partly protests against the business-oriented sophistication of urban church authorities who had supposedly lost their "souls" by becoming too comfortable with middle-class urban culture. Religion itself, such critics were saying, could be corrupted by the city.

American religion and the American city grew up together. Whether in its city-building and urban-adapting functions or in shaping civic culture, religion has been central to American urban identities and interests. Whatever the promise of Winthrop's religious vision of building a unified "City upon a Hill" in America, religion, in the words of urban historian Kathleen Conzen, "has been and remains a structuring and enculturating factor in American urban life."

—Randall M. Miller

**See also**
Addams, Jane; Catholicism; Downing, Andrew Jackson; Gladden, Washington; Henry Street Settlement; Hull House; Judaism; Kelley, Florence; Matthews, Mark Allison; McPherson, Aimee Semple; Mormons; Playgrounds; Rauschenbusch, Walter; Settlement House Movement; Shaker Villages; Social Gospel; Strong, Josiah; Sunday, Billy; Wald, Lillian D.

**References**
Boyer, Paul S. *Urban Masses and Moral Order in America, 1820–1920.* Cambridge, MA: Harvard University Press, 1978.
Conzen, Kathleen Neils, et al. "Forum: The Place of Religion in Urban and Community Studies." *Religion in American Culture* 6 (1996): 107–129.
Marsden, George M. *Religion and American Culture.* New York: Harcourt Brace Jovanovich, 1990.
Miller, Randall M., and Thomas D. Marzik, eds. *Immigrants and Religion in Urban America.* Philadelphia: Temple University Press, 1977.
Moore, R. Laurence. *Selling God: American Religion in the Marketplace of Culture.* New York: Oxford University Press, 1994.
Noll, Mark A. *A History of Christianity in the United States and Canada.* Grand Rapids, MI: William B. Eerdmans, 1992.

# Religion in Suburbs

In the twentieth century, suburbanization has keenly affected the character of religious activity in the United States. The story of religion in suburbs is one of small beginnings in which suburban churches were, from the viewpoint of their denominations and sister churches in the cities, insignificant, and synagogues were virtually nonexistent. What began almost as an afterthought on the American religious landscape came to be one of religion's areas of greatest strength by the 1970s.

The crucial years for understanding the shift of religious organizational vigor from cities to suburbs are the early years after World War II, from 1945 to 1965. During that time, and to a lesser extent even to the present, many issues for American religious bodies could be framed in terms of a tension between cities and suburbs, or between the concerns of city dwellers and suburbanites more generally.

The first suburbs began with the self-consciousness of small towns. At one level this was natural because many of the early suburbs that developed near older cities such as New York, Boston, Philadelphia, and Chicago had existed as small towns before 1900. Early suburban growth was fed by the desire of upper-middle-class people to escape crowded city living in favor of a small-town or more parklike setting while still retaining incomes linked to the nearby city. Since these people maintained vital and immediate economic ties to the urban center, their movement to small towns and farming communities began the process of suburbanization and did not reverse the long-standing nineteenth-century movement from rural to urban areas. Nevertheless, in rhetoric and outlook, the first residents of suburbs thought in terms of town and village, not in terms of suburb.

This proved important for churches and other religious organizations because the major Protestant denominations tended to classify these new suburban churches as "town and country" ministries. The tendency of Protestant denominations to erect a church in every community was only partially countered by the ecumenical spirit of the social gospel movement during the Progressive Era, which emphasized "deeds over creeds." Suburban churches physically resembled small-town or rural churches and paralleled their membership size as opposed to larger, more complex city churches.

Roman Catholic, fundamentalist Protestant, and Jewish congregational growth in suburbs during the first half of the twentieth century lagged far behind that of mainline Protestant congregations, partly due to restrictive housing covenants that barred Jews and Roman Catholics from some communities. An even greater reason for the lag, however, was that adherents of those religions remained more firmly attached to cities.

Since religious leaders followed their secular counterparts in thinking of suburbs as small towns, they misunderstood or misinterpreted some of the features that distinguished early suburban churches. Compared to small-town churches of similar size, members of suburban churches had greater per capita wealth and income. Thus, they could pay ministers more highly than could rural churches. Also, since many suburban churches were new and adjacent to newer houses occupied by relatively young families, a higher proportion of their members was still in the prime years of life and available for lay leadership as compared to city, small-town, or rural churches. In the long run, the availability of money and leadership gave suburban congregations power in their national denominations and regional church bodies. That these latent possibilities went mostly unnoticed is less surprising when one realizes that this was also the heyday of the "institutional church," a city church that occupied a large piece of land and offered activities seven days a week for its members and its neighbors, activities that ranged from sewing groups to athletic teams.

In nearly all respects, the 20 years after World War II constitute a high point for religion in the United States. Never before had as many Americans belonged to, attended, or associated with religious institutions. Not only in adherence, but also in status, religion experienced an unparalleled position. Contemporaries used terms like "religious revival" and "theological renaissance" to describe the phenomena. The religious resurgence of the 1950s was fueled in no small measure by the contemporaneous suburbanization. All of the ways in which suburbanization had changed and strengthened organized religion in earlier years now became major factors in American religious life as the period took shape.

The new suburbanites of these years had a "frontier" experience as they conducted the rituals of marking out and defining their living spaces. Just as earlier pioneers had marked out spaces for laundry, waste disposal, food production, marketing, government, worship, and social interaction in each new "wilderness," so too did suburbanites. If the settlers of each new suburb had most of their physical needs for roads and public services planned for them, then they emphasized their social needs even more strongly. Family, motherhood, the Parent-Teacher Association, the block club, the playground and parks committees, and, of course, the church or synagogue were all aspects of the exciting process of community building. The high level of churchgoing was related to the phenomenon of belonging to an institution's first generation and therefore feeling a higher degree of responsibility for its success.

Many of the same economic realities faced church building that affected domestic construction. It has been calculated that, in 1929, roughly 10 percent of the money donated to religion was spent on building; between 1932 and 1936, the figure dropped to only 2.5 percent. This low number continued through the war years when construction material was diverted to defense; of the more than $7 billion given to religious organizations during World War II, only $131 million, or 1.8 percent, was spent on construction despite the significant increase in religious contributions during the war. Religious building, like home construction, failed to keep pace with society's needs. Quite naturally, when building began again at the end of the war, the greater part of the new religious construction took place in outlying and suburban areas.

Although the most famous suburbs were in the Boston to Washington corridor, southern California, and the industrial Midwest, suburbanization was a national phenomenon, and building churches in new outlying residential areas was part of the process. For example, at the beginning of the 1950s, Omaha had 35 major religious building projects under construction, including 7 new Protestant churches but not counting 11 more that had been recently completed. Nearly all of Omaha's residential growth in this period occurred within the municipal limits of Omaha, meaning that it was not considered "suburban" by the federal government. Yet, although the owners of the new homes and members of the new churches belonged to the same political jurisdiction as the people in the central city, their experience resembled that of residents in the actual suburbs of the nation's older cities. Just like Levittowners, they banded together to lobby for the extension of services—schools, sewers, utilities—to their neighborhoods and engaged in community building on the fringe of established urban areas.

Suburbanization during the 1950s was primarily a Protestant and Jewish phenomenon because of who moved to the suburbs. Those who bought a station wagon and a house with a picture window were, initially, overwhelmingly middle to upper-middle class, concentrated in the Northeast, Far West, and industrial Midwest, white, of British or German ancestry, and college educated. These were precisely the same demographic characteristics associated with liberal or mainline Protestantism and Reform Judaism. Early sociological studies of suburbs also revealed the propensity of intellectuals and professionals—academics, doctors, dentists, lawyers—to move to suburbs. A large number of Jews also practiced these occupations, so that while Jews were only a small part of the total number of people moving to suburbs, a sizable proportion of the American Jewish population made the transition from urban to suburban living and did so early on. Therefore, suburbanization was a dominant social reality in the institutional life of mainline Protestantism and Ameri-

can Judaism from the early 1950s on. This fact proved not always pleasant for some representatives of these groups.

In their 1950 series "Great Churches of America," the editors of *The Christian Century* presented the promises and dilemmas of suburbia as they saw them. "The residents of Suburbia are, by and large, Protestant in tradition and by natural addiction. They want to have Protestant churches in their communities and will support them generously. They send their children to Protestant church schools, and more often than not they maintain a church membership for themselves. But in too many instances Suburbia breeds a sense of self-satisfaction, of complacency, on occasion even of self-congratulation, which tends to look on the church as little more than a social convenience. Suburbia is the home of those who have arrived."

Suburbia also concerned Jewish social observers. In 1955 Morris Freedman wrote a feature article for *Commentary* magazine about a new Jewish community being formed in the Hillcrest section of Queens (one of the five boroughs of New York City). Located in the inner ring of new suburbs on Long Island, and the only sizable pocket of wealth between Forest Hills and Great Neck on Long Island, Hillcrest was the site of booming residential construction, with some houses costing as much as $100,000. The ethos of homeownership immediately impressed Freedman. He quoted the Hillcrest Jewish Center's rabbi, Dr. Israel Mowshowitz. "It's very important in understanding our character to realize that this is a congregation of homeowners. But even more important is the fact that these are their *first* homes—and probably their last. They don't have the sense of being apartment dwellers who might move away any time. Our members feel that for the first time in their lives they have let roots down here." In putting down roots in a neighborhood of single-family houses, Freedman discovered that many Jewish families also formally affiliated with a Jewish community institution for the first time, but he believed that the attraction was mostly social and not religious. Freedman hoped that because the Hillcrest Jewish Center was new and its patterns for the future were not yet fixed, "a close and sober look now may offer an opportunity for those deeply concerned to help shape those patterns before the mold hardens." Freedman's worries paralleled those of Marshall Sklare, who concluded that while the congregation had become increasingly influential in Jewish life as it broadened its range of activities, the attitudes and life patterns of Jews in all three major branches of Judaism "depart[ed] markedly from ideal norms."

These criticisms from religious journalists and commentators did not stop suburban residents from founding churches and synagogues nor prevent those institutions from being tremendously popular. Suburbanization resulted in homogeneous communities that, far from being the sterile wastelands their worst critics feared, became the locus of incredible vitality.

Suburban churches shared in this vitality, for they too were settings in which nearly all participants ranged in age from newborn to 35. These were times and places when and where everything seemed possible; veritable utopias from which death, cancer, and poverty had been banished. A typical suburban church or synagogue could go years without a funeral or memorial service. On the other hand, the joyful, life-affirming rituals of baptism, first communion, confirmation, bar mitzvah, bat mitzvah, and marriage were frequently celebrated. Moreover, though the suburban family of faith might go to meetings in an elementary school gymnasium and listen to the reading of scripture while sitting on metal folding chairs, the prospects for the future were bright: ecclesiastical budgets were rising, never going down or being tied to the declining incomes of aging or retiring members; building programs were under way (the family proud of their new split-level house would soon be attending a church equally new and worthy of pride); and the typical suburban church or synagogue had exactly what most prospective members sought in a religious home—people exactly like themselves.

The religious building boom in the suburbs changed the landscape of America and redefined what churches and synagogues looked like. Here, the churches were popular objects of art and architectural endeavor. *McCall's* magazine's adoring coverage of new churches was typical. Under the title "The Churches Rise Again," *McCall's* proudly proclaimed, "Not since Solomon have people lavished so much on housing for God and those who would worship Him." God's new housing displayed all the features of modern design and took advantage of the creative energy of the era's architectural innovators. The number of dollars spent on commissions for church buildings in the 1950s were second only to those for hospitals, and of all the possible kinds of construction, perhaps only art museums offered more symbolic possibilities and freedom from functional concerns. It was estimated that 25 percent of all new Christian houses of worship were of completely contemporary design. For Jewish synagogues, estimates went as high as 85 percent. But one did not need Frank Lloyd Wright or Marcel Breuer to build a church appropriate to the spirit of the age. For those many Americans so inclined, the *Saturday Evening Post* printed an article entitled "How to Build Your Own Church," which neatly allowed them to combine two of the most popular activities of the 1950s in a single experience. Indeed, the easy functionality of space outside the sanctuary bore striking resemblance to that found in modern suburban tract homes. The Sunday school had moved from a dank basement underneath an urban sanctuary into a wing of its own with lots of light; little fiberglass and plywood laminate tables and chairs—even tiny toilets—made especially for God's smaller children, reinforcing the impression that here, too, the prevailing culture was child-centered. Boy Scouts, Girl Scouts, teen clubs, square dances, B'nai B'rith, meetings of the temple sisterhood, pancake dinners, potluck suppers, hobby clubs, and choirs for all ages filled the calendar and the space of the typical suburban church or synagogue.

All this activity seemed to be fueled by refreshments. The coffee hour, the new member's group, the emphasis on children, and the endless round of social activities all indicated that the church or synagogue of the 1950s was serving a great variety of felt needs. A religious congregation's popularity derived from multiple sources, but not to be discounted was the role it played as a *de facto* community center.

In the 1950s critics who had focused on America's failure to feed and clothe its people in the 1930s now took material goods for granted and began asking the moral question, "affluence for what?" So social critics worried more about the distorting psychological effects of conformity, the meaninglessness of work, and the trivialization of leisure time than about the absence of political alternatives, the ownership of the means of production, and economic inequity. Not surprisingly, they found more than enough to criticize in suburbanization and suburban religion. The intellectual critics of the 1950s, writers such as William H. Whyte, David Riesman, C. Wright Mills, and Dwight Macdonald, viewed American society as a lonely crowd of white-collar workers and organization men, housed in lookalike suburban homes and dominated by mass culture and a power elite.

For religious elites—including Reinhold Niebuhr, John Courtney Murray, Abraham Heschel, Will Herberg, Peter Berger, and Gibson Winter—the numerical growth of churches and synagogues, and the popularity of prayer and piety, represented a hollow success. In their eyes it was not real religion that was succeeding, but rather something less than faith in the God of Abraham, Isaac, and Jacob. In the language of the Bible, the critics believed the people had "gone off after idols and false gods." By the end of the decade they were calling the nation's true faith "the American Way of Life" and comparing the suburbanization of middle-class churches to the Babylonian captivity of the ancient Israelites. They even suggested that God did not appreciate the sounds rising up to him from America's solemn religious assemblies.

Of all the social critics of religion, Gibson Winter was most trenchant in his critique of the suburban impact on religion. For Winter, suburbia was the ultimate extension of two centuries of industrialization and a very real peril to the soul of the Christian church. Winter first published his indictments about the suburban captivity of churches in *The Christian Century* in 1955 and later extended his argument in a popular book, *The Suburban Captivity of the Churches.* When it came to church life, Winter maintained, suburbia had introduced its conception of success into every aspect of the church's being. In spite of infusing the church and its programs with energy and enthusiasm, and filling the offering plates, pews, and educational facilities to overflowing, suburbia had, Winter believed, brought the churches into captivity—with all the negative connotations that the term implied. Suburbia had imposed its mind-set on the church. Financial prosperity and numerical growth had crowded out more traditional measures of Christian success—salvation, redemption, care of the poor, and witness to the power of the cross. Indeed, the very success of suburban churches threatened the identity of Christian churches. With church members being added more quickly than clergy and dedicated laypeople could assimilate and train them, it was virtually guaranteed that more of the world would be brought into the church of Christ than Christ would be taken by the church into the world. Finally, for Winter, suburbia undermined the life of the church insofar as it had "nailed up an impenetrable layer of insulation between the churches and the world of work, community, housing, and daily bread." Winter recognized that the isolation of the church from daily life was not created by suburbia, but even so he argued that secularization had found its fullest and final expression in suburbs. This, he believed, constituted a national tragedy for it was happening at a time when America's world leadership necessitated a prophetic church. And the suburban church was anything but prophetic. "Suburban domination may well be God's word of judgment upon us as his church," Winter wrote. "For our trespasses and complacency we have been delivered to Babylon."

Since 1965, American suburbs have continued to grow, and organized religion has continued to move its center of gravity into the suburbs. Where elites once worried about the suburbs' moral and religious significance, suburbs are now increasingly taken for granted. This shift was not accomplished without pain, however, and most of the transitional burden has been shouldered by city dwellers and urban congregations.

By the middle of the 1960s, two decades of postwar suburbanization had depleted white urban churches and synagogues of the young and left behind older congregants. In the 1950s, the majority of the remaining urban members had been in their late middle age or early retirement years. Consequently, they were often still married, had high disposable incomes, and were able to sustain downtown congregations without noticeable strain—despite the fact that they were not adding younger members. But when older, urban congregations of Christians and Jews continued to age and

their resident members moved increasingly into periods of widowhood, infirmity, and declining financial resources in the later 1960s, numerous congregations fell on hard times. Endowments allowed some "large steeple" churches to support exciting preaching ministries, but the relocation of younger adults to suburbs virtually assured a dramatic religious decline among whites in cities. The prophets who had wailed about suburbia during the 1950s seemed more prophetic as the years wore on.

African-American religion in cities was relatively untouched by suburbanization in the 1950s or by its religious critics. Fleeing the cities and their problems was not a moral issue for black Christians since they were largely excluded from suburbs. Residential segregation meant that moving to suburbs and leaving the poor behind was not an available option. Later, when residential opportunities for African Americans became obtainable, they did so mostly in formerly all-white neighborhoods of cities themselves.

But the crisis in cities during the 1960s—collapsing tax bases, departing white middle classes, declining city jobs, diminishing city resources to fight crime, fires and decay, rioting, and intensifying institutional racism—did change the ethos in which black urban churches existed. On the positive side, the rising proportions of black to white voters in cities meant the election of more black governmental officials; big city mayors and members of the Congressional Black Caucus frequently had church backgrounds and related well to religious constituencies. On the negative side, the decay of schools and economic opportunities in cities meant that political freedoms were often rendered hollow by the inability of African Americans to afford the fruits of freedom. After white flight, the black church in many urban places continued to play its historic role of assisting the black community in bearing adversity and maintaining hope, while taking on responsibility as well for the larger institutions of government and education.

In the last 15 years, suburban populations have become more diverse, and with ethnic and racial diversity has come greater religious diversity. Thus, there are suburbs like New Rochelle, New York, with a large African-American population and a number of well-established churches associated with historically black denominations. Once all-white and overwhelmingly Christian, Dearborn, Michigan, is now home to a substantial Muslim population from the Near East. Lawrenceville, Georgia, a suburb of Atlanta, boasts fast-growing Korean-language churches associated with both the Methodist and Presbyterian denominations. These changes have forced religious groups to adjust to the suburbs in different ways than they had in the past. The seemingly easy equation of suburbs with a privileged life devoid of cultural diversity has evaporated. Compared to the 1950s and 1960s, religious congregations of the 1990s in both cities and suburbs are more apt to be engaged in social ministries that extend beyond their neighborhoods and primary class identifications.

—*James Hudnut-Beumler*

**References**
Hudnut-Beumler, James. *Looking for God in the Suburbs: The Religion of the American Dream and Its Critics, 1945–1965.* New Brunswick, NJ: Rutgers University Press, 1994.
Winter, Gibson. *The Suburban Captivity of the Churches: An Analysis of Protestant Responsibility in the Expanding Metropolis.* Garden City, NY: Doubleday, 1961.
Wuthnow, Robert. *The Restructuring of American Religion: Society and Faith since World War II.* Princeton, NJ: Princeton University Press, 1988.

## Rent Control

Rent control, government restrictions on the amount of rent that can be charged for private housing, developed during wartime emergencies when municipalities tried to stem the political and social consequences of inflation in war production centers. During World War I, many cities reacted to threats of rent "profiteering" by establishing voluntary "fair play" compliance among landlords or authorizing magistrates to review rent increases or sometimes both. In 1920, New York State enacted Emergency Rent Laws for New York City, which allowed tenants to challenge "unjust" increases in court; these were then extended until 1928. During World War II, the Office of Price Administration (OPA) "froze" the rent that could be charged in multiple dwellings in "war rental areas" like Los Angeles, Seattle, and the four-county Chicago district and imposed voluntary compliance in "defense rental areas" like New York City. In the aftermath of rioting in Harlem in August 1943, which was blamed on rent grievances, the OPA froze the allowable rents on 1.4 million units in New York City. Landlords could appeal to the OPA for 15 percent "hardship" increases, but tenant groups remained vigilant against landlord grabs, payments for "fixtures," and other evasions.

After Congress let the OPA rent controls expire in 1947, ten states, including Illinois and Wisconsin, adopted supplementary provisions whose coverage and legality were contested by real estate lobbies and tenant politicians. In New York City, a vehement tenant lobby forced Governor Thomas E. Dewey to inaugurate a state-run system that retained rent controls on apartments built in the city before July 1, 1947. Every three years, state officials certified that vacancy rates under 5 percent meant a continued emergency, and the legislature dutifully renewed controls with an occasional 15 percent "catch-up" for landlords. In the 1960s, city politicians bowed to demands to "stabilize" rents on units built after 1947, and in the 1970s they bowed to fears of landlord "abandon-ment" by enacting "vacancy decontrol." Then they reversed course and put the decontrolled housing back in the stabilized category. During the inflationary 1970s, cities as widespread and as diverse as Boston, Massachusetts, Berkeley, California, and Fort Lee, New Jersey, controlled rents on apartments in multiple-dwelling buildings.

The largest stock of rent-controlled housing remains in the New York region where there are 124,000 rent-controlled and 800,000 rent-stabilized apartments in New York City and 82,000 units in both categories in suburban cities like Yonkers and White Plains. This system, which rests on when an apartment was built rather than on an income test (which the legislature modified in 1993 to decontrol apartments whose occupants earn more than $100,000 annually), remains rife with inequities. While controls restrain rents 15 percent below market levels citywide, the greatest boon benefits tenants of Manhattan's semiluxury "prewar" apartments. Controls have been blamed for problems that range from housing abandonment to lagging property tax collections, and critics contend that they give the least protection to those who need it most—recent, impoverished migrants.

—*Joel Schwartz*

**See also**
Rent Strikes; Tenant Unions.
**References**
Lawson, Ronald. *The Tenant Movement in New York City, 1901–1984.* New Brunswick, NJ: Rutgers University Press, 1986.
Lebowitz, Neil H. " 'Above Party, Class or Creed': Rent Control in the United States, 1940–1947." *Journal of Urban History* 7 (1981): 403–438.
Lett, Monica. *Rent Control.* New Brunswick, NJ: New Jersey Center for Urban Policy Research, 1976.

## Rent Strikes

Rent strikes, the withholding of rent by tenants of multiple-unit dwellings as a way of expressing grievances, have occasionally forced concessions from landlords and municipal governments. (Property law, which afforded tenants the "right" to quit premises made uninhabitable by a "constructive eviction," did not recognize the rent strike, and magistrates usually dismissed strikes as extortion or racketeering.) Strikes broke out on the Lower East Side of Manhattan and in Brownsville in Brooklyn between 1904 and 1908, and again after World War I when Jewish socialists organized rent withholding, forced landlords to rescind rent increases, and compelled the New York State legislature to impose municipal rent controls. During the Depression, strikes occurred again on the Lower East Side, and also in the Bronx and in Harlem in conjunction with working-class protests and Black Nationalist movements. Neighborhood lawyers, scrounging for fees and cooperating with left-wing supporters, fought evictions in local courts, winning leeway among magistrates who feared political turmoil. Few withholdings, however, reached a neighborhood scale. By far the most successful occurred in 1934 and involved several hundred tenants in middle-class Manhattan apartments, London Terrace, and in Knickerbocker Village, a quasi-cooperative redevelopment project financed by the Reconstruction Finance Corporation and therefore vulnerable to political pressure.

Rent controls during World War II reduced rent strikes to a sporadic phenomenon until the community-power fervor of the 1960s when the Congress of Racial Equality and Jesse Gray, a Harlem activist, organized tenants for direct action against "slumlords," and New Left visionaries saw massive strikes as "the weight of the poor" against the power structure. The results were exaggerated by activists who never convinced more than a few score tenants to withhold rent at any one time. However, they did unnerve white liberals, who demanded that payments of withheld rent into escrow accounts administered by courts to be used to make repairs and improvements be legalized. Into the late 1960s, many cities redirected rent strikes toward the practice of tenant "ownership" under court auspices. Even so, the most spectacular rent strike was against the largest institutional landlord of all, the New York State Mitchell-Lama housing program, and was spearheaded in the early 1970s by 15,000 residents of Co-op City in the Bronx, who withheld their rent and forced the state to intervene with larger subsidies for operating costs.

—*Joel Schwartz*

**See also**

Rent Control; Tenant Unions.

**References**

Lawson, Ronald. *The Tenant Movement in New York City, 1901–1984.* New Brunswick, NJ: Rutgers University Press, 1986.

Lipsky, Michael. *Protest in City Politics.* Chicago: Rand McNally, 1970.

Schwartz, Joel. "The Consolidated Tenants League of Harlem: Black Self-Help vs. White, Liberal Intervention in Ghetto Housing, 1934–1944." *Afro-Americans in New York History and Life* 10 (1986): 31–51.

## Resettlement Administration

During the 1920s and 1930s American farmers were in dire financial straits. Plagued by falling prices, high costs of production, and dwindling domestic and foreign markets, farmers produced more in hopes of increasing their sales and incomes. In fact, all they accomplished was raising their costs while pushing prices even lower, resulting in bankruptcies. As a result, poverty and migration from farms to cities took place, and the problems of tenancy and sharecropping multiplied. Moreover, land erosion was reaching serious proportions. After the Depression set in, the farm situation reached a critical stage, even resulting in widespread violence during Herbert Hoover's presidency. By 1932 traditional farm remedies such as higher tariffs had failed to alleviate the crisis while schemes to sell produce abroad cheaply, give subsidies to farmers, and pay them to reduce their production were never implemented.

Franklin D. Roosevelt addressed the farm crisis quickly by asking Congress to pass the Agricultural Adjustment Act (AAA). Designed to control production, the AAA relied on the principle of domestic allotment whereby farmers voluntarily agreed to limit production in return for a federal subsidy. The plan eventually failed because farmers violated their contracts, administrators of the AAA such as George Peek and Secretary of Agriculture Henry Wallace disagreed on how to implement the program, and publicity for the program failed to convince Americans of the need for scarcity economics.

One of the New Dealers most responsible for realizing domestic allotment and helping to implement the AAA was Rexford G. Tugwell. An economics professor at Columbia University, Tugwell was part of Roosevelt's Brain Trust and later served as assistant and undersecretary of Agriculture. Mistakenly perceived as a collectivist, Tugwell emphasized the need to control farm production, to move farmers off of marginal land, and to reconsider the role of the small farmer. Throughout the New Deal, he championed the idea of a long-term land use program. When Roosevelt issued Executive Order 7027 creating the Resettlement Administration (RA) on May 1, 1935, Tugwell was given the chance to do something about his ideas.

A hodgepodge creation, the RA consolidated a number of programs from the Department of Interior (Subsistence Homesteads), the Federal Emergency Relief Administration (state Rural Rehabilitation Corporations), and the Department of Agriculture (Submarginal Lands Committee) that overlapped and duplicated each other. Receiving its funding directly from the president under the terms of the Federal Emergency Relief Act of 1935, the RA was to conserve land by retiring submarginal lands and putting them to forestry or recreational use, to resettle farmers living on poor land, and to help farmers on productive land who, for whatever reason, needed assistance. Dividing the country into 11 regions, the RA had four main divisions: Suburban Resettlement, Rural Rehabilitation, Land Utilization, and Rural Resettlement. Highly capable individuals were given responsibility for carrying out the RA's principal programs, and Tugwell served as overall director.

During its brief existence, the RA resettled more than 4,400 farm families, developed sanitary camps for migrants, and set up several cooperative farming communities. However, its most ambitious, and highly controversial, endeavor was Tugwell's attempt at suburban resettlement. Strongly influenced by the idea of garden cities for full-time industrial workers, the RA designed and constructed three greenbelt towns to accommodate 500–800 families each, provide useful work for men on unemployment relief, and offer low-rent housing for low-income families and healthful surroundings for the urban poor. Although Tugwell had initially planned on building 25 greenbelt communities, only three were completed: Greenbelt, Maryland (outside of Washington); Greenhills, Ohio (outside of Cincinnati); and Greendale, Wisconsin (outside of Milwaukee).

Critics attacked the towns as being too expensive, foreign to America's traditions, and incapable of dealing with urban problems. By the fall of 1936, the attacks on Tugwell himself had become so intense that he submitted his resignation and was replaced by Will Alexander.

In 1937, Congress passed the Bankhead-Jones Farm Tenancy Act to help tenants, farm laborers, and small landowners, and that same year, Henry Wallace set up the Farm Security Administration (FSA) with Alexander as its director to take over the RA's programs. FSA continued some of the RA's initiatives, such as rural rehabilitation, resettlement of farm families, and helping migrant workers, but it never considered building more greenbelt towns. And, in 1946, the FSA was replaced by the Farmers Home Administration.

—*Michael V. Namorato*

See also
Greenbelt Towns; Tugwell, Rexford Guy.
References
Baldwin, Sidney. *Politics and Poverty: The Rise and Decline of the Farm Security Administration.* Chapel Hill: University of North Carolina Press, 1967.

Conkin, Paul. *Tomorrow a New World: The New Deal Community Program.* Ithaca, NY: Cornell University Press, 1959.

Holley, Donald. *Uncle Sam's Farmers: The New Deal Communities in the Lower Mississippi Valley.* Urbana: University of Illinois Press, 1975.

Namorato, Michael V. *Rexford G. Tugwell: A Biography.* New York: Praeger, 1988.

———, ed. *The Diary of Rexford G. Tugwell: The New Deal, 1932–1935.* Westport, CT: Greenwood Press, 1992.

## Residential Community Association

Created by real estate developers and subject to the approval of local government officials, residential community associations provide homeowners in single-family housing developments, condominium developments, and cooperatives a governing mechanism to manage the commonly owned property in their neighborhood, such as streets, parking lots, tennis courts, and swimming pools. Also, they often provide various services for their members, such as street maintenance, trash collection, and snow removal; assess and collect fees to pay for these facilities and services; and create and enforce various covenants, rules, and regulations (CR&Rs) that control their members' behavior. The CR&Rs can, among

other things, determine whether homeowners may own pets, paint their house a certain color, or place a basketball hoop over their garage door.

There are more than 160,000 residential community associations in the United States, and more than 9,000 are formed every year. Although they are most prevalent on the East and West Coasts, residential community associations now exist in every state. Over 40 million Americans currently belong to some kind of residential community association, and many members consider the association as important as their municipal government.

Local government officers generally like residential community associations because these organizations relieve them of providing many services. This lets them either reduce taxes and fees or expand services in other areas of a town or city. Many prospective home buyers like residential community associations because they value the cost savings that result from having commonly owned recreational facilities and other amenities. They also like the leisure time gained by having chores such as lawn care handled by the association.

Because residential community associations furnish services traditionally provided by government, some scholars have suggested that they should be subject to the same legal standards applied to government. Among other things, this would mean giving all adults residing within an association's boundaries the right to vote at meetings and be elected to the association's governing board. Most residential community associations currently base voting rights on homeownership, not on residence. Thus, renters cannot usually vote at the association's meetings or run for office on the board of directors.

Some scholars have also suggested that residential community associations are causing broad social and political changes that are undermining the vitality of American cities. They argue that residential community associations encourage social exclusiveness and class divisions by letting homeowners create a community within a community, effectively "seceding" from the town or city in which they are located. Although this argument is subject to debate, it is clear that members of residential community associations are becoming more politically active. Worried about urban encroachment and undesirable activities near their neighborhoods, they are a vital part of the NIMBY (Not in My Back Yard) movement. They are also increasingly vocal in their opposition to local taxes used to pay for services such as snow or trash removal that they already provide for themselves.

The number of residential community associations in the United States is increasing rapidly. As their numbers continue to grow, so will their influence on American lifestyles, American politics, and American cities.

—*Robert Jay Dilger*

References

Barton, Stephen E., and Carol Silverman. *Common Interest Homeowners' Associations Management Study.* Sacramento: California Department of Real Estate, 1987.

Dilger, Robert Jay. *Neighborhood Politics: Residential Community Associations in American Governance.* New York: New York University Press, 1992.

McKenzie, Evan. *Privatopia: Homeowner Associations and the Rise of Residential Private Government.* New Haven, CT: Yale University Press, 1994.

U.S. Advisory Commission on Intergovernmental Relations. *Residential Community Associations: Private Governments in the Intergovernmental System?* Washington, DC: Government Printing Office, 1989.

## Residential Construction

Residential construction has often been described as backward—"the industry that capitalism forgot." There is some truth to this. Technological change has been steady, but slow in the industry, and small businesses still account for a significant amount of activity, especially in the growing renovation sector. Nevertheless, over the past century or so, cumulative changes have been significant.

For the most part, dwellings are assembled on the site from parts that have been manufactured elsewhere. This distinguishes houses from most other goods and helps disguise the fact that the production of building materials is as streamlined as that of auto parts. Bricks, cut lumber, pipes, nails, wire, drywall, and shingles, not to mention bathroom fittings, kitchen appliances, windows, and doors, are mill- or factory-made in large quantities. Some of these materials—bricks and lumber, for example—may be regarded as traditional, but their production has steadily been standardized and made more efficient. The introduction of grade-marking in lumber between the world wars had an enormous impact on its marketing, distribution, and use. Other materials are comparatively recent innovations—concrete only became widely used in residential construction around the turn of the twentieth century; drywall after World War II.

Any revolution in construction technology in North America, however, occurred in the mid-nineteenth century with the adoption of the technique of balloon framing. This simultaneously reduced the cost of construction and the skills required. By the early twentieth century, it had become widespread throughout most of North America while bricks and mortar was still the more costly norm in Europe.

In the twentieth century, some on-site experiments have been made with industrial assembly techniques as workers put together preassembled wall units that incorporate doors, windows, and wiring. Such techniques have never been used as widely in North America as in Europe, however, mainly because they offer few cost advantages over balloon framing. Instead, the comparative cheapness of wood encouraged companies to manufacture entire house kits. With detailed assembly instructions, these can be shipped anywhere by manufacturers.

In the early twentieth century, kits became a common and distinctive feature of North American construction. Since World War II, some of the same market has been met by the manufacturers of mobile homes. The name seems especially appropriate in a mobile nation like the United States today. Even though only about 10 percent are moved annually, mobile homes account for about one-fifth of the annual production of new dwelling units today.

The builders of the remaining four-fifths of new homes usually operate in one of three ways: on speculation, on contract, or for themselves. Speculative builders erect dwellings without having particular buyers in mind. Like the manufacturers of most consumer goods, they read "the market" and target particular segments that are always defined by income, and sometimes by age, family characteristics, ethnicity, and—less obtrusively—race. They pitch their advertising accordingly. Using an innovation developed in the 1920s, they build "model" homes to impress potential buyers.

In contrast, contractors are employed to do particular jobs for a specified sum. The employer may be a speculative builder, who "contracts out" instead of doing the work in-house, or a governmental agency wishing to produce publicly subsidized housing. The use of contractors is necessary for small builders whose scale of operation cannot support the profitable use of expensive equipment, such as backhoes. It is also widely used by larger builders who maximize their flexibility by minimizing their permanent workforce. Contractors are influenced by the same considerations, and the large ones subcontract particular jobs. These in turn may be further distributed in a complex social division of labor.

Some contractors are employed directly by the eventual homeowner, or the owner's agent, frequently an architect. In this manner, the owner is able to exert direct control over the construction process and get a house that suits his or her particular needs. Recognizing that "control" can be a selling point, and in an effort to reduce the risks of speculative construction, in recent years large builders have begun to offer customized versions of otherwise standard designs. Typically, buyers sign a contract and pay a deposit before the foundation is dug. In return, they are able to specify particular features and materials, and they are also able to monitor the construction process.

Together, speculative builders and contractors make up the building industry. In addition, many people build their own homes. This is especially true in the fringe areas of cities, in smaller towns, and in rural areas where building regulations are less stringent. Owner-builders operate in many different ways. At the extreme, they do everything themselves:

purchasing the land and materials, arranging the financing, designing their dwelling, shaping and assembling the materials. More typically, they purchase plans, seek advice from dealers, and contract out particular jobs, especially those that require special skills or equipment. At the extreme, they simply direct the work of others. The line between owner building and contractor building, then, easily becomes blurred.

These three methods of construction are associated with different segments of the housing market. Customized contractor building is most common at the top end of the market where prospective homeowners can afford the inefficiencies of having a unique home built for them, often under the supervision of an architect. In contrast, most of those who have built homes for themselves have done so because they could not afford to acquire a home in any other way. Erecting dwellings that can begin as shacks, many have very low incomes indeed. Speculative builders have always been most active in the middle segment of the market, where households can afford not to work on their own home, but where limited budgets have compelled them to accept fairly standard designs.

Over time, speculative building has grown at the expense of the alternatives. Owner building was common even in cities until the 1920s and made a brief but strong resurgence in the late 1940s and 1950s. A survey undertaken by the Bureau of Labor Statistics in 1949 found that one-third of new homes were owner-built that year. This was one of the most distinctive features of residential construction in Canadian and U.S. cities. It enabled many blue-collar workers who otherwise would have been unable to afford new homes in suburbs to settle there. The introduction, and eventual enforcement, of building regulations slowly eroded the practice. In the 1950s and 1960s, and to a lesser extent in more recent decades, the needs of some low-income home buyers were met by speculative builders who erected "shells." Buyers finish all or part of the interior when their time and money allow. This sort of building activity shades into home renovations, some of which are intended to make dwellings that the original builder had thought to be finished more livable.

The expanding operations of some speculative builders have made it possible to realize economies of scale. In developments like Levittown, builders make a small margin on each unit but thrive by building whole subdivisions at a time. Combined with the refinements to residential financing that were sponsored by the federal government during the 1930s, this speculative activity brought mortgaged homeownership within reach of many moderate-income households after World War II. The greater efficiencies of larger-scale production, and vertical integration, have also allowed speculative builders to move upmarket, especially by offering limited custom features to more affluent clients. One of the benefits that large builders have been able to offer well-to-do families is the planned, controlled, residential subdivision. These controls include standards for building and service, zoning, and large lots. In recent years, these have been supplemented by the construction of controlled-access subdivisions that are walled, gated, and privately policed. The growth of speculative construction has depended in part upon the integration of home building with land development, and many of the larger speculative builders are more properly regarded as land developers.

Although speculative building has become the norm, sweat equity and contracting remain important. One of the reasons that they have persisted in the face of competition from developers and from manufacturers of kits and mobile homes are the services provided by building-supply dealers. The construction industry is unusual in that, except for the largest companies, most producers of housing rely upon retailers for their raw materials. In the early twentieth century, competition from mail-order companies compelled lumber dealers to diversify, in effect providing a one-stop service to small builders. By the late 1940s, their services included not only a wide range of building supplies but also credit, job and product information, estimates on contracts, and house plans. They helped small builders compete with larger competitors.

Another strength of small builders in general is their greater flexibility. Construction is highly cyclical. It is more than usually dependent upon the general state of the economy, mainly because houses are durable and flexible in their use. In any year, construction adds only a small amount to the total stock of housing. For months, and even years, an increase in the demand for housing can be met by using the existing stock more intensively—by taking in lodgers or by subdividing existing dwellings. During boom periods, speculative activity expands in absolute and relative terms, as

*A young couple surveys a new house being built with balloon frame construction.*

erstwhile contractors become ambitious. During severe downturns, all builders are hurt, but those with substantial capital investments have usually been affected most of all. The share of speculative construction drops as builders go bankrupt or shed their workforce and return to contract work. This cyclical pattern places a premium on flexibility, and on subcontracting in particular. As long as severe economic downturns continue to occur, large builders are never likely to dominate the construction industry for very long.

This is especially true because so many Americans own their own homes. This virtually guarantees that some form of owner-labor, even if only in the form of do-it-yourself repairs and improvement, will remain common. Owners, as opposed to tenants, can easily repair their own home. They are also able to extend, or adapt, their dwelling to changing family needs, creating new space for a small business, elderly relatives, or paying tenants. For demographic reasons, and because of the recent growth of interest in historic preservation, an increasing proportion of all construction is being devoted to renovation rather than the production of new dwellings. Owners are able to do much of this themselves; pride in being handy, or the prospect of saving money, provide many with the incentive. For the remainder, the only alternative is to hire a contractor. In active renovation markets there have been local attempts to franchise residential contracting services, and speculative renovations of multiunit dwellings have been undertaken. Even here, however, it is usually the owner of the apartment building who takes the risk, not the company that actually undertakes the renovations. In general, the growth of home renovation favors the owner-builder and small contractor. Speculative activity may sometimes become the norm for home building, but it is unlikely to dominate residential construction activity as a whole.

—*Richard Harris*

**See also**
Balloon Frame Construction; Homeownership; Levittown; Mobile Home Communities; Single-Family Detached House.

**References**
Checkoway, Barry. "Large Builders, Federal Housing Programs, and Postwar Suburbanization." In Rachel G. Bratt, Chester Hartman, and Ann Meyerson, eds., *Critical Perspectives on Housing*. Philadelphia: Temple University Press, 1986.

Doucet, Michael, and John Weaver. *Housing the North American City*. Montreal and Kingston: McGill-Queen's University Press, 1991.

Harris, Richard. *Unplanned Suburbs: Toronto's American Tragedy, 1900–1950*. Baltimore: Johns Hopkins University Press, 1995.

Owen, David. *The Walls around Us: The Thinking Person's Guide to How a House Works*. New York: Random House, 1991.

Schlesinger, Tom, and Mark Erlich. "Housing: The Industry Capitalism Didn't Forget." In Rachel G. Bratt, Chester Hartman, and Ann Meyerson, eds., *Critical Perspectives on Housing*. Philadelphia: Temple University Press, 1986.

Warner, Sam Bass, Jr. *Streetcar Suburbs: The Process of Growth in Boston, 1870–1900*. Cambridge, MA: Harvard University Press, 1962.

## Residential Differentiation

Residential areas differ from one another in a number of ways, most notably in their social composition and the character of their housing stock. Such contrasts are closely related to social segregation. If one social group is segregated from the rest of the urban population, then there exists (at least) one neighborhood that contains a concentration of that group and that is therefore thought to be "different." Although segregation and differentiation may be viewed as two sides of the same coin, they should not be confused. It matters that a social group is segregated, for segregation can reflect and influence its relation to the larger society. What also matters, however, is where that group is segregated, for this affects its members' access to jobs, open space, and other urban resources.

In the United States, "segregation" often implies "racial segregation," but in fact it can refer to the separation of social groups of all kinds, including racial, ethnic, class, and gender. The same is true of residential differentiation. A district that contains an especially high concentration of a particular group may be referred to as a ghetto. In contemporary American usage, this term almost invariably has racial connotations, but in its European origins, and in America until about World War II, it was mainly used to denote a concentration of Jews. In the face of these changing popular images, it is useful to retain segregation and differentiation as general concepts that together define the social geography of the city.

Within any metropolitan area, similar types of neighborhoods tend to be clustered together. As a result, it is often possible to identify broad patterns of differentiation, for example between city and suburbs, or east side and west side. It has sometimes been said that North American cities differ from those in Latin America and many of those in Europe, in their characteristic pattern of inner-city poverty and suburban affluence. In fact, this pattern has emerged most strongly only in the past 50 years. It is not characteristic of every American city and in a number of cases is being halted, and even reversed, by gentrification.

The patterns of differentiation evident in contemporary cities are the outcome of diverse and changing processes. The most important of these are the changing importance and location of different types of workplaces; the availability and cost of different modes of transportation; and the changing assessments that Americans have made of inner-city, as opposed to suburban, living. Over the past century or so, employment has moved out of the central city into the suburbs, and beyond. This occurred first in "heavy," capital-intensive industries that required large sites; later in the case of lighter manufacturing industries, many of which clustered in industrial districts or parks; and last of all among offices. To some extent, this phased process of decentralization has drawn workers in its wake. In many cases, however, employees moved to suburbs while retaining jobs downtown. This suburban trend was made possible by the development of the horsecar and the commuter railroad in the mid-nineteenth century. Since these forms of transportation were affordable only for the middle and upper-middle classes, they tended to create suburbs that were more affluent than the city. The balance shifted with the widespread adoption of the electric streetcar during the 1890s and the automobile after World War I. These made commuting affordable to the masses and encouraged the growth of quite modest residential suburbs.

What made the suburban movement inevitable was the widespread preference among Americans, both native-born and immigrant, for suburban living. The ideal for the majority has long been to own a freestanding dwelling on as large a lot as possible. This ideal depends on fairly abundant, and comparatively cheap, suburban land. The preference for suburban life has long been combined with an active aversion for the city, expressed above all by affluent, white, native-born Americans. At the beginning of the twentieth century, this aversion was based upon the dirt, noise, and congestion of industrial cities; the corruption of city government; and disquiet about the rapid growth of immigration. Since World War II, "white flight" has reflected concerns about the expansion of inner-city African-American ghettos, high crime rates, and a deteriorating urban infrastructure. It has been facilitated by the exceptionally fragmented structure of local government, which has made possible the creation and maintenance of affluent suburban ghettos. It has also been tacitly encouraged by the federal government through homeowner tax subsidies.

These processes have been described, more or less adequately, in various influential "models"—or simplified accounts—of the social geography of the city. The first was that elaborated by Ernest W. Burgess in 1925 and based, in part, upon his knowledge of Chicago. Assuming that employment was concentrated downtown and that only quite affluent employees could afford to commute from new suburban homes, he suggested that the resulting pattern of residential differentiation would be one of successive rings of settlement. The poor would live close to the center while the affluent would cluster at the periphery. This model was tied to the assumption that an open border allowed a steady stream of immigrants to settle in poor, inner-city districts. As these immigrants, and their descendants, were assimilated and got better jobs, they would move into better housing in more peripheral neighborhoods. Thus, Burgess's rings described not only a class but also an ethnic geography.

It also implied an understanding of the housing market. Burgess assumed that as the city grew outward, new homes would be built for the affluent, who would thereby vacate more modest homes and neighborhoods closer in. These neighborhoods would be taken over by households with slightly lower incomes who had moved out of slightly less expensive districts. These, in turn, were resettled by families with still lower incomes, and so on. Burgess referred to this process as one of residential "succession." In its essentials, succession implies a process that later writers have referred to as "filtering"—over a period of decades, houses (and neighborhoods) filter down as they are occupied by a sequence of households with progressively lower incomes.

Although he did not use the term, Burgess, like many observers since, assumed that "filtering" is the process by which lower-income families are housed. As an account of the processes shaping the urban geography of his day, Burgess's model has been criticized on a number of grounds. The most significant of these is the unrealistic assumption that employment is concentrated downtown, coupled with the belief that low-income families are housed only by a process of filtering and succession. In fact, by the mid-1920s, a great many manufacturing jobs had already moved to the suburbs, while owner building allowed many workers to follow suit.

A more descriptively accurate model was presented by Homer Hoyt in 1938. Based on extensive analysis of rent patterns in numerous cities, Hoyt concluded that residential differentiation often followed a sectoral, as well as a partial ring, pattern. He found high- and low-rent sectors (or wedges) extending, in some cases, from the center of the city all the way out to the fringe. High-rent sectors might follow an attractive topographic feature, such as Chicago's North Shore along Lake Michigan, while low-rent sectors often followed radial rail routes and their attendant industries. Interpreting his results, Hoyt showed a clear understanding of the geography of transportation and employment, but his references to filtering failed to account either for the persistence of older high-rent areas or for the emergence of new low-rent districts in the suburbs. Subsequently, Walter Firey explained the former in terms of the influence of enduring social prestige, while Chauncy Harris has interpreted the latter in terms of owner-building by lower-income workers.

As urban growth continued in the twentieth century, the declining rate of annexation meant that city-centered urban areas became polycentric metropolitan regions. The early stages of this development were interpreted by Harris and E. L. Ullman in 1945 when they recognized that subsidiary centers of employment might be older towns that had been absorbed by the expansion of an adjacent city or by entirely new spin-offs of urban growth. The implication was that patterns of residential differentiation were becoming very complex. This has been extensively documented by a generation of scholars who have employed computers to analyze tract data published in the decennial census. One of the most comprehensive analyses ever undertaken, however, shows that zonal patterns have persisted to a surprising extent in terms of homeownership levels, home values, income, family status, and, to a lesser extent, race. Occupation tends to show a sectoral pattern, while ethnicity, immigrant status, and also race show appreciable clustering. Although Burgess's model may still have some relevance to our understanding of residential differentiation, the links between class and ethnicity are evidently far more complex than he assumed.

Over the past half-century, the creation of entirely new centers of suburban employment, dubbed "Edge Cities" by Joel Garreau in 1991, has proceeded apace. The amount of segregation has not changed much. Residential areas are still most clearly differentiated on the basis of race, to a lesser extent ethnicity, and least of all in terms of occupational class. A comparatively recent development in a few larger cities is the emergence of gay and lesbian ghettos. This development, coupled with the polycentric decentralization of jobs, and the effects of the ubiquitous automobile, have created a more complex pattern of residence, one that defies simple description.

A further complication has been the recent emergence of a taste for inner-city living on the part, especially, of affluent professionals. This has led to the selective gentrification of inner-city neighborhoods in a number of places. Gentrification entails the renovation of old dwellings as well as the construction of new. The associated process of "filtering up" has reversed the dominant trend. It has stabilized, and in some cases begun to reduce, the social contrasts between city and suburb. The extent of gentrification varies greatly from place to place depending, to a large extent, on the health of the local economy and, in particular, the rate of growth of downtown office employment. It depends as much upon the convenience of being close to work as it does upon a preference for urban lifestyles, and it is not clear that the latter will spread, or even endure. As the baby-boom generation of once-young professionals belatedly has children, safer and more spacious suburbs have begun to exert an attraction. The residential geography of the city is still shaped by the popular appeal of the suburban frontier.

—*Richard Harris*

**See also**
Desegregation of Housing; Gentrification; Ghetto; Housing Segregation.
**References**
Burgess, Ernest W. "The Growth of the City." In Robert E. Park, Ernest W. Burgess, and R. D. MacKenzie, *The City.* Chicago: University of Chicago Press, 1925.
Firey, Walter. *Land Use in Central Boston.* Cambridge, MA: Harvard University Press, 1947.
Garreau, Joel. *Edge City: Life on the New Urban Frontier.* New York: Doubleday, 1991.
Harris, Chauncy, and E. L. Ullman. "The Nature of Cities." *Annals of the American Academy of Political and Social Science* 242 (1945): 7–17.
Harris, Richard. "Self-Building and the Social Geography of Toronto, 1901–1913: A Challenge for Urban Theory." *Transactions of the Institute of British Geographers* NS 15 (1990): 387–402.
Harvey, David. "Social Processes and Spatial Form: The Redistribution of Real Income in an Urban System." In *Social Justice and the City,* ch. 2. London: Arnold, 1973.
Hoyt, Homer. *The Structure and Growth of Residential Neighborhoods in American Cities.* Washington, DC: Federal Housing Administration, 1939.
Smith, Neil, and Peter Williams, eds. *Gentrification of the City.* Boston: Allen & Unwin, 1986.
White, M. J. *American Neighborhoods and Residential Differentiation.* New York: Russell Sage Foundation, 1987.

## Residential Mobility

In modern times, the residential relocation of families and individuals has been the prime generator of urban population growth. Birthrates in American cities were low, compared to those in rural areas, and were usually offset by death rates, so natural increase explains very little of the population explosion that caused a city like Chicago to grow from 3,000 people to more than 1 million in just over 50 years. Annexations, particularly in the late nineteenth and early twentieth centuries, accounted for some of the new residents, but net migration, more than any other factor, contributed the most. But focusing just on net migration masks the extraordinary amount of total movement that has characterized American cities. An increase in a city's population of, say, 10,000 people over one decade may have resulted from the total movements of 50,000 or more individuals who flowed into and out of that city during the decade. And even this number represents only the tip of the iceberg because it does not include the enormous numbers of people who moved from one residence to another inside the city.

The issue of residential mobility divides into three analytical questions: How many people moved? Why did they move? What effects did their movements have? Measuring residential change has challenged American historians because of the phenomenal frequency with which urban dwellers have moved. Unlike some European countries, no American government agency, federal or otherwise, has kept registers that historians could use to tabulate the frequency of movement from one place to another or within the same place. Still, by using nineteenth- and early-twentieth-century decennial censuses to estimate how many of a city's residents at one point in time still lived there ten years later, historians have discovered that between 40 and 60 percent of the urban population left their community over the course of a decade. In 1940, the U.S. Census Bureau estimated that one in five Americans moved every year, and historians have generally agreed that this ratio has been constant for much of recent

American history, and many believe the ratio was closer to one in four before the twentieth century.

Using annual city directories, a few historians have been able to trace the moves that individuals and families made within one city. In places as diverse as Omaha, Nebraska, and Providence, Rhode Island, in the late 1800s and early 1900s, people normally occupied three or more dwellings in a 20-year period. Similar studies suggest that this frequency of residential mobility was constant in other cities at other times. Some people moved many more times, but generally instability was a common phenomenon among all neighborhoods and all social, economic, and ethnic groups.

Determining why people move is a difficult and complicated issue. Demographers explain migration in terms of "push" factors, such as overpopulation and economic distress, that drive a person or family away from one place, and "pull" factors, such as job opportunities and relatives who have already moved, that lure a person or family someplace else. Historians, unable to ask people why they moved, have focused on the kinds of people who moved most frequently: the young, the unmarried, the unskilled, and those who rented rather than owned their homes. The result has been the identification of a "floating proletariat" in American cities, a group of low-status persons who moved from place to place many times without ever improving their lot in life. Sociologists, using more sophisticated methods on more recent patterns of residential change, have developed more elaborate models to explain movement. Adopting the assumption that most people act rationally, sociologists have applied a "stress-threshold" interpretation, according to which a person first determines his or her satisfaction with the current residence, then examines the alternatives, and ultimately decides to move or stay on the basis of the comparison between the current residence and the alternatives. This model would appear to work with regard to the history of American cities, but historians have yet to apply it.

The effects of residential mobility have made American cities extraordinarily dynamic places. The constant turnover of their populations has enabled cities and neighborhoods to receive and exchange new ideas, new capital, and new institutions. In this way, cities like Philadelphia in the eighteenth century, Chicago in the nineteenth century, and Miami in the twentieth century became burgeoning centers of opportunity. Moreover, in the American vernacular, movement has always implied improvement, and the residential shifts made by countless families have taken them to better quarters and better neighborhoods. When other avenues to social betterment were closed, the possibilities of more space and improved facilities still beckoned. In places as diverse as Newburyport, Massachusetts, in the nineteenth century and Boston in the early twentieth century, many working-class families increased their wealth by acquiring property even when their occupational status did not rise.

But there have been costs as well as benefits from residential change. Some people, protective of the results of their own movement, have resented attempts by others, particularly racial and ethnic minorities, to seek the same advantages. Residents of colonial New England towns passed laws to prohibit unwanted individuals from moving in, violence erupted along the borders of immigrant neighborhoods in Philadelphia in the 1850s, and in the twentieth century wealthier urban groups have used zoning laws and restrictive covenants to prevent African Americans from moving into certain districts. The resulting segregation and conflict have disrupted American urban life for three centuries. In some instances as well, urban political and labor organizations have had difficulty mounting sustained campaigns because their constituents were constantly changing, although in other instances, constant membership turnover enabled a stable core to retain power over the organization. Frequent residential change, especially from urban centers to the periphery and suburbs, has also resulted in the removal of human and capital resources from older, inner-city neighborhoods, thereby accelerating the process of economic and physical decline that has plagued American cities in the late twentieth century. Perhaps most importantly, the continuous American tradition of freedom of movement has nurtured the notion of housing as a commodity, to be freely bought and sold (with hope of profit), occupied and used up, rather than as a resource that might attract some kind of relatively permanent commitment. Urban real estate markets and residential mobility have been mutually reinforcing forces throughout American history.

Until recently, most analysts viewed residential change unfavorably. Influenced by the ideas of early sociologists at the University of Chicago, historians and other social scientists identified the residentially mobile as "marginal" people who were disorganized in their attitudes and behavior and whose constant movement disrupted neighborhood stability, making it difficult for viable urban communities to form. But other scholars have begun to assert that a community need is not necessarily a place-based phenomenon; in spite of all their movements, residents of places like mid-nineteenth-century New York and mid-twentieth-century Los Angeles formed "unbounded communities" with relatives and/or friends who provided means of support and association that were more important than those that people could obtain—or which eluded them—in their immediate neighborhoods. Clearly many urban dwellers had their lives disrupted by residential change and suffered loneliness, lack of attachment, and other distresses. But residential mobility more often was a rational and desired action, bringing people into more comfortable living spaces and leading them to better security and a deeper understanding of city life. American urban societies benefited from the new resources and ideas of population turnover more than they suffered. In this way, residential change was more of a *re*-organizing than a *dis*-organizing factor that gave American cities their most dynamic quality.

—*Howard P. Chudacoff*

**See also**
Migration from Rural to Urban Areas.
**References**
Chudacoff, Howard P. *Mobile Americans: Residential and Social Mobility in Omaha, 1880–1920.* New York: Oxford University Press, 1972.
Knights, Peter R. *Yankee Destinies: The Lives of Ordinary Nineteenth-Century Bostonians.* Chapel Hill: University of North Carolina Press, 1991.
Rossi, Peter H. *Why Families Move.* 2d ed. Beverly Hills, CA: Sage Publications, 1988.
Speare, Alden, Jr., Sidney Goldstein, and William H. Frey. *Residential Mobility, Migration, and Metropolitan Changes.* Cambridge, MA: Ballinger, 1975.
Thernstrom, Stephan. *Poverty and Progress: Social Mobility in a Nineteenth-Century City.* Cambridge, MA: Harvard University Press, 1964.

## Resort Towns

Resorts represent a unique form of urban development and structure. They are "landscapes of leisure" created the world over by the growth of tourism, and have developed within both historical and geographical contexts.

The story of modern tourism and resorts is the story of a social revolution. The progressively broadening participation in the trek to the sea or the mountains for recreation occurred in the middle decades of the nineteenth century due to the coincidence in timing of technological and social changes. Railroads brought recreational sites within reach of most classes and satisfied the demand for recreation by an ever-growing sector of society who had increased leisure and the means to enjoy it.

Before the Industrial Revolution, resorts were relatively small, based as they were on the patronage of leisured classes. Preindustrial European resorts were usually inland towns located near a mineral spring. People went to the springs, or spas, for recreation in addition to seeking relief from various physical ailments; the spas provided socialization among the leisure classes and featured music and other entertainment. The medicinal aspects of these springs may have been simply an excuse for having a good time in societies that then frowned on travel for pleasure alone.

In the late eighteenth and early nineteenth centuries, the popularity of inland spas began to be supplanted by seashore and mountain resorts. The seashore, once an exposed front line of defense, and therefore vulnerable to attack, became relatively safe at the end of the Napoleonic Era in Europe and after the War of 1812 in America. Mountain resorts began to appeal as the Romantic movement in literature and the arts produced a new appreciation of wild, untamed nature.

At about the same time, transportation contributed to the development of new leisure sites. Tourism obviously requires movement across space and therefore demands transportation. The Industrial Revolution produced two great innovations in the steamboat and the railroad, both of which greatly reduced the amount of time and money needed to travel. It became easier, faster, and cheaper to go somewhere for pleasure, and a day by the sea or mountain lake came within the financial reach of a great many people. Industrialization not only provided faster transportation that linked growing urban, industrial populations with expanding resorts, but it also generated rising incomes that enabled many to become tourists, at least for a day.

The inland spas, tightly focused on a mineral spring, were not readily expandable to accommodate increasing hoards of tourists. The pretension that one was traveling for medical treatment, rather than for fun, did not long persist in the age of mass tourism. Although some doctors did prescribe sea bathing and even drinking salt water for their supposedly curative effects, it quickly became clear that treats rather than treatments motivated most seashore visitors.

As the development of transportation technology and systems reduced the time and distance costs of travel, progressively lower-income groups were able to patronize any particular resort. For example, when Coney Island first became a major seaside resort, it catered almost exclusively to those wealthy enough to own carriages. By 1847, a steamboat connected Manhattan with Coney Island, bringing more middle-class passengers. During the Civil War, horsecars brought Manhattan even closer to the beach in terms of time and cost; electric trolleys followed, further diminishing costs. The extension of New York City's subway system to Coney Island completed the process of transforming that resort into one accessible to virtually the entire population of the metropolitan area. Thus, the socioeconomic orientation of any particular resort is often tied directly to its relative accessibility, in both contemporary and historical contexts. The specific technology changes, but the relationship between increased accessibility and decreased time and distance costs, on the one hand, and the specific socioeconomic traits of tourists, on the other, continues in evidence. Each new form of transportation helps to promote development of an array of resorts. Just as the railroad "created" resorts like Atlantic City, the automobile and the jet plane were instrumental in the development of such resorts as Disney World, Las Vegas, Cancun, and Honolulu.

*The reliance of Aspen, Colorado, on skiing and other winter sports becomes obvious when the finish of a skiing race is situated in the very center of town.*

All resorts exhibit one salient morphological feature. The part of town that proclaims its social and economic nature and, at the same time, marks it as a resort is the character of its tourist-oriented business district. For example, in seaside resorts the area immediately adjacent to the water has been the linear focus of visitors' interests and activities; the seafront is the central economic zone of a seaside resort. Lakeside mountain resorts have a similar linear aggregation of hotels, eating establishments, entertainment facilities, and specialized vacationer-oriented retail shops. Here, as elsewhere, form and function interact.

The social qualities of a resort town are reflected in its "face"—the leisure-oriented facade. Middle-class summer cottage communities may present a sedate, small-town appearance, while upper-income resorts might be typified by a complex of luxury hotels, expensive restaurants, and, perhaps, exclusive casinos. In resorts that appeal to the working class, the leisure-oriented business district is commonly developed very intensively. Inexpensive food and souvenir stalls stand side by side with mechanical amusements, candy, and novelty shops.

The blend of retail establishments and their distribution among districts indicates a town's status as a resort and the degree of dominance of its resort functions. Most sizable towns possess a central business district (CBD), suburban malls, shopping thoroughfares, neighborhood shopping districts, minor centers, and isolated retail nodes. To this long array of urban retail trade districts, the recreational business district or RBD must be added in a resort town. This area is the seasonally busy, linear complex of restaurants, specialty food stands, candy stores, and novelty and souvenir shops that cater to tourists' demands for leisurely shopping and entertainment. Tourists and seasonal residents provide, in varying degree, business for most of a resort's retailers; the RBD, however, exists almost completely on patronage by tourists. The almost total seasonal closing of RBD establishments in the "off season" attests to this specific tourist orientation.

The RBD is a social phenomenon as well as an economic one. It provides a means of entertaining, as a unit, family members who might not otherwise participate together in various forms of amusement or shop with each other in a relaxed atmosphere. To the prevalent desire to take home visible evidence of visits to a resort must be added the social activity of casual shopping for resort clothing and decorative items. Vacationers spend a considerable portion of their leisure time, particularly in evenings, shopping for such goods, resulting in a concentration of gift and variety stores in RBDs. The relative dominance of luxury shopping versus commercial amusements and inexpensive fast-food restaurants within various RBDs is an indicator of the social status and image of different resorts.

Several geographers have documented the evolution of resorts or tourist regions. The cycle begins with an exploration stage in which a few adventurous tourists "discover" the resort potential of an area not yet equipped with facilities for visitors. In the involvement stage, local people perceive that tourism is a desirable, logical, and likely profitable use of local environmental resources, a beach for example. Basic recreational facilities and visitor accommodations are created. If the involvement phase is the "takeoff" of an area's career as a resort, then the third stage, development, is the period of accelerating investment in expansion. Typically in the development stage, outsiders control the tourist trade through large-scale investment and providing more experienced management. The tourist hinterland or customer supply area is expanded with better access to transportation and by advertising. By the fourth stage, consolidation, tourism has triumphed as a major (sometimes, the only) industry, but growth rates have begun to level off from the hectic expansion of development. Some older facilities have become obsolete and inferior. In the fifth stage, stagnation, peak numbers of visitors arrive. This stage, which is not inevitable, marks a crisis for any resort because it means that the resort is losing appeal. No longer fashionable, the resort no longer attracts consistent reinvestment to modernize the visitor-service infrastructure, much less new facilities.

The nature of seaside or lakeside tourism, based as it is on shorelines, tends to create strongly linear resort zones. When these attractive shores are accessible to nearby cities with high average incomes that facilitate leisure and recreation away from home, an intensely developed strip of resorts may follow. Such seashore resort strips may be termed a "leisureopolis." Examples of leisureopolis can be found on the New Jersey shore, Cape Cod, portions of Long Island, the southeast coast of England, and the French and Italian Rivieras. A leisureopolis also possesses the characteristic of filling empty areas between older urban centers, which now form a continuous urbanized region.

—*Charles A. Stansfield, Jr.*

**See also**
Coney Island; Disneyland.
**References**
Funnell, Charles. *By the Beautiful Sea: The Rise and High Times of That Great American Resort, Atlantic City.* New York: Knopf, 1975.
Jakle, John. *The Tourist: Travel in Twentieth-Century North America.* Lincoln: University of Nebraska Press, 1985.
Matheson, Alister, and Geoffrey Wall. *Tourism: Economic, Physical and Social Impacts.* London: Longman, 1982.
Pearce, Douglas. *Tourist Development.* London: Longman, 1981.
Stansfield, Charles. *New Jersey: A Geography.* Boulder, CO: Westview Press, 1983.
Theroux, Paul. *The Kingdom by the Sea.* Boston: Houghton Mifflin, 1983.

## Restaurants

In the simplest terms, restaurants are places to buy and eat meals, but restaurants are more than that. From the perspective of management, a restaurant is part of the larger industrial web of manufacturing and employment. Restaurants and restaurant-support industries contribute nearly 5 percent to the gross national product of the United States. Today, as in years past, restaurants offer jobs to unskilled immigrants, older adolescents, or native-born populations. For customers, a restaurant can mean anything from "fast food" to "gourmet" food. A restaurant can be pleasing because of its atmosphere or a friendly face.

The restaurant scene is a canvas on which to view the American city, its people, and its connections to the hinterland over time and space. Cities have been a place of opportunity; some cities have always been rich and have always attracted a wide variety of ethnic groups. Americans have always been mobile, and in terms of restaurants, these facts have translated into a clientele with money to spend, new tastes to satisfy, and a wide variety of available dining experiences.

Spatially, urban macroscale variations are obvious as regional restaurant fare is still popular. From barbecue pits in the Southeast and beef houses in the Great Plains to fish houses in the Pacific Northwest, eating out has not been totally flattened by mass communications. Diverse opportunities in dining allow Americans to choose from as many as 50 ethnic menus in large cities and as many as 100 different restaurant cuisines.

In urban areas, the restaurant landscape has continually evolved to meet the demands of changing tastes and needs. While dining rooms for the rich established themselves by the middle of the nineteenth century, the popularity of inns and taverns in early America made way for the pushcart, cafe, and fast-food franchise. On this changing landscape, types of eateries have endeared themselves to different parts of the population. The classic diner stirs feelings of nostalgia for people of the Northeast. Its very existence mirrored technology and innovation—America on the move. Yet, diner operators state unequivocally that it was primarily the food that pulled people in, not the classic car of media fame; therefore, the structure changed periodically to keep up with taste and technology. After all, they will tell you, "business is business," and they are right.

The restaurant business is highly competitive. Nationally, approximately 92 percent of all restaurants fail. What's new in the restaurant arena? Fast food is more popular than ever, but there is also a trend developing for moderately priced, family-oriented, chain restaurants. Family dining, ethnic cuisine, and a reaffirmation of regional specialization have all taken hold. This is obvious by noticing chains that specialize in steaks, Mexican food, or California cuisine.

Finally, the restaurant in the heart of the city is ultimately connected to the broader geography of the agricultural hinterland. Whether or not the corn or wheat belt provides a topic of conversation for the 50 percent of American adults who eat out once a day, it must be remembered that most Americans have rarely had to ask, "Will there be enough food?"

—*Joseph T. Manzo*

**References**
"Dining through the Decades: Special Commemorative Issue—75 Years." *Restaurant News.*
Luxenberg, Stan. *Roadside Empires: How the Chains Franchised America.* New York: Penguin Books, 1986.
Manzo, Joseph T. "From Pushcart to Modular Restaurant: The Diner on the Landscape." *Journal of American Culture* 13 (1990): 13–23.
Pillsbury, Richard. *From Boardinghouse to Bistro: The American Restaurant Then and Now.* Boston: Unwin Hyman, 1990.
Tangires, Helen. "American Lunch Wagons." *Journal of American Culture* 13 (1990): 91–109.

## Reston, Virginia

Reston, Virginia, located 18 miles west of Washington, D.C., promotes itself as a "decidedly urban, even sophisticated, new town." Placed in Fairfax County, Virginia, this model of urban/suburban development has gone through three phases since its founding in 1962 while still remaining faithful to the original plans of its mastermind, Robert E. Simon, Jr. (1914– ). Simon persuaded the county to adopt radically new zoning, the first of its kind in the nation, for a "residential planned community" with mixed densities and uses.

In 1956, the A. Smith Bowman family realized that their huge farm was sitting on a major urban corridor in the Metropolitan Region's Year 2000 Plan, and they hired a Washington firm to plan a satellite city for 30,000 people there. The project failed because the projected town's sewerage would have polluted the Potomac River and the capital's water supply. Shortly afterward, the federal government announced plans to build a new international airport nearby and an access road that would cut the property in half. In 1960, the Bowmans sold their property for $20 million to Lefcourt Realty, which immediately sold it to Simon.

Simon's family owned large amounts of land in New York City, including Carnegie Hall, an area he considered the ideal of vibrant urban living. His father had played a role in financing Radburn, New Jersey, the first "garden city" in 1929, and the idea of developing a satellite city captured his imagination. In 1961, with a small down payment from the sale of Carnegie Hall, Simon entered the Reston project as part of a deal involving almost $13 million. Gulf Oil was the chief lender, and no government money was involved.

Simon hired Harland Bartholomew & Associates of St. Louis, the nation's largest planning firm, to design a master plan that met his specifications. The new town was to have 13 neighborhoods designed for 5,000 residents each, but county officials balked. Simon complained that "present zoning ordinances [were] largely responsible for the diffusion of our communities into separate, unrelated hunks without focus, identity, or community life" and produced "chaos on our highways, monotony in our subdivisions, ugliness in our shopping centers . . . because of the subdivision's separation from commercial and recreational facilities." In response to the county's negative reply, Simon hired the New York firm of Whittlesey & Conklin to "flesh out" the Bartholomew plan. Julian Whittlesey, who had previously worked with Clarence Stein and Lewis Mumford, reduced the number of village clusters to seven, each housing 10,000 residents to achieve an urban feel but with each having its own motif.

In July of 1962, Fairfax County accepted the new idea of "density zoning" (11 people per acre). Work began on the first village center on Lake Anne, "a boldly urban statement" not to be confused with suburbia. Washington Plaza featured the 15-story Heron House (1964), "an architectural exclamation point" with apartments, shops, restaurants, and an art gallery to satisfy Simon's insistence on public art. The first family moved to Reston in 1964, as did Simon, no longer a distant CEO. A nursery school/kindergarten opened in 1965 and an elementary school in 1967.

Reston blends different types of residence with service areas, cultural amenities, and businesses to provide local jobs for one-third of its residents, thus satisfying one of Simon's primary aims. Houses, townhouses, and apartments cluster in neighborhoods arranged around four man-made lakes. They are interspersed with glades of trees amid rolling hills and lawns and united by systems of pedestrian paths and bicycle trails that lead to common recreational facilities. Reston has 19 swimming pools; uncounted tennis courts, playgrounds, and tot lots, not to mention baseball, soccer, and football fields; two golf courses; and a community center. Trails converge on a nature center that is part of the 850 acres of open space—one-ninth of the entire town and part of Simon's commitment to allocate ten acres of parks for every 1,000 residents, twice the national standard.

Reston was Simon's baby, and his Seven Goals, a manifesto, emphasized leisure and privacy, permanency and heterogeneity, natural and structural beauty, financial stability, unity of life and work, individual dignity, and all amenities provided from the start. He even wanted to include and blend compatible light industry into Reston, but the county refused. During its first decade, Reston housed only small businesses.

In 1963 social policy was added to the goals of "Reston's Proposed Income Mix"; it now included diversity of age and family composition with mores and taste as the criteria for those who desired "urban living in a rural setting." The Reston Community Fund, later the Reston Foundation for Community Programs, set up churches, schools, libraries, health care, housing for the elderly, and special environmental education, theatrical, and music programs—utopian social planning achieved slowly during the 1980s. The Common Ground Foundation provided community services such as local buses, space for religious services, youth employment, counseling, and a coffeehouse. Simon and his associates promoted and emphasized volunteerism as central to the "Reston Spirit."

Simon also stipulated architectural creativity. The cubistic three-story townhouses with bright accents near the tin roofs and pastel hues of the Waterview Cluster took their inspiration from the Dutch modernist de Stijl movement; Chloethiel Smith had designed it to resemble a Mediterranean fishing village. Charles Goodman's colorful Hickory Cluster is urban contemporary. Conklin and Rossant embellished 47 townhouses in the quayside with Chimney House gothic detail. Tall Oaks, atop ravines, is inspired by European hill towns. Hunters' Woods has an equestrian theme, linked to shopping by horse paths, although the "horsy" ideal never caught on.

Reston did not grow in the late 1960s and provided housing for only 2,500 residents in 370 houses and 370 apartments. Simon had undertaken more than he could handle, and in 1967 Gulf Oil, his primary creditor, ousted him and claimed that Reston was just too big for him to supervise alone. Gulf Reston, Inc. (GRI) installed managers to tighten finances and market aggressively, an action that spurred early residents to organize to preserve Simon's ideals, including nondiscrimination in housing, bringing in health care, and establishing express commuter buses to Washington, D.C. GRI also consolidated the Home Owners Associations of Lake Anne and Hunters' Woods, claiming its goal was unifying the town. It developed the Forest Edge section with standardized, marketable designs, and it opened the Hunters' Woods Village Center, as multifunctional as a settlement house, and the Reston International Center by 1973. Nevertheless, by 1977 GRI had to sell some buildings and apartment clusters.

During these hard times, conflicts began to develop between GRI and town residents. Gulf Reston resisted popular desire to form a limited town government because it feared that a government would tax businesses more heavily. Also, residents often clashed with GRI's CEO, William H. Magness, who was experienced in developing oil company towns abroad. However, Magness did put Reston on a solid financial footing while retaining most of Simon's plans.

But Gulf, itself in financial crisis, retrenched and sought to sell Reston in 1979. The Mobil Corporation purchased 3,700 acres of undeveloped land for $31 million. Gulf sold the rest to Donatelli and Klein and Mark Winkler Management of Alexandria, Virginia, for an additional $40 million. Mobil created the Reston Land Company (RLC) and launched an era of explosive growth. It subcontracted marketing to Coldwell Banker Real Estate, which attracted the first of many large companies to the town. At that time, Virginia had just funded a new toll road to Dulles International Airport (completed in 1984), and the bulk of Reston's industry clusters on the south side of the highway, only five miles away. International computer and telecommunications firms have made Reston their corporate headquarters and a major high tech center on the East Coast. The Reston Board of Commerce lured them with good transportation systems, protective covenants, architectural controls, and promises of a highly educated female workforce eager for part-time work. By 1991, 2,100 companies were employing 34,000 residents of Reston, and it was projected that 3,000 firms and 50,000 jobs would make Reston Virginia's second largest business center. More than 40 percent of the residents worked in Reston, surpassing Simon's goal. In the meantime, Mobil has sold most of its original land, some at 25 times the purchase price.

By 1986, Mobil considered the original Village Center too small and outdated, more in terms of the amenities marketable to corporate clients than for residents. RTKL Associates of Baltimore along with Sasaki Associates of Boston won the design competition for a new town center, and its first phase was completed by 1990. Centering on Fountain Square, Market Street has the feel of an old-fashioned Main Street transformed by postmodernism. By 1991 Reston's 22 churches, two synagogues, 47 restaurants, 28 banks, 12 hotels, and 24 child-care centers served 54,000 residents living in 18,600 units. Projections at "buildout" are for 62,000 people in 22,000 units.

—*Blanche M. G. Linden*

### References

Grubisich, Tom, and Peter McCandless. *Reston: The First Twenty Years.* Reston, VA: Reston Publishing, 1985.

Hays, Allison Feiss. "Reston, Virginia, 1964–1984: An Evaluation of the New Town in Terms of Robert E. Simon's Original Goals." Master of Urban and Regional Planning thesis, George Washington University, 1985.

Klauber, Martin, et al. *Reston, Virginia.* Washington, DC: George Washington University, 1967.

Kulski, Julian E. *Reston, Virginia: Analysis of a New Community.* Washington, DC: Graduate Program in Urban and Regional Planning, George Washington University, 1967.

Larson, Nancy. *A History of Reston, Virginia's Unique Community.* Reston, VA: New Town Publications, 1981.

McCandless, Peter. *A Brief History of Reston, Virginia.* Reston, VA: Gulf Reston, 1973.

Netherton, Nan, *Reston: A New Town in the Old Dominion: A Pictorial History.* Norfolk, VA: Donning Company, 1989.

Simon, Robert E., Jr. *The Reston Story.* Fairfax, VA: Victor Weingarten, 1962.

Stone, Kathryn H. *Reston: A Study in Beginning: A History of Reston from the Purchase of Land in 1961 to the Period of First Occupancy in 1964.* 2 vols. Washington, DC: Washington Center for Metropolitan Studies, 1966.

## Restrictive Deed Covenants

Restrictive deed covenants (also known as *deed restrictions* or *restrictive covenants*) are those obligations that limit or control the use of a piece of property and that have been written into the deed conveying that property. Because they have been inserted into a deed of property, restrictive covenants are part of the contract between two private individuals—the seller and the buyer of the property. As such, they are essentially a private means to control land use; by inserting them the seller determines some aspect of how the land may be used by other owners in the future. These restrictions are inserted into deeds when the ownership of land is transferred, and their effectiveness at controlling development stems from their application to all the lots in a subdivision. Although they are often viewed as a precursor to public land use control by zoning, the two techniques of controlling land use may exist simultaneously and have no legal relationship to each other.

Their provisions may differ, but property owners are bound by both the private contract and the public law.

Restrictive covenants have appeared in American property deeds since early times, but their greatest impact dates from the late nineteenth century. Realizing that the value of property hinges at least partly on its surroundings, land developers began using deed restrictions for three primary purposes: to prevent waste (so that buildings were not erected in a dedicated right-of-way or easement), to stabilize land value, and to provide amenities. Initially, developers used restrictive covenants to prevent nuisances such as tanneries, saloons, or slaughterhouses. They then expanded their use of restrictions to prohibit all business activity in areas intended for residential development or to designate specific lots in a subdivision for particular uses, such as single-family homes, duplexes, apartments, or small shops. By determining land use before construction, developers shaped urban and suburban spatial structure.

Land developers have controlled more than a structure's use. Deed restrictions can also specify a building's size (by height, lot coverage, or floor area), its placement on a lot, construction materials or design, and cost. Moreover, for decades land developers also controlled who could own or use land and could bar people and uses they considered undesirable. Until the U.S. Supreme Court ruled these deed restrictions not legally enforceable in *Shelley v. Kramer* in 1948, developers routinely inserted covenants prohibiting certain individuals from owning, leasing, renting, or even occupying property on the basis of race, ethnicity, religion, national origin, or citizenship.

Being part of a deed, restrictive covenants became part of the public record of the property itself and were thus binding on all future purchasers. To shape development effectively and withstand legal scrutiny, restrictive covenants had to apply to all lots in a subdivision according to some identifiable plan, not contradict public policy, and be "reasonable" (in the sense of being what an "average" person would expect in similar circumstances). Restrictions were on safer legal ground if they specified an expiration date (by month, day, and year) or period (such as 25 or 50 years after the subdivision was filed or the property transferred). To effect what was essentially perpetual control, some developers provided for the automatic renewal of covenants for successive periods unless a majority of the property owners covered voted otherwise. Since they were a part of private contracts, enforcing deed restrictions required legal action by either the seller of the property or by other property owners covered by the same restrictions. Although legal scholars have debated the use of municipal power to enforce deed restrictions (which amounts to using a public authority for a private purpose), municipal enforcement has been the principal means in at least one major American city (Houston).

Deed restrictions initially gained great popularity in the late nineteenth and early twentieth centuries. In a time of rapid urban growth and increasing immigration, developers sought to stabilize land values by stabilizing land use. At the same time, middle- and upper-income people sought sanctuary from the noise, dirt, and congestion of cities. Developers thus planned exclusive subdivisions in picturesque locations; provided curving avenues, spacious lots, forested parkland, and reserves; and used restrictive covenants to ensure that upper-income families built attractive homes. Riverside, Illinois, Roland Park, Maryland, Shaker Heights, Ohio, and Kansas City's Country Club District all benefited from extensive deed restrictions. With stability ensured, developers also used restrictions as a marketing device and charged a premium for lots in restricted subdivisions; they assured prospective buyers that the value of property would not fall due to the presence of people or activities they considered unpleasant. By earmarking parts of the city—or even entire suburbs—for restricted subdivision development, developers shaped the social structure of urban areas as well as their spatial structure, for they determined who would and would not live in certain places.

Although restrictive deed covenants had no legal relationship to zoning, developers who used them often supported the adoption of municipal zoning to gain a second layer of security for property values and to protect tracts that they themselves did not own. Even after zoning was adopted and annexation policies after World War II brought more undeveloped land under municipal control than before, land developers continued to insert restrictive covenants into deeds. Instead of developing primarily for exclusivity, however, they were planning some developments for upper- or upper-middle-income households and others for moderate income families who might be buying their first home with an FHA- or VA-backed mortgage. They were thus planning for segregation by socioeconomic class.

Through the use of restrictive deed covenants over several decades, land developers stabilized property values while shaping metropolitan areas, frequently not in accordance with professed American social and political values.

—*Patricia Burgess*

### References

Burgess, Patricia. *Planning for the Private Interest: Land Use Controls and Residential Patterns in Columbus, Ohio, 1900–1970.* Columbus: Ohio State University Press, 1994.

Delafons, John. *Land-Use Controls in the United States.* 2d ed. Cambridge, MA: MIT Press, 1969.

Ellickson, Robert C. "Alternatives to Zoning: Covenants, Nuisance Rules, and Fines as Land Use Controls." *University of Chicago Law Review* 40 (1973): 681–781.

Monchow, Helen. *The Use of Deed Restrictions in Subdivision Development*. Chicago: Institute for Research in Land Economics and Public Utilities, 1928.

Siegan, Bernard H. *Land Use without Zoning*. Lexington, MA: D. C. Heath, 1972.

Sies, Mary Corbin. "American Country House Architecture in Context: The Suburban Ideal in the East and Midwest." Ph.D. dissertation, University of Michigan, 1987.

Worley, William S. *J. C. Nichols and the Shaping of Kansas City: Innovation in Planned Residential Communities*. Columbia: University of Missouri Press, 1990.

## Retail Workers

One out of every six workers in the United States works in retail trade, surpassing the proportion of the population employed in manufacturing. More than 20 million clerks, managers, shelf-stockers, and burger flippers work in 1.5 million retail establishments throughout the country. Department stores, places to eat and drink, discount houses, drugstores, gas stations, furniture stores, supermarkets, mail-order houses—these are only a few of the kinds of establishments in which retail workers are employed.

Because retail establishments sell directly to the public, they are as dispersed geographically as the population itself. From classy downtown boutiques or restaurants, to suburban mall stores or fast-food joints, to rural general stores or lunch counters, the location and character of retail businesses reflect changes in the location, lifestyle, and income of consumers. Urban downtowns, once the center of retail trade, declined as consumers increasingly moved to the suburbs. Urban retail activity has revived somewhat in major cities with the development of urban malls and retail centers, and will always be central to the urban economy. Indeed, in the years since World War II, most large cities in the United States have changed from having a majority of their employment in manufacturing to a majority in services, including but not limited to retail trade. Downtown retailers, however, continue to suffer strong competition from regional shopping malls in the suburbs. Suburban malls are more convenient for many shoppers and can generate the same sales per square foot as urban locations but at lower costs to retailers.

Two major segments of retailing, department stores and places for eating and drinking, have undergone dramatic growth and differentiation in the second half of the twentieth century. Challenged by discounters like the early outlet stores, most department stores, which once relied on skilled selling and knowing their customers, have responded by embracing self-service and reducing their dependence on labor to cut costs. While skilled selling remains in expensive boutiques, in some small, family-owned establishments, and to a lesser extent in other parts of retailing, the typical clerk is now young, female, part-time, and has a low attachment to the industry.

Changing strategies in department stores—particularly the move to intense, price-based competition and self-service—have produced significant changes in employment conditions. As self-service and electronic point-of-sale terminals made it easier for employers to hire relatively unskilled labor, as cost-cutting became more acute, and as longer store hours increased the need for evening and weekend workers, the department store workforce became increasingly young, part-time, and low paid, and it had a high rate of turnover. Today, the majority of retail employees work part-time, and since the early 1970s at least half the employees of department stores have been younger than 25. Jobs are relatively stratified by age and gender, with prime-age men overrepresented in management, especially at the upper levels, and women and the young overrepresented in lower-level positions.

Employee turnover in retailing is also extremely high. In the six New England states in 1969, for example, employers hired 92, 000 workers and achieved a net decline in employment of 8,100. Many of the jobs at the nonsupervisory level are paid at or near the minimum wage.

Similar trends have taken place in other kinds of retailing, such as eating and drinking places. These changes are reflected in the declining number of hours worked per week and in declining real hourly earnings for retail workers. The average number of hours worked per week for all employees in retail trade shrunk from 38 in 1960 to 29 in 1993, and average hourly earnings, adjusted for inflation, had fallen from $5.70 per hour in 1980 to less than $5.00 by 1993 for nonsupervisory employees. Today, slightly more than half of the retail labor force is female, compared to 46 percent in the workforce as a whole. Nine percent of the retail labor force is black and 8.5 percent is Hispanic, slightly less and slightly more, respectively, than their proportions of the national labor force. Like the department store labor force, employment in retail trade is stratified by age, gender, and race. Low wages, high turnover, and low levels of unionization make these jobs suitable as a temporary way station for young workers, but not as the basis for a lifetime career opportunity for most employees.

—*Sarah Kuhn*

**See also**
Department Stores; Franchises and Franchising; Mail-Order Merchandising; Retailing.

**References**
Benson, Susan Porter. "Women in Retail Sales Work." In Karen Brodkin Sacks and Dorothy Remy, eds., *My Troubles Are Going to Have Trouble with Me*. New Brunswick, NJ: Rutgers University Press, 1984.

Bluestone, Barry, Patricia Hanna, Sarah Kuhn, and Laura Moore. *The Retail Revolution: Market Transformation, Investment and Labor in the Modern Department Store*. Boston: Auburn House, 1981.

Frieden, Bernard J., and Lynne Sagalyn. *Downtown, Inc.* Cambridge, MA: MIT Press, 1989.

Noyelle, Thierry. *Beyond Industrial Dualism*. Boulder, CO: Westview Press, 1987.

# Retailing

Retailing refers to the activities associated with selling goods to consumers. It differs from wholesaling, which refers to an intermediate stage between the producer and the consumer of a good.

Retailing differs from the processes of production, although often, and certainly in its earliest guises, retailers often produced the goods they sold. Although the word retailing dates only from the fourteenth century, the actual activity it denotes must far predate it. Whenever and wherever individuals or cultures produced more goods than they could consume themselves, they inevitably traded their surplus for other goods, and presumably this constitutes retailing activity.

However, the more contemporary use of the term itself places the origins of retailing in the cities of early medieval Europe, where outdoor markets were usually established for the sale of local agricultural produce and crafts. These markets were often periodic, and in the beginning their locations may not have been fixed. But since the markets were held only under the jurisdiction and protection of the crown or church, market areas were located close to the centers of authority, that is, within the walls of medieval cities. Geographer Harold Carter suggests that in their most primitive stages, markets required only the space created by the widening of a main street, where merchants could construct temporary stalls or lay mats on the ground. These emerging market areas were relatively insignificant compared to the usually large structures that housed the dominant religious and political orders. Early medieval cities were centered around the church and the castle or town hall—markets and merchants existed only at the sufferance of these powers.

These markets sold local agricultural produce and, in certain cities, goods brought from afar by itinerant merchants. These items had to be procured from long-distance trade, and therefore the sale of these goods was carried out by people not engaged in their production. Here, then, we see the distinction between the producer and the seller, a type of retailing more akin to our contemporary notions of selling, in which the consumer rarely deals with the actual producer of a good but instead buys from a merchant. In early medieval cities, these two types of retailing (local and long distance) most often took place side by side in the open markets of the city.

The expanding population of cities like Paris and London in the fourteenth and fifteenth centuries, and the concomitant need for more and more produce to feed the population, produced an explosion of markets in Europe. A large network of market towns evolved in England in the fifteenth century, extending from Scotland to the English Channel, with each region specializing in particular goods to supply the growing market. As the geographer Johann von Thunen would later describe, a series of belts of commercial agricultural activity began to develop around London, with farmers in each belt specializing in the type of agriculture that would command the highest market value. The areas immediately surrounding London supplied it with fruits and vegetables, those slightly further out but still within the Thames Valley supplied grain, while the regions furthest from London became dedicated to animal grazing. Thus, the growing population of such large medieval cities as London and Paris led gradually to the incorporation of rural areas into a market economy and to the establishment of merchants as a new but increasingly powerful socioeconomic class within the city.

As the power of merchants increased relative to the other dominant powers of the medieval city, the location of the market within the city also took on greater significance. The first step in such a process was the construction of a permanent covered market or hall. These buildings were usually constructed for specific trades, such as the cloth trade, and examples of the construction of cloth halls abound in the fourteenth, fifteenth, and sixteenth centuries. Other common types of halls were built to house the corn markets and for the wine, leather, and shoe trades. These halls, of course, were not shops per se; many different producers and merchants sold their goods under one roof. But the halls do represent the first permanent structures that housed the retailing trade.

Most of these market halls were built fairly close to the centers of medieval cities, despite the havoc they wreaked in surrounding streets by virtue of the congestion and waste they created. But locations central to the economic life of the city were as important to this early form of retailing as they are today, and halls with surrounding open-air markets began to form the nuclei of what became the central business districts of Western cities. Yet not all economic activity took place in the center. Even in early medieval cities, distinctive microregions of specialized crafts and retailing activity could be found. Blacksmiths, for example, were positioned near the main gates of the city where their services and goods were most needed, and tanners needed to be located near water sources. Crafts that did not require specialized locations could operate near the center, but they too began to cluster together within the main market areas, forming economic districts that are still noted in the street names of many medieval cities.

In the medieval city, and probably up until the eighteenth century, it is impossible to separate the making and selling of goods, and it is therefore difficult to speak of a retail district per se. From the few detailed studies we have of medieval urban land use, however, it is possible to suggest that those craftspeople engaged in retail sales did in fact locate themselves in the city differently from those not engaged in retailing. Geographer John Langton notes in his study of late medieval Gloucester that cloth and leather craftsmen who did not manufacture for retail sale lived further away from the city center. By the late medieval period, craftsmen-retailers were generally located closer to the city center than those just engaged in craft, foreshadowing the industrial patterns of urban land use. In general, then, the medieval city had no distinct retail district, but did have a central market, often symbolized by a market hall or guildhall, where foods were sold as well as some luxury goods, surrounded by an area of craftsmen-retailers clustered together in specialized districts.

As long-distance trade became more prevalent in the late medieval, preindustrial world, retailing became more defined around the sale of imported goods. This, of course, makes clear the separation of retailing from production but obscures the distinction between retailing and wholesaling. The new merchants were involved in importing, exporting, and selling, and they often used the same urban space for both storing their goods and selling them. Because control of the Atlantic trade gave English merchants ample opportunity for trade, the docks and wharves along the Thames River in London were cramped with buildings to house the multitude of goods being brought into the country. Those goods were often sold at the same site to consumers, or were purchased by other merchants and sent elsewhere to be sold. By the first decades of the seventeenth century, the areas further inland from the docks became spotted with small shops selling many of the goods, forming specialized retailing districts. These shops were often located on the first story of a building with the floors above used as small warehouses for storage.

The linkage between wholesaling and retailing was replicated in the spatial structure of the mercantile cities on the eastern seaboard of the United States. The major ports, Boston, New York, Philadelphia, Charleston, and New Orleans, followed similar commercial patterns, with emergent retailing districts located just inland from the densely settled dock and warehouse areas, gradually moving to a location more central to the city's other business activities and closer to the upper-class residential areas that provided the retailers' best customers. Geographer Martyn Bowden suggests that completely separate retailing districts were formed in New York and Boston in the last decades of the eighteenth century. These districts were relatively small and contained shops where customers met with merchants in the front room or on the first floor to negotiate the item and its price, while the goods themselves were kept either in the back or on upper stories. Since this type of retailing predates the Industrial Revolution, neither the goods nor their prices were standardized, and customers were therefore personally involved in assessing the quality of goods and in negotiating with the merchant about an appropriate price. This, of course, is a different type of selling procedure from our contemporary world as it involved direct encounters with the actual owners of the shops over price and quality.

This type of retailing characterized American cities until the middle of the nineteenth century, when the full impact of industrialization was felt in the retailing trade. With industrialization, a much larger range of commodities was available to an expanded class of customers since mass production made most commodities cheaper and therefore more affordable. This expansion of goods and consumers made it difficult to continue selling in the same small shops that had characterized the eighteenth and early nineteenth centuries. Many of these shops expanded by adding more rooms to house the new commodities and appeal to the new customers. In addition to these changes, the standardization of prices meant that haggling over cost was now removed from retailing. In fact, as shops grew larger, most consumers dealt not with the owner but with a salesclerk, whose job was not to haggle but to help shoppers choose from the array of goods being offered. Thus, purchasing goods was now less about bargaining and much more about comparative shopping. This meant that goods needed to be displayed in a manner appealing to customers.

The combination of these factors helps explain the development of the department store. The first department store, Stewart's Marble Palace, opened in New York City in 1848, but it was really not until after the Civil War, with America's industrial powers seeking new outlets for their products, that department stores reached their heyday. These new department stores differed from their predecessors not only in size but also in their emphasis on creating an environment conducive for consumption by the major class of consumers, middle- and upper-income women. With their husbands busy producing and managing, women's work switched from home production to consumption. Department store owners did their best to cater to these new customers by providing what was considered an environment appropriate for the Victorian woman. The stores were organized into clearly marked departments, filled with beautiful displays of goods, and decorated to appear more as cultural adornments than commercial markets. These department stores were usually located close together, in an area central to the city, yet close to the middle- and upper-class residential enclaves. In New York, an area on Broadway and Fifth Avenue, between Union and Madison Squares became known as Ladies' Mile, and contained within it such stores as Macy's, Stern's, James McCreery's, and Lord and Taylor. Similar retailing districts were formed in most major American cities, and these districts remade the downtown area into a new type of space, one inhabited by women and occupied by the activities of consumption. In the 1870s, the development of plate glass and iron framing allowed the viewing of goods in display windows, thus transforming the experience of walking on the newly paved and lit streets into a type of shopping fantasy. Increasingly throughout this period, retailers incorporated elements of fantasy into their advertisements and displays, stimulating the desire for more commodities and thus more sales.

These new retailing districts continued to be located in central business districts, but as the upper and middle classes began to move away from the downtown, retailers followed. The development of streetcar systems in the late nineteenth and early twentieth centuries allowed for the movement of residences out of an increasingly congested downtown. With the introduction of the automobile in the early decades of the twentieth century, the pace and scale of residential as well as commercial suburbanization increased. Small shops that offered services and goods to local populations were constructed close to the new residential communities. Often, these convenient grocery and service shops were located together in a strip with access to a parking lot, thus creating the first shopping centers. Urban historians identify the first planned shopping center as Country Club Plaza, constructed in 1922 in Kansas City as part of developer Harvey Nichols's planned suburban community.

Most early shopping centers, however, were far less elaborate, consisting of a strip of stores laid out in one of three schemes (linear, U-shaped, or L-shaped) and centered around a parking lot. Although these centers represent the first significant movement of retailing activity out of the downtown, they did not replace the downtown retail district. Department stores, for example, relied on access to a large population, and the central city still provided the best location for such accessibility.

This began to change with the new suburban construction following World War II. The explosion of mass-produced suburban housing communities and the construction of the interstate highway system, combined with federal housing policies that encouraged suburban development, reshaped American metropolitan areas. Throughout the 1950s and 1960s, large expanses of agricultural land on the fringes of American cities were converted into large-scale residential communities whose inhabitants commuted to work in the city on the new highways or, by the late 1960s, commuted to work in another suburban area. Industries and offices, too, were relocating to suburbs to avoid the congested inner city and take advantage of cheaper suburban land made accessible by automobiles and trucks. This radical shift in population often led to the almost complete abandonment of the central city by the middle and upper classes of America. As has always happened in retailing, stores followed their customers.

The movement of department stores out of the downtown required a different spatial solution than the shopping center. Department stores needed to draw on a very large population base to succeed, and therefore store owners looked to locations accessible to the major highways. The undeveloped land just beyond the fringe of suburban residences, yet close to the interstate, provided an ideal location. The land was much cheaper, and large expanses could be bought by a developer who could use department stores as anchors for a new type of retailing form that came to be known as the mall. These enclosed retailing spaces surrounded by large parking lots created entire environments dedicated to retailing. In their simplest and earliest form (in the early 1960s), malls consisted of two department stores linked by smaller shops, with a central walkway often lined with benches or other conveniences for customers. But, as the economic potential of suburbs was realized by developers and retailers, malls grew in size and complexity. According to geographer Peter Muller, the suburban share of retail sales in the United States rose from 48.5 percent to 65 percent between 1963 and 1972; by 1990, shopping malls alone accounted for 55 percent of retail sales, excluding automobiles.

The new malls of the 1980s and 1990s have been called superregional malls, since the range from which they draw customers often exceeds one metropolitan area. The largest of these malls have become tourist destinations in and of themselves, drawing customers from long distances. These malls include many more activities than traditional retail shopping, with food courts, entertainments, arcades, hotels, and cinema complexes. The Mall of America, for example, which opened in 1992 in Bloomington, Minnesota, and is considered the largest mall in the world, covers 4.2 million square feet and contains over 400 stores, six dining establishments, 14 movie screens, a large food court, and a seven-acre amusement park with a roller coaster. In effect, malls have taken on many of the functions of the nineteenth-century downtown, acting as the entertainment and social centers of many metropolitan areas.

As a result of this postwar explosion of residential and commercial suburban growth, many American downtown retail districts have been almost completely abandoned. Yet the process of gentrification—the movement of middle- to upper-income people into downtown areas that has occurred in the past 20 years—has created, particularly in large cities, small pockets of urban retail growth. According to Jon Goss, that growth has taken two generalized forms. The first is the urban shopping mall, often referred to as a galleria and containing the usual elements of a suburban shopping mall, combined with an architectural style reminiscent of Victorian shopping arcades. These malls provide urban dwellers with the security and order of the suburbs in an urban setting. The second type, often called festival marketplaces, are commonly attempts to gentrify a decaying area of a city by re-creating it in the image of its nineteenth-century commercial past. These retail environments, such as Boston's Faneuil Hall and Baltimore's Inner Harbor, rely on proximity to a historical section of the city or to an old waterfront in order to capture the nostalgia for a lost urban community that seems to attract customers, the upper-income urban dwellers.

These latest forms of retailing in America continue to rely on factors that were central to the earliest forms: proximity to their best customers and a mixing of civic with commercial space. Yet the scale of retailing has changed considerably as has its importance to American life. Today, the shopping mall is the place where Americans spend more of their time than any other place except for home and work or school.

—*Mona Domosh*

**See also**
Chain Stores; Commercial Strips; Department Stores; Franchises and Franchising; Gasoline Stations; Mail-Order Merchandising; Pedestrian Malls; Retail Workers; Shopping Malls in Suburbs; Supermarkets.

**References**
Bowden, Martyn J. "Growth of the Central Districts in Large Cities." In Leo Schnore, ed., *The New Urban History,* 75–109. Princeton, NJ: Princeton University Press, 1975.

Braudel, Fernand. *The Wheels of Commerce.* Berkeley: University of California Press, 1992.

Carter, Harold. *An Introduction to Urban Historical Geography.* London: Edward Arnold, 1989.

Goss, Jon. "The 'Magic of the Mall': An Analysis of Form, Function, and Meaning in the Contemporary Retail Built Environment." *Annals of the Association of American Geographers* 83 (1993): 18–47.

Langton, John. "Late Medieval Gloucester: Some Data from a Rental of 1455." *Transactions of the Institute of British Geographers* 2 (1977): 259–277.

Muller, Peter. *The Outer City: Geographical Consequences of the Urbanization of the Suburbs.* Washington DC: Association of American Geographers, 1976.

## Retirement Communities

Retirement communities are a widely known housing option for older people, and they include a wide variety of specialized housing. Broadly defined, they are aggregations of housing units and at least a minimal level of services planned for older people who are predominantly healthy and retired. Five types of retirement communities have been identified: new towns, villages, subdivisions, congregate housing, and continuing care retirement communities.

Retirement new towns are large, privately developed, self-contained communities offering a leisurely and active lifestyle, targeted at the functionally independent preretirement and young retirement market. New towns attract people moving long distances and are commonly found in Sunbelt and western states where the climate is conducive to year-round outdoor activity. Examples of retirement new towns are Sun City and Sun City West near Phoenix, Arizona; Sun City Center near Tampa, Florida; and Leisure World in Laguna Hills, California.

New towns are the largest retirement communities. They have populations of at least 5,000, although many are considerably larger. For example, Arizona's Sun City is the world's largest retirement development with a population of 46,000 residents, and the adjacent Sun City West is to house 25,000 more. Another new town, Leisure World in Laguna Hills, California, has 21,000 residents.

New towns also offer the most extensive network of recreation, retail, financial, and medical facilities and services of all the retirement community types. Opportunities for active and passive recreational pursuits are abundant. Two distinct philosophies of security are reflected in the physical design of new towns. The closed, self-contained community is characterized by perimeter walls and security gates restricting access to the development, as in Leisure World, California. The open community is undifferentiated from its surroundings and has unrestricted access, as in Sun City, Arizona, and Sun City Center, Florida.

Retirement villages are privately developed communities offering a leisurely and active lifestyle targeted toward the preretirement and young retirement market that largely draw on the surrounding area for support services such as shopping and health care instead of providing them internally. Although commonly found in Sunbelt states, villages have also been developed in northeastern states. Examples of retirement villages are Leisure World in Montgomery County, Maryland; Leisure Village in Camarillo, California; Leisure Village West in Ocean County, New Jersey; and Hawthorne near Leesburg, Florida.

Retirement villages are smaller than new towns and generally range in size from 1,000 to 5,000 residents. Residence in many of these villages is limited to people at least in their early fifties, although some are age-integrated. Residents of retirement villages are generally retired couples in their late sixties, who are college educated and financially comfortable. Recreational and communal facilities and programs are prevalent in retirement villages. Because retirement villages are not planned to be self-contained, the extent to which they provide shopping facilities either on-site or on the perimeter of the village varies. As in the case of new towns, retirement villages differ in the extent of their security, although many are surrounded by walls with guarded entrances.

Retirement subdivisions contain few services and amenities and are planned by profit-seeking developers to be incorporated into a surrounding community that is usually rich in services and amenities. The lifestyle offered by the host community is the major attraction for prospective residents, who are functionally independent preretirees or young retirees. Retirement subdivisions tend to be located in urban Sunbelt areas to take advantage of the attractive climate. Examples of retirement subdivisions are Bradenton Trailer Park and Trailer Estates, both in Bradenton, Florida; Orange Gardens in Kissimmee, Florida; and Riviera Mobile Home Park in Scottsdale, Arizona.

Retirement subdivisions are composed of conventionally built homes (Orange Gardens) or mobile homes where tenure arrangements vary. Residents with mobile homes may either own their lot (Trailer Estates) or rent one (Bradenton Trailer Park and Riviera Mobile Home Park). Ownership of mobile home and lot is a relatively new option, with Trailer Estates being the first to offer this possibility in 1955. Although many subdivisions impose age limitations for their residents, many do not or only restrict residents under 18 years of age. Households generally consist of married couples in their early seventies, both in good health. Residents tend to be less affluent than those in new towns and villages. Since retirement subdivisions contain fewer amenities and many are mobile home parks, they are more affordable than other types of large-scale retirement communities.

Congregate housing has no precise definition since it is referred to deferentially depending on the state, sponsor, and type of structure. In most cases, congregate housing refers to a multiunit apartment building that is targeted toward the older elderly whose health is at risk. Its goal is to provide a physical and social environment that will extend the time older residents can live independently in comfort and safety. Apartments have bathrooms and kitchenettes, and some support services are provided such as a dining room for at least one main meal a day, optional housekeeping, transportation, and 24-hour watch service. Usually there is common space for social, educational, and other group activities.

The typical resident is a single woman over 75 years old whose health is at risk and formerly lived near the congre-

*Senior citizens play shuffleboard in the retirement community of Century Village in Florida.*

gate housing site. Factors influencing a person's decision to move to congregate housing include poor or declining health; reduced ability to perform such basic activities of daily life as housework, shopping, laundry, and meals; constriction of social networks of friends, family, and neighbors; worries about neighborhood security; and increased concern about the ability to obtain help in any emergency.

Congregate housing has traditionally been sponsored by nonprofit groups or the government. In the 1980s two major private developers entered the market, a subsidiary of Hyatt Hotels that began constructing its Classic Residences in Maryland, Texas, New Jersey, and California, and Leisure Technology, Inc., which had previously developed several retirement villages named Leisure Village. The cost of living in congregate housing varies greatly. Lower-cost housing in these developments is subsidized by federal, state, and local programs. Religious and fraternal organizations sponsor many higher-cost congregate developments nationally. The highest-cost congregate housing is provided by profit-making corporations and emphasizes a wide assortment of amenities.

Continuing care retirement communities (CCRCs) offer housing, medical services, preventive health care, and an array of social and recreational services to an initially healthy, older clientele who usually pay an entrance fee and a monthly charge. The provision of a continuum of health care distinguishes CCRCs from other forms of retirement housing.

There are two versions of CCRCs—the life-care community and the life-care lookalike. Life-care communities guarantee residents nursing care if they need it, while the life-care lookalikes guarantee only priority on the waiting list for a nursing bed. Thus, the lookalikes offer a continuum of care rather than continuing care. CCRCs offer numerous opportunities for social and recreational pursuits. Many have facilities and programs for arts and crafts, games, and classes. As congregate housing, they rarely have facilities for active recreation such as golf, tennis, or swimming. Most of them contain amenities such as a common dining area, a chapel, beauty and barber shops, snack bars, a library, a convenience grocery shop, gift shop, and lounges for informal gatherings.

The average CCRC resident is in her early eighties and did not move to the community until she reached her late seventies. Females outnumber males by two to one. It has been estimated that only 15 to 20 percent of the people older than 75 can afford these retirement communities, and CCRCs have traditionally been developed by nonprofit sponsors. In recent years, large for-profit companies have been entering the market. Most notable of these is the Marriott Corporation, the hotel developer.

The five types of retirement communities can be collapsed into two broad categories: recreation-oriented communities composed of retirement new towns, villages, and subdivisions and service-oriented communities composed of congregate housing and CCRCs. The two categories are differentiated by their target markets and market areas. The target market of recreation-oriented communities is typically active couples who are young retirees or preretirees seeking a maintenance-free home that offers recreational opportunities. In contrast, the target market of service-oriented communities is typically people over 75, the vast majority of them women living alone, who are functionally and socially independent most of the time but are beginning to recognize their physical limitations and questioning their ability to maintain an independent household.

The market area refers to the geographic area from which residents move. Recreation-oriented communities often have market areas that are regional or even national in scale. Service-oriented communities have a much smaller market area. The only exception to this rule is the Southeast, where retirement communities attract relatively large numbers of people from out of state. It has been said, for example, that parts of Florida are suburbs of New York City.

The future of retirement communities is partly related to demographic trends in the United States. According to population projections, the most rapid growth in the elderly population over the next 25 years will be among those at least 85 years old, most of them women living alone. In the following 20 years, however, the most rapid growth will be among those aged 65 to 74, most of whom will be married and physically active. The first group will be attracted to service-oriented communities, and the second group to recreation-oriented communities. Responding to both of these markets at the appropriate time will be a challenge for retirement communities in the future.

—*Michael E. Hunt*

**See also**
Naturally Occurring Retirement Communities.
**References**
Hunt, Michael E., et al. *Retirement Communities: An American Original.* New York: Haworth Press, 1984.
LaGreca, Anthony J., Gordon F. Streib, and W. Edward Folts. "Retirement Communities and their Life Stages." *Journal of Gerontology* 40 (1985): 211–218.
Marans, Robert W., et al. "Retirement Communities: Present and Future." In Eric Smart and Nancy Stewart, eds., *Housing for a Maturing Population.* Washington, DC: Urban Land Institute, 1983.
Marans, Robert W., Michael E. Hunt, and Katherine L. Vakalo. "Retirement Communities." In Irwin Altman, M. Powell Lawton, and Joachim F. Wohlwill, eds., *Elderly People and the Environment.* New York: Plenum Press, 1984.
Streib, Gordon F. "Retirement Communities: Linkages of the Locality, State, and Nation." *Journal of Applied Gerontology* 9 (1990): 405–419.
Streib, Gordon F., Anthony J. LaGreca, and W. Edward Folts. "Retirement Communities: People, Planning, Prospects." In Robert J. Newcomer, M. Powell Lawton, and Thomas O. Byerts, eds., *Housing an Aging Society.* New York: Van Nostrand Reinhold, 1986.

## Revenue Sharing

Revenue sharing gained considerable prominence in the 1970s when a series of national programs returned federal tax revenue to state and local governments. The philosophical justification for revenue sharing was that the federal government raised money more efficiently than states or cities but that decisions about expenditures should be made by local officials. Politically, two factors prompted general acceptance of revenue sharing—the "peace dividend" resulting from the end of the Vietnam War and the need of many American cities for more money to meet the rapidly escalating cost of social services.

Congress enacted two broad revenue sharing programs in the 1970s. The first, called "general revenue sharing" (GRS), was passed in 1972 and terminated in the late 1980s. GRS provided funds to more than 38,000 state and local general-purpose governments and distributed more than $30 billion to them for a wide range of public expenditures. Its supporters (including President Richard Nixon) hailed GRS for providing significant funds to state and local decision-makers who knew best how to spend the money.

GRS was supposed to solve two problems—the size and power of the federal bureaucracy and the inability of state and local officials to respond to the needs they considered most pressing. After initially receiving widespread public and political support, subsequent efforts to renew the program resulted in more restrictions and limitations on the use of the money. While sometimes expended on new initiatives, in most cases GRS grants supplemented local money and support programs already in place. Most of the money was spent on politically acceptable programs that already existed, such as those in public safety.

A second type of revenue sharing was labeled "special revenue sharing" (sometimes called block grants) and took the form of combined grants to state and local governments for broad purposes. Special revenue sharing was supposed to simplify and reduce federal bureaucratic requirements and provide funds directly for programs rather than administrative costs. The most important of these special revenue sharing programs was the Housing Community Development Act of 1974, which proved very popular with elected officials.

Both general and special revenue sharing programs stressed decentralization of government and local responsibility for decision making. It does not appear that either produced a widespread increase in public participation. Both were seen as ways of reducing the size of the federal bureaucracy and increasing the responsiveness of state and local governments.

By the mid-1980s, both programs had either been cut off or significantly reduced by increased political opposition to the idea that federal tax revenue should be used for such programs. This resulted in some contentious and difficult times for state and local leaders as they openly disagreed with President Reagan and prominent Republicans in Congress. The shifting budgetary situation and the changed political climate of the late 1980s made it difficult to justify revenue sharing as a viable policy. The emphasis on reducing government expenditures and curtailing the role of federal programs in particular, but on all government activity in general, increased. Revenue sharing remains, however, a powerful policy approach that could be reborn in the future since it is popular with state and local leaders and is seen as contributing to decentralization.

—*David A. Caputo*

**See also**
Community Development Block Grants; Nixon Administration: Urban Policy; Reagan Administration: Urban Policy.

**References**
Brazer, Harvey E., and Michael A. Conte. *The States and General Revenue Sharing.* Ann Arbor, MI: Institute for Social Research, 1975.
Caputo, David A., and Richard L. Cole, eds. *Revenue Sharing.* Lexington, MA: Lexington Books, 1976.
Cole, Richard L., and David A. Caputo. *Urban Politics and Decentralization: The Case of General Revenue Sharing.* Lexington, MA: Lexington Books, 1974.
Dommel, Paul R. *The Politics of Revenue Sharing.* Bloomington: Indiana University Press, 1974.
Institute for Social Research. *The Economic and Political Impact of General Revenue Sharing.* Ann Arbor: University of Michigan, 1977.
Nathan, Richard P. *Monitoring Revenue Sharing.* Washington, DC: Brookings Institution, 1975.
Scheffer, Walter F., ed. *General Revenue Sharing and Decentralization.* Norman: University of Oklahoma Press, 1976.
U.S. Executive Office of the President. *History of Revenue Sharing.* Washington, DC: Domestic Policy Council, 1971.

## Richardson, Henry Hobson (1838–1886)

Acclaimed by many historians as America's most important nineteenth-century architect, Henry Hobson Richardson transformed the course of American architecture, only to have his career cut short by an early death.

A native of Louisiana, Richardson graduated from Harvard College in 1859. After 1860, he studied at the *Ecole des Beaux-Arts* in Paris, returning to the United States after the Civil War. He settled in New York, where he opened his own practice in 1866. From 1867 to 1878, he practiced in partnership with Charles Dexter Gambrill, whose primary role seems to have been managing the firm.

Richardson based his early buildings on contemporary European and American Gothic Revival and Second Empire precedents. However, beginning about 1870, his designs revealed a broader exploration of possible sources and thereafter his works, such as the Brattle Square Church, Boston

(1869–1873), the New York State Hospital, Buffalo (1869–1880), and the Hampden County Court House, Springfield, Massachusetts (1871–1874), showed his experimentation with a design framework based on Romanesque precedents. In 1872, Richardson won the competition for Trinity Church in Boston (1872–1877) with a Romanesque Revival design, and his successful completion of this project propelled him to the front ranks of American architects and set the course for the remainder of his career.

Richardson moved to Brookline, Massachusetts, in 1874 to be closer to the work on Trinity Church; in 1878, he dissolved his partnership and moved his office to Brookline as well. Over the next eight years, Richardson was responsible for a series of exemplary works. Although the largest number of his buildings were institutional, he was also responsible for significant commercial and residential projects. His mature works show a refinement of style that resulted from his eliminating specific historical references and details so that his works depended upon their own sense of gravity, order, repose, and appropriate use of materials for their character.

Richardson's contribution to the creation of an institutional framework for urban life is evident in the series of small public libraries he designed between 1876 and 1885 for the Boston suburbs of Woburn, North Easton, Quincy, and Malden; his series of railroad stations, including nine for the Boston & Albany Railroad; and the educational buildings, Sever Hall (1878–1880) and Austin Hall (1881–1884), which he designed for Harvard University. His most significant institutional work was the Allegheny County Court House and Jail in Pittsburgh (1883–1888).

Richardson's urban commercial architecture included works such as the Cheney Block in Hartford, Connecticut (1875–1876), several store buildings in Boston for the Ames family, and his masterpiece in this genre, the Marshall Field Wholesale Store in Chicago (1885–1887).

Richardson's suburban and rural houses are particularly noteworthy as they influenced the evolution of the Shingle Style and introduced the "living hall" plan, which created a more open interior. Examples include the Sherman House in Newport, Rhode Island (1874–1876), the Bryant House in Cohasset, Massachusetts (1880–1881), and the Stoughton House in Cambridge, Massachusetts (1882–1883). His urban houses often featured plans that reflected the planning innovations he had developed in his suburban works, but their monumental exteriors of brick or stone, as exemplified by the Glessner House in Chicago (1885–1887), also demonstrate a relationship to his institutional designs.

In the last years of his career, Richardson was inundated with commissions. Although he had been plagued by ill health throughout his life, he practiced at a hectic pace until his death in April 1886 at the age of 47. His chief assistants continued his office as Shepley, Rutan & Coolidge and supervised the completion of his unfinished buildings.

The breadth of Richardson's achievement was reflected in the influence he exerted on the next generation of American architects, and his works served as models for almost a decade of Romanesque Revival designs across the country. Many of his assistants, including Charles McKim, Stanford White, George Shepley, Alexander W. Longfellow, and John Galen Howard, were leading figures in the emergent generation of academic eclectic architects, and his late buildings were critical examples that inspired the Chicago School of architects, such as Louis Sullivan, in the 1880s and early 1890s.

—*Jeffrey Karl Ochsner*

**References**

Hitchcock, Henry-Russell. *The Architecture of H. H. Richardson and His Times.* 2d ed. Cambridge, MA: MIT Press, 1966.

Ochsner, Jeffrey Karl. *H. H. Richardson: Complete Architectural Works.* Cambridge, MA: MIT Press, 1982.

O'Gorman, James F. *H. H. Richardson: Architectural Forms for an American Society.* Chicago: University of Chicago Press, 1987.

———. *H. H. Richardson and His Office: Selected Drawings.* Boston: David R. Godine, 1974.

———. *Three American Architects: Richardson, Sullivan and Wright, 1865–1915.* Chicago: University of Chicago Press, 1991.

Scully, Vincent J., Jr. *The Shingle Style and the Stick Style.* New Haven, CT: Yale University Press, 1971.

Van Rensselaer, Marianna Griswold. *Henry Hobson Richardson and His Works.* Reprint ed. New York: Dover, 1969.

## Riis, Jacob August (1849–1914)

What catapulted Danish-born Jacob A. Riis to fame and established his credentials as an urban reformer was his 1890 exposé *How the Other Half Lives: Studies among the Tenements of New York.* As poet James Russell Lowell put it in a congratulatory letter to the author, "I had but a vague idea of these horrors before you brought them home to me." By making slum residents more comprehensible to his readers, Riis also made them not quite so fearful. His popular book helped usher in a generation of examination into urban institutions.

Riis's background had equipped him well for the task of bridging the chasm of communication between rich and poor. Reared in the preindustrial town of Ribe, Denmark, he was nurtured by the primary bonds of family, church, and community and developed an idealistic, adventurous, optimistic personality, which was sorely tested when he arrived in New York at the age of 21. For seven years he drifted in semipoverty from job to job and place to place, searching for a creative outlet for his formidable energies before he became a police reporter for the *New York Tribune.* His beat was in Manhattan's Lower East Side slum district, Mulberry Bend, where 250,000 people resided in one square mile, often 20 to a room in foul, poorly lit dwellings.

For Riis journalism served two functions: to secure for himself a comfortable place in American society and to give him a forum for venting his outrage at the tragic scenes that he witnessed daily. The squalor and human misery, in his words, "gripped my heart until I felt I must tell of them, or burst or turn anarchist, or something." While Riis's descriptions of New York's polyglot populace were somewhat condescending, especially toward nonwhites, he was virtually an environmental determinist who believed that decent housing, parks, playgrounds, and schools could save the offspring of the poor. In the 1880s, he had put together a display of photographs which, using the latest flash technology, showed the dark interiors of apartments, lodging houses, cellars, stale beer dives, and back alleys. After his illustrated book put him in demand, he toured the country for many years with his stereopticon and slides.

During the 1890s Riis participated in many crusades to reconstruct the urban environment. He advised New York Mayor William L. Strong and Theodore Roosevelt, Strong's appointee as president of the Police Board. He attempted to organize good-government neighborhood clubs, became secretary of the Mayor's Advisory Committee on Small Parks, and built up a settlement house that later bore his name. In 1902, Riis selected the title *The Making of an American* for his autobiography. The following year he published a paean to his hero entitled *Theodore Roosevelt the Citizen.* That same year, fellow muckraker Lincoln Steffens wrote a sympathetic piece about his colleague for *McClure's* magazine entitled "Jacob A. Riis, Reporter, Reformer, American."

During the final decade of his life he remained a prolific writer and became somewhat of a maverick elder statesman of Progressivism, criticizing professional altruists, advising President Roosevelt on making Washington, D.C., a "model city," and sustaining several of his favorite charities, including the Boy Scouts and the Sea Breeze Tuberculosis Hospital for children. A believer in social reform rather than social control, he represented the humanitarian tradition within Progressivism.

—*James B. Lane*

**References**

Alland, Alexander Sr. *Jacob A. Riis, Photographer and Citizen.* New York: Aperture, 1973.

Fried, Lewis, and John Fierst. *Jacob A. Riis: A Reference Guide.* Boston: G. K. Hall, 1977.

Lane, James. *Jacob A. Riis and the American City.* Port Washington, NY: Kennikat Press, 1974.

Meyer, Edith. *"Not Charity but Justice": The Story of Jacob A. Riis.* New York: Vanguard, 1974.

## River Towns

Many of the largest cities in the United States—New York, Boston, Philadelphia, Baltimore, Washington, Chicago, San Francisco, Los Angeles, and Seattle—are located on rivers that empty into a bay or estuary that flows to the ocean. Because of their locations, these cities were ports that first served as entrepots and later as industrial centers for a regional or national hinterland. As they developed, however, each of these cities expanded beyond its initial riverside location, and as transportation technologies changed, rivers became less important in determining cities' economic function. For many years, residents in most of these cities turned away from the port and river, and they became peripheral. Even though urban planners and residents in the 1980s and 1990s once again recognized the recreational and scenic value of old riverfront districts or ports (often leading to significant commercial and residential refurbishing and construction), rivers no longer define urban economies, societies, cultures, or spatial orders.

In the United States, the term, "river town" refers not just to any city or town located on a river but to a specific type of city or town located at a strategic site alongside one of the great interior rivers of North America. River towns were founded and laid out as urban development spread west with the "urban frontier" in the early nineteenth century. Initially, as town developers moved ahead of settlement, they platted many towns at sites on rivers that seemed to possess the "natural advantages" necessary for urban development. Usually, however, the competition among newly born river towns was short-lived. A town that possessed an elevated site and a superior location relative to water flow or the economics of steamboating, or had a better wharf for ferries and boats, or had more aggressive civic leaders and local businessmen to stimulate trade quickly developed into the local entrepot. In time, some of these local entrepots developed first into regional entrepots or river cities, then became railroad and industrial centers, and finally emerged as modern metropolises. Prominent among these successful river towns have been Pittsburgh, Cincinnati, Louisville, St. Louis, Memphis, New Orleans, Kansas City, Omaha, and St. Paul. Other towns settled back into secondary roles as centers of local commerce and industry. Wheeling, West Virginia; Marietta, Ohio; Madison and Evansville, Indiana; Cairo, Alton, Quincy, Rock Island, and Peoria, Illinois; Keokuk, Davenport, and Dubuque, Iowa; Cape Girardeau and Hannibal, Missouri; and Baton Rouge, Louisiana, are all quintessential river towns.

The economy of each of these towns and cities relied on the steamboat, which enjoyed its heyday as the primary means of transporting goods between 1811 and about 1860. Likewise, the function, size, spatial arrangement, and social composition of river towns and cities were remarkably similar in different regional urban systems.

Though some cities initially benefited by becoming a railroad terminus in the 1860s, railroads, interstate highways, and airplanes drew passengers and freight away from rivers and eroded the entrepot function of many river towns. As one historian has noted, these towns gradually lost "their window on the world." In time, the term *river town* connoted an older, secondary place in the regional urban system that had been overtaken economically and culturally by a newer inland city or by a growing regional river metropolis that became a railroad center. These towns and cities either adjusted to a local or regional market and grew moderately or they declined and stagnated, struggling to survive while the importance of river transportation declined and rivers became simply corridors to move bulky goods or places for water recreation and tourism.

The economy, society, culture, and life of a river town was suffused with and nurtured by its river; the ecology, hydrology, and environment of the river shaped and dominated the lives of people who resided in river towns. Initially, the layout of the city itself was oriented to the river. As one historian put it, "All these settlements . . . deriv[ed] their importance and prosperity from water connections. Early planners, for that reason, made the river the central street, so to speak, in their design. Plats tended to be long rather than wide, allowing maximum access to the water . . . the waterfront became commercialized . . . while residential building retreated inland . . . [and] soon, travelers coming down the river spoke of the business of the city, not its beauty."

John Reps has shown, however, that many artists and lithographers were indeed interested in portraying the appearance of these towns. As long as steamboats remained the primary form of transportation, river towns were depicted from a riverine or river-centric perspective. The warehouses and commercial buildings along wharves lined with steamboats presented a "facade" to river travelers; depending on the slope of the site, other buildings extended behind the wharf and onto the bluffs above.

During the steamboat era, the river was the front door or entrance to a river town, the place where traffic converged and strangers arrived and departed, thus introducing river towns to a transient social element with its concomitant disorderly behavior. As one historian noted, "during trading seasons, the waterfront presented a picture of intense activity and confusion." To arrive there was to arrive in the center of town. A bit farther away from the wharf, most business and social activity concentrated along Main Street, which frequently was an extension of the wharf. In some towns, a town square not far from the river served as the central stage for public life. In time, the urban elite exhibited their power by

*This 1870 map of Memphis, Tennessee, illustrates the effect of the Mississippi River on the physical structure of the city.*

building impressive residences or "villas" on the bluffs over-looking the commercial district and the residential districts of the middle and working classes in the town below.

Over time, as the business district expanded and the center of town moved back from the river, the middle class and the elite separated themselves into specific residential districts farther away from the river. When that happened, the riverfront was abandoned in favor of facilities for railroads, which had surpassed steamboats as the primary form of transportation by 1870, and which were built to reach strategically located river towns. New industries quickly sprang up in the railroad right-of-way along the river. Industrial workers, railroad workers, and workers on the river formed ethnic and racial enclaves in nearby working-class neighborhoods. As this spatial transformation occurred, the riverfront district of most cities and towns became an area apart, separate, even isolated, from the life of the larger community. Not unlike an area of "transition" near the urban core, the district along the riverside became a kind of frontier at the border of organized society.

As riverside areas deteriorated, transience, disease, and social disorder increased, and a subculture of violence developed there. Given the smaller population of a typical river city, the native-born white majority responded in different ways to these developments. Though some river towns developed a reputation for tolerating deviant social behavior and more equitable race relations, white residents also drew on the subcultures of violence and corruption to segregate black neighborhoods and institutions, discriminate against black workers, and maintain social control over the black community with police intimidation and brutality. The ensuing tense race relations erupted into major race riots in Memphis and New Orleans in 1866, Evansville in 1903, East St. Louis in 1917, and Omaha in 1919, just to name a few. These clashes poisoned race relations for decades.

For ethnic and black residents, the riverfront district became the focal point of a vibrant local society supported by a variety of institutions. Economically, ethnic and black residents found employment and cultural expression within entertainment or vice districts that had developed near the riverfront since the earliest days of settlement. These entertainment and vice districts often acquired sobriquets or nicknames such as the Swamp or, between 1897 and 1917, Storyville (New Orleans), Under-the-Hill (Natchez), the Levee or the Reservation (Louisville), Pinch or Pinch Gut (Memphis), and the Midway (Evansville). For many blacks in the entertainment business, these districts provided a venue for the vibrant jazz culture that emerged and then migrated north; it went first to St. Louis and Kansas City after Storyville (New Orleans) was closed in 1917 and then centered in Chicago and New York during the 1920s.

But these entertainment and vice districts were mostly places of exploitation within a transient subculture of crime and violence. The predominant exploiter was often a ward boss who controlled saloons, gambling halls, nightclubs, and brothels. In some cases, a ward boss used control over entertainment and vice as a foothold from which to increase his citywide power; it was common to develop a political machine that expanded its power from the vice district to the police department to the courts and then to City Hall. Strangely enough, a few bosses developed their influence by breaking the power of a ward boss or councilman from the vice district and trying to clean up the city.

In general, though, river towns and cities gained reputations as "wide open" towns, ruled over by a provincial, even parochial, oligarchy of elite families who sanctioned or tolerated the corrupt political bosses and machines as long as they maintained control of the city's ethnic and black populations. Among these river city bosses were the brothers "Big Jim" and Tom Pendergast of Kansas City, George B. Cox of Cincinnati, John Whallen of Louisville, and Tom Dennison of Omaha.

Many river cities or towns, in the past and today, are viewed as unprogressive examples of American urbanization where stagnation and economic decline, social complacency, political and cultural backwardness, vice, crime, and decay prevail. In large part, this image, which has pervaded the way in which the outside world has viewed river towns and their residents, has been reinforced by the fateful locations of some river cities on the floodplains of the Ohio, Mississippi, Missouri, and other large tributary rivers. Though some river towns and cities—Memphis, Natchez, St. Louis, St. Paul, Kansas City, and Omaha, for example—prospered because their situation on higher ground protected them from the periodic flooding of nearby towns, every so often many river cities and towns experience great floods, which marked the history of the town. In addition to burdening residents with damages and insurance costs, and regularly compelling them to recover rather than develop further, floods have motivated many residents to relocate or leave altogether. Thus, the aftermath of a great flood often included considerable transience and out-migration. In addition, massive federal investment in locks and dams, levees, and barriers to control the river or protect the town from it further eroded local autonomy. Along the Mississippi and Ohio Rivers, six great floods during the nineteenth century and eight more during the twentieth century before 1994 left indelible marks on the

economy, society, culture, pattern of land use, and nearby environment of different river cities and towns. In a true river town or city, as Ron Powers noted in *White Town Drowsing*, the town and the river were and are indivisible, the river both a blessing and a curse. This fact remains a defining characteristic of every American river town or city.

—*Timothy R. Mahoney*

### References

Abbott, Carl. *Boosters and Businessmen: Popular Economic Thought and Urban Growth in the Antebellum Middle West.* Westport, CT: Greenwood Press, 1981.

Bigham, Darrel E. *An Evansville Album: Perspectives on a River City, 1812–1988.* Bloomington: Indiana University Press, 1988.

Biles, Roger. *Memphis in the Great Depression.* Knoxville: University Press of Tennessee, 1986.

Changnon, Stanley A. *The Great Flood of 1993: Causes, Impacts, and Responses.* Boulder, CO: Westview Press, 1996.

Chudacoff, Howard P. "Where Rolls the Dark Missouri Down." *Nebraska History* 52 (1971): 1–30.

Dorsett, Lyle W. *The Pendergast Machine.* Lincoln: University of Nebraska Press, 1968.

Hiller, Ernest Theodore. *Houseboat and River-Bottoms People.* Urbana: University of Illinois Press, 1939.

Mahoney, Timothy R. *River Towns in the Great West: The Structure of Provincial Urbanization in the American Midwest, 1820–1870.* New York: Cambridge University Press, 1990.

Miller, Zane L. *Boss Cox's Cincinnati.* New York: Oxford University Press, 1968.

Muller, Edward K. "From Waterfront to Metropolitan Region: The Geographical Development of American Cities." In Howard Gillette and Zane Miller, eds., *American Urbanism, A Historiographical Review.* New York: Greenwood Press, 1987.

Powers, Ron. *White Town Drowsing.* New York: Penguin Books, 1984.

Primm, James Neal. *Lion of the Valley: St. Louis, Missouri.* Boulder, CO: Pruett, 1981.

Reps, John W. *Cities of the Mississippi: Nineteenth-Century Images of Urban Development.* Columbia: University of Missouri Press, 1994.

Teaford, Jon C. *Cities of the Heartland: The Rise and Fall of the Industrial Midwest.* Bloomington: University of Indiana Press, 1993.

Wade, Richard C. *The Urban Frontier.* Chicago: University of Chicago Press, 1964.

Wright, George C. *Life behind the Veil: Blacks in Louisville, Kentucky, 1865–1930.* Baton Rouge: Louisiana State University Press, 1985.

## Riverside, Illinois

In 1868 a group of eastern investors (constituted in 1869 as the Riverside Improvement Company) headed by E. E. Childs purchased 1,600 acres of land called "Riverside Farm" for purposes of subdivision and speculation. Nine miles southwest of Chicago, the land flanked a station of the Burlington railroad line leading directly to the city. Frederick Law Olmsted, commissioned to assess the group's plans for the site, found them "abominable." He and his partner Calvert Vaux then produced a preliminary report, which established the principles on which the new suburban community would be laid out. The next year, Olmsted and Vaux issued a promotional plan showing a tract divided into four parts by the rail line and the Des Plaines River. The new suburb would have miles of curving drives "to suggest and imply leisure, contemplativeness and happy tranquility." The roads led past building plots at least 100 feet wide and 200 feet deep, as well as 700 acres of landscaped grounds reserved for public use; the largest single portion was a preserve of 160 acres along the river.

The preliminary report, noting the growing tendency in urban design toward "a separation of business and dwelling streets, and toward rural spaciousness," proposed turning the rural site into a community that would combine "urban and rural advantages." In addition to rail access, Olmsted recommended building a broad carriageway from Riverside to Chicago, while the developers promised to introduce all "the conveniences of the city—viz, Gas, Water, Roadways, Walks and Drainage." Rural landscape and leisure space would be melded in a series of public areas having "the character of informal village-greens, commons and playgrounds." Echoing the nineteenth-century celebration of bourgeois domesticity, Olmsted proposed that his design for the community would foster not only the "harmonious association" of all the like-minded individuals who would settle there, but also accentuate the separation of this realm of domesticity and leisure from that of work, capital, and politics in the city. Furthermore, Olmsted thought that the design also would serve—far better than Llewellyn Park, New Jersey, which he criticized—to spatialize the identity of each family as a distinct, private entity within the overall community. "The essential qualification of a suburb is domesticity," he wrote, and so it should emphasize "the idea of habitation." To that end he proposed enhancing the "seclusion" of individual houses by setting them back a minimum of 30 feet from the road, requiring owners to have two trees between the house and the road, and encouraging fences as a way of making apparent "the independence of the freeholder relative to the public" and creating a "private outside apartment" for each family.

As a speculative enterprise, the venture was a failure. Already in 1869 Olmsted's relations with the company had soured, and he terminated his association with them in 1870. The company itself went bankrupt following the Panic of 1873. But the village—particularly before 1900—stayed close to Olmsted's original recommendations, and it generally remains a showpiece of nineteenth-century suburban design: idyllic in articulating the identity of the domestic realm as a succession of private sanctuaries in nature; utopian in professing to unite features of city (defined in terms of "modern conveniences" and "congenial society") and country (idealized as pastoral, with sweeping lawns and cultivated woods); and socioeconomically homogeneous in its restriction to single-family houses, substantial lot sizes, and residents employed in professional, managerial, and entrepreneurial pursuits.

—John Archer

**See also**
Llewellyn Park, New Jersey; Olmsted, Frederick Law.
**References**
Bassman, Herbert J., ed. *Riverside Then and Now*. Riverside, IL: Riverside News, 1936.
Creese, Walter L. *The Crowning of the American Landscape: Eight Great Spaces and Their Buildings*. Princeton, NJ: Princeton University Press, 1985.
Olmsted, Frederick Law. *The Papers of Frederick Law Olmsted. Volume VI: The Years of Olmsted, Vaux & Company, 1865–1874*. David Schuyler and Jane Turner Censer, eds. Baltimore: Johns Hopkins University Press, 1992.
Olmsted, Vaux & Company. *Preliminary Report upon the Proposed Suburban Village at Riverside, near Chicago*. New York: Sutton, Bowne & Company, 1868.
Riverside Improvement Company. *Riverside in 1871 with a Description of Its Improvements*. Chicago: Riverside Improvement Company, 1871.
Schuyler, David. *The New Urban Landscape: The Redefinition of City Form in Nineteenth-Century America*. Baltimore: Johns Hopkins University Press, 1986.

## Roads

Humans have learned a great deal by observing animal behavior, whether in the wilderness or sophisticated scientific laboratories. This has held true from prehistoric times, when cavemen realized that animal trails through otherwise impenetrable jungles, forests, and mountain terrain invariably followed the easiest, most natural, efficient course. Centuries, even millenniums later, when humans finally began building roads, some of the most famous highways followed routes chosen by prehistoric herds and predators.

For thousands of years, there was little or no improvement of beaten-down paths. In his incessant wanderings that yielded the famous multivolume accounts of the Persian wars, the Greek historian Herodotus mentioned well-established trade routes, and archaeological evidence reveals the existence of improved roads around the Mediterranean Sea in Greek times. The Romans, of course, gained fame as road builders. Roman roads served many purposes. They stretched to the farthest frontiers of the empire, allowing rulers to move armies from one region to another quickly, thereby maintaining political, economic, and military control. Pliny the Elder observed that roads facilitated movement of commercial goods and often served as boundaries between private estates. French historian Raymond Chevallier described the "road culture" in ancient Rome; the roads accommodated

military leaders and their forces, emperors with their train, high dignitaries accompanied by their staff, envoys from afar or the provinces, messengers

. . . sailors from the fleet . . . and, of course, private citizens. These included people traveling on business (merchants in search of supplies or fairs, itinerant craftsmen such as masons, sculptors and mosaicists, gangs of seasonal farm-workers . . . theatrical performers, teachers or lecturers. . . . There were the sick on their way to drink healing waters or to breathe healthier air, pilgrims seeking a holy place . . . and a host of quacks.

In the fourth century A.D., one contemporary source claimed that 372 main roads covering 53,638 miles united the Roman Empire. Italy, naturally, was covered by the most extensive network of roads.

Roman engineering was unmatched for a millennium or more following the fall of the empire. By the Middle Ages, thousands of miles of Roman roads had fallen into ruin, and not until the emergence of European nation-states would road building on such a grand scale begin to reemerge. Between the Renaissance and the end of the eighteenth century, nations with imperialistic ambitions possessed the greatest incentive to build roads.

Decision-makers in the American colonies and, later, the United States appeared nearly oblivious to these events. At the beginning of the nineteenth century, the new nation was poorly served by public thoroughfares. The handful of adequate roads were constructed almost exclusively by private companies. The Philadelphia-Lancaster turnpike, chartered in 1792, was for many years the finest road in the United States. The overwhelming majority of public roads in the new nation were little more than unimproved cart paths, not distinguishable from the byways travelers had used since prehistoric times.

By the early nineteenth century, inventors had effectively harnessed steam power, which was rapidly adapted to transporting passengers and goods. Although there were abortive attempts to attach steam engines to heavy wagons traversing overland routes, the earliest vehicles were so cumbersome that they quickly broke down or became mired in mud on the unimproved roads outside of urban areas. Even in cities, rough cobblestone streets quickly destroyed the axles and wheels of such experimental devices. Engineers quickly determined that steam power could be applied commercially only to seagoing and river vessels or locomotives chugging along smooth iron or steel rails. Technological constraints, then, limited the application of steam power to steamships and railroads until later in the nineteenth century.

In 1803, President Jefferson ordered "improvements" in the famous Natchez Trace. Little more than an Indian trail, the Trace was an important route taken by many pioneers seeking opportunities west of the Allegheny Mountains.

Albert Gallatin, Jefferson's secretary of the Treasury, was so unused to the concept of actually building or improving roads in a nation of trails that he called them "artificial" in his 1808 "Report on Roads and Canals." Nevertheless, Gallatin was extraordinarily farsighted, proposing construction of a turnpike from Maine to Georgia, with four cuts from east to west through the Alleghenies. The projected cost was $2 million a year. But Congress rejected his plan, due to state rivalries and funding demands created by the War of 1812. The only major road project underwritten by the federal government was the National Road, from Cumberland, Maryland, to Wheeling, Virginia (now West Virginia), which was completed in 1817. Beyond Wheeling, travelers had to strike out alone across the Ohio and Indiana prairies or ride flatboats down the Ohio River.

The years that followed marked the triumph of commercial conveyances on river, ocean, and rail routes. Government policy at both the state and federal levels clearly favored steamships and railroads. Henry Clay's highly touted program of "internal improvements," designed in part to promote interstate trade and commerce, provided subsidies for canals and port improvements. Another generation of politicians extended Clay's vision to include subsidies for railroads during the remainder of the nineteenth century. Given this climate of opinion, investors in steam power had little incentive to advocate public road building, even in the decades following the Civil War.

As the nineteenth century wound down, inventors made significant strides in developing lightweight steam- and electric-powered automobiles. The 1890s marked the successful introduction of the first practical internal-combustion engines, and by the turn of the century several thousand Americans owned automobiles powered by one of these three energy sources. In towns, they were generally free to putter along over paved or semi-improved local byways, although local ordinances sometimes restricted their use severely. However, beyond city limits, they had almost nowhere to go. As late as 1903, there were more than 2 million miles of so-called "roads" in the United States, but more than 90 percent of them were almost impassable, "horse-belly deep in mud in spring and thick with dust in summer, frozen in iron-hard ruts in winter."

If the United States was ever to boast decent public roads, identifiable political constituencies had to step forward. The initial boost for improved public roads came from several sources. The bicycle craze had arrived in full force by the late 1880s as millions of Americans took up riding the new "safety" models featuring equal-sized chain-driven wheels. Active riders found city streets confining, and the League of American Wheelmen formed a powerful interest group by the 1890s. Representatives of this somewhat elitist organization pressured local governments to improve country roads, at least those within a day's outing from cities and towns. Publications such as *The Carriage Monthly* and *The Horseless Age* also lobbied for better roads.

However, at the turn of the century, roads were almost exclusively the responsibility of local government. This largely explains why there was little or no coordinated road building over long distances. One county might provide gravel or even macadam roads, but travelers often found roads disappearing into mud tracks as they crossed a county line.

Energetic Americans possessing enthusiasm for long-distance automobile travel realized that they would need to coordinate their demands for better roads. In the first years of the new century, several intrepid individuals set out on coast-to-coast automobile trips, partly from a sense of adventure, but also to show that such journeys were possible. Horatio N. Jackson and Sewell K. Croker were the first to complete the trip, covering 4,500 miles of primitive roads from San Francisco to New York City in 61 days. A year later, Boston millionaire Charles J. Glidden sponsored the first of his famous "Glidden tours," in which convoys of automobiles traversed hundreds of miles for several weeks, competing for various prizes. Although the chief focus was the automobiles themselves, and which might be the most comfortable and reliable, these tours eventually reached every part of the country and highlighted the desirability of improved roads.

A decade after Jackson's and Croker's transcontinental journey, the automobile mania was in full swing. Several manufacturers had built racing cars that circled oval tracks at speeds over 100 miles per hour, and drivers like Barney Oldfield were among the nation's prime sports heroes. More to the point, automobile ownership was no longer a mark of distinction. Henry Ford had introduced the Model T in 1908, and his highly efficient assembly-line production system rapidly reduced the price of reliable transportation. From a few thousand vehicles owned by wealthy adventurers in 1900, registrations nationwide approached the half-million mark a decade later. Capitalizing on public enthusiasm for the "Tin Lizzie," promoter Carl Fisher (who later fathered the Florida land boom of the 1920s) initiated the idea of building the first all-weather, toll-free transcontinental highway in 1912. In order to generate widespread enthusiasm and support from local and state road-building authorities, the huge project was named the Lincoln Highway. Fisher raised about $4 million from various contributors, including automobile companies, parts suppliers, local booster groups, and thousands of individuals. However, many additional millions would be needed to bring Fisher's dream to fruition. Several hundred miles of improved road were built along the proposed trek, but progress was erratic. According to historian Stephen Sears, long stretches "remained rutted dirt tracks bogged down in local politics." The federal government finally provided the funding required to pave the unimproved sections, and the Lincoln Highway was completed in 1923.

As American entry into World War I loomed, even the most sanguine enthusiasts realized that federal funds were critical if all-weather national highways were to become a reality. In 1916 and 1921 the federal government finally enacted two landmark pieces of legislation. A total of $150 million in matching funds was set aside, to be administered through state highway departments. The chief objective was developing the first truly interstate highways. As automobile ownership multiplied exponentially in the 1910s and 1920s (from 8 million in 1920 to 23 million a decade later), state and local funding likewise escalated rapidly.

Most of the money was raised through gasoline taxes. Oregon passed the first gasoline tax of a penny per gallon in 1919, and every state in the union had followed suit a decade later. Americans willingly accepted "user" fees, as drivers paid in direct proportion to their use of roads. Expenditures on construction and maintenance of roads escalated from $1.38 billion in 1921 to $2.85 billion in 1930.

Almost all Americans benefited directly or indirectly from the boom in road building before the Depression, none more so than farmers. In the first years of the automobile, many farmers either feared and despised them or dismissed their potential for ever replacing horses. Some rural Americans argued that gasoline-powered cars frightened horses and disrupted the delivery of goods to markets. Other more opportunistic farmers hooked up teams of horses to drag stranded motorists out of mud holes—for a stiff fee. However, in response to Populist pressures, the federal government had introduced Rural Free Delivery of mail in 1896, and twentieth-century farmers quickly warmed to the idea that thousands of miles of roads were being improved to permit the easier delivery of their mail. These same byways also facilitated their access to more distant, and more competitive, markets for their commodities. Farm families could enjoy shopping excursions to larger towns, bypassing local general stores and taking advantage of volume pricing in chain stores. Before the onset of the Depression, farmers purchased millions of Model Ts. These versatile cars not only carried farm families into nearby towns and cities but powered much of their machinery, thus saving hours of backbreaking labor. Perhaps more than any other changes in the early twentieth century, the automobile and improved roads ended the farmers' isolation.

The Depression forced severe budget cuts at state and local levels, and many road systems suffered neglect. Few local roads were built, and repairs were routinely postponed. In an effort to create jobs for the unemployed, the federal government piped some funds into road building through the

Works Progress Administration, Public Works Administration, Civilian Conservation Corps, and similar programs. Federal workers blacktopped thousands of miles of roads; in fact, paved road mileage more than doubled between 1933 and 1941, a remarkable fact given the state of the nation's economy.

Perhaps most notable were several brand new, state-of-the-art parkway systems. The New York City metropolitan region had provided a glimpse of the future as early as 1907, when construction began on the Bronx River Parkway. Within three decades, the Saw Mill, Hutchinson, and Cross County Parkways were added, and by 1932 Westchester County boasted 160 miles of parkways. By the end of the 1930s, Long Island's Meadowbrook Parkway, the Henry Hudson Parkway, and the Taconic Parkway essentially completed one of the most sophisticated metropolitan parkway systems in the world. In masterminding this system, road-building czar Robert Moses integrated ideas from nineteenth-century planner Frederick Law Olmsted to some of the most advanced techniques introduced by the designers of Germany's celebrated Autobahn system. In several other eastern states, federal officials underwrote the Blue Ridge Parkway and Skyline Drive. Following World War II, new federally sponsored road projects included the Palisades and the Garden State Parkways.

During both world wars, public officials realized that the nation's highway networks were wholly inadequate for defense purposes. In retrospect, each conflict marked a watershed in federal policy. Federal lawmakers' response to critical needs was almost immediate after World War I, but their reaction following World War II was delayed for more than a decade, for several reasons. Many highway planners placed their faith in tollways, funded largely by state bonds. In 1935, the Pennsylvania legislature had authorized construction of an east-west tollway, to traverse the entire length of the state. The engineering challenge was formidable, and construction encountered delays and difficulties. Pessimists feared that it would be a financial bust. When the first section of 160 miles opened in 1940, traffic experts predicted a daily volume of 715 vehicles; within two weeks, volume reached 26,000 per day, and 2.4 million cars used the road in 1941, its first full year in operation. Other states, mostly in the East, copied Pennsylvania's initiative. By 1959, drivers could accept a toll ticket in eastern New Jersey and not encounter a traffic signal until they reached the outskirts of Chicago.

Patterns of vehicle movement changed significantly in the 1920s and 1930s, including the emergence of commercial trucking, but between 1929 and 1945 the number of vehicles on the road increased very slowly. Between 1945 and 1955, motor vehicle registrations doubled to 52 million. Shortcomings in the nation's highway system quickly reached crisis proportions. Highway engineers, as always placing great faith in technological fixes and design improvements, believed that one answer was widespread construction of limited access superhighways. New York's parkway system boasted highly sophisticated design features. In the Los Angeles region, the Arroyo-Seco Parkway (later renamed the Pasadena Freeway) opened in 1940 as the first link in the massive Los Angeles freeway system. At the New York World's Fair that opened in 1939, Norman Bel Geddes had presented General Motors" "Futurama" exhibit, projecting a vision of the United States in 1960. His design dazzled visitors. One historian described an urban landscape "criss-crossed by nonstop, 100 mph turnpikes: great sparkling metropolises pierced by 14-lane expressways. . . . There were no accidents, no traffic jams, no roadside clutter—and no parking spaces either."

The Germans had constructed the famous Autobahn in the 1930s, and its advanced design features deeply influenced Dwight D. Eisenhower, who was elected president in 1952. Following years of planning and intense lobbying by powerful interest groups, Congress passed the Federal Aid Highway Act in 1956. This landmark bill authorized construction of 41,000 miles of limited-access, toll-free highways across the nation. The federal government assumed 90 percent of the construction costs. Original projections were that the interstate system would be complete in 15 years at a cost of $27 billion. In fact, it took 20 years to construct the first 38,000 miles of interstate highways, at a cost of $62 billion. Eisenhower, thinking at least partly in Keynesian terms, considered such massive projects as "the right way to regulate the economy." Indeed, many business groups worshiped the interstates: construction, the automobile and oil industries, truckers, auto parts accessories, and a host of highway user groups. Funds collected from federal fuel and use taxes and imposts on the purchases of tires, buses, trucks, and trailers were administered by the Highway Trust Fund.

For the first few years, Americans accepted the interstates uncritically. By using wide medians and employing the latest safety features, the smooth concrete ribbons drastically reduced accident rates. Truckers not only moved their loads far more quickly, but they operated their massive rigs more economically and with far less stress. Numerous roadside services established franchises at interchanges, reaping millions of dollars in profits. American families found themselves able to travel across far more countryside during annual vacations and holidays, even if their impressions were dulled by the monotony of Stuckey's oases and Holiday Inns.

By the 1960s, however, voices of protest began to be heard. As originally designed, 12 percent of the interstate system passed through America's cities. Urban planners originally welcomed interstates and other freeways, believing that they would ease the flow of traffic. However, it quickly became apparent that freeways simply generated more traffic, and that benefits in easing traffic congestion were temporary at best. In Los Angeles and other sprawling metropolitan regions, air pollution, caused largely by automobile emissions, reached crisis proportions. Many new freeways passed through the hearts of established cities, ripping apart entire neighborhoods. Social critics pointed out that it was usually the poor and powerless whose neighborhoods were "invaded," and freeway politics took on increasingly nasty, divisive racial and class overtones. Other critics charged that the Highway Trust Fund had assumed a life of its own, that vested interests had created a sacred cow, and that it was nearly impossible to divert funds from massive road-building projects to other transportation needs.

In the 1950s and 1960s, freeway designers almost always achieved their goals. By the 1970s and 1980s, however, critics of the automobile culture frequently celebrated the termination of freeway projects, and even today, some urban landscapes feature uncompleted freeway ramps projecting jaggedly into the sky. At the end of the twentieth century, highway planners appear willing to share rights-of-way with urban mass transit, but vehicular traffic on the open road will probably dominate interurban travel and transport for the foreseeable future.

—*Mark S. Foster*

**See also**

Automobiles; Benjamin Franklin Parkway.

**References**

Chevallier, Raymond. *Roman Roads.* Berkeley: University of California Press, 1976.

McShane, Clay. *Down the Asphalt Path: The Automobile and the American City.* New York: Columbia University Press, 1994.

Patton, Phil. *Open Road: A Celebration of the American Highway.* New York: Simon and Schuster, 1986.

Rae, John B. *The Road and Car in American Life.* Cambridge, MA: MIT Press, 1971.

Rose, Mark H. *Interstate: Express Highway Politics, 1940–1956.* Lawrence: Regents Press of Kansas, 1979.

Sears, Stephen W. *The American Heritage History of the Automobile in America.* New York: American Heritage, 1977.

## Robinson, Edward G. (1893–1973)

During a long and varied career, Edward G. Robinson (who was born Emanuel Goldenberg) made more than 80 films. He is best known for his portrayals of tough-guy gangsters or befuddled victims—two extremes he was able to represent with equal aplomb. Among his most noted films are *Little Caesar* (1930), *Double Indemnity* (1944), *The Woman in the Window* (1944), *Scarlet Street* (1945), and *Key Largo* (1948). In 1972 he received a special Academy Award honoring his long and distinguished career.

*Little Caesar* was Robinson's star-making performance, and in some ways it served to typecast him, at least for a while, as a gangster and psychopath. The film was one of the "Big Three"

in the early 1930s that established the gangster genre (along with *Scarface* and *The Public Enemy*), and Robinson walked the mean city streets with a sneering cockiness that established his character as tough, dangerous, and seemingly on the edge of insanity. Other gangster roles followed, usually set in the tough neighborhoods of a big city where crime bosses ruled and the streets were never safe, especially at night.

Equally interesting were nongangster roles that Robinson played in the 1940s—some in which he was on the right side of the law (*Double Indemnity* and others) and especially a pair of classics directed by Fritz Lang, *The Woman in the Window* and *Scarlet Street.* In these two films, made only a year apart and featuring the same leading cast (Robinson, Joan Bennett, and Dan Duryea) and strikingly similar plots, Robinson moved away from the persona of tough gangster and presented vivid, haunting portrayals of meek, downtrodden, essentially decent fellows who are overwhelmed by the lure of glamour and excitement until they lose control of their own lives. *Woman* and *Scarlet* are exceedingly bleak, although *Woman* hedges its bets with a happy ending of sorts. Both present dark, depressing visions of American city life as a trap designed to ensnare anyone too weak to resist its temptations. The suburbs never looked more inviting as an escape from the trouble waiting around every corner in the urban world of booze, women, and murder.

In the later stages of his career, Robinson played more varied dramatic roles (*All My Sons*, for example), but he will be best remembered for two character types—gangsters who ruled the city streets (at least for a while) and everyday, hardworking men who let the temptations of the urban world take control of them.

—*Robert P. Holtzclaw*

**See also**

Bogart, Humphrey; Gangster Films.

**References**

Hirsch, Foster. *Edward G. Robinson.* New York: Pyramid Publications, 1975.

Robinson, Edward G. *All My Yesterdays: An Autobiography.* New York: Hawthorn Books, 1973.

## Rockefeller Center

Rockefeller Center is a complex of office buildings, theaters, and commercial retail space between 48th and 51st Streets and Fifth and Seventh Avenues in Manhattan, which was erected at various times after 1929. Its primary architects were Raymond Hood and Reinhard & Hofmeister. The principal building period ended in 1940, and subsequent buildings have been erected intermittently since then, including a triad of skyscrapers on Sixth Avenue that opened in 1973. The center is important to American urban development because it

*The skating rink at Rockefeller Center is one of its most popular attractions, perhaps since an open-air skating rink is so unexpected in the heart of a great city.*

presents a model of private, comprehensive building that is both artistic and profitable, a purely commercial enterprise that managed to attain the status of a beloved public place.

While there had been earlier balanced and axial architectural groups, often associated with Beaux-Arts planning principles and the City Beautiful movement, they were almost always built for governmental or cultural rather than commercial sponsors. Rockefeller Center's closest prototype, the office buildings, clubs, and hotels erected near Grand Central Terminal by the owners of the New York Central Railroad (1903–1931), were monotonous in design and lacked popular appeal.

John D. Rockefeller, Jr. (1874–1960), leased the three blocks from 48th to 51st Streets between Fifth and Sixth Avenues from their owner, Columbia University, in 1928, intending to erect impressive high-rent office buildings around a plaza fronted on one side by a new Metropolitan Opera House. When the opera's owners could not finance a new building after the financial crash of 1929, Rockefeller and his development adviser, John R. Todd, proposed a mix of high and low office buildings toward fashionable Fifth Avenue, with theaters on the north and south blocks along Sixth Avenue. The city's height and zoning regulations, and the dismal rental prospects in 1930, were critical in determining such aspects as the building heights (some of them agreeably low), the insertion of a private street on which more office windows could face, and the retention of the plaza, which made it possible to construct a high tower on the same block. In the central RCA (now GE) Building, Rockefeller and major tenants had their offices; this building replaced the opera house and was embellished with materials of high quality and murals by international artists. The plaza was depressed in order to provide retail (now restaurant) space around it, which zoning rules would have forbidden at street level. By 1936, when many shops had failed, the plaza floor was made into an ice-skating rink, a successful experiment later imitated at commercial centers in other cities. Amenities at the center included benches for the public, plazas and small parks (products of zoning rules, but better designed than some others), and displays of plants, fountains, and abundant works of art. Most important for the city as a functioning mechanism is the provision underground for a network of shop-lined walkways linking all of the Center's buildings and the subway, and tunnels for off-street truck loading and delivery.

These improvements were gifts to the city, but made with the understanding that only premises of high quality had any chance of attracting tenants during the 1930s. They go well with the finely crafted limestone surfaces, the staggering of building heights that guarantees ventilation and views, and the artistry seen in the spectacular Radio City Music Hall, the surviving theater. The post-1940 buildings are generally considered artistically inferior.

—*Carol Herselle Krinsky*

**References**
Balfour, Alan. *Rockefeller Center: Architecture as Theater.* New York: McGraw-Hill, 1978.
Krinsky, Carol Herselle. *Rockefeller Center.* New York: Oxford University Press, 1978.

## Roebling, John Augustus (1806–1869)

The world-famous engineer and bridge builder John Augustus Roebling was born in Muhlhausen, Thuringia, in Germany in 1806. Twenty years later, he graduated from Berlin's Royal Polytechnic Institute where he was said to be the favorite student of the great philosopher Hegel. He spent the next three years doing required work for the government of Prussia. In particular, he was assigned to road construction projects, but he dreamed about building mighty bridges. In the aftermath of the revolutions of 1830 in the German states, Roebling abandoned plans for an engineering career in his native land and sailed for the United States in 1831. There, he and his brother Karl founded the agrarian community of Saxonburg, Pennsylvania.

Following his marriage to Johanna Herting, Roebling resumed his engineering career in 1837, the year that he became an American citizen. For the next three years he worked for the state of Pennsylvania on canal, dam, and railroad projects. Observing the problems inherent in moving canal boats over the Allegheny Mountains, Roebling came up with the idea of replacing the hemp ropes then in use with a new type of rope made from twisted wire. This durable product, which Roebling manufactured first in Saxonburg and then in Trenton, New Jersey, was used extensively in the shipping industry, and before long it became an integral part of the suspension bridges he constructed.

Roebling's first bridge, completed in 1846, spanned the Monongahela River in Pittsburgh. By 1850 he had built four

suspension aqueducts for the Delaware and Hudson Canal to transport coal to the Hudson River. In 1855, in his greatest undertaking to date, the railroad suspension bridge at Niagara Falls was completed, whereupon Roebling headed for the Midwest to begin building a bridge over the Ohio River, linking Cincinnati and Covington, Kentucky. This span opened in 1867. In the meantime, in 1860 Roebling and his son, Washington Augustus Roebling, completed a bridge over the Allegheny River, also at Pittsburgh.

Throughout this entire period, Roebling was formulating plans for the most challenging construction project of his career, the great East River Bridge linking Manhattan with Brooklyn. This project was approved in 1869, but Roebling did not live to see the inception of the project. In the early summer of 1869, he was severely injured while doing preliminary fieldwork. As he stood on pilings at the water's edge and performed calculations, one of his feet was crushed by a ferryboat approaching the Brooklyn shore. Carried to his son's house in Brooklyn Heights, Roebling underwent surgery to amputate several toes. Despite excruciating pain, he took full charge of his medical treatment and insisted upon hydropathy, or water cure. Although Roebling was determined to complete the design work for the Brooklyn Bridge, his drawings and instructions remained unfinished when he succumbed to tetanus or lockjaw less than a month after the accident. His death on July 22, 1869, came at the height of a brilliant career that had begun nearly a half-century earlier in his native Germany. At the time of his death, Roebling was at the pinnacle of his career. In addition to his fame as an engineer, he was known internationally for his entrepreneurial success as a manufacturer and as the author of articles dealing with engineering and construction. The Brooklyn Bridge was completed by his son, Washington Augustus Roebling.

—*Marilyn Weigold*

**See also**
Roebling, Washington Augustus.
**References**
McCullough, David. *The Great Bridge.* New York: Simon and Schuster, 1972.
Neidle, Cecyle S. *Great Immigrants.* Boston: Twayne, 1973.
Schuyler, Hamilton. *The Roeblings: A Century of Engineers, Bridge-builders and Industrialists.* Princeton, NJ: Princeton University Press, 1931.
Steinman, David B. *The Builders of the Bridge.* New York: Arno Press, 1972.

## Roebling, Washington Augustus (1837–1926)

As a child growing up in the western Pennsylvania community of Saxonburg, where he was born in 1837, Washington Augustus Roebling had no way of knowing that he would one day become famous as the builder of the Brooklyn Bridge, the span designed by his father, John Augustus Roebling. The oldest of John Roebling's nine children with his first wife, Johanna Herting Roebling, Washington's education consisted of private tutoring until the family moved to Trenton, New Jersey, where his father had established a wire rope manufacturing business. Washington attended the Trenton Academy for four years and was then accepted by the nation's most rigorous college of engineering, Rensselaer Polytechnic Institute. Upon receiving his degree in 1857, he joined the family's wire rope business but soon accepted an invitation to assist his father in constructing the Allegheny River Bridge.

When the Civil War broke out, Washington Roebling volunteered for service in the Union army. As an engineer, he spent the war years building bridges, but he also saw action and was honored for heroism. While assigned to the staff of General Gouverneur Kemble Warren, Roebling met the general's sister, Emily Warren, whom he married a year later. The couple had one son, John Augustus Roebling II, born in Germany while Washington Roebling was abroad studying European bridge-building techniques in preparation for assisting his father with the great East River Bridge linking Manhattan and Brooklyn. Before going abroad, Washington Roebling had worked with his father on construction of the bridge across the Ohio River that connected Cincinnati and Covington, Kentucky. When John Roebling died following an accident before the start of construction on the Brooklyn Bridge, his son succeeded him as chief engineer of the project.

A thoroughly hands-on engineer, Washington Roebling spent long hours in the caissons or foundations of the bridge's gigantic towers. Following two attacks of caisson disease or the "bends," Roebling became an invalid confined to his home in Brooklyn Heights overlooking the construction site. Roebling, who had completed the design and engineering work for the bridge following his father's death, nevertheless continued to supervise the mammoth project until 1883 when the bridge was opened to the public. His wife Emily assisted him by acting as liaison with the assistant engineers in the field, materials suppliers, and the bridge's board of trustees.

In 1884 Washington and Emily Roebling moved to Troy, New York, and later to Trenton, New Jersey, site of the family's wire rope business. Washington Roebling's health gradually improved but he remained a semi-invalid for many years. During that time he devoted himself to his expanding mineral collection, which was donated to the Smithsonian Institution following his death. Toward the end of his life he also served as the president of the Roebling wire rope company.

—*Marilyn Weigold*

**See also**
Roebling, John Augustus.
**References**
McCullough, David. *The Great Bridge.* New York: Simon and Schuster, 1972.

Neidle, Cecyle S. *Great Immigrants.* Boston: Twayne, 1973.
Schuyler, Hamilton. *The Roeblings: A Century of Engineers, Bridgebuilders and Industrialists.* Princeton, NJ: Princeton University Press, 1931.
Steinman, David B. *The Builders of the Bridge.* New York: Arno Press, 1972.

## Rouse, James (1914–1996)

Entrepreneur, civic activist, community builder, and philanthropist, James Rouse addressed many of the most compelling issues facing urban America in the second half of the twentieth century. Although the diversity of his activities, from developing shopping centers, to building the new town of Columbia, Maryland, to promoting affordable housing in inner-city areas, gave his career an eclectic quality, it was informed by a consistent philosophy. Like many of the planners and social activists he was associated with over time, Rouse sought to mold the physical environment in an effort to improve social conditions.

Orphaned at the age of 16 in 1930, Rouse survived hard times during the Depression. He made his way through night law school at the University of Maryland and into the banking business in Baltimore, where he began selling the new and controversial FHA mortgages. During the 1940s, he became active with the Citizens Planning and Housing Association, which pioneered what became known as the "Baltimore plan" to improve slum conditions with aggressive neighborhood campaigns to enforce housing codes strictly. Rouse became an aggressive proponent of this approach as chairman of a housing advisory council to Mayor Thomas D'Alesandro. Subsequently, he helped promote the redevelopment of Baltimore's downtown business district as a founder of the Greater Baltimore Committee, which developed a plan to convert a decaying waterfront section of the city into an entirely reconstructed area known as Charles Center.

Rouse's visibility in Baltimore and his support for the Republican national ticket in 1952 prompted President Dwight Eisenhower to appoint him chair of the urban redevelopment subcommittee of the President's Advisory Committee on Government Housing Policies and Programs. In stating the necessity for "developing a much broader approach to slum elimination," the subcommittee endorsed rehabilitation in order to create "sound healthy neighborhoods out of the existing housing inventory." The subcommittee's recommendations proved influential in shaping the Housing Act of 1954. In addition to requiring cities to coordinate their planning efforts by establishing a "workable plan" for redevelopment, the report stressed Baltimore's approach to neighborhood conservation through rehabilitation. Rouse put these ideas into effect quickly in preparing a workable plan for the District of Columbia as the 1954 act required. Titled "No

Slums in Ten Years," this plan, released in January 1955, reiterated the congressional testimony that Rouse had given a year earlier in which he defined urban renewal as "making the city into a community of healthy neighborhoods where people want to live and raise families."

Even as he prepared the Washington plan, Rouse helped form a national citizens committee to promote this new concept of urban renewal. Announced in a major address by President Eisenhower in November 1954, the American Council To Improve Our Neighborhoods, or ACTION, represented a growing commitment by the private sector to work with government and planning officials to revitalize blighted urban areas. The organization envisioned seeking $100 billion, mainly from private sources, to eliminate slums, a goal Rouse personally pursued when he assumed the presidency of ACTION in 1958. Never a supporter of public housing, Rouse promoted the goal of making existing housing fit and livable.

As his own business interests took him into the development of shopping centers, Rouse appeared to move away from his earlier concerns. Yet, following closely a philosophy pioneered by the architect Victor Gruen, he envisioned bringing into suburban malls some of the same sociability he had espoused in urban renewal. In the first of three dozen shopping centers he designed, Mondowmin, three miles from downtown Baltimore, and in collaboration with Gruen in New Jersey's Cherry Hill shopping center, Rouse sought to create the lively social interactions associated with the city but to avoid the attendant nuisances of traffic congestion and lack of parking. Noting that suburbanites probably spent more time in shopping centers than anywhere else except home or school, Rouse argued that the shopping center should relax and replenish the families who used it and promote friendly contact among the people of the community.

Rouse conceived the new town of Columbia, Maryland, on the outskirts of Washington as the next step in building community by creating designs that "develop better people." By emphasizing open housing and a range of building types to assure affordable prices for a large part of the population, Rouse hoped to relieve urban housing problems with a metropolitan-wide approach. In the effort to promote community sentiment, he divided Columbia into carefully planned and defined neighborhoods, each with its own limited shopping facilities, primary schools, and playgrounds. The heart of the city, however, was the Columbia Mall. Here were the same facilities for special events and the same visual elements tested in earlier suburban centers.

From Columbia it was but a short step to Rouse's innovative inner-city malls, starting with Faneuil Hall in Boston (1976) and Harbor Place in Baltimore (1980). These festival marketplaces, as they became known, demonstrated the economic viability of mixed-use projects downtown while at the same time incorporating Rouse's belief, stated in 1956, that the enclosed regional mall had the potential for "a massive reorganization of the urban community." As the Rouse Company's chairman and president, Mathias J. DeVito, described it, "The suburban mall is perceived as attractive, safe, comfortable, and dependable with lots of greenery, lots of light and entertainment. These things work . . . because a mall has one management that controls the environment. . . . Our mission is to do downtown what has been done in the suburbs."

As Rouse neared retirement in the late 1970s, he sought other means of directing his efforts to improve the urban environment. Building on his experience of providing affordable housing in an inner-city section of Washington, D.C., through his involvement with the Church of the Savior, Rouse announced creation of the Enterprise Foundation in 1981. Promising to raise $15 million a year to support the purchase and renovation of slum buildings, Rouse combined his expertise as both an entrepreneur and a philanthropist to introduce the concept of using a moneymaking real estate development corporation to invest in commercial enterprises in inner cities as a way of helping to revive depressed areas. Any profits from the enterprise were to be reinvested in housing in poor neighborhoods. This retail effort faltered, and the company sold its interest in the first group of centers in Norfolk, Virginia; Toledo, Ohio; and Flint, Michigan. Sufficient corporate donations, however, allowed the foundation to expand broadly. By the middle of the 1980s, Rouse had designated a decaying inner-city neighborhood in Baltimore, Sandtown-Winchester, as the location for a pilot program to combine public and private sponsorship to transform a neighborhood from decay to self-sufficiency. Two years of planning with the community produced a corporation with a very Rouse-like name, Community Building in Partnership. In addition to promoting new and rehabilitated housing for the area, the neighborhood plan embraced an ambitious range of social programs. While this latest experiment in community building seemed far removed in time and space from Rouse's first venture into inner-city revitalization, he described the effort in terms that could summarize much of his career. Speaking in 1991 he called for "a united effort to lift the physical conditions of the neighborhood from dilapidation and oppressive rents . . . and, at the same time, to lift the human condition from hopelessness and fear to self-respect, growth, and a sense of well-being."

—*Howard Gillette, Jr.*

### References
Gillette, Howard, Jr. "The Evolution of the Planned Shopping Center in Suburb and City." *Journal of the American Planning Association* 51 (1985): 449–460.
Landers, Robert K. "The Conscience of James Rouse." *Historic Preservation* 37 (1985): 60–63.

# Row House

The row house has been the predominant form of urban housing in many American cities, especially in larger metropolises along the East Coast. Row houses typically are understood to be attached to other dwellings by party walls, are relatively low-rise (usually two to four stories), and are built as residences for one household (although they are sometimes later subdivided into separate apartments). Initially, row houses were often erected separately, adjoining other structures, but as the pace of urban development accelerated, they were constructed as units in longer rows, sometimes encompassing entire blocks. Historically, upscale versions of row houses might be called "town houses" to distinguish them from the "country houses" of wealthy residents; in recent decades, the term *townhouse* is often employed to evoke associations of status and prestige for new row house developments, whether in suburb or city.

The American version of the urban row house has its roots in medieval European cities where defensive and commercial needs dictated compact, dense living areas. Its immediate antecedents derived especially from the Netherlands and England, where the rise of a new urban middle class created a demand for in-town dwellings rather than country residences. In the seventeenth and eighteenth centuries, English "terraced" houses with regular facades set the standard for elite urban residences, London and Bath providing especially grand examples.

The rise of towns, then cities, in England's Atlantic coastal colonies made the row house a natural export, especially in urban areas where dense population created pressure on residential space near city centers. Row houses have been documented in Philadelphia from the early eighteenth century onward, and by 1800 they were common in Baltimore, New York, and Boston. While these cities became most associated with this housing type, it also appeared in smaller places, from New England to Georgia; examples include Savannah, Georgia; Richmond and Alexandria, Virginia; and Georgetown (later D.C.). In the later colonial and early national period, the essential row house form—usually of brick construction—served all classes. Elegantly designed row houses, with embellishments reflecting the latest in architectural taste, typically facing a main street or square, housed the wealthy; artisans, professionals, and lesser merchants inhabited more modest but still substantial versions, often on side streets or in less prestigious locations; while the working class (including urban slaves or freedmen) lived in small, crude attached houses on alleys.

As an urban housing type serving diverse social groups, the row house peaked after the Civil War. In New York's Manhattan, "brownstones" represented the most elegant of American row houses until rapid population growth and accelerating land values led to the exodus of wealthy New Yorkers to new railroad suburbs and to the erection of large tenement-style dwellings for the less well-off. In New England, triple-deckers, detached and built of wood, were that region's answer to the urban housing needs of working-class immigrants. However, in cities with firmly entrenched traditions of row house living for middle- and working-class families, like Philadelphia and Baltimore, the modest row house predominated as an urban housing type until World War II.

The row house made optimum use of urban land, yet on a scale that afforded grade-level entry and individual household privacy. It seemed especially well suited to the gridiron street systems that dominated American city plans. Economies of cost in terms of construction, heating, and upkeep appealed both to builders and home buyers. Initially the product of artisan builders on a small scale, row house construction eventually was dominated by large-scale speculative developers. On both scales, it tended to foster homeownership.

Row house design reflected popular architectural trends. The narrow facade limited opportunities for expression, which had to be conveyed through the treatment of doors, windows, and cornices. Early styles reflected the clean, classical lines of Federal, then Greek Revival, motifs. In the mid–nineteenth century, the romanticism of Italianate forms heightened the degree of ornamentation, especially in high-style examples. Technological innovation also played a role—steam cutting made brownstone available as a replacement for brick; plate glass allowed for large, uninterrupted panes; wood, metal, and stone trim could be mass-produced. Prior to 1900, typical row house proportions were narrow and deep, but turn-of-the-century concern about the density of urban living, especially the lack of light and ventilation, produced an important evolution of dimensions with the development of the "Airlite" or "Daylight" design, a more boxlike floor plan that gave every room a window.

In cities where row houses continued to predominate as the choice of the middle and working classes in the twentieth century, demand eventually led speculative builders to develop same-style housing on a massive scale that critics would find monotonous, especially when little consideration was given to open, public spaces. After World War II, when suburban development produced detached housing options in a variety of price ranges, the urban row house lost its appeal. Recent years, however, have experienced a revival of interest in row houses, whether as the renovation of historic row houses in neighborhoods near the center of the city, part of a return to the city movement often termed gentrification, or as new construction of clustered "townhouses," in recognition of the need for more economical land use in suburbs as well as cities.

—W. Edward Orser

**References**

Daunton, Martin J. "Cities of Homes and Cities of Tenements: British and American Comparisons, 1870–1914." *Journal of Urban History* 14 (1988): 283–319.

Hayward, Mary Ellen. "Urban Vernacular Architecture in Nineteenth-Century Baltimore." *Winterthur Portfolio* 16 (1981): 33–63.

Lockwood, Charles. *Bricks and Brownstones: The New York Row House, 1783–1929, an Architectural and Social History.* New York: McGraw-Hill, 1972.

Murtagh, William John. "The Philadelphia Row House." *Journal of the Society of Architectural Historians* 14 (1957): 8–13.

Orser, W. Edward. *Blockbusting in Baltimore: The Edmondson Village Story.* Lexington: University Press of Kentucky, 1994.

Shivers, Natalie W. *Those Old Placid Rows: The Aesthetic and Development of the Baltimore Rowhouse.* Baltimore: Maclay and Associates, 1981.

## San Antonio, Texas

San Antonio has always relied on the kindness of strangers for its prosperity. Unlike other cities that have actively, even aggressively, sought to promote local development, San Antonio has adopted a passive role in determining its destiny. It is a city to which things happen, rather than a city that makes things happen.

Such passivity is not typical of American cities. Many settlements with unpromising sites and prospects, like Dallas, Denver, or Los Angeles, have developed into major cities by consciously and deliberately ignoring their disadvantages and pursuing aggressive growth strategies. Yet, for almost exactly 250 years, native-born businessmen in San Antonio failed to produce a single initiative to promote development. Indeed, considering that urban historians have frequently marveled at the energy and success of local businessmen in building large, dynamic cities, the absence of such energy and dynamism in San Antonio offers one of the more interesting reasons to examine its history. Its distinctiveness may reveal something important about the ways in which some American cities have managed to grow without employing the traditional tools of aggressive boosterism.

The key to San Antonio's growth has always been outside subsidy, and the military has been the primary source of those subsidies. Indeed, this relationship dates from the city's founding in 1718. At that time, Spanish imperial officials, worried about a potential threat from France's expanding North American empire, needed a supply base for their projected defense line in east Texas. They chose the site that became San Antonio because its river and fertile soil would support an agricultural village to supply food to troops in east Texas. Farmers would sell their surplus to the local presidio, which would store the crops for future use by the military.

That arrangement, and the designation of San Antonio as a provincial capital during the Mexican Era, sustained the town until the Texas Revolution. During the 1840s German immigration to central Texas began transforming San Antonio into an important regional agricultural service center, but

it was the American military that provided cash to stimulate economic development. Borrowing the Spanish idea of a logistical center, the U.S. Army established a supply base in San Antonio during the Mexican War. Afterward, the army established a line of frontier defense posts stretching north from San Antonio to Fort Worth and west to El Paso. San Antonio's businessmen organized freight companies dependent on army contracts to transport supplies to those forts.

In the second half of the nineteenth century, San Antonio enjoyed sufficient growth to make it the largest city in Texas by 1900. That short-lived triumph occurred primarily because a railroad arrived in 1877 and created links to outside markets for the first time. Oddly, though, local San Antonians initially refused to entice a railroad to town. The army, concerned about transportation costs, forced the city to acquire a rail line by threatening to leave otherwise. Once completed, the railroad created an economic boom that attracted thousands of new residents, but businessmen neglected to seize on this opportunity to launch any significant city building. By contrast, at the same time, Dallas was busily transforming itself into a major center for manufacturing agricultural machinery.

San Antonio's reliance on the military and agriculture, and its resolute refusal to sponsor local growth, eventually damaged its ability to compete with regional rivals. At the outset of the twentieth century, when Houston, Dallas, and Fort Worth launched major growth initiatives, San Antonio chose to focus on developing tourism, an "industry" that required little local investment and relied on the city's store of historic missions and its "colorful" Mexican-American culture for success.

Local businessmen even turned a deaf ear to potentially important opportunities. When truck farmers in the Rio Grande Valley pleaded for a rail connection that would have given San Antonio control over a mushrooming business, local businessmen ignored them. Population growth occurred largely, although not entirely, because of the steady flow of refugees from the Mexican Revolution that began in 1910.

Largely poor and unskilled, these refugees arrived in a city that offered them extremely limited economic opportunities.

In these circumstances, military subsidies continued to play a significant role in the local economy. During World War I, San Antonio acquired two new, permanent air bases and a host of temporary bases, all of which gave a major boost to the economy, but only for the duration of the war. During the years between the two world wars, a serendipitous and fierce debate over the importance of airpower to national defense led Congress to authorize another training base. Assuming that this new base simply had to be located in San Antonio, local businessmen and politicians initially refused to help the Army Air Forces locate and develop a site. Finally forced to reconsider their indolence by a hostile Congress, the local leadership barely met the deadline for acquiring land for the Army Air Corps training center, now Randolph Air Force Base, in early 1927.

By 1940, San Antonio, with roughly 250,000 residents, had slipped into third place in the state's urban hierarchy. Its unemployment rate stood officially at 19 percent, and it had

The museum at the historic compound of Mission San Antonio de Valero, known as the Alamo, where 188 Texans died in an 1836 battle against 5,000 Mexican troops.

recently been pilloried in the national media for having the worst slums and the worst health problems in the country, both resulting from massive indifference to the plight of the city's Mexican-American population.

In the late 1930s, San Antonio stood to benefit significantly from President Franklin D. Roosevelt's national defense program, but local community leaders showed a distinct preference for training rather than manufacturing initiatives. In 1939, when military policy dictated the dispersal of aircraft manufacturing around the nation, San Antonio's Chamber of Commerce refused to ask for production plants, preferring to emphasize training as the city's contribution to the military buildup. After Pearl Harbor, this policy accidentally created an economic boon when Army Air Force officials decided to transform Kelly Air Force Base into a major logistical center. Civilian employment at Kelly mushroomed from 800 in 1938 to 37,000 in 1945. For the first time in its history, San Antonio suddenly had a large, highly skilled, civilian workforce.

The long Cold War ensured that Kelly Air Force Base would be the single largest employer in the city until the 1990s. With the military firmly entrenched as the most important pillar of the economy, local businessmen began, for the first time, an active campaign to develop San Antonio. In 1954, they organized the Good Government League (GGL), a political machine that seized control of local government to implement its growth agenda. That agenda included a massive investment of federal and state money in a vastly expanded road and highway system, federal subsidies to sponsor an international exposition (HemisFair in 1968) to boost local tourism, state subsidies to establish a medical research facility, and a new branch of the University of Texas.

San Antonio was hardly unique in seeking these subsidies. Many other cities, inside and outside of Texas, benefited from federal largesse during the Cold War. What distinguished San Antonio, however, was its resolute refusal to risk local capital to develop or attract manufacturing as a natural corollary to subsidized development.

That task was left to a new group of outsiders, businessmen not born in San Antonio, who founded the Economic Development Foundation (EDF) in 1974. Although they lacked broad support among their peers, these businessmen implemented a systematic, relatively successful, long-term effort to bring manufacturing to the city. In effect, the EDF represented the first break with the tradition of relying on outside subsidies for local development.

In the meantime, the GGL's agenda had promoted massive growth on the city's north side, but it had also ignored the needs of inner-city minority neighborhoods. That favoritism finally provoked a political crisis between 1975 and 1977 that resulted in a more equitable distribution of political power but that also undermined public support for continuing economic development. Many San Antonians felt that redeveloping older neighborhoods and the downtown should take precedence over further northside growth.

As mayor from 1981 to 1989, Henry Cisneros managed to bridge the political, ethnic, and racial divisions within the city to implement a dynamic growth program. Cisneros used federal programs such as Community Development Block Grants to redevelop inner-city neighborhoods while simultaneously cooperating with the EDF to attract new businesses to San Antonio. He encouraged tourism by convincing several hotel chains to construct major new facilities and by expanding meeting space for conventions (culminating in the Alamo Dome project at the end of his mayoralty). Cisneros was also instrumental in helping establish a fledgling biotechnology research park in the city.

Despite all these efforts, San Antonio remained firmly third within the Texas urban hierarchy. That, however, was impressive enough to earn a place among the largest cities in the nation (with a metropolitan area population of 1.2 million in 1990). In a perverse—and certainly slow-paced—way, San Antonio represents, at least until recently, how well a city can prosper through the kindness of strangers.

—*David R. Johnson*

### References

Blackwelder, Julia Kirk. *Women of the Depression: Caste and Culture in San Antonio, 1929–1939.* College Station: Texas A & M University Press, 1984.

Garcia, Richard A. *Rise of the Mexican American Middle Class: San Antonio, 1929–1941.* College Station: Texas A & M University Press, 1991.

Green, Peyton. *San Antonio: City in the Sun.* New York: McGraw-Hill, 1946.

Johnson, David R. "The Failed Experiment: Military Aviation and Urban Development in San Antonio, 1910–40." In Roger Lotchin, ed., *The Martial Metropolis: U.S. Cities in War and Peace,* 89–108. New York: Praeger, 1984.

———. "Frugal and Sparing: Interest Groups, Politics, and City Building in San Antonio, 1870–85." In Char Miller and Heywood T. Sanders, eds., *Urban Texas: Politics and Development,* 33–57. College Station: Texas A & M University Press, 1990.

———. "San Antonio: The Vicissitudes of Boosterism." In Richard M. Bernard and Bradley R. Rice, eds., *Sunbelt Cities: Politics and Growth since World War II,* 235–254. Austin: University of Texas Press, 1983.

Johnson, David R., John A. Booth, and Richard Harris, eds. *The Politics of San Antonio: Community, Progress, & Power.* Lincoln: University of Nebraska Press, 1983.

Poyo, Gerald E., and Gilberto M. Hinojosa, eds. *Tejano Origins in Eighteenth Century San Antonio.* Austin: University of Texas Press, 1991.

## San Diego, California

San Diego, California, is located in the far southwest corner of the continental United States—or, as one nineteenth-century observer put it, "on the edge of the earth." In 1990 the population of San Diego passed 1 million, and it became the sixth largest city in the nation. This modern city is a major center for the U.S. Navy, tourism, and aerospace and biotech research and manufacturing. Formerly more of a collection of suburbs than a "city," since the 1980s San Diego has begun to acquire an impressive skyline, a revived downtown, and increasingly mature cultural institutions. A city that traditionally was overwhelmingly middle class and Anglo-American in its ethnic composition, it has become a multicultural community perched on the edge of the Pacific Rim and on the Mexican border.

Every city is the result of its history and its geography. Modern San Diego bears this out to a greater extent than most, as much of the contemporary city can be explained by its geographical setting or the community's historical development. For instance, geography prevented San Diego from becoming a major industrial or commercial center. The area has no significant natural resources (no extensive agricultural lands, no coal, petroleum, iron ore, or other minerals), and this fact prevented the development of an industrial or commercial base. Because of the difficulty of penetrating the mountain barrier to the east, the city was unable to draw upon a hinterland for its resources and trade, as had Boston, New York, Philadelphia, or Baltimore in their growth years. Since San Diego never developed heavy industry, large-scale agriculture, mining, or extensive commerce, it has never had a large blue-collar population or a strong labor movement.

At the same time, the Mediterranean-like climate and the access to the sea has meant that the city has attracted health seekers since the beginning of the American period. When tourism emerged as a major part of American life, San Diego developed a huge visitor and recreation industry. When aviation entered the picture, San Diego's mild climate helped it become a major aviation research, design, manufacturing, and training center. The same dependable weather made San Diego attractive as a military training site, and as a base for a large portion of the navy's fleet. And the city's location on the Pacific Rim and the Mexican border positions it for major development in the future that taps into those geographical areas.

The city that developed in this geographic setting planted roots in 1769 when Spain, to protect its claims to the northern Pacific coast, established a mission and a presidio, or fortified settlement, on San Diego Bay, making San Diego the first European settlement in the present state of California.

During the Spanish Era (1769–1821), the presidio remained minor, with its population probably not exceeding several hundred non-Indians. The mission, San Diego de Alcala, developed into a sizable enterprise to convert the local Native Americans, make them act like Hispanics to the greatest degree possible, and develop an economic base to support them and other Spanish enterprises in the area. The mission system was extremely destructive to the Indians of the area (the Kumeyaay), virtually imprisoning them as laborers, destroying much of their native culture, compromising the natural environment in which they had functioned effectively, and killing a high percentage of them.

At about the time the Mexicans won independence from Spain and California became a Mexican province (1821), residents of the presidio of San Diego began to spill over into the small coastal plain nearby and formed the town of San Diego, which was laid out in traditional Spanish-Mexican style around a central plaza. Some residents of the town became rancheros as the Mexican government issued large land grants, which provided minor wealth and a hacienda lifestyle that novelists and moviemakers have much romanticized. Many of the ranchos remained intact until recent times; others became the source of towns, state parks, military bases, and housing developments. Many local place-names reflect the ranchos of the Mexican Era.

When California became part of the United States in 1848, San Diego was a sleepy village of adobe houses, with a population of perhaps 350 non-Indians. The aggressive, individualistic, entrepreneurial, Anglo-Americans quickly transformed the community, introducing U.S. laws and government, building a courthouse, establishing a newspaper and a school, and improving transportation and communication facilities. Anglo-Americans also displaced the Mexican population politically and overshadowed Hispanic culture. In terms of numbers and political, social, and economic impact, the Hispanic role in San Diego remained small until recently.

After the removal in the 1860s of San Diego to its present location on the shores of San Diego Bay, the modern city began to emerge. It boomed slightly in the early 1870s with the rumor that the city was to be the western terminus of the Texas Pacific Railroad, but that small boom collapsed in the Panic of 1873. When the railroad finally did arrive in the 1880s, the city experienced an even greater boom as people imagined tremendous prosperity created by commerce and industry. The city's population soared to 40,000, and land prices skyrocketed as well. But the expected good times never arrived as Los Angeles became the effective destination of the railroad, and San Diego nothing but a spur.

Land values plummeted, and the population dwindled to 15,000. The city entered a period of stagnation. However, during that period, San Diego established most of the foundations and infrastructure needed by a modern city: public utilities and facilities, social and cultural clubs, religious institutions, the library, internal and regional transportation systems, and many businesses. In addition, most of the towns in the surrounding area were founded, creating for the time

a limited hinterland to feed into San Diego and, for the future, suburbs to serve an expanding city.

The population that transformed San Diego into a small American city came primarily from the northern and midwestern United States. It was over 80 percent Anglo-American, mostly Republican, and overwhelmingly Protestant. This Yankee population brought with it a vision of a community of economic opportunity with a quality of life represented by churches, schools, libraries, parks, and many philanthropic and service organizations. It also brought its mainstream American cultural values and tastes. This is illustrated by the architecture of the era; from the 1850s through the 1910s San Diegans built white frame Victorian residences, red brick commercial buildings, and a few Beaux Arts public buildings. Until the mid-1910s, the community looked like a midwestern town; in fact, it was derisively called "Omaha-by-the-Bay."

That self-confident Anglo population provided strong, progressive civic leadership between the boom of the 1880s and World War I. With extremely weak political institutions, most of the developments that transformed San Diego into the unique city it is today have resulted from private initiative. This included establishing such institutions as the public library, the San Diego Zoo, virtually all charitable institutions, and the Scripps Institution of Oceanography, in addition to the development of many parks. Private leadership secured the navy installations in the area, and private enterprise built most of the early transportation, water facilities, and utilities.

Private leadership also produced the Panama-California Exposition of 1915–1916, designed to celebrate the completion of the Panama Canal and to remind the world that San Diego was the first American port of call on the Pacific Ocean. This spectacularly successful world's fair drew upon a romanticized version of the city's Spanish past to stress its Mediterranean-like climate and lifestyle. This was part of a larger California movement between 1880 and 1910 to use its Hispanic past to create a special identity for California. It was manifest in the development of mission revival architecture and in the use of Spanish themes in advertising, in naming towns, and later, in naming streets. San Diego drew deeply from its Spanish past to displace its early Victorian appearance with one celebrating its own roots. Thus, the Spanish revival buildings of the Exposition of 1915 in Balboa Park became a permanent statement of the area's history, as did many other buildings of the era—the railroad station, the Marine Corps Recruit Depot, the City/County Administration Building, San Diego State University and the University of San Diego, many commercial buildings, and thousands of residential bungalows with white walls and red-tiled roofs. In addition, the citizens restored the old mission and preserved the site of the Spanish presidio; in time the state made the original townsite Old Town State Park in order to preserve it. Thus, from about 1915 on, much of the look and identity of San Diego has been Hispanic—a phenomenon created by an overwhelming Anglo leadership class drawing primarily upon a mythical past.

Between World War I and World War II, the town grew rapidly, doubling its population each census. After World War I, many navy installations were moved to San Diego; from that time on, the military has been a major factor in San Diego's economic and social life. The city also drew upon its early aviation history to develop a major aviation manufacturing industry, which matured in the 1930s and expanded in World War II and during the Cold War. Although the Depression had some effect on San Diego, it was minor compared to many places, and it ended quickly with the military buildup prior to World War II.

With World War II, San Diego moved from being a small city to its status as a major city when its population skyrocketed, never to decline again. With growth fed by manufacturing for the war (primarily in aviation and related industries), the tremendous number of navy and marine corps bases, plus additional army facilities established for training purposes, the city suffered massive problems in housing, education, transportation, and public services. After the war, many people who had passed through during the conflict returned, and for a generation a large portion of San Diegans traced their first contact with the area to their war experiences.

After World War II, it was assumed that the city would shrink back to its prewar size; that never happened. As one observer put it, the Cold War saved San Diego from the ravages of peace. Because of the Cold War, the city continued to be a major center for aviation (and later aerospace) research and manufacturing; it also remained a major military center. Thus, with some ups and downs the city not only did not shrink, it continued to grow steadily. In the 1970s and 1980s the city's population increased 86 percent, making it the sixth largest city in the nation, with, after 1990, over 1 million people in the city and 2.5 million in the metropolitan area.

As the city grew it did so by creating a series of freeways, suburban shopping malls, and suburban industrial parks that pulled the population into a large series of suburbs (by 1980 more people lived in the suburbs than in the city proper). This enabled the city to maintain a lifestyle of individual homes, swimming pools, and greenery; it also led to a serious decline of the inner city. In the 1960s the city fought back with a downtown civic center (which won it an All American city designation) and early attempts to make downtown into a financial center. These efforts did not pay off until the 1980s when the construction of a unique downtown shopping mall (Horton Plaza), which, with the creation of the Gaslamp District, construction of a major convention center, and development of downtown residential units, began to revitalize the inner city. Among other things, this led to the construction of skyscrapers that have transformed the skyline, giving San Diego, for the first time, the look of a big city.

Along with the new focus on downtown, San Diego's cultural life matured in the 1980s and 1990s. It has an extremely active theater scene, a very successful opera company, a major symphony with its own hall, and innumerable art galleries and museums. The area's universities (two major ones, San Diego State University and University of California at San Diego, plus a number of smaller colleges) help San Diego maintain its ranking as the major city with the highest percentage of college graduates; they also add to the intellectual life of the community and support the research-oriented economy. Popular institutions such as the San Diego Zoo and Wild Animal Park, Sea World, and Cabrillo National Monument, coupled with the area's beaches, harbors, and parks, serve both the local population and the tourist industry.

Economically, in the 1990s the city manufacturing and commercial sectors grew, which should continue to with North American Free Trade Agreement (NAFTA) and Pacific Rim trade. San Diego continues to stress high tech research and manufacturing, especially in aviation and biotechnology. Although the downsizing of the military has cost San Diego some military bases, the consolidation of others into local bases has actually increased the military foundation of San Diego. If the city can tap into the potential of its location on the Mexican border and its Pacific Rim connections, San Diego's economic future would seem bright.

One major change in San Diego since the 1970s has been the displacement of the overwhelmingly Anglo population with a growing Spanish-speaking, Asian, and African population; there has also been a continual stream of European immigrants. By the 1990s, nonwhites have become a majority in the public schools, indicating the future ethnic makeup of the city. San Diego has been slow to respond to these changes, with limited integration of nonwhites into the economic, political, or cultural life of the city. Perhaps that failure is but part of a larger failure of political leadership, which has also been unable to address major problems, such as airport relocation, construction of a suitable public library, and control of growth.

San Diego in the 1990s is a beautiful city, with a distinct character and identity shaped by its physical location and its use of Hispanic traditions. It can anticipate an increasingly diversified and colorful cultural and social life if it can integrate its new populations into the mainstream, and unlimited economic growth if it capitalizes on its location on the Pacific Rim.

—*Raymond G. Starr*

### References

Engstrand, Iris H. W. *San Diego: California's Cornerstone*. Tulsa, OK: Continental Press, 1980.

Garcia, Mario T. "Merchants and Dons: San Diego's Attempt at Modernization, 1850–1860." *Journal of San Diego History* 21 (1975): 52–80.

Hennessey, Gregg R. "San Diego, the U.S. Navy, and Urban Development: West Coast City Building, 1912–1929." *California History* 72 (1993): 128–149, 209–212.

Lotchin, Roger W. "The City and the Sword through the Ages and the Era of the Cold War." In Robert B. Fairbanks and Kathleen Underwood, eds., *Essays on Sunbelt Cities and Recent Urban America*. College Station: Texas A & M University Press, 1990.

Pourade, Richard W. *The History of San Diego*. 7 vols. San Diego, CA: Union-Tribune Publishing Company, 1960–1977.

Starr, Raymond G. *San Diego: A Pictorial History*. Norfolk, VA: The Donning Company, 1986.

## San Francisco, California

According to archaeological evidence, human settlement on the peninsula where the San Francisco Bay meets the Pacific Ocean dates to 3,100 B.C. The Spanish established the first European settlement nearly 5,000 years later in 1776, when members of an expedition dispatched from Mexico City established a presidio and mission there. The Ohlone, or Costanoan, people living in the area at the time numbered about 500. The first municipal survey was performed in 1835, when the village was known as Yerba Buena, and the hamlet became part of a coastal trading network that brought Yankee Americans, English, and other Europeans—some from South America—to the Pacific Coast.

The American flag was first flown at Yerba Buena's Plaza in July 1846, symbolizing the transfer of the settlement from Mexico to the United States. The change of names from Yerba Buena to San Francisco occurred in January 1847. Only one year later, gold was discovered near Sacramento, California, on land owned by John A. Sutter, a Swiss immigrant. Because of the virtual flood of men rushing through the port of San Francisco on their way to find gold, the city's population soared from 1,000 to 25,000 between January 1848 and December 1849, and the city joined the front ranks of American cities.

During the second half of the nineteenth century, San Francisco became the dominant urban settlement of the western United States. The city profited from its port facilities, which the business community developed under the watchful eye of the state government after California achieved statehood in 1850. Banking also developed in San Francisco from the time of the gold rush, and benefits derived from the city's role as a depository for Mother Lode gold and Comstock Lode silver allowed its business elite to furnish the frontier outpost with mansions and hotels that rivaled those in New York City. The Palace Hotel, built by the banker William C. Ralston and opened in 1875, was the largest great hostelry in the nation.

From the start of the gold rush, San Francisco attracted a diverse array of Asians, Central Americans, and South Americans, as well as Europeans and Americans of European ancestry. (African Americans did not comprise more than a fraction of 1 percent of the population before World War II.) The city's Chinatown, until recently the nation's largest, originally provided services to Chinese immigrants employed in the gold mines and expanded when unemployed Chinese construction workers moved to its crowded streets adjacent to the city's old Plaza after the nation's first transcontinental railroad was finished in 1869. By the early 1870s, Irish and German newcomers, especially from New York, many of them Roman Catholic with a sizable Jewish minority, had established themselves in the upper echelons of San Francisco business and society. With the notable exception of the years after 1856, when the nativist Committee of Vigilance dampened Irish-Catholic participation in local politics for nearly a decade, Catholics and Jews enjoyed relative freedom from public displays of prejudice and discrimination. The Chinese population, on the other hand, experienced both routine and riotous racist attacks, particularly during the hard times of the middle to late 1870s, when a demagogic politician and small-business owner, Denis Kearney, led his Workingmen's Party of California in a campaign against Chinese immigration, which culminated in passage of the Exclusion Act of 1882.

Between 1860 and 1890, San Francisco's population increased from 57,000 to 299,000, and the city moved from being the fifteenth largest to the eighth largest in the United States. By the beginning of the twentieth century, the city still stood as the dominant metropolis of the West, with commercial ascendance over Alaska, Hawaii, and much of the Pacific Coast and intramountain region. Also, a new generation of business leaders, born in the 1860s and 1870s, began to take control of the city's economy. Michael H. DeYoung, a newspaperman, had been advocating a major exposition for nearly a decade, and the Midwinter International Fair of 1894 emulated the World's Columbian Exposition held in Chicago the year before as a way of advertising San Francisco's mild winter climate. James D. Phelan, a banker, a bon vivant, and later a U.S. senator, worked unsuccessfully to modernize San Francisco according to the prescriptions of the City Beautiful movement and successfully headed a municipal reform movement that gave the city a new charter in 1900. William H. Crocker, son of one of the magnates who constructed the first transcontinental railroad, forged a business empire that embraced banking, manufacturing, mining, and utilities throughout the West. Other local businessmen also invested widely, and much of the financial and commercial life of the West focused on San Francisco's financial district.

While business leaders planned for a multistate region, most San Franciscans concerned themselves with more immediate concerns. The anti-Chinese racism of the late nineteenth century subsided slightly, Chinatown became a major tourist attraction, and mutual tolerance usually characterized relations among the numerically dominant Irish, German, British, Italians, Scandinavians, and native-born Americans.

Labor organizations emerged and developed great strength in the early twentieth century, making San Francisco unusual among American cities with respect to the power of organized labor. A major strike by teamsters and waterfront workers in 1901 led to formation of the Union Labor Party, an organization dominated by unions that captured City Hall and shattered James D. Phelan's dream of a city run by enlightened and cultured businessmen.

The Union Labor Party was nearly destroyed by a graft prosecution financed partly by Phelan. However, the party revived under the leadership of Mayor Patrick H. McCarthy, a building trades leader, who saw city government as appropriately run by political brokers who represented wage earners. San Francisco's labor movement also sought to extend the reach of unions to workers in other parts of California; McCarthy, for example, also headed the statewide council of building trades unions.

On April 18, 1906, an earthquake measuring somewhere between 7.9 and 8.25 on the Richter scale and lasting 48 seconds hit San Francisco and the surrounding region. Current estimates place the death toll at more than 3,000, a number in sharp contrast to the city's official estimate in 1906 of 674. The earthquake started fires that destroyed over 28,000 buildings and leveled four square miles, including the entire downtown and about two-thirds of the city's commercial, industrial, and residential neighborhoods.

Recovery after the disaster of 1906 coincided with the forging of San Franciso's version of Progressivism. In the immediate aftermath of the catastrophe, all segments of the community experienced a brief sense of unity in facing the need to rebuild. Major disagreements over the role of planning divided the business leadership, however, and the City Beautiful plan that Phelan had commissioned from Daniel H. Burnham was never implemented. The graft prosecutions of 1906 created additional discord as prosecutors sought to indict prominent business leaders for bribery. Although city voters established the first municipally owned streetcar line in the nation, construction lagged because brokers boycotted its bonds.

In 1911 a coalition of leading businessmen and a few conservative labor organizations elected James Rolph, the self-proclaimed "mayor of all of the people." He became one of the first mayors of a large city to attempt to build civic unity through a program of public construction. The cornerstone of this effort was the Panama-Pacific International Ex-

position of 1915, a world's fair intended to express both the city's phoenixlike recovery and its hope of continuing to exercise dominance over the commerce of the Pacific. However, attempts to create a Greater San Francisco, modeled on the consolidation of New York City a few years before, foundered when they met opposition from Oakland in the East Bay and from other municipalities outside the city.

Civic unity altogether proved elusive during the first decades of the twentieth century, particularly after July 22, 1916, when terrorists bombed a parade in support of Britain and its allies during World War I. Two socialist labor organizers were convicted of the crime after the chamber of commerce launched a law and order campaign targeting organized labor and left-wing radicals generally. Beginning in 1921, an Industrial Association led a formidable campaign in favor of open shops that received financing from nearly all the city's businesses and banks. The city's politics continued to be polarized between business and labor, and conflict over government ownership of municipal utilities added to the division. Republican voters dominated San Francisco as they

*The Golden Gate Bridge and San Francisco.*

did other great cities. While businessmen supported Herbert Hoover strongly in his 1928 presidential campaign, unions backed their longtime favorite Hiram Johnson, former governor of California, as the city's deep polarization extended to presidential politics.

Although Los Angeles passed San Francisco in total population in 1920, the city continued to grow, from 506,676 in 1920 to 634,394 in 1930, and landmarks such as the Mark Hopkins Hotel remade the city's skyline during that decade. Amadeo P. Giannini's Bank of America, a pioneer in branch banking, emerged as the leading banking institution in California, one of the most important in the nation, and an important source of capital for the growth of the film industry in southern California. A new city charter, which took effect in 1932, incorporated many innovations based on a corporate model of decision making, including a chief administrative officer derived from the city manager model. New civic construction projects—an opera house, museum, streetcar lines—generated popular support but failed to restore the unity fostered by Mayor Rolph's pre–World War I construction activities. Efforts at regional planning drew slight support, although the automobile contributed to growth all around the bay.

The Depression made it clear to San Franciscans that their economic well-being had become more dependent on conditions beyond local control than ever before. Agencies of the federal government began to play a much larger role in the economy and urbanization of the Bay Area. Section 7 of the National Recovery Act revived organized labor in 1933. Militants, led by Harry Bridges, won control of a revitalized longshoremen's union; in 1934 shipping companies' intransigence produced a coastwide maritime strike and a brief citywide general strike. Employers slowly made accommodations with labor militancy. A loan from the federal Reconstruction Finance Corporation funded construction of the Oakland–San Francisco Bay Bridge. The Works Progress Administration and the Public Works Administration provided funds to resume civic construction, and a regional authority established by the state paid for the Golden Gate Bridge. Even so, some civic projects were still financed by local bond issues supported by city voters. In 1939, San Francisco celebrated completion of the two great bridges with an international exposition (the cost underwritten in part by the WPA), but the Golden Gate Exposition failed to ignite the enthusiasm of the 1915 World's Fair.

By the end of the 1930s, San Francisco contained proportionately more Communist Party members than any other American city, laying part of the foundation for a radical subculture after World War II. However, the movement had little immediate impact on city politics. Angelo Rossi, a prominent businessman who succeeded Rolph as mayor, retained the mayor's office through the 1930s, but Upton Sinclair's EPIC campaign in 1934, together with the New Deal, began to change voter alignments that resulted in the election of New Deal Democrats to some city, state, and federal offices. Since 1964, mayors of the city have generally come from the liberal to moderate wings of the Democratic Party.

The production of military goods for World War II enlarged San Francisco's historical shipbuilding facilities into one of the largest complexes in world history. Wartime expansion of bases, repair yards, and manufacturing sites in the city followed two decades of efforts by local boosters to attract military investment, and the war contributed to the regional dispersion of such activities. Severe labor shortages stimulated tremendous migration to the city, and a dramatic expansion of the African-American population from less than 1 percent to more than 5 percent brought the city a significant black population for the first time.

Wartime migration swelled the population from some 635,000 in 1940 to over 775,000 in 1950. After the city's population peaked at nearly 784,000 in 1953, it gradually declined to 759,300 in 1995. The city's residential patterns began to change as large numbers of blue-collar and white-collar white families moved to racially homogeneous districts in outlying parts of the city or to newly constructed sections of San Mateo County to the south or Marin, Alameda, and Contra Costa Counties to the north and east. By the end of the 1960s, following the federal immigration reforms of 1965, Asian and Pacific Island immigrants began flocking to San Francisco and further altering the already complex social geography of the city's ethnic minorities. Refugees from the political instability of Central America during the 1970s and 1980s joined the other Hispanic residents of the city. The white population declined from 89 percent to 47 percent of the total between 1950 and 1990, while the African-American share of the population increased from 5 percent to 10 percent, the Asian from 4 percent to 36 percent, and the Hispanic from about 2 percent to 14 percent.

During the years after World War II, San Francisco's economy changed dramatically as it experienced the full force of regional and metropolitan economic transformations associated with the rise of the global economy. By the end of the 1970s, in a pattern that has continued, the city became predominantly a service center for regional and Pacific Basin economic development, with government, education, finance, insurance, real estate, and (during the 1990s) multimedia commanding a greater share of the workforce. Economic transformation expressed itself in the dramatic alteration of the city's built environment. High-rise office buildings in the central business district turned the downtown area into a mini-Manhattan. Abandonment of the finger piers along the Embarcadero, and the demolition of the

Embarcadero Freeway because of damage caused by the Loma Prieta earthquake of 1989, allowed redevelopment of the waterfront in connection with the city's most important service business, tourism. Retailing reminders of the city's colorful history—the cable cars and Fisherman's Wharf, for instance—have allowed the hotel and restaurant business to thrive as San Francisco has become a prime destination for both recreational visitors and convention goers.

Supporters of the civil rights movements of the 1950s and 1960s and subsequent environmentalist, feminist, and gay rights social reform movements of the 1970s, 1980s, and 1990s successfully coalesced with culturally conservative supporters of economic reform to transform San Francisco into one of the most liberal cities in America during the 1960s, and they have kept it on the political left throughout the years of the nation's turn to conservatism during the 1980s and 1990s. Residents have debated redevelopment, gentrification and displacement, district election of supervisors, and access to political power by black and gay activists since the 1960s.

City politics turned deadly in 1978 when Dan White, a disgruntled conservative and former member of the board of supervisors, murdered liberal Democratic Mayor George Moscone and Harvey Milk, the city's first openly gay supervisor. In the years since the murders, a variety of reform campaigns has continued, from limiting downtown high-rise construction to municipal government protecting the rights of all citizens regardless of race, gender, sexual orientation, age, or disability. Many San Franciscans would undoubtedly regard the late 1990s sobriquet "Left Coast City" as a compliment rather than an epithet.

—*William Issel*

### References

DeLeon, Richard Edward. *Left Coast City: Progressive Politics in San Francisco, 1975–1991.* Lawrence: University Press of Kansas, 1992.

Godfrey, Brian J. *Neighborhoods in Transition: The Making of San Francisco's Ethnic and Nonconformist Communities.* Berkeley: University of California Press, 1988.

Issel, William, and Robert W. Cherny. *San Francisco 1865–1932: Politics, Power, and Urban Development.* Berkeley: University of California Press, 1986.

Lotchin, Roger W. *San Francisco 1846–1856: From Hamlet to City.* New York: Oxford University Press, 1974.

Shilts, Randy. *The Mayor of Castro Street: The Life and Times of Harvey Milk.* New York: St. Martins Press, 1982.

Wirt, Frederick M. *Power in the City: Decision Making in San Francisco.* Berkeley: University of California Press, 1974.

## Satellite City

Simply defined, a satellite city is a smaller city on the periphery of a larger city, independent of its political influence but within its economic and social orbit. Its distance from the central city varies with the quality of the transportation system, rate of growth, access to large tracts of land, and amount of dependence. Above all, a satellite has to be far enough from the central city to have a distinct physical identity. The term can also be applied to a number of different types of suburbs: incorporated communities surrounding a central city, dormitory suburbs, or industrial suburbs. A large number of a satellite's inhabitants work in the larger city and take advantage of its recreation, retail, medical, educational, and other services typically not available in the satellite. Characteristics of a satellite city include a largely independent economic base; an independent local government with some ties to other governments in the area; strong ties with the larger city; functioning within the orbit of the larger urban area; often, but not always, containing an industrial center; good transportation conduits to the larger city; and only partial dependence on commuting to the larger city. The satellite is not permanently attached to the larger city and can evolve into a central city or devolve into a suburb. Often, the central city is expanding by creating suburbs and satellites as steps in the process.

Satellite cities are sometimes perceived as one solution to the modern urban crises of the inner city. If residents of the city move there, the community on the outskirts of the larger urban area will help lessen traffic congestion, air and water pollution, municipal finance, poverty, education, housing, crime, and unemployment. As satellite cities are created by either government or private enterprise and people move out to them, the population of the inner city decreases, even though poor people are left behind and continue to face the problems just mentioned.

The origin of the term *satellite city* is associated with the British New Town movement. Advocates of garden cities used the term in 1918 to describe communities that were largely self-contained and separated from central cities by greenbelts of farms, parks, and woodlands. In 1930, the London City Council used the term *quasi-satellites* to describe the development of housing in suburban areas surrounding a large city. By 1944, new towns in England were known as satellite cities or towns. In the United States, Graham Romeyn Taylor used the term in 1915 in his study of emerging smaller communities on the outskirts of larger towns. Taylor considered these new communities "made to order" cities and not just offshoots of the larger urban area.

The satellite city is often associated with other urban entities like the greenbelt towns built during the New Deal, private projects that create new communities, and large-scale residential and industrial developments located on the urban fringe of large cities. The term is often used interchangeably with "new towns," "new town-in-town," "regional growth center," "new communities," "planned communities," "new cities," "greenbelt towns," and "garden cities."

—*Craig Pascoe*

**See also**
Greenbelt Towns; Levittown; Reston, Virginia.

**References**
Brodsky, Harold. "Land Development and the Expanding City." *Annals of the American Association of Geographers* 63 (1973): 159–166.

Clapp, James A. *New Towns and Urban Policy: Planning Metropolitan Growth.* New York: Dunellen, 1971.

Gans, Herbert. *The Levittowners: Ways of Life and Politics in a New Suburban City.* New York: Random House, 1967.

Garreau, Joel. *Edge City: Life on the New Frontier.* New York: Doubleday, 1991.

Golany, Gideon. *New Town Planning: Principle and Practice.* New York: Wiley, 1976.

King, Leslie J., and Reginald G. Golledge. *Cities, Space, and Behavior: The Elements of Urban Geography.* Englewood Cliffs, NJ: Prentice-Hall, 1978.

## Scarsdale, New York

Located in central Westchester County, the town of Scarsdale, New York, acquired a railroad connection to mid-Manhattan in 1846 and entered the suburban phase of its history in 1891 when the Arthur Suburban Home Company laid out a subdivision. Other subdivisions followed quickly thereafter, many geared to the emerging upper-middle-class market of business managers and professionals. In 1915 Scarsdale's residents voted to incorporate as a village to fend off the threat of annexation from the neighboring city of White Plains. Armed with a new sense of their suburb's distinctiveness, and with the increased powers accorded villages as compared to towns in New York State, local leaders embarked on a creative 15 years. They established high-quality essential services (especially in the areas of water and waste disposal), exclusionary zoning and building codes (the former upheld by the highest court in the state), and a progressive public school system with an individualized plan of instruction that attracted national interest.

Eager to see their village used as a model, Scarsdale's residents spearheaded numerous campaigns in the middle decades of the twentieth century. Scarsdale served as a center for anti–New Deal sentiment in the 1930s, and it won renown as the "Thunderbolt Town" for selling enough bonds to finance 125 fighter planes during World War II. From 1949 to 1954 the board of education, with broad community support, fended off charges of Communist infiltration. And in the late 1960s, even as residents proposed the racial integration of local housing and schools, Scarsdale became a symbol for radical youth of the meaninglessness of modern life. "You Have to Grow Up in Scarsdale to Know How Bad Things Really Are" announced the title of a *New York Times Magazine* article.

Two sensational murders, one in 1977, the other in 1980, kept Scarsdale in the public eye. But although Scarsdale was changing in terms of its ethnic population (from a predominantly WASP community in 1940 to a largely Jewish community with, by 1990, a significant minority of Asians), it remained a well-to-do suburb of fewer than 20,000 residents with expensive houses, exorbitant taxes, and excellent services and schools.

*—Carol A. O'Connor*

**Reference**
O'Connor, Carol A. *A Sort of Utopia: Scarsdale, 1891–1981.* Albany: State University of New York Press, 1983.

## Sector Theory

The sector theory is an idealized model of the internal structure of urban areas developed by Homer Hoyt in 1939. Analyzing detailed housing data for nearly 150 cities in the United States, Hoyt rejected Ernest W. Burgess's concentric zone theory and concluded that variations in socioeconomic status conformed to a pattern of sectors extending outward from the central business district (CBD).

Hoyt argued that the sectoral pattern of land uses reflected the expansion of "high-grade residential areas" away from the financial and retail side of the CBD where most upper-income residents worked. These residents sought the most desirable residential sites away from crowded neighborhoods near the CBD, creating an axial pattern of growth along the city's best transportation routes toward wide-open areas with high ground or natural amenities. The streetcar and the automobile accelerated the expansion of affluent sectors, drawing the locations of new office buildings, banks, and upscale retail outlets in the same direction. Lower-income groups, meanwhile, crowded into less-desirable sectors on low-lying land or near industrial districts.

Hoyt's theory provided an influential alternative to Burgess's model, but both formulations relied on the controversial notion of filtering to explain neighborhood change. The urban ecologists of the Chicago School of Sociology had described the process by which established neighborhoods tended to "filter down" with age, as higher-income residents left and were replaced by poorer arrivals, but Hoyt refined the concept and applied it to residential mobility at the urban fringe. Since upper-income groups are unlikely to find existing housing better than their own, they construct new homes at the leading edge of the expanding high-grade sector. The outward movement of the highest income groups releases their former homes to those with lower incomes, setting in motion a succession of households through the housing stock, rippling away from the least-desirable housing (usually closest to the center) and toward the newest and best homes.

While many scholars accept filtering as a descriptive concept, they also challenge the implication of Hoyt's theory that constructing housing for upper-income groups benefits all households. Hoyt's work also influenced the early development of mortgage lending practices of federal agencies, which institutionalized patterns of segregation in the housing market, particularly along racial lines.

—*Elvin Wyly*

**See also**
Concentric Zone Theory; Multiple Nuclei Theory.
**References**
Adams, John S. "Housing Submarkets in an American Metropolis." In John Fraser Hart, ed., *Our Changing Cities,* 108–126. Baltimore: Johns Hopkins University Press, 1991.
Boddy, Martin, and Fred Gray. "The Origins and Use of Theory in Urban Geography: Household Mobility in Filtering Theory." *Geoforum* 10 (1979): 117–127.
Bourne, Larry S. *The Geography of Housing.* Silver Spring, MD: V. H. Winston & Sons, 1981.
Hoyt, Homer. *The Structure and Growth of Residential Neighborhoods in American Cities.* Washington, DC: U.S. Federal Housing Administration, 1939.
Park, Robert E., Ernest W. Burgess, and Roderick D. McKenzie. *The City.* Chicago: University of Chicago Press, 1925.

## Sennett, Mack (1880–1960)

Mack Sennett, the producer of silent comedy films, was born Michael Sinnott in Quebec, Canada. After working as a boilermaker and performing in vaudeville, he was hired as an actor for the Biograph Motion Picture Company in 1908. Unable to convince his director, D. W. Griffith, that policemen could be funny, Sennett started directing comedies himself for Biograph in New York and Los Angeles.

In 1912, he founded the Keystone studios, and the company moved into a small lot that had previously been used to shoot westerns. The lot was located at what is now 1712 Glendale Boulevard in Edendale, a suburb three miles northwest of what was then downtown Los Angeles (and sometimes erroneously assumed to be part of the city of Glendale). Because a good portion of the 28-acre lot was hillside, Sennett only had enough room to build interior sets (houses, restaurants, etc.); for exterior sets, Sennett and his crews took to the streets of Los Angeles. His comic actors, including the Keystone Kops (who disproved Griffith's notion that policemen were not funny), performed surreal activities on very real streets. Cars and people stretched into unlikely contortions as Sennett's films exploded the conventions of late Victorian society.

Sennett effectively used the variety of locations available in Los Angeles. For his first comedy feature, *Dillies Punctured Romance* (1914), Sennett found both the rural settings in the early part of the picture and the city settings of the latter part within a few miles of his studio. Echo Park, the city park where Charlie Chaplin and Mabel Norman stroll in the film, was only a few blocks from the studio and appears in several Sennett films. Sennett's crews also used the activities of the city as subject matter for his films. The best-known example is *Kid Auto Races,* the 1914 short that introduced Charlie Chaplin to moviegoers as the Tramp. In this film, Chaplin's famous character interrupts a cameraman filming midget auto races near the beach at Venice, California.

Chaplin was not the only major talent to pass through Sennett's studio. Silent comedy greats such as Harold Lloyd and Harry Langdon worked for Sennett, as did such later dramatic stars as Gloria Swanson and Wallace Berry; Frank Capra was the best known of the many directors who worked for Sennett. Sennett's use of Los Angeles city streets set a pattern followed by many silent comedies and comedians. Harold Lloyd's *Safety Last* (1923) and *Girl Shy* (1924) and Buster Keaton's *Seven Chances* (1925) all have spectacular sequences filmed in the city. Ironically, Sennett's most famous protégé, Chaplin, preferred to build his own exterior sets at the studio.

Sennett continued making films in the early years of "talkies," but they were not as successful as his earlier films. He appeared as himself in the 1939 film *Hollywood Cavalcade,* and Dan Ackroyd portrayed him in the 1992 film *Chaplin,* which includes an accurate reconstruction of Sennett's original Keystone lot.

—*Tom Stempel*

**See also**
Chaplin, Charlie; Keaton, Buster.
**References**
Brownlow, Kevin, and John Kobal. *Hollywood: The Pioneers.* New York: Knopf, 1979.
Capra, Frank. *The Name above the Title.* New York: Macmillan, 1971.
Fowler, Gene. *Father Goose.* New York: Crown, 1934.
Lahue, Kalton C., and Terry Brewer. *Kops and Custards: The Legend of the Keystone Films.* Norman: University of Oklahoma Press, 1968.
Sennett, Mack, with Cameron Shipp. *King of Comedy.* New York: Doubleday, 1954.

## Service Labor

Traditional theory distinguishes between work in three major industrial sectors: agriculture, manufacturing, and services. Each is considered to reflect the modal work associated with a particular stage of social and economic development. Thus, in the writings of Daniel Bell (1973), services reflect an end point in development—the so-called postindustrial society.

Service workers are commonly defined by the industrial context of their work. These definitions are residual, specifying service workers as those not employed in manufacturing or agriculture. Doctors and waiters, in this view, are both service workers; machine operators and farmers are not.

Using this industrial definition, statistics indicate that in the United States in 1992 approximately 87 million workers were employed in the service industry; this represents 74 percent of the labor force. By contrast, the proportion of service workers in the labor force was approximately 65 percent in 1970 and 23 percent in 1870. It is important to note that more women than men work in the service sector of the economy. Indeed, much of the recent growth in the number of women employed outside their homes parallels the growth of service-sector employment.

The reference to *service labor* calls attention to important trends in American society. First, owing to the continued decline in the number of agricultural workers, to the increased productivity in manufacturing, and to the movement of manufacturing to less-developed countries, the size of the labor force employed in the service sector will unquestionably continue to grow. Second, the expanding proportion of service workers testifies to the enormous resources allocated to health, education, and welfare in modern societies. Both trends confirm the importance of service workers in the growing use of knowledge and in the increased attention to the "flow of information" rather than the "flow of things" in the economy.

In spite of the popularity of the concept of a *service worker,* considerable ambiguity mars the utility of this term. As a consequence, many social scientists are critical of an unqualified reference to service workers. For example, although service workers are popularly defined by industry, others define service workers by occupation: those paid to perform an activity—or provide a service—for somebody else. In this view, service workers like accountants, CEOs, or mail room clerks are found in all industrial sectors. Both occupational and industrial referents are inconsistent in labeling different workers as providing services. Both terms also are exceedingly general, cut across levels of occupational skill and industrial location, and lump together very different kinds of jobs and occupations. The terms classify as service workers both those in the public and private sectors as well as those at disparate ends of social power and occupational prestige.

To complicate this ambiguity, the U.S. Bureau of the Census explicitly uses a narrow categorization of "service workers" to refer to semiskilled and unskilled labor employed primarily in the hospitality industry—hotels, food, and beverage services—and amusement facilities. Hamburger flippers, for example, are service workers, according to the census classification.

Social scientists also have criticized the association of services with economic affluence or an advanced stage of economic development such as postindustrialization. Studies indicate a lack of any clear association between industrialization and service-sector employment. In this view, service workers are abundant in underdeveloped societies—although they typically perform menial labor in the informal sector of the economy. The informal economy refers to workers hired to do various tasks on an informal basis; they are not counted in employment statistics by governmental agencies. Such service workers are widespread in underdeveloped countries.

Others question the common identification of services with skilled employment in advanced, industrial societies. These critics argue that service workers in the informal sector are prevalent throughout both the industrialized and nonindustrialized world. Sassen, for example, argues that service workers in informal economies of economically advanced societies cluster in large metropolitan areas, where they provide the servant class for national and international elites and perform an array of tasks from caring for children to doing housework and gardening. These workers are typically denied access to social security, health and safety regulations, and other fringe benefits, as well as guarantees of minimum wages. They are the invisible workers in an underground economy.

Recent work recognizes the ambiguities inherent in the "service sector" designation and uses these ambiguities to highlight the multiple, contradictory, and divergent implications of service-sector employment. As an example, various writers have noted that the growth in service-sector employment is responsible for bifurcation of the stratification structure resulting from: (1) the continued trajectory toward professional training and the importance of educational credentials and (2) the proliferation of lesser-skilled jobs in delivering consumer goods—particularly in retail trade and the food and beverage industry. In this view, service workers, however defined and identified, are portrayed as a new force in economically advanced societies—in polarizing the stratification structure of society and in exacerbating disparities in income and wealth.

—*Joel I. Nelson*

## References

Bell, Daniel. *The Coming of Post-Industrial Society.* New York: Basic Books, 1973.

Bluestone, Barry, and Bennett Harrison. *The Deindustrialization of America: Plant Closings, Community Abandonment, and the Dismantling of Basic Industry.* New York: Basic Books, 1982.

Clark, Colin. *Conditions of Economic Progress.* London: Macmillan, 1940.

Drucker, Peter. "The Economy's Power Shift." *The Wall Street Journal* (September 24, 1992): A16.

Kravis, Irving. "Services in World Transactions." In Robert Inman, ed., *Managing the Service Economy: Prospects and Problems,* 135–160. Cambridge, England: Cambridge University Press, 1985.

Kravis, Irving, Alan Heston, and Robert Summers. "The Share of Services in Economic Growth." In F. Gerard Adams and Bert Hickman, eds., *Global Econometrics,* 188–218. Cambridge, MA: MIT Press, 1983.

Machlup, Fritz. *The Production and Distribution of Knowledge in the United States.* Princeton, NJ: Princeton University Press, 1962.

Mills, Peter. *Managing Service Industries.* Cambridge, MA: Ballinger, 1986.

Nelson, Joel. *Post-Industrial Capitalism.* Thousand Oaks, CA: Sage Publications, 1995.

Sassen, Saskia. "Economic Restructuring and the American City." *Annual Review of Sociology* 16 (1990): 465–490.

Stanback, Thomas, Peter Bearse, Thierry Noyelle, and Robert Karasek. *Services: A New Economy.* Totowa, NJ: Allanheld, Osman, 1981.

## Settlement House Movement

The settlement house movement reached the United States in 1886 with the establishment of Neighborhood Guild (soon renamed University Settlement) on New York's Lower East Side. Its founder, Stanton Coit, a minister of Ethical Culture, had spent several months as a resident at the first settlement house in the world, Toynbee Hall in London, founded in 1884. By the late nineteenth century, city dwellers were increasingly sorting themselves out by social class by moving into more highly stratified neighborhoods. The well-to-do no longer associated with the poor on a daily basis as they had when rich and poor lived more or less jumbled up in cities of the preindustrial period. The purpose of the settlement house was to provide a place where the well-to-do could reestablish contact with the poor, learn firsthand about their problems, assist in bringing about fundamental social changes to alleviate those problems, and also provide a daily round of cultural, recreational, and social activities for the poor in neighborhoods where the settlements were located. The method was for the well-to-do to actually live in the settlement house or "settle" in the neighborhood. Those well-to-do who preferred not to change their lifestyles so drastically could participate as volunteers at the settlement house, perhaps teaching a class or leading a neighborhood children's club once a week.

Settlement houses soon began to proliferate. In 1889, some women graduates of elite eastern women's colleges opened College Settlement near University Settlement. Within weeks, Jane Addams founded Hull House in Chicago. Other famous settlements included Robert A. Woods's South End House (1892) in Boston, Lillian Wald's Henry Street Settlement (1893) in New York, and Graham Taylor's Chicago Commons (1894). By 1895, when John Lovejoy Elliott founded Hudson Guild in New York City's Chelsea neighborhood, around 50 settlement houses existed in American cities. By World War I, the number was between 200 and 400, depending on how readily church-sponsored settlement houses were counted. Strictly speaking, a settlement house was a secular organization. However, the practicalities of fund-raising meant that some of them relied on church support. These houses ranged from those that did no religious proselytizing to those that were more accurately classified as city missions.

The Progressive Era was the period in which settlement houses enjoyed their greatest prestige and influence. As new and innovative institutions, they attracted some of the leading urban reformers of the times. The Progressive Era also saw the heaviest immigration the United States had ever experienced. Settlements were at their best as well-to-do residents reached out to ambitious immigrants while furthering Progressive reforms. Settlement workers actively supported mothers' pensions; ending child labor; better working conditions in factories; establishing playgrounds, kindergartens, and home economics and industrial education classes; English and citizenship classes for immigrants; and adopting housing codes. Their reform methods included studying and documenting bad conditions; publicizing problems through books, articles, and speeches; personally lobbying influential citizens; and staging "demonstration" projects. For example, Cleveland's Hiram House privately established and ran a model playground in 1900; 12 years later, it actively campaigned for a bond issue extending city-financed playgrounds throughout the city.

By the 1920s, the settlement house movement had reached the peak of its influence. The new social work education promoted hiring Master of Social Work professionals, not the well-to-do amateurs settlement houses attracted. Also, the wave of immigrants that had dominated many settlement house neighborhoods declined to a trickle when Congress limited the number who could enter the United States after 1921 and, again, after 1924. Many settlement house leaders whose houses were now funded by the Community Chest found it more difficult to engage in controversial reform activities. Furthermore, support for reform was generally absent in the country.

That changed sharply during the Depression. As slum-based social agencies seeking solutions to poverty, settlement house expertise was once again in demand. The National Federation of Settlements, formed in 1911, had sponsored a 1928 study of people who were unemployed because of technological change and stoppages in industry. Helen Hall, the head of University Settlement in Philadelphia, gathered this research together in an account of 150 situations that analyzed not just the economic but the physical and psychological effects of unemployment. The federation's annual conferences were occasions when settlement workers from around the country gathered to pass resolutions urging adequate welfare programs.

In 1933, Hall became head of Henry Street Settlement in New York. The following year, she served on the Advisory Council of the President's Committee on Economic Security. That group provided citizen input for the landmark 1935

Social Security Act, which established the federal welfare system. Besides social insurance, the act established the unemployment compensation program, Old Age Assistance, Aid to the Blind, Aid to Families with Dependent Children, and some minor medical programs, such as the Crippled Children's Services. The Aid to Families with Dependent Children was undone in the welfare reform legislation enacted in 1996.

By 1935, Hall was also president of the National Federation of Settlements. That organization helped to publicize the idea of national health insurance by sponsoring a study of the British system. In addition, Hall and other settlement workers were ready to testify in Washington whenever liberal politicians in the Roosevelt (and later the Truman) administration wanted a witness with professional standing who could support progressive social legislation with human interest stories of people they actually knew. In turn, the settlements supplemented their staffs during the mid- and late 1930s with all the Works Progress Administration workers they could manage to supervise.

After World War II, the settlement house movement underwent major changes. Settlements began replacing their resident heads with holders of the Master of Social Work degree. These professionals were likely to be married men with families who thought of themselves as interacting with the settlement's members or clientele as professionals, not as neighbors. By the 1950s men outnumbered women as head workers for the first time since the movement began. The practice of living in settlement houses became virtually extinct. In fact, many of the old settlement house buildings were torn down as part of urban renewal. Some settlements moved at least part of their operations into the community space of burgeoning new public housing projects. The National Federation of Settlements added "and Neighborhood Centers" to its name in 1949, and 30 years later it dropped the word "settlement" as anachronistic and adopted the name, United Neighborhood Centers of America. Also by 1970, African Americans and Latinos dominated most settlement neighborhoods as well as settlement director positions. Walter Smart's appointment as head of the national organization in 1971 reflected this shift from white to minority leadership in the majority of settlements.

The post–World War II settlement house movement did maintain some influence, but it also suffered from attacks that it was elitist. Henry Street Settlement originated the prototype program for the War on Poverty, Mobilization for Youth. However, the settlement lost control of that program by the time the federal government funded it because of charges that settlement workers did not really represent the wishes or desires of their neighbors. To try to bolster the influence of the movement with the federal government, the organization moved its headquarters from New York to Washington in 1985.

As settlements approached their centennials, some, like Henry Street, capitalized heavily on their history. Others, like South End House, whose neighborhood had changed from white to African American, chose to downplay their connection with the settlement house movement altogether. By 1996, settlement houses were better known as neighborhood centers or neighborhood houses, and they could be difficult to distinguish from more lightly staffed community centers. Nevertheless, settlement houses remained significant urban social institutions.

—*Judith Ann Trolander*

**See also**
Addams, Jane; Henry Street Settlement; Hull House; Kelley, Florence; Wald, Lillian D.

**References**
Carson, Mina. *Settlement Folk: Social Thought and the Settlement Movement, 1885–1930*. Chicago: University of Chicago Press, 1990.

Davis, Allen F. *Spearheads for Reform: The Social Settlements and the Progressive Movement, 1890–1914*. New York: Oxford University Press, 1967.

Hall, Helen. *Case Studies of Unemployment*. Philadelphia: University of Pennsylvania Press, 1931.

Lasch-Quinn, Elisabeth. *Black Neighbors: Race and the Limits of Reform in the American Settlement House Movement, 1890–1945*. Chapel Hill: University of North Carolina Press, 1993.

Trolander, Judith Ann. *Professionalism and Social Change: From the Settlement House Movement to Neighborhood Centers, 1886 to the Present*. New York: Columbia University Press, 1987.

———. *Settlement Houses and the Great Depression*. Detroit: Wayne State University Press, 1975.

## Sewerage and Sanitation Systems

In the days before sewers, household liquids and wastewater often found their way to on-site cesspools or dry wells in many communities, but all too frequently they were simply cast on the ground. Under the best circumstances, the wastes were recycled on farmland or sold to reprocessing plants as fertilizers. More problematic was the impact of wastewater once it left private property and the flow of storm water through the streets. While the "cesspool–privy vault–scavenger" system provided rudimentary handling of some residentially derived wastes, existing "sewers" offered increasingly little help in controlling drainage problems as cities grew. As early as the end of the eighteenth century, major cities such as New York and Boston had sewers. However, a sewer in this period was intended to carry off storm water or to drain stagnant pools rather than to handle wastewater, and it was most often a street gutter rather than an underground drain.

By contrast with the strides made in the development of water supply systems, the development of adequate sewerage systems was slight through the late nineteenth century. Private companies had paid for the early development of water supply systems—with the support of city and state governments. But a similar outcome for sewerage was highly unlikely because sewers generated little revenue in comparison to water systems. In addition, as primitive as they may appear today, privy vaults and cesspools operated as effective disposal options for much of the nineteenth century.

The breakdown of the old methods began to occur when water pipes brought greater volumes of water into homes and businesses, and it needed to be removed. Demand for improved sanitation was on the rise, and flooding problems encouraged the development of better storm-water discharge. Once the need for sewerage systems became clear, their growth was steady. Indeed, 100 years after the first major sewer systems were developed in American cities in the 1870s and 1880s, approximately 600,000 miles of sewer lines had been installed.

The primary technical issues revolved around a debate over combined as opposed to separate sewers. The English had wrestled with this controversy since the 1840s, but it did not surface in the United States until the 1880s. Combined systems came first. They handled both liquefied waste and storm water in a single large pipe. A separate system used two pipes—a small one for household waste and a larger one for storm water. Only combined systems were successfully built in the United States in the 1860s and early 1870s, largely due to cost and the lack of a successfully operating separate system.

However, the deep concerns over combating epidemic disease through environmental sanitation techniques kept the debate over sewer design alive for several years. Memphis built the first major separate system in the United States in the wake of a devastating yellow fever epidemic. It had been promoted with the argument that the city could avoid future health risks by trapping "sewer gas" and other harmful miasmas in sanitary pipes. By 1892, 22 systems of this kind had been constructed. Yet, by the turn of the century, it was clear that a choice between a combined and a separate system depended upon the size of a city and its available resources, not on the relative sanitary value of either. Both were deemed equally hygienic.

The ultimate disposal of sewage proved to be an additional dilemma in the building of new systems. Sanitary engineers were aware that rivers could become overloaded with raw sewage and present health hazards and nuisances, but they did not know how much pollution constituted a problem for downstream users or how far downstream a hazard might persist. Adequate disposal—especially at the turn of the century when disease transmission was now clearly linked to bacteria rather than filth—revolved around questions of the purification of water versus the treatment of sewage. In other words, should upstream disposers treat their sewage before dumping it, or should downstream water users purify their supply before using it?

High death rates from typhoid motivated enactment of stream pollution laws after 1903 in states such as Pennsylvania, New Jersey, and Ohio. However, legislation did not apply to sewerage systems constructed before enactment of the laws, only to extensions. The debate continued, nevertheless, over how best to deal with the pollution from municipal sewage. Many engineers tended to emphasize water filtration, arguing that disposing of wastewater by dilution often mitigated against the more costly process of treatment. Individuals in the medical profession argued that health was better protected by not allowing municipalities to discharge any raw sewage into rivers and streams.

Nonetheless, experiments in a variety of treatment and filtration methods continued to be explored. One approach, which became widespread in the United States, was the activated sludge process developed shortly before World War I. Raw sewage was combined with heavy concentrations of aerobic microorganisms to stimulate bacterial reduction of organic pollutants. After World War II, oxidation ponds or stabilization lagoons gained widespread use, especially in smaller urban areas with sufficient available land. In these shallow bodies, wastewater interacted with sunlight, algae, and oxygen, resulting in water that in many cases was restored to equal or better quality than water from treatment plants.

The treatment methods of the late nineteenth and early twentieth centuries had a prolonged life. Although improved and modified, they essentially consisted of separating solids, disposing of sludge, and neutralizing suspended organic matter. In the late 1960s, as environmental consciousness deepened, efforts were made to develop waste treatment systems that provided a higher degree of purification.

The administration of wastewater control and treatment systems has varied widely over time and throughout the country. The first public sewer works normally were built and managed by state and local commissions. Today, the sewage unit is usually part of an omnibus public works agency that coordinates planning, operations, and maintenance. Some cities divide sanitary and storm-water service units. The more recent trend concerning water reuse has led many cities to combine water supply and wastewater agencies into a single organization. As metropolitan areas spread outward, intergovernmental or multicommunity approaches have been implemented. State and federal water pollution control legislation has added major environmental responsibilities to local sewerage development and sewage disposal entities, especially since the 1970s.

—*Martin V. Melosi*

**See also**
Garbage and Garbage Collection.
**References**
Peterson, Jon A. "The Impact of Sanitary Reform Upon American Urban Planning, 1840–1890." *Journal of Social History* 13 (1979): 83–103.

Schultz, Stanley K. *Constructing Urban Culture*. Philadelphia: Temple University Press, 1989.

Tarr, Joel A., and F. C. McMichael. "Historical Decisions about Wastewater Technology, 1800–1932." *Journal of Water Resources Planning and Management* 103 (1977): 47–61.

## Shaker Villages

The Shakers, a religious society whose members devoted themselves to communal lives of work and worship and who foreswore marriage and sexual relations, successfully established 19 villages in the eastern United States between 1787 and 1836. Formally named the United Society of Believers in Christ's Second Appearing, a small group of Shakers—so known because of their inspired religious dance and also apparently from a contraction of the terms *Shaking Quakers*—that included Ann Lee, the society's founder, emigrated to New York from England in 1774. Within a year, they secured land in Watervliet, New York, where they founded a pioneering settlement.

In 1787 the first Shaker society was formally organized at New Lebanon (later Mount Lebanon), New York, and set the pattern for the development of Shaker villages in all the remaining societies. In their mature phases, each village contained subunits called families, self-contained communities that served individual functions such as overseeing a mill or housing the novitiate order. At the hub of these families was the First Family at Mount Lebanon, the center of authority and spiritual life of the society. The community at Mount Lebanon was the largest Shaker village, containing eight families with a total population of 550 at the height of its membership in the 1850s.

Shaker villages have a distinctive appearance that reflects the Shaker way of life. The Shakers lived communally on large tracts of rural land assembled from a nucleus of the converts' farms. This unity of purpose allowed the Shakers to cluster their buildings so that scores of people could live and work together most efficiently, leaving relatively larger expanses for farming, timber stands, or millponds. Shaker villages are also distinctive for their unity of design, with the style of construction responsive to a central authority and informed by Shaker beliefs that form follows function and that simpler is better. Buildings designed to accommodate Shaker "brothers" and "sisters" jointly were distinguished by paired sets of doorways and staircases so that the members of this celibate sect might work and worship together without coming into physical contact.

*What remains of the Shaker Village near Pleasant Hill, Kentucky.*

In the years after the Civil War, fewer converts chose this way of life, and in 1875 the first Shaker village closed for lack of membership. Today, only one active Shaker society remains, at Sabbathday Lake, Maine. Several communities have been restored as museum villages, notably at Pleasant Hill, Kentucky; Canterbury, New Hampshire; and Hancock, Massachusetts. Other Shaker villages have been used as schools, prisons, or group homes for the elderly. The Shaker village at North Union, Ohio, disappeared virtually without a trace under the suburban development of Shaker Heights near Cleveland.

The 18 villages successfully established by the Shakers are: Watervliet (or Niskayuna) (1787–1938); Mount Lebanon (or New Lebanon) New York (1787–1947); Hancock, Massachusetts (1790–1960); Harvard, Massachusetts (1791–1918); Tyringham, Massachusetts (1792–1875); Enfield, Connecticut (1792–1917); Canterbury, New Hampshire (1792–1992); Shirley, Massachusetts (1792–1909); Enfield, New Hampshire (1793–1923); Sabbathday Lake, Maine (1794–still active); Union Village, Ohio (1805–1912); Watervliet, Ohio (1806–1900); Pleasant Hill, Kentucky (1806–1910); South Union, Kentucky (1807–1922); West Union, Indiana (1810–1827); North Union, Ohio (1822–1889); White Water, Ohio (1822–1916); and Groveland, New York (1836–1892).

Shaker villages were established briefly at five additional sites: Gorham, Maine (1808–1819); Savoy, Massachusetts (1817–1825); Sodus Bay, New York (1826–1836); Narcoossee, Florida (1896–ca. 1920); and White Oak, Georgia (1898–1902).

—*Robert Emlen*

### References
Emlen, Robert P. *Shaker Village Views.* Hanover, NH: University Press of New England, 1987.
Nicoletta, Julie. *The Architecture of the Shakers.* Woodstock, VT: Countryman Press, 1995.
Stein, Stephen. *The Shaker Experience in America: A History of the United Society of Believers.* New Haven, CT: Yale University Press, 1992.

## Shopping Malls in Suburbs

When Southdale Mall, the first indoor suburban shopping mall in the United States, opened its doors outside of Minneapolis in 1956, it launched a new era of retailing in North America. Today, the continent's 1,500 regional shopping malls by themselves, mostly located in suburbia, are major players and account for nearly one-fourth of all retail sales. (The share of all retail sales, except automobiles, for all malls in the United States exceeded 55 percent in 1990.) The culmination of suburban mall development may have occurred in 1992 with the opening of 4.2 million square feet at the Mall of America, just a few miles from Southdale Mall.

Suburban malls generally contain several large department stores that are strategically situated and act as anchors. Connecting these anchors along interior pedestrian streets are groups of smaller specialty shops that are usually associated with national chains; independent local stores are the exception. Many of these shops are geared toward impulse buying, not necessities, and tend to sell items such as clothing, shoes, jewelry, books, music, and gifts.

Malls are oriented toward their inside, and access to most shops (not the anchor stores) and restaurants in the mall is limited to a single entrance approached from an interior court. Malls are also climate-controlled environments where the mix and location of stores, services, and activities is carefully planned and coordinated by a single management organization. To be successful, a mall must have good highway access—an interstate interchange or the junction of two major arterial roads is ideal—and must provide abundant free parking encircling the mall.

The design and management of suburban malls create a controlled environment whose purpose is encouraging shoppers to maximize the amount of time and money they spend in shops, restaurants, and movies. Circulation patterns within a mall (e.g., location of escalators) are designed to bring patrons past the maximum number of stores as they make their way around. Clocks and exterior windows are rare so that shoppers are less aware of the time of day. Interior lighting is soft to enhance the natural colors of the merchandise displayed. Music is carefully selected to stimulate shoppers to be in a purchasing mood. Plants and other landscaping are arranged to help patrons relax. Food courts have proven successful in prolonging the length of mall visits. Private security officers are highly visible and actively enforce appropriate mall behavior (which, among other things, prevents the mall from serving as true public space).

In suburbia, malls have become much more than mere shopping centers. They serve as town centers for many suburban communities that lack traditional hearts as they host civic functions and social events. In fact, the local mall may represent the most well known landmark in many suburbs. They serve as entertainment centers because malls often house movie theaters, restaurants, health clubs, and arcades; the Mall of America even includes an amusement park, and others contain hotels and ice-skating rinks. Malls serve as a meeting place for groups ranging in age from teenagers to senior citizens, and they provide a familiar environment where people can hang out, socialize, and people-watch. They provide a place to keep warm when the weather is cold or to keep dry when it is raining, and they afford a year-round exercise facility (the number of people who regularly walk malls for exercise is rapidly increasing). And some critics of the suburban lifestyle suggest that the mall provides

*Ample parking, such as can be found at this shopping mall in Pasadena, California, characterizes shopping malls in suburbs.*

an escape—"somewhere to go"—in an otherwise boring and antisocial environment.

Many malls built during the 1960s and 1970s have been renovated or redesigned in the 1990s for several reasons. First, malls that date back 15 or 20 years are beginning to show their age; they often look dark, dingy, and outdated when compared to newer shopping facilities. Second, increased competition from newer malls, outlet centers, and discount stores is forcing older malls to rethink the design and retail-mix formulas that were so successful at one time. Third, renovation and redesign provide malls with an opportunity to get rid of unwanted tenants and change their retail mix. For example, a number of malls are trying to attract value-oriented stores to help them compete for shoppers attracted to large discount chains (such as Wal-Mart and K-Mart) and mail-order catalogs. Fourth, many mall tenants are demanding renovation in order to maintain their store's image and profit level. Finally, mall renovation usually permits the mall's management to charge higher rents.

—*Kent A. Robertson*

### References

Gillette, Howard, Jr. "The Evolution of the Planned Shopping Center in Suburb and City." *Journal of the American Planning Association* 51 (1985): 449–460.

Goss, Jon. "The Magic of the Mall: An Analysis of Form, Function, and Meaning in the Contemporary Retail Built Environment." *Annals of the Association of American Geographers* 83 (1993): 18–47.

Jacobs, Jerry. *The Mall.* Prospect Heights, IL: Waveland Press, 1984.

Thomas, Ian F. "Reinventing the Regional Mall." *Urban Land* 53 (1994): 24–27.

## Sinclair, Upton (1878–1968)

Upton Sinclair wrote his classic muckraking novel, *The Jungle,* before he was 30 years old. Its publication assured that for the rest of his long career he would write with fervor against many of the manifestations of urban life, if not against cities themselves. A number of his works of fiction, from the parable *Samuel the Seeker* (1910) or the Prohibition novel *The Wet Parade* (1931) to the very late *Affectionately, Eve* (1961), use the city to underscore a schematic passage from innocence to experience. Even prior to *The Jungle,* before class consciousness began to play a part in his own thinking, Sinclair had written luridly in his Nietzschean *Prince Hagen* (1903) of a New York City floundering in its own excess of wealth and vanity.

*The Jungle* itself was best known, of course, for its portrayal of the Chicago meatpacking industry, which Sinclair investigated firsthand in 1905. The reportorial detail of the stockyards played against a much more generalized background of life in one of the city's immigrant ghettos, where the horrors of the meat plants give way to a picture of stifling desperation marked by predatory business schemes and corrupt authorities. While his American audience, including President Theodore Roosevelt, devoured *The Jungle* to learn if it was safe to eat their sausage, Sinclair's foreign readers were more inclined to read the novel as an indictment of the American city itself, a dark mirror to contrast with conventional promises of wealth and success in the New World. Sinclair's vision of the city may well have influenced parts of Franz Kafka's *Amerika,* and it unquestionably informs several plays of Bertolt Brecht, such as *Die heilige Johanna der Schlachthöfe* (Saint Joan of the Stockyards) or *Im Dickicht der Städte* (Jungle of Cities).

Sinclair himself had initially considered expanding his novel into a broader exposé of Chicago's urban ills. But after 1906, in the glow of *The Jungle*'s large sales, he turned instead to muckraking New York City in three novels intended to treat, in order, Fifth Avenue society, Wall Street manipulations, and political racketeering. The first two, *The Metropolis* and *The Moneychangers* (both 1908), sold poorly. The third, and potentially most interesting of the set, only appeared as a stage play, *The Machine,* in 1911. Thereafter, Sinclair delivered his strongest indictments of America's large cities by implication in nonfiction reformist tracts, e.g., *The Brass Check* (1920) on journalism and *Money Writes!* (1927) on commercial publishing, or in his semidocumentary *Boston* (1928) on the Sacco and Vanzetti trial.

As an adoptive Californian after 1917, his novels set in Los Angeles, *They Call Me Carpenter* (1922) and *Oil!* (1928) are less rancorous. On the other hand, his political campaign for the governorship of California in 1934, the famous EPIC campaign, which marked the zenith of Sinclair's personal activism, might well be seen as "taking on the city bosses" in a number of ways, and is so described in his rueful memoir, *I, Candidate for Governor, and How I Got Licked* (1935).

—*John Ahouse*

**References**
Harris, Leon. *Upton Sinclair: American Rebel.* New York: Crowell, 1975.
Herms, Dieter. *Upton Sinclair, Amerikanischer Radikaler.* Berlin, Germany: Maerz-Verlag, 1978.
Westbrook, Wayne W. *Wall Street in the American Novel.* New York: New York University Press, 1980.

## Single-Family Detached House

So fundamental is the single-family detached house to the morphology of American suburbs in the late twentieth century that we tend to forget how singularly this house type reflects current definitions of the family and its appropriate relationship to the larger community. Since the end of World War II, the separate, domestic structure, isolated from its neighbors and the street by a broad expanse of lawn and often differentiated from adjacent houses by its seemingly unique architecture, has become a principal icon of American middle-class urban life. Its historic precedents, however, accommodated different and mixed social classes and reflected varying definitions of the family. Earlier versions of the detached family house in America, in fact, represented interdependence and community values, rather than the blatant individualism that the single-family detached house has advanced during the twentieth century.

Seventeenth-century houses in America reflected the landscapes from which the settlers had come, as well as some regional characteristics of the new land. Throughout the North and South, seventeenth-century homes were detached, in that they were not connected to their neighbors' dwellings. However, the arrangement of Puritan homes in New England around a village green that pastured common livestock emphasized the importance of community life and expressed a clear social hierarchy among the settlers. Strip fields surrounded the settlement, and at its center was the all-important meetinghouse.

This expression of the shared control of the landscape and a community focus fundamentally differed from the tradition of aristocratic country houses in England, which was to become extremely influential in America. The most important British precedent was the eighteenth-century country house, which was typically surrounded by picturesque gardens that emphasized the landscape's aesthetic, rather than its productive, potential. These large mansions were often designed in a so-called Neo-Palladian style, a revival patterned after the work of the Italian Renaissance architect Andrea Palladio as translated in the work of the British architect Inigo Jones (1573–1652) and such significant treatises as Colen Campbell's *Vitruvius Britannicus.*

In the United States, the classical villa in a picturesque landscape was at the center of Thomas Jefferson's utopian visions for the new nation. The American version of the Neo-Palladian villa, however, had a completely different relationship to its context. Jefferson's own home, Monticello, constructed near Charlottesville, Virginia, in 1768–1782 and remodeled in 1796–1809, differed from any English precedent in its effort to reach beyond the confines of its immediate site. It also showed an early near-obsession with technological efficiency, which as several scholars have noted marked a distinction between British and American domestic ideals.

Through his architecture and his writings, Jefferson put forth his powerful vision of an agrarian society of white farmers controlling individual plots of arable land. He realized many of these ideals with passage of the national Land Ordinance of 1785, which subjected most of the land between the Appalachian Mountains and the Mississippi River to a regular grid, ignoring the natural topography and encouraging both an agricultural economy and the speedy occupation of the West. Square townships six miles on each side were subdivided into sections of one square mile, which were then divided into quarter-sections. This uncompromising grid was adopted for all new towns in the West and for the expansion of existing cities. It was a perfect setting for the proliferation of isolated domestic architecture.

This notion of the detached house was in direct opposition to the tradition of row housing in large European cities. In contrast to the multifamily housing on the continent, the houses of English cities largely consisted of attached dwellings, built either with party walls or with walls constructed side by side, and with little setback from the street to accommodate an area well with the service entrance.

Row housing was also a significant American building type that flourished in crowded cities like New York, Boston, Philadelphia, and Baltimore where high land values favored high-density residential development. The popularity of the row house began to diminish after about 1850 when wealthy city dwellers moved to the outskirts of cities in their attempt to escape industrialization and the attendant crowded city living, increased racial strife, and spreading diseases like tuberculosis. In subsequent decades, the row house was largely replaced in the English-speaking world, particularly in North America, by the single-family detached house. Although less efficient in terms of land use, heating and cooling, and the use of building materials, the freestanding house emphasized the nuclear family and sanctioned homeownership, factors that had been obscured by row housing and apartments.

Whereas row housing had been built mostly of brick or masonry due to fire regulations, the single-family detached house in America was constructed of wood. This was not the heavy timber, hand-tooled construction of the seventeenth-century house built by house wrights; rather, Americans built their houses using the "balloon frame" that developed in Chicago in the 1830s after machine-made nails became widely available. The balloon frame meant that relatively unskilled workers could erect houses quickly, and it was the system used to construct most housing in North America until it was replaced by platform framing.

The individual family as the center of moral reform, facilitated by the popularity of the detached house, was touted both by the professional architectural press and the women's press in the second half of the nineteenth century and received particular emphasis in the evangelical movement. Ladies' magazines praised the home and institutionalized the wife and mother as its queen. The house itself, beginning at mid-century, took on important didactic nuances. It was widely believed that a woman could instill virtue in her husband and children, for example, through careful choice of architecture and furniture. In this way, the detached house became the symbol of proper family life.

In the architectural press, the most powerful supporter of the isolated middle-class family dwelling was Andrew Jackson Downing (1815–1852), whose books *The Architecture of Country Houses* (1850) and *Cottage Residences* (1842) featured plans and perspectives of cottages in various architectural styles, mostly Gothic Revival, invariably set amidst mature trees and gardens. Downing's books were a widely read and codified domestic ideology for architecture. Perhaps his most lasting contribution to American domestic architecture was his suggestion that residents could express their own personalities in their houses. This notion has been widespread from Downing's time to the present, and since then a plethora of architectural forms and materials has been employed to express the individual tastes and personal territory of the family.

Catherine Beecher (1800–1878), too, promoted the single-family detached house in her book *The American Woman's Home* (1869). She detailed the moral superiority of women based on their highly developed capacity for self-sacrifice, suggesting that the detached house was the primary sphere in which to express this characteristic. She hoped that her radical reforms to the middle-class house, including the omission of servants' quarters and a rational reconfiguration of the kitchen, would raise the status of American women working at home to professional.

The late nineteenth century witnessed several formal changes to house plans that foreshadowed the modern suburban house. Many of the so-called Shingle Style houses, for example, introduced open, flowing plans. The well-known architects of these houses—firms like Henry Hobson Richardson and McKim, Mead & White—emphasized the individual needs of their clients by responding directly to the physical and cultural contexts of the sites.

Agitated silhouettes, asymmetrical plans with variously shaped rooms, and spacious living "halls" brought back memories of colonial houses in the area and the dramatic seacoast that many of them faced. Vincent Scully has suggested that these houses were the first examples of a truly American architecture.

The form of the typical Victorian detached dwelling, however, was far more conservative. Set back from the street, these houses were enclosed by lawns, hedges, and fences with gates. The front porch, entry lobby, and corridor of the house functioned as part of an elaborate filtering system that underlined the class and gender differences in the family and its relations to the outside world. The front parlor, one of a series of specialized rooms in the house, was usually expressed on the building's facade by a bay window; the large, undifferentiated kitchen, the heart of the servants' quarters, was located in the rear of the house. Servants were essential to the proper functioning of the household and were accommodated spatially by separate stairways, sleeping quarters, and entrances.

The architect most frequently credited with the proliferation of single-family detached houses is Frank Lloyd Wright (1869–1959), mostly because of the revolutionary houses he designed for the suburbs outside Chicago just before World War I. These "prairie houses," ground-hugging dwellings sheltered by hipped roofs and illuminated by bands of ribbon windows, reflected what Wright described as the total "destruction of the box." Rather than a series of specialized rooms accessible from a corridor, Wright's houses featured a pinwheel-like plan where rooms spun off from a central living room and massive hearth. A classic example of a prairie house is the Frederick C. Robie House of 1906–1909 in Chicago. These houses were widely copied and influenced, to a great extent, the ubiquitous ranch house after World War II. Wright's faith in the family as the ideal living unit and the detached house as its proper architectural expression were confirmed in his utopian "Broadacre City" of 1931–1935. This project revealed his deep-rooted, decentralist tendencies and foreshadowed postwar suburbs in many ways, particularly in its vision of small houses on one-acre plots.

Catherine Beecher's pleas for more rational, smaller, servantless houses were answered, to some extent, by the popularity of the bungalow in the Progressive Era. Distributed by companies like Sears and Aladdin, the bungalow was a relatively modest, detached single-family dwelling—the first to exclude any provisions for servants. For the first time, the kitchen became an integral part of general living spaces in the middle-class house. To a great extent, bungalow kitchens were inspired by methods of efficient factory production, like Taylorism. The development of home economics as a discipline, too, had encouraged the use of factories and laboratories as models for middle-class kitchens. In general, bungalows were less formal and smaller than their Victorian predecessors.

The single-family detached house was thrust to the front rank of American middle-class culture in the suburbs that developed after World War II. In response to the postwar housing crisis, automobile suburbs were constructed on the edges of cities, farther away from the central city than they had ever been. Since they were mostly developed by tract or "merchant" builders, the houses showed great stylistic conformity, which distinguished them from both nineteenth-century suburban houses and those constructed during the 1920s. Most postwar suburbs comprised streets of detached houses on clearly defined lots, with spacious front and back yards and driveways leading to double garages. The isolation of these suburbs and the pro-family sentiments that were common after World War II encouraged many women to stay at home and raise families, rather than working in the labor force as many of them had during the war. The planning of many detached houses reflected this era of the "baby boom," particularly in California where the thousands of modern ranch houses constructed by the developer Joseph Eichler featured open plans with central kitchens at the core of large, multipurpose rooms (living and dining). This design of the kitchen as the technological control center of the home was intended to allow stay-at-home mothers to cook and watch their children simultaneously, since the kitchen provided views of both an enclosed atrium and a spacious backyard, in addition to the multipurpose room. The sleek, undecorated surfaces of the modern house comprised a showcase for housekeeping standards, which were raised considerably by the concurrent mania for domestic appliances.

Despite environmental and feminist concerns about the single-family detached house, it continues to be the preferred house type as the twentieth century reaches its close. An emphasis on family values, personal freedom, and anti-urban living remain a powerful index of American middle-class culture and urban life.

*—Annmarie Adams*

**See also**
Balloon Frame Construction; Bungalow; Homeownership; Lawn; Suburban Ideal.
**References**
Adams, Annmarie. *Architecture in the Family Way: Doctors, Houses, and Women, 1870–1900.* Montreal, Quebec: McGill-Queen's University Press, 1996.
———. "The Eichler Home: Intention and Experience in Postwar Suburbia." In Elizabeth Cromley and Carter L. Hudgins, eds., *Gender, Class, and Shelter: Perspectives in Vernacular Architecture, vol. V.* Knoxville: University of Tennessee Press, 1995, 164–178.
Cummings, Abbott Lowell. *The Framed Houses of Massachusetts Bay, 1625–1725.* Cambridge, MA: Harvard University Press, 1979.
Handlin, David P. *The American Home: Architecture and Society, 1815–1915.* Boston: Little, Brown, 1979.
Hayden, Dolores. *The Grand Domestic Revolution: A History of Feminist Designs for American Homes, Neighborhoods, and Cities.* Cambridge, MA: MIT Press, 1981.
Jackson, Kenneth T. *Crabgrass Frontier: The Suburbanization of the United States.* New York: Oxford University Press, 1985.
Kostof, Spiro. *America by Design.* New York: Oxford University Press, 1987.
———. *A History of Architecture: Settings and Rituals.* New York: Oxford University Press, 1985.
Scully, Vincent, Jr. *The Shingle Style.* Rev. ed. New Haven, CT: Yale University Press, 1971.
Stilgoe, John R. *Common Landscape of America, 1580–1845.* New Haven, CT: Yale University Press, 1982.
Weiss, Marc A. *The Rise of the Community Builders: The American Real Estate Industry and Urban Land Planning.* New York: Columbia University Press, 1987.
Wright, Gwendolyn. *Building the Dream: A Social History of Housing in America.* New York: Pantheon, 1981.
———. *Moralism and the Moral Home: Domestic Architecture and Cultural Conflict in Chicago, 1873–1913.* Chicago: University of Chicago Press, 1980.

## Skid Row

The origin of the term *skid row* is murky, but it may have come from the logging industry of Seattle. The street on which logs were skidded to the sawmill (Skid Road) became associated with the loggers who went on drunken sprees after their isolation in the woods came to a temporary end. The term stuck, eventually becoming associated with seedy areas of the city known for public drunkenness, the presence of disreputable men, general rowdiness, prostitution, and poverty.

Skid row has been a constant irritant to moralists, social reformers, and the more genteel citizens. It has been viewed as a center of vice, a threat to morality, and a stain on a city's reputation. Sociologists who studied skid row in the 1950s and 1960s found that it was functional for its inhabitants. Much less disorganized than it appeared to outsiders, skid row provided institutions that met the needs of the downwardly mobile: a low-rent district with stores that sold secondhand goods, pawn shops, cheap bars, barber colleges, day-labor offices, blood banks, and rescue missions.

By the late 1970s, the land on which skid row was located had become too valuable to ignore. With the onslaught of national urban renewal programs, skid row began to disappear from cities in the United States, and its residents were dispersed instead of clustered into a single area.

Some analysts thought that skid row was destined to become only a memory of the past, but the area was counted out too soon. By 1990, its reappearance was evident—but with a changed face. Today's isolated, urban homeless are younger and as likely to be addicted to crack or other drugs as to alcohol, to be minority rather than white. Today's skid row is more dispersed and more violent.

As long as there are isolated people trapped in poverty and substance abuse, some form of skid row will exist, for this part of the city, though distasteful, meets and serves many needs of its residents and habitues.

—*James Henslin*

**References**
Miller, Ronald J. *The Demolition of Skid Row.* Lexington, MA: Lexington Books, 1982.
Siegal, Harvey A., and James A. Inciardi. "The Demise of Skid Row." *Society* 39 (1982): 39–45.
Whitman, David. "The Return of Sid Row." *U.S. News & World Report* 108:2 (January 15, 1990): 27–29.

## Skokie, Illinois

A suburb of about 70,000 residents located approximately 15 miles north of Chicago's Loop, Skokie was founded in 1888. Originally a small enclave primarily settled by German Lutherans and Catholics, Skokie first took shape as a depot along the plank road running from Chicago to Milwaukee. The town (then known as Niles Center) developed relatively slowly, and attempts to spur development along electric rail lines foundered during the Great Depression. In the 1930s, surrounded by such thriving bedroom communities as Evanston, Wilmette, and Park Ridge, local boosters spearheaded a campaign to change the name of their town to "Skokie"—a Pottowatami term for "big swamp" that they thought was more modern, up-to-date, and attractive to investors and future home buyers.

With the end of World War II, Skokie finally realized the dreams of these pro-growth forces and became a sizable residential suburb. The demand for new housing after the war fueled the rapid construction of single-family homes in Skokie, and construction of the Edens Expressway, a key link for automobile transportation, made them readily accessible. Village leaders consciously aimed to distinguish Skokie by restricting the construction of new multifamily apartment buildings to specific zones. With home builders energetically reclaiming land from the swamp that "Skokie" commemorated, the population of 7,172 before World War II skyrocketed to 65,000 by 1960.

By the mid-1950s, Skokie had become a prime destination for Jewish out-migrants from Chicago. Constituting about half of the population in 1955, this concentration of Jewish residents—including thousands of Holocaust survivors—led to the most notorious event in Skokie's history, a proposed march by Chicago's branch of the American Nazi Party in 1977. Attempts by the village to block these plans caused bitter and emotional debates about First Amendment issues. After a year of court battles and public outcry, the American Nazi Party abandoned its plans; in 1987, Skokie became the first municipality in the country to install a Holocaust memorial on its village green.

Its location just across the city border and its mix of apartments and moderately priced single-family homes have made Skokie perennially attractive to upwardly mobile immigrant families. In 1995, an article about suburbanization and immigration in the *Chicago Tribune* identified Skokie as the suburb of Chicago with the highest concentration of foreign-born residents, a very diverse population drawn from Eastern Europe, Southeast Asia, and Latin America. Known primarily as a residential community, Skokie is also the eighth largest industrial and commercial center in Illinois. One of the nation's first shopping malls, Old Orchard, was built there in 1956; Skokie also houses an array of light industry and the headquarters of corporations such as G. D. Searle and Rand McNally.

—*Karen Sawislak*

**References**
Chamberlin, Everett. *Chicago and Its Suburbs.* Chicago: T. A. Hungerfield, 1874.
Mayer, Harold M., and Richard C. Wade. *Chicago: Growth of a Metropolis.* Chicago: University of Chicago Press, 1969.
Whittingham, Richard. *Skokie, 1888–1988: A Centennial History.* Wilmette, IL: Raspail Productions, 1988.

## Skyline

From at least medieval times, many towns could be identified at a distance by the distinctive appearance of cathedral towers. The term *skyline* is of recent origin, however, referring specifically to the profile of a skyscraper city. William R. Taylor found the first use of the term in May 1896, but it had appeared in isolated instances during the previous two decades. This term indicates the heightened awareness of the vertical city of skyscrapers, and it was frequently used to refer to the view of Chicago seen from Lake Michigan or from across the plains, or of Manhattan seen from its harbor or rivers. In 1897, Montgomery Schuyler was among the first critics to admit that the silhouette of Manhattan had a symbolic quality, an "immense impressiveness" that was not a conscious intent of architects but a concatenation of the whole. His generation was responding to the creation of an artificial horizon, a completely man-made substitute for the geology of mountains, cliffs, and canyons, as cities began to make their distinctive mark on the sky. Arnold Bennett found that the skyline of New York, "seen from the New Jersey shore, is stupendous, and resembles some enchanted city of the next world rather than of this." In short, the skyline reduced the complexities of the urban scene to a beautiful pattern that seemed orderly and promising, and a city's skyline soon became one of its central features, reproduced in photographs

*The Brooklyn Bridge and New York City from across the East River.*

and postcards, and used to represent the modern city in paintings and advertisements.

—*David E. Nye*

### References

Nye, David E. *American Technological Sublime.* Cambridge, MA: MIT Press, 1994.
Schuyler, Montgomery. "The Sky-line of New York, 1881–1897." *Harper's Weekly* 41 (March 20, 1897): 295.
Taylor, William R. "New York and the Origin of the Skyline." *Prospects* 13 (1988): 225–248.
van Leeuwen, Thomas A. P. *The Skyward Trend of Thought.* Cambridge, MA: MIT Press, 1988.

## Skyscraper

Tall buildings were invented in America in the 1870s in both New York and Chicago. If the use of structural iron or steel (rather than masonry) is taken to be a defining characteristic, then Chicago's Home Insurance Building of 1885, designed by William Le Baron Jenney, clearly was the first skyscraper. The virtual absence of such buildings from major European capitals such as London and Berlin for several generations afterward suggests that population density was less impor-

tant than cultural factors in calling the skyscraper into being. While it seems plausible to assume such buildings were a logical economic development, forced into existence by the demand for the limited land available in Chicago between Lake Michigan and the railway yards (and in New York by the limited area of the island of Manhattan), this explanation is not substantiated by empirical research. Rents alone did not justify the expense of building additional floors; rather, publicity value did.

Tall buildings entailed high risks for their builders, who faced demanding standards for safety, wind sheer, ventilation, and internal transportation. In practical terms, such buildings were not feasible until several new technologies were in place during the last decades of the nineteenth century. A safe and reliable elevator was one requirement; a steam-driven apparatus came into regular use at New York's Fifth Avenue Hotel in the 1860s. Such elevators were replaced by electrical models after about 1885. Just as important were steel construction techniques that reduced the volume of the building needed for supporting walls.

Two of the most important architects of early tall buildings in Chicago, Louis Sullivan and Jenney, learned the potentials of structural steel from the Eads Bridge in St. Louis. Another Chicagoan, John Root, was one of the first to develop a foundation that he termed a "floating raft," which was "a solid mass of cement webbed with a mesh or grill of steel, giving it very great transverse as well as crushing strength." By the end of the century, skyscrapers were understood to be steel buildings with elevators that were ventilated and lighted by electricity.

From their inception, skyscrapers had symbolic uses as corporate icons and, indeed, in New York they emerged partly as an outgrowth of competition among newspapers. In 1875, the *New York Tribune* completed the city's tallest structure, 260 feet, prompting *The Observer, The Herald,* and Joseph Pulitzer's *World* to erect taller buildings. In the 1890s, life insurance companies quickly surpassed the newspapers, as they discovered the advertising value of landmark buildings. In contrast, banks often built ostentatiously low structures, preferring classical models of conservative horizontality. Eventually, the genteel elite gave up on the horizontal city, but not without a fight. The horizontal city had been the ideal of the 1893 Chicago World's Fair, which presented the city of the future as a series of Beaux Arts structures of uniform height, surmounted by a few Neoclassical domes. To the dismay of Sullivan, the "White City" proved popular with the public. This contradiction between vernacular and European taste encouraged a good deal of eclecticism after the initial phase of skyscraper construction, characterized by the functional designs of Sullivan and Root, notably the former's Carson Pirie Scott Building (1889–1904). After about 1890, however, for 40 years many architects tried to assimilate elements of Palladian, Gothic, and Classical styles before they shifted first to Art Deco in the 1920s, then to the international style from the later 1920s, and in the 1960s to a postmodern playfulness, which led back to a revived appreciation for turn-of-the-century eclecticism.

Between 1902 and 1931 New York experienced a feverish competition to build the highest structure in the world. In 1902, the Flatiron building at 307 feet high presented an edge almost as sharp as the bow of a ship at the intersection of Broadway and Fifth Avenue, prompting the photographer Alfred Stieglitz to write, "it appeared to be moving toward me like the bow of a monster ocean steamer—a picture of new America still in the making." But this impressive structure was quickly overshadowed by others, notably the Singer Building (1908), the 792-foot Woolworth Building (1913), the 1,048-foot Chrysler Building (1929), and finally, the 1,250-foot Empire State Building (1931). This remained the world's tallest structure until a new boom began in the 1960s, when the twin towers of the World Trade Center in New York went up to 1,350 feet, overtaken in the following decade by Chicago's Sears Tower at 1,453 feet. Today, virtually every major American city has at least one structure over 500 feet high that provides a dramatic panoramic view to tourists and to executives on the upper floors. By the 1920s, the Olympian perspective from a corporate office had become a cliché in advertising images that was immediately recognized as a visualization of economic power.

Yet for all their popularity, skyscrapers have undesirable social effects. They concentrate a mass of people in certain locations and weaken the sense of neighborhood. The proliferation of tall buildings destroys the human scale of the city and cuts off much of the sunlight, turning the street into a dark canyon with new kinds of winds and downdrafts from the towering structures overhead. And urban transportation systems, usually taxed to the limit before skyscrapers appeared, often cannot cope with the increased traffic these buildings bring. A city full of skyscrapers can seem massive, crowded, and impersonal.

Objections to skyscrapers, abetted by conflicting interests among property owners, also produce zoning restrictions. In the early years, these concerned height limits. Chicago, for example, briefly lowered the limit from 260 to 200 feet in 1911. In New York, even architects who had designed skyscrapers often felt that they should not exceed a certain limit. Its zoning law of 1916, which resulted in the famous regulations regarding setbacks from the street, dictated that "no building shall be erected in excess of twice the width of the street, but for each one foot that the building or a portion of it sets back from the street line, four feet shall be added to the height limit."

For many years, these restrictions forced architects to design buildings with a zigzag profile that maximized the enclosed space, which necessarily diminished as the building rose higher. During the 1930s, Walter Dorwin Teague and others foresaw widely spaced skyscrapers located amid gardens, parks, and playgrounds, but these garden city visions were only partially realized in the growth of "edge cities" a generation later.

In the post–World War II Era, large cities, notably New York, passed new zoning laws that allowed property owners to build higher in exchange for civic improvements, such as putting a public passageway through a building or placing a subway entrance inside it. Starting in the mid-1970s, another innovation permitted owners to buy and sell "unused" columns of air, so that one site could be developed to its maximum if sufficient "air rights" to an adjacent property were purchased. Thus, the Museum of Modern Art sold its "air rights" for high-rise condominium construction. These changes in zoning gave architects more latitude in their designs during the same time that the minimalist orthodoxies of the international style gave way to the new eclecticism of postmodernism.

More and taller skyscrapers continue to be erected despite the exodus to suburbia and the decline of inner cities. Their value as public relations statements, combined with their economies of scale, have made them the central, symbolic structures of a capitalist economy.

*—David E. Nye*

**See also**
Chrysler Building; Elevators; Empire State Building; Height Restrictions; Jenney, William Le Baron; World Trade Center.
**References**
Domosh, Mona. "The Symbolism of the Skyscraper: Case Studies of New York's First Tall Buildings." *Journal of Urban History* 14 (1988): 320–345.
Goldberger, Paul. *The Skyscraper.* New York: Knopf, 1981.
Schleier, Merrill. *The Skyscraper in American Art, 1890–1931.* New York: Da Capo, 1986.
van Leeuwen, Thomas A. P. *The Skyward Trend of Thought.* Cambridge, MA: MIT Press, 1988.

## Skywalks for Pedestrians

Elevated pedestrian skywalk systems are becoming an increasingly popular element of the downtown streetscape in the United States and Canada. A skywalk system can be defined as a network of elevated interconnecting pedestrian walkways. The network consists of sky bridges over the street, second-story corridors within downtown buildings, and various activity hubs. For the most part, they are enclosed and climate-controlled, and connect a body of retail and service establishments that oftentimes has no direct access to the street level.

When the first skywalks were erected in the early 1960s, their primary function was to protect downtown pedestrians from the harsh winter climate in cities such as Minneapolis and St. Paul. However, over the years cities have increasingly been attracted to skywalks because of their downtown development potential. Skywalks serve to promote densities, create a new level of commercial activity, and link large downtown development projects such as retail centers, hotels, and office towers. Moreover, they facilitate pedestrian mobility, allowing most trips to be made in less time and in more comfort, and they improve pedestrian safety by physically separating pedestrians from vehicular traffic.

As a result of their downtown development potential, together with their tremendous popularity with the general public, particularly suburbanites, numerous downtown systems have been constructed in North America. The most extensive systems have been built in medium-sized northern cities such as Des Moines, Milwaukee, Minneapolis, Rochester (New York), Spokane, and St. Paul in the United States, and Calgary, Winnipeg, and Edmonton in Canada. Smaller cold weather cities, such as Duluth (Minnesota), Fargo (North Dakota), and Sioux City and Cedar Rapids (both in Iowa) have

built systems as well, as have several cities that enjoy relatively mild weather, such as Charlotte (North Carolina), Cincinnati, Dallas, Ft. Worth, and Portland (Oregon).

Despite their popularity with city officials, downtown businessmen, and the general public, skywalks pose a number of problems to the downtown environment. Economically, they often reduce the value of street-level space and of buildings not connected to the network. Aesthetically, they can damage the architectural integrity of the facades of older buildings and interrupt sight lines of downtown landmarks and vistas. Socially, they possess the potential to segregate people based on social class, as skywalks are often perceived to be reserved for white-collar office workers and patrons of upscale stores and hotels. Finally, the tendency for skywalks to reduce substantially the volume of street-level pedestrian traffic and activity can hurt the overall image of a downtown.

These problems notwithstanding, it is likely than an increasing number of downtowns across the United States and Canada will implement skywalk systems during the 1990s.

*—Kent A. Robertson*

**References**
Lasser, Terry J. "The Pros and Cons of Downtown Skywalks." *Urban Land* 47 (1988): 2–6.
Maitland, Barry. "Hidden Cities: The Irresistible Rise of the North American Interior City." *Cities* 9 (1992): 62–69.
Robertson, Kent A. *Pedestrian Malls and Skywalks.* Brookfield, VT: Avebury Press, 1994.
———. "Pedestrian Skywalk Systems: Downtown's Great Hope or Pathways to Ruin?" *Transportation Quarterly* 42 (1988): 457–484.

## Slavery in Cities

At no time during the long history of slavery in North America did the phrase "plantation slavery" encompass the experience of all slaves or slaveowners. Nor was urban slavery a phenomenon limited to the nineteenth century or an area south of the Mason-Dixon line. During periods long and short, urban slavery shaped much of the social and economic life in such places as Baltimore and New Orleans, New York and Norfolk, Savannah and Mobile, Richmond and Nashville. Slavery emerged in New York before there was a Charleston, and it thrived in Philadelphia and ended in Boston before there was a Washington, D.C. Slavery ended in northern cities by the early nineteenth century—at about the same time that it began to flourish in Memphis and Louisville.

In the Old South, the social geography of black slavery differed from that of black freedom. Most slaves lived in rural areas. By contrast, free black residents of Georgia tended to live in Augusta or Savannah, just as their counterparts in Virginia tended to live in Richmond, Norfolk, or Petersburg. Free blacks and urban slaves did not necessarily view each other as colleagues and equals; especially in Charleston and New Orleans, "free persons of color" might distinguish themselves by color and class from black slaves.

Just as some black southerners were free—though not remotely as "free" as white southerners—some slaves lived in cities. While slavery was bondage everywhere, it varied by time and place. Urban slavery in the eighteenth century resembled urban slavery in the nineteenth—and slavery in New York resembled that in Norfolk—more than any of these resembled the rural varieties found on plantations, colonial or antebellum, that grew cotton, tobacco, rice, and sugar.

Cities in the antebellum South provided a wider range of possible jobs than did farms and plantations, especially for men. Men might work in ironworks like Tredegar in Richmond, women in textile mills in cities of the Deep South, and both men and women in tobacco factories. Men might work on railroads in any antebellum city and as stevedores in any of the cities along the coast or a river.

Perhaps more important than the types of employment available in the cities was the likelihood, especially in the upper South, that slaves might hire themselves out. Those who located their own employment had greater autonomy in their work lives than did most slaves; and if they also found their own housing, they had much more control over their social lives, too. Moreover, as Frederick Douglass reported from observing slave life in Baltimore, slaves who hired themselves out were more likely than most slaves to save money for purchasing their own freedom or that of family members.

Yet, most urban slaves remained slaves into the 1860s. Moreover, most slave women in cities worked as domestics, much as many of them might have done on a plantation or farm. Women's responsibilities revolved around cooking, cleaning, and child care, though urban slavery tended to add marketing as an additional important function.

Life as an urban slave did not protect a person from the slave trade, either local or interstate. The threat of being sold remained a fact of life for slaves, whether they lived in cities of the upper South like Baltimore, Alexandria, and Norfolk or cities of the Deep South like Charleston and New Orleans. Living in Richmond, Henry Brown hired himself out, found his own housing, married, and had three children, but the slave trade invaded his world and sent his wife and children out of state. With his previous advantages no longer of value, Brown grasped his only remaining advantage, the greater opportunity of successfully running away to freedom that life in a city of the upper South afforded.

Urban slaves tended to have greater freedom to engage in community activities than their plantation and farm counterparts. Considerable numbers of slaves and free blacks lived in southern cities, and both groups enjoyed greater freedom of movement and behavior than they would have had in rural areas. Black churches developed in southern cities, and slaves and free blacks tended to worship together. These African-American churches provided opportunities for organizational leadership, for learning how to read and write, and for establishing mutual aid and other benevolent societies. Black churches and other organizations, like the leadership experience that they provided black southerners, did not wait until slavery ended to become important parts of the social landscape in southern cities.

Urban slavery differed from rural slavery in its pattern of growth as well as in the conditions of life. The absolute and relative number of African-American slaves declined in cities even as American society experienced rapid urbanization. This was most evident in northern cities, to be sure, whose population growth was extraordinary but where slavery virtually vanished, yet it was generally true in the South, too. The District of Columbia supplies an example. The District contained three cities in the early nineteenth century, and in all three—Georgetown, Alexandria, and Washington—the number of slaves peaked no later than the early 1830s, as did the ratio of slaves to free black residents and their percentage of all city residents. The same was true in Baltimore. Given the demand for plantation labor, slaves with few skills might well be sent out of cities to work on farms or plantations, either near their cities of origin or somewhere far to the south and west.

Yet, not everywhere did the number of urban slaves decline before the 1860s, and the numbers remained substantial even for those southern cities where they did drop. The 1860 census showed the largest number of slaves ever recorded for Richmond, Savannah, and Mobile. The number of slaves in Charleston peaked at 19,532 in 1850, but 13,909 slaves still lived there in 1860; the number in New Orleans peaked at 23,448 in 1840, but 13,385 slaves resided there in 1860. Richmond's figure for 1860, 11,699, was the highest ever recorded for that city and placed it third among all American cities that year. Moreover, the number of slaves in major southern cities mushroomed during the Civil War as urban industries grew to meet wartime military demands.

Freedom came to all slaves in the 1860s, and three groups of African Americans emerged in disproportionate numbers among the black leaders of the postemancipation years. Free blacks from the North constituted one such group, and free blacks from southern cities constituted another. Former slaves from southern cities were the third. Slavery in the cities, restrictive though it was, provided opportunities and experiences that permitted slaves to acquire skills that served them and other African Americans well when they finally became their own masters.

—*Peter Wallenstein*

**References**

Goldfield, David R. "Black Life in Old South Cities." In Edward D. C. Campbell, Jr., with Kym S. Rice, eds., *Before Freedom Came: African-American Life in the Antebellum South,* 123–154. Charlottesville: University Press of Virginia, 1991.

Goldin, Claudia Dale. *Urban Slavery in the American South, 1820–1860: A Quantitative History.* Chicago: University of Chicago Press, 1976.

Green, Constance McLaughlin. *The Secret City: A History of Race Relations in the Nation's Capital.* Princeton, NJ: Princeton University Press, 1967.

Miller, Elinor, and Eugene D. Genovese, eds. *Plantation, Town, and County: Essays on the Local History of American Slave Society.* Urbana: University of Illinois Press, 1974.

Nash, Gary B. *Race, Class, and Politics: Essays on American Colonial and Revolutionary Society.* Urbana: University of Illinois Press, 1986.

Powers, Bernard E., Jr. *Black Charlestonians: A Social History, 1822–1885.* Fayetteville: University of Arkansas Press, 1994.

Wade, Richard C. *Slavery in the Cities: The South, 1820–1860.* New York: Oxford University Press, 1964.

White, Shane. *Somewhat More Independent: The End of Slavery in New York City, 1770–1810.* Athens: University of Georgia Press, 1991.

## Sloan, John (1871–1951)

John Sloan began his professional career in 1892 as a newspaper illustrator in Philadelphia, and he continued to support himself primarily as an artist and illustrator for the next 25 years. In 1892, he took a night class in drawing at the Pennsylvania Academy of the Fine Arts, his only formal art training, and became associated with a small circle of artists around Robert Henri, who encouraged Sloan to devote himself to painting. Henri also advised his protégés to draw from fresh visual perception rather than to imitate the conventional forms and subjects of academic idealism. As a result, Sloan's earliest works on canvas feature urban landscapes and architecture that the artist observed firsthand.

In 1902 a commission for a large series of etchings to illustrate a deluxe edition of the novels of Charles Paul de Kock encouraged Sloan to focus on the subject matter for which he is best known—narrative figural compositions. Shortly after moving to New York in 1904, he began a series of etchings called City Life in which he translated his narrative compositions from the nineteenth-century French settings of de Kock to the contemporary urban environment. Two of the ten City Life prints were deemed too "vulgar" to be included in an exhibition at the American Watercolor Society. This incident and his frank portrayal of everyday life, particularly of the working classes, confirmed Sloan's association with the antiestablishment activities of his mentor and colleague Robert Henri, who had also moved to New York City.

In 1906 Sloan began producing urban genre pictures in oil on canvas. Like much of his graphic work, these paintings were based on direct observation of the daily lives of ordinary people in New York City. By depicting gatherings of young, working-class men and women without chaperones, new forms of commercialized entertainment such as movie theaters, or prostitutes stepping into notorious nightspots, Sloan was confronting, without judgment or sentimentality, the changing social structures of modern urban America. Though several progressive critics admired the honesty and vitality of paintings by Sloan and other insurgent realists in the Henri circle, conservative jurists frequently refused to admit their pictures into major exhibitions at the National Academy of Design. Henri and his colleagues retaliated by organizing a highly publicized exhibition of their work at the Macbeth Gallery in 1908 that became a landmark event in the independent exhibition movement in the United States.

The Armory Show of 1913, which introduced European modernism to many Americans, reinforced Sloan's growing interest in formal issues and the abstract elements of painting. He questioned his long-standing attachment to an idea—typically a narrative idea that had some level of resonance for him emotionally—as the basis for his work. While he was working in Gloucester, Massachusetts, during the summer of 1914, Sloan no longer waited for a subject to inspire him but painted directly from nature. In a few years, however, the artist was once again casting about for meaningful subject matter. His search took him to Santa Fe, New Mexico, where he found motifs in the daily lives of the Pueblo Indians, and to them he responded much as he had responded to vignettes of urban working-class life more than ten years earlier. By the date of Sloan's first trip, 1919, this southwestern pilgrimage was nothing new or unusual. During an era of increased and critical awareness of the routine artificiality of urban America, a number of writers and painters from New York City made pilgrimages to the Southwest, seeking to connect with a culture and a way of life that they perceived as more authentic than their own. Sloan became a prominent member of the artists' colony in Santa Fe, summering there regularly until 1950, one year before his death.

—*Marianne Doezema*

**References**

Brooks, Van Wyck. *John Sloan: A Painter's Life.* New York: Dutton, 1955.

Elzea, Rowland. *John Sloan's Oil Paintings: A Catalogue Raisonné.* 2 vols. Newark, NJ: University of Delaware Press, 1991.

Hills, Patricia. "John Sloan's Images of Working-Class Women: A Case Study of the Roles and Interrelationships of Politics, Personality, and Patrons in the Development of Sloan's Art, 1905–16." *Prospects* 5 (1980): 157–196.

Holcomb, Grant. "John Sloan in Santa Fe." *American Art Journal* 10 (1978): 33–54.

Kinser, Suzanne L. "Prostitutes in the Art of John Sloan." *Prospects* 9 (1984): 231–254.

Loughery, John. *John Sloan: Painter and Rebel.* New York: Henry Holt, 1995.

Scott, David W., and E. John Bullard. *John Sloan, 1871–1951.* Exhibition catalog. Washington, DC: National Gallery of Art, 1971.

Sloan, John. *Gist of Art: Principles and Practise Expounded in the Classroom and Studio,* recorded with the assistance of Helen Farr. New York: American Artists Group, 1939.

St. John, Bruce, ed. *John Sloan's New York Scene, from the Diaries, Notes, and Correspondence, 1906–1913.* New York: Harper & Row, 1965.

## Smith, Alfred E. (1873–1944)

Although only his maternal grandparents had migrated from Ireland and his maternal grandmother had converted to Catholicism, Al Smith, a third-generation American, symbolized the emergence of urban Irish Catholics in American political life. Like many ethnics, he grew up on New York's Lower East Side and found an avenue of upward mobility in politics even though he failed to complete the eighth grade. He gained his political education at a Democratic club reminiscent of the world of George Washington Plunkett, where Smith often "took the contract" to deliver tangible aid to constituents. He was rewarded first with a patronage job as a process server and subsequently with nomination to the New York State Assembly.

Through 12 successive terms between 1904 and 1916, he came under the influence of Progressivism and its programs to improve state and local government. Like many new-stock politicians, Smith opposed the Progressives' moralistic reforms that threatened the machine that was promoting his career. At the same time, he gladly embraced their humanitarian measures, which enhanced the well-being of the working-class population of his district. In 1911, reacting to the Triangle Shirtwaist Company fire, the New York state legislature created the Factory Investigating Commission and named the Democratic leaders from New York City, Senator Robert F. Wagner and Assemblyman Al Smith, as chair and vice-chair respectively. In the Empire State, social progressivism culminated in the enactment of their commission's recommendations.

Smith gained wider recognition at the 1915 New York state constitutional convention in Albany. In the referendum on the new constitution, he advocated rejection, primarily because the apportionment provisions gave upstate districts an unfair advantage over New York City. Smith served a term as sheriff of New York County and a year as president of the New York City Board of Aldermen before being elected governor of the state.

Except for the Republican interregnum of 1921–1922, Smith's administration spanned the entire decade from 1919 to 1929. As chief executive, he adopted the Progressive agenda, not only for labor legislation but also for structural reform of state government, perhaps his most substantial achievement. Nowhere was his sensitivity to the needs of New York City more apparent than in his proposals to subsidize affordable housing and his successful fight to locate state parks on Long Island that would be accessible to the urban multitudes. The variegated metropolis bred in Governor Smith the open-mindedness with which he championed civil liberties during the Red Scare of 1919. After the death of Charles F. Murphy, chief of Tammany Hall, the governor exercised his influence in the organization to deny renomination to Mayor John F. Hylan, a protégé of William Randolph Hearst whom Smith held in contempt.

Contemporaries believed that Murphy's death handicapped Smith in his quest to become the first Catholic president of the United States. He ran on his record as a Progressive governor but was defeated by Herbert Hoover in 1928. Smith, with his immigrant forebears, Catholic faith, and antagonism to Prohibition, represented the threat of the city, with all its negative connotations for Middle America. His candidacy did, however, contribute to the electoral transformation of large cities from Republican to Democratic that would make them a major component of the New Deal coalition.

Meanwhile, Smith himself switched from the Democratic to the Republican party. Enforced retirement from politics made him "a most tragic case of unemployment." During the Depression, he consorted with wealthy businessmen, condemned a New Deal that alleviated the hardships of the less fortunate unemployed, and committed the cardinal sin of deserting his party in 1936 and 1940. With his vituperation, Smith, in the words of one observer, "was presenting Roosevelt with the sidewalks of New York one brick at a time."

—*Paula Eldot*

### References

Eldot, Paula. *Governor Alfred E. Smith: The Politician as Reformer.* New York: Garland Publishing, 1983.

Josephson, Matthew, and Hannah Josephson. *Al Smith: Hero of the Cities.* Boston: Houghton Mifflin, 1969.

Neal, Donn C. *The World beyond the Hudson: Alfred E. Smith and National Politics, 1918–1928.* New York: Garland Publishing, 1983.

Perry, Elisabeth Israels. *Belle Moskowitz: Feminine Politics and the Exercise of Power in the Age of Alfred E. Smith.* New York: Oxford University Press, 1987.

Smith, Alfred E. *Up to Now: An Autobiography.* New York: Viking Press, 1929.

## Social Gospel

The social gospel was an ideology and reform movement within Protestant churches at the turn of the century that arose in response to social turmoil in America's industrializing cities. As industry and cities expanded in the Gilded Age, the gap between rich and poor widened dramatically; workers and employers became embroiled in bitter, sometimes violent, labor disputes; and poverty and despair haunted the tenement districts of major cities in the United States. These conditions prompted many to question the belief that hard work and self-control would yield success. Moreover, churches that clung to this individualistic ideal seemed to condone business practices that tore families apart, perpetuated starvation wages, necessitated unwholesome living quarters, and generated cynicism about economic opportunity and fundamental morality. In short, Protestant churches' continued insistence on spiritual individualism led many Americans—both inside and outside the churches—to question the Protestant commitment to the teachings of Jesus Christ.

Not all churchmen and churchwomen, however, were contented with the idea of Protestant individualism. Those who ministered to urban congregations recognized that economically and spiritually individuals could not rely exclusively on their own efforts to obtain satisfaction. When Washington Gladden, a minister in Columbus, Ohio, published *Applied Christianity* in 1886, he voiced this concern and the need for a social ethic that would apply Christianity to modern life.

In the next two decades, Gladden and others worked out more completely what this social gospel implied. Most importantly, those who accepted the social gospel believed that individuals could not be assured of salvation until they dedicated themselves to the redemption of others. Redemption, however, was not limited to proselytizing. Adherents of the social gospel insisted that spiritual and material needs went together and called for an extensive array of social programs that addressed problems of hunger, disease, child neglect, and inadequate sanitation. People who struggled for mere survival, they argued, lacked the energy and will to seek solace in church. Those who received material assistance from churches, however, would see immediately the compelling power of the Christian message. Salvation thus came to have temporal as well as otherworldly meaning.

As an ideology, the social gospel found expression in books by Gladden, Walter Rauschenbusch, Charles Stelzle, George Herron, Lyman Abbott, and Shailer Mathews, to name but a few of the prominent writers and theologians who became its advocates. Elizabeth Stuart Phelps and Charles M. Sheldon also promoted social consciousness in many novels published in the 1890s and early 1900s. The Religious Education Association, based in Chicago and influenced by Shailer Mathews, devised a line of Sunday school instructional materials that reflected social gospel ideas. In the 1890s, the relationship between social problems and Christian action became a central subject in many schools of theology, and George Herron founded a department of applied Christianity at Grinnell College in Iowa. By the 1910s, social gospel ideas had become pervasive in American Protestant circles.

As a reform movement, the social gospel enjoyed a strong reciprocal relationship with programs founded by Progressive reformers. Both religious and secular reformers shared an interest in improving the quality of life for all Americans—especially those living in urban squalor. Social gospelers supported and participated in the settlement house movement, of which Jane Addams's Hull House was the most famous. They converted their own churches from centers of Sunday worship to "institutional churches" that were open seven days a week and provided free or inexpensive meals, medical services, and child care for people who lived nearby. Caroline Bartlett's People's Church in Kalamazoo, Michigan, served as a model institutional church in the 1890s. Some followers of the social gospel held public offices from which they could encourage the state to shoulder responsibilities for social services. With Walter Rauschenbusch, they hoped to "Christianize" economic, political, and social life, and they saw their movement as a way to usher in the "Kingdom of God" on earth. This dimension of the social gospel was responsible for greater activism and social concern on the part of Protestant churches in twentieth-century America.

Although the ideas of social gospel have not disappeared from American Protestantism, the social gospel as a coherent movement enjoyed its greatest influence between the mid-1880s and World War I. While its influence was felt in small towns as well as industrial cities, the social gospel owed its existence to rapid social change and the problems associated with urban and industrial conditions. It was an important Protestant response to changes wrought by cities and industry, and it became one of the cornerstones of a modern American social ethos.

—*Susan Curtis*

**See also**
Gladden, Washington; Matthews, Mark Allison; Rauschenbusch, Walter; Strong, Josiah.

**References**
Abell, Aaron. *The Urban Impact on American Protestantism, 1865–1900.* Cambridge, MA: Harvard University Press, 1943.
Curtis, Susan. *A Consuming Faith: The Social Gospel and Modern American Culture.* Baltimore: Johns Hopkins University Press, 1991.
Gorrell, Donald K. *The Age of Social Responsibility: The Social Gospel in the Progressive Era, 1900–1920.* Macon, GA: Mercer University Press, 1988.
Handy, Robert T. *The Social Gospel in America, 1870–1920.* New York: Oxford University Press, 1966.
Hopkins, Charles H. *The Rise of the Social Gospel in American Protestantism, 1865–1915.* New Haven, CT: Yale University Press, 1940.
May, Henry. *Protestant Churches in Industrial America.* New York: Harper, 1949.
White, Ronald C., Jr., and C. Howard Hopkins. *The Social Gospel: Religion and Reform in Changing America.* Philadelphia: Temple University Press, 1976.

## Social Mobility

Social mobility involves the movement of people from one social position to another. Such movement may be studied by comparing changes in social position within an individual's lifetime (career mobility), by comparing the social attainment of an individual to that of the individual's parent or parents (intergenerational mobility), or by assessing the social attainment of an ethnic, racial, or other type of subpopulation as a whole relative to the rest of society (group mobility). Because the concept of social position (status) contains subjective as well as empirical components, social scientists have most often measured it through proxies of income, occupation, and property holding. Because of the variety and multitude of these phenomena in cities, most studies of social mobility have focused on urban patterns.

Several factors historically have influenced the extent of social mobility in American urban society. Many are personal, including birth (parents' status), religion, race, ethnicity, education (including level of skill), and physical or mental impairment. Other influencing factors are social, such as the type of community (egalitarian versus authoritarian) or the extent of industrialization and/or modernization. It is apparently the case that urbanization, which resulted in the decline of agricultural employment, the emergence of new occupations, and an increase in the amount of education, enhanced opportunities for social mobility in both directions, down as well as up. Thus, cities have traditionally been identified as places with well-defined social (class) structures.

Assumptions about class status and upward and downward movement among different positions within the status system imply a strict rank order of the factors that define social position. In the analysis of urban social mobility, occupation has served as the most accessible defining characteristic for such a rank order, especially because income information for individuals long dead is difficult to obtain. While agreement on the ranking of fine gradations in occupation has been difficult to achieve, historians have generally accepted six major distinctions: unskilled, semiskilled, skilled, clerical, proprietor, and professional. And although there has been some difficulty distinguishing relative status between and within some categories, such as semiskilled and skilled or proprietors and professionals, distinctions between manual (the first three categories) and nonmanual (the latter three categories) are recognized as significant. Meaningful mobility is said to have occurred when persons move upward or downward between the two.

Throughout American urban history there has been both a myth and a reality of social mobility. The myth is of rags-to-riches. The reality is that most studies have concluded that the path from the lowest to the highest status is seldom trod. Those individuals at the top, especially of the occupational and wealth scales, were either there from the start because of advantages of birth or they did not travel far to reach their perch. Moreover, only a very few at the absolute bottom of the social scale ever made significant moves upward. Their family background, race, ethnicity, or access to capital stacked the deck against them. On the other hand, widespread incremental movement was a reality. In every era, there were generally high frequencies of minor improvements in job status and property holding, improvements that almost always outnumbered the cases of those falling from a higher rank to a lower one. And even if such advances did not occur within an individual's career, there remained a strong chance that the person's offspring, usually sons, could reach slightly higher status than their parents. Only with the onset of the worldwide recession of the late 1980s and early 1990s, and a mature postindustrial society, was this general pattern interrupted.

Widespread social mobility usually occurs in an open society, one characterized as egalitarian and democratic. Low rates of social mobility occur in a closed society, one characterized by authoritarianism and rigid social castes. American cities have contained elements of both types. For most white ethnic groups (including the native-born), urban society has been open. The commercial growth of the eighteenth and early nineteenth centuries, the industrialization of the early and middle nineteenth century, and the expansion of white-collar and service occupations from the late nineteenth century through the twentieth created many opportunities for social advancement. For some ethnic groups and most racial minorities, however, urban society has been relatively closed because prejudice has constricted avenues of opportunity.

Several other issues confound the study of the already complicated issue of urban social mobility. First, although occupation is a necessary representation of socioeconomic status, scholars have not yet developed a full understanding of the process of job recruitment in the past. Presumably, in an open society, access to most occupations would be based on qualification and merit. This ideal has seldom been attained, but exactly how individuals obtained their jobs and advanced in them is not always clear.

Second, almost all studies of social mobility have focused on the career, intergenerational, and group patterns of urban men. Yet the social mobility patterns of urban women have often followed different paths. Various cultural impediments, both overt and subtle, have blocked careers for women in professional, commercial, and artisanal occupations, causing a woman's social status to be defined in terms of the men—husband, father, brothers—with whom she was associated. Moreover, historians often have excused women from mobility studies because the sudden change of name due to marriage made it difficult to trace individual women through a succession of records such as censuses and directories.

Yet women, particularly those living in a city, have manifested patterns of status change that provide insights into the dynamics of urban life. In colonial times, some local governments allowed women, especially widows, to acquire and manage property. Throughout the eighteenth and nineteenth centuries, artisans sometimes taught their craft to their wives and daughters. Even though surveys and records did not list these women as skilled workers, they often toiled as such in assisting the so-called main breadwinner and replaced him when he was ill or otherwise incapacitated. Similar patterns occurred within families of small merchants. More than men, women experienced sudden shifts of social status, downward when a spouse or parent died and upward through marriage or inheritance. In the late nineteenth and early twentieth centuries, expansion of professions such as teaching, social work, and nursing provided women with new opportunities for career mobility. And the entry of increased numbers of women into higher education enabled some women—though disproportionately few compared to men—to enter managerial and other professional ranks in the mid- and late twentieth century.

Third, the larger meaning of social mobility remains open to debate. Many scholars have linked the phenomenon with American exceptionalism, suggesting that the frequency of upward movement, no matter how short the distances traveled, inhibited challenges to the capitalist system. That is, there were enough incremental improvements in status to prevent socialism from gaining as much of a foothold in the United States as it did in other industrializing countries. Even if a person's own status did not improve, the persuasive character of mobility in the society and the hope for improvement in the next generation acted to soften major protests or attempts to change the system.

This conclusion may well have some substance, but its underlying assumption—that there has been only weak anticapitalist ideology in American history—has not been fully proven. Recent studies of American laborers, and even some white-collar workers, have identified a stronger undercurrent of resistance to capitalism than analysts had previously believed. Moreover, even if the notion that American political protest has been relatively tame is accepted, it does not necessarily follow that social mobility is the explanatory factor. Ethnic and racial divisions, the ubiquity of geographical mobility, the myth of political democracy, and other factors may have exerted equal, if not greater, influence.

Finally, the equation between social mobility and success may not be a balanced one. The American success ethic, in which social mobility was inherent, was a middle-class concept and contained an element of risk. To many groups and individuals, especially those living in cities, security rather than mobility defined success. In a world where frequent swings of the business cycle buffeted workers among the uncertainties of wage cuts and layoffs and where the frequency of small business failures was high, a secure job and the steady income it would bring could have more relevance

for success than climbing a precarious occupational ladder. Thus, social mobility was not a completely pervasive ideal; cultural preferences also influenced patterns of movement.

The belief in social mobility nevertheless has had a strong influence on American culture. Inspirational and prescriptive literature overflows with admonitions to improve. And those who achieved material success exploited the myth of mobility to justify their position and salve their consciences. Poverty, according to the myth, was no barrier to wealth; to some, such as Horatio Alger and Andrew Carnegie, poverty was a prerequisite, a quality that gave a person the incentive to rise in status. But though social mobility retains a firm hold in popular ideology, scholars have shown that it is a much more complex phenomenon than it appears to be.

—*Howard P. Chudacoff*

### References

Barton, Josef. *Peasants and Strangers: Italians, Rumanians, and Slovaks in an American City, 1890–1950.* Cambridge, MA: Harvard University Press, 1975.

Bodnar, John, Roger Simon, and Michael P. Weber. *Lives of Their Own: Blacks, Italians, and Poles in Pittsburgh, 1900–1960.* Urbana: University of Illinois Press, 1982.

Griffen, Clyde, and Sally Griffen. *Natives and Newcomers: The Ordering of Opportunity in Mid-Nineteenth Century Poughkeepsie.* Cambridge, MA: Harvard University Press, 1978.

Thernstrom, Stephan. *The Other Bostonians: Poverty and Progress in the American Metropolis, 1880–1970.* Cambridge, MA: Harvard University Press, 1973.

———. *Poverty and Progress: Social Mobility in a Nineteenth-Century City.* Cambridge, MA: Harvard University Press, 1964.

Zunz, Olivier. *The Changing Face of Inequality: Urbanization, Industrial Development, and Immigrants in Detroit, 1880–1920.* Chicago: University of Chicago Press, 1982.

## Social Services

Social services, a wide range of programs designed to meet the social needs of individuals, families, and groups, are an important component of urban areas. Generally, social services are those programs that employ social workers or related professionals and are directed toward achieving social welfare goals. A different definition describes social services as intangible benefits provided by agencies and institutions to ameliorate social dysfunctioning and prevent problems in social functioning. Both definitions link social services to the broader field of social welfare services, which are generally considered to be society's attempt to meet basic human needs such as income, housing, education, health care, and employment. Social services include counseling, information and referral, education, socialization, and rehabilitative group programs, as well as associated support services.

Social services are delivered by social service agencies, in which social workers are the primary professionals, or through social welfare organizations, such as hospitals, in which social workers are only one of many occupational groups involved in providing these services. For example, public child welfare services, under the auspices of state governments, attempt to ensure the safety of children with a variety of programs designed to protect children in abusive or neglectful families or situations and to restructure those families or situations to ensure the future safety of the children. Programs such as foster care, residential group treatment, adoption, and family preservation services reflect the responsibility government has assumed for the care and safety of children. In the field of child welfare, social workers provide the bulk of these services, but in the field of mental health, social workers collaborate with psychiatrists, psychiatric nurses, psychologists, art therapists, and a variety of other professionals to provide comprehensive services to the mentally ill.

Social services are common in urban areas in which the traditional methods of satisfying social needs have broken down. Families, kinship systems, churches, and other informal helping systems are often unable to solve the overwhelming problems of poverty, inadequate and unsafe housing, drug

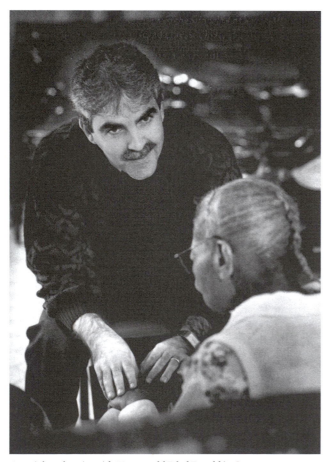

*A social worker sits with 88-year-old Ethel Engold in Germantown, Pennsylvania, 1994.*

addiction, and serious health disorders. Many people who use social service systems have tried to meet their social needs through informal systems, but either those systems have failed to meet the demand or the attempts to obtain assistance have been inadequate. In either case, the social service system has supplanted more informal traditional systems and has become an essential aspect of urban life.

Social services implement social welfare policy in the United States. Social welfare policy is broadly defined as anything government chooses to do, or not to do, that affects the quality of people's lives. That policy is determined by legislation that establishes the disposition of society with respect to a particular problem or issue, governmental guidelines for implementing that legislation, and judicial decisions. Because of the highly political nature of policy development, social welfare services in the United States have developed incrementally, rather than in a comprehensive, rational way, resulting in a system that is sometimes rife with overlapping, sometimes even contradictory, services.

One classic description of social welfare services identifies two different conceptions of social welfare—the residual and the institutional. The first holds that social welfare institutions should come into play only after traditional structures of supply—the marketplace, voluntary associations and organizations, and the family—break down. Only when these informal channels fail to help individuals meet their needs, as in illness, economic depression, and so on, should the social welfare system step in. Thus, this notion considers welfare services, including social services, as temporary. The second conception of social welfare, in which social services are perceived as normal, "first line" functions of a modern industrial society, believes that providing services to assist individuals achieve self-fulfillment is a legitimate function of society. Thus, services that not only meet an individual's basic survival needs but also those that aim at relational, educational, and rehabilitative needs are seen to be necessary components of modern urban life. These two very different beliefs about the role and place of social welfare in today's society are often in the center of the ongoing political debate about social welfare.

Most social services are dispensed or made available within the context of an agency or organization, and the type of sponsor is one characteristic that defines social service agencies. There are both public and private agencies, and private agencies can be either for-profit or not-for-profit. Most nonprofit agencies rely on several different sources of funding—contracts with public agencies, grants from corporations, and donations from private individuals, churches, and small businesses. Agencies can be sectarian or nondenominational, but they usually have a board of directors who are fiscally and legally responsible for the agency. Private for-profit agencies are owned by people or corporations who expect to realize a gain in return for providing services. They actively seek clients who can pay for services or who have insurance that covers the costs.

Other characteristics used to describe social service agencies are the age of the client population (youth organizations or programs for the elderly), the setting (is the agency community-based or does it provide institutional services), and the type of services offered (emergency housing, counseling and advocacy, legal aid, and so on).

In today's society, the clients of social services include not only the poor and other vulnerable populations but also individuals who are able to pay for services and may do so when seeking help from certain agencies. For example, social services provided by a hospital are available to all patients, those covered by insurance as well as those who are indigent. Social services in a hospital will assist a middle-class family obtain home health services for a patient after discharge as well as locate a nursing home for a patient on Medicaid. In private, nonprofit counseling agencies, families at certain income levels may be asked to pay a fee for family therapy based on a sliding scale determined by the agency, but it provides services to poor families at no charge.

Although a number of disciplines provide social service functions, social work is the primary professional field associated with delivering these services. The roots of social work lie in two nineteenth-century movements to confront the problems of urbanization and industrialization—charity organization societies and the settlement house movement. The "friendly visitors" of charity organization societies sought to dispense charity to needy individuals and families in a scientific and systematic manner and were predecessors of caseworkers and individual social work practitioners. They tended to believe that some defect or flaw in the individual caused the problems that a person experienced.

On the other hand, settlement house workers, who lived in the communities where they worked, tended to view social and economic problems as the result of society's inability to care for its people. They concentrated their efforts on collective action and reform. These workers inspired succeeding generations of social workers to assist individuals in groups and to persuade communities to provide more nurturing environments for individuals and families. Today, social work education focuses on training professionals to work with individuals, families, communities, and other groups to improve the relationship between individuals and the world in which they live.

Social services evoke a number of different political responses. Radical sociologists and social workers often believe that social services contribute to the denial of real social problems and serve to pacify people. One of them, for example, suggests that social services reflect the values and norms of the larger society and deny the greatest potential for life to their clients. He says that social services require clients to accept behaviors and roles for themselves that conform to traditional, conservative visions of the good society. Conservatives. on the other hand, object to the money spent on social services and insist that programs should only be residual. Preventive programs such as funding "night basketball" to provide urban youth with alternatives to crime incur the greatest opposition from many conservatives. Liberals often despair of the social service system as well, agreeing that the system only provides "Band-Aids" and does not address the fundamental issues of society.

Urban problems, such as homelessness, domestic violence, AIDS, substance abuse, crime, limited health care, and unemployment, will continue to overwhelm the structures of our cities and suburbs. The family will continue to change its structure, requiring new conceptions of raising and caring for children. Social services, as they exist today, cannot sufficiently address all of these problems, nor is it certain, in the current political climate, that social services will be viewed as important to the solution of those problems.

—*Nancy J. Harm*

**See also**
Charity; Settlement House Movement; Social Welfare.
**References**
Brieland, Donald. "History and Evolution of Social Work Practice." In *Encyclopedia of Social Work.* 18th ed., 739–754. Silver Spring, MD: National Association of Social Workers, 1987.
DiNitto, Diana M. *Social Welfare: Politics and Public Policy.* Englewood Cliffs, NJ: Prentice-Hall, 1991.
Galper, Jeffry H. "The Political Functions of the Social Services." In George T. Martin and Mayer N. Zald, eds., *Social Welfare in Society,* 167–193. New York: Columbia University Press, 1991.
Johnson, H. Wayne. *The Social Services: An Introduction.* 3d ed. Itasca, IL: F. E. Peacock Publishers, 1990.
Johnson, Louise C., and Charles L Schwartz. *Social Welfare.* 3d ed. Needham Heights, MA: Allyn & Bacon, 1994.
McInnis-Dittrich, Kathleen. *Integrating Social Welfare Policy and Social Work Practice.* Pacific Grove, CA: Brooks/Cole Publishing, 1994.
Wilensky, Harold L., and Charles N. Lebeaux. *Industrial Society and Social Welfare.* New York: Free Press, 1958.

## Social Structure of Cities

The spatial organization of the American city has long mirrored the social structures of its inhabitants. First characterized by small-scale ethnic clustering in otherwise undifferentiated areas, the division between work and residence and, ultimately, the articulation of class that developed in nineteenth-century neighborhoods still exists in the era of modern suburb and exurb.

At the outset, American cities were ethnically diverse but unified by the common social and religious backgrounds of their founders, ranging from Puritans coming from East Anglia in Boston to English Quakers in Philadelphia and from Dutch Reformed Calvinists in New Amsterdam to Anglicans in Charleston. This unity of purpose did not survive the late seventeenth and early eighteenth century arrival of significant numbers of immigrants from Germany, Ulster, and the West Indies. It is certainly true that early New York City retained much of the identity of the earlier New Amsterdam because English conquerors, out of practicality, came to tolerate the culture and religion of Dutch settlers. By the early eighteenth century, however, Dutch Creoles, French Huguenots, and Jews had coalesced into ethnic groups, each with its own distinct identity and institutions. Philadelphia, with its proclaimed policy of religious toleration, was even more diverse socially, boasting 14 separate religious denominations and eight ethnic groups by 1800.

Through the early eighteenth century class boundaries remained somewhat fluid and many humble artisans could aspire to modest wealth by speculating in urban real estate or military supply during the many colonial wars. Increasingly, however, wartime inflation, postwar economic downturns, and the growing number of widows all swelled the ranks of the poor. Leaders of corporate bodies that governed cities resorted to the practice of "warning-out" (in which town fathers took paupers to the edge of town and denied any further responsibility for them) and building almshouses and workhouses to control the strolling (or homeless) poor by requiring them to work in return for minimal sustenance. Poverty was also common among the nontransient residents, ranging from a fifth of Philadelphia's population to almost half of Newport, Rhode Island's adult males who were too poor to appear on tax assessors' rolls. Ethnicity and poverty converged for free black residents who faced restricted opportunities eking out livings surrounded by their enslaved brethren. Following the Revolution, class divisions widened even further, culminating in widespread urban misery, mortality, and criminality usually associated with later periods of immigration and industrial change.

Social stratification, first by ethnicity and subsequently by class, came to be expressed through place of residence. The origin of the neighborhood as a meaningful social unit can be traced to the late seventeenth century. Though cities remained small unified places based on face-to-face relations between members of an essentially classless society, the distribution of institutions such as markets, churches, and taverns began to transform wards into neighborhood communities. Early in the eighteenth century, clustering led to the formation of rudimentary ethnic communities anchored by neighborhood churches. Throughout the eighteenth century, residents lived in small spatial clusters inhabiting homes that combined residence and workplace. Nonetheless residential areas remained mixed in ethnic and economic composition until quite late.

By the eve of the American Revolution, many cities were divided into residential neighborhoods differing in characteristics, with upper-class residents living within or adjacent to commercial districts, artisans residing and working in broad bands across the center of cities, and the poor transient population clustering on the fringes. The formation of distinctive residential neighborhoods intensified in the late eighteenth and early nineteenth centuries with the replacement of older integrated house-shops with single-family dwellings. Although the bottom two-fifths of Philadelphia's taxpayers had lived scattered evenly throughout the city before the Revolution, growing population densities and the deterioration of life in lower-class neighborhoods dispersed the poor in outlying wards while concentrating the wealthy in the commercial core. During the eighteenth century, weak ethnic communities were replaced by neighborhoods divided by trade and by class. In the early nineteenth century, systematic location of industry helped create industrial districts along fringe areas that expanded as cities grew. At the same time, developers who combined Georgian private parks imported from London with restrictive residential covenants created areas like New York's Gramercy Park and Boston's Louisbourg Square, surrounded by blocks of uniform, single-family houses that catered to the wealthy. By the second quarter of the century, affluent residents had begun the wholesale abandonment of central area homes in favor of newly constructed exclusive residential areas on the urban periphery.

In the nineteenth century, the tightening supply of housing and the clustering of immigrants established ethnic background and employment as predictors of residential location, thus making neighborhood an important badge of social rank. Indeed, for many historians of industrial capitalism, neighborhoods have held a special importance in defining working-class community, serving as material manifestations of class formation comparable to the division of labor and the debasement of crafts in the workplace. Traditional household modes of labor organization that had integrated work and living space declined as master craftsmen ceased to provide accommodations for their workers. This gave rise to a bifurcated housing market in which large property owners lived apart from their tenants. Displaced journeymen and unskilled workers became more transient. In this new social environment, tenant areas became collections of slums while developers constructed genteel districts of middle-class houses offering health and family comfort.

While these changes in residence were important to the development of neighborhoods, many historians have exaggerated the extent of residential segregation. Save for a small elite who purchased homes in exclusive residential neighborhoods, class-based segregation remained weak in American cities. The pattern of differentiation that did exist proved highly unstable due to uncertain business cycles and the rapid explosion of the urban population. Economic differences showed themselves chiefly between buildings and blocks rather than between neighborhoods, with rich and poor still living next to one another. Exclusively residential areas catering to the needs of the lower-middle class and, eventually, to more secure working-class inhabitants were not constructed until the middle or end of the nineteenth century.

For most of those who settled in industrializing cities during the nineteenth century, work location shaped where one lived regardless of ethnic background. Occupational rank and, to a lesser extent, the quality of housing stock became badges of status on their own. Despite the existence of rich and poor areas, class was not an unambiguous predictor of neighborhood type. Working-class neighborhoods remained heterogeneous in character. This fact should temper efforts to locate class consciousness in the residential patterns of neighborhood.

Even segregation among the foreign-born population was less striking than often described. The proportion of German and Irish residents—the two most common immigrant groups residing in many American cities before the Civil War—often varied little from one area to the next. (Ironically, the standard description of segregated ghetto neighborhoods applied best to areas inhabited by native-born residents.) Immigrants did not settle in a single large concentration but rather formed many small residential clusters scattered uniformly throughout the city. While Germans tended to cluster more than the Irish, as could be seen in such heavily German boom towns as Milwaukee, the overall rate of dispersal for both groups was remarkably uniform. Not until the second great wave of immigration later in the nineteenth century would two ingredients essential to the formation of immigrant ghettos exist in sufficient quantities to foster ethnic segregation: (1) a generous supply of vacant centrally located housing and (2) jobs for unskilled labor in the central business district. High population turnover and an ethnic labor mix actually delayed the formation of tight concentrations until later in the century.

The relationship between ethnicity and residence was also highly fluid over time, fluctuating with changes in residential taste and shifts in the availability of housing. These changes reflected variations between successive waves of migrants and immigrants over several decades, while at the same time presaging the development of "zones of emergence" that drew more established immigrants. To the extent it existed, the segregation of immigrants in shantytowns on urban peripheries or in downtown areas of declining respect-

ability resulted from many factors: the withdrawal of native-born residents to exclusive enclaves, internal demographic cleavages among ethnic groups, abrupt changes in residential fashion, the development of a central business district, and the workings of a tight rental market strained to its limit by the influx of newcomers. Ethnic historians have emphasized the creation of "ghetto" neighborhoods as a natural product of ethnic affinities that operated at the national, parish, and even village level corresponding to the old country. Revisionist students of ethnic residence, together with many new labor historians, have treated ethnic neighborhoods as the result of industrial location, reflecting decisions made within the local, regional, and national economies. But the fact remains that the typical ethnic community was the small ethnic enclave rather than the exclusive immigrant "ghetto."

The level of homeownership within a city had an important impact on the formation of neighborhoods, promoting both class and ethnic homogeneity. Cities composed disproportionately of renters had higher levels of transience and higher rates of heterogeneity. For example, fewer than 10 percent of New York City residents owned homes in most areas of the city, making its ownership rate half that of many other cities. The wave of speculative building that swept New York within its established borders was almost entirely composed of tenements. Single-family housing, residences most likely to be owner-occupied, was built mainly for the middle and business classes in suburban wards where few New Yorkers lived. But even here it was common to see much of this new housing constructed for the rental market. Cities with higher levels of homeownership, such as Chicago or Philadelphia, came to show more marked and stable neighborhood patterns, with even many working-class ethnics becoming homeowners.

Among the lowest classes, the homeless lumpenproletariat were temporarily housed on floors and benches of police stations, and here social rank meant the difference between poverty in a tenement house and utter destitution. Not belonging to any set neighborhood, lodgers and vagrants floated from one address to another, slept outdoors, or sought shelter in police stations. Even before the increase in immigration of the 1850s, as many as 50,000 of New York's 350,000 permanent residents lacked house or home. By the 1860s an average of 86,214 lodgers per year sought refuge on naked wooden platforms in city-run police stations. Many of these were women beyond the prime ages of domestic employment. The older age of many vagrants compared with that of other residents suggests that for some immigrants, inopportune timing and the lack of adaptability may have hampered their life chances and doomed them to destitution on the streets.

The emergence of residential neighborhoods, then, involved a number of factors, including the shift from central to peripheral residence by the wealthy, the separation of commercial from residential functions, and the development of axes of differentiation in residence corresponding to class, ethnicity, and family status (e.g., neighborhoods with high numbers of boarders compared to those with more young families). Furthermore, the residential attraction of any given area of a city depended upon the availability of employment, the cost of housing, and the existence of established residents with whom the newcomer could feel secure. For immigrants, decisions about where to settle were restricted by their newness to the city and the degree to which their group had been assimilated into the dominant culture. Age was also an important factor, because the networks of friends, coworkers, and relations who supplied much of the information required for finding a job or moving were age-specific. These network ties, combined with the cultural background of the newcomer, promoted "consciousness of kind," a shared group identity that applied equally well to natives as to immigrants.

The industrialization of older port cities was accompanied by the development of new industrial cities, some of which, like Newark, New Jersey, were peripheral to a large metropolis while others were situated near sources of hydropower or fossil fuel needed to drive their machines. The emergence of textile cities like Lowell, Lawrence, and Fall River in Massachusetts and Manchester in New Hampshire attracted short-term workers, some of them women migrating from the countryside to escape the stagnant rural economy. Rather than ethnicity, these mill towns reflected the paternalistic ideals of mill owners, who organized their cities to reflect the stratification of the factory, ranging from mill superintendent on the high ground, to master mechanics in less substantial homes, to operatives living in barracks-like boarding houses adjoining the mills. This same paternalism and the desire of the Amoskeag Corporation to foster an institutional identity led workers and overseers to share neighborhoods near the mills in Manchester. Where paternalism was absent, as in Fall River, neighborhoods were organized first by class and secondarily by ethnic background.

By the late nineteenth century, the clustering of large factories in industrial districts attracted growing numbers of immigrants, who created residential communities that were more institutionally complete than before. Though homogeneous ethnic districts were exceptional, the magnitude of immigration led newcomers to cluster around ethnic parishes and social clubs. Often, the small ethnic pockets created by Southern and Eastern European immigrants sought to emulate the European peasant villages from which they had come. Such was the case in cities like Milwaukee, Detroit, and most notably Chicago with ethnic communities like the Back of the Yards, where families of workers in packinghouses formed segmented communities divided by church, corner grocery,

and community thrift institutions. It was these specific conditions that created the spatial typology of neighborhood immortalized by the Chicago sociologists like Ernest W. Burgess in the 1920s.

Workshops for craftsmen, small industries, and sweatshops survived into the twentieth century, but urban workers increasingly were employed in large factories that might have thousands of workers. The new corporate capitalism stabilized and regionalized wage scales while promoting long-term maximization of profits for their managers. The workers also benefited because these new corporations were less likely to fail and offered more opportunities for career advancement. And unlike small family-run manufacturing, these factories were less subject to economic downturns and wide swings of seasonal employment. By the 1920s large employers had begun to implement corporate welfare programs designed to decrease worker turnover through profit sharing, management-worker consultation, and employee benefits. Many of these programs fell victim to the Depression of the 1930s, but organizational efforts by unions such as the Congress of Industrial Organizations won higher wages, job security, and seniority rules in the late 1930s and 1940s.

As historian Thomas J. Sugrue has noted, the differentiation by class that occurred in the early twentieth century produced a corresponding segmentation of urban geography within the American metropolis. The departure of native-born residents from immigrant sections of cities accelerated toward the end of the nineteenth century. The expanding number of corporate managers and middle-class workers preferred the privacy and spaciousness to be found in suburbs and, with the development of new rail transportation systems, could afford the time and money needed to commute to exclusive suburban communities. Blue-collar workers could not afford suburban homes and were further concentrated in working-class areas by restrictive covenants and zoning. Where earlier neighborhoods had been jumbles of different classes and ethnic clusters, the homogeneity of worker-based housing surrounding large industrial complexes greatly intensified residential segregation. The new industrial geography thus subsumed earlier patterns of residence based on ethnicity to residence based on class as workers from diverse backgrounds congregated in tract housing built close to their places of employment.

The growing separation between blue-collar industrial neighborhoods and middle- and upper-class suburbs was further exacerbated by federal government policies and decisions made in the 1930s and after World War II. Recovery measures during the Depression created long-term, fully amortized mortgages to replace the earlier practice of five-year mortgages and hefty down payments. The Home Owners' Loan Corporation bought short-term loans from savings and loan institutions and consolidated them into the first federal loan program to underwrite 20-year mortgages. This program was extended and further liberalized under the Federal Housing Administration (FHA), an agency whose low requirements for down payments largely subsidized the explosive growth of American suburbs in the decades following World War II. Coupled with massive federal subsidies for road construction that made suburbs more accessible, the number of Americans who owned homes rose from half prior to the Depression to nearly two-thirds at the peak of the postwar boom.

Postwar industrial development also fostered uneven urban development. Manufacturing firms abandoned urban location for suburbs or even exurban locations, many located in the Sunbelt areas of the West and the South. Many other jobs were exported from the country altogether. Meanwhile, the social structure of cities began to show symptoms of these changes. Economic uncertainty, together with the outmigration of urban population, led to major population shifts within neighborhoods. By the 1970s, the falling incomes of those who remained in central cities depressed rent incomes for landlords and fostered widespread abandonment of housing. Practices such as redlining denied mortgage credit for urban real estate while, at the same time, subsidizing suburban development. Even when downtown areas seemed to be revitalized by the relocation of corporate headquarters and business services, the accompanying movement of professionals from downtowns into gentrified areas actually continued the overall decline in the availability of low-income urban housing.

These changes have become most apparent to Americans through the racial character of class divisions. Although blacks constituted only a small proportion of the urban population during most of the last three centuries, by the early nineteenth century free slaves from rural areas and the upper South had become perhaps the most highly segregated group living in cities. Much of this resulted initially from self-segregation fostered by a desire to be near their own churches and institutions, but growing racism made predominantly African-American areas difficult to escape. Blacks in northern cities were restricted to a narrow range of menial jobs and lacked the resources to support the range of businesses found in other ethnic communities. With a ready supply of immigrant labor available later in the century, industrial employers could systematically exclude African Americans from factory jobs. Even within the service sector, black workers were squeezed out of jobs they had once dominated, including catering and barbering.

This began to change during World War I when employers coped with wartime labor shortages by recruiting cheap black labor from the South. If these new migrants prospered relative to rural southern blacks, they fared little better than earlier recruits who had been brought in as strikebreakers. They faced racial discrimination in hiring and were often the first fired. The second Great Migration that began with World War II and continued through the 1950s coincided with the major exodus of industrial jobs from northern cities. Those blacks who did find industrial employment were unable to move beyond unskilled jobs, and employers continued to show an unwillingness to hire nonwhite employees. Industrial exodus, the growing surplus of unemployed blacks and Hispanics, and technological change dried up job opportunities and "deproletarianized" minority residents by permanently excluding them from the urban economy. Tightly segregated by racial discrimination in housing, federal discrimination in lending, and practices such as blockbusting, high-poverty inner-city neighborhoods became synonymous with black ghettos.

Modern urban America thus reflects continuing social divides. If strip cities and decentralized corporate headquarters give an appearance of sameness that blurs differences between suburbs in different areas of the country, the stark division between urban slum and affluent suburb hardly masks what many see as deepening social divides in postindustrial America. That the roots of these divisions are not new, going back to the early social divisions in seaport cities, is little reassurance. As urban growth trends become more regional in scope, and as counterurbanization (the movement of people away from cities) threatens to undermine not only inner cities but also the older suburbs, class continues to be reflected in urban social geography—although the automobile has widened the scale by which such divides are measured. Even ethnic divisions, once seen as a throwback to an earlier history, continue to flourish with new clusters of immigrants, from the Vietnamese in Westminster and Chinese in Monterey Park near Los Angeles, to Hispanics in Jamaica Plain in Boston, to Portuguese in Newark, to Poles in Chicago, and South Asians in New York City's borough of Queens. Yet underneath the sprawling growth of an Atlanta, Seattle, or Jacksonville, it is unclear whether the social patterns found in cities will resemble those with which Americans are now familiar or the new patterns of twentieth-century Third World cities plagued by transportation gridlock and sharp class divisions. Or perhaps the patterns of inner-city abandonment will continue to appear, albeit on a larger scale, as employers leave cities in one region for those in another, or even move abroad. Regardless, chances are that cities will continue to express familiar divisions, even if the forms of its expression seem new.

—*Kenneth A. Scherzer*

See also
Middle Class in Cities; Upper Class in Cities; Working Class in Cities.

**References**

Goodfriend, Joyce. *Before the Melting Pot: Society and Culture in Colonial New York City, 1664–1730.* Princeton, NJ: Princeton University Press, 1992.

Katz, Michael B., ed. *The "Underclass" Debate: Views from History.* Princeton, NJ: Princeton University Press, 1993.

Nash, Gary B. "The Social Evolution of Preindustrial American Cities, 1700–1820: Reflections and New Directions." *Journal of Urban History* 13 (1987): 115–145.

Scherzer, Kenneth. *The Unbounded Community: Neighborhood Life and Social Structure in New York City, 1830–1875.* Durham, NC: Duke University Press, 1992.

Zunz, Olivier. *The Changing Face of Inequality: Urbanization, Industrial Development, and Immigrants in Detroit, 1880–1920.* Chicago: University of Chicago Press, 1982.

## Social Structure of Suburbs

Social structure refers to the classification and arrangement of the various social and economic groups that form a society. In the popular image, American suburbs are thought to have social structures characterized by homogeneity in contrast to urban diversity. Although uniformity is often the case within individual suburbs, when taken as a whole the suburbs that make up a metropolitan region often display as much variation as that contained in urban neighborhoods.

Some development took place beyond city limits even before the American Revolution, but the first true U.S. suburbs did not appear until the three decades preceding the Civil War. Even these early suburbs showed considerable diversity. Historians have identified several forms of nineteenth-century suburban development, although these archetypes smooth over considerable individual variety.

Designed suburbs, such as Llewellyn Park, New Jersey (1857), and Riverside, Illinois (1868), were attempts to establish exclusive preserves of wealth and privilege from which the poor and lower-middle class would be excluded. Few were actually realized. More common were the various railroad suburbs that ringed New York, Chicago, Philadelphia, Boston, and many other cities by 1890. Communities such as Evanston, Illinois, Bryn Mawr, Pennsylvania, and Brookline, Massachusetts, contained large numbers of families headed by upper-middle-class commuters who caught the train each day to downtown jobs. Despite their prominence, however, commuters rarely formed a majority of the male workforce. Railroad suburbs were home to large numbers of servants, laborers, construction workers, farmers and farm workers, gentlemen of means, and local tradesmen and professionals. Often they included significant numbers of poor immigrants or blacks, who frequently—but not consistently—were concentrated in segregated neighborhoods.

If not formally designed, many railroad suburbs were founded by purposeful upper-middle-class men and women determined to craft environments that would embody their preferences and exclude undesirable aspects of urban life. Good public schools and libraries, efficient municipal services and amenities, and the absence of heavy industry and saloons became as characteristic of railroad suburbs as the well-dressed men who assembled each workday morning at the depots. In order to maintain this control, most railroad suburbs resisted annexation by the central cities they surrounded. Even suburbs, like Chestnut Hill, Pennsylvania, that found themselves within city limits possessed sufficient economic and political power to obtain services similar to those enjoyed by communities beyond the municipal boundaries.

Horse-drawn street railways, which appeared in many American cities before 1860, rapidly became more common in the years following the Civil War. By 1900 virtually every major American city featured a network of car lines, by then mainly powered by electricity, that fanned out from the downtown business district. Numerous speculative subdivisions—often developed by the same men who had built the street railways—sprang up along the routes. These streetcar suburbs, such as Roxbury and Dorchester, often were within city limits (in this case, Boston), and today are thought of as typical urban neighborhoods. But in their heyday at the end of the nineteenth century, streetcar suburbs represented the locale of choice for the burgeoning lower-middle classes, the one social class largely excluded from the railroad suburbs. Many of the male household heads rode the horsecars (after 1890, electric trolleys) to white-collar jobs in downtown offices and stores. The streetcar suburbs also housed large numbers of skilled workers, some factory workers and laborers, and even a few upper-middle-class professionals, proprietors, and executives.

Streetcar suburbs contrasted sharply with the crowded tenements of older urban neighborhoods. Most buildings housed only one to three families and were set amid small yards on tree-lined streets. (The automobile would alter these suburbs; today, the large number of parked cars in the streets and the loss of lawns to garages and driveways make it difficult to visualize how they appeared a century ago.) If the amenities did not measure up to those of the most prestigious railroad suburbs, the schools, municipal services, utilities, police and fire protection, and parks were superior to those of the inner city, aside from a few elite enclaves. In the late nineteenth century the vast majority of streetcar suburb residents were native-born whites (although many had immigrant parents), in contrast to the foreign-born majorities of most of the older city districts outside of the South.

In the latter part of the nineteenth century, industry, looking for low-cost land on which to expand, began to relocate to the suburbs. Some manufacturers built their own communities to house their workers, most notably Pullman, Illinois (on the far south side of Chicago), and Gary, Indiana.

These were part of a long tradition of paternalistic company towns that stretched back to Lowell, Massachusetts. More typical were the cases of Norwood and Oakley in suburban Cincinnati, two districts to which various factories relocated around the turn of the century. Here, employers let the private housing market provide for their employees. Some factory hands found quarters nearby, but many workers rode streetcars from their homes in inner Cincinnati each day.

By World War I most cities had one or more of these satellite cities; some were of recent origin while others, like Lynn and Waltham outside Boston, were older industrial centers that had been engulfed by the expanding metropolis. These industrial suburbs featured large numbers of blue-collar factory workers, although they also usually included at least a few streets of middle- and even upper-middle-class residents. Although physically removed from the inner city and built at a lower density, satellite cities in most respects resembled older urban neighborhoods more than streetcar or railroad suburbs. Many residents of satellite cities were immigrants (except in the South), living on the margin of poverty with limited skills. Saloons were common.

At the end of the nineteenth century the suburban scene was already a mosaic of considerable diversity. The steady expansion of the transit network into older railroad suburbs in many cases blurred the distinction between streetcar and railroad suburb, and the development of industrial satellite cities was promoting even greater variety. Nearly every social class, ethnic or racial group, and religion that could be found in the city was now represented, to a greater or lesser degree, in the suburbs as well.

The basic trends of nineteenth-century suburbanization continued into the next century, but technological change and economic growth produced a massive physical expansion of suburbia into the hinterlands. The discipline that fixed-route mass transit had imposed on suburban growth was eroded as the private automobile replaced legs, the streetcar, and the railroad coach as the preferred means of traveling to and from work. Cheap secondhand automobiles were becoming obtainable to all but the poor as early as 1915; by the end of the 1920s, roughly half of all American households had access to a car. New and improved roads promoted the development of huge tracts of land that lay beyond railroads and streetcars.

Working-class housing accounted for a significant portion of this growth. Developers operating beyond city limits and outside of incorporated suburbs (or in isolated corners of cities) were free to design and market their subdivisions as they saw fit. While some offered finished houses on paved streets with all the latest amenities to the affluent, many other developers sold unimproved lots on dirt streets. Thousands of blue-collar workers left the city to build their own homes—often with their own hands—in these crude subdivisions,

where low taxes and lax regulation kept costs down, and where they could supplement their incomes with vegetables and poultry they raised in their own backyards. Eventually, most of these suburbs were incorporated, following the pattern set earlier by the satellite cities.

Working-class suburbanization was most common around newer southern or western cities, such as Los Angeles, or near rapidly growing industrial cities like Detroit. Older seaboard cities like Boston, New York, or Philadelphia had little accessible land that had not been incorporated, and nearly all of the new suburban development there before 1930 catered to the middle and upper classes. But even in these older metropolitan regions, the presence of older industrial satellite cities helped maintain suburban variety.

Nineteenth-century suburbs contained few blacks, but greater racial diversity characterized early-twentieth-century suburbs. Black-majority suburbs appeared around some southern cities, often developing out of older rural black settlements. In a number of northern cities, including Chicago, Detroit, Cincinnati, and Cleveland, small numbers of urban blacks established suburban settlements that resembled those of working-class whites. Some older elite railroad suburbs, like Evanston, Illinois, and New Rochelle, New York, acquired significant numbers of black residents who worked as servants to wealthy white households. Many of the newer industrial satellite cities, like Gary, Indiana, and Hamtramck, Michigan, had substantial black populations by 1930.

But working against the tendency toward greater diversity were powerful forces that ultimately imposed order on the suburban scene. Driven by racism, white Protestants kept minorities out of their communities whenever possible, or at least segregated them into isolated neighborhoods. The primary tool was the restrictive covenant, whereby the buyer of a house agreed at the time of purchase never to convey it to blacks, Hispanics, Asians, Jews, or other minorities (depending on the mores of the particular community). Even without legal restrictions, most suburban real estate brokers and developers refused to sell homes or lots to members of minority groups except in neighborhoods in which nonwhites already lived. If all else failed, violence was employed.

The federal government was the single greatest force promoting order in the suburbs. Under the leadership of Herbert Hoover, the Commerce Department encouraged greater standardization within the residential construction industry. In 1921 Hoover established an Advisory Committee on Zoning, which promoted the adoption of zoning by publishing a model state zoning act. Zoning, along with subdivision controls and other land-use regulations, proved to be a popular and powerful tool that enabled suburban governments to direct the kind of development that would occur within their communities. Newer suburban districts increasingly were characterized by homogeneity, restricted to a single use (commercial, apartments, single-family residential) and often featuring housing of nearly identical size and value.

The Depression and the election of Franklin Roosevelt in 1932 ushered in a new era in American suburbanization. The sudden collapse of the suburban housing boom left the metropolitan landscape littered with partially built subdivisions containing thousands of vacant lots. In 1933, the Home Owners Loan Corporation (HOLC) was created to refinance existing home mortgages, and the Federal Housing Administration (FHA) was set up the following year to guarantee mortgages and building loans. With the help of the FHA the housing industry had largely revived by 1942, when World War II put the brakes on most residential construction. In 1944, however, Congress enacted the Servicemen's Readjustment Act (the GI Bill), which established the Veterans Administration (VA) housing program that enabled millions of veterans to purchase homes with minimal down payments. The FHA-VA housing programs, when combined with the greatest surge of prosperity in American history, produced a massive explosion in the suburban population. In 1950 the census found 41 million people—27 percent of the nation's total—living in suburban areas (within metropolitan areas but outside of central cities). Twenty years later there were 66 million (37 percent). More Americans now lived in suburbs than in either central cities or rural areas.

The federal government, which promoted this boom through the FHA-VA housing programs, tax subsidies, agricultural policies that encouraged rural depopulation, and highway construction, also brought order. The FHA (and later the VA, which followed FHA practices) set minimum building standards for homes and lots whose financing it would guarantee, and backed them up with inspections. Since it was difficult to sell houses not eligible for FHA-VA financing, most builders complied. The FHA-VA also practiced redlining, whereby loans were seldom or never insured in black-majority or racially changing neighborhoods. Builders discovered that federal agencies smiled on developments that excluded blacks and were conventionally middle-class suburban. Large-scale builders, such as the Levitts, typically built communities in sections, each one featuring streets of similar single-family homes. Within each section, house prices were largely the same, although the sections themselves might differ considerably in price and appearance. Smaller-scale builders constructed a single subdivision at a time, with similarly priced houses on nearly identical lots.

Federal assistance and prosperity made it possible for most of the white middle class to afford a suburban house in the 1950s and 1960s (in the South, even some black suburbs were allowed). But the building standards imposed by the FHA-VA, combined with the spread of zoning and building codes, virtually ended self-building as a means for poorer families to leave the city. Mobile homes provided a low-cost substitute, but most suburbs outlawed their use. Suburban resistance kept nearly all low-income public housing confined to the cities. Many suburbs would not even permit apartments. Never before had suburbia been so successful in keeping out the poor.

Zoning and the automobile enabled newer elite suburbs to exclude all but the wealthy. In earlier times these communities required resident servants, government workers, storekeepers, and service providers. Widespread ownership of the automobile now enabled these workers to commute from homes in cities or lower-income suburbs.

By 1984 more than 105 million Americans lived in the suburbs (45 percent of all persons). A century and a half of suburbanization has produced a metropolitan landscape of great variety. Suburbia, with its burgeoning malls, office and industrial parks, and megaplexes, has become increasingly urban, while within city limits are solid middle-class districts of single-family homes on large lots fronting tree-lined streets. Some observers have argued recently that these new urbanized suburbs represent a new type of city that should not be thought of as suburban at all.

Compared to the central cities, suburbs are more affluent and whiter. In 1980, blacks represented 6 percent of the suburban population but 23 percent of those in central cities. Even within suburbia, many blacks reside in segregated neighborhoods or black-majority suburbs. A plethora of economic and discriminatory barriers work to keep suburbs segregated. Despite open housing laws, investigations continue to find mortgage lenders and real estate agents discriminating against blacks and other minority groups. Resistance against blacks is strongest in the old industrial metropolises of the Northeast and Midwest, where cities find themselves ringed with suburbs determined to exclude minorities. Racism is scarcely confined to the suburbs, however; many of these cities contain neighborhoods even more segregated.

As the nation deindustrialized in the 1980s and early 1990s, wealth and income became increasingly maldistributed. Upper-class elite suburbs became even more exclusively inhabited by a single economic class (even if more racially and ethnically diverse). Rising house prices and declining real wages made it difficult for blue-collar families to afford suburban homes in many cities (particularly on the East and West coasts), even in what traditionally had been working-class suburbs. Diversity still characterizes the social structure of the suburbs as a whole, but within individual communities the trend is clearly toward greater class homogeneity.

—*Ronald Dale Karr*

See also
Middle Class in Suburbs; Working Class in Suburbs.
References
Binford, Henry C. *The First Suburbs: Residential Communities on the Boston Periphery, 1815–1860.* Chicago: University of Chicago Press, 1985.
Ebner, Michael H. *Creating Chicago's North Shore: A Suburban History.* Chicago: University of Chicago Press, 1988.
Fishman, Robert. *Bourgeois Utopias: The Rise and Fall of Suburbia.* New York: Basic Books, 1987.
Jackson, Kenneth T. *Crabgrass Frontier: The Suburbanization of the United States.* New York: Oxford University Press, 1985.
Taylor, Graham Roemyn. *Satellite Cities: A Study of Industrial Suburbs.* New York: Appleton, 1915.
Teaford, Jon C. *City and Suburb: The Political Fragmentation of Metropolitan America, 1850–1970.* Baltimore: Johns Hopkins University Press, 1979.
Warner, Sam Bass, Jr. *Streetcar Suburbs: The Process of Growth in Boston, 1870–1900.* Cambridge, MA: Harvard University Press, 1962.

## Social Welfare

From their inception in the seventeenth century, cities in the British colonies of North America concerned themselves with the social welfare of their residents, although the term *social welfare* itself did not come into general use until the twentieth century, with the rise of the social work profession and the development of modern government welfare policies. Instead, earlier generations talked about the problems of "pauperism" or the dependent, defective, and delinquent classes. The *Encyclopedia Britannica* provided an expansive modern definition of social welfare as "the attempts made by governments and voluntary organizations to help families and individuals by maintaining incomes at an acceptable level, by providing medical care and public health services, by furthering adequate housing and community development, by providing services to facilitate social adjustment . . . by furnishing facilities for recreation . . . [by protecting] those who might be subject to exploitation, and [by caring] for those special groups considered to be the responsibility of the community." But city government officeholders and the officers of private charities in the seventeenth, eighteenth, and nineteenth centuries talked much more narrowly about how to deal with those who were unable to support themselves and who could not rely upon their families for support—the poor, infirm, aged and disabled, orphans, and abandoned or neglected children. This narrower definition is the one used in this essay.

Several themes characterize the history of social welfare in American cities. First, although a majority of Americans did not live in cities until 1920, and there was much poverty in rural areas and small towns, in urban places the problems of the poor and dependent appeared most visibly and seemed to pose the greatest threat to social order. Therefore, cities led the nation in developing social welfare programs. Second, cities have had a disproportionately large share of the nation's poor but have seldom had resources adequate to address their needs. Third, city officials and leaders of private organizations that provided welfare services generally had both benevolent feelings for those receiving aid and also a deep-seated concern for social control of the poor. And finally, welfare policy has maintained a sharp separation between assistance for the poor and incapacitated and broad social insurance for working citizens, old age pensions and unemployment compensation, for example.

American colonies closely followed the principles established by the Elizabethan poor laws, codified in the Law of 1601. This English precedent made poor relief a *public* responsibility of *local* government, with each parish responsible for its own poor. Only those with no immediate relatives to support them received public assistance. The overseers of the poor regularly apprenticed poor children to farmers and artisans who trained and cared for them.

Following these traditions, American colonies passed laws that made poor relief a local responsibility, and the larger towns and cities soon established workhouses where the able-bodied poor lived and were put to work. Cities had other forms of poor relief also, including auctioning off paupers for their labor, providing apprenticeships for pauper children, and poor relief outside the workhouse (outdoor relief). Despite these alternatives, institutionalization was generally thought best, and the resulting financial pressure soon strained local city budgets. Cities, which naturally attract transients, also passed laws against vagrancy and tried to exclude those who might become public charges. During the American Revolution, some state governments started to depart from the principle of local responsibility. New York, for example, established a state agency to assist those away from their normal residence because of the war. In 1796, the state provided funds to New York City for relief of persons without a local residence.

A variety of private charities developed alongside this public system. Groups like the Scots Charitable Society of Boston, founded in 1657, dispensed charity to Scotsmen and others in need. Likewise, every Quaker meetinghouse in Philadelphia maintained a poor fund.

As capitalist development proceeded in the nineteenth century, demand for poor relief soared. As the extent of pauperism increased, the dominant Protestant elites increasingly viewed poverty as the result of individual moral failure, and they sharply distinguished between the worthy poor (those disabled and unable to work) and the unworthy able-bodied. Therefore, city and state governments sought to limit outdoor relief and rely on institutionalization as a means of moral reeducation and a disincentive to laziness. Reports by state officials in New York City, Baltimore, Boston, Providence, and Philadelphia all called for increased indoor relief. In 1824 Massachusetts had 83 almshouses, in 1839 it had 180, and in 1860 it had 219. By the end of the Civil War, 80 percent of those receiving extended public aid in Massachusetts lived in institutions. States also began to establish specialized institutions for children, the mentally ill, the feeble-minded, and the deaf. New York opened the first state institution for juvenile delinquents, the House of Refuge, in Manhattan in 1824.

Private charities also sought to dispense a mixture of material aid and moral uplift. The New York Association for Improving Conditions Among the Poor, established in 1843, placed recipients of aid under the "paternal guidance" of upstanding male citizens. In 1853, Charles Loring Brace founded the New York Children's Aid Society to counteract the growth of the city's "dangerous classes." The society provided schools, training programs, and outings for lower-class youth, but its major effort was to remove these youngsters from the city and place them as farm laborers with families in the West. In 25 years, the Children's Aid Society removed 50,000 children from New York City.

Rapid industrialization after the Civil War and the severe effects of periodic depressions increased the pressure on the welfare apparatus of cities and produced greater bureaucratic centralization and specialization and more outdoor relief. After the war, states set up centralized boards of charity, and private charities banded together into charity organization societies. Reinforced by Social Darwinist thought in the belief that the cause of poverty was individual inadequacy, charity workers created centralized bodies, staffed by volunteer women—"friendly visitors"—to investigate requests for aid, separate the worthy from the unworthy, and coordinate dispensing aid by numerous specialized private agencies. The first charity organization society began in Buffalo in 1877; by 1883 similar societies operated in 25 cities, and by 1900 in 138. By 1920 trained social caseworkers began replacing friendly visitors. States and cities continued to develop specialized welfare institutions, including enlarged orphanages, mental hospitals, and flophouses for homeless men, eventually transforming traditional poorhouses into old age homes.

Some private welfare agencies remained quite apart from the charity organization movement. Political machines dispensed emergency assistance as a way of winning the loyalty of low-income voters. As George Washington Plunkitt, a Tammany ward heeler, explained, "If a family is burned out I don't ask the charity organization society, which would investigate their case in a month or two and decide that they were worthy of help about the same time they are dead from starvation. I just get quarters for them, buy clothes for them if their clothes are burned up, and fix them up till they get things running again." Immigrant groups formed numerous burial, insurance, and loan societies, providing mutual assistance to their members. African-American leaders and white elites formed the National Urban League in 1910, with chapters in many cities, to provide social services to black migrants arriving from the South.

By the beginning of the twentieth century, charity workers came to recognize that social factors played a significant role in explaining urban poverty. In 1907 Edward Devine, general secretary of New York's charity organization society, asserted, "we may quite safely throw overboard, once and for all, the idea that the dependent poor are our moral inferiors." This view was reinforced by research on the causes of poverty and other social ills undertaken by settlement houses starting in the late 1880s and by social scientists.

Settlement house workers and other reformers of the Progressive Era attempted to create a more expansive government welfare system. During the depression of 1893, many city governments established elaborate programs of emergency employment and relief. The women of Hull House in Chicago helped win establishment, in Illinois, of the first juvenile court and the first Mothers Pension law, which provided state support for widowed or deserted mothers so they could raise their children at home. Forty states passed similar legislation in the next decade. States also passed workers' compensation laws in this period.

The federal government played a modest role in providing social welfare services during the Progressive Era. After the Civil War, Congress set up pensions for veterans and their widows, and some scholars argue that this pension program laid the foundation for the American welfare state. In the early twentieth century, progressive reformers won establishment of a federal Children's Bureau and of a federal program of infant and maternal nutrition. They fought unsuccessfully for broad-based federal old age, unemployment, and disability insurance. Still, welfare remained primarily a state and local responsibility.

Local governments, state but especially city, felt the brunt of the Depression in its early years. Per capita spending on welfare had remained low through the 1920s, but was highest in cities—$0.25 for the federal government in 1929, $1.85 for state governments, and $3.12 for cities. With the onset of the Depression, public and private relief in 81 cities soared from about $42 million in 1929 to $70 million in 1930 and $170 million in 1931. In Detroit, the cost to city government of relief skyrocketed from $116,000 in 1930 to $1,582,000 in 1932. But cities had extremely limited resources. By early 1930, nearly 1,000 local governments had defaulted on their debts.

The governor of New York, Franklin D. Roosevelt, led the nation in providing state unemployment relief. The Wicks Act, passed in 1931, provided grants to localities for unemployment relief. Within a year, 24 states followed suit. When he became president, Roosevelt quickly established a variety of emergency work programs, including the Civilian Conservation Corps, the Works Progress Administration, and the National Youth Administration. The Federal Emergency Relief Act also provided substantial federal assistance to states for relief programs.

The Social Security Act of 1935 embodied the permanent welfare reforms of the New Deal. The act provided two major pieces of social insurance—a federally administered program of old age pensions funded jointly by employee and employer contributions, and federally financed state programs of unemployment compensation. The Committee on Economic Security, which wrote the law, wanted to include national health insurance in the legislation, but the president withdrew that provision because of opposition from physicians and others. The act also provided federal support for state "outdoor relief" programs for dependent women and children ("mothers pensions") and for crippled youngsters and the blind.

By 1940, argues historian Michael Katz, the United States had developed a "semi-welfare state." In 1913 local, state, and national governments spent $21 million on public aid (1 percent of all government expenditures); by 1939 the figure had increased to $4.9 billion (27.1 percent of all government expenses). Government had assumed unprecedented responsibility for economic security. Still, Katz argues, "It compromised with, rather than superseded, the local basis of relief. It modified but did not erase the archaic distinctions between the worthy and unworthy ... poor; it created walls between social insurance and public assistance that preserved class distinctions and reinforced the stigma attached to relief or welfare."

During the 1940s and 1950s politicians and policy analysts paid relatively little attention to welfare and economic security. But as the size of public assistance roles began to escalate in the 1960s and as the civil rights movement addressed the economic needs of black citizens, America rediscovered poverty. The number of people receiving public assistance rose from 7.1 million in 1960 to 14.4 million in 1974. Scholars cite many reasons for the increase. Southern agriculture mechanized, driving poor black farmers into northern cities. Activists encouraged poor people to apply for aid, and the courts struck down many eligibility restrictions. The number of female-headed families increased as a result of separation, divorce, and the birth of children to unmarried women. Poor people with limited education faced increasing difficulty getting jobs, and nonwhites confronted racial barriers in employment.

The new interest in poverty focused particularly on large cities. Rapid suburbanization and housing discrimination tended to concentrate the poor and nonwhites in central cit-

ies and the middle class in suburbs. In a widely heralded study of poverty, *The Other America* (1962), author Michael Harrington wrote that, "The very development of the American city has removed poverty from the living, emotional experience of millions upon millions of Americans. Living out in the suburbs, it is easy to assume that ours is, indeed, an affluent society." City governments, with declining tax bases, had to provide welfare services for an ever-increasing number of poor people. A series of riots in black urban ghettos in the middle and late 1960s highlighted the problems of the urban poor and intensified public concern about the social control of poor people in cities.

The federal government, often in partnership with state and city governments, addressed these problems with a panoply of new programs designed to encourage the poor to work and to provide aid to poor children: the 1962 amendments to the Social Security Act, which greatly increased federal support to states for job training and placement services; the Manpower Development and Training Act of 1962; the Area Redevelopment Act of 1961 and the Economic Development Act of 1965, which sought to induce new industries to move into economically depressed areas; the Economic Opportunity Act of 1964 (popularly called the War on Poverty), creating the Job Corps, Upward Bound, Neighborhood Youth Corps, Head Start, and the Community Action Program; the Food Stamp program (1964); the Demonstration (Model) Cities Act of 1965; the Work Incentive Program (1967), designed to force public assistance recipients to work; the Concentrated Employment Program (1967), providing grants to community groups for comprehensive approaches to employment; and the Nixon administration's consolidation of most of the job programs in the Comprehensive Employment and Training Act (1973).

The provision of medical care for the elderly under social security, known as Medicare and enacted in 1965, was the most important new social insurance program of the postwar years. Congress also passed in that year the Medicaid program, which provided federal grants to states for medical services for the indigent. A series of amendments to the Social Security Act between 1969 and 1972 substantially raised old age benefits.

Despite the rash of new programs in the 1960s and early 1970s aimed at the urban poor, two New Deal programs still consumed the lion's share of federal social welfare dollars: (1) Aid to Families with Dependent Children (AFDC), the old "mothers pensions" section of the Social Security Act, now popularly known as "welfare," and (2) old age payments under the same act. In 1970 the federal government spent $30.3 billion on payments to the elderly and $5.1 billion on AFDC. By 1984, the figures were $180.9 billion and $8.3 billion, respectively. As Michael Katz explains: "Social security cut

*A lumber mill worker who got laid off in the northwest United States and his family wait for a social worker to arrive.*

across class lines. . . . Its constituency, therefore, was broad, articulate, effective, and above all, respectable." The federal government, Katz concludes, "spent most of its social welfare dollars . . . on the nonpoor."

Beginning in the late 1970s, welfare expenditures in cities declined substantially. Cities continued to lose jobs and middle-class population to the suburbs, and the transition from an industrial to a service economy also took a toll on urban jobs. Cities faced severe fiscal austerity, and along with fiscally strapped state governments they cut back on welfare and social service expenditures. After Ronald Reagan, who was ideologically opposed to the welfare state, was elected president in 1980, the federal government drastically reduced expenditures for education and training, nutrition programs, Medicaid, and public service employment. Both state and federal government sought to reduce eligibility for AFDC and food stamps. By the early 1990s, poverty in central cities had worsened dramatically, homelessness was at its highest level since the Depression, and the country was vigorously debating the growth of a permanently impoverished "underclass" and a seeming epidemic of violent crime and drug abuse in the cities. Finally, in 1996, Congress ended AFDC as an entitlement program and drastically reduced benefits in a highly publicized "welfare reform" bill signed by President Bill Clinton.

As in the past, poverty in the early 1990s was most pronounced and posed its greatest social threat in the cities, which lacked the resources to combat it. Social control remained a major objective of welfare policy.

—*Steven J. Diner*

**See also**
Social Services.
**References**
Axxin, June, and Herman Levin. *Social Welfare: A History of the American Response to Need.* New York: Harper & Row, 1975.
Brock, William R. *Welfare Democracy and the New Deal.* New York: Cambridge University Press, 1988.
Davis, Allen F. *Spearheads for Reform: The Social Settlements and the Progressive Movement, 1890–1914.* New York: Oxford University Press, 1967.
Gordon, Linda. *Pitied but Not Entitled: Single Mothers and the History of Welfare.* New York: Free Press, 1994.
Jansson, Bruce S. *The Reluctant Welfare State: A History of American Social Welfare Policies.* 2d ed. Pacific Grove, CA: Brooks/Cole Publishing, 1993.
Katz, Michael B. *In the Shadow of the Poorhouse: A Social History of Welfare in America.* New York: Basic Books, 1986.
Lieby, James. *A History of Social Welfare and Social Work in the United States.* New York: Columbia University Press, 1978.
Lubove, Roy. *The Struggle for Social Security: 1900–1915.* Cambridge, MA: Harvard University Press, 1968.
Mohl, Raymond A. *Poverty in New York: 1783–1825.* New York: Oxford University Press, 1971.
Rothman, David J. *The Discovery of the Asylum: Social Order and Disorder in the New Republic.* Boston: Little, Brown, 1971.

## South Side of Chicago

Chicago's South Side began as an outgrowth of the original city center, and neighborhoods developed south of the Loop as early as the 1850s. After the Chicago Fire of 1871, the South Side expanded quickly as both the rich and the poor moved south. In the late 1860s and 1870s industry relocated from the downtown to the South Side.

The growth of the South Side was connected to the development of public transportation. The white middle class made its way south from the expanding Loop. African Americans also located their institutions on the South Side, and the city's Black Belt developed a complex institutional, social, cultural, and economic life. The African-American population doubled from approximately 50,000 to 100,000 between 1915 and 1920 and doubled again in the 1920s. With the end of World War I, social, residential, political, and economic pressures reached a peak, and in July 1919 a race riot broke out and resulted in 38 deaths and hundreds of injuries.

In 1945 the South Side actually included many distinct ethnic and socioeconomic communities and neighborhoods. These had continued to thrive despite the Depression and World War II. A transformation, however, took place after the war, when economic prosperity led many residents, especially white middle-class families, to seek new housing and job opportunities. The automobile made it possible for people to move further out into new neighborhoods and suburbs, leading to white flight and the expansion of African-American neighborhoods. This resulted in conflict as race riots broke out. The South Side also witnessed a great expansion of the Mexican community from its base in the stockyard and steel mill districts. Other Hispanics, too, settled on the South Side, including a small Puerto Rican community.

Older South Side neighborhoods, especially the traditional Black Belt, saw new housing after 1945. For the most part, this was public housing built and administered by the

Chicago Housing Authority. The new South Side, however, remained very familiar as it retained segregated housing patterns and huge pockets of poverty and wealth. One major change was the loss of industry. In the mid-1950s and early 1960s Chicago witnessed the shutting down of most of the large meatpacking houses. The late 1970s and early 1980s saw the further erosion of the city's industrial base. Empty factories and warehouses symbolized the shift in Chicago's employment base from manufacturing to the service industries.

The South Side, however, has continued to attract investment. By the 1990s over 100 firms had located at the site of the old Union Stock Yard. The developers of the Dearborn Park residential area in the South Loop pushed south of Roosevelt Road. Chinatown has also expanded. A new residential development, Central Station, along the lakefront south of Roosevelt Road has also been built. In 1991 the Chicago White Sox began to play baseball in a new Comiskey Park. The South Side continues to play an important role in the social, cultural, political, and economic life of Chicago.

—*Dominic A. Pacyga*

### References

Hirsch, Arnold. *Making the Second Ghetto: Race and Housing in Chicago, 1940–1960.* New Yok: Cambridge University Press, 1983.

Holt, Glen E., and Dominic A. Pacyga. *Chicago: A Historical Guide to the Neighborhoods: The Loop and South Side.* Chicago: Chicago Historical Society, 1979.

Pacyga, Dominic A., and Ellen Skerrett. *Chicago: City of Neighborhoods.* Chicago: Loyola University Press, 1986.

Philpott, Thomas Lee. *The Slum and the Ghetto: Neighborhood Deterioration and Middle-Class Reform, Chicago, 1880–1930.* New York: Oxford University Press, 1978.

Spear, Allan. *Black Chicago: The Making of a Negro Ghetto, 1880–1920.* Chicago: University of Chicago Press, 1967.

## Southern Cities

Glitzy towers, sleek expressways, state-of-the-art concert halls and art museums, and restaurants serving up dishes ranging from soul food to tofu characterize the urban South today. When Americans picture the "new South" in their mind's eye, it is the vision of the southern city that comes into focus. And well it might. The urban South epitomizes the transformation of a region from the nation's "Number One economic problem" a half-century ago to the locus of postindustrial economic prosperity.

The southern city did not always epitomize the region or feature a trend-setting economy. Before the Civil War, the commercial plantation that produced cotton, tobacco, or rice and bred slaves dominated the southern economy. The South's major cities, New Orleans, Mobile, Savannah, Charleston, and Norfolk, hugged the Gulf or South Atlantic coasts and functioned primarily as collection points for staple crops. Interior cities such as Richmond and Louisville boasted some manufacturing, but they too mainly served to transfer agricultural products to northern cities. The most prevalent urban place in the Old South remained the county seat or crossroads hamlet with a few lawyers, perhaps a physician, and a scattering of merchants standing guard along a river or, by the 1850s, a railroad depot. It might be an exaggeration to state, as did one frustrated Richmond entrepreneur, that southern cities were mere "hewers of wood and drawers of water" for the great cities of the North, but the urban South did function as junior partner in the emerging national urban system by the time of the Civil War. Among southern cities in 1860, only New Orleans appeared among the nation's ten most populous cities.

Both the nature and location of southern urbanization changed after the Civil War. The decline of seaports, the rise of major rail terminals such as Dallas, Atlanta, Nashville, and Charlotte, and the emergence of the textile industry in a broad band along the southern Piedmont fueled urban growth in the interior South. Unlike their antebellum predecessors, these cities soon became the hub of a new southern economy that emphasized commercial and industrial development.

Although migration from the overpopulated and impoverished countryside expanded urban populations, the South lagged behind the rest of the country in urban growth. Industrial development tended to concentrate in small towns or company towns, and the South's struggling agricultural sector demanded few services of its market towns. By 1920 the United States was an urban nation; more than one-half of the population lived in towns and cities, but less than one-quarter of the South's inhabitants resided in urban places at the same time. No southern city appeared among the nation's ten most populous in 1920, and only New Orleans, ranked seventeenth, cracked the top twenty. And, in terms of the volume of commerce, the amount of bank deposits, and the value of industrial output, the urban South also remained in a secondary position in relation to the rest of the nation.

Despite their modest size, southern cities set the tone for much of the South in the early twentieth century. Racial segregation emerged and flourished in the urban South and became the most characteristic form of southern race relations. Urban reformers, especially the growing number of middle-class white women unburdened by the rigors of farm life but still thwarted by regional traditions against working outside the home, attacked child labor, corrupt government, alcohol, and illiteracy. They also promoted black disfranchisement and segregation, a peculiarly southern version of the Progressive movement. New technologies, such as the electric trolley, electric power, and air-conditioning (a prerequisite for urban growth in the subtropical South), made their first national appearances in the urban South. Imaginative chemists devised formulae for such diverse products as Coca-Cola and Vick's Vapo-Rub. But by the 1920s boosterism overcame the reform impulse as urban promoters prattled incessantly about significant economic gains, even as their embrace of cheap, segregated, nonunion labor limited more significant economic development. They also did not deviate much if at all from the political and racial orthodoxy of the rural elite that still controlled most state politics in the South.

The New Deal and World War II changed the landscape of the urban South. New Deal agricultural policies, mechanization, and the "green revolution" of soybeans and peanuts drastically reduced the need for agricultural labor. While millions of rural southerners migrated to the urban North, tens of thousands also left the farm for Atlanta, Birmingham, Charlotte, Memphis, and other southern cities. The rapid expansion of the wartime economy swelled urban populations even more as defense plants, military bases, and other new employment opportunities provided the first real alternatives to farm work in more than a generation. Newly returned white veterans demanded more services and favored economic development over the maintenance of white supremacy. They won local offices and shaped policies that occasionally recognized the blacks in their midst. For their part, black newcomers found rich institutions, especially the black church, established neighborhoods, jobs, and even political activism, in the cities of the South. Without this significant urbanization of the black population in the decade after World War II, the civil rights movement might not have occurred when and how it did.

The diversified economy, primed by vast government expenditures during World War II, the racial accommodations of the 1960s that dismantled segregation in the urban South, and the decline of northern industrial cities contributed to the rapid growth of southern cities after 1965. By 1980, the South counted two cities in the nation's top ten, and five in the top twenty, even as the South continued to lead the nation in the number of urban places with fewer than 10,000 people. By the 1990s the urban South was setting national trends in banking, geographic expansion, and higher education. Crime, poverty, and pollution accompanied the benefits of growth, and with a historical legacy of minimal government and low taxes, the prospects for addressing some of these costs remain uncertain.

More certain is that four aspects of contemporary southern urban growth will shape both the region and nation in the coming decades. First, the urban South is becoming more diverse. Through much of the twentieth century, the signs "white" and "colored" divided and explained life in the urban South. Now, however, immigration from Asia, Latin America, and the North is changing the nature of the southern city and of the South. The influx of Hispanic migrants to Texas and Florida is well known. As they become citizens, they will become a potent political force. They are already an economic force, developing small businesses and entering service occupations at menial levels.

Less well documented is the filtering of Hispanic and Asian migrants into some southern cities. During the 1980s the Atlanta metropolitan area, for example, experienced an influx of 4,000 Vietnamese, 10,000 Asian Indians, 25,000 Koreans, 30,000 Chinese, and 100,000 Hispanics. By 1994, Hispanics comprised roughly 10 percent of the southern population, the vast majority living in cities. The Asian and Hispanic populations are settling primarily in the metropolitan South, and their numbers are growing faster than those of blacks or whites. In a region where race has served as the traditional dividing line for jobs, neighborhoods, and politics, the growing presence of diverse ethnic groups will change the physical and political landscapes of the urban South.

Second, southern cities have benefited and will continue to profit from the regionalization of the American economy during the past two decades. The deregulation of the American airline industry in 1979 encouraged carriers to open regional hubs. Charlotte, Raleigh-Durham, Atlanta, Dallas, and Memphis function as regional hubs for one or more major airlines. Efficient air connections promote sustained economic development in much the same way that railroads boosted urban growth in the nineteenth century. Also, the trend toward uncoupling corporate activities has favored southern metropolitan areas. Major corporations with headquarters in cities such as New York, Chicago, and Pittsburgh are separating certain activities from their main offices. Cheap land, lower taxes, nonunion labor, good climate, and reasonable utility costs attract these activities to the urban South. Southern cities led the nation in generating service-related employment during the 1980s. While low-wage occupations continue to dominate, the South is receiving its share of research and development firms, with the Research Triangle Park in the Raleigh-Durham-Chapel Hill metropolitan area of North Carolina serving as both a regional and a national prototype.

The rapid growth of the southern urban service sector has reinforced a third trend evident in southern urbanization through much of the twentieth century. Southern cities tend, on the average, to be half as dense as cities in other parts of the country. Much of southern urban growth has occurred since World War II, when the automobile, not mass transit, ruled the streets, encouraging low density and sprawl. Spatial imperialism, aided by relatively easy annexation laws in most southern states, has reinforced the expansive landscape of the southern metropolis. "Edge cities"—urban developments on the metropolitan periphery—are often within city boundaries in the South. The ability of southern cities to capture their fleeing population and economic base has not only made those cities more attractive to outside investors, but it has also tended to dilute the impact of race and poverty.

The specters of race and poverty (and their coincidence in most southern cities) haunt the prosperity of the urban South and constitute the fourth major trend of southern urbanization. The generous geography of southern cities exacerbates the separation between the location of jobs (the periphery) and the location of those without employment (the core). The emphasis on low taxes and modest service levels reduces funding for social services. Fortunately, southern cities have a long tradition of voluntarism, especially from the churches. While religion, especially evangelical Protestantism, continues to grow as a major spiritual, political, and economic force in many cities, the demands of a growing underclass outstrip both the ability and the desire of congregations to fund charitable organizations. Finally, persistent poverty in the rural South and continued out-migration to southern cities, combined with growing numbers of foreign immigrants, will test both the charity and tolerance of urban southerners.

The urban South today, more than ever, defines the region. It is appropriate in this context to ask if that definition implies an end to southern regional distinctiveness. On the face of it, there is little to distinguish Dallas, Charlotte, or Atlanta, for example, from comparable cities in other regions. The dumbbell spatial arrangement—a strong, vibrant, high-rise downtown and equally strong edge cities on the periphery flanking inner-city neighborhoods in various stages of decay—is a common geography in urban America. The growing ethnic diversity also moves southern cities more toward the national norm. In politics, the emergence of black political power, although belated in some southern cities, reflected in the growing numbers of black mayors and other officials, also parallels national trends. The days of one-party Democratic rule that set off southern cities and the entire region from the rest of the nation are long gone. The urban South is in the forefront of a Republican resurgence regionally and nationally. Shopping malls, fast-food emporia, and architectural styles, both suburban and urban, scarcely distinguish southern cities from those elsewhere. Throw in several million "Yankees" who have migrated to the metropolitan South since the early 1970s (thereby reversing a long-standing migration trend), and it is easy for native southerners to become disoriented.

But the interplay of region and city persists in the South. While sushi joints and espresso bars may jostle them for space, barbecue and fried chicken establishments abound and thrive. Regional cooking is alive and well in the urban South. Social graces—"manners," if you will—still control interpersonal relations in shops, in offices, and in neighborhoods. Although growth has sorely tested the culture of courtesy, it nevertheless remains a hallmark of southern urban life, where the pace is slower even if the profits come more quickly, than in cities elsewhere. Evangelical Protestantism reigns in southern cities, even as Roman Catholics, Jews, and Muslims expand their respective denominations. Evangelicals still control much of the social debate, letters to the editor of the local newspapers, and patterns of church attendance. Affiliates of other religious groups discover their own church- or synagogue-going habits change and become more regular and dutiful within the religious context of the urban South.

It is also important to keep in mind that even the most thriving southern cities remain off the top-twenty list of the most populous cities in the nation. The medium- and small-sized city dominates the urban South. These environments are more likely to adhere to regional cultural patterns than the diverse metropolis of the North and West. And, as sociologist John Shelton Reed has demonstrated, urban southerners often become stronger in their regional attachments as they become more cosmopolitan and can compare themselves to urban cultures in other parts of the country. As for the Yankee invasion, Reed has argued that many, if not most, northerners are lured into the southern urban lifestyle and become regional patriots as well.

Adherence to regional culture does not imply that urban southerners do not welcome national and global contacts and prosperity. But it may be most accurate to depict the contemporary southern city as having a layered look—the patina of modernity over a deep stratum of regional tradition.

—*David Goldfield*

**See also**
Charleston, South Carolina; Dallas, Texas; Houston, Texas; Jacksonville, Florida; Memphis, Tennessee; Miami, Florida; Nashville, Tennessee; New Orleans, Louisiana; San Antonio, Texas; Tampa, Florida.
**References**
Bartley, Numan V. *The New South, 1945–1980: The Story of the South's Modernization.* Baton Rouge: Louisiana State University Press, 1995.
Button, James W. *Blacks and Social Change: Impact of the Civil Rights Movement in Southern Communities.* Princeton, NJ: Princeton University Press, 1989.
Cobb, James C. *Industrialization and Southern Society, 1877–1984.* Chicago: Dorsey Press, 1988.
Goldfield, David. *Cotton Fields and Skyscrapers: Southern City and Region, 1607–1980.* Baton Rouge: Louisiana State University Press, 1989.
Miller, Randall M., and George E. Pozzetta, eds. *Shades of the Sunbelt: Essays on Ethnicity, Race and the Urban South.* Westport, CT: Greenwood Press, 1988.
Rabinowitz, Howard. *Race Relations in the Urban South, 1865–1890.* New York: Oxford University Press, 1978.
Schulman, Bruce J. *From Cotton Belt to Sunbelt: Federal Policy, Economic Development, and the Transformation of the South, 1938–1980.* New York: Oxford University Press, 1991.

## Spanish Colonial Towns and Cities

At the end of the eighteenth century, Spain exercised jurisdiction over what are now Florida, Alabama, Texas, most of the southwestern states, and California; the total area of these colonies exceeded 50 percent of today's continental United States. However, only a very small number of Spaniards lived in this vast domain. The number of residents descended from Europeans living in this huge area before the Mexican-American War is estimated to have been between 50,000 and 80,000, mostly in small villages and towns.

Two conditions adverse to urban growth were the generally hostile attitude of the Indian population, which never developed the centralized political structures of the Mayas or Incas, and the lack of gold, silver, and precious stones, which forced the development of agriculture as the economic base of the towns and villages. To Spanish colonists, that prospect was not nearly as attractive as the economic opportunities in Mexico and South America.

Spanish colonization and the initial settlement of parts of the continental United States by Spain took place in four regions: Florida, Texas, New Mexico, and California. Juan Ponce de León was the first Spanish explorer to reach Florida when his expedition landed near present-day St. Augustine, on the day of Pascua Florida (Easter Sunday) in 1513. He returned again in 1521, trying to discover the legendary Fountain of Youth, but the legend died with him. After a group of French Huguenots settled on the St. Johns River, north of St. Augustine, the Spanish king ordered Don Pedro Menéndez de Avilés to reconquer the land, which he did. He destroyed the French settlement and in 1565 founded St. Augustine, the first permanent European settlement in the present-day United States.

For more than two centuries, Spain tried to develop Florida but could never control the entire peninsula and ended up settling two main towns—St. Augustine and, in 1698, Pensacola. When Spain sold Florida to the United States for $5 million in 1819, the European population was estimated to be fewer than 10,000 residents.

Álvar Nuñez Cabeza de Vaca, one of only four survivors of Pánfilo de Narváez's Florida expedition, was a Spanish nobleman. He and three others, two Spaniards and a black slave, spent about eight years wandering from the coast of Texas, where Narváez's expedition shipwrecked, to a village in Mexico near the Pacific Ocean. They walked through territory that is today Texas, New Mexico, and Arizona. In 1536 Cabeza de Vaca recounted the existence of the Seven Cities of Cibola, which had extraordinary wealth and were centers of a rich civilization. Three years later, Father Marcos de Niza, an Italian priest, led an expedition to find the fabled Seven Cities. He used as his guide Estebanico de Orantes, the black slave who had survived and wandered with Cabeza de Vaca.

After the explorer suffered several military defeats, he returned to Mexico saying that he had seen the cities and that its buildings had golden walls and roofs of gold. He also related stories that the Indians used utensils of pure gold for cooking and that their civilization was extraordinary.

These accounts attracted the attention of Hernán Cortés and Antonio de Mendoza, governor of Nueva Galicia. They asked the King of Spain for permission to conquer this rich land and add it to the glory of Spain. Apparently Mendoza did not await the king's permission, and he organized an expedition of 1,000 soldiers under the leadership of Francisco Vásquez de Coronado in 1539. After a few months, Coronado captured the first city, a small group of stone houses with thatch roofs. This was Hawikuh, just minutes away from today's Zuñi, New Mexico. In spite of his disappointment, Coronado continued the expedition, discovering Arkansas, the Colorado River, the Grand Canyon, the Continental Divide, and the vast regions of the Southwest. At the end of the expedition, Coronado concluded that the region's future would be agricultural. He returned to Mexico in defeat and never occupied another official position. This failure also ended Spain's interest in the region.

Spain organized the huge territories explored by Vásquez de Coronado as the province of Nuevo México. Its first capital, San Juan de los Caballeros, was founded by Juan de Oñate in 1598 near the Indian pueblo of Caypa on the Chama River. Later, a new governor, Pedro de Peralta, moved the capital to a new settlement, La Cuidad Real de la Santa Fé de San Francisco, known today as just Santa Fe, New Mexico. Despite the discovery of limited amounts of gold and silver and the existence of a large Indian labor force, the region did not prosper under Spanish rule. At the beginning of the 1800s, the Spanish estimated that there were fewer than 30,000 Europeans in the province. The only settlement that even remotely had the character and name of a city was Santa Fé. Others, like Albuquerque and Santa Cruz, were small towns at best.

Spain showed more interest in the area between Florida and Mexico. As early as 1519, the governor of Jamaica sent Alonso Álvarez de Pineda to explore the entire Gulf coast, and his company was probably the first group of Europeans to visit Texas. Many years later, the Spanish colonization of Texas was organized as a protective strategy against French encroachment. In reaction to the French presence, the Viceroy of Mexico, the Count of Galve, ordered Alonso de León to investigate the French presence as a potential threat to Spain. León discovered the ruins of a French fort and the bodies of some French settlers, and in 1690 he founded the mission of San Francisco de los Texias. Between 1690 and 1731, Spain sent more than 90 expeditions into Texas, but they were small and had few accomplishments of any importance.

The mission in San Antonio de Valero, settled in 1718, was near the presidio, or fort, of San Antonio de Bexar. The two were consolidated on a nearby site to create the city of San Antonio, which became the capital of Texas in 1772. When Mexico won its independence from Spain, the European population of the region was estimated at about 3,000, most of them living in or around San Antonio.

Farther west, the Spanish initiated explorations of California in 1542–1543, but the first permanent settlement did not occur until establishment of the mission in San Diego in 1769. In 1777, the Spanish government actively promoted development of the region, but in California Spain assigned a leading role to Catholic priests backed by small military forces based in presidios. A system of missions was the backbone of Spanish colonization on the Pacific coast. California was organized into four provinces: Monterey, San Diego, Santa Barbara, and San Francisco, and the missions benefited from a generally peaceful relationship with the Indian population. At the end of Spanish rule in California in 1821, the European population was estimated at 25,000, living in more than 30 settlements. Most of the sites selected for missions and presidios became cities of the United States, another indication of the Spaniards' ability to select the best location for new cities.

The Spanish colonization of territory within what is now the continental United States cannot be evaluated in terms of its size or the richness of its cities and towns because the main goal of Spain was using this region as a buffer to protect Mexico, her primary source of wealth. Compared with the urbanization of the Caribbean, Mexico, and Central and South America, no settlement compared in scale and complexity to La Habana, Santo Domingo, or Cuidad Mexico. However, the settlement and survival of a network of towns and villages were remarkable, especially when the scale, limited resources, continuous resistance of the native population, and geographical characteristics of the region are considered.

—*Felipe J. Prestamo*

### References

Reps, John W. *Cities of the American West.* Princeton, NJ: Princeton University Press, 1979.

———. *The Forgotten Frontier: Urban Planning in the American West before 1890.* Columbia: University of Missouri Press, 1981.

## Sports in Cities

A recent survey of American sport history is aptly titled *City Games,* for the author begins with a bold statement, "Nearly all contemporary major sports evolved, or were invented, in the city." There is much truth in this. Although English traditions have dominated, America's growing cities provided the critical frameworks and markets for the amalgamation of diverse immigrant pastimes and customs into today's most popular sports. In the first place, cities had the concentrated material conditions—in particular, dense populations, communications and transportation networks, and higher concentrations of discretionary time and income—to aid promotion and competition. Entrepreneurs of sports, like their counterparts in dry goods, hardware, religion, or law, quickly saw growing towns and cities as their most productive and profitable markets.

But cities offered more than a material base. They were ripe with symbolic and cultural conditions that gave value and meaning to games that were otherwise childlike, self-indulgent, or violent. Thus, boxing could accentuate ethnic, class, and racial struggles that wrenched at the core of urban life. One group's hero was another's villain. Likewise, bicycling could focus issues of female liberation and sexuality in public space. Football could crystallize the contradictions of masculine science, organization, brutality, and violence. Golf at a country club offered a safe haven of homogeneity in a swirling polyglot population. And baseball or basketball promised to turn ethnic (and later, racial) rivals into "American" teammates. For many, sports held the promise of both escaping and resolving the anxieties and conflicts of urban-industrial life.

The urban roots of American sports are buried deep in the colonial period. By the eighteenth century, tavern owners—the first sports promoters—were continuing English traditions by providing the equipment, advertising, and facilities for contests in bowling, cricket, cockfighting, and bear-baiting. At the same time, elites in Philadelphia organized private sporting clubs like the Colony in Schuylkill (1732) and the Jockey Club (1766). Chesapeake jockey clubs brought races, gambling, and swollen populations to Williamsburg, Annapolis, and Richmond. By 1779, when the Pennsylvania Assembly aimed at Philadelphia an "Act for the Suppression of Vice and Immorality," sports were already a lightning rod for tensions between mechanics and merchants, Quakers and Anglicans, moderates and radicals.

In the nineteenth century, both the quantity and quality of population growth heightened the symbolic value of competition. For example, by the 1840s bare-knuckle boxing (despite its illegal status) captured widespread attention. The first major boxing spectacle was the 1849 "championship" fight between James (Yankee) Sullivan, an Irish immigrant, and Tom Hyer, a "native" butcher, brawler, and gang hero. Sparked in New York and fought on an island in the Chesapeake Bay, the match was widely followed by an urban press, which used the newest technology—the telegraph—to send instant results to crowded newsrooms. The boxers' fists flashed with the sparks that Irish immigration brought to the worlds of housing, work, religion, and politics. Although hounded underground for decades, bare-knuckle spectacles enjoyed popularity precisely because they gave meaning to urban life.

Before the Civil War, public events in boxing, rowing, running, and horse racing reached wide audiences through daily newspapers and specialty journals like the *American Turf Register,* the *Spirit of the Times,* and the *Clipper.* Still, the contests were irregular; nothing like today's daily calendar. And respectable families had little use for these sports, which dripped with the drinking, gambling, and rowdiness of the "Fancy," an old British term for the odd mix of gentry and robust workers who comprised the sporting crowd. By the 1850s and 1860s, however, a loose coalition of reformers, clergymen, and journalists began to craft an emerging defense of some sports on the basis of their contributions to health and morality, both critical to orderly and prosperous cities.

Cricket and baseball began to share the supposed salutary benefits of water cures, bran diets, and home gymnastics. Henry Chadwick, an immigrant journalist and the "father" of baseball, captured most of the ideology in his myriad columns, reports, and guidebooks. Cricket, he argued, "teaches a love of order, discipline and fair play." He was more glowing in his conversion to baseball, which, he claimed in 1866, "merits the endorsement of every clergyman in the country" as "a remedy for the many evils" that stemmed from "immoral associations" in city life.

If the city's "immoral" associations resided in saloons, brothels, and theaters, the "moral" associations of sport were private clubs, the standard organization throughout the nineteenth century. Such groups offered more than health and character; they promised identity and community, often through discrimination. Some clubs, like New York's Knickerbocker Base Ball Club (1845), were strictly bourgeois, but skilled workers organized numerous ball clubs by the 1850s. Ethnicity was the obvious unifying factor for Scots Caledonian clubs, whose competitions fueled interest in track and field. Likewise, German *turnvereins* and Bohemian *Sokols* promoted both ethnicity and gymnastics in cities like Cincinnati, Milwaukee, and Chicago, while Gaelic Athletic Associations and hurling clubs transported "invented" traditions from the old country to the new. Young Men's Hebrew Associations advanced boxing and basketball along with Jewish identity. In the 1920s, the South Philadelphia Hebrew Association sponsored one of the most dominant teams in the history of basketball.

Sports clubs were halfway houses for many urbanites who sought more clearly defined communities amid the polyglot swirl. This was especially true for the growing number of athletic clubs, which created a new kind of sport called "amateurism" in the last quarter of the century. As increasing numbers of the emerging professional and clerical classes sought the benefits of active sports, they erected clubs, facilities, and restrictive memberships in cities around the country. In the 1880s and 1890s suburban sport and country clubs offered an even more exclusive refuge. As one observer remarked in 1905, country clubs brought together "persons of similar tastes and means." By nurturing common traits and behaviors through tennis, golf, or debutante balls, such clubs could bring "order to the chaos created by sudden prosperity."

While sports clubs and heroes often aggravated differences among urban groups, baseball emerged as the "national pastime" partly because professional promoters shrewdly positioned their clubs to represent entire cities and not just special or particular interests. Many club owners were local bosses and politicos like "Boss" Cox of Cincinnati or traction magnates like Stanley Robison of Cleveland. Public interest and private profit blended early in the history of baseball, when urban rivals fought for bigger stakes in railroads and markets. Newspapers like the *St. Louis Republican* were quick to boost the significance of victory. "Chicago has not only been beaten in baseball, but outrageously beaten. . . . In this, as other things, St. Louis proves stronger. . . . Chicago came, saw, and was conquered" (1875). Stories of widespread interest evolved into an ideology of community, as baseball and the ballpark became the city's true melting pot. In 1909 Rollin Hartt captured the mythology of baseball in a book entitled *The People at Play.* "Mickey O'Houlighan," he claimed, "sees more of America at a baseball game, and hears more of it than anywhere else." Supposedly, an Irish laborer could bond through baseball—by rooting or discussing statistics—with chance plutocrats, rabbis, local policemen, settlement house workers, scabs, or ward bosses. Such sporting interaction brought "always a glow of fellow feeling" that offered a glimpse of "that noble American ideal, the brotherhood of man."

Such themes fit together well in the anxious decades at the beginning of the twentieth century; the stakes were higher for burgeoning cities like Chicago, New York, Pittsburgh, and Detroit, where staggering population growth understated the actual turnover of migrants who included increasing numbers of Slavs, Italians, Catholics, and Jews. Reform-minded clergy, journalists, politicians, and philanthropists pondered the prospects of a fragmented society, drifting with the erosion of its traditional (read WASP) values and leadership. Many promoted the benefits of sports, especially team sports, which could supposedly nurture discipline, obedience, hard work, and success through the balance of individual and team effort.

Baseball, football, and basketball became perfect analogies to urban industrial life. Jane Addams, Jacob Riis, and Joseph Lee led a national call for public playgrounds and professional curriculums of "organized play." In 1905 they helped

*A game of stickball on 42nd Street in New York City, January 1943.*

celebrate the birth of the Playground Association of America. The reports of playground committees in the nation's cities typically echoed that of the Massachusetts Civic League in 1900: "hockey and football teams ignored, to a great extent, the race lines between Irish, Jews, and Italians, which are so marked at the north End." Such sentiments fueled the expansion of public school sports in the same period. Public urban high schools offered more than academic preparation; their mission equally entailed training for commerce, trades, and "citizenship." Administrators were quick to embrace or annex student-run teams.

This powerful ideology about the value of sports is now commonplace, but it can be understood only in the context of urban growth and problems. It has been forcefully promulgated and propagated by generations of journalists, teachers, coaches, politicians, merchants, and boosters, who all advocated major investments of public money in the first three-quarters of the twentieth century.

Athletics are also a flash point in the recent tax revolts that have squeezed public education and recreation programs.

Urban problems continue to haunt America. Many find solace in an old ideology that somehow sports can fuse the broad range of urban cultures into one, but reality has often lagged behind this vision. As Steven Riess has carefully documented, newer immigrant groups were slow to enjoy the promise of sports. Adult workers had little time for weekday games, and Sunday ball was illegal in many cities. Working-class and immigrant youth had less space for play, and even public playgrounds and schools could not overcome all the obstacles, especially parental opposition. As one Jewish boy named "Jim" told an interviewer in Los Angeles in the late 1920s, "My father won't allow us to play ball on the lot. He says it's a waste of time and a disgrace to make a lot of noise over nothing."

Women faced stiffer resistance when they ventured into the public space of sports. To be sure, antebellum reformers like Catherine Beecher and Dio Lewis had promoted exercise for women of the "sedentary" classes. And in the 1860s, bourgeois women played croquet on lawns across the expanding suburbs of American cities. *The Nation* concluded in 1866 that "of all the epidemics that have swept over our land, the swiftest and most infectious is croquet."

Baseball was more strenuous. Despite being ridiculed, women formed their own baseball clubs in places ranging from New Orleans and Cincinnati to Chester, Pennsylvania. By 1918, the Cleveland Recreation Survey claimed that 44 percent of the city's female employees played baseball in their leisure time. Factories and companies in places as disparate as Wilmington, Akron, Dallas, and Oakland sponsored women's sports programs in the 1920s and 1930s. Such open competition challenged the masculine traditions of sport. Journalists lampooned women who competed in Madison Square Garden's indoor "marathons" in the 1870s; male physicians especially fretted that strenuous cycling (called "scorching") or ball playing threatened health as well as morality. Nonetheless, in the first third of the twentieth century, women ventured aggressively into the public space of sports. The Depression and fascism, however, appeared to threaten masculinity along with democracy; as a result, female athletes and their history slid into relative oblivion during World War II.

African Americans have had an even tougher road; the public agenda of sport held little out to them through the first half of the twentieth century. Therefore, they built a separate and vibrant world of clubs, teams, leagues, and heroes who grew in stature along with the waves of urban arrivals in the twentieth century. Organized black baseball clubs had long existed in urban areas; Philadelphia's Pythians and Brooklyn's Monitors date back to the 1860s. By 1875, New Orleans had 13 black clubs. With the Great Migration, however, came markets that attracted entrepreneurs like Chicago's Rube Foster, who founded the Negro National League in 1920, and Pittsburgh's Cumberland Posey, whose career as an important sports entrepreneur crossed four decades (1910–1946) and two sports. His Leondi "Big Five" and Homestead Grays rank among the strongest teams in the history of professional basketball and baseball.

Basketball particularly thrived in the cauldrons of cities. Along with their Jewish counterparts (in an alliance that was both collaborative and antagonistic), African Americans developed special languages in picks and weaves and slam dunks that rung with the cadence of city life. The "Hoop Dreams" of 1995 are not the product of a stagnant "ghetto" culture; they have deep roots in the great urban migrations of the first half of the twentieth century.

Most of today's beliefs about sports grew in the dynamic and turbulent developments of an urbanizing America. The rise of movies, radio, and television in the twentieth century cast such narratives and ideologies across a wide range of Americans and, at the same time, raised the value of the sport product. Promoters, franchise owners, and entrepreneurs rec-

ognized this, especially in the major team sports. Under their prods and threats, cities in the 1960s began to invest huge amounts of public money in stadiums and arenas, ostensibly as part of "urban renewal" campaigns. As Indianapolis Mayor (and later Indiana Senator) Richard Lugar argued in 1972, the Market Square project "will offer new hope for the heart of the city. Sports, along with the theater and the arts, must be a focal point for the renewal of the city." A new narrative emerged, one suggesting that cities could not afford not to build the vast infrastructure needed to attract or retain "big league" teams. Owners had more leverage than ever.

Few objective analysts see economic payoffs in these investments. As Charles Euchner concludes, even "winning" cities lose because the "zealous pursuit of gypsy franchises distracts city leaders from the more important job of building a viable political and economic base. Substituting a vicarious community for a more sturdy community promotes the illusion of progress while the city as a whole declines." In the end, of course, the importance of sport is an illusion. But in the life of American cities, such illusions have sometimes seemed to matter more than life itself.

—Stephen Hardy

See also

Ballparks; Baseball; Basketball; Boxing; Country Clubs; Playgrounds.

References

Adelman, Melvin. *A Sporting Time: New York City and the Rise of Modern Athletics, 1820–1870*. Urbana: University of Illinois Press, 1986.

Carter, Gregg Lee. "Baseball in Saint Louis, 1867–1875: An Historical Case Study in Civic Pride." *Missouri Historical Society Bulletin* 31 (1975): 253–263.

Euchner, Charles. *Playing the Field: Why Sports Teams Move and Cities Fight to Keep Them*. Baltimore: Johns Hopkins University Press, 1993.

George, Nelson. *Elevating the Game: Black Men and Basketball*. New York: HarperCollins, 1992.

Gorn, Elliott J. *The Manly Art: Bare-Knuckle Prize Fighting in America*. Ithaca, NY: Cornell University Press, 1986.

Hardy, Stephen. "The City and the Rise of American Sport, 1820–1920." *Exercise and Sports Sciences Reviews* 9 (1981): 183–229.

———. *How Boston Played: Sport, Recreation, and Community, 1865–1915*. Boston: Northeastern University Press, 1982.

Jable, J. Thomas. "The Pennsylvania Sunday Blue Laws of 1779." *Pennsylvania History* 40 (1973): 413–426.

Kuklick, Bruce. *To Everything a Season: Shibe Park and Urban Philadelphia, 1909–1976*. Princeton, NJ: Princeton University Press, 1991.

Rader, Benjamin. *American Sports from the Age of Folk Games to the Art of Televised Sports*. 2d ed. Englewood Cliffs, NJ: Prentice-Hall, 1990.

Riess, Steven. *City Games: The Evolution of American Urban Society and the Rise of Sport*. Urbana: University of Illinois Press, 1989.

Ruck, Rob. *Sandlot Seasons: Sport in Black Pittsburgh*. Urbana: University of Illinois Press, 1987.

Somers, Dale. *The Rise of Sports in New Orleans, 1850–1900*. Baton Rouge: Louisiana State University Press, 1972.

Struna, Nancy. "Sport and Society in Early America." *International Journal of the History of Sport* 5 (1988): 292–311.

## Sprague, Franklin Julian (1857–1934)

Franklin Julian Sprague, the inventor of the electrified streetcar, or trolley, was born in 1857 in Milford, Connecticut. After excelling in science in high school, Sprague studied engineering at the U.S. Naval Academy; in 1882, while in the Navy, he officiated at the Crystal Palace Electrical Exhibition in London. His frequent trips on London's smoky, steam-powered subway motivated him to invent an electric motor that would obviate the use of steam in urban transportation.

In 1883, Sprague resigned from the Navy and began working for the Edison Electric Light Company in New York. A year later, he formed the Sprague Electric Railway and Motor Company, fulfilling the goal he had set in London, and in 1886 he demonstrated an electric railway in New York. He first undertook to apply electricity to an entire streetcar line in Richmond, Virginia, where he electrified a 12-mile-long, 40-car track, which began service in February 1888.

Unlike the few other electric traction systems then in place, Sprague's system involved two motors mounted beneath each car, a single overhead conductor, and a controller at each end of the cars, allowing them to be operated from either end. Within two years, Sprague's system had spread across the country, and the number of electric railways increased from 8 in 1885 to 200 in 1890.

After inventing the first electric traction system capable of widespread use, Sprague developed devices that controlled a group of elevator cars with a single switch. Still keenly interested in urban transportation, he soon applied this idea to traction. In 1897, he invented a multiple-unit control system that allowed an entire train to be controlled from either end of any car. This breakthrough allowed for lighter cars, longer trains, and unprecedented acceleration speed.

Sprague was a risk-taker and a visionary inventor. He was also an astute entrepreneur and scientist, continuing his work in electrical invention until 1934, when he died of pneumonia. Although some of his later inventions were notable, none of them had the importance or impact of the electric trolley.

—*Martha J. Bianco*

### References

Hammond, John Winthrop. *Men and Volts: The Story of General Electric*. Philadelphia: J. B. Lippincott, 1941.

Jackson, Dugald C. "Frank Julian Sprague 1857–1934." *Scientific Monthly* 57 (1943): 431–441.

Miller, John Anderson. *Fares Please! A Popular History of Trolleys, Horse-Cars, Street-Cars, Buses, Elevateds, and Subways*. Reprint ed. New York: Dover, 1960.

Passer, Harold C. "Franklin Julian Sprague: Father of Electric Traction, 1857–1934." In William Miller, ed., *Men in Business: Essays on the Historical Role of the Entrepreneur*, 212–237. New York: Harper & Row, 1962.

Sprague, Franklin Julian. "Application of Electricity to the Propulsion of Elevated Railroads." *Electrical World* 12 (1886): 27, 36, 118.

———. "Lessons of the Richmond Electric Railway." *Engineering Magazine* 7 (1894): 789.

———. "The Multiple Unit System for Electric Railways." *Cassier's Magazine* 16 (1899): 460.

## St. Louis, Missouri

More than two centuries before municipal officials celebrated completion of the gateway arch, St. Louis was already becoming a gateway city. In its early days, this frontier trading post marked the boundary between European and Indian territories in North America, and St. Louis has served as an important border city even as political and economic forces have redefined regional lines. At various times, the river city has been the gateway to Missouri and Osage territories, to the French and Spanish empires in the Mississippi valley, to the Far West, and to the Old South. More recently, St. Louis has emerged as the commercial capital of the "central-south" region. The city's role as a point of commercial exchange between regions has shaped the economic character of St. Louis and has invigorated local culture, but it has not spared the city from deep-seated social and racial tensions.

French traders established a permanent settlement at St. Louis in 1764 to serve as a trading post at the border between Indian and European territories. The first Europeans to arrive recognized the potential of a site close to major waterways but shielded from floodwaters and nestled in an area rich with natural resources. When Pierre de Laclede arrived in the vicinity, he announced that the place would soon be "one of the finest cities in America."

The fur trade shaped St. Louis for more than a half-century. During the late 1700s, Indian trappers brought pelts to the city and sold them to French merchants, who shipped them to New Orleans. By 1800, St. Louis had nearly 1,000 residents, almost all of them involved in the fur trade. The purchase of the Louisiana Territory by the United States in 1803 accelerated the pace of growth. American troops arrived to protect U.S. interests in the region and added to the population. The scale of the fur trade also increased during the early nineteenth century. Each spring hundreds of "mountain men" returned from western trapping grounds, met in St. Louis, sold their goods, and celebrated their success and survival, giving the town a rough-hewn, "frontier" reputation.

When the first steamboats plied the Mississippi River in 1816, the importance of St. Louis was assured. Located just south of the confluence of the Mississippi and Missouri rivers and just north of where the Ohio flowed into the Mississippi, St. Louis also neighbored a "break in the waters" of the Mississippi River. Because the depth of the river changed abruptly near the city, river cargo had to be unloaded and reloaded in St. Louis. Thus, during the 1820s the steamboat transformed St. Louis into a bustling commercial center.

St. Louis became the heart of a western economy based on—and dependent on—rivers. In 1830, 278 steamboats docked there, and by the end of the decade more than 2,000 steam-powered vessels stopped at its levee every year. Settlers heading for the Far West used the city as their "jumping-off point," and St. Louis, with a population of 16,000 in 1840, began attracting large numbers of easterners who considered it an ideal place for young newcomers to make their mark in the world. Virtually everything that happened in the West seemed to generate activity and energize the local marketplace. St. Louis, for example, became a staging area for troops preparing to invade Mexico, and the gold rush in California brought thousands of travelers to the city, all needing food and lodging and many of them buying wagons, guns, and other supplies in local stores.

With nearly 80,000 residents in 1850, St. Louis was the eighth largest city in the nation. Although an old elite ruled over cultural affairs and newcomers from the Northeast dominated commercial ranks, St. Louis attracted huge waves of European immigrants. During the 1830s, a group of German intellectuals settled in the region and established a strong cultural presence. Reports of high wages and plentiful work added to the city's appeal during the 1840s, and by 1850 more than 22,000 Germans lived there. Predictions that St. Louis would soon become the "New York of the West" also attracted nearly 10,000 Irish newcomers. Immigrants comprised nearly 60 percent of the city's population at mid-century, and the river city emerged as the great metropolis of the West.

St. Louis's regional supremacy, however, proved short-lived as Chicago increasingly challenged it for control of western commerce. Each city's leaders recognized the importance of the railroad and pursued money to forge an empire held together with track. Eastern capital flowed into both cities until the middle of the 1850s, when political conditions jeopardized the future of the city in Missouri. As the sectional crisis erupted and political violence exploded in western Missouri, the location of St. Louis in a slave state and its ties to the South dampened eastern enthusiasm for financing its transportation system. These tensions, along with the rapid economic development of the upper Midwest, enabled Chicago to overtake its rival in Missouri. Each city gained about 80,000 residents during the 1850s, and St. Louis had a larger population until the 1870s even though Chicago gradually captured the commerce of the West.

The Civil War recharted the river city's economic future. In 1861, Confederate troops blockaded the Mississippi, severing St. Louis's ties to its long-established markets and prostrating the local marketplace. With its northern hinterland lost to Chicago and its reputation on Wall Street linked to the war-ravaged South, St. Louis became dependent on markets in the lower Mississippi valley. The renewed rail construction after the war connected the Missouri entrepot to the Southwest. When cotton production surged in Arkansas, Oklahoma, and Texas in the late nineteenth century, for example, St. Louis emerged as the third largest cotton market in the nation.

The city became the commercial gateway to the central-south region and an important manufacturing center during the closing decades of the nineteenth century. In 1890, for example, St. Louis was fourth nationally in the gross value of manufactured products and fifth in capital invested in manufacturing. Similarly, local factories were among the national leaders in tobacco and metal products, not to mention the output of beer.

Although more prosperous cities attracted larger numbers of immigrants during the late nineteenth century, St. Louis's reputation as a German city blossomed. German intellectuals found the Missouri metropolis particularly attractive, and St. Louis became renowned as a center for the study of Hegelian philosophy. In addition, German workers assumed a prominent role in the city's labor movement, and St. Louis unions had great influence in the national labor movement.

Other immigrants, particularly those from Southern and Eastern Europe, found St. Louis less attractive. In 1910, for example, just 18 percent of the city's residents were foreign-born (compared to 36 percent in Chicago and 40 percent in New York), ranking St. Louis only thirtieth among large cities in the proportion of foreign-born in the population. Only modest numbers of Italian, Slavic, and Jewish immigrants arrived, and in 1910 St. Louis had six times as many German as Italian residents and more Scots than Greeks.

St. Louis's rail and river ties to the South did draw many African Americans to the city. Until the late nineteenth century, few African Americans settled there, and in 1860 African Americans comprised only 2.3 percent of the population. Four decades later, members of the group made up 6.2 percent of the population. By 1920, African Americans comprised 9 percent of the city's inhabitants, compared to only 4.1 percent in Chicago and 4.3 percent in Cleveland. On the one hand, these newcomers provided an important component of the local workforce and made significant contributions to local culture. On the other hand, white residents, as in many other cities, reacted in hostile fashion to the immigrants, and the city's racial climate deteriorated.

As the infrastructure of St. Louis aged and its economy sputtered during the middle of the twentieth century, the local population became increasingly polarized. Whites moved in great waves to the western parts of the municipality and to the suburbs. Federal and local funds accelerated this process by funneling highway and housing dollars to outlying sections of the metropolitan area. White-collar and light-manufacturing jobs followed, and unemployment racked the inner city, which included a growing number of African Americans. During the 1940s, the suburban population grew at six times the rate of the city's population. Development became still more uneven during the 1950s; the urban population fell by more than 12 percent, while the suburban population surged by almost 52 percent. During the late 1970s, barely one-third of the jobs in the metropolitan area were located inside the city limits. At the same time, African Americans, who comprised 45.6 percent of the urban population in 1980 (compared to 5.9 percent of the suburban population), clustered in the declining inner city; the average African American in St. Louis lived in a neighborhood where more than 80 percent of the residents were also African American, making St. Louis one of the ten most segregated cities in the nation. Between 1940 and 1980, the population of St. Louis declined by 44 percent, and the city plunged to being only the twenty-sixth largest in the United States. Once among the fastest-growing urban places in the country, St. Louis was among the most rapidly declining cities of the United States in the middle of the twentieth century. Its population in 1980 was virtually identical to its population in 1890.

The Pruitt-Igoe housing project symbolized the decline of St. Louis and the failure of urban policy. Planned during the early 1950s as an innovative response to the housing crisis in inner cities, St. Louis's Pruitt-Igoe complex consisted of 33 buildings scattered across 70 acres, with a capacity of almost 3,000 families. Featuring communal porches and recreation areas, the development was supposed to create "vertical neighborhoods" where a sense of community would flourish in a concrete environment. But Pruitt-Igoe turned out to be a monumental failure. Located far from public transportation, health services, shopping facilities, and jobs, it experienced immediate problems. By 1971, 16 of the 33 buildings were vacant, and the project held only 600 families; as a result, total demolition of Pruitt-Igoe began in 1975. The housing and economic crises in St. Louis worsened. Close to a fourth of downtown land sat vacant, jobs continued flowing to outlying areas, and African Americans remained disproportionately isolated from adequate housing and employment opportunities.

During the turbulent life of Pruitt-Igoe, however, St. Louis also experienced a renaissance of sorts. New alliances of business, labor, and government spearheaded a redevelopment campaign. Offering tax abatements to developers who invested in downtown projects and relying on bond issues to finance slum clearance and highway projects, St. Louis officials spearheaded the creation of new commercial areas. The city seemed poised for recovery; even property tax valuations began to climb.

*The great arch in St. Louis symbolizes that city's claim to being "Gateway to the West."*

In many ways, St. Louis has fulfilled its destiny. Just as Pierre de Laclede predicted in 1764, St. Louis has become one of the finest cities in the nation. But the modern renaissance has produced uneven results. The "New St. Louis" campaign brought in tax dollars and facilitated the creation of fashionable shopping areas. The rebirth, however, failed to solve the vexing housing and employment crises of the inner city. Although the local economy has enjoyed new prosperity and St. Louis remains an important commercial center, not all residents of the city have participated in the renaissance. Just as St. Louis in the eighteenth century flourished and suffered from competition among Indian nations and successive European empires, and just as St. Louis in the nineteenth century grew as Americans moved west and endured economic difficulties because of regional boundary shifts, St. Louis in the twentieth century, like many "snow-belt" cities, contains pockets of high-technology prosperity and upscale wealth, but the city also struggles to overcome long-standing racial and economic problems.

—*Jeffrey S. Adler*

**See also**
Pruitt-Igoe Housing Complex.
**References**
Adler, Jeffrey S. *Yankee Merchants and the Making of the Urban West: The Rise and Fall of Ante-bellum St. Louis.* New York: Cambridge University Press, 1991.
Mormino, Gary Ross. *Immigrants on the Hill: Italian-American in St. Louis, 1882–1982.* Urbana: University of Illinois Press, 1986.
Primm, James Neal. *Lion of the Valley: St. Louis, Missouri.* Boulder, CO: Pruett, 1990.
Wade, Richard C. *The Urban Frontier: Pioneer Life in Early Pittsburgh, Cincinnati, Lexington, Louisville, and St. Louis.* Cambridge, MA: Harvard University Press, 1959.

## States and Cities

Municipal government must be understood at least partly within a context that includes county governments, special districts, and most especially state governments. All of these different levels of government play important roles in delivering services to communities and help determine many local policies. In delivering services and determining policies, all of these governments affect city government, none more so than state government, which has the authority to charter municipal corporations and which often had the power to act directly for cities despite the existence of urban governments.

The U.S. Census Bureau defines a city as a municipal corporation providing general local government for an identified population within a defined geographic area. Cities are legally organized by states under charter systems, and these charters vary widely and both grant and restrict municipal authority. Unlike many local governments, municipal governments are normally incorporated, allowing them some of the same characteristics as other legal corporations (e.g., entering into contracts).

Many city services are not provided by city governments themselves but by special districts or counties. Special districts are the fastest-growing category of local government, increasing in number by over 61 percent since 1962. They are often established to provide needed services in an area that does not correspond to existing government boundaries, and so they play an increasingly critical role in local service delivery. In addition, special districts sometimes shape policy decisions made by other local governments. Special districts are usually created by state action and receive their authority from the state. Because special districts often overlap other local governments, are often not very visible, and have some administrative and fiscal autonomy, critics worry that special districts are inadequately accountable to the state, other local governments, or even the public.

The authority of county governments is granted by the state. Unlike municipal governments, counties are usually not incorporated and therefore have less legal autonomy to address the service demands of citizens. Historically, county governments have been considered rural, but with the population growth in many locales, in some cases counties have become focal points for urban service delivery and government access.

The U.S. Constitution mentions only the national and state governments specifically, and much of the legal basis for local government authority is shaped by judicial interpretation of state policy. Dillon's Rule provides a legal framework for the relations between states and localities. According to this rule, the authority of local government is limited to specifically granted powers, clearly implied powers, and those powers essential to performing designated functions of local governments. As a consequence, state government plays a major role in making local policy as local officials who feel uncertain about their authority may defer decisions to states to avoid potential legal problems. Also, if local government either does not have clear authority or chooses not to act, citizens may turn to the state or national government to address local needs. Finally, in the case of disagreement between a state and a local government, the state's position is typically stronger in court.

The legal weakness and vulnerability of cities has led many reformers to advocate home rule, which enables local governments to adopt new structural arrangements and, in some cases, grant themselves new authority (usually subject to voter approval). Although most states now grant home rule to at least some of their cities, the results have been varied. Home rule has given cities more flexibility and autonomy, but in cases of disagreement between a city and a state, states continue to have a stronger legal position.

Since 1890, the population of the United States has almost quadrupled, and over 77 percent of that population now live in urbanized areas as defined by the U.S. Census Bureau. The shift in population to cities, and later into the suburbs, has changed the demands made upon municipal governments that serve city populations, and special districts and counties that may, in conjunction with municipal governments, provide services to urban and suburban populations. In fact, urban and suburban growth has produced an explosion in the number of local government "units" within a metropolitan area. The complexity of intergovernmental relations is staggering when multiple municipalities, special districts, and counties attempt to coordinate service delivery to a contiguous urban area.

John Harrigan notes that a major shift from rural to urban areas occurred by 1920 and an even more interesting shift of urban population to suburban areas by the 1970s. The shifting population patterns are complicated by what Harrigan calls a dual migration. Comparatively affluent persons are migrating out of cities to suburban areas, while most recent migrants to central cities are less affluent individuals seeking economic opportunity. So local government has faced dramatic changes in the types and quantity of local services its citizens request. The change in quantity and types of local services is a result of these shifting population patterns and is complicated by reduced revenues for local government from traditional revenue sources like property taxes.

Local governments in all forms are directly delivering more services to citizens and are charged with forming policy to address future needs. However, state governments still influence local government policymaking and service delivery in a number of ways. State governments have grown substantially during this century in terms of employees, revenue, and expenditures and serve both as a conduit and a source of local aid. Local governments increasingly depend on money from the state and national governments; outside aid for local governments grew from 6 percent in 1902 to almost 33 percent in 1990.

Mandates drawn from the extensive legal authority that states wield over local governments can be used to encourage a variety of policy choices and modes of service delivery. State mandates can be useful in encouraging policy uniformity, which is particularly important when problems cross boundaries. Mandates can also ease coordination problems for local governments. The growing complexity of relations between different local governments may be streamlined through the use of state mandates.

Unfortunately, mandates also have drawbacks. They can be very costly, particularly when a local government is expected to fulfill a mandate without receiving funds from the state for implementation. Mandates are not only a tool of the state; mandates from the federal government to both states and localities are increasing, leading to regulatory requirements for service delivery, often without the funds to provide these services. The Clinton administration has called for innovation to address the contradictions inherent in the "mandates without money" facing both states and local government. These mandates are often passed along to the local government. Finally, a mandate may be offensive to a local government that disagrees with a particular state policy, but the mandate could, conversely, serve as a political scapegoat for a local politician.

Although mandates are a direct and common method of influencing local action, state governments use a variety of other approaches to influence local governments. Some of the more common methods include consultation, technical assistance, reporting, inspections and investigations, grants, state review and approval, removal of officials, and direct state control.

Local governments relate to state government within a complex legal and fiscal environment. Since legal authority for local action usually comes from the states and varies with the type of local government, actions taken by municipal governments may vary dramatically from those by counties. These local governments are charged with serving their constituency, a single population that may sometimes be shared by counties, municipalities, special districts, and even two states. With shifts in the location and composition of citizen populations changing public opinion, and changing problems, local governments must often react to dramatic swings in service demands or needs. These changes do not always occur when local governments have sufficient revenues, legal latitude, or technical resources to address citizen concerns. The complexity of service delivery in metropolitan areas with multiple jurisdictions prompts calls for a national urban policy, but the complex and varying needs of our cities has made that goal elusive.

—*Patricia J. Fredericksen and David C. Nice*

**See also**
Fragmentation of Municipal Government; Home Rule.
**References**
Adrian, Charles, and Michael Fine. *State and Local Politics.* Chicago: Lyceum Books/Nelson-Hall, 1991.
Berman, David R. *State and Local Politics.* 7th ed. Dubuque, IA: Brown & Benchmark, 1994.
Caraley, Demetrios. *City Government and Urban Problems.* Englewood Cliffs, NJ: Prentice-Hall, 1977.
Glendening, Parris, and Mavis Reeves. *Pragmatic Federalism.* 2d ed. Pacific Palisades, CA: Palisades, 1984.
Grant, Daniel R., and Lloyd B. Omdahl. *State and Local Government in America.* 6th ed. Dubuque, IA: Brown & Benchmark, 1993.
Harrigan, John J. *Political Change in the Metropolis.* 5th ed. New York: HarperCollins, 1993.
Morgan, David, and Mei-Chiang Shih. "Targeting State and Federal Aid to City Needs." *State and Local Government Review* 23 (1991): 60–68.
Nice, David C., and Patricia J. Fredericksen. *The Politics of Intergovernmental Relations.* 2d ed. Chicago: Nelson-Hall, 1995.
Pagano, Michael, and Ann O'M. Bowman. "The State of American Federalism 1992–1993." *Publius* 23 (1993): 1–22.
Sokolow, Alvin, and Keith Snavely. "Small City Autonomy in the Federal System: A Study of Local Constraint and Opportunity in California." *Publius* 13 (1983): 73–88.
Stanley, Harold W., and Richard G. Niemi. *Vital Statistics on American Politics.* 4th ed. Washington, DC: Congressional Quarterly Press, 1994.
Walker, David B. "American Federalism from Johnson to Bush." *Publius* 21 (1991): 105–119.
Zimmerman, Joseph. *Contemporary American Federalism.* New York: Praeger, 1992.

## Steamboats

Except for the railroad, no other form of technology did more to shape America's urban growth during the nineteenth century than the steamboat. While its influence was felt nationally and lingered into the twentieth century, the steamboat's greatest impact occurred in the trans-Appalachian West where the rise of important urban centers coincided with the heyday of steamboat transportation between 1815 and 1860.

An American creation, the steamboat resulted from the enterprise of rival inventors James Rumsey of Virginia and the Pennsylvania artisan John Fitch during the 1780s. By 1790, Fitch had perfected his designs sufficiently to establish regular commercial passenger service on the Delaware River between Trenton, New Jersey, and Philadelphia. Though Fitch's line lasted less than a year, the steamboat era had begun.

In the first decade of the next century, the pioneering work of Fitch and Rumsey was advanced by new designers, most notably John Stevens and Robert Fulton. In 1806, Stevens's boat *Phoenix* journeyed from New York to Philadelphia and became the first steam vessel to complete a deep-sea voyage. That same year, Fulton built his famous *Clermont*, which began navigating the Hudson River between New York and Albany in August 1807. With their initial emphasis on passenger service, steamboats dramatically improved intercity travel on the East Coast of the United States and made the growth of commuter suburbs possible around sheltered waters like New York Harbor, Long Island Sound, and Delaware Bay.

In 1811, Fulton and his partner Robert Livingston inaugurated steamboat service west of the Appalachians by launching the *New Orleans* on the Ohio River at Pittsburgh. Piloted by Captain Nicholas Roosevelt, the first steamboat to ply western waters took two and one-half months to travel downstream to New Orleans. It did not, however, possess the horsepower required to make the return trip upstream. That feat was soon accomplished by boat builders Daniel French and Henry M. Shreve of Brownsville, Pennsylvania. By 1817, their improved vessels had successfully completed several round-trips between Pittsburgh and New Orleans, removing all doubts about the ability of steamboats to sail against the powerful currents of the Ohio and Mississippi rivers.

Led by Shreve, Oliver Evans, and Stephen Long, engineers and craftsmen quickly introduced a series of innovations designed to adapt the steamboat to the shallow, upper reaches of the Ohio and Mississippi river system. Rejecting the deep-draft hulls and side wheels used by Fulton's boats and early oceangoing steamships, they built vessels featuring low, flat hulls, large stern wheels, and towering superstructures. With the engine and cargo holds raised above the waterline, the reconceived western riverboat assumed the classic form that enabled it to ride on the water rather than through it. Western steamboats navigated in remarkably shallow currents, and captains frequently boasted that they could pilot their vessels in nothing more than a heavy dew. This was only a slight exaggeration. By 1860 many boats built specifically for upriver traffic drew as few as 11 inches when empty and could carry 50 to 100 tons of freight in just two feet of water. These vessels were significantly smaller than their deepwater counterparts downstream. Boats on the Mississippi above St. Louis, for example, ranged in size from 118 to 200 tons, while the celebrated "floating palaces" operating on the river's main stem between St. Louis and New Orleans varied between 220 and 500 tons.

The steamboat revolutionized transportation in the American West. With its rough and primitive wagon roads, the trans-Appalachian frontier had always relied heavily on the Mississippi and its tributaries for efficient long-distance shipping. Commercial farm produce flowed south on simple makeshift flatboats to New Orleans, which served, until the Erie Canal opened in 1825, as the virtually uncontested outlet for the region's export trade. Likewise, New Orleans stood as the entrepot for almost all goods imported to the West from the East Coast or overseas. These traveled upriver on small keelboats, laboriously propelled by sturdy boatmen like the legendary Mike Fink, who used oars, poles, towropes, or, whenever they possibly could, sails to move against the current. Travel on such craft was painfully slow. At a rate of ten to twenty miles per day, keelboats took three or four months to venture from New Orleans to Louisville and about three months to reach Pittsburgh from St. Louis.

The advent of the steamboat thoroughly transformed this picture. In 1817 transporting goods from Cincinnati to New York City by keelboat to Pittsburgh, and then via wagon through Philadelphia required at least 50 days. By the 1850s freight sent from Cincinnati to New York via steamboat to New Orleans took only 28 days. If directed by way of the Ohio and Erie canals, interconnected by steamboats plying Lake Erie and the Hudson River, the same shipment arrived in just 18 days.

Greater speed, coupled with the steamboat's larger carrying capacity, dramatically lowered shipping costs. Between 1820 and 1860, steamboats cut the expense of transporting goods downstream by 75 percent, while the reduction of upriver rates was even greater, a stunning 90 percent or more. The obvious superiority of the steamboat made it the dominant form of commercial transportation in the West between the War of 1812 and the Civil War.

The spread of commercially viable railroads after 1827, however, put steamboat companies on the defensive by the mid-1850s and foreshadowed their eventual demise. Despite much greater costs of construction and maintenance, the faster and more reliable railroad possessed advantages that emphasized the deficiencies inherent in steamboat service. Geographically, the range of the steamboat was fixed by the natural extent and distribution of navigable waterways. For the eastern half of the country, well endowed with large rivers and bounded by the Mississippi, the Atlantic Ocean, the Gulf of Mexico, and the Great Lakes, this limitation was not overly constraining. In the more arid trans-Mississippi West, however, it meant that steamboating was confined to a small number of widely scattered waterways. These included large western tributaries of the Mississippi such as the Minnesota, Red, Arkansas, and, most importantly, the Missouri; Puget Sound; the Columbia River and its two great feeders, the Snake and Willamette; and, in California, San Francisco Bay and the Sacramento and San Joaquin rivers.

But even where navigable water was plentiful, other geographic and climatic obstacles to steamboating abounded. In many northern climes, for example, ice impeded or halted navigation for extended periods each winter. Similarly, the onset of low water during the summer typically reduced or eliminated shipping on the upper reaches of navigable streams. Hazardous shoals, sandbars, and rapids also increased the dangers and difficulties of river-borne commerce. Especially feared by river pilots were the snags, planters, and sawyers that often protruded from the beds and banks of streams. Added to the alarming frequency of exploding boilers, these natural obstructions burdened steamboat companies and their clients with high levels of risk and unpredictability.

Even despite these drawbacks, steamboat traffic on America's rivers continued to flourish long past its antebellum golden age. Not surprisingly, steamboats remained prosperous wherever rail service remained unavailable, but

steamboats often thrived in the presence of railroads. Where rail lines terminated at navigable water, steamboats served as vital feeders and adjuncts. And, although they almost always lost out in head-to-head competition for passenger traffic, steamboats towing barges competed successfully with railroads for carrying bulky cargoes like grain, lumber, and coal, which did not require quick delivery.

Consequently, steamboats provided many communities with an important check against railroad monopolies. Because navigable waters constituted public thoroughfares, and because a medium-sized steamboat could be built for as little as $20,000, local merchants and even farmers could launch independent "tramp" vessels or regularly scheduled packet lines to compete with railroads. The ability of boats to challenge railroads was strengthened, moreover, by the improvement of barge-towing techniques after the Civil War, which greatly expanded their capacity to carry cargo.

Their extended vitality meant that steamboats continued to shape the nation's urban landscape. After 1815 steamboat technology had greatly intensified the already powerful tendency of navigable water to attract urban concentrations. Especially in the trans-Appalachian West, old towns boomed, and new ones sprang up at locations made

*Paddle steamers lined up in New Orleans to move the cotton crop, around 1862.*

strategic by the interacting dynamics of river navigation and steamboat engineering. Thus, Cairo, Illinois, flourished at the confluence of the Mississippi and Ohio Rivers, while St. Paul, Minnesota, grew up just below the Falls of St. Anthony, the head of high water navigation on the Mississippi.

Louisville, Kentucky, derived a tremendous commercial advantage from its location at the Falls of the Ohio River, where boats often had to stop and portage their passengers and cargoes around the falls to vessels waiting further up or downstream. Despite the opening of a canal around the falls in 1830, Louisville managed to preserve much of its importance as a storage and forwarding point for the Ohio trade. On the Mississippi, Davenport and Keokuk, Iowa, became prominent as transshipment depots at the upper and lower rapids that segmented the northern half of the river into three distinct zones of navigation.

Finally, St. Louis, the Gateway to the West, earned its nickname by virtue of its commanding position on the Mississippi just south of the mouth of the Missouri, which could be navigated 3,100 miles north and west to Fort Benton in the heart of the Montana Territory. The city's location also enabled St. Louis, which pays homage to the steamboat on its official seal, to serve as the point at which goods moving up and down the Mississippi and its northern tributaries changed transportation if needed. Shallow waters above St. Louis forced the deep-draft boats plying the lower Mississippi to stop and transfer their cargoes to lighter draft upriver vessels. Since the latter could not effectively compete with the larger craft operating below St. Louis, the Gateway City became the recognized division point between downriver and upriver boats.

With a few notable exceptions, steamboat service in America ceased by 1940. The passing of the steamboat did not, however, spell the end of commercial river navigation. Today, many cities such as St. Paul and St. Louis retain their importance as river ports and cater to vigorous barge and tugboat traffic. Propelled by the powerful diesel engines that eventually replaced steam, these modern vessels continue the legacy of their more colorful predecessors on the Mississippi and Ohio system.

—*Michael Magliari*

### References

Hunter, Louis C. "The Invention of the Western Steamboat." *Journal of Economic History* 3 (1943): 201–220.

———. *Steamboats on the Western Rivers: An Economic and Technological History.* Cambridge, MA: Harvard University Press, 1949.

Mahoney, Timothy R. *River Towns in the Great West: The Structure of Provincial Urbanization in the American Midwest, 1820–1870.* New York: Cambridge University Press, 1990.

———. "Urban History in a Regional Context: River Towns on the Upper Mississippi, 1840–1860." *Journal of American History* 72 (1985): 318–339.

Oliver, John W. *History of American Technology.* New York: Ronald Press, 1956.

Taylor, George Rogers. *The Transportation Revolution, 1815–1860.* New York: Rinehart and Company, 1951.

Winther, Oscar O. *The Transportation Frontier: Trans-Mississippi West, 1865–1890.* New York: Holt, Rinehart and Winston, 1964.

## Steffens, Lincoln (1866–1936)

Lincoln Steffens (born Joseph Lincoln Steffens), the journalist and muckraking author of *The Shame of the Cities* (1904), was born in San Francisco but raised in semirural California. His *Autobiography* (1931), the opening section of which is titled "Boy on Horseback," frames his life in an implicit rural-urban dichotomy, for as the boy becomes a man he moves from the country to big European cities—on a "grand tour" of Continental universities—and eventually back to New York and the other metropolises of his own country. Rural America is idyllic, he seems to say; European cities like Berlin, Munich, Paris and London are clean, cultured, and dull, and New York is filthy, corrupt, and exciting.

Steffens reported police and financial news for the *New York Evening Post* from 1892 to 1897 and then became city editor of the *Commercial Advertiser.* In 1901, he joined the staff of *McClure's Magazine* as managing editor and in the next few years built a national reputation, along with Ida M. Tarbell and Ray Stannard Baker, as a muckraker.

*Shame of the Cities,* serialized between 1902 and 1904, reported on Steffens's tour of St. Louis, Minneapolis, Pittsburgh, Chicago, Philadelphia, and New York and made three points about political corruption in American cities: first, businessmen's private needs always take precedence over the public good; second, the guilt for corruption lies less with the grafters and boodlers than with their victims, the citizens who cannot be bothered to rise against them; and third, all cities must pass through a series of stages from "miscellaneous loot with a boss for chief thief" at one end, to "absolutism" at the other. Steffens's essays had the look of close and careful research, as though he were the prototype of the modern investigative journalist, but mostly he just summarized information available in local newspapers.

Steffens's real skill was his ability to create memorable stereotypes of bosses and reformers and make his readers feel like the reporter's companions as he walked the streets of cities or bearded his villains in saloons and boardrooms. Steffens followed *Shame* with *The Struggle for Self Government* (1906), on state corruption (but with cameos of Cincinnati and Cleveland), and *The Upbuilders* (1909), an optimistic account of reformers in Jersey City, San Francisco, and Denver.

By 1914, Steffens's eye was attracted to foreign affairs, as he covered the Mexican and Russian Revolutions and the

Paris Peace Conference of 1919. In the 1920s, he was in semiretirement but increasingly and happily persuaded that the world faced a socialist future. In 1931, he published his best book, *The Autobiography of Lincoln Steffens,* which details, rather creatively, how Steffens got the inside dope on cities. It also contains a 175-page evocation of New York life in the 1890s, including the hilarious story "I Make a Crime Wave," about his attempts to scoop Jacob Riis at a rival newspaper by stealing secret files of daily crime reports at police headquarters.

*—Robert Stinson*

### References

Kaplan, Justin. *Lincoln Steffens: A Biography.* New York: Simon and Schuster, 1974.

Steffens, Lincoln. *The Autobiography of Lincoln Steffens.* New York: Harcourt, Brace, 1931.

Stinson, Robert. *Lincoln Steffens.* New York: Frederick Ungar, 1979.

## Stein, Clarence S. (1882–1975)

Inspired by a Progressive social consciousness, the planner Clarence S. Stein believed that constant mobility in dense yet dispersed, "obsolete," "dangerous," "unworkable" cities full of "ugliness" and devoid of nature mitigated against "moral communities" and led to the "waste of time, money, and energy," anomie, deviance, "dangers to life and health," and all manner of "evils." To counter these negative characteristics and tendencies, Stein used design theory to create a "primary" or holistic sense of place in neighborhoods, which he expected would restore a sense of village life. Inspired by Ebenezer Howard's *Garden Cities of Tomorrow: A Peaceful Path to Real Reform* (1898), he advocated planned "new towns" as an antidote and alternative to contemporary urban places; he visualized the creation of planned communities or "clustered cities" of manageable size, mixed uses, and social diversity within a context of preserved nature called "greenbelts" and interspersed with green common areas.

A central member of the Regional Planning Association of America (RPAA), Stein joined the social critic Lewis Mumford, the architect and planner Henry Wright, the naturalist and planner Benton MacKaye, the economist Stuart Chase, housing advocates Catherine Bauer Wurster and Edith Elmer Wood, and Charles Harris Whitaker, the editor of the *Journal of the American Institute of Architects,* in rehabilitating and reconfiguring Howard's ideas for use in the United States. Meeting and studying together regularly from 1923 to 1933, the group applied the principles they developed to help create the Appalachian Trail, the Civilian Conservation Corps, the Rural Electrification Administration, and the Tennessee Valley Authority. They used Stein's own "Radburn Idea" to decentralize "dinosaur cities" through town and regional planning in the name of "contemporary good living."

An early RPAA experiment was a housing development on Long Island (in the borough of Queens) known as Sunnyside Gardens (1924–1928). With its 1,201 units built on 55 acres, the developers intended to provide low-cost urban housing surrounded by green space. Stein worked actively on Sunnyside and the Phipps Garden Apartments there. Restricted by the city to a grid layout, Sunnyside had blocks that intermingled single-family houses, duplexes, and apartments around central park areas—six acres of commons and three and one-half acres devoted to playgrounds and recreation. Appointed chairman of the New York State Commission on Housing and Regional Planning by Governor Al Smith, Stein affirmed that population dispersal was more economical than city life and more conducive to the growth of a "democratic community."

Backed by private developers, Stein worked with architects and landscape architects to design Radburn, New Jersey (1928–1929), "a town for the motor age," located 16 miles from New York City. The absence of zoning permitted innovation on 2 square miles of farmland near Paterson, New Jersey. The plan called for three "neighborhoods," each intended for 10,000 people, and each with its own shopping center and elementary school. Without being constrained by a preexisting urban grid, "superblocks" of clustered "moderate income," single-family, two-story, detached houses flanked an elongated central green. Six superblocks comprised a neighborhood of about 960 homes. "Collector roads," service ways (alleys), and cul-de-sac access freed residential streets from through traffic, and an internal system of pedestrian paths could be reached from every street.

The innovative "Radburn Idea" stipulated coherent neighborhoods, separation of pedestrians from vehicles, and plentiful park areas—social planning through design to create an ideal place for raising children. The initial plans also included a large commercial town center to serve the entire region as well as industry to create jobs for local residents. However, implementing these plans ran into a snag over attracting industry to provide local jobs. Even if that had been possible, it would have eaten into the surrounding "greenbelt."

Suspended by the Depression, only two of Radburn's neighborhoods were built as the developers went bankrupt after 1935. Housing in Radburn became joined as duplexes and triplexes, and real estate pressures ate into common land; only internal parks were preserved in trust. Stein regretted that Radburn had "to accept the role of a suburb" that housed commuter residents more affluent and homogeneous than the RPAA had hoped, but throughout the 1930s residents praised the "desirable, economical place to live" with amenities "not found in all suburban communities," and they formed active local voluntary organizations.

Stein also served as a consultant to the Henry Buhl, Jr., Foundation of Pittsburgh, Pennsylvania, in choosing a site and making recommendations for developing Chatham Village (1932, expanded 1936). This development contained 197 row houses for rent that were arranged in three pedestrian blocks. The entire complex was located on 16 acres of land and was surrounded on three sides by an additional 29 acres of wooded hills crisscrossed by two miles of paths. According to one commentator, it was "a plan of such brilliance as to be universally accepted even decades later as one of the country's most charming and successful housing projects."

Stein also advised on the development of Baldwin Hills Village (1938–1941), an apartment complex of 627 units on 80 acres of unincorporated land surrounded by Los Angeles. Four architects initiated the project and secured private financing through the Federal Housing Administration and the Reconstruction Finance Corporation. The landscape architect, who had gotten experience working on Radburn, insisted on a large superblock around a central "Village Green" with no through streets. Stucco buildings two stories high contained between three and six units each and were clustered together with a few small "bungalows" to form three neighborhoods. Los Angeles annexed the project to provide public utilities.

Radburn's legacy can be seen in the greenbelt towns built by the New Deal between 1935 and 1938: Greenbelt, Maryland, north of Washington, D.C.; Greenhills, Ohio, near Cincinnati; and Greendale, Wisconsin, near Milwaukee. Rexford G. Tugwell, the director of the Resettlement Administration (later the Farm Security Administration), consulted with Stein about these "greentown" projects, aiming to provide housing for people with moderate incomes. Another design team drew lessons from Radburn when they planned Norris, Tennessee (1933–1934), which was originally meant to provide temporary housing for Tennessee Valley Authority construction workers but became a permanent settlement.

Stein's ideals also influenced Robert E. Simon, Jr.'s design, utopian plan, and early private development of Reston, Virginia (1962); his father had helped finance Radburn. James Rouse also embraced many of Stein's principles and applied them to Columbia, Maryland (1963), another private project designed as a "village" of housing clustered into neighborhoods in a setting of groves, lakes, and permanent open space. Likewise, Stein's legacy of community planning is clearly visible in Fresh Meadows (1948), a development of 175 acres set on a country club in New York City. It is unfortunate that more developers after World War II did not follow Stein's lead in applying "new town" design principles to mitigate against the anomie of the suburban, automobile landscape.

—*Blanche M. G. Linden*

**See also**
Bauer, Catherine; Greenbelt Towns; Mumford, Lewis; Perry, Clarence Arthur; Regional Planning Association of America; Reston, Virginia; Tugwell, Rexford Guy.
**References**
Cautley, Marjorie S. "Planting at Radburn." *Landscape Architecture* 31 (1930): 23–29.
Christensen, Carol A. *The American Garden City and the New Towns Movement.* Ann Arbor, MI: UMI Research Press, 1986.
Newton, Norman T. *Design on the Land: The Development of Landscape Architecture.* Cambridge, MA: Harvard University Press, 1971.

## Stockyards

Stockyards are extensive facilities for the unloading, enclosure, care, sale, and transshipment of livestock. Facilities include pens arranged in a network of numbered alleys, unloading chutes for trucks and railway cars, cattle scales, and one or more auction-sale rings. The term *stockyard* refers to both small locally oriented "country yards" or "auction marts" in agricultural service towns and to large-scale metropolitan yards at strategic points in the railway network known as "public terminal stockyards."

The impetus for stockyards arose with the long-distance shipment of livestock that became possible when railway networks expanded deep into the continental interior in the 1860s. At their inception, many stockyards functioned as transshipment points to feed and water cattle destined for rail shipment further east. But as time progressed, yards that were situated at strategic nodes in the rail grid evolved into terminals and livestock markets as meatpacking facilities were attracted to adjacent sites.

Established in 1865, Chicago's Union Stock Yard was the first large terminal yard to take advantage of a strategic railroad situation and became the model for nearly 100 stockyards in the Midwest and Plains of the United States and Canada. The largest of these public stockyards included Kansas City (1871), St. Louis (1872), Omaha (1884), Fort Worth (1902), and Toronto (1903). The establishment of these and many other stockyards catalyzed investment in large-scale slaughterhouses and the development of a basic livestock and meat industry that served national markets.

Some stockyards (e.g., Omaha) were geared to local slaughter while others (e.g., Oklahoma City) functioned primarily as markets for stocker cattle at the midpoint of the commodity chain. Since many livestock producers did not produce full carload lots, the large public terminal stockyards induced growth in local market facilities such as country livestock dealers and packer buying stations. Thus, the major public terminal stockyards sat atop a hierarchy of western country yards and agricultural service centers in cattle breeding and feeding regions.

During World War I public outcry concerning profiteering and collusion by the "Big Four" meatpackers prompted an investigation by the Federal Trade Commission. In 1921 this led to the Packers and Stockyards Act to curb the packers' oligopoly power. Among its other provisions, the legislation regulated the operation of stockyards as quasi-public utilities, prevented them from dealing in the livestock they handled, prohibited their ownership by meatpackers, and required employees to be registered with the U.S. Department of Agriculture. Thus, public terminal stockyards were closely regulated, which put them at a disadvantage relative to country yards.

The stockyard was significant to many midwestern cities as the nucleus of an agro-industrial complex that propelled rapid urban growth at the turn of the century. There was a close symbiosis between railroads, stockyards, livestock exchanges, slaughter and packing concerns, animal by-products processors, and a host of specialist suppliers. The shared savings accruing from the proximity of vertically linked operations that processed every component of the carcass, the availability of a large semiskilled butcher workforce, and tacit acceptance of noxious environmental externalities was the source of localization economies that made stockyards the heart of the midwestern and Plains agro-industrial complex.

Beginning in the 1940s and accelerating in the 1950s, stockyards began to decline. There were some 100 public terminal stockyards in the United States and Canada in 1940 but this number had dropped to about 15 in 1995. There were four main reasons for the gradual disappearance of stockyards from the metropolitan scene:

1. Metropolitan packing plants began closing in significant numbers in the 1950s as the industry shifted to smaller centers in cattle-feeding regions. The exodus of meatpacking plants from Chicago's Packingtown began in 1954. All of the major plants had closed by 1970, prompting the closure of Chicago's Union Stock Yard in 1971.
2. Packers began to procure their cattle direct from feedlot operators. By 1973 direct farm to packer sales had become the norm, and only 12 percent of U.S. slaughter cattle were purchased at terminal markets. Electronic auctions are replacing the sale ring in the price discovery system for stocker cattle and bulls.
3. Railway transportation of livestock declined in the 1950s and had all but disappeared by the 1970s in favor of highway "cattle liners," which are less efficient on congested inner-city streets. Thus a strategic location in the rail network no longer conferred an advantage on terminal yards.
4. Finally, the noxious sights, smells, and sounds of the stockyard had become an increasing source of friction with downwind residents in metropolitan areas.

The passing of the public stockyard left two issues in its wake. First, the closure of stockyards and associated packing plants released large quantities of industrial land with rail access in the center of midwestern cities. This presented a prime opportunity for inner-city redevelopment. Chicago has a huge industrial park on the former site of its stockyard that awaits investment. Following the closure of the Ontario Stockyards in 1993, Toronto's stockyard district is being redeveloped for large-scale industrial and retail space. Second, a web of small-scale country yards has arisen to replace terminal public stockyards. These have helped to reinforce the agricultural service functions and economic base of smaller cities and towns across the Midwest and Plains.

—Ian MacLachlan

**See also**
Armour, Philip Danforth; Hammond, George Henry; Swift, Gustavus Franklin; Union Stock Yard.
**References**
Ives, J. Russell. *The Livestock and Meat Economy of the United States.* Washington, DC: American Meat Institute, 1966.
McDonald, D. R. *The Stockyard Story.* Toronto, Ontario: NC Press Limited, 1985.
Pate, J'Nell L. *Livestock Legacy: The Fort Worth Stockyards 1887–1987.* College Station: Texas A & M University Press. 1988.
Skaggs, Jimmy M. *Prime Cut: Livestock Raising and Meatpacking in the United States, 1607–1983.* College Station: Texas A & M University Press, 1986.
Williams, Willard F., and Thomas T. Stout. *Economics of the Livestock Meat Industry.* New York: Macmillan, 1964.

## Street Lighting

Street lighting is simultaneously one of the most taken-for-granted and one of the most visible urban utilities. People just assume that cities (of any size) will be well lit artificially; to many, "bright lights" are one of the most vivid images of the "big city." A closer look reveals that these assumptions and the path to modern street lighting were paved with a series of conscious choices about whether street lighting would exist, what its purpose was, and how it would be provided.

For much of the history of cities, questions about street lighting went unasked. Outdoor activity generally ceased after dusk; reasons ranged from simple fear of darkness and what it might harbor, to religious injunctions against tampering with the "natural" cycle of day and night, to ingrained habits of work and play. Traditional guild strictures against lengthening the workday tended to reinforce the sharp decline in nighttime activity. Travelers who did wish to go abroad at night often carried a source of light with them, whether a simple torch, a "link" (a wax-coated brand), or a lantern. Moonlight was also a source of light; on into the twentieth century many cities reduced public street lighting during moonlit periods, presumably as a cost-saving measure.

By the eighteenth century, however, demand for better lighting had become widespread. The reasons generally fall into three categories: utility, security, and urbanity. All were pinned to the growing pace of economic activity in cities, to the new diversity of the population, to the struggle to maintain public order, and to the increasing use of nighttime for leisure or shopping. "Utility" simply refers to the need of the growing pedestrian and wheeled traffic for a visible path through muddy, obstructed streets. In the twentieth century, the rise in automobile traffic provided an additional reason for lighting; studies have shown a marked decrease in automobile-related fatalities if there is public lighting.

"Security" reasons for lighting are clearly shown in Ralph Waldo Emerson's oft-quoted dictum that "a good lamp is the best police." From the time when night watchmen were responsible for lighting lamps at night to the desires of modern policemen and citizens to illuminate high-crime areas intensively, the strong feeling has existed that better lighting means less crime. (Some argued in the nineteenth century that better lighting only afforded criminals a clearer field of play, and some recent studies sponsored by the U.S. Justice Department began to question the generally unexamined relationship between lighting and crime.) As an "urbane" lifestyle began to flourish in the nineteenth century, lights also began to acquire a role as elements of public architecture, especially in high-income districts, at public assembly points, and in downtown areas that were especially conscious of their design image. It should be noted that these three reasons sometimes conflict; for example, should parkways that carry automobile traffic through well-designed spaces, like Lake Shore Drive in Chicago, be lighted for utility or for ornament? Until the 1990s, the trend has been to favor automobiles, though more attention is now being paid to architectural alternatives.

How, then, should the streets be lighted? In 1751 Benjamin Franklin proposed and organized the first scheme for public lighting in the United States in Philadelphia, where the municipality provided lanterns. As the demand for light burgeoned, technology advanced, and various methods of finance and organization developed. It is characteristic of street lighting in the nineteenth and twentieth centuries that new inventions and techniques have been widely and rapidly adopted by cities across the nation. Lighting with coal gas rapidly replaced oil lamps after the first system was established in Baltimore in 1821. Cities strapped for cash normally preferred long-term franchise arrangements with private companies who built and operated the utilities, but by the start of the

twentieth century many cities turned to full municipal ownership. Kerosene lamps were popular briefly in the middle of the nineteenth century until advances in electric street lighting began to appear, first with Charles Brush's arc lighting of the Cleveland Public Square in 1878 and later with Thomas Edison's incandescent lighting system in the financial district of New York in 1882. Gas lighting was rejuvenated following the American patent of the Welsbach incandescent mantle in 1890, and these three forms—arc electric, incandescent electric, and incandescent gas—dominated until the 1930s. After 1907, improved tungsten filament, incandescent electric "Mazda" lamps were preferred for "urbane" situations, a preference that coincided with the integration of lighting systems into City Beautiful design schemes.

In the 1930s, a number of gas vapor lamps came on the market that were widely adopted after World War II. At roughly the same time, pole designs were changed to a "cobra head" type in which lamps were hung over traffic lanes from a transverse arm. Some situations, such as freeway interchanges, call for a collar of lamps to be suspended from tall poles, a system also tried in some arc lighting systems during the nineteenth century. Gas lamps are now generally found in consciously "historical" districts, while incandescent and arc lamps have been replaced by gas vapor lamps. Today, the most widely used lamps are mercury vapor, metal halide, fluorescent, and high-pressure sodium vapor. Controversy has accompanied introduction of the latter; while it offers the most lumens per watt of any lamp type, concerns have been raised on aesthetic grounds about its harsh yellowish light, and by astronomers who claim that "light pollution" from places such as San Diego, Los Angeles, and Tucson diminishes the view from nearby observatories.

—*Mark J. Bouman*

### References

Bouman, Mark J. " 'The Best Lighted City in the World': The Construction of a Nocturnal Landscape in Chicago." In John Zukowsky, ed., *Chicago Architecture and Design, 1923–1993: Reconfiguration of an American Metropolis*, 32–51. Munich, Germany: Prestel, 1993.

———. "The 'Good Lamp Is the Best Police' Metaphor and Ideologies of the Nineteenth Century Urban Landscape." *American Studies* 32 (1991): 63–78.

———. "Luxury and Control: The Urbanity of Street Lighting in Three Nineteenth Century Cities." *Journal of Urban History* 14 (1987): 7–37.

Schivelbusch, Wolfgang. *Disenchanted Night: The Industrialization of Light in the Nineteenth Century*. Berkeley: University of California Press, 1988.

## Streetcar Suburbs

Before 1815, the American city was a "walking city" in which most people lived and worked within two miles of the city center. The well-to-do were less inclined to walk even that far, so their residences tended to be closest to the center while the poor and the working class lived on the outskirts of town.

After 1815, however, changes in transportation technology gave people a way to live at slightly greater distances from the center but still be able to get back and forth. Between 1815 and 1880, some combination of steam ferry, omnibus, commuter railroad, horsecar, elevated rail, and cable car was introduced in virtually every major city in the United States.

These transportation improvements allowed people to move away from the city center to suburban developments spreading beyond the two-mile radius of the old walking city. First the wealthy and then the middle class, enticed by real estate developments along the routes of the new transportation carriers, left the congested, crowded city behind for the more genteel lifestyle of the suburbs.

Suburbanization was fueled by a combination of technological, cultural, social, and economic factors. The new transport technologies—particularly the horsecar and then the electric streetcar—provided the means, but not necessarily the motivation, for suburbanization. Technological revolution was not limited exclusively to transportation; advances in other urban services—street lighting, water supply, sewerage, and paved roads—were also essential for suburbanization to occur.

Cultural forces were important in providing the impetus for suburbanization; two that particularly shaped the pursuit of the American dream were the ideal of autonomy and the desire for homogeneity. The ideal of autonomy meant a single-family detached home with a lawn providing a boundary between private hearth and public street. This ideal could be realized only on the spacious lots of the suburban subdivisions. The desire for homogeneity expressed itself as a resistance among Americans to living in the same neighborhood with people of lower incomes or different ethnic backgrounds. Established American families of Northern European descent were inclined to put a geographical distance between themselves and new immigrants from Southern and Eastern Europe. These forces, along with rising incomes and the fear of epidemic diseases, promoted suburbanization during the nineteenth century.

It was, however, streetcars that made widespread suburbanization possible. The first horse-drawn streetcar, or horsecar, followed a route between Prince and 14th Streets in lower Manhattan in 1832. Horsecars did not become widespread until the middle of the century, however, with the advent of grooved rails lying flush with the pavement. This arrangement allowed horsecars, carriages, wagons, and pedestrians to share streets.

Rails also allowed for a relatively smooth ride and speeds of up to eight miles per hour. By 1870, a city well blanketed with horsecar lines—such as New York, Philadelphia, Chicago,

or Boston—now had a radius of about seven miles. The physical arrangement of the walking city was now reversed, with the well-to-do living away from the city center in suburbs, and the working class and immigrants living closest to the heart of the city. Smaller, younger cities such as Portland or Seattle still had the characteristics of advanced walking cities, with steam ferries providing interurban transportation.

By the end of the 1870s, most cities had a horsecar transit system consisting of several competing transit companies who provided linked crosstown service from one suburb to another. This geographical breadth allowed for a decentralization of activities and a gradually developing segregation of land use, with the city center increasingly devoted to business, commerce, and other economic activities.

The new urban form became even more clearly defined as a result of the next technological breakthrough in transportation—the electrification of street railways. The first major electrical streetcar system was placed in operation in Richmond, Virginia, in 1888 by Franklin J. Sprague. His technological innovations allowed urban transportation to operate as a true system, with scores of electric cars operating along miles and miles of track.

By 1903, 98 percent of America's 30,000 miles of street railway had been electrified. Each mile of extension allowed a larger percentage of the population to live in suburbs. Streetcar suburbs defined the transition from the urban to the rural, as automobile suburbs would do in the decades to follow.

—*Martha J. Bianco*

**See also**
Streetcars.

**References**
Foster, Mark S. *From Streetcar to Superhighway: American City Planners and Urban Transportation, 1900–1940*. Philadelphia: Temple University Press, 1981.
Jackson, Kenneth T. *Crabgrass Frontier: The Suburbanization of the United States*. New York: Oxford University Press, 1985.
Muller, Peter O. "Transportation and Urban Form: Stages in the Spatial Evolution of the American Metropolis." In Susan Hanson, ed., *The Geography of Urban Transportation*, 24–48. New York: Guilford Press, 1986.
Schaeffer, K. H., and Elliott Sclar. *Access for All: Transportation and Urban Growth*. Baltimore: Penguin Books, 1975.
Stilgoe, John R. *Borderland: Origins of the American Suburb, 1820–1939*. New Haven, CT: Yale University Press, 1988.
Warner, Sam Bass, Jr. *Streetcar Suburbs: The Process of Growth in Boston 1870–1900*. Cambridge, MA: Harvard University Press, 1962.

## Streetcars

For most of the first half of the twentieth century, the electric streetcar (often called the trolley) was the dominant mode of transportation in urban America. By the 1870s, the shortcomings of the horsecar were universally recognized, and a purely mechanical system in the form of the cable car had proved itself seriously flawed by the late 1880s. Various inventors had tried to develop electric locomotion from the 1830s, and two of them, Leo Daft and Charles J. Vandepoele, had received contracts for installations throughout the United States and Canada. Vandepoele's installation at Montgomery, Alabama, in April 1886 was the first citywide electric railway system in the United States, but none of these installations had proved superior to the cable car; Daft's technology, in particular, was highly unreliable.

What became the standard technology of the electric streetcar was developed by Frank J. Sprague, a young graduate of the U.S. Naval Academy, in installations in St. Joseph, Missouri, in September 1887 and Richmond, Virginia, in February 1888. Sprague developed a means of spring-mounting motors on trucks that insulated them against the shocks of irregular track, and he adopted a system of direct current electrification—eventually almost always at 600 volts—that was ideal for vehicles that started and stopped continually.

Early installations suffered from imperfect means of admitting electric power to the motors, but by 1892 the controller had been developed for this purpose. The controller was a device for regulating speed by varying the resistance and shifting the motors between series and parallel. On the typical 600-volt car with four motors, motors one and four (numbered from the front) were permanently wired in parallel, and motors two and three were rigged in the same fashion. As the operator faced the controller, he could set the handle at a succession of points. At the first four or five, resistances were cut until the two pairs of motors operated in series at the full 600 volts. The next point put the two pairs of motors in parallel, but reintroduced resistances. At the remaining points, the resistances were cut out until the motors operated in parallel to produce the highest speed possible for the car. Largely because of this device, Sprague's system was demonstrably superior to its rivals, and by 1893, in spite of the depression of the 1890s, it rapidly swept through the industry.

The onset of the great Edwardian prosperity in 1899 marked the beginning of a decade of massive investment in transportation facilities of all kinds, including street railways. The industry, which had initially operated mainly with single-truck equipment, converted in this period to heavy, double-truck wooden cars, built to the order of individual companies on the presumption (probably incorrect) that conditions were different everywhere. Brill of Philadelphia, Pullman of Chicago, the St. Louis Car Company, the American Car Company (also of St. Louis), the Cincinnati Car Company, and several smaller firms specialized in producing equipment for the industry. The cars were either single-ended or double-ended. Single-ended cars were cheaper to build and could be de-

signed with higher passenger capacity, but they required more land for terminals. Some cities—notably Philadelphia, Detroit, and Cleveland—became identified with single-ended equipment, but most companies opted for double-ended cars.

In densely populated portions of New England, street railways spread into suburban and rural areas. The electric streetcar contributed greatly to the proliferation of suburbs outside Boston, and the street railways of the Connecticut Company, which operated in virtually every major city in that state, were connected by rural trolley lines. In the Midwest, the intercity electric railways became the more substantial interurbans.

From the outset, there were strong economies of scale in electric street railways. These increased after 1907 when the industry's system of electric power distribution improved. Thereafter, the standard method was generating three-phase alternating current at a central powerhouse, with transmission to a series of substations about the city for conversion with motor-generator sets to direct current to feed into the overhead wire. Cincinnati required a dual overhead, but other cities were satisfied with positive in the wire and negative in the rails. Portable substations could be moved about the system to boost the direct current output when there was temporary heavy demand in a specific area—as when the circus came to play on the edge of the city, for example.

The optimal economic organization for such a system was a citywide monopoly. Kansas City, the metropolitan area that had converted most fully to the cable car, had 11 cable powerhouses serving six operators, including one line that never worked properly. The introduction of the electric streetcar quickly brought about consolidation of the system into the Metropolitan Street Railway with a single electric powerhouse. The monopolization of street railway systems coincided with introduction of electric power systems and telephone networks, both of which shared the same characteristic of technological monopoly. All three became regulated industries with monopoly rights established by franchise and discriminatory fare structures, which is to say with prices set on the basis of relative elasticities of demand.

In the instance of street railways, the fare remained 5 cents, as it had been on horsecars and cable cars. The technological improvement manifested itself not in falling fares, but rather in fares becoming citywide, as distinct from being restricted to a single line. That is, in return for receiving a citywide monopoly, the street railway obligated itself to issue transfers whereby the passenger could make trips of any length for a nickel. In Chicago, which became a quintessential streetcar city, one could travel 37 miles for 5 cents. The flat nickel fare was, in fact, a discriminatory pricing structure, selling the service to long-distance passengers at a lower fare per mile than to short-distance passengers. This was a rational form of discrimination, for passengers who jumped on streetcars for short distances were presumed of higher value of time than longer-distance passengers, and thus of higher income or wealth.

The electric streetcar had an unprecedented effect on urban patterns because it traveled substantially faster than the horsecar. Partly for this reason, but also because the nickel fare subsidized longer-distance passengers, the distance between home and work greatly increased. Adversely, the electric car was very loud, and its overhead wires were considered unsightly. The streets along which it ran became unattractive for residences and were typically zoned commercial. Apartments above the shops along these streets were usually cheap, frequently inhabited by broken families.

An urban pattern emerged in which ordinary retailing—groceries, cheaper clothing, inexpensive restaurants, hardware, and the like—was carried out along streetcar lines in what came to be known as strip shopping streets; more specialized retailing, along with central office employment, a financial community, and a restaurant and entertainment complex, was provided in a central business district. Municipal governments typically liked this arrangement because central business districts provided a major source of tax revenues, and the street railways paid taxes, either explicitly or implicitly, by maintaining streets, providing street lighting, and transporting police and fire personnel without charge. The industry prospered in this economic organization, and by 1906 it was handling over 90 percent of urban trips. Steel equipment was introduced, mainly after 1912. The number of passengers moved on street railways rose from about 2 billion in 1890 to more than 11.3 billion in 1917.

The economic organization of the industry carried an incentive for its own destruction, however. Because the monopoly gain in the industry was generated by people who traveled under 2.5 miles, and subsidized longer-distance passengers, operators had an incentive to be what was called a "cream-skimmer," a company that could perform the service in which gains were earned without providing losing services. The cream-skimmer first appeared in Los Angeles in mid-1914 in the form of the jitney, a Ford Model T automobile used as a common carrier by an owner-operator. The idea spread rapidly across the country, menacing street railways in every major city except Cleveland, which had an uneconomic 3-cent fare with which the jitney could not compete, and Denver, which required a franchise for operation. Jitneys provided a competitive market in urban transportation, operating demand-responsively without fixed routes. They drove street railways out of business in Bay City, Michigan; Newburgh, New York; and Everett, Washington, but elsewhere they were suppressed to protect the established pattern of the industry. Although some jitneys survived into the 1920s, most had been done in by franchise and insurance requirements by the end of 1916. Had they been allowed to survive, they would probably have been able to destroy most of the other street railways by the mid-1920s.

The street railway industry considered eliminating jitneys as simply dealing with an aberration in urban transport. Actually, putting down the jitneys had two major consequences, neither of which was foreseen. First, society turned to the automobile as a private carrier, not as a common carrier. Second, as costs in the transit industry moved in favor of the bus relative to the streetcar, the conversion of transit systems was made within the economic organization of the street railways: a city- or area-wide monopoly, a flat fare regardless of distance, a vehicle with a capacity of about 40 passengers operating on a fixed route with a published schedule, and a unionized operator. The industry continued to provide service, mainly at the overall speed of eight to ten miles per hour. The service was so time-consuming that virtually everyone had an incentive to turn away from it, but because the automobile could be used only as a private carrier, the result was an excessive number of automobiles with a low rate of occupancy.

The industry's long-run problems were not immediately apparent because of the temporary problems of World War I. Street railways were caught between a rigid 5-cent fare—which was frequently written into their franchise—and costs of labor and materials that nearly doubled during the war. The rate of return for the industry sank to 90 percent in 1918. By May 31, 1919, 62 companies were bankrupt, including the operators in New York, St. Louis, and Pittsburgh, and 60 others had left the industry. Thereafter, the industry's situation improved, partly because restraints on fare increases were dropped in most cities and partly because of technological improvements. In 1916, Charles O. Birney, the engineer in charge of car design for the Stone & Webster utility syndicate, developed a lightweight, four-wheel, one-man streetcar that he called the Safety Car, but which has always been known simply as the Birney Car. Although Birney intended the car for more frequent service on major lines, it had its principal use on light-density lines of major systems and on systems in medium-sized communities. Birney developed a double-truck version of his car for medium-density routes. The Cincinnati Car Company developed both single- and double-truck versions of a rival lightweight car. J. G. Brill brought out a more substantial standard double-truck car, the Master Unit, in the 1920s.

The American urban transit industry peaked in ridership in 1926 with 17.2 billion passengers, 12.9 billion of whom were still on streetcars. About 2.4 billion were on rapid transit, some 80 percent of them on New York's subway and elevated lines. Thus, by the mid-1920s, the bus, as it had been organized following the jitney episode, had made limited progress in the industry.

This situation changed rapidly after the onslaught of the Depression. This period saw the first complete conversion from streetcars to buses in a major city, San Antonio, in 1933. By 1940, the bus carried 4.2 billion passengers and the streetcar 5.9 billion. World War II generated a great revival in urban public transport, but the trend in favor of the bus continued, and the bus passed the streetcar in total passengers in 1944. The combination of diesel engines, rear-mounting of engines, and automatic transmissions, beginning in the late 1930s, amounted to a major technological advance in buses.

The bus would probably have been able to annihilate the streetcar, except in special situations, by the mid-1940s, except for the war and a technological innovation of the Depression years. In 1929, Thomas Conway, a Philadelphia financier and the head of two electric railways, initiated a joint effort to design a new streetcar. Conway and Charles Gordon, editor of the *Electric Railway Journal,* believed that the standard method of ordering cars from builders to individual specifications of operating companies had stultified design. The builders simply chose from available components to assemble something that, except for its steel construction, represented essentially the state of the engineering knowledge of the Edwardian period. The typical car was about 20 years old, and most of the first generation of double-truck wooden cars still remained in service. A few operators had attempted to install innovative equipment, but in the main the industry remained technologically stagnant. A meeting in 1929 authorized Conway to convene a conference at which a committee was appointed to design a new car. In an effort to go outside the narrow fraternity of car builders and transit operators, the committee chose Clarence F. Hirshfeld, director of research for the Detroit Edison Company, as head of the design team. The intention was explicitly to draw on the current state of knowledge of electrical engineering generally, as distinct from the conventional wisdom of car building. The design had many novel elements of which two were preeminent. First, the car would be controlled by a rheostatic accelerator of 99 points, actuated by a pedal used by a seated operator. Second, the design entailed regenerative magnetic track brakes, coupled with other electric, manual, and, in some installations, air brakes. This combination gave the car better acceleration and deceleration than conventional streetcars. As a consequence, when new cars were introduced on a line, all of the remaining conventional equipment had to be phased out, otherwise the new cars would catch up with any conventional cars on the line and thus fail to realize their advantage in speed. The car was about the size of the single-ended cars long associated with Detroit and Cleveland; thus, it was suitable only for long routes of high traffic density.

The vehicle—the President's Conference Committee Car or, more familiarly, the PCC—emerged for its first commercial installation in Brooklyn in 1936. It succeeded instantaneously, quickly becoming almost universal for new equipment. Washington, Pittsburgh, and several other major cities converted almost completely to the PCC. Cities as small as Johnstown, Pennsylvania, adopted them. The last models were delivered as late as 1952.

Immediately after World War II, dominant opinion in the American transit industry was that PCC units were suitable for major routes, most of which radiated from central business districts; trolley buses were appropriate for intermediate traffic densities, especially on lines with major grades; and buses were preferable for lighter-density lines. Costs rapidly moved in favor of the bus, however. The bus had various advantages relative to a streetcar of any sort. It could fan out into newly populated areas of low population density. It could avoid obstructions on the street. It was not limited to a fixed order of vehicles; notably, it could return empty to the central business district to take a second trip out in the evening rush hour in situations that the streetcar could not. It had no heavy fixed investment in rails and electrical distribution systems. The growing practice of spreading salt on streets to melt snow was very destructive to rails, and even more so to the conduit of lines that used underground pickup. Following municipalization of its system in 1947, Chicago estimated that conversion to buses would save some 48 cents per vehicle mile. The Chicago Transit Authority set about converting the entire system to buses, mainly with Twin Coach equipment. Trucks, electrical equipment, and interior fittings from the fleet of 683 PCC cars were reused for rapid transit equipment. Completion of Chicago's conversion in 1958 provides an approximate date for the end of the streetcar as a general carrier in America. The system in Milwaukee, which never adopted PCC cars, ended its conversion that same year. A few lasted longer; Los Angeles did not go out until 1963.

Streetcar lines that survived did so as special cases. The principal reason was ventilation problems in tunnels. Other lines survived because of narrow streets, and the St. Charles line in New Orleans continues partly because it uses a long private right-of-way and partly because it has become a major tourist attraction. As the only remaining line with pre-PCC equipment, it serves as a museum piece of traditional electric streetcar operation, parallel to the cable car system in San Francisco.

The economic organization characteristic of the industry, an area-wide monopoly, was unchanged through the conversion in technology. Such systems became successively more unprofitable after World War II, and all major systems were converted to municipal ownership. Even this proved inadequate to enable them to survive, and area-wide transit systems, in which suburbs subsidized cities, replaced them in the largest metropolitan areas. A large number of small cities simply lost all public transportation.

The streetcar has had a mild revival from purely political calculations in the form of the limited tram line. The Urban Mass Transportation Assistance Program, inaugurated in 1961, was based on the assumption that the transit industry was starved for capital. It sought to revive the industry by making it more capital-intensive, partly by accelerating the replacement of buses and partly by substituting rail transport for bus lines. The program accelerated the conversion of transit systems to public ownership, especially in smaller cities. Heavy rail rapid transit proved extremely expensive and limited in its benefits. As an intermediate, public policy hit upon light rail, essentially streetcar lines on a mixture of city streets in central areas and private right-of-way elsewhere.

The movement began with a line on existing railroad tracks from central San Diego to the Mexican border in 1981. Although the San Diego metropolitan area is extremely automobile dependent, the border crossing impedes automobile use, and the line's performance was favorable. The movement spread to Buffalo in 1984, Portland, Oregon, in 1986, and to Sacramento and San Jose in 1987. More than 20 other cities developed plans for similar systems. Typically, the lines are equipped with relatively heavy articulated units fitted for multiple-unit operation. Surviving streetcar lines in San Francisco and Pittsburgh have been refitted with such equipment, and these units have replaced the PCC as the standard urban rail vehicle. Because the lines, like rail transit systems generally, are highly oriented toward central business districts, which are declining, the light rail lines are likely to have only a minor impact on metropolitan regions. As long as federal funds are available to make urban transit more capital-intensive, such lines are likely to proliferate, however.

—*George W. Hilton*

**See also**
Buses; Cable Cars; Elevated Railways; Horsecars; Interurban Transit; Omnibuses; Sprague, Franklin Julian; Subways.
**References**
Carlson, Stephen P., and Fred W. Schneider, III. *PCC: The Car That Fought Back.* Glendale, CA: Interurban Press, 1980.
Eckert, Ross D., and George W. Hilton. "The Jitneys." *Journal of Law & Economics* 15 (1972): 293–325.
Hilton, George W. *Federal Transit Subsidies: The Urban Mass Transportation Assistance Program.* Washington, DC: American Enterprise Institute, 1974.
———. "The Rise and Fall of Monopolized Transit." In Charles A. Lave, ed., *Urban Transit: The Private Challenge to Public Trans-*

*portation.* San Francisco: Pacific Institute for Public Policy Research, 1985.
Middleton, William D. *The Time of the Trolley.* Milwaukee, WI: Kalmbach, 1967.
Miller, John Anderson. *Fares Please! A Popular History of Trolleys, Horse-Cars, Street-Cars, Buses, Elevateds, and Subways.* Reprint ed. New York: Dover, 1960.
Rowsome, Frank, Jr. *Trolley Car Treasury.* New York: McGraw-Hill, 1956.

## Strong, Josiah (1847–1916)

Josiah Strong, an influential Congregational leader, was born in Naperville, Illinois, and graduated from Western Reserve College in 1869. He then attended Lane Theological Seminary before being ordained a minister in 1871. He was called to several pulpits before he wrote *Our Country* in 1885, a manual for the Congregational Missionary Society of Cincinnati. This popular book proposed revolutionary ideas by applying statistical data to try resolving the social and economic problems of urban industrial America.

After he moved to New York City in 1886, Strong wrote *The New Era* (1893), which affirmed a philosophy called Christian Socialism and made Strong a leader of the expanding social gospel movement. Although a proponent of imperialism who preached that civilized nations should Christianize inferior peoples, Strong inspired reformers of all sorts.

*The New Era* was translated into many languages and launched Strong's career on the lecture circuit. He became secretary of the American Evangelical Alliance, which hoped to unite churches as a national reply to social responsibility. When orthodox clergy resisted this call, Strong resigned and founded the League for Social Service in 1898, renamed the American Institute for Social Service in 1902. Under its aegis, Strong lectured, wrote pamphlets and books, traveled to Britain and South America, and launched the Safety First campaign to prevent industrial accidents. He also established the Institute for Social Service in Britain, and he promoted the Federal Council of Churches of Christ, later to become the National Council of Churches of Christ in the United States.

Among his many influential books were *Religious Movements for Social Betterment* (1900) and the yearbook, *Social Progress,* which he edited between 1904 and 1906. Strong died in New York City in 1916 at the end of the social gospel era he had personified.

—*Peter C. Holloran*

**References**
Hopkins, Charles H. *The Rise of the Social Gospel in American Protestantism, 1865–1915.* New Haven, CT: Yale University Press, 1940.
White, Ronald C., Jr., and C. Howard Hopkins. *The Social Gospel: Religion and Reform in Changing America.* Philadelphia: Temple University Press, 1976.

# Subdivision

Subdivision is the process of transforming the use, ownership, and monetary value of a large tract of land through division into smaller building lots for sale and development. It is also the term used to designate a parcel of land that has been divided for these purposes. Even though undeveloped, rural and agricultural acreage can be subdivided for industrial, commercial, and residential uses, but typically it is the latter that is most often called a subdivision.

Along with annexation, subdivision has been one of the principal ways for towns and cities to expand. Whether removed from city limits, or at the urban fringe, creating elite suburbs by subdivision has produced incremental growth. Although residential subdivisions may extend a preexisting urban grid, one or more devices have been used frequently since the late nineteenth century to define subdivisions visually and spatially as separate neighborhoods, including lot size, street pattern, signage, street furniture, green spaces and plantings, and house size and design. Before the U.S. Supreme Court declared them unconstitutional, deed restrictions often mandated these regulations in middle- and upper-middle-class subdivisions; they also were used to exclude minority home buyers. In the twentieth century, it has become more common for single-family houses to be built on speculation by large-scale developers of subdivisions.

Historically, landowners, real estate speculators, and developers have been the principal subdividers, relying upon their personal judgment of a city and local market forces to determine the direction and extent of its growth. Without the guidance of comprehensive plans or controls, subdividers in the nineteenth and early twentieth centuries achieved some coordination of their efforts by taking their cue from, and then influencing, the network of existing transportation and utility lines. Extension of the urban infrastructure and subdivision development often proceeded in tandem. Although not all subdivisions in this period consciously and deliberately improved the infrastructure, these improvements had become standard by the period's end.

At the same time, the lure of profits in real estate speculation produced periodic waves of excess subdivision and transformed productive agricultural acreage or natural woodlands into vacant areas of unneeded building lots. A mania for speculative subdivision gripped the nation in the early 1920s, typified by the dramatic, runaway speculation in Florida that peaked in 1926. The financial turmoil and physical blight stemming from premature subdivision stimulated discussion of controls and led to formulation of the Standard City Planning Enabling Act in 1928 under the auspices of the Department of Commerce.

This initiative, produced through collaboration of the Home Builders' and Subdividers' Division (later the independent National Association of Home Builders) of the National Association of Real Estate Boards (later the National Association of Realtors) and the American City Planning Institute (later the American Institute of Planners), codified informal subdivision practices that leaders of the real estate and planning professions had pioneered. It sought to regularize them within the framework of municipal and regional master plans. It encouraged planning agencies to review subdivision proposals on the basis of continuity with existing street plans, the size of building lots, and the provision of infrastructure improvements, parks, and recreation spaces. Local subdivision and zoning regulations have continued to build upon and refine these features.

The first systematic discussions of subdivision practices took place among a group of real estate developers in the early twentieth century. They characterized their activities as community building and tried to forge a new identity for realtors as planning and development professionals. In the 1910s and 1920s these exchanges were joined by studies of subdivision practices conducted by planners and economists who were concerned with the destabilization caused by excess subdivision and the inefficiency and cost of poorly designed or unimproved subdivisions.

In the years after World War II, discussions of subdivisions were displaced by socioeconomic analyses of suburban homogenization, the impact of zoning, the fragmentation of metropolitan government, and critiques of suburban sprawl. The greatest expansion of subdivision development, characterized by the total transformation of previously agricultural land to fully improved lots for single-family houses and landscaping, took place during these years and incorporated interwar experiences. The three Levittowns (built from the 1940s to the 1960s in New York, Pennsylvania, and New Jersey) became emblematic of this period.

Since the 1970s, detailed historical studies of local subdivision practices have enriched the contemporary picture of city-building processes. These typically consider the interrelationships among real estate speculators, subdividers, local governments, transportation systems, utility companies, housing designers, and consumers, and analyze the ways that their private decisions shaped urban spatial and social structures. From these, a more complex understanding of the historical and cultural construction of land use patterns is emerging.

—*Carolyn Loeb*

**See also**
Land Developers and Development; Levittown.
**References**
Burgess, Patricia. *Planning for the Private Interest: Land Use Controls and Residential Patterns in Columbus, Ohio, 1900–1970.* Columbus: Ohio State University Press, 1994.

Fisher, Ernest M. *Real Estate Subdividing Activity and Population Growth in Nine Urban Areas.* Ann Arbor: Michigan Business Studies, 1928.

Keating, Ann Durkin. *Building Chicago: Suburban Developers and the Creation of a Divided Metropolis.* Columbus: Ohio State University Press, 1988.

Monchow, Helen Corbin. *Seventy Years of Real Estate Subdividing in the Region of Chicago.* Evanston, IL: Northwestern University Press, 1939.

Nichols, Jesse Clyde. *Real Estate Subdivisions.* Washington, DC: American Civic Association, 1912.

Shuler, Irenaeus. "Subdivisions." In Blake Snyder, ed., *Real Estate Handbook.* New York: McGraw-Hill, 1925.

Weiss, Marc A. *The Rise of the Community Builders: The American Real Estate Industry and Urban Land Planning.* New York: Columbia University Press, 1987.

## Suburban Crime

Crime seems to be an inevitable part of civilization; hardly an inhabited place on earth has not been touched by crime. Even suburban "havens" have been affected by this traditional scourge of urban areas, spurred by the rapid influx of people into suburbs. Violent crime, traffic problems, deteriorating living conditions, aging housing, concentrations of poor people, and other characteristics of cities drive more residents and business establishments out of central cities to the open spaces of "satellite cities" in suburbia.

Suburbanization has increased since the late 1940s, and it accelerated through the 1950s and 1960s. As more highways linked central cities and suburbs, virgin land was developed and new homes were built. The increased number of people and the greater amount of wealth in suburbs, their relatively easy accessibility, the fairly poor protection of suburban homes, and the scarcity of police protection encourage criminals to extend their activities to suburban areas. The U.S. Bureau of the Census defines a suburban area as "a county or group of counties containing a central city, plus any contiguous counties that are linked socially and economically to the center city." Thus, the suburbs are distinct entities that cities encompass; at the same time, however, they remain separate and autonomous from those cities.

Because of this unique, almost paradoxical condition and the suburban physical environment, the types of crimes committed in suburbs differ from those in central cities. The main type of crime occurring in suburbs involves property rather than acts of personal violence, which occur more frequently in cities. Unfortunately for law enforcement agencies, the traditional ways of combating and counteracting crime in inner cities are rarely appropriate in suburbs and may be ineffective in a suburban setting.

Under these circumstances, suburban crime has become a new subject of interest. In fact, suburban crime has interested researchers from a wide spectrum of fields: economics, geography, demography, regional science and planning, and political science, as well as criminology. The geographical aspect of suburban crime is not the only salient point, however. The ecological approach was pioneered by Shaw and McKay (1942), who divided Chicago into equal statistical regions and discovered that there is a gradient of crime as one moves farther from the central city. They found that this gradient has not changed over time even when the socioeconomic conditions of the population have changed. This suggests that central cities export crime to outlying neighborhoods. Thus, the ecological approach asserts that crime and the place of its occurrence are interrelated.

Observing suburban crime also reveals that crime spills over city boundaries. For instance, crime in close proximity to a city's boundaries is high and diminishes as distance increases. However, crime diminishes less rapidly along major arterial roads than along secondary roads, which are less likely to be used by criminals. Also, the probability of property crime occurring is greater at accessible homes and businesses than at less convenient but still physically similar properties. Suburban crime also depends upon the attributes of the "boundary area" between the city and suburbia.

Still another consideration is that increased penalties for criminal offenses and greater expenditures for law enforcement in central cities raise the level of crime in the surrounding suburbs. This phenomenon may be caused by potential criminals who try to avoid the higher costs of committing crime by going to places where lower expected costs more than offset the cost of transportation and becoming familiar with a new location. This implies that while increased police expenditures might lower the rate of crime *in a particular place,* they do not lower the overall rate of crime. Rather, better coordination among police departments of different municipalities within the same metropolitan area would be more efficient in tackling crime than initiatives taken unilaterally by one area.

The most practical results of distinguishing crime in suburbs from crime in cities are determining the characteristics of the most susceptible properties and suggesting ways of preventing crime. One of the more innovative ways considering these topics is applying economic models to explain criminal behavior. Many scholars characterize the decision of a rational individual to commit a crime in the language of economics—when the expected payoff of a potential crime exceeds the perceived opportunity cost, then a potential criminal is motivated to actually commit the crime. Opportunity costs include both the monetary costs and the time used to acquire the necessary knowledge, tools, transportation to and from the target, inability to do other jobs or illegal activities, the expected probability of being caught, and expected punishment if that happens. Payoffs may include the value of stolen assets, personal emotional satisfaction, and recognition gained from peers and others. Understanding the pattern of crimes and the behavior of criminals helps determine the opportunity costs of committing crimes as they are understood by potential criminals. Increasing the expected costs could deter them from committing crimes and thus lower the crime rate.

Much of the available literature has found a correlation between geographic location in suburbs and crime. This subdivision goes beyond the simple demarcation between urban and suburban. One study found that proximity to drug treatment centers, schools, convenience stores, and other places where juveniles gather increases the risk of burglary in suburbs. Another recently discovered that property close to woods, stores, parks, and schools has a higher risk of being burglarized. For instance, locating a business within three blocks of a school increases the likelihood of being burglarized by almost 70 percent.

There is also a correlation between the probability of being burglarized and proximity to "attractors." A possible explanation offered for this correlation is that woods, for example, offer concealment for burglars, and stores, parks, and schools are gathering places for juveniles. Therefore, property close to these attractors potentially faces a larger criminal population. In the first case, woods lower a criminal's chance of being detected, and they therefore lower the expected cost of committing the crime (there is a lower probability of being caught). The other attractors also increase exposure to crime. This has implications for both the suppliers and the users of real estate. A business that wants to lower its exposure to burglary should avoid these attractors when choosing to start or relocate its activities.

Having decided that location is a major determinant of who gets burgled, the question becomes how businesses can protect themselves, even if they are located in a "danger zone." The answer may lie in the presence of alarm systems. At the same time, social optimization requires coordinated efforts by different law enforcement agencies. As previously mentioned, intensive policing by one locality may increase the level of crime in an adjacent one; the current structure of independent police departments causes a relocation of crime and requires coordinated efforts by all localities to minimize it. Generally, however, increasing the expected opportunity costs of committing crime does deter potential criminals and lowers the crime rate. This method must be vigorously pursued.

—*Simon Hakim and Yochanan Shachmurove*

**See also**
Crime Mobility; Drinking, Alcohol Abuse, and Drunkenness; Drugs, Drug Abuse, and Drug Addiction; White-Collar Crime.

**References**
Becker, Gary Stanley. "Crime and Punishment—An Economic Approach." *Journal of Political Economy* 76 (1968): 169–217.
Boggs, Sarah Lee. "Urban Crime Patterns." *American Sociological Review* 30 (1965): 899–908.
Brown, Marilyn A. "Modeling the Spatial Distribution of Suburban Crime." *Economic Geography* 58 (1982): 247–261.
Figlio, Robert M., Simon Hakim, and George F. Rengert. *Metropolitan Crime Patterns.* Monsey, NY: Criminal Justice Press, 1986.
Hakim, Simon, and Yochanan Shachmurove. "Spatial and Temporal Patterns of Commercial Burglaries: The Evidence Examined." *American Journal of Economics and Sociology* 56 (1996): 443–456.
Shaw, Clifford R., and Henry D. McKay. *Juvenile Delinquency and Urban Areas.* Chicago: University of Chicago Press, 1942.
Stabura, J. M., and C. Ronald Huff. "Crime in the Suburbs: A Structural Model." *Urban Affairs Quarterly* 15 (1980): 291–316.

## Suburban Ideal

The suburban ideal, distilled to its essence, consists of the belief that the best form of shelter is the single-family detached house with a garden and ample open space located in a homogeneous, locally controlled community on the periphery of a city. As a historical concept, the suburban ideal is Anglo-American in origin and emerged in some form in England by the late eighteenth century. It has altered constantly over time and space, but the version familiar to twentieth-century Americans was codified around 1900 by upper-middle-class residents of planned, exclusive suburbs in the United States and Canada. Thereafter, the suburban ideal assumed something of a standardized formula that realtors and community builders have recapitulated to guide the mass production of a limited variety of very popular tract subdivisions and suburban housing developments across the nation.

A comprehensive definition and description of the suburban ideal must include not only ideas—those values and benefits to health, spirit, moral character, and social acquaintance thought to accompany suburban living—but also material culture—the characteristic forms of architecture and landscape that have expressed those ideas in the suburban built environment. Both dimensions are best understood as cultural propositions generated and modified over time by particular individuals or groups responding to their historical circumstances. The concept of suburban *retirement*—a gentleman's temporary retreat from the urban world of business to the pleasures and informalities of country life—was well established in Britain by the beginning of the eighteenth century. The suburban ideal, however, was bourgeois rather than aristocratic in origin, the creation of London merchants and bankers seeking a more controlled, more family-centered life in a community of like-minded social equals. In new suburbs like Clapham, as early as the 1790s, they began to work out a residential ideal that embodied and promoted an entire lifestyle of private domesticity, the health-restoring and intellectually revitalizing powers of nature, social homogeneity, and the display of economic standing. Those qualities were expressed most characteristically in small, low-density, planned, and gated suburbs of detached or semidetached villas in verdant settings, designed according to a picturesque aesthetic; Calverly Park, Tunbridge Wells (1827–1828), and Victoria Park, Manchester (1837) are good examples. Suburban dwellers embraced the picturesque for its qualities of rusticity, irregularity, movement, and variety, those aspects of nature deemed most suitable for fashioning an environment meant to serve as a residential alternative to the city.

In the United States, the suburban ideal was first articulated during the 1840s in commuter suburbs like Cambridge and Somerville, Massachusetts, and in the writings of architectural theorist Andrew Jackson Downing. In his two pattern books, *Cottage Residences* (1842) and *The Architecture of Country Houses* (1850), Downing, following the British architectural theorist John Claudius Loudon, repeated many elements of the British suburban ideal: the value of dwelling close to nature, an emphasis on comfort and utility in the home, a preference for the picturesque aesthetic, and a strong faith in the moral force generated by an artistically designed residential setting. Downing adapted these precedents to American climate, geography, and society, promoting the republican ideal of every citizen residing in a cottage of his own in sylvan villages carefully designed to remove all traces of corrupt urbanity. Together with the commuting suburbs' insistence on domestic technological amenities and political self-determination, these principles formed the core of what would emerge after the Civil War Era as the predominant American suburban ideal.

In basic outline, the suburban ideal that has come to dominate the twentieth-century residential environment of North America evolved between the Civil War and World War I in planned, exclusive suburbs designed by and for an emerging urban upper-middle class of business managers, professionals, and cultural workers. Like its British predecessor, the American suburban ideal formalized the status of a privileged social stratum, but it was more self-consciously prescriptive in character. Upper-middle-class architects, developers, housing reformers, clubwomen, and new suburban residents self-consciously promoted their own domestic ideal as the model for modern middle-class living most likely to guarantee social, moral, and economic progress for the nation as a whole. Their suburban ideal, in essence, was a proverbial middle landscape; part ideology, part physical environment, it balanced the values and qualities its privileged constituents held dear and accommodated precisely their needs for daily living.

Those values and qualities included an intensely domestic and child-centered style of living, dedication to the self-expression of the individual, and cultivation of the society and benefits of association with like-minded peers. The turn-of-the-century suburban ideal both sheltered families from the uglier consequences of urban growth while encouraging ties to the city's social, cultural, and occupational opportunities. It enfolded suburban dwellers in a bower of healthful landscaped greenery while also supplying them with energy and every technological amenity available downtown. Central to the suburban ideal in America as well as in Great Britain was a belief in the advantages of social homogeneity; residence in an ideal suburb would reify social status, guarantee social exclusivity, and enable suburbanites to control their social, physical, and, to the extent possible, political environments.

By the beginning of the twentieth century, the physical landscape fashioned to engender the model middle-class lifestyle consisted of a well-planned suburban community of single-family houses set back from the street on large lots along picturesque, winding streets. Compared to Great Britain, the ideal suburban landscape in the United States was greener and more spacious, dedicated substantially more acreage to recreation and pleasure grounds, and devoted more attention to integrating architecture with the natural surroundings. As in Great Britain, the standard suburb was modest in size, excluded commercial land uses, and carefully demarcated its boundaries, the better to advertise its social prestige. The model suburban home, a new post–Civil War building type, featured an informal plan that accommodated family and neighborly gatherings while still affording private spaces for family members. Designed for efficiency and economy, the suburban home, nonetheless, attended to every domestic comfort, including the indoor/outdoor living that the suburban location so favored. The suburban ideal offered an environment that, through its artistry and imagined possibilities for romantic self-fulfillment, promised to refresh, replenish, and elevate the spirit and taste of all who lived there.

That sense of promise, resting on the dual belief in the power of the environment to shape human behavior and the therapeutic pleasures of consumerism, encapsulates the crucial element of fantasy that Lewis Mumford found at the heart of the suburban ideal. As a cultural proposition for guiding ordinary living, however, the suburban ideal has maintained tremendous popular appeal in the United States throughout the twentieth century. This is evident in the degree to which middle-class consumers still embrace its package of cultural values and demand the opportunity to live in suburban subdivisions patterned to embody them, as well as in the official supports that favor the suburban lifestyle. Raising a family in a well-fitted home of one's own in the suburbs remains at the center of the American Dream. This is so despite dramatic economic and demographic changes during the second half of the twentieth century. The traditional lifestyle for which the suburban ideal was tailored—nuclear families with husbands working and wives at home, short commutes to work from suburb to downtown, suburban homes affordable on one middle-class income—is an anomaly today. The lifestyle and form of residential development prescribed by the suburban ideal are intensely consumption-oriented and environmentally prodigal. As the contemporary metropolis expands, and patterns of work, residence, and commuting increasingly intermix, the suburban ideal begs to be transformed or reconstituted to accommodate the domestic circumstances of the twenty-first century.

—*Mary Corbin Sies*

**References**
Archer, John. "Ideology and Aspiration: Individualism, the Middle Class, and the Genesis of the Anglo-American Suburb." *Journal of Urban History* 14 (1988): 214–253.
————. *The Literature of British Domestic Architecture 1715–1842.* Cambridge, MA: MIT Press, 1985.
Binford, Henry C. *The First Suburbs: Residential Communities on the Boston Periphery, 1815–1860.* Chicago: University of Chicago Press, 1985.
Downing, Andrew Jackson. *The Architecture of Country Houses.* New York: Da Capo Press, 1969.
Fishman, Robert. *Bourgeois Utopias: The Rise and Fall of Suburbia.* New York: Basic Books, 1987.
Jackson, Kenneth T. *Crabgrass Frontier: The Suburbanization of the United States.* New York: Oxford University Press, 1985.
Marsh, Margaret. *Suburban Lives.* New Brunswick, NJ: Rutgers University Press, 1990.
Sies, Mary Corbin. "The City Transformed: Nature, Technology, and the Suburban Ideal." *Journal of Urban History* 14 (1987): 81–111.
————. "God's Very Kingdom on the Earth: The Design Program for the American Suburban Home, 1877–1917." In Richard Guy Wilson and Sidney K. Robinson, eds., *Modern Architecture in America: Visions and Revisions,* 2–31. Ames: University of Iowa Press, 1991.
Wallock, Leonard, and William Sharpe. "Bold New City or Built Up 'Burb? Redefining Contemporary Suburbia." *American Quarterly* 46 (1994): 1–30.

## Suburban Railway Service

At one time, every major city in the United States had some form of rail commuter service. Short-distance trains carried passengers to and from the central business district, with most trains running during the morning and evening rush hours. Some of these trains operated over mainline tracks on fairly fast schedules, considering their many stops. Others ran slowly over lightly built suburban lines that were often constructed by real estate developers as a way of attracting commuters to distant suburbs. Most of these smaller operations were abandoned around 1890 when electric streetcars came into service.

Mainline commuter operations, however, have survived into modern times, at least in a few of the larger urban areas, and they remain a vital part of the local transportation system. New York City has the largest of these operations. Rail commuter lines radiate into New Jersey, Long Island, and Connecticut. The largest commuter railroad in the nation, the Long Island Rail Road, terminates in Pennsylvania Station and annually carries over 100 million passengers. It was taken over by New York State in 1966, and today all other commuter lines are controlled by state or regional authorities.

Chicago boasts the second largest rail commuter system in the United States and operates half a dozen lines. The largest goes south for about 30 miles and runs on tracks formerly belonging to the Illinois Central Railroad. Low fares and high operating costs (mainly because the equipment is fully utilized only twice a day and only on weekdays) made even the well-patronized Illinois Central a money loser, and government subsidies have been required to keep this badly needed service in operation.

Public funding has revived suburban trains into a few cities in recent years: Washington, D.C., is only one example. These suburban commuter trains should not be confused with subways, light rail, or other rapid transit systems that are generally built on a much lighter and more compact scale. Commuter trains tend to go longer distances and in most places are built to full-size, mainline standards.

—*John H. White, Jr.*

**See also**
Dummy Lines (Steam Street Railways); Interurban Transit; Streetcars.

**References**
Grove, Lawrence. *On the 8:02.* New York: Mayflower Books, 1979.
Hilton, George W. *American Narrow Gauge Railroads.* Stanford, CA: Stanford University Press, 1990.
Middleton, William D. *When the Steam Railroads Electrified.* Milwaukee, WI: Kalmbach, 1975.

## Suburbanization

From the vantage point of the end of the twentieth century, the basic vocabulary employed to define the American metropolis is changing. This rhetorical alteration corresponds to the shifting residential and employment patterns of the nation's population. As a result, such key words as *city* and *suburb* have become inadequate.

The demographic transformation since 1900 alone is striking. As of 1900, 20 percent of Americans lived in urban places and another 6 percent in suburban settings. Since 1970, statistically speaking, the United States has been a suburban nation. While 75 percent of all Americans lived in a metropolis that year, even more significant has been their preference for suburbs over cities. As of 1990, 44 percent of the population lived in a suburb, while only 31 percent lived in a city. The presidential election of 1992 was the first time a majority of voters in the United States probably considered themselves suburbanites.

Kenneth T. Jackson, preeminent among students of the suburban experience, offers an important addition—urban population deconcentration—to historians' language of metropolitan development. This demographic process constitutes a causal explanation encompassing the vast sweep of American urban history since the beginning of the nineteenth century.

The suburban tradition is most often attributed to the surging and inventive forces of the nineteenth century, but to appreciate what has happened in the United States, it is necessary to step back at least to the late Middle Ages and examine suburbia's antecedents in England as well as on the European Continent. The earliest image conveyed by the word *suburb* was a setting described by H. J. Dyos, an English historian, as an extramural (literally outside the walls) settlement. "In the suburbes of toun," wrote Geoffrey Chaucer in *The Canterbury Tales,* were places of "fereful residence" frequented by "thise robbours and thise thives." A peripheral zone south of London about 1580 has been termed on the fringe of urban society. The modern word "slum" has been invoked to characterize suburbs as they existed in the eighteenth century. In Central and Eastern Europe, the poor inhabited the outlying regions of principal cities, including Gdansk, Prague, Poznan, Lublin, Warsaw, and Riga.

The origin of modern suburbs, it is generally agreed, was set in the seventeenth century and evolved over the next 400 years. A key date for London was 1735, when a network of new bridges and turnpikes began to transform the economy of the rural landscape; to this would be added, starting in 1774, the rudiments of a public transportation system. By 1800, several communities had been launched outside of London. Although the size of their populations was minuscule, they established noteworthy precedents. Residents of London considered Clapham, five miles to the southeast, a "serious paradise." Its middle- and upper-class inhabitants had physically and morally separated themselves from the perils of the urban core. Regents Park and Park Village, each five miles northwest of London, were commissioned in 1811. The former was proposed as a haven for the upper classes, the latter as a model suburb for the middle classes. John Nash designed them to emphasize the rural landscape. Only Park Village would reach fulfillment, designed as an alternative to city life. Yet as late as the middle of the 1830s, it was difficult to ascertain where the economy of the countryside ended and that of the suburb had taken hold.

To comprehend the origins of the movement to the suburbs in the United States, it is necessary to return to the first quarter of the nineteenth century. Spurred by the Industrial Revolution, the pace of urban growth exceeded almost every expectation. Congestion, filth, and disease exerted a significant force in prompting city residents to consider alternatives. We learn from Margaret Marsh, moreover, that the impulses underlying the earliest American ideology of suburbanism took root in male—not female—concerns that equated democracy with rural life; the dominant concern of women, by contrast, entailed fostering domesticity ("In her home, a spiritual and emotional oasis, she succored her husband and nurtured her children"). In turn, this understanding helps explain the popularity of what became known as commuter suburbs by means of perfecting three corresponding (but not simultaneous) transportation systems between 1815 and 1830: steam-powered ferryboats, various horse-drawn conveyances, and steam railways. Ultimately, the steam railway proved dominant; in Chicago alone, 3,600 miles of new track were laid between 1848 and 1856. The steam railway enabled people who worked in the city to live in newly established railroad suburbs.

Commuter railways swiftly became the most influential agent of change. Here were the origins of the phenomenon that John R. Stilgoe terms "metropolitan corridors," recasting physical landscapes and cultural patterns. The new form first took hold in Boston. Overcrowded as early as 1820, in part resulting from the scarcity of real estate, rudimentary commuting service became available in 1838. By late 1849, daily passenger trains entering or departing its seven depots numbered 208, with 118 of them moving within a 15-mile radius; Henry David Thoreau wrote at mid-century how the "startings and arrivals" of trains disturbed his beloved village of Concord. A railway was constructed north of New York City into Westchester County in the 1840s; 7 weekday trains visited Croton Falls, 6 more stopped at White Plains, and 15 at Williamsbridge. A combination of steam railways and ferryboats brought residents of several counties in northeastern New Jersey into Manhattan via Jersey City. Pittsburgh's commuter service commenced in 1851, when the Ohio & Pennsylvania Railroad was completed as far west as New Brighton. In Chicago and its environs, only 10 miles of track entered the city in 1848, but within eight years the figure exceeded 3,600 miles as 11 new lines were constructed.

By the second quarter of the nineteenth century, the North American pattern of spatial change—"peripheral affluence and central despair" are the words used by Kenneth T. Jackson—was already evident in the nation's largest metropolises. For instance, as of 1830 Brooklyn was growing more quickly than Manhattan; by mid-century a journalist rued the exodus of population across the East River, claiming that it was resulting in "the desertion of the city by its men of wealth."

As of the 1850s, Boston boasted of its Chestnut Hill, Philadelphia its Germantown, San Francisco its Nob and Russian Hills, and Chicago its North Shore. And increasingly apparent was the romantic suburb—Newark's Llewellyn

Park, Cincinnati's Glendale, Chicago's Lake Forest—whose artful designers preserved pastoral landscapes for their upper-class clients. Gunther Barth, in studying the cultural transformation of cities, cites these amenities as fostering "the isolationist features of modern city life," whereby people's place of residence was determined by their class status.

In post–Civil War America, the configuration of the metropolis underwent a dramatic reordering. Several factors contributed: heightened industrialization; massive new waves of immigration, increasingly from Southern and Eastern Europe after 1880; significant innovations in sanitary engineering during the early 1880s; and further technological advances, none more important than the telephone (1876) and the gasoline-combustion automobile (1893). While promoters sought to convey images of the romantic suburb, what architectural historians regard as Victorian suburbs were actually being democratized, with large tracts of land divided into small, affordable plots. Gender figured tellingly in this process as middle-class women exerted intensified influence upon their communities. Brightwood, east of Indianapolis on the Bee Line Railroad, was a speculative venture launched in the early 1870s on a conventional gridiron plat; absentee landowners allowed residential property owners to construct homes as they wished without stipulations as to land use or design. In West Philadelphia, once "genteel estates" gave way after 1880 to a pattern of land development premised on the sensitivity of prospective residents to achieving a "uniformity of appearance, of price, and of situation." Tellingly, the federal census report of 1880 heralded the advent of the nation's first metropolitan district: New York City and its environs, a two-state region including Manhattan Island and the autonomous cities of Brooklyn, Jersey City, Hoboken, and Newark.

During the second half of the nineteenth century, suburban residents found their communities coveted by metropolitan imperialists. Leaders of several major cities designed to centralize administrative control over adjacent territories through annexation. Jon C. Teaford explains that annexation campaigns constituted an explicit understanding among urban leaders as to the enviable circumstances of adjacent suburbs. The first effort occurred in Philadelphia, which with one swoop in 1854 expanded its municipal boundaries from 2 square miles to 129 square miles; the previously independent suburb of Spring Garden had ranked as the nation's ninth largest city in the preceding decennial census. Chicago added 133 square miles to its existing 43 square miles in 1889 (including the thriving municipalities of Lakeview and Hyde Park); it was the largest single addition of outlying land in Chicago's history. Most significant of all was the formation in 1898 of Greater New York City, in which its square mileage leaped from 40 to 300, its population growing instantaneously by 2 million. Included in the consolidation was Brooklyn,

heretofore the nation's fourth largest city. Similar annexations occurred in St. Louis, Boston, New Orleans, Baltimore, Minneapolis, Cleveland, and Pittsburgh.

Not that urban imperialism proceeded unimpeded. In some long-established suburbs on the borders of major cities, people prized their local autonomy and distinctive identities. Citizens of Brookline, Massachusetts, thwarted plans for annexation by Boston as early as 1873, a decision now regarded by urban historians as the first significant setback to the consolidation mania sweeping the nation. When other suburban communities—Cambridge (1892) and Somerville (1893) north of Boston as well as Evanston (1894) north of Chicago—faced similar questions, their citizens rejected annexation. These residents, and their counterparts elsewhere, demonstrated a dogged determination (still very much evident today) to differentiate their communities, politically and culturally, from the central city.

The firm opposition to imperialist designs within well-established suburbs is evidence that closed social cells—a hallmark of the North American pattern of metropolitan life as we know it today—were being set in place during the 1890s. When annexations occurred thereafter, they tended to be in southern, southwestern, or western cities. Los Angeles grew from 108 to 440 square miles between 1915 and 1930 by annexing the San Fernando Valley; Dallas expanded in physical size, from 1940 to 1960, from 45 to 350 square miles. For the most part, however, each suburban community would view itself as separated physically and culturally from the central city, as well as from neighboring suburbs.

A technological innovation in transportation—the electrified street railway or streetcar—added to the complexity of metropolitan life in the last decade of the nineteenth century. Known as the trolley, it radically transformed urban mass transit. Adna Ferrin Weber, deservedly acknowledged as the pioneer scholar of American cities, wrote in 1899 that the key to his faith in suburbanization as a democratizing force was the electrified trolley. First launched experimentally by Frank J. Sprague in Richmond, Virginia, in 1888, it ran immediately thereafter in the western suburbs of Boston and soon caused a revolution in mass transportation that quickly attained international proportions. Its instant success has been attributed to its economy, cleanliness, speed, and geographic radius. By 1895, 85 percent of all street railways in the United States had been electrified; in 1902, the figure was 97 percent. Although suburban preserves of the elite—Chicago's Lake Forest and New York City's Tuxedo Park among them—continued to rely primarily on steam railroads for commuting, electrified trolleys proved a boon to the middle class. Stimulating the home construction industry, they created what Sam Bass Warner, Jr., has labeled "streetcar suburbs." Builders of the new transit lines, faced with their own economic imperatives, laid track on whatever suburban property became available rather than along well-designed and well-chosen coordinates. Instead of new communities or neighborhoods, and the public life associated with them, by 1900 there had evolved a fragmented pattern of civic life best defined as centerlines.

Not that electric street railways won universal approbation. In Newark, New Jersey's affluent suburbs, a protracted campaign encouraged by local politicians temporarily prevented trolleys from penetrating the long-established communities of Orange, East Orange, and Montclair. Their suburban residents, already fearful about the influx of new ethnic immigrants, created legal obstacles to franchise petitions. Along the North Shore of Chicago, substantial opposition prevented completion of a new line for nine years until 1899. Contributing to such delays—which also occurred in Toronto (1893) and Paris (1902)—was concern over preserving local autonomy, fear of encroachment by people and corporations deemed foreign because of their urban addresses and corporate ties, and uncertainty about how this advance would affect the urban landscape.

The 1890s saw the emergence of another revolutionary innovation, the automobile. Initially a technological novelty enjoyed by the rich, the possibilities offered by the automobile dramatically affected trolleys after 1900. Although the balance did not shift toward the automobile until the 1920s, a variety of factors figured in the trolley's decline: diminishing profits for transit companies, political criticism over fare structures, overcrowding, and deteriorating rolling stock.

The marriage between suburb and automobile was consummated during the 1920s. Vehicle registration reached 8 million in 1920; in 1927, there was one car for every five Americans. By 1929, 26 million vehicles were on the nation's roadways, and the United States manufactured 85 percent of the world's cars. Highway and road construction mounted, stimulated in part by federal legislation dating back to 1916; in 1925, the cost of highway construction nationally surpassed $1 billion a year. Key linkages were also erected: the Benjamin Franklin Bridge tied Philadelphia to Camden, New Jersey (1926); the Holland tunnel joined lower Manhattan to Jersey City (1927); and the George Washington Bridge did the same for upper Manhattan and Bergen County, New Jersey (1931). Stimulated in large part by these transportation developments, by the first third of the twentieth century the suburban experience encompassed a broad range of Americans, not just residents of long-established upper-class enclaves. But masculine domesticity was waning. Women colored communal sensibilities by organizing child-centered as well as family-oriented pursuits, often attended by dutiful fathers, in affluent suburbs such as Palos Verdes, California, Scarsdale, New York, and Winnetka, Illinois.

Meanwhile, the nation's 40 largest industrial counties suffered a net loss of 617,965 jobs at the expense of peripheral localities over a seven-year period beginning in 1919. In retailing, highway clutter was becoming common along major arteries leading into cities. Strips of businesses catered to retail customers, advertising their wares with neon-illuminated signs and billboards.

But the effect of automobiles on suburbanization during the 1920s should not be overestimated. What was happening reflected a process whose social and demographic origins extended back into the nineteenth century. Industrial plants located in suburbs (Allis Chalmers established its Norwood, Ohio, operation in 1898 on the northeastern edge of Cincinnati) took hold as management sought to avoid the costly land acquisitions and high tax rates of cities; correspondingly, workers found it more convenient to relocate in close proximity to their jobs. Retailers also found it essential to decentralize. Between 1910 and 1920, Chicago department stores such as Wiebolts, Sears, Roebuck, and Marshall Field's, as well as Filene's in Boston, established suburban branches.

Further contributing to the exodus from the urban core was the modernization of commuter transit lines. As early as 1911, more than 50 percent of all the practicing lawyers in Boston lived beyond the city's corporate limits. The figure reached 40 percent for Newark, New Jersey, as early as 1925.

Accompanying the supposed triumph of the American suburb during the 1920s were doubts and outright criticism about its influence and its effects. To be sure, Harlan Paul Douglass could write a much-acclaimed book, *The Suburban Trend* (1924), in which he portrayed his topic (not uncritically) as an integral dimension of "urban civilization." He defined suburbs in this way: "It is an urban society trying to eat its cake and keep it too." The introduction and widespread acceptance of zoning codes, whatever the original intention of such legislation, contributed to the practice of codifying the restrictiveness of affluent suburbs. Euclid, Ohio, in a landmark policy later sustained by the U.S. Supreme Court (*Euclid v. Ambler,* 1926), prohibited the construction of multiple-family residences in a suburb north of Cleveland, Ohio.

The prominent urban analyst Lewis Mumford advocated an alternative vision of suburban America during the 1920s that was rooted in the ideal of planning rather than entrepreneurship. Although not fully realized, his ideas merit attention. Influenced by decentralist thinkers of the late nineteenth century, Mumford's goal was to create tightly organized planned communities within the metropolis ("fully equipped for work, play, and living"). This aspiration was partially realized in 1928 in the establishment of Radburn, a 1,350-acre planned community in New Jersey with a projected population of 25,000 that was designed by Clarence Stein and Henry Wright. Located 12 miles west of the George

Washington Bridge (then under construction) in Bergen County, Radburn's completion was sidetracked by the Depression. During the 1930s the concept of planned communities was briefly revived by the federal government, but its plans met opposition from virulent antistatist critics. Even though Mumford's idea was never fully achieved, its influence on the American suburban tradition has endured among intellectuals as well as progressive planners. Alexander Garvin claims that the cul-de-sac is the most enduring design element of Radburn. Other evidence of its persistence is also found in Palos Verdes Estates, California (which in fact predates Radburn), as well as in the rise of a handful of experimental new towns (e.g., Reston, Virginia; Columbia, Maryland; and Irvine, California) during the 1960s. Nonetheless, deeply embedded opposition to large-scale planned community developments persists as a hallmark of American political and economic systems.

The 1930s exacerbated the complex and uneasy relationship between suburb and city. The Depression affected the urban core with enormous severity. Unemployment soared in major cities: 1 million in New York City, 600,000 in Chicago, and 298,000 in Philadelphia. Yet the gross effects do not tell all. Puzzling as it initially appears, suburbs prospered at the expense of cities because of New Deal policies! This effect is curious in that Franklin Delano Roosevelt is widely regarded as a politician with an urban electoral base.

Two pieces of New Deal housing legislation explain this circumstance. The Home Owners Loan Corporation (HOLC), created in 1933, sought to curtail the enormous number of foreclosures on private home mortgages, and the Federal Housing Administration (FHA), established in 1934, boosted the home construction industry by subsidizing the improvement of existing dwellings and the initiation of new starts. If conventional wisdom once instructed us that such laws restored faith and prosperity, historians offer a revised interpretation: the policies of these agencies undermined the well-being of housing stock in the urban core while enhancing conditions in the suburbs. Real estate appraisers developed the nefarious practice we now know as redlining, wherein loans are not granted in portions of the city classified as physically or economically deteriorated or in neighborhoods populated by African Americans and working-class ethnics. The FHA favored what it thought were low-risk loans: new units rather than existing dwellings, open spaces rather than built-up locales, white collar rather than working class, whites rather than blacks, and native-born rather than immigrant stock. (A bank appraiser, working for a federal agency, favorably described Kenilworth, Illinois, 17 miles from the Loop and part of Chicago's network of North Shore suburbs, "Except for a few poor units adjacent to the railroad on the west side, the entire community is very uniform and

high grade throughout.") Of course, neither housing agency possessed a legislative mandate to defend or revive central cities. Rather, their housing programs fit a classic New Deal mold by utilizing public funds to induce a return to economic health in the private sector. Whatever the motives of those who designed the HOLC and FHA, they best served suburban, middle-class homeownership.

After 1945 the suburban trend seemed inevitable, as if it amounted to a self-fulfilling prophecy abetted by the federal government. Housing starts between 1946 and 1955 doubled over the preceding 15 years. Many new homes were situated on the metropolitan periphery, constructed inexpensively, and subsidized by federal loan programs. Best known were the Levittowns (first on Long Island at Strathmore-on-Manhasset, then in suburban Philadelphia in Bristol, and later in central New Jersey in Willingboro), mass-produced, low-cost, detached single-family houses, 750-square-feet large, of a Cape Cod style, built on concrete slabs on 60 foot by 100 foot lots in parklike subdivisions. Although purchasers had their choice among five styles (which changed annually), each contained two bedrooms, one bathroom, a kitchen, a Bendix washing machine, and unfinished attic space. Kenneth T. Jackson reports that no African Americans lived among the 82,000 inhabitants of the Levittown on Long Island as late as 1960. Highway construction also flourished, reaching $2 billion in 1949 and $4 billion by 1955. A suburban life inspired two-car families, as did rising numbers of women remaining in the labor force. In 1953 *Glamour* magazine linked homeownership and the two-income household.

Los Angeles County experienced a larger population increase (1,887,084) than any other county in the country during the 1950s, comprising the center of a multicounty and multinucleated megalopolis that Kevin Starr aptly describes as "the continuous sub/urb." Population deconcentration within the city realized its zenith in the San Fernando Valley, northwest of the historic downtown, which grew from a population of 150,000 in 1945 to 739,000 in 1960. The Interstate Highway Act of 1956 projected a transcontinental network of superhighways stretching 42,500 miles and costing $60 billion.

By 1970 some 14,000 shopping centers served retail consumers, diverting them from older central business districts. When Woodfield Mall opened in 1971 in Chicago's northwestern suburb of Schaumburg, it featured four major department stores, 230 smaller retail establishments, and 11,000 parking spaces spread over nearly 200 acres. Whether the destination was Woodfield or such counterparts as Garden State Plaza in Paramus, New Jersey (1957), Fashion Island in Newport Beach, California (1967), or Gwinnett Place Mall northeast of Atlanta, Georgia (1984), their collective presence decreased the necessity and the likelihood of a shopper traveling to an urban central business district. By the end of 1958, for instance, retail sales in the declining industrial city of Paterson, New Jersey (four miles west of Paramus), had decreased by half of what they had been four years earlier. The proliferation of suburban malls affirmed the fundamental fact that Americans live and shop in the suburbs.

Whether the vantage point is social or economic, the suburban trend since World War II has seriously damaged the nation's older cities. A key aspect of this harm has been a regional demographic shift away from the Northeast and upper Midwest. Among the 29 fastest-growing cities in the country (with populations of at least 100,000) between 1980 and 1990, 22 were actually suburbs in the shadows of larger central cities; 16 were in California, 4 in Texas, and 3 in Arizona. Only one was east of the Mississippi River (Virginia Beach, Virginia). Contributing to this demographic movement, beginning in the 1950s, was the widespread existence of air-conditioned residences as well as workplaces, ease of airplane travel, advances in communications technologies, and federally supported highway improvements. The transfer of the previously hapless California Angels baseball team from Los Angeles to Anaheim in 1966 merits notice as the first time a suburb could boast of having its own major league baseball franchise. A modicum of local disappointment did result from the initial decision by management to retain the team's identity as the California Angels, but that decision has since been reversed, and the team now plays in the American League as the Anaheim Angels.

Meanwhile, Sharon Zukin has metaphorically, but accurately, identified the nation's oldest urban places as "the hollow center." Between 1950 and 1960, cities grew 11 percent as contrasted with suburban growth of 46 percent. Similar shifts occurred in employment patterns. Between 1948 and 1963, the number of industrial jobs declined 7 percent in the nation's 25 largest cities while the number of industrial jobs in suburbs was increasing by 61 percent. From 1970 to 1977, the number of suburban industrial jobs increased 48 percent in Washington, D.C., 41 percent in Baltimore, 31 percent in St. Louis, and 22 percent in Philadelphia. The U.S. Conference of Mayors balefully itemized the myriad problems afflicting cities in 1986: population loss, poverty, racial concentration, deindustrialization, unemployment, homelessness, crime, poor schools, and high taxes. William Julius Wilson has said as much in explaining how the underclass or poorest residents of inner cities suffer disproportionately from the compound effects of their environs as one affliction builds upon another.

At the end of the twentieth century, a new suburbanization phenomenon is emerging: edge cities. Among their key characteristics are locations along highway corridors far removed from central cities; an almost total reliance on au-

tomobiles for transportation; population homogeneity; and swift economic development led by technology-related industries, computer-linked enterprises, and retail businesses located in shopping malls. Revolutionary advances in information technology early in the 1980s resulted in proliferation of so-called wired offices that rely on networked computers that permit corporate centers located in suburbs to receive, analyze, and transmit data essential to the daily transactions of far-flung, large-scale, corporate and research enterprises. People work, live, and pursue many of their leisure activities in these settings. Edge cities are situated along interstate highways as much as 40 miles from the urban core on the peripheries of large-scale metropolitan systems. In 1991, Joel Garreau of the Washington Post calculated the existence of some 200 edge cities including Bellevue, Washington; Gwinnett County, northeast of Atlanta; Naperville, Illinois; Overland Park, Kansas; Princeton, New Jersey; and Tyson's Corner, Virginia.

Naperville, 30 miles from Chicago near the western edge of its metropolis, dates back to 1831. Residents long have cultivated local pride because they live in DuPage County's oldest community. They strive, down to the present day, to maintain Naperville's distinct character as a small midwestern town. Nonetheless its economy, over more than 150 years, has experienced no fewer than four major phases: (1) agricultural and horticultural production; (2) small-scale industrial center; (3) commuter suburb; and (4) center for high technology. Even before construction of the East-West Tollway (a segment of Interstate 88) in 1958 linking Naperville to the central city, the seeds of change had been planted. Key was the decision in 1947 by the Atomic Energy Commission, tied to 3,600 acres of available land and low population density, to establish the Argonne National Laboratory in nearby Lemont. In its contemporary form, Naperville evolved into Chicago's "technoburb" (a term coined by Robert Fishman), a process that took hold early in the 1960s. The tollway, designated by boosters in 1985 as the Illinois Research and Development Corridor, is its economic center. Its corporate roster included Amoco Research Center (1,600 employees); Bell Telephone's (now AT&T) Indian Hill Laboratories (9,000); the Hewlett-Packard Company (360); Nalco Chemical Company (1,154 employees); Northern Illinois Gas Company (700); and Travelers Insurance Companies (700). As of 1980, 40 percent of Naperville's female population were active in the civilian labor force; 30 percent worked in professional or managerial occupations (an advance of nearly 11 percent since 1970) as contrasted with 22 percent in the entire Chicago Standard Metropolitan Statistical Area. By 1990 its population had grown to more than 85,000 from only 5,000 in 1950.

During the 1980s Naperville distinguished itself as the fastest-growing municipality in Illinois. A survey conducted in 1982 ranked it first in the amount of new-home construction in a six-county region. In physical size, it expanded from 5.8 square miles in 1960 to 28 square miles on December 31, 1990, the result of approximately 370 separate annexations. A savvy journalist, decoding the rhetorical strategies devised for marketing its residential real estate, maintains that its elevated reputation as a suburb—abundant employment, school-centered inhabitants, congenial residential character, high-quality public services—is as significant to the prospective purchaser as the actual home. Residents find their environs repeatedly examined, regionally and nationally, in the company of other centers of growth across the United States. Then again, they also must contend with the problems induced by growth: traffic, facilities, schools, housing, and water.

But like so many of its homogeneous suburban counterparts, in one characteristic Naperville did not change much at all. Among its 5,272 residents in 1940, 99.9 percent were white. Fifty years later, fewer than 10 percent of its total population were Asians or Pacific Islanders (4.8 percent), African Americans (2.1 percent), or of Hispanic origin (1.8 percent). Moreover, Naperville was singled out, based on data compiled for 1992, as having the lowest rate of poverty (1.5 percent) among cities nationally with a population of at least 50,000. Yet Naperville's heritage as a small residential suburb remains an active force in the lives of its inhabitants. Sustaining some sense of the past is an ambitious 13.5 acre living history museum, organized in 1971 and financially assisted by the municipal government. It has realized a measure of the public's approbation because it provides people with a semblance of small-town intimacy in a community that otherwise would be known only as a center of phenomenal growth.

Robert Fishman, a rare historian willing to cast an eye toward the future, forecasts how such edge cities might differ "radically" in form and function from their traditional precursors, "too congested to be efficient, too chaotic to be beautiful, and too dispersed to possess the diversity and vitality of a great city." Edge cities, contrary to what some optimistic observers foresee, do not represent the nation's urban future. Rather, they constitute the most recent chapter, avowedly anti-urban, in the evolution of our suburbs. And there is even the prospect, raised by Fishman, that edge cities will eradicate the traditional suburban culture and replace it with mindless metropolitan sprawl.

The dual metropolis, encompassing our decaying inner cities and our glittering suburbs within a single geographic system, is a useful contemporary depiction of the relationship between cities and suburbs. It is premised on the notion of unbalanced development (e.g., technologically oriented job opportunities requiring high levels of skill in suburbs and poorly educated, underemployed labor pools in cities). Replete with the starkest of contrasts, such instances are symptomatic of national political structures and economic systems that too often have proved themselves to be disdainful of the inner city, its depleted resources, and its beleaguered inhabitants.

To cite a single benchmark statistic, federal spending on cities diminished from 15 percent of the budget to 6 percent between 1980 and 1990, a direct result of the new federalism associated with the presidency of Ronald Reagan (1981–1989). As early as 1982 Richard C. Wade foresaw that the outcome would benefit the American suburban majority. Indeed, when urban experts from Europe recently visited American cities, reports Derek Bok in *The State of the Nation* (1996), they expressed wonderment at encountering circumstances akin to a nation in the Third World. Central cities housed 43 percent of Americans below the poverty line in 1991 as contrasted with only 27 percent in 1959.

Representative of the dual metropolis are two divergent examples. Gwinnett County, north of Atlanta, the nation's fastest-growing county in 1985, prospered in considerable part because of a mixture of expansive job opportunities in technology and science-related industries with benefits derived from the network of interstate highways constructed within its borders beginning in 1958. As the nation's sixth largest edge city based on a 1993 analysis, its economic focal point was Gwinnett Place Mall. During the 1980s Gwinnett ranked first among Georgia's 159 counties in the percentage of new homes constructed. Gwinnett County also led the state in the growth of its executive and managerial employment sector, which increased 197 percent between 1980 and 1990; Fulton County's increased only 48 percent. As of 1990, 3.95 percent of Gwinnett County's population lived below the poverty line, placing it second lowest in the state; Fulton County's figure stood at 17.8 percent. Yet despite strong political support from business leaders in Gwinnett County as well as Atlanta, who envisioned long-range opportunities to broaden and diversify the county's labor force, Gwinnett's electorate decisively rejected referendum questions in 1971, and again in 1990, that would have connected it to Atlanta's rapid transit system. Indicative of their priorities, during 1988 residents of the county launched dual campaigns squarely aimed at Atlanta. One sought to entice the owners of the Atlanta Braves baseball team, without success, to construct a new major league baseball stadium in the county after their existing lease with the operators of Atlanta-Fulton County Stadium expired. The other undertook a $25 million airport expansion of Gwinnett County-Briscoe Field. Almost entirely funded by the Federal Aviation Authority, its purpose was to accommodate local corporations whose employees wished to avoid traveling across Atlanta to Hartsfield Atlanta International Airport. As the expansion project drew to its finish in 1990, boosters anticipated the day when this facility might offer commercial service and possibly attain designation as Atlanta's second major airport. (Joel Garreau claims that upgrading satellite airfields to operate at some level of commercial capacity—citing Islip, Newburgh, and Westchester County as alternatives to the three major airports serving New York City—counts as an essential characteristic of edge cities.)

Chicago offers another case in point. Between 1970 and 1990 the city was losing 17 percent of its population as its suburbs grew by 24 percent. As of 1990 the city's share of private-sector employment in the metropolitan region had fallen slightly below 40 percent for the first time; 18 years earlier the city's share had been 56 percent. The 1990 statistic also reflected a precipitous 12-month decline for the city, a loss of more than 8,000 jobs occurring at the very time that the six-county suburban region had added almost 66,000 positions. Ranking first in suburban job growth, no doubt spurred by Naperville's expansion, was DuPage County. *The Economist* has reported that within Chicago some 2,000 manufacturing sites were vacant in 1994. The decision by Sears, Roebuck to relocate its corporate headquarters away from its downtown Sears Tower to the northwestern suburb of Hoffman Estates in 1992 affected 5,000 workers. Underlying these changes is the fact that in 1990 Chicago ranked second nationally—exceeded only by Detroit—in an analysis of the 100 largest cities in the country that measured concentrations of poverty and distressed neighborhoods.

If the dual metropolis represents the bleakest of contemporary realities, what better prospect exists for our metropolitan future at the close of the twentieth century? The most optimistic expression, rooted in an abiding faith in our capacity as a democratic nation to foster renewal and change, is that future suburban residents might yet find reason to reorient their sensibilities. This would require a series of political and economic imperatives fostered by our leaders—in the public and private sector, in the neighborhoods, in the giant corporations, in small enterprises, in labor unions—at the local, state, and national levels. David Rusk, a former mayor of Albuquerque, New Mexico (1977–1981), received considerable attention in 1993 when he urged state governments to enact legislation easing prospects for realizing city-county consolidations ("Redeeming inner cities and urban underclasses requires reintegration of city and suburb"). Indeed, when the occasional city-county consolidation was consummated—Nashville, Tennessee (1962), Jacksonville, Florida (1968), and Indianapolis, Indiana (1972)—more often than not it reflected the lines of the regional demographic shift away from older urban centers largely dependent upon smokestack industrial economies. Escaping the scourge of the dual metropolis is a goal worthy of our self-respect as a great and powerful nation.

Contemporary examples of what might be achieved by linking corporate interests to metropolitan initiatives for urban revitalization have been launched in Atlanta, Boston, and Pittsburgh. Writing in 1993 about the imperiled urban condition, Paul E. Peterson championed what amounts to a reversal of the new federalism—"a national political and policy commitment that sees urban needs as an intimate part of the country's broader social agenda." Achieving this, of course, would require broad-based recognition of a new set of imperatives obliging Americans to redirect their metropolitan lives—geographically, economically, and culturally—away from the edge and back toward the core.

Zane L. Miller has wisely reminded us that key words such as *suburban* and *metropolitan* are themselves the products of perpetual recasting that reaches back to the very beginning of urban population deconcentration in the first quarter of the nineteenth century. Each word, moreover, continues to inspire a range of sensibilities. Some of them are noble and others less so. A *suburb* can be construed as an interdependent element within a functional metropolitan system, inextricably linked culturally and economically to the central city as well as to adjacent places; alternately, viewed through another set of eyes, a suburb is a place to which people furtively escape in their quest to avoid urban problems and dangers. *Metropolitan* has been used to depict a pluralistic agency for programmatic efforts designed to amend some of the perplexing issues encompassing cities and suburbs. But it also may be cast pejoratively to peremptorily cast away blueprints drawn up to guide the construction of useful conjunctures between the core and the periphery.

—*Michael Ebner*

**See also**

Annexation; Automobiles; Dummy Lines (Steam Street Railways); Federal Housing Administration; Levittown; Multicentered Metropolis; Mumford, Lewis; New Federalism; Omnibuses; Redlining; Reston, Virginia; Sprague, Franklin Julian; Stein, Clarence S.; Streetcar Suburbs; Streetcars; Urban Rivalry and Urban Imperialism.

**References**

Binford, Henry C. *The First Suburbs, Residential Communities on the Boston Periphery, 1815–1860.* Chicago: University of Chicago Press, 1985.

Birkner, Michael J. *A Country Place No More: The Transformation of Bergenfield, New Jersey, 1894–1994.* Rutherford, NJ: Fairleigh Dickinson University Press, 1994.

Blumin, Stuart M. "When Villages Become Towns: The Historical Contexts of Town Formation." In Derek Fraser and Anthony Sutcliffe, eds., *The Pursuit of Urban History,* 54–68. London: Edward Arnold, 1983.

Bok, Derek. *The State of the Nation.* Cambridge, MA: Harvard University Press, 1996.

Burgess, Patricia. *Planning for the Private Interest: Land Use Controls and Residential Patterns in Columbus, Ohio, 1900–1970.* Columbus: Ohio State University Press, 1994.

Cisneros, Henry G., ed. *Interwoven Destinies, Cities and the Nation.* New York: W. W. Norton, 1993.

Cohen, Lizabeth. "From Town Center to Shopping Center: The Reconfiguration of Community Marketplaces in Postwar America." *American Historical Review* 101 (1996): 1050–1081.

Douglass, Harlan Paul. *The Suburban Trend.* New York: Century, 1924.

Dyos, H. J. *Victorian Suburb: A Study of Camberwell.* Leicester, England: University of Leicester Press, 1961.

Ebner, Michael H. *Creating Chicago's North Shore: A Suburban History.* Chicago: University of Chicago Press, 1988.

Fishman, Robert. *Bourgeois Utopias: The Rise and Fall of Suburbia.* New York: Basic Books, 1987.

Frey, William H. "Metropolitan America: Beyond the Transition." *Population Bulletin* 45 (1990): 3–47.

Garreau, Joel. *Edge City: Life on the New Frontier.* New York: Doubleday, 1991.

Garvin, Alexander. *The American City: What Works, What Doesn't.* New York: McGraw-Hill, 1996.

Jackson, Kenneth T. *Crabgrass Frontier: The Suburbanization of the United States.* New York: Oxford University Press, 1985.

Keating, Ann Durkin. *Building Chicago, Suburban Developers and the Creation of a Divided Metropolis.* Columbus: Ohio State University Press, 1988.

Kling, Rob, et al., eds. *Postsuburban California: The Transformation of Orange County since World War II.* Berkeley: University of California Press, 1990.

Marsh, Margaret. *Suburban Lives.* New Brunswick, NJ: Rutgers University Press, 1990.

Miller, Zane L. *Suburb, Neighborhood and Community in Park Forest, Ohio, 1935–1976.* Knoxville: University of Tennessee Press, 1981.

O'Connor, Carol A. *A Sort of Utopia: Scarsdale, 1891–1981.* Albany: State University of New York Press, 1983.

Rose, Mark H. *Interstate: Express Highway Politics, 1939–1989.* Rev. ed. Knoxville: University of Tennessee Press, 1990.

Rusk, David. *Cities without Suburbs.* Baltimore: Johns Hopkins University Press, 1993.

Schaffer, Daniel. *Garden Cities for America: The Radburn Experience.* Philadelphia: Temple University Press, 1981.

Schuyler, David. *The New Urban Landscape: The Redefinition of City Form in Nineteenth-Century America.* Baltimore: Johns Hopkins University Press, 1986.

Starr, Kevin. *The Dream Endures: California Enters the 1940s.* New York: Oxford University Press, 1997.

Stilgoe, John R. *Borderland: Origins of the American Suburb, 1820–1939.* New Haven, CT: Yale University Press, 1988.

———. *Metropolitan Corridor: Railroads and the American Scene.* New Haven, CT: Yale University Press, 1983.

Teaford, Jon C. *City and Suburb: The Political Fragmentation of Metropolitan America, 1850–1970.* Baltimore: Johns Hopkins University Press, 1979.

———. *Post-Suburbia: Government and Politics in the Edge Cities.* Baltimore: Johns Hopkins University Press, 1996.

Wade, Richard C. "The Suburban Roots of the New Federalism." *New York Times Magazine* (August 1, 1982): 20–21.

Wallock, Leonard, and William Sharpe. "Bold New City or Built Up 'Burb? Redefining Contemporary Suburbia." *American Quarterly* 46 (1994): 1–30.

Warner, Sam Bass, Jr. *Streetcar Suburbs: The Process of Growth in Boston 1870–1900.* Cambridge, MA: Harvard University Press, 1962.

Weber, Adna Ferrin. *The Growth of Cities in the Nineteenth Century: A Study in Statistics.* New York: Macmillan, 1899.

Wilson, William Julius. *When Work Disappears: The World of the New Urban Poor.* New York: Knopf, 1996.

Zukin, Sharon. "The Hollow Center: U.S. Cities in the Global Era." In Alan Wolfe, ed., *America at Century's End,* 245–261. Berkeley: University of California Press, 1991.

## Subways

A subway is a mode of transporting passengers that operates along its own right-of-way, runs wholly or partially underground, has regular schedules, makes frequent stops, and has a set fare. Today, there are subways in 11 American cities: Atlanta, Baltimore, Boston, Buffalo, Chicago, Los Angeles, New York City, Newark, Philadelphia, the San Francisco Bay area, and Washington, D.C.

Subways were a European, not an American, innovation. The world's first subway was the Metropolitan Railway in London, which opened on January 10, 1863. This subway was designed to alleviate traffic congestion in the center of London, where narrow streets were jammed with slow-moving horse-drawn vehicles. By building an underground railway with a separate right-of-way, the Metropolitan Railway avoided delays on the surface and traveled much faster.

One shortcoming of the Metropolitan Railway was the environmental pollution caused by its steam locomotives. Steam engines spewed forth smoke and cinders that discomfited passengers and crews in the enclosed tunnels. This air pollution helped slow the proliferation of subways beyond London, and no other city inaugurated an underground railway until 1886, when Glasgow, Scotland, introduced a cable-powered route.

The adoption of electricity solved the power problem. On November 4, 1890, the City and South London Railway became the first electrically powered subway. Although many surface railways had recently been electrified, the City and South London proved that this new power source could handle a subway's dense traffic. The adoption of electricity, together with the development in 1898 of a multiple-unit control that enabled trains to be operated as an integrated system, precipitated a boom in subway construction. The Budapest subway opened in 1896, the Paris metro in 1900, and the Berlin subway in 1902.

The first subway in North America was inaugurated in Boston on September 1, 1897. Built to relieve traffic congestion in the central business district, the Boston subway consisted of a tunnel that ran below Tremont and Washington Streets. This tunnel gave the trolleys of the West End Street Railway Company easy access to downtown and allowed streetcar tracks to be removed from Boston's most crowded streets.

Despite its relatively short length, the Boston subway was expensive, with a cost of $4.2 million. Because subways cost more to build per mile of track than elevated or street railways, the Boston subway changed how mass transit was financed in the United States. Most earlier urban railways had been privately financed and owned, but the Boston subway involved a combination of private and public control. A public agency, the Boston Transit Commission, financed and built the subway, while a private corporation, the West End, leased and operated it. This formula of public-private cooperation was followed in other American cities, including New York City.

New York City's subway was built in three separate stages. The first stage, the Interborough Rapid Transit Company's line, opened on October 27, 1904, and served two of the city's five boroughs, Manhattan and the Bronx. The second stage, known as the dual system, was authorized in 1913. Operated by the Interborough Rapid Transit Company and a second company, the Brooklyn-Manhattan Transit Corporation, the dual system was the largest of the three stages and extended to outlying areas of the Bronx, Queens, and Brooklyn. By the time it was completed in the 1920s, New York had the longest and most heavily traveled rapid transit system in the world.

These first two stages had been developed in a framework that resembled that of Boston's subway—a public agency owned and regulated the subways and a private corporation operated them. A political backlash against this public-private framework led to creation of new arrangements for the third stage of subway construction, the Independent Subway System. Completed in 1940, the Independent was owned and operated by the municipal government. The major period of subway construction ended in 1940; only a few lines have been added since then.

New York's subway became the fastest urban mass transit railway in the world. Its express trains traveled at speeds in excess of 40 miles per hour, three times faster than the city's steam-powered elevated railways and six times faster than its electric trolleys. By allowing New Yorkers to live farther from their jobs in downtown Manhattan without having to spend any additional time commuting, the subway stimulated residential construction in sections of northern Manhattan, the Bronx, Queens, and Brooklyn that had previously been undeveloped. This construction boom resulted in the deconcentration of Manhattan's population. In 1910, 49 percent of New Yorkers had lived in Manhattan, a long, narrow island that constituted only 14 percent of the city's total land area. By 1940, only 25 percent resided there.

Following the lead of Boston and New York, several other major American cities—including Philadelphia, Chicago, and Newark—also built subways. But subways were affected by the general decline of mass transit that began in the 1920s. Chronic financial problems that emerged after World War I prevented the construction of new subways and lowered the quality of maintenance on existing networks. These financial problems were caused by competition from the automobile, by political reactions to the subway companies' monopolistic business practices and poor passenger service, and by the absence of public subsidies.

Financial constraints also ended the private operation of subways. By the 1950s, public agencies operated most subways in the United States. The most important public takeover occurred in New York City in June 1940. After the financial integrity of the city's subways was threatened during the Depression by the bankruptcy of the Interborough Rapid Transit Company and the near collapse of the Brooklyn-Manhattan Transit Corporation, the City of New York acquired the facilities of the transit corporations and began direct operation of municipal transit. This municipal ownership did not lead to significantly larger public subsidies, however. Most city politicians and transit officials retained the existing definition of rapid transit as a business entity that should support itself. The result of municipal ownership was a publicly owned subway system with old, deteriorating facilities that could not compete with private automobiles.

In the 1960s the federal government recognized that mass transit could no longer be dealt with on a local level. The Urban Mass Transit Act of 1964 defined mass transit as a national priority for the first time. This act represented a response to two concerns: first, that transit planning should be undertaken in a broad regional context not restricted by municipal boundaries; and second, that rapid transit could free metropolitan areas from excessive dependence on automobiles. The Urban Mass Transit Administration was subsequently created as an agency of the Department of the Interior and charged with implementing the federal mass transit program.

The 1964 act was also significant for initiating federal funding of rapid transit construction. Even though the availability of federal grants was an important departure from rapid transit's previously local orientation, the principal emphasis of the federal legislation was on developing new lines rather than operating existing ones. The availability of federal funding spurred another boom in subway construction. On October 11, 1972, the San Francisco Bay Area Rapid Transit System (BART) became the country's first new regional rail system to be unveiled in six decades. Since the 1970s, new subways have opened in Atlanta, Washington, D.C., Pittsburgh, Buffalo, Baltimore, and Los Angeles. A rapid transit system was also built in Miami that consisted of elevated and surface track.

Despite this recent construction, subways have not become a major means of urban transportation. Except in New York City, where nearly half the workforce uses the subway to reach their jobs, relatively few Americans ride subways with any regularity. Outside of New York City, the private automobile continues to be the dominant form of urban and suburban transportation in the United States.

—*Clifton Hood*

**References**

Cheape, Charles W. *Moving the Masses: Urban Public Transit in New York, Boston, and Philadelphia, 1890–1912.* Cambridge, MA: Harvard University Press, 1980.

Cudahy, Brian J. *Cash, Tokens, and Transfers: A History of Urban Mass Transit in North America.* New York: Fordham University Press, 1990.

Hood, Clifton. *722 Miles: The Building of the Subways and How They Transformed New York:* Simon and Schuster, 1993.

## Sullivan, Louis H. (1856–1924)

Louis Sullivan never designed an entire city and never formulated a cohesive urban design theory. However, Sullivan's architectural theory and practice, motivated by his search for an American style grounded in nature, address the problems of integrating architectural naturalism into a modern urban context. In particular, he conceived the ornamented skyscraper in relation to a culture of commerce and industry and a geography of gridiron streets and building structures.

*Undated photograph of Louis Henri Sullivan.*

What makes Sullivan's solutions "American" are his philosophical adherence to Ralph Waldo Emerson's aesthetic agenda and his artistic alignment with the Emersonian poet *par excellence,* Walt Whitman.

Emerson's transcendentalist writings on art and nature put artists at the center of realizing America's Manifest Destiny as "Nature's nation." In essays dating from 1836 to 1860, Emerson maintained that America's vast and varied landscape provides both a record of the nation's past and also the setting for its moral, spiritual, and technological growth in the future. To ensure this growth and, in turn, an indigenous artistic culture, Emerson instructed the artist to copy the poet's example of reading and translating all things natural and man-made as symbols of the divine mind. To this end, each artist—whether painter, sculptor, or architect—was mandated to reconcile the apparent contrasts or oppositions between the real and ideal. For Emerson, this poetic reading of nature guaranteed not only a spiritual reconciliation between the fine arts and the mechanical or utilitarian arts but also a harmonizing of country and city. Indeed, Emerson's aesthetic agenda enabled every man and woman to regard "the land as a commanding and increasing power on the American citizen, the sanative and American influence" that provides a remedy for whatever is false in our culture. Assuming this Emersonian duty, Sullivan created what he called "the true, the Poetic Architecture" as a means of bringing nature into the city.

Although Sullivan has been identified as the preeminent designer of the Chicago School of Architecture with its skyscrapers and functionalist form, his primary concern was developing an architectural symbolism comprised of simple geometric, structural forms and organic ornamentation. For the latter, he intertwined native botanical motifs with abstract curvilinear patterns that denoted the vital processes of nature. He identified both geometric abstraction and botanical realism as symbols of primal, dialectical forces: the "Objective" and "Subjective" and their generative source, the "Infinite Creative Spirit." Sullivan first demonstrated this symbolism in the Wainwright Building (St. Louis, Missouri, 1890). Here he juxtaposed the objective-tectonic and the subjective-organic as the essence of the ornamented skyscraper in its poetic form.

In formulating this architectural symbolism, Sullivan modeled his role as architect-poet upon Whitman's role as "divine literatus." In doing so, Sullivan joined Whitman in solving one of the most urgent cultural problems cited in Emerson's aesthetic agenda, integrating material and technological progress with a national identity rooted in a pastoral ideal and its attendant spiritual freedom. Beginning with *Democratic Vistas,* a theoretical exegesis published in 1871, Whitman disclosed his poetic techniques for repairing the decidedly industrialized American society. As "divine literatus," he converted apparently contradictory images of rural and urban existence, organic and mechanical forces, and individual and collective experiences into symbols representing the "Kosmos" and its contingencies, the "Me" and the "Not-Me." To this end, Whitman used juxtaposition, parallelism, and repetition of word symbols and syntax, first to set up and then to dissolve oppositions between man-made and natural forms. In such poems as "Give Me the Splendid Silent Sun," "Crossing Brooklyn Ferry," and "Eiddlons," he intwerwove verbal patterns and word images of the city and industry with the organic rhythms and scintillating surfaces of nature's processes and physical forms.

Sullivan responded to Whitman's poems by naturalizing the technology of skyscraper construction. In "The Tall Office Building Artistically Considered" (1896) Sullivan distinguished between the technological/economic and the metaphysical problems of the skyscraper. He argued that the speculator, engineer, and builder had made the skyscraper an object of physical forces and materialist values, what he considered "the perversities" of American culture. To reverse this process, Sullivan restated the skyscraper problem from the perspective of a poet: "How shall we proclaim from the dizzying height of this strange, weird, modern housetop the peaceful evangel of sentiment, of beauty, the cult of higher life?" Having equated the technological with the divine, Sullivan insisted that "the true architect" must give the skyscraper "its full justification and higher sanctification. . . . [He] must realize . . . that the problem of the tall office building is one of the most stupendous, one of the most magnificent opportunities that the Lord of Nature in His beneficence has ever offered to the proud spirit of man." Here, Sullivan moved from "coarser to finer considerations" and, in the process, returned to nature where the problem of reconciling the physical and spiritual aspects of the skyscraper "dissolved."

In his most Whitmanesque skyscraper, the Guaranty Building (Buffalo, New York, 1894–1896), Sullivan fused his symbols of the "Objective" and "Subjective" into an image of the "Infinite Creative Spirit." In this building, he adorned the entire geometric composition of steel-cage construction, primary structural elements, and building mass with low relief organic ornament, what he called the garment of poetic imagery. At the same time, he exaggerated the ascending and descending directions of the unbroken vertical piers, carried by half-circle arches, to symbolize nature's incessant rhythms of growth and decay. Sullivan thus fully realized an "image of our poetic art: utilitarian in foundation, harmonious in superstructure."

Viewed as a poetic means of architectural expression, the repeated structural patterns and scintillating surface textures of the building evoke a process of dematerialization compa-

rable to Whitman's verbal interweaving of urban imagery with the organic rhythms of natural phenomena. But while Whitman obliterated distinctions between city and country, Sullivan realized that in fulfilling his Emersonian task as an urban architect only a self-contained poetic image of naturalized technology could provide the city dweller with a transcendental return to nature and a spiritual escape from the constraints of the late-nineteenth-century urban existence.

—*Lauren S. Weingarden*

**See also**
Skyscraper; Whitman, Walt.
**References**

Machor, James L. "Pastoralism and the American Urban Ideal: Hawthorne, Whitman, and the Literary Pattern." *American Literature* 54 (1982): 330–340.

Sullivan, Louis H. "Emotional Architecture as Compared with Intellectual: A Study in Subjective and Objective." In Isabella Athey, ed., *Kindergarten Chats and Other Writings*. New York: Wittenborn, 1947.

———. *Louis H. Sullivan: System of Architectural Ornament*. Chicago: Rizzoli, Art Institute of Chicago, Ernst Wasmuth Verlag, 1990.

Weingarden, Lauren S. *Louis H. Sullivan: The Banks*. Cambridge, MA: MIT Press, 1987.

———. "Naturalized Nationalism: A Ruskinian Discourse on the Search for an American Style of Architecture." *Winterthur Portfolio* 24 (1989): 43–68.

———. "Restoring Romanticism to the World's Fair: The Sullivan-Olmsted Collaboration." In Gustavo Curiel, et al., eds., *XVII Colloquio Internacional de Historia del Arte: Arte, Historia e Identidad en America: Visiones Comparativas*, vol. II, 375–386. Mexico City: Universidad Nacional Autonoma de Mexico, 1994.

———. "Sullivan's Emersonian Reading of Whitman." In Geoffrey Sill and Roberta Tarbell, eds., *Walt Whitman and the Visual Arts*. New Brunswick, NJ: Rutgers University Press, 1991.

## Sunday, Billy (1862–1935)

Billy Sunday became one of the foremost urban evangelists in American religious history. Born William Ashley Sunday on a farm near Ames, Iowa, Sunday spent much of his early life in a Civil War orphanage and received little formal education. He became a major league baseball player in 1883, and three years later he made a formal commitment to Christianity at Chicago's Pacific Garden Rescue Mission. In 1891, he quit baseball and devoted himself to the ministry full-time. He worked for the Young Men's Christian Association and traveled with another popular evangelist of the day, J. Wilbur Chapman. By 1896, he was receiving invitations to preach throughout Iowa and other parts of the upper Midwest.

In 1908 Sunday began to receive invitations from larger cities throughout the country. His wife, Helen Amelia Thompson, known more affectionately as "Ma Sunday," worked to make arrangements with local churches and organize the campaigns ahead of Sunday's arrival. Beginning in Spokane, Washington, but soon extending to Chicago and New York,

Sunday held evangelistic revivals until his death in 1935. Millions of people heard Sunday's version of the gospel.

Billy Sunday had a distinctive preaching style that was meant to appeal more to the working class than the middle class. A typical Sunday sermon included acrobatic stunts performed atop a chair and earthy criticisms of almost everything and everyone. The evangelist once proudly exclaimed, "I don't know any more about theology than a jack-rabbit knows about ping-pong, but I'm on my way to glory."

Although not always approved by the religious establishment, Sunday clearly hoped to change the basic lifestyle of the unchurched working class. Best known for his "booze" sermon, which he preached hundreds of times, he is often credited with helping bring prohibition to many communities. Sunday also preached on topics ranging from laziness to swearing. In still other sermons, Sunday argued that the urban environment needed to be improved and that there was a direct connection between the environment and sin.

Sunday's career began to decline in the 1920s, and he ceased to receive invitations for multiweek revivals from the major cities of the nation. Nevertheless, until he died in 1935 he continued to preach in communities throughout the United States. Sunday ranks among the most important revivalists in American history, along with Charles G. Finney, Dwight Moody, and Billy Graham. His career peaked during a period of rapid urbanization and at a time when middle-class and working-class values were contending with each other. In some sense, Sunday bridged those class divisions. He appealed to the working class because of his folksy uncomplicated style; he appealed to the middle class because he vigorously opposed the use of alcohol and embraced the virtue of hard work. He reflects the importance of religious influences on the process of urbanization in American history.

—*Dale E. Soden*

### References

Dorsett, Lyle W. *Billy Sunday and the Redemption of Urban America.* Grand Rapids, MI: William B. Eerdmans, 1991.

McLaughlin, W. G., Jr. *Billy Sunday Was His Real Name.* Chicago: University of Chicago Press, 1955.

## Supermarkets

Supermarkets are large grocery stores, doing over $2.5 million a year in retail business and comprising approximately 30,000–40,000 square feet of floor space. As many as 30,000 individual items may line the shelves of a typical outlet. There are about 23,000 supermarkets, and though they comprise only 10 percent of the grocery outlets, they sell three-fourths of the food not purchased for use in restaurants.

The development of supermarkets as a major sales and cultural influence in American urban society can be traced to their creation in the 1920s on the West Coast and the early days of the Great Depression in the East. The first Eastern supermarket opened in 1932 at Elizabeth, New Jersey. Supermarkets were originators of the mass-merchandising concept where the seller relies on low prices and breadth of inventory to produce rapid merchandise turnover, large sales volume, and adequate profits. Total supermarket sales first topped $1 billion in 1938.

Historically, several factors converged to allow early supermarkets to meet potential customers' needs and succeed as a marketing phenomenon. Price structure, urbanization, transportation networks, and population mobility allowed the growth of these large, centralized shopping facilities. Early supermarkets used several pioneering strategies to control overhead and keep prices low. Initially, they were located in vacant warehouses, and unlike traditional, neighborhood grocery stores of the era, fledgling supermarkets supplanted personalized service with less costly self-service. Ongoing cost-containment measures maintained low pricing practices, and today, efficiency of operation is still a hallmark of the supermarket industry. Supermarkets maintain the lowest profit margins of any major business category, at about 1 percent of sales.

The continued success of supermarkets has facilitated changes in the way people purchase food items and, indirectly, has affected lifestyles. With all food items at one location it was no longer necessary to shop several specialty stores. Because of quick stock turnover, customers could expect a predictable supply of fresh food that contributed to the trend away from daily visits to grocery stores. People began making purchases two or three times a week, instead of daily. The parallel, technical development of refrigeration allowed more goods to be purchased and stored at one time, for longer periods. With less time spent gathering foodstuffs, time was freed for other activities. With fewer shopping visits to perform, consumers became willing to frequent more distant supermarkets, depending on the ubiquitous automobile to get there. Ultimately, even our urban landscapes have been shaped by supermarkets. To further facilitate the trend toward large numbers of shoppers driving to a relatively small number of stores, supermarkets provided large parking lots, which we now take for granted as icons of city and suburban life.

Though a wide assortment of grocery items has always been the mainstay of the supermarket, in recent years they have expanded their offerings to include other goods, including pharmaceuticals, clothing, flowers, stationary supplies, and even light hardware and automotive items. Other product distributors were quick to notice the success of the supermarket concept and began patterning their operations after these grocery outlets. Mass merchandising, instigated by the supermarkets of 60 years ago, has produced retail giants like Wal-Mart and K-Mart. Today the blossoming superstore concept may be considered a direct descendant of the original grocery supermarkets.

—*Barlow Soper*

References

Berman, Barry, and Joel R. Evans. *Retail Management: A Strategic Approach.* 5th ed. New York: MacMillan, 1992.

McCarthy, E. Jerome, and William D. Perreault, Jr. *Basic Marketing: A Global Managerial Approach.* 11th ed. Homewood, IL: Irwin, 1993.

Phillips, Charles F., and Delbert J. Duncan. *Marketing Principles and Methods.* 6th ed. Homewood, IL: Irwin, 1968.

## Swift, Gustavus Franklin (1839–1903)

Gustavus Swift, American meatpacker and agroindustrialist, is best known for commercializing the refrigerated shipment of fresh beef by rail from Chicago to New York. Raised in Massachusetts, Swift rose from butcher boy at age 14 to cattle buyer and eventually founder of Chicago-based Swift and Company in 1885, North America's largest fully integrated meatpacking firm.

Swift arrived in Chicago in 1875, about the same time as Philip Armour, George Hammond, and the other emergent meat barons who became the millionaire scions of Chicago's industrial elite. The rapid growth of the industry after the establishment of the Union Stock Yard in 1865 encouraged the in-migration of these merchant capitalists. They were opportunists both in their selection of growth industries and in their adoption of Chicago—"hog butcher to the world"—as home, headquarters, and locus of capital accumulation.

Involved at all stages of cattle procurement, slaughter, and meat retailing, Gustavus Swift recognized the enormous profitability of large-scale meatpacking if only some means could be found to prevent fresh beef from spoiling. The refrigerated rail shipment of fresh beef from the Midwest to the East Coast had been inaugurated by George Hammond. Swift's major achievement was in retaining Andrew Chase to engineer an improved reefer design. The shipment of large quantities of beef in "Swift-Chase cars" began in 1877. With iceboxes at both ends of the car and a ventilation system that ensured a constant flow of air around each carcass, the design was soon used by all of Swift's major competitors, including George Hammond himself.

One of Swift's greatest achievements was his command of logistics. Under nineteenth-century refrigeration technology, fully integrated meatpackers required winter ice harvesting operations. Swift developed a network of ice stations in northern Illinois and Wisconsin to supply the two tons of ice required to keep each carload of meat chilled during its four-day journey to eastern markets.

Swift pioneered a Canadian alternative to the hegemony that the northeastern pikes (led by the New York Central) attempted to exert over the Chicago–East Coast shipment of beef. Routing eastbound refrigerated beef traffic through southern Ontario on the Grand Trunk Railway broke this attempt to control captive shippers. By 1885 over 60 percent of Chicago's dressed meat output was shipped via Canada and the Grand Trunk, benefiting from lower freight rates and lower ice consumption.

Swift was also an innovator in retailing. At a time when traditional butchers cut each piece of meat to order from carcasses kept hidden in the cooler, Swift recognized that sales would increase if carcasses were cut and displayed ahead of time in an apparently hygienic meat case. In Swift's words, "The more you cut, the more you sell." Swift's injunction is still the guiding principle of supermarket meat-counter management.

Gustavus Swift died on March 29, 1903, in Chicago, leaving Swift and Company as his legacy. The firm endured until it transformed itself into Esmark, a conglomerate holding company, in 1973. Fresh meat operations were spun off as Swift Independent Packing Company (SIPCO) in 1981, which contracted and collapsed as a meatpacking enterprise in the mid-1980s. While the enterprise has disintegrated, the "Swift's Premium" brand name has maintained the essential value built up by its founder.

—*Ian MacLachlan*

References

Skaggs, Jimmy M. *Prime Cut: Livestock Raising and Meatpacking in the United States, 1607–1983.* College Station: Texas A & M University Press, 1986.

Swift, Louis F., and Arthur Van Vlissengen, Jr. *The Yankee of the Yards: The Biography of Gustavus Franklin Swift.* Chicago: A. W. Shaw, 1927.

Wade, Louise Carroll. *Chicago's Pride: The Stockyards, Packingtown, and Environs in the Nineteenth Century.* Urbana: University of Illinois Press, 1987.

## Tammany Hall

New York City's Tammany Hall epitomizes urban political machines. A political machine is a party organization that gains electoral support by controlling and distributing patronage and services. As a result, it is capable of reliably centralizing power within its jurisdiction.

The Democratic machine in Manhattan originated as the Tammany Society or Columbian Order, a local patriotic society, in May 1789. The society took these names from its two patron saints, Christopher Columbus and St. Tammany, a great chief of the Delaware Indians, and it appropriated several Indian terms. The society's clubhouse was known as the Wigwam, and Tammany itself was popularly called "the Tiger." Its governing body, the grand council, consisted of the grand sachem and 13 subordinate sachems. After 1812, when the general committee of the city's Democratic Party began meeting in a hall owned by the Tammany Society, the city's dominant Democratic organization became known as Tammany Hall.

Tammany has often been considered an "unofficial" welfare agency for the city's poor, and its association with patronage and corruption has long been part of New York politics. The Tweed Ring Scandal of 1871 was a celebrated case implicating Tammany's boss, William Marcy Tweed, and his closest associates. But Tammany has not always supported the public provision of social services for the poor. In 1877 the Tammany administration itself, for internal party reasons, slashed the municipal outdoor relief program for the city's poor. And it was only toward the 1890s that Tammany centralized power within the organization; eliminated rival factions of the Democratic Party, notably Irving Hall and the County Democracy; and dominated government and politics in New York City.

An essential element of Tammany's political power was controlling primary elections in the city. The state Democratic Party's recognition that Tammany was New York City's "regular" Democratic organization gave Tammany tremendous power. It was able to exert influence not only in the city but also in the determination of platforms and candidates in state party conventions. Control of the nation's largest city and tremendous sway in its largest state allowed Tammany to play an important role in national Democratic politics as well.

Tammany Hall's political structure evolved through the years. At its top was the party boss who chaired the powerful Committee on Organization, or Executive Committee, which included the city's assembly district or ward leaders. Each ward had its own ward committee that represented the ward's election districts. When combined, these ward committees formed Tammany Hall's General Committee for the entire city. At the bottom were the election district committees headed by local leaders or captains.

Following the Tweed Ring debacle, the organization that had once been dominated by Yankees came under Irish rule; its new boss, John Kelly (1871–1886), laid the foundation of the modern Tammany machine. The Wigwam established its hegemony by creating a coalition among major political forces in the city—business, labor, and the poor—that also cut across class lines. By 1890 Tammany, under Boss Richard Croker (1886–1902), had extended its sway beyond the city into state politics. After 1888, the city's Board of Aldermen was at the command of the boss, and in 1892 and 1893 Croker dictated state legislation in Albany by telephone from Tammany headquarters. After the election of Robert Van Wyck as mayor in 1897, the boss drew up the entire slate of mayoral appointments. The extraordinary power of the machine and its boss is revealed by the fact that Croker's successor, Charles Murphy (1902–1924), secured the impeachment of the incumbent Governor William Sulzer for his insubordination on patronage issues.

Nevertheless, Tammany's power was never as absolute as opponents believed nor was its rule in the city uninterrupted. Between 1894 and 1933, Tammany briefly lost control of City Hall four times to fusion candidates who favored reform. Then, in 1933, the election of Fiorello La Guardia as mayor banished the Tiger to 12 years in the political wilderness. The Depression unleashed anti-Tammany insurgencies, from Jews and Italians in particular, and the national political realignment under the New Deal further undermined Tammany's power by freezing the Tiger out of both state and federal patronage. The machine staged one last comeback under Carmine de Sapio (1949–1961), its first Italian-American boss. But in 1961 the boss lost a hotly contested election for district leadership in Greenwich Village to Village Independent Democrats.

The failure in the years after World War II to genuinely incorporate new ethnic groups, particularly blacks and Hispanics, into the organization; the rise of new political forces organized as independent interest groups, such as the Liberal Party and the municipal employees; and the challenge from reformers within the Democratic Party itself all contributed to the demise of Tammany Hall as a citywide political machine and the central influence in New York City politics.

—*Adonica Y. Lui*

### References

Breen, Mathew P. *Thirty Years of New York Politics.* New York: John Polhemus Printing Company, 1899.

Erie, Steven P. *Rainbow's End: Irish Americans and the Dilemmas of Urban Machine Politics, 1840–1985.* Berkeley: University of California Press, 1988.

Garret, Charles. *The La Guardia Years, Machine and Reform Politics in New York City.* New Brunswick, NJ: Rutgers University Press, 1961.

Hammack, David C. *Power and Society: Greater New York at the Turn of the Century.* New York: Russell Sage Foundation, 1982.

Hirsch, Mark D. *William D. Whitney: Modern Warwick.* New York: Dodd, Mead, 1948.

Lui, Adonica Y. "Party Machines, State Structure and Social Policies: The Abolition of Public Outdoor Relief in New York City, 1874–1898." Ph.D. dissertation, Harvard University, 1993.

Rhadamanthus [C. A. Brown '97 and G. H. Dorr '97]. *A History of Tammany Hall.* Privately printed, 1955.

Riordon, William L. *Plunkitt of Tammany Hall.* New York: Dutton, 1963.

Shefter, Martin. "The Emergence of the Political Machine: An Alternative View." In Willis D. Hawley and Michael Lipsky, eds., *Theoretical Perspectives on Urban Politics.* Englewood Cliffs, NJ: Prentice-Hall, 1976.

———. *Political Crisis, Fiscal Crisis: The Collapse and Revival of New York City.* New York: Basic Books, 1985.

———. "Trade Unions and Political Machines: The Organization and Disorganization of the American Working Class in the Late Nineteenth Century." In Ira Katznelson and Aristide Zolberg, eds., *Working Class Formation: Nineteenth Century Patterns in Western Europe and the United States,* 197–296. Princeton, NJ: Princeton University Press, 1986.

Windhoff-Heritier, Adrienne. *City of the Poor, City of the Rich: Politics and Policy in New York City.* New York: Walter de Gruyter, 1992.

## Tampa, Florida

Nature endowed the vast estuary known as Tampa Bay with remarkable vitality and variety. The bay's 212 miles of shoreline support a complex ecosystem, made possible by ample supplies of freshwater from rivers, springs, and aquifers.

The region surrounding Tampa Bay has been the scene of human habitation for 10,000 years, making it one of the oldest inhabited sites in North America, but in an astonishingly brief period contact with Europeans proved fatal to the Tocobaga Indians. Pánfilo de Narváez and Hernando de Soto, who led the first European invasions into the American mainland, landed at Tampa Bay in 1528 and 1538, respectively. De Soto was one of the last Europeans to observe large, cohesive, and populous groups of natives in the American Southeast as the local Indians vanished soon after 1600. The encounter, though disastrous to Native Americans, left a rich legacy in what scholars call the "Columbian Exchange."

Modern Tampa owes its origin to Fort Brooke. In 1821, centuries of Spanish power in Florida ended with transfer of the territory to the United States. The American government attempted to solve the Indian "problem" by forcing several thousand Seminole Indians to leave north Florida for reservations around Tampa Bay, and in 1823 the War Department ordered construction of a military cantonment to check the Indian threat. Fort Brooke took hold on the east side of the Hillsborough River, where the river met the bay. When the Second Seminole War ended in 1842, a city began to emerge around the fort. Fort Brooke served as fortress and gateway for thousands of soldiers, symbolizing for present and future generations the power of the federal government as maker of cities and source of prosperity.

The city of Tampa, having already served as the seat of Hillsborough County since 1834, was officially incorporated in 1849, although Fort Brooke was not deactivated until the early 1880s. The city's antebellum fortunes rose and fell in an irregular cycle of war and peace, boom and bust, mercantile boosterism and natural disaster. Its population approached 1,000 in the 1840s and 1850s with development of its port and settlement of its hinterland. While voices from Europe and the Caribbean could be heard, the predominant accent was southern, especially Georgian. Captain James McKay, a Scottish immigrant, began a lucrative cattle trade with Cuba in 1859, rounding up longhorns on Florida's open range and shipping them from Ballast Point. By 1850 the population of Hillsborough County had climbed to 2,377, and it grew to 2,981 in 1860. Approximately one-fourth of the county residents were slaves, although the percentage was smaller in the city itself.

The Civil War brought grief and suffering to Tampans. In May 1864, following bombardment and blockade by Union gunboats, Tampa surrendered. The town's population had fallen to only a few hundred during the war, and they were almost certainly dissatisfied as they watched federal troops spike the cannons at Fort Brooke and liberate the remaining slaves. They almost certainly preferred the prompt departure of the Union army.

Hard times continued in Tampa during Reconstruction. Friction between freedmen and whites generated conflict and violence, and federal troops, including African Americans, were needed to help keep the peace. Economically, Tampa languished in the 1860s and 1870s. Demographically, the city was losing people; its population in 1880 had declined to only 720. Periodic outbreaks of virulent yellow fever further dimmed confidence in the city's future.

The direction and character of Tampa changed drastically in the 1880s. In 1884, Henry Bradley Plant brought the railroad to the city and made it the hub of his vast transportation empire, which by 1900 included more than 2,000 miles of railroad track and a steamship line. The Plant System integrated Tampa into national and international transportation and communications networks. The railroad also made a flourishing agricultural industry possible. The discovery of phosphate east of Tampa boosted Plant's fortunes even more, and the robber baron created a new city, Port Tampa, to facilitate the flow of phosphate and other cargo from the region. Plant's railroad also brought new waves of northern tourists. Many of them stayed at his opulent hotels, none grander than the Tampa Bay Hotel, a $3 million Byzantine jewel that opened in 1891.

Plant's railroad buoyed Tampa's hopes and its population. By 1885 the city had grown to 2,376 residents. The demographic character and composition of the city changed dramatically in 1886, when Spanish entrepreneur Vicente Martinez Ybor moved his cigar factory to Tampa and thousands of Cuban, Spanish, and Italian immigrants made Ybor City—then a separate town on Tampa Bay that was soon joined to the larger city—their home. Tampa's prosperity was linked to the sales of fine, hand-rolled cigars, and hundreds of cigar factories dotted Ybor City and West Tampa (an immigrant enclave begun in 1895 and incorporated into Tampa in 1925). Ten thousand Spaniards, Cubans, and Italians—collectively called "Latin" in the vernacular—rolled millions of cigars annually, making Tampa synonymous with Hav-a-Tampas, Tampa Nuggets, and Tampa Girls.

Ybor City and West Tampa existed as islands in the Deep South. They hosted a Latin workforce in a region dominated by native southerners, and they supported an industry characterized by handicrafts in a nation increasingly oriented to clocks, schedules, and mass production. By the 1930s, a WPA writer observed that "Tampa is politically southern, industrially northern, and has a distinct Spanish atmosphere." When strikes interrupted the supply of cigars—and savage, protracted strikes occurred in 1899, 1901, 1920, and 1931—Tampa was paralyzed.

In 1900, Tampa boasted a population of 15,839, a figure that soared over 100,000 by 1930. Increasingly, decisions in New York, Washington, and abroad affected local fortunes. In the spring of 1898 Tampa served as the port of debarkation for 66,000 soldiers bound for Cuba to fight in the Spanish-American War, Tampa's neighborhoods reflected the race, class, and ethnicity of their inhabitants. Virtually all of the Latin immigrants (except the owners, of course) resided in Ybor City or West Tampa. African Americans (more than 21,000 by 1930) lived in proscribed ghettos, such as Dobyville, the Scrub, Belmont Heights, and College Hill. Anglo-Americans chose neighborhoods such as Hyde Park, Tampa Heights, Sulphur Springs, and Seminole Heights, according to their family's status.

A well-defined color line determined the nature of race relations in Tampa. The census reported that virtually all of Tampa's 4,200 servants, maids, and laundresses were black. The city's 20,000 African-American workers included just 18 teachers, four dentists, and two lawyers. Only as stevedores did blacks gain a meaningful economic niche.

The decade of the 1920s left an indelible mark on Tampa and on Florida. A wave of new tourists—Tin Can Tourists they were called—arrived in their Model T Fords. By the end of the 1920s, tourists could drive to Miami via the newly opened Tamiami Trail. The construction of the Gandy Bridge in 1924 facilitated travel between Tampa and St. Petersburg and reduced the 43-mile excursion around Tampa Bay to only 19 miles. Developer David P. David engineered a remarkable accomplishment when he created Davis Island out of muck and landfill in 1925.

The Depression smashed Tampa's economy, especially the slumping cigar industry. The New Deal provided some relief, and government projects included building or improving major roads, a state park, and an airport. It was World War II that truly galvanized Tampa, and the city's industries, ports, and farms turned out cigars, oranges, phosphate, and ships for the crusade. Employment at shipyards reached 16,000, and the yards generated payrolls exceeding $750,000 a week. MacDill Air Field and Drew Air Field—the latter destined to become Tampa International Airport—trained thousands of B-17 and B-29 fliers during the war. To ease transportation between MacDill and Drew fields, the government constructed Dale Mabry Highway. Today, Dale Mabry symbolizes the lack of mass transit and the traffic woes of modern Tampa; the last streetcar had made its final journey in 1946.

Tampa stood at a crossroads in 1945, and many civic leaders demanded reform and change. To the rest of the world, Tampa was synonymous with cigars (a dying industry) and sleaze (scores of unsolved gangland slayings had prompted one writer to describe Tampa as "Sin City of the South") in the 1940s. Bolita, a local variant of the numbers racket, had corrupted local politics, making a farce of the franchise and some elections. But as Bolita slowly lost influence, Tampa politics became cleaner, if less interesting.

The betrayal of Ybor City marked one of the great tragedies of Tampa after World War II. In 1965, the Great Society unfurled its sails, and Tampa leaders—Anglo and Latin—eagerly accepted federal funds. Under the guise of urban renewal, they demolished much of the Latin quarter. Where factories, cottages, and cafes had once stood, 51 acres still sit vacant 30 years later. Today, the vestige of Ybor City flourishes as an exotic collection of restaurants, art studios, and nightclubs.

Most Tampans shed few tears over the destruction of Ybor City because new industries have promised a brighter future than Hav-a-Tampas. Lured by sunshine, aggressive recruiting, ample industrial parklands, and low taxes, hundreds of new businesses have moved to Tampa since World War II. These new businesses bring diversity to the regional economy: brewing, steel, shrimp processing, insurance, and services, for example. Clearly, the scarcity of Fortune 500 companies that have located their corporate headquarters in Tampa weakens the city's economic base. This weakness can also be felt in the region's persistent difficulty supporting philanthropic and social causes, such as orchestras, universities, and other social institutions.

Technology has dramatically changed Tampa's relationship to the world and even to nature. Air conditioning lures tourists and migrants to the Sunshine State, paralleling the population boom after World War II. As late as 1960, only one of every six households in Tampa was cooled by air conditioning; today scarcely one in ten is not served by the new technologies of heating and cooling. Air conditioning, accompanied by other new technologies, has also altered skylines and neighborhoods. The ubiquitous ranch house and concrete block structure have replaced environmentally adaptable bungalows and cottages. Glass-paneled skyscrapers, depressingly similar to structures in Atlanta and Seattle, dominate the corporate city's skyline.

Air conditioning has also helped create a year-round tourist industry. The central focus of Tampa's tourist industry during the last several decades has been Busch Gardens. In 1959, when the park adjoining the Busch brewery opened, only 70,000 tourists visited Tampa annually. Within a dozen years, the amusement park had become the state's leading tourist attraction, drawing a million and a half tourists annually. The opening of Disney World near Orlando in 1971 quickly forced many of the smaller attractions out of business. Busch Gardens itself has survived, drawing 3.7 million tourists in 1994 compared to the 30 million flocking to Disney's Magic Kingdom, Epcot, and MGM Studios.

Tampa and the Tampa Bay area have devoted enormous energy and capital to attracting professional sports. Since 1915, Tampa has been home to baseball teams during spring training, but only since the 1980s have Florida cities offered "Grapefruit League" teams attractive tax and development packages. In 1947, Tampa hosted the Cigar Bowl in a brief flirtation with postseason college football. In 1976, the National Football League awarded Tampa a franchise. The Tampa Bay Buccaneers have for most of their history been a miserable failure on the field, but civic leaders insist that the resulting publicity finally gave the city a "major league" image. In 1996, taxpayers narrowly decided in a bitterly contested referendum to build a new, publicly financed football stadium. In 1998, the city also became home to a new major league baseball team, the Tampa Bay Devil Rays.

Downtown Tampa began declining in the 1950s, and few buildings were constructed there between 1950 and 1970. Since the 1970s, hundreds of millions of dollars, courtesy of federal, state, local, and private sources, have been spent to rejuvenate the downtown core. This tremendous amount of money has generated a curious phenomenon. On the one hand, the downtown "appears" to be booming—scores of expensive new buildings dominate the skyline, highlighted by a performing arts center, hockey arena, aquarium, convention center, and plethora of banking complexes. On the other hand, the city seems to have lost control of its urban destiny. Deregulation has meant that almost all of the banking complexes are owned and controlled by outside interests. Tampa's leadership, once selected from among the city's own banks, utilities, newspapers, and corporations, has been challenged by new demands for inclusiveness and change.

—*Gary R. Mormino*

**References**
Grismer, Karl. *Tampa: A History of the City.* St. Petersburg, FL: St. Petersburg Printing Company, 1950.
Mormino, Gary R., and George E. Pozzetta. *The Immigrant World of Ybor City: Italians and Their Latin Neighbors in Tampa, 1885–1985.* Urbana: University of Illinois Press, 1987.
Mormino, Gary R., and Tony Pizzo. *Tampa: The Treasure City.* Tulsa, OK: Continental Heritage Press, 1983.
*Tampa Bay History* (1979– ).

## Telegraph

The telegraph revolutionized communication during the nineteenth century. Instrumental in settling the American West, it became the most important communications link between towns and cities that developed alongside the expanding railroad system.

Invented in the United States by Samuel F. B. Morse and his associates Leonard Gale and Alfred Vail in 1837, and in Great Britain later that same year by Sir Charles Wheatstone and Sir William Cooke, the telegraph was the most expeditious way of reporting news and business activities for most of the nineteenth century. Morse's invention used electric current that passed through a single long-distance wire; the sending operator controlled a simple switch (called a key) that interrupted or activated the flow of current in order to form codes that represented characters of the English alphabet. At the receiving station, the bursts of current were converted to audio tones or marks on moving paper tape that allowed the receiving operator to decipher the transmission. The codes used by Morse consisted of short bursts and long bursts called dots and dashes. This code, known as the Morse code, is still used throughout the world for many types of communication.

Morse received a patent for the telegraph in 1840, and Congress provided $30,000 to construct a trial telegraph line between Baltimore, Maryland, and Washington, D.C., in 1843. In this experiment, Morse discovered that telegraph signals could not be transmitted successfully for more than 30 kilometers so he developed a relay station that used battery power to regenerate signals over longer distances. By cascading relay stations at 30-kilometer intervals, it was possible to transmit messages over great distances. In 1844 Morse successfully completed the Baltimore-Washington line, and he demonstrated its capability by announcing the presidential and vice-presidential nominees in Baltimore well before local delegates returned from Washington with the same news. This feat captured the attention of both the federal government and the railroad industry, which required a means for dispatching trains and supplies.

Telegraph cables were strung parallel to railroad tracks throughout the United States, and railroads used them first, primarily to schedule and control train traffic. Operators in train stations routinely reported train accidents and robberies on the telegraph. In those cases where only a single set of tracks connected two distant towns, the telegraph was used to indicate track usage and prevent head-on collisions while increasing railway efficiency.

Like radio and television later, the telegraph experienced exponential growth in just over a decade. In 1846, only 40 miles of telegraph wire connected cities in the United States. By 1848, 2,000 miles of wire had been hung. Approximately 12,000 miles of wire connected American cities by 1850, and in 1852, just six years after the telegraph was introduced, more than 23,000 miles of wire serviced towns and cities across the country. During this time, a variable fee was charged for transmitting a message of ten words or less. From Washington to Baltimore, the typical fee was 20 cents. From Washington to New Orleans, it was $2.40.

The telegraph quickly became the most important means of communication between American cities in the nineteenth century. While horse couriers and railroads still carried routine personal communications, the telegraph was used to send news throughout the country, for business correspondence, and for urgent personal messages. The tele-

graph was the world's first long-distance communications device, and it enabled American business and the western frontier to expand at a time when no other rapid communications mechanism existed. However, due to the use of Morse code, and the need for special operating equipment, the telegraph was never meant to provide a personal means of communication for every American citizen. Eventually, the popularity of the telegraph yielded to the telephone, which was first developed by Alexander Graham Bell in the late 1860s and which provided a means of personal communication in cities, using much of the existing telegraph infrastructure, toward the end of the nineteenth century.

—*Jason Hale and Theodore S. Rappaport*

**See also**
Telephone.
**References**
Andrews, Frederick T. "The Heritage of Telegraphy." *IEEE Communications Magazine* (1989): 12–18.
Ault, Phil. *Wires West.* New York: Dodd, Mead, 1974.
Rappaport, Theodore S. *Wireless Communications.* New York: Prentice-Hall, 1996.
Thompson, Robert. *Wiring a Continent.* New York: Arno Press, 1972.

## Telephone

The telephone has traditionally been defined and used as an instrument to reproduce articulate, comprehensible speech and other sounds at a distance using electrical waves. This is still its main function, although in recent decades telephone systems have become an integral part of modern telecommunications systems in general through the use of their circuits to transmit and process telephoto, television, facsimile, and computer signals. Also, the spread of cellular phone technology has substantially enhanced locational flexibility in transmitting phone messages. Overall, since the phone's invention in 1876, technological developments have progressively extended the geographical range of its signals from the local to the regional, then to the national, and then to the global. Concomitantly, the speed and cost of sending telephone messages long distances, either nationally or internationally, have both declined, especially during the 1980s and 1990s.

The invention of the telegraph in the 1840s had created a space-transcending technology that allowed the virtual separation of communication from transportation (except for the physical intervention of telegraphers and telegram deliverers, the whole message was moved electronically). However, the telephone took this separation an important step further by offering the possibility of instant long-distance verbal communication without the necessity of preliminary encoding or decoding. Nevertheless, despite this manifest advantage, early technical limitations combined with high costs and limited perceived consumer need to restrict the telephone's spread. Thus, for the first 30 years of its history, the phone remained largely an urban phenomenon and, within cities, the early diffusion of the instrument was restricted mainly to the homes and offices of professionals and businesspeople.

This limited penetration was gradually expanded as the majority of middle-class urban households outside the South adopted the phone by the 1920s. However, for most of the North American urban working class, as well as many middle-class urbanites in the South, ready access to a household phone only occurred during and after World War II. This relatively recent "social democratization" of the phone has effectively made it universal, although the instrument's overall household penetration rate of 93 percent in 1990 remains lower than the 98 percent penetration of television sets.

The gradual spread of the telephone has stimulated more speculation than research about the centrality of its influence in shaping urban ecology and social structure. In some areas, it was clearly a first cause of urban change. In others, it was one factor among many, but the specific nature of its impact may have been exaggerated by technological determinists. Finally, some hypothesized impacts should be regarded as doubtful. Thus, as a first cause, the maze of overhead wires that changed city streetscapes in the late nineteenth century was the most visible reminder of the new technology. More subtly, the thousands of messengers who traveled the streets were gradually rendered obsolete by the technology, as were most telegraphers. In the demise of such occupations, and in the rise of new ones such as telephone operators (50,000 women in 1907), one can see the most obvious direct impact of the phone in the urban setting. However, more far-reaching, and also more controversial, is the telephone's purported role in both the centralization and decentralization of urban settlement.

In the view of Ithiel de Sola Pool, "the modern city in its present form, with its traffic jams, its high-rise office blocks downtown, and its sprawling suburbs, is a direct consequence of telecommunications developments at the turn of the century." In a nutshell, he argues that the telephone contributed to the growth of downtown business districts—that is, to centralization—by allowing the separation of company offices from their production facilities. Company offices moved downtown to be close to customers, suppliers, and financiers, and their executives used the telephone to communicate with plant managers rather than, as earlier, themselves being located on the factory premises. And when offices relocated, they moved into one of the new skyscrapers, which, so the argument goes, were also made possible only by the telephone. Thus, according to an early AT&T engineer, without the telephone every message would have had to be carried personally and the necessary banks of elevators would have

swamped available office space and rendered the concept of skyscrapers economically impossible.

This view of the telephone as facilitating the physical development of skyscrapers is accepted by a number of scholars, notably Pool, who also argues that the ability to build upwards led to the existence of more commodious and cheaper office space. Thus, the business phone helped create the demand for high-rise buildings downtown and the dense, congested downtown. With this final proposition, that the telephone facilitated downtown concentration, there can be little quarrel.

However, one scholar has correctly called the notion that the telephone made the skyscraper possible an "unexamined assertion." One might just as easily claim that the elevator made the skyscraper possible; and, as Claude Fischer asks, why would messengers have had to be used in the absence of the telephone? Why could pneumatic tubes not have been used instead? Telephones undoubtedly facilitated communication within high-rise buildings, but they were not the only available option.

Nonetheless, recognizing that the telephone played an initial role in favoring downtown concentration counterbalances the widespread notion that it, along with the automobile, was responsible for the growth of suburbs and the urban sprawl that typifies North American cities. Suburbanization was originally stimulated by transportation improvements, with the automobile amplifying the process greatly. However, the slow social diffusion of the telephone, as well as the fact that, even today, the great majority of calls are local, suggests that its role in suburbanization was probably limited. By the same token, the view that the automobile and telephone were major factors in the decline of local community life in small towns, as citizens extended their contacts beyond town boundaries, is also dubious. In a rare empirical study of localism in three California towns between 1890 and 1940, Claude Fischer concludes that both technologies did enable Americans to participate more easily and frequently in activities outside their communities, but they also encouraged and assisted the growth of local activities. Implicitly for Fischer, and explicitly for Jean Gottman, the telephone has linked people in towns and cities, and even in a *megalopolis,* Gottman's term for such huge conurbations as the Boston-Washington corridor. The megalopolis is geographically dispersed, but its numerous interconnected centers and subcenters are, in his view, linked and fostered by the telephone.

Yet, there is still an alternative vision of the impact of contemporary telecommunications on urban ecology: Marshall McLuhan's view that they can make the large city "dissolve like a fading shot in a movie." This view causes Alvin Toffler and others to place such developments as the fax, e-mail, telecommuting, and telemarketing at the center of *antipolis* (again Gottman's term), characterized by the dissolution of the nucleated city. In this scenario, urban centers and subcenters are attenuated and diminished as people linked by communications technology reside wherever they want. They live, work, and consume to a far greater extent within their "electronic cottages" and immediate communities than in cities. If this is the future urban scenario—and some scholars consider it one of the myths of the information age—the telephone will be the basic technology underlying the recent processes of decentralization. Paradoxically, it will also be a potent force against the social isolation and anomie that may arise.

—*Robert M. Pike*

### References

Fischer, Claude. *America Calling: A Social History of the Telephone to 1940.* Berkeley: University of California Press, 1992.

———. "Studying Technology and Social Life." In Manuel Castells, ed., *High Technology, Space and Society,* 284–301. Beverly Hills, CA: Sage Publications, 1985.

Gold, J. "Fishing in Muddy Waters: Communications Media and the Myth of the Electronic Cottage." In Stanley Brunn and Thomas Leinbach, eds., *Collapsing Time and Space: Geographical Aspects of Communication and Information,* 327–341. London: HarperCollins, 1991.

Gottman, Jean. "Megalopolis and Antipolis." In Ithiel de Sola Pool, ed., *The Social Impact of the Telephone,* 303–317. Cambridge, MA: MIT Press, 1977.

McLuhan, Marshall. *Understanding Media: The Extensions of Man.* London: Sphere Books, 1964.

Pool, Ithiel de Sola. *Forecasting the Telephone: A Retrospective Technology Assessment of the Telephone.* Norwood, NJ: Ablex Publishing, 1983.

———. *Technologies without Boundaries: On Telecommunications in a Global Age.* Eli Noam, ed. Cambridge, MA: Harvard University Press, 1990.

Toffler, Alvin. *The Third Wave.* London: Pan Books, 1990.

## Television

The etymological roots of the word *television* are the Greek *tele* (far off, from, or to a distance) and the Latin *visio* (the act of seeing, or that which appears). Technologically, television involves the transmission and synchronization of electronic sounds and images by frequency-modulated audio signals and amplitude-modulated video signals. In receiving these images, an electron scanning beam reads the image (constructed of pixels, lines, fields, and frames), which is then displayed on a receiver's picture tube. Television channels are allocated in both VHF and UHF bands. In the last 10 to 20 years, terrestrial (e.g., cable, telephone wire, fiberoptic) and satellite distribution systems have proliferated, generating renewed attention to the technology of television.

Integral to television's historical and cultural significance in the United States since World War II is its thorough entanglement with every aspect of daily home life. Since the 1920s, television's centrality to domestic life has been standardized through commercial and regulatory negotiations by corporate-industrial and governmental agencies. American television is uniquely positioned between commercial (in advertising, subscription, and as an entertainment medium) and public service applications (exemplified by the Public Broadcasting Service, public access television, and as an information medium regulated by the Federal Communications Commission).

From the dawn of the "electric age" in the middle of the 1800s, there has been active experimentation with the transmission of wireless images. Mechanical television—which scanned and synchronized images with rapidly spinning flat metal discs—was invented in Germany in 1884 by Paul Nipkow and was central to most experiments with television technology through the 1920s. By the 1930s, however, emerging electronic systems offered significantly clearer images. An American, Philo T. Farnsworth, developed successful synchronization of reception—which eliminated the ghostly afterimages of earlier experiments—while a Russian émigré, Vladimir Zworykin, patented the electronic camera pickup tube in 1928.

In 1934 Congress created the Federal Communications Commission and gave it the responsibility of coordinating several agencies then overseeing telegraph, telephone, and radio operations and of granting and revoking television licenses to broadcasters. After 1935, the Radio Corporation of America (RCA)—a leader in the development of television—was demonstrating the new technology to the trade press. In 1939, the company presented television to the public in the "Land of Tomorrow" exhibit at the New York World's Fair. By then, RCA, competing companies, and a curious public were exerting constant pressure on the government to allocate channels for television transmission and allow the marketing of television sets. By 1941, the FCC had approved regulations for black-and-white television, including the 525-line standard that is still used today. Television sets could now be purchased without the threat of possible obsolescence.

The FCC moved early to prevent broadcast monopolies in specific locations by arguing against NBC (one of the powerful radio networks that had acquired television broadcast licenses) that networks could own and operate only one station in a community. By 1943 this decision led NBC to sell its less profitable "Blue Network," which later became ABC. From 1940 to 1942, only a few dozen television stations were broadcasting in the United States, and the country's entrance into World War II froze further development.

At that time, broadcasters serviced eight major cities located primarily in the Northeast. In 1946, the first relay circuit between cities ran from New York City to Washington,

D.C., but not until 1948 did coaxial cables allow network relays from New York to the Midwest. Immediately after the war, the FCC rapidly issued new broadcast licenses (400 in 1946 alone), but it had allowed insufficient geographic separation between stations on the same channel causing considerable interference. From 1948 to 1952, the FCC "froze" the granting of new licenses while it resolved the issues. During these years, coaxial cable joined the East and West coasts allowing the creation of national networks.

While only a third of American homes—mostly urban and affluent—had television sets in the 1940s, television appeared in nearly two-thirds of the nation's homes between 1948 and 1955. By 1960 almost 90 percent of American households had at least one television set. Although receivers were readily available in 1946, the expansion of commercial television and the sale of sets grew most explosively in 1948 when television sales increased more than 500 percent over the previous year.

Television was promoted and standardized in concert with utopian hopes and dystopian fears about the ability of electronic media to transcend barriers of time and space. It could make the previously unseen visible and literally bring new visions home, directly into the secure domestic environment. Its broadcasts could "unite" regional and national communities of viewers. Television's negotiation of public and private space was enhanced by its dual "public service" role—inscribed and regulated by the federal government in the name of "public" airwaves—and its status as a privately controlled, commercial medium. Following radio's success (i.e., profitability) with sponsored programming, television incorporated advertising into its broadcasts. This was—and still is—a source of consternation to some as it implies the intrusion of the public market into the family hearth. However, utopians, who favored television's apparent ability to fuse radio's live address and motion pictures' ability to capture moving images, argued that television might erode monopolies of knowledge and open limitless vistas to citizens, regardless of whether families lived in an urban center or a rural farming community.

Television's domestication moved the new media away from being a spectacular novelty available only to a limited few and brought it into millions of American homes. Significantly, at first those homes belonged predominantly to white suburban families as television's conventional presentation of American life coincided with the suburban expansion that took place between 1946 and 1960. While the programs of the 1940s and early 1950s emphasized the locations where they originated (e.g., Philadelphia's *Kovacs on the Corner*) and presented comedy series about predominantly urban and immigrant, ethnic, working-class people (e.g., *The Goldbergs, Life with Luigi, Mama*), as television became a national me-

dium seeking national audiences, networks and sponsors favored programs that might appeal to a more "homogenous," commercially attractive, and increasingly suburban audience (e.g., *Father Knows Best, Ozzie and Harriet, Leave It to Beaver,* and *The Donna Reed Show*).

The critiques of suburbia that became popular in the middle of the 1950s (such as William Hyde Whyte's *The Organization Man* and John Keats's *The Crack in the Picture Window*) raised fears about television's rapid rise and naturalized role inside the home. Concerns often focused on gender roles and behavioral changes in "proper" socialization when technology entered private, domestic space. In the era of economic and ideological "reconversion" after World War II, which asserted that white, middle-class women belonged in the home, popular magazines and literature depicted them competing with television sets for their husbands' attention or as captives of daytime television who were unable to focus on their motherly and household duties because of their absorption in daytime shows. Equally, this threat to the proper functioning of private life was shown to affect fathers, who were inept when faced with television technology or lifeless while watching broadcast sporting events. Finally, children were portrayed as potentially threatened with permanently warped posture, violent hyperactivity, or severe eyestrain due to excessive exposure to television and its "rays."

The television set became equally crucial in advertising and in media representations of family togetherness, gender roles, child socialization, and the division of space within the suburban house. For instance, television was promoted as a consumer good that could entertain a "homemaker" while she simultaneously cleaned, cooked, and laundered. For the hardworking family patriarch in this dynamic, television offered a relatively inexpensive mode of easily accessible and varied entertainment. Finally, for teens and children, television offered a controlled space for socializing and for play within the view of their parents. Television was promoted and sold as a medium that could keep the family together at home, and yet, its "live" and "far-seeing" images allowed the same family to "go out on the town" or travel around the world. Within suburban neighborhoods, television offered communal reasons for neighbors to get together—to watch a political convention, important government events like the Army-McCarthy hearings, or a favorite sports team.

As planned communities began to dot the national landscape, television became, both literally and figuratively, "built in" to American life; by 1949, a television was one of the appliances included in Levitt and Sons's prefabricated homes. If the technology of war had capitalized on the destructive potential of harnessing natural power with science and mechanics, suburban domestic architecture (as epitomized by the ranch home) and consumer commodities (including television, but also electric dishwashers, vacuum cleaners, washing machines, and so on) reasserted an ethos of benevolent equilibrium between people and their mechanical and natural surroundings. If television technology threatened to annihilate the borders of time and space in everyday life, "domesticating" television within the suburban neighborhood could attempt to reinstate the hearth as the benefactor of technological progress and be an example of its containment and familiarization.

While television was not necessarily received in exactly the ways its promoters wished, the medium's deep connections to a mythical suburban and metaphoric ideal of community, and its contributions to the familiarization and standardization of American life, cannot be underestimated. This is particularly underscored by the fact that the manufacture and sale of the television set became a cultural phenomenon and, eventually, an assumed household artifact in conjunction with the development of suburbia.

—*Victoria Johnson*

### References

Boddy, William. *Fifties Television: The Industry and Its Critics.* Urbana: University of Illinois Press, 1990.

Carey, James W. *Communication as Culture: Essays on Media and Society.* New York: Routledge, 1992.

Covert, Catherine L. "We May Hear Too Much." In Catherine L. Covert and John Stevens, eds., *Mass Media between the Wars: Perceptions of Cultural Tension, 1918–1941,* 199–220. Syracuse, NY: Syracuse University Press, 1984.

Folkerts, Jean, and Dwight Teeter. *Voices of a Nation: A History of the Media in the United States.* New York: Macmillan, 1989.

Gomery, J. Douglas. "The Coming of Television and the Lost Motion Picture Audience." *University Film and Video Journal* 38 (1985): 5–11.

Head, Sydney, and Christopher J. Sterling. *Broadcasting in America: A Survey of Electronic Media.* 5th ed. Boston: Houghton Mifflin, 1987.

Lipsitz, George. "The Meaning of Memory: Family, Class, and Ethnicity in Early Network Television Programs." *Camera Obscura* 16 (1988): 79–118.

Marvin, Carolyn. *When Old Technologies Were New: Thinking about Electric Communication in the Late Nineteenth Century.* New York: Oxford University Press, 1987.

Spigel, Lynn. *Make Room for TV: Television and the Family Ideal in Postwar America.* Chicago: University of Chicago Press, 1992.

Williams, Raymond. *Television: Technology and Cultural Form.* London: Fontana, 1974.

## Temperance Movement

Dr. Benjamin Rush, a Philadelphia physician and signer of the Declaration of Independence, launched the temperance movement in 1784 when he attacked the overuse of hard liquors such as rum and whiskey as ruinous to health. At that time cities such as Philadelphia had many poor, sick, or mentally ill residents, most of whom, Rush noted, drank heavily.

Unlike Quakers and Methodists, who had earlier banned strong beverages for members on moral grounds, Rush sought to lengthen life and improve health and work habits by changing the entire society's drinking practices. Followers called the campaign one of temperance because they wanted Americans voluntarily to replace straight liquor with lighter beverages such as wine, beer, and cider or even with diluted rum and whiskey. Rush's campaign failed, and while the Massachusetts Society for the Suppression of Intemperance, founded in 1812, did urge moderation in drinking, alcohol consumption rose during the early decades of the century. Just as important, the heavy consumption of whiskey occurred simultaneously with growing urban slums, vice, and crime, all of which reformers blamed on liquor.

By the 1820s Protestant ministers in the North, amid the largely rural Second Great Awakening, had adopted temperance. Unlike Rush, who had stressed that the overuse of hard liquor impaired health, evangelicals argued that any use of distilled spirits, which they began calling the Demon Rum, led inevitably to crime, sin, and hell. Acting through the American Temperance Society, founded in 1826, they insisted that their followers renounce hard liquor to demonstrate their religious sincerity. This campaign enjoyed considerable success, especially in New England and in western areas settled by New Englanders, but few conversions to evangelicalism or temperance occurred in large cities. Blaming their partial success on the inconsistency of attacking only hard liquor, temperance leaders in the 1830s demanded that Americans become teetotalers and give up all alcoholic beverages. Wine was expensive, and wealthy wine drinkers had failed to persuade poorer whiskey drinkers to stop while the rich continued to imbibe. Now, in order to be consistent, evangelical churches began to use grape juice during communion. At the time, most Americans lived on farms, and few drank beer.

During the 1840s temperance leaders stressed renouncing alcohol voluntarily, and as many as half of all Americans, especially in rural areas and small towns, stopped drinking. Populous cities, however, remained notoriously wet, despite some success by the Washingtonian self-help movement, which had been organized in 1841 by former drinkers in Baltimore. By the 1850s temperance supporters increasingly urged prohibition to change the behavior of those immune to evangelical appeals. Statewide prohibition, first enacted in Maine in 1851, was advocated to dry out the cities and especially the newly arrived immigrants, such as whiskey imbibing Irish and beer drinking Germans. Abstinence became an important sign that they had assimilated, and it was also argued that poor immigrants who gave up liquor could join the middle class, which used teetotalism to define respectability. Many immigrants, however, continued to drink. After the Civil War, the temperance movement, which had always

*An 1880 woodcut of women in Kyana, Indiana, destroying a cargo of liquor as part of the temperance movement.*

stressed personal, voluntary abstinence, gave way to the more coercive prohibition movement.

—*W. J. Rorabaugh*

**See also**
Nation, Carry Amelia Moore; Prohibition.

**References**

Abzug, Robert H. *Cosmos Crumbling: American Reform and the Religious Imagination.* New York: Oxford University Press, 1994.

Dannenbaum, Jed. *Drink and Disorder: Temperance Reform in Cincinnati from the Washingtonian Revival to the WCTU.* Urbana: University of Illinois Press, 1984.

Tyrrell, Ian R. *Sobering Up: From Temperance to Prohibition in Antebellum America, 1800–1860.* Westport, CT: Greenwood Press, 1979.

Walters, Ronald G. *American Reformers, 1815–1860.* New York: Hill and Wang, 1978.

## Tenant Unions

Tenant unions have sprouted periodically in cities, particularly when wartime inflation inflicted hardship on renters and where working-class militancy provided models of collective protest, as in New York City. Jewish socialists on the Lower East Side of Manhattan and in Brownsville in Brooklyn or-

ganized tenant unions and staged protests (including rent strikes) between 1904 and 1908 and in the aftermath of the rent inflation of World War I, which led to scores of short-lived unions. Another outbreak occurred between 1934 and 1939 when Black Nationalists from Harlem and united-front activists harangued tenants to fight evictions, withhold rents, and contest landlord authority in local court. While some citywide alliances were formed, they were undermined by federal and state rent controls during World War II, which made tenant protection the mainstay of local politics in Chicago, Los Angeles, and, particularly, New York.

Tenant unions got their second lease on life during the community-action fervor of the 1960s, when local organizers like Jesse Gray in Harlem, the Congress of Racial Equality in Brooklyn, and the Students for a Democratic Society in Newark, New Jersey, saw tenant power as a springboard to community control. Unions organized by Gray, CORE chapters, and SDS aroused tenants in scores of buildings to withhold rents between 1963 and 1965. The movement spread to other cities, notably Berkeley, California, and Cambridge, Massachusetts, where the liberal (and large college student) populations campaigned for rent control. The movement scored notable successes in public housing projects in Chicago (Taylor United Tenants) and in East Harlem (where CORE organized the Robert A. Taft Houses) among residents protesting unfair evictions and for the rights of welfare recipients to stay in public housing.

Despite New Left expectations for tenant unions as the basis for community power, they proved to be short-lived, single-issue institutions that were dependent on the liberal programs they were organized against. Most sprung up with rent grievances in large projects, whether philanthropic limited dividend projects like Knickerbocker Village, long the mainstay of New York's citywide tenants council in the 1930s, or the public projects in Harlem where Jesse Gray found his most loyal following. The largest tenant action ever occurred in the early 1970s at the middle-class Co-op City in the Bronx, where tenants struck for greater New York State subsidies under the Mitchell-Lama program. When rents were scaled back, fuel pass-alongs rescinded, and state intervention pledged, tenant union membership melted away.

—*Joel Schwartz*

**See also**
Rent Control; Rent Strikes.
**References**
Lawson, Ronald. *The Tenant Movement in New York City, 1901–1984.* New Brunswick, NJ: Rutgers University Press, 1986.
Lipsky, Michael. *Protest in City Politics.* Chicago: Rand McNally, 1970.
Schwartz, Joel. "The New York City Rent Strikes of 1963–1964." *Social Service Review* 57 (1983): 544–564.

## Tenement

The curious history of the word *tenement* over the past two centuries reflects the evolution of housing into a matter of public policy and the controversies surrounding housing improvement. Until the nineteenth century, the term referred to any dwelling unit, including both houses and parts of buildings, and it carried no negative connotations. By the end of the nineteenth century, it had become a pejorative term for multifamily structures purposely built to house poor residents, and tenements were at the center of a burgeoning movement for housing reform. By the middle of the twentieth century, the word was seldom used in discussions of housing policy and had been replaced by terms such as *substandard housing* and *slum.*

The forces that shaped this etymology arose from changes in the stock of urban housing and changes in the way Americans thought about poverty. Three important stages can be discerned in the history of tenements: first, the emergence of multifamily housing as an "evil" to be abated; second, the crusade for restrictive legislation to curb the abuses; and third, the effort to clear slums and replace tenements with publicly subsidized housing. These stages overlapped each other to some extent, and the legacies of all three still shape policymaking today.

Changes in urban housing, the rise of environmentalist thinking about poverty, and enthusiasm for sanitary reform all contributed to the rising perception that multifamily housing was a policy problem in the middle of the nineteenth century. Starting in the late eighteenth century, a number of forces had combined to create a large class of tenants and an extensive rental housing market. Commercial and industrial expansion undermined the position of propertied artisans and increased the number of wage laborers who were frequently migrants to the city who owned no property. Because employment for these workers was intermittent and unpredictable, they had to live within easy reach of multiple potential employers. This burgeoning population of wage earners in need of housing encouraged propertied households to take in boarders or rent rooms, and entrepreneurs to invest in rental property. The geographical concentration of renters in the central city encouraged the subdivision of older dwellings and eventually the construction of new multifamily structures intended to be rented to the working class. By the middle of the nineteenth century, these structures had become known as "tenant houses" or "tenement houses," labels that carried undesirable connotations of crowding and degradation.

The largest number of tenement houses, and the most notorious examples, were in New York City. There, the transformation of the housing market eventually led builders to erect buildings five to seven stories high that covered as much as 90 percent of their land. Whole parts of the city, the Lower East Side for example, became districts in which almost every lot was covered by a tenement structure. Although other cities had examples of this type of structure, no other American city had tenement districts quite like New York's. The poorest residents of other cities occupied a rich array of housing types, ranging from multistory buildings, to clusters of subdivided frame houses crammed onto lots meant for a single house, to shanties on marginal land. However, the general process of creating a rental housing market that concentrated the working class and the poor in low-quality, multifamily housing did occur in varied ways in most large cities. And while New York was not a model for other cities in terms of housing types, it was the major source of ideas about the tenement as an evil and about potential remedies. By 1900 ideas about tenements emanating from New York were being applied to all the varied forms of multifamily, working-class housing in cities.

This diffusion of ideas began in New York and Boston in the middle of the nineteenth century when educational reformers, charitable visitors, and writers of sensational fiction popularized an environmental explanation for the allegedly deviant behavior of the poor. Devotees of Horace

Mann believed that common schools would provide an antidote to the corrupting influences of big city streets and tenements. Evangelical Christian agents saw themselves as bearers of uplifting moral influences that would counter the corrosive milieu of geographically concentrated poverty. The often lurid and highly popular works of authors such as George Foster and E. C. Judson were full of sentimental narratives in which characters either succumbed to or narrowly escaped the evil influences and "dens of iniquity" supposedly so common in tenement districts.

In an atmosphere characterized by the explosive growth of rental housing and a growing belief in environmental explanations for character and behavior, some city residents gradually began to consider tenements a legal and political issue. Tenement houses became a focus of public policy largely through discussions of urban sanitation and health. From the 1840s through the 1860s, sanitary reformers in America's largest cities conducted surveys of local conditions, especially among the concentrated populations of wage earners and immigrants. Beginning with New York, Dr. John H. Griscom's "Brief View of the Sanitary Condition of the City" (1842), and continuing with similar reports on Boston (1846), Philadelphia (1849), and Baltimore (1850), investigators presented dramatic evidence to the public. Initially, these reformers were more interested in conditions that fostered epidemic disease than in housing per se. But their reports demonstrated that thousands of city residents were living in dark, filthy, verminous, unventilated rental units, without adequate water or toilets, at the mercy of exploitative landlords. By the late 1850s many sanitary reformers had concluded that the tenement itself was a major source of disease—a "nuisance" akin to rotting garbage or contaminated water.

With the widespread conviction that tenements were both an "evil" and a "nuisance," the way was open for the second major stage in their history, a quest for legal remedies to the problems. From the 1860s into the Progressive Era, tenement reformers pursued a regulatory approach to correcting the problems they saw and promoted legislation that would regulate the construction of new multifamily housing. In 1865 the New York Council of Hygiene and Public Health issued a report on sanitary conditions that led directly to enactment of the nation's first tenement law, the Tenement House Act of 1867. Among its main provisions, this law required that every room in new tenements should be ventilated, that the building should have a fire escape, that there should be one privy for every 20 occupants, and that cellar or underground rooms could not be occupied without a permit from the Board of Health. Although the law had limited impact on the 15,000 tenement houses already existing, was not effectively enforced in cases of new construction, and said nothing about the problem of lot coverage, it provided a model for the regulatory approach to tenement reform that prevailed into the twentieth century.

Ironically, the law also created new problems. In 1878, the *Plumber and Sanitary Engineer* sponsored a competition for tenement house designs that met the regulatory standards. The winning design met the requirement for ventilation with a "dumbbell" floor plan in which buildings were pinched on both sides to provide interior bedrooms with windows that opened onto an air shaft between adjacent buildings. The design led New York officials to require windows for bedrooms, and they effectively made the dumbbell plan the standard for thousands of tenements constructed in the next 20 years. But the air shafts were only 28 inches wide, and in five- or six-story buildings they provided almost no light or ventilation. Instead, the shafts became garbage dumps, fire hazards (they acted as flues), and dangers to children playing on roofs.

Nevertheless, regulatory reformers persisted, organizing a series of state commissions and sponsoring new legislation to extend and improve the regulatory process. Some reformers, following a proposal first advanced by the New York Association for Improving the Condition of the Poor in the 1850s, promoted "model tenements" intended as patterns for investors. The few model tenements actually built were indeed far superior to most existing structures, but they were also too expensive for all but skilled workers, and they did not generate enough profit to lure investors away from cheaper and poorer structures. Restrictive regulation remained the focus, and New York's attempts to reform tenements became the model for investigations and reports produced in other cities during the 1880s and 1890s. The regulatory crusade also gained powerful support from the writings and photographs of Jacob Riis, whose *How the Other Half Lives* (1890) won legions of reform advocates across the country.

Regulatory reform reached its climax with passage of the New York Tenement House Law of 1901, whose main architect was Lawrence Veiller, a hardworking, detail-oriented reformer bent on correcting all the flaws in previous regulation. This act prohibited dumbbell tenements, capped new construction at five stories, required toilets in each unit, and committed resources to inspection and enforcement. Veiller pursued the regulatory process relentlessly. Two years after the 1901 act, he joined another reformer, Robert W. DeForest, to edit *The Tenement House Problem,* a two-volume collection of essays that summarized the progress in New York since 1901 and surveyed the state of regulatory reform in two dozen other cities. He also wrote housing reform manuals and helped organize the National Housing Association. Through his efforts and those of his followers and admirers, regulatory legislation modeled on the 1901 New York act was adopted in many other cities by the 1920s.

The third stage of tenement history arose partly in response to Veiller's kind of tenement reform. Throughout the regulatory crusade, some critics had pointed out the limitations of restrictive legislation. It primarily affected new construction, leaving in place thousands of existing tenements, and it did nothing to ensure an adequate supply of housing for lower-income people. From the 1880s on, some writers called attention to British and European experiments with slum clearance in which governments razed whole districts of poor housing. A few advocated public subsidy or construction of improved housing for the poor. Supporters of these approaches called them "constructive" reform.

But in the United States, slum clearance and public housing required decades to receive even minimal support. In the 1890s, New York and Boston both undertook a few small municipal projects of tenement condemnation and demolition to make way for parks and playgrounds. But the use of state power and money to shape the housing market directly was anathema to the many who saw such measures as a form of socialism. Restrictive reformers like Veiller often opposed clearance or subsidy vigorously. Some had faith in the private market's ability to meet the problem of supply. Some assumed that improved transportation technology would one day allow many tenement dwellers to move to suburban homes. Many believed that the "natural" expansion of central business districts would gradually remove the worst of the old housing and that even the poorest tenants would then move into dwellings a notch up the quality scale.

These assumptions, however, increasingly ran up against the mounting evidence accumulated in the regulatory reformers' numerous and extensive surveys of housing in many locales. Progressive Era studies showed that the stock of tenement housing was not shrinking and that "new-law" tenements built to satisfy the regulatory standards were too expensive for unskilled workers. In the early twentieth century, some of the participants in national housing and planning conferences began to promote the ideas of systematic clearance and subsidy more vigorously.

Among the most influential advocates of these solutions was Edith Elmer Wood, whose Columbia University Ph.D. dissertation was published in 1919 as *The Housing of the Unskilled Wage Earner: America's Next Problem.* This work surveyed the history of regulatory reform and model tenements and highlighted the limits of both. Emphasizing the problem of supply, she became a leading promoter of subsidized housing throughout the 1920s and 1930s, influencing New York Governor Al Smith in his introduction of state support for limited dividend housing corporations in 1926.

Wood and other housing and planning experts brought the ideas of clearance and subsidy into the New Deal. As part of its effort to stimulate the construction industry, the Public Works Administration (PWA) supported a few small programs of demolition and rebuilding, but the principles of federal entrance into the low-income housing market were not truly defined until passage of the Wagner Housing Act of 1937. This act established the mechanisms of acquisition and clearance that became the basis of federal policy until the 1960s. Under its auspices, the federal government also subsidized 300 projects of low-income housing before World War II, and opened the way to more extensive public housing construction under the Housing Act of 1949.

By the middle of the 1960s, the combined mechanisms of clearance and subsidy had generated more than 500,000 units of federally subsidized public housing in more than 3,600 projects. In the process, thousands of units of tenement housing were destroyed, and the "tenement problem" became the "housing problem." Twentieth-century redevelopment efforts did not come close to eliminating all of the housing that had been labeled as tenements at the beginning of the century, nor did they displace the regulatory strategy—which indeed became more effective as building codes grew tougher and inspection more systematic. The combined influence of decades of regulation plus dramatic redevelopment projects shifted the focus away from tenements and onto housing.

A variety of problems with clearance and subsidy made those strategies just as controversial as regulation had once been. Thus, at the end of the twentieth century, debate centered not on structures called tenements but on the more general problem of housing the poorest residents of large cities.

—*Henry C. Binford*

See also
Dumbbell Tenement; Riis, Jacob August; Veiller, Lawrence Turnure.
**References**
Birch, Eugenie Ladner, and Deborah S. Gardner. "The Seven-Percent Solution: A Review of Philanthropic Housing, 1870–1910." *Journal of Urban History* 7 (1981): 403–438.

Blackmar, Elizabeth. *Manhattan for Rent, 1785–1850.* Ithaca, NY: Cornell University Press, 1989.

Daunton, Martin J. "Cities of Homes and Cities of Tenements: British and American Comparisons, 1870–1914." *Journal of Urban History* 14 (1988): 283–319.

Ford, James. *Slums and Housing, with Special Reference to New York City.* 2 vols. Cambridge, MA: Harvard Universiyt Press, 1936.

Lubove, Roy. *The Progressives and the Slums: Tenement House Reform in New York City, 1890–1917.* Pittsburgh, PA: University of Pittsburgh Press, 1962.

## Theme Parks

The idea of structuring outdoor amusement in terms of cultural themes was born at the 1893 World's Fair in Chicago. Sol Bloom, a young entrepreneur hired to run the Midway Plaisance, the mile-long strip of entertainment concessions on either side of the Ferris wheel, came up with the village reproduction concept. What emerged was a hodgepodge of different ethnic or national villages containing exotic shops, eateries, theaters, performers, and costumed people to amuse the millions who thronged to the Columbian Exposition. So successful was this approach to amusement that virtually all succeeding expositions and parks had a midway of ride, game, and food offerings.

A decade later, Frederick Thompson created Luna Park in New York's Coney Island, history's first amusement park with historical, geographical, and cultural themes. Thompson—a former carnival worker, architecture student, and inventor of illusion rides—realized more than any other showman of his day the importance of building design, spectacle, and ambiance in entertainment. At that time, amusement parks were little more than a collection of disparate mechanical rides, catchpenny games, and circus-type activities. Luna's rides and attractions, however, were arranged around a German Village, Chinese Theater, Japanese Garden, Eskimo Village, Dutch Windmill, and the Canals of Venice. Thompson literally built a fantasy land, an "other world" of gaiety and excitement. In 1904, on the heels of Luna's enormous success, a copycat park, initially called Wonderland but renamed Dreamland, opened right across the street. Dreamland—with its foreign architecture, Lilliputian village, Grand Ballroom, display of infant incubators, chariot races, and wild animal shows—was more aesthetically appealing than Luna Park and had bigger and better attractions but garnered smaller crowds.

During the next half-century, no other amusement park in America resembling a Luna Park or Dreamland was built. Regrettably, these two early parks with thematic structures had short life spans. Dreamland burned down in 1911, and Luna Park, after Thompson's death in 1919, faltered both creatively and financially. A much curtailed, almost themeless Luna itself succumbed to fire in 1944. Only the 1939 New York World's Fair, with its World of Tomorrow and exhibitions on technology and the future, significantly advanced the art and science of themed entertainment at this time.

The term *theme park* was first applied in connection with Disneyland in southern California. In the early 1950s Walt Disney sought to create a totally new kind of amusement park, a place where children and adults could find happiness and knowledge, a place free of cheap thrills and the tawdry, honky-tonk atmosphere characteristic of Coney Island and other parks of the day. The Disney Corporation's initial design and ideas for an unnamed amusement park referred to various "themes" or "motifs" that would transport people from the present day to the more pleasurable worlds of yesterday, tomorrow, and fantasy. The five themed areas originally proposed—a Main Village, Western Village, Indian Village, Old Farm, and Carnival section—evolved into Main Street, a sani-

tized replica of turn-of-the-century America, and four "lands" (Fantasyland, Adventureland, Frontierland, Tomorrowland) with particular motifs. Disney naturally capitalized on his own media products by using stories and characters from his cartoons and feature films as foci for the park's rides, attractions, and staged events. Press releases from corporate officials stressed Disneyland as a theme park, not to be confused with the far less attractive amusement parks of the day.

In the creation of Disneyland, Disney both borrowed from and extended patterns of amusement extant in society. He resurrected the long-forgotten notions that a park's attractions could be grouped in terms of thematic structures and that architecture, illusion, and fantasy greatly enhance the playful spirit. Disney essentially technologized Thompson's recipe for entertaining large crowds and built a modern and more permanent version of Luna Park and Dreamland. His development of audio-animatronics, coupled with the park's futuristic look, bears witness to the obvious influence of the New York Fair on the design of Disneyland. While Disney's "lands" were simply by-products of his 30-year film career, the Main Street theme area was highly innovative, undoubtedly the most significant new idea in amusement since Luna Park. There was nothing like a Main Street in Luna or Dreamland, as turn-of-the-century park operators amused people with a taste of foreign lands and a peek into the future. By drawing on his own boyhood experiences and Americans' feelings of nostalgia, Disney derived entertainment value from a reverence for the past and a yearning for idyllic small-town life. In the latter part of the twentieth century Main Street had great mass appeal.

Disney developed a model for financing and managing his park that became the industry standard. He exacted cash and secured loans for construction from a television studio in exchange for programs, enlisted sponsorship of particular exhibits and attractions from large corporations, received advance payments from Disneyland businesses, and collected licensing fees for Disney merchandise sold in the park. The Disney formula included an emphasis on total control over park design, movement of people, visual images, and guest behavior. Disneyland was thus the prototypical theme park, and its impressive early success induced Disney officials to predict that within five years 20 facsimile parks would appear throughout the country.

That prediction, even in twice the time, was not realized. The first decade of Disneyland's operation, 1955 through 1964, saw only a handful of other theme parks, mostly failed business ventures. Denver's Magic Mountain—with plans for a cable car ride up a mountain, a boat ride on a river, a western town, and a train ride—was scheduled to open in 1958 but never did because of financial problems. That same year,

Pacific Ocean Park in Santa Monica, California, was redesigned with aquatic themes at a cost of $16 million only to go bankrupt a decade later. Pleasure Island near Boston lacked the Disney expertise and attention to detail. Its whaling harbor and western town motifs left crowds unimpressed; thrill rides were soon introduced, and the erstwhile theme park only survived by scaling down to a small traditional amusement park. In 1960 Freedomland opened in New York, after investors spent $33 million and advertised their new park as the Disneyland of the East. Shaped like the United States and with American history as its theme, some of the major attractions were Little Old New York (circa 1850), a New England fishing village, the Chicago fire, a Santa Fe train robbery, the San Francisco earthquake, Civil War battlegrounds, and New Orleans Mardi Gras. With the public bored by poorly planned amusements and concerned about safety after a well-publicized accident, attendance dropped sharply, and Freedomland was forced to close in 1964.

The first successful non-Disney theme park was Six Flags Over Texas, located between Dallas and Fort Worth. The park opened in 1961 with its rides, attractions, and staged events thematically keyed to the six flags that have waved, or authorities that have ruled, over Texas: Spain, France, Mexico, the Republic of Texas, the Confederacy, and the United States. The historical sections circled a 300-foot-high lookout tower shaped like an oil derrick. Six Flags followed the Disney model by paying careful attention to the park's design and the placement of shops and restaurants, but departed from it by including many thrill rides. Its financial backers, buoyed by their success the very first year of operation, formed a corporation and built two new parks, Six Flags Over Georgia near Atlanta in 1967 and then Six Flags Over Mid-America near St. Louis. The new parks' architecture and atmosphere reflected, conveniently if not always accurately, six historical influences on the Southeast and Midwest.

The three Six Flags' enterprises demonstrated that regional theme parks could be financially successful. In the 1970s, corporate conglomerates got in on the act, and by the end of the decade there were two dozen major theme parks around the country that attracted over 60 million visitors a year and took in 70 percent of amusement industry revenues. Taft Broadcasting opened Kings Island north of Cincinnati with European country sectors (including a half-scale Eiffel Tower), a safari tour, a HappyLand, and a midway with the flavor of a traditional amusement park. In 1975, after the success of its first venture, Taft built Kings Dominion, a similar theme park near Richmond, Virginia. Like Disney, Taft utilized their own cartoon characters (from the Hanna-Barbera television shows) as integral parts of the parks' attractions.

The Anheuser-Busch Corporation's interest in theme parks dates back to the 1904 St. Louis World's Fair, where they reproduced an Alpine mountain village. Busch Gardens was developed near the brewery in Tampa with an animal habitat, later expanded into various African sectors and dubbed the Dark Continent. In 1974 a new park, the Old Country, opened in Williamsburg, Virginia, and exploited the colonial atmosphere with seventeenth-century European hamlets. In 1976 the Marriott Corporation introduced two identical Great America parks, one south of San Francisco and the other between Chicago and Milwaukee. The five theme areas—Hometown Square, Yukon Territory, Yankee Harbor, County Fair, and Orleans Place—were planned to ensure authenticity. Bally Manufacturing's Great Adventure in New Jersey was divided into two theme areas—the Safari, where wild animals roam freely and automobiles drive through, and Enchanted Forest, containing the thrill rides.

Other theme parks were financed by nonconglomerates or individual investors and likewise serve regional markets. Astroworld in Houston, Worlds of Fun in Kansas City, Marco Polo Park north of Daytona Beach, Carowinds on the North Carolina state line, Opryland in Nashville, and Knott's Berry Farm in southern California are notable examples. Popular ideas such as space travel, explored worlds, local history, country music, or agricultural products are made entertaining and serve as foci for the park's rides and attractions. The theme of ocean life is explored in the Sea Worlds and Marinelands in California, Florida, and other states. Holyland in Mobile, Alabama, and Bible World in Orlando, Florida, depict religious stories and feature a Jerusalem marketplace, a Garden of Eden, a Tower of Babel slide, and animated talking biblical figures. With these and similar theme parks, Americans' penchant for adventure, travel, and excitement is exploited in the guise of an educational experience.

None of these other theme parks surpassed Disneyland in terms of variety of amusements, size, capital, attendance figures, or international reputation. Only Walt Disney World in central Florida, unveiled in 1971, was more impressive than its older sibling. The Disney Corporation purchased more than 27,000 acres of land and secured public authority from the state over the vast tract for its largest venture yet. Disney World was not meant to be an East Coast version of the earlier park but rather was planned as the ultimate vacationland, complete with themed attractions, resort hotels, recreational sports, and residential communities. EPCOT Center appeared next door in 1982 but was not, as Disney initially envisioned, an experimental prototype of a futuristic city. EPCOT's two theme areas, pavilions representing countries of the world and scientific wonders, were criticized as too commercial and vacuous. Over the years, both the California and Florida parks apparently have conceded to popular tastes and added roller coasters and other thrill rides not part of Disney's original plan. In this respect, the Disney parks have followed the pattern established by its own copiers, the regional theme parks.

Theme parks, from Luna Park to Disney World, the first to the foremost, have become an American institution. Turn-of-the-century Coney Island parks created a new cultural product, an enclosed park for fun and fantasy via illusion rides, visual attractiveness, blend of foreign cultures, staged events, and pleasant atmosphere. A half-century later, Walt Disney revived the idea of a themed amusement park, added his own touches to its cultural content and style of presentation, and significantly enhanced its appeal to all audiences. The plethora of theme parks built in recent decades has cemented their place on the American landscape, influencing the hundreds of millions who have visited them plus countless more who participate vicariously in their brand of popular culture through the mass media. The successful parks have defined what outdoor amusement should be like and captured the imagination of people throughout the world. In recent years American-built theme parks have been in great demand in other countries.

Theme parks are complex cultural products and often affect people and society in contradictory or opposing ways. For example, they opened up new entertainment vistas but displaced older forms of amusement. Television, film, theater, museums, air travel, scientific expositions, world's fairs, etc., are now closely tied to our theme parks, while local carnivals, circuses, fairs, amusement parks, and midways stand isolated from them. The parks also shape our vision of the future as well as our recollections of the past. They apply the latest technology in transportation and architecture to environmentally controlled communities, shoring up images of twenty-first-century living, and at the same time replay historical events and situations, forcing us to rethink our heritage. It is clear that theme parks remain, in terms of the effect on people's consciousness and behavior, an important part of contemporary American society.

—Raymond M. Weinstein

**See also**
Amusement Parks; Coney Island; Disneyland.
**References**
Adams, Judith A. *The American Amusement Park Industry: A History of Technology and Thrills.* Boston: Twayne, 1991.
Griffin, Al. *"Step Right Up, Folks!"* Chicago: Henry Regnery Company, 1974.
King, Margaret J. "The New American Muse: Notes on the Amusement/Theme Park." *Journal of Popular Culture* 15 (1981): 56–62.
Kyriazi, Gary. *The Great American Amusement Parks: A Pictorial History.* Secaucus, NJ: Citadel Press, 1976.
Weinstein, Raymond M. "Disneyland and Coney Island: Reflections on the Evolution of the Modern Amusement Park." *Journal of Popular Culture* 26 (1992): 131–164.

## Thompson, William Hale (Big Bill) (1867–1944)

If any one word describes William Hale Thompson, mayor of Chicago from 1915 to 1923 and 1927 to 1931, it is "mercenary," for Thompson spent his public life cultivating and discarding blocs of voters as circumstances demanded. And, like any good soldier of fortune, Thompson ignored the matter of issues and chose to focus on the promise of victory, along with the attendant spoils.

Thompson was a wealthy Chicago sportsman who was elected mayor in 1915 by fashioning himself as the candidate of middle-class white Protestant Chicago; he was a Republican who promised to enforce Sunday closing laws for saloons and break the public school teachers' union. Then, in 1918, Thompson ran for the U.S. Senate and recast himself as another Robert M. LaFollette by criticizing American entry into World War I and advocating a windfall profits tax on business. He lost the nomination by 60,000 votes.

Despite the controversy about his wartime remarks, Thompson won a second term as mayor in 1919. He spent his next term as mayor building public works and advocating American isolationism. However, a school board scandal forced him to retire in 1923.

Yet Thompson returned for a third term in 1927. Demagogic attacks on Prohibition and the local business elite helped him put together a coalition of blacks, ethnics, and organized labor. In office once again, Thompson dispensed jobs to unions as he long had to blacks, and he instructed that the contributions of immigrant Americans be discussed in the history textbooks used in public schools. Thompson entertained notions of running for president, but a nervous breakdown in 1928 ended any national political ambitions he might have had. By the time he recovered, the Depression had begun and Chicago no longer had a disposition for incumbent Republicans. Thompson lost his bid for a fourth term in 1931, but he had the consolation of seeing Democrats appropriate his strategy of public works and group coalitions to control City Hall for close to a half-century.

—Douglas Bukowski

**References**
Allswang, John M. *Bosses, Machines and Urban Voters.* Rev. ed. Baltimore: Johns Hopkins University Press, 1986.
Buenker, John D. "Dynamics of Chicago Ethnic Politics." *Journal of the Illinois State Historical Society* 67 (1974): 175–199.
Kogan, Herman, and Lloyd Wendt. *Big Bill of Chicago.* Indianapolis, IN: Bobbs-Merrill, 1953.
Luthin, Reinhard H. *American Demagogues: Twentieth Century.* Boston: Beacon Press, 1954.
Schottenhamel, George. "How Big Bill Thompson Won Control of Chicago." *Journal of the Illinois State Historical Society* 45 (1952): 30–49.
Thurner, Arthur W. "The Mayor, the Governor and the People's Council." *Journal of the Illinois State Historical Society* 66 (1973): 125–143.

## Tin Pan Alley

Tin Pan Alley is a designation used for the American popular song industry from about 1885 to 1929. Tin Pan Alley—whose actual location traveled over time from New York's Union Square, to West 28th Street, and finally to the corner of Broadway and West 46th Street—sprang up in response to a sharp nationwide demand for new songs, itself a product of the mass production of pianos and the rise of new forms of popular entertainment, like music halls and vaudeville.

The developing industry was vertically organized. A publishing company's staff composer created the product, which then went to the staff arranger, who prepared it in notation suitable for America's amateur pianists, to the "song plugger," who stoked demand by convincing singers and orchestras to include it in their repertoire, and then to the publisher, who reaped the profits from sheet-music sales. When the young George Gershwin signed on with one firm as a staff composer in 1918, he was paid $35 a week plus a 3 percent royalty on sales.

Charles K. Harris is generally considered to have been the first Tin Pan Alley composer in the classic mold; his sentimental "After the Ball" (1892) sold more than 5 million copies. Irving Berlin, almost certainly the most successful composer in the years after the turn of the century, wrote topical songs and rags that typified Tin Pan Alley's lightning-quick responsiveness to catchphrases and fads, as well as its appropriation of black musical forms.

Tin Pan Alley waned in the 1920s, the victim of several forces. The first was a new generation of songwriters, like Gershwin, Jerome Kern, and the team of Richard Rodgers and Lorenz Hart, whose talents were too sophisticated and individual for Tin Pan Alley's assembly-line approach. Technological innovations like the radio and phonograph dramatically diminished the demand for sheet music, the industry's *raison d'être*. And, beginning in the late 1920s, the Hollywood musical became the principal market for new songs, eventually attracting every top songwriter to the West Coast. By the early 1930s Hollywood studios had bought all the major music publishing firms, and Tin Pan Alley was a thing of the past.

—*Ben Yagoda*

### References
Bergreen, Laurence. *As Thousands Cheer: The Life of Irving Berlin.* New York: Viking, 1990.
Goldberg, Isaac. *Tin Pan Alley: A Chronicle of the American Music Racket.* New York: John Day, 1930.
Tawa, Nicholas. *The Way to Tin Pan Alley: American Popular Music, 1866–1910.* New York: Schirmer Books, 1990.

## Township

The Land Ordinance that Congress passed in 1785 mandated that all federally owned land be surveyed and divided into townships that were squares of six miles on each side, and then into 36 squares of one square mile each called sections, some of which were reserved for specific purposes. Initially, the thrust of the ordinance encouraged settlement by community as suggested in the name *township* and in the reservation of certain land for schools and government buildings.

As early as 1776, the Continental Congress promised land to soldiers who fought in the Revolution and considered the sale of land in the region north and west of the Ohio River as a way of raising money to finance the war and military pensions. After the war ended and that land was acquired piecemeal from Native American tribes and ceded to the federal government by states with claims to western lands, Congress appointed two committees. The job of one was planning governments for the new territory, and the task of the other was locating and mapping the lands and devising methods for their disposal. The Land Ordinance of 1785, which those committees drafted, established the Northwest Territory, defined the means of surveying new public land, structured an apparatus to transform it into private property, and created a mechanism of local governance by establishing the township. The ordinance also sought to determine how the newly independent states would colonize the rest of the continent, and the legislation contains an early attempt to articulate the rights of American citizens that served as a precursor to the Bill of Rights. The Homestead Act of 1862 modified the pattern of settlement onto the scale of individual ownership, but the initial surveying and division of land into the grid of 36 square miles became universal outside the original 13 states and the southern states formed from land south of the Ohio River and east of the Mississippi River.

In many places, though by no means all, the township—which provided for schools, roads, poor relief, keeping peace, assessing taxes, and collecting them—has withered away and been replaced by the larger units of metropolis, city, and county. But in many rural and some suburban areas, the township still frequently functions as the primary form of government. The legacy of townships can be read in the skeletal grid of many larger towns and cities where the main arteries evolved from the original township roads, and the blocks within the urban area are oriented along these same axes.

—*Michael Martone*

## Trade and Commerce

In American history, cities and commerce have been inextricably linked. With modest governmental and ecclesiastical establishments, urban areas emerged primarily as sites for economic activity. The forms of this activity varied over time; for the first two centuries after European settlement, trade determined the pace and pattern of city growth. In the middle of the nineteenth century, commerce gave way to manufacturing as the dynamic element driving urbanization in the East and, to a lesser extent, in the West. Nevertheless, along the expanding frontier, commercial opportunities fostered new cities. By the twentieth century, much of the dynamism attributable to trade was spent; commercial needs explained at best only a part of the expansion of the Sunbelt cities. In the last two decades of the twentieth century, however, the linkages between cities and commerce have again become front-page news. But the nature of the relationship has shifted; commerce is increasingly international, and trade is more likely to be in services than goods.

Trade created cities. In 1826, German economist Johann Heinrich von Thunen hypothesized that even on a featureless plain towns would form to meet the needs of trade. As long as some individuals wanted to specialize and rely upon local markets to purchase the goods given up by specializing, towns would arise to facilitate exchange. Of course, the United States was not featureless, and most cities that grew to appreciable size were located on waterways. For much of American history, shipment by river, lake, or open sea was much cheaper than transportation on land, so cities on waterways could tap much larger hinterlands. The largest cities were located at breaks in transport, i.e., where the means of transportation could no longer continue and had to be changed, where the cities mediated trade between extensive hinterlands and the world beyond.

Commerce also shaped the relationships among cities. From the colonial "array of cities" with modest interurban trade, by the nineteenth century cities were participating in a dense trading network. They sought to extend their hinterlands, often at the expense of neighboring urban areas, and they planned transportation systems to garner more of the trade flowing through the region. The very largest cities captured even more trade—even measured on a per capita basis—with larger market areas, and they rose to the top of a fairly stable urban hierarchy.

Trade vitally affected the physical and societal relationships within cities. Immigration tended to mirror trade so that who came to America and where they landed depended upon the patterns of international commerce. The physical layout of cities was shaped initially by the demands of commerce and altered repeatedly as increases in scale and the introduction of new transportation modes forced the expansion and relocation of business districts. Commerce affected the social and political landscapes as well. Merchants have been among the wealthiest urban residents, and their business interests have often dictated that they participate actively in local politics.

Growth in the colonial economy stemmed from the ability to exploit abundant natural resources for sale in international markets. What goods, what markets, and who handled the trade determined the number, size, and structure of American cities. This trade underwrote urban growth but not urbanization; that is, the number and size of colonial cities increased, but the proportion of the colonial population living in cities may have actually fallen as time went on. As long as cities existed primarily to assemble cargoes for export and to distribute imports, the share of the population so employed was quite modest. Widely accepted estimates place the urban share at less than 7 percent in 1700; 70 years later the portion had fallen to perhaps 5 percent.

Agglomeration economies, those that result from related activities locating close to one another, favored concentration at a few sites, usually along the seaboard at the mouth of a river. Once a city launched commercial exchange with Europe or the West Indies, others nearby found it difficult to compete for long-distance trade. In 1790, for example, some 54 percent of the urban population of the entire country lived in only five cities; by way of contrast, in 1960, the five largest American cities contained a mere 14 percent of the nation's urban population.

The size of individual cities depended upon the patterns of overseas trade. This emphasis on long-distance waterborne trade accurately reflected its importance; as late as 1790, 19 of the 20 cities identified in the first federal census were located on tidal waters. As these cities extended the range of their overseas trade, they passed population thresholds. Thus, the largest cities, general entrepots that traded with the entire globe, had populations exceeding 15,000 on the eve of the American Revolution. Those that exchanged goods only with Southern Europe and the West Indies numbered their inhabitants at 8,000 or more, while those with connections only to the West Indies contained around 4,000 individuals. As much as one might be tempted to see an urban system emerging here, the levels of interurban colonial trade were too small to permit such an inference. The fundamental orientation of American ports was toward Atlantic markets located beyond the original 13 colonies.

One of the most fascinating aspects of colonial urbanization is the absence of cities in two of the richest, most populous, and most export-dependent colonies, Virginia and Maryland. Historian Jacob Price has attributed this to the British domination of tobacco marketing. Forced by the Navigation Acts to export the "stinking weed" directly to England, tobacco planters relied on English, and later on Scottish, traders who benefited from cheaper capital and better information to market the crops and purchase imports. Moreover, tobacco required little processing before export so towns of only several thousand inhabitants could meet all the needs of trade. Only after 1740, when these southern colonies developed new staples for new markets, did cities grow to any appreciable size. Norfolk and Baltimore boomed as colonial merchants undertook direct trade with Southern Europe and the West Indies based on the export of grains and forest products.

This southern example serves as a reminder that even in the early years cities served as more than funnels for the movement of goods into and out of the colonies. When local merchants handled foreign trade, they generated mercantile and maritime employment. They also spurred the growth of subsidiary industries such as printing, publishing, shipbuilding, cooperage, milling, and distilling. The indispensable role of commerce in economic life can be seen in the early history of the colonies. In the depressed 1640s, merchants rescued Boston by opening trade in local goods with the West Indies market. The resident mercantile community there and in other ports provided much of the economic dynamism in the colonies as they were the source of the information and often the capital necessary to underwrite new activities.

The wars ignited by the French Revolution ushered in a golden age of commerce for American ports. With British and French shipping fully employed in the fighting, American merchants stepped in to handle much of the trade between European countries and their Atlantic colonies, as well as the swelling trade in American goods bound for transatlantic markets. Demonstrating the close connection between commerce and business services, this burgeoning trade facilitated a business revolution—dramatic improvements in finance, insurance, law, communications, and transportation. The beneficiaries of this commercial boom were the great eastern seaports; their populations more than doubled, and the wealth generated by trade financed both the extension and renovation of their commercial and residential structures.

The era of international trade and specialization ended abruptly. First the Embargo and then the War of 1812 interrupted trade with Europe, and the impact of this sudden stoppage of international exchange was quickly apparent. In the 1810s, the urban share of the U.S. population actually fell; never again would the census record a decline in the percentage of urban population. Before 1808, international exports had taken some 10 to 20 percent of colonial or national product; in the next 150 years, it would absorb only 5 to 8 percent. The nation would now look inward, and the cities that grew most rapidly were those that could facilitate trade within and among the regions of the United States.

In the century after the Peace of Paris in 1815, Americans built a transportation and communications system that enabled them to create an integrated national market. First,

the great eastern seaports competed to tap not just their own backcountry trade but also the trade of the growing Midwest. New York won this competition and in the process created the beginnings of an urban system. Second, cities spread across the continent. Formed to link the periphery so rich in resources to the developing core, these new cities prospered in proportion to their ability to capture regional trade. By the end of the nineteenth century, an urban hierarchy was in place, determined primarily by the reach of commercial and financial hinterlands. But city size and location were not due solely to commerce. The urbanization of the nation during the last two-thirds of the nineteenth century owed more to manufacturing as cities became the sites of the Industrial Revolution.

Perhaps the most striking accomplishment of the era could be observed at its outset. Around 1803 New York surpassed Philadelphia as the nation's largest city and never relinquished its title. Its success stemmed from its increasing shares of the nation's foreign and domestic trade. In the late 1790s it became the leading port in the country's foreign trade, and the gap between New York and its seaboard rivals widened. By 1860 more than 60 percent of the nation's imports entered the United States through New York. Not surprisingly, since most foreign vessels landed at New York, some two-thirds of foreign immigrants disembarked there as well.

New York also used its foreign connections to cement its position as the hub of domestic trade. By the 1790s New Yorkers had replaced English and Scottish merchants in the southern staple trade, although now they were marketing cotton in Liverpool and not tobacco in London. By the 1840s New York had captured most of the foreign trade of Boston, Baltimore, and Philadelphia. While Boston maintained a modest direct commerce with Asia and Baltimore with Latin America, most of the outbound foreign trade from the East would leave by way of New York's harbor. The hungry 1840s brought realization of the enormous carrying capacity of the Erie Canal as millions of bushels of midwestern grain flowed into New York en route to famished Europe. With dozens of regular packet services to European and southern ports, thousands of canal boats plying interregional canals, and tens of thousands of small coastal vessels arriving annually, New York enjoyed superior access to regional, sectional, and international markets.

In this era, information followed the same channels as trade, and New York became the hub of the nation's information flows. It led the nation not only in shipping but also in the number of business visits, newspaper circulation, telegraph messages, and post office receipts. Whenever an event of importance occurred, New Yorkers were among the very first to find out. Superior information, transportation, and communications supported a dominance in finance and business services. Philadelphia's loss of federal deposits when President Andrew Jackson killed the Second Bank of the United States (1836) signaled the shift of banking preeminence from Chestnut Street to Wall Street. The widespread use of the telegraph facilitated the emergence of the New York Stock Exchange as the primary brokerage institution in the nation, weaning potential business away from the Boston and Philadelphia markets, which became little more than local stock exchanges. As the most efficient site for a range of services, New York assumed top rank in an urban system. The other eastern cities had to assume lesser positions while they depended on New York for a range of services; they could exercise only regional or subregional dominance.

In other sections of the country, urbanization followed different paths. While new cities would be formed as cotton production moved west, southern urbanization languished. The section's ports, even in the prosperous years before the Civil War, generated negligible levels of intercity trade. Engaging in virtually no intraregional specialization, southern cities served primarily as funnels through which to export staple crops. Without resident commercial decision-makers, without extensive financial and business services, and without appreciable manufacturing, the South had little reason to build cities. So the section's urban population, while increasing from 10 to 20 percent between 1860 and 1910, remained less than half the national average. And its cities failed to coalesce into a well-defined urban hierarchy.

Meanwhile, midwestern cities flourished as their percentage of urban population rose from less than 5 in 1840 to more than 50 in 1910. From the earliest years of settlement, its cities maintained impressive levels of interurban trade and specialization. Along the Ohio and Mississippi Rivers, an identifiable urban system emerged from Pittsburgh to St. Louis. With the completion of an extensive system of canals to the Great Lakes, a parallel trading network formed between Buffalo and Milwaukee. Much of the urban employment in the Midwest was devoted to processing and shipping western agricultural staples, thereby underwriting sizable commercial, manufacturing, and transportation sectors in the cities.

In the second half of the nineteenth century, Chicago became the dominant city in the interior of the country. Its initial success derived from Chicago's location as the western terminus of all-water and all-rail routes to the Midwest. It then became the eastern terminus of an extensive network of railroads that stretched north, south, and particularly west. A classic example of a city located at a break in transportation, Chicago became the point for the transshipment of western products and, given the economics of manufacturing and transportation, the processing point for many of these staples as well. Other cities in the region never had much of a chance. Chicago bested St. Louis in the 1850s when the axis of trade shifted from north and south along the Mississippi River to east and west on the railroad. The Civil War solidified the city's advantage by closing the Mississippi River trade to New Orleans and by the federal government's designation of Chicago as the exclusive entrepot for western trade. Cities located further west, such as Kansas City, Omaha, and Minneapolis, grew to appreciable size only after Chicago had achieved metropolitan status. Much as New York had done earlier in the century, Chicago used superior transportation and communications to become the heartland's primary center for wholesaling, finance, and business services. By the 1890s, it was the nation's second city, supervising an urban hierarchy that extended from the Appalachians to the Sierra Nevadas.

For much of the twentieth century, the commercial relationships among cities have changed little. The dynamic impact of internal trade was spent. The basic transportation network had been built and the enduring patterns of regional specialization established. New modes of transportation in the twentieth century (the airplane, automobile, and truck) have not radically reduced domestic transportation costs nor have they changed the basic flows of goods and services among regions. While cities may have changed rank, the urban hierarchy has remained remarkably stable.

But in recent years, changes have occurred that may portend a fundamental alteration in the American urban system. Increased speed and declining costs of transportation and communication, along with widespread reductions in tariff barriers, have inaugurated a new era of vastly expanded world trade and specialization. One critical manifestation of this has been the growth of trade with the Pacific Rim; in 1982 the United States for the first time exchanged more with Pacific than with Atlantic nations. While rapid urbanization of the West Coast predated this boom in international trade, Pacific commerce hastened the growth of the largest cities, particularly Los Angeles, which supplanted Chicago as the nation's second largest metropolitan center in the 1980s.

But the real competitive opportunity for the largest metropolitan areas at the end of the twentieth century is to be found in providing services. As the *New York Times* noted in 1994, most urban centers have historically manufactured goods for export and produced services for local consumption. But places such as New York now manufacture for the local market and peddle "cutting edge services—finance, law, communications, popular culture, and medicine—internationally. . . . Its leading competitors are no longer Chicago, Miami, and Houston but London and Tokyo."

Particularly after the first half of the nineteenth century, the urbanization of the United States owed little to trade and commerce. Other economic activities, especially manufacturing and noncommercial services, explain why most Americans live in cities today. But the system of cities, that is, the rank-size hierarchy and the interrelationships among cities, depended upon trade and its complement, specialization. The largest cities had the densest trading networks, providing both goods and services for lesser cities and their hinterlands. The decline in transportation and communication costs during most of the last 300 years has increased the scope of trade as well as the variety of goods and services exchanged. In American history, this has had two ramifications: the emergence of regional centers located at a "respectful" distance from each other across the continent and the impressive, although sporadic, growth in the wealth and population of the cities at the top of the hierarchy.

—*Diane Lindstrom*

**See also**
Hinterland; Urban Rivalry and Urban Imperialism.
**References**
Conzen, Michael. "The Maturing Urban System in the United States, 1840–1910." *Annals of the Association of American Geographers* 67 (1977): 88–108.
Cronon, William. *Nature's Metropolis: Chicago and the Great West.* New York: W. W. Norton, 1991.
Lampard, Eric. "The Evolving System of Cities in the United States: Urbanization and Economic Development." In Harvey S. Perloff and Lowden Wingo, Jr., eds., *Issues in Urban Economics,* 81–138. Baltimore: Johns Hopkins University Press, 1968.
Lindstrom, Diane, and John Sharpless. "Urban Growth and Economic Structure in Ante-bellum America." In Paul Uselding, ed., *Research in Economic History* 3 (1978): 161–216.
Pred, Alan R. *Urban Growth and the Circulation of Information: The United States System of Cities, 1790–1840.* Cambridge, MA: Harvard University Press, 1973.
Price, Jacob. "Economic Function and the Growth of Port Towns in the Eighteenth Century." *Perspectives in American History* 8 (1974): 123–186.

## Traffic

Modern cities in the United States rely almost exclusively on cars and trucks for the circulation of people and goods. Cars provide unprecedented mobility, privacy, flexibility, comfort, and—in some places and moments—speed. The side effects include congestion, noise, and conflict with pedestrian movement. Half of Americans now live in urban regions of over 1 million people. The "suburbs" have nearly twice the population of central cities, and there are about twice as many work trips from suburb to suburb as from suburb to central city. Many once-bucolic streets in small towns are now part of metropolitan areas and gridlocked by commuters. Nonwork trips (80 percent of total urban trips) produce considerable traffic during nonpeak hours and weekends.

Traffic patterns and problems in the United States have five interrelated causes:

1. High automobile ownership and use. The United States has more cars than workers; a typical American family owns two or more cars, and teenagers drive cars to school. Trips, even for a loaf of bread, are seldom made by any other form of transport.

2. The car's voracious appetite for space. Cars can transport only about 150 persons/hour per meter of width of a city street with traffic signals, given the requirements for parking and the average of 1.15 occupants per car. On a freeway, capacity per meter width increases to about 650 persons/hour. Other modes have far higher capacities and thus require less space. Per meter of width of the passageway, bikeways can move 1,500 cyclists/hour; sidewalks, 4,500 pedestrians/hour; modern bus and rail systems with exclusive right-of-way, 6,000 passengers/hour. Paradoxically, building more streets to reduce congestion and promote energy efficiency lowers the density of residential and other activities and further separates the origins and destinations of trips, increasing travel and energy consumption. Streets and parking can take up 50 percent of central areas, but still not be built fast enough to accommodate the growing number of cars.

3. Dispersed residential and activity patterns. In the nineteenth century, American city dwellers walked to work and carried or carted most of their goods. Activities were located near ports or sources of steam and water power, and population densities sometimes reached 30,000 persons per square kilometer. The car eventually lowered residential densities to levels that could not support frequent bus or train service. Today, New York, with 8,700 persons per square kilometer in its urban area, is America's only city with moderately dense population by historical or international standards; as a consequence, New York alone accounts for one-third of all commuting by train and bus. Chicago follows with 5,000 persons per square kilometer; other large cities in the United States

*A familiar scene on a Los Angeles freeway with cars jammed in both directions.*

quickly fall to densities nearer that of Houston—1,100 persons per square kilometer.

4. Tax, expenditure, and transport policies that favor cars. About one-third of traffic-related expenditures come from general funds not covered by taxes on fuel and motor vehicles. Low-interest federal loans have long subsidized single-family housing, promoting urban sprawl; tax policies subsidize free employee parking and tax company-provided transit tickets. Car taxes in the United States add a mere 5 percent to their prices, versus 47 percent in Holland and 186 percent in Denmark; the U.S. gasoline tax is about 5 cents per liter, compared to 40 cents per liter in England and Japan. Since the early 1900s transport planning has meant roadbuilding, with little thought for pedestrians, cycling facilities, or buses bogged down in automobile traffic.

5. The related mind-set. People in the United States regard central cities as places to be fled, rather than historic and cultural centers to be nurtured; as a nucleus of crime rather than the source of civilization. A big lawn and multiple-car garage are synonymous with the American dream; coupled with residential-only zoning, this translates into a 10-kilometer round-trip to buy milk or do almost anything else. Like Pogo, Americans have met the enemy and he is us. What politician would touch the transport economists' proposals of a dollar-a-liter fuel tax and electronic road pricing?

Decreasing and calming motor vehicle traffic require awareness of the experiences of other countries by transport planners and citizens. The Dutch walk or bike on nearly half their urban trips. Curitiba, Brazil, offers a comprehensive, modern bus network whose comfort and ease of boarding rival those of fine metro systems; buses account for 70 percent of motorized trips, are privately operated, receive no subsidies, and are profitable.

To solve traffic problems, innovative urban planners and residents need to find paths to healthier lives and more neighborly communities with fewer cars. Mixed and higher-density land use patterns can make walking and cycling viable for many common errands. These traits can be enhanced by creating environments friendly to pedestrians and cyclists that are linked to quality bus and train services. Tax and expenditure policies can help create a more balanced urban transport system and encourage companies and other entities to promote ride sharing. Such measures are, of course, easier to enumerate than to implement in the absence of major economic changes such as a prolonged oil shortage.

—*Charles L. Wright*

### See also
Congestion.

### References
Cervero, Robert. *Suburban Gridlock.* New Brunswick, NJ: Center for Urban Policy Research, 1986.
Litman, Todd. *Transportation Cost Analysis: Techniques, Estimates and Implications.* Victoria, British Columbia: Victoria Transport Policy Institute, 1995.
Newman, P. W. G., and J. R. Kenworthy. *Cities and Automobile Dependency.* Aldershot, England: Ashgate Publishing Company, 1989.
Pisarski, Alan E. *Commuting in America II.* Washington, DC: Eno Foundation for Transportation, 1996.
Wright, Charles L. *Fast Wheels, Slow Traffic: Urban Transport Choices.* Philadelphia: Temple University Press, 1992.

## Train, George Francis (Citizen) (1829–1904)

George Francis (Citizen) Train was one of nineteenth-century America's great eccentrics, a larger-than-life character whose legend far exceeded his considerable accomplishments. A prolific author and world traveler, Train's public career spanned 50 years of dramatic social and economic reorganization following the Civil War. A self-proclaimed genius and disciple of psychic energy, as well as an oddball and declared lunatic, Train's occasionally less-than-brilliant career touched the major movements of his times and fascinated a generation of Americans who delighted in his antics.

Born into modest circumstances and orphaned during the yellow fever epidemic in New Orleans in 1833, Train rose to prominence and wealth investing in shipping and railroads. He was an early backer of the Union Pacific Railroad, and he played an active role in organizing the scandal-plagued Credit Mobilier. His real estate holdings in Omaha brought Train considerable wealth, but legal entanglements prevented him from realizing the full return on a modest investment. Far less probable was Train's assuming credit for the Emancipation Proclamation, the rise of Irish Fenianism, and the fall of the Paris Commune.

Train was an early enthusiast of urban development during the Gilded Age. In his speeches and writings, he envisioned a "magnificent [transcontinental] highway of cities" along the Union Pacific tracks, eventually extending all the way from San Francisco to Boston. On separate occasions, Train predicted that Denver or the Seattle-Tacoma area represented the future of urban America. Although investors to his Credit Foncier scheme never appeared, and his personal life became mired in controversy, Train remained an unabashed booster of transcontinental and municipal transportation systems as the arteries of urban progress in the United States and Europe.

Train likewise took an interest in reform issues, especially the struggle for women's equality, spiritualism, and free love. He supported Susan B. Anthony's campaign for suffrage, and he befriended the Woodhull sisters during their obscenity trial in 1871. In this latter episode, Train insinuated himself into the Woodhulls' conflict with Anthony Comstock, an intrusion that brought him censure from the *New York Times,* a brief incarceration, and a magistrate's pronouncement that he was insane. Train's subsequent 80-day trip around the world became an inspiration for H. G. Wells's famous satire.

In the afterglow of the Woodhull controversy, Train retreated from public life for two decades. He reappeared in New York City in 1893 with a harebrained scheme to rescue the Chicago World's Fair from potential disaster. The fabled White City had fallen victim to the Panic of 1893, and some investors feared their great civic pageant would be a financial disaster. Train arrived in Chicago at midseason and promised to exert his psychic energy to turn the fortunes of the Exposition around. Though no one took him seriously, attendance figures began rising dramatically while Train was in Chicago, and the fair showed a final profit of $400,000.

Thereafter, Train retired into anonymity and died in New York in 1904 from complications brought on by nephritis. Hero or humbug, apostle of urban fantasies and unorthodox ploys, George Francis Train managed to delight a generation of Americans with his mischievous pranks and outlandish eccentricities.

—*Dennis Downey*

### References

Downey, Dennis B. "George Francis Train: The Great American Humbug." *Journal of Popular Culture* 14 (1980): 251–261.

Glaab, Charles N., and A. Theodore Brown. *A History of Urban America.* New York: Macmillan, 1967.

Train, George Francis. *My Life in Many States and Foreign Lands.* New York: D. Appleton, 1902.

———. *Young America in Wall Street.* London: S. Low, 1857.

## Transportation

Had Socrates been able, by some sort of magic, to step onto a street in colonial Boston, little would have confounded him. In the two millennia separating the heyday of Greek civilization and the emergence of the New World colonies, advances in urban transportation were virtually nonexistent. The Romans had proven themselves to be superior civil engineers, particularly as road builders. Various practical inventors had experimented with numerous paving materials, attempting to create durable surfaces for streets, roads, and highways. Yet the fact remained that, at least outside of downtown areas, almost all byways remained little more than dirt paths, unchanged since biblical times. Wagons and carriages were powered by animals used back then, oxen and horses. Nor had the speed of travel, or level of comfort, improved significantly over that period.

Three decades ago, urban historian Sam Bass Warner, Jr., characterized early-nineteenth-century urban enclaves as "walking cities." The term has many implications, and two are manifestly obvious. Cities were confined to small areas, most of which could be traversed on foot in less than an hour. Thus, dwellers could conduct their daily business while depending only on their two feet for transportation. Streets were narrow and congested. In addition, transportation technology had not advanced to the point where faster, affordable means of movement around cities were available.

The rich, of course, had always managed to move around with comparative ease. A wealthy colonial merchant might finish a sumptuous breakfast and, if not inclined to walk off his repast, order his livery servant to bring his carriage for a short ride to his office. Lean, hardy dock workers and others who were less affluent took to the streets on foot without considering alternative modes of transport. Adventurous schoolboys and rough street urchins might hitch rides on the back of the rich man's carriage until warned off by the coachman.

As many historians have astutely noted, the nineteenth century marked a revolution in urban transportation. Rapid urban growth, advances in transportation technology, and emerging capitalism created a dynamic symbiosis in which new opportunities for urban mobility developed and were rapidly adopted. In the early nineteenth century, alert observers noticed that it was becoming easier to move between cities and towns than within them. By the late eighteenth century, a number of successful privately owned turnpikes had been opened, most notably the Philadelphia-Lancaster Turnpike, chartered in 1792. Turnpikes were graded and often paved, and despite their tolls they lowered transportation costs by as much as 50 percent. The turnpike craze peaked in the 1820s, by which time they were beginning to experience competition from the first railroads.

Other civilizations had been constructing canals for centuries, but the necessary combination of need, opportunity, and available capital created a surge in long-distance canal building in the United States only in the 1820s and 1830s. The harnessing of steam power to riverboats and locomotives between 1810 and 1830 was a harbinger of great forward leaps in speed, economy, and comfort in interurban transportation. By mid-century, a long-distance journey that formerly required weeks could be completed in a matter of days, and goods could be transported at a fraction of the rates charged in 1800.

However, overcoming challenges of increasing mobility within cities appeared more problematic. This was not necessarily due to lack of foresight or effort. Oliver Evans tried to build a viable steam automobile beginning in 1787 when he received a patent to develop such a device from the state of Maryland. He struggled to bring his concept to fruition for the next 18 years. Discouraged by some of the nation's foremost engineers, including the renowned Benjamin Latrobe, Evans nevertheless persisted. In 1805 he finally unveiled his contraption, a boat-shaped device that chugged about the streets of Philadelphia at four miles per hour. Unfortunately, cobblestone streets broke the wheels the first day. Viable self-powered street vehicles were still a century into the future.

The first significant, widely accepted innovation in urban transportation was the omnibus, a French import. The omnibus was essentially a long, oversized stagecoach, capable of seating about 20 passengers. First introduced on Broadway in New York in 1829, omnibuses operated on fixed routes at scheduled intervals. Passengers hailed them anywhere along their routes. However, these devices were not for the common man, as fares usually ranged between 10 and 15 cents (a considerable sum in the 1830s, roughly an hour's wages). Still, omnibus travel grew rapidly in the first half of the nineteenth century. Used heavily in large eastern cities, their numbers surged, and by 1854 New York had 683 omnibuses that carried 120,000 passengers a day.

Omnibuses did not revolutionize urban transportation. On rough cobblestone streets, they could only travel five to six miles per hour; with frequent stops for passenger exchanges, average speed was even slower. Hence, their capacity for expanding the commuting radius of cities was negligible. Fares were prohibitively steep, horses sometimes panicked and got out of control, and service shut down in severe weather. Accidents were all too common, and overworked horses sometimes dropped dead in summer heat, further hampering service.

In the early 1820s, almost simultaneously with omnibuses, the first horse-drawn street railway experiments occurred. Copying rail-drawn carts used in some mining operations, promoters tried horse-drawn vehicles on wooden rails, switching later to more durable iron rails. By the early 1830s, horse-drawn railways appeared in Baltimore and New York. In the latter city, promoters initially experimented with grooves cut for the wheels, allowing private carriages with similar axle widths to also use the grooves. However, private carriers quickly realized the commercial value of their lines and the necessity of monopoly control over their rights-of-way.

Early railway operators lobbied for the right to elevate iron tracks a few inches above street level, making them accessible only to their own cars using specially designed wheels. However, private citizens with carriages and teamsters drawing wagons for competing carriers fought these developments. Competition with other vehicles for use of road space became a serious problem in the 1830s and would be a major reason for the decline of public transportation before the onslaught of the automobile a century later.

Nevertheless, the 1830s marked a period of considerable promise for new forms of urban transportation. By the late 1830s promoters were bringing steam locomotives into the centers of cities. In Boston, Philadelphia, and elsewhere, railway promoters began to serve affluent suburban dwellers who chose to live away from noisy, bustling urban cores and the sudden "influx" of new and different sorts of immigrants. Steam-drawn railroad cars offered riders a pleasant trip of a half-hour or so from downtown offices to sylvan estates several miles away.

As early as 1850 some 2,000 passengers commuted into Boston by train daily. But townspeople along the routes often objected, partly from class resentment. Steam railroads clearly enhanced the lifestyles of the wealthy, but at the expense of the less fortunate. Noisy engines exacerbated the increasing urban din, locomotives spewed noxious smoke that spread soot onto their hanging laundry and into open windows, and sparks created severe fire hazards. Anxious residents also feared boiler explosions, which were not infrequent in the early years of railroad technology. Finally, the trains intruded into social space; early-nineteenth-century urbanites considered streets their proper venue for informal social visits and children's' games. Fast-moving, dangerous machinery was an ominous new development to be feared and resisted.

Public protest gradually won the battle against steam railroads operating along residential streets. Similar confrontations would be waged against elevated steam railroads, electric elevateds, and freeways in future decades, with mixed results. However, advances in transportation technology continued. While unified neighborhood groups might prevent unwelcome intrusions into their areas, new transportation forms were destined to penetrate the cores of American cities. Railroads were sometimes directed above ground through industrial and commercial districts, and then through cuts or tunnels into downtown areas.

While steam railroads accommodated suburban commuters and the intercity transportation of goods and passengers, the challenge of meeting intraurban transit needs remained. In 1832, New York chartered the first horsecar railway lines independent of steam railroads. The iron rails greatly reduced friction and increased the speed of travel, and patrons enjoyed rides that were far more comfortable than those provided by omnibuses. Faster horse-drawn lines increased the half-hour commuting radius on city streets from about two to three miles. This in turn made it possible for downtown workers to seek improved housing on the city's fringes.

Although not as flexible as omnibuses due to their need for fixed rail routes, horse-drawn lines had essentially driven their competitor off most urban streets by 1870. The smooth-riding cars had become a fixture in the lives of modern urban dwellers. New Yorkers used the devices an average of 100 times a year. Women in outlying locations used them for shopping excursions downtown. Whole families piled into them on holidays for trips to distant amusement emporiums, baseball stadiums, or picnics in outlying parks.

Horsecars, although an improvement over omnibuses, were still no panacea for nineteenth-century urban transportation needs. The usual speed of about six miles per hour was hardly brisk, and the nickel fare was still beyond the reach of ordinary laborers, except for special occasions. Even so, many riders complained about overcrowding and rude, offensive behavior by both fellow passengers and conductors. As the ethnic and racial mixes in many American cities intensified in the decades after the Civil War, many citizens found commuting long distances in close quarters distasteful.

By the end of the Civil War, most American cities were notoriously unhealthy, plagued by foul smoke and soot. They typically faced severe problems with garbage, sewage removal and disposal, and densely packed housing. Streets were filthy, and frequent deadly epidemics created severe health hazards. While horse-drawn trolleys speeded up traffic flow, the animals contributed a great deal to the filthy environment. In large cities, public health officials measured annual manure deposits in the thousands of tons. Street cleaning was inefficient, expensive, and often confined to commercial districts and elite neighborhoods. In wet weather, streets often resembled cesspools, and in hot, dry weather, manure dust soiled clothing and hampered breathing. Horses that dropped dead in the line of duty often remained for days before being removed by public works departments.

Thus, transportation engineers had enormous incentives to invent a viable substitute for animal power. In 1872, Alexander Halladie introduced the cable car. A centrally located steam engine powered a system of endless cables through conduits located under city streets. Vehicles moved by physically gripping the cables, then releasing them when stopping for passengers. Cable cars were a major improvement over steam-powered trains, since passengers were spared from smoke, flying sparks, and excessive noise. Somewhat faster than horse-drawn lines, the cable car averaged roughly ten miles per hour. They were also able to pull heavier loads, a critical consideration in hilly cities like San Francisco, which up to that time had relied on hooking up extra teams of horses to pull cars up steep grades.

Like other innovations, however, cable cars had drawbacks. Most important was cost. Installation of cable cars ran about $100,000 per mile, ten times as expensive as horsecar lines. Because the cable car industry was highly capital intensive, it was profitable only in densely settled areas. Cable cars suffered frequent dangerous mechanical breakdowns. Consequently, no more than 15 of the largest American cities

adopted them, and service was confined almost exclusively to downtowns. At their peak in the early 1890s, there were only about 600 miles of cable car lines in the United States.

In the late nineteenth century, urban America experienced explosive growth. Structural steel and mechanical elevators permitted the construction of skyscrapers. Incandescent light and telephones revolutionized commerce, retailing, and the length of workdays. Electricity also provided the last major innovation in urban transportation before the emergence of the internal-combustion engine. In 1887, Frank J. Sprague began laying electric trolley lines in Richmond, Virginia, and he completed his 12-mile, 40-car system the following year. The concept was not new; various inventors had experimented with electric-powered transit conveyances for the previous half-century, but until the invention of the dynamo in the 1870s they had to rely on battery-powered electric motors, and battery power was 20 times as expensive as steam power. Thus, cost alone made application to street transit impossible. But Sprague's system incorporated the dynamo in generating and transmitting electricity from a central power source directly to the trains through overhead wires.

Sprague's initial contract in Richmond brought a financial reversal, as unforeseen technical problems inflated costs to twice the revenue guaranteed by his contract. However, he recouped his financial losses many times over in the next few years through sales of his equipment. The triumph of electric streetcars over alternative devices was swift and dramatic. By 1890, just two years after Sprague debuted his system in Richmond, 51 cities had installed electric railways. Five years later, there were 850 such systems operating in the United States. Horses were quickly relegated to pulling delivery wagons and carriages. As late as 1890 almost 70 percent of all mass transit mileage in cities had been operated under horse power, but by 1902 that figure had dropped to a minuscule 1.1 percent, whereas electric power was employed on 97 percent of all urban tracks.

At the turn of the century, the future of electric street railways appeared limitless, and the wondrous new technology transformed urban mobility. Although hampered by interference from slower-moving vehicles, pedestrians, and other obstacles in crowded downtowns, electric streetcars nevertheless averaged about 12 miles per hour. This breakthrough expanded the potential for spreading American cities horizontally. Because they were detached from underground cables, all cars did not have to travel at the same comparatively slow speed. Cars with sufficient headway could make up lost time, and when routes passed through uninhabited or open areas, they could move along at a brisk 35 to 40 miles per hour.

In the hands of farsighted real estate developers, interurban street railway franchises were valuable assets indeed.

Direct, fast trolley service to urban cores made distant single-family home lots far more valuable. In southern California and elsewhere, real estate and utility syndicates used cheap water and interurban transportation to open huge tracts to private suburban development many miles from urban cores.

In more densely settled areas, the electric trolley's impact was not quite as dramatic, but this innovation permitted urban transportation experts to consider new ways of speeding up intracity mobility and overcoming chronic congestion. Like cable cars, electric trolleys emitted neither sparks nor smoke. Thus, urban residents were less resistant to the prospect of elevated or submerged lines. Naturally, few homeowners relished the thought of elevated lines passing close to second-story windows. In addition, the steel elevated structures were ugly. Thus, it came as no surprise that elevated lines seldom intruded into wealthy neighborhoods. Subways were far more expensive to build, and the underground ride was less pleasant than one above street-level crowds; however, the important point was that electrification permitted engineers in the nation's most densely populated cities to separate urban transit along three horizontal planes.

The rapid development of mass transit tempted engineers to place too much faith in technological fixes for any future challenges. The flaws of such thinking would become evident in the new century with the head-on clash of mass transit, automobiles, and highway-building technologies. However, in 1900 electric railway technology appeared triumphant. Urbanites took to the bell-clanging cars with a passion, whether they be street-level trolleys, elevateds, or subways. Naturally, streetcars dominated the development of new transit systems. Unless congestion demanded elevateds or subways, private investors and/or local governments had no reason to bear the huge expense of separating planes of transport. Between 1890 and 1920, most urban dwellers commuted to work, ran errands, and enjoyed family outings on trolleys. During those 30 years, the nation's urban population grew 150 percent, while trolley patronage expanded almost 700 percent, from 2.2 billion to 15 billion patrons annually. In several cities, the typical resident rode the trolley more than once each day. Electric street railways were ubiquitous, celebrated in music, fiction, art, vaudeville, and even the emerging motion picture industry.

As electrified transportation systems dominated urban transportation, they required huge investments of capital for maintenance and expansion. However, as long as cities remained densely settled and patronage increased, the electric street railroad industry prospered. Even in medium-sized, prosperous towns of 8,000 to 10,000 persons, conservative bankers sagely advised spinster librarians and others to invest $5 monthly in local streetcar company bonds. In the years before World War I those investments looked very secure.

However, beneath the facade of nearly universal public use and gilt-edged bonds lay seeds of decay for the electric transit industry. A riding public whose parents had welcomed trolleys as miraculous inventions viewed the rumbling devices with mounting suspicion by the second decade of the twentieth century. A major reason was that many riders, and urban politicians, believed that electric traction magnates had violated the public trust. In the opinion of many knowledgeable urban critics, city officials had awarded overly generous franchises to street railway companies in order to ensure prompt installation of service. Only too late did they realize their mistake. In some cases, trolley companies enjoyed perpetual or 99-year franchises to operate on city streets under near-monopoly conditions.

In many cities, street railway companies were highly profitable, their ownership groups extremely arrogant. With dominance over city streets, some critics charged that street railway companies treated both patrons and those seeking to control or regulate them with contempt. As ridership multiplied, company profits mushroomed, yet operators seemingly defied public demands for service extensions into thinly settled "nonprofitable" areas or crosstown routes. Crosstown routes might significantly cut commuting time, but they were seldom profitable. Some progressive "reformers" fought to lower trolley fares, or at least hold the line on increases. These campaigns enhanced their images in the eyes of virtually all working-class constituents. Progressives believed their battles against street railway monopolies were justified in light of increasing ridership, fat profits, and liberal franchises. In many cities, "machine" politicians were sympathetic to the operators, winking at abuses of franchise agreements in exchange for patronage for "deserving" party men and generous "kickbacks." Novelist Theodore Dreiser brilliantly captured the flavor of the struggle between "corrupt" traction interests, machine politicians, reformers, and the riding public in the first two volumes of his renowned trilogy about Frank Cowperwood. These volumes, *The Financier* (1912) and *The Titan* (1914), featured the rise to power of a brilliant, ruthless streetcar magnate. Astute critics knew the protagonist was a thinly disguised representation of Chicago's traction king, Charles T. Yerkes.

World War I marked the peak of mass transit operations above, below, and on the streets of American cities. From then on, public transit declined, almost imperceptibly at first, then conspicuously after World War II. In fact, patronage of public transit peaked in 1923, as Americans were turning to other means of transit, particularly automobiles.

Gasoline-powered automobiles and electrics had appeared on city streets in the last decade of the nineteenth century, but they were initially playthings for the rich. Trolley operators arrogantly dismissed them as a mere nuisance on city streets. However, Henry Ford's inexpensive Model T, plummeting in price to under $300 by the mid-1920s, placed privately operated vehicles within financial reach of the masses.

Eighty years ago, automobile makers enjoyed widespread admiration from American consumers, who perceived them as pioneering risktakers. In contrast to the street railway magnates, who were widely reviled by many as bloated, arrogant capitalists, auto makers like Henry Ford and the Dodge brothers symbolized the persevering "little guy" who had triumphed against long odds. Time would drastically alter these perceptions. By the 1930s most street railway companies were either publicly owned or operated by colorless salaried managers; in contrast, some automobile manufacturers (including Ford) were revealing their ugly sides (both individual and corporate). By then, however, most of the critical commitments regarding urban transportation had already been made, and in most American cities the automobile emerged triumphant. The public images of electric transit operators and automobile producers between the world wars had played significant roles in the car's victory in hundreds of cities and towns across the United States.

Widely held negative perceptions of electric traction operators during the World War I Era weakened the industry at the worst possible juncture. As the automobile was fast gaining widespread acceptance and popularity, the straphanging public was transferring their cynicism toward trolley operators against mass transit in general. In the first decade of the twentieth century, trolley operators had appeared all-powerful, virtually impervious to public opinion. A decade or so later, they increasingly sought public sympathy and support as their industry faced unprecedented financial problems.

Between 1914 and 1920, the cost of living in the United States doubled. Rampant inflation struck the transit industry heavy blows. Most companies were locked into long-term franchise agreements that set fixed fares, usually between a nickel and a dime. By World War I, any politician who succumbed to corporate pressure to raise fares faced almost certain defeat in the next election. However, operating costs rose inexorably, with or without fare increases. Workers forced pay increases; construction materials were more expensive, insurance costs increased. At the turn of the century, trolley operators often received favors they did not need or deserve; by the 1920s, they collectively paid the price, frequently being denied concessions that were critical to their long-term health.

Another particularly pesky problem was the jitney, a new form of competition that appeared on city streets on the eve of World War I. Jitneys were private automobiles, whose owners cruised major boulevards, providing rides for passengers waiting at trolley stops. Trolley operators cried foul, claiming that jitney operators were siphoning off the "cream" of their

ridership. In Los Angeles, as many as 150,000 persons rode jitneys every day.

Whatever the cause of those problems, profits for trolley companies fell, and their bonds soon had to be discounted in order to be sold. In response, street railway operators had little choice but to postpone purchasing new equipment and extend intervals between periodic maintenance of tracks and equipment, cutting corners wherever they could. Passengers showed neither sympathy nor understanding. In the first few years of the century, they tolerated cars with windows jammed shut on hot summer days, or cold, drafty cars in winter. By 1920, however, they complained vehemently about such annoyances; no longer would they tolerate discomfort.

In part, this was due to the unprecedented upsurge in American prosperity that was accompanied by rapidly escalating material comforts for the masses in the first three decades of the twentieth century. Automobile manufacturers had contributed significantly to the rising expectations. The 1920s were years in which the "American dream" of a detached, single-family home in a suburb with a small fenced-in yard and a garden appeared reachable for millions of middle-class citizens. Owning an automobile became an integral part of this dream. Wages had risen to the point that millions of immigrants could afford to ride trolleys, and many "native" Americans found even more reasons to avoid riding them when possible. Driving was far more appealing than trolleys for other reasons as well. Automobile owners did not have to conform to schedules, so there was no waiting time on street corners. One could run several errands on a trip to scattered locations without numerous waits and multiple fares. In addition, drivers could either ride alone or choose their companions, avoiding potentially unpleasant contacts with strangers.

The 1920 census reported that for the first time in American history half of the population resided in urban enclaves. Metropolitan areas continued to expand in the 1920s, as rural America continued to lose population. Most of the urban growth occurred in fringe areas and in new suburbs. The automobile was a critical contributing factor as increasing numbers of workers found it more convenient and pleasant to live in suburbs and commute to downtown jobs in their automobiles. As late as World War I, suburban development in most American cities had been limited to land located no more than a few blocks from either steam railway or streetcar lines. Real estate advertisements for new subdivisions up to that time usually emphasized the convenience of rail service to adjacent urban cores. A decade later, their advertising focus had shifted markedly, stressing detached one- or even two-car garages, rarely mentioning trolley service.

Shifting settlement patterns encouraged metropolitan leaders to accommodate automobiles rather than mass transit. In part, this was a response to sheer necessity. Between 1920 and 1929 the number of automobiles in the country almost tripled, from 8 million to 23 million. As more and more cars crowded city streets, traffic congestion quickly became problematic. Urban decision-makers had to accommodate drivers, or they risked their political futures.

The interwar years were a period of feverish experimentation with technological and engineering fixes for traffic problems created by automobiles. Civil engineers experimented with new paving techniques, street widening, multilevel highways, limited-access highways, and freeways. Within the profession, there existed a profound faith in the ability to solve traffic problems; surely the next breakthrough would magically solve the congestion riddle. They thought that innovative traffic regulation would also help—stop signs, traffic lights, and synchronized lights along wide boulevards. Elevated pedestrian crosswalks and other structural designs would enhance the flow of all forms of traffic.

By the mid-1920s mass transit officials were complaining that public officials were ignoring their needs. They argued that subways, elevateds, and streetcars were far more efficient carriers of passengers than automobiles because they occupied far less street space per passenger carried. Thus, public funds should be devoted to subsidies to improve mass transit rather than street widening and new parkways. However, their pleas fell mostly on deaf ears. Not only had they generated ill will in previous years but their proposed solutions were enormously expensive. The 1920s witnessed the presentation of elaborate mass transit consolidation schemes in many cities; with few exceptions, they met defeat. Too often, they promised to improve traffic movement in very limited areas (usually central business districts) and serve only small numbers of vested interests. Not only were street and parkway improvement plans far more economical, but by providing tangible benefits to every district in a city, they were far more appealing to elected officials.

Public transit officials also realized that fixed rail systems were in trouble because of high overhead costs and lack of flexibility. By the early 1920s, they developed the strategy of supplementing rail service with "feeder" bus service. Buses could be used to extend mass transit into thinly settled areas where fixed rail service could not operate profitably. In addition, buses might provide crosstown service, the lack of which inconvenienced and irritated many people who still depended on public transportation. The census did not list buses as public carriers until 1922, when they transported 404 million patrons, but by 1930 they accounted for 2.5 billion riders out of a total of 15.6 billion transit passengers.

There were short-lived, hopeful efforts to revive rail service through the marketing of sleek, new, comfortable cars, most notably the highly touted PCC car, introduced in the mid-

1930s. The Depression of the 1930s and World War II forced some Americans out of their cars and back onto mass transit. Wartime mobilization between 1940 and 1945 brought suspension of automobile production along with strict rationing of gasoline and rubber tires. In the early 1940s, many prosperous workers remained committed straphangers, willingly or otherwise.

After World War II, public transportation companies in all but the most densely settled cities rapidly switched from rail to bus service. In some cities, transportation executives experimented with electric-powered buses, or "trackless trolleys," which were connected to overhead wires but had the advantage of greater maneuverability in congested traffic. Many urban critics, however, complained of overhead wires as visual blight, and by the end of the 1950s most of the wires had been removed. Manufacturers of buses provided improved diesel-powered engines, and by the early 1960s only a few nostalgia buffs lamented the disappearance of clattering streetcars.

By then, it was obvious to the most casual observer that automobiles were the overwhelming choice of urban commuters in all but the most densely settled cities. Passage of the Federal Highway Act in 1956 initiated the process of pumping billions of federal dollars into superhighways, including urban freeways. Mushrooming suburban developments 20 to 40 miles from city cores, and the simultaneous emergence of highly decentralized shopping centers, industrial parks, sports complexes, universities, and other metropolitan amenities, fundamentally altered commuting patterns. Urban dwellers without access to automobiles felt increasingly isolated and alienated.

Yet the triumph of "automobility" provoked a spirited reaction. In many areas, neighborhood groups battled proposals to build new freeways that they perceived as sinister attempts to reinforce de facto segregation. In some cases, they triumphed, and in reformers' eyes half-completed, abandoned multilevel freeway skeletons symbolized the failure of a misguided, soulless public policy. Some also charged that back in the 1930s, automobile manufacturers (most notably General Motors) had conspired to destroy mass transit by buying certain bus operations and then purposely allowing them to deteriorate, wither, and die. In many respects, the issue was moot, since by then tens of millions of urbanites had already committed themselves to the automobile, and such a strategy could only marginally have affected the decline of mass transit.

Ironically, Lyndon Johnson's Great Society programs of the mid- to late 1960s also generated funds for the revival of mass transit. The initial Urban Mass Transit Act (UMTA) of 1964 opened the spigot of federal funding for new responses to unmet public transportation needs. The most publicized triumphs in mass transportation were sparkling, massive new rail systems: San Francisco's Bay Area Rapid Transit (BART), Washington's Metrorail system, and a handful of others. Even Los Angeles, long considered the nation's benchmark "autopia," planned a new subway under one of its key arterial boulevards in the early 1990s. Some critics dismiss these enormously expensive projects as unnecessary boondoggles, but transportation expert George Smerk wisely cautions that it would be unfair to indict most mass transit projects for their failure to meet costs solely from revenues, especially in the short run. Clearly they will require large subsidies. Most were designed to meet broader social agendas, and, in addition, many were pilot projects, intended to guide transportation over future decades.

Predictions are always risky. Many experts discounted rail transit 30 years ago, but it now appears to have a future. Still, it would be misleading to assume that the masses will soon throng back to the big cars on fixed rails. At an international conference on the future of mass transit in the early 1980s, a dozen or so experts from the automobile industry, mass transit companies, and public agencies were surprisingly consistent in their predictions for the future of mass transit in the United States. Asked to predict what percent of daily trips American urbanites would take on mass transit by the year 2000, most predicted a figure close to 6 percent; the most "optimistic" was 12 percent. This was when memories of OPEC muscle-flexing during the 1970s were vivid and American policymakers were working frantically to promote alternatives to petroleum-powered vehicles. By the mid-1990s awareness of the "energy crisis" had receded, and Detroit automobile manufacturers were producing more efficient new products. In light of all these important recent adjustments, it is hard to imagine American citizens abandoning their cherished chariots in the foreseeable future, and the trend in the late 1990s to larger, less-efficient vehicles confirms its unlikelihood.

—*Mark S. Foster*

**See also**
Airports; Automobiles; Buses; Cable Cars; Canals; Dummy Lines (Steam Street Railways); Elevated Railways; Horsecars; Interurban Transit; Jitneys; Journey to Work; Mass Transit; Omnibuses; Railroads; Rapid Transit; Roads; Steamboats; Streetcars; Suburban Railway Service; Subways; Traffic; Walking City.

Barrett, Paul. *The Automobile and Urban Transit: The Formation of Public Policy in Chicago, 1900–1930.* Philadelphia: Temple University Press, 1983.
Davis, Donald F. *Conspicuous Production: Automobiles and Elites in Detroit, 1899–1933.* Philadelphia: Temple University Press, 1988.
Foster, Mark S. *From Streetcar to Superhighway: American City Planners and Urban Transportation, 1900–1940.* Philadelphia: Temple University Press, 1981.
Hood, Clifton. *722 Miles: The Building of the Subways and How They Transformed New York.* New York: Simon and Schuster, 1993.
McShane, Clay. *Down the Asphalt Path: The Automobile and the American City.* New York: Columbia University Press, 1994.
Smerk, George M. *The Federal Role in Urban Mass Transportation.* Bloomington: Indiana University Press, 1991.

## Tugwell, Rexford Guy (1891–1979)

Rexford Guy Tugwell, an important adviser of President Franklin Roosevelt as head of the Resettlement Administration and sponsor of the Greenbelt towns, was born in Sinclairville, New York, in 1891. He attended the Wharton School of Finance and received a Ph.D. in economics at the University of Pennsylvania in 1922. He then taught at Columbia University where he was promoted to full professor in 1931.

In 1932 President Roosevelt recruited Tugwell to be part of his "Brain Trust," and in 1933 the president appointed him assistant secretary of Agriculture. In 1935, he appointed Tugwell head of the Resettlement Administration. In this position, Tugwell oversaw the creation of three "greenbelt" towns, the cooperative planned communities of Greenbelt, Maryland, Greenhills, Ohio, and Greendale, Wisconsin. Critics of the New Deal found him an excellent target, and he left the government when Roosevelt dismantled the Resettlement Administration at the end of 1936.

In 1938, Tugwell became the first chairman of the New York City Planning Commission and promptly experienced major difficulty fulfilling the commission's mandate in the presence of Mayor Fiorello La Guardia and Robert Moses. He resigned from the commission in 1940 when Roosevelt appointed him chancellor of the University of Puerto Rico; a year later Roosevelt appointed him governor of the island. In 1946, Tugwell moved to Chicago to head the graduate program in planning at the University of Chicago where he remained until his retirement in 1957. In his later years he served as visiting professor at a number of universities before he settled in Santa Barbara, California, where he died in 1979.

Tugwell's planning goals evolved during his days in graduate school, where he was influenced by men such as Thorstein Veblen and Simon Patten. Tugwell believed that man must use a rational planning process to shape the institutions of society for the common good. Throughout his entire life he saw himself as an advocate of this process, whether working on greenbelt towns, on the New York City Planning Commission, or with students at the University of Chicago. In our capitalistic, individualistic culture, Tugwell's vision of society met resistance at every turn. He thought his goals for society were entirely reasonable and rational; in actuality, his desire for a system in which planning can achieve economic and environmental benefits for the good of all was utopian. He deserves to be remembered for the perseverance with which he worked throughout his career to achieve his vision of a better life for all.

—*Cathy Knepper*

**See also**
Greenbelt Towns; Resettlement Administration.

**References**
Namorato, Michael V. *Rexford G. Tugwell: A Biography.* New York: Praeger, 1988.
Sternsher, Bernard. *Rexford Tugwell and the New Deal.* New Brunswick, NJ: Rutgers University Press, 1964.
Tugwell, Rexford G. *The Diary of Rexford G. Tugwell: The New Deal, 1932–1935.* Michael V. Namorato, ed. Westport, CT: Greenwood Press, 1992.

## Tunnels

A tunnel is a long horizontal passage constructed underground for the transit of people, vehicles, goods, or services. Tunnels are usually constructed for three reasons: first, to provide an easy route for a railroad or highway through a mountain range; second, to allow safe passage across a river or estuary; and third, to enable rapid movement of passengers beneath busy city streets.

The construction of tunnels is as old as cities, and as early as 1200 B.C. galleries were driven beneath the ancient fortified cities of Syria and Palestine to intercept underground springs and provide a secure water supply. The Greeks and Romans also constructed tunnels for supplying water to their cities; the Romans were also the first people who regularly constructed tunnels as part of their road system.

In the United States, one of the early tunnels was the four-and-one-quarter-mile Hoosac Tunnel, constructed through the Hoosac Mountain in northwestern Massachusetts between 1855 and 1876. The tunnel was driven to provide a rail link between Boston, Massachusetts, and Troy, New York, on the Hudson River. It is important in the annals of tunneling because of its pioneering use of mechanical rock drilling and nitroglycerin explosives. The Hoosac Tunnel is an example of a tunnel driven through mountains to provide passage for a railroad.

The Detroit River Tunnel is an example of a tunnel to provide transit across a waterway. It was constructed between 1906 and 1910 to carry the Michigan Central Railroad across the Detroit River between Detroit, Michigan, in the United States and Windsor, Ontario, in Canada. Before the tunnel was built, railcar ferries transported trains across the river with a service frequently interrupted during winter by ice in the river. The Detroit River Tunnel is an example of an immersed-

*The First Street tunnel in Los Angeles, California, seen often on television and in motion pictures.*

tube tunnel, that is to say, one constructed by dredging a trench across the river bottom, laying a tube in the trench, and then backfilling it.

The third type of tunnel—to provide more rapid movement of people below city streets—is probably the one most relevant to cities. The first urban underground railroads were built in London from 1863 on, but other cities soon followed: Paris in 1898 and New York (from the Battery in Manhattan to Joralemon Street in Brooklyn) in 1902. The importance of the urban underground railroad (tube, metro, subway) to the development of cities cannot be overemphasized. Long before the construction of subways, city streets had become choked with traffic, and this made anything but short journeys difficult and time-consuming.

But underground railroads had another, perhaps even more important, role to play beyond easing travel within the city itself; in many cities where they were built, underground railroads were soon extended to suburbs (often coming up to the surface to do so) and provided commuter routes for city workers. This development helped make possible the modern city with its central business core surrounded by an outlying suburban residential fringe. It is generally considered that any city whose population exceeds 1 million can justify constructing a subway system.

—*Graham West*

**References**
Carrington, B. "Mass Transit 1989: Worldwide Metro Guide." *Mass Transit* 16 (1989): 4–40.
Sandström, G. E. *The History of Tunnelling.* London: Barrie and Rockliff, 1963.
West, Graham. *Innovation and the Rise of the Tunnelling Industry.* Cambridge, England: Cambridge University Press, 1988.

## Unemployment

Unemployment gained a new quality with the onset of industrialization. Before industrialization occurred, a person destitute because of joblessness had been classified with the poor at large and was considered no differently from anyone else. Under the impact of industrialization, however, it was gradually realized that individuals were often helpless in an empty labor market when no jobs were available.

This revision of long-held ingrained beliefs, of course, did not come overnight. It was the increasingly widespread unemployment in the decades after the Civil War that caused the beginnings of this reorientation. Continuously heavy immigration, peaking occasionally when cyclical unemployment reached higher levels, accounted for much of the excess labor. In a way, then, this shift in the appreciation of the problem paralleled an increase in numbers. A change of terminology also occurred. Hitherto, words like *nonemployment* or *lack of employment* had been applied, and the afflicted had generally been designated as *tramps* or *vagrants*. By the late 1880s, however, words like *unemployment* and *the unemployed* came into use, signaling the adoption of the new environmental viewpoint.

At any rate, people who had this new understanding believed that if society had caused the distress, society should also alleviate it. But it was not clear at the outset which segment of society should directly bear the burden. Private charity made a heroic effort, helped by the professionalization of social work in the twentieth century, but in the 1930s, in the face of the catastrophic joblessness of the Depression, private welfare agencies had to acknowledge their essential powerlessness and inability to solve the massive problems.

Less eager, but equally on the front lines, were municipal services. Traditions dating back as far as the English Poor Law gave them the ultimate responsibility for the welfare of the impecunious. On the other hand, the acceptance of the view that the environment and not the individual caused unemployment might mean that the Poor Law no longer applied. This point was not lost on most local authorities. Often chafing under the many difficulties that rapid urban growth and inadequate administrative structures caused them, as a rule they would have been happy to surrender the mandate. That they could not immediately do so was due to the unwillingness of potential substitutes. The state and possibly the federal governments might have taken over, but until the problem reached statewide and then nationwide proportions, senior governments saw little reason to assume a costly and onerous undertaking. In other words, only during the tremendous unemployment of the 1930s did they seriously lend a hand in alleviating the evil.

Until then, the care of the unemployed remained chiefly a task of municipalities. Their active involvement thus stretched from the time when industrialization had a noticeable impact until the Depression. Obviously, the volume and the detail of activities differed vastly according to the location and condition of the specific towns and cities. Nevertheless, the very nature of the problem imposed a general pattern. Authorities had to sort out the individuals worthy of help, they had to get an understanding of the size of the problem, and they had to decide what remedial measures to employ.

Not the least problem was initially defining *unemployment* and then designating those entitled to aid. Most local authorities had some difficulty distinguishing between the *voluntarily idle* (i.e., the improvident paupers) and those unemployed through no fault of their own. While the time-honored work test, which meant an offer of work instead of relief, recommended itself for various reasons, it was not applicable in many instances. Work had to be available, and the applicant had to be suited for it; neither was necessarily the case. Thus, prospective recipients' worthiness to obtain support more often than not rested upon their assurance of being ready to work but unable to secure jobs, upon the fulfillment of some residence requirement, and possibly upon the recommendation by caseworkers who knew the person or the family.

Partially as a result of this uncertainty about definitions, no city ever had reliable figures about the number of the unemployed within its boundaries. Only the advent of unemployment insurance would change this. In the decades before it was introduced, authorities had to rely on impressionistic indicators such as charity welfare rolls, trade union reports, the occasional police count, or even scenes in the streets. If this kind of evidence presented an unmistakable picture of distress, as it did in most larger and many smaller places during the various depressions, then the time for action had apparently arrived.

As often as not, this action began with the creation of a committee or commission whose task it was to get a grip on the problem and, if warranted, plan remedial activities. If the emergency had not passed by the time the committee reported, definitive measures had to be taken. These measures commonly belonged to one of three categories, or a combination of them. The unemployed might be assisted in their search for work, work might be provided for them, or simple handouts might be given to tide them over the period of need.

The establishment of temporary (and in a few instances permanent) employment agencies was a step most municipalities took readily and without much delay. These exchanges could help the unemployed help themselves, they reduced human waste and enhanced productivity, and they were relatively inexpensive, by no means their least important advantage. Unfortunately, these agencies at best rationalized the job market somewhat, but they could not create new opportunities for employment. Often enough, therefore, additional measures appeared to be in order.

Job creation for relief purposes, though, was a difficult task. As a rule, municipalities did not possess the funds, or the ready plans, to start projects of sufficient size in an emergency. Even when they did possess money and ideas, other problems remained. If relief workers received substandard wages, regular employees and trade unions were up in arms because of the unwanted competition; paying standard wages, however, was usually too hard on the treasury. Moreover, few municipalities had any public works possibilities other than construction projects, but these, as mentioned previously, did not suit all the unemployed. As a result, most of the jobs offered were make-work, such as leaf raking or snow removal.

Under these circumstances, in many instances local authorities saw no way other than doling out relief directly. They could pay subsidies to private charities that had the apparatus to dispense aid adequately. Or the municipality could assume the distribution function itself, be it by running soup kitchens or food banks or by opening agencies to apportion small sums of cash.

All these activities were normally taken as emergency measures, and the haphazardness of their administration, as well as the weakness of their impact, limited their value. Over time, therefore, the demand grew louder for more substantial action. Almost by definition, these actions had to be long-range in character, and by the 1920s there was general agreement that this meant introducing unemployment insurance. As early as the 1890s, some European cities had dabbled with such schemes, but not much had come of them. American municipalities therefore wisely—and impatiently—waited for higher levels of government to take the first step. They were finally let off the hook when passage of the Social Security Act in 1935 signaled the federal government's readiness to assume responsibility for taking care of the unemployed.

—*Udo Sautter*

### References

Feder, Leah Hannah. *Unemployment Relief in Periods of Depression: A Study of Measures Adopted in Certain American Cities, 1857 through 1922.* New York: Russell Sage Foundation, 1936.

Keyssar, Alexander. *Out of Work: The First Century of Unemployment in Massachusetts.* New York: Cambridge University Press, 1986.

Leiby, James. *A History of Social Welfare and Social Work in the United States.* New York: Columbia University Press, 1978.

Lubove, Roy. *The Struggle for Social Security, 1900–1935.* Cambridge, MA: Harvard University Press, 1968.

Sautter, Udo. *Three Cheers for the Unemployed: Government and Unemployment before the New Deal.* New York: Cambridge University Press, 1991.

*Men examine job postings outside an unemployment office in the late 1940s.*

## Union Stock Yard

The Union Stock Yard in Chicago opened on Christmas Day 1865. The market, built and operated by the Union Stock Yard & Transit Company, originally covered 320 acres and contained pen space for 21,000 cattle, 75,000 hogs, 22,000 sheep, and 200 horses. Located in the suburban four miles south of the city, it became a catalyst for Chicago's growth. Earlier, in 1861, Chicago had become the center of the meatpacking industry, and in the 1870s Chicago's leading packers moved just west of the stockyard. During the market's first year of operation, 1,564,293 head of livestock passed through its gates. In 1900, that number reached 14,622,315; in 1924, the market reached an all-time high, processing 18,643,539 head. The original 320-acre site grew to 475 acres with pen space for 75,000 cattle, 300,000 hogs, 50,000 sheep, and 5,000 horses.

Technological advancements in refrigeration enabled Chicago's packers to dominate the nation's meat supply with the development of refrigerated railroad cars. Armour, Swift, Morris, Hammond, and Wilson became familiar names to consumers as Chicago's meat flooded local markets. In 1905, Upton Sinclair's famous muckraking novel, *The Jungle,* made the Stock Yard district even more well known throughout the nation.

The huge plants attracted thousands of workers; by 1900, some 32,000 employees worked in the packinghouses, and their number rose to 40,000 during World War I. Almost from its opening, and especially with the growth of this huge labor force, the Union Stock Yard attracted labor organizers. First the Knights of Labor, later the Amalgamated Meat Cutters and Butcher Workmen of the American Federation of Labor, and finally the United Packinghouse Workers of the Congress of Industrial Organizations came to organize the "yards." By the end of World War II, workers in all of Chicago's major plants had union contracts.

After 1945 technology again transformed the meat industry. As the Union Stock Yard benefited from Chicago's position as a rail center, so too the decline of the rail industry harmed it. New refrigerated trucks and the growing highway system allowed the industry to decentralize. Furthermore, packers increasingly chose to purchase animals directly from producers, making central stockyards obsolete. From the early 1950s through the mid-1960s, Chicago lost most of its packers. On August 1, 1971, the Union Stock Yard closed, ending an era in industrial history.

—*Dominic A. Pacyga*

### References

Barrett, James R. *Work and Community in the Jungle: Chicago's Packinghouse Workers, 1894–1922.* Urbana: University of Illinois Press, 1987.

Holt, Glen E., and Dominic A. Pacyga. *Chicago: An Historical Guide to the Neighborhoods, The Loop and South Side.* Chicago: Chicago Historical Society, 1979.

Jablonsky, Thomas J. *Pride in the Jungle: Community and Everyday Life in Back of the Yards, Chicago.* Baltimore: Johns Hopkins University Press, 1993.

Pacyga, Dominic A. *Polish Immigrants and Industrial Chicago: Workers on the South Side, 1880–1922.* Columbus: Ohio State University Press, 1991.

Slayton, Robert. *Back of the Yards: The Making of a Local Democracy.* Chicago: University of Chicago Press, 1986.

Wade, Louise Carroll. *Chicago's Pride: The Stockyards, Packingtown, and Environs in the Nineteenth Century.* Urbana: University of Illinois Press. 1987.

## Unions

Unions first appeared in American cities in the late eighteenth century. According to the rhetoric of early unionists and workingmen's advocates, the masters of some large shops took advantage of their wealth to legislate unfair monopolistic privileges, cheapen honest labor, and above all lengthen and intensify the workday, thereby threatening the competencies and independence of upstanding citizen-journeymen. Urban craft workers, most prominently journeyman carpenters, cordwainers (shoemakers), and tailors, organized into hundreds of local labor societies in the United States from the 1790s to the 1820s. A citywide Mechanic's Union of Trade Associations was formed in Philadelphia in 1827, and a General Trades Union was created in New York City in 1833. These early crafts unions demanded high dues from their members and generally excluded African Americans, women, and unskilled factory operatives. The depression of 1837 to 1842 had a disastrous effect on the nascent union movement.

From their beginnings, unions have had to contend with a legal and political ideology that holds that unions are conspiracies that undermine property rights and entrepreneurial freedom. From this perspective, unions promote invidious "class" distinctions in a society otherwise without significant barriers to economic advancement for meritorious workingmen. Throughout the nineteenth century and until the 1930s, local and state courts and legislatures employed the doctrine of conspiracy to limit strikes. They generally upheld the right of unions to exist, while declaring that most of the methods used by unions to accomplish their aims, including picketing and various kinds of boycotts, were unlawful infringements on commercial and property rights.

Beginning in the late nineteenth century, debates within the union movement over aims and methods revolved around questions of craft versus industrial unionism, local versus centralized control, and the pursuit of "utopian" social and political objectives versus incremental organization and using strikes as the most effective recourse for grievances.

The Knights of Labor, founded in Philadelphia in 1869, endorsed some goals beyond the workplace, such as currency and land reform. Consistent with its "producerist" ethos, the organization admitted all manual workers and even some merchants and manufacturers, but excluded bankers, stockbrokers, lawyers, liquor dealers, gamblers, and others suspected of idle parasitism, intemperance, or corruption. In its platforms, the Knights called for moderate means, cooperative production, and land reform to achieve a radical end, "the abolition of the wages system." Even so, the Knights of Labor was involved in several of the most violent large-scale strikes of the era, especially against railroads and shops associated with them. The organization declined rather precipitously after the Haymarket tragedy of 1886 and the ensuing repression. "Respectable" opinion associated the Knights with anarchism and violent rebellion. Disagreements and lack of coordination between national and local leadership also weakened the organization, and its credibility suffered because of many successful lockouts by employers after 1886.

Samuel Gompers, who founded the American Federation of Labor (AFL) in 1886, derided the Knights of Labor, with its diffuse membership and larger social reform objectives, as an "educational" organization. Gompers and his associates, influenced by Marxian ideas, focused on the careful development of union organization and working-class control in the workplace; they generally eschewed political objectives and alliances in favor of strikes to achieve limited, job-related goals. The officers of AFL unions were generally unwilling to risk their organization's resources and credibility by initiating comprehensive and ideologically freighted organizing campaigns in large-scale industry. These campaigns provoked state repression and also compromised the rather insular, "manly," highly ritualized, and exclusive culture of the "labor aristocracy." Thus, AFL-style pragmatism generally meant neglecting women, African Americans, and transient semiskilled laborers. Except for the radical Industrial Workers of the World (IWW), which kept the idea of industrial unions alive well into the twentieth century, and the significant but unsustainable appeals of some socialist and Communist unionists, Gompers's model of craft unionism predominated among American workers until the 1930s. The ideal of class- and job-conscious unionism remains a powerful current in the organized labor movement.

However, as technological change and organizational consolidation eroded the craft system of production in the twentieth century, Gompers's conception of "pure and simple" unionism had serious shortcomings, especially in meeting the needs of workers in the great urban industrial centers. AFL unions in the mining and clothing trades did have an industrial organization. However, with its chronic jurisdictional rivalries and inherent fragmentation, the AFL was unable to maintain an effective presence in primary industries like automobiles and steel.

The large industrial unions established during the Depression and World War II represented a significant departure from earlier republican, reformist, socialist, or "pure and simple" models. There was an undeniable strain of old-time militancy in the movements to organize workers in such industries as steel, automobiles, rubber, electrical, and meatpacking. However, a new culture of unionism emerged, pragmatic and organizationally sound for logistical reasons, but at the same time somewhat more inclusive, less deferential, and more politically active. Workers in the great industrial states of the North seized plants in massive sit-down strikes, switched political affiliation *en masse* to the Democratic Party in response to appeals based loosely on class, occasionally allowed Communists to achieve leadership of their unions, and helped organize large numbers of African Americans and women.

New Deal reforms helped create a favorable legal and political atmosphere for organizing workers in basic industry in the 1930s and 1940s. As a result, the unions founded under the aegis of the Congress of Industrial Organizations (CIO) in 1935 developed a closer relationship with the state than had any previous union movements. Liberal labor "statesmen" like Sidney Hillman (Amalgamated Clothing Workers), Philip Murray (CIO and Steel Workers), and Walter Reuther (United Auto Workers) cultivated close alliances with the Democratic Party; this reflected the preferences of their constituents as well as pragmatic recognition of the increasing legal and political role in collective bargaining.

Organizing basic industries increasingly depended on pronouncements of the National Labor Relations Board established under the Wagner Act (1935), and later, wartime regulatory agencies. The Taft-Hartley Act (1948) outlawed mass picketing, secondary strikes of neutral employers, and sit-down strikes. It also permitted employers to challenge some union initiatives in court. This further "legalized" collective bargaining. In addition, Supreme Court decisions in the 1960s and 1970s cast unions in the roles of arbitration and disciplinary agents by restricting the right to strike during the life of a contract. In the United Auto Workers, precedent-setting contracts signed after World War II granted union security and prosperity in exchange for increased managerial control. Unprecedented gains in productivity and wages after the war era meant that these developments went largely unchallenged.

In the 1980s, as wages stagnated and employment in heavy industry declined, migrated to nonunion areas, or moved abroad, labor unions' political and economic power ebbed dramatically. The percentage of workers belonging to unions remained consistently below 20 percent, half the portion of the early 1950s. In the 1980s and 1990s, unions faced a number of challenges as firms established nonunion productivity teams, strikes became increasingly rare, and employers hired permanent replacements for striking workers more frequently. Unions continue to face criticism for harming efficiency and competitiveness, although there is evidence that they promote productivity and innovation in most firms. Increasing the power and influence of unions continues to depend on their ability to challenge legal and political obstacles to organizing unorganized workers. This ability, in turn, requires that unions reassert a coherent vision of social and economic justice both within and beyond the workplace.

—*Edward Johanningsmeier*

### References

Dubofsky, Melvyn. *The State and Labor in Modern America*. Chapel Hill: University of North Carolina Press, 1994.

Fraser, Steven. *Labor Will Rule: Sidney Hillman and the Rise of American Labor*. Ithaca, NY: Cornell University Press, 1993.

Licht, Walter. *Industrializing America: The Nineteenth Century*. Baltimore: Johns Hopkins University Press, 1995.

Lichtenstein, Nelson. *Walter Reuther: The Most Dangerous Man in Detroit*. New York: Basic Books, 1995.

Zieger, Robert H. *The CIO: 1935–1955*. Chapel Hill: University of North Carolina Press, 1995.

## Upper Class in Cities

Defining the urban upper class is a difficult task in a country as large and diverse as the United States. Urban upper classes come in many forms and often have very different histories. Still, despite this varied character, urban upper classes do share basic traits: high social status, substantial wealth, and community-wide power. Taken together, these three characteristics define an upper class. The absence of any one of them compromises possession of the other two and eventually undermines the upper class in a community.

Equally important, the upper class as a group sustains intense loyalty and commitment among its members and their families. Wealth, power, and status bring the members of the upper class together in many venues, from the business office or the bank to evening dinners and gala celebrations. Club membership, church affiliation, and common cultural activities reinforce membership in the upper class.

Members of the upper class often select spouses from other families who have the same social status in the community. This pattern, repeated often among families in the upper class, produces strong kinship ties that intimately bind those in the upper class. Inevitably, these kinship ties serve as the basis for legal, business, and financial partnerships that strengthen the economic power of the upper class. These relationships, as Frederic Jaher points out, generate "shared lifestyles, experiences, and expectations among the members of the upper class and their families."

Exclusiveness certainly marks the upper class. Still, to be viable, an upper class must mediate between exclusivity and interaction with their fellow citizens. To sustain their position, the upper class must address the key values of their locality as a whole, provide dynamic leadership that benefits a substantial portion of the community, and maintain ongoing relationships with other groups in their city. The greater the extent to which an upper class loses its ties to the rest of the community, the more real is the danger of isolation and irrelevance.

After the American Revolution, the upper class certainly demonstrated the traits of an upper class. Yet, it also incorporated many social habits of pre-Revolutionary society.

Known as the "Better Sort" in earlier years, the upper classes in urban ports had constructed social institutions, economic bases, political positions, and dense kinship and friendship networks that bound its members and families into a cohesive group clearly apart from the vast majority of the population. Dominated by merchants, the upper class depended on the overseas trade that fueled economic growth and distributed highly valued European goods throughout the colonies. By the time of the Revolution, these groups had matured into an upper stratum that counted the wealthy, economically powerful, and socially sophisticated among its ranks.

This sophistication made itself manifest in the powerful notion of "refinement." Refinement provided all-encompassing rules for every aspect of behavior, from personal appearances and posture to dinning habits and polite conversation. By the late eighteenth century, genteel families resided in lavish mansions marked by impressive staircases and extravagant furniture. The mansion also served as the site of the "parlor," which, more than any other place in the house, epitomized refinement. Essential for the "Better Sort," whether

*Eighteenth-century chandeliers hang high over debutantes and their escorts in the Astor Hotel ballroom during the 1964 International Debutante Ball.*

in Portsmouth, New Hampshire, or Philadelphia, Pennsylvania, a parlor implied civil behavior, breeding, and a moral superiority unattainable by common people. Reserved for polite exchange, it served as the central and most costly room for the upper class.

This segment of society, as Gordon Wood demonstrates so powerfully, remained connected to the common people primarily through patronage relationships. These reached down through the various ranks and categories of colonial society to provide favor, and favors, to ordinary people. Sail makers who depended on a specific merchant for business or an artisan who relied on a member of the "Better Sort" for credit or political patronage provide examples of these relationships. In this way, the "Better Sort" demonstrated their centrality to the lives of lesser people who relied on them for a myriad of essential economic, occupational, financial, and other benefactions vital to their own survival.

Polite society of the colonial era also showed an appetite for social space devoid of the coarse and vulgar, whose rude intrusions into the daily lives of the "Better Sort" shattered the serenity and elegance they had worked so hard to build. In ports from New York City to Philadelphia to Charleston, the "Better Sort" generally confined their residence to particular neighborhoods. In New York City, they congregated along Wall Street, and by the late eighteenth century they were clustering on Broadway near the governor's residence. Churches, elaborate taverns reserved for the best people, and appropriate housing created polite space for formal social gatherings, worship, and informal exchanges.

The world of the "Better Sort" would, as all of colonial society, experience dramatic changes as the Revolution transformed the colonies into a republic dedicated to ideals at odds with the presumptions of the "Better Sort." Ironically, a substantial proportion of the "Better Sort" had worked tirelessly to realize victory in the war and had risked all that they were and all that they owned to achieve this success.

The world they helped create after independence immediately threatened their once-uncontested leadership. The revolutionaries proclaimed the new country a self-governing republic free of social distinctions and the hierarchy they created. Simplicity reigned, and equality and independence replaced patronage and dependency. The upper classes shared this new rhetoric and helped build the new political institutions to govern the Republic. Few of those in the upper strata dared label themselves the "Better Sort," now a term of contempt quickly abandoned by its once-proud holders.

Did the urban upper classes, then, embrace the very simplicity and equality so prominent in the wake of the Revolution? In fact, nothing of the sort occurred. Mansions, the most visible sign of gentility, sprouted up all over New England, the very home of the Revolution. In fact, the demand for large and imposing houses helped spark the emergence of the architect as a true professional. Similarly, painters who copied European styles flourished in the Connecticut Valley, where proprietors of the new mansions wished their likeness portrayed in subdued but European fashion.

The urban upper classes continued to fashion genteel spaces in their communities. Imitating their English and French counterparts, they planted extravagant gardens and built walks secure from the vulgar. Luxury shops continued to meet their special tastes, and their habits of consumption still distinguished them from the rest of urban society. Lavish carriages sheltered them from the dirt, mud, and dung that littered urban streets as well as from the general population that traveled the city on foot.

The upper classes also continued to expand their associational ties. In Boston, the Brahmin leaders founded libraries, historical societies, and journals for the exchange of ideas. Similarly, Philadelphia's nobility established an academy of science and a philosophical society that exist today. Such activity nurtured and solidified the cohesiveness that maintained the upper class in positions of community leadership.

Secure economically in their mercantile base, the urban upper classes made their mark in politics. In New England, for example, they continued to control regional politics. Upper-class merchants represented communities throughout the region. They successfully developed policies that favored mercantile interests from tariffs to credit, and they dominated the Federalist Party, which held sway in New England into the nineteenth century.

The decades after 1820 witnessed the transformation of American society and the urban economies that fueled industrial growth. The mercantile elite especially faced new challenges in the industrial environment. In Boston, mercantile leadership responded by developing a new manufacturing base, textiles. Members of the upper class in Boston established the most sophisticated textile factories in the world. Their profits greatly enhanced their wealth and secured them a place in the new industrial order. Boston entrepreneurs complemented this central industry with canals and railroads that provided the transportation necessary to bring in raw materials and distribute finished products.

In New York City, new men largely propelled the metropolitan economy into national prominence, surpassing all competitors including Boston. These men made New York the chief transportation hub of the country, the major center of finance, and the main site for the thriving cotton trade.

In the interior of the country, newly emerging upper classes engineered significant industrial expansion that turned small towns into major commercial and mining sites. In Wilkes-Barre, Pennsylvania, the upper class developed the coal industry and turned a small village into the major regional center for much of northeastern Pennsylvania by 1860. In Chicago, an infant upper class prompted innovations in transportation and trade that transformed an early-nineteenth-century small town into a major metropolis by 1860.

The upper classes in North American communities clearly remained business enclaves. As Frederic Jaher points out, they embraced values consonant with the market. These included "thrift, industry, prudence, personal restraint, and self-dependence," essentially the Protestant work ethic. From newly emerging industrial communities to older cities, upper classes made their way by succeeding in the market revolution. Successful entrepreneurs continued to move into the ranks of these groups.

Participation in the marketplace inevitably drew members of the upper classes into the world of antebellum politics, both at local and state levels. In Chicago, access to political decision making proved essential to securing company charters, grants of land, limited liability, or government subsidies. The upper class dominated politics and political parties in many communities such as Chicago or Boston. Brahmins from the Massachusetts capital extended their influence into the state arena, where they ruled the Whig Party and dictated its state platforms. The Whig Party itself ruled Massachusetts for most of the antebellum years, a circumstance that enhanced the influence of the Brahmin class.

Distinctive upper-class institutions remained the bedrock of these urban leadership groups. Unitarian churches continued to serve the Boston Brahmins, while Episcopal institutions persisted as a hallmark of the wealthy in New York City, Philadelphia, and Charleston. Even in newly developing Chicago, the emergent upper class usually affiliated with the Episcopal Church. The upper classes enhanced their exclusivity by creating a series of new cultural institutions. Mindful of their eastern counterparts, the Chicago upper class founded historical, literary, and intellectual societies that enhanced their prestige. The Athenaeum in New York City, the North American Review in Boston, and the Academy of Sciences in Chicago depended on upper-class patronage and participation. In Wilkes-Barre, the Wyoming Historical and Genealogical Society reminded everyone in the community of the deep roots of upper-class families in the city's past. Not surprisingly, admission weighed heavily on such familial ties.

The upper classes also continued to carve out and sustain genteel living space. In cities of the Northeast, city halls and statehouses inexorably drew the families of the upper class. New York's City Hall anchored upper-class residential quarters. In this same neighborhood a host of the finest hotels and shops serviced upper-class families and their guests. Similarly, the elegant domiciles of Boston's upper class flanked the state capitol building at the center of Beacon Hill. In Philadelphia the upper class transformed a number of squares, such as Rittenhouse and Franklin Squares, into refined space for the genteel.

The women in upper-class families assumed power in the homes located in these neighborhoods. Separated from their husbands' world of work and decision making, women found themselves in charge of the household and its myriad of servants and workmen. They increasingly took responsibility for maintaining "taste, sensibility, and delicacy." Wives in the upper class directed entertainment, selected dinner guests, sent invitations for balls, and controlled the social activities that involved upper-class families and friends.

These newfound duties enhanced their standing in society, but they operated in a world truly divorced from the emerging centers of power. Men studiously kept women away from company offices, the workplace, and the new boardrooms. While women handled a myriad of household chores, they accomplished these tasks at the beckoning of societal norms and their husbands, whose control over money remained unchallenged.

Within elegant upper-class homes, parlor culture continued to expand and intensify. Capitalizing on nineteenth-century technology, the upper class adorned their parlors and surroundings with lush carpets, fancy tablecloths, and expensive upholstery. The parlor remained the chief site for social exchange among the genteel and served no economic or utilitarian functions, but it spoke volumes about refinement, that singular mark of the upper class. "The walnut furnishings, the finished porcelains, the gilt clocks . . . the flowers and shrubs," described so powerfully by Richard Bushman, demonstrated little or no "productive value." The parlor represented ease and comportment that seemingly challenged the work ethic so prominent in the elite business enclaves.

Social power appeared in the spread of parlor culture to the willing, and perhaps even eager, middle classes of the cities. Their domestication of refinement demonstrated the very real and unspoken ways that the upper classes had provided a model of behavior and respectability for those who sought to stand as social pillars. At the same time, the democratization of parlor culture fit nicely into the republican ethos, still the pervasive ideological norm in the United States. The shift also reversed suspicions held by many in the early Republic toward an upper-class culture that traced its origins to Renaissance courts and appeared to embody aristocratic pretensions, all supposedly cast aside by the Revolution.

While upper-class parlor culture silently touched those of comfortable means, those with wealth, status, and power actively reached out to the rest of society in a series of benevolent and charitable institutions. In Chicago, Wilkes-Barre, and Boston, the upper class sponsored Bible study groups, city missions, and Sunday schools that attempted to meet what they perceived as the spiritual needs of the population.

Wealthy members of the upper class also bequeathed substantial sums of money to mechanics' institutes for the benefit of working-class populations, and sponsors often waved tuition charges to encourage working-class participation. The upper classes clearly attempted to instill their own values in those who singularly seemed to lack them.

Still, social distance continued to separate the upper classes from the rest of society. These appeared most powerfully in fissures that increasingly undermined popular culture before the Civil War. Then, Americans shared a common popular culture that featured opera, symphony, and, above all else, the plays of William Shakespeare. His works stood out as one of the most cherished forms of entertainment for all citizens of the Republic. From an early age, Americans encountered the English bard in common school. Here, they learned Shakespeare "as declamation or rhetoric not as literature." But, profound tensions existed between the upper classes and ordinary Americans who regularly attended the theater, and actors often set these tensions into stark relief. The widely known Edwin Forest, for example, used his interpretation of Shakespeare to appeal to the democratic sensibilities of ordinary people. Other actors, most notably the Englishman William Charles McCready, appealed to the upper class and its refined tastes. Pronunciation, word choice, and overall appearances and gestures distinguished some actors and divided audiences on the basis of class. This division manifest itself most powerfully in the increasing unhappiness of the upper classes, who expressed profound dissatisfaction about sharing theaters and entertainment in general with common people. The appearance of theaters designed specifically for the upper classes marked the widening gulf between the wealthy and the common.

The upper classes worked tirelessly to shield cultural affairs, such as Shakespearean performances, from the general public in the years after the Civil War. The upper classes devoted much of their time to redefining these art forms and removing them from the public sphere. For example, upper-class observers denounced the common habit of breaking up Shakespearean plays with vaudeville acts and condemned the custom of injecting American vernacular into the bard's plays, practices that appealed to ordinary Americans. Commentators vigorously advocated using only the original dialogue and even began to argue that academic tutoring best suited audiences who wanted to appreciate the author's texts. Of course, only those in the upper class had access to such preparation.

Ordinary people repeatedly heard the message that commoners lacked the capacity to grasp Shakespeare or understand other forms of art. The shift in audience was clear in comments of the *San Francisco Chronicle* when it reviewed a performance by the Mapleson Opera Company. With some satisfaction, the paper noted the presence in the audience of "a bright representation of San Francisco society comprising the beauty, youth, and elegance of its fair sex . . . [and] almost all the leading men who had made a mark in their various professions." It also had sharp words for commoners who failed to match genteel standards set by the best people. Similarly, in Atlanta, the community's best families sponsored the opera, attended the performances, and paid the steep bills to bring the very best talent available to town. Here, too, local newspapers praised the people who made these performances such special events. The upper class could safely enjoy the pleasures of the arts free from the undesirable and unwanted segments of the population.

The effort to segregate cultural activities mirrored the success of the urban upper classes in building a more formal institutional structure that distinguished the well-off from the rest of society. The appearance of an elaborate club structure in the late nineteenth century epitomized this trend. In metropolitan areas upper classes developed a complex club system that always operated in a clear social hierarchy and catered both to men and women. The first clubs were men's downtown clubs. Typically, men's luncheon clubs provided exclusive surroundings for those in the upper class to meet socially as well as to talk business. Social accomplishments matched business prowess at these clubs. Usually, young men of significant social standing and who were related to current members were admitted every year. Just as important, these clubs frequently took in only those who had won prominence in the business world. Once introduced to club members, newcomers found that a host of positions in the leading cultural, civic, and other community organizations were offered to them. These ties embedded them in the upper class while sustaining its economic and its community power bases.

In larger cities, these clubs appeared in sufficient numbers to form a clear hierarchy. The most prestigious in Philadelphia, the Philadelphia Club, included members of the oldest, most illustrious families among its ranks. The Rittenhouse Club also attracted some of the best-known men, but not the most distinguished, and occupied second place. After those two, aspiring young men who sought citywide recognition often began their social climb in the Union League Club, the least prestigious of the men's clubs, and they hoped some day to gather sufficient prestige to gain membership in the Philadelphia Club.

Other kinds of high-status clubs also existed in larger cities. Men's athletic clubs, university clubs, and women's clubs appeared in New York, Philadelphia, and Atlanta. Athletic clubs generally ranked far behind luncheon clubs in terms of prestige. University clubs catered to graduates of the leading Ivy League schools, namely Harvard, Princeton, and Yale. Admission to these clubs still depended on a vote of the membership to safeguard against the socially unfit. Unlike other local clubs, university clubs also served out-of-town residents and facilitated ties among members of upper classes from different cities.

Women's clubs also performed important functions for those in the upper class. Often, as in the case of Pittsburgh's Twentieth Century Club, organizers intended the club for intellectual as well as social purposes. Members inevitably came from prestigious families, and their husbands belonged to the appropriate equivalent male organizations. The Acorn Club in Philadelphia and Boston's Chilean Club were counterparts to the Twentieth Century Club.

These clubs also exercised a profound influence on upper-class social life. Debutante balls, holiday dances, afternoon teas, annual cotillions—all the major social events on the entertainment calendar—depended on the organizational skills of upper-class women. Debutante balls, for example, were coming-out events for young woman on the verge of marriage who needed an introduction to the eligible young men of the upper class. The financial sponsorship of these events often remained the preserve of the men's clubs, but they still remained within the dominion of the women.

On the other hand, many women's clubs dedicated themselves to community improvement. The Woman's Club in Los Angeles, for example, worked in the interests of women employees in the area and engaged in social crusades such as demanding juvenile courts and women's suffrage. In Nashville, upper-class female members of the Centennial Club promoted city cleanup, beautification, and other reform projects. Similarly, in Chicago, the Chicago Political Equality League concentrated on women's suffrage and the increased participation of women in government.

On one hand, activist women's clubs reached out to the community. On the other, social clubs reinforced the exclusivity of the upper class. Upper-class social and familial institutions generally divorced the private lives of the upper class from the rest of the community. Kinship and family, religious denominations, church affiliation, and educational choices created a private social world for elites. Kinship ties also joined many prominent families together. In Pittsburgh and Philadelphia, for example, a high degree of intermarriage among old, prestigious families persisted throughout this period. Such intimate ties enhanced the cohesiveness of the upper class. Kinship also worked effectively to buoy up family members who experienced financial disaster from the 1860s to the 1940s. Marriage alliances also secured upper-class control over local companies and banks and ensured family longevity, so important to many in the upper strata.

The urban upper classes increasingly affiliated with the Episcopal Church in the Northeast and Midwest. The Episcopal Church stressed an intellectual dimension wholly absent in evangelical denominations. This singularity specifically appealed to the urban upper classes. The Episcopalians relied on long-standing doctrine, a clear hierarchical order in its organization, and an elaborate dress and decorum for its priests and religious services. These naturally appealed to conservative, affluent residents, such as those in Philadelphia, who felt threatened by the egalitarianism of other denominations. As members of the Episcopalian denomination, the upper class generally attended churches located in the center of their communities. St. Mark's, Holy Trinity, and St. James Episcopal churches, for instance, all sat in the Rittenhouse Square district where Philadelphia's "best" families resided well into the twentieth century. Belonging to exclusive churches like these marked the high social standing of the communicants and their families. Vestrymen, church board members, and financial support all came from the upper class, a pattern repeated in many cities in the United States.

The denominations of the upper class also sponsored educational institutions for the children of the best families. In Philadelphia their sons attended the Episcopal Academy located in the Rittenhouse Square area. The upper class firmly believed that an education acquired in privately funded schools operated by those of their own kind guaranteed appropriate socialization, conditioned marriage choices, and ensured adequate training.

Wealth generated from the activities of entrepreneurs in the upper classes often sustained local colleges. In the South, members of the upper strata established Vanderbilt University and Emory University in Nashville and Atlanta, respectively. Admittedly both depended, in part, on northern money. Still, local wealth provided some money for these institutions and sustained them once in operation. Of course, the sons of upper-class families matriculated at these universities, where they acquired the educational and social skills so vital later in their lives.

These educational institutions were crucial in allowing children of the upper class to develop careers that ensured persistence of their families at the top of society. They often went into law or medicine—fields that generated substantial income, power, and status—law since it proved vital in business, and medicine because it affected the community so dramatically. Increasingly, both of these professions called for the university training that was available only to a handful of young men who had both the time and the funds necessary for graduate preparation. In the majority of these cases, career choices depended on their fathers' resources, background, and contacts crucial to sustaining university training. None of these were in short supply among upper-class families.

Even more commonly, young men in the upper classes selected business for their careers, sometimes aiming their effort at their fathers' pursuits or what the social class as a group chose. In Pittsburgh, for example, many opted for manufacturing products related to iron and steel. In Wilkes-Barre, they chose mining. Similarly, Detroit's upper class initially chose carriage, carriage-related, stove, and railroad car manufacturing and then shifted to automobile production.

The upper class continued to express a strong interest in politics, especially in government. Its members could hardly ignore an institution that provided so many resources, levied taxes, granted urban franchises, regulated businesses, granted tax exemptions, and issued professional licenses; government actions clearly touched issues that directly affected the fortunes of the upper class and demanded their involvement. Yet the upper classes faced challenges in localities where political machines backed by immigrants supported urban political bosses and their followers. In most cities, contending parties reached a compromise that usually kept members of the upper class in the executive branch and in cultural arenas such as parks and fine arts, while immigrants secured places in the legislative branches.

Beginning as early as the 1850s, and intensifying throughout the rest of the century, the urban upper classes began to flee downtown neighborhoods. The changing composition of downtown populations as immigrants and workers crowded into limited space, the demands business placed on prime real estate in central cities for their company headquarters, and the inability of the upper class to control land use near their homes and neighborhoods pushed many of them outside the city boundaries. Suburban migrants discovered that state laws would protect their new residences. Armed with this legal protection, the upper class built neighborhoods safe from annexation by cities and free of unwanted neighbors. At the same time, developers had acquired the capacity to provide the urban services necessary to sustain such communities.

Just as important, urban transportation improved dramatically in speed, regularity, and flexibility. Railroad lines opened the possibility for suburban communities even before the Civil War, and electric traction provided new options for suburban transportation by the end of the 1890s. In Chicago, the wealthy trekked to North Shore communities such as Evansville. In Philadelphia, they followed the Pennsylvania Railroad line to the west where they settled in a series of communities collectively known as the Main Line. In New York City they journeyed north along the Hudson River to secluded communities within an hour's commute on the train.

These new residences attempted to recapture the rural atmosphere lost in the central city. Once established in these suburban communities, the upper class re-created their downtown neighborhoods. Churches, private schools, family networks, and clubs all appeared in the suburbs and acted as stabilizing influences on upper-class life.

Clubs proved to be an especially formidable influence on the new suburban upper class, which established the suburban country club, a hallmark of these communities. These organizations served the entire family and provided a place for members to meet, dine, and engage in sporting events. All of these clubs featured golf as one of their key activities. The sport had acquired an unrivaled popularity among the urban upper classes, many of whom responded to the opportunities for conspicuous consumption offered by the sport. It demanded considerable time to play a round and outrageous expenses for clothing and equipment, items that were affordable only to the upper class and that only it possessed.

While country clubs catered primarily to local leadership, members of the urban upper classes devoted much of their energy to securing interurban ties among leadership groups. The increasing presence of the corporation acted as a unifying influence among those in the upper class. This new form of business organization often brought together directors, officers, and business agents drawn from upper-class communities all over the region. Coal companies located in either New York or Philadelphia regularly included members of upper-class groups from other major metropolitan communities and smaller industrial cities such as Wilkes-Barre. These men met at board meetings, business activities throughout the year, and clubs such as the Westmoreland Club of Wilkes-Barre or the Philadelphia Club. Often, the families of these men intermarried, thus strengthening the bonds that stretched across the industrial landscape of the Northeast and the Midwest.

Education often sparked the first contacts among those who would seize the reins of power in their respective communities. Upper-class families often sent their sons to prestigious schools, where they encountered the offspring of upper-class families from other cities. These institutions reinforced the values and perceptions of the upper classes and created the basis for associations among the members of these groups, often followed by matriculation at an Ivy League university such as Princeton. Upon arriving at one of the big three—Harvard, Yale, and Princeton—first-year students began seeking the right clubs, the ones that maintained proper social standing and common class origins among their members. Admission to these clubs ranked as an important goal of these new students. The ties generated by such affiliations sustained the networking they had begun in boarding school and would extend beyond college and continue into business or professional life.

The Ivy League schools served as an ideal environment for the sons of upper-class families. Even old-line families like the Roosevelts, who patronized institutions other than the three Ivy League schools, shifted their money and support to these institutions. Sons of families whose members had amassed unheard-of fortunes in the late nineteenth century, such as the Morgans and Goulds, joined the Roosevelts in their four years at Princeton, Yale, or Harvard. Among Pittsburgh's upper class, the vast majority dedicated their resources to a single institution, Princeton University. This decision grew out of the close ties developed between Princeton's administration and the wealthy in Pittsburgh.

One sign that members of the upper class were developing even closer ties was most visible in the *Social Register,* a national guide for those of high social status. The *Social Register* first appeared in New York City in the late 1880s, but it spread throughout the metropolitan United States during the next two decades and reached San Francisco in 1906. The *Social Register* even drew subscribers from medium-sized industrial communities such as Wilkes-Barre, Pennsylvania, and Youngstown, Ohio. Regardless of where one lived, to appear in the *Social Register* required letters of support from existing members who could verify one's social pedigree and acceptability. Last, these cosmopolitan families often spent the warmer months of the year in summer colonies such as Bar Harbor, Maine, which catered to upper classes from all over the Northeast.

Despite the similarities shared by all the urban upper classes, they each confronted different local conditions that shaped their configuration and even determined their fates. Understanding the dynamics of these groups and their relationship to the growth of their communities proves crucial in explaining the diversity among the urban upper classes as they faced dramatic economic changes from the late nineteenth century to the 1930s.

Rapid economic growth involved urban upper classes in a variety of ways during those years. In Detroit, the early automobile producers in the upper class dramatically reshaped the economy of the metropolitan area. Once dependent on carriage manufacturing, the lumber industry, and specialty iron and steel, the Detroit upper class turned the city into a one-industry community. By the 1910s the Detroit upper class had transformed the automobile into the chief symbol of the emerging consumer culture in twentieth-century America.

Yet Henry Ford, an outsider, would again change that symbol as he developed an inexpensive car that ordinary Americans could afford and one that drove upper-class automobile producers out of business. Ford overtook his upper-class competitors, who by 1933 desperately sought financial help from him, their bitter enemy. His refusal only placed the last nail in their coffin.

Chicago's upper class proved as capable as Detroit's had been in developing new economic activities that transformed the city from a small town in the middle of the nineteenth century into a major manufacturing and railroad center by

the 1920s. Its members built some of the largest retail and mail-order businesses in the country. In Atlanta, Georgia, the upper class played an identical role. Built on the wealth of successful newcomers, the upper class proved central in establishing the new industrial economy of the city and its region. In both cases, the upper class acted as the key agent in promoting growth and economic development. Both thrived into the twentieth century without facing a competitor such as Ford.

Upper classes often resisted innovation and growth. In New York, an older mercantile upper class failed to capitalize on the opportunities and technologies in new industries. Instead, they remained wedded to their established commercial activities. As a result, newcomers could cash in on the potential of new industries and technologies to build a new, dynamic economy. These men built new manufacturing corporations that depended on vertical integration and the array of professional and managerial talent available in the city. None of these reflected the traditional institutions and kinship system that had sustained the commercial upper class. By 1900 this growth fragmented the upper class into multiple groups, each of which had its own business and social organizations. The older upper class retreated to its wealth, its genealogies, and its social exclusivity.

In Boston, growth proved the undoing of the Brahmins. The increasing scale of economic activities demanded the same corporate bureaucracies that threatened New York's mercantile upper class. At the same time, textiles faded as a central part of Boston's economy and undermined the dynamic part of Brahmin fortunes. Fearful of new economic imperatives, the upper class hid much of its money in trusts rather than in risky ventures and technological innovation. Much like their New York counterparts, the Brahmins took refuge in museums, private social activities, and clubs.

Ironically, the very growth that marginalized Boston's Brahmins sustained the upper class in Wilkes-Barre. It, too, depended on families, traditional institutions, and exclusive social clubs. Yet, coal proved more durable than textiles, and the members of the city's upper class kept a measure of control despite the intrusion of New York money. The families in the upper class continued to maintain ties of blood and marriage into the 1920s, and they often reinforced business relationships. Ironically, Wilkes-Barre's upper class also began to develop similar connections to the leadership groups in metropolitan centers. These ties enhanced their power in the region since it gave them access to metropolitan companies and banks by virtue of their family connections. The upper class in Wilkes-Barre retained its wealth, its social standing, and its economic dominance in the city's and region's economy. Only the collapse of the anthracite industry, first challenged by new energy sources in the 1920s and then devastated by the Depression of the 1930s, unhinged the community's upper class and impoverished the entire region by the 1950s.

Charleston's upper class also maintained its kinship base into the twentieth century, but it barely resembled Wilkes-Barre's upper class. Charleston's upper strata clung desperately to its antebellum past and, in the process, rejected industrialization, whereas Wilkes-Barre's upper class prospered only while mining anthracite coal thrived. For Charleston's leaders. their plantation origins revealed themselves in leisurely workdays and unhurried noontime dinners on verandahs or in the serenity of shuttered mansions. The city's upper class fiercely resisted intrusions by successful newcomers, who remained outsiders despite their sometimes considerable economic achievements. In fact, the antebellum past provided the essential core of existence for Charleston's elite. Wilkes-Barre's upper strata behaved very differently. While they often looked to the past to provide identity, they remained firmly rooted in the economic realities of the twentieth century, and they drew vitality from participating in the regional and national economies. Wilkes-Barre's upper class often embraced new arrivals, particularly those sent by coal and railroad officials to oversee their operations in the city.

In the years after World War II, urban upper classes often faced an economic world of unparalleled economic growth. More than any other city, Los Angeles embodied the phenomenal economic explosions that occurred. The city benefited from the development of a myriad of new defense-related industries such as aerospace and the rise to national and even international prominence of the motion picture industry. People successful in volatile new industries and the mercurial world of entertainment crowded into an increasingly fragile and changing upper class. In this fluid world, sheer wealth and public notoriety often proved vital to securing social status.

Insecure over their relative youth and frequently unorthodox routes to prominence, movie stars and corporate executives contributed substantial resources to local institutions. Donations from wealthy Angelenos, for example, established law, medical, and theater arts schools. Similarly, these new patrons funded museums, music and performing arts centers, and purchased superb art collections, all of which gained national prominence for the city. Their philanthropies helped legitimize an upper class characterized by large numbers of arrivistes and marked Los Angeles as a major metropolitan and cultural center of the United States.

Significantly, the city's upper class generously funded science, the symbol of the future. As a group with few of their own traditions and only a short past, the wealthy in Los Angeles had little time for history or genealogy. Instead, they developed an outlook that eagerly anticipated the future. This

openness enabled many groups, for example Eastern European Jews who were usually excluded from upper classes that harbored anti-Semitic attitudes, to play a major role in philanthropic efforts and secure a place in the new and unstable upper class.

The social changes that shaped a new kind of upper class in Los Angeles undermined prominent groups in other cities. New York and Chicago witnessed the demise of their upper classes. The rise of impersonal corporate bureaucracies and absentee owners dislodged many leading families from their traditional moorings. In both of these cities, and others, too, many upper-class families faced bankruptcy as investments and business activities soured. Bereft of economic power, they often confronted irrelevance in their communities. At the same time, increasing personal instability and a growing estrangement from particular cities produced a wealthy class no longer wedded to their place of residence. Short-lived marriages wreaked personal havoc with individual lives and weakened a pillar of upper-class cohesion, namely the family.

In the years after World War II, members of the upper class ceased to identify with both New York and Chicago. In New York, the cafe society of the 1920s had positioned many members of the upper class in a transatlantic world stretching from London and Paris to New York. Among those who came of age in New York during the post–World War II era, the vast majority rejected the old upper-class rituals such as debutante balls and elaborate dinners. Instead, they opted for discotheques, social causes, and environmentalism. As a result, New York society ceased to function as it had previously, thus marking an end to the upper class as an integral part of the community. Similarly, in Chicago, extended departures from the city along with the shift of resources elsewhere undermined ties to the city. By the 1960s, the members of the faded upper class no longer operated in the world of metropolitan Chicago.

This loss of identification with a particular community seemed to peak during the 1990s when the national economy that once housed the urban upper classes gave way to a new global economy. The new technologies that facilitated instantaneous communication and rapid global transportation produced a truly international economy that spanned continents with ease. In the process, it created a new global setting for the upper class. Their investments and much of their daily business take place in a world without borders. Capital flows electronically across national boundaries, and the corporations for which they work or share ownership transact a considerable amount of business overseas, especially in the Pacific Rim. The global, integrated workplace capitalizes on inexpensive labor and weak government regulations of many countries.

A new, rootless upper class draws from members of the northeastern establishment, wealthy entrepreneurs, managers of major multinational corporations, and the successful grandchildren of European immigrants who arrived in the United States around 1900. Those who belong to this new, globally oriented class wear two visible badges: an outrageously expensive college degree, usually from an Ivy League institution, and a professional certificate such as a law degree. This validation derives its legitimacy from the power of agencies such as the American Bar Association. Typically, these most prominent individuals preside over three-parent families, two professionals and a nanny, who rears the children, unlike most American families. The long-term implications of this new upper class remain unclear; yet if the sketch proves accurate, it may have profound implications for upper classes that have always functioned within, and been key parts of, nation-states. Wealth, status, and power may have moved beyond this community to a new international sphere.

—*Edward J. Davies, II*

### References
Baltzell, E. Digby. *Philadelphia Gentlemen: The Making of a National Upper Class.* Chicago: Quadrangle, 1971.
Bushman, Richard L. *The Refinement of America: Persons, Houses, Cities.* New York: Knopf, 1992.
Davies, Edward J., II. *The Anthracite Aristocracy: Leadership and Social Change in the Hard Coal Regions of Northeastern Pennsylvania, 1800–1930.* DeKalb: Northern Illinois University Press, 1985.
Davis, Donald F. *Conspicuous Production: Automobiles and Elites in Detroit 1899–1933.* Philadelphia: Temple University Press, 1988.
Doyle, Don H. *New Men, New Cities, New South: Atlanta, Nashville, Charleston, Mobile, 1860–1910.* Chapel Hill: University of North Carolina Press, 1990.
Ingham, John N. *The Iron Barons: A Social Analysis of an American Elite, 1874–1960.* Westport, CT: Greenwood Press, 1978.
Jaher, Frederic Cople. *The Urban Establishment: Upper Strata in Boston, New York, Charleston, Chicago and Los Angeles.* Urbana: University of Illinois Press, 1982.
Levine, Lawrence W. *High Brow/Low Brow: The Emergence of Cultural Hierarchy in America.* Cambridge, MA: Harvard University Press, 1988.

## Urban
Throughout human history, people have acknowledged a difference between urban and rural areas, between the city and the country. Even in America today, where cities sprawl formlessly outward so that their physical boundaries become blurred, the term *urban* is widely used. The fact that it is frequently linked with *problems*—such as *crime* and *underclass*—says something about the attitudes of Americans toward cities and also, not surprisingly, the type of city that Americans have made.

Widespread use of the term has been associated with widespread disagreement about its meaning and significance.

One of the oldest definitions of an urban place is one that is primarily devoted to nonagricultural activities and that, as a result, is almost wholly a human artifact. This may be viewed positively; as a complex artifact, a city embodies civilization. Civilization, however, imply elites, and as the home of religious, economic, and political elites, cities have often been viewed critically as centers of power and even exploitation.

The artificiality of the urban environment itself has often been viewed critically. In the United States, for example, a strong anti-urban tradition has manifested itself in literature and in the long-standing movement to suburbs. In recent years, negative images of the city have been reinforced as people become more aware of the environmental consequences of economic growth. The excesses of industrialism have always been most apparent in urban places, but they once seemed localized. Now it is possible to see cities as the main sources of the blight that encircles the planet.

Urban land uses—manufacturing, commerce, and finance—require little space. Often, they derive economic advantages from being carried out in close proximity, and in any event they are tied to a local labor force. Urban centers, then, are quite densely settled. Density and size are additional defining elements of the urban scene. Although land use can be categorized as being either urban or not, size and density are continuous variables. Farms shade into hamlets and then villages, and then on to towns, cities, and global metropolitan areas. For at least two reasons, larger centers may then appear to be more urban than smaller ones. First, competition for urban space tends to create the highest land prices in the largest cities. Such prices can be supported only by multistory buildings, and so a city's size is often manifested in its skyline. Manhattan is the epitome. Second, places that fall toward the upper end of this continuum are likely to have a finer division of labor and to perform a wider range of urban functions. A village might have a gas station, but not a supermarket; a town will have a bookstore, but not a symphony orchestra; a city might boast a major league baseball team, but not a commodities market. In an age when Americans, especially, are highly mobile, the relationship between city size and function is not perfect. Quite small places, like Aspen, Colorado, or Stratford, Ontario, can specialize by attracting visitors from a wide area. Conversely, medium-sized centers that exist in the shadow of a larger city may offer fewer services than would otherwise be available. In general, however, larger centers perform a wider range of functions and services.

The economic and functional diversity of large cities is mirrored in their social composition. Social diversity can be created either by migration or through the differentiation of an existing population. Cities encourage both forms. Those that are growing attract migrants, and for much of the past five centuries most American cities have been growing. Rural areas, too, have attracted migrants as large areas opened to immigrants through the displacement of the native population. But the phase of rural settlement and population growth was quite limited. Only cities have been able to attract new immigrants, decade after decade, thereby renewing (and changing) their racial and ethnic mix. Then, too, cities allow for the internal diversification of their populations. A village might contain only one bookworm; a town can support a book club. In many towns, even today, a gay person might feel isolated. A city might support a gay book club whose members offer and receive mutual support. A city like New York might support gay book clubs that are differentiated by politics, ethnicity, or both. In large part, the emergence of such diverse communities within the city is a matter of simple arithmetic. With enough people, a community can form. In addition, and especially in the case of those who are viewed skeptically, or with disapproval, by the social mainstream, the very size of the large city offers an appealing anonymity. Where people do not know you, they cannot easily compel you to conform. Cities tolerate, and therefore attract, social minorities. As particular cities gain particular reputations, they attract social minorities accordingly. The movement of aspiring actors to Los Angeles exemplifies the pattern.

Being more urban may make a place more interesting but also less pleasant. Larger centers are likely to be more congested, noisy, and polluted. Their very size can make it difficult for people to get into the country, at least on day or weekend trips. One of the few redeeming features of early industrial towns was that open country lay only a few minutes' walk away. Today, a two-hour drive may be required to escape from downtown Los Angeles and reach open country. For many Americans, parks, tree-lined streets, and backyards provide a convenient substitute for open country. In larger cities, the price of land limits yard space, and open space becomes especially significant. We are attracted to green parks because they recall the country. This attraction, of course, reflects an urban sensibility—there is nothing more urban than a park.

If size, density, and diversity vary continuously, there is no agreement about the threshold at which a settlement should be considered urban. As in most countries, the U.S. census offers a precise definition in terms of population size and density. For statistical purposes, such precision is necessary. Using these criteria, we can trace the emerging dominance of urban centers within any nation. England became the first urban nation in about 1850, when people who lived in urban centers began to outnumber their rural counterparts. At that time, only 14 percent of Americans lived in urban areas, and the 50 percent threshold was crossed as late as the 1920s. It is a sign of the rapid decentralization of American metropolitan areas that, within another half-century,

more Americans (40 percent of the total) were living in suburbs than in cities or rural areas. In that sense, the United States has become the world's first suburban nation.

Although precision is necessary for some purposes, in sociohistorical terms it is spurious. Census definitions do not reflect a clear or agreed-upon understanding of the effects of population size and density. Indeed, there is no agreement that these aspects of urban life have any independent significance. The classic argument on this issue was developed by the sociologist Louis Wirth. Characterizing cities as large, dense, and socially heterogeneous, he suggested that these environmental features of the city might promote what he called the "urban way of life." In cities, Wirth argued, we continually meet strangers whom we know, and who know us, in only a single role—as bus driver, customer, plumber, or busker. It is the typically fragmentary nature of urban relationships that provides the impression and reality of personal freedom: one's behavior in one social setting (a gay club) will not carry over into another (a workplace). Alone, however, fragmentary relationships can be impersonal and unsatisfactory, producing a sense of alienation and anomie.

The freedoms of city life have each produced what might be called "urban" controls. One person's freedom is the source of a neighbor's annoyance. As cities grow, their citizens develop regulations that limit what their anonymous neighbors can do. Zoning controls prevent your neighbors from using their property in a noxious way, building regulations prevent them from building a fire trap, building codes discourage them from letting it fall into disrepair, noise bylaws prevent their teenage children from playing a stereo loudly in the middle of the night. Behind these regulations lies an administrative apparatus—planners, building inspectors, and, above all, police. To the extent that they are a response to uniquely urban freedoms, these can be regarded as "urban" institutions.

So, in a different way, are many forms of urban association. In the anonymous city, people seek community self-consciously by forming associations. Many of these are geographically defined, such as residents' associations that, typically, defend their turf against outsiders and set standards of acceptable behavior to define themselves. The majority, however, are wider in scope and include interest groups that are defined in a variety of ways, from sexual preference to fossils. Commercial interests have also tapped the need for community. A notable example is professional sports, which emerged in the late nineteenth century in larger cities. Ball teams typically mobilize and shape a community of interest that is citywide. In many ways, these teams represent their host communities more effectively than local government, which helps to account for the willingness of municipalities to build stadiums for local teams.

Competition between cities produces civic boosterism. Its most visible form has been the provision of direct tax subsidies to businesses, although cities also compete with one another to provide an urban infrastructure—roads, schools, and so forth—to support an efficient workforce. This competition arguably plays an important role in the process of capital accumulation as companies are able to play one off against another. As capital becomes ever more mobile and global in reach, competition between cities (as, indeed, between regions and countries) is likely to become progressively more significant.

The spate of interest in "urban" problems during the 1960s renewed the debate about the extent to which the personal experience of freedom and alienation within cities can be attributed to processes that are specifically "urban." Following Wirth, many have assumed that they can. In contrast, critics have argued that freedom and alienation are features of capitalist society in general, and of the labor market in particular. Problems may occur *in* cities, but they are not *of* cities. The implication is that problems cannot satisfactorily be addressed with merely urban solutions.

It is not necessary to adopt one or the other of these points of view. There is a long tradition of viewing cities as places in which the characteristics of the wider society are concentrated and heightened. Their features are those of the wider society, but caricatured. In that sense, the modern American metropolitan area can be regarded as a peculiar sort of place where, for good and ill, capitalism is made incarnate.

—*Richard Harris*

### References

Abrams, Philip. "Towns and Economic Growth: Some Theories and Problems." In Philip Abrams and E. A. Wrigley, eds., *Towns in Societies,* 9–33. Cambridge, England: Cambridge University Press, 1978.

Barth, Gunther. *City People: The Rise of Modern City Culture in Nineteenth-Century America.* New York: Oxford University Press, 1980.

Cronon, William. *Nature's Metropolis: Chicago and the Great West.* New York: W. W. Norton, 1991.

Fischer, Claude. *To Dwell among Friends: Personal Networks in Town and Country.* Chicago: University of Chicago Press, 1982.

Harvey, David. *The Urbanization of Capital.* Baltimore: Johns Hopkins University Press, 1985.

Mumford, Lewis. *The City in History.* New York: Harcourt, Brace and World, 1961.

White, Morton, and Lucia White. *The Intellectual versus the City: From Thomas Jefferson to Frank Lloyd Wright.* Cambridge, MA: Harvard University Press, 1962.

Wirth, Louis. "Urbanism as a Way of Life." *American Journal of Sociology* 44 (1938): 1–24.

# Urban Beautification

Founded in 1866, the New York Board of Health embodied and shared the concerns of a rapidly urbanizing nation, including the appearance of the city. One writer described the city that confronted the board as a place where "not only were large tracts [of the city] covered with densely crowded, ill-ventilated, and filthy tenement-houses, but, scattered everywhere, were individual nuisances of the most aggravated character contributing their noxious exhalations to the deteriorated atmosphere." Due to the lack of regulation, New York, like most American cities of that time, had become a squalid incubator of disease. Largely due to the findings of health organizations, Americans of the late nineteenth century therefore slowly began to reshape their cities with more responsibility and care. They soon discovered that making a city more beautiful enhanced residents' health while also creating a monument to American society.

The earliest manifestations of urban beautification came in confined areas such as parks and cemeteries. Planners such as Andrew Jackson Downing and Frederick Law Olmsted believed that nature's beauty was crucial to the human character, and its absence was leading to the "demoralization" of city dwellers. Therefore, what began in parks and around public buildings was slowly incorporated into planning on a larger scale.

Because of the commercial value of urban space, planners felt that they had to protect it aggressively. Landscaping the World's Columbian Exposition of 1893 in Chicago was their chance to attempt this kind of planning. The fairground of Olmsted and Daniel H. Burnham consisted of grand vistas, exquisite landscaping, and a previously unknown sensitivity to the human visitor. The landscape was much superior to that of actual North American cities—it presented an ideal to which cities could strive.

In 1909 Burnham published a plan to construct and incorporate such an ideal landscape throughout Chicago. His effort went beyond superficial beautification to consider matters of industry, transportation, and future urban development. Although Burnham's plan was never implemented, the effort to combine beauty and utility would recur noticeably in the developing cities of the West and Midwest as they planned civic centers and state capitols during the City Beautiful movement of the early twentieth century, and then again during the New Deal.

—*Brian Black*

### See also
Burnham, Daniel H.; City Beautiful Movement; City Efficient Movement; Downing, Andrew Jackson; Olmsted, Frederick Law.

### References

Ciucci, Giorgio, et al. *The American City: From the Civil War to the New Deal.* Barbara Luigia La Penta, trans. Cambridge, MA: MIT Press, 1979.

Fein, Albert. *Frederick Law Olmsted and the American Environmental Tradition.* New York: Van Nostrand Reinhold, 1967.

Gilbert, James. *Perfect Cities: Chicago's Utopias of 1893.* Chicago: University of Chicago Press, 1991.

Relph, Edward. *The Modern Urban Landscape.* Baltimore: John Hopkins University Press, 1987.

Roth, Leland M. *A Concise History of American Architecture.* New York: Harper & Row, 1980.

Schaffer, Daniel. *Garden Cities for America: The Radburn Experience.* Philadelphia: Temple University Press, 1982.

Schuyler, David. *The New Urban Landscape: The Redefinition of City Form in Nineteenth-Century America.* Baltimore: Johns Hopkins University Press, 1986.

Spirn, Anne Whiston. *The Granite Garden.* New York: Basic Books, 1984.

Warner, Sam Bass, Jr. *The Urban Wilderness: A History of the American City.* New York: Harper & Row, 1972.

## Urban Development Action Grant Program

The Urban Development Action Grant Program (UDAG) was authorized by amendments made in 1977 to the Housing and Community Development Act of 1974 and placed in the U.S. Department of Housing and Urban Development (HUD). The UDAG program was intended to complement the revised Community Development Block Grant (CDBG) program that had been enacted by the 1974 act as part of the effort to consolidate six categorical urban programs (urban renewal, Model Cities, water and sewer facilities, open space, neighborhood facilities, and public facilities loans).

Revisions to the CDBG program were enacted in 1977 because of criticisms made during its first three years of operation. In particular, detractors questioned the extent to which spending had reached targeted groups (low- and moderate-income people), and they expressed frustration with the actual accomplishments of the program. In reviews of the CDBG program and in subsequent policy discussions, critics also expressed a need for additional funding if distressed cities were to attempt meaningful redevelopment.

The result was a proposed amendment to the original CDBG legislation providing additional grants for "special opportunities." The HUD secretary at the time, Patricia Harris, argued convincingly for this new program in testimony before Congress. She said that it would allow the federal government to respond to unique opportunities. Her testimony before the House Committee on Banking, Finance, and Urban Affairs in February of 1977 reveals some of the program's original philosophical intent.

> [L]ocal government, like a business, must be able to move quickly to take advantage of opportunities for coordinated economic and community development when and where such opportunities arise.... I am proposing initiation of an urban development action grant program . . . to provide this much needed capability.

Grant applications were to be developed locally, and federal funds were to be released only after stringent program requirements had been satisfied. These included meeting eligibility requirements before applying, satisfying the requirement for a minimum leverage of funds, and accepting the implied pressure to coordinate UDAG funds with other government money to assure maximum benefit. The program was unique because grant agreements contained contractual provisions designed to prevent the private sector pullouts that had occurred in other large urban renewal projects. It also mandated a "but for" clause that required federal officials to certify that the planned development would not have been implemented without the UDAG funds. In addition, the program was an early example of a fast-track program in which decisions on grant applications were rendered in relatively short order.

The specific procedures for determining application eligibility and adjudication evolved from the initial implementation of the program. These included meeting various physical and economic criteria measured by lags in economic growth, the extent of poverty, and the adjusted age of housing in an area. The statute also allowed the HUD secretary to determine any other relevant factors and listed several that should be included. One other early issue was the call for a reasonable balance between industrial, commercial, and neighborhood projects.

In what has been called the honeymoon phase of the program, UDAG became the centerpiece of federal urban policy. However, the program was not executed without controversy. In addition to doubts about the goals and effectiveness of the program as a whole, there were frequent assessments of, and objections to, the spatial impacts of targeting mechanisms (through the rules for eligibility and the procedural requirements) and criticism of the potential political nature of UDAG contract negotiations.

After the election of Ronald Reagan as president in 1980, members of the new administration repeatedly questioned the program and reevaluated and changed its goals, targeting mechanisms, and achievements. They shifted the focus of the program in a number of ways. First, they changed the major purpose of UDAG to emphasize economic recovery and job creation in a broader sense. They altered the emphasis from cities suffering physical distress to those suffering severe economic distress. Second, they relaxed the balance required among different types of projects, and, at one point, they almost denied eligibility to housing or neighborhood projects. Third, over a period of years, they so broadened and redefined eligibility requirements that by the middle of the 1980s more than half of the largest cities and more than 10,000 small cities qualified as "severely distressed." Some of these changes revolved around ideological shifts in the federal government; others around a perceived need to broaden the distribution of funds to ensure broad political support for UDAG in an era of tight budgets.

From its inception until its cancellation in 1988, the legitimacy and effectiveness of UDAG were questioned. During the Reagan years particularly, the program was consistently attacked. By its end, even with alterations to broaden its appeal, the program had lost all but a few supporters. Appropriations fell from their high of $675 million in 1980 to nothing in 1988.

In summary, the UDAG program was unique in encouraging and assisting public-private partnerships for the redevelopment and economic recovery of urban areas, in requiring leveraging, in demanding intergovernmental coordination and cooperation, and in placing responsibility for proposals on local government. Additionally, individual UDAG projects reveal much about relations between the public and private sectors. The unusual nature of the program—the tensions between its goals and achievements on the one hand and its strange position as a government program meant to influence private investment in a strongly pro-business administration on the other—have attracted wide attention and investigation that disclose insights into the nature of urban redevelopment during the era.

—*Richard Stephen Kujawa*

**See also**

Community Development Block Grants; Housing and Urban Development, Department of; Reagan Administration: Urban Policy.

**References**

Harris, Patricia R. "Recent Trends in the Community Development Grant Program." *Urban Law Annual* 15 (1978): 3–14.

Jacobs, Susan S., and Elizabeth A. Roistacher. "The Urban Impacts of HUD's Urban Development Action Grant Program, or, Where's the Action in Action Grants?" In Norman J. Glickman, ed., *The Urban Impacts of Federal Policies*, 335–362. Baltimore: Johns Hopkins University Press, 1981.

Nathan, R. P., and J. A. Webman, eds. *The Urban Development Action Grant Program.* Princeton, NJ: Princeton Urban and Regional Research Center, 1980.

Otte, G. "National Urban Policy in Action: Saint Louis, Urban Development Action Grants, and Adjustment to Change." *Saint Louis University Law Journal* 28 (1984): 929–958.

Watson, D. J., J. G. Heilman, and R. S. Montjoy. *The Politics of Redistributing Urban Aid.* Westport, CT: Praeger, 1994.

# Urban Ecology

The notion of urban ecology comes originally from the writings of central figures in the Chicago School of Sociology. The key person in this group of scholars was Robert E. Park who, according to Amos Hawley, was the first person to coin the term *human ecology.* Hired by the Department of Sociology at the University of Chicago in 1916, after years of other pursuits such as journalism, Park helped to found a school of scholars that became exclusively devoted to studies of the city.

Park came to believe that in many respects life in the city paralleled life among plants and animals. Both kinds of life (human and nonhuman) displayed a characteristic competition among different orders to become the dominant form of life in a particular place. It was the homology of competition, and also conflict, that invited Park to seek parallels between how forces in cities worked among human beings and how the web of life functioned among plants and animals. Here, like so many aspiring scientists of the natural world, Park found his greatest inspiration in many of the ideas of Charles Darwin.

Park argued that there were two distinctive levels of life in the human, urban community. The first was the biotic, or biological, level. At this level, the struggle among different human groups was over the use and exercise of resources in a place. Park maintained that one could speak of urban economics at this level, in particular, how goods were exchanged, prices developed, and the like. Moreover, at this level a social division of labor eventually emerged among human beings, a division of labor that developed because competition intensified as ever-larger numbers of people congregated in a city. In this respect, Park linked his ideas to those of the French sociologist, Emile Durkheim, who made a similar argument about why the division of labor emerged in human communities.

The second important level of life among human beings in a community was the cultural level. At this level, Park maintained, the forces and agents creating moral consensus emerged. Moreover, Park argued, it was the socially created fact of consensus that distinguished human beings from lower levels of natural life. Other forms could not create such a uniformity of opinion and ideas in the midst of the natural competition for survival that occurred among them. Park further insisted that the key problem for sociologists to study was the formation of consensus—or, in other words, the nature of cultural forms in the city.

Colleagues and students of Park took up the banner of human ecology and developed its ideas at length. Roderick McKenzie was one such figure, and he helped explore the nature of ecological patterns formed in metropolitan communities. Ernest W. Burgess, a close collaborator of Park's, helped to develop the ecological agenda for studying the city, and he was particularly successful in articulating the notion of natural areas of the city. Other followers of Park did in-depth studies of the dominant groups in particular natural areas, such as those who lived in the Gold Coast of Chicago and hoboes.

More sophisticated conceptions of the human ecological paradigm were developed later. Amos Hawley changed the field by tightly analyzing how the human ecological paradigm applied to all facets of human life. He further integrated a wide variety of materials, including those dealing with the nature of population aggregates, issues of fertility and mortality, and the nature of transportation routes and their impact on metropolitan areas. Park had argued that transportation and communication were perhaps the key dimensions of the city that required intensive study, but Hawley took that analysis to a new level.

In the 1970s the human ecological paradigm came under heavy attack through a series of withering criticisms developed in particular by Manuel Castells, a product of the French school of structuralism. Castells maintained, among other things, that the human ecologists had misunderstood the nature of the city, especially by arguing for its parallelism to biological forms. Instead, Castells insisted, the forces and engine of the city lay in the economic realm and, in particular, in the nature of modern capitalism. Other critics soon advanced similar ideas, eventually displacing the dominance of the human ecological paradigm, at least among sociologists, and replacing it with other concepts, many of them building on central conceptions of Karl Marx.

—*Anthony M. Orum*

**See also**

Burgess, Ernest W.; Chicago School of Sociology; Park, Robert Ezra; Wirth, Louis.

**References**

Castells, Manuel. *The Urban Question: A Marxist Approach.* Cambridge, MA: MIT Press, 1977.

Frisbie, W. Parker, and John D. Kasarda. "Spatial Processes." In Neil J. Smelser, ed., *Handbook of Sociology,* 629–666. Beverly Hills, CA: Sage Publishers, 1988.

Hawley, Amos H. *Human Ecology: A Theory of Community Structure.* New York: Ronald Press, 1950.

Katznelson, Ira. *Marxism and the City.* Oxford, England: Clarendon Press, 1992.

Park, Robert E. *Human Communities: The City and Human Ecology.* Glencoe, IL: Free Press, 1952.

Park, Robert E., Ernest W. Burgess, and Roderick D. McKenzie. *The City.* Chicago: University of Chicago Press, 1925.

## Urban Fauna

The Europeans who settled the New World dramatically altered its natural environment. Nowhere is this transformation more obvious than in America's villages, towns, and cities, especially after rapid industrialization and urbanization in the nineteenth century. In the process of carving urban areas out of the wilderness, Americans worked feverishly to remove vegetation, drain wetlands, channel streams, pave roads, and construct buildings. These activities devastated the habitat on which native wildlife had long depended to live and reproduce.

Soon it became clear that the environmental consequences of concentrating human populations in dense settlements extended deep into the hinterlands. As early as the late seventeenth and early eighteenth centuries, observers began to lament the obvious decline of many game species and extensive deforestation of vast areas surrounding America's largest cities. By the mid-nineteenth century, overharvesting, dam construction, and pollution had also severely depleted the abundant fish that once inhabited the rivers of the northeastern United States.

The introduction of exotic species wreaked further havoc on the fauna of urban areas and their surroundings. Whether by accident or design, European settlers brought with them a hodgepodge of plants, animals, and pathogens. For example, early settlers routinely imported pigeons along with their dogs, cats, cows, goats, sheep, and other domesticated animals. Many of these species established feral populations that succeeded in outcompeting with native fauna. Later, in the mid-nineteenth century, New Yorkers introduced the European house sparrow in an unsuccessful attempt to control the cankerworms that were defoliating their trees. Following repeated releases, the house sparrow finally took hold and began expanding its range along rail lines, driving out native species like the bluebird, the purple finch, and the indigo bunting in the process. In 1890 a wealthy drug manufacturer named Eugene Schieffelin introduced European starlings into New York's Central Park as part of a misguided effort to establish all the birds mentioned in Shakespeare. Within seven decades, the aggressive species had extended its range into every continental state and Canadian province. Today, pigeons, sparrows, and starlings make up as much as 95 percent of the typical urban bird community.

*Pigeons are one of the most common, and most maligned, forms of urban wildlife.*

Many other animals commonly associated with urban areas first arrived in America as stowaways. The common house mouse, the Norway rat, and the black rat are all Old World species that thrive almost everywhere dense human settlement occurs. As one of the most abundant mammals in central city districts, the Norway rat often reaches a population density exceeding one for every twenty human inhabitants. The many species of cockroach typically found in urban areas originated in the tropics. As the hubs of vast transportation networks, American cities have accumulated plant and animal species from the far corners of the globe. No one knows for sure why a handful of these organisms have succeeded so well amid the hustle and bustle of modern metropolitan environments, but many of today's most characteristic urban animals—pigeons, sparrows, rats, and mice—have long been associated with human populations in Europe.

In less-disturbed urban areas, the number of native species and faunal diversity more generally tend to increase. Diurnal tree squirrels (especially the gray squirrel) are among the most visible native metropolitan mammals. In parks, cemeteries, and other areas that have large canopy trees and where supplemental feeding by humans occurs, gray squirrels can achieve much greater population densities than their rural counterparts. Larger city parks also provide suitable habitats for many native birds. Bird watchers in New York's Central Park have spotted no less than 275 species, leading one expert to dub this oasis one of the best birding locations in the United States. If supplied with the appropriate vegetation, even relatively small parks can attract significant wildlife populations.

Despite the pervasive practice of cultivating environmentally unfriendly lawns, the suburbs surrounding America's cities also continue to support a moderately diverse range of native fauna. Raccoons, squirrels, bats, opossums, deer, skunks, rabbits, chipmunks, woodchucks, coyotes, and foxes remain common in many suburban areas. In the Southwest peccaries and in the Southeast armadillos must be added to the list of abundant suburban mammals. The practices of planting ornamental shrubs and setting out feeders attract many birds, including ground-foraging seed eaters and omnivores—like robins, blue jays, grackles, and mourning doves—as well as many fruit-eating omnivores—like cardinals, catbirds, and mockingbirds. Several species of fish, reptiles, and amphibians also frequent suburbs. As in the central cities, species that are habitat generalists seem to fare best.

Until recently, those who maintained bird feeders were among the few Americans who paid much attention to urban and suburban wildlife. Scientists seemed far more interested in studying game species and wildlife populations that were relatively untainted by human interference. During the widespread environmental awakening of the late 1960s and early 1970s, this long-standing neglect finally began to be addressed. Biologists moved to create a new discipline, urban ecology, that sought to increase our knowledge of the relationships between urban-based organisms and their highly disturbed environments. In 1973, they also established a new organization—the National Institute for Urban Wildlife—to promote research on and greater appreciation of wild animals residing in cities and suburbs.

Scientists and conservationists have also begun to recognize the possibility of reintroducing some native species into urban environments. One of their greatest success stories to date is the peregrine falcon, a raptor whose populations were decimated through habitat destruction and the introduction of harmful synthetic pesticides after World War II. Thanks to the efforts of conservation biologists and concerned citizens, the majestic bird once again soars above the skylines of Boston, New York, and other large metropolitan areas. As urban sprawl continues to transform the American landscape, cities and suburbs may represent the only hope of survival for many other threatened species.

—*Mark V. Barrow, Jr.*

### References

Adams, Lowell W. *Urban Wildlife Habitats: A Landscape Perspective.* Minneapolis: University of Minnesota Press, 1994.

Adams, Lowell W., and Daniel L. Leedy, eds. *Integrating Man and Nature in the Metropolitan Environment.* Columbia, MD: National Institute for Urban Wildlife, 1987.

Cronon, William. *Changes in the Land: Indians, Colonists, and the Ecology of New England.* New York: Hill and Wang, 1983.

Crosby, Alfred W. *Germs, Seeds, and Animals: Studies in Ecological History.* Armonk, NY: M. E. Sharpe, 1994.

Dorney, Robert S. "Bringing Wildlife Back to Cities." *Technology Review* 89 (1986): 48–56.

Garber, Steven D. *The Urban Naturalist.* New York: Wiley, 1987.

Martin, Douglas. "Central Park Is a Festival of Odd Birds." *New York Times* 145 (January 25, 1996): B1, B4.

Rome, Adam W. "Building on the Land: Toward an Environmental History of Residential Development in American Cities and Suburbs, 1870–1990." *Journal of Urban History* 20 (1994): 407–434.

Whitney, Gordon G. *From Coastal Wilderness to Fruited Plain: A History of Environmental Change in Temperate North America, 1500–Present.* Cambridge, England: Cambridge University Press, 1994.

## Urban Flora

Urban flora is both the spontaneous and the cultivated vegetation that characterizes urban areas. It is created directly by manipulating the structure and composition of vegetation (e.g., planting, maintaining, removing) and indirectly by altering the local environment. Human activities and artifacts such as buildings, cars, and the combustion of fossil fuels alter soils and water cycles, making cities warmer and more polluted than natural environments. These environmental modifications, along with direct human disturbances and vegetation management, change natural floristic compositions to create the plant growth characteristic of urban areas. Urban flora is highly variable both within and among cities, although there are some common characteristics.

Urban vegetation is a dominant component of greenspace (i.e., proportion of area covered with vegetation or soil) within a city. In the United States, city greenspace averages around 60 percent but varies with such factors as population density, historical development patterns, land use functions, and human preferences and objectives. Greenspace occupies the largest proportion of vacant lands (96 percent), followed by parks (86 percent), "other" lands (i.e., agriculture, transportation, etc., 70 percent), institutional land (56 percent), residence (48 percent), and commercial-industrial areas (26 percent).

The proportion of greenspace covered by trees varies in different parts of the United States according to a region's natural environment. On average, about one-half of urban greenspace in forested regions is filled with trees, one-third in grasslands, and one-sixth in the desert shrublands of the Southwest.

Parks and residential lands, along with vacant lands in forested areas, usually have the greatest amount of tree cover among the land use types. The remaining greenspace typically supports grass and other herbaceous coverings. Of the ground surface greenspace area (exclusive of trees) in Chicago, Illinois, for example, two-thirds is grass, 17 percent bare or covered soil (e.g., mulch), 10 percent other herbaceous cover, and 7 percent low-lying shrubs. Cities in desert regions usually have the largest part of their greenspace occupied by bare soil.

In forested regions, tree canopies cover, on average, about 31 percent of a city; in grasslands, about 19 percent; and in desert regions, about 10 percent. However, within a region, tree cover varies significantly among individual cities, ranging from 15 to 55 percent in forested areas, 5 to 39 percent in grasslands, and 1 to 26 percent in deserts. This variation within a region is largely due to differences in the proportion of a city occupied by each type of land use, the density of development, and the management of vegetation practiced in various locations

Along with variations in the amount and type of vegetative cover within and among American cities, the composition of floristic species also varies. Urbanization affects the combination of spontaneous plant communities, particularly herbaceous communities, by generally decreasing the proportion of native species, increasing the number of species adapted to heat and dryness (xerothermic plants), increasing the number of species adapted to frequently disturbed sites (ruderals), and increasing the floristic homogeneity among cities.

Unmanaged segments of each type of land use allow spontaneous vegetation to generate. Species composition varies within and among cities depending on the natural environment of a region, the local source of seeds, and such site factors as moisture, nutrients, and light. Tree species that commonly occur in urban areas where vegetation is not managed include acacia *(Acacia spp.)*, ailanthus *(Ailanthus altissima)*, black cherry *(Prunus serotina)*, black locust *(Robinia pseudoacacia)*, boxelder *(Acer negundo)*, buckthorn *(Rhamnus spp.)*, cottonwood *(Populus deltoides)*, elm *(Ulmus spp.)*, green ash *(Fraxinus pennsylvanica)*, Norway maple *(Acer platanoides)*, and willow *(Salix spp.)*.

Species of ground cover that commonly occupy unmanaged inner-city sites include crabgrass *(Digitaria spp.)*, peppergrass *(Lepidium spp.)*, bromegrass *(Bromus spp.)*, sow thistle *(Sonchus oleraceus)*, and prickly lettuce *(Lactuca scariola)*. Unmanaged sites that are frequently disturbed are often inhabited by species such as ragweed *(Ambrosia artemisiifolia)*, goldenrod *(Solidago canadensis)*, fleabane *(Erigeron spp.)*, Queen Anne's lace *(Daucus carota)*, and black medic *(Medicago lupulina)*.

The management and maintenance of vegetation are dominant factors throughout much of urban areas and create various cultivated floristic types. Practices such as mowing, using herbicides, and planting can inhibit or encourage various floristic types. These management practices vary by type of land use and are usually basic forces in creating and sustaining local configurations of vegetation. These structures often contain numerous exotic species that increase plant diversity but can sometimes cause management problems.

Tree species commonly planted in managed urban areas in the northeastern United States include red maple *(Acer rubrum)*, honey locust *(Gleditsia triacanthos)*, pin oak *(Quercus palustris)*, Norway maple, green ash, and crab apple *(Malus spp.)*; in the North Central region green ash, red maple, river birch *(Betula nigra)*, crab apple, sugar maple *(Acer saccharum)*, and honeylocust; in the South, callery pear *(Pyrus calleryana)*, red maple, flowering dogwood *(Cornus florida)*, river birch, and redbud *(Cercis canadensis)*; and in the West, Norway maple, green ash, little-leaf linden *(Tilia cordata)*, Amur maple *(Acer ginnala)*, and honey locust. Common ground cover species in managed lawn areas include Kentucky bluegrass *(Poa pratensis)* and red fescue *(Festuca rubra)*.

In more heavily used areas, such as parks and lawns, common cultivated or spontaneous herbaceous species include perennial ryegrass *(Lolium perenne)*, white clover *(Trifolium repens)*, knotweed *(Polygonum spp.)*, and plantain *(Plantago spp.)*. Herbaceous species such as Kentucky bluegrass and dandelions *(Taraxacum officinale)* are common in both managed and spontaneous urban landscapes.

Along with the high degree of spatial variability because of local differences in environmental and anthropic factors, urban flora also tends to have a high degree of temporal variability due to urban development, human disturbance of sites, and changes in vegetation management. Although there are various costs associated with urban flora, both spontaneous and cultivated vegetation provide a wealth of benefits to an urban environment and its inhabitants. These include climatic modifications (e.g., reductions in air temperature and wind speed), reductions in the use of air within buildings, the improvement of air and water quality, aesthetics, wildlife habitat, and individual and community well-being.

—*David J. Nowak*

### References

Dwyer, John F., et al. "Assessing the Benefits and Costs of the Urban Forest." *Journal of Arboriculture* 18 (1992): 277–324.

Nowak, David J. "Urban Forest Structure: The State of Chicago's Urban Forest." In USDA Forest Service General Technical Rep. NE-186. Washington, DC: Government Printing Office, 1994.

Nowak, David J., and T. Davis Sydnor. "Popularity of Tree Species and Cultivars in the United States." In USDA Forest Service General Technical Rep. NE-166. Washington, DC: Government Printing Office, 1992.

Nowak, David J., et al. "Measuring and Analyzing Urban Tree Cover." *Landscape and Urban Planning* 36 (1996): 49–57.

Sukopp, H., and P. Werner. "Urban Environments and Vegetation." In W. Holzner et al., eds., *Man's Impact on Vegetation.* The Hague, Netherlands: Dr. W. Junk Publishers, 1983.

Whitney, G. G. "A Quantitative Analysis of the Flora and Plant Communities of a Representative Midwestern U.S. Town." *Urban Ecology* 9 (1985): 143–160.

## Urban Forestry

Urban forestry is "the planning, establishment, protection and management of trees and associated plants, individually, in small groups, or under forest conditions, within cities, suburbs and towns." In its broadest sense, urban forestry involves managing multiple systems, including wildlife, landscape design, outdoor recreation, watershed, and general tree care. Urban forestry differs from arboriculture, which is managing and caring for individual trees. Arboriculture, however, is a major portion of urban forestry, with a large percentage of the urban forester's time devoted to caring for and maintaining street trees. Urban foresters, however, manage the whole system, not just individual trees.

Although the term *urban forestry* is relatively new, the concept of forest management in urban areas is very old. Trees have been used to enhance the environment of cities and towns since early civilizations. In ancient times, trees were primarily used in developing gardens and groves to enhance temple settings and to complement statues and buildings. During the Middle Ages, botanical gardens became popular, primarily due to the widespread use of plants as medicines. As civilizations developed and the Renaissance occurred, increased travel and trade from country to country increased. During this time, transplanting trees from other countries and developing large gardens became common.

Much of our early knowledge about trees and tree care in cities comes from seventeenth-century England. By the eighteenth century, the use of trees in urban settings and knowledge of their growth and maintenance were well developed. In the early settlement of North America, however, trees were often considered detrimental. Although they provided shade and wood for housing and heating, forests also "housed" real and imagined dangers. Fear of forests and the need for space to grow crops caused their removal. As urban areas developed, trees were planted in town squares whose main functions were for assembling the militia and protecting livestock if the town were attacked.

As the United States industrialized, three major events produced the realization that its urban areas needed management: first, the expansion of urban centers into forested areas; second, shifting social values reflecting urban living; and third, the view that urbanization negatively affects vegetation and therefore requires management. Urban forestry was first practiced in large metropolitan areas of the northeastern United States, and practitioners generally concentrated on individual tree management (arboriculture). Now, urban forestry, or management of the entire system, is becoming more widespread. People want more greenspace, wildlife amenities, forested areas, and so on. In addition, urban forest management is spreading throughout the country and into smaller cities and towns.

—*Art Chappelka*

### References

Chadwick, Lewis C. "3000 Years of Arboriculture—Past, Present and Future." In International Shade Tree Conference, *Proceedings of the 46th International Shade Tree Conference,* 83a–87a. Urbana, IL: International Shade Tree Conference, 1970.

Grey, Gene W., and Frederick J. Deneke. *Urban Forestry.* 2d ed. New York: Wiley, 1986.

Jorgensen, E. "Urban Forestry in Canada." In International Shade Tree Conference, *Proceedings of the 46th International Shade Tree Conference,* 43a–51a. Urbana, IL: International Shade Tree Conference, 1970.

Miller, R. W. *Urban Forestry: Planning and Managing Urban Greenspaces.* Englewood Cliffs, NJ: Prentice-Hall, 1988.

## Urban Fringe

The urban fringe is a complex landscape composed of farms, forests, idle land waiting for development, scattered home sites, isolated subdivisions, strip development, and small towns and hamlets. There are many conceptualizations of the urban fringe. Economist Richard Muth's is the landscape where undeveloped land is valued more for urban uses than for agriculture, forest, or other rural uses. Planner John Friedmann's is a landscape outside the contiguously developed urban area to the edge of the "urban field." Geographers Brian J. L. Berry's and Quinten Gillard's is the landscape beyond the contiguously developed area to where 10 percent of the workers commute to the urban area. Although using different definitions, architect Hans Blumenfeld, engineer Kenneth J. Decker, sociologist Marvel Lang, and policy analyst Arthur C. Nelson conceptualize the urban fringe as the landscape beyond the contiguously developed area as far out as there are people who have any direct economic link to the urban area, such as through commuting or telecommuting. Although there is no formal government definition, the U.S. Census Bureau seems to conceptualize it as the region within metropolitan statistical areas with fewer than 1,000 people per square mile but where rural, nonfarm households live and any subcounty-subparish-subtownship area, such as a census tract, that would be linked to a metropolitan statistical area although the county or parish or township as a whole is not.

The urban fringe is an area undergoing conversion from rural to urban land uses. Before World War II, the urban fringe was a narrow landscape adjacent to the contiguously built urban area—the next ring beyond urban ecologist Ernest W. Burgess's "commuter ring" in his concentric zone theory. Since the war, federal and state highway programs, heavily subsidized sewer and water systems, and heavily subsidized home purchase programs have facilitated development much farther into the countryside. Edge cities, decentralized employment, telecommuting, and exurban residential development since the 1970s have pushed the urban fringe tens and sometimes more than 100 miles farther out.

Under proper planning and management, areas of the urban fringe become efficiently urbanized. Improperly managed, urban fringe development leads to the scattered and isolated (leapfrog), strip, and land-extensive low-density development characterized as urban sprawl. Unmanaged urban fringe development leads to costly development patterns subsidized mostly by urban and suburban residents. It also undermines agriculture and forestry, the nation's largest export sectors, and adversely impacts on watersheds, recharge areas, and other sensitive landscapes. Because of greater subsidies for urban than rural land uses in the urban fringe, combined with negative urban externalities imposed on resource land, the value of land in the urban fringe for resource uses is artificially low while the value of such land for urban uses is artificially high. In the absence of proper planning and management, the urban fringe becomes a landscape composed of conflicting and inefficient land uses.

—*Arthur C. Nelson*

### References

Berry, Brian J. L., and Quinten Gillard. *The Changing Shape of Metropolitan America.* Cambridge, MA: Ballinger, 1977.

Blumenfeld, Hans. "Have the Secular Trends of Population Distribution Been Reversed?" Research Paper 137. Toronto, Ontario: Centre of Urban and Community Studies, University of Toronto, 1982.

———. "Metropolis Extended." *Journal of the American Planning Association* 52 (1983): 346–348.

Burgess, Ernest W. "The Growth of the City." In Robert E. Park, Ernest W. Burgess, and Roderick D. McKenzie, eds., *The City.* Chicago: University of Chicago Press, 1925.

Dueker, Kenneth J., et al. "Rural Residential Development within Metropolitan Areas." *Computers, Environment and Urban Systems* 8 (1983): 121–129.

Friedmann, John. "The Urban Field as Human Habitat." In S. P. Snow, ed., *The Place of Planning.* Auburn, AL: Auburn University Press, 1973.

Lang, Marvel. "Redefining Urban and Rural for the U.S. Census of Population: Assessing the Need and Alternative Approaches." *Urban Geography* 7 (1986): 118–134.

Muth, Richard F. "Economic Change and Rural-Urban Land Conversions." *Econometrica* 29 (1961): 1–23.

Nelson, Arthur C. "Characterizing Exurbia." *Journal of Planning Literature* 6 (1992): 350–368.

U.S. Bureau of the Census. *Proceedings of the National Geographic Areas Conference.* Washington, DC: Government Printing Office, 1986.

## Urban Frontier

Ever since urban history began to develop, historians have used the concept of the "urban frontier" to argue for and examine the role of urbanization in the expansion and settlement of the frontier, in the regional development of the Midwest and the West, and in the creation of an American character. The shifting meanings of the term in the last 40 years therefore parallel the debates about the validity and usefulness of the frontier theory of American history, the definition and thematic focus of midwestern and western regional history, as well as the goals, methods, and nature of urban history as a separate field.

The term first emerged as urban and social historians sought to articulate the field of urban history. They challenged the rural emphasis of the Turner thesis and its argument that the frontier had determined the course of American history and the nature of the American national character. They did this by pointing out that frontier towns and cities were actually the "spearheads of the frontier" and did not develop only after its passing. Historians of cities argued that urban outposts and towns accelerated and shaped not only the interactions of European Americans with Native Americans but also the settlement of the West by European Americans and the development of markets, transportation systems, and institutions that connected the frontier to the national economy, society, culture, and political system.

Although the term *urban frontier* was conceived by previous social and urban historians, the key book that articulated this interpretation was Richard C. Wade's *The Urban Frontier: Pioneer Life in Early Pittsburgh, Cincinnati, Lexington, Louisville, and St. Louis,* which was published in 1959. Even though it was resisted at the time, Wade's urban perspective of the frontier reinforced the notion of the frontier as a place and also encouraged closer scrutiny of it as a process across space that extended out from the core of a national system.

By its influence, then, the book opened or reinvigorated, or both, two new types of study among historians. On the one hand, Wade's thesis about the existence of an "urban frontier" (which soon acquired quotation marks and continues to be referred to, as a buzzword, in this way) focused on examining the dynamics of community organization and politics. In particular, Wade focused on the efforts of elite leaders, or "boosters," to establish social order within communities on the competitive urban frontier. Subsequent works in this tradition addressed similar questions about the impact of the social, economic, and political context of the frontier as a place on the dynamics and structures of urban economies, societies, and political cultures as they were reflected by geographic mobility, social mobility, and democratic political activity—all central conceptual concerns of urban historians in the 1970s. Because most urban historians initially focused on the nineteenth-century city, the intersection of urban history and the frontier under the rubric of the "urban frontier" produced a number of community studies, case histories, or biographies of towns in the trans-Appalachian West, the Midwest, the Great Plains, and the Far West. In doing so, their recognition of the "urban frontier" also enabled urban historians to penetrate and reinvigorate two regional fields whose dominant conceptual frameworks were structured and, as some historians have argued, restricted by the traditional frontier approach.

But as some have observed of early urban history in general, so it was with these early monographs; the frontier, like the city, was conceived as a historical context, a place or setting, rather than a process. Thus, it served merely as a backdrop for the social and historical analysis of the structure of frontier communities and the nature of frontier politics and culture. Nevertheless, the framework of studying a town or a city's development during the frontier stage or period of the Midwest (roughly 1830 through 1860) or the West (through about 1880)—including the mining and cattle frontiers as well as the urban frontier—or Far West (to about 1900) developed and remains a vibrant field of inquiry that has created a framework of analysis from which to make even broader comparisons, two of which recently encompassed both North America and Australia.

"Urban frontier," as a general term whose definition and meaning most historians now accept, thus continues to pros-

per, despite its limited, even narrow, scope and is apparently unaffected by, indifferent to, and even oblivious to the academic "boxing match" over the word "frontier" (the "f-word") within western history in particular and American history in general. Perhaps the centripetal, interactive, and integrating nature of urbanization, which remains the basis of the field's interdisciplinary approach, accounts for this agreement. In any case, the notion of the "urban frontier" now forms the basic framework for both midwestern and western history, while it simultaneously navigates along the parallel discourses in urban, frontier, and regional history that examine cities, frontiers, or regions as either places or processes.

This has been especially true regarding the twentieth-century West where the "urban frontier" has become the "metropolitan frontier" and the study of urbanization has been established as a vigorous field of inquiry that promises to shape, redesign, or mediate many of the debates over competing perspectives, frameworks, and agendas.

Some historians and historical geographers followed the trail broken by the monographs that followed Wade's *Urban Frontier* and, drawing from historical, geographical, and economic approaches to urban history, sought to examine more closely the dynamics of frontier urbanization as both local and regional systemic processes. The frontier became, from this systemic perspective, an outer edge, a peripheral zone, or a hinterland within a system whose functional core was located in the East. Though some historians eschewed the term *frontier,* the concept shaped the discussion of paper towns, urban outposts, gateway cities, and boom towns, all of which emerged as rival towns competed to establish themselves as nodal points, entrepots, river towns, and central places all viewing the frontier as extensions of dynamic, regional, mercantile-based urban systems that drove the frontier west. This more systemic approach naturally focused attention on the structure and dynamics of regional networks or systems, for it was at the regional level that economic-geographic dynamics and structures could be observed and understood most effectively. This inquiry paralleled the analysis of the "frontier as process" that some frontier and western historians adopted as they defined the frontier as a "zone of interpenetration."

At about the same time, this emphasis on urban systems fused with other regional formulations and contributed to the emergence of the "New Regionalism." According to this interpretation, a traditional provincial regionalism was not seeking to resist, define, or differentiate regional characteristics from national trends. Rather, a systemic and functionally defined regionalism was set on exploring how regional urban systems worked and how systemic forces and dynamics shaped local social experience and development. From this perspective, local and regional reality reflected the interpenetration or intertwining of certain local, regional, and national forces with other local, regional, and national (and even global) processes to create much more complex contexts and structures within which to understand urban and regional society. This line of inquiry, which also has adherents among western historians, remains the less traveled road when compared to viewing the frontier as a context of urbanization in which local and regional society developed.

Other urban historians followed the systemic approach on a more micro level by seeking the "frontier" within the process of urbanization itself. Following the almost universal use of the word "frontier" since the 1960s as a "metaphor for promise, progress, and ingenuity," the city itself has been heralded as the new frontier. For some, this urban frontier is more specifically located *within* the metropolis, where the city interacts with nonurban phenomena on the urban "fringe," edge, or periphery, or in the "urban shadow." For others, it is where individuals and groups, whether as "pioneers" in exurbia or in the urban core, have struggled to establish order and forge communities within an impersonal, pathological, or discursive urban environment. Whether they live in the "borderlands," the "crabgrass," the "scruffy and ... cultureless" suburban frontier, or even in the exurban "edge city" or megalopolis, all urbanites collectively live on the "urban frontier."

Thus, as points of intense interaction and convergence, cities unleash both powerful centripetal forces of agglomeration, efficiency, innovation, and creativity, as well as centrifugal forces of differentiation, separation, disintegration, conflict, and disequilibrium. They therefore constitute a "new frontier." In the metropolis, the focal point of innovation, development, and hegemony, modern Americans most aggressively confront and respond to change by creating or exploring new ideas, values, identities, and cultures. Whether these responses occur at the urban edge, on the periphery, in zones of transition, at points of interaction among groups or functions, or in the metropolis in general, modern city people, pushed by the urban environment to the individualistic aesthetic, cognitive, experiential, and social extremes, encounter their own fragmented sense of self-identity.

Through such a general interpretation of the "urban frontier," urban historians who aspire to "explain" modern American life through the filter of urbanization have repeatedly argued that an urban interpretation of American history is the rightful heir to the Turner thesis in explaining the American character.

These four predominant uses of the concept have been, and promise to remain, in the realm of postmodern cultural discourse that focuses so heavily on the interactions, convergence, and border management among the diverse groups who live in urban cultures, useful to urban historians who explore regional and locational variations in urban development as a way of focusing on the process, rather than the place, of urbanization. The term "urban frontier" has thus helped to sharpen and consolidate the definition of the fragmented field of urban history. By intertwining urban history with local and regional history, it has also sustained the dialogue between urban historians and economic, social, political, and cultural historians within a broader attempt to define and understand the general development of modern American economy, society, political system, and culture.

—*Timothy R. Mahoney*

**See also**
Boom Towns; Cattle Towns; Ghost Towns; Mining Towns; River Towns; Western Cities.

**References**
Abbott, Carl. *Boosters and Businessmen: Popular Economic Thought and Urban Growth in the Antebellum Middle West.* Westport, CT: Greenwood Press, 1981.

Frost, Lionel. *The New Urban Frontier: Urbanisation and City Building in Australasia and the American West.* Kensington, Australia: New South Wales University Press, 1991.

Goodstein, Anita Shafer. *Nashville, 1780–1860: From Frontier to City.* Gainesville: University of Florida Press, 1989.

Hamer, David. *New Towns in the New World: Images and Perceptions of the Nineteenth-Century Urban Frontier.* New York: Columbia University Press, 1990.

Jackson, Kenneth T. *Crabgrass Frontier: The Suburbanization of the United States.* New York: Oxford University Press, 1985.

Larsen, Lawrence H. *The Urban West at the End of the Frontier.* Lawrence: Regents Press of Kansas, 1978.

Limerick, Patricia. "The Adventures of the Frontier in the Twentieth Century." In James Grossman, ed., *The Frontier in American Culture,* 67–101. Berkeley: University of California Press, 1994.

Lotchin, Roger W. *San Francisco, 1846–1856: From Hamlet to City.* New York: Oxford University Press, 1974.

Luckingham, Bradford. "The American Southwest: An Urban View." In Raymond Mohl, ed., *The Making of Urban America,* 252–267. Wilmington, DE: Scholarly Resources, 1988.

———. "The Urban Dimension of Western History." In Michael P. Malone, ed., *Historians and the American West.* Lincoln: University of Nebraska Press, 1983.

Mahoney, Timothy R. *River Towns in the Great West: The Structure of Provincial Urbanization in the American Midwest, 1820–1870.* New York: Cambridge University Press, 1990.

Mohl, Raymond. "The Transformation of Urban America since the Second World War." In Robert B. Fairbanks and Kathleen Underwood, eds., *Essays on Sunbelt Cities and Recent Urban America,* 8–32. College Station: Texas A & M University Press, 1990.

Monkkonen, Eric H. *America Becomes Urban: The Development of U.S. Cities and Towns, 1780–1980.* Berkeley: University of California Press, 1988.

Nash, Gerald D. "The West as Urban Civilization, 1890–1990." In *Creating the West, Historical Interpretations, 1890–1990,* 159–195. Albuquerque: University of New Mexico Press, 1991.

Pomeroy, Earl. "The Urban Frontier of the Far West." In John G. Clark, ed., *The Frontier Challenge, Responses to the Trans-Mississippi West.* Lawrence: University Press of Kansas, 1971.

Reps, John W. *The Forgotten Frontier: Urban Planning in the American West before 1890.* Columbia: University of Missouri Press, 1981.

Smith, Duane A. *Rocky Mountain Mining Camps: The Urban Frontier.* Bloomington: Indiana University Press, 1967.

Teaford, Jon C. *Cities of the Heartland: The Rise and Fall of the Industrial Midwest.* Bloomington: Indiana University Press, 1993.
Wade, Richard C. *The Urban Frontier: Pioneer Life in Early Pittsburgh, Cincinnati, Lexington, Louisville, and St. Louis.* Chicago: University of Chicago Press, 1959.

## Urban Law

As Arnold Toynbee and others have shown, urban law arose out of cities' advantages and problems. Notwithstanding the opportunities that cities allow their residents, distaste for them has long permeated religious literature, constitutional edifices, and legal practices. This hostility toward cities is reflected in policies that are rooted deeply in our legal and constitutional history and in the relationships among colonies that evolved in British North America well before 1776. At Philadelphia in 1787, Madison and his coadjutors institutionalized relationships between the federal and state governments and among states in ways that were almost certainly superior to what had existed before. But by attending only to nation, states, and territories, the Constitution's framers continued the states' habitual domination, indifference, or worse concerning urban needs.

In nineteenth-century legal theory, parent states created "municipal corporations" by issuing charters and, exercising what lawyers later labeled "police powers," were responsible for residents' health, safety, welfare, and morals. But realities differed from the theory. Cities grew quickly where trade, finance, defense, culture, or entertainment promised livelihoods and excitement. States belatedly chartered these growths, but they also allowed overrepresented nonurban voters to decide on state and county tax rates that rarely met even traditional urban needs, much less the many novel and expensive requirements of the burgeoning urban populations.

City life involved government functions that were unglamorous and foreign to a rural population in both kind and cost. Few rural justices of the peace, constables, or coroners had to cope with the chemistry of water purification, firefighting hydraulics, police forensics, mass transit logistics, antiepidemiology medicine, or schoolchildren's truancy. Costly, specialized attention to these issues and concerns by a full-time technical staff was essential for urban life. As a result, city residents paid more in taxes to counties and states than counties and states spent to build, manage, and staff aqueducts, sewers, hospitals, transit lines, schools, commodity exchanges, libraries, parks, zoos, and museums, just to mention a few.

Urban public works and services attracted demagogues and profiteers and evoked their censure. These critics increasingly identified malefactors as ethnic or religious newcomers to America. Spokesmen for older, displaced urban elites, including lawyers, retreated to metaphorical and actual suburbias from which, as reform activists, they spewed forth their vitriol and exposed municipal "ring" corruptions.

In the 1860s lawyers in northern states contributed impressively to a consensus that the North's cities and the South's states were twin cancers in American public life. Just as from the Northwest Ordinances (the Land Ordinances of 1784, 1785, and 1787) and the Constitution, cities benefited little from Civil War public policies establishing the U.S. Department of Agriculture or subsidizing homesteading and higher education. The singular, public-funded state colleges and universities conceived by these laws matured not in cities but in bucolic Ann Arbor, Michigan; Berkeley, California; Madison, Wisconsin; and Urbana, Illinois. Ivy-covered private schools had set a pattern for the upstart state universities, Yale in then-new New Haven, Columbia in far-uptown Morningside Heights, and Harvard in suburban Cambridge rather than in Hartford, Manhattan, or Boston.

Nevertheless, in the early 1870s, a new style of degree-granting law school sprouted up at universities in these small towns, many of them state law schools. The improvisation, teaching law by using the case method, was first introduced at Harvard Law School by Professor Christopher Columbus Langdell, and spread quickly throughout the growing number of university campuses across the nation. In them, full-time academic professors of law (who were often practicing lawyers, although sometimes not) taught from published reports of high court decisions that, increasingly, issued forth as textbooks from the West Publishing Company, itself located in forested Minnesota. From such textbooks, law professors derived proofs for the proposition that the northern cities and the southern states both destabilized political morality and private property. For example, classes in tort law, a newish specialization, studied Chicago's efforts in the 1850s to prevent endemic flooding by raising its downtown ground level and reversing the flow of its major river. Numerous buildings suffered damage from this heroic improvement of the city's infrastructure, and contract violation, malfeasance, and misfeasance litigation, in addition to tort claims, were filed against the city. Studying these cases in law school reinforced the idea that cities were hostile and disagreeable places.

Even more dramatic proof of cities' evil nature emerged in 1863, when, simultaneously with the climactic Gettysburg and Vicksburg cases, antidraft riots with racist and pro-Confederate undertones erupted in Boston, New York, and Chicago. Close in their wake, the U.S. Supreme Court decided *Gelpcke v. Dubuque*, a case that the Court reporter asserted was its initial enforcement of the "high moral duties . . . upon a whole community [i.e., a city] seeking apparently to violate them."

*Gelpcke* arose because Dubuque's civic boosters tried to attract railroad termini there. In order to finance relevant and necessary urban improvements, the city issued bonds that in total exceeded the limit on public indebtedness for the entire state set by Iowa's constitution. State lawmakers had initially approved the bond issue, but a subsequent reform legislature repudiated it. Bondholders sued. Successive Iowa Supreme Court judges who had been popularly elected contradicted one another on the validity of the original bond issue and on its repudiation. Losing parties appealed to the federal Supreme Court. In 1864 it voided the repudiation despite contrary recent judgments of Iowa's Supreme Court.

The controversy surrounding the Dubuque case had profound implications for public law and money markets. Attorneys nationwide found that neither the Constitution of 1787 nor the professional literature on *Gelpcke* adequately clarified the limits of urban initiatives. The important New Orleans lawyer Louis Janin later complained to Lincoln's favorite constitutional scholar, Francis Lieber, that "lawyers in . . . commercial and industrial communities seldom find application for the principles of ethical and philosophical law which arise out of the relations of government, and their libraries are but scantily supplied with works upon these . . . unpractical branches of the law." Sensing that they were no longer "unpractical," law writers quickly remedied this deficiency after Appomattox. Some of their publications became textbooks that many state law schools required well after World War I.

One of the most important of these publications, John Dillon's *Law of Municipal Corporations* (1872), was intensively studied and its principles widely applied for more than 50 years by law students and practitioners. Lawyers also discovered that important professional income was available to those who knew the law of municipal bond issues. Himself a former Iowa Supreme Court judge who bemoaned the *Gelpcke* decision, Dillon wrote the later constitutional scholar Charles Fairman to "know *everything* about municipal bonds." In another of his books, *Municipal Corporations,* Dillon concluded that a city was merely a tenant that existed at the will of its state legislature, which had the right to control or even destroy its urban progeny. Especially in appeals courts, Dillon's anti-urban influence was quick, large, and persistent.

Thomas McIntyre Cooley's *Constitutional Limitations Which Rest upon the Legislative Power of the States of the American Union* first appeared in 1868, but, like Dillon's book, its numerous succeeding editions became standard law school textbooks nationwide through the 1920s. In them, Cooley modified Dillon's views by emphasizing the inherent right of individuals (not cities) against arbitrary actions by state legislatures, a right greatly reinforced after 1868 when the country ratified the Fourteenth Amendment to the Constitution.

Exploited endlessly by advocates of nonpartisan municipal politics, both Dillon's "Rule" and the treatises by Cooley and Dillon justified states in further tightening and narrowing the charters that defined the organization and the powers of major cities (not to mention their shifting attention away from the denial of black residents' civil rights by southern states and onto election wrongs committed in northern cities). Despite the adoption in the early 1900s by some states of "home rule" and other efforts to protect cities, Dillonesque views prevailed in the contemporary legal world, as in the Supreme Court's exaltation of the absolute discretion of a state over its cities.

More recently, the "Second Reconstruction" after World War II partially redirected the legal community's attention away from constraints on municipal governments and toward positive efforts to secure the rights of both individuals and municipalities against fiscal inattention or other wrongs committed by states. Partial breakthroughs have occurred in remedying the voting inequities of urban and nonurban voters. Yet legitimate concerns persist that the highly urbanized America of the 1990s still keeps its cities and suburbs relatively powerless, largely through legal doctrines that derived from unneutral legal principles.

Although many have emphasized cities' contagious corruption to justify their legal subordination, no one ever wrote a song asking: "How're You Gonna Keep 'Em Down in the City?" Talent, inventiveness, and drive keep moving toward the metropolis, an inflow whose effects are eddied as suburbs swell in number and become a haven for white flight simultaneously with the decline in rural population. In the twenty-first century, will the cities so enriched remain willing to serve the law as both villains and victims?

—*Harold M. Hyman*

**See also**
The Legal Basis of Municipal Government.
**References**
Burke, Albie. "Federal Regulation of Congressional Elections in Northern Cities, 1871–1894." Ph.D. dissertation, University of Chicago, 1968.
Fox, Kenneth. *Better City Government: Innovation in American Urban Politics, 1850–1937.* Philadelphia: Temple University Press, 1977.
Frug, Gerald. *Local Government Law.* 2nd ed. St. Paul, MN: West Publishing Co., 1994.
Teaford, Jon C. *City and Suburb: The Political Fragmentation of Metropolitan America, 1850–1970.* Baltimore: Johns Hopkins University Press, 1979.
———. *Municipal Revolution in America: Origins of Modern Urban Government, 1650–1825.* Chicago: University of Chicago Press, 1975.
———. *The Unheralded Triumph: City Government in America, 1870–1900.* Baltimore: Johns Hopkins University Press, 1984.

# Urban Renewal

Urban renewal is one of the most important and also controversial federal urban programs in twentieth-century America. More than 20 years after its formal demise, scholars continue to write about the dramatic, contradictory effects of a program that was born to improve deteriorating cities but that caused its own special kind of destruction.

The program began under the Housing Act of 1949. Title I of that law authorized loans and capital grants to help selected localities undertake what was called "slum clearance and urban redevelopment." During congressional hearings preceding passage of the legislation, several interest groups openly disagreed about the best way to carry out urban redevelopment. Labor unions and proponents of public housing were primarily concerned about the urban poor and favored a residential program that focused on building housing for people with low incomes. Financial and real estate institutions, such as the National Association of Real Estate Boards, opposed building public housing, and they lobbied for a redevelopment program that safeguarded the development rights of the private sector.

The legislation that emerged in 1949 resulted from political compromise. On the one hand, Title I required that localities undertake redevelopment projects that were primarily residential, either before or after clearance. On the other hand, Title I did not require the construction of public or low-income housing, and it decreed that only private developers could undertake redevelopment. It provided for the federal government to pay two-thirds of redevelopment costs and the locality to pay the rest; neither, however, could construct replacement housing without involving the private sector. Essentially, this provision left localities at the mercy of private developers who sometimes refused to buy land that the city had cleared at great cost.

Although this basic structure remained intact for the next 25 years, several acts of legislation modified the program. The Housing Act of 1954 required local community planning and allowed local communities to prevent the spread of deterioration with selective rehabilitation rather than clearance. After this act, the program's official name became "Slum Clearance and Urban Renewal," more popularly known simply as urban renewal. This term continued to connote clearance rather than rehabilitation or conservation, since the sheer size of, and controversy surrounding, clearance activities always overshadowed the more modest preservation activities. The act of 1954 also provided that up to 10 percent of the total money allocated for urban renewal could be used for nonresidential projects, thereby allowing redevelopment for commercial purposes.

The Housing Act of 1959 increased the maximum amount of money that could be used for nonresidential construction to 20 percent of the total, and it authorized localities to assist colleges and universities without regard to residential requirements. The Housing Act of 1961 extended this favorable status to hospitals, increased the allowable non-residential portion of the money to 30 percent, and permitted limited dividend corporations, nonprofit corporations, cooperatives, and public bodies to buy land cleared through urban renewal and then construct rental housing. Thus, projects that cities began in the 1960s often helped educational institutions or hospitals expand their boundaries or helped revive central business districts. At the same time, those projects sometimes included subsidized housing supported by nonprofit corporations and other groups.

Later housing acts continued to authorize and adjust the program, but in 1966 federal attention turned to the new Model Cities (Demonstration Cities) program. President Lyndon Johnson devised Model Cities as a way to improve urban renewal by making redevelopment citizen-directed and by combining physical and social renewal. Under the Housing and Community Development Act of 1974, Congress officially merged Model Cities and urban renewal into the Community Development Block Grant program. Many previously established urban renewal projects received federal, state, or local funding for some years thereafter.

The negative effects of urban renewal, which one author called "the federal bulldozer," first emerged when cities started acquiring land through eminent domain. It soon became apparent that Title I did not sufficiently safeguard the rights of people who had been residents before redevelopment. Localities were supposed to help relocate families displaced by projects and ensure that they received decent, permanent dwellings that they could afford. The reality was far different. The experiences of New York, one of the first cities to implement urban renewal, were repeated throughout the nation. There, city officials notified residents that they had to move in a short period of time, sometimes in only 30 days. Notices implied that residents were expected to use their own resources and contacts to find other places to live. When those tactics did not work quickly enough, the city sometimes used petty harassment techniques such as disconnecting utilities.

Part of the problem was the failure of Congress to provide enough resources for families and businesses to relocate without suffering significant financial losses. Although localities paid market rates for the housing they acquired by eminent domain, during the early years of the program the federal government gave residents only a token amount, $100, to move. Scant attention to the rights of residents by federal officials left local administrators relatively free to carry out relocation as they saw fit, and many of them abused the privilege.

Another fundamental problem was that one person's "slum" was another person's "community." Although some cities emphasized clearing the most dilapidated housing, others used urban renewal to wipe out viable housing located on valuable land that local officials were eyeing for other purposes. Officials especially targeted African-American communities, leading civil rights groups to call urban renewal "Negro removal." European ethnic communities also suffered. The close quarters, rental housing, and small neighborhood businesses that characterized these areas often offended middle-class bureaucrats more than residents who lived nearby.

One of the first scholars to document the sad results was Herbert Gans, who conducted an ethnographic study of one Italian-American community in Boston. The ethnic community he studied was not a disorganized and loathsome "slum" but instead consisted of proud residents bound by tradition and friendship who happened to have low incomes. To destroy their neighborhood was, in effect, to destroy a lively and productive "urban village." Jane Jacobs was another early writer who argued that cities were destroying the healthiest communities in their midst. She lauded the strong social bonds, mixed residential/commercial uses, and informal oversight of children and strangers that characterized urban neighborhoods like Greenwich Village in New York.

Even where it was difficult to suggest that such a "village" or community existed, the insensitivity with which redevelopment officials treated low-income residents caused considerable hostility. Central city housing was scarce in those years, and residents forced out of areas by urban renewal projects often had nowhere to go. As a result, many of them were crowded into surrounding residential areas that quickly declined from the strains of having too many residents. In cities where redevelopment officials targeted adjacent project areas, people were sometimes obliged to relocate their homes twice, or even more often. In its first 12 years, urban renewal demolished 126,000 dwelling units but provided only 28,000 to replace them. The resulting upheaval caused particular distress and instability in African-American communities since blacks made up the majority of those who had to move despite their limited housing choices due to racism.

Ironically, city officials who had moved so quickly to relocate residents of projects and tear down existing housing sometimes found themselves with vacant land and no developer willing to buy it. And so sites designated for urban renewal often sat vacant for years, becoming eyesores overgrown with weeds and strewn with garbage that constantly reminded nearby residents that urban renewal was not renewing the city. When residential reconstruction did take place, developers quickly realized that they could make more money by building middle-income or high-income housing rather than low. The result was obvious; former residents often could not afford to move back into a project area.

Over a period of years, this manifest injustice generated social protest that swept across the country. Some writers believe that this protest produced significant changes in national as well as local politics. In essence, urban citizens rebelled against the pro-growth coalition that destroyed neighborhoods, displaced residents and businesses, provided little low-income housing, and recaptured land for the favored few. Sometimes, peaceful protest initiatives ensued, but the Kerner Commission suggested in 1968 that the discontent and displacement also fueled black civil rebellion during the middle and late 1960s. Small wonder that urban renewal was controversial.

After such a historical overview, some might wonder what could possibly have been positive about this program. In fact, urban renewal did make a number of contributions to American cities, and throughout its existence the program remained fairly popular with local officials. The federal government never forced localities to accept urban renewal funds, and in fact they continued to apply for project approval and expansion for many years after urban renewal had become controversial.

From the perspective of these officials, urban renewal was a route to salvation. The middle class had begun leaving central cities much earlier, but after World War II the flight of both commerce and people became clearly evident. Faced with declining tax bases—a loss aggravated in no small part by federal highway, tax, and mortgage insurance policies, such as those administered by the Federal Housing Administration (FHA)—city officials fought to reclaim key areas of central cities by turning low-income neighborhoods to more lucrative uses. They hoped that areas previously overgrown with low-income housing would attract new capital and retain middle-income people, businesses, and institutions.

And they did. Private developers tended to favor housing for high- rather than low-income people. Although this left low-income people almost literally out in the cold, it also encouraged greater income mixing within cities. Redevelopment created attractive inner-city areas that sometimes generated additional development, particularly near central business districts.

When cities began working more closely with institutions such as hospitals and universities, as encouraged by the Housing Acts of 1959 and 1961, they cleared land with the assurance that a ready party would actually redevelop it. Although institutional projects were just as likely to cause community distress as other projects, the results sometimes produced economic benefits in the long run. For example, in Detroit, Michigan, the Detroit Medical Center caused significant displacement and sparked major protests. When completed, however, the complex became an important center of health sector employment. In some years during the 1980s, the Detroit Medical Center was the city's largest private employer, outranking both General Motors and the Chrysler Corporation.

In addition, the availability of money for subsidized housing allowed states, cities, and nonprofit corporations to construct some affordable housing for low-income city residents on cleared land. This construction peaked in the 1960s and 1970s when townhouse complexes sprang up on land that had been vacant for years.

Urban renewal also increased the capacity of local governments. It accomplished this largely by financing community planning, provided in the Housing Act of 1954, which required that all local redevelopment activities take place in the context of "workable programs." These workable programs were, in effect, community plans. They allowed municipalities to coordinate their efforts and ensure that all improvements took place in the context of an overall scheme of municipal investment. For years, subsequent urban renewal authorizations included funds to support community planning in their budgets.

In the early 1970s the federal government finally passed legislation to safeguard the rights of citizens forced from their homes or businesses by federal actions. At that time, however, urban renewal was fading fast, as was Model Cities. Funding for subsidized housing was in serious jeopardy because of the conservative national backlash. By the time cities received the tools required to undertake more enlightened redevelopment, they had lost many of their powers for redevelopment. The contemporary Community Development Block Grant program, in many ways an improvement over urban renewal, contained its own flaws.

The physical improvements produced by urban renewal survive in many American cities in the form of redeveloped central business district, residential, and institutional projects. Urban renewal also improved cities' fiscal positions, removed dangerously dilapidated housing and business structures, and expanded local planning ability. But the program also harmed tens of thousands of people for the sake of physical and economic redevelopment. The program leveled viable neighborhoods that bureaucrats considered "slums." Cities used urban renewal as a tool to accommodate local business and institutional interests with scant regard for the rights of low-income people and minority communities. These injustices fomented social protest that affected even the most complacent local officials. The gradual reforms that Congress implemented were inadequate to save the program, and when urban renewal "died" it left few mourners.

Between 1949 and 1971, the federal government authorized more than $10 billion for urban renewal. But in 1949 alone, Congress had authorized $6 billion in mortgage insurance just for the FHA program. For all the hue and cry about urban renewal, it was among the least funded of several federal programs that definitively shaped the cities of the United States. While the federal government parsimoniously paid for the small-scale redevelopment of inner cities with urban renewal programs, it generously financed the dramatic expansion of suburbs with FHA, federal highway, and federal tax policies. These latter policies helped decentralize the metropolis and contributed to the very drain of people and capital that central city redevelopment leaders sought to counteract.

—June Manning Thomas

**See also**
Community Development Block Grants; Pruitt-Igoe Housing Complex; Public Housing; Urban Revitalization.
**References**
Anderson, Martin. *The Federal Bulldozer.* Cambridge, MA: MIT Press, 1964.
Bauman, John F. *Public Housing, Race, and Renewal: Urban Planning in Philadelphia, 1920–1974.* Philadelphia: Temple University Press, 1987.
Caro, Robert A. *The Power Broker: Robert Moses and the Fall of New York.* New York: Random House, 1975.
Fried, Marc. "Grieving for a Lost Home: Psychological Costs of Relocation." In James Q. Wilson, ed., *Urban Renewal: The Record and the Controversy,* 359–379. Cambridge, MA: MIT Press, 1966.
Gans, Herbert. *People, Plans, and Policies: Essays on Poverty, Racism, and Other National Urban Problems.* New York: Columbia University Press, 1993.
———. *The Urban Villagers: Group and Class in the Life of Italian Americans.* Rev. ed. New York: Free Press, 1982.
Gelfand, Mark I. *A Nation of Cities: The Federal Government and Urban America, 1933–1965.* New York: Oxford University Press, 1975.
Greer, Scott. *Urban Renewal and American Cities.* Indianapolis, IN: Bobbs-Merrill, 1965.
Jacobs, Jane. *The Death and Life of Great American Cities.* New York: Random House, 1961.
Levin, Melvin R. *Planning in Government: Shaping Programs That Succeed.* Chicago: American Planning Association Planners Press, 1987.
Mollenkopf, John H. *The Contested City.* Princeton, NJ: Princeton University Press, 1983.
U.S. Congress. Committee on Banking, Currency, and Housing. Subcommittee on Housing and Community Development. *Evolution of the Role of the Federal Government in Housing and Community Development: A Chronology of Legislative and Selected Executive Actions, 1892–1974.* Washington, DC: Government Printing Office, 1975.
U.S. Kerner Commission. *Report of the National Advisory Commission on Civil Disorders.* New York: Bantam Books, 1968.

## Urban Revitalization

*Urban revitalization* is a generic term applied to a wide range of situations in urban areas that somehow deal with urban improvement. There seems to be no formal definition for the term, and users have employed it in many different ways, ranging from a specific type of urban improvement to some, or all of them combined. The geographical scale associated with the term also varies, ranging from improvements to a small area such as one city block or a single street, to larger urban districts, the city as a whole, and cities in general. An approximate synonym is *urban renewal;* however, *renewal* often seems to have a narrower meaning that involves slum clearance projects that began in the 1950s as part of federal housing programs.

The term *urban revitalization* first became common in the literature in the 1970s. The context seems to be the population and economic declines that have troubled central cities, particularly since the 1950s and 1960s, as well as the large-scale suburbanization that is said to have sapped central cities of vitality. Consequently, the various improvements associated with urban revitalization seem to have the common goal of attracting people back into cities, in part from the suburbs, and stimulating urban economies.

When applied to residential neighborhoods, the term refers to a mix of improvements that, in combination, are intended to raise an area from substandard conditions to being a good place to live or do business. Specific improvements might include rehabilitating dilapidated housing or replacing it with new dwelling units; finding new uses for vacant buildings and empty lots; upgrading neighborhood facilities such as schools, recreation centers, parks, and streets and sidewalks; and improving services such as police and fire protection, health care, and public transportation. Revitalization also applies to neighborhood shopping centers and commercial strips. For example, neighborhood commercial revitalization might include programs that are intended to attract new businesses to vacant stores, as well as programs that strengthen existing businesses by helping with physical improvements (e.g., "paint up–fix up" projects) and improvements to local services. Whether they are aimed at the residential parts of neighborhoods or their commercial areas, neighborhood-based revitalization efforts can be performed by either the public sector (e.g., the city government) or by private interests (e.g., neighborhood residents themselves or private developers). Most often, urban revitalization at the neighborhood scale involves a combination of efforts by government and private interests.

Another widespread usage of *urban revitalization* has to do with efforts to bring new life to a city's downtown or central business district (CBD). This type of revitalization commonly involves partnerships between city government and urban business leaders, and employs the expertise of urban planners and architects, economic development specialists, and others. Examples of downtown revitalization projects that have been instituted in American cities include constructing new convention centers and hotels to stimulate tourism, improving transportation such as better highway access and new rail or subway lines, developing modern office towers and shopping centers (often as part of large, multiuse redevelopment projects that cover at least one whole city block), developing sports facilities such as stadiums for baseball or arenas for basketball and ice hockey, and improving the historic ambiance of older sections of the downtown or waterfront districts, often to stimulate nighttime and weekend entertainment. In many cities, urban revitalization has been linked closely with historic preservation efforts in and near the downtown.

*Urban revitalization* has also been used in conjunction with the type of neighborhood change known as gentrification. In fact, some of the early literature about gentrification in American cities during the 1970s and 1980s used *revitalization* and *gentrification* interchangeably. However, this is problematic, because gentrification often involves replacing one group of people in a neighborhood (usually the poor) with another group (such as middle-class "young professionals") and is not seen as revitalization from the perspective of the former group and their supporters. Therefore, this particular use of *urban revitalization* has declined in recent years.

Similarly, there is controversy about applying *urban revitalization* to downtown development projects whose benefits are targeted to one part of the population at the expense of another. For example, residents of flophouse districts on the edge of downtown or owners of small businesses in the CBD might not agree that a massive redevelopment project such as a new corporate headquarters tower that displaces them is properly called *revitalization*.

—*Roman Cybriwsky*

**See also**
Central Business District; Gentrification; Urban Renewal.
**References**
Barnekov, Timothy K., and Mary Helen Callahan, eds. *Neighborhoods: Changing Perspectives and Policies.* Newark: College of Urban Affairs, University of Delaware, 1980.
Gittell, Ross J. *Renewing Cities.* Princeton, NJ: Princeton University Press, 1992.
Laska, Shirley Bradway, and Daphne Spain, eds. *Back to the City: Issues in Neighborhood Renovation.* New York: Pergamon Press, 1980.
Palen, J. John, and Bruce London. *Gentrification, Displacement and Neighborhood Revitalization.* Albany: State University of New York Press, 1984.
Teaford, Jon C. *The Rough Road to Renaissance: Urban Revitalization in America, 1940–1985.* Baltimore: Johns Hopkins University Press, 1990.

## Urban Rivalry and Urban Imperialism

Urban rivalry, a central element in the growth and development of cities in the United States, can be defined as competition between cities for people, business, and technology. Often led by urban elites, these rivalries have gathered strong support for urban growth from local citizens.

Urban rivalry has played a prominent role in the United States for three reasons. First, the country's capitalist economy encouraged entrepreneurs to build cities as a profit-making activity. Second, the nation's democratic political institutions eliminated most governmental constraints on the establishment of towns. Third, the existence of vast expanses of land provided many suitable locations for cities and encouraged speculators to champion their town as the best home for newcomers settling in the West.

While some of these early settlements grew into permanent towns, many others failed to prosper and disappeared. The rapid rise and decline of cities in these struggles made urban elites especially anxious about meeting the competitive threats posed by rivals. In response, urban elites strove constantly to improve their city's prospects. To ensure urban expansion, they introduced new transportation and manufacturing technologies and launched promotional campaigns. They touted statistics that traced growth in population, construction, commerce, and industrial output as indicating their city's success in its struggles against rivals.

Cities along the Atlantic Coast competed for the movement of people and goods between Europe and the interior of North America and for the processing of manufactured goods. While Boston took the lead during the sixteenth century and Philadelphia in the seventeenth century, New York surged ahead in the early eighteenth century after the establishment of regular transatlantic shipping service between the city and Europe and changing the conduct of trade by instituting the mandatory auction system. New York solidified its dominance in 1825 by reaping great benefits from the Erie Canal, which allowed the city to capture control of marketing the agricultural production of the Great Lakes region and the Ohio Valley. In response, Boston, Philadelphia, and Baltimore constructed their own transportation networks in hopes of increasing their own share of western agricultural processing.

The construction of canals in the early nineteenth century generated many battles between western towns for control of regional development. These rivalries intensified with the coming of railroads in the 1840s. Railroads heightened competition among urban places because they could be built almost anywhere and because railroad officials forced towns to purchase company stock, provide free rights-of-way, and offer additional inducements to prevent the railroad from locating elsewhere. Town leaders acquiesced to guarantee that the lines would pass near or through their areas. In the Midwest in the 1850s, the construction of the Illinois Central south from Chicago created intense struggles between many towns desiring rail links.

Before the Civil War, St. Louis and Chicago engaged in a heated competition for control of the Midwest's growing trade. In the early nineteenth century, St. Louis had been settled as an outpost that later developed into a city by controlling the shipment of goods down the Mississippi River to New Orleans. But during the Civil War, when many Missourians supported the Confederacy, easterners shied away from

investing in St. Louis just long enough for Chicago to gain the upper hand in their conflict. Because it adopted the railroad early on, Chicago became a transportation and processing center and flourished by moving goods and products between western farmers and eastern markets. In another intense rivalry, Kansas City surpassed Leavenworth in the 1860s after its prominent citizens wooed the Hannibal and St. Joseph Railroad by granting the company land, purchasing stock, and bridging the Missouri River.

During westward expansion, city leaders also battled over the location of state capitols, universities, and military installations. All of these rivalries gave rise to imaginative city promotional campaigns as leaders sought to place their own city in the best light. Boosters hired artists to draw lithographic bird's-eye view maps, and journalists wrote grandiose descriptions that detailed their city's rapid growth and foretold its prosperous future based on the analysis of migration trends, weather, and proximity to ports, rivers, railroads, mountain passes, or fertile plains.

While inland communities competed for railroad stops, port cities on the Atlantic and Pacific continually strove to augment their positions by expanding shipping facilities. Urban rivalries over transportation continued into the era of highways as cities vied with each other for federal and state highway construction money. Throughout the second half of the twentieth century, increased air travel made the location of airports, especially hubs, a major issue of contention among cities.

In the last two decades of the twentieth century, the decline in American manufacturing has altered the source and style of urban rivalry. Cities can no longer depend on advantages from proximity to natural resources that were previously required by manufacturers. The deterioration of manufacturing has lessened the volume of shipping and thus increased the competition between port cities for what remains. With a greater proportion of the economy devoted to processing information, central cities must now compete with suburbs for companies that can locate anywhere within a metropolitan area. City officials lure companies by cutting taxes, providing low-interest loans, and selling land for less than market price. City officials have responded to suburban competition by launching urban renewal programs that include leveling tenements and other structures and by constructing freeways and parking lots to accommodate suburban motorists who make the trek downtown.

Beginning with World War I, but especially after World War II, the loss of heavy industry increased the importance of military spending as a spur to urban growth. This was especially true of western cities that lacked the industrial base of eastern and midwestern cities. War brought the expansion of military bases in the West and the rapid growth of the aerospace industry in the Southwest. The influx of military spending contributed to urbanization around Seattle, San Jose, Los Angeles, San Diego, and Albuquerque. A highly competitive battle developed as eastern and midwestern city leaders fought against the movement of defense spending away from their areas. From New York to San Diego, urban boosters argued that national defense necessitated spending defense money in or near their communities.

Now that the transportation network is in place, rivalries increasingly focus on the service sector. Central cities compete for convention trade by expanding hotels and conference halls or by building new ones altogether. City officials struggle to lure tourists by creating new downtown shopping districts, often in renovated warehouses or factories that recall the bygone era of urban predominance. Cities vie for professional sports teams and a "major league" image by constructing new stadiums with public money and using tax breaks to keep or lure clubs. With the growth of the global economy, urban boosters try to entice foreign corporate tenants into their office buildings. Finally, immigration and the multiplication of ethnic centers has affected minority groups and increased the importance of ethnic enclaves to cities. In the San Francisco Bay Area, for instance, the old Chinatown in San Francisco faces stiff competition and strong challenges from the new "Asiatowns" in Oakland and San Jose, and all three enclaves now compete for tourists, businesses, residents, and foreign investment.

Closely related to the concept of urban rivalry is urban imperialism. Urban imperialism refers to urban expansion and a city's economic dominance over a larger and larger geographic area. The growth of population, trade, and manufacturing motivated urban elites to call for the extension of transportation links from cities into the hinterland. These leaders endeavored to tap nearby agricultural production so that their cities could serve as processing centers. They also sought to exploit nearby deposits of natural resources like timber, coal, and oil.

One of the most important resources for cities was water. Particularly in the arid West, urban leaders realized that growing cities required large supplies of freshwater. In California, San Francisco, Oakland, and Los Angeles took the lead in constructing reservoirs and canals throughout the state. In Los Angeles, the civil engineer William Mulholland oversaw construction of the largest transfer system in the world as the city siphoned water from distant sources, creating political controversies over urban growth and the rights of cities versus the needs of agricultural users. Similar events occurred in Arizona and Colorado.

Another form of urban imperialism was the growing influence of cities over the lives of rural Americans. The growth of large cities created enormous demand for meat, grain, fruit, and vegetables, and this demand caused changes in the scale of agriculture in the late nineteenth century. Farmers used new technologies like the McCormick reaper, manufactured in Chicago, and dozens of other machines to meet the demands of urban residents for food. Railroad companies developed the refrigerator car to ship fruits and vegetables from Florida, Texas, and California to the growing cities. New and larger-scale agriculture also brought about the use of low-paid migrant workers to harvest the crops.

Advances in communication technologies caused the diffusion of urban culture from cities to rural areas. The mass printing of magazines and mail-order catalogs allowed rural consumers to participate vicariously in cities and urban life, no matter how far removed. Later, the radio, motion pictures, and television distributed urban culture to the countryside even more widely. The arrival on the train of consumer goods from large cities sent untold numbers of local store owners into bankruptcy because they could not sell goods as cheaply as huge retailers with access to vast, cheap transportation networks.

Another aspect in the history of urban imperialism was annexation and the consolidation of small towns and large cities. Throughout the nineteenth century, one means used by major cities to grow was spreading horizontally and engulfing small towns. Larger cities succeeded in augmenting their population while smaller cities and towns increased the level of municipal services without incurring additional tax burdens, and they also gained the prestige of being part of a larger city.

The creation of the New York borough system in 1898 became a model for metropolitan consolidation, and the process occurred over and over again during the late nineteenth and early twentieth centuries. Yet, beginning in the 1920s, a countertrend became evident as smaller cities rejected consolidation and retained their autonomy. This reversal resulted from the growing independence of suburbs resulting from use of the automobile, suburban fears of larger tax burdens, and the increasingly negative image of cities that stressed the crime, poor schools, and political malfeasance supposedly inherent in them.

—*Joseph A. Rodriguez*

**See also**
Annexation; Boosterism; Consolidation.
**References**
Albion, Robert Greenhalgh. *The Rise of New York Port. 1815–1860*. New York: Scribners, 1939.
Belcher, Wyatt W. *The Economic Rivalry between St. Louis and Chicago, 1850–1880*. New York: Columbia University Press, 1947.
Cronon, William. *Nature's Metropolis: Chicago and the Great West*. New York: W. W. Norton, 1991.

Fogelson, Robert M. *The Fragmented Metropolis: Los Angeles, 1850–1930.* Cambridge, MA: Harvard University Press, 1967.

Kahn, Judd. *Imperial San Francisco: Politics and Planning in an American City, 1897–1906.* Lincoln: University of Nebraska Press, 1979.

Lotchin, Roger. *Fortress California, 1910–1961: From Warfare to Welfare.* New York: Oxford University Press, 1992.

———. "The Origins of the Sunbelt-Frostbelt Struggle: Defense Spending and City Building." In Raymond A. Mohl, ed., *Searching for the Sunbelt,* 47–68. Knoxville: University of Tennessee Press, 1990.

Scheiber, Harry N. "Urban Rivalry and Internal Improvements in the Old Northwest, 1820–1860." *Ohio History* 71 (1962): 227–230, 289–292.

Wade, Richard C. *The Urban Frontier, 1790–1830.* Cambridge, MA: Harvard University Press, 1959.

## Urban Sprawl

The very term *urban* seems to imply a higher population density as people converge for commerce, services, and proximate residence. Much of the history of cities fits just that pattern. Yet there is another side to the city that complicates how we think about it and how it relates to the land. A city may grow and spread to encompass a good deal of space, even to the point where its density declines. But as this happens, it may remain a single unit of sorts, with daily interactions covering a broader area and including a larger number of people despite the lower density.

This is the phenomenon called *urban sprawl.* That term seems to be an oxymoron for the word *urban* implies density while the term *sprawl* implies reduced density. How, then, can urban sprawl exist? The answer lies in the changing transportation technology of modern society. When people could only move about on foot, a few kilometers of travel was the limit for carrying out daily obligations and then returning home in the evening. Later in history, animals provided motive power, widening the possible distance of daily travel. The use of fossil energy to drive all kinds of vehicular transportation expanded everyday movements still farther, making possible the inclusion in the same community of many more people distributed over far more space. Hence, the possibility of urban sprawl developed. Towns surrounding a city could contribute workers and shoppers, who traveled into the center during the day and then returned home at night. The suburb gained its name because it was urban but subordinate to a larger entity, in time called the metropolis.

This was not yet urban sprawl, since reliance upon public transit, particularly trains, focused travel within limited corridors. Towns could only participate in the larger metropolis if they were located along train routes and their residents could get in and out of the city quickly, despite the distances involved. These towns became part of a "corridorized metropolis," whose outward spokes were defined by railroad routes. The high cost of railroad construction limited the amount of space that could be included within the urban system. Even though true urban sprawl did not yet exist, a step in that direction had been taken since areas of lower density than the central city could now be part of a metropolitan system. Streetcars provided connections to more areas and thus

*The sprawl of New York City is clear from the observation deck of the World Trade Center.*

made it possible for the urban system to expand beyond railroad lines.

The automobile made cities sprawl in the full sense of the word for it enabled people to fill the gaps between public transit lines. They could spread over vast spaces and still live within reach of the city and its jobs. Although road construction was still necessary, the car was especially suited to metropolitan life at a moderate density. At first, work and major shopping remained central activities while residence spread outward. In time, work and shopping, too, dispersed away from the core. Industrial zones near the city lost jobs to suburban factories. With jobs at the periphery, residence could move out still farther. The result was a "great metropolitan reef," its new parts growing like new coral building upon that part of the reef just a bit older. This metro-reef proliferates because it does not rely on concentrated public transit. Thus, urban sprawl shifts from oxymoron to modern reality.

—*Marcus Felson*

**References**

Felson, Marcus. "Routine Activities and Crime Prevention in the Developing Metropolis." *Criminology* 24 (1987): 911–931.

Hawley, Amos H. *The Changing Shape of Metropolitan America: Deconcentration since 1920.* New York: Free Press, 1956.

———. *Urban Society: An Ecological Approach.* New York: Ronald Press, 1971.

## Urban Systems

The concept of an urban system refers to any set of functionally interdependent urban places. Urban systems are often discussed and analyzed in relation to national territories, but the concept can be applied to any geographic scale, from the subregional to the global. The formal analysis of urban systems is based on the premise that the spatial organization of any territory depends on a series of urban-centered regions: towns and cities (or central places) and their hinterlands. Flows of labor, capital, goods, services, and information within each hinterland are assumed to center on, and be organized by, its town or city. Meanwhile, movements and transmissions between towns and cities are seen as a function of their relative size and the degree of specialization within their economies. It is thus possible, as Brian J. L. Berry put it, to conceptualize cities "as systems within systems of cities."

Berry was the first to apply systems analysis and general systems theory to the study of cities, showing how urban systems exhibit certain attributes and regularities. Thus, for example, territory can be seen as organized through hierarchies of towns and cities of different sizes and with different sets of social and economic functions. This observation was the basis of the central place theory elaborated by Walter Christaller. His study of towns in southern Germany became the basis for much of the conventional wisdom about towns and cities as "central places" or nodal markets around which territory is organized into a nested set of hinterlands. In essence, Christaller theorized that the provision of lower-order goods and services (e.g., groceries, dairy goods) is organized through a series of small central places, each dominating only a small market area, or hinterland. This, of course, is because the "range" of lower-order goods and services—the distance people are willing to travel to obtain them—is short, and their commercial "threshold"—the size of the population needed to sustain them—is small.

Each small central place and its hinterlands is, in turn, embedded within the hinterlands of larger central places that, because they dominate a larger market area, sustain a greater variety of goods and services, including some of a higher order, i.e., more specialized goods and services. The number of levels in the hierarchy of towns and cities, and their size and spacing relative to each another, depends on assumptions made about the nature of functional interdependencies between places, and the importance of market principles *vis-à-vis* other influences, such as the administrative organization of space and the configuration of transportation routes. Christaller himself produced a series of urban systems geometries that illustrate this idea.

Christaller's view of cities as central places, of course, values their function as market centers over their function as centers of production, governance, or cultural significance—a questionable supposition. Moreover, there are relatively few regions of the world where marketing still dominates the functions of most towns and cities. Nevertheless, the urban systems of most subregions do exhibit a hierarchical structure, as do the socioeconomic subsystems within metropolitan areas.

The functional interdependence between places within urban systems results in a distinctive relationship between the population of cities and their rank within an overall hierarchy. This relationship has been expressed as the rank-size rule:

$$Pf = Pg / Rf$$

where Pf is the population of city f, Pg is the population of the largest city in the urban system, and Rf is the rank of city by population size.

Thus, if the largest city in a particular system has a population of 1 million, the fifth largest city should have a population one-fifth as big (200,000), the hundredth-ranked city should have a population one one-hundredth as big (10,000), and so on. This relationship produces a linear plot on a graph with a logarithmic scale for population sizes. The actual rank-size relationship for the urban system of the United States, for example, has always come close to this.

This does not mean, however, that individual cities have always maintained their relative position within the rank-order of cities. The growth of some cities (e.g., Los Angeles) has sent them from the lower end of the hierarchy to the very top, while other cities (e.g., Charleston, South Carolina) have grown much less rapidly and have slipped down the hierarchy. It is the overall relationship between city sizes and their rank within the urban system that has tended to stay fairly constant.

In some urban systems, the top of the rank-size distribution is distorted by the disproportionate size of the largest (and sometimes the second largest) city. In Argentina, for example, Buenos Aires is more than ten times the size of Rosario, the second largest city. In the United Kingdom, London is more than nine times as large as Birmingham, and in France, Paris is more than eight times larger than Marseilles. In Brazil, both Rio de Janeiro and Sao Paulo are five times the size of Belo Horizonte, the third largest city. This condition is called "primacy." Primacy is not simply a matter of sheer size. Some of the largest metropolitan areas in the world—Karachi, New York, and Bombay, for example—are not primate. Furthermore, primacy is a condition found in both the core and the periphery of the world system.

This suggests that primacy results from the roles played by particular cities within their own national urban system. There is, however, a relationship to the world economy. Primacy in peripheral countries tends to be a consequence of primate cities' early roles as gateway cities. Primacy in developed countries tends to be a consequence of primate cities' roles as imperial capitals and centers of administration, politics, and trade for a much wider urban system than that of their own nation.

When cities' economic, political, and cultural functions are disproportionate to their population, the condition is known as centrality. Very often, primate cities exhibit this characteristic, but cities do not have to be primate in order to be functionally dominant within their urban system. Bangkok, for instance, with around 16 percent of Thailand's population, accounts for approximately 50 percent of the country's overall gross domestic product, over 85 percent of the country's gross national product in banking, insurance and real estate, and 75 percent of its manufacturing.

In addition to this centralization, the spatial division of labor resulting from economic development means that many medium and larger-sized cities provide highly specialized economic functions and so acquire distinctive characters. Thus, for example, one can point to steel towns (e.g., Pittsburgh, Pennsylvania; Sheffield, England), textile towns (e.g., Lowell, Massachusetts; Manchester, England), and auto-manufacturing towns (e.g., Detroit, Michigan; Oxford, England; Turin, Italy; Toyota City, Japan; Togliattigrad, Russia). Meanwhile, of course, some towns and cities do evolve as central places, providing an evenly balanced range of functions for their own hinterlands. This has prompted the analysis of urban systems in terms of functional taxonomies.

Such approaches have typically rested heavily on quantitative methodologies using cross-sectional economic data from national data sets. They have provided useful "snapshots" of the composition of particular urban systems. They have also provided useful taxonomies within which to analyze other attributes of cities: crime rates, fiscal health, or employment growth, for example. But they have been of limited value in uncovering any regularities in the structure and evolution of urban systems, largely because data limitations have precluded comparative or diachronic analyses, as well as analyses of the most significant economic flows between cities.

Finally, it should be noted that—since the functional interdependence of towns and cities is itself a function of transportation and communications technologies and infrastructures and of corporate and governmental structures that are increasingly international in scope—studies of national and regional urban systems are of increasingly limited value. Interlocking urban systems now link regional, national, and international flows in a complex web of interdependence. Economic and cultural globalization has produced a global urban system, with a hierarchy of "world cities" that, between them, have reorganized global space. At the top of this global urban hierarchy are three cities—London, New York, and Tokyo—whose corporate and financial influence is truly global in scope. The second tier of world cities includes places with some functions that are global in scope: Frankfurt, Hong Kong, Paris, and Los Angeles, for example. The third tier includes places like Bombay, Miami, Johannesburg, and Sydney that have important international linkages and close functional ties to the higher-order world cities. What is particularly interesting and significant about all these world cities is that in some ways they have acquired a greater affinity for one another than to other cities within their own national urban systems.

—*Paul L. Knox*

**See also**
Central Place Theory; Gateway Cities; Hinterland.

**References**
Berry, Brian J. L. "Cities as Systems within Systems of Cities." *Papers and Proceedings of the Regional Science Association* 13 (1964): 147–163.

Christaller, Walter. *Die zentralen Orte in Suddeutschland.* C. W. Baskin, trans. Englewood Cliffs, NJ: Prentice-Hall, 1966.

Dunn, E. S., Jr. *The Development of the U.S. Urban System. Vol. 1: Concepts, Structures, Regional Shifts.* Baltimore: Johns Hopkins University Press, 1980.

Knox, Paul L., and P. J. Taylor. *World Cities in a World-System.* Cambridge, England: Cambridge University Press, 1995.

Marshall, J. U. *The Structure of Urban Systems.* Toronto, Ontario: University of Toronto Press, 1990.

Novella, T. J., and T. Stanback, Jr. *The Economic Transformation of American Cities.* New York: Conservation of Human Resources, 1981.

# Urban Technologies

Urban technologies provide the sinews of the modern city: its road, bridge, and transit networks; its water and sewer lines and waste disposal facilities; and its power and communications nets. These technological systems allowed cities to function as centers of commerce, industry, entertainment, and residence. In the hands of politicians and public works officials, entrepreneurs, and developers, they have stimulated urban growth and diversification, created and destroyed communities, altered the urban landscape, and reorganized political life. These technologies have sometimes been publicly owned and administered, sometimes privately, or occasionally constructed and operated by public-private coalitions. Over time, service provision has frequently shifted back and forth between private and public delivery because of dissatisfaction over costs and the quality of service. In the design and construction of urban technologies, technical experts played important roles, although oftentimes political factors, or factors such as real estate speculation, were the determining factors.

The technological history of the American city can be divided into four approximate periods: 1790 to 1880, 1880 to 1920, 1920 to 1960, and 1960 to the present. The period from 1790 to 1880 is that of the walking or pedestrian city, a period of foundations. The decades between 1880 and 1920 witnessed the rise of the networked or wired, piped, and tracked city, and the construction of the core infrastructure. Between approximately 1920 and 1960, the technologies of the motor vehicle—the automobile and the truck—became the predominant shaping elements in the metropolis, with suburban growth and a concomitant decline of the central city. Since 1960, facilitated by increased auto and truck use and new telecommunications technology, the United States has experienced the rise of a new urban form, the outer or edge city.

Until the last decades of the nineteenth century, most cities were pedestrian or walking cities. With the exception of large cities such as New York, Baltimore, Philadelphia, and Chicago, American cities were compact, densely populated, and composed of a jumble of residences and small businesses, although a few cities such as Cincinnati, Philadelphia, and Pittsburgh had growing industrial sectors. Dramatic urban structural changes, however, commenced in the 1840s and 1850s due to value shifts on the part of urban populations

and the development and application of technologies related to transportation, water supply, and sanitation. In these decades, the concept of municipal government acting as a service provider was relatively new. Commercial elites, professionals, and sanitarians often joined together to form coalitions pushing for public construction of water and sewerage systems or for policies making possible private provision of services. A new breed of urban politician based their careers on appeals to a recently enlarged electorate and promised to deliver public works and services as a response to voting constituencies or the needs of specific interest groups.

Some of the most extensive developments occurred in regard to transportation, thus facilitating alterations in patterns of work and residence and expansion of the city's boundaries. Until the 1850s public transportation was minimal. In the 1820s and 1830s horse-drawn buses called omnibuses appeared in a few cities, such as New York, Philadelphia, and Baltimore; during the 1830s commuter railroads first carried passengers in Boston; and in 1852 the first horse-drawn street railway began operating in New York. By 1880 the streetcar was becoming a ubiquitous part of the urban infrastructure. In the 1870s elevated railways and cable-driven systems appeared in the largest cities. Growing numbers of urbanites utilized these transport forms, although the large majority of working-class urbanites continued to walk to work through the end of the century.

Commercial elites, industrialists, and sanitarians, concerned about the public order and the public health (i.e., preventing the spread of epidemic disease) and motivated to spur economic development, drove technology implementation. The interaction of the various forces generating construction of these systems is clearly illustrated with regard to water supply. Until the last quarter of the nineteenth century, the majority of American urbanites depended on local sources such as wells, ponds, cisterns, or vendors for water. Local supplies, however, proved inadequate to provide for the needs of growing cities as wells and ponds became visibly polluted and groundwater levels receded. The desire of urbanites for more copious and cleaner water supplies for household and industrial uses, concern over threats to the public health from polluted local sources and filthy streets, and the insufficiency of water to control fires led to a search for nonlocal sources of supply. Water supply therefore represents a situation in which a number of interests—businesses and industries, homeowners, fire insurance companies, and sanitarians—joined to demand the construction of large public works in order to secure more adequate supplies at a reasonable cost. City boosters considered waterworks crucial in the competition with other municipalities for population, trade, and industry, and emphasized their possession in touting their cities.

The first large city to construct a municipal water supply system was Philadelphia (1799–1801). Cincinnati installed a water system in the 1820s, New York opened the Croton Aqueduct in 1841, and Boston the Cochituate Aqueduct in 1848. By 1860 the nation's 16 largest cities all had waterworks, with a total of 136 systems—57 public and 79 private—although most small towns and cities still relied on private supplies. By 1880, however, waterworks technology had rapidly diffused, and the number of systems had increased to 598, of which 293 were public and 305 private. The larger cities were more likely to have publicly owned waterworks and the smaller cities to have privately owned, many with relatively few users. The large capital requirements of waterworks and frequent inadequacies of the private companies often resulted in a preference for public ownership. A number of cities that began with privately owned waterworks, such as New York, Chicago, and San Francisco, shifted to public ownership because private companies refused to provide adequate water for such civic purposes as street flushing and fire hydrants, nor would they eliminate pollution, enlarge their works in anticipation of population growth, or service distant districts. Water supply provision, therefore, especially in large cities, presents a triumph of technology and administration in the construction of large public works to provide a needed service. A capital-intensive and centralized technological system replaced a decentralized and labor-intensive method of delivery.

Other urban technologies also developed in this period. Cities constructed integrated sewerage systems as replacements for the decentralized and labor-intensive privy vault/cesspool systems and for private sewers. The larger cities adopted centralized fire alarm telegraph systems and lit their streets with gas in order to protect public safety. By the 1880s these technologies, combined with the growing transportation networks, were changing the compact walking city into the much more extensive technologically networked city.

The growth of a body of trained engineers made possible the construction of these new technological systems. Before the latter part of the century, relatively few persons had received formal engineering training. Most belonged to the "craft" tradition and had learned their engineering from direct, practical experience, especially on the large public works and railroad projects of the antebellum period. A number of civil engineers who were trained on these projects became municipal engineers. In the years after the Civil War the expansion of engineering education provided a body of talent for the explosion of infrastructure construction that occurred after 1890.

Equally important for the construction of large-scale technological systems was the development of new methods of public finance. Since city tax revenues were usually insufficient to cover capital costs, many cities followed the practice of having abutters pay for infrastructure improvements. This often resulted in an undersupply of infrastructures for poorer districts. Increasingly, however, in the late nineteenth century, cities financed capital-intensive projects, such as water and sewerage systems and street lighting, with municipal bonds. Large-scale debt financing was new to American municipalities, and many citizens feared financial disaster. Some defaults did occur, especially during recessions, but cities continued to spend and municipal debt burdens greatly increased, leading to state legislative caps on spending.

The period from 1880 to 1920 was one of great city growth in the United States, as millions of immigrants and rural migrants chose urban destinations. The shift of population from country to city, natural increase, and immigrant absorption produced large urban population increases and stimulated incentives to introduce new approaches to control the urban environment. Some of these changes involved the more systematic application of techniques, such as sewerage and water supply, that had been developed in the earlier period. Others, such as electrical supply or telephone systems, differed from older infrastructure systems and were often rooted in new science-based concepts. Over time, these systems became increasingly networked and centralized, providing important economies of scale but also vulnerability in cases of system failure.

Engineers working with these technologies believed that systems such as gas, electricity, or water ought to be large and widely dispersed, and yet carefully regulated from a central office staffed by experts like themselves. Beginning around 1880, moreover, civic-minded elites and professionals became concerned over existing approaches to city building. These concerns were reflected by a new interest in the planning of cities, as typified by the City Beautiful movement. By the 1910s, members of this group also helped codify a new set of norms and procedures, which usually included a prominent role for engineers who spoke in the language of large-scale systems and centralized control.

As in the period before 1880, transport systems proved central to the development of the modern city and the thinking of planners. Beginning around 1890, electrically powered streetcars, as well as subways, elevated railways, and commuter railroads, provided the essential framework for the expansion of urban areas. From 1890 to 1907, for instance, streetcar mileage (almost all privately supplied) increased from 5,783 to 34,404 miles, most of it electrical. Annual rides per urban inhabitant jumped from 111 to 250, as the use of public transit far outdistanced population increases and vast areas surrounding central cities were opened for residential development. Streetcar suburbs proliferated along the transit routes while commuter rails transformed small towns into commuter suburbs. In many cases, the entrepreneurs behind streetcar development were themselves heavily invested in suburban real estate development. In addition to extending the fringe of the urbanized area, public transit, which focused on the downtown, accelerated the transformation of the urban core from an area used for mixed residential, commercial, and industrial purposes into a true central business district devoted primarily to commercial and business uses, including great department stores such as Hudson's and Macy's.

The building of other urban technological systems made this period the most intensive in regard to construction of the core urban infrastructure. Included was the extension and diffusion of water and sewerage systems, the development and construction of water filtration and sewage treatment facilities, the building of large-scale electrical power networks, and the extension of telephone services. In more quantitative terms, the number of waterworks increased from 1,878 to 9,850 between 1890 and 1920, and the population served by filtered water increased from 310,000 to 17,291,000 between 1890 and 1914. Meanwhile, the miles of sewers grew from 6,005 to 24,672, approximately half the urban population acquired home electric service, and the portion of households (urban and rural) with telephones increased to about one-third.

Construction and operation of great technological systems, such as streetcars and electrical power networks, affected not only the city's physical landscape but also eventually encouraged substantial changes in social and political relationships. Because of the monopolistic nature and great power of these systems, many citizens concluded that only regulation or even municipal ownership would provide the necessary controls. Some of this rhetoric and the accompanying political action represented the efforts of a disinterested elite anxious to secure the benefits of administrative efficiency. They were also part of a broader effort by suburbanites who wished to secure the benefits of urban technologies such as electric trolleys at a low and uniform rate.

Although members of these diverse coalitions viewed the city from different perspectives, they agreed on many aspects of the city-building process. Modern urban technologies required regulatory frameworks, including strong building and sanitary codes as well as zoning, to control new land uses. In many respects, their image of the city was one of neat statistical categories. Such technical rhetoric and analytic categories helped fix the framework within which the politics of urban technology was played out. By 1920 the logic and rhetoric of administration used by engineers and other experts had come to assume a prominent place in political discourse and deliberations, although not always determining the exact policies followed.

Two factors, one technological and the other governmental, largely shaped urban infrastructure developments after 1920. The critical technological innovation was the automobile (along with the motor truck and the bus), first made widely available by Henry Ford's assembly-line production techniques. This innovation encouraged a host of social, spatial, and administrative developments that sharply altered technological priorities and patterns. The crucial expansion of governmental policy with implications for cities first occurred in the 1930s during the New Deal, continued in the postwar period at a reduced level of investment, rose again in the 1960s and 1970s, and declined in the 1980s. Although numerous technological and administrative innovations affected cities and their technological systems during these years, these two—the explosion of automobile usage and the altered role of the federal government—were most critical.

During the period between 1910 and 1930, the nation's automobile registrations rose from 458,000 to nearly 22 million, or from one car to every 20.1 persons to one car to every 5.3 persons. The automobile initially was most adopted in rural areas, but urban use of automobiles, trucks, and buses expanded in the 1920s. The automobile dramatically impacted the urban fabric and the city's technological systems. Cars facilitated out-movement toward the city's periphery and suburbs, permitted settlement of land between radial transit lines, greatly increased downtown congestion because of a growth in commuter traffic, and jammed existing road networks.

In a nation lacking a central planning capability, responses to the automobile varied according to commercial and professional interests. All agreed that highway building and remodeling was desirable, but disagreements arose as to who would pay for the improvements and who would actually benefit from them. Road-building advocates proved especially effective in securing highway improvements. The needs of the automobile, motor truck, and bus for improved roads and highways expressed by automobile clubs, business organizations, and engineering associations resulted in extensive construction. Between 1914 and 1929, the mileage of surfaced roads increased 157 percent and the mileage of high-grade surfaced roads increased 776 percent, reflecting the need of motor vehicles for smooth surfaces. The Bureau of Public Roads, aided by the American Road Builders' Association, the American Society for Municipal Improvements, and the American Society of Civil Engineers, developed standards and specifications that were often used in designing new roadways and the rebuilding and resurfacing of highways and streets.

Planners and members of the new discipline of traffic engineering concentrated on improving automobile circulation in the central business district. They promoted the widening and double-decking of streets, elimination of grade crossings, and the development of a variety of traffic controls. In addition, street surfacing with smooth pavements (mostly asphalt) took place throughout urban areas. Cities and counties built hundreds of bridges and tunnels to facilitate cross-river transportation, while Chicago, New York, Pittsburgh, and Los Angeles even constructed costly limited-access roadways into the downtown area.

The problems of financing road and street construction encouraged innovations in taxation and intergovernmental cooperation. The state gasoline tax (first implemented in Oregon in 1919 and in all states by 1929) was the most important automobile-related funding innovation of the 1920s, providing funds for highway construction. Municipal expenditures for streets and highways also rose, although cities depended largely on conventional means of financing, such as bonds, the property tax, or special assessments, to provide improvements. In the 1920s municipal operating and capital expenditures for streets and highways were exceeded only by spending for education. Cities, counties, and other governmental authorities cooperated to improve transportation infrastructure, such as Westchester County's Bronx Parkway, Philadelphia's Benjamin Franklin Parkway, or Pittsburgh's Liberty Tunnel, Liberty Bridge, and Boulevard of the Allies improvement.

The New Deal evolved as a governmental response to the Depression and had major impacts upon the urban infrastructure. From 1933 to 1938, the federal government accounted for approximately 60 to 65 percent of all public construction through agencies such as the Public Works Administration. These projects included almost one-half of all new sewer and water supply construction, over three-quarters of all new municipal sewage treatment plants (1,165 of 1,310), and numerous airports, parks, hospitals, dams, and public buildings. Such federal spending prevented what was almost the collapse of spending for urban public works during the decade and provided essential infrastructure necessary to keep cities operating.

In World War II, as in World War I but on a larger scale, the strains of war affected American cities. War production produced a massive expansion of industrial work in cities such as Baltimore, Detroit, and Pittsburgh. In addition, it accelerated growth in Sunbelt cities such as Phoenix and San Diego and in cities that had lacked major industry, such as Portland and Oakland. An influx of workers generated enormous pressure on housing and transportation facilities. Federal public works investment was largely for factories and equipment, although some public housing was constructed. Municipal spending for construction and maintenance was sharply reduced, and roads and streets deteriorated rapidly, as heavy trucks and even tanks heading for war crisscrossed pavements constructed for fewer and lighter vehicles.

Following World War II, large numbers of urban Americans joined the movement to the suburbs. During the period from 1946 to 1950, truck, bus, and auto registrations increased from 34.3 million to 49 million. Simultaneously, retail sales in central business districts declined, as merchants, shoppers, and executives sought prosperity and convenience in distant subdivisions, in suburban shopping malls, and in modern office buildings featuring free parking and air conditioning. Suburbanization increased the formation of municipalities in many metropolitan areas, often because of the perception among many suburbanites that large-city government was unresponsive to the specialized needs of their group and locale. In suburban St. Louis County, for instance, the number of municipalities grew from 21 in 1930 to 83 in 1950; in Los Angeles County, the number went from 45 to 68 in the 1950s.

One reason for the proliferation of governmental units was the desire among many new suburbanites for closer control over services such as schools, roads, water supply, and sewerage, as well as other land uses. In turn, suburban policymakers, faced with providing costly technologies, often tried to cope with fragmentation by expanding old and creating new special purpose metropolitan districts for services such as water supply and sewage disposal. The functions of county government also expanded in the postwar period. By 1972, of the 150 major urban counties, more than one-half provided public libraries and recreational facilities, over one-third sewage disposal, and about one-fifth solid waste collection and water supply.

Faced with rapid suburbanization and central city decline, downtown business interests and urban politicians in cities like Pittsburgh and Atlanta joined in private-public partnerships in an attempt to revitalize their cities. These "growth machines" hoped to revive the central business districts, stimulate the return of the middle classes back to cities, and improve the economic climate of central cities. Their programs largely involved a combination of private-sector investment in office structures with public-sector investment in supporting infrastructure.

Those seeking explanations for central city decline often blamed congestion and access problems, and they were especially attracted to the promise of an interstate highway system. Beginning after World War II, truckers, automobile clubs, highway contractors, the automobile industry, engineering associations, and business groups lobbied Congress to provide federal funding for expanded and accelerated highway construction. At the center of their plans stood the interstate highway system, a network of 40,000 miles (eventually 42,500) of limited-access roadway. The advisory committee on a national highway program, headed by retired General Lucius D. Clay, recommended that both national security and the health of the economy depended on rapid construction of the highway network, and in 1956 Congress finally approved the bill. The final legislation provided for federal assumption of 90 percent of the costs of building the interstate highway system, with gasoline tax revenues placed in a highway trust fund to prevent diversion to nonhighway purposes.

The interstate highway system was the nation's largest and costliest public works project ever. The Clay Committee had sold the interstate system to Congress as a carrier of long-haul traffic and a vital component in the defense system, but municipal leaders had visualized the highways as a means to solve traffic congestion problems and to revitalize central business districts. Because highway construction through congested urban areas was exceedingly expensive, cities received a large percentage of the total allocations. The interstate system, however, failed to reverse central city decline. Its construction often destroyed established inner-city neighborhoods, falling with special severity on African-American communities. The interstate carried a great deal of traffic, but only rarely did suburban residents drive it for shopping and recreation located downtown. In fact, it played a key role in continuing and even accelerating the out-migration to the suburbs of businesses and householders. Developers promoted large malls located miles from downtown, usually at the confluence of several interstate highways. Reliance on the interstate system to resuscitate the downtown, then, represented a considerable miscalculation on the part of urban leaders who had been among the system's leading enthusiasts.

Throughout the 1960s, 1970s, and into the 1980s, other urban technological systems, often environmentally related, benefited from federal programs. Under various acts such as the Federal Water Pollution Control or Clean Water Act (1972), federal dollars poured into sewer and sewage treatment projects. Between 1967 and 1977, federal expenditures for sewerage systems increased from $150 million to $4.1 billion and, by 1986, 90 percent of the wastewater treatment plants required to meet the requirements of the Clear Water Act had been constructed. Federal support for urban mass transit was also provided through the Urban Mass Transit Administration, and between 1973 and 1977 federal funds to localities for transit systems grew from $275 million to $1.3 billion. The increasing dependence on Washington for infrastructure dollars, however, resulted in serious problems for states and localities when federal funds were reduced or programs canceled, as occurred in the 1980s under the administrations of Presidents Reagan and Bush.

In the decades since completion of most of the interstate's urban mileage, several overlapping demographic, fiscal, and social trends have shaped the design and location of costly urban technologies. The loss of central city population and the movement to the suburbs continued at a rapid rate, producing decline for the metropolitan region. Accompanying central city losses was a massive regional population shift from the older cities of the Northeast and Midwest toward Sunbelt cities. One of the most important consequences of these population trends has been a decline in tax revenues to support maintenance and renewal of the urban infrastructure.

While the inner city has often experienced dramatic population declines, most sections of the outer city are undergoing a continuing boom, forming a new urban construction called the outer or edge city. Traditional suburbia as well as exurbia have attracted a mass of urban activities that were formerly a central city monopoly. Most prominent in the outer city are the new multiple-purpose centers (or suburban downtowns) such as Naperville, Illinois (northwest of Chicago) or Cumberland/Galleria (in suburban Atlanta), which provide concentrations of retailing, entertainment, and employment activities. In addition, by the 1960s airports had begun to facilitate creation of a host of traditionally downtown-type activities in their normally outer-city locales, including hotels, conference centers, office buildings, and retail shops. Developers located modern industrial parks and distribution centers along airport corridors and in close proximity to the interstate highway system. In many cases, special purpose authorities provided infrastructure systems whose initial capital costs were aided by federal and state funds, leaving users to finance the costs of operation and maintenance.

These outer-city areas, like inner-city central business districts, are very infrastructure dependent, requiring major road systems for effective circulation and power and communications lines to meet not only residential but also commercial and industrial needs. In the outer city, however, development is also quite dispersed, raising important questions concerning the applicability of infrastructure originally developed to fit the needs of a more concentrated environment. New urban forms have evolved, but technological innovation has lagged behind with the exception of advances in telecommunications. One major trend in the 1980s and 1990s was to privatize urban services, or, if they remained public, to impose user fees. Clearly, urban technologies, whether developed and implemented by public or private authorities, will continue to shape the lives of our urban inhabitants and the forms of our metropolitan areas.

—*Joel A. Tarr*

**See also**
Elevators; Telegraph; Telephone; Television; Transportation.
**References**
Armstrong, Ellis L., Michael C. Robinson, and Suellen M. Hoy, eds. *History of Public Works in the United States, 1776–1976.* Chicago: American Public Works Association, 1976.
Condit, Carl W. *Chicago: Building, Planning, and Urban Technology, 1910–1970.* 2 vols. Chicago: University of Chicago Press, 1973–1974.

Hood, Clifton. *722 Miles: The Building of the Subways and How They Transformed New York.* New York: Simon and Schuster, 1993.

McShane, Clay. *Down the Asphalt Path: The Automobile and the American City.* New York: Columbia University Press, 1994.

Ogle, Maureen. *All the Modern Conveniences: American Household Plumbing, 1840–1890.* Baltimore: Johns Hopkins University Press, 1996.

Platt, Harold L. *The Electric City: Energy and the Growth of the Chicago Area, 1880–1930.* Chicago: University of Chicago Press, 1991.

Rose, Mark H. *Cities of Light and Heat: Domesticating Gas and Electricity in Urban America.* University Park: Pennsylvania State University Press, 1995.

Tarr, Joel A., and Gabriel Dupuy, eds. *Technology and the Rise of the Networked City in Europe and America.* Philadelphia: Temple University Press, 1988.

## Urbanization

Urbanization has long been recognized as a major theme in the history of the United States. Standard textbooks have traditionally included a chapter on "the rise of the city" placed after "the closing of the frontier" and before "the United States becomes a world power." The growth of cities and the concentration of population in urban hubs has been seen, then, as a vital element in the progressive triumph of the nation, an element as significant as westward migration and flexing American muscle on the international scene. Defined by historian Blake McKelvey as the "progressive concentration of the population into cities" and "the development of increasingly complex patterns of urbanism," urbanization unquestionably transformed the politics, economy, society, and culture of America.

From the very beginning of European settlement in North America, people have congregated in villages and cities. New York City dates from 1625, and Boston was founded five years later. Yet, during the colonial period, the prevailing tendency was toward the dispersion of population rather than its concentration. It has been estimated that in 1700 about 7.7 percent of the population of the British colonies in North America lived in the five principal port cities of Boston, Massachusetts; Newport, Rhode Island; New York; Philadelphia, Pennsylvania; and Charleston, South Carolina. But by 1760 this figure had dropped to 4.5 percent. Population data for the colonial period are unreliable, but cities clearly did not yet exert a magnetic attraction on rural dwellers. Most newcomers to North America did not seek their fortunes in nascent cities. Instead, they sought to cultivate the rural expanses of the eastern seaboard.

Yet those who did populate the colonial cities were developing new patterns of urban life. Though their city governments initially resembled those of Great Britain, by the middle of the eighteenth century the focus of municipal rule was shifting. Managing the municipal corporation's wharves and other property and regulating markets and trade practices remained significant responsibilities of city government, but municipal records also reveal a growing interest in fire protection, street lighting, and regulating nuisances. Moreover, by the 1760s the residents of colonial America's cities were growing more restive. Frustrated in part by the increasing social and economic inequities of urban life, Boston's mob proved especially unruly, becoming notorious for its protests against the Stamp Act and other policies of the British Parliament. Although no colonial city had more than 40,000 inhabitants at the time of the American Revolution, the small commercial hubs along the Atlantic seaboard proved to be festering sores for the ailing British Empire.

Following the Revolution, the pace of urban growth quickened somewhat, although the new nation remained overwhelmingly rural. From 1790 to 1810, the rate of population growth for towns of 2,500 or more inhabitants far outpaced that of the nation as a whole. Whereas the country's population rose 84 percent, the urban population soared 160 percent. Moreover, during these two decades New York City was already proving to be the most dynamic of the Atlantic seaboard hubs. During the second half of the eighteenth century, Philadelphia had been the largest city in English-speaking North America, but by 1810 New York City had surpassed the Philadelphia metropolitan area. It boasted a population of 96,373, securing it top position on the list of American cities, a position it retained throughout the nineteenth and twentieth centuries.

The pace of urbanization, however, slowed notably during the decade from 1810 to 1820. Reversing the pattern of the previous 20 years, the urban population grew slightly more slowly than the population of the nation as a whole. The War of 1812 disrupted trade in the formerly burgeoning port cities, momentarily inhibiting commercial development and blasting the hopes of profit seekers in urban America. As of 1820, then, still only 7.2 percent of Americans lived in communities with populations over 2,500.

But during the next 40 years, the United States experienced an unprecedented wave of urbanization as millions of newcomers congregated in booming cities. By 1860 the urban population constituted 19.8 percent of the nation's total. In 1820 only two urban areas could boast of more than 100,000 inhabitants; by 1860 there were nine cities in that population category. Philadelphia had surpassed the half-million mark and the population of New York City and Brooklyn combined approached 1.1 million. The completion of the Erie Canal in 1825 ensured that western produce would be funneled into New York City, further fueling its already impressive growth spurt earlier in the century.

Between 1820 and 1860 the wave of urbanization also moved west of the Appalachian Mountains. No longer was location on the Atlantic seaboard a prerequisite for urban growth. Of the twenty largest cities in the United States in 1860, ten were in the Mississippi River valley or Great Lakes basin and one was on the Pacific coast. As steamboat traffic expanded on the inland waterways and millions of farms produced a bountiful surplus for the market, communities along the Mississippi and Ohio Rivers boomed. Moreover, from the 1830s on, the most favorable anchorages along the Great Lakes exploded with thousands of newcomers and hordes of land speculators. By 1860 New Orleans ranked sixth in the nation, followed closely by Cincinnati in seventh place, St. Louis in eighth position, and a booming Chicago ranking ninth. In 1820, Chicago had been a frontier trading post, and as late as 1840 it could claim only 4,470 residents. But in the next two decades its growth was the marvel of the nation, and its population exceeded 109,000 in 1860.

Even more phenomenal was San Francisco. In 1848 it had fewer than 1,000 inhabitants, but four years later, in the wake of the gold rush, its population had risen to almost 35,000. In 1860 the California metropolis had 56,802 residents and already held fifteenth place in the hierarchy of American cities. Deemed by some observers an "instant city," San Francisco was startling evidence of the powerful wave of urbanization that was transforming wilderness sites into major cities almost overnight.

The impact of urbanization, however, was not uniform throughout the nation. Though New Orleans emerged as a leading city, urban growth was least pronounced in the South. Charleston, South Carolina, which ranked as the nation's fifth largest city in both 1800 and 1810, suffered relative stagnation during the half-century before the Civil War. By 1860 it was not even among the twenty largest cities in the United States. In fact, only five of the twenty largest cities were in slave territory; of them, three were in border states and another was the District of Columbia. New Orleans was the only major city in the 11 states of the Confederacy. Thus, a regional pattern had developed that would persist into the twentieth century. The story of urbanization in the South would differ from that in the North, for urban growth would be less pronounced in the nineteenth-century South than in the northern states. The relative decline of Charleston sharply contrasted with the mushrooming of San Francisco and Chicago, reflecting the different regional scenarios of urbanization.

A sharp rise in immigration from Ireland and Germany during the 1830s and 1840s added to the surge of urbanization and flooded the growing cities with newcomers from abroad. Thus, urbanization in nineteenth-century America entailed not only increased population concentration but also a change in the urban ethnic composition. Many impoverished Irish immigrants lacked the resources to move west or acquire farms. Consequently, they tended to cluster in the eastern seaports, taking whatever menial jobs were available. By 1860 both Boston and New York City were heavily Irish. Better-off Germans migrated to interior cities or invested in rural land. Cincinnati, St. Louis, and Milwaukee became centers of Teutonic influence, complete with German schools, singing societies, gymnastic groups, and beer gardens.

The ethnic changes that accompanied mid-nineteenth-century urbanization stirred new tensions and unrest among the urban population. Anti-immigrant riots broke out periodically in Boston and Philadelphia, as native-born city dwellers expressed their distrust and hatred of the newcomers violently. During the 1850s the nativist Know-Nothing political movement had momentary success in one city after another. Even after the Know-Nothing Party had disappeared, ethnic cleavages strongly influenced local politics. The native-born middle class in eastern cities associated the Irish with political corruption and bossism, and in midwestern cities teetotaling American-born residents clashed with imbibing Germans over temperance.

Rapid urbanization not only fostered ethnic animosities, it also exacerbated a number of other long-standing ills. Epidemic disease had swept through colonial cities, but the magnitude of the problem increased as more Americans congregated in urban areas. Disease could spread more readily in population centers where people lived in close proximity to one another. Moreover, sanitary conditions worsened as thousands of newcomers crowded into cities without modern water or sewer systems. Devastating cholera epidemics in 1832 and 1849 made Americans grimly aware of the health hazards in cities. Sewage-laden water supplies facilitated the rapid spread of the disease, which killed thousands of urban dwellers throughout the nation.

Similarly, the problem of fire became more serious in the urbanizing nation. Flames could spread readily among the closely packed buildings of American cities during the mid-nineteenth century. In 1835 a fire swept through lower Manhattan, destroying 674 buildings. In the 1840s both Pittsburgh and St. Louis suffered great fires that devastated the most valuable urban real estate. In the minds of many Americans, violence, disease, and destructive fires were inevitable consequences of the rapid urbanization transforming the United States.

Reacting to these undesirable by-products of urbanization, municipal leaders introduced reforms aimed at making city life more bearable. In the 1850s, the steam-powered fire engine and the paid firefighting force began to supplant hand pumpers and volunteer fire companies in the larger cities. Technology and professionalism seemed to be one answer to the problem of urban fires. Likewise, municipalities seeking to supply urban residents with pure water from rural sources invested in new water systems such as New York

City's Croton Aqueduct. And beginning in the 1840s cities hired 24-hour police forces to replace the traditional night watch. By 1860 many urban police forces had adopted badges, uniforms, and military titles, all symbols of the increased concern for law enforcement in America's troubled cities.

The increased population of America's cities also created a demand for public transportation. Before the 1820s the American city was a walking city with a radius of no more than two miles, and walking was the principal means for getting around these compact hubs. But in the late 1820s, omnibuses began to appear on the streets of New York City, and by 1850 every urban center worthy of mention could claim a fleet of these horse-drawn coaches. For a fare ranging from 5 to 10 cents, urban dwellers could now move about the city without destroying their shoe leather.

In the 1850s, however, a new means of public transportation began to eclipse the omnibus. Horse-drawn streetcars appeared in one city after another. The streetcar moved along iron rails, enabling horses to pull more passengers at higher speeds than the old-fashioned omnibus. By 1860, then, the streetcar era had begun, and one consequence was the physical expansion of cities. No longer dependent on walking, urbanites could live farther from their jobs and the city's shops and markets. Thus, while unprecedented urbanization concentrated population in cities, new means of transportation seemed to pose the possibility of deconcentration in the future.

Though the pace of urbanization in the United States would never again match the phenomenal rate of the 1840s, from 1860 to 1890 the migration to America's cities continued, and the nation grew increasingly urban. Whereas less than 20 percent of the nation's population lived in cities in 1860, by 1890 this figure had surpassed 35 percent. According to the 1890 census, both Chicago and Philadelphia had more than 1 million residents, and New York City and its environs could boast of more than 2.5 million people. In 1860 only 9 American cities had over 100,000 inhabitants; 30 years later, 28 cities were that large. Among these 28 was Denver, a city not even founded until 1858. Booming populations were the norm in cities throughout the country, and few urban centers escaped the flood of newcomers. After experiencing phenomenal growth in the antebellum period, Cincinnati was considered a laggard among the cities of the era after the Civil War; yet even its population rose almost 40 percent between 1870 and 1890. So rapid was the pace of urbanization that a city whose population grew only 20 percent each decade was deemed stagnant.

Despite this pattern of growth, regional discrepancies in urbanization persisted after the Civil War. In 1890, New Orleans was the only city in the 11 states of the former Confederacy with a population over 100,000, and even the great Louisiana metropolis had dropped from sixth rank among the nation's cities in 1860 to the twelfth position 30 years later. Whereas in 1890 more than one-half the population of Massachusetts, Rhode Island, New York, and New Jersey lived in communities larger than 10,000, fewer than 4 percent of the people in North Carolina, Arkansas, and Mississippi lived in such places. In the late nineteenth century, as in the years before the Civil War, urbanization was primarily a northern phenomenon. The nation as a whole was not moving in lockstep toward the cities, and the South remained a region apart.

Influencing urbanization after the Civil War were changes in transportation. During the second half of the nineteenth century, the railroad became the preeminent means of transportation in America, robbing waterways of much of their previous commercial importance. A location on a navigable body of water was no longer a prerequisite for urban growth, as such landlocked cities as Indianapolis, Denver, and Atlanta were to prove in the late nineteenth century. Instead, rail lines were essential elements in the formula for urban growth. Those cities with the best rail connections would win the race for commercial supremacy and population growth. Thus, the nation's greatest rail hub, Chicago, was the wunderkind of the world, doubling its population each decade. Cincinnati and St. Louis, its chief midwestern rivals, owed their initial growth to locations on the Ohio and Mississippi rivers, respectively. As the railroad eclipsed the steamboat, so Chicago eclipsed Cincinnati and St. Louis, establishing itself as the unchallenged capital of mid-America.

Manufacturing also fueled the rapid growth of cities in the late nineteenth century. An increasing portion of the urban population found work in manufacturing, as new shops and factories offered jobs to the millions of migrants converging on America's metropolises. Shoe and clothing manufacturing were especially common in eastern cities, and thousands of clothing workers crowded lofts in Manhattan. The production and fabrication of metals spurred the economies of Pittsburgh, Cleveland, Detroit, and Milwaukee. Chicago was the great meatpacker of the world, and Minneapolis the renowned flour miller. Whereas trade had once been the foundation of America's urban economy and the wholesale merchant the preeminent economic figure, by 1890 manufacturing had supplanted commerce as the principal source of urban prosperity. The production of goods was the mainstay of many cities; the distribution function had become secondary.

Among those working in the new factories were many immigrants from abroad. Between 1870 and 1890, 8 million newcomers arrived in America from other nations, and a large proportion of them congregated in cities. In 1890 over 40 percent of the population of New York City and San Francisco were foreign-born. Germans and Irish still predominated, but by 1890 more Eastern and Southern Europeans were arriving in the largest cities. Italians, Poles, and Czechs were no longer a rarity, as the ethnic composition of American cities became increasingly diverse. Some cities (e.g., Washington, D.C., Indianapolis, and Kansas City) remained overwhelmingly native-born, attracting primarily migrants from rural America, but they were the exceptions to the rule.

Rapid growth, an exploitative factory system, and ethnic diversity together spelled trouble in the minds of many Americans. American cities were growing larger and wealthier, but their success was not an object of unalloyed pride. Increasingly, urbanization was considered one of the greatest problems facing the nation. According to many observers, the burgeoning cities threatened morality, good government, civilization, and the psychological and physical welfare of their citizenry. The massing of people in urban centers seemed fraught with multiple dangers.

For moral reformers the city was the scene of vice and corruption, a place with too many saloons, brothels, and gambling dens. By the close of the nineteenth century, Storyville in New Orleans and the Levee in Chicago had become notorious as vice districts. Such districts seemed to pose a serious threat to the moral rectitude of vulnerable young men coming to the city. To provide wholesome recreation for urban newcomers, moral reformers opened new branches of the Young Men's Christian Association (YMCA) in cities across the country. Throughout the late nineteenth century, upright reformers also sought a viable substitute for the saloon. These drinking establishments often served as workingmen's clubs, filling a social void in the life of the blue-collar male. But in the minds of temperance advocates, the saloon was a prime means by which city life was corrupting the populace and endangering the very future of the nation.

Much to the chagrin of middle-class reformers, saloons were also frequently centers of neighborhood politics, and saloonkeepers had a disproportionate role in municipal government. Many editorials decried the number of liquor sellers who won seats on city councils, lowering the moral and social stature of the municipal legislature. In fact, middle-class Americans repeatedly complained of the baneful effect of urbanization on government in the United States. As people massed in urban hubs, the level of government seemed to decline, with unworthy plebeian barflies securing public office and profiting from it. The saloonkeeping Irish ward boss was a commonplace character in reform diatribes authored by members of the so-called better class. These respectable citizens were not reluctant to express their disgust at the political rise of those they considered to be their social inferiors. The British observer James Bryce summed up the views of his upper-middle-class American acquaintances when he labeled city government "the one conspicuous failure of the United States." Viewing the past through rose-colored glasses, Bryce's American informers contrasted the supposed moral virtue and political rectitude of yesterday's village with the corrupt realities of their present city.

Other admirers of the rural past identified additional dangers arising from rapid urbanization. Some resented the rising power of Roman Catholicism as Catholics from Ireland, Germany, Poland, and Italy eroded the traditional hegemony of Protestantism. The prevalence of foreign tongues and customs also appeared to threaten Anglo-American culture. And the perceived devotion of some immigrants to radical political creeds was thought to endanger property and capital. Rumors of German anarchists and Czech socialists plotting to destroy the existing economic system spread through American cities in the last decades of the nineteenth century.

Urban growth, however, not only seemed to threaten morality, government, religion, and property but also the very sanity of millions of people who congregated in the crowded cities. The fast pace, noise, and tension of urban life supposedly had an insidious effect on the human nervous system. According to some nineteenth-century commentators, urbanization was driving Americans mad. To soothe the jangled nerves of the urban dweller and create a tranquil oasis of rural scenery, municipal fathers in one city after another invested in park systems during the late nineteenth century. Great believers in the tranquilizing effect of natural scenery on harried city residents, landscape architect Frederick Law Olmsted and his partner, Calvert Vaux, designed New York's Central Park in the 1850s. The success of this first major park brought Olmsted other commissions, and by the close of the century he had worked on the development of parks in Chicago, Brooklyn, Boston, Buffalo, Detroit, Hartford, and Louisville.

Moreover, to escape the supposed mental exhaustion caused by city life, an increasing number of affluent Americans were building homes in picturesque suburban communities. In 1868 Olmsted designed Riverside on the outskirts of Chicago, a community of large lots along gently curving streets. The curvilinear pattern of streets was intended to suggest a more leisurely and contemplative way of life, in sharp contrast to the nerve-wracking pace of the big city.

The increasing concentration of population in America's cities seemed to threaten the physical health of urbanites as well as their psychological well-being. A growing corps of public health officials attacked the crowded tenement houses of the eastern cities, and in every major metropolis poor housing and inadequate sanitation continued to pose a health hazard. The Lower East Side of Manhattan was supposedly the most densely populated place in the world with some blocks having more than 800 residents per acre. Thousands jammed into five- or six-story tenement houses, airless structures with few windows and primitive plumbing at best. Bathtubs were a rarity, and streets were the only available play space for the many neighborhood children. During the last decades of the nineteenth century, municipal boards of health stepped up their efforts to fight disease, and after the 1860s periodic cholera epidemics no longer wreaked havoc in American cities. But in the minds of many Americans, health conditions remained deplorable, hideous by-products of rapid urban growth.

Violence and social unrest appeared to be yet another heavy toll exacted by the forces of urbanization. Police departments expanded, and an increasing number of officers patrolled the city streets. But rioting and disorder persisted. Labor unrest proved especially threatening to the existing order. No nineteenth-century city grew as dramatically as Chicago, but this preeminent exemplar of rapid urbanization also achieved international renown for its violence and rioting. In 1886, Chicago's Haymarket Riot unnerved many middle-class Americans and raised new fears of foreign anarchists, who seemed especially numerous in the Illinois metropolis. Then, in 1894, the destructive Pullman Strike reinforced Chicago's reputation as a hotbed of revolution. Rapid urban growth had seemingly destroyed the supposed social harmony of the past and abetted the forces of chaos.

While many Americans increasingly regarded urbanization as a major problem, the fast-growing cities also nurtured some of the marvels of the age. Thus, urbanization produced triumphs as well as trouble. Among them was the skyscraper. In the 1880s builders in Chicago erected the first office structures supported by steel-beam frames, and by 1890 a 21-story behemoth that claimed to be the world's tallest building was rising there. Nothing better symbolized the impact of urbanization than these new skyscrapers. As more people vied for space in the congested downtown, land prices soared, and it became profitable to build skyward. In America's emerging urban areas, people were literally stacked on top of each other. The greater the pressures from urbanization, the higher the buildings rose.

Meanwhile, the department store was retailing's response to urbanization. Marshall Field's in Chicago, Wanamaker's in Philadelphia, and Macy's in New York City offered an unprecedented variety of merchandise in giant emporiums. To the avid shopper, these fascinating bazaars were as impressive manifestations of urban growth and prosperity as the soaring skyscrapers.

Urban growth spawned other wonders as well. In the late nineteenth century, baseball became a professional sport and secured its position as the national pastime. One of the proudest adornments of any big city was a winning baseball team. Even though a city might have fallen behind its rivals in the race for population and commerce, it could partially compensate by defeating its rivals on the baseball diamond. High culture also was a by-product of urbanization as an increasing number of cities sought to prove that they were civilized as well as big. City dwellers sponsored music festivals and raised funds for symphony orchestras. Moreover, they founded art museums in Boston, New York, Chicago, Cincinnati, and Detroit to expose their fellow urbanites to the benefits of the visual arts. Music, painting, and sculpture were deemed antidotes for the ugly maladies fostered by urbanization. The fast-growing cities seemed to breed rampant materialism, class and ethnic hatred, and a general indifference to the commonweal. Art would supposedly tame the crass barbarians of the city and nurture the finer sensibilities threatened by the urban hordes.

Perhaps the ultimate celebration of urban growth in the late nineteenth century was Chicago's Columbian Exposition of 1893. Officially intended to commemorate the five hundredth anniversary of Columbus's landing in America, this world's fair was as much a paean to the marvelous development of Chicago as it was a tribute to the legacy of the Italian explorer. With its grand statuary, noble vistas, gigantic Neoclassical exhibition halls, and entertaining midway, it appeared to sum up in one location all the wonders of America's rapidly emerging urban culture.

Moreover, the Chicago world's fair expressed confidence that Americans could cope with urbanization and create a better city environment. As such, it ushered in an age dedicated to correcting the wrongs of the city. From 1890 to 1920, urban reformers grabbed the headlines in cities across the nation, decrying the flaws of urban society and proposing solutions. The late-nineteenth-century pattern of urban growth persisted in the early twentieth century. A flood of migrants from Europe continued to boost urban populations, and by 1920 a majority of Americans lived in urban places. The tide of urbanization was unabated, but in the years from 1890 to 1920 there was a heightened commitment to confronting the ills arising from this growth. Americans believed something had to be done to solve the problems of the city, and increasingly they believed that something could be done.

An emerging corps of city planning advocates were among those proposing solutions. Rather than tolerating the helter-skelter expansion of cities, a growing number of urban leaders believed that municipal governments should intervene to ensure a more beautiful and efficient city. During the first decade of the twentieth century, the City Beautiful movement won many adherents, and in one city after another those seeking to beautify the urban environment presented plans for grand boulevards, monuments, fountains, and park systems. The Chicago architect Daniel H. Burnham was in the forefront of the City Beautiful cause, preparing influential plans for the improvement of San Francisco and Chicago and serving on commissions for the beautification of Washington, D.C., and the development of a civic center in Cleveland. Burnham and other City Beautiful planners sought to draw together the heterogeneous population of urban America by creating monuments of civic pride that would instill a unifying civic loyalty. Aesthetic harmony would supposedly foster social harmony and quell the chaos wrought by fast-paced urbanization.

City governments employed new tools to realize the benefits of planning. In 1907 Hartford, Connecticut, created the first city planning commission, a municipal agency that would become a fixture in the governmental structure of communities throughout the nation. In 1916 New York City adopted the first comprehensive zoning ordinance, which regulated land use and building heights throughout the metropolis. During the following decade, zoning spread throughout the country as municipal leaders assumed the prerogative of determining which areas would be devoted to commerce and which to residence. Again, the goal was order and harmony to improve the quality of urban life and preserve the value of urban property. Uncontrolled urbanization had supposedly burdened American cities with manifold problems. Through the regulation of urban development, cities could purportedly avoid many of these troubles.

Planning, however, was not the sole panacea for urbanization. Among those who proposed additional reforms was Jane Addams. In 1889 Addams founded Chicago's Hull House, a settlement house that provided a wide variety of educational and social opportunities for poor residents of the city's near West Side. Moreover, the middle-class settlement house workers learned firsthand about the problems of their less affluent brothers and sisters. Basically, Hull House and the hundreds of other settlement houses founded in cities across the nation were intended to bridge the gap between the classes. Rapid urban growth had widened this gap, isolating the social segments of the city and encouraging mutual animosity. The settlement house of the 1890s and early twentieth century would supposedly reunite urban dwellers and remedy the social fragmentation of the city.

Others sought to solve the problem of the city through promoting wholesome recreation and combating vice. In one city after another, reformers successfully advocated the creation of playgrounds in slum neighborhoods, places where children from poor families could enjoy the recreational facilities formerly available only to the more affluent. Meanwhile, committees on public morals and leagues for law and order demanded a crackdown on the "dens of iniquity" that had long flourished in American cities. In 1912, Chicago police closed down the notorious Levee, and five years later New Orleans authorities suppressed prostitution in Storyville. Although temperance forces had never been as successful among urban voters as the rural electorate, a number of city dwellers did yearn for a dry America and supported a Prohibition Amendment to the federal Constitution. Through stringent government action, moral reformers thus endeavored to eradicate the blight of sin that had purportedly accompanied the emergence of the big city.

Many city residents, however, believed that immorality and corruption in the city was simply a by-product of the deplorable living conditions endured by the poor. Sin was just a symptom, and slums were the ultimate problem. In 1890 the crusading New York City photojournalist Jacob Riis published *How the Other Half Lives: Studies among the Tenements of New York*. Riis's exposé opened the eyes of many Americans to urban conditions and heightened demands for tenement house reform. In 1901 New York State enacted a new tenement house law that required a private toilet for each household in newly constructed tenements and a window in every room, thereby ensuring at least a minimum of ventilation and light. Elsewhere, housing reform groups lobbied successfully for similar legislation aimed at raising the housing standards of the urban poor. Some believed that new regulations and tougher legislation were not enough, and some reformers invested in limited-dividend corporations created to build model tenements. In other words, they believed that by foregoing excessive profits, private developers could build low-rent housing and improve the living environment of those deemed victims of urbanization.

City government, though, was the primary focus of reform efforts. Every city had its cadre of crusaders dedicated to fighting the so-called urban bosses and cleansing the body politic. Good-government associations were commonplace, and in 1893 municipal reformers from throughout the country gathered in a convention and organized the National Municipal League.

The reform agenda was long and varied. Some reformers proposed strengthening the office of mayor and limiting the authority of the board of aldermen or city council. Good-government advocates also favored a smaller council elected at-large to replace larger boards elected by ward. This would supposedly limit the opportunity for plebeian saloonkeepers and other representatives of working-class neighborhoods to win a place in the municipal legislature. Under the at-large election scheme, a successful candidate would have to win support from a broad range of the electorate and establish a broad base of various classes from various neighborhoods.

Civil service reform was yet another major goal. Devotees of the merit system sought to reduce the role of the party boss in the hiring of city employees. A system of civil service examinations would purportedly ensure a more professional, less partisan bureaucracy that would administer municipal functions efficiently and effectively.

Some municipal reformers sought to discard the whole mayor-council structure of rule and replace it with the commission plan or city manager government. In 1901 Galveston became the first city to adopt the commission plan. Under this scheme, all legislative and executive authority rested in the hands of a small commission, with each commissioner in charge of a single area of municipal service. Thus, the commissioner of public works would join with the commissioner of public safety and a few other commissioners to run the city. The commissioners would not represent specific wards but would be elected at-large, and consequently the working-class ward boss would have only a muted voice in the operation of urban government. During the second decade of the twentieth century, the city manager plan began to eclipse the popularity of the commission scheme. The city manager plan retained an elected council to determine municipal policy, but a manager appointed by the council had charge of administering city services. This manager was expected to be a nonpartisan professional recruited from outside the community who could apply his expertise to local government.

Through these reforms, urban leaders sought to accommodate the local polity to the changes engulfing America. Rapid urbanization had supposedly rendered the older forms of government obsolete. Saloonkeepers and neighborhood favorites were not adequate to rule the modern big city. Only the best citizens and professional experts could meet the challenges that urbanization posed.

Some reformers not only wanted to revise the structure of urban government, they also sought to expand its role. Most notably a number of crusading mayors believed that city governments had to act to protect urban consumers from grasping public utility companies. Detroit's Hazen Pingree, Cleveland's Tom Johnson, Toledo's Samuel Jones, and Chicago's Edward Dunne attacked streetcar corporations, which monopolized urban transit, and urged municipal ownership of these utilities. During the 1890s the widespread introduction of the electric streetcar had transformed the industry, and by the early twentieth century millions of Americans could travel farther from the city center more rapidly because of this technological advance. But consumers paid a price for the new technology, and many felt the toll was excessive. They thought that in the new age of the big city, a laissez-faire attitude toward utilities was no longer satisfactory. According to Pingree, Johnson, and others, local government had to assume a more activist stance and take control of the vital transportation lines. In most cases, the utility corporations blocked efforts to achieve municipal ownership, but thousands of urban voters believed that urbanization necessitated greater government control over private business.

Between 1890 and 1920, then, the problems of the city seemed more tractable. Americans increasingly believed that something could and should be done. Not every reform produced the intended results, and reformers' expectations often exceeded realities. But Americans were making a strenuous effort to tame the beast of urbanization.

By the 1920s and 1930s, however, some new trends became evident. Whereas urbanization had previously transformed the Northeast and Midwest, the most dramatic growth now appeared in the South and Southwest. During the 1920s the five metropolitan areas with the fastest rates of population growth were Miami, Los Angeles, Oklahoma City, Houston, and San Diego. Moreover, 18 of the 25 metropolitan districts with the highest rates of population increase were in the former Confederacy, California, or Oklahoma. *Sunbelt* was a term coined in the 1960s, but as early as the 1920s Americans were witnessing the phenomenon of rapid growth along the country's southern fringe. In 1920 Houston was the forty-fifth largest city in the United States; by 1940 it ranked twenty-first. Los Angeles rose from tenth position to fifth. After decades of only moderate urban development, the predominantly rural South was finally feeling the impact of migration to cities. In 1900 only 18 percent of southerners lived in urban places; 40 years later almost 37 percent did so. By 1940 a majority of Floridians were urban dwellers and over 40 percent of Louisiana and Texas residents lived in cities.

Meanwhile, in many older urban areas, new forces of deconcentration were becoming more powerful than those of concentration. The advent of the automobile encouraged a new wave of suburbanization as many Americans left central cities for outlying municipalities removed from the soot, smoke, and class and ethnic discord of urban hubs. Whereas in 1920, 66 percent of America's metropolitan population lived in central cities, 20 years later the figure had dropped to 62.7 percent. *The Suburban Trend,* published in 1925 by Harlan Paul Douglass, recorded this new demographic pattern. Moreover, like many of his contemporaries, Douglass believed this suburban trend a desirable alternative to the horrors of urbanization. "A crowded world must be either suburban or savage," Douglass concluded. Fortunately, the centripetal forces of urbanization finally appeared to be losing ground to a centrifugal tendency to move beyond the central city limits and find a new way of life that combined the best of city and country.

In fact, during the 1930s the forces of urbanization seemed to be waning and losing their long-standing grip on the nation. In the United States as a whole, the proportion of people living in urban places rose only 0.3 percent, the smallest gain recorded since 1820. During the 1930s, for the first time since the federal government had begun to collect population figures in 1790, the percentage of people living in urban places actually declined in New England. The urban population lost ground to rural dwellers in the Middle Atlantic and East North Central regions as well. As more people in Massachusetts, New York, Pennsylvania, Ohio, and Michigan abandoned cities in favor of unincorporated areas, they boosted the rural population and reversed what had seemed to be an irreversible trend toward urbanization.

Real estate developers exploited the growing anti-urban sentiment, spreading the suburban gospel in brochures and newspaper advertisements. Advertising copy exalted the clean air, sunshine, and sylvan tranquillity of suburbs. Page after page of ads emphasized the nonurban advantages available to prospective homeowners within commuting distance of the big city. Moreover, developers effused about the "good neighbors" found in suburban villages. These outlying communities were intended to be socially and ethnically homogeneous, places of refuge for like-minded respectable citizens who sought to avoid the undesirables of the city. Throughout the 1920s and 1930s, real estate brokers presented and sold suburban communities as havens from the big city and the worst effects of urbanization.

Less mercenary promoters shared these anti-urban biases. At the turn of the century, the British idealist Ebenezer Howard had formulated the concept of the garden city, a community of limited size that seemingly combined the best of both town and country. By the 1920s Howard's ideas were winning adherents in the United States. In 1928–1929 garden city enthusiasts laid out Radburn in northern New Jersey. Though the community fell short of expectations, in part because of the Depression of the 1930s, it reflected the growing interest among intellectuals as well as entrepreneurs in an alternative to the existing city.

During the 1930s, some New Deal programs similarly promoted an alternative to existing cities. Under the leadership of Rexford Tugwell, the Resettlement Administration created subsistence homestead communities across the nation. These provided mini-farms where part-time industrial workers could supplement their wages with homegrown produce. Since the depressed manufacturing sector no longer provided enough jobs, the Resettlement Administration believed that blue-collar workers needed to return to the land and support themselves partly through small-scale farming. Tugwell's agency also sponsored the greenbelt communities program. Influenced by the ideas of Ebenezer Howard, the Resettlement Administration built three greenbelt towns. These were outlying communities surrounded by a green belt of farms and forests. In Tugwell's mind, deconcentration was

*The growth of suburbs like Levittown on Long Island, New York, has become an important part of urban development in the twentieth century.*

an answer to the nation's ills. Government agencies should tear down urban slums and move the residents to subsistence homesteads and outlying communities where they could escape the miseries wrought by massive urbanization.

America's most innovative and outspoken architect shared this anti-urban attitude and proposed a futuristic scheme for a radically different mode of settlement. In 1932, in *The Disappearing City*, Frank Lloyd Wright presented his Broadacre City scheme. With only 1,400 families inhabiting its 16 square miles, the proposed community was a sprawling mixture of town and country and expressed Wright's rejection of the centripetal forces of urbanization that had transformed the United States in the nineteenth and early twentieth centuries. Dispersion of population, rather than concentration, characterized the great architect's utopia. Though no developer ever literally translated the Broadacre plan into reality, Wright's ideals reflected an anti-urban bias that many shared and that would influence the metropolitan future. For Wright and others, the city was not just a problem; it was a failure that was best discarded.

After World War II, the prewar pattern of urbanization persisted. The pace of urban growth was most dramatic in the Sunbelt, and cities in the South and Southwest continued rising on the list of America's largest metropolises. By 1970, 11 of the 30 largest American cities were in the former Confederacy or the Southwest. Los Angeles had moved up to third place, Houston ranked sixth, and Dallas was the eighth largest city in the nation. In 1950, 48.6 percent of the South's population was urban; 20 years later 64.6 percent lived in cities. In every Confederate state at least 40 percent of the people were urban dwellers. According to the federal census, then, the South, like the rest of the nation, had become predominantly urban, with only a few states such as Mississippi and South Carolina still having a rural majority.

During the middle of the twentieth century, urbanization also transformed the way of life of African Americans. From the early twentieth century on, blacks migrated from the rural South to cities in both the North and South. The shift to urban areas, however, was especially marked in the 1940s and 1950s. In 1910, only 8 percent of African Americans resided in one of the nation's 25 largest cities; by 1960, 32 percent did so. More than 1 million blacks lived in New York City, and there were 810,000 African Americans in Chicago and over 500,000 in Philadelphia. Although 75 percent of blacks were rural in 1910, 50 years later 72 percent lived in cities. In fact, a higher proportion of blacks lived in urban areas than did whites.

While the South was growing more urban and African Americans were migrating in large numbers to urban hubs, many of the older central cities in the Northeast and Midwest experienced declining populations. Ringed by suburban

municipalities and unable to annex outlying territory, these cities suffered the consequences of continuing migration to suburbs. Of the nation's ten largest cities in 1950, eight lost population during the next two decades. Between 1950 and 1970, the population of St. Louis plummeted 27 percent, Pittsburgh's head count fell 23 percent, and the number of Boston's inhabitants dropped 20 percent. The trend toward deconcentration evident in the 1920s and 1930s was accelerating, leaving the historic hubs with fewer people and lower ranks in the hierarchy of American cities. In 1950, St. Louis was the eighth largest city in the nation; 20 years later it ranked eighteenth. Meanwhile, Pittsburgh dropped from twelfth to twenty-fourth, Buffalo from fifteenth to twenty-eighth, and Minneapolis from seventeenth to thirty-second.

While this trend toward population dispersion was depopulating central city neighborhoods, it sharply increased the pace of growth in surrounding suburbs. During the two decades following World War II, developers transformed thousands of pastures and cornfields into housing subdivisions, and builders erected millions of single-family dwellings. In the course of a few years, rural villages became suburban cities. Whereas 57 percent of the metropolitan area population of the United States lived in central cities and only 43 percent resided outside these cities in 1950, 20 years later the central city component had fallen to 46 percent and the outlying proportion had risen to 54 percent, almost a precise reversal. In other words, by 1970 a majority of metropolitan area Americans lived in the suburbs. The United States was neither predominantly urban nor predominantly rural. Instead, the largest segment of the population was suburban.

Accompanying this boom in residential development along the metropolitan fringe was an outward flow of business. During the 1950s, suburban shopping centers transformed retailing, bringing branches of downtown stores to outlying areas. Once primarily a downtown experience, shopping was becoming increasingly a suburban phenomenon. In the late 1960s and early 1970s the proliferation of enclosed malls anchored by major department stores accelerated the centrifugal flow of retail dollars. By 1970 fewer shoppers found it necessary to travel downtown; one could find ample merchandise much closer to home in a suburban mall.

Jobs also migrated to the suburbs. During the post–World War II era, manufacturers were abandoning multistory mill buildings in the central cities for sprawling one-story structures better adapted to modern assembly-line production. Moreover, they were increasingly dependent on truck transportation and needed space for employee parking. Industrialists thus turned to the open spaces of suburbia where ample land was available for low-rise buildings and parking lots, and where trucks did not have to battle traffic on narrow central city streets. In one suburb after another, developers laid out

*An important part of urbanization in the twentieth century has been the growth of suburbs, which attract families with backyard activities such as barbecuing, playing, swimming, and socializing.*

industrial parks to attract manufacturing plants, and by 1970 the bedroom suburb inhabited primarily by commuters to the central city was disappearing. An increasing number of Americans did more than sleep in the suburbs; they also shopped and worked there.

The loss of people, jobs, and retail dollars alarmed central city leaders, and during the years from 1945 to 1970 they launched a counterattack to reverse the prevalent wave of dispersion. In order to bolster the central business district's traditional position as the metropolitan hub, they advocated a system of expressways radiating from the downtown. Just as all streetcar lines had once converged on the central business district, now all the great automobile arteries would also meet there. Financed in large part with federal funds, these superhighway systems were constructed during the 1950s and 1960s, cutting large swaths through older neighborhoods but providing multilane access to the urban core. The automobiles that had been agents of deconcentration would now supposedly prove a means for achieving a reconcentration of urban America.

To further bolster the aging hubs, central cities also embarked on urban renewal programs. Again with large-scale funding from Washington, local renewal authorities bulldozed supposedly blighted areas in the core as a necessary step in revitalization. Once cleared, this land would be available for private developers who supposedly would erect office buildings, apartments, and stores that would reverse the flow of population and money to the suburbs.

Neither the superhighway program nor the urban renewal efforts succeeded, however, in reversing the outward trend. Despite the new superhighways converging on the core, American consumers did not flock back to downtown stores, restaurants, or movie theaters. Instead, the outer-belt freeways, constructed to allow bothersome interstate truck traffic to bypass cities, attracted an increasing number of businesses. Thus, outlying highways proved to have a magnetic attraction for commerce while the centripetal links converging on downtown failed to funnel the bulk of suburban dollars into the central business district. Likewise, many urban renewal sites remained vacant for years as the expected investors did not materialize. Many new downtown structures did arise, and during the 1960s one city after another experienced a boom in the construction of high-rise office buildings and hotels. But the much ballyhooed renaissance of some cities was misleading. Developers were investing in the central business district, but the prevailing trend was still outward. The deconcentration of urban America remained unabated.

In fact, by the early 1970s some experts on urban America were writing about the counterurbanization of the nation. The demographic wave had reversed, and urbanization seemed to be a phenomenon of the past. Certainly the census data demonstrated a continuing dispersion of population. Northeastern and midwestern central cities continued to lose population and drop in rank among America's urban hubs. By the mid 1990s St. Louis ranked only forty-third among the nation's cities, Pittsburgh forty-fifth, Cincinnati forty-sixth, and Minneapolis forty-seventh. On the other hand, cities in the South and Southwest continued to advance in the urban hierarchy. Six of the ten largest cities were in California, Texas, or Arizona, and little-known newcomers such as Virginia Beach, Virginia, and Mesa, Arizona, were moving up the list, surpassing the major hubs of the past. Migration to the suburbs and the Sunbelt remained the most important demographic fact of American life.

During the last three decades of the twentieth century, the shift of jobs and retailing to the suburbs also proceeded uninterrupted. Office parks joined industrial parks in the suburbs, and millions of executives, accountants, and secretaries no longer commuted to the central city; instead, they found employment on the metropolitan fringe. Shopping malls became a magnet for freshly minted office buildings and hotels, and new outlying "downtowns" appeared in metropolitan areas across the country. In the typical American metropolis, there was no longer a single commercial focus; instead, there were multiple nuclei of business, reflecting the ongoing suburbanization of population and money. Given this migration of commerce to the fringe, many observers questioned the continued validity of the term *suburb*. The so-called suburb had become a center of business and employment in its own right and was no longer a subordinate satellite of a dominant central city downtown. Commentators referred to the new pattern of settlement as postsuburban and labeled the emerging hubs of the late twentieth century "edge cities" and "technoburbs." Reality no longer conformed to the traditional concepts of city and suburb, and a new lexicon was needed to describe the demographic patterns of the United States.

In fact, by the last decades of the twentieth century the whole notion of urbanization seemed increasingly anachronistic. The sharp line that had differentiated urban and rural in the nineteenth and early twentieth centuries had grown so blurred that it was almost indistinguishable. The American population was spread across the countryside with millions of people living and working in areas that failed to conform to traditional definitions. In scattered enclaves such as Manhattan an urban milieu survived, but only a minority of Americans actually experienced this environment. Likewise, rural America survived, remote and isolated, in a few areas such as the prairies of North Dakota. But relatively few people experienced this either. The majority of Americans lived in nonurban metropolitan areas, and urbanization was no longer drawing them into densely populated hubs. Migration continued and business clustered in certain choice locations. But the linear freeway had a stronger attraction for commerce and investment dollars than the old-fashioned downtown hub. Highway sprawl had become the prevailing pattern of development rather than urban concentration. Broadacre City was no longer a futuristic utopia; it more closely resembled a blueprint of the present.

At the close of the twentieth century, then, the age of urbanization in the United States had come to a close. The concept was no longer relevant for a nation that was metropolitan but not urban. Unimaginative data collectors in the Bureau of the Census still embraced the outdated concepts of urban and rural, but such concepts masked rather than illuminated reality. The urban frontier had closed, and the term *urbanization* should have been retired to that conceptual attic frequented primarily by students of the past.

—*Jon C. Teaford*

**References**

Brownell, Blaine A., and David R. Goldfield. *Urban America: A History.* 2d ed. Boston: Houghton Mifflin, 1990.

Chudacoff, Howard P., and Judith E. Smith. *The Evolution of American Urban Society.* 4th ed. Englewood Cliffs, NJ: Prentice-Hall, 1994.

McKelvey, Blake. *American Urbanization: A Comparative History.* Glenview, IL: Scott, Foresman, 1973.

Monkkonen, Eric H. *America Becomes Urban: The Development of U.S. Cities and Towns, 1780–1980.* Berkeley: University of California Press, 1988.

Teaford, Jon C. *Cities of the Heartland: The Rise and Fall of the Industrial Midwest.* Bloomington: Indiana University Press, 1993.

———. *The Twentieth-Century American City.* Baltimore: Johns Hopkins University Press, 1993.

Weber, Adna Ferrin. *The Growth of Cities in the Nineteenth Century: A Study in Statistics.* New York: Macmillan, 1899.

## U.S. Housing Authority

The United States Housing Act of 1937 established the United States Housing Authority (USHA) to create a permanent public housing program. It followed the experimental public housing programs of the Housing Division of the Public Works Administration (PWA) and, like its predecessor, was placed under the direction of the Department of the Interior. The purpose of the USHA was to make grants, long-term loans, and annual contributions to local public housing authorities to develop, acquire, and manage low-income housing and slum clearance projects. Establishment of the USHA was a major triumph for supporters of public housing, who also persuaded President Franklin D. Roosevelt to appoint their candidate, Nathan Straus, to head the Authority. Straus in turn hired such leading public housers as Catherine Bauer, Boris Shishkin, and Warren Vinton.

Improving on the PWA's slow rate of production, the USHA and local housing authorities were developing over 50,000 units per year by 1939. By mid-1941, the USHA had begun or completed construction of over 132,000 dwelling units.

The USHA experienced serious problems, however, which prevented the public housing program from being successful in the United States. Bureaucratic rigidity hampered its operations. The Washington office of the USHA imposed numerous regulations concerning architecture, building costs, and limits on tenant incomes. These rules alienated local housing authorities and discouraged imaginative designs. Although the USHA financed no tall elevator buildings outside of New York City, most USHA projects had a recognizably uniform and grim appearance.

In addition, Straus was an arrogant and abrasive administrator, who quarreled with key staffers and alienated congressmen so much that Roosevelt suggested that Straus avoid Capitol Hill altogether. His inability to develop good relations with Congress became critical after conservative victories in the congressional elections of 1938, 1940, and 1942. Not until 1949 did Congress approve any additional funds for the public housing program.

In January 1942, Roosevelt succeeded in forcing Straus to resign, and later that year he combined the USHA with other federal housing agencies into a consolidated organization, the National Housing Agency. In 1947, control of its operations were shifted to the Housing and Home Finance Agency, now the Department of Housing and Urban Development.

—*Alexander von Hoffman*

### References
Biles, Roger. "Nathan Straus and the Failure of Public Housing, 1937–1942." *The Historian* 53 (1990): 33–46.
Keith, Nathaniel S. *Politics and the Housing Crisis since 1930.* New York: Universe Books, 1973.
Straus, Nathan. *The Seven Myths of Housing.* New York: Knopf, 1944.

## Utopian Towns and Communities

The New World has proven to be a fertile ground for utopian experimentation, both religious and secular. While certain religious groups formed utopian communities in the eighteenth century and the formation of such communities continues to this day, the period of greatest enthusiasm for these experimental forms was the first half of the nineteenth century. One of the first to arrive were the Shakers, sometimes thought to have been named because their body movements resembled a kind of ecstatic dance when they were praying,

other times thought to have been named by contracting "Shaking" with "Quakers." Ann Lee and her eight followers moved to New York State in 1774 and proclaimed a Millennial Church, a belief that Christ had come a second time in female form, and that celibacy would prepare his followers for the coming millennium. Attracting a number of followers, the Shakers formed 18 communities in New England and the frontier West. These communities became quite successful economically, but their inability to attract new members after the Civil War meant an inevitable decline, especially given their beliefs.

Three other religious communities originated from German pietistic groups: the Rappites, the Separatists of Zoar, and the Amana Colony (the Community of True Inspiration). The Rappites, led by George Rapp, came from Wurtemberg in 1804 and established Harmony, Pennsylvania. They moved on to Harmony, Indiana, in 1815, but left ten years later because they feared corruption by success and moved to Economy, Ohio. The Separatists of Zoar, led by Joseph Michael Bimeler, came to Zoar, Ohio, from Bavaria, Wurtemberg, and Baden in 1817. The two groups held similar universalistic and antisacramental views; both declined after their founders died. Not so the Amana Society, made up of migrants from the Rhineland, who built Ebenezer, a community near Buffalo, New York, in 1843. Fearing the attractions of that area, they moved to eastern Iowa in the 1850s, where they prospered and maintained communal living until the group became a cooperative in 1932.

An even more successful religious community was Oneida, founded in 1839 by John Humphrey Noyes in Putney, Vermont. Noyes had become a Christian perfectionist who believed in shared property, but his advocacy of "complex marriage" scandalized the larger community and forced Noyes to move to Oneida. The community prospered first by making steel traps and later silverplated flatware. It became a corporation in 1881.

Two very short-lived utopian communities are famous because of their association with the reform impulse of the 1840s. One was Hopedale, founded by Adin Ballow, a Universalist minister, in Milford, Massachusetts, in 1841. Designed to promote "practical Christianity" through social reform, Hopedale lasted 15 years. Even more short-lived was Brook Farm in Roxbury, Massachusetts, probably the most famous utopian experiment in American history. George Ripley, a former Unitarian minister and editor of the *The Dial,* the principal journal of the Transcendentalists, and other Transcendentalists envisioned a society where they could create "a more natural union between intellectual and manual labor than now exists." These ideas attracted a number of prominent literary figures, including Nathaniel Hawthorne and Bronson Alcott as residents and Ralph Waldo

Emerson and Margaret Fuller as frequent visitors. Within two years, Ripley had been attracted by the social theories of François-Marie-Charles Fourier, which resembled those of Brook Farm in their social and organizational structures and ideals. Like Fourier, Ripley advocated working in organized groups rather than individually and thought that all members should live together in a single building called a "phalanstery." In 1844, despite objections from some of the residents, Brook Farm was renamed the Brook Farm Phalanx, Fourier's term for that kind of group. The reorganization of Brook Farm accelerated its financial problems, and it formally disbanded in 1847.

Brook Farm was not the first completely secular utopian community in the United States. In 1825, Robert Owen, a British industrialist and social reformer, bought Rapp's community and renamed it New Harmony. Here he tried to realize his principles of fair labor, intellectual stimulation, and improved education. The experiment lasted only two years. More famous than New Harmony were other Fourieristic "phalanxes"; they were designed to promote the ideas that labor was the ultimate source of wealth and that all humans had an equal right to property. Although Fourier never came to America, his ideas were popularized by Albert Brisbane in the 1840s and resulted in the formation of several dozen phalanxes. None lasted very long because of the appeal of the speculative society around them.

That religious utopian communities lasted longer than secular ones seems to have resulted from the charisma of their leaders. Nor did the demise of so many of these communities end experiments with communal life. Utopian societies continued to emerge after the Civil War and continue to do so.

—*Dwight W. Hoover*

**See also**
Bellamy, Edward.
**References**
Fogarty, Robert S. *All Things New: American Communes and Utopian Movements, 1860–1914.* Chicago: University of Chicago Press, 1990.
Guarneri, Carl J. *The Utopian Alternative: Fourierism in Nineteenth-Century America.* Ithaca, NY: Cornell University Press, 1991.
Harrison, John F. C. *The Second Coming: Popular Millenarianism, 1780–1850.* London: Routledge & Kegan Paul, 1979.
Hayden, Dolores. *Seven American Utopias: The Architecture of Communitarian Socialism, 1790–1875.* Cambridge, MA: MIT Press, 1976.
Lasky, Melvin. *Utopia and Revolution: On the Origins of a Metaphor.* Chicago: University of Chicago Press, 1976.
Manuel, Frank E., and Fritzie P Manuel. *Utopian Thought in the Western World.* Cambridge, MA: Harvard University Press, 1979.
Veysey, Laurence. *The Communal Experience: Anarchist and Mystical Counter-Cultures in America.* New York: Harper & Row, 1973.

## Vaudeville

In the first two decades of the twentieth century, vaudeville was the unrivaled sovereign of American entertainment, boasting some 2,000 theaters scattered throughout the United States and Canada that played nothing else. At its height in the early 1920s, vaudeville was seen by 1.6 million men, women, and children daily, and more than 12,000 performers played on the vaudeville circuits—no surprise considering that it was one of the highest-paid professions in the world. Remarkably, no matter where a vaudeville performance was seen, from Boston to Los Angeles, it had a recognizable character, style, and form—a type of entertainment that had formulated a consistency and a loyalty to a set structure—the vaudeville bill.

Vaudeville descended from the nineteenth century theater forms of the minstrel show and the saloon burlesque. The solidifying of vaudeville as a new theatrical form with corporate control and regulations resulted from the work of three dominant figures: Tony Pastor (who cleaned up the acts and opened his theater/saloon to women and children) and B. F. Keith and E. F. Albee, two museum theater operators who developed the vaudeville bill, created a national corporation, and established the circuit that linked vaudeville houses to a central booking agency.

The goal of Keith and Albee was to enhance the appeal of vaudeville and provide an entertainment whose structure satisfied metropolitan audiences. They accomplished this by offering a bill consisting of nine acts, all able to be presented twice a day. The diversity and number of these acts helped broaden vaudeville's commercial marketability.

Albee recognized early that "New York tastes" and theatrical uniformity were the keys to profit. Yet in spite of his monetary concerns and his ruthless management of performers, Albee deserves credit for ensuring that vaudeville's best talent and brightest stars appeared in all cities. For performers, the rule was simple: if you were going to play the Keith-Albee circuit, you played vaudeville theaters in every city that had one. This imposed the hardship of travel on the actors, and it also demanded their adaptation to the tastes and morals of each city and town. However, most vaudevillians resigned themselves to the road because it was "big time" and paid well.

As the West grew and industrialized, more cities became viable centers of cultural distribution. People left farms for cities to become laborers, domestics, clerks, and even professionals. With the increasing number of people gainfully employed, a demand for more leisure-time outlets arose. Vaudeville was there to meet the demand, and it became an integral part of urban entertainment.

According to historian Albert McLean, the most successful vaudeville theaters were generally located near metropolitan areas. The quality of a city's vaudeville offerings were shaped by the population, economic life, and social structure of a city (small towns = limited facilities = small-time vaudeville = limited talents). The local cultural values and moral perceptions of a town's patrons were reflected and revealed in their reactions and acceptance of certain vaudeville acts (nonverbal acts were popular in small towns). Sex appeal became more acceptable in metropolitan areas as humorous ethnic portrayals lost favor. Continuous vaudeville performances throughout the day harmonized with a city's round-the-clock employment schedules.

McLean observes that there were definite relationships between a city's population, industrial expansion, and the emergence of new theaters. In sheer numbers, there was extensive growth. In 1901, *Billboard* listed 12 vaudeville theaters in New York, 34 elsewhere in the East, 7 in Chicago, 24 elsewhere in the Midwest and the South, and 2 on the West Coast. These theaters needed 650 to 700 acts a year, and they drew them from a supply of 1,500. Within five years, the figures doubled.

By using railroads for travel and handling bookings by telegraph and telephone, the Keith-Albee organization tightly controlled the movement and employment of vaudeville acts. The New York office regulated most of the complex financial aspects of the system, but ultimate responsibility and decisions about the bill rested with the manager of each individual theater. It was felt that the manager better knew what acts would "sell" in his area. He was often a successful businessman who was active in the political, social, and cultural affairs of the community, and it was thought that a manager's reputation could bring respectability to vaudeville in places where it had been morally suspect.

One man who understood the circuits better than either Keith or Albee was a former local manager from the West Coast, Martin Beck. Unlike Albee, who was disliked by vaudeville performers, Beck sought to better their treatment and improve theater facilities. Beck also hoped that vaudeville would develop "class," patterned after the best in New York. Beck joined Morris Meyerfield, another entrepreneur, and together they founded the Orpheum chain, which included 17 houses between Chicago and California.

The Orpheum was the only successful big-time vaudeville circuit in the East other than the original Keith-Albee circuit. It boasted some of the best and newest theater technology, and it paid top salaries to performers. Beginning with the original Orpheum theater in San Francisco, Beck opened houses up and down the West Coast. One of Beck's crowning achievements was the Los Angeles Orpheum (still standing, though used for different purposes), where every major vaudeville star appeared at least once.

The leading vaudeville center outside of New York was Chicago. All the major vaudeville circuits (including the Orpheum and Keith-Albee) and several smaller ones (the Bert Levy circuit, the Gus Sun Booking Exchange, and others) booked acts there. Chicago was also the railway stopping-off point en route to many smaller towns that booked acts through the Western Vaudeville Managers Association. In spite of the city's weather, most vaudeville performers liked playing Chicago because audiences were so receptive.

Every city of any size, from Lowell, Massachusetts, to Knoxville, Tennessee, and from Toronto, Ontario, to Los Angeles, California, had at least one major theater owned and managed by Keith-Albee or Orpheum. Generally, these theaters accommodated 1,200 to 1,600 spectators. The Orpheum boasted the largest capacities, ranging from 916 in Champaign, Illinois, to 2,774 at the State-Lake theater in Chicago. The average seating for the Orpheum circuit theaters was approximately 1,500.

From 1925 to 1932 vaudeville rapidly declined from its position as one of America's most successful entertainment forms. The invention of radio, increased popularity of motion pictures (spurred by the invention of the "talkie" by 1927), stagnation of creativity, rising costs, and a lack of foresight all contributed to vaudeville's demise. By the end of 1928 only four theaters in the United States were playing vaudeville without film—Keith's in Philadelphia, Chicago's Palace, the Palace in New York, and the Orpheum in Los Angeles. By 1932 the Mecca of vaudeville, New York's Palace, had itself become strictly a theater for film. This was the final blow to vaudeville, indicating to the rest of the country that even New York, long recognized as the center of vaudeville, had capitulated to the new form of entertainment. This marked the definite end of the vaudeville era.

—Stan Singer

**See also**
Brice, Fanny; Burlesque; Nickelodeons.
**References**
Cahn, Julius. *Julius Cahn's Official Theatrical Guide.* New York: Empire Theater Building, 1909–1919.
Di Meglio, John E. *Vaudeville USA.* Bowling Green, OH: Bowling Green University Popular Press, 1973.
Gilbert, Douglas. *American Vaudeville: Its Life and Times.* New York: McGraw-Hill, 1940.
Green, Abel, and Joe Laurie, Jr. *Show Biz: From Vaude to Video.* New York: Holt, Rinehardt and Winston, 1951.
McLean, Albert F., Jr. *American Vaudeville as Ritual.* Lexington: University of Kentucky Press, 1965.
Sobel, Bernard. *A Pictorial History of Vaudeville.* New York: Citadel Press, 1961.

## Veiller, Lawrence Turnure (1872–1959)

Lawrence Veiller was the Progressive Era's most influential advocate of restrictive tenement house legislation, and more than any other individual, he was responsible for abolition of the dumbbell tenement in New York City. He illustrates a particular type of Progressive Era activist—the technician as reformer.

Veiller was born in Elizabeth, New Jersey, and graduated from City College in New York City. During the depression of 1893, he worked with the East Side Relief Work Committee, and this experience convinced him that the primary target of any attack on poverty had to be housing. He believed that everybody deserved minimum standards of safety and sanitation in their residence and that government had to mandate the standards. In 1898, at Veiller's urging, the New York Charity Organization Society (COS) formed a Tenement House Committee with Veiller as its secretary and executive officer. The committee's chief concern was New York's notorious dumbbell tenements, ubiquitous buildings of five or six stories consisting of front and rear apartments connected by halls and featuring narrow air shafts as the only source of light and air for many tenants.

In 1900, after he had schooled himself in building practices and the intricacies of building codes, Veiller organized a Tenement House Exhibition sponsored by the COS. Its photographs, maps, and cardboard models illustrated New York City's densely populated immigrant working-class neighborhoods at their worst. Governor Theodore Roosevelt of New

York viewed the exhibition, and he and Veiller successfully used the show's publicity to seek restrictive legislation prohibiting construction of dumbbells in the future. The Tenement House Law of 1901 was Veiller's greatest triumph.

The law's requirements for light and air ended the construction of dumbbells and created a Tenement House Department to enforce it. Veiller was a deputy commissioner of the department during the reform administration of Mayor Seth Low (1902–1903), and he directed the efficient enforcement of the law. His term expired with Low's defeat in 1903, but he continued to head COS efforts to resist builders' attempts to modify the law. In 1916, when the COS surrendered and accepted a law permitting air shafts in private homes that had been converted to tenements for three families, Veiller resigned from the COS Tenement House Committee in protest.

Recognizing the need for organized opposition to slum housing throughout the country, Veiller persuaded the Russell Sage Foundation to establish the National Housing Association (NHA) in 1910, and he became its director. From that position, Veiller emerged as the country's most influential housing reformer. His books, *A Model Tenement House Law, Housing Reform,* and *A Model Housing Law,* guided reformers as they drafted and implemented restrictive housing legislation. Most tenement house laws bore his imprint in one way or another.

Veiller quickly outlived his youthful radical reputation. He considered housing reform to be a kind of social control; society, he thought, would not be safe while millions of people lived in substandard, unhealthful housing. Restrictive legislation marked the limit, rather than the beginning, of his reform impulse. He derided private model housing schemes as too few and wasteful. The building industry could provide housing for the poor; regulation alone would ensure minimum standards. Veiller opposed public housing throughout his life, but this did not differentiate him from most Progressive reformers. But by the 1920s, as the building industry proved unable to produce enough adequate low-income housing, many reformers began calling for a stronger, more direct government role. Veiller disagreed, and several former colleagues increasingly considered him irrelevant to housing reform. As early as the 1920s, John Ihlder, his former field secretary at the NHA, called him "the greatest handicap to housing in America." Although Veiller criticized New Deal housing programs, that did not diminish his prior accomplishments as the nation's premier advocate for legislating minimum standards of safety and sanitation in urban housing.

—*John F. Sutherland*

**See also**
Dumbbell Tenement; Tenement.

**References**
Jackson, Anthony. *A Place Called Home: A History of Low-Cost Housing in Manhattan.* Cambridge, MA: MIT Press, 1976.
Lubove, Roy. *The Progressives and the Slums: Tenement House Reform in New York City, 1890–1917.* Pittsburgh, PA: University of Pittsburgh Press, 1962.
Plunz, Richard. *A History of Housing in New York City: Dwelling Type and Social Change in the American Metropolis.* New York: Columbia University Press, 1990.
Sutherland, John F. "A City of Homes: Philadelphia Slums and Reformers, 1880–1918." Ph.D. dissertation, Temple University, 1973.

## Villages

A village, a focal place in rural space, connotes neither country nor city, but something in between. It expresses community, exclusivity, and mutual obligation. Community, exclusivity, and obligation are the supposed virtues of a village, which for many people sustain interest in villages as places of settlement separate from country and city today.

Villages form part of a settlement-size continuum and hierarchy of interconnected service centers: homestead to hamlet to village to town to city. Each offers a larger and more complex, or higher-order, set of economic, social, and political functions and houses an increasingly larger population than the one below it. Of these places, homesteads, hamlets, and villages are the least urban. Villages are largely a preurban settlement form, though many were proto-urban and eventually represented anti-urbanism as well. Town, in contrast, has often been used interchangeably with large village and with small city to connote something separate and different from country.

In a preindustrial economy, villages were places where full-time farm families clustered together, usually but not always in close proximity. Villages were both basic organizational units of community and also their corresponding settlement forms. In the European tradition, they were the source of a family's economic competence as well as its social obligations, political expressions, and religious associations.

Access to land was economically critical for families; without land, no family could support itself well. In turn, the morphology or form of the village often reflected the distribution of land. Farmsteads in close proximity, often focused on a single point, including a manor, church, or common, clustered within surrounding open, common, or fragmented fields. Farmsteads arrayed in a linear fashion, along a stream or a road, for example, and forming a street or row village, commonly reflected the distribution of land into long strips running perpendicularly away from the line of farmsteads, stream, or road and thereby could encompass a variety of land types in a single plot. Villages of loosely dispersed farmsteads, or open-country neighborhoods, as exist in parts of East Anglia and much of New England, derived from enclosed farmlands. Variations among and between these three primary forms were manifold.

Agricultural villages in the American colonies, as well as in immigrant and utopian villages during the nineteenth-century, survived only where they continued as the source of a right to land. Where land rights were vested in fee-simple ownership, and as division of labor became more complex, villages disappeared as congregations of farmers. In the nineteenth century, moreover, market and mill or factory villages proliferated. Such proto-urban places, usually with fewer than 2,500 people, still suggested the scale of the settlement form and something of its supposed social and economic virtue.

Nineteenth-century literature romanticized villages. No longer was the village a place of cloying familiarity, suffocating strictures, and little opportunity—the very things that encouraged flight to cities. Rather, villages became a supposed antidote to cities in a period of growing anti-urbanism, places where one might find pastoral pleasures and supportive communal values.

Such romanticism led to placemaking. Suburban design has appealed partly because it has been perceived to produce settlement forms, like villages, that are neither country nor city, but something in between. They also suggest exclusivity. Even urban villages, comprising a culturally homogeneous population within a residential district of a city, are meant to seem removed from the city. Most explicitly, however, neotraditional planning evokes the virtue, scale, and, ideally, sense of place of the romantic nineteenth-century village.

—*Joseph S. Wood*

See also
Community; New England Towns and Villages; Township.
References
Lingeman, Richard. *Small Town America: A Narrative History 1620–the Present.* Boston: Houghton Mifflin, 1980.
Smith, Page. *As a City upon a Hill: The Town in American History.* Cambridge, MA: MIT Press, 1966.
Stilgoe, John R. *Borderland: Origins of the American Suburb, 1820–1939.* New Haven, CT: Yale University Press, 1988.
———. *Common Landscapes of America, 1580–1845.* New Haven, CT: Yale University Press, 1982.

# Violence

Many Americans associate cities with high levels of violence and believe that violent crime characterizes urban society. In particular, because homicide is the least ambiguous type of violence, analysts often study homicide rates to measure rates of violence. However, the history of violence in American cities is much more complex than that. In fact, the nature of urban violence has changed dramatically during the last two centuries, reflecting rapid shifts in the development of urban society. Contrary to popular perception, urbanization actually reduced rates of violence during much of this period even though urban violence reached epidemic proportions in some places at some times. Both the rate and the character of violence have been sensitive to shifts in political, social, demographic, gender, economic, class, and race relations. Therefore, historians have charted changes in urban violence as a way of understanding central facets of the American urban experience.

Just as industrialization and demographic pressures in the early nineteenth century revolutionized cities and city life, the same processes transformed urban violence, beginning a trend that lasted for nearly 150 years. According to many scholars, the rate of urban violence has followed a U-shaped pattern. Cities experienced high rates of homicide during the antebellum period, representing the left side of the "U." A number of factors combined to generate these high levels of violence. The early stages of industrialization strained social and class relations; moreover, millions of native-born farmers and European immigrants arrived in American cities between 1820 and 1860. This influx of newcomers exaggerated group affiliations and sparked ethnic, political, religious, and racial tensions. Friction over neighborhoods—turf wars—and political power triggered approximately 80 major riots and hundreds of gang wars between 1830 and 1865. Baltimore, for example, experienced 12 major riots, and Philadelphia 11 during these years. The wave of disorder crested in New York in 1863, when workers, particularly Irish immigrants, rioted for five days. Begun as an effort to prevent local men from being drafted into the Union army, the protest exploded into a rampage against African Americans and prominent Republicans. More than 100 people died in the New York Draft Riots.

Popular culture in cities during the middle of the nineteenth century also contributed to the violence. Blending traditions based on ethnicity, class, and gender, urban working-class culture glorified toughness, prized ferocity, and nurtured a nightlife emphasizing bars, misogyny, and rowdiness. Workers embraced activities such as drinking and brawling and rejected the values of middle-class employers and moral reformers. Not surprisingly, in a cultural atmosphere in which bare-knuckle boxing was wildly popular, rates of homicide were also high. A typical urban murder during the middle of the century occurred as the result of a brawl between two young, immigrant, male workers. In a disproportionate number of homicides, the participants were friends or acquaintances, belonged to the same ethnic group, had been drinking, and responded impulsively and violently to a trivial dispute.

By the 1870s, however, homicide rates in American cities had begun to plummet—reflecting the downward slope of

One of the most common forms of violence in cities in recent years has resulted from conflicts between college students and law-enforcement officials.

the U-shaped curve. A series of related circumstances produced this decrease. The urban police, established partly in response to rioting, discouraged raucous behavior. Very important were public schools, which taught children to be orderly and obey rules. However, the regimen of the workplace may have been the most powerful force. Factories demanded industrious workers, and supervisors punished drunken or volatile laborers. To secure and maintain jobs, workers had to conform to the needs of the factory. Dovetailing with middle-class values that emphasized restraint and self-control, these conditions discouraged impulsive and aggressive behavior. As urban-industrial society matured, rioting became much less common and homicide rates plunged, falling as much as 75 percent in some cities. Immigrants who arrived in urban America during the final decades of the century quickly encountered institutions that encouraged restraint, and newcomers experienced declining homicide rates. Despite the widespread poverty, transience, and inequality, cities became increasingly peaceful and orderly as the century ended. A similar process, also linked to urban-industrial growth, reduced violence in European cities.

Two exceptions to this pattern confirm that industrial society reduced urban conflict. First, southern cities, which were less industrialized and thus had weaker forces inculcating discipline and order, typically experienced homicide rates at least three times higher than northern cities. Second, surging levels of racism during the late nineteenth century generated increased violence among African-American city dwellers. During the middle of the century, black and white homicide rates were similar in northern cities. But when race relations in northern cities deteriorated, African Americans were excluded from schools and industrial jobs. Because of this discrimination, they often lived apart from the social and economic conditions that discouraged urban violence. By the start of the twentieth century, homicide rates among African Americans were far higher than those of other city residents, and black violence rose in an era when white violence fell. Just as exposure to urban-industrial life reduced violence among European immigrants, exclusion from the same pressures—because of racism—contributed to increasing violence among African Americans.

The level of urban violence remained low until after World War II, when it ballooned once again—forming the right side of the U-shaped curve. During the last half of the twentieth century, two far-reaching changes occurred. First, overall rates of urban violence spiraled between the early 1960s and late 1970s, doubling and tripling in many cities. Second, large cities became particularly violent. During the early 1970s, for example, the average homicide rate for cities with more than 1 million residents was double that of cities with between 100,000 and 250,000 residents—and more than three times that of even smaller cities. For most of American history, the rural South had the highest rates of homicide; that distinction now belongs to the nation's largest cities.

Urban historians have urged observers to analyze modern trends in the context of long-term patterns. The fact that homicide rates have often fallen as cities have grown should dispel the notion that urban society is intrinsically violent. Some experts have linked the high levels of violence in modern cities to the collapse of the industrial economy. The urban-industrial factors that once discouraged aggressive behavior appear to be ineffective as factories close, inner-city schools deteriorate, industrial jobs disappear, employment prospects for inner-city youth become bleak, and America experiences the shift to a postindustrial economy. In sum, urban violence reflects powerful, macrocosmic economic and cultural changes. The city itself does not generate violence, nor does increasing population density cause aggressive behavior. Rather, the character of urban society—such as the nature of economic institutions and the tenor of social, class, and race relations—shapes the degree of conflict. As cities grow and change, urban violence is likely to assume new forms and new levels. Perhaps the maturation of the postindustrial city will be accompanied by a new array of social and cultural circumstances that will, as in the late nineteenth century, discourage conflict and reduce urban violence.

—*Jeffrey S. Adler*

**See also**

Crowds and Riots; Public Disorderliness; Race Riots.

**References**

Feldberg, Michael. *The Turbulent Era: Riot and Disorder in Jacksonian America*. New York: Oxford University Press, 1980.

Lane, Roger. "On the Social Meaning of Homicide Trends in America." In Ted Robert Gurr, ed., *Violence in America*, 55–79. Newbury Park, CA: Sage Publications, 1989.

———. *Roots of Violence in Black Philadelphia, 1860–1900*. Cambridge, MA: Harvard University Press, 1986.

Monkkonen, Eric H. "Diverging Homicide Rates: England and the United States, 1850–1875." In Ted Robert Gurr, ed., *Violence in America*, 80–101. Newbury Park, CA: Sage Publications, 1989.

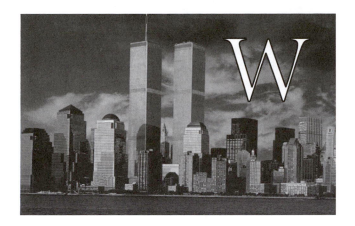

## Wald, Lillian D. (1867–1940)

Lillian D. Wald, the settlement house founder, social reformer, and pioneer of the visiting nurse service, was born in 1867 to German-Jewish, upper-middle-class parents in Cincinnati, Ohio. As a young woman, Lillian Wald studied nursing and also taught a home nursing class on New York's Lower East Side. While there, a neighborhood girl took Wald to her wretched tenement to see her dying mother. Wald was deeply moved by the experience, and in 1893 she decided to make the Lower East Side her home, become a visiting nurse to her neighbors, and try to improve their lives in other ways. She would charge only what her patients could afford. Joining her in this enterprise was her friend and fellow nursing student, Mary Brewster. Wald did not invent the idea of the visiting nurse service, but she was among its earliest pioneers and its best publicist. She did originate the term "public health nurse," and in 1902 she began public school nursing in New York City. By 1921, she had several hundred women working for her as visiting nurses in branch offices throughout New York City.

At the same time Wald was beginning her visiting nurse service, she established one of the earliest and most successful settlement houses in the United States, Henry Street Settlement. At first called Nurses Settlement, the program of clubs, classes, and other activities received a permanent home in 1895 when the philanthropist Jacob Schiff gave Wald an early-nineteenth-century row house at 265 Henry Street. She added a "little theater," other arts programs, and expanded the settlement's social, recreational, and educational activities.

Wald attracted other settlement house residents to Henry Street, such as the nurse and social reformer Lavinia Dock and the activist for better working conditions Florence Kelley, who headed the National Consumers League. Wald herself became involved in numerous reform causes. In the area of child labor, Wald helped found the National Child Labor Committee to gather data and lobby for legislation in 1904. The following year, she suggested forming the U.S. Children's Bureau, which was established in 1912. She also was successful in getting New York City to create badly needed public parks on the congested Lower East Side. Wald formed an effective partnership with Florence Kelley in promoting better working conditions. She supported labor unions, vocational education, public health campaigns, and better housing for low-income people. She was an active suffragist and joined Jane Addams in campaigning for peace during World War I.

Like Addams, her counterpart in Chicago, Wald was a talented writer. Her account of settlement life, *The House on Henry Street,* was well received and led to a sequel, *Windows on Henry Street.* Because of her ill health, Wald relinquished formal control of the settlement in 1934 but remained on the Henry Street board until her death. She is second only to Jane Addams as the most prominent settlement house leader in the United States.

—*Judith Ann Trolander*

**See also**
Henry Street Settlement.
**References**
Daniels, Doris. *Always a Sister: The Feminism of Lillian D. Wald.* New York: Feminist Press, 1989.
Duffus, Robert Luther. *Lillian Wald: Neighbor and Crusader.* New York: Macmillan, 1938.
Siegel, Beatrice. *Lillian Wald of Henry Street.* New York: Macmillan, 1983.

## Walking City

A walking city is an urban area in which the dominant mode of transportation is by foot. Through the first decades of the nineteenth century, urban areas in the United States shared many features with European cities: they were compact, dense agglomerations of population, craft production, and small-scale goods-processing industries that extended only a few miles in diameter. Over the middle third of the nineteenth century, cities in both the United States and Western Europe experienced profound spatial reorganization as industrialization concentrated economic activity in urban places while transportation innovations allowed residences to decentralize. Suburbanization was particularly rapid in the United

States, where rapid industrialization combined with the land development interests of transportation companies to expand the urban fabric far beyond the confines of the walking city.

Kenneth Jackson has identified five significant features of the walking city. First, the walking city was congested, with high population densities, small lot sizes, and narrow streets. Second, the walking city was marked by a clear distinction between city and country. American cities were not as rigidly demarcated as their European counterparts (which retained medieval walled fortifications well into the nineteenth century), but "before the age of industrial capitalism, a sharp-edged dot on the map was an accurate symbol for a city."

Third, the walking city contained a mixture of functions. Before the rapid industrial growth of the mid-nineteenth century, most urban production was dispersed among small shops, creating a diverse mosaic of activities on each block and often within the same building. As historical geographer James E. Vance, Jr., has noted, "in the long history of cities, the distinction [of land uses] has lain more among the uses of various stories within buildings than in simple ground space." The horizontal separation of land uses within urban areas began in the 1830s and 1840s as horsecars and railroads permitted the separation of newly expanding residential areas from the emerging central business district. Within the CBD, clearly defined districts for financial, retail, and warehousing emerged only after the Civil War in most cities.

Fourth, the walking city was characterized by short journeys to work with the vast majority of urban workers living less than a mile from their places of employment. Finally, the most prestigious residential areas in walking cities were located near its center while undesirable land uses and lower-status residents were pushed onto less desirable sites at the periphery. As rapid growth filled the nation's cities with factories and wage laborers, however, the wealthy and the new middle classes were the first to flee the congestion and pollution of the industrial city for the suburbs.

The walking city represented the prevailing form of urban structure in medieval European cities, and capitals in Europe, the Middle East, and Latin America retain significant portions of their original high-density pedestrian cores. In contrast, only a few cities in the United States retain remnants of their preindustrial form, and American cities that have developed since the steam locomotive developed without walking cities.

—*Elvin Wyly*

### References

Adams, John S. "Residential Structure of Midwestern Cities." *Annals of the Association of American Geographers* 60 (1970): 37–62.
Jackson, Kenneth T. *Crabgrass Frontier: The Suburbanization of the United States*. New York: Oxford University Press, 1985.
Sjoberg, Gideon. *The Pre-Industrial City, Past and Present*. New York: Free Press, 1960.
Vance, James E., Jr. "Human Mobility and the Shaping of Cities." In J. F. Hart, ed., *Our Changing Cities*, 67–85. Baltimore: Johns Hopkins University Press, 1991.
Ward, David. "The Emergence of Central Immigrant Ghettoes in American Cities, 1840–1920." *Annals of the Association of American Geographers* 48 (1968): 343–359.
Warner, Sam Bass, Jr. *Streetcar Suburbs: The Process of Growth in Boston, 1870–1900*. Cambridge, MA: Harvard University Press, 1962.

## War on Poverty

In his State of the Union message in January 1964, President Lyndon Johnson declared "unconditional war" on poverty, and in a message to Congress the following March, he called for a "national war on poverty." In August of 1965, the Johnson administration proposed and Congress passed the Economic Opportunity Act (EOA). This legislation established the Office of Economic Opportunity (OEO) in the Executive Office of the President with two roles. First, it was to coordinate the work of existing federal bureaucracies charged with implementing some EOA programs. And second, it was to administer other EOA programs directly.

The legislation also allocated funds for the War on Poverty to more than 1,000 cities and rural areas during the 1960s. However, the money spent to implement EOA programs actually constituted a relatively small part of all the federal funds appropriated for antipoverty programs and constituted only a minuscule part of the federal budget.

The EOA included several education and job training programs intended to provide opportunities for low-income citizens to better themselves and achieve upward mobility. These included the Neighborhood Youth Corps, the Jobs Corps, and Adult Basic Education. The law also authorized Volunteers in Service to America (VISTA), which was often referred to as a domestic Peace Corps, and established programs to aid migrant workers, make loans to small businesses, and assist rural areas. The Head Start education program for preschool children became part of the antipoverty program early in 1965, and the OEO also began funding the Legal Services program in many communities.

The component of the Economic Opportunity Act that received the most attention was Title II. This section of the law called for local areas to establish community action programs (CAPs) to be administered by local organizations to be known as community action agencies (CAAs). According to the EOA, these community action programs were to be "developed, conducted and administered with the maximum feasible participation of residents of the areas and members of the groups served." Different communities interpreted this goal in a variety of ways. Residents of target areas often received jobs in the CAAs and the programs they funded. Also, most community organizations began to include representatives of poverty areas on the governing boards of the CAAs, a procedure soon required by the OEO. Initially, however, representatives of the social welfare community and political officeholders generally made the major decisions. Although CAAs in some communities mobilized residents of poverty-stricken areas to protest the established practices of political and social welfare institutions, these actions were prominent in relatively few cities.

The Office of Economic Opportunity lost its political support during the later 1960s and early 1970s. The administration of Head Start was removed from OEO and transferred to the Department of Health, Education, and Welfare; the Job Corps was moved to the Department of Labor; and VISTA was transferred to the new ACTION agency. In 1974 OEO was renamed the Community Services Administration. Although this federal agency was abolished in 1981, some local CAAs found enough financial support to continue.

—*Robert Kerstein*

**See also**
Community Action Program.
**References**
Donovan, John C. *The Politics of Poverty.* 3d ed. Washington, DC: University Press of America, 1980.
Greenstone, J. David, and Paul E. Peterson. *Race and Authority in Urban Politics: Community Participation and the War on Poverty.* New York: Russell Sage Foundation, 1973.
Lemann, Nicholas. *The Promised Land: The Great Black Migration and How It Changed America.* New York: Knopf, 1991.
Piven, Frances Fox, and Richard A. Cloward. *Regulating the Poor: The Functions of Public Welfare.* New York: Vintage Books, 1993.

## Warner, W. Lloyd (1898–1970)

Lloyd Warner pioneered the research method of doing community studies based on fieldwork in his studies of a number of smaller cities in the 1930s and 1940s. The best known of these, the Yankee City (Newburyport, Massachusetts) research, became a standard for subsequent generations of urban scholars.

A social anthropologist by training, Warner applied techniques he first developed in his studies of Australian aborigines to patterns of community life in the United States. His method was distinctive for adopting the viewpoint of the people being studied, rather than imposing the external, abstract, interpretive perspectives of the analyst.

Warner's main substantive contribution to urban studies was his inductive model of community stratification. Beyond the obvious criterion of wealth, interviews with citizens of Yankee City revealed that they ranked each other according to the source of their wealth (i.e., inherited or earned), the neighborhood where they lived, their education (extent and source), and their lineage (family name and ethnicity). The resulting model included six distinct classes (upper-

upper to lower-lower) that functioned to delineate parameters of work, marriage, worship, and voluntary association. Subsequent research generally corroborated Warner's model, but the upper-upper (old aristocracy) stratum was less distinct outside New England.

A more durable legacy of Warner's work is his insight into the symbolic mechanisms of community life—how physical symbols and public ceremonies both integrate an otherwise disparate local community. For example, the town cemetery has complementary functions. The size and placing of tombstones reflect the local status hierarchy, but the consecrated area containing the graves of veterans transcends all strata and links the local community to the entire nation. As for ceremonies, Memorial Day rites symbolically unite "the living and the dead" of a community by reminding contemporaries of the sacrifices made by departed citizens. Similarly, the observance of Yankee City's tercentenary reified the entire history of the town, enabling the present generation to absorb the values and heritage of their collective identity.

Warner paid scant attention to physical patterns of urban growth or to conventional spatial depictions of the city. Rather, he always focused on the purely social and cultural manifestations of residential life. But as long as the quest for community remains a salient theme in urban studies, Warner's exemplary fieldwork provides a methodological and conceptual foundation for understanding contemporary urban settlement.

—*M. Kenneth Brody*

**See also**
Lynd, Robert S. and Helen M.; Middletown.
**References**
Warner, W. Lloyd. *Yankee City.* Abbreviated ed. New Haven, CT: Yale University Press, 1973.
Warner, W. Lloyd, et al. *Democracy in Jonesville.* New York: Harper & Row, 1949.
Warner, W. Lloyd, and Paul S. Lunt. *The Social Life of a Modern Community.* New Haven, CT: Yale University Press, 1941.

## Washington, D.C.

Historically and socially, Washington, D.C., is a city of contradictions. It began with an orderly plan conceived and executed amid controversy and compromise. In almost 200 years as the capital of a great democracy, Congress has never granted residents of the District of Columbia the same political rights enjoyed by other citizens of the United States. The movement for total self-government continues in the effort to persuade Congress to designate Washington the fifty-first state of the United States, New Columbia.

Following the American Revolution, Pennsylvania's unpaid troops mutinied and were perceived to have threatened the Confederation Congress, which then met in Philadelphia.

Pennsylvania's Supreme Executive Council refused to use state militia to quell the revolt, persuading Congress that the federal government needed a national capital that it controlled. The federal Constitution, adopted on September 15, 1787, mandated such a city.

On July 16, 1790, Congress authorized President George Washington to select a site on the Maryland side of the Potomac River, between the Eastern Branch (Anacostia River) in the south and Conococheague Creek (Williamsport) in the north, for the new nation's new capital. He designated a diamond-shaped area, ten miles long on each side, that included land on both the Maryland and Virginia sides of the Potomac River and started south of the mouth of the Anacostia River. It included the busy seaports of Alexandria, Virginia, and Georgetown, Maryland. Washington persuaded Congress to amend the Residence Bill to legitimize boundaries that included land in Virginia, but Congress decreed that all federal buildings would be on the Maryland side of the Potomac.

In the following year, Washington picked three prominent residents, Thomas Johnson and Daniel Carroll representing Maryland and Dr. David Stuart representing Virginia, as commissioners to supervise development of the federal city. He also selected Pierre (Peter) Charles L'Enfant, a French immigrant, to lay out the city and site the public buildings and Andrew Ellicott to survey the federal district. In 1792, after continual conflict between L'Enfant and the commissioners, Washington fired the Frenchman. Following this, Major Ellicott modified L'Enfant's plan for the city and prepared it for publication. The Washington family coat-of-arms, three red stars over two red stripes on a white field, is in the upper right corner of this plan, and in 1938 Congress selected this symbol to be on the District of Columbia's flag.

After a decade of planning, construction, land speculation, and financial disaster, the federal government officially moved from Philadelphia to Washington on December 1, 1800. One of the first actions taken by Congress in the new capital was to divide the district into Washington County on the Potomac's northeastern bank (in Maryland) and Alexandria County on the southwestern bank (in Virginia). This act stipulated that the laws of Maryland then in force would be the laws of Washington County while those of Virginia would prevail in Alexandria County. After much petitioning by residents of the federal city, Congress granted the City of Washington a charter in 1802.

The new city's government resembled others of that time, with a mayor and a legislative council divided into two houses. At first, the president of the United States appointed the mayor, but by 1820 the mayor and both councils were elected by popular vote. President Thomas Jefferson appointed Robert Brent to be the first mayor of Washington, and he served from 1802 to 1812. In retaliation for the burning of Fort York (now Toronto), the capital of Upper Canada, by American forces during the War of 1812, the British invaded Washington and burned the public buildings on August 24, 1814. At that moment, the District of Columbia was probably more in danger of ceasing to be the national capital than ever before or ever since; however, the private and public interests of the city united to persuade Congress to remain in Washington.

After the slave rebellion led by Nat Turner in 1831 in Virginia, racial tensions increased in Washington. "Black Laws" that had been laxly enforced were revised, made more restrictive, and enforced much more rigidly. In one case, a young physician and botanist, Dr. Reuben Crandall, moved to the District of Columbia from Peekskill, New York. While he was unpacking his books and scientific equipment, a new acquaintance noticed an abolitionist pamphlet among his possessions. He asked Crandall if he could borrow the pamphlet and read it; Crandall reluctantly agreed. Word soon circulated throughout the city that an abolitionist was distributing literature. As no specific law outlawed the distribution of abolitionist literature, Dr. Crandall was charged with seditious libel, arrested, and held in the city jail. A gang composed primarily of "mechanics" from the Navy Yard tried breaking into the jail and lynching Crandall. Frustrated in their attempt, the white mob roved the streets of Washington burning the homes and businesses of free blacks. Beverly Snow, a free African American who owned and operated a successful restaurant, was accused of speaking disrespectfully about some of the mechanics' wives. This charge became the excuse for actions that came to be known as the Snow Riots or "Snow Storm." In the meantime, Crandall remained in jail awaiting trial from the time he was imprisoned on August 10, 1835, until April 26, 1836, when he was acquitted. After spending more than eight months in jail, Crandall's health was broken; he contracted tuberculosis and died in early February 1838.

This was the first trial in the United States dealing with the distribution of literature concerning the condition of the black population, either slave or free, and it presaged events of the next 200 years. Slavery and race issues have always been near the surface in Washington and have had a serious impact on the city. As early as 1846 the conflict over slavery in Virginia produced a request for Congress to cede Alexandria County back to its original state. Congress complied and reduced the size of the District by 40 percent.

Racial tensions flared again on April 13, 1848, when the sailing schooner *Pearl* docked in Washington with a load of wood. Two nights later, 77 slaves who belonged to some of the most prominent families of Washington, Georgetown, and Alexandria attempted to escape aboard the ship. The *Pearl* was pursued by the steamship *Salem,* carrying a party of 30 heavily armed men. Early the next morning, the *Salem* overtook and captured the *Pearl* while it was anchored near Point Lookout, Maryland, about 140 miles from Washington.

The *Salem* returned to Washington with the *Pearl* in tow. Fearful of a lynching, the white crew was taken to jail in a closed vehicle while the slaves were paraded through the streets. A mob, frustrated in their attempt to lynch the crew, turned its attention to a nearby abolitionist target, the offices of the *National Era,* a moderate antislavery newspaper. By ten o'clock that evening, hundreds of people surrounded the *National Era's* offices. Most of Washington's populace considered the mob a collection of the most undesirable elements; only strong pro-slavery champions like Senator John C. Calhoun and the future President of the Confederacy Jefferson Davis considered them outraged citizens trying to protect themselves against abolitionist aggression. The mob smashed and destroyed a sign, then it forced open the door of the newspaper before local police arrived and dispersed them with help from a heavy rain.

The census of 1860 showed that Washington's population had increased more than 64 percent since 1850. This population growth resulted primarily from foreign immigration. Since this phenomenon was national, the nativist reactions that took place in Washington resembled those that occurred across the country. The antiforeign, anti–Roman Catholic American Party (commonly called the Know Nothings) was formed and gained immediate strength. By 1855 the Know Nothings controlled Washington's city government, but in June 1856 a combination of Democrats, Conservative Whigs, Free Soilers, and Republicans unified behind Dr. William Beans Magruder and defeated the Know Nothing candidate for mayor. Magruder won by only the slimmest of margins, 13 votes out of 5,841 cast; however, the Know Nothings still controlled the city councils.

The 1857 election for council members was therefore critical to controlling the city. The Know Nothings imported the Plug-Uglies, a squad of goons from Baltimore, to intimidate immigrants trying to vote. The resulting riot was suppressed only when President James Buchanan called out 110 marines from their Washington barracks. After someone in the crowd fired a pistol and wounded one marine, the soldiers opened fire, killing at least eight people and wounding many more. In the election, the anti–Know Nothing candidates won a sweeping victory.

During the Civil War and the years immediately after, the population of Washington increased by more than 75 percent, from 75,080 in 1860 to 131,700 in 1870. Although no improvement in the infrastructure necessary for urban living accompanied this increased population, there were several improvements in the condition of African Americans. On April 16, 1862, the District of Columbia legally abolished slavery, nearly a year before President Lincoln issued the Emancipation Proclamation. Slaveowners were compensated with up to $300 for each slave freed. At the beginning of 1867, over the strenuous objection of the white population, Congress granted the franchise to black males who lived in the nation's capital.

At war's end, the streets planned by L'Enfant had neither been graded nor paved, and the dirt, or at best cobbled, streets were not illuminated at night. Along a few downtown streets, pedestrians could avoid the mud by sticking to wooden sidewalks, but even there they had to compete with fire engines that frequently found the roadways impassable. Natural stream channels and canals functioned as sewers. Most of the trees in the city at the start of the war had either been cut down for fortifications or used for firewood. Parks and government reservations remained unimproved and were frequently swampy and malarial. Drinking water came from springs, wells, cisterns, and public pumps. Animals, particularly pigs, roamed freely in the streets and posed an unsightly hazard to health.

*A wide pedestrian pathway leads through a section of The Mall between the Capitol and the Washington Monument.*

In 1871, as a result of pleading by community leaders, Congress abolished the municipal governments of Washington, Georgetown, and Washington County and created a unified territorial government for the District of Columbia. The plan featured a governor appointed by the president; a secretary (a combination of lieutenant governor and secretary of state); an 11-member council; a legislative assembly of 22 popularly elected members; and a nonvoting delegate to the U.S. House of Representatives, also elected by popular vote. The same legislation created a board of public works and a board of health, both appointed by the president. This new bureaucracy began a massive program of city improvements.

Together, the government and the public boards transformed Washington from a mud hole into a real city in only three years. It graded 260 miles of road and paved 116. The streets were illuminated with 3,000 gaslights. The board of public works established a parking commission of professional arborists to reforest the city. The commission created "parking" between roadways and walkways, and it also permitted residents to plant gardens on land that the city owned between their homes and the sidewalks. The commission planted over 50,000 street trees, and as a result, Washington became known as the "city of trees."

Swamps, some more than 100 acres large, were drained, and sewage was routed into 123 miles of conduits that ranged in diameter from six inches to 30 feet. For the first time, city wastes were treated before being dumped into the Potomac River. Treated water was piped into individual homes through 34 miles of mains. In spite of creating a stringent and comprehensive building code, this government created a favorable climate for building, both public and private, and many of Washington's most substantial homes, office buildings, schools, and markets date from this period.

The first governor of the territory was Henry David Cooke, a banker and the brother of the financier Jay Cooke. Alexander Robey Shepherd was appointed to the first board of public works and, after Cooke resigned, became the city's governor. He is the single individual considered most responsible for the modern city of Washington.

The most important achievement of the territorial government, aside from constructing the city's infrastructure, was passing the Civil Rights Acts of 1872 and 1873, which provided precedents for important court decisions made in the 1950s. Congress, no longer sympathetic to President Grant and angered by the large debt that the urban improvements had generated, abolished the territorial government in June 1874. For the next 93 years, Congress, with only slight modifications, governed the District of Columbia through three commissioners appointed by the president.

Because the suburbs of Washington were developing without any discernible pattern toward the end of the nine-teenth century, in 1888 Congress decreed that no future subdivisions would be approved unless they conformed to the original plans of L'Enfant and Ellicott. Early in the 1890s, reform arrived in Washington, and employees of the District were forbidden to take "gifts" from contractors or kickbacks from subordinates under the penalty of immediate discharge. Congress occupied itself with such "vital" questions of national interest as whether children in Washington should be allowed to fly kites on the mall (it was ultimately prohibited), while the commission dealt with matters of such gravity as the morality of playing baseball on Sunday (it was determined to conflict with the fourth commandment and therefore outlawed).

The commission's lack of authority and the absence of a popular voice in local affairs produced persistent calls for self-determination. During the years of commissioner government, District of Columbia residents, deprived of all participation in national elections, periodically petitioned Congress to establish a democratically elected government for the city. This political discontent produced nothing more than several congressional studies of the appropriate form of appointed government, even though presidents from Harry S Truman to Richard Nixon all favored greater democratic participation for local citizens. This movement, known by many names, did not achieve a victory until 1956 when an election was allowed in Washington for the first time since 1873, but even then it was only for party offices.

President John F. Kennedy appointed the first African-American member of the commission, John Bonner Duncan, in 1961. That same year, the 50 states ratified the Twenty-Third Amendment to the Constitution giving residents of the District of Columbia the right to vote in presidential elections for the first time since 1800. President Lyndon Johnson modified the appointed commissioner government in 1967 to have a single commissioner/mayor and an appointed council. And he appointed Walter Washington, an African American, to the highest post.

On April 4, 1968, only hours after Dr. Martin Luther King, Jr., was assassinated, looting and burning broke out in sections of Washington. Most of the damage was done on 14th and 7th Streets, N.W., and H Street, N.E. The rioting continued for three days during which the city's government imposed a curfew and requested troops from the federal government. Ultimately, 900 businesses and 677 dwelling units suffered $24 million in damage.

In the next few years, the city's board of education became elective, and Congress allowed the city to have nonvoting representation in the national House of Representatives. This law of 1970 restored representation, which had been lost in 1875. And on Christmas Eve 1973, President Nixon signed into law the District of Columbia Self-Government and Governmental Reorganization Act, which finally provided limited "home rule" for the city. Under this "charter," Washington residents elect a mayor, a city council of 13 members, and a board of education. Congress retains control of the city budget and can invalidate any local laws. In 1974 the voters elected Walter Washington the first mayor of the city since 1870. In 1978 (elections for mayor occur every four years), Marion S. Barry, Jr., succeeded Washington, and he was reelected in 1982 and 1986.

In 1982 the citizens of Washington convened a constitutional convention and produced a constitution that was subsequently approved by voters and then submitted to Congress. However, the House of Representatives rejected statehood for the District of Columbia by a vote of 153 to 277 on Sunday, November 21, 1993. This was the first floor vote since the bill's introduction in 1983.

In 1990 Mayor Barry was convicted of a misdemeanor charge of drug possession and served six months in federal prison. Before his conviction, Barry had decided not to run for reelection, and the first woman to be elected mayor of Washington, Sharon Pratt Dixon Kelly, succeeded him. But four years later, in the 1994 Democratic primary, Barry ran once again and defeated the incumbent Mayor Kelly; in the general election, he defeated his Republican and Independent opponents and won his fourth term as mayor of the District of Columbia.

—*Philip Ogilvie*

**See also**
Barry, Marion S., Jr.; L'Enfant, Peter Charles.
**References**
Borchert, James. *Alley Life in Washington: Family, Community, Religion, and Folklife in the City, 1850–1970.* Urbana: University of Illinois Press, 1980.
Brown, Letitia Woods. *Free Negroes in the District of Columbia: 1790–1846.* New York: Oxford University Press, 1972.
Bryan, Wilhelmus Bogart. *A History of the National Capital: From Its Founding through the Period of the Adoption of the Organic Act.* 2 vols. New York: Macmillan, 1914–1916.
Green, Constance McLaughlin. *The Secret City: A History of Race Relations in the Nation's Capital.* Princeton, NJ: Princeton University Press, 1969.
———. *Washington: A History of the Capital, 1800–1950.* Princeton, NJ: Princeton University Press, 1976.
Porter, John Addison. *The City of Washington: Its Origin and Administration.* Baltimore: Johns Hopkins University Press, 1885.

# Water

The quest for pure and abundant water supplies is as old as American cities themselves. The town site for Boston was selected mainly because of the area's springs. Newark's original residents received much of their water from a stream-fed pond near the center of the town, which satisfied the thirsts of both cattle and people.

As towns expanded, residents who did not live within walking distance of potable water sources had to rely on other citizens and the government for water. To meet this need, enterprising citizens dug wells on their own property or on sites leased from the municipal government. A few public wells were put in service for the poor and for firefighting. Some householders dug their own wells or placed rain barrels under roof gutters. A visitor to Philadelphia in 1744 commented that its water was excellent and no one had to walk more than 50 paces to a pump. On the eve of the Revolution, Philadelphia had nearly 500 wells, of which about one-fourth were publicly owned.

With urban growth, Philadelphia's groundwater became saturated with seepage from privies, breweries, and slaughterhouses. Residents began to complain about the unpleasant taste and odor of the city's water and wondered if polluted wells had exacerbated the deadly yellow fever epidemic of 1793, which killed 4,000 people. When yellow fever struck again in 1794, 1797, and 1798, municipal leaders decided to end the city's dependence on well water and to develop a municipally owned water supply system.

The city went to the Schuylkill River for its water supply. Two huge, lumbering steam engines pumped water from the river to a reservoir located on Center Square from which it was distributed to consumers through bored wooden logs. The waterworks failed miserably, mainly because the primitive steam engines consumed enormous amounts of coal and broke down frequently. In 1822 this waterworks was abandoned for a new system that used giant waterwheels to lift water from the river. For the next 20 years, Philadelphia had, arguably, the best water supply system in the nation.

By the early 1800s, the nation's largest cities had outgrown their cisterns, wells, and springs, and private aqueduct companies sprang up to develop communal water supply systems. But the use of private enterprise to satisfy urban water needs proved unsatisfactory. Urban residents were unhappy because the aqueduct companies would make water available only where it was profitable, and thus did not furnish water to lightly populated or poor areas or use it for important civic purposes, such as washing the streets and fighting fires. The aqueduct companies and city dwellers viewed water differently. The companies regarded water as a private asset, while the public increasingly saw it as a community resource. Public dissatisfaction grew as a result of a number of disastrous conflagrations and the appearance of cholera, a dread new epidemic disease. Firefighters were greatly hampered by the low pressure of water delivered by the companies. Businessmen who needed pure water for their enterprises, such as brewers and confectioneries, also complained.

In New York City the refusal of the local aqueduct company to abandon its very small and polluted water supply led the city government to embark on an audacious venture. The city decided to go to the mountains for its water supply and to anticipate future growth by developing a system that greatly exceeded existing needs. A dam was built on the Croton River in the highlands 40 miles north of the city, and the water was conveyed by a complex system of masonry aqueducts and tunnels. The system took seven years (1835–1842) and $13 million to build, and was considered one of the greatest engineering accomplishments of the period. New York's success induced other cities to construct their own water supply systems, and by 1860, 12 of the 16 largest waterworks were municipally owned.

The nineteenth century witnessed unprecedented urban growth and increased water use. In 1790 the nation's largest city, Philadelphia, had 43,000 inhabitants. By 1890 there were 22 cities with more than 100,000 residents and 3 cities whose population exceeded 1 million. In the three decades following the Civil War, the number of urban water supplies increased from 136 to over 3,000.

Nineteenth-century municipal waterworks had to serve many more persons, each of whom used far more water than earlier urban inhabitants. In the years after the Civil War, water closets and other water-using fixtures were widely adopted by the urban middle class. Also, as American cities industrialized, the need for water grew. In Philadelphia, per capita consumption of water increased from 8 gallons a day in 1810 to 55 in 1870. In Chicago and Detroit, residents used more than 100 gallons per day.

Cities had two options in choosing a water supply. They could bring in water from the mountains, as did New York, Boston, and Baltimore, or they could use improved steam engines to pump water from nearby, low-lying rivers and lakes. Since the latter option was less expensive, this is what most cities did, frequently with tragic results. At the very same time cities began to tap nearby freshwater rivers and lakes, they also started to use them as sinks to dispose of their wastes. Thus, numerous cities drank their own sewerage or that of their neighbors upstream. Typhoid fever and other waterborne diseases became endemic. In Newark, which drew its water from the heavily polluted Passaic River, the typhoid fever mortality rate in 1891 was 107 per 100,000 population. In the following years, Newark abandoned the Passaic for a pure mountain water supply system, and its typhoid fever mortality rate fell to less than 30 per 100,000 population.

Bringing in water from distant highlands was very expensive, so most cities looked for other alternatives. Some cities tried to prevent factories and persons who lived alongside rivers and lakes from using them as repositories for sewage and industrial effluents, but the courts frequently negated these efforts. Courts generally viewed the nation's waterways as natural resources that individuals and businesses could use and abuse as they saw fit. Chicago in the years 1892 to 1900 spent $45 million to prevent the sewage-contaminated Chicago River from infiltrating the city's water crib in Lake Michigan. To accomplish this, the city had to reverse the flow of the Chicago River and redirect it to the Illinois River system. In Memphis, a huge aquifer was found that provided copious amounts of pure water at little cost.

Most cities were not as fortunate as Memphis and had to look for other solutions to their water problems. In the 1870s a few cities began to filter their water, but it was not until the advent of bacteriology and the germ theory of disease that water treatment methods became effective. In 1893 the Lawrence Experiment Station of the Massachusetts State Board of Health designed a slow sand filter plant for the Lawrence waterworks that effected a 70 to 80 percent reduction in the city's typhoid fever mortality rate. Other improvements were rapidly introduced, notably chlorination, which was first used in 1908 by the privately owned Jersey City Water Company. By 1923 nearly all water supplies were being treated, and the typhoid fever death rate for the nation's largest cities was 3.6 per 100,000 population, about 90 percent less than what it had been in 1890.

Throughout the first half of the twentieth century, cities had to seek new sources of water to keep up with population growth. In 1913, over the strenuous opposition of John Muir and the Sierra Club, Congress authorized San Francisco to dam the Hetch Hetchy Valley in Yosemite National Park. In the arid southern half of the state, Los Angeles went 238 miles to the Owens River Valley in the Sierra Nevada Mountains to quench its thirst. New York City reached out to the water-rich Catskill Mountain watershed 100 miles to the north and by 1927 had raised its daily water supply to 525 million gallons. And still the nation's largest cities needed more water. Therefore, Los Angeles, after depleting the Owens River Valley of its water, laid claim to a portion of the water of the Colorado River, while New York tapped the upper Delaware River Valley, precipitating a fight with Pennsylvania, which also wanted to tap the Delaware River.

As cities went further and further afield for their water supplies, the state and federal governments became involved. State water agencies were established, and interstate water compacts were negotiated. During the Depression, federal work-relief programs enabled many small communities to construct wholesome water supply systems. Beginning with the establishment of the Bureau of Reclamation in 1902 and the construction of federal multiple-purpose dams and reservoirs in the 1930s and 1940s, the federal government has played a key role in providing water for the arid and semiarid Southwest. Especially notable in this regard was the opening of the Colorado River Aqueduct in 1941.

The last decades of the twentieth century have presented new water challenges to the nation's cities. Whereas before, cities only had to consider the technical and economic feasibility of proposals to dam free-flowing rivers, they must now contend with the desire of sportsmen, environmentalists, and ecologists, backed by federal legislation, to preserve wilderness areas. As it becomes harder to augment existing water supplies, cities may be compelled to put greater emphasis on conservation. They will also have to spend billions of dollars to meet new federal water quality standards that are being imposed because of concern about pesticides, industrial wastes, and toxic chemicals seeping into the nation's groundwater and surface water supplies from waste dump sites and from nonpoint sources of pollution, such as city streets and agricultural fields and orchards.

*—Stuart Galishoff*

**See also**

Sewerage and Sanitation Systems; Water Pollution.

**References**

Armstrong, Ellis L., Michael C. Robinson, and Suellen M. Hoy, eds. *History of Public Works in the United States, 1776–1976.* Chicago: American Public Works Association, 1976.

Blake, Manfred Blake. *Water for the Cities: A History of the Urban Water Supply Problem in the United States.* Syracuse, NY: Syracuse University Press, 1956.

Galishoff, Stuart. "Triumph and Failure: The American Response to the Urban Water Supply Problem, 1860–1923." In Martin Melosi, ed., *Pollution and Reform in American Cities, 1870–1930,* 35–59. Austin: University of Texas Press, 1980.

O'Connell, James C. "Technology and Pollution: Chicago's Water Policy, 1833–1930." Ph.D. dissertation, University of Chicago, 1980.

Rosen, Howard, and Ann Durkin Keating, eds. *Water and the City: The Next Century.* Chicago: Public Works Historical Society, 1991.

Weidmer, Charles H. *Water for a City: A History of New York City's Problem from the Beginning to the Delaware River System.* New Brunswick, NJ: Rutgers University Press, 1974.

## Water Pollution

The conception of water pollution has changed over time, and those changes are reflected in legal change. Attempts to cope with polluted water predate development of the germ theory of disease in the late nineteenth century, even though the notion that contaminated water could cause disease contradicted the miasmatic theories then popular. The desire for "cleanliness" that emerged under the miasmatic theory led to wastes being removed from houses and streets, but they were then dumped in lakes and rivers that provided cities with their water. People believed that moving bodies of water would purify the wastes, but a firm, scientific basis for this idea lay in the future.

Urban growth in the nineteenth century produced levels of pollution far beyond what those bodies of water could purify. This pollution was reduced for two reasons. In the eighteenth century, demographic research produced some understanding of the correlates of disease and, earlier, urban dwellers had begun to demand drinking water that tasted good. Today, the impetus for pollution control derives more from an environmental aesthetic than from the concern for public health.

Primary responsibility for controlling water pollution now resides with the federal government, but until recently it was a local matter. The first recorded pollution law enacted in the United States was adopted by Massachusetts in 1647. This act made it "unlawful for any person to cast any dung, draught, dirt or anything to fill up the Cove . . . upon penalty of forty shillings." Similar statutes can be found throughout the period in which the miasmatic theory prevailed.

Even with development of the germ theory of disease, attempts to identify and eliminate sources of water pollution remained a local responsibility. In most states, city governments paid for water supply and sewage disposal. Any necessary construction was financed with bonds that were ultimately retired with local tax revenues or special assessments. Operating costs were typically met by user fees.

Most cities also created a board of health and made it responsible for maintaining water quality. This board was charged with inspecting the water supply and waste disposal facilities (including wells and cesspools) and with evaluating alternatives for expansion as urban growth created an almost continuous demand for increased capacity. The focus, however, remained on taste and odor until instrumentation was developed that identified individual pollutants. Consequently, throughout most of the nineteenth century, urban death rates from waterborne diseases such as typhoid and cholera remained high.

During the nineteenth century, state legislatures simply passed laws that established penalties for polluting water and delegated authority to local governments to enforce them. But by the beginning of the twentieth century, state governments had become more active. Industrialization and urban growth had created unprecedented problems of pollution for water and wastewater systems, but the early twentieth century was also a time of great technological development in regard to water and waste treatment. Scientists and engineers discovered relatively inexpensive methods of purifying water such as filtration and, especially, chlorination. Wastewater, particularly that which contained industrial wastes, proved more difficult to treat. State laws prohibited the disposal of specific materials, such as dead animals, in sources of water supply, and state boards of health were created to enforce these laws. Even without this compulsion, cities adopted the new technologies because of their positive effect on public health.

Beginning in the middle of the 1950s, states adopted a broader definition of pollution that recognized and took into

*An undated photograph of a trash-strewn stream in the Bronx, New York.*

account the recreational uses of water. This new definition, in turn, broadened the state's regulatory role from simply prohibiting pollution to protecting water supplies from contamination. As a result, new state agencies specifically charged with environmental protection were created.

Before World War I, the federal involvement was limited primarily to laws prohibiting obstructions in navigable waterways. Some agencies, precursors of the U.S. Public Health Service, studied water quality and the linkages between pollution and waterborne disease, but their involvement was indirect as they conducted their studies in conjunction with state boards of health. When the Public Health Service was created in 1912, it was authorized to study "the pollution either directly or indirectly of the navigable streams and lakes of the United States." As part of its first study, the agency determined what types of waste were being discharged into the Ohio River, the effects of these pollutants on the "stream," and the effect of pollution on the health of people who lived adjacent to the river or drew water from it. Although World War I significantly slowed the agency's research, it continued to publicize its findings. After the war, public awareness of the potential health effects of pollution caused many cities to construct wastewater treatment works. States on major rivers also attempted to control pollution in the river basin. The Ohio River Valley Water Sanitation Commission (ORSANCO),

set up to monitor the water in the Ohio River, received the federal government's blessing in the 1940s, but it was supplanted by the uniform federal approach that emerged after World War II.

The Water Pollution Control Act of 1948 is the basis for subsequent federal legislation concerning water quality. While its basic ideas had first been introduced in the middle of the 1930s, the Depression and war delayed legislation. The law of 1948, reflecting the concern for public health, authorized funding to plan and financially assist local governments to construct sewage treatment plants and state agencies to foster interstate cooperation.

When the act was amended in 1965, public opinion supported a broader definition of pollution, which reduced the emphasis on public health. The new law stressed the quality of life and the need to preserve the environment for aesthetic purposes. The Water Quality Act of 1965 mandated state governments to establish minimum standards of water quality, which the federal government would then review.

The National Environmental Policy Act of 1969 established the Environmental Protection Agency as the body to enforce this legislation. Symbolic of the new emphasis was the environmental impact statement that all federal agencies were required to include "in every recommendation or report on proposals for legislation and other major federal actions significantly affecting the quality of the human environment." Executive orders issued in 1970 effectively expanded the use of these statements when agencies issued contracts, licenses, loans, or grants to, among others, municipalities.

While the broader definition of pollution was retained, the path to abatement changed once again several years later. With funding authority under the 1965 statute due to expire, the Senate passed a bill in 1972 that would have required eliminating all water pollution by 1985. The Water Pollution Control Act that finally passed in 1972 softened this demand simply to eliminating the discharge of pollution. It required municipalities to use secondary sewage treatment by the middle of 1977, and it instructed the private sector to use the "best available technology economically achievable" by the middle of 1983. The Clean Water Act of 1977 attempted to reduce the vagaries of the 1972 act without abandoning the goal of zero discharge. Other federal statutes that affect water pollution are the Safe Drinking Water Act of 1974 and the Toxic Substances Control Act of 1976.

Because water pollution is partly a natural phenomenon, the goal of eliminating all water pollution was unreachable, but the country has not yet reached even the less stringent goal of the 1972 statute. As the determination of standards for acceptable levels of pollution has moved from municipalities to the federal government, and as the funds and enforcement to achieve them now come largely from the federal government, the interaction between an urban government and its constituents has weakened. If water pollution as currently conceived is to be effectively lessened, these links will have to be strengthened.

—*Louis Cain*

**References**
Armstrong, Ellis L., ed. *History of Public Works in the United States, 1776–1976.* Chicago: American Public Works Association, 1976.
Callan, Scott J., and Janet M. Thomas. *Environmental Economics and Management: Theory, Policy, and Applications.* Part V. Chicago: Irwin, 1996.
Melosi, Martin V., ed. *Pollution and Reform in American Cities, 1870–1930.* Austin: University of Texas Press, 1980.

## Wesleyan Grove and Oak Bluffs, Massachusetts

The nineteenth-century Methodist camp meeting on Martha's Vineyard, Massachusetts, turned the wilderness revival site into a permanent community of considerable fame and aesthetic appeal. Around 1860 anonymous designers devised a new building type, the campground cottage, which collapsed images of house, church, and tent into tiny cottages fitted onto tent sites, thus making single-family housing available to participants in the densely packed revival; at any one time, 500 cottages might be crammed onto less than 30 acres. With the grounds owned and controlled by an association, there were no private exterior yards, leaving the paths and spaces between cottages to trees and people, creating a "city in the woods."

Because of the startling design results, Wesleyan Grove became famous in the 1870s and was visited by enthusiasts from all over the Northeast and Midwest, who joined the original southern New Englanders who went there. Soon there were hundreds of imitations, such as the cottage-based camp meeting resorts at Round Lake, New York; Fair Point (Lake Chautauqua), New York; Lakeside, Ohio; Ocean Grove, New Jersey; Bay View, Michigan; and Pacific Grove, California. As a group, these places functioned as predecessors or parallels to other kind of resorts, to developing suburbs, and to many aspects of urban reform design during the late nineteenth century.

Wesleyan Grove was laid out in 1835 in a single circle around a preaching space, and its subsequent growth took the form of larger concentric circles, radial paths, and smaller tangential radial-concentric circles. The result was a "mazy" confusion that helped create a sense of magical dislocation and was considered, along with the miniature cottages, part of its charm. In 1867 developers purchased the adjacent land and built the popular resort of Oak Bluffs. Wishing to extend the remarkable formal system of the campground, the developers hired Robert Morris Copeland, a landscape gardener experienced in designing romantic cemeteries with curving

paths, to plan it. His design, along with the campground cottages that also filled Oak Bluffs, expanded the area's architectural and planning language to make a stunning Victorian resort. Oak Bluffs is now also known as "the Inkwell" and is the most favored of all seaside resorts by African Americans.

—*Ellen Weiss*

**References**
Stoddard, Chris. *A Centennial History of Cottage City.* Oak Bluffs, MA: Oak Bluffs Historical Commission, 1981.
Vincent, Hebron. *A History of the Camp Meeting and Grounds at Wesleyan Grove, Martha's Vineyard, for the Eleven Years Ending with the Meeting of 1869.* Boston: Lee, 1870.
———. *History of the Wesleyan Grove Camp Meeting from the First Meeting Held There in 1835 to That of 1858.* Boston: George C. Reed & Avery, 1858.
Weiss, Ellen. *City in the Woods: The Life and Design of an American Camp Meeting on Martha's Vineyard.* New York: Oxford University Press, 1987.

## Western Cities

Shortly after taking the census of 1890, federal officials declared that it was no longer possible to draw a distinct frontier line on a map of the United States. Equally important was the statement in the same census that "the urban element in the western division . . . has gained somewhat more rapidly than the total population." In fact, the extent of urbanization in the Rocky Mountain and Pacific states (30 percent of the population lived in cities) had passed that of longer-settled parts of the nation by 1880. Throughout the twentieth century, the western states have continued to be the most highly urbanized part of the nation.

In the broadest perspective, cities have been central to the European-American conquest of the western United States since the seventeenth century. From then until the early nineteenth century, European nations used frontier cities to connect the vast expanses of western North America to the system of mercantile capitalism and trade that centered on the North Atlantic. These first western towns were small outposts around the margins of what is now the western United States. They included Spanish Santa Fe (founded first in 1609 and again in 1692), San Antonio (1718), and Los Angeles (1781); the French outpost of St. Louis (1764); the Russian post at Sitka (1804); and the British fur trading center at Fort Vancouver (1825). These communities were small, counting their European populations in the hundreds, but they were clearly urban in function—seats of government, centers of administration, focal points for trade, workplaces for skilled artisans.

The second stage in western city building coincided with the industrialization of the United States. From the 1840s to the 1870s, Anglo-American settlers brought the urban frontier west with their surveying gear and printing presses. Settlement and economic activity spread into the western territories from spearhead cities such as San Francisco, Portland, Denver, and Salt Lake City. All but San Francisco were new creations, founded on high hopes and sustained by the need to organize and supply the farmers and miners who were beginning to transform western nature into raw materials for the American economy.

As railroad builders completed the western transportation system in the 1880s and 1890s, they linked isolated metropolitan regions more and more closely to the national hierarchy of cities that focused on New York and Chicago. New western cities supplemented and sometimes supplanted the original spearheads. The result by the end of the century was distinct sets of cities that stretched north to south across the continent. The gateways for ocean-borne trade were Pacific coastal and river ports: Seattle, Tacoma, Portland, San Francisco, Sacramento, Stockton, Los Angeles, and San Diego. The railroad gateways from the East straddled the ninety-seventh meridian, the very approximate boundary between the middle western corn belt and the cattle and wheat country of the Great Plains; these gateways included Minneapolis and St. Paul, Minnesota; Fargo, North Dakota; Omaha, Nebraska; Kansas City, Kansas, and Kansas City, Missouri; Wichita, Kansas; Oklahoma City, Oklahoma; and Dallas, Fort Worth, and San Antonio, Texas. A third set of cities developed as immediate entries to the stock-raising and mining regions, often at access points to the western mountains: Great Falls and Billings, Montana; Cheyenne, Wyoming; Denver and Pueblo, Colorado; Albuquerque, New Mexico; and El Paso, Texas. Finally, some communities were at the end of the line—final distribution points locked between the great mountain systems of the West—such as Salt Lake City, Utah; Spokane, Washington; Reno, Nevada; Butte, Montana; and Boise, Idaho.

The outlines of a western urban system were largely complete by the early twentieth century. In the northern and central West, the years from 1900 to 1940 were an era of urban maturity and slowing growth. Ethnic variety declined with the curtailment of Chinese migration after 1882 and the slowing of European immigration in the 1920s. The "instant cities" of the frontier now provided the amenities and public services that made them settled communities. Denver is a case in point. Despite the depression of the 1890s, the local economy had diversified, government services had matured, and socially distinct neighborhoods were firmly established. The census of 1900 reported for the first time that women outnumbered men, and Denverites of both sexes could choose among scores of literary groups, fraternal organizations, charitable societies, churches, and clubs. Visitors arrived looking for the Wild West and found a city not terribly different from Indianapolis. By the 1920s and 1930s, maturity had sometimes turned to stodginess, with journalists calling Denver "prematurely gray" and Portland a "spinster city."

The story was different in the southern third of the West, where oil and sunshine combined to provide a preview of the southwestern Sunbelt. Houston, Beaumont, and Dallas, Texas, as well as Oklahoma City and Tulsa, Oklahoma, boomed with the petroleum industry. Phoenix began to market its climate, its boosters coining the phrase "Valley of the Sun" in the 1930s. Los Angeles capitalized on both factors to surge past San Francisco as the largest metropolis of the western states in the early 1920s.

The last half of the twentieth century has again restructured the American economy, introducing a third era of urbanization in the West. New technologies and institutions of communication have brought much of the world into a single marketplace for ideas as well as goods. Urban growth in the western United States has responded to a complex of economic forces, including (1) the expansion of the metropolitan-scientific-military complex, (2) the reinternationalization of the American economy, and (3) the global shift from manufacturing to services (especially those involved in the leisure economy of recreation and retirement). At the same time, the communications revolution has driven explosive decentralization of metropolitan areas, a process that is especially obvious in the western supercities of Houston, Dallas–Fort Worth, the San Francisco Bay region, and southern California.

Between 1940 and 1990 the West contained three of the nation's premier military cities: Honolulu, Hawaii; San Diego, California; and San Antonio, Texas. Military bases and employment were also a powerful presence in Salt Lake City, Utah; Sacramento and San Francisco, California; and smaller cities such as Colorado Springs, Colorado; Corpus Christi, Texas; and Grand Forks, North Dakota. The Pentagon was also the single best customer for the aerospace, nuclear, and electronics industries from the 1940s through the 1980s. In the aftermath of World War II, airframe production was heavily concentrated in Wichita, Kansas; Dallas–Fort Worth, Texas; San Diego and Los Angeles, California; and Seattle, Washington. Nuclear weapons development and production fueled the growth of Albuquerque, New Mexico; Denver, Colorado; Richland, Washington; and Las Vegas, Nevada. Efforts to devise weapons control systems triggered the takeoff of the postwar electronics industry in California's "Silicon Valley" between San Francisco and San Jose in the 1950s. As the industry moved on to civilian applications, advanced semiconductor and computer production diffused to new industrial complexes around Austin, Texas; Phoenix, Arizona; Albuquerque, New Mexico; and Portland, Oregon.

Since the 1960s western cities have been leaders in reintroducing the United States to the world. Immigration reform legislation in 1965 has led to a steady increase in the volume of documented migration. The majority of the newcomers have been Asians and Latin Americans who have settled disproportionately in southwestern and Pacific cities. The same cities have been in the forefront of changing patterns of American trade. The development of Mexican *maquiladora* manufacturing (which uses cheap labor to manufacture parts assembled in another country) in the 1970s and 1980s and the North American Free Trade Agreement (NAFTA) of 1993 are powerfully affecting the economic base of southwestern border cities. In the same years, the value of American trade across the Pacific passed that across the Atlantic.

One result was a new internationally oriented hierarchy of western cities. At the top was Los Angeles, a "world city" for trade, transportation, and finance and a "new Ellis Island" for immigration. The San Francisco–Oakland–San Jose area, Seattle, and Dallas competed as global gateways. Specialized international cities included Houston, El Paso, and Honolulu. In contrast, other large cities, such as Denver, Salt Lake City, and Portland, retained their strongest economic orientation to their traditional hinterlands of the "Rocky Mountain Empire," the Mormon culture region, and the Columbia River Basin.

The impact of the American leisure economy is obvious in the growth of large tourism sectors in cities like Reno, Las Vegas, and Honolulu. The effects can also be seen in the ongoing transformation of the resource-producing backcountry. Only a small fraction of westerners are now needed to run cattle, cut trees, grow crops, or mine and process ore. The West will continue to see metropolitan influence filter down the urban hierarchy and incorporate the sparsely settled farm and rangelands into the use zones of metropolitan areas. Low costs and amenities attract small, footloose manufacturing and service businesses to small cities and towns of the rural West. These towns also serve as commuting, recreation, and retirement zones for western metropolises. Some communities (such as Aspen and Telluride, Colorado) have been completely transformed into jet-set suburbs of the metropolis. Other communities (such as Hood River, Oregon, or Sandpoint, Idaho) maintain an uneasy balance between traditional and new economies. Still others (particularly places on the Great Plains) lack the amenities to attract either tourists or small businesses.

The results of the several economic forces can be read from census data. In 1940, 43 percent of the people of the 19 western states lived in metropolitan areas; by 1990 the figure was 80 percent. Four of the ten largest metropolitan complexes in the country were western in 1990. Residents of western metropolitan areas accounted for 25 percent of all Americans, up from 9 percent in 1940.

In adding 51 million residents from 1940 to 1990, western metropolitan areas have been experimental sites for new forms of metropolitan geography. Since the 1950s, it has become a cliché to read the future of American cities and American society from the urban West. Critics have variously offered Los Angeles, Orange County, and San Jose in California, Las Vegas, and Houston as models for the emerging city. Their evaluations range from strongly positive (Reyner Banham, *Los Angeles: The Architecture of the Four Ecologies*) to deeply pessimistic (Mike Davis, *City of Quartz: Excavating the Future in Los Angeles*), but common themes are the formative power of highways and automobiles and the fragmentation of metropolitan areas into nearly independent subregions.

The multicentered metropolis has been manifested in the proliferation of "suburban activity centers" or "edge cities" and in fully planned new cities in the largest scale. Examples of the latter include Irvine, California, and Las Colinas and The Woodlands in Texas. The new pattern is also seen in the development of intensively urbanized corridors. Such "linear cities" can be identified in Denver (downtown to Tech Center), Los Angeles (the Wilshire Boulevard corridor), and East Bay (Richmond to Fremont, California).

The political or policy adjustment to the multicentered metropolis has been comparatively effective in the West. The region's institutional openness has allowed western cities to adapt their political structures and organizational responses to new realities of social and economic geography. For example, "supersuburbs" with populations of 100,000 or more provide a full range of public services without relying on central cities. In 1960 there were 6 such supersuburbs in the western states and 6 in the eastern states. By 1990, the figures were 39 for the West and only 16 for the rest of the country. Examples are Arlington, Texas; Tempe, Arizona; and Concord, California. Cities like Bellevue, Washington, and Aurora, Colorado, have pushed their own development agendas as rivals and peers of their central cities.

Finally, during this third era of growth since 1945, western cities have gone through three cycles of political reform. The period 1945 to 1965 brought a cycle of "businessmen's reform," in which local civic leaders tried to position western cities to take advantage of new economic forces by modernizing city administrations and investing in public infrastructure. The late 1960s and 1970s brought political reactions in which ethnic minorities and middle-class neighborhoods revolted against large-scale urban renewal and permanently widened the terms of political debate. The Voting Rights Act, amended in 1974, has been a particularly important tool for expanding minority representation in city governments across the Southwest. The 1980s and early 1990s saw a new stage of "rainbow growth coalitions." Hispanic and African-American politicians in cities such as Denver, San Antonio, Oakland, and Seattle reasserted the importance of economic growth with greater attention to the equitable distribution of jobs and other benefits.

—*Carl Abbott*

**See also**

Dallas, Texas; Denver, Colorado; Houston, Texas; Los Angeles, California; Multicentered Metropolis; Phoenix, Arizona; San Antonio, Texas; San Diego, California; San Francisco, California.

**References**

Abbott, Carl. *The Metropolitan Frontier: Cities in the Modern American West.* Tucson: University of Arizona Press, 1993.

———. *Portland: Planning, Politics and Growth in a Twentieth Century City.* Lincoln: University of Nebraska Press, 1983.

Banham, Reyner. *Los Angeles: The Architecture of Four Ecologies.* New York: Harper & Row, 1971.

Barth, Gunther. *Instant Cities: Urbanization and the Rise of San Francisco and Denver.* New York: Oxford University Press, 1975.

Cherny, Robert, and William Issel. *San Francisco, 1865–1932: Politics, Power, and Urban Development.* Berkeley: University of California Press, 1986.

Davis, Mike. *City of Quartz: Excavating the Future in Los Angeles.* New York: Verso, 1990.

Findlay, John M. *Magic Lands: Western Cityscapes and American Culture after 1940.* Berkeley: University of California Press, 1992.

Fogelson, Robert. *The Fragmented Metropolis: Los Angeles, 1850–1930.* Cambridge, MA: Harvard University Press, 1967.

Kling, Rob, Spencer Olin, and Mark Poster, eds. *Post-Suburban California: The Transformation of Orange County since World War II.* Berkeley: University of California Press, 1991.

Lotchin, Roger. *Fortress California: From Warfare to Welfare, 1910–1961.* New York: Oxford University Press, 1992.

Luckingham, Bradford. *Phoenix: The History of a Southwestern Metropolis.* Tucson: University of Arizona Press, 1989.

McComb, David G. *Houston: A History.* Austin: University of Texas Press, 1981.

Moehring, Eugene. *Resort City in the Sunbelt: Las Vegas, 1930–1970.* Reno: University of Nevada Press, 1989.

Noel, Thomas J., and Stephen J. Leonard. *Denver: From Mining Camp to Metropolis.* Niwot: University Press of Colorado, 1992.

Quiett, Glenn. *They Built the West.* New York: Appleton-Century, 1934.

Reps, John W. *Cities of the American West.* Princeton, NJ: Princeton University Press, 1979.

Sale, Roger. *Seattle: Past to Present.* Seattle: University of Washington Press, 1976.

# White-Collar Crime

The United States is unique among Western nations for the crime it sustains every year. It is the premier Western country in violent crime, drug crime, organized crime, juvenile delinquency, and white-collar crime. Why the United States exceeds other civilized nations in most kinds of criminality cannot be explained easily, but several factors must be noted.

The United States has been built on immigration. Over the years, wave after wave of immigrants—English, Irish, Jewish, Polish, German, Italian, Scandinavian, Asian, and Hispanic to name a few—have come ashore with the result that American communities embrace a wide variety of ethnic, religious, and racial groups. Some have fallen victim to ethnic or religious conflicts, which in turn have undermined communal solidarity and cooperation—qualities essential to crime prevention. Nevertheless, as immigrants formed communities, they established their own institutions and social groups and often lowered their levels of criminality below that of older American communities. These ethnic communities encountered the same incessant, undermining pressures as older communities—for example, a sizable migration of families as well as a flight of youth to more promising areas.

This differed sharply from the more settled communities of Europe, for example, where solidarity and custom acted informally to channel human enterprise along established pathways and curbed much deviance. In the absence of such structures in both old and new communities, mobile families faced minimal social restraint, and American communities were forced to use laws and formal rules whereas European communities relied more on informal traditions and customs.

The resulting web of city ordinances and laws in the United States sometimes fixed in the legal system bitter antagonisms that had long been only informal. It was, for example, illegal in antebellum Boston to bury an Irish Catholic with religious ceremonies in a public cemetery. Many other examples could be cited of laws discriminating against other groups, especially African Americans. Although the Constitution explicitly forbade the use of law as a means of racial or religious discrimination, many local and regional laws did just that. Many ethnic groups, including blacks, were convinced that America was not a land of civil liberty and economic opportunity.

The lack of coherent social controls in immigrant communities, together with divisive ethnic antagonisms and a deep suspicion that government is oppressive, has led many ethnic groups to pursue their destinies in an underworld economy. Blacks and Hispanics are the most recent examples, but Italians, Jews, and Irish Catholics have also run along this path in the past. Many have prospered despite obstacles, but many more have perished, with the result that lower-class people, whether white or black, often harbor bitter feelings toward the upper classes and the agents of government.

Communal weakness and ethnic or racial conflict have contributed to an isolated, marginal status for many minority groups and have in turn made antisocial paths that much easier. The crimes that resulted followed traditional crime patterns: juvenile delinquency, organized crime, and drug and street criminality.

It was not white-collar crime. Though white-collar crime was every bit as common in the United States as more traditional crime patterns, it involved older, better educated, socially established groups from distinctly privileged circumstances. White-collar crime—crime committed during the course of legitimate, upper-status occupations and shielded by the respect and trust that such occupations receive—has mainly been the preserve of older American groups who have been thoroughly socialized to civic culture. Lower-status occupations (unskilled workers or sales clerks) shield their share of criminality, too, but lower-status occupations lack the broad opportunity to become involved in occupational criminality. They have no control over large funds, have little access to strategic information, and make few decisions about marketing or recruitment. It is simply not possible for lower-status workers to use their occupations for sizable illegal gains.

White-collar crime occurs primarily among people in upper-status occupations who use their authority, expertise, or technical knowledge (that is also the basis of upper-status occupations) to violate the laws and standards regulating their occupation. It often takes the form of violating professional rules. Physicians may sometimes prescribe certain procedures because they have a strong financial stake in doing so; lawyers representing a plaintiff may recommend a settlement favorable to the defendant in return for a sizable but under-the-table fee; key financial columnists leak information to associates who anticipate market fluctuations.

It may also take the form of using technical knowledge inappropriately. Managers of uranium processing plants or metal pickling firms must supervise dangerous procedures to produce usable goods, but if workers are asked to perform dangerous tasks unknowingly, it is a (white-collar) crime. Careful laboratory testing for safety and effectiveness is required of all foods and drugs to be widely distributed, but it is not uncommon for laboratory scientists to misrepresent their results in order to persuade the Food and Drug Administration that the products are safe and effective. Since an almost infinite variety of standards governs white-collar positions, virtually an infinite number of violations occurs.

Further, as the sophistication and number of authoritative, technical positions increase, the opportunity for new violations expands dramatically. Thus, white-collar crime is almost certainly the most prevalent and most rapidly growing form of crime in the West. It is also the most intricate and intriguing variety of crime. Why do highly respected professionals, with so much to lose, do it? Why are they punished so lightly? How much recidivism is there?

The laws that govern white-collar crime must evolve at a furious pace. The technical processes that govern medicine, bioengineering, manufacturing, marketing, or the financial industry, for example, are all developing rapidly, and the laws regulating new procedures must keep pace. As these processes become more intricate and technical, they also become more arcane. Laymen cannot fully appreciate them, and legislatures are often at sea. It is very difficult to formulate effective laws that will regulate most white-collar activity in a free enterprise system, and when the United States began to focus on this problem in the late nineteenth century, it ignited controversy.

The Interstate Commerce Act (1887) and the Sherman Antitrust Act (1890) detailed specific offenses for the Justice Department and the courts, but the Federal Trade Act (1914) gave the Federal Trade Commission a very broad mandate, and the same was true later for the Securities and Exchange Commission (1933). Traditionally, the lawful regulation of commerce and businesses depended on the legislature and its ability to enact laws that prohibited specific acts. If a particular facet of business required regulation, it had always been the legislature's responsibility to formulate statutes to curb specific behavior. Regulatory agencies needed laws to define their jurisdiction, and they needed laws outlining specific offenses to be curbed within that jurisdiction. Criminal law had always evolved this way, and this was how laws governing white-collar crime initially evolved. Without laws that justified their regulatory acts, commissions would be ignored, and their authority to issue restraining orders would be challenged. Without legislation defining their actions, the agencies would be controlled mainly by the idiosyncrasies of their administrators.

Nevertheless, legislatures were incapable of formulating timely regulatory legislation because processes that needed regulating were usually novel, solving troublesome problems, and supported by powerful interests. New legislation needed to be framed and evaluated by all of the responsible parties in legislative debate. If it was worthy, it still needed to make sense to specific legislators and to the public in the current political climate. Finally, after months of debate and compromise, legislation that regulated the unwanted activity might be forthcoming. By then, however, other innovative activities needed regulatory attention. While a legislature was working on one problem, business had sidestepped new laws by finding novel ways of dealing with problems in ways not yet regulated. The processes in business and professional life are complicated by the many different ways of doing and accomplishing the same thing. Focused, controlling legislation can be enacted, but in a fast-moving field it quickly becomes obsolete. When organized opposition to legislation makes itself felt, it takes twice as long. As a result, white-collar activity is difficult to control with specific legislation.

The path that John D. Rockefeller followed in the late nineteenth century is instructive. In 1862, at the age of 23, he saw the potential of oil refineries. Within ten years he had acquired 80 percent of the refineries in Cleveland and established Standard Oil of Ohio. By 1882 he controlled 90 percent of the oil industry in the United States and had reorganized Standard Oil as a vertically integrated trust. As a monopoly, Standard Oil dictated its terms to the railroads, its competitors, and its customers. Its economic power was enormous, and if left unchecked it threatened the commercial and democratic foundations of society. Nevertheless, it wasn't until July

2, 1890, that the Sherman Antitrust Act was signed into law by President Cleveland. But the act was awkwardly phrased, and the courts were unwilling to enforce it. Moreover, trusts had already given way to holding companies that were not in violation of the act. The Sherman Antitrust Act was obsolete almost before it had been enacted.

The only alternative to specific legislation detailing the nature of unacceptable behavior is a broad legislative mandate providing a regulatory agency with a specific jurisdiction but with broad authority to define controls and issue directives within its jurisdiction. The specific controls devised by the agency then become administrative law and must be obeyed, even though no legislature has enacted specific laws to deal with the problems.

Suppose, however, that a firm contests the right of an agency to issue an administrative order under its legislative mandate. The firm must show that the activity in question is beyond the jurisdiction of the agency. The order may well be legitimate, but if it is not within the agency's jurisdiction, it is not authoritative. If the order is authoritative and the firm continues to defy it, the firm can be ordered to pay a fine that increases as long as the firm remains defiant.

Suppose that in addition to violating the order, the firm has also caused losses to competitors or employees. It can be sued for damages in civil court by these plaintiffs. Or suppose the firm has lied to the agency in documenting its activities or in testimony by its officers; then it can be prosecuted by state or federal district attorneys for fraud or perjury. The agency itself can also initiate civil or criminal prosecutions because violations of its lawful directives are often civil or criminal offenses.

Regulatory agencies develop administrative law to govern firms within their jurisdiction. They can enjoin firms against specific practices and punish them with fines. Should a firm's activities simultaneously create grounds for civil suits, it can be sued both by the agency and by private parties. If it simultaneously violates the criminal law via fraud, reckless behavior, or willful defiance of lawful directives, it can be prosecuted accordingly. All three actions can proceed at the same time, although they are usually dealt with one by one, with the most serious issues settled first. But who gets prosecuted, the firm or its individual officers? This is a major question.

The agency can withdraw enabling licenses or order fines against the firm, which the firm must obey. But who gets charged when the matter is a civil or criminal complaint? The firm's activity can be examined in civil court, and it can be ordered to comply with an order of either the court or of the agency. But in criminal court, the complaint often turns on a willful decision to violate the criminal law and therefore must name specific officers who had both the will and the authority to commit a criminal offense. Ignorance by the firm's officers of its activity in violating a law is not an appropriate defense. Attempts have been made to find firms guilty of manslaughter or to incapacitate them, but these attempts have not been successful for the most part. When specific corporate officers have been charged with serious crimes, prosecutors have had more success.

Administrative law is an intensely political arena within which the lines of authority are neither precise nor inexorable. Both sides maneuver, and the outcome often turns on politics. This imprecision has bothered legal scholars since the 1880s because it could serve personal vendettas by mean-spirited directors. Responsible observers have opposed broadening the authority of administrative agencies on these grounds, but as their critics have pointed out, there is no alternative except self-regulation.

Does self-regulation work? Like most citizens, most business firms obey the law routinely. They are staffed with responsible citizens who follow regulations without much concern as to their authority. Occasionally they may not be aware of a particular regulation, or they may misunderstand its intentions and as a result fall into noncompliance.

In these cases, only simple guidance is needed, and many regulatory agencies view education as their major responsibility. But sometimes there is a significant financial advantage to ignoring a directive. When they are made aware of the penalties, most firms accept agency guidance and quickly comply, but occasionally the financial incentive is so large, or the firm's officers are so greedy, that the firm willfully seeks ways of sidestepping the directive. This behavior is considered criminal by the agency, the courts, and the public at-large and may require prosecution. Without a public regulatory agency to control such firms, all manner of economically predatory behavior could become common.

Regulation provides a degree of order that is vital to the well-being not only of individual firms and citizens but to the economy as a whole. Anticipating the actions of others is the basis of growth in the marketplace. Regulatory agencies serve to control irresponsible behavior, and judicious regulation buttresses responsible, efficient free enterprise. Reasonable regulation enhances the ability of effective entrepreneurs to predict the reactions of honest peers, customers, shareholders, competitors, and suppliers and reap deserved rewards by doing so. Effective entrepreneurs support the efforts of regulators to maintain responsible order in the economy.

—*Theodore N. Ferdinand*

### References

Braithwaite, John. "Taking Responsibility Seriously: Corporate Compliance Systems." In Brent Fisse and P. A. French, eds., *Corrigible Corporations and Unruly Law*, 39–61. San Antonio, TX: Trinity University Press, 1985.

Cullen, F. T., W. J. Maakestad, and G. Cavender. *Corporate Crime under Attack: The Ford Pinto Case and Beyond.* Cincinnati: Anderson Publishing, 1987.

Fisse, Brent. "Sanctions against Corporations: Economic Efficiency or Legal Efficacy?" In W. Byron Groves and Graeme Newman, eds., *Punishment and Privilege.* New York: Harrow and Heston, 1986.

Horwitz, Morton J. *The Transformation of the American Law.* 2 vols. New York: Oxford University Press, 1992.

Magnusson, Dan, ed. *Economic Crime—Programs for Future Research.* Stockholm, Sweden: National Council for Crime Prevention, 1985.

Simpson, Sally. "Corporate-Crime Deterrence and Corporate-Control Policies." In Kip Schlegel and David Weisburd, eds., *White Collar Crime Reconsidered,* 289–308. Boston: Northeastern University Press, 1992.

Skowronek, L. S. *Building a New American State: The Expansion of National Administrative Capacities, 1877–1920.* New York: Cambridge University Press, 1982.

Walt, Steven, and William S. Laufer. "Corporate Criminal Liability and the Comparative Mix of Sanctions." In Kip Schlegel and David Weisburd, eds., *White Collar Crime Reconsidered,* 309–331. Boston: Northeastern University Press, 1992.

Weisburd, David, Stanton Wheeler, Elin Waring, and Nancy Bode. *Crimes of the Middle Classes.* New Haven, CT: Yale University Press, 1991.

# White Flight

White flight refers to the residential movement of whites to avoid levels of racial integration that they find unacceptable.

Historically, white flight is primarily a twentieth-century urban phenomenon. Prior to this century, African-American population in cities was relatively small. However, when African-American numbers increased substantially, in part as a consequence of major migration from rural areas, whites typically responded with resistance and with restrictions intended to segregate areas of settlement. When exclusion failed, whites often took the recourse of out-migration, a process sometimes resulting in racial turnover of individual blocks or whole neighborhoods. The tendency toward residential homogeneity was part of an urban trend that also involved class, religion, or ethnicity, but the salience of race led to the identification of relocation related to racial difference as white flight.

In the decades following World War II, housing demand, held in check by the Depression and the emergency of World War II, produced development of outer-city and suburban areas on an unprecedented scale, yet prevailing social practice and institutional policy continued to govern the housing market on a racially restrictive basis. The attraction of the new suburbs, primarily available only to whites, and the pent-up housing needs of African Americans combined to produce an era of unprecedented racial turnover of urban neighborhoods, sometimes triggered by blockbusting that specifically preyed on white racial fears to induce panic. Challenges to the racial status quo—through judicial decisions, legislation, and changing institutional policies—seemed to contribute to the out-migration of whites from older urban areas, especially those experiencing racial integration. These episodes of white flight greatly expanded areas of African-American residence, but usually resulted in high degrees of residential resegregation.

Scholars generally have agreed about the phenomenon of neighborhood turnover, but they have sometimes differed on whether race was a sufficiently singular factor to justify use of the term white flight as a primary explanation. Theories by sociologists associated with the University of Chicago in the 1920s and 1930s implied that race was one factor among others in "ecological succession," interpreted as a natural process whereby older and less desirable housing stock filtered down to lower-status social groups. However, the great episodes of neighborhood turnover after World War II prompted social scientists to focus specifically on the racial dimension, attempting to determine a "tipping point," the percentage of nonwhite presence that would trigger white exodus.

Some scholars sought to downplay the role of white flight as the primary cause of postwar residential change. One argument took the position that such nonracial factors as the attraction of the suburbs were largely responsible; a second contended that white avoidance of racially mixed or changing areas, not white flight per se, represented the chief explanation. Analysts also have stressed that the role of institutional factors may have been more determinative than individual attitudes for variable degrees of response to residential integration.

The controversy regarding white flight has had special relevance for school desegregation policy. In the mid-1970s, the influential James S. Coleman suggested that court-ordered desegregation, under certain conditions, might accelerate white flight from urban schools. Some challenged this contention, while others used it to argue for metropolitan solutions. Mandatory busing programs ordered by courts in such localities as Boston, Massachusetts, and Norfolk, Virginia, received special scrutiny regarding whether they contributed to white flight and therefore were counterproductive in achieving desegregation. To a great degree, the debate about the specific role of racial factors in changing school demographics mirrored the debate about race and residence.

Recent studies of residential patterns based upon data from the 1980 and 1990 censuses reveal a slower pace of racial turnover in metropolitan areas, a slight decline in indices of residential segregation, and some degree of variation by region. These results have led some scholars to suggest that the particularly acute episodes of racial change during the postwar decades may have been time and place specific, phenomena especially evident in large, older, northeastern and midwestern cities. Recent surveys of white attitudes also show a gradual increase in willingness to accept residential integration, although a continued pattern of heightened reservations as African-American numbers rise.

Fair housing advocates long have argued that the abolition of housing discrimination (through such measures as the U.S. Fair Housing Act of 1968 and similar state and local statutes) should dampen the propensity for racially motivated flight because all residential areas would be available to diverse racial and social groups. Nevertheless, while recent decades certainly have witnessed a cooling of these episodes, the general phenomenon of white flight remains a persistent challenge to residential racial integration.

—*W. Edward Orser*

**See also**
Blockbusting; Busing.

**References**
Aldrich, Howard. "Ecological Succession in Racially Changing Neighborhoods." *Urban Affairs Quarterly* 10 (1976): 327–348.
Farley, Reynolds, and William H. Frey. "Changes in the Segregation of Whites and Blacks during the 1980s: Small Steps toward a More Integrated Society." *American Sociological Review* 59 (1994): 23–45.
Farley, Reynolds, et al. " 'Chocolate City, Vanilla Suburbs': Will the Trend toward Racially Separate Communities Continue?" *Social Science Research* 7 (1978): 319–344.
Goering, John. "Neighborhood Tipping and Racial Transition: A Review of the Social Science Evidence." *American Institute of Planners Journal* 44 (1978): 68–78.
Orser, W. Edward. *Blockbusting in Baltimore: The Edmondson Village Story.* Lexington: University Press of Kentucky, 1994.
Wood, Peter B., and Barrett A. Lee. "Is Neighborhood Racial Succession Inevitable? Fifty Years of Evidence." *Urban Affairs Quarterly* 26 (1991): 610–620.

## Whitman, Walt (1819–1892)

After growing up in rural Long Island and the busy village of Brooklyn, the great American poet Walt Whitman spent his adult life living in and writing about the American city. He resided in New York during the 1840s and 1850s (except for a brief stay in New Orleans), writing articles about city politics and the cultural scene, stayed in Washington during and after the Civil War, serving first as a volunteer nurse in hospitals and then as a minor government official, and finally settled in Camden, New Jersey, writing poetry and prose and receiving visitors come to pay homage to America's bard. Whitman's lifelong immersion in American urban milieus renders him the first great poetic celebrant of metropolitan life, a sensitive recorder of urban experience, ever fascinated by street scenes, by "the blab of the pave," by the pageantry of Broadway at noon, and by the expectant rush of commuters on the Brooklyn ferry.

But what makes Whitman important to the history of American cities is not so much his poetic catalogues of ur-

ban characters and settings or his factual descriptions of parades on Pennsylvania Avenue as it is his visionary conception of city life in the New World. For the American city to Whitman is much more than a mere concentration of persons, dwellings, and marketplaces. It is an idyllic realization of what Whitman calls the "paradox" of "Democracy": "the eligibility of the free and fully developed individual with the paramount aggregate." That is, while the American city brings people together as social and economic functions (boss, employee, merchant, consumer, bus driver, neighbor, policeman, etc.) contributing to the overall liveliness and prosperity of the city, these identities highlight the singularity of every individual. In the metropolis, American citizens become lost in the crowd, submerged in a "countless prodigality of locomotion, dry goods, glitter, magnetism, and happiness." Yet because American society ideally is organized on egalitarian principles, every laborer and consumer feels equally valuable in the city's bustling operations and thereby stands out as a unique personality at the same time he or she stands for a portion of humanity. The city is the site of representative democracy, where the crowd *(demos)* has a legitimate political voice, but no more than that of each individual member.

A theater of passions and incidents, teeming with conflict and conciliation, mixing classes, races, occupations, nationalities, and sexualities, Whitman's American city is the social analogue of Whitman's own inclusive democratic poetry: "I will not have a single person slighted or left away" and "This is the city and I am one of the citizens, / Whatever interests the rest interests me." Like Whitman's poetics of integration, the city levels those distinctions of persons (wealth, title, privilege) that lead to artificial hierarchies and privileges. However, in massing citizens together indiscriminately in the same streets and stores and parks, the city does not sink individuals into an anonymous, powerless existence. Citizens' close socioeconomic relations signify a natural fellowship that enlivens people's lives, a communal bond that guarantees their participation in democracy. The only threat to this municipal pastoral is if urban relations become disconnected from the natural attachment of souls they should represent; if, say, business relations rest not upon a spirit of cooperation but upon a drive of competition. To Whitman, the best antidote to the decay of urban ideals would be to maintain intimate ties with nature:

> American Democracy, in its myriad personalities,
> in factories, work-shops, stores, offices—through
> the dense streets and houses of cities, and all their
> manifold sophisticated life—must either be fibred,
> vitalized, by regular contact with outdoor light and
> air and growths, farm-scenes, animals, fields, trees,

birds, sun-warmth and free skies, or it will certainly dwindle and pale.

—*Mark Bauerlein*

**References**
Allen, Gay Wilson. *The Solitary Singer: A Critical Biography of Walt Whitman.* New York: New York University Press, 1955.
Dougherty, James. *Walt Whitman and the Citizen's Eye.* Baton Rouge: Louisiana State University Press, 1993.
Keller, Elizabeth Leavitt. *Walt Whitman in Mickle Street.* Rev. ed. New York: Haskell House Publishers, 1971.
Rubin, Joseph Jay. *The Historic Whitman.* University Park: Pennsylvania State University Press, 1973.

## Willard, Frances Elizabeth Caroline (1839–1898)

Frances Willard, the renowned temperance reformer, was born in Churchville, New York, near Rochester, the daughter of Josiah Flint Willard and Mary Thompson Hill. Her parents, devout schoolteachers who had both been born in Vermont and attended Oberlin College, homesteaded in Wisconsin where Frank, as she preferred to be called, was a tomboy. A lifelong Methodist who had had a conversion experience, Willard had a bookish side and graduated in 1859 from what would later become Northwestern University. After a brief engagement ended abruptly, she taught school and then traveled in Europe and the Holy Land from 1868 to 1870 with a friend. After returning to the United States, she became a professor and dean of the female division of Northwestern University from 1871 to 1874, but she quarreled with the president, her onetime fiancé, and resigned.

In 1874, a women's crusade against liquor swept over the United States, and Willard became president of the Chicago Woman's Christian Temperance Union. In 1879, she was elected head of the national WCTU, a position she held until her death. An effective organizer, speaker, and writer, she and her confidante, Anna A. Gordon, turned the WCTU into the largest women's organization in the country, with 200,000 members. Willard attacked liquor from all directions, a policy called "Do Everything." Thus, the WCTU examined health, labor, welfare, prisons, and prostitution, and it persuaded public schools to adopt antiliquor materials. Considering alcohol primarily a threat to the family, Willard called for "home protection." While emphasizing the personal and moral dimensions of abstinence, she did support prohibition.

In 1884 Willard abandoned her lifelong commitment to the Republican Party and endorsed the Prohibition Party. At a time when many antiliquor leaders thought the suffrage issue divisive, she demanded that women be given the vote. Her autobiography, *Glimpses of Fifty Years* (1889), sold 50,000 copies and secured her financial independence. In 1891 she took charge of the World's WCTU. With her health declining, she spent much time in Britain, where she was influenced by Fabian socialism and drew close to the temperance leader Lady Henry Somerset. Willard's early death made her a martyr, and Illinois honored her with a statue in the U.S. Capitol.

—*W. J. Rorabaugh*

**References**
Bordin, Ruth B. A. *Frances Willard.* Chapel Hill: University of North Carolina Press, 1986.
James, Edward T., et al., eds. *Notable American Women: The Modern Period, A Biographical Dictionary.* Cambridge, MA: Harvard University Press, 1971.
Leeman, Richard W. *"Do Everything" Reform: The Oratory of Frances E. Willard.* New York: Greenwood Press, 1895.
Willard, Frances E. *Woman and Temperance; or, the Work and Workers of the Women's Christian Temperance Union.* Reprint ed. New York: Arno Press, 1972.
———. *Writing Out My Heart. Selections from the Journal of Frances E. Willard.* Carolyn De Swarte Gifford, ed. Urbana: University of Illinois Press, 1995.

## Williams, William Carlos (1883–1963)

The American poet William Carlos Williams was born in Rutherford, New Jersey, about seven miles from New York City. He attended the University of Pennsylvania where he met and was influenced by the premier modernist poet Ezra Pound. After he graduated, Williams continued his studies, earned a medical degree, practiced medicine, and wrote poetry for much of his adult life. Living in the New York area, he had easy access to the city and became a leading modernist thinker.

Williams's poetry, written in free verse, follows the rules of the Imagist school; it is direct, economical, and rhythmic. Williams himself contributed to the understanding of this poetic style with his statement, "No ideas but in things." Though many of his short lyrics generally meet the strictures of Imagism, Williams, like Pound himself, struggled with conventions. His most famous short poem, "The Red Wheelbarrow" (1923) shows this battle. In its entirety, the poem is:

so much depends upon
a red wheel barrow
glazed with rain water
beside the white chickens.

Here, despite the obvious rhythm and sparseness, Williams forces meaning into the poem by using the abstract "so much depends," thereby violating his own rule about providing ideas only through objects.

Williams's most famous long poem is *Paterson,* published between 1946 and 1962. Williams wrote this open field poem in the tradition of Walt Whitman's *Leaves of Grass*. In it, Williams uses free verse to convey the richness of everyday things, events, and places while using simple language, cogent images, and allusions to the local history of Paterson, New Jersey, near his own home in Rutherford. There are three major symbols in this book-length poem: the Passaic River, a symbol of generative power; Garret Mountain Park, a symbol of femininity; and the mill area of the city, a symbol of masculinity. To Williams, Paterson symbolized all American cities, and his poem shows the change from pastoral beauty before settlement to grime and hucksterism during industrialization. Like other modernist poems, "Paterson" shows the degrading effects of man's arrogance on the land and on his fellow men.

Williams's poem and his depiction of Paterson brought the city grants and other funding from federal urban renewal programs during the 1970s. As a result, the scuzzy urban area that Williams describes in the poem has changed to one of gentrified respectability, and filthy textile factories have become cute little museums. Williams writes of the people in the area as once "eating and kissing, / spitting and sucking, speaking" (37), but the area now, in his own words but in a different context, is "cleaner / and freer of disease" (23), partly because of the poem itself.

*—William R. Klink*

### References

Guimond, James. *The Art of William Carlos Williams: A Discovery and Possession of America*. Urbana: University of Illinois Press, 1968.

Klink, William R. "Paterson Forty Years after 'Paterson.'" *Sagetrieb* 6 (1987): 96–108.

Mariani, Paul. *William Carlos Williams: A New World Naked*. New York: W. W. Norton, 1990.

Riddel, Joseph. *The Inverted Bell: Modernism and the Counter-Poetics of William Carlos Williams*. Baton Rouge: Louisiana State University Press, 1974.

## Wirth, Louis (1897–1952)

Born in Gemunden, Germany, in 1897, the great urban sociologist Louis Wirth was brought to the United States as a child by a relative and stayed here to receive his education. Trained as an undergraduate at the University of Chicago, he returned there in 1931, on the invitation of Robert E. Park, to become a member of the Department of Sociology. There he would stay for the remainder of his life.

Wirth was a very active writer and teacher. He participated in a wide variety of public pursuits in Chicago and served on the boards of a number of important national organizations. He held strong political points of view, and early in his life he was drawn to radical causes at the university. In the 1940s and early 1950s he participated in a number of social and political activities in Chicago, including groups active in human relations and on the University of Chicago Roundtables, radio broadcasts that covered important topics in a lively and informative way for a lay audience. Wirth helped begin a number of important organizations, including the International Sociological Association, of which he was the first president. He also was elected president of the American Sociological Association in 1947.

Wirth's greatest accomplishments, according to his daughter, lay mainly in his ability to provide stirring lectures and to excite people with his splendid oratorical skills. These proved helpful in a number of ways, including the establishment of the first social science courses in the College of the University of Chicago. He also worked hard to improve race relations in the United States. He was particularly insistent on making blacks full members of the American mainstream, and he wrote and argued persuasively on the topic.

Wirth also became a second-generation member of the Chicago School of Sociology. Like Robert E. Park and Ernest W. Burgess, key members of this school, Wirth devoted a great deal of his attention to studying cities and helping to formulate key policies to correct urban ills. In the course of this work, Wirth produced what would become a classic piece of theoretical analysis on the city, "Urbanism as a Way of Life." This article, first published in *The American Journal of Sociology* in 1938, would become perhaps the most widely cited work ever written by an urbanist. It reflected not only the original ideas of Wirth but served as a touchstone for the urban agenda of the Chicago School of Sociology. And it also deeply reflected the influence of German thinkers, particularly the writings of Georg Simmel on the city.

In this essay, Wirth argues that by the early part of the twentieth century the city had become the central locus of cultivation and of new ideas. It stood as the empirical and conceptual contrast to the village. Here he invoked parallel polarities that would become discussed in other contexts, particularly the contrast between the folk and urban society. There were three central features to the city, he argued: the size of the population, the density of the population, and the heterogeneity of the population. He proceeded to relate each of these key variables to certain distinctive social, political, and psychological patterns in the city. For example, he maintained, as cities grew larger the relationships between people inevitably grew more impersonal, ephemeral, and in some sense based sheerly on objective rather than subjective criteria. People knew one another in cities not as individuals but as members of categories. In addition, as cities grew more densely populated, individuals were forced to become both more specialized and more differentiated in terms of their occupational pursuits and careers. As cities became more diverse and heterogeneous, people were compelled to seek one another out, creating new social bonds in the form, among other things, of new voluntary associations. This theoretical portrait was brilliantly conceived and compellingly developed. Because of its clarity, it seemed to capture all the distinctive features of newly emergent American cities, especially as they differed from rural areas.

But later analysts pointed to serious flaws and unexamined assumptions in Wirth's analysis. For example, Wirth insisted that neighborhoods would disappear as cities grew. Yet that proved not to be the case. Ironically, it was Wirth who helped oversee the publication of the first of several Community Fact Books for the city of Chicago, works that revealed in rich detail the nature and variety of subcommunities in the city. In addition, later analysts also pointed out that many of Wirth's urban characteristics, particularly of the disorganization among individuals and of the "predatory" character of commercial life, were not so much features of urban life as they were of the growth of capitalism.

Wirth had enormous energy and a rapacious interest in efforts to reform and improve American society. Unfortunately, his premature death at the age of 55 cut short his activities and probably deprived sociology of an even richer and more illustrious heritage of theoretical writings on the city.

—*Anthony M. Orum*

### References

Bulmer, Martin. *The Chicago School of Sociology.* Chicago: University of Chicago Press, 1984.

Reiss, Albert J., Jr., ed. *Louis Wirth: On Cities and Social Life.* Chicago: University of Chicago Press, 1964.

## Women in Cities

For women, perhaps even more than for men, cities have been places of opportunity. Across the history of American urban development, both sexes migrated to cities in search of employment, education, and better prospects than the countryside or their native lands offered. As Americans began leaving farms for cities and as immigration accelerated in the nineteenth century, women found some cities especially attractive places to live. Cities offered many more advantages to women than did rural areas. Better-paying jobs; possibilities for recreational, cultural, and leisure activities; and an end to the isolation that frequently accompanied rural life all drew women to cities.

Urbanization and industrialization were closely linked in the United States, with certain industrial environments being specially attractive to women. In the early nineteenth century, for example, small Massachusetts towns developed into cities with a predominance of women working in textile mills and shoe factories and residing in the districts surrounding them. By 1860 women outnumbered men in some

of the largest eastern cities, including Boston, New York, Philadelphia, and Baltimore, while men were more numerous in western cities such as Cincinnati, Chicago, and St. Louis.

Over the twentieth century, cities continued to exert a particular attraction for women. Of the large cities (those with more than 100,000 residents) in 1900, three-fifths had more women living in them than men. Men tended to predominate in cities whose economies were based on heavy industry, mining, or logging, mostly in the West. Women clustered in eastern and southern cities, those with large textile and garment industries or where the service sector was particularly well developed. This trend has continued throughout the twentieth century, resulting in a higher proportion of American women living in cities than men. Most (but not all) cities at the end of the twentieth century have unbalanced sex ratios favoring women.

As immigration and migration altered the composition of the urban population in the early twentieth century, the sex ratio teetered back and forth, favoring women in 1900 and men until 1930. From the Depression on, cities have had more female residents. Although the definition of *city* in the U.S. census changed to exclude places with smaller populations, by the middle and late twentieth century urbanized areas, and particularly central cities, tended to have a greater preponderance of women, who found rural and suburban areas less attractive, especially for women without partners.

A comparison of urban women and urban men in 1890 (the first year for which marital status was disaggregated by city size) shows that urban dwellers were more likely than the country as a whole to be single and that there were more single men in cities than single women. By the late twentieth century, nonmarried women outnumber single men in many cities. Two processes are at work here: more women survive the death of a partner than vice versa, and widowed, divorced, and never-married women have always been attracted to cities as a means of keeping body and soul together and finding others in similar circumstances. As the twentieth century progressed, the proportion of never-married women declined, but cities still held more attraction for them than rural or suburban areas. The urban trend for widows to outnumber widowers by large numbers continued in cities. Divorce rates also rose so that, overall, cities had a greater proportion of unmarried women than either rural areas or suburbs. In the late twentieth century, the number of unmarried women in urban areas exceeded that of men, as did the number of older women whose partners have died.

The economic opportunities available to women in cities exerted a significant urban impetus quite early in the nation's history. While women on their own and in families could and did farm, for some of them the city offered a surer or more straightforward way to earn a living. Women with young children who inherited the family farm on their husband's death might move to a nearby city to open a boarding house or a small shop. Alternatively, widows with older or grown children might continue to operate the farm as a family venture. In the late eighteenth and early nineteenth centuries, many urban widows continued the businesses their husbands had owned and in which they might have already worked. As long as home and workplace were located together, women participated in family businesses and knew enough about them to continue after their husband's death. Urban women also engaged in shopkeeping, peddling, seamstressing, and similar occupations on their own behalf.

Evidence from both northern and southern urban areas in the early nineteenth century shows the extent to which white and free African-American women were economically active in cities in their own right. They grew fruit and vegetables to sell at markets; sold eggs, butter, and dairy products; and generally entered a variety of income-producing activities. Even when women did not live in cities or towns, they might still use them as a market for their products, journeying there to sell whatever commodities they processed or produced. For married women, at least, such productivity declined by the middle of the nineteenth century, succumbing to the emphasis on female domesticity and competition from commercial producers.

As home and workplace separated, business activities expanded, and production of goods in factories increased, it became more difficult for married women to engage in production for market. The Cult of True Womanhood, which emphasized piety, purity, submissiveness, and domesticity as appropriate female behaviors, hindered married middle-class white women from taking advantage of the new economic opportunities cities offered. While married African-American women continued to work on the land or as domestic servants in cities, this became less common for married white women by the middle of the nineteenth century. Nevertheless, urban women from all races and ethnic groups had sporadic employment outside the home. They did casual labor, took in washing or sewing, or cleaned offices, shops, and homes, but census officials rarely included their part-time or occasional work in official statistics of employment.

Married women also used their homes to generate income by taking in boarders. This form of generating income fell out of favor with middle-class women by the end of the nineteenth century and with working-class women by the second quarter of the twentieth. Some married women also toiled in the "sweated" trades of tenement house districts in large cities of this era. They sewed garments, rolled cigars, and made artificial flowers for many hours a day, at low wage rates for piecework, frequently combining their work with looking after their children. The employment of married

women increased throughout the century, accelerated by the opportunities of World War II, improved education and training, and a desire to participate in the post–World War II consumer culture that increasingly required two incomes to provide the desired standard of living and education for the family and its children.

While the rate of married women participating in the urban labor force did not rise markedly until the twentieth century, that of single women surged in the nineteenth. The new factories paid better wages than were available to women as servants, hired hands, or working at other rural endeavors. This drew women, particularly young, single, native- and foreign-born white women into cities that housed factories. At first, textile mill owners felt obliged to provide a quasi-familial environment for their young female employees (usually in company-supervised boarding houses), but as increased immigration led to a more diverse hiring policy, more women workers lived with their own families. Increasingly in the twentieth century, women migrated to cities seeking work and living in boarding houses, shared apartments, or (in the late twentieth century) on their own. This gave them freedom to structure their leisure time as they wanted, to retain their wages (frequently quite low), and spend their money in accordance with their own priorities rather than their families'.

During the early twentieth century, the cities with the greatest proportion of women workers had economies dominated by producing textiles, or they were located in the Deep South where African-American poverty meant that a very high proportion of African-American women took jobs as servants and laundresses. While African-American men received little encouragement from employers to move to cities, African-American women found readily available, if poorly paid, work as domestics. As a result, many cities with large African-American populations had an excess of women over men.

World War II provided opportunities for African-American and Mexican-American women to work in defense plants, just as it did for European-American women. This brought even more women into cities searching for relatively well paid jobs. After the war, as marriage rates soared, many new couples abandoned cities for suburbs, obtaining mortgages through federally subsidized programs. While the new housing developments attracted white women and their families, women of color found that racial prejudice virtually barred them from the flight to the suburbs that occurred after World War II.

Cities provided jobs for many women after World War II, but many women workers now live outside the city, residing instead in the suburbs. The urban core has become an increasingly problematic place to live, raise a family, and feel safe. As whites and the middle class of all races fled from cities, their tax dollars followed them, leaving poor central cities surrounded by more affluent suburbs. The deterioration in urban services that resulted has had serious consequences for women who did not wish to, or were unable to, join the suburban exodus. Changes in social mores have meant that more women are raising children without partners, frequently on low incomes or Aid to Families with Dependent Children. Many urban women live in areas rife with crime, drug abuse, and serious health problems such as AIDS and tuberculosis. Competition for federal, state, and even city tax dollars means that the social services needed to support women and their children are underfunded and overstretched.

One consequence of the growth of cities and women's interest in affairs outside the home in the nineteenth and early twentieth centuries was their increased participation in a wide range of reform endeavors. Spurred on by a belief that individual moral responsibility meant that women, no less than men, should work on behalf of the less fortunate, many women went out from their churches into the community to undertake a variety of reform and welfare activities. Urban women in the North joined antislavery societies, and when their speaking out was not welcomed, they formed their own, exclusively female, organizations to work against slavery and for moral reform, temperance, and charity. Affluent women raised money to help the poor and formed societies to reform their behavior. In the nineteenth century, they acted on the belief that women had a unique role to play in providing guidance to the less fortunate, acting as friendly visitors and, toward the end of the nineteenth and beginning of the twentieth centuries, establishing settlement houses such as that pioneered by Jane Addams at Hull House in Chicago.

In the latter decades of the nineteenth century and early decades of the twentieth, women also played vital roles in reform movements. They tried to improve municipal government, develop protective legislation, and improve public health, especially for women and children. The women of most religious, ethnic, and racial groups worked actively on behalf of their less fortunate sisters and brothers. Bound together by ties of sentiment, national origin, religion, or race, and possibly excluded from other groups by racial, religious, or ethnic prejudice, women labored to ameliorate the worst aspects of urban life. Many of the organizations established in the late nineteenth century continued their efforts into the 1920s, only to see them collapse during the Depression. Female volunteers were supplanted by professional social workers, themselves mostly female, with the overall result that women continued to play a major part in urban social and professional services, but as trained, paid employees rather than as genteel volunteers.

In addition to providing economic opportunities and serving as venues for reform, cities have enabled women to participate in recreational and leisure activities that rural areas (and later suburbs) lacked or provided meagerly. Depending upon social class, ethnic or cultural background, and personal interests, women joined benevolent societies, church missionary societies, literary and discussion clubs, and reform organizations in the nineteenth century, while in the twentieth century the range of urban leisure activities spans the artistic, cultural, and sporting endeavors.

In the nineteenth century, most women's recreational time was spent with other women, while in the twentieth century women increasingly engaged in mixed-sex leisure-time pursuits. Women participated in a wide variety of commercial recreational opportunities in the early twentieth century, some of which met with extreme disapproval from Progressive reformers who felt that dance halls, nickelodeons, and amusement parks were sordid places. These venues, along with the cinema in the twentieth century, provided an escape from the humdrum world of work. They also facilitated unsupervised contact with men, which appealed to many women in the twentieth century.

Cities continue to be places of opportunity, recreation, and culture for women, but they also pose very serious problems for those who encounter racial prejudice, suffer from chronic ailments, or lack the education to obtain better-paying jobs. For many women, urban employment at the end of the twentieth century occurs in "McJobs," poorly paid, marginal, and without the health insurance and other benefits so necessary to survival in the late-twentieth-century city. The gap between rich and poor women in cities has widened since World War II, as it has for men. A more equitable sharing of resources between city and suburb, greater investment in basic services, and affordable heath care would all improve the quality of urban life for women and their families.

—*S. J. Kleinberg*

**See also**

Amusement Parks; Fertility; Women's Clubs; Women's Work.

**References**

Blackwelder, Julia Kirk. *Women of the Depression: Caste and Culture in San Antonio, 1929–1939.* College Station: Texas A & M University Press, 1984.

Glenn, Susan A. *Daughters of the Shtetl: Life and Labor in the Immigrant Generation.* Ithaca, NY: Cornell University Press, 1990.

Jones, Jacqueline. *Labor of Love, Labor of Sorrow: Black Women, Work, and the Family from Slavery to the Present.* New York: Basic Books, 1985.

Lopata, Helena Znaniecki. *Widowhood in an American City.* Cambridge, MA: Schenckman Publishing Company, 1973.

Lynd, Robert S., and Helen Merrell Lynd. *Middletown: A Study in Modern American Culture.* Reprint ed. New York: Harcourt, Brace & World, 1950.

Meyerowitz, Joanne J. *Women Adrift: Independent Wage Earners in Chicago, 1880–1930.* Chicago: University of Chicago Press, 1988.

Peiss, Kathy. *Cheap Amusements: Working Women and Leisure in Turn-of-the-Century New York.* Philadelphia: Temple University Press, 1986.

## Women's Clubs

American women have formed voluntary organizations for social interaction, educational improvement, and civic reform activism, particularly between the middle of the nineteenth century and the 1930s. The most influential and the earliest of these were founded in 1868, Sorosis in New York City and the New England Woman's Club in Boston. The concept was rapidly embraced by women of other cities and their suburbs, and the club movement expanded nationally. By 1890 the General Federation of Women's Clubs (GFWC) formed to unite club interests, provide a clearinghouse for club ideas, sponsor conventions, and offer publications for the use of members. By 1910 the GFWC asserted that almost 1 million members belonged to women's clubs, and by the 1920s membership had peaked at about 2 million. Not until the 1920s, when the growing availability of labor-saving devices eased their household and farm burdens, did rural women contemplate participating.

The women attracted to club life tended to be the privileged, white, educated, middle-class wives of successful business and professional men of their communities; their children had grown, and they had servants to ease their domestic responsibilities. Often, when a club limited the size of

*Women working for their Women's Club in Cleveland, Ohio, collect household waste to be recycled in an effort to counteract supply shortages caused by World War II.*

its membership, these women had to wait until a vacancy occurred and they received an invitation from friends and neighbors to join. This kept most early clubs small and, equally important, it kept them exclusive and desirable.

African-American women, Jewish women, and women of other ethnic and racial minorities were often excluded from these clubs and responded by forming parallel groups of their own that undertook many similar self-improvement and civic reform projects. For example, the National Association of Colored Women (formerly the National Association of Colored Women's Clubs) developed from the merger in 1896 of the National Federation of Afro-American Women and the National League of Colored Women. The National Council of Jewish Women was founded two years before, in 1894.

In the middle of the nineteenth century, women were not welcome in most men's clubs and organizations. Nevertheless, they were eager to expand their roles outside the household and so they formed these clubs. The groups met weekly or monthly, from September to June, in gatherings as small as a dozen, in the homes of members. Literary study was frequently the initial reason for meeting. The members selected a single topic each year, such as Shakespeare's plays, American history, Asian art, or current events, and each member was responsible for researching, writing, and delivering a talk to the whole group, answering questions, and generating debate. Refreshments generally rounded out the meeting. Some clubs emphasized gracious hospitality and sent reports of the menu and decor to the women's club page of their local newspaper, perhaps leaving the false impression that only social activity had occurred.

That understanding was incorrect. Many women's clubs addressed social issues, investigating such problems as the need for libraries, parks, playgrounds, art galleries, vocational training and music instruction in the schools, public health clinics, day care facilities, improved educational opportunities for women, and shelters for aged, homeless, abused, or pregnant women. Members often proposed solutions by initiating, funding, and maintaining programs to meet social needs and lobbying for local, state, and federal legislation to regulate child labor, working conditions, mothers' pensions, maternal and infant health care, and the environment.

These clubs became an interest group to be reckoned with. Government bureaucrats, officeholders, and politicians routinely spoke at their meetings and sought support. Recognizing this, and hoping to increase their influence in the public arena, clubs in the twentieth century tended to invite increased numbers to join. By the middle of the 1920s the Friday Morning Club and the Wilshire Ebell of Los Angeles each had 2,500 members.

With this larger size, clubs could offer their members specialized study or a variety of departments with which members could ally themselves. A large women's club had sufficient members to maintain regular Spanish-language classes, a women's chorus, or field trips to the studios of local painters. The Chicago Woman's Club, founded in 1876 for "mutual sympathy and counsel, and united effort toward the higher civilization of humanity," organized itself around six departments: reform, home, education, philanthropy, art and literature, and philosophy and science. Similarly, the Atlanta Woman's Club, founded in 1895, divided its volunteer work around literature, art, science, education, philanthropy, home, civics, and business.

While some critics objected to the clubs' growing voice in the public arena, restating the age-old dictum that "a woman's place is in the home," women continued cooperating to change their communities. Clubs offered leadership positions and organizing skills to large numbers of women who had few other training schools for civic leadership and no significant outlets to express civic activism. The clubs not only offered a place for women to develop these skills, the members developed them well as they achieved many of their municipal goals for reform and improvement.

Membership peaked in the 1920s. By then, women had been admitted into other arenas for political, economic, and social expression, and clubs were no longer the only vehicle that provided them with a public voice. Women's clubs have continued to exist, however, and to employ many of the same structures and goals as they have throughout their history.

—*Karen J. Blair*

### References

Baker, Paula. "Domestication of Politics: Women and American Political Society, 1780-1920." *American Historical Review* 89 (1984): 620–647.

Blair, Karen J. *The Clubwoman as Feminist: True Womanhood Redefined, 1868–1916.* New York: Holmes and Meier, 1980.

———. *The History of American Women's Voluntary Organizations, 1810–1960: A Guide to Sources.* Boston: G. K. Hall, 1989.

———. *The Torchbearers: Women and Their Amateur Arts Associations, 1890–1920.* Bloomington: Indiana University Press, 1994.

Croly, Jane Cunningham. *The History of the Woman's Club Movement in America.* New York: Henry G. Allen, 1898.

## Women's Work

Urban development multiplied women's employment opportunities. From the colonial period on, American farm women brought dairy and poultry products, garden yields, and home manufactures to market. The cash value of these products rose as the number of city-dwelling consumers increased. Women also carried their skills in housekeeping, cookery, needlework, and the like to the city as they migrated in search of employment, and demand for female workers rose steadily with industrialization.

Industrialization altered the nature and the location of women's work as the factory production of textiles, shoes, garments, paper products, and other nondurable goods replaced home and artisanal manufactures. Textile factories dotted the rivers and streams of the Northeast and mid-Atlantic states in the mid-nineteenth century. In early textile centers such as Lowell, Massachusetts, villages formed about the mills, and the villages soon grew into towns and cities. In emerging textile centers, women dominated the labor force, and their presence defined living arrangements and the cultural and social life that flourished in and about the mills. In other locations, the growth of garment and shoe factories, which followed from the broad adoption of Singer sewing machines in the 1860s, centered in existing commercial and manufacturing centers in which similar numbers of men held jobs in heavy industry.

Whether women worked in small towns or major cities, factories and sweatshops exposed them to unhealthful conditions. Factories had emerged as notorious centers of women's exploitation by the end of the nineteenth century. In the first decade of the twentieth century the U.S. Senate authorized a study of the wages and working conditions of women and children in the nation's factories, a measure that culminated in volumes of data on the low wages and dangerous environments of female employment and the persistence of child labor in factories throughout urban America. After 147 workers, mostly women, died in a 1911 fire at the Triangle Shirtwaist Company in New York City, the state of New York adopted a comprehensive factory safety code, and other states followed New York's initiative. Protective legislation removed some hazards from the workplace, but these gender-based employment codes also worked to depress women's earnings.

Movement to cities transformed women's unpaid tasks as well as their wage-earning activities and exposed them to different living arrangements. Dense housing, crowded apartments, and the dangers of city streets complicated housekeeping and child care. The interdependence of urbanites and the influence of environmental conditions on individual health and welfare propelled women into cooperative ventures and political action from the late nineteenth century on. Social and welfare workers like Jane Addams in Chicago and Lillian Wald in New York campaigned to improve the living and the working conditions of the urban poor and simultaneously forged new careers for themselves and other educated women. Settlement workers set the stage for women's entry into mainstream politics in the twentieth century through their individual efforts to make their voices heard at City Hall and in the legislature.

Historically, women have outnumbered men in most urban places as urban economies offered women superior em-

*Urban women have often been able to find only menial work in unpleasant conditions. Here, women at the W.A. Burpee Seed Company fill orders in cramped quarters.*

ployment options to rural settings and drew women from the American countryside and from other nations. Although factory employment was a mainstay of the working woman through the 1950s, service jobs employed more women in the twentieth century than did manufacturing, and service jobs were firmly tied to the urban economy and infrastructure. Demand for female labor increased steadily as urban commercial classes gained wealth and disposable income. The middle and upper classes employed domestic servants and patronized hotels, commercial laundries, and sewing and millinery shops that employed women as charwomen, washerwomen, needleworkers, and clerks. City-dwelling women comprised the primary market for women's magazines, an industry that specifically catered to the growing middle class. While men generally dominated the business end of publishing, magazines such as *Godey's Lady's Book and American Ladies' Magazine,* founded in 1837 and edited by Sarah Josepha Hale, opened the world of journalism to educated women. Technological change and urban consumer tastes paved the way for new jobs in the beauty industry. The number of hairdressers and beauty schools grew rapidly in the 1920s, and beauty salons continued to expand through the 1950s. Employing many more women than men, the retail beauty trade, like other fashion-based industries, catered to particular class-based and race-based clienteles and thus provided entrepreneurial opportunities to immigrant and minority women.

The labor shortage that accompanied the Civil War induced the federal government to employ thousands of female office clerks in the nation's capital. In the years following the war, female office employment caught on in other cities. The adoption of communication technologies such as the typewriter and the telephone and new standards of record keeping generated urban jobs for women beginning in the late-nineteenth century. By the 1920s female typists, stenographers, and switchboard operators predominated in public and private workplaces. Industrialization and urbanization also drove the expansion of skilled service industries such as medicine and education that used female labor to fill vacancies in teaching and nursing at substantially lower costs than those required to employ men. In the twentieth century, teaching and nursing provided avenues of social mobility for working-class women who were fortunate enough to pursue high school and postsecondary training.

Regardless of the nature of their work, occupational segregation by gender and by race or ethnicity has characterized women's work during the modern era, and the segmentation of the labor market has worked to depress women's earnings. The steady expansion of city-based jobs for women since the early nineteenth century has permitted women to sustain themselves through wage earning, but most urban employers of the nineteenth and early twentieth centuries paid women so little that independent women were doomed to poverty. From the late nineteenth century into the late twentieth century, women have earned between 50 and 70 cents for every dollar earned by men. Through labor unions and strikes, women steadily fought low wages, but protest had minimal effect on women's earnings until after World War II. In the last four decades of the twentieth century, women have fought occupational segregation and succeeded in marshaling the force of law behind their efforts. Although occupational segregation persists at the close of the century, its intensity has diminished as women have gained footholds in occupations such as firefighting and the law, and separate pay scales for women have been abolished. Market forces, legal remedies, and affirmative action policies have all worked to narrow the wage gap since 1980.

In the long run, the evolution of wage work for women increased their ties to the urban setting and transformed American family life. As reliance on goods grown or produced within the household decreased or disappeared, the cash needs of families rose steadily. Working children initially provided the majority of earnings that supplemented the profits or wages of household heads, but child labor declined as employers' needs for skilled workers escalated; the increasing wage gap between unskilled youthful workers and well-educated adults diminished the importance of working children. In time, wives' earnings replaced those of sons and daughters who spent more time in school than had their parents. As families increasingly relied on wives to earn wages, the advantages of urban economies with complex employment opportunities stood in clear contrast with single-industry towns and rural settings in which one family member's earning potential was severely restricted. Urban economies thus worked continuously to draw women and families into settings that maximized their earning potential, although employment at the urban periphery gradually replaced the importance of central manufacturing and business districts as the core of the nation's cities declined after World War II.

—*Julia Kirk Blackwelder*

**See also**
Office Work; Retail Workers.
**References**
Blackwelder, Julia Kirk. *Now Hiring: The Feminization of Work in the United States, 1900–1995.* College Station: Texas A & M University Press, 1997.
Blewett, Mary H. *Men, Women, and Work: Class, Gender, and Protest in the New England Shoe Industry, 1780–1910.* Urbana: University of Illinois Press, 1988.
Dublin, Thomas. *Transforming Women's Work: New England Lives in the Industrial Revolution.* Ithaca, NY: Cornell University Press, 1994.
———. *Women at Work: The Transformation of Work and Community in Lowell, Massachusetts, 1826–1860.* New York: Columbia University Press, 1979.
Ewen, Elizabeth. *Immigrant Women in the Land of Dollars: Life and Culture on the Lower East Side, 1890–1925.* New York: Monthly Review Press, 1985.
Goldin, Claudia. *Understanding the Gender Gap: An Economic History of American Women.* New York: Oxford University Press, 1990.
Kessler-Harris, Alice. *Out to Work: A History of Wage-Earning Women in the United States.* New York: Oxford University Press, 1982.
Matthaei, Julie A. *An Economic History of Women in America: Women's Work, the Sexual Division of Labor, and the Development of Capitalism.* New York: Schocken Books, 1982.
Stansell, Christine. *City of Women; Sex and Class in New York City.* New York: Knopf, 1986.

## Workhouses

Institutions to provide for the indigent date back to English laws of the fourteenth century that were codified in 1601. The Elizabethan Poor Laws established the principle of local responsibility for the poor and needy, and they authorized parish church wardens and a board of respectable householders to serve as Overseers of the Poor. Vagrants and sturdy but unemployed beggars were confined to workhouses to control poverty and crime. Transplanted to America by the 1660s, the municipal workhouse became a refuge of last resort for the urban sick, elderly, homeless, and petty criminals of all ages.

Boston built America's first workhouse in 1660, replaced by a larger building in 1662 near Boston Common. Mixing children with adults, especially the unfortunate inmates commonly found there—the insane, senile, handicapped, pregnant, diseased, drunken, and disorderly—was deplored as

unwise, but the practice continued until 1735. Outdoor poor relief (at home) was limited to respectable local residents, and indoor relief in the workhouse provided for all others. Despite every effort to control and contain them, both types of public welfare were one of the most costly items for American city governments in the eighteenth century.

The unclassified workhouse was considered obsolete by 1800, but the traditional alternatives—indenture, apprenticeship, outdoor relief, warning out, and whipping—were not always practical in expanding urban places. Philanthropic citizens who founded penitentiaries and congregate asylums in the 1820s were confident that the new publicly supported institutions would replace workhouses (or poorhouses and almshouses) in towns and cities. But when the number of paupers did become burdensome to cities, Americans isolated the poor to discourage pauperization. In 1849 Boston built a new workhouse on Deer Island in Boston Harbor to separate the indigent from the rest of the community. By the 1860s the number of county workhouses had increased greatly and remained a common urban institution until the early twentieth century.

Although Charles Dickens had exposed the cruelty of workhouses in *Oliver Twist* (1838), this bleak asylum persisted. During hard times or economic depressions, especially in the 1870s and 1890s, the "tramp menace" (the migrating unemployed) caused some workhouses to overflow and drain the public purse. Governments used vagrancy and loitering laws to discourage the nonresident poor from begging or lingering. As public hospitals and prisons became more common, the workhouse collected the noncriminal poor and elderly. Not until the New Deal reformed public welfare programs in the 1930s did workhouses disappear from most American cities.

—*Peter C. Holloran*

**See also**
Almshouses.
**References**
Bremner, Robert H. *From the Depths: The Discovery of Poverty in the United States.* New York: New York University Press, 1956.
Holloran, Peter C. *Boston's Wayward Children: Social Services for Wayward Children, 1830–1930.* Rutherford, NJ: Fairleigh Dickinson University Press, 1989.
Poynter, John R. *Society and Pauperism: English Ideas on Poor Relief, 1795–1834.* Toronto, Ontario: University of Toronto Press, 1969.
Trattner, Walter I. *From Poor Law to Welfare State: A History of Social Welfare in the United States.* New York: Free Press, 1974.

## Working Class in Cities

The origins and composition of the American working class have been matters of intense debate for several centuries. Politicians have often proclaimed that America is a classless society, but scholars have shown that lines of wealth and social status have always divided the nation. Although the United States may be a nation without a clearly articulated sense of class consciousness, classes, and especially the working class, have always played a significant role in the United States.

The urban centers of colonial America—especially port cities such as Boston, New York, and Philadelphia—had significant numbers of artisans and common laborers. These skilled craftsmen (cabinetmakers, silversmiths, carpenters, masons, tailors, and so on) and unskilled workers (teamsters, cart men, ditchdiggers, and so forth) were essential to the physical and economic growth of colonial cities. During the Revolutionary Era, a wide range of urban workers resisted British authority. Groups like the Sons of Liberty often drew their members from local trade societies of bakers, butchers, painters, and other craftsmen. Poorer urban workers from nearby docks, warehouses, and construction sites filled the crowds that tormented British tax collectors and other officials.

Urban workers also figured prominently in the campaign to ratify the Constitution in 1789. Most cities on the East Coast strongly favored ratification, and many workers considered the Constitution crucial to the nation's economic stability and growing export economy. The laboring people of Philadelphia literally marched front and center in a grand parade to celebrate ratification in July 1788. Numerous groups carried the tools of their trades in the procession and proclaimed that workers had physically and politically laid the foundations of the new nation.

By the end of the eighteenth century, many artisans and laborers considered themselves a distinct group within the larger society. They began to enunciate the idea of a working-class republicanism in which those who labored were deemed virtuous by their serving the commonweal, deserved an equal stake in the nation's government, and were entitled to equitable laws that would narrow the gap between rich and poor. The very future of the republic was said to rest on the strength, independence, and unity of the producing class—the working majority of farmers, shopkeepers, and urban laborers.

The nation's urban population soared from barely 200,000 in 1790 to 3.5 million in 1850. Thousands of migrants from surrounding rural regions poured into cities such as New York looking for new job opportunities as land started to wear out in older farming communities. New western cities like Pittsburgh, Cincinnati, St. Louis, and Chicago grew up around canals, water-powered machine shops and mills and, later, railroad terminals. Starting in the late 1840s, an enormous wave of Irish immigrants escaping the potato famine filled port cities from Boston to Savannah. A smaller group of Germans fleeing political persecution after the failed revo-

lutions of 1848 added highly skilled and highly politicized workers to cities as far west as Chicago and Milwaukee.

Workers in cities saw many of their occupations—especially shoemaking, tailoring, and furniture building—broken down into discrete and repetitive tasks that could be performed by semiskilled rural migrants and recent immigrant workers. Wages often fell while working conditions deteriorated, and it became nearly impossible for a journeyman to save enough money to open his own shop.

Workers responded to these dramatic changes by forming the first "modern" labor unions in American history—organizations usually organized around a single trade in a single city, and agitating for a living wage and workers' control of their own crafts. These unions—often called journeymen's societies—negotiated with employers over price lists, closed shops, and apprenticeship rules; they also served as important outlets for the expression of workers' culture. Within these organizations, workers drank, sang, marched, and toasted each other, they raised money for sickness and death benefits, and they sponsored reading rooms and lecture series on mechanical arts and contemporary political issues.

The political and cultural life of workers was not confined to union halls; the late 1820s and early 1830s also experienced the rise of workingmen's political parties. These parties campaigned to end imprisonment for debt, to lower the property requirement for male suffrage, and for access to public schools for working-class children. Within a few years, much of the membership and platform of these parties was absorbed and appropriated by the Jacksonians or deflected into renewed union organizing and early efforts to build alliances for labor reform that crossed class lines.

As cities grew in population, their physical size also increased through expansion, annexation, and construction. Working-class neighborhoods often became more distinct and in some cases physically isolated from wealthier districts. Although many workers in this period were known to share a taste for opera, symphony, and Shakespeare with the elite, the laboring community also began to be interested in sports such as baseball and boxing, and to develop a male-centered (and sometimes ethnically centered) culture around saloons.

The links between urbanization, industrialization, and immigration were especially strong from 1880 to 1920 when more than 20 million immigrants (many of them from Southern and Eastern Europe) entered the United States. Although newcomers from Scandinavia and parts of Central Europe often went to the Midwest and Great Plains in search of farmland, millions of unskilled European peasants filled the factories, sweatshops, warehouses, docks, and freight yards of American cities.

These immigrants often lived in congested neighborhoods where sanitation was lacking or nonexistent, and mortality rates from communicable diseases (especially diphtheria, typhus, cholera, and tuberculosis) were quite high. In smaller cities, a variety of ethnic groups might crowd into a single immigrant neighborhood, often close to the factories or rail yards where many immigrant men and their children found employment. In larger cities, distinctive neighborhoods for particular immigrant populations—Poles, Italians, Russian Jews—might cluster near each other. As a result, there could be interethnic group contact and sometimes conflict, especially near the unmarked borders of a neighborhood where the boundaries between immigrant populations often blurred.

Within these ethnic enclaves, immigrants struggled to retain crucial links with Old World customs and traditions, and to earn enough money to support their families in America. In churches and synagogues, clergy often served as important mediators between the community and urban authorities such as police and politicians. There were local merchants and shopkeepers who spoke the immigrants' native languages, stocked familiar foods and other products, and provided credit during hard times (something that the new department stores downtown would never extend to a poor immigrant). There were ethnic fraternal lodges—the Sons of Italy, Polish Falcons, Ancient Order of Hibernians, Knights of Pythias—which often provided essential health and burial insurance in addition to male camaraderie.

Newly arrived immigrants used networks of family, friends, neighbors, and townsfolk within these enclaves to help them find jobs and places to live. Certain immigrant groups developed virtual monopolies over particular occupations in the urban industrial economy. Italians dominated many construction jobs, especially excavating and tunneling; Eastern European Jews controlled many of the "sweated" trades in the garment industry; Poles and Central Europeans filled the steel mills; and Irish immigrants often held longshoring jobs at major ports along the East Coast.

American cities at the beginning of the twentieth century were vibrant centers of working-class culture, even beyond individual ethnic neighborhoods. Working men continued to base much of their social life around fraternal lodges, saloons, and sporting events. Women and children often used neighborhood streets, front stoops, and local parks for their recreation and socializing. Everyone seemed to take part in revelry, some of it quite rowdy, associated with holidays such as Labor Day, Christmas, and especially the Fourth of July. Even recent immigrant groups gathered in lodges and churches to link the celebration of American independence with their own concepts of freedom, play, and ethnic pride. By the early 1900s new forms of popular entertainment—amusement parks, dance halls, and movie houses (nickelodeons)—attracted literally millions of working-class people (particularly younger people) to spend their hard-earned money and their hard-won free time on commercial leisure.

American cities were also the site of enormous conflicts between labor and capital. The railroad strikes of 1877—fueled in part by radical German immigrants in alliance with native-born activists—spawned general uprisings that nearly shut down Chicago and St. Louis. In 1886 a nationwide campaign for the eight-hour workday led to widespread strikes and violent conflict in cities such as Milwaukee (at the Bayview Rolling Mills) and Chicago (the infamous Haymarket bombing that led to the execution of four anarchists). The Homestead strike of 1892 brought labor protest close to Pittsburgh, and the Pullman boycott of 1894 once again nearly brought the economy of Chicago to a halt. In the years before World War I, the syndicalist labor movement, led by the Industrial Workers of the World (IWW), waged long battles against the textile magnates of Lawrence, Massachusetts (1912), and Paterson, New Jersey (1913).

Urban workers also became deeply enmeshed in the complex urban politics of the period. Some laborers supported radical organizations such as the Socialist Labor Party led by Daniel DeLeon. Others flirted briefly with creating their own labor parties, especially during the heyday of the Knights of Labor in the late 1880s. Many recent immigrants used urban political machines, in conjunction with their own ethnic networks, to find jobs, housing, and aid in hard times. Given the often nativist and moralistic biases of private charities (sometimes linked with Protestant churches and viewed with great suspicion by Catholic and Jewish immigrants), and the lack of established public welfare agencies, favors such as free coal in winter or Christmas turkeys or a city job for a relative were often seen as an eminently reasonable quid pro quo for a worker's support and vote in a coming election.

The years between the world wars saw several significant changes in the world of the urban worker. Stringent immigration controls stopped much of the population influx from Europe and elsewhere. Ethnic neighborhoods remained a strong presence in many cities, but for American-born children and grandchildren the city seemed to offer a myriad of temptations and opportunities outside familiar streets and shops. Popular culture—in the form of films, radio, recordings, advertising, chain stores—penetrated deep into these ethnic enclaves. The forces of assimilation, of "Americanization," were overtaking the desire to preserve Old World folkways and values (again, especially for younger people born in America and attending American schools). Yet, this pattern was not an all or nothing "victory" for American mass culture. Rather, a complex and sometimes tenuous process was unfolding as tightly knit immigrant communities constantly had to accommodate the surrounding cultural and economic pressures, even as they continued to resist some ideas they still considered alien and dangerous.

The Great Migration of African Americans from the rural South to the urban North—starting in World War I and accelerating dramatically during World War II—also profoundly shaped the experience of urban workers. Millions of blacks fled the poverty and brutal segregation of the South and satisfied the demand for industrial workers in war industries. The urban black population of the United States more than quadrupled from 850,000 in 1880 to 3.5 million in 1920, then nearly tripled again to 9.5 million in 1950. Though many African Americans lost their factory jobs when white servicemen returned home after the wars, others clung to even lower-skilled industrial employment or menial jobs in the urban economy as an improvement from the meager existence of sharecroppers in the rural South. African Americans were usually shunted into urban ghettos, sometimes displacing older ethnic neighborhoods through a complex process by which bankers and speculators manipulated the price of real estate, blocked investment in the black community, and scared older residents into "white flight," a process that accelerated in the 1950s and 1960s as the black urban population doubled once again, to 19 million in 1970.

Life in the North was often harsh for African Americans. They constantly faced discrimination in jobs and housing, sometimes enforced by laws (as in the South) and covenants, and sometimes propped up by the sheer force of prejudice. Brutal race riots scarred many northern cities throughout the twentieth century. But the opportunity to vote and to get a job that paid cash wages (no matter how menial the work or meager the money) continued to draw relatives, friends, neighbors, and townsfolk of early migrants into the burgeoning black communities of Chicago, Detroit, Pittsburgh, New York City, and elsewhere. Like European immigrants before them, African Americans built strong community networks and institutions to protect their rights and interests when the surrounding white community turned a cold shoulder to their needs in hard times and their demands for equal treatment in the public arena.

The half-century following World War II brought even more dramatic shifts in the composition and location of the urban working class. The growing suburbs surrounding most American cities have siphoned off population, especially from old European immigrant neighborhoods. Most of the descendants of the original urban "pioneers" in these ethnic enclaves moved away from cities, attracted by the promise of single-family homes and a backyard of one's own, financed often by the federal government's GI Bill. These new generations are often better educated than their parents or grandparents, upwardly mobile in their economic and social aspirations, and physically mobile in their imported automobiles on interstate highways built with federal dollars. The old neighborhoods (or what remains of them after urban renewal and inner-city freeway construction) have been left to a rear guard of the elderly, the disabled, and the chronically underemployed, if not abandoned entirely to new migrants and immigrants—especially African Americans, Hispanics, and Asians.

The rise of the megalopolis in the South and West—Atlanta, Houston, Dallas, San Francisco, San Diego, and especially Los Angeles—has also meant that jobs and workers have moved to these locales and away from "rust belt" cities such as Buffalo and Cleveland. Cities in the West are also home to enormous numbers of new immigrants—especially from Latin America and the Pacific Rim. These urban immigrant workers once again pose fundamental questions about class, power, employment, exploitation, geography, and politics in the urban environment. The newcomers also trigger powerful emotions about racial identity in an increasingly intertwined global economy.

The world of the American urban working class has changed a great deal over the past three centuries. Yet, the struggle of people to make a living and a life for themselves in the urban economy and society is still a fundamental part of America's historical development.

—*David Zonderman*

### References

Bodnar, John. *The Transplanted: A History of Immigrants in Urban America*. Bloomington: Indiana University Press, 1985.

Cohen, Lizabeth. *Making a New Deal: Industrial Workers in Chicago, 1919–1939*. Cambridge, England: Cambridge University Press, 1990.

Nash, Gary. *The Urban Crucible: The Northern Seaports and the Origins of the American Revolution*. Cambridge, MA: Harvard University Press, 1986.

Oestreicher, Richard. *Solidarity and Fragmentation: Working People and Class Consciousness in Detroit, 1875–1900*. Urbana: University of Illinois Press, 1986.

Peiss, Kathy. *Cheap Amusements: Working Women and Leisure in Turn-of-the-Century New York*. Philadelphia: Temple University Press, 1986.

Rock, Howard B. *Artisans of the New Republic: The Tradesmen of New York City in the Age of Jefferson*. New York: New York University Press, 1979.

Rosenzweig, Roy. *Eight Hours for What We Will: Workers and Leisure in an Industrial City, 1870–1920*. Cambridge, England: Cambridge University Press, 1983.

Ross, Steven. *Workers on the Edge: Work, Leisure, and Politics in Industrializing Cincinnati, 1788–1890*. New York: Columbia University Press, 1985.

Schultz, Ronald. *The Republic of Labor: Philadelphia Artisans and the Politics of Class, 1720–1830*. New York: Oxford University Press, 1993.

Stansell, Christine. *City of Women: Sex and Class in New York, 1789–1860.* Urbana: University of Illinois Press, 1982.

Wilentz, Sean. *Chants Democratic: New York City and the Rise of the American Working Class, 1788–1850.* New York: Oxford University Press, 1984.

## Working Class in Suburbs

This topic might seem to be a contradiction in terms. In popular American mythology, suburbs are middle-class places. This is usually meant to imply one of two things. First, and this is a characteristically (although not uniquely) American line of argument, it suggests that the simple fact of living in a suburban, owner-occupied home makes a person middle class. This downplays the importance of the workplace as a determinant of class and instead emphasizes the economic and social significance of homeownership. Alternatively, a second argument is that the price of entry to the suburbs is sufficiently high to require a "middle-class" income, thereby precluding workers.

For different reasons, neither argument is very satisfying. Although owning a home does provide certain economic advantages—many of them fiscal in origin—it is difficult to argue that these are anywhere near as important as the inequalities of the workplace. Buying a suburban home, in itself, does not really change one's class position. The second line of argument is empirically wrong. As it happens, many workers, some with very modest incomes, have moved to the suburbs. This is not a recent development. Indeed, large numbers of workers and their families have been settling in American suburbs for well over a century.

Cheap land has long enabled fringe areas to offer blue-collar workers an attractive alternative to city living. Until at least the middle of the twentieth century, cities dominated their surrounding suburbs. Central sites were the most accessible, and the most expensive. Despite rapid decentralization, in most metropolitan areas this is still true. By comparison, suburban land has been cheap, permitting lower densities and higher levels of homeownership. In many suburbs, restrictions imposed by developers and local governments have compelled households to occupy expensive homes on large lots, thereby excluding all but the best-paid workers. In many others, however, such restrictions have been weaker, or altogether absent. As late as the 1940s, many districts at the urban fringe provided limited services and imposed few building or zoning regulations. This was especially true of unincorporated areas, and workers were able to acquire modest homes, often by building their own.

The main limitation on this process was the need to stay within commuting distance of work. Until the electric streetcar became widespread in the 1890s, workers walked to work.

In the largest cities, as long as blue-collar employment—in factories, warehouses, and on the railroads—remained downtown, workers found it difficult to move to the suburbs. In smaller cities and towns, however, it was possible for employees to work downtown and live at the urban fringe. This was even true of a place as large as Toronto, whose population was approaching 500,000 by 1914.

More important, and although the fact is still not widely recognized, some industries began to establish themselves at the urban fringe from the mid-nineteenth century on, and quite a number of workers followed. After 1900 this trend gathered momentum, and many industrial suburbs and satellite towns had grown up by World War I. Pittsburgh was an extreme case, where many working-class mill communities, such as Homestead, sprang up.

As early as World War I, however, not all blue-collar suburbs were overshadowed by industry. Many workers were willing to travel two or three miles to work. This became easier with the introduction of the ten-hour and later the eight-hour day, and with the rapid growth of streetcar and subway routes before World War I. This meant that even in large cities, residential suburbs of workers could develop at some distance from suburban industry. In New York, by far the largest city on the continent, after 1905 the subway permitted the early movement of skilled blue-collar workers into Brooklyn and the Bronx. Although these were boroughs of the city, in other respects they had a suburban character.

During the years between the world wars, mass production brought automobiles within the reach of better-paid workers. This made it possible for them to travel further to work. During the 1920s, builders took advantage of this fact by creating workers' subdivisions both within and beyond city limits. A good example was Brightmoor in Detroit, where B. E. Taylor laid out extensive subdivisions, building some houses speculatively and selling many single lots to prospective owner-builders. During the 1930s and 1940s, mobile workers moved still further out, scattering across an exurban countryside. Many chose to supplement their wages with part-time farming.

By the late 1940s, however, a variety of circumstances made it possible for a new generation of builder-developers to provide houses for workers. The creation of federal mortgage insurance through the agency of the Federal Housing Administration (FHA) was of critical importance because it established the long-term amortized mortgage as the norm. It increased workers' demands for mortgaged homeownership and encouraged institutional lenders to meet this demand. In areas that received wartime industry, mass suburbs were built during the early 1940s. Elsewhere, they did not become common until later in the decade, when the demand for new homes soared.

For many years scholars assumed that large-scale development and FHA financing made the blue-collar suburb possible. In fact, in some respects, they destroyed it. Until the 1940s, most of the fringe areas occupied by workers were inferior in their amenities, and many were quite homogeneous in social composition. This was especially true of industrial suburbs and satellite communities, where workers clustered around factories and mills. Even residential suburbs, however, often took on a class character. In contrast, the mass suburbs of the postwar years were usually targeted to a specific income range. The union drives of the 1930s had brought the wages for many manual workers well into the salary range of white-collar workers. Some of the early mass suburbs were dominated by blue-collar workers, especially in smaller communities like Milpitas, California, where the opening of a large factory meant that new homes for a specific group of workers would dominate the local housing scene for a time. Typically, however, and certainly in larger urban centers, the new suburbs were socially mixed. Today, although workers of all kinds live at the urban fringe, it is rarely possible to speak of the working-class suburb.

Because the history of working-class settlement in suburbs has been neglected, its meaning to the people involved and its larger significance remain unclear. Suburbs have long offered a variety of advantages over the city: lower residential densities, cheaper land, more affordable housing, cleaner air, less-crowded streets, and better access to open country. These amenities have long been valued by all types of people, but not equally. One study of Detroit has argued that workers cared more than the middle classes about homeownership. This is consistent with evidence for Canadian and other U.S. cities. Opportunities for homeownership have always been greatest in the suburbs, and workers, especially, seem to have viewed suburban residence as a means of acquiring a home. In Toronto, for example, in the early part of the century, they made enormous sacrifices in order to acquire suburban homes: they were willing to commute long distances, sometimes on foot; they were prepared to dispense with basic municipal services, such as running water and paved streets; they worked evenings and weekends building their own homes. If workers' suburbs are comparatively modest in character, then, they also once expressed a distinctive set of cultural values.

These values have eroded since World War II. The greater occupational diversity of the mass suburbs has been associated with a decline in working-class consciousness. It is hard to say which is the cause and which the effect. In part, the geographical integration of workers into mass suburbs has reflected a desire for personal social mobility. At the same time, however, living in areas of mixed occupations probably helped erode their class consciousness.

The manner in which workers acquired homes has also become less distinct. Traditionally, of course, many workers had rented. Those who acquired homes built their own, borrowed from private individuals, or from Savings and Loan societies. Financially, then, the mechanisms by which workers saved for and acquired homes were rather distinctive. This began to change rapidly in the 1930s. After a short renascence in the late 1940s and early 1950s, the possibilities for owner building were reduced by municipal regulation and the imposition of standardized FHA lending guidelines. These same guidelines steadily squeezed out private lenders and brought Saving and Loans in line with other institutional lenders. Increasingly, then, workers acquired homes in much the same way as everyone else—by buying on long-term credit from approved institutions.

The larger implications of blue-collar settlement in the suburbs are also unclear. One effect of suburbanization has surely been to improve the living conditions of American workers. Although many suburbs were unregulated, unplanned, and unhealthy, most were preferable to the inner city. By striving to move to the suburbs, workers made it clear which place they preferred. Suburban reality may often have fallen short of the ideal, but on the whole most of those who moved to suburbia were apparently pleased with their decision. Few returned.

One of the more likely political consequences is that, having acquired their own suburban homes, workers have been less inclined to challenge the inequities of the workplace. The evidence on the latter issue is thin, although it is clear that employers and governments have often assumed that they were discouraging radicalism by encouraging suburban homeownership. The "Bolshevik" scare after 1917 provoked many employers into providing better housing for their workers, and one of the motives behind state housing initiatives during the 1930s was the attempt to defuse labor unrest.

Even if it is true that suburban homes make for more contented workers, this can be interpreted in different ways. Conservatives have tended to view working-class settlement in the suburbs as a sign that capitalism works—workers, after all, are staking a claim to part of the American dream. Left-leaning observers have been more inclined to dismiss this, arguing that suburban homeownership has bought off workers while doing little or nothing to redress the class inequalities of American society.

—*Richard Harris*

**See also**
Homeownership; Industrial Suburbs; Satellite City; Suburban Ideal; Working Class in Cities.

**References**
Berger, Bennett. *Working-Class Suburb: A Study of Auto Workers in Suburbia.* Berkeley: University of California Press, 1960.

Gans, Herbert. *The Levittowners: Ways of Life and Politics in a New Suburban Community.* New York: Random House, 1967.

Halle, David. *America's Working Man.* Chicago: University of Chicago Press, 1984.

Harris, Richard. "Industry and Residence: The Decentralization of New York City." *Journal of Historical Geography* 19 (1993): 169–190.

———. *Unplanned Suburbs: Toronto's American Tragedy, 1900–1950.* Baltimore: Johns Hopkins University Press, 1995.

Taylor, Graham Roemyn. *Satellite Cities: A Study of Industrial Suburbs.* New York: Appleton, 1916.

Zunz. Olivier. *The Changing Face of Inequality: Urbanization, Industrial Development and Immigrants in Detroit, 1880–1920.* Chicago: University of Chicago Press, 1982.

## World Trade Center

Skyscrapers are built because they fulfill important social and economic needs. Perhaps most significant in an urban society is the need to bring people and facilities together to transact business. The skyscraper allows a city to gather into a central core a large amount of space organized and equipped for work. In this respect, it can be seen as the product of an open competitive economy that requires immense amounts of space to accommodate huge numbers of people.

The massive dimensions of the World Trade Center testify vividly to this observation. One hundred and ten stories and 1,350 feet high, the twin towers of the trade center are the tallest structures in New York City (surpassing the Empire State Building) and the second tallest in the United States (the tallest is now the Sears Tower in Chicago). The average daily population consists of 50,000 employees and 100,000 visitors. The entire complex consists of seven buildings providing 10 million square feet of office space on 16 acres of lower Manhattan. It includes an elevated plaza 5 acres large, an underground retail concourse, 250 express and local elevators, and a hotel with 820 rooms. "Topped out" in December 1970 at an initial cost of $900 million, it is owned by the Port Authority of New York and New Jersey. Its sponsor has described it as a "central international trade market place."

Initially proposed by banking and investment interests as a strategy to upgrade real estate values in lower Manhattan, it can be argued that no other building project has been subject to so many intricate negotiations or so many trade-offs to accommodate competing public and private interests. Business groups, labor groups, and city, state, and federal agencies were all involved. Underlying much of this was concern over the scale of the development and its probable effects on the city and region. Even more important was the fact that the Port Authority of New York and New Jersey had

*The World Trade Center seems to dwarf the other skyscrapers of New York City.*

been selected as the sponsor of the proposed project. As a quasi-public agency with special responsibilities in transportation and port development, its selection posed additional policy questions that were difficult to resolve.

Accountable to the governments of New York and New Jersey, the Port Authority had to assure comparable benefits to both states. If New York was to get the Trade Center, New Jersey wanted improved commuter transportation services. Thus, the site of the World Trade Center was shifted from the East Side of Manhattan to the West Side where the Port Authority could redevelop railroad facilities used by New Jersey commuters. This was subsequently linked to improving other commuter facilities in New Jersey.

A major issue that had to be settled with New York City was payments by the Port Authority in lieu of taxes. This opened the broader question of the "proper role" of the Port Authority. In exchange for granting street closings that allowed construction to proceed, the administration of Mayor John Lindsay and the City of New York received a new West Side passenger terminal, new port facilities in Brooklyn, a refurbished subway station, the widening of streets, the complete reconstruction of new on-site utilities, and a 28-acre shoreline landfill that later became the site for the World Financial Center.

The size and height of the proposed project posed further controversy. Realty interests feared the effects of 10 million square feet of rental space on the rental market. Many tenants and businesses that were relocated from the 16-acre site contended that they were being dislocated. Broadcasters complained of television interference from the two 1,350-foot towers. Negotiations on these questions were greatly limited in scope, and many of the issues were never fully resolved to the satisfaction of challenging parties. Ultimately, however, the trade center did bring about a resurgence of development and land values in lower Manhattan. It is estimated that some 350,000 workers make the area the nation's third largest business center, after midtown Manhattan and Chicago.

In 1993 the World Trade Center was back in the news when a homemade 1,000-pound bomb, delivered in a van by terrorists, exploded in the underground garage. Six people were killed, and thousands of other lives were disrupted. The explosion destroyed the emergency command center of the complex, disabled its backup generators, and sent thick smoke up into the two towers. With few instructions to guide them because loudspeakers had no power, tens of thousands of workers had to flee down dark stairways. Interestingly, structural damage to the towers was not extensive. The World Trade Center has since undergone a $300 million renovation and, with improvements, is reportedly safe and running smoothly with a very low vacancy rate.

*—Leonard I. Ruchelman*

### References

Bennett, David. *Skyscrapers: Form and Function.* New York: Simon and Schuster, 1995.

Danielson, Michael N., and Jameson W. Doig. *New York: The Politics of Urban Regional Development.* Berkeley: University of California Press, 1982.

Huxtable, Ada Louise. *The Tall Building Artistically Reconsidered: The Search for a Skyscraper Style.* Berkeley: University of California Press, 1992.

Ruchelman, Leonard I. *The World Trade Center: Politics and Policies of Skyscraper Development.* Syracuse, NY: Syracuse University Press, 1977.

Schachtman, Tom. *Skyscraper Dreams: The Great Real Estate Dynasties of New York.* Boston: Little, Brown, 1991.

## World's Fairs and Expositions

Cities in the United States have hosted more than 30 major world's fairs and international expositions from the first (New York in 1853) to the most recent (New Orleans in 1984). Interspersed have been dozens of other commercial and commemorative expositions of national or regional importance. These events have served simultaneously as devices for economic development and ways to communicate new ideas. Their planning has been tied to intercity rivalries for economic growth and to specific needs for urban land development. The displays and programming of the major expositions have been used to justify American imperialism and express the national faith in progress through science and technology.

American international expositions are best understood in their world context. The international exposition originated as an expression of the North Atlantic economy of the mid-nineteenth century, undertaken by those nations and cities that claimed both cultural and economic leadership. They have overwhelmingly been planned and organized in French and in English, whether with North American, British, or Australian accents. Following the standard model for the diffusion of innovations, they spread from London and Paris to provincial cities around the North Sea and the Mediterranean; to the dominant centers for newer English-speaking settlement such as Melbourne, New York, and Philadelphia; to provincial English-speaking cities such as San Diego, Seattle, and Wellington; and to cities in the nascent "Third World" such as Hanoi and Guatemala City.

The origin of the world's fair is customarily traced to the Great Exhibition of the Works of Industry of All Nations, held in London in 1851 and notable for the vast glass-walled Crystal Palace. New York soon imitated London with an Exhibition of the Industry of all the Nations in 1853. Major events followed in Paris (1867) and Vienna (1873). These initial decades coincide with what historian Eric Hobsbawm calls the "Age of Industry." The 1850s and 1860s were the flush years of adolescent European capitalism, which began to fully realize the possibilities of urban factory production and to integrate much of the world into a single market for European industry. Most of the early international expositions were European and straightforward, grander versions of scores of smaller manufacturing exhibitions and commercial fairs that took place in the same years. They were marked by simple delight in the display and exchange of new products.

The first concentrated era of American expositions lasted from 1876 to 1915. Inside and outside the United States, this was the era that produced the emblematic expositions that historians use as symbols of the maturing nineteenth century—especially Philadelphia's Centennial International Exposition in 1876, Melbourne's International Exposition in 1880, the Exposition Universelle in Paris in 1889, the World's Columbian Exposition in Chicago in 1893, and the Panama-Pacific International Exposition in San Francisco in 1915.

One factor behind the proliferation of international fairs was the changing structure of the world economy. The great deflation of the late nineteenth century triggered increasingly bitter competition within industrialized Europe, leading to the use of expositions as competitive devices. At the same time, the resource-rich peripheries of Australasia and North America were enjoying at least a partial countertrend to the deflationary cycle, generating capital with which the provinces could stage their own festivals of self-promotion.

An additional factor was the second industrial revolution after 1875, involving the rise of the chemical and electrical industries. The emergence of an economy based increasingly on scientific and technical marvels could be effectively illustrated, publicized, and explicated through international expositions. These fairs are remembered in part for their new technologies—the telephone and the Corliss steam engine at Philadelphia, Gustav Eiffel's tower, the profligate use of electric lights that became a cliché by the start of the new century. They are also remembered for architectural styles that attempted to express urban and national maturity, especially in the case of the Neoclassical buildings of the Columbian Exposition in Chicago.

A third factor was the broadening of middle-class tourism as the comfort of rail travel increased and costs fell. It was far easier and cheaper to travel long distances across North America in 1905 than it had been in 1880, making long summer tours a real possibility for the middle class. Without this widening market, cities like Seattle could never have hoped to stage a successful exposition. In turn, major expositions were viewed as important devices for promoting increased tourism.

The entire set of American fairs from 1876 to 1915 was one major product of urban boosterism, and fairs were complex elements in systems of interurban rivalry. They were ways to rise above one's rival cities by proving maturity, stability, and competence (and therefore attractiveness to investors and immigrants). They were also rites of passage. Southern fairs of the 1880s and 1890s were closely tied to the imagery of the entrepreneurial New South. Western fairs were intended to confirm the transition from frontier to region, with Portland, Seattle, San Diego, and San Francisco all imitating Chicago and St. Louis.

Turn-of-the-century fairs had a second role in local agendas as tools for enhancing the usability of undeveloped or underdeveloped public lands. Expositions created or improved Piedmont Park in Atlanta, Forest Park in St. Louis, Jackson Park in Chicago, and Balboa Park in San Diego. The design for the campus of the University of Washington is another exposition legacy.

As national events, the fairs of the late nineteenth and early twentieth centuries were also apologists for American imperialism. Both sideshows and educational exhibits justified the prevailing racial hierarchy. Native Americans, Filipinos, and other overseas peoples appeared at best as practitioners of quaint customs, at worst as primitives on display in an anthropological zoo. The fairs thus confirmed Eurocentric assumptions about the superiority of the white race and American civilization.

The messages changed with a new set of expositions in the 1930s. Chicago's Century of Progress Exposition in 1933–1934, San Francisco's Golden Gate International Exposition in 1939–1940, and the New York World's Fair of 1939–1940 all tried to fight the Depression of the 1930s by building confidence in the underlying strength of scientifically grounded capitalism. Their sleek Art Deco buildings seemed to claim the future as a high-tech utopia. The best-known exhibit was the General Motors Futurama in New York, which communicated the wonders of the automobile age. Several expositions in the United States since 1960 presented themselves more narrowly as sophisticated scientific theme parks, such as Seattle's Century 21 Exposition in 1962, Spokane's International Exposition on the Environment in 1974, and Knoxville's International Energy Exposition in 1982.

Since World War II, public investment in expositions has frequently been justified as an opportunity for land redevelopment. Picking sites on the immediate fringe of their downtowns, Seattle, Spokane, San Antonio (1968), Knoxville, and New Orleans cleared large tracts, constructed new public facilities, and hoped for additional private reinvestment.

Finally, modern fairs have also been justified in economic development terms as ways to reposition a city within the world urban system. A case in point was Montreal, whose Expo '67 was part of a comprehensive "international city" strategy for economic development. The same was true of San Antonio's Hemisfair, Osaka's Japan World Exposition in 1970, and Vancouver's Expo '86. In this manner, the booster impulse of the nineteenth century survived at least to the 1980s.

In the 1980s, the world's fair met hard times in the United States. The Knoxville and New Orleans fairs were considered aesthetic and financial failures; they neither stirred the public nor attracted enough visitors to break even. The Vancouver Expo was a popular success but a major money loser. These experiences helped convince Chicagoans to shelve plans for a Columbian quincentennial exposition for 1992 and have discouraged fair enthusiasts in other cities.

—*Carl Abbott*

**See also**

Boosterism; Centennial Exposition of 1876; Chicago World's Fair of 1893 (World's Columbian Exposition); Urban Rivalry and Urban Imperialism.

**References**

Badger, Reid. *The Great American Fair: The World's Columbian Exposition and American Culture.* Chicago: N. Hall, 1979.

Findlay, John M. *Magic Lands: Western Cityscapes and American Culture after 1940.* Berkeley: University of California Press, 1992.

Findling, John, and Kimberly Pelle. *Historical Dictionary of World's Fairs and Expositions, 1851–1988.* New York: Greenwood Press, 1990.

Gilbert, James. *Perfect Cities: Chicago's Utopias of 1893.* Chicago: University of Chicago Press, 1991.

Rydell, Robert. *All the World's a Fair: Visions of Empire at American International Expositions, 1876–1916.* Chicago: University of Chicago Press, 1984.

———. *World of Fairs: The Century-of-Progress Expositions.* Chicago: University of Chicago Press, 1993.

## Yellow Journalism

Now a general term of disapprobation for almost any kind of journalism that one dislikes, *yellow journalism* really applies to big city dailies during the closing decades of the nineteenth century. Although its exemplars were Joseph Pulitzer's *New York World* and William Randolph Hearst's *New York Journal,* its tone rubbed off on other dailies, especially those published in large cities. Why "yellow"? Philologists trace the color's long association with depravity and decadence, and some point to another possible source—"the Yellow Kid" was the first color comic in these same newspapers.

Although some historians have attempted to limit the term to Hearst's paper, while reserving "new journalism" for Pulitzer's, in the years leading up to and including the Spanish-American War, the content and appearance of the two papers was similar. *The Journalist,* a New York–based trade journal, detected few differences between them. Because Pulitzer scored his initial journalistic triumph in St. Louis and Hearst in San Francisco, American contemporaries often referred to their innovations as "western journalism," while publishers in Europe called them both "new journalism." Not only did their page layouts, news, and features look alike, their editorial positions resembled each other. On foreign policy both were nationalistic, on domestic issues mildly reformist and pro-Democratic.

During the half-century before Pulitzer arrived in New York in 1883, American metropolitan newspapers had become a major force in politics, economics, and social life. Once written for and about the upper crust of society, they now served a broad cross-section of the growing populace. Printing technology (most notably typesetting machines and faster presses) coupled with much less expensive paper derived from pulpwood slashed production costs. Retail advertising, a large share derived from department stores, tripled revenues. Larger local staffs were augmented by news from afar, sped by the telegraph and undersea cables. As always, the largest units were in the best position to exploit the changed conditions. In the newspaper business, that meant the New York dailies.

In terms of both circulation and advertising, James Gordon Bennett, Jr.'s *Herald* had been the undisputed leader for decades, but Pulitzer's *World* soon surpassed it. Once a radical organ, the *Herald* had become a voice of conservatism. With a steady stream of stories about crime and vice and full of sexual innuendo, a generous sprinkling of illustrations, and screaming headlines, Pulitzer's paper became king of the New York newspaper hill. He also sponsored contests and charity events to promote his paper.

Meanwhile, he championed such popular causes as taxing the rich and raising tariffs. In 1890 his declining health forced him to give up active direction of his paper, and he spent the rest of his life firing off cables from his soundproof yachts and summoning editors to him anywhere in the world. His success bred emulation, and in 1896 Hearst purchased the moribund *New York Journal,* determined to defeat Pulitzer at his own game. He shamelessly copied the look and style of his rival, serving up the same mixture of crime and exposé at half the price. Whereas Pulitzer had promoted his paper with giveaways (such as ice for the poor in summer and soup in winter), Hearst sought a grander scale. By offering previously unheard-of salaries, Hearst lured the city's best reporters and editors. Not surprisingly, Pulitzer was incensed when Hearst hired away his entire Sunday staff in one week. By then, Sunday editions had become the largest and most profitable of the week. Separate staffs produced society sections for women, sports sections for men, and comics sections for children. Retail advertisers had begun to learn about demographics.

The battle joined, both egocentric millionaire owners urged their writers, illustrators, and headline composers to exploit every juicy angle. Pulitzer claimed legitimacy by insisting that he was using sensationalism in his news sections to attract readers for his editorials, but Hearst made no such assertions. Eventually, their lieutenants forged secret agreements to limit expenditures on promotion and to cooperate in distribution and other matters.

The competition to cover the Spanish-American War is often considered the lowest point in American journalism.

However, considering the nation's long-standing discontent with Spanish rule in Cuba, it is a gross distortion to blame the war on Hearst and Pulitzer. Many Americans, fearful of being excluded from the contest for overseas colonies, were spoiling for a war. Ironically, all the major New York dailies spent far more on covering the war than they gained in circulation revenues. Although the *Journal* finally passed the *World* in circulation, Hearst was soon turning his attention to expanding his multimedia empire, while Pulitzer vowed to give up gutter journalism and return to the high ground. (Many of his contemporaries did not believe he had ever occupied it.) By the time Pulitzer died in 1913, the *World* was respected, especially for its forceful editorials.

What, then, is the heritage of yellow journalism? On the positive side, it led to a broadened definition of news and a more readable writing style; on the negative, it trivialized the news and blurred the line between fact and fiction.

—*John D. Stevens*

**See also**
Hearst, William Randolph; Pulitzer, Joseph.
**Reference**
Milton, Joyce. *The Yellow Kids.* New York: Harper & Row, 1989.

## Young, Brigham (1801–1877)

A well-known leader of the Church of Jesus Christ of Latter-day Saints (also known as the Mormon Church), Brigham Young was also distinguished as a successful city builder who played a major role in founding several hundred cities and towns throughout the Great Basin and Far West.

Born on June 1, 1801, in Whittingham, Vermont, Young grew up in an unsettled frontier environment marked by frequent family moves that took him to upstate New York. He received only a limited formal education and as a young man was apprenticed to be a carpenter, painter, and glazier. Young met and married his first wife, Marian Works, in 1824, and they had two daughters.

In 1832, Young joined the fledgling Mormon Church that Joseph Smith had founded two years earlier in the "burned-over district" of upstate New York. Young rose quickly through Mormon ranks and in 1835 was appointed to the church's ruling elite, the Council of Twelve. He also played an important role in building Mormon communities in Kirtland, Ohio, and later in Missouri. In 1838, as the senior member of the Council of Twelve, Young directed the Mormon exodus to Illinois in the wake of their expulsion from Missouri. Young also helped establish Mormonism's new metropolis, or gathering place, of Nauvoo, Illinois. In 1840 Young traveled to England, where he promoted an extremely successful missionary program. While he was there, the grinding poverty in London and other English cities during the so-called "hungry forties" appalled Young and made a deep and lasting impression on him.

Joseph Smith was murdered by an anti-Mormon mob in 1844, and Young, who had returned to America in 1841, emerged as the most important Mormon leader. From this position, he directed the mass movement of Mormons from Illinois to the Far West that began in 1846. With careful planning and preparation, he presided over the largest, best-organized migration in American history. Over the next 30 years, Young supervised the movement of thousands of Mormons to the Far West by various means of transportation, including covered wagons, handcarts, church teams, and finally the railroad.

He also supervised the establishment of some 350 Mormon cities and towns of different sizes, not just in Utah but throughout the Far West, including Nevada, Idaho, Wyoming, Arizona, Colorado, and California. In addition to his roles as preeminent community builder and principal Mormon leader, Young was appointed Utah's first territorial governor. He held this post until he was removed in 1857 because of escalating tensions over the Mormon practice of plural marriage. Young himself helped fuel the controversy by marrying 55 women with whom he fathered 57 children. Brigham Young, having died on August 29, 1877, did not live to see this controversy finally resolved when the Mormon Church officially renounced polygamy in 1890.

—*Newell G. Bringhurst*

**See also**
Mormons.
**References**
Arrington, Leonard J. *Brigham Young: American Moses.* New York: Knopf, 1985.
———. *Great Basin Kingdom: An Economic History of the Latter-day Saints.* Cambridge, MA: Harvard University Press, 1958.
Bringhurst, Newell G. *Brigham Young and the Expanding American Frontier.* Boston: Little, Brown, 1986.
Campbell, Eugene E. *Establishing Zion: The Mormon Church in the American West, 1847–1869.* Salt Lake City, UT: Signature Books, 1988.
Hunter, Milton R. *Brigham Young, the Colonizer.* Salt Lake City, UT: Deseret News Press, 1940.
Ricks, Joel E. *Form and Methods of Early Mormon Settlement in Utah and the Surrounding Region, 1847 to 1877.* Logan: Utah State University Press, 1964.

## Young, Coleman A. (1919–1997)

Coleman Alexander Young, the first African-American mayor of Detroit, was born in Tuscaloosa, Alabama, on May 18, 1919, and arrived in Detroit at the age of five. In grade school, he gained a reputation as a precocious child who excelled at his studies. After he graduated from high school in 1936, Young worked at the Ford Motor Company, where he later became a labor organizer. From labor politics, he moved into city politics and radical left social movements. In 1952, he gained notoriety by refusing to cooperate with the House Un-American Activities Committee investigation of the National Negro Labor Council, a group he headed as executive director.

After Young's recalcitrance at the hearings, the organized labor movement shunned him. For the next decade he worked several jobs, most notably selling insurance. In 1961 he returned to politics as a delegate to the Michigan Constitutional Convention. Three years later, he won election to the state senate, and in 1968 he became the first black member of the Democratic Party National Committee.

In 1973 Young defeated John Nichols and became the first black mayor of Detroit. During his tenure, the city experienced an economic transformation. Once home to the Big Three auto makers, the city was declining as the automobile industry lost a large market share to foreign makes. Young's attempt to diversify the city's economy had only mixed results, and with the loss of jobs, Detroit also began losing population to suburbs and Sunbelt cities.

Young remained popular despite several scandals involving his appointees. Known as a strong advocate of affirmative action and a booster of downtown development, Coleman Young served as mayor for two decades. In 1993, after serving an unprecedented fifth term, he declined to seek another term for health reasons. He was 75 when he retired.

—*Wilbur Rich*

### Reference

Rich, Wilbur C. *Coleman Young and Detroit Politics: From Social Activist to Power Broker.* Detroit: Wayne State University Press, 1989.

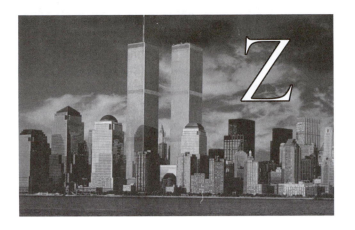

## Zone in Transition

In the 1920s Ernest W. Burgess developed the concentric circle or zonal model to describe spatial patterns of American cities. Burgess's model consists of five concentric zones: the central business district (CBD), the zone in transition, the zone of workingmen's homes, the zone of better residences, and the commuter's zone. The zone in transition is a belt that surrounds the CBD and acts as a buffer between the CBD and the innermost residential areas. This zone is not homogeneous but is composed of different sections experiencing different degrees of activity and different forms of transition simultaneously. Within the zone, there are concentrations of activities and establishments like wholesaling, storage, light and heavy industry, transportation, offices, parking, financial establishments, and transient residences. Originally the zone was an area of upper-class residence, but as the city center expanded and immigration increased, houses were converted into apartments, businesses, and professional offices.

The zone in transition contains an outer area of residence deteriorating because of encroachment from the CBD and an inner industrial area serving the CBD. Housing is in different stages of obsolescence; public facilities and industrial districts are run-down and have high rates of vacancy, and while population might be increasing numerically, it tends toward a racial or ethnic makeup with lower levels of education and income.

The zone in transition contains sectors of active assimilation, passive assimilation, and general inactivity. Active sectors are constantly encroaching on older, more established, higher-quality residential neighborhoods with viable commercial enterprises and successful multifamily residences. The passive area experiences continual change and even growth, but the quality of growth is lower than in the active zone. The sector of inactivity usually separates the active from the passive zones and is characterized by gradual change and a lack of land conversion. This area usually experiences growth in low-quality, multifamily housing. The sector of inactivity also contains some heavy industry connected to transportation facilities such as harbors and railroad terminals.

—*Craig Pascoe*

**See also**
Burgess, Ernest W.; Central Business District.
**References**
Burgess, Ernest W. "Growth of the City." In Robert E. Park, Ernest W. Burgess, and Roderick D. McKenzie, eds., *The City,* 47–62. Chicago: University of Chicago Press, 1925.
———. "Urban Areas." In Thomas V. Smith and Leonard D. White, eds., *Chicago: An Experiment in Social Science Research,* 113–138. Chicago: University of Chicago Press, 1929.
Nelson, Howard J. "The Form and Structure of Cities: Urban Growth Patterns." *Journal of Geography* 68 (1969): 198–207.
Preston, Richard E. "The Zone in Transition: A Study of Urban Land Use Patterns." *Economic Geography* 42 (1966): 236–260.

## Zone of Discard

As central business districts (CBDs) migrate and expand into new areas, they leave behind an area that they no longer encompass and that is usually declining as a result; this is the zone of discard. It is part of a model of CBD structure and specifically a counterpoint to the zone of assimilation into which the CBD is expanding. The zone of discard is usually regarded as an area of physical decay and socioeconomic deprivation that is characterized by low-grade retail and service activities such as pawnshops and bars; bus stations; and run-down residential areas associated with poverty, delinquency, and the "red-light district." The area has also been seen as an appendage to the core of the CBD in which central functions insensitive to appearance and unable to pay high rent can cluster, particularly wholesaling, warehousing, and parking. The idea of the zone of discard was a central contribution to successive models of the CBD, including "core-frame" and "transition zone" that were part of the preoccupation with urban modeling in the 1960s.

The conceptualization of the zone of discard has created a paradoxical situation. It is exactly the area of the inner city in which the oldest buildings are likely to have survived because there has been no incentive for redevelopment; thus, an area frequently considered undesirable becomes commonly identified as a prime heritage resource around which the "tourist-historic city" is developing as a pivotal component of the contemporary urban economy. The relevance of the zone of discard to the sort of revitalization that emphasizes history and heritage was recognized in the 1970s. It is particularly applicable to port cities in North America that have experienced extensive migration of the CBD away from constricted waterfronts and the widespread development there of maritime "discard" characteristics. These areas have subsequently offered major possibilities for heritage exploitation, including adaptive uses of warehouses (following the decentralization of wholesaling), and have been associated with a reevaluation of the waterfront's recreational possibilities (as in Boston, Baltimore, Montreal, and Vancouver). However, extensive discard revitalization also occurs elsewhere, as in the tourist-historic development of Ottawa, Canada.

—*John E. Tunbridge*

**See also**
Central Business District.
**References**
Ashworth, Gregory J., and J. E. Tunbridge. *The Tourist-Historic City.* London: Belhaven, 1990.
Griffin, Donald W., and Richard Ellis Preston. "A Restatement of the Transition Zone Concept." *Annals of the Association of American Geographers* 56 (1966): 339–349.
Horwood, Edgar M., and Ronald R. Boyce. *Studies of the CBD and Urban Freeway Development.* Seattle: University of Washington Press, 1959.
Murphy, Raymond E., James E. Vance, Jr., and Bart J. Epstein. "Internal Structure of the CBD." *Economic Geography* 31 (1955): 21–46.
Nader, George A. *Cities of Canada.* 2 vols. Toronto, Ontario: Macmillan, 1975–1976.
Tunbridge, J. E. "Clarence Street, Ottawa: Contemporary Change in an Inner-City 'Zone of Discard.'" *Urban History Review* 14 (1986): 247–257.
Tunbridge, J. E., and Gregory J. Ashworth. "Leisure Resource Development in Cityport Revitalization: The Tourist-Historic Dimension." In B. S. Hoyle and David A. Pinder, eds., *European Port Cities in Transition.* London: Belhaven, 1992.

## Zoning

Beginning with New York in 1916, 48 of the 68 largest cities in the United States adopted "comprehensive building zone laws" that put zoning into effect. Hundreds of smaller cities and towns followed suit, and by 1926 the 426 municipalities with zoning laws had a total population in excess of 27 million, more than half the total urban population of the United States.

These zoning laws divided cities into districts according to designated land uses—residence, business, or manufacturing—and according to advisable building height and ground area. Zoning was said "to guarantee to the home owner that the area in which his home is located shall not be subjected to uses which might have a tendency to destroy the area for home purposes; and likewise to protect the business man from industrial intrusion which might destroy the area in question for business purposes."

Zoning was one of the first attempts by local governments to regulate a private market intensively. In 1927, the U.S. Supreme Court upheld its constitutionality as a valid exercise of the "police power" in the case of *Village of Euclid v. Ambler Realty Company.*

For its first 40 years, zoning was criticized only in muted tones. Naysayers pointed out that zoning, as implemented, sometimes fell short of achieving laudable objectives. Commentators were particularly concerned that corrupt deals between developers and local officials sometimes resulted in permissive "spot zoning."

Over the past several decades the pendulum has completed a half swing. Critics from across the political spectrum now agree that zoning does mischief. The attack from the left springs from the belated realization that zoning has been used to discriminate on the basis of wealth, race, and national origin. The centrist critique of zoning questions its efficacy as a tool of city planning. Rightists charge that zoning confiscates private property and promotes inefficient land use.

Most liberal criticism has focused on zoning's negative impact on the affordability of housing. Empirical studies indicate that "excess" zoning drives up the cost of new housing by 15 percent, thereby excluding people of low or moderate incomes from developing suburbs and slowing the rate at which older housing becomes available to them in cities. The centrist critique is a product of planners. When zoning was first enacted, planning was a fledgling profession, and city planners felt that zoning, a product of lawyers, was usurping their rightful job. They had three basic objections: first, zoning laws were enacted before development of a comprehensive city plan; second, there was little planning justification for separating land uses; and third, the zoning districts devoted too much land to some uses and failed to provide enough for others.

Planning's basic notion was that government ought to dictate the future, and city planners sought to use scientific methods to ordain the course of physical urban development. Imposing legal controls before public choices had been made about the location and size of streets, rapid transit lines, sewers, public utility plants, parks, playgrounds, and public buildings put the cart before the horse. To them, zoning was the antithesis of planning. The conservative criticism views zoning as confiscatory and inefficient. In broad terms, it argues that our system of limited government and private property ought not be elastic enough to accommodate zoning. Private property is perceived as a barrier to government regulation that zoning transgresses, thereby violating the constitutional prohibition against taking property.

Notwithstanding these criticisms, zoning remains popular and almost universally employed by local governments. It is the essence of home rule, and meets the "demand for self-government in the daily lives of people." The extent to which regulations should be permitted to curtail freedom of individual choice, in the real estate market or elsewhere, will remain a vexing problem of constitutional law and public policy.

—*Garrett Power*

**See also**
City Planning; Height Restrictions; Master Plan.
**References**
Downs, Anthony. *Opening Up the Suburbs.* New Haven, CT: Yale University Press, 1973.
Epstein, Richard A. *Takings: Private Property and the Power of Eminent Domain.* Cambridge, MA: Harvard University Press, 1985.
Haar, M. Charles. "In Accordance with a Comprehensive Plan." *Harvard Law Review* 68 (1955): 1154–1175.
Pollard, W. L. "Outline of the Law of Zoning in the United States." In *Zoning in the United States: The Annals of the American Academy of Political and Social Science* 155 (1931): part II, 15–33.
Scott, Mel. *American City Planning since 1890.* Berkeley: University of California Press, 1969.
Siegan, Bernard H. *Land Use without Zoning.* Lexington, MA: Lexington Books, 1972.
Toll, Seymour I. *Zoned American.* New York: Grossman, 1969.
U.S. Department of Commerce. *A Standard State Zoning Enabling Act.* Washington, DC: U.S. Department of Commerce, 1926.
*Village of Euclid v. Ambler Realty Company,* 272 U.S. 365 (1926).

## Zoos

Zoos have evolved through four distinct stages. Those stages do not, however, fit a neat temporal sequence. All of the stages exist today, many in the same zoo but in separate exhibits. The most primitive method of keeping animals can be characterized as close captivity, frequently behind bars or in shackles. This is the traditional menagerie; its only element of aesthetic appeal occurs if the exhibit buildings have been designed to reflect a relevant cultural context, e.g., Indian architecture for an elephant building. The death of animals after a short period of captivity under these conditions has been a major worry, both humane and economic, for management. This concern lead to improved care for the animals' health and physical comfort and resulted in a second way of displaying animals, the "bathroom" school of architecture. Animals were still penned and kept behind bars, but everything inside the barred cage was lined with ceramic tile that was easily kept clean with a high-pressure hose. The emphasis on animal health and well-being also brought about improved veterinary medicine and a better understanding of the nutritional needs of the captive clientele.

At the beginning of the twentieth century, a European animal dealer and circus owner, Carl Hagenbeck, constructed a zoo near Hamburg, Germany, that displayed animals in naturalistic settings without bars. While showing African antelope with lions in the background did not dramatically improve the animals' condition, it made patrons much more comfortable with the zoo experience. The most recent stage in zoological parks results directly from the work of a Swiss zoologist, Heini Hediger, in the 1930s and 1940s. Hediger demonstrated that the quality of space provided for animals was more important than either the appearance or quantity of the space. He contended that for animals to be truly healthy, their behavioral as well as their physical needs had to be met. Many traditional exhibits met these needs, at least to some limited extent: flight cages for birds; bear pits, with dead trees to climb and tear up; and the then-new monkey islands, but it was Hediger who first expounded a biological justification for this kind of zoo.

While a number of menageries preceded it (for example, the one in New York's Central Park), the first American zoo to be organized on the European model of a learned society sponsoring a zoological garden opened in Philadelphia in 1874. One way of measuring the constantly expanding size of animal displays is to compare the sizes of this entire Philadelphia zoo with a single exhibit at the New York Zoological Gardens in 1985 called "Jungle World"; they are both about 40 acres.

Many municipal zoos in the United States developed quite by accident; for example, a circus went broke, and the only appropriate space in town for the animals belonged to the park department. Carnival rides were always part of the package. The town zoo became part of the local parks organization, and a merry-go-round, Ferris wheel, and miniature train became integral parts of the new attraction. There was no thought of either education or research.

This close association with recreation hindered the professional development of American zoos for many years; not until 1972 did the American Association of Zoological Parks and Aquariums (AAZPA) become independent of the American Institute of Park Executives and its successor organizations. Only after the AAZPA became independent did codes of ethics, professional certification, zoo accreditation, conservation initiatives, and academic curricula develop, all under its aegis.

The Brookfield Zoo, developed by the Chicago Zoological Society on land owned by the Cook County Forest Preserve District in 1934, was the first American zoo to be built entirely on the principles enunciated by Carl Hagenbeck at the turn of the century. In the 1960s Dr. Charles R. Schroeder of the San Diego Zoo dreamed of a great breeding ground for exotic animals where the public could see them in much more natural surroundings. The San Diego Wild Animal Park on 1,800 acres in San Pasqual Valley resulted. This innovation

*Visitors of all ages watch a hippo and her baby at the San Diego zoo in 1984.*

showed the way, and several other institutions followed. The most recent major presentation to incorporate all of the most modern principles of both zoo and museum practice is "Amazonia," which opened at the National Zoological Park in Washington, D.C., in 1992. This exhibit of 15,000 square feet is designed to allow the visitor to experience one of the world's most complex ecosystems, the Amazon Basin, and not just see the relevant animals.

In spite of all the changes in zoos and the professional concerns of zoo personnel, a portion of our society believes that all animal captivity is cruel and favors the abolition of zoos. Michael Fox of the Humane Society of the United States has written that if the public ever became aware of the basic brutality of captivity, the National Zoo, "like all zoos, would be demolished and the animals liberated by a compassionate humanity." But, regardless of all the criticism, zoos have progressed in the past 20 years. Today, there are 140 fully accredited zoos and 26 aquariums in the United States. The public votes their approval with their attendance; almost 120 million persons visited North America's zoos in 1993.

—*Philip Ogilvie*

### References

Conway, William. "How to Exhibit a Bullfrog." *Curator* 11 (1968): 4.

Fischer, James. *Zoos in the World.* London: Aldus, 1966.

Gold, Don. *Zoo: A Behind-the-Scenes Look at the Animals and the People Who Care for Them.* Chicago: Contemporary Books, 1988.

Hahn, Emily. *Animal Gardens.* Garden City, NY: Doubleday, 1967.

Hancocks, David. *Animals and Architecture.* New York: Praeger, 1971.

Hediger, Heini. *Man and Animal in the Zoo: Zoo Biology.* London: Routledge & Kegan Paul, 1969.

Hoage, R. J., and William A. Deiss, eds. *New Worlds, New Animals: From Menagerie to Zoological Park in the Nineteenth Century.* Baltimore: Johns Hopkins University Press, 1996.

Livingston, Bernard. *Zoo: Animals, People, Places.* New York: Arbor House, 1974.

Lumpkin, Susan. "Glimpses of Amazonia." *Zoogoer* 21 (1992): 5–12.

Luoma, Jon R. *A Crowded Ark: The Role of Zoos in Wildlife Conservation.* Boston: Houghton Mifflin, 1987.

Wade, Robert, ed. *Wild in the City: the Best of ZOONOOZ.* San Diego, CA: Zoological Society of San Diego, 1985.

# Selected Bibliography

The following bibliography is not comprehensive, nor was it meant to be. It was created from the references found at the end of entries by separating out all references listed in more than one entry and then arranging those references into the subject categories below. The bibliography is simply intended to serve as a useful tool for someone who wants to investigate a broader subject than the entries contained in the encyclopedia and needs some direction about where to begin. Although these lists are not all-inclusive, and though many outstanding (even classic) books and articles are omitted, the fact that more than one authority recommended a work indicates that these works will, at the very least, guide researchers toward the relevant literature.

The bibliography is arranged according to the following subect categories:

**Entertainment, Leisure, Recreation, and Sports**—including specific manifestations such as opera and museums, as well as theme parks

**The Growth of Urban Places**—including urbanization, suburbanization, and studies of individual cities and suburbs

**The Physical Nature of Urban Places**—including architecture, city planning, housing, and urban infrastructure

**Race and Ethnicity, Racism and Ethnocentrism, and Religion**—including specific racial, ethnic, and religious groups, how they have affected cities, and how cities have affected them

**Technology**—focusing on transportation and communications, including streets and bridges and technology that makes communication possible without face-to-face contact

**Urban Economics**—including all sectors of the urban economy and the people involved in the urban economy

**Urban Government**—including politics, types of government, political bosses and machines, reformers, and the governmental response to crime

**Urban Society**—including studies of class, social structure, segments of society, community structure, education, and criminal behavior, but excluding studies of race and ethnicity, technology, and leisure

## Entertainment, Leisure, Recreation, and Sports

Armstrong, Louis. *Satchmo: My Life in New Orleans.* New York: Prentice-Hall, 1954.

Badger, Reid. *The Great American Fair: The World's Columbian Exposition and American Culture.* Chicago: Nelson Hall, 1979.

Blesh, Rudi, and Harriet Janis. *They All Played Ragtime: The True Story of an American Music.* New York: Knopf, 1950.

Gorn, Elliott J. *The Manly Art: Bare-Knuckle Prize Fighting in America.* Ithaca, NY: Cornell University Press, 1986.

Hardy, Stephen. *How Boston Played: Sport, Recreation, and Community, 1865–1915.* Boston: Northeastern University Press, 1982.

Kasson, John F. *Amusing the Millions: Coney Island at the Turn of the Century.* New York: Hill and Wang, 1978.

Kuklick, Bruce. *To Everything a Season: Shibe Park and Urban Philadelphia, 1909–1976.* Princeton, NJ: Princeton University Press, 1991.

Kyriazi, Gary. *The Great American Amusement Parks: A Pictorial History.* Secaucus, NJ: Citadel Press, 1976.

Levine, Lawrence W. *High Brow/Low Brow: The Emergence of Cultural Hierarchy in America.* Cambridge, MA: Harvard University Press, 1988.

Nasaw, David. *Going Out: The Rise and Fall of Public Amusements.* New York: Basic Books, 1993.

Peiss, Kathy. *Cheap Amusements: Working Women and Leisure in Turn-of-the-Century New York.* Philadelphia: Temple University Press, 1986.

Rader, Benjamin G. *American Sports: From the Age of Folk Games to the Age of Televised Sports.* Englewood Cliffs, NJ: Prentice-Hall, 1990.

Riess, Steven A. *City Games: The Evolution of American Urban Society and the Rise of Sports.* Urbana: University of Illinois Press, 1989.

———. *Touching Bases: Professional Baseball and American Culture in the Progressive Era.* Westport, CT: Greenwood Press, 1980.

## The Growth of Urban Places

Abbott, Carl. *Boosters and Businessmen: Popular Economic Thought and Urban Growth in the Antebellum Middle West.* Westport, CT: Greenwood Press, 1981.

———. *The Metropolitan Frontier: Cities in the Modern American West.* Tucson: University of Arizona Press, 1993.

Adler, Jeffrey S. *Yankee Merchants and the Making of the Urban West: The Rise and Fall of Ante-bellum St. Louis.* New York: Cambridge University Press, 1991.

Albion, Robert Greenhalgh. *The Rise of New York Port, 1815–1860.* New York: Scribners, 1939.

Allen, James B. *The Company Town in the American West.* Norman: University of Oklahoma Press, 1966.

Arnold, Joseph L. *The New Deal in the Suburbs: A History of the Greenbelt Town Program, 1935–1954.* Columbus: Ohio State University Press, 1971.

Bender, Thomas. *Toward an Urban Vision: Ideas and Institutions in Nineteenth-Century America.* Lexington: University Press of Kentucky, 1975.

Bigger, Richard, and James D. Kitchen. *How the Cities Grew: A Century of Municipal Independence and Expansionism in Metropolitan Los Angeles.* Los Angeles: Haynes Foundation, 1952.

Biles, Roger. *Memphis in the Great Depression.* Knoxville: University Press of Tennessee, 1986.

Binford, Henry C. *The First Suburbs: Residential Communities on the Boston Periphery, 1815–1860.* Chicago: University of Chicago Press, 1985.

Buder, Stanley. *Pullman: An Experiment in Industrial Order and Community Planning, 1880–1930.* New York: Oxford University Press, 1967.

Burgess, Ernest W. "Growth of the City." In Robert E. Park, Ernest W. Burgess, and Roderick D. McKenzie, eds., *The City,* 47–62. Chicago: University of Chicago Press, 1925.

Caro, Robert A. *The Power Broker: Robert Moses and the Fall of New York.* New York: Knopf, 1974.

Ciucci, Giorgio, et al. *The American City: From the Civil War to the New Deal.* Barbara Luigia La Penta, trans. Cambridge, MA: MIT Press, 1979.

Contosta, David R. *Suburb in the City: Chestnut Hill, Philadelphia, 1850–1990.* Columbus: Ohio State University Press, 1992.

Cronon, William. *Nature's Metropolis: Chicago and the Great West.* New York: W. W. Norton, 1991.

Doyle, Don H. *New Men, New Cities, New South: Atlanta, Nashville, Charleston, Mobile, 1860–1910.* Chapel Hill: University of North Carolina Press, 1990.

Dykstra, Robert R. *The Cattle Towns.* New York: Atheneum, 1979.

Ebner, Michael H. *Creating Chicago's North Shore: A Suburban History.* Chicago: University of Chicago Press, 1988.

Findlay, John M. *Magic Lands: Western Cityscape and American Culture after 1940.* Berkeley: University of California Press, 1992.

Fishman, Robert. *Bourgeois Utopias: The Rise and Fall of Suburbia.* New York: Basic Books, 1987.

Fogelson, Robert M. *The Fragmented Metropolis: Los Angeles, 1850–1930.* Cambridge, MA: Harvard University Press, 1967.

Frost, Lionel. *The New Urban Frontier: Urbanisation and City-Building in Australasia and the American West.* Kensington, Australia: New South Wales University Press, 1991.

Gans, Herbert. *The Levittowners: Ways of Life and Politics in a New Suburban Community.* New York: Random House, 1967.

Garner, John S. *The Model Company Town: Urban Design through Private Enterprise in Nineteenth-Century New England.* Amherst: University of Massachusetts Press, 1982.

Gottman, Jean. *Megalopolis: The Urbanized Northeastern Seaboard of the United States.* Cambridge, MA: MIT Press, 1961.

Hamer, David. *New Towns in the New World: Images and Perceptions of the Nineteenth-Century Urban Frontier.* New York: Columbia University Press, 1990.

Harris, Chauncy D., and Edward L. Ullman. "The Nature of Cities." *Annals of the American Academy of Political and Social Science* 242 (1945): 7–17.

Harris, Richard. *Unplanned Suburbs: Toronto's American Tragedy, 1900–1950.* Baltimore: Johns Hopkins University Press, 1995.

Holt, Glen E., and Dominic A. Pacyga. *Chicago: A Historical Guide to the Neighborhoods, The Loop and South Side.* Chicago: Chicago Historical Society, 1979.

Hoyt, Homer. *The Structure and Growth of Residential Neighborhoods in American Cities.* Washington, DC: Federal Housing Administration, 1939.

Jackson, Kenneth T. *Crabgrass Frontier: The Suburbanization of the United States.* New York: Oxford University Press, 1985.

Jacobs, Jane. *The Death and Life of Great American Cities.* New York: Random House, 1961.

Keating, Ann Durkin. *Building Chicago: Suburban Developers and the Creation of a Divided Metropolis.* Columbus: Ohio State University Press, 1988.

Kling, Rob, Spencer Olin, and Mark Poster, eds. *Post-Suburban California: The Transformation of Orange County since World War II.* Berkeley: University of California Press, 1991.

Lingeman, Richard. *Small Town America: A Narrative History, 1620– the Present.* Boston: Houghton Mifflin, 1980.

Lotchin, Roger. *Fortress California, 1910–1961: From Warfare to Welfare.* New York: Oxford University Press, 1992.

———. *San Francisco, 1846–1856: From Hamlet to City.* New York: Oxford University Press, 1974.

Lubove, Roy. *Twentieth Century Pittsburgh.* 2 vols. New York: Knopf, 1969.

Luckingham, Bradford. "The Urban Dimension of Western History." In Michael P. Malone, ed., *Historians and the American West.* Lincoln: University of Nebraska Press, 1983.

Mahoney, Timothy R. *River Towns in the Great West: The Structure of Provincial Urbanization in the American Midwest, 1820–1870.* New York: Cambridge University Press, 1990.

Mayer, Harold M., and Richard C. Wade. *Chicago: Growth of a Metropolis.* Chicago: University of Chicago Press, 1969.

McComb, David G. *Houston: A History.* Austin: University of Texas Press, 1981.

Miller, William D. *Memphis during the Progressive Era.* Memphis, TN: Memphis State University Press, 1957.

Miller, Zane L. *Boss Cox's Cincinnati.* Chicago: University of Chicago Press, 1968.

Monkkonen, Eric H. *America Becomes Urban: The Development of U.S. Cities and Towns, 1780–1880.* Berkeley: University of California Press, 1988.

Muller, Peter O. *The Outer City: Geographical Consequences of the Urbanization of the Suburbs.* Washington, DC: Association of American Geographers, 1976.

Mumford, Lewis. *The City in History.* New York: Harcourt, Brace and World, 1961.

O'Connor, Carol A. *A Sort of Utopia: Scarsdale, 1891–1981.* Albany: State University of New York Press, 1983.

Park, Robert E., Ernest W. Burgess, and Roderick D. McKenzie. *The City.* Chicago: University of Chicago Press, 1925.

Pred, Allan R. *Urban Growth and City Systems in the United States, 1840–1860.* Cambridge, MA: Harvard University Press, 1980.

Reps, John W. *Cities of the American West.* Princeton, NJ: Princeton University Press, 1979.

———. *The Forgotten Frontier: Urban Planning in the American West before 1890.* Columbia: University of Missouri Press, 1981.

———. *The Making of Urban America: A History of City Planning in the United States.* Princeton, NJ: Princeton University Press, 1965.

Schaffer, Daniel. *Garden Cities for America: The Radburn Experience.* Philadelphia: Temple University Press, 1981.

Smith, Page. *As a City Upon a Hill: The Town in American History.* Cambridge, MA: MIT Press, 1966.

Stansell, Christine. *City of Women: Sex and Class in New York, 1789–1860.* Urbana: University of Illinois Press, 1982.

Stilgoe, John R. *Borderland: Origins of the American Suburb, 1820–1939.* New Haven, CT: Yale University Press, 1988.

———. *Common Landscape of America, 1580–1845.* New Haven, CT: Yale University Press, 1982.

———. *Metropolitan Corridor: Railroads and the American Scene.* New Haven, CT: Yale University Press, 1983.

Still, Bayrd, ed. *Urban America: A History with Documents.* Boston: Little, Brown, 1974.

Taylor, Graham Roemyn. *Satellite Cities: A Study of Industrial Suburbs.* New York: Appleton, 1915.

Teaford, Jon C. *Cities of the Heartland: The Rise and Fall of the Industrial Midwest.* Bloomington: Indiana University Press, 1993.

———. *City and Suburb: The Political Fragmentation of Metropolitan America, 1850–1970.* Baltimore: Johns Hopkins University Press, 1979.

———. *The Rough Road to Renaissance: Urban Revitalization in America, 1940–1985.* Baltimore: Johns Hopkins University Press, 1990.

Vance, James E., Jr. "Human Mobility and the Shaping of Cities." In J. F. Hart, ed., *Our Changing Cities,* 67–85. Baltimore: Johns Hopkins University Press, 1991.

Wade, Richard C. *The Urban Frontier: Pioneer Life in Early Pittsburgh, Cincinnati, Lexington, Louisville, and St. Louis.* Cambridge, MA: Harvard University Press, 1959.

Wallock, Leonard, and William Sharpe. "Bold New City or Built Up 'Burb? Redefining Contemporary Suburbia." *American Quarterly* 46 (1994): 1–30.

Warner, Sam Bass, Jr. *Streetcar Suburbs: The Process of Growth in Boston, 1870–1900.* Cambridge, MA: Harvard University Press, 1962.

———. *The Urban Wilderness: A History of the American City.* New York: Harper & Row, 1972.

Weber, Adna Ferrin. *The Growth of Cities in the Nineteenth Century: A Study in Statistics.* New York: Macmillan, 1899.

Worley, William S. *J. C. Nichols and the Shaping of Kansas City: Innovation in Planned Residential Communities.* Columbia: University of Missouri Press, 1990.

Zunz, Olivier. *The Changing Face of Inequality: Urbanization, Industrial Development, and Immigrants in Detroit, 1880–1920.* Chicago: University of Chicago Press, 1982.

## The Physical Nature of Urban Places

Armstrong, Ellis L., Michael C. Robinson, and Suellen M. Hoy, eds. *History of Public Works in the United States, 1776–1976.* Chicago: American Public Works Association, 1976.

Arnold, Joseph L. "Housing and Resettlement." In Otis L. Graham, Jr., and Meghan Robinson Wander, eds., *Franklin D. Roosevelt, His Life and Times: An Encyclopedic View.* Boston: G. K. Hall, 1985.

———. *The New Deal in the Suburbs: A History of the Greenbelt Town Program, 1935–1954.* Columbus: Ohio State University Press, 1971.

Biles, Roger. "Nathan Straus and the Failure of Public Housing, 1937–1942." *The Historian* 53 (1990): 33–46.

Blackmar, Elizabeth. *Manhattan for Rent, 1785–1860.* Ithaca, NY: Cornell University Press, 1989.

Bluestone, Daniel. *Constructing Chicago.* New Haven, CT: Yale University Press, 1991.

Boyer, M. Christine. *Dreaming the Rational City: The Myth of American City Planning.* Cambridge, MA: Harvard University Press, 1983.

Buder, Stanley. *Pullman: An Experiment in Industrial Order and Community Planning, 1880–1930.* New York: Oxford University Press, 1967.

Burg, David F. *Chicago's White City of 1893.* Lexington: University of Kentucky Press, 1976.

Burgess, Patricia. *Planning for the Private Interest: Land Use Controls and Residential Patterns in Columbus, Ohio, 1900–1970.* Columbus: Ohio State University Press, 1994.

Cervero, Robert. *Suburban Gridlock.* New Brunswick, NJ: Center for Urban Policy Research, 1986.

Christaller, Walter. *The Central Places in Southern Germany.* C. W. Baskin, trans. Englewood Cliffs, NJ: Prentice-Hall, 1970.

Clapp, James A. *New Towns and Urban Policy: Planning Metropolitan Growth.* New York: Dunellen, 1971.

Condit, Carl. *The Chicago School of Architects and Their Critics: A History of Commercial and Public Building in the Chicago Area, 1875–1925.* Chicago: University of Chicago Press, 1964.

Cranz, Galen. *The Politics of Park Design: A History of Urban Parks in America.* Cambridge, MA: MIT Press, 1982.

Creese, Walter L. *The Crowning of the American Landscape: Eight Great Spaces and Their Buildings.* Princeton, NJ: Princeton University Press, 1985.

Cullingworth, J. Barry. *The Political Culture of Planning: American Land Use Planning in Comparative Perspective.* New York: Routledge, 1993.

Daunton, Martin J. "Cities of Homes and Cities of Tenements: British and American Comparisons, 1870–1914." *Journal of Urban History* 14 (1988): 283–319.

Doucet, Michael, and John Weaver. *Housing the North American City.* Montreal, Quebec, and Kingston, Ontario: McGill-Queen's University Press, 1991.

Fein, Albert. *Frederick Law Olmsted and the American Environmental Tradition.* New York: Van Nostrand Reinhold, 1967.

Foster, Mark S. *From Streetcar to Superhighway: American City Planners and Urban Transportation, 1900–1940.* Philadelphia: Temple University Press, 1981.

Frieden, Bernard J., and Lynn B Sagalyn. *Downtown Inc.: How America Rebuilds Cities.* Cambridge, MA: MIT Press, 1989.

Friedman, Lawrence M. *Government and Slum Housing: A Century of Frustration.* Chicago: Rand McNally, 1968.

Garner, John S. *The Model Company Town: Urban Design through Private Enterprise in Nineteenth-Century New England.* Amherst: University of Massachusetts Press, 1982.

Giedion, Siegfried. *Space, Time, and Architecture.* Cambridge, MA: Harvard University Press, 1954.

Gilbert, James. *Perfect Cities: Chicago's Utopias of 1893.* Chicago: University of Chicago Press, 1991.

Gillette, Howard, Jr. "The Evolution of Neighborhood Planning: From the Progressive Era to the 1949 Housing Act." *Journal of Urban History* 9 (1983): 421–444.

Goldberger, Paul. *The Skyscraper.* New York: Knopf, 1981.

Goss, Jon. "The 'Magic of the Mall': An Analysis of Form, Function, and Meaning in the Contemporary Retail Built Environment." *Annals of the Association of American Geographers* 83 (1993): 18–47.

Hayden, Dolores. *Seven American Utopias: The Architecture of Communitarian Socialism, 1790–1875.* Cambridge, MA: MIT Press, 1976.

Hays, Forbes B. *Community Leadership: The Regional Plan Association of New York.* New York: Columbia University Press, 1965.

Hines, Thomas S. *Burnham of Chicago: Architect and Planner.* New York: Oxford University Press, 1974.

Hirsch, Arnold. *Making the Second Ghetto: Race and Housing in Chicago, 1940–1960.* New York: Cambridge University Press, 1983.

Hoch, Charles, and Robert A. Slayton. *New Homeless and Old: Community and the Skid Row Hotel.* Philadelphia: Temple University Press, 1989.

Jackson, Anthony. *A Place Called Home: A History of Low-Cost Housing in Manhattan.* Cambridge, MA: MIT Press, 1976.

Keating, Ann Durkin. *Building Chicago: Suburban Developers and the Creation of a Divided Metropolis.* Columbus: Ohio State University Press, 1988.

Kuklick, Bruce. *To Everything a Season: Shibe Park and Urban Philadelphia, 1909–1976.* Princeton, NJ: Princeton University Press, 1991.

Laska, Shirley Bradway, and Daphne Spain, eds. *Back to the City: Issues in Neighborhood Renovation.* New York: Pergamon Press, 1980.

Losch, A. *The Economics of Location.* W. H. Woglom and W. F. Stolper, trans. New Haven, CT: Yale University Press, 1954.

Lubove, Roy. *The Progressives and the Slums: Tenement House Reform in New York City, 1890–1917.* Pittsburgh, PA: University of Pittsburgh Press, 1962.

McCullough, David. *The Great Bridge.* New York: Simon and Schuster, 1972.

Meehan, Eugene J. *Public Housing Policy: Myth versus Reality.* New Brunswick, NJ: Center for Policy Research, 1975.

Melosi, Martin V. *Garbage in the Cities: Refuse, Reform, and the Environment, 1880–1980.* College Station: Texas A & M University Press, 1981.

Miller, Donald L. *Lewis Mumford: A Life.* Pittsburgh, PA: University of Pittsburgh Press, 1992.

Muller, Peter O. *The Outer City: Geographical Consequences of the Urbanization of the Suburbs.* Washington, DC: Association of American Geographers, 1976.

Muth, Richard F. *Cities and Housing.* Chicago: University of Chicago Press, 1969.

Newton, Norman T. *Design on the Land: The Development of Landscape Architecture.* Cambridge, MA: Harvard University Press, 1971.

Palen, John J., and Bruce London, eds. *Gentrification, Displacement and Neighborhood Revitalization.* Albany: State University of New York Press, 1984.

Philpott, Thomas Lee. *The Slum and the Ghetto: Neighborhood Deterioration and Middle-Class Reform, Chicago, 1880–1930.* New York: Oxford University Press, 1978.

Platt, Harold L. *The Electric City: Energy and the Growth of the Chicago Area, 1880–1930.* Chicago: University of Chicago Press, 1991.

Plunz, Richard. *A History of Housing in New York City: Dwelling Type and Social Change in the American Metropolis.* New York: Columbia University Press, 1990.

Reps, John W. *The Forgotten Frontier: Urban Planning in the American West before 1890.* Columbia: University of Missouri Press, 1981.

———. *The Making of Urban America: A History of City Planning in the United States.* Princeton, NJ: Princeton University Press, 1965.

Robertson, Kent A. *Pedestrian Malls and Skywalks.* Brookfield, VT: Avebury Press, 1994.

Rosenzweig, Roy, and Elizabeth Blackmar. *The Park and the People: A History of Central Park.* Ithaca, NY: Cornell University Press, 1992.

Roth, Leland M. *A Concise History of American Architecture.* New York: Harper & Row, 1979.

Schuyler, David. *The New Urban Landscape: The Redefinition of City Form in Nineteenth-Century America.* Baltimore: Johns Hopkins University Press, 1986.

Scott, Mel. *American City Planning since 1890.* Berkeley: University of California Press, 1969.

Scully, Vincent J., Jr. *The Shingle Style and the Stick Style.* New Haven, CT: Yale University Press, 1971.

Siegan, Bernard H. *Land Use without Zoning.* Lexington, MA: D. C. Heath, 1972.

Steinman, David B. *The Builders of the Bridge.* New York: Arno Press, 1972.

Stilgoe, John R. *Common Landscape of America, 1580–1845.* New Haven, CT: Yale University Press, 1982.

Sutherland, John F. "A City of Homes: Philadelphia Slums and Reformers, 1880–1918." Ph.D. dissertation, Temple University, 1973.

Tatum, George Bishop, and Elisabeth Blair MacDougall, eds. *Prophet with Honor: The Career of Andrew Jackson Downing, 1815–1852.* Philadelphia: Atheneum of Philadelphia; Washington, DC: Dumbarton Oaks Research Library and Collection, 1989.

Toll, Seymour I. *Zoned American.* New York: Grossman, 1969.

Turak, Theodore. *William Le Baron Jenney: A Pioneer of Modern Architecture.* Ann Arbor, MI: UMI Research Press, 1986.

van Leeuwen, Thomas A. P. *The Skyward Trend of Thought.* Cambridge, MA: MIT Press, 1988.

Wade, Louise Carroll. *Chicago's Pride: The Stockyards, Packingtown, and Environs in the Nineteenth Century.* Urbana: University of Illinois Press, 1987.

Weiss, Marc A. *The Rise of the Community Builders: The American Real Estate Industry and Urban Land Planning.* New York: Columbia University Press, 1987.

Worley, William S. *J. C. Nichols and the Shaping of Kansas City: Innovation in Planned Residential Communities.* Columbia: University of Missouri Press, 1990.

Wright, Gwendolyn. *Building the Dream: A Social History of Housing in America.* New York: Pantheon, 1981.

Zaitzevsky, Cynthia. *Frederick Law Olmsted and the Boston Park System.* Cambridge, MA: Harvard University Press, 1982.

## Race and Ethnicity, Racism and Ethnocentrism, and Religion

Armstrong, Louis. *Satchmo: My Life in New Orleans.* New York: Prentice-Hall, 1954.

Bennett, David H. *The Party of Fear: From Nativist Movements to the New Right in American History.* Chapel Hill: University of North Carolina Press, 1988.

Bernstein, Iver. *The New York City Draft Riots: Their Significance for American Society and Politics in the Age of the Civil War.* New York: Oxford University Press, 1990.

Biles, Roger. *Richard J. Daley: Politics, Race, and the Governing of Chicago.* DeKalb: Northern Illinois University Press, 1995.

Bodnar, John, Roger Simon, and Michael P. Weber. *Lives of Their Own: Blacks, Italians and Poles in Pittsburgh, 1900–1960.* Urbana: University of Illinois Press, 1982.

Borchert, James. *Alley Life in Washington: Family, Community, Religion, and Folklife in the City, 1850–1970.* Urbana: University of Illinois Press, 1980.

Button, James W. *Blacks and Social Change: Impact of the Civil Rights Movement in Southern Communities.* Princeton, NJ: Princeton University Press, 1989.

Capeci, Dominic J., Jr. *The Harlem Riot of 1943.* Philadelphia: Temple University Press, 1977.

Chan, Sucheng. *Asian Americans: An Interpretive History.* Boston: Twayne, 1991.

Curtis, Susan. *A Consuming Faith: The Social Gospel and Modern American Culture.* Baltimore: Johns Hopkins University Press, 1991.

———. *Dancing to a Black Man's Tune: A Life of Scott Joplin.* Columbia: University of Missouri Press, 1994.

Formisano, Ronald P. *Boston against Busing: Race, Class, and Ethnicity in the 1960s and 1970s.* Chapel Hill: University of North Carolina Press, 1991.

Gans, Herbert. *The Urban Villagers: Group and Class in the Life of Italian Americans.* New York: Free Press, 1962. Rev ed., 1982.

Garcia, Maria Cristina. *Havana, USA: Cuban Exiles and Cuban Americans in South Florida.* Berkeley: University of California Press, 1996.

Green, Constance McLaughlin. *The Secret City: A History of Race Relations in the Nation's Capital.* Princeton, NJ: Princeton University Press, 1967.

Greenberg, Cheryl Lynn. *"Or Does It Explode?" Black Harlem in the Great Depression.* New York: Oxford University Press, 1991.

Greenstone, David J., and Paul E. Petersen. *Race and Authority in Urban Politics.* Chicago: University of Chicago Press, 1973.

Handlin, Oscar. *Boston's Immigrants: A Study in Acculturation.* Rev. and enlarged ed. New York: Atheneum, 1977.

Handy, Robert T. *The Social Gospel in America, 1870–1920.* New York: Oxford University Press, 1966.

Hirsch, Arnold. *Making the Second Ghetto: Race and Housing in Chicago, 1940–1960.* New York: Cambridge University Press, 1983.

Hopkins, Charles H. *The Rise of the Social Gospel in American Protestantism, 1865–1915.* New Haven, CT: Yale University Press, 1940.

Jaynes, Gerald David, and Robin M. Williams, Jr. *A Common Destiny: Blacks and American Society.* Washington, DC: National Academy Press, 1989.

Lane, Roger. *Roots of Violence in Black Philadelphia, 1860–1900*. Cambridge, MA: Harvard University Press, 1986.

Lemann, Nicholas. *The Promised Land: The Great Black Migration and How It Changed America*. New York: Knopf, 1991.

Lewis, David Levering. *When Harlem Was in Vogue*. New York: Oxford University Press, 1979.

Massey, Douglas S., and Nancy A. Denton. *American Apartheid: Segregation and the Making of the Underclass*. Cambridge, MA: Harvard University Press, 1993.

McNickle, Chris. *To Be Mayor of New York: Ethnic Politics in the City*. New York: Columbia University Press, 1993.

Miller, Jerome G. *Hobbling a Generation: Young African-American Males in Washington, D.C.'s Criminal Justice System*. Alexandria, VA: National Center on Institutions and Alternatives, 1992.

Mormino, Gary R., and George E. Pozzetta. *The Immigrant World of Ybor City: Italians and Their Latin American Neighbors in Tampa, 1885–1985*. Urbana: University of Illinois Press, 1987.

Neidle, Cecyle S. *Great Immigrants*. Boston: Twayne, 1973.

Orser, W. Edward. *Blockbusting in Baltimore: The Edmondson Village Story*. Lexington: University Press of Kentucky, 1994.

Osofsky, Gilbert. *Harlem, the Making of a Ghetto: Negro New York, 1890–1930*. 2d ed. New York: Harper & Row, 1971.

Pacyga, Dominic A. *Polish Immigrants and Industrial Chicago: Workers on the South Side, 1880–1922*. Columbus: Ohio State University Press, 1991.

Philpott, Thomas Lee. *The Slum and the Ghetto: Neighborhood Deterioration and Middle-Class Reform, Chicago, 1880–1930*. New York: Oxford University Press, 1978.

Powers, Bernard E., Jr. *Black Charlestonians: A Social History, 1822–1885*. Fayetteville: University of Arkansas Press, 1994.

Trotter, Joe William, Jr., ed. *The Great Migration in Historical Perspective: New Dimensions of Race, Class and Gender*. Bloomington: Indiana University Press, 1991.

Tucker, David M. *Memphis since Crump: Bossism, Blacks, and Civic Reformers, 1948–1968*. Knoxville: University of Tennessee Press, 1980.

White, Ronald C., Jr., and C. Howard Hopkins. *The Social Gospel: Religion and Reform in Changing America*. Philadelphia: Temple University Press, 1976.

Wilson, William Julius. *The Truly Disadvantaged: The Inner City, the Underclass, and Public Policy*. Chicago: University of Chicago Press, 1987.

Zunz, Olivier. *The Changing Face of Inequality: Urbanization, Industrial Development, and Immigrants in Detroit, 1880–1920*. Chicago: University of Chicago Press, 1982.

## Technology

Adams, Judith A. *The American Amusement Park Industry: A History of Technology and Thrills*. Boston: Twayne, 1991.

Barrett, Paul. *The Automobile and Urban Transit: The Formation of Public Policy in Chicago, 1900–1930*. Philadelphia: Temple University Press, 1983.

Cheape, Charles W. *Moving the Masses: Urban Public Transit in New York, Boston, and Philadelphia, 1890–1912*. Cambridge, MA: Harvard University Press, 1980.

Cudahy, Brian J. *Cash, Tokens, and Transfers: A History of Urban Mass Transit in North America*. New York: Fordham University Press, 1990.

Davis, Donald F. *Conspicuous Production: Automobiles and Elites in Detroit, 1899–1933*. Philadelphia: Temple University Press, 1988.

Eckert, Ross, and George W. Hilton. "The Jitneys." *Journal of Law and Economics* 15 (1972): 293–325.

Foster, Mark S. *From Streetcar to Superhighway: American City Planners and Urban Transportation, 1900–1940*. Philadelphia: Temple University Press, 1981.

Hanson, Susan, ed. *The Geography of Urban Transportation*. 2d ed. New York: Guilford Press, 1995.

Hilton, George W. *American Narrow Gauge Railroads*. Stanford, CA: Stanford University Press, 1990.

Hood, Clifton. *722 Miles: The Building of the Subways and How They Transformed New York*. New York: Simon and Schuster, 1993.

Juergens, George. *Joseph Pulitzer and the New York World*. Princeton, NJ: Princeton University Press, 1966.

McCullough, David. *The Great Bridge*. New York: Simon and Schuster, 1972.

McKelvey, Blake. "The Erie Canal, Mother of Cities." *New York Historical Quarterly* 35 (1951): 55–71.

McShane, Clay. *Down the Asphalt Path: The Automobile and the American City*. New York: Columbia University Press, 1994.

Middleton, William D. *Time of the Trolley*. Rev. 2d ed. San Marino, CA: Golden West Books, 1987.

Miller, John Anderson. *Fares Please! A Popular History of Trolleys, Horse-Cars, Street-Cars, Buses, Elevateds, and Subways*. Reprint ed. New York: Dover, 1960.

Rose, Mark H. *Interstate: Express Highway Politics, 1939–1989*. Rev. ed. Knoxville: University of Tennessee Press, 1990.

Rowsome, Frank, Jr., and Stephen D. Maguire, eds. *Trolley Car Treasury: A Century of American Streetcars, Horsecars, Cablecars, Interurbans, and Trolleys*. New York: McGraw-Hill, 1956.

Sears, Stephen W. *The American Heritage History of the Automobile in America*. New York: American Heritage, 1977.

Smerck, George M. *The Federal Role in Urban Mass Transportation*. Bloomington: Indiana University Press, 1991.

Steinman, David B. *The Builders of the Bridge*. New York: Arno Press, 1972.

Stilgoe, John R. *Metropolitan Corridor: Railroads and the American Scene*. New Haven, CT: Yale University Press, 1983.

Taylor, George Rogers. *The Transportation Revolution, 1815–1860*. New York: Holt, Rinehart and Winston, 1951.

Warner, Sam Bass, Jr. *Streetcar Suburbs: The Process of Growth in Boston, 1870–1900*. Cambridge, MA: Harvard University Press, 1962.

## Urban Economics

Abbott, Carl. *Boosters and Businessmen: Popular Economic Thought and Urban Growth in the Antebellum Middle West*. Westport, CT: Greenwood Press, 1981.

Adams, Judith A. *The American Amusement Park Industry: A History of Technology and Thrills*. Boston: Twayne, 1991.

Adler, Jeffrey S. *Yankee Merchants and the Making of the Urban West: The Rise and Fall of Ante-bellum St. Louis.* New York: Cambridge University Press, 1991.

Albion, Robert Greenhalgh. *The Rise of New York Port, 1815–1860.* New York: Scribners, 1939.

Arrington, Leonard J. *Great Basin Kingdom: An Economic History of the Latter-day Saints.* Cambridge, MA: Harvard University Press, 1958.

Barrett, James R. *Work and Community in the Jungle: Chicago's Packinghouse Workers, 1894–1922.* Urbana: University of Illinois Press, 1987.

Berman, Barry, and Joel R. Evans. *Retail Management: A Strategic Approach.* 5th ed. New York: Macmillan, 1992.

Biles, Roger. *Memphis in the Great Depression.* Knoxville: University Press of Tennessee, 1986.

Bluestone, Barry, and Bennett Harrison. *The Deindustrialization of America: Plant Closings, Community Abandonment, and the Dismantling of Basic Industry.* New York: Basic Books, 1982.

Castells, Manuel. *The Urban Question: A Marxist Approach.* Cambridge, MA: MIT Press, 1977.

Chandler, Alfred D., Jr. *The Visible Hand: The Managerial Revolution in American Business.* Cambridge, MA: MIT Press, 1975.

Dublin, Thomas. *Women at Work: The Transformation of Work and Community in Lowell, Massachusetts, 1826–1860.* New York: Columbia University Press, 1979.

Gillette, Howard, Jr. "The Evolution of Neighborhood Planning: From the Progressive Era to the 1949 Housing Act." *Journal of Urban History* 9 (1983): 421–444.

Goldin, Claudia. *Understanding the Gender Gap: An Economic History of American Women.* New York: Oxford University Press, 1990.

Goss, Jon. "The 'Magic of the Mall': An Analysis of Form, Function, and Meaning in the Contemporary Retail Built Environment." *Annals of the Association of American Geographers* 83 (1993): 18–47.

Harvey, David. *Social Justice and the City.* Baltimore: Johns Hopkins University Press, 1975.

Hershberg, Theodore, ed. *Philadelphia: Work, Space, Family and Group Experience in the Nineteenth Century.* New York: Oxford University Press, 1981.

Losch, A. *The Economics of Location.* W. H. Woglom and W. F. Stolper, trans. New Haven, CT: Yale University Press, 1954.

Luxenberg, Stan. *Roadside Empires: How the Chains Franchised America.* New York: Penguin Books, 1986.

McCarthy, E. Jerome, and William D. Perreault, Jr. *Basic Marketing: A Global Managerial Approach.* 11th ed. Homewood, IL: Irwin, 1993.

Meyerowitz, Joanne J. *Women Adrift: Independent Wage Earners in Chicago, 1880–1930.* Chicago: University of Chicago Press, 1988.

Noyelle, Thierry J., and Thomas M. Stanback, Jr. *The Economic Transformation of American Cities.* New York: Rowman and Allanheld, 1983.

Pacyga, Dominic A. *Polish Immigrants and Industrial Chicago: Workers on the South Side, 1880–1922.* Columbus: Ohio State University Press, 1991.

Padilla, Felix M. *The Gang as an American Enterprise.* New Brunswick, NJ: Rutgers University Press, 1992.

Phillips, Charles F., and Delbert J. Duncan. *Marketing Principles and Methods.* 6th ed. Homewood, IL: Irwin, 1968.

Rock, Howard B. *Artisans of the New Republic: The Tradesmen of New York City in the Age of Jefferson.* New York: New York University Press, 1979.

Rosenzweig, Roy. *Eight Hours for What We Will: Workers and Leisure in an Industrial City, 1870–1920.* Cambridge, England: Cambridge University Press, 1983.

Skaggs, Jimmy M. *Prime Cut: Livestock Raising and Meatpacking in the United States, 1607–1983.* College Station: Texas A & M University Press, 1986.

Taylor, George Rogers. *The Transportation Revolution, 1815–1860.* New York: Holt, Rinehart and Winston, 1951.

Wade, Louise Carroll. *Chicago's Pride: The Stockyards, Packingtown, and Environs in the Nineteenth Century.* Urbana: University of Illinois Press, 1987.

Wilentz, Sean. *Chants Democratic: New York City and the Rise of the American Working Class, 1788–1850.* New York: Oxford University Press, 1984.

Zunz, Olivier. *The Changing Face of Inequality: Urbanization, Industrial Development, and Immigrants in Detroit, 1880–1920.* Chicago: University of Chicago Press, 1982.

## Urban Government

Allswang, John M. *Bosses, Machines and Urban Voters.* Rev. ed. Baltimore: Johns Hopkins University Press, 1986.

Argersinger, JoAnn E. *Toward a New Deal in Baltimore: People and Government in the Great Depression.* Chapel Hill: University of North Carolina Press, 1988.

Barrett, Paul. *The Automobile and Urban Transit: The Formation of Public Policy in Chicago, 1900–1930.* Philadelphia: Temple University Press, 1983.

Bennett, David H. *The Party of Fear: From Nativist Movements to the New Right in American History.* Chapel Hill: University of North Carolina Press, 1988.

Bernstein, Iver. *The New York City Draft Riots: Their Significance for American Society and Politics in the Age of the Civil War.* New York: Oxford University Press, 1990.

Biles, Roger. *Big City Boss in Depression and War: Mayor Edward J. Kelly of Chicago.* DeKalb: Northern Illinois University Press, 1984.

———. "Nathan Straus and the Failure of Public Housing, 1937–1942." *The Historian* 53 (1990): 33–46.

———. *Richard J. Daley: Politics, Race, and the Governing of Chicago.* DeKalb: Northern Illinois University Press, 1995.

Caro, Robert A. *The Power Broker: Robert Moses and the Fall of New York.* New York: Random House, 1975.

Clapp, James A. *New Towns and Urban Policy: Planning Metropolitan Growth.* New York: Dunellen, 1971.

Conlan, Timothy. *New Federalism: Intergovernmental Reform from Nixon to Reagan.* Washington, DC: Brookings Institution, 1988.

Cranz, Galen. *The Politics of Park Design: A History of Urban Parks in America.* Cambridge, MA: MIT Press, 1982.

Cullingworth, J. Barry. *The Political Culture of Planning: American Land Use Planning in Comparative Perspective.* New York: Routledge, 1993.

Davis, Allen F. *Spearheads for Reform: The Social Settlements and the Progressive Movement, 1890–1914.* New York: Oxford University Press, 1967.

Dorsett, Lyle W. *Franklin D. Roosevelt and the City Bosses.* Port Washington, NY: Kennikat Press, 1977.

Fogelson, Robert M. *Big-City Police.* Cambridge, MA: Harvard University Press, 1977.

Fox, Kenneth. *Better City Government: Innovation in American Urban Politics, 1850–1937.* Philadelphia: Temple University Press, 1977.

Friedman, Lawrence M. *Government and Slum Housing: A Century of Frustration.* Chicago: Rand McNally, 1968.

Gelfand, Mark I. *A Nation of Cities: The Federal Government and Urban America, 1933–1965.* New York: Oxford University Press, 1975.

Gosnell, Harold F. *Machine Politics: Chicago Style.* Chicago: University of Chicago Press, 1968.

Greenstone, David J., and Paul E. Petersen. *Race and Authority in Urban Politics.* Chicago: University of Chicago Press, 1973.

Grumm, John G., and Russell D. Murphy. *Governing States and Communities: Organizing for Popular Rule.* Englewood Cliffs, NJ: Prentice-Hall, 1991.

Haas, Edward F. *DeLesseps S. Morrison and the Image of Reform: New Orleans Politics, 1946–1961.* Baton Rouge: Louisiana State University Press, 1974.

Handy, Robert T. *The Social Gospel in America, 1870–1920.* New York: Oxford University Press, 1966.

Harrigan, John J. *Political Change in the Metropolis.* 5th ed. New York: HarperCollins, 1993.

Harvey, David. *Social Justice and the City.* Baltimore: Johns Hopkins University Press, 1975.

Hawkins, Brett W. *Nashville Metro: The Politics of City-County Consolidation.* Nashville, TN: Vanderbilt University Press, 1966.

Hopkins, Charles H. *The Rise of the Social Gospel in American Protestantism, 1865–1915.* New Haven, CT: Yale University Press, 1940.

Kessner, Thomas. *Fiorello H. La Guardia and the Making of Modern New York.* New York: McGraw-Hill, 1989.

Kluger, Richard. *Simple Justice.* New York: Knopf, 1975.

Lawson, Ronald. *The Tenant Movement in New York City, 1901–1984.* New Brunswick, NJ: Rutgers University Press, 1986.

Lipsky, Michael. *Protest in City Politics.* Chicago: Rand McNally, 1970.

Lubove, Roy. *The Progressives and the Slums: Tenement House Reform in New York City, 1890–1917.* Pittsburgh, PA: University of Pittsburgh Press, 1962.

———. *The Struggle for Social Security, 1900–1935.* Cambridge, MA: Harvard University Press, 1968.

McKenzie, Evan. *Privatopia: Homeowner Associations and the Rise of Residential Private Government.* New Haven, CT: Yale University Press, 1994.

McNickle, Chris. *To Be Mayor of New York: Ethnic Politics in the City.* New York: Columbia University Press, 1993.

Meehan, Eugene J. *Public Housing Policy: Myth versus Reality.* New Brunswick, NJ: Center for Policy Research, 1975.

Melosi, Martin V. *Garbage in the Cities: Refuse, Reform, and the Environment, 1880–1980.* College Station: Texas A & M University Press, 1981.

Miller, Jerome G. *Hobbling a Generation: Young African-American Males in Washington, D.C.'s Criminal Justice System.* Alexandria, VA: National Center on Institutions and Alternatives, 1992.

Miller, Zane L. *Boss Cox's Cincinnati.* Chicago: University of Chicago Press, 1968.

Monkkonen, Eric H. *Police in Urban America, 1860–1920.* New York: Cambridge University Press, 1981.

Namorato, Michael V., ed. *The Diary of Rexford G. Tugwell: The New Deal, 1932–1935.* Westport, CT: Greenwood Press, 1992.

Peterson, Paul. *The Price of Federalism.* Washington, DC: Brookings Institution, 1995.

Philpott, Thomas Lee. *The Slum and the Ghetto: Neighborhood Deterioration and Middle-Class Reform, Chicago, 1880–1930.* New York: Oxford University Press, 1978.

Rose, Mark H. *Interstate: Express Highway Politics, 1939–1989.* Rev. ed. Knoxville: University of Tennessee Press, 1990.

Schiesl, Martin J. *The Politics of Efficiency: Municipal Administration and Reform in America, 1880–1920.* Berkeley: University of California Press, 1977.

Shefter, Martin. *Political Crisis, Fiscal Crisis: The Collapse and Revival of New York City.* New York: Basic Books, 1985.

Slayton, Robert. *Back of the Yards: The Making of a Local Democracy.* Chicago: University of Chicago Press, 1986.

Smerck, George M. *The Federal Role in Urban Mass Transportation.* Bloomington: Indiana University Press, 1991.

Smith, Douglas L. *The New Deal in the Urban South.* Baton Rouge: Louisiana State University Press, 1988.

Sutherland, John F. "A City of Homes: Philadelphia Slums and Reformers, 1880–1918." Ph.D. dissertation, Temple University, 1973.

Svara, James H. *Official Leadership in the City: Patterns of Conflict and Cooperation.* New York: Oxford University Press, 1990.

Teaford, Jon C. *City and Suburb: The Political Fragmentation of Metropolitan America, 1850–1970.* Baltimore: Johns Hopkins University Press, 1979.

———. *The Municipal Revolution in America: Origins of Modern Urban Government, 1650–1825.* Chicago: University of Chicago Press, 1975.

———. *Post-Suburbia: Government and Politics in the Edge Cities.* Baltimore: Johns Hopkins University Press, 1996.

———. *The Rough Road to Renaissance: Urban Revitalization in America, 1940–1985.* Baltimore: Johns Hopkins University Press, 1990.

———. *The Unheralded Triumph: City Government in America, 1870–1900.* Baltimore: Johns Hopkins University Press, 1984.

Tucker, David M. *Memphis since Crump: Bossism, Blacks, and Civic Reformers, 1948–1968.* Knoxville: University of Tennessee Press, 1980.

Wendt, Lloyd, and Herman Kogan. *Bosses in Lusty Chicago: The Story of Bathhouse John and Hinky Dink.* Bloomington: Indiana University Press, 1974.

White, Ronald C., Jr., and C. Howard Hopkins. *The Social Gospel: Religion and Reform in Changing America.* Philadelphia: Temple University Press, 1976.

## Urban Society

Anderson, Nels. *The Hobo: The Sociology of the Homeless Man.* Chicago: University of Chicago Press, 1923.

Baltzell, E. Digby. *Philadelphia Gentlemen: The Making of a National Upper Class.* New York: Quadrangle, 1971.

Barrett, James R. *Work and Community in the Jungle: Chicago's Packinghouse Workers, 1894–1922.* Urbana: University of Illinois Press, 1987.

Barth, Gunther. *City People: The Rise of Modern City Culture in Nineteenth-Century America.* New York: Oxford University Press, 1982.

Beard, Rick, and Leslie Cohen Berlowitz, eds. *Greenwich Village: Culture and Counterculture.* New Brunswick, NJ: Rutgers University Press, 1993.

Bender, Thomas. *Toward an Urban Vision: Ideas and Institutions in Nineteenth-Century America.* Lexington: University Press of Kentucky, 1975.

Blackwelder, Julia Kirk. *Women of the Depression: Caste and Culture in San Antonio, 1929–1939.* College Station: Texas A & M University Press, 1984.

Boggs, Sarah Lee. "Urban Crime Patterns." *American Sociological Review* 30 (1965): 899–908.

Borchert, James. *Alley Life in Washington: Family, Community, Religion, and Folklife in the City, 1850–1970.* Urbana: University of Illinois Press: 1980.

Boyer, Paul S. *Urban Masses and Moral Order in America, 1820–1920.* Cambridge, MA: Harvard University Press, 1978.

Bremner, Robert H. *American Philanthropy.* 2d ed. Chicago: University of Chicago Press, 1988.

———. *From the Depths: The Discovery of Poverty in the United States.* New York: New York University Press, 1956.

Brown, Marilyn A. "Modeling the Spatial Distribution of Suburban Crime." *Economic Geography* 58 (1982): 247–261.

Bulmer, Martin. *The Chicago School of Sociology.* Chicago: University of Chicago Press, 1984.

Burg, David F. *Chicago's White City of 1893.* Lexington: University of Kentucky Press, 1976.

Clark, Norman H. *Deliver Us from Evil: An Interpretation of American Prohibition.* New York: W. W. Norton, 1976.

Curtis, Susan. *A Consuming Faith: The Social Gospel and Modern American Culture.* Baltimore: Johns Hopkins University Press, 1991.

Davis, Allen F. *Spearheads for Reform: The Social Settlements and the Progressive Movement, 1890–1914.* New York: Oxford University Press, 1967.

Davis, Donald F. *Conspicuous Production: Automobiles and Elites in Detroit, 1899–1933.* Philadelphia: Temple University Press, 1988.

Dublin, Thomas. *Women at Work: The Transformation of Work and Community in Lowell, Massachusetts, 1826–1860.* New York: Columbia University Press, 1979.

Duis, Perry. *The Saloon: Public Drinking in Chicago and Boston, 1880–1920.* Urbana: University of Illinois Press, 1983.

Fabian, Ann. *Card Sharps, Dream Books, and Bucket Shops: Gambling in Nineteenth-Century America.* Ithaca, NY: Cornell University Press, 1990.

Feldberg, Michael. *The Turbulent Era: Riot and Disorder in Jacksonian America.* New York: Oxford University Press, 1980.

Findlay, John M. *Magic Lands: Western Cityscape and American Culture after 1940.* Berkeley: University of California Press, 1992.

Formisano, Ronald P. *Boston against Busing: Race, Class, and Ethnicity in the 1960s and 1970s.* Chapel Hill: University of North Carolina Press, 1991.

Gans, Herbert. *The Levittowners: Ways of Life and Politics in a New Suburban Community.* New York: Random House, 1967.

———. *The Urban Villagers: Group and Class in the Life of Italian Americans.* New York: Free Press, 1962. Rev. ed., 1982.

Gilbert, James. *Perfect Cities: Chicago's Utopias of 1893.* Chicago: University of Chicago Press, 1991.

Gilfoyle, Timothy J. *City of Eros: New York City, Prostitution and the Commercialization of Sex, 1790–1920.* New York: W. W. Norton, 1992.

Goldin, Claudia. *Understanding the Gender Gap: An Economic History of American Women.* New York: Oxford University Press, 1990.

Hall, Jacquelyn Dowd, et al. *Like a Family: The Making of a Southern Cotton Mill World.* Chapel Hill: University of North Carolina Press, 1987.

Harvey, David. *Social Justice and the City.* Baltimore: Johns Hopkins University Press, 1975.

Hawley, Amos H. *Human Ecology: A Theory of Community Structure.* New York: Ronald Press, 1950.

Hays, Forbes B. *Community Leadership: The Regional Plan Association of New York.* New York: Columbia University Press, 1965.

Hershberg, Theodore, ed. *Philadelphia: Work, Space, Family and Group Experience in the Nineteenth Century.* New York: Oxford University Press, 1981.

Hoch, Charles, and Robert A. Slayton. *New Homeless and Old: Community and the Skid Row Hotel.* Philadelphia: Temple University Press, 1989.

Johnson, Paul E. *A Shopkeeper's Millennium: Society and Revivals in Rochester, New York, 1815–1837.* New York: Hill and Wang, 1978.

Katz, Michael B., ed. *The "Underclass" Debate: Views from History.* Princeton, NJ: Princeton University Press, 1993.

Leiby, James. *A History of Social Welfare and Social Work in the United States.* New York: Columbia University Press, 1978.

Levine, Lawrence W. *High Brow/Low Brow: The Emergence of Cultural Hierarchy in America.* Cambridge, MA: Harvard University Press, 1988.

Marsh, Margaret. *Suburban Lives.* New Brunswick, NJ: Rutgers University Press, 1990.

McKenzie, Evan. *Privatopia: Homeowner Associations and the Rise of Residential Private Government.* New Haven, CT: Yale University Press, 1994.

Meyerowitz, Joanne J. *Women Adrift: Independent Wage Earners in Chicago, 1880–1930.* Chicago: University of Chicago Press, 1988.

Mintz, Stephen, and Susan Kellogg. *Domestic Revolutions: A Social History of American Family Life.* New York: Free Press, 1988.

Noel, Thomas J. *The City and the Saloon: Denver, 1858–1916.* Lincoln: University of Nebraska Press, 1982.

Padilla, Felix M. *The Gang as an American Enterprise.* New Brunswick, NJ: Rutgers University Press, 1992.

Palen, John J., and Bruce London, eds. *Gentrification, Displacement and Neighborhood Revitalization.* Albany: State University of New York Press, 1984.

Park, Robert E. *Human Communities: The City and Human Ecology.* Glencoe, IL: Free Press, 1952.

Rock, Howard B. *Artisans of the New Republic: The Tradesmen of New York City in the Age of Jefferson.* New York: New York University Press, 1979.

Rosen, Ruth. *The Lost Sisterhood: Prostitution in America, 1900–1918.* Baltimore: Johns Hopkins University Press, 1982.

Rosenzweig, Roy. *Eight Hours for What We Will: Workers and Leisure in an Industrial City, 1870–1920.* Cambridge, England: Cambridge University Press, 1983.

Rosenzweig, Roy, and Elizabeth Blackmar. *The Park and the People: A History of Central Park.* Ithaca, NY: Cornell University Press, 1992.

Rothman, David J. *The Discovery of the Asylum: Social Order and Disorder in the New Republic.* Boston: Little, Brown, 1971.

Rydell, Robert. *All the World's a Fair: Visions of Empire at American International Expositions, 1876–1916.* Chicago: University of Chicago Press, 1984.

Scherzer, Kenneth. *The Unbounded Community: Neighborhood Life and Social Structure in New York City, 1830–1875.* Durham, NC: Duke University Press, 1992.

Shaw, Clifford R., and Henry D. McKay. *Juvenile Delinquency and Urban Areas.* Rev. ed. Chicago: University of Chicago Press, 1969.

Smith, Neil, and Peter Williams, eds. *Gentrification of the City.* Boston: Allen & Unwin, 1986.

Stansell, Christine. *City of Women: Sex and Class in New York, 1789–1860.* Urbana: University of Illinois Press, 1982.

Symanski, Richard. *The Immoral Landscape: Female Prostitution in Western Societies.* Toronto, Ontario: Butterworths, 1981.

Thernstrom, Stephan. *The Other Bostonians: Poverty and Progress in the American Metropolis, 1880–1970.* Cambridge, MA: Harvard University Press, 1973.

———. *Poverty and Progress: Social Mobility in a Nineteenth-Century City.* Cambridge, MA: Harvard University Press, 1964.

Trolander, Judith Ann. *Professionalism and Social Change: From the Settlement House Movement to Neighborhood Centers, 1886 to the Present.* New York: Columbia University Press, 1987.

Wilentz, Sean. *Chants Democratic: New York City and the Rise of the American Working Class, 1788–1850.* New York: Oxford University Press, 1984.

Wilson, William Julius. *The Truly Disadvantaged: The Inner City, the Underclass, and Public Policy.* Chicago: University of Chicago Press, 1987.

# Entries by Subject

The following lists, which compile the names of entries into lists determined by subject, are not exhaustive. Almost all of the entries in the encyclopedia concern more than a single subject, and each of the terms can be conceived and interpreted in more than one way, depending on the user's own concerns and interests. For example, "Daley, Richard J." could be listed under "Politics and Government" in addition to "People (Individuals)." Some entries are listed by more than one subject, but this is when they do not fit easily into any one subject. Therefore, these lists should be used simply as a relatively easy way into obvious larger topics for anyone who would like some assistance in entering the enormous subject of cities and urban life. They are meant more for novices in the field than for experts.

The entries have been arranged according to the following subjects:

- Arts
- Buildings, Building Types, and Construction
- Cities, Suburbs, and Sections of Cities
- Concepts and Terms
- Economics
- Infrastructure, Services, and Related Topics
- Institutions
- Law, Crime, and Law Enforcement
- People (Groups)
- People (Individuals)
- Politics and Government
- Race, Ethnicity, and Religion
- Recreation and Leisure
- Reform and Reform Movements
- Transportation
- Types and Sections of Cities, Towns, Suburbs, and Communities

## Politics and Government

Omnibuses
Railroads
Rapid Transit
Roads
Skywalks for Pedestrians
Steamboats
Streetcars
Suburban Railway Service
Subways
Traffic
Transportation
Tunnels

## Types and Sections of Cities, Towns, Suburbs, and Communities
African-American Towns
Boom Towns
Broadacre City
Cattle Towns
Coal Towns
College Towns
Company Towns
French Colonial Towns
Gateway Cities

German Colonial Towns
Ghost Towns
Greenbelt Towns
Hoovervilles
Industrial Suburbs
Levittown
Mill Towns
Mining Towns
Mobile Home Communities
Naturally Occurring Retirement Communities
New England Towns and Villages
Railroad Suburbs
Red-Light District
Resort Towns
Retirement Communities
River Towns
Satellite City
Shaker Villages
Skid Row
Spanish Colonial Towns and Cities
Streetcar Suburbs
Utopian Towns and Communities
Walking City
Western Cities

# Illustration Credits

| | | | | | |
|---|---|---|---|---|---|
| 14 | Library of Congress/Corbis | 252 | Corel Corporation | 595 | Library of Congress/Corbis |
| 15 | Joseph Sohm; ChromoSohm, Inc./ Corbis | 258 | Morton Beebe-S.F./Corbis | 603 | UPI/Corbis-Bettmann |
| 19 | UPI/Corbis-Bettmann | 263 | Hulton-Deutsch Collection/Corbis | 608 | Library of Congress/Corbis |
| 24 | Kelly-Mooney Photography/Corbis | 277 | Library of Congress/Corbis | 609 | UPI/Corbis-Bettmann |
| 41 | Corbis-Bettmann | 288 | Corel Corporation | 623 | UPI/Corbis-Bettmann |
| 46 | Roger Word/© Corbis | 296 | Corbis-Bettmann | 625 | Corbis-Bettmann |
| 54 | Corbis-Bettmann | 301 | UPI/Corbis-Bettmann | 634 | Morton Beebe-S.F./Corbis |
| 56 | The Purcell Team/Corbis | 308 | The Purcell Team/Corbis | 648 | Corbis-Bettmann |
| 68 | Robert Holmes/Corbis | 318 | Minnesota Historical Society/Corbis | 654 | Marc Muench/Corbis |
| 71 | Corbis-Bettmann | 325 | Corel Corporation | 664 | Earl Kowall/Corbis |
| 75 | Courtesy of Matt Kincaid | 337 | Hulton-Deutsch Collection/Corbis | 669 | Library of Congress |
| 82 | Library of Congress | 359 | Corel Corporation | 676 | Marc Muench/Corbis |
| 88 | Corel Corporation | 367 | Corel Corporation | 684 | Wolfgang Kaehler/Corbis |
| 98 | Corbis-Bettmann | 373 | Dean Wong/Corbis | 689 | Phil Schermeister/Corbis |
| 106 | Corbis-Bettmann | 380 | UPI/Corbis-Bettmann | 698 | Kevin R. Morris/© Corbis |
| 109 | Library of Congress/Corbis | 387 | Corbis-Bettmann | 700 | Courtesy of Matt Kincaid |
| 112 | Courtesy of Matt Kincaid | 392 | Corbis-Bettmann | 705 | Corbis-Bettmann |
| 117 | Corel Corporation | 404 | Hulton-Deutsch Collection/Corbis | 714 | David H. Wells/Corbis |
| 122 | Library of Congress/Corbis | 408 | Colorado Historical Society | 726 | Ted Strehinsky/Corbis |
| 126 | Library of Congress/Corbis | 417 | Paul Almasy/© Corbis | 733 | UPI/Corbis-Bettmann |
| 129 | UPI/Corbis-Bettmann | 434 | Library of Congress/Corbis | 737 | Corel Corporation |
| 135 | Courtesy of Matt Kincaid | 440 | Richard A. Cooke/Corbis | 741 | U.S. Army Military History Institute/ Corbis |
| 140 | Lynn Goldsmith/© Corbis | 447 | Richard T. Nowitz/Corbis | | |
| 156 | Corbis-Bettmann | 453 | Sandy Felsenthal/Corbis | 766 | Corbis-Bettmann |
| 160 | Corel Corporation | 462 | Michael Boys/Corbis | 780 | Corbis-Bettmann |
| 164 | Courtesy of Matt Kincaid | 470 | Corel Corporation | 791 | Nik Wheeler/Corbis |
| 166 | Johnathan Blair/Corbis | 476 | UPI/Corbis-Bettmann | 800 | Courtesy of Matt Kincaid |
| 171 | Courtesy of Matt Kincaid | 479 | David G. Houser/Corbis | 802 | Corbis-Bettmann |
| 183 | Library of Congress | 492 | Library of Congress/Corbis | 805 | UPI/Corbis-Bettmann |
| 190 | Phil Schermeister/Corbis | 502 | Lee Snider/Corbis | 818 | UPI/Corbis-Bettmann |
| 196 | James L. Amos/Corbis | 511 | David Muench/Corbis | 833 | Gail Mooney/© Corbis |
| 205 | Corel Corporation | 521 | Corbis-Bettmann | 848 | UPI/Corbis-Bettmann |
| 208 | Corel Corporation | 537 | Corbis-Bettmann | 850 | Rob Rowan; Progressive Image/Corbis |
| 215 | Tony Roberts/Corbis | 547 | UPI/Corbis-Bettmann | 859 | UPI/Corbis-Bettmann |
| 224 | Corbis-Bettmann | 552 | Kelly-Mooney Photography/Corbis | 865 | Mark Thiessen/Corbis |
| 226 | Kelly-Mooney Photography/Corbis | 557 | Dave G. Houser/Corbis | 870 | Corbis-Bettmann |
| 231 | UPI/Corbis | 568 | Corel Corporation | 884 | Hulton-Deutsch Collection/Corbis |
| 243 | Kelly-Mooney Photography/Corbis | 571 | Jeffry Myers/Corbis | 886 | Corbis-Bettmann |
| 246 | Ted Strehinsky/Corbis | 585 | UPI/Corbis-Bettmann | 893 | José F. Poblete/Corbis |
| | | 588 | UPI/Corbis-Bettmann | 904 | Morton Beebe-S.F./Corbis |

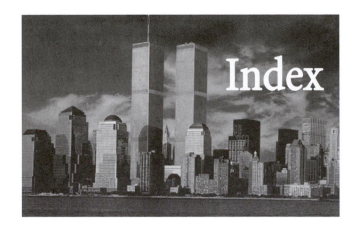

# Index

*Page citations in bold denote encyclopedia entries of the same, or very similar, name.*